The Graphic Designer's Digital Toolkit

ALLAN B. WOOD

CENGAGE
Learning·

Australia · Brazil · Japan · Korea · Mexico · Singapore · Spain · United Kingdom · United States

The Graphic Designer's Digital Toolkit, 7th Edition
Allan Wood

VP, General Manager, Skills and Planning: Dawn Gerrain

Product Director, Computing: Kathleen McMahon

Director, Development, Global Product Management, Skills: Marah Bellegarde

Senior Product Manager: Jim Gish

Senior Product Development Manager: Larry Main

Senior Content Developer: Meaghan Tomaso

Product Assistant: Gillian Daniels

Senior Marketing Manager: Eric La Scola

Senior Production Director: Wendy Troeger

Production Director: Andrew Crouth

Senior Content Project Manager: Glenn Castle

Senior Art Director: Jack Pendleton

> For product information and technology assistance, contact us at
> **Cengage Learning Customer & Sales Support, 1-800-354-9706**
> For permission to use material from this text or product, submit all requests online at **www.cengage.com/permissions**.
> Further permissions questions can be e-mailed to **permissionrequest@cengage.com**

Unless otherwise noted, screenshots are courtesy of Adobe®.

Adobe® Photoshop®, Adobe® InDesign®, Adobe® Illustrator® Adobe® Creative Cloud® Adobe® Acrobat® are trademarks or registered trademarks of Adobe Systems, Inc. in the United States and/or other countries. Third party products, services, company names, logos, design, titles, words, or phrases within these materials may be trademarks of their respective owners. Adobe product screenshots reprinted with permission from Adobe Systems Incorporated.

Library of Congress Control Number: 2014941557

ISBN-13: 978-1-305-26365-9

Cengage Learning
200 First Stamford Place, 4th Floor
Stamford, CT 06902
USA

Cengage Learning is a leading provider of customized learning solutions with office locations around the globe, including Singapore, the United Kingdom, Australia, Mexico, Brazil, and Japan. Locate your local office at: **www.cengage.com/global**

Cengage Learning products are represented in Canada by Nelson Education, Ltd.

To learn more about Cengage Learning, visit **www.cengage.com**

Purchase any of our products at your local college store or at our preferred online store **www.cengagebrain.com**

Notice to the Reader
Publisher does not warrant or guarantee any of the products described herein or perform any independent analysis in connection with any of the product information contained herein. Publisher does not assume, and expressly disclaims, any obligation to obtain and include information other than that provided to it by the manufacturer. The reader is expressly warned to consider and adopt all safety precautions that might be indicated by the activities described herein and to avoid all potential hazards. By following the instructions contained herein, the reader willingly assumes all risks in connection with such instructions. The publisher makes no representations or warranties of any kind, including but not limited to, the warranties of fitness for particular purpose or merchantability, nor are any such representations implied with respect to the material set forth herein, and the publisher takes no responsibility with respect to such material. The publisher shall not be liable for any special, consequential, or exemplary damages resulting, in whole or part, from the readers' use of, or reliance upon, this material.

Printed in China
5 6 7 8 9 19 18 17 16

TABLE OF CONTENTS

ANYONE WILL FIND THIS BOOK HELPFUL

Welcome to the *Graphic Designer's Digital Toolkit!* Here you will learn the essential skills and design techniques to get you comfortable using the newest versions of the premier graphics programs in the industry today: Photoshop, Illustrator, and InDesign. This book is set up as a challenging hands-on, project-based classroom book with which students will complete useful, real-world projects from start to finished product in a structured format that a designer would normally create for a client. All files used for all exercises can be downloaded from the publisher's website at www.cengagebrain.com; downloading these is also one of the first exercises in Chapter 1. The tutorials are set for the user to start from concept to completion. This book also contains terminology or language used in the graphics today to give the learner an understanding of terms and techniques. It is created for college students who are taking introductory to intermediate classes in computer graphics applications, digital media, graphic design, or as a supplementary text providing projects for courses in Photoshop, Illustrator, and InDesign. Many colleges have adopted the text as the main text directly for multiple courses in digital imaging, digital illustration, digital (desktop) publication, digital media, or graphic design instead of purchasing different books for each course. It can also be used for a half-year course in digital media for college-bound upper-class students at the high school level, and can be used not only in the traditional classroom, but in hybrid and online courses as well.

For the professional who may need a refresher course in one or more of the applications, or for the individual looking for an edge in making a career change into the graphics industry, this book can be used as a self-paced study. It also makes a great reference text for professionals already in the field. The business owner who wants to create his or her own logo, business cards, promotional pieces, advertisements, newsletters, and brochures or to adjust and retouch a photograph can also use this book.

EMERGING TRENDS

With new versions of applications coming out constantly, most individuals do not need to learn every function and command, but they can learn the most essential of these to be productive in creating most types of projects. This is the focus of the book: to make the reader comfortable in each graphic application to be able to create the projects that a designer might be asked to produce, and to speak the language used in the graphics industry today. Current new important useful tools, processes, and techniques are used realistically in each application and are integrated in each chapter tutorial.

BACKGROUND OF THIS TEXT

After spending many years as an instructor and Program Chair at the college level and evaluating books to be used by faculty, I was disappointed by the lack of depth in many of the project-based learning books. I also could not find a suitable book that was an introduction to the major graphic applications used in the industry today—Photoshop, Illustrator, and InDesign—and how they are used individually and together in creating quality projects. I wanted to design a book that not only addresses the essential skills a designer would need in each application without having to be bombarded with countless commands and functions that may never be used, but a book that also shows the design process involved in creating a project from start to finish, and the language of the graphics industry. Each hands-on project in this book builds upon the functions of select tools and commands with basic, similar concepts to show the reader what happens in the real world of graphics. This book assumes the reader knows the basics of working with computers.

TEXTBOOK ORGANIZATION

Welcome to a project-oriented, real-world approach to learning the three categories of graphics applications used in the industry today. Specifically, this book focuses on Adobe Photoshop for digital image editing, Adobe Illustrator for digital illustration, and Adobe InDesign for digital desktop publishing as the standards in their respective fields. Before introducing these applications, the book provides a foundation of Macintosh OS X Marvericks, and Windows 7 and 8 computer operations, terminology, and design elements, principles, typography, imagery, and color concepts, along with an understanding of the process of design from concept to completion in the first two chapters. Each chapter provides insight on the design fundamentals, terminology, and technical aspects that a designer needs to know for each application. Although the book uses the newest versions of each program, previous versions are also explained in many cases. The projects and information given for each application provide the essential skills a designer needs to feel comfortable using that application, no matter what version they are working with. The text then provides the added demonstrated knowledge of current new tools, techniques, and processes that may be useful in their everyday work flow by showing how they are integrated in each chapter tutorial and exercise. This book can be used with either Macintosh or Windows computers.

The book is divided into four units, and each unit is divided into chapters with projects or assignments a designer could actually create for a client from concept to final completion for print or web media. Each chapter builds upon skills learned from the previous chapter to enhance the learning process. You will walk through and create a project from each chapter assignment using the necessary online files (which can be downloaded from the publisher's website at www.cengagebrain.com), learning the process from concept to completion of the project, including technical "Toolkit Tip" suggestions, special design tips, and help on what to do if you run into a specific problem.

The first unit, Getting Ready for Production, focuses on getting comfortable using both Macintosh and Windows computers and understanding the design principles and elements that go into the creation of a good design. The other three units are set for each of the three graphic applications: Photoshop, Illustrator, and InDesign. In each chapter, there is also an Advanced Users section to further challenge the learner and a Digital Toolkit Extra section for mini projects to demonstrate additional concepts or techniques. At the end of each chapter are review questions that could also serve as a chapter quiz to test the reader's knowledge of fundamental material. Each unit contains a Unit Review Project Challenge that ties together all the chapters within the unit and provides a few additional functions, tools, and techniques to explore.

In the first unit, Getting Ready for Production, you will become familiar with both Macintosh OS X and Windows 7 and 8 environments, managing files and folders, creating shortcuts, learning keyboard shortcuts, creating electronic slide shows, using widgets (Mac), using iTunes, setting up for online with iCloud, fun tools and techniques for organizing your desktop, and burning data, music, and photo CDs. You will also be exposed to design elements and principles, typography basics, imagery basics, and understanding color and how to use color to create posters.

In the second unit on Photoshop CC, assignments involve adjusting poorly exposed or badly colored graphics, using Adobe Bridge and Mini Bridge to locate and manage files, completely changing the color of a sports car image for a realistic effect using selection techniques, creating a well-toned black-and-white image from a color image, creating a black and white and color composite image, using actions to create special effects and copyright info, fixing off-color images, combining images into one suitable image using layer techniques, digitally restoring an old image, creating a multicolor product ad from a single product, and combing images and special techniques to create a realistic front and back cover for a music CD. Other tutorials involve working in 3D with text and creating 3D shapes, color replacement in products, managing files and application settings online using Creative Cloud, adjusting an image's vantage point, and working with shapes in creating a basic figure illustration. You will also learn about working with camera raw files as the new digital negative from digital cameras.

In the Illustrator CC unit, you will create an electronic game board, a 3D wine bottle with a perfectly fit label, special design symbols, a logo, playing cards, company business cards with logo, a clock face, and a tourism map, as well as create an advanced figure illustration, sync files and application settings between multiple computers, and using actions for repetitive projects like laying out eight business cards on a sheet. You will also create radio station web banners that combine both Photoshop and Illustrator images, and a promotional label on a 3D mug. You will also learn to use the Image Trace and Live Paint features, and creating multiple artboards using one logo for various media.

The fourth and final unit demonstrates how to use InDesign CC as a desktop publishing tool. It provides assignments in creating a direct mail coupon ad, a photo or art desktop calendar, a four-page newsletter, interactive PDF documents, developing alternate layouts for digital devices and print sizes using the same design, and a tri-fold brochure to get you right into the most familiar projects a designer might find, along with an understanding of the process from preflighting or checking documents and graphics to packaging your project for the service provider.

You will find many of these same projects coming up in your design career. Enjoy the ride!

ALL STUDENT FILES FOR ALL TUTORIALS CAN BE DOWNLOADED ONLINE

Online at www.cengagebrain.com, you will find all image and text files used in all the assignments and projects. You will find some extra goodies like additional information, more projects (yes, more!), and resource information that may be useful, too, in the "*Extras & Goodies*" folder online. To access the online files for this book, take the following steps:

1. Open your browser and go to the publisher's website at http://www .cengagebrain.com

2. Type the author, title, or ISBN of this book in the Search window. (The ISBN is listed on the back cover.)

3. Click the book title in the list of search results.

4. When the book's main page is displayed, click the Access Now button under the Free Materials tab.

5. To download files, select a chapter number and then click on the Student Files tab on the left navigation bar to download the files.

6. To access additional material, click the *Extras & Goodies* link next to the *Student Data Files* link to download the files. For those not very comfortable with downloading material, there is also a detailed exercise in Chapter 1 on the process.

FEATURES

The following list provides some of the salient features of the text:

- Over 50 projects and tutorials in the text, more additional projects, tutorials, and info in the online *Extras & Goodies* folder.
- Objectives clearly state the learning goals of each chapter.
- All files needed for projects are included online at www.cengagebrain.com for download.
- Client Assignments involve multiple tools and techniques and resemble those that a designer might encounter on the job to complete a useful project.
- Toolkit Tips in each chapter explain tools and techniques and additional info.
- Design Tips in each chapter show how to master design fundamentals with each software application.
- Digital Toolkit Extra and Advanced Users sections at the end of each chapter provide added challenges and additional tools, techniques, and mini projects.
- Review questions reinforce material presented in the each chapter.

- Unit Review Project Challenges tie together all the chapters within the unit and provide a few additional functions or techniques to explore.
- All kinds of terms used in the graphics industry today so you can understand the designer's lingo.

 CourseMate

The Graphic Designer's Digital Toolkit, 7e includes a CourseMate, which helps you make the grade!

This CourseMate includes:

- An interactive eBook, with highlighting, note-taking, and search capabilities
- Interactive learning tools including:
  - Chapter quizzes
  - Flashcards
  - Crossword Puzzles
  - And more!

Go to login.cengagebrain.com to access these resources.

NEW TO EDITION

- Text provides a comprehensive overview of new functions, tools, techniques, and panels used in Adobe Illustrator CC, Adobe InDesign CC, and Adobe Photoshop CC. Many additional tutorials have been added in the Advanced Users and Digital Toolkit Extra sections and new images have been added to replace others in some of the tutorials for a refreshing look.

- Nearly all figure artwork is updated to the current Macintosh, Windows 7, and Windows 8 operating systems in Chapter 1, and to the Adobe Creative Cloud format, with over 700 figures redesigned to meet the new darker interface for Illustrator, Photoshop, and InDesign and for even better comprehension for the user. New current menus, tools, techniques, and additional tutorials using Adobe Creative Cloud applications Photoshop CC, Illustrator CC, and InDesign CC. Updated Windows 7 and Mac OS X Mavericks operating systems, and an all new section in using the Windows 8 operating system.

- Navigating the Macintosh OS X Mavericks desktop and having fun organizing and playing on your desktop using Widgets, Launchpad, Mission Control, iCloud, iTunes, and Dashboard programs. Using Tabs and Tags to organize your files. Electronic slide shows using Quick Look and Preview.

- Updated end-of-chapter projects will help reinforce tools and techniques taught throughout each chapter.

- The reader will find complete tutorials in using Windows 8 with its Start Screen of tiles and apps, ribbon interface, navigation, and organization. Updated Windows 7 techniques provided and comparisons made between Windows 7 and 8. Electronic slide shows using Pictures Library, Photos App (Windows 8), and Windows Media Center are also updated.

- There are new images, tutorials, and projects offered in the Photoshop CC unit. Updated tutorials of new masking techniques and selection technologies with the Refine Edge function, the Properties panel, along with various color and black and white presets and enhancements. Additional tutorials include adjusting vantage points with the Perspective Warp function, managing and syncing files and settings using Creative Cloud, and moving subjects with Content Move for precise blending. Additional tutorials involving tools not discussed in previous editions are introduced like using the Color Replacement and Eyedropper tools to sample and replace colors in products, and as corrective tools in removing stains and rust in architecture, along with creating shapes on different layers in the development of a basic figure diagram. There are updated exercises on enhanced Camera Raw effects, and using the new Camera Raw Filter with new images. Finally, a large tutorial in creating and working with 3D text and shapes in creating special materials-based objects that can be ready for 3D print.

- Illustrator CC showcases reconstructed Pen, Pencil, Smooth and Direct Selection Tools. The Pen and Direct Selection tools have a Path Segment Reshape function for precise curve adjustment. There is also a Live Corners function used with the Direct Selection Tool for creating precise curves from corner points. There is the ability to convert text into individual objects with the new Touch Type Tool, and updates with color and swatches, panels, packaging, and creating smart objects. Additional tutorials involve creating an advanced figure illustration that showcases the Live Corners feature, syncing files and settings in Creative Cloud, and creating an action to convert one business card into a layout of eight business cards on a sheet.

- InDesign CC figure artwork has been updated to accommodate the current dark interface preferred by professionals using Adobe Photoshop CC and Illustrator CC for consistency. InDesign CC contains many new features that help in production workflow. Exploring enhanced font management techniques, syncing files and settings, generating QR codes, color and packaging updates, and EPUB updates. There is the ability to work seamlessly with integration of hyperlinks and create scalable effects.

- Additional tutorials and handouts are also offered in the *Extras & Goodies* folder that can be found online at www.cengagebrain.com.

- Accompanying website offers additional projects, expanded tutorials, and other valuable learning tools.

COMPLETED PROJECTS AND TUTORIALS FROM EACH CHAPTER IN APPENDIX A

You will find all completed projects and tutorials at the end of this book as Appendix A. It provides a great visual reference of the depth of these challenging projects and tutorials that you will be creating, and having fun while learning!

Find All Your Completed Projects in Appendix A

HOW TO USE THIS TEXT

OBJECTIVES

Learning Objectives start off each chapter. They describe the competencies readers should achieve once they understand the chapter material.

DESIGN AND TOOLKIT TIPS

These tips are located throughout the text. Design Tips show readers how to master design techniques, and Toolkit Tips demonstrate how to work more efficiently and effectively within each software application.

CLIENT ASSIGNMENTS

These projects involve multiple tools and techniques and resemble assignments that a designer might encounter on the job.

REVIEW QUESTIONS

Review Questions are located at the end of each chapter and allow readers to assess their understanding of the material.

ADVANCED USERS AND DIGITAL TOOLKIT EXTRA SECTIONS

These tutorials are located at the end of each chapter and provide added challenges using additional tools and techniques.

UNIT REVIEW PROJECTS

These projects link together all chapters within a unit and utilize a few additional functions or techniques.

THE LEARNING PACKAGE

INSTRUCTOR RESOURCES

The online instructor resources were developed to assist instructors in planning and implementing their instructional programs. They include all the files needed for the projects and assignments, PowerPoint presentations, and some extra projects and information in an "*Extras & Goodies*" folder. These resources also include exams, review questions and answers from each chapter, syllabi, web references, additional assignments, and concept information. These resources can be found online at: **http://login.cengage.com**. Once you login or create an account, search for the title under "My Dashboard" using the ISBN. Then select the instructor companion site resources and click "Add to my Bookshelf."

WHO IS THE AUTHOR?

Allan B. Wood served 12 years as Associate Professor and Program Chair of the Graphic Design and Professional Photography degree programs at McIntosh College in New Hampshire, until its closure a couple of years ago. He recently was awarded a second place standing for Educator of the Year in the Computer Design: Graphics and Photography category among 80 colleges participating. Allan currently teaches a full load of college level courses independently as an adjunct Professor in digital media and business at New Hampshire's Great Bay College and Manchester Community College, along with an online multimedia course each semester for DeVry. He is also involved with corporate training as well. He has nearly 30 years of teaching experience and many years working in graphic design and photography environments, including 6 years as full-time portrait photographer and graphics lab business owner. Over the last 17 years while teaching college level courses, as a Program Chair for 12 of those years at McIntosh College, Allan created the professional project-based curriculum for college-level courses in Photoshop, Illustrator, Web Page Fundamentals, and Desktop Publishing. He developed the curriculum for all courses in the Professional Photography program, including the computer graphics applications Photoshop, Illustrator, and InDesign used in this book. Allan also has a master's degree in Instructional Design and Online learning, continues to assist in curriculum development for digital media and computer technology departments, and is a beta tester for Adobe products.

Allan is a member of the National Association of Photoshop Professionals, and has been a member of the New Hampshire Professional Photographer's Association. He is a New England lighthouse enthusiast and has had a 16-month lighthouse wall calendar published of just his images. His images have and will be published for 2013, 2014, and 2015 calendars with Brown Trout calendar publishers for worldwide distribution. He has also published two front-cover magazine photos, has won various photography awards, and has had many of his images downloaded worldwide on stock photo agency sites like Shutterstock, Alamy, and Fotolia.

As Allan enjoys teaching many college level courses each semester, he continues to employ the project oriented approach he emphasizes in this book. All the while maintaining the importance of integrating traditional design concepts and techniques. He has recently completed photographing all 170 lighthouses in New England, then designed and created an extensive (300 page) New England lighthouse tourism website at www.nelights.com using the lighthouses as guides for exploring local attractions, and has written a book on famous shipwrecks, rescues, and hauntings around New England's lighthouses.

ACKNOWLEDGMENTS

I'd like to thank the great folks at Delmar-Cengage for their patience and inspiration: James Gish, acquisitions editor, for his positive attitude, sincerity, and willingness to take a chance on this book in breaking some new ground; and to Meaghan Tomaso, my supreme coordinator and rudder for all her help and encouragement with the book; Tara Botelho for her keen eyes in reviewing the book, and great sense of humor; Glenn Castle (supreme production coordinator), Jack Pendleton, and the crew in the art and production departments (love the front cover design!); Suwathiga Velayutham, Harold, and the folks at Integra for producing the highest quality text, and everyone else who helped me out on this project. You are all awesome!

I'd also like to thank the following individuals, who made contributions to the success of this book:

Thanks to Carla Clancy for providing an image for the Photoshop chapter on retouching images and to Michael Magoon for lending his 1964 Rambler for the CD cover project. Thanks also to Greg Tenhover for helping out with layout for the newsletter and tri-fold brochure projects, and to Shelly Britton, who wrote and photographed what it's like to be on a lobster boat for the newsletter project. Check out a little slice of life in New England!

I also need to thank the most important people in my life for their support, especially my wife Chris, for supporting me while I spent countless hours, weekdays, and weekends on the book. Her keen understanding and continued support of the importance in the creation of this seventh edition has helped me keep focus, and still have fun. Thanks to my two sons, Bryan and Steven, for dragging Chris and I away once in a while to go out to dinner as our weekly family tradition (time to eat!) and allowing me to work at home without complaining, our dog Spot for forcing me to walk her before I work in the mornings, and to Ma and Pa Wood (Kay and Larry) for giving me the positive attitude over the years to achieve anything I put my mind to.

The book and lighthouse images are also dedicated to the memory of my buddy Lisa Johnson.

Allan Wood, 2014

QUESTIONS AND FEEDBACK

Delmar Cengage Learning and the author welcome your questions and feedback. If you have suggestions that you think others would benefit from, please let us know, and we will try to include them in the next edition.

To send us your questions and/or feedback, you can contact the publisher at:

Delmar Cengage Learning
Executive Woods
5 Maxwell Drive
Clifton Park, NY 12065
Attn: Graphic Communications Team
800-998-7498

Or contact the author at:

alwood@nelights.com

UNIT

1

Welcome to the Land of OS

CHAPTER OBJECTIVES: To understand how to be productive in a graphics environment, in this chapter you will:

▷ Learn the basics of the Mac OS X Mavericks, Windows 7, and Windows 8 operating systems and techniques that allow Mac OS X and Windows to work together.

▷ Use basic file management techniques to help organize workflow.

▷ Learn keystroke combinations to increase productivity.

▷ Use new fun applications and techniques to keep your desktop from becoming too cluttered.

▷ ADVANCED USERS: Create electronic slide shows of images using special applications within Macintosh OS X and Windows operating systems.

▷ DIGITAL TOOLKIT EXTRA: Burn music, photo, and data CDs on Mac OS X and Windows platforms using free programs within each. Use iCloud to manage your music, images, and documents.

CREATIVE
CLOUD
EDITION

Before we get into the various graphics applications, we will start by getting comfortable with Macintosh and Windows operating systems. An **operating system**—sometimes referred to as an *OS*—makes sure hardware and software work together nicely. **Applications** are software programs for a particular use, such as Photoshop, which is an application used for digital image editing. For instance, if you want to print an image created in Photoshop, you click on the command to print, and the operating system sets up the communications between the application and the printer to print the document accurately. This chapter will familiarize you with the basics of the **Macintosh OS X,** or *Mac OS X*, and **Windows 7** and **Windows 8** operating systems and some of their included special applications. There are tips on using both systems together to manage your files and downloading the student data files for the chapter exercises, which will help you develop skills to improve your productivity as a designer or photographer.

THE MAC OS X ENVIRONMENT

Welcome to the operating system of the graphics industry: Mac OS X. You will notice similarities between the Mac OS X **desktop**—the screen displayed when the system has loaded—and the Windows 7 and Windows 8 desktop screens. Both Macintosh and Windows operating systems display your drives, portable media devices, and most frequently used applications, files, and folders on your computer screen as small picture representations, called **icons** (see Figure 1-1). When you double-click on an icon, it opens up that file, folder, or application; it is actually a link, or shortcut, that you can create as an **alias** on your desktop.

At the bottom of the Mac desktop—or sometimes to the left or right side, depending on your System Preferences settings—is the **Dock**, which is used to display applications, files, and folders. The **Trash** icon is used to remove and restore files. The **Finder** menu (sometimes referred to as the desktop menu) at the top of the screen lets you navigate the computer; it also appears as a square, smiling face on the Dock. Each application has its own menu bar and commands to perform tasks. You can also transfer and store folders and their contents on the desktop for quick access, or you can click on the icon in the Dock.

▷ FIGURE 1-1

The Macintosh OS X Mavericks desktop.

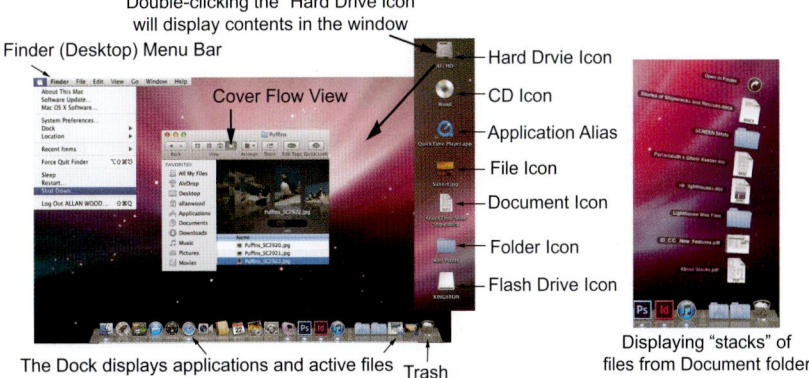

Finder (Desktop) Menu Bar

Double-clicking the "Hard Drive icon will display contents in the window

Cover Flow View

- Hard Drvie Icon
- CD Icon
- Application Alias
- File Icon
- Document Icon
- Folder Icon
- Flash Drive Icon

The Dock displays applications and active files Trash

Displaying "stacks" of files from Document folder

THE DOCK

The Dock can be set to reside at the bottom, side, or even out of view off the edge of your screen (see Figure 1-2). It can contain images, minimized windows, folders, applications, documents, and even links to websites. Each item stored on the Dock has its own icon. Click on the icon and the Dock restores the window in your workspace or launches the application. When you open an application, that application's icon appears on the Dock. You'll find a white dot displays underneath when an application is active. Your favorite applications can be set to remain on the Dock, even after the computer has been turned off. You will also see the Trash icon on the right side or bottom of the Dock. Besides using it to remove and restore files, it can be used to eject drives, portable media devices, and CDs. On the left side of the Dock is the smiling Finder interface; its desktop menu commands are also at the top of the screen. You will find that most standard Mac OS X application icons—except for the Trash icon—will be displayed on the left side or top of the Dock, and minimized files will appear to the right. The Mac OS X version displays a "Documents" folder for your most recent documents to retrieve, or you can simply create your own folder. Any folder placed on the Dock's right side can be used as part of a feature called "**stacks**." When you click a stack folder, it springs from the Dock to display the folder contents. To open a file in a stack, just click on it. To remove it, just drag it into the Trash. You may also find, on the right side of the Dock, a Downloads folder designated by the downward pointing arrow for quick access to downloaded applications or files. On the left side of the Dock you'll find an application called the **Launchpad**, which displays all the Mac's current installed applications when you click on it.

▷ FIGURE 1-2

The Dock displays applications, folders, files, and functions. Icons on the leftmost side are applications in Mac OS X, while "stacks" and minimized windows reside on the right side.

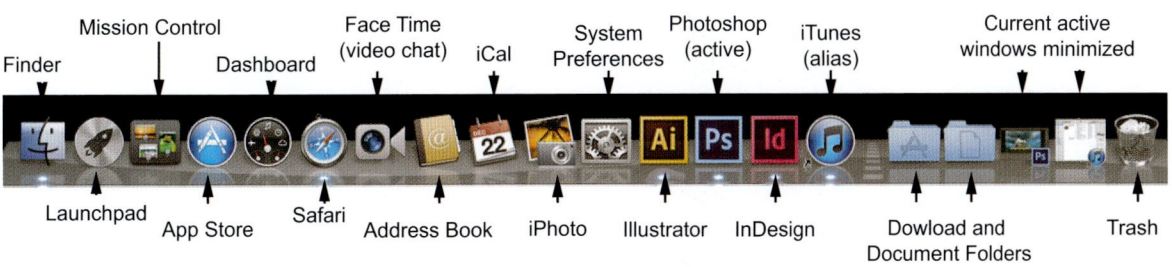

Finder | Mission Control | Dashboard | Face Time (video chat) | iCal | System Preferences | Photoshop (active) | iTunes (alias) | Current active windows minimized

Launchpad | App Store | Safari | Address Book | iPhoto | Illustrator | InDesign | Dowload and Document Folders (click to expand as stacks) | Trash

TOOLKIT TIP To remove an application from the Dock, click the application icon and hold it until a pop-up menu appears; when the menu bar displays for that application, select Remove from Dock. If a shortcut or alias is created, it will have a broken arrow under the icon and can simply be dragged off the Dock; the icons are just links and do not affect the original application, which can be found in the Applications folder (Go > Applications).

MAC OS X WINDOWS

In Mac OS X, windows that are opened to locate contents in folders or drives display a weblike page (default view), where you can use back and forward arrow buttons to move between windows and previous documents (see Figure 1-3). You can also select one of four View buttons to choose how you want the content displayed. These functions appear on the window **toolbar**, which shows special commands and functions for each application.

All windows have a **title bar** that contains the file or function name and three colored buttons on the left side that control how the window displays. The red button closes the window, the yellow button minimizes the window to an icon on the Dock, and the green button increases the window to its full size or restores it to its original state. To resize the window, click and drag the lower right corner. Sometimes when you select a command or function, indicated by a gearlike icon called the Action button, a **dialog box** appears to provide more commands or functions. In current Mac OS X versions, you can observe a full screen preview of any image or document by selecting the document, and clicking the eye icon on the Toolbar called "**Quick Look**." To customize your toolbar with specific actions, with your cursor over the toolbar, hold down the CTRL key and select Customize from the display panel.

▷ FIGURE 1-3

Mac windows used to locate and modify files and folders.

Display contents (Column View)

THE HARD DRIVE

To display the contents of your hard drive, double-click on the Macintosh HD or hard drive icon on the desktop. On the toolbar, you will notice the View button, which lets you choose between displaying in Icon View, List View, Column View, and Cover Flow View. Column View makes it easy to navigate between drives, folders, and files; the contents of whatever is highlighted are displayed in the next column to the right (see Figure 1-4). When you select a folder, you will notice its contents are displayed. Cover Flow View shows graphic thumbnail representations of your files and documents.

The left side column of the window displays Documents links and storage media—such as your hard drive and network connections—and organizes specific links to your desktop, your "Home" space for your personal files on the computer, and available applications, including those that were included with Mac OS X. There are specific media categories for your files and folders, such as Movies, Music, and Pictures to maintain peak computer performance. You can also search for previously used documents and applications. There is a category called **All My Files**, which puts all your personal music, images, documents, etc., in specific categories for quick access.

Now, we will learn to navigate around the Macintosh HD or hard drive icon.

1. Double-click on the Macintosh HD or hard drive icon on your desktop.
2. Select the Home icon (next to your username) link for your personal settings, files, and so on; locate a folder and display its contents, then use the back and forward arrow buttons to move around.
3. Select the All My Files and Applications buttons to display their contents.
4. Select the Desktop and Documents buttons and select the four different views on the toolbar to see how contents are displayed.
5. Navigate around a little, then close the window.

DESIGN TIP

To resize a window proportionately when it is not displayed as a full screen on your monitor, hold down the Shift key while you drag from the window's lower right corner point.

▷ FIGURE 1-4

Options to locate, edit, and organize files and folders of various media on your hard drive or device.

TOOLKIT TIP If you are not sure what some of the icons mean on the toolbar, press the CTRL key, then click to display a menu, then choose "Icon and Text" to display both.

MAC OS X FINDER DESKTOP MENUS

The Mac OS X Finder interface on the desktop works much the same way as the Start menu does in Windows. It provides access to particular functions for applications, files, folders, and computer using a **Menu bar,** which contains commands from various menus specific to the Finder desktop interface shown here (see Figure 1-5) or for any other application, such as Photoshop.

The Apple Menu

The **Apple menu** is where you can find information about your Mac system ( > About This Mac) and files, which includes a listing of the most recently opened applications and files; you can also set global, System Preferences here and check for software updates. Use the About My Mac link to check what version you are using. If you are using the current Mavericks version, you'll find it reads 10.9 version. To avoid damaging data and software by turning off the power to your Mac, use the Restart or Shut Down commands under this menu to power down your Mac safely.

The Finder Menu

The Finder menu lets you organize how icons are displayed and set desktop preferences. This is where you find the Empty Trash command to permanently remove files dragged into the Trash.

▷ FIGURE 1-5

Apple, Finder, and File menus in Finder desktop menu bar.

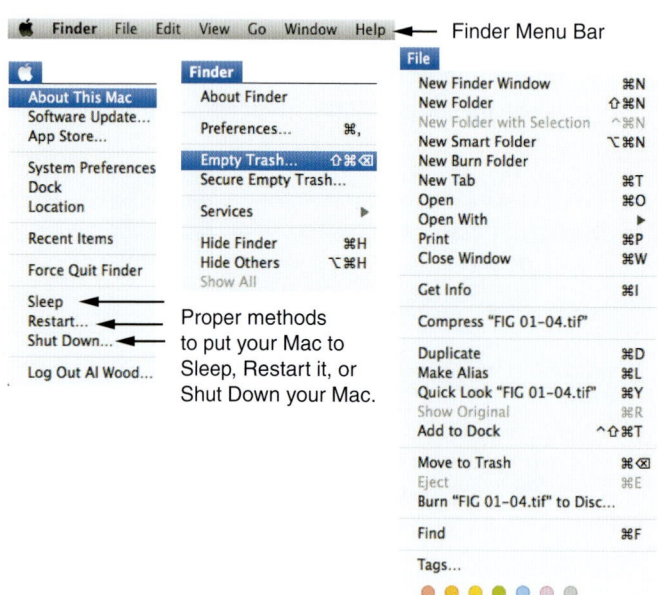

The File Menu

The **File menu** allows you to create new folders, search for and get info about folders and files, duplicate items, and create links or shortcuts to files and folders, called *aliases*. In this menu, you can eject discs, burn CDs, and move files to the Trash.

Some of the special commands in the File menu are described below.

- **Get Info** gives details, such as date and size, about a selected icon.
- **Make Alias** makes an alias, shortcut, or *link* to a file, document, or folder, which can be dragged onto the desktop.
- **New Smart Folder** helps you to organize files by what they have in common based on criteria you set.
- **New Burn Folder** allows you to create a collection of files to be burned or written onto a CD or DVD multiple times.
- **New Tab** allows you to consolidate various open Finder windows into one.
- **Add to Dock** allows you to add files, folders, and applications to the sidebar for quick access. To remove, press down the CTRL key and select Remove From Sidebar. This is similar to adding favorites on the Internet Explorer web browser.
- **Move to Trash** moves selected files and folders to the Trash icon on the Dock.
- **Find** locates files and folders through specific criteria in Home through category links.
- **Tags** (or **Label** in earlier versions) helps to organize groups of files by assigning color labels and keywords.

The Edit Menu

The **Edit menu** allows you to work with text and graphics, which includes selecting all components in a document (see Figure 1-6). It allows you to undo, copy, cut and paste, and see what is copied on the clipboard. The **clipboard** is a temporary memory site for storing text and graphics that have been cut or copied before pasting them into another document or to another location. Since the clipboard only "remembers" one thing at a time, anytime you cut or copy something else, the content of the clipboard is replaced by the new data.

▷ FIGURE 1-6

Edit, View, and Window menus on Finder desktop menu bar.

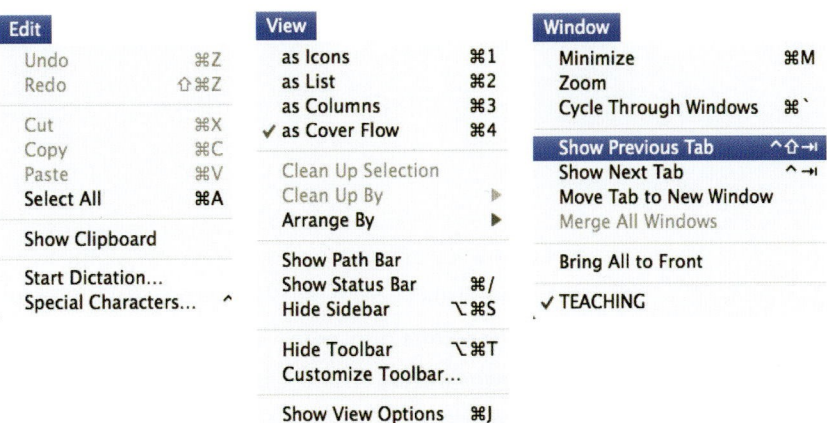

The View Menu

The **View menu** on the desktop displays files and folders on various drives and discs. It lets you customize the toolbar and change the way files look and are arranged on your system. Folders and files can be displayed as icons, either listed by name with additional data or arranged in columns to display contents inside folders and drives. The fourth view, Cover Flow View, is also used in iPods.

The Window Menu

The **Window menu** allows you to minimize any open window and place it in the Dock. Anything minimized in the menu will show a black triangle beneath the icon on the Dock. To restore the window to the Desktop at its original size, click the icon on the Dock. Tabs can also be navigated.

The Go Menu

The **Go** menu lets you view your applications, favorite places and folders, and connect to a server to share information with other computers (see Figure 1-7). You can jump to any location on your computer, the Internet, or on your network. The Go menu also lists recently used folders.

▷ FIGURE 1-7

The Go menu helps to navigate around the computer.

Some of the Go commands follow:

- **Computer** opens a window to display all the items on your desktop.
- **Home** displays contents of your personal Home folder.
- **Applications** displays all programs in the Applications folder.
- **Recent Folders** shows a list of recently used folders.
- **Go to Folder** allows you to go to a particular folder.

- **Connect to Server** allows you to connect to a local or remote server.
- **Airdrop** allows you to share files over WiFi in any office or home network.
- **All My Files** displays files in specific categories from music, to images, to spreadsheets.

Get Mac Help

Mac Help Center, in Mac OS X, provides answers to questions and also gives instructions on how to perform various functions by clicking underlined links; it also lets you type a question, phrase, or term to display a list of topics to look for further information (see Figure 1-8). You can also use the help of an alphabetical index to narrow your search. You can get help from information stored on the hard drive, particularly all the Mac functions, or you can get help from the Apple website with an Internet connection. All applications have a Help command on their menu bars to bring up topics that pertain directly to that application, and you'll find a link to all help for your Mac's applications in the Help Center. There is also a Help viewer menu bar to aid in searching for information.

▷ FIGURE 1-8

Mac Help Center provides you with information for your computer, or application.

Mac Help Center

Use Mac OS X Help tutorials to help you familiarize yourself with Mac OS X. In this exercise, you will learn about iTunes, review navigating around the Mac desktop, and explore some new ways to use your Mac.

1. Select Help > Help Center (under the search bar) from your Finder desktop menu.

2. First, select the "Learn the Basics" link, to use as a review.

3. Type "iTunes" in the upper right blank box and press the Return key; a list of related topics appears. Also type in "Widgets," "iCal," and "Safari" for some other useful features included in Mac OS X.

4. Click on links that interest you, or try other variations or phrases, and print the pages on these topics (File > Print). You will be learning more about this at the end of this chapter.

5. Hit the red Close button to close the window when you are finished.

A Program's Application Menu

When you are working with a particular application, such as Photoshop, its menu bar contains various menus and commands for functions specific to Photoshop. Each program has a special Application menu in Mac OS X to the right of the Apple icon in its menu bar (see Figure 1-9). This **Application menu** contains commands for information about the application, changing settings, preferences, syncing settings, and quitting the application.

▷ FIGURE 1-9

The Application menu on the menu bar provides commands for that particular application.

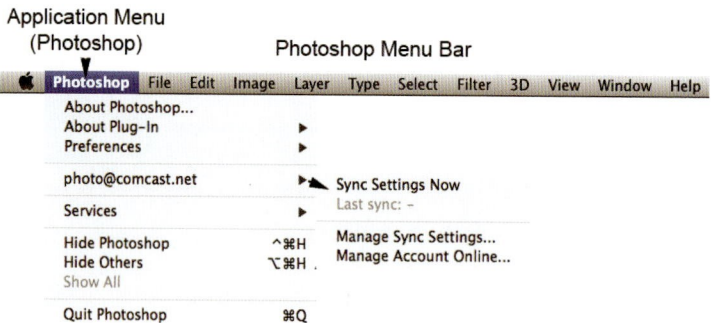

SYSTEM PREFERENCES IN THE APPLE MENU

The **System Preferences** program in the Apple menu on the far left allows you to make modifications within your computer, like adding hardware, adding and removing programs, updating applications, and modifying system functions and monitor displays (see Figure 1-10). Here is where you can change Internet options, adjust Accessibility options, and set network connections.

▷ FIGURE 1-10

System Preferences in the Mac allows you to make changes and adjustments within your computer.

THE WINDOWS 7 ENVIRONMENT

DESIGN TIP

To resize a window proportionately, hold down the Shift key while dragging from a window's corner point.

The Windows 7 desktop functions much like the Mac desktop; it has icons for files, applications, and special functions (see Figure 1-11). One of the special functions, the **Recycle Bin**, stores and restores deleted files much like the Mac's Trash icon. Windows uses what is called the **taskbar** to display minimized active files and applications, which is similar to the Dock on the Mac. To restore the application or file to original size, click on its minimized taskbar button. In Windows 7, the taskbar allows you to preview "**Jump Lists**" to navigate around recent files, images, or tasks. Another feature called **pinning** allows you to pin your favorite programs or files to the taskbar.

▷ FIGURE 1-11

Windows desktop displays icons for shortcuts to common applications and special functions, the taskbar, and the Start menu, which is the control center for Windows.

All computers that use the Windows operating system are called **PCs**. Windows on a PC are adjusted much the same way as windows on the Mac, but with the sizing buttons on the top right side of the title bar instead of on the left. The dash button minimizes the window to the taskbar, the center button maximizes and restores the window, and the red X button closes the window. You can resize a window by clicking and dragging on the window's edge or corner. Sometimes when you select a command or function, a dialog box appears to provide more commands or functions. The Start menu is used in the same way as the Finder interface on the Mac; in Windows, the Start button is the control center.

THE START MENU, WINDOWS EXPLORER, AND THE COMPUTER FUNCTION

As the control center for Windows, when you click on the **Start menu** you can select from the most recently used applications, documents, stored images, and music; you can select and launch any programs on your computer, connect to the Internet, access email, or use the Search command to locate files and folders and look for help. You can also open the Start menu by pressing the special Windows key on your keyboard. In Windows 7, you can select the All Programs link in the Start Menu display window to display the application programs on your hard drive. You can also locate and find information about outside hardware, such as portable drives, printers, and digital cameras; these devices are called **peripherals**.

The Start menu in Windows 7 also contains the Shut Down command to perform a proper shut down operation on your PC. Within the Start menu options, the **Computer** function provides access to information about disk drives, files, and folders, and it also provides special commands so you can choose what to do with those files (see Figure 1-12). You can use the forward and back arrow buttons in the toolbar to navigate between windows and previous documents in the same way you would navigate between web pages on the Internet. When a window is selected, its file or function name is displayed on the window's title bar.

▷ FIGURE 1-12

The Start menu is the control center for Windows operations. Selecting the Computer option, or the Windows Explorer icon, helps you locate files and folders in drives, special links, and libraries.

Selecting "Computer" displays drives and contents

Address Bar
Toolbar
Hard Drive (C)

Start Menu   Windows Explorer   Shut Down

Links to your file libraries, special links, and drives   Drive contents displayed

Windows 7 uses the Windows Explorer icon on the taskbar to locate files and folders in specialized **libraries**. These libraries can be used to gather content for special folders from various locations to be placed in certain categories of files. Lists of recent documents and applications can also be found using Windows Explorer.

TOOLKIT TIP You can create a shortcut to place the Computer link on the desktop by selecting the Start menu, and then the Computer link; right-click with your mouse to select Show on Desktop. This way, with the shortcut on the desktop, you can simply double-click on it to open the Computer dialog box.

Next, we will navigate around the Start Menu and use the Computer function to locate files.

1. From the desktop on your Windows computer, select the Start Menu (Windows icon).

2. Select Computer to display the drives (see Figure 1-12). Select the Local Disk (C:) to show folders, files, and applications on your hard drive, and use the back and forward arrow buttons to move between previous windows. Play with this feature until you are comfortable looking for files.

3. With folders displayed, select the View tab to display choices of various layouts, then select the view most comfortable for you.

4. You will see various links to libraries and locations on the left side of the display window; feel free to click on these links. If you are not sure where you are, click on the down arrows in the address bar or on the navigation arrows up top to display previous locations to go back to (see Figure 1-13).

▷ FIGURE 1-13

You can select from categories of file libraries on the right side to locate personal files; click the down arrow to return to a previous location.

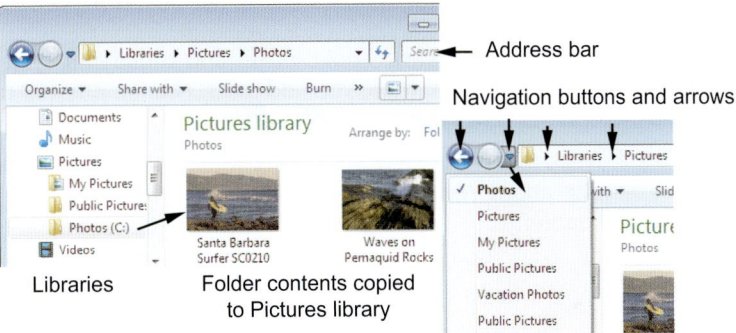

Libraries   Folder contents copied to Pictures library

5. Select Start > All Programs to display applications on your computer.

6. To restart the computer, select Start and click the right arrow icon next to the Shut down icon (shown in Figure 1-12); then select Restart to restart the computer.

7. To shut down completely by powering off, select Start, then select Shut down. *Always shut down your computer in this manner;* never try to power off by removing the plug, or shutting off the power, because this may damage data on your PC.

8. Click on the Windows Explorer icon on the taskbar and navigate around the libraries and folders within to see the ease of this function. The Pictures library, for example, is where you would locate and organize folders of images.

WINDOWS 7 HELP AND SUPPORT, AND CONTROL PANEL

The **Help and Support** center in the Start menu is where you will also find all kinds of tutorials, troubleshooting, and maintenance information to help keep your computer performing optimally and to customize your settings; a box area also allows you to search for information (see Figure 1-14). The **Control Panel** lets you make modifications within your computer, like adding and removing

The Help and Support center helps you to troubleshoot or fine-tune your computer and search for information. The Control Panel allows you to make changes within your computer.

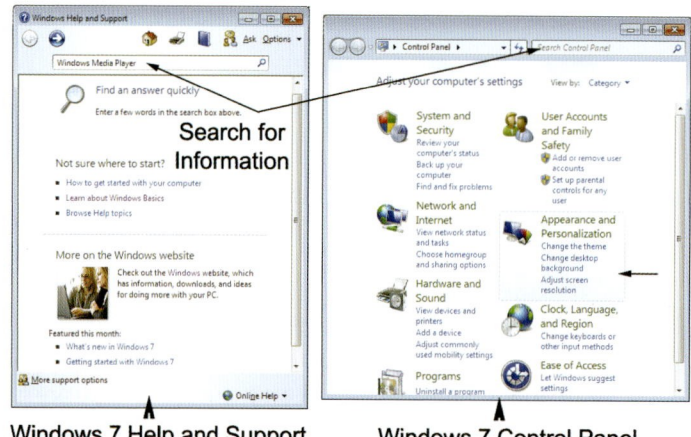

Windows 7 Help and Support   Windows 7 Control Panel

programs, updating applications, and modifying system functions and monitor displays. Here is where you add fonts, change Internet options, adjust Accessibility options, and set network connections.

Next, we will review your skills with the Windows 7 tutorials and get information about Windows Media Player for the Toolkit Extra section at the end of this chapter.

1. From the Start menu, select the Help and Support link; feel free to click on the Windows Basics link (see Figure 1-14) and browse through the tutorials.

2. After you feel comfortable working in Windows basics, in the Help and Support section, select the What's New link to get a peek at the new Windows 7 experience. Check out Using Windows Flip 3D, Side Bar, and Aero Peek; these programs make life more interesting and spice up your desktop. You can also type keywords in the Search box. Enjoy!

3. Back in Help and Support, type "Windows Media Center" in the Search box, then press Enter.

4. Look through the topics and navigate using the back and forward buttons to read about copying music from CDs and creating your own CDs.

5. Print out pages on these topics and on how to use Windows Media Player to play music, Internet radio, and videos by clicking in the print icon in the Navigation bar on top. Close the window when you have finished.

6. To check out your computer's display settings, select Start > Control Panel > Appearance and Personalization; observe your current settings. Note: If you are on a secure network, you probably will not be able to access Control Panel for security reasons.

7. Close the window when you have finished.

THE WINDOWS 8 ENVIRONMENT

Windows 8 is Microsoft's current operating system with a consistent, yet different graphical user interface for consistent use on personal computers, laptops, smart phones, and tablets. Users will find that when their Windows 8 computer starts, it displays a series of squares or "tiles" that display as applications, or are referred to as **apps**. This is called the **Start Screen**, which is a layer of favorite applications over the desktop screen, which looks familiar to the Windows 7 desktop. The **Desktop Screen** is accessed by clicking on the Desktop tile found on the Start Screen, or by pressing the Windows four-square logo key on the keyboard next to the ALT key. To return to the Start Screen press the key again, it acts as a toggle between screens.

This new interface can also be used with devices that use touch screen technology, where the user would create swipe and gestures to move between screens, and tap once to select files or commands, instead of using a mouse to click. Tapping twice on a screen would be the same as double-clicking with a mouse to open a folder. *Note: In the exercises mentioned, only mouse operations are described, although with touch screen devices, the same operations are completed with simple tapping, gestures, and swiping.*

WINDOWS 8 START SCREEN

In Windows 7, the Start Menu is a button on the bottom left of the desktop where you select applications, documents, stored images, and music from a menu list. In Windows 8, these menu items or icons are part of that "layer" of selections over your Desktop Screen referred to as the Windows 8 Start Screen where your applications are displayed as individual **tiles**, replacing the Start Menu button used previously in Windows 7 (Figure 1-15). The Start Screen is the control center for Windows 8, and is used the same way as the Finder interface on the Mac.

▷ FIGURE 1-15

Windows 8 Start Screen and Desktop Screen.

Start Screen (tiles)

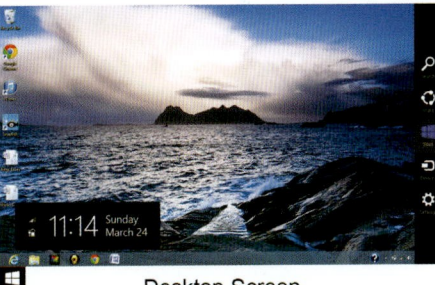
Desktop Screen

- Some of the applications are part of what are called **live tiles**, which display information without clicking on the application tile, like the Weather tile or the News tile. To see more details of your live application tile, just click on that tile. Doing that with the weather app tile displays it full screen. To close, click the "X" on the far right, or click the four-square Windows logo key on your keyboard to toggle back to the Start Screen.

- To start an app, just click on the app's tile.

- You can also remove unused apps and add your most frequent apps on the Start Screen.

- To view all of your applications, right-click the Start Screen background (not the tiles) and select "All apps" on the bottom toolbar. You can also select an arrow that displays downward on the background to display all apps, or swipe from the middle of the screen.

- To toggle between the Start Screen and the Desktop Screen layer underneath, hover your mouse on the bottom left corner to display the Windows (four-square) icon and click. It's simply a toggle to move between both screens (Figure 1-16). Right-click on the icon to display a shortcut context sensitive menu. You can also press the Windows icon on your keyboard next to the ALT key to toggle between screens.

▷ FIGURE 1-16

The Start Screen in Window 8 replaces the Start Menu button in Windows 7.

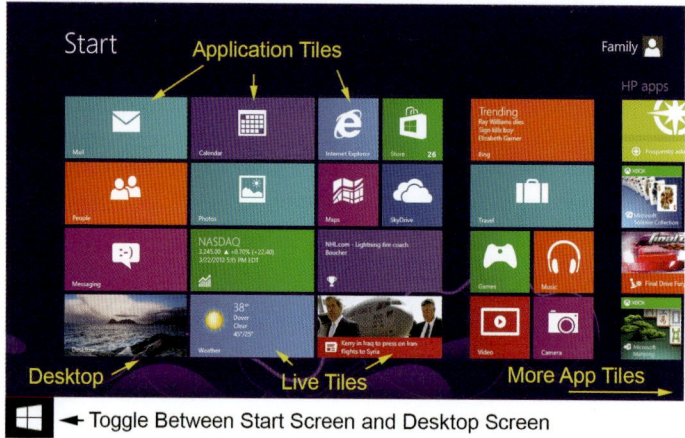

◄ Toggle Between Start Screen and Desktop Screen

For viewing more tiles, scroll using your mouse on the bottom scroll bar from right to left, or if you have touch screen capabilities, like with a tablet, use your fingers as gestures to swipe right to left.

CUSTOMIZING YOUR START SCREEN APPLICATION TILES

Start Screen apps are different from the "classic" Windows apps you may be used to using. Applications fill the entire screen instead of opening in a window. If you don't like the way your apps are arranged on the Start screen, you can rearrange them by moving them wherever you want. You may also find that the animated live tiles are too distracting, and you can easily turn them off so that they will display a plain background with no animations. Closing an app involves dragging from the top of the screen to the bottom.

In Windows, when you right-click on any app tile, a **Tile Control bar** displays on the bottom with options related to the app you are selecting. If you right-click on any open area of the desktop screen, or on a file or folder icon on the screen, a shortcut context sensitive menu appears to give you some basic choices relating to what you are selecting.

Opening, Moving, Closing, and Turning Off Application Tiles

Here you will complete some of the basic operations with Application tiles (be wary that your network security may not allow you to try these exercises). In this exercise you will open, move, close, and turn off an app tile on the Start Screen.

1. On the Start Screen, locate and click the application tile that you want to open. If you hover your mouse over a tile, it will display the tile name. Choose the "News" or "Sports" live tile, for instance.

2. The app will open and fill the entire screen.

3. To display options on the bottom control bar, right-click on the screen.

4. You can also right-click on an app tile to display control options, like resizing your tile to help organize your Start Screen (Figure 1-17).

5. To close the open app tile, hover your mouse at the top screen area of the open application where you'll see the cursor change to a hand icon.

6. Click, hold, and drag from the top edge of your screen with the hand cursor icon to the bottom of the screen, the open application will shrink and close, and you'll be returned to the Start Screen.

7. To move an application tile, click and drag the application tile to the desired location on your Start Screen. Try moving the tile "Navigating in Windows 8," or pick any tile.

8. Release the mouse and your tile will be moved to its new location.

9. To turn a live tile off, right-click the application tile you want to change. A Control bar will appear at the bottom of the screen.

10. Click Turn live tile off, and the graphic tile will change to a plain background.

▷ FIGURE 1-17

Start Screen control options at bottom of screen for selected application tiles.

NAVIGATING THE WINDOWS 8 DESKTOP AND USING "HOT" CORNERS

The Windows 8 desktop functions much like the Windows 7 (and Mac) desktop, it has icons for files, applications, and special functions like the Recycle Bin, which stores and restores deleted files much like the Mac's Trash icon. Windows uses what is called the taskbar on the Desktop Screen to display minimized active files and applications, similar to the Dock on the Mac. You can access the desktop by selecting the displayed tile on the Start Screen, by pressing the Windows logo key on your keyboard next to the ALT key, and by clicking the Windows icon in the bottom left corner of the Start Screen.

In Windows 8, moving your mouse in each corner (or using your fingers if you have touch screen capabilities) and dragging outwards provides access to switching between applications, switching between the Start Screen and the desktop, and access to the **Charms bar** which provides quick access to special related applications, tools, and features.

- With the Desktop Screen displayed (click the desktop tile in the Start Screen if needed), move the mouse to the upper right or lower right corner to display the Charms bar. For touch screens, use simple swipe gestures.

- To switch between any open applications or files (or if you were in Start Screen display, it would display the desktop), hover your mouse over the top left corner.

- To switch back to the Start Screen, hover your mouse over the bottom left corner.

- If you have several applications open, you can switch between them by hovering the mouse in the upper left corner and then moving the mouse down. This displays a list of all of your open applications, and you can click the desired app to switch to it.

- Note: For quick access of the Start Screen, press the "Windows" four-squared logo key on your keyboard, located next to the ALT key.

WINDOWS 8 CHARMS BAR

The Charms bar contains several icons, which are called charms, and each one contains different options (Figure 1-18):

▷ FIGURE 1-18

Windows 8 Desktop Screen.

Hover cursor over top or bottom right corner
and drag to swipe to the left for Charms bar

Taskbar displays minimized active applications and files   Charms bar
(No Start Menu button)

- The **Search charm** lets you find applications, files, or settings on your computer.

- The **Share charm** is basically a copy and paste feature that is designed to be as convenient as possible. It allows you to "copy" information (such as a photo or web address) and "paste" it into another app. For example, if you're reading an article online, you can share the address with the Email application, which lets you email the article to a friend.

- The **Start charm** switches to the Start screen. If you're already on the Start screen, it will open the most recent app.

- The **Devices charm** shows any hardware devices or peripherals that are connected to your computer, such as printers, monitors, or digital cameras.

- The **Settings charm** lets you access general settings for your computer, as well as settings for the app you're currently viewing. For example, if you're in Internet Explorer, you can go to the Settings charm to access your Internet Options. This is where you want to correctly power down or shut off your computer without damaging data.

To Shut Down Your Computer in Windows 8—Using the

Settings Charm

It's very important not to just turn off or unplug your computer as data on your drive can become corrupted. In earlier versions of Windows, you would shut down your computer correctly from the Start menu button. In Windows 8, you use the Settings charm for power options on your computer.

▷ FIGURE 1-19

Using the Settings charm Windows 8 to shut down your computer.

In this exercise, you will shut down or restart your computer properly.

1. Hover the mouse in the upper or lower right corner of your screen to access the Charms bar.

2. Select the Settings charm (Figure 1-19).

3. Click Power and select Shut down if you are taking a break, otherwise, select Restart to leave on for the next exercise.

WINDOWS 8 DESKTOP: USING FILE EXPLORER, LIBRARIES, AND RIBBONS

On the Desktop Screen in Windows 8, **File Explorer**, previously named Windows Explorer in earlier versions, is the central place where you can access any content on your computer to make changes, adjustments, retrieve information, or make deletions. Here you can also find recent downloads, places you've been on the Internet, access to your desktop icons, and information on your computer hard drive, flash drives, and other devices connected to your computer. Files and folders are placed in and can be located in specialized **libraries**. These libraries don't actually store your files and folders, they are used to gather content and keep them organized in certain categories (Documents, Pictures, Videos, and Music categories). For instance, photos would be found in the Pictures library, but you may have a folder of photos on your desktop for quick access.

The Windows 8 interface has an integrated feature called a **Ribbon**, used in Microsoft Office applications, which groups similar functions, tools, and commands together and provides special tabs with more options or features on selected images, videos, music, and documents. For instance, select a photo, and you'll find a Picture Tools tab with lots of options in its ribbon you can select in regards to that selected image. Click on a music icon and you'll find a Music Tools tab with options for enjoying your favorite music. Selecting just folders provides options for just the content within the folder. In the Pictures library, a folder of images could be set up for a slide show. On each Windows ribbon, the Home tab is always the default tab that displays basic functions first.

The icon for File Explorer is displayed as a "folder" icon on the Desktop Screen's taskbar. In Windows, when a window opens within the desktop, you have options in the top right corner of minimizing the window to an icon in the taskbar, maximizing or restoring the window to its original size, or closing the window all together using the red X button. Underneath these buttons you will find an inverted "V" which is a toggle to hide or display the Ribbon. The question mark button is Windows help for the application. You can also resize a window by clicking and dragging on the window's edge or corner.

You will use File Explorer to navigate and look for images in the Pictures library.

1. Make the sure the Desktop Screen is displayed, and then click on the File Explorer icon on the Desktop taskbar.

2. When it opens, you will see where you can navigate to different spots or recent places on your computer, and the various libraries displayed on the left side of the display window.

3. Click on the Pictures library icon once on the left side of the display window to bring up folders with images. Notice the Library Tools and Pictures Tools tabs appear over the Manage tab, with specific settings for your folder and its contents with other tabs (Figure 1-20A).

4. Double-click on one of the folders to open up choices for photos or images.

5. Click once on one of the images and notice the Picture Tools tab again over the Manage tab, and other tabs. Note: If you double-click by mistake the image will open up in the default graphics program assigned to it. Close that program if that occurs.

6. Click on the tabs (Home, File, Share, View, Manage) to see various options and commands you can choose for your selected image.

7. If you lose the screen you're on, try to move your cursor up to the left corner of your computer and select the thumbnail, which should bring you back to the previous open screen or open app, or in our case, File Explorer.

8. Feel free to explore the Music and Documents libraries. Leave open for the next exercise.

▷ FIGURE 1-20A

Windows 8 File Explorer, Libraries, and Ribbons.

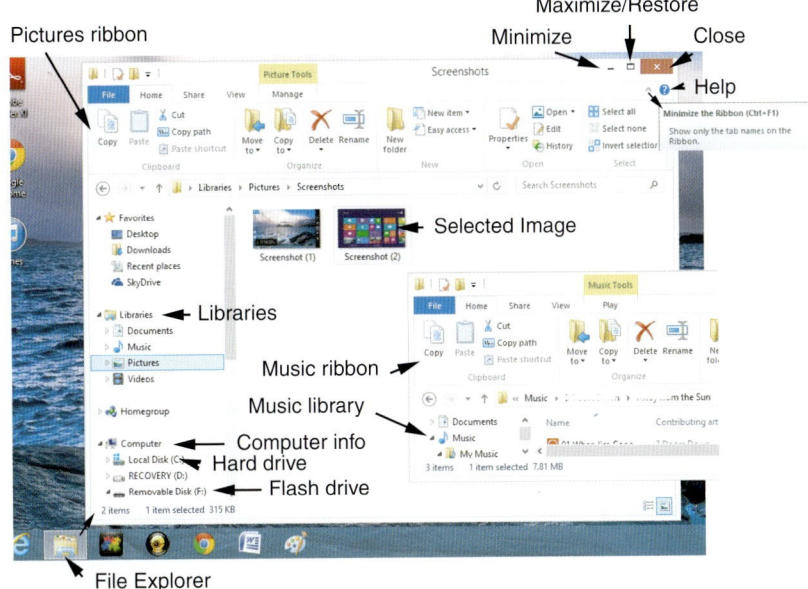

To Change the Content View and Sorting

When using File Explorer, the ribbon's **View tab** makes it easy to change the way files are displayed and sorted within a folder. For example, you may prefer to see your files as a list when viewing documents and as large icons when viewing pictures. Depending on the folder, you may also want to sort your files using various methods. You can sort files by size, name, date created, date modified, file type, and much more.

Here, you will use the ribbon's View tab to display files as large thumbnails.

1. As was done in the previous exercise, click on the Pictures library icon once on the left side of the display window to bring up folders with images.

2. Select the View tab and then choose large icons from the Layout group (Figure 1-20B).

3. Click the Sort by button and then choose your preference from the drop-down menu.

4. Close when done and return to the Desktop Screen for the next optional exercise.

Optional Exercise: To Add Folders to Libraries

Some folders, such as Documents, Pictures, and Music, are included automatically in your Libraries. You can also add additional folders in your Libraries group. Note: If you are on a secure network, you may not be allowed to perform this exercise.

For this exercise you will create a folder of images on the desktop and also one in the Pictures library without changing the folder's location.

1. Create a folder of images from the Internet or another source on your desktop, then right-click or hover your mouse over the folder.

▷ FIGURE 1-20B

View options in Ribbon for Picture Library. Use CTRL-click to create additional new Library.

View Options in Pictures Library Ribbon

2. Right-click on the folder and select Include in library, then choose Pictures to select the Pictures library.

3. The new folder will now be included in the Pictures library. The photos will also be viewable in the Photos app from the Start screen.

4. You can also create a new library, just right-click on Libraries, and then select New > Library. Another way to create a new library of your folder of images is to right-click on the folder, and select Include in library > Create new library. Afterwards, highlight and rename your new library.

FILE EXPLORER'S COMPUTER FUNCTION

When you first click on the File Explorer icon on the desktop, the default Computer tab displays on a special Ribbon entitled "This PC" that allows you to find direct information about your computer. On this Ribbon you can find information about your hard drive, and any information on portable drives and flash drives connected to your computer, along with files and folders, and observe their contents. It also provides special commands so you can choose what to do with files you've found.

Here you'll locate the files and folders on your drive.

1. Select the File Explorer icon on the Desktop Screen to open up the This PC Ribbon (may not display on a network drive for security reasons). Notice the Computer tab displays with specific commands related to your computer. Notice you can also remove or install programs here as well. Select the system properties link if displayed to view info about your computer's processor and RAM. Leave as is and select the backward arrow to return to the Ribbon.

2. With the File Explorer window open, place your flash drive in your computer's slot. It may display as an "F" drive and may be named. In most cases, Windows 8 senses the flash drive and opens a Ribbon window as "Drive Tools" with options for the contents on the drive (Figure 1-21). Observe the flash drive contents.

▷ FIGURE 1-21

Windows 8 Computer function used to display folders and files, and organized Ribbon of commands.

File Explorer

Drive ribbon

Flash drive

Click drive to display folders and files

3. Click the drive you want to look at, and the folder and files of that drive will be displayed. Double-click folder icons to open and view files and contents. Notice the Drive Tools tab above the Manage tab in the drive's ribbon. Click on the other tabs to view options and other commands.

4. If you right-click on your flash drive, or the Local Disk (C:) drive, you'll find another shortcut menu.

5. Select Properties to see information on your drive.

6. You can also click on the Search box to look for files if you want to try.

7. Click on the red "X" when done to close File Explorer.

TOOLKIT TIP To select something, click on the icon or thumbnail once, to open something double-click the icon or thumbnail, and to view a shortcut or context sensitive menu of limited choices, right-click.

WINDOWS 8 HELP AND SUPPORT, AND THE CONTROL PANEL

The Help and Support center is where you'll find access to all kinds of information, tutorials, troubleshooting, and maintenance information to help keep your computer performing optimally, and provide helpful information as you navigate and learn to work in this operating system. You'll find a box area to search for specific information. The Control Panel lets you make modifications within your computer, like adjusting screen display, installing or removing applications, and modifying system functions. Here is where you can add fonts, change Internet settings, adjust Accessibility options, and set network connections. Both of these functions are found in the Settings charm in the Start Screen or Desktop Screen. In the Settings charm, you'll also find controls to make all kinds of adjustments and network connections, and a PC Info link to find out about your PC's hardware and software.

▷ FIGURE 1-22

Windows 8 Help and Support, and Control Panel.

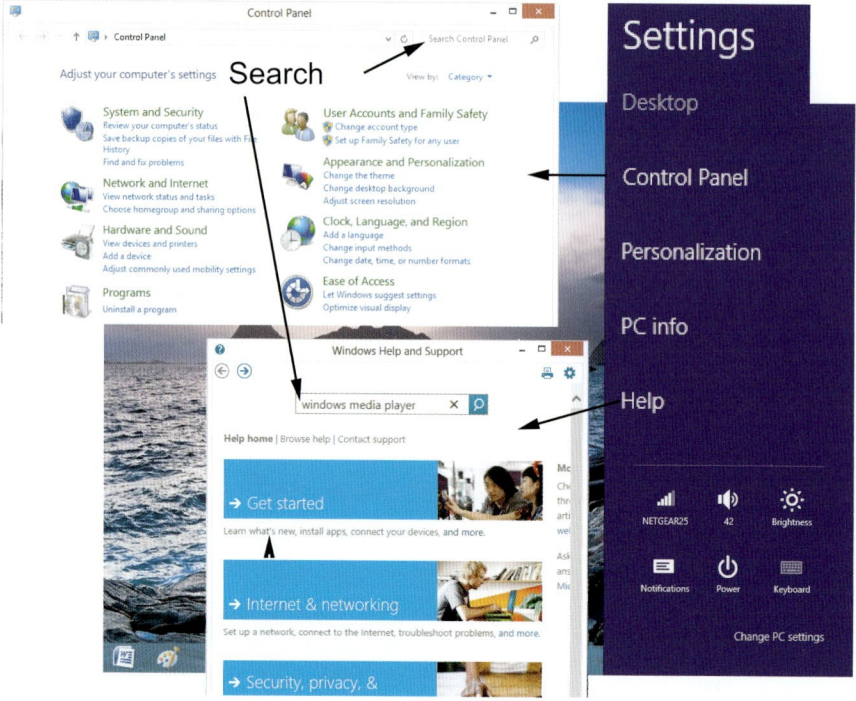

Using the Settings charm to access Windows 8
Help and Support, and the Control Panel

Next, we will review your skills with the Windows 8 tutorials and get information about Windows Media Player for the Toolkit Extra section at the end of this chapter.

1. From the Desktop Screen, or from the Start Screen, hover your mouse in the upper or lower right corner to access the Charms bar, then select Settings.

2. Locate and select Help from the Settings charm. The Windows Help and Support Panel will appear (Figure 1-22).

3. Select the Get started section, and select Get to know Windows to help as a review of some of the features and techniques in using this new graphic interface.

4. Back in Help and Support, or in the current screen you're on, type "Windows Media Center" in the Search box, then press Enter.

5. Look through the topics and navigate using the back and forward buttons to read about Getting Started with Windows Media Player. Close the window when you have finished.

6. Locate the Control Panel from the Settings charm. Select Settings > Control Panel > Appearance and Personalization, to check out your computer's display settings. Note: If you are on a secure network you probably will not be able to access Control Panel for security reasons.

7. Close the window when you have finished. You can also type keywords in the Search box to look for information. Enjoy!

MACS AND WINDOWS WORKING TOGETHER

You will find that functionally both Mac OS X and Windows are very similar and can work together with a few helpful tips to keep documents consistent and universally acceptable to both systems.

SAVING AND READING MAC OS X AND WINDOWS FILES

DESIGN TIP

If you have difficulty reading another computer's graphic images on either Mac or Windows platforms, you can have the file saved with more universal or cross-platform extensions, such as .JPG, .TIF, .EPS, .GIF, or .PDF, depending on the type of file you are using. Graphic extensions all have specific purposes, which we will discuss in the following chapters.

Since you will be designing in the graphics industry, you will be working mostly in a Mac environment. Microsoft's Office suites for both Mac and Windows systems allow Office users to read each other's documents regardless of what type of computer created the file. Files can be saved with universal graphic and text file extensions so that they may be read by either Macs or PCs. Files or applications that can be read by different operating systems are called **cross-platform** files.

The **Save** command saves the file as the same name, with the same extension, and to the same location. The **Save As** command allows the designer or photographer to save files with different names and extensions for various purposes, to save them to different locations, and to create different file names for the same file. When using the Save As command in Mac OS X, the dialog box displays columns as a directory of files within folders to navigate, reading from left to right (see Figure 1-23). Creating folders and saving files within those folders creates an organized path, or directory structure, like having file cabinets with drawers where you organize your files and folders (see Figure 1-24). When saving files in Windows, icons on the toolbar are used to help navigate the directories in a vertical format.

▷ FIGURE 1-23

Save As dialog boxes within Mac OS X and Windows from the Photoshop application.

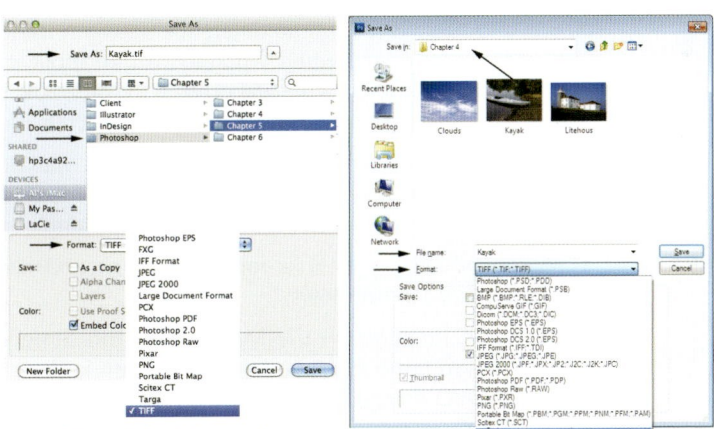

Mac OS X Save As (TIFF or TIF)

Windows Save As (TIFF or TIF)

TOOLKIT TIP When naming and saving a file, avoid naming files using the following characters: / \ : " ? * < >

▷ FIGURE 1-24

Directory structure displayed in Windows Address Bar and Mac OS X Column View of files in Chapter 4 folder.

SAME FUNCTION, DIFFERENT NAME

You will find there is really little difference between using a Mac or Windows operating system, especially when working within applications that can be used by both systems, like the ones we will present in this book. Photoshop, Illustrator, and InDesign are the graphic standards in their respective industries today.

- The Macintosh HD or hard drive icon on the Mac desktop functions much the same as the Computer command or Windows Explorer function in Windows 7, or File Explorer function in Windows 8, for locating contents of drives and folders.

- Aliases, which create links for applications and files on the Mac, are called *shortcut icons* in Windows.

- The Trash function on the Mac is used the same way as the Recycle Bin in Windows to remove deleted files. The Trash icon also serves as an eject button for CD/DVD drives, external hard drives, memory cards, and flash drives.

- The Find command in the desktop Finder application (File > Find) locates files and folders, as does the Search command in Windows.

- The Dock in Mac OS X functions about the same as the taskbar in Windows 7 and 8. They display multiple applications that are running and store minimized documents or files. To work with a running application or active file, just click the icon on the Dock or the tab button on the taskbar.

- The System Preferences application allows you to change settings on your Mac the same way as the Control Panel in Windows.

MAC AND WINDOWS KEYSTROKES

You will find that many basic keystrokes are close to or the same for both Mac and Windows platforms. These keys are mainly used with other keys for certain commands. The key name may be different, but the function is the same. Here are the main ones.

- The Option key on the Mac functions like the ALT key on the Windows keyboard. It can be used to copy files, folders, or object selections.
- The Command key (marked with the beside a loop-cornered square) on the Mac selects multiple nonadjacent items the same as the CTRL (Control) key in Windows.
- The Shift key on both the Mac and Windows keyboards selects a range of the same adjacent items within a group. It is also used to resize graphics proportionately.
- The Return key on the Mac functions the same as the Enter key in Windows; it accepts a command or operation.
- To display pop-up menus that list commands depending on where you click, the Control key on the Mac can be used in conjunction with the mouse. The Windows mouse uses a right-button click to display pop-up menus.

KEYSTROKES TO INCREASE PRODUCTIVITY

Mac and Windows computers use specific keys that perform the same functions or commands. Some of these commands are used universally with Mac and PC platforms. Others are specific to one or the other. Special keyboard shortcuts are also used for special functions within an application. To perform a particular

TO DO THIS	MACINTOSH	WINDOWS
Create a new document	Command + N	CTRL + N
Save a file	Command + S	CTRL + S
Find	Command + F	CTRL + F
Select everything in document	Command + A	CTRL + A
Cut	Command + X	CTRL + X
Copy	Command + C	CTRL + C
Paste	Command + V	CTRL + V
Print a selected document	Command + P	CTRL + P
Bold text	Command + B	CTRL + B
Italicize text	Command + I	CTRL + I
Quit	Command + Q	CTRL + Q
Undo previous action	Command + Z	CTRL + Z
Redo action	Command + Y	SHIFT + Y
Move between menus	(F9 shows all open windows to choose from)	ALT, Arrow keys
Create alias or shortcut to link file or application	Command + L	Right-click mouse to create shortcut

function, hold down the first key mentioned—the *function* key—and then press the *secondary* key. The table on the previous page shows the universal keyboard shortcuts that can be used with any application.

OPTIONS FOR VIEWING AND TRANSPORTING PORTABLE MEDIA

Removable media are CDs, DVDs, memory cards, or portable external hard drives and USB flash drives that can be transported to other computers. Most Mac and Windows computers today have USB and Firewire connections that allow hardware portable drives to plug into any computer to transfer data.

- When you place a CD, DVD, flash or USB drive, or memory card from your digital device—like your camera—into a PC with Windows, a dialog box displays that allows you to choose what you would like to do with the drive; this feature lets you choose whether to copy images to a folder, view the images as electronic slides, view the drive contents, or burn a blank CD or DVD, depending on the type of files you have and the media used.

- Windows: To eject DVD or CD drives, press button beneath the drive tray.

- Macs: When you place a disc or CD, DVD, flash or USB drive, or memory card from your digital device into a Mac, an icon displays on the desktop. You can double-click the icon to display the contents.

- Macs: When using a Mac to eject portable drives, such as USB flash drives, memory cards, CDs, and DVDs, the selected icons must be dragged to the Trash icon first, otherwise your data may become corrupted or not open properly. Afterwards, you can then remove or physically eject the device.

- Macs: You can open and close the CD or DVD tray on an older Mac by pressing the **Media Eject key** (press to simply eject CDs or DVDs on newer Macs), which looks like a triangle with a line under it; this key is located on the upper right corner of the Mac keyboard (see Figure 1-25).

- On a Mac, you can also use the File Menu (File > Eject) to eject selected discs and drives. The Trash icon located on the Dock is also used for ejecting by dragging the drive icon into the Trash icon (see Figure 1-25).

- Both PCs and Macs provide different ways to view files and folders. In both, you can choose between viewing as lists with details or small icons, or as various sizes of icons. On a Mac you can use the Cover Flow View, which allows you to flip through your files, folders, and images as large thumbnail images for quick reference.

Here, you will learn to insert and then eject a CD on either the Mac or PC.

1. Mac users: Press the Media Eject key on the keyboard to open the CD tray and insert the CD or DVD (Figure 1-25). If your Mac has a Superdrive, you do not have to press the eject key: simply insert the disc in the drive.

2. Notice a CD icon displays on the desktop.

3. Double-click the CD icon on the desktop to view the contents. Select the various view options on the toolbar, from lists to icons to Cover Flow, which allows you to move graphic thumbnails across the screen (see Figure 1-26).

▷ FIGURE 1-25

Options for digital media and ejecting discs on Macintosh and Windows computers.

Options using digital media with Finder's desktop menu on Mac

Windows provides a "What to do" display when removable media are inserted in the computer. Windows 8 displays the Drive Tools ribbon when media consists of files and folders.

4. On the Mac, close the window, then select the CD icon on the desktop and drag it to the Trash icon on the Dock to open the tray again.

5. For Macs with a standard CD drive, press the Media Eject key again to close the CD tray.

6. Windows (PC) users, press the button under the CD drive to open the tray and place a CD in the drive; then press the button again to close the tray.

7. Windows users, when the dialog box displays, choose "Open folder to view files." Take a look at the contents, select the Views tab to see what options suit your tastes—whether to view as icons, as a list, or showing details—and then close the window display when you have finished (see Figure 1-26).

TOOLKIT TIP On the Mac, when removing USB drives, memory cards, or portable hard drives, do not remove them physically until they have been dragged into the Trash to be ejected and the icon does not display on the screen, otherwise the data on the drive could get corrupted. You can also click the "up" arrow next to the icon at the left of any open window, where the graphics for drives and folders are, or select the icon on the desktop and use the eject button.

▷ FIGURE 1-26

Options for Mac OS X and Windows to view files, thumbnails, and folders.

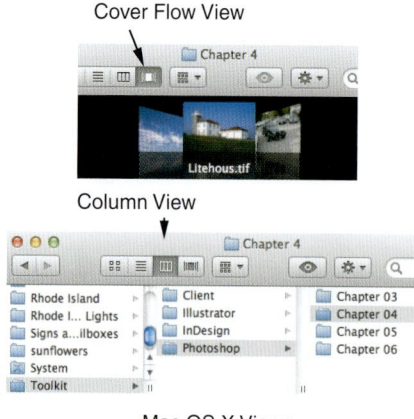

Cover Flow View

Column View

Mac OS X Views

Windows 8 View Menu

Windows 7 Views

CLIENT ASSIGNMENT

In each chapter, this is where you will be given an assignment from a potential client in which the thought process is discussed along with a list of action items for you to follow throughout the chapter. In this first chapter, you are the designer, and your assignment is to create specific folders on your hard drive that will be used to copy text assignment files which you will download from the publisher's website. You will be able to retrieve, edit, and save files in these special folders.

Designers need to keep organized by managing files and folders to maintain productivity. These folders will help you manage files within these folders to keep you organized as you proceed through the chapters. You will be given the basics in Mac OS X, Windows 7, and Windows 8 platforms to familiarize you with their similarities and differences. You will also be shown various fun applications and techniques that both operating systems use to keep your desktop from being too cluttered with files and open windows. At the end of the chapter, in the Advanced Users section, you will create electronic slide shows of chosen images. In the Digital Toolkit Extra section, you will learn to burn music, photo, and data CDs using special applications in both Mac OS X and Windows.

PROJECT: TEST DRIVE MAC OS X AND WINDOWS

ACTION ITEMS

Each chapter will provide a bulleted list of "Action Items" that will give you an insight as to what main exercises you will be completing throughout the chapter, including an Advanced Users section you can try at the end.

- Create an initial folder called *Toolkit* on your hard drive or portable drive.

- Inside the *Toolkit* folder, create *Client, InDesign, Photoshop,* and *Illustrator* folders for the book exercises.

- Copy chapters downloaded from the publisher site to the folders you created.

- Create a shortcut (Windows) or an alias (Mac) on the desktop to the *Toolkit* folder for quick access and search for files and applications.

- Keep your desktop from getting too cluttered using special fun applications and techniques.

- Advanced Users: Create an electronic slide show of your images.

MANAGING FILES AND FOLDERS

One of the most important things a designer or photographer can do to be productive is to get organized. Creating folders and placing files within those folders saves time spent searching later on. You can also create shortcuts or aliases (Mac) for files and applications on the desktop, which also provides quick access to current files but be careful; having too many can create quite a mess on your desktop.

You can use the Dock on your Mac or the taskbar in Windows for shortcuts or aliases to software applications. Using commands to locate files eliminates the guesswork of having to manually look around. Understanding how to download files, and how to move and copy files to another location helps you build a logical directory of files and folders. Learning the basics of both Mac and Windows operations will help familiarize you with their similarities and differences.

MAC OS X AND WINDOWS: DOWNLOADING THE STUDENT DATA FILES FOR ALL THE BOOK EXERCISES

In this 7th edition, you can download all the "Student" files needed to complete the exercises in each chapter from the book publisher's website at *www.CengageBrain.com*. In addition, you'll also find a special link, *Extras & Goodies,* for additional tutorials and information for each chapter beyond the exercises in the text to broaden your knowledge. When you select a file to have it downloaded to your computer, they are automatically placed in a *Downloads* folder. On Macs, the *Downloads* folder is located in the Go menu, or under the Hard Drive > Favorites > Home sidebar. In Windows, the *Downloads* folder is located in the My Computer > Favorites section. You can also choose to save the file to a specified location.

You will find all files are in a compressed format to keep the file size down and to combine multiple files together as one file, which makes it more convenient to download. They will have a ".zip" extension to indicate they are compressed files. Your compressed files can be opened automatically to show individual student data files using the applications WinZip for Windows, or ZipIt for Mac. These free applications can also be downloaded from the site as well, if you need them.

For this exercise you will download and save your student data files on your desktop.

1. First, you need to create a folder on your desktop called *Student Files*. This will be your main folder to place all downloaded files into. To create a folder on the Mac, select File > New Folder from desktop Finder menu (or press the CTRL key and click). You will see a highlighted "untitled folder" on the desktop and type "Student Files" over it, then press the Return key to accept the change. Using Windows, right-click and select New > Folder, and then type "Student Files" over the highlighted text.

2. Open your browser and go to *www.CengageBrain.com*.

3. Type my name as the author (Allan Wood), and either the title of this book (7th edition) or the ISBN of this book in the Search window (the ISBN is listed on the back cover).

4. Click the book title in the list of search results. When the book's main page is displayed, click the Access Now button under Free Materials.

5. To download files, select a chapter number and then click on the Student Files Chapter link on the left navigation bar to download the files (Figure 1-27). Click on the file to be downloaded. On the Mac, it will go to the specified Downloads folder. In Windows, a dialog box will open to allow you to choose to open or save the file to a location. For our purposes, choose to save the file to your Desktop. Leave at defaults.

▷ FIGURE 1-27

Downloading the student data files needed to complete book projects and assignments from the *www .cengage.com* publisher website.

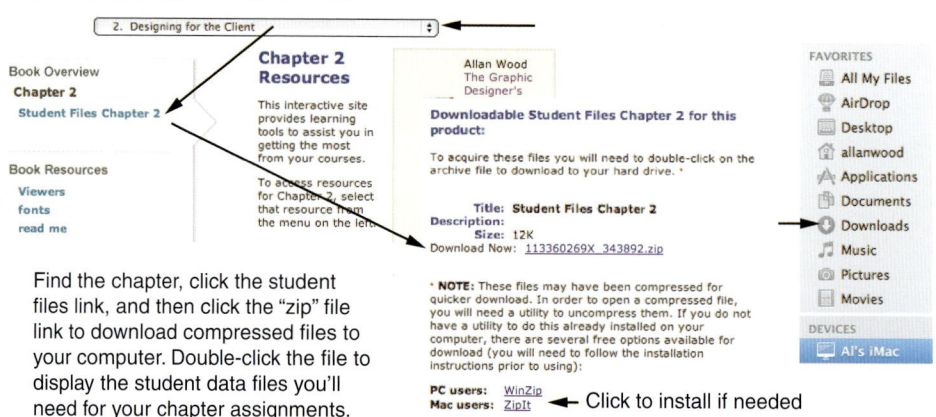

The Graphic Designer's Digital Toolkit

Find the chapter, click the student files link, and then click the "zip" file link to download compressed files to your computer. Double-click the file to display the student data files you'll need for your chapter assignments.

6. To unzip your files, just double-click the file and the computer's compression (decompression) application will display the chapter number folder and its contents.

7. Drag the labeled chapter folder (Chapter 1, Chapter 2, etc.) into the *Student Files* folder you created and continue downloading files for each chapter. Note: If your files will not unzip, just download the free application (WinZip for Windows, ZipIt for Macs) shown at the book site, follow easy instructions, and try again. You'll organize these folders and files in the next exercises. Most computers have these already installed.

8. With the files unzipped and chapters dragged into the *Student Files* folder, you can drag the compressed zipped files into the Trash (Mac) or Recycle Bin (Windows) and delete.

9. Optional: Create a *Goodies* folder on your desktop for additional tutorials outside the text exercises. To access the additional material, on the same web page you downloaded the student data files, click the *Extras & Goodies* tab under Book Overview to download the files. Download at least the first two chapters, unzip, and drag into your *Goodies* folder.

10. You'll find an abbreviated set of instructions on the back page or cover of this book for future reference.

ORGANIZING TEXT CHAPTERS ON YOUR COMPUTER

After downloading the student data files needed to complete the text exercises, it is important to create an organized group of folders on your hard drive, assigned network drive, or flash drive to place these files in, as a work area. In either environment, you will create the main folder, called Toolkit, where all your work exercises from the text will be stored: This will act as a digital file cabinet, and help to serve as a backup of your files. You will then create folders for the text units inside the *Toolkit* folder similar to drawers in a file cabinet; this directory of folders will help you keep track of the files used in the exercises. Chapter folders will be placed inside the unit folders.

TOOLKIT TIP You can use the files for these exercises on your computer's hard drive, network drive, or on removable portable media like USB drives. If you are on a network drive at a school, ask your instructor about setting up your space on the network, where you may need to create a folder to store your work.

MAC OS X: CREATING A FOLDER DIRECTORY

Using the Finder menu on the Mac is one way to create and manage folders on drives (see Figure 1-28). To navigate files and folders, you can set the View, from the Finder toolbar, to Columns; when you are opening or looking for a file on your Mac, you will find in Column View a blue horizontal scroll bar that displays the directory structure from left to right. You can also use the new Cover Flow View to quickly flip through images or documents.

▷ FIGURE 1-28

Creating a directory of folders in Mac OS X for text exercises.

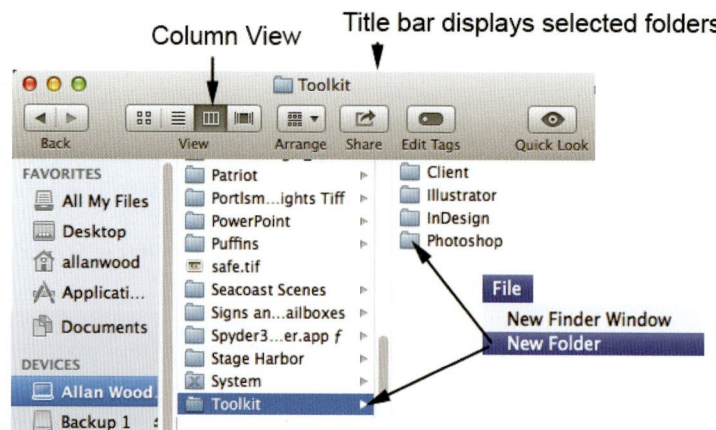

Using Mac OS X, you will create the main *Toolkit* folder and then add the four unit folders (*Client, Photoshop, Illustrator,* and *InDesign*) within the *Toolkit* folder.

1. To create folders on just the desktop, click on any blank area. If you are placing folders on your hard drive or USB flash drive, double-click on the drive icon to open the display window, which shows its contents on the right side (Figure 1-28), then click on the white background to make sure no folders are selected.

2. To create a folder, select File > New Folder from the desktop Finder menu. You will see a highlighted "untitled folder" on the hard drive. You can also right-click with your mouse, or press the CTRL key and click with the mouse, and select New Folder from the display menu.

3. With the words "untitled folder" highlighted in blue, type "Toolkit" over it, then press the Return key to accept the change, or click outside the text area to save the folder name. If it becomes deselected, press the Return key to make the folder name editable. To change a name, you can also click and drag the mouse over the text and type in the new name.

4. Double-click on the *Toolkit* folder icon to display an empty window with the name *Toolkit* in the title bar. This is where you will create your unit folders and store all the files you will be working on in the book.

5. Click in the blank area under "Name," then select File > New Folder from the desktop Finder menu and create four more folders: *Client, Photoshop, Illustrator,* and *InDesign*. Make sure the *Toolkit* folder is selected and displayed in the title bar (see Figure 1-28). If you are having a problem with the placement of these folders, just select them, drag them to the Trash icon on the Dock, and try again.

6. With the four folders displayed inside the *Toolkit* folder window, leave the window display open for the next exercise (see Figure 1-29).

TOOLKIT TIP As mentioned, an easy method of creating and organizing folders is on the desktop itself. When you select CTRL + click on the desktop (or right-clicking if you are using a two-button mouse), a content dialog box displays. Select New Folder to create the folder. Double-click the folder to open it, and create other folders inside as described in Step 5 of the previous exercise. Be wary that if you are on a network such as a school network, and you need to restart the computer, the security setting may wipe out anything left on the desktop. This is a safer method on a home or local computer.

MAC OS X: COPYING FILES AND FOLDERS

First you will set the View on the Finder toolbar to Columns which helps display files and folders for copying. Next, you will select and drag chapter folders that contain the exercise files from the *Student Files* folder on your desktop to the unit folders you created inside the main *Toolkit* folder on your drive. On the Mac, you can drag folders and files right onto the desktop as a temporary holding place, and then drag it into a folder on your drive; or you can drag them into folders between the two open windows.

Here you will drag the chapter folders from the *Student Files* folder containing the text files downloaded from the publisher's website to the window of unit folders you created, or you can drag them to the desktop and then into the unit folders.

1. To place the chapters inside the unit folders, you can drag each chapter folder onto the desktop from the *Student Files* folder first, then drag it onto the *Toolkit* window, or open both the *Student Files* folder and *Toolkit* folder and adjust the windows to both fit your screen, and simply drag between the *Student Files* window and the *Toolkit* window. When the appropriate folder you want to put the contents in is highlighted, you can release the mouse to place the contents into the designated unit folder (Figure 1-29).

▷ FIGURE 1-29

To copy files and folders from one place to another, drag between open windows, or drag folders and files to the desktop, then to the destination folder.

Copying (dragging) folders from *Student Files* folder of downloaded files

Folders copied to desktop

Folders copied to destination folder

TOOLKIT TIP To move a file or folder to another location on any writable drive, select it and drag it to its new destination. if you are copying to create a duplicate of a folder or file, you can create duplicates by holding down the Option/ALT key and dragging between windows on either platform. Copying leaves the original in its original location.

2. Drag Chapter 2 and Unit 1 Review to the *Client* folder, Chapters 3 through 6, and Unit 2 Review folders to the *Photoshop* folder, Chapters 7 through 10, and Unit 3 Review folders to the *Illustrator* folder, and Chapters 11 and 12, and Unit 4 Review folders to the *InDesign* folder. Release the mouse to drop the file in. Note: There are no files needed in Chapter 7.

3. To see how the Mac's new "stacks" function works, drag the *Toolkit* folder to the right side of the Dock *next to* the Trash icon. Click on the folder to expand the *Toolkit* folder contents, and click on any unit folder and its file contents that you may be interested in.

4. When you're done, close the window; you can easily drag your new *Toolkit* folder you created on the desktop to a flash drive as well. Remember to drag the flash drive's icon into the trash to eject it, or you will receive an error message. Keep the *Goodies* folder of additional tutorials separate from the *Toolkit* folder.

PROBLEM If you place a file or folder in the wrong place, you can try to drag it out and over to the correct folder, or simply delete it and try again.

TOOLKIT TIP On the Mac, when you drag and hold the file icon over the folder to place the file, the folder will open to display the contents.

TOOLKIT TIP When you select your drive from your home Mac computer, you'll notice a sidebar on the left with an area designated as Favorites. This contains icons for folders that you can access as the most frequently used, or wish to store as works in progress, and a search area for recently used files. If you are working from a home computer, to make it easier to locate your *Toolkit* folder, you can simply drag (or hold down the Option key to copy) your *Toolkit* folder with its contents and store it inside either the Documents icon as there are image and text files, or within the Favorites icon. Neither choice will harm your computer. To remove, just drag outside the Places onto the desktop or another location. If you are on a secure network this option may not be allowed.

WINDOWS 7 AND WINDOWS 8: CREATING A FOLDER DIRECTORY

Windows 8 uses File Explorer when selected on the Desktop Screen to display drives, folders, and files. When selected they open a ribbon of choices. Windows 7 uses the Computer function command, or Windows Explorer, to display drives, folders, and files. On the left side window display is a list of media libraries or options to locate your files, as in Mac OS X systems. Windows uses libraries to store different types of media. These libraries can be used as another method to organize and gather content for special folders from various locations. You can create various folders in each library. You can use the Views tab to choose the best method of display to copy the downloaded student data files (see Figure 1-30).

▷ FIGURE 1-30

To create new folders, select New Folder from the Tools menu (Window 7) or Ribbon (Window 8), then highlight and name the folder, or right-click, then select New, > Folder.

In Windows, you will create the main *Toolkit* folder and then add unit folders within the *Toolkit* folder. For our purposes, you will create the Toolkit and other folders on the desktop or on your USB drive if you are using your home computer.

1. In Windows 8, select the Desktop tile from the Start Screen to display the Desktop. Select the File Explorer icon to display drives and contents. Using Windows 7, select the Start menu icon on the desktop and then select the Computer function command to display various drives and contents. You'll find "C" usually designates the hard drive, and "E" or "F" is usually a "Removable Disk" or USB flash drive, or other portable drive.

2. If you want to store your work on your portable hard drive or USB drive, double-click on the drive letter to display its contents.

3. If you are creating a folder on the drive, with the display window open, click on the white background on the right side to make sure no folders are selected. If you are using the desktop, go to step 4.

4. In Windows 8, select Home > New Folder. If you are using Windows 7, select New Folder from the Tools menu window display. You will see a highlighted "untitled" folder on the hard drive.

5. Click and drag the mouse over the highlighted blue text and name your folder *Toolkit*; then press the Enter key or click outside the text area to save the folder name.

6. Double-click on the *Toolkit* folder icon to display an empty window on the right side with the name *Toolkit* in the Title bar. This is where you will create your unit folders and store all the files you will be working on in the book.

7. This time, right-click on a blank area on the right side display window; then select New, then select Folder from the content menu and create four more folders: *Client, Photoshop, Illustrator,* and *InDesign.* Make sure the *Toolkit* folder is selected and displayed in the title bar (Figure 1-30). If you are having a problem with placement of the folders, just select the folder and press the delete key on your keyboard and try again. (Note: You can also create new folders using the methods described in Step 4 instead.)

8. Next, you will copy the contents of each chapter you downloaded onto your *Student Files* folder into these organized folders. Leave everything open on your screen for the next exercise.

 TOOLKIT TIP In Windows, if you saved one of the folders incorrectly, drag the folder to the desktop; select the back button on the window display to locate the *Toolkit* folder, then drag the folder back inside the *Toolkit* folder. Another method of creating and organizing folders is on the desktop itself by right-clicking on the desktop. When the content dialog box displays, select New, then Folder. You can then drag the folder and its contents from the desktop to one of the Library icons (Desktop or Documents) on the hard drive's sidebar, or onto the drive list itself. Be wary that if you are on a network such as a school network, if you need to restart the computer, the security setting may wipe out anything left on the desktop. This is a safe method on a home or local computer.

WINDOWS 7 AND 8: COPYING FILES AND FOLDERS

The downloaded student data files you placed in the *Student Files* folder contain all the files you will need to complete the real-life projects and assignments in this book. In this exercise, you will copy those files over to the unit folders you created on your drive or desktop by selecting and dragging each chapter folder into the appropriate unit folders (see Figure 1-31). This way, you can open, edit, and save files to your drive. Use the Views tab to display the folders.

There are many ways to create and store folders with files. Here you will drag the chapter folders from the *Student Files* folder containing the text data files downloaded from the publisher's website to the windows of unit folders you created, or you can drag them to the desktop then into the unit folders.

1. If you have closed the window display, locate the *Toolkit* folder you created and double-click to open the folder to display the four unit folders: *Client, Photoshop, Illustrator,* and *InDesign.* Or if the display is showing the four unit folders from the previous exercise, continue to the next step.

2. Select the View tab and make sure you are in List, Tiles, or Medium Icon View on the toolbar. Then, drag the title bar (top area of open window) over to the right side until your cursor meets the screen edge, making a half window. This will be the "copy to" window.

3. Double-click the *Student Files* folder to display the chapters; resize the window by dragging the bottom right corner. Click and drag the title bar to place the *Student Files* window on the left next to the *Toolkit* window. This will become the "copy from" window.

4. To place the chapters inside the unit folders, click and drag each chapter folder from the *Student Files* window to each unit folder in the *Toolkit* window described below. When it is highlighted, you can release the mouse to place the contents into the designated unit folder. You can also drag each chapter onto the desktop from the *Student Files* folder first, and then drag it into the *Toolkit* window.

5. Drag Chapter 2 and Unit Review 1 to the *Client* folder, Chapters 3 through 6, and Unit Review 2 folders to the *Photoshop* folder, Chapters 7 through 10, and Unit Review 3 folders to the *Illustrator* folder, and Chapters 11 and 12, and Unit Review 4 folders to the *InDesign* folder (Figure 1-31). Release the mouse to drop the file in.

▷ FIGURE 1-31

The easiest way to copy folders from one place to another is between open windows of each.

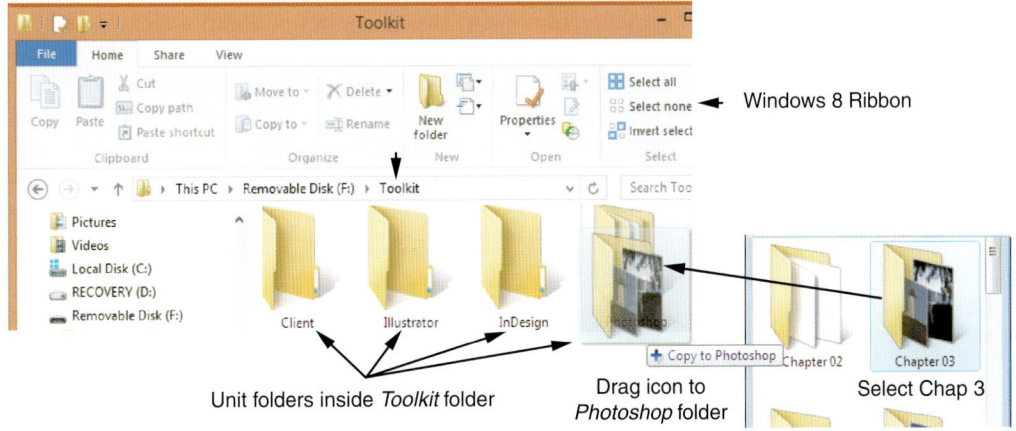

Unit folders inside *Toolkit* folder

Drag icon to *Photoshop* folder

Select Chap 3

Chapter contents downloaded from publisher's website

6. If you have problems or are not sure where you are, or if you are curious and want to look at the files dragged over, you can click on the back or forward arrows to view previous actions, or click on the down arrows in the address bar to display folder contents (Figure 1-32).

7. When you're done, close the windows. Keep the *Goodies* folder of additional tutorials you may have downloaded from the publisher's site separate from the *Toolkit* folder.

▷ FIGURE 1-32

The arrow pointing downward next to the back and forward arrow buttons displays a history of visited locations. To display a folder's contents, click on the downward arrow next to the folder (highlighted) in the Address bar.

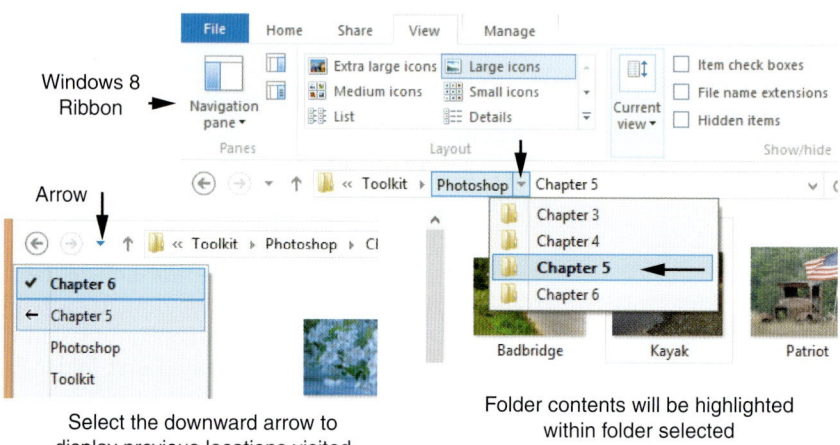

Select the downward arrow to display previous locations visited

Folder contents will be highlighted within folder selected

 TOOLKIT TIP In Windows, as with Macs, you can create or drag folders and files right onto the desktop as a temporary holding place, and then drag them onto a folder on your drive. If you are using your own home computer, another method of storing and organizing your folders and files allows you to copy the folder and its contents into one of the categories of libraries located on the left sidebar. To copy the contents of the *Toolkit* folder you created into the Documents library, for instance, right-click the *Toolkit* folder, then select Include in library > Documents. You'll see the *Toolkit* folder with its contents inside the chosen library. To quickly view and access libraries and their contents, you can click on the File Explorer (Windows 8) or the Windows Explorer icon (Windows 7) on the Taskbar to grab the files you need for your exercises. You can also choose to keep the folder just on your local drive. Your choice.

 TOOLKIT TIP In either platform, click once with the mouse to select an item, and double-click to open it. When opening a Windows file on the Mac, you can double-click the files to open them, or launch the application first, and then select File > Open to display the file instead of double-clicking on the file icon.

MAC OS X AND WINDOWS 7: SEARCHING FOR FILES

Both Mac OS X and Windows provide commands to locate folders and files (see Figure 1-33). Mac users select the File > Find command in the desktop's Finder menu to locate files and folders on a computer or network. You can also locate the contents of these files by searching for words or phrases, based on criteria as a kind or type of file, or media. Windows 7 uses a Search command in the Start menu to focus your searches with an advanced search feature that can be used by typing in specific criteria. In Windows 8, you can search from either the Start Screen using the Search Charm, or from the Desktop Screen (Figure 1-34).

▷ FIGURE 1-33

Using Mac OS X desktop Finder menu, select File > Find, Go > Computer, or use Search for box to locate files. In Windows 7, use the Start menu Search box, Windows Explorer, or use the Computer link to locate files and folders.

Here you will look for the *Toolkit* folder you just created on the hard drive and for the *Goodies* folder you downloaded; it contains additional assignments and information for you to practice with. Check it out!

Macintosh OS X

1. Select File > Find from the Finder toolbar on the desktop.

2. Select Search This Mac and type "Toolkit" in the Search box. You will come up with a list display indicating where the *Toolkit* folder is located. Close the Search when done.

3. Locate the *Goodies* folder on your desktop, or flash drive if you saved the files there. Take a look at some of the additional projects and assignments in the various chapter folders. Close the window when finished.

Windows 7

1. Click Start button, then type "Toolkit" in the Start Search box. The matching folder will display as a list. Close the Search when done.

2. In the Start menu display, you can also select Recent Items (located above the Computer button) to view a list of the last files you worked on. You can use it to locate the *Toolkit* folder you just created. When the folder is displayed, you can double-click the folder to view the contents.

3. Test the Search command to find the *Goodies* folder. Take a look at some of the additional projects and assignments in the various chapter folders. Try using Advanced Search in the Search window display for specific criteria, or click on Windows Explorer icon on the taskbar to locate the Goodies folder, or your *Toolkit* folder. Close the window when finished.

 TOOLKIT TIP For Mac searches, you can also use the Go > Computer command on the desktop Finder toolbar, and type the file name in the Search box. For more advanced users, Mac OS X also has a sidebar that contains a Search For function to locate recently used files, movies, and images. This section also contains icons for creating "Smart Folders" that can collect files, folders, and applications that meet a specific criteria for fast access. For a Windows 7 search, you could also select the Computer function command, or click on the Windows Explorer icon in the taskbar. For advanced users, you can also search on the left sidebar under Favorites for Recent Places to find previously created documents and files to search all drives.

WINDOWS 8 SEARCH (START SCREEN AND DESKTOP SCREEN)

Windows 8 has some built-in search features, which can help you find files, apps, or almost anything else on your computer, or on the Internet. You can search from either the Start Screen using the Search charm, or the Desktop Screen.

To Search from the Start Screen

1. To access the Start Screen, press the Windows logo key on your keyboard. From the Start Screen, click on the screen and just type what you're looking for. Type "weather" and you'll find the search function may default to Everywhere allowing you to search a combination of apps, files, folders, and websites. Sometimes it's easier to change the search to say, apps, to minimize selections.

2. Your search results will appear on the right side of the screen, defaulted as Apps first, and you should find the app you are looking for. You can also choose options for Settings or Files (Figure 1-34).

3. Select Files and try searching for one of the *Toolkit* folder files.

4. You can also use a specific app to search. For example, you can search the People app to find a friend's contact info.

▷ FIGURE 1-34

Windows 8 Search methods for locating applications, files, and folders from the Start Screen and Desktop Screen.

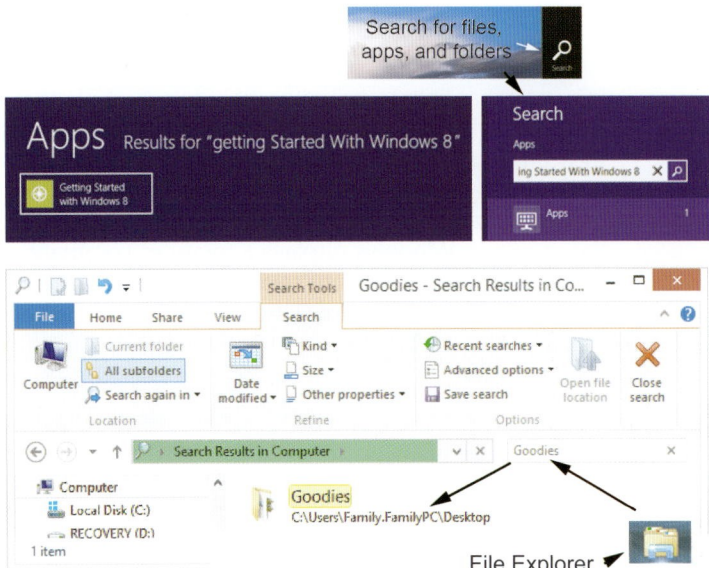

Figure 1-34

Selecting Search Charm from the Desktop

If you are in the Start Screen, select the Desktop Icon or toggle the Windows icon on the bottom left of the screen or press the logo key on your keyboard. Move the mouse to the upper or lower right corner of your screen to display the charms. Select the Search charm and type in what you are looking for. You can choose the default setting "Everything" to search files, folders, apps, and websites, or Settings, or Files to search.

Searching with File Explorer on the Desktop

In addition to the Search feature found on the Charms bar, you could also search for files directly from File Explorer using the Search bar. Whenever you enter something into the search bar, the **Search Tools** tab will automatically open the Ribbon for more advanced searches (Figure 1-34). This can be especially helpful if you are looking for recent searches, a specific file, file type, file by date, or even find file sizes.

Here you will use File Explorer to search for the *Goodies* folder you created.

1. Click the File Explorer folder icon on the taskbar in Desktop view to open File Explorer.

2. Locate and click in the Search bar in File Explorer.

3. Type "Goodies" to locate the *Goodies* folder you had created previously to take a look at some additional projects and assignments in the various chapter folders, or try to locate the *Toolkit* folder (Figure 1-34).

4. Try some advanced searches like largest file size, or a specific file.

CREATING AN ALIAS OR SHORTCUT

You can create a link on your desktop called an *alias* (for Mac users) or a *shortcut* (for PC users) that links to an application, folder, or file that you plan to use frequently (see Figure 1-35). An alias or a shortcut is usually designated by a bent arrow on the icon. You can rename it, duplicate it, or remove it, and it will not harm the original; it is only a link. Mac users can also place documents or files into the original folder by dragging the items on top of the alias of that folder. Right-clicking with the mouse in Windows displays a menu of commands depending on where you click, including shortcuts of selected files and folders. This can also be done with Macs by holding down the Control key and clicking with the mouse.

▷ FIGURE 1-35

Creating a link on the desktop to the *Toolkit* folder.

Creating an alias in Mac OS X

Creating a shortcut in Windows

Here you will create a link to the *Toolkit* folder to work on the exercises in this book.

Macintosh OS X

1. If you used a flash drive or network drive for your files, or created the *Toolkit* folder on your desktop, locate and select the *Toolkit* folder.

2. With the *Toolkit* folder selected, select File > Make Alias in the Finder menu bar. A copy with the label *Toolkit alias* will display in the window. You can also CTRL + click the folder and choose the Make Alias link.

3. Drag the Toolkit icon to the desktop: now you have a link to that folder. If you change the desktop location to the Dock, you can simply drag the folder/icon to the dock and it creates an alias automatically.

4. Double-click the alias on the desktop, and the *Toolkit* folder will open, displaying all the folders you created to work on.

TOOLKIT TIP For Mac OS X users, if you need to locate the original folder, you can select the alias by clicking once to highlight it; then select File > Show Original from the Finder menu.

Windows 7 and 8

1. If you created the *Toolkit* folder on your desktop, or if you used a flash drive or network drive, locate and select the *Toolkit* folder you created.

2. Select the *Toolkit* folder and right-click to get a shortcut display box.

3. Select Send To > Desktop to create a shortcut; this will automatically put it on the desktop as a link. To remove shortcuts, files, and folders, right-click the selected icon and then select Delete, and they will be sent to the Recycle Bin.

4. Double-click the Toolkit shortcut on the desktop to display all the folders you created to work on.

MAC OS X AND WINDOWS: ORGANIZING YOUR DESKTOP

Sometimes your desktop becomes cluttered with windows of open applications and files that you are working on. Both Mac OS X and Windows provide applications and functions to help keep you organized and productive, and still have fun.

MAC OS X DESKTOP

To organize your folders, Mac OS X has a Stacks feature mentioned earlier in the chapter that allows you to create folders of various types of documents, applications, and images, so that when you click on a stack folder, it springs open in an arc or a grid, depending on the number of items. There you just select what you want to work with. To see what version you have, select "About This Mac" from the Finder's Apple desktop menu.

Using the Dock

As you open applications (or open files to launch applications), their respective icons appear in the Dock, even if they weren't there originally. The Dock keeps applications on its left side, while "Stacks" for files and folders, and minimized windows are kept on its right, separated by a vertical line between them. If you want to rearrange where the icons appear within their line limits, just drag a docked icon to another location on the Dock and drop it. To remove an item from the Dock, drag its icon an inch or more off the Dock and wait a couple seconds, then release; the icon will disappear in a poof of smoke. There are some icons that you can't remove from the Dock, such as the Trash and the Finder.

The Dock provides a lot of flexibility in organizing what applications, files, and folders you want to leave to work on, and what to remove or rearrange to adjust to your workflow. Adobe applications have an ".app" extension. In addition to the applications that automatically are included with the Dock in Mac OS X, you can also add your own applications, files, and folders to the Dock, and you can choose to have them removed as well. By CTRL-clicking or right-clicking on the application on the left side of the dock you have options to keep it on the Dock when the computer restarts, remove it from the Dock (not uninstall), and other options. On the right side you have additional options for adding and removing files and folders.

In this exercise you will launch the Photoshop application on the Dock, create a stack of files, and minimize the Photoshop application using the Dock.

1. Launch the Photoshop application. If it is not displayed on the Dock, select Go > Applications > Adobe Photoshop CC > Adobe Photoshop CC.app. As the application opens, you'll see its icon displayed on the left side of the Dock with a white dot underneath to indicate it is active (Figure 1-36).

2. CTRL-click or right-click on the active Photoshop "Ps" icon and select Options > Keep in Dock so that Photoshop remains on the dock when the computer restarts.

3. Insert your flash drive, and drag a folder of images or contents, or even your *Toolkit* folder, onto the right side of the dividing line on the Dock.

4. To display the contents, just click on the folder, and the Stacks feature will spring open the contents for you to view. If you have a folder of other folders, like the *Toolkit* folder, you will find the stack of multiple folders will display, and when you click on one of the stacked folders, the contents are displayed in a separate window.

5. You can also select one of the documents or image files you have displayed in the Stack and drag it to the appropriate application, to open that application, and have it displayed in that application's window. Let's say you have a folder of images, click on an image and drag it onto the Photoshop icon and it will appear on Photoshop's desktop. A document would be opened in Word, for example, if you dragged it onto the "W" icon if it displays on the Dock. Go ahead and play.

6. You can also click and rearrange applications on the left side of the Dock, and folders on the right side. To remove folders and files, just click and drag away from the Dock. You can do the same with many applications.

7. With Photoshop open, or any application open, click the yellow minimize button on the top left and watch it shrink to a thumbnail on the right side of the Dock. To open it, just click on it and it fills your monitor screen.

▷ FIGURE 1-36

Options for keeping and removing applications on the Dock. Using Stacks to help with your workflow.

Displaying "Stacks" of files
from *Document* folder

8. To close the Photoshop application, right-click on the icon on the Dock and select Quit, or, in Photoshop, select Photoshop > Photoshop Quit. You can see how this can keep your workflow organized.

Using Finder to Create Tags and Tabs to Organize Your Projects

In the current Mavericks version of Mac OS X, there is an organizing feature in the Finder called **Tags**. Tags are a powerful way to organize and find your files, even documents stored in iCloud (see Digital Toolkit Extra). Simply tag the files you want to keep together with a keyword or phrase, or designated color, to identify the tagged files. Then when you want to find those files, just select File > Find in the Finder menu, and click the keyword tag in the Finder sidebar or enter it in the search field. All the files with that tag will appear together in one Finder window, even if they are being stored in different locations. You can tag a file once, or give it multiple tags to assign it to multiple projects.

For those who are tired of multiple open windows of folders or files from different places on your computer, Mac OS X Mavericks also has a **tabs** feature that allows you to locate folders and files from different locations and create tabs for quick access. This operates the same way as if you were navigating to different websites, and your browser would display those recently visited websites on different tabs for quick reference. You can move and copy files and folders from one tab to another, and you can move your tabs around too. Another great organizing tool!

Here you will create and label tags to a couple of files, and use the tabs feature to access files from different locations of your computer.

1. Find a file or document that you would like to create a new Finder Tag for and CTRL-click, or right-click on it. Then click on Tags... in the popup menu.

2. Type in the name of the new Finder Tag you'd like to create and then click on Create New Tag directly below that (Figure 1-37A).

▷ FIGURE 1-37A

Creating tags of files and folders for quick access.

Tagging File on Desktop

Tagging Folder on Drive

Finding All Related Tagged Files

3. That's it! The new Finder Tag is created and will then be added to the navigation under Tags in Finder for you to use.

4. Find an image file, document, or folder, repeat Step 1, and assign the Tag you created to keep all your work together.

5. To find your tagged work, in the Finder menu on the desktop, select File > Find and click on the associated labeled tag or color. If you use colors for tagging, the related color dot will display whenever you observe a list of files and folders.

6. All tagged files and folders will display in the Finder window. Close when done.

 TOOLKIT TIP Whether you are using Adobe applications like Photoshop, or Microsoft applications like Word, when you select File > Save As, you will find you can also assign your document or image file to a color tag or text tag that you may have previously created, or you can start a new tag. This provides another method for quick access to your files.

7. Optional: To create a tab, from the Finder desktop, insert your flash drive or use your existing computer and select File > New Tab > and select a folder either on your flash drive, or any folder available on your computer or desktop. The folder name will appear on the tab (Figure 1-37B).

8. To create another tab, double-click the preferred drive, either your flash drive or your computer's drive, or a file or folder on your desktop, click on the Action button and select Open in New Tab. A second tab will appear. Note: Right-clicking the folder will also allow you to open the file or folder in a new tab.

9. You can now click on each tab to locate files and folders. Create more tabs if you want. To move them just click the tab and drag between other tabs.

▷ FIGURE 1-37B

Creating tabs to access files and folders in different locations on your computer.

10. You can copy or move files from one to another; to copy, just select a file from one tab, hold down the Option/ALT key, and drag to another tab. You'll find the file or folder copy in the other tab.

11. To close a tab, hover your mouse over the left side of the tab, and select the X. Go ahead and play! Close all your tabs when done.

Using the Launchpad, Mission Control, Launchpad, Dashboard, and Widgets

Dashboard (Figure 1-38) is a feature in Mac OS X that contains small programs called widgets. These programs provide a wide variety of tasks, such as checking stock prices and finding weather information, and may provide links or aliases to larger applications, or info about your printer. For example, a weather widget provides web-based information without opening the web browser. To find special widgets to fit your needs, go to the Apple website at www.apple.com, click on the Downloads tab, and select or type in widgets.

In the current version, you can use various gestures with your fingers to interact with your Mac. You can use this technique with a special Apple mouse (magic mouse), or by using the track pad of your laptop to tap, scroll, pinch, and swipe your way through your Mac using simple finger gestures to move between pages and applications. If you don't have the available mouse or track pad, clicking also works as well. **Mission Control** creates an overview of all your open windows. In Mission Control, you'll find a row of thumbnails across the top of the screen representing Dashboard, desktop spaces, and your full-screen apps. The lower part of the screen shows an uncluttered view of the open windows on your desktop grouped by app (Figure 1-38). To get where you want to go, just swipe left or right, or simply click a thumbnail. You can add and remove spaces with ease. Create a new space by dragging an app to the top row. **Launchpad** (Figure 1-38) is also a feature in Mac OS X that displays on screen every launchable app that is in the Applications folder in the Finder's Go menu. To scroll through to move between pages, simply swipe your mouse sideways with two fingers, or use your track pad if you are using a laptop.

To give you an idea of the power of these features, you'll open up multiple windows and use Mission Control and Launchpad to organize your open windows, and then observe stacks from a folder of documents. You'll also be able to check the weather using a weather widget on Dashboard.

1. With your Mac OS X turned on, open or create a set of documents using your word processor or other application. If you have a flash drive or have access to images, double-click on them to open them up in the default application on your computer. You'll get a better overview with different applications open.

2. To see how Launchpad works, click on the icon on the Dock and select a few applications like App Store, Safari, and iTunes, if you have access to them, and leave the applications open. You may find you are limited due to security at your school, or check with your instructor.

Launchpad   Mission Control   Dashboard

Weather Widget

▷ FIGURE 1-38

**MAC OS X has
Launchpad to view all
your applications at
once; Mission Control
to view all your
open windows; and
Dashboard for special
apps called widgets.**

3. To see how Mission Control works, select the icon on the Dock (F3), or click on it in System Preferences, if it is not available, to see all the open windows of applications and documents, and thumbnails of Dashboard. You'll notice the application icon displays at the bottom of each matching open document window.

4. Select one of the open windows and drag to the top with the Dashboard thumbnail. It becomes its own separate Desktop, which comes in quite handy if you are working on a particular project and want to keep documents grouped together. Click the Mission Control icon again on the Dock to close, and resume the desktop.

5. To check out the Dashboard with its widgets, click on the Dashboard icon on the Dock (if it is missing on the Dock, select Go > Applications > Dashboard), or use Mission Control (F3), and click on the Dashboard thumbnail to see what widgets are displayed. If there is a weather widget, set up for your area. Usually simply click on "i" to change the information.

6. To find other widgets, go to the Apple website at http://www.apple.com/downloads/dashboard/ to see what is available. Go ahead and download one to see how it works.

7. Close down your computer when finished by selecting the Apple icon in the Finder menu bar, then select Shut Down. Do not just turn off or unplug your computer.

WINDOWS 7 DESKTOP

To organize open windows, Windows 7 provides features called Snap, Peek, and Shake. The **Snap** feature allows you to resize open windows, simply by dragging them to the edges of your screen. You can make your windows expand vertically, take up the entire screen, or appear side-by-side with another window. The

Peek (show desktop) function gives you the opportunity to watch open windows instantly disappear to display only the Windows 7 desktop. On the far right edge of the taskbar you'll find a small rectangle; just click to show the desktop, and click again to toggle back to your open windows. If you just want to focus on one open window, use the **Shake** function by clicking the window you want to focus on and give your mouse a shake. All other open windows will disappear except for your chosen window. Go ahead and open a bunch of windows and try these features out!

For quick access to most used applications and files Windows 7 has created a **Pin** function to pin programs to the taskbar and the ability to pin files with a matching application as part of that application's jump list. A **jump list** allows you to navigate around recent files, images, tasks in an application, and even websites. To pin an application, right-click on its icon either in the Start menu and select Pin to Taskbar, or just drag the program's icon if it is on the desktop to the taskbar and select to Pin to Taskbar. You can then just click on the icon much like the dock to open the application, and then click on the icon again to close. The pinned icons stay on the desktop until you unpin them. You can view the jump list to a program by right-clicking on its icon in the taskbar, or by dragging the icon to the desktop. To pin files to applications, simply create an icon on the desktop and drag to the program's icon or the taskbar, which may select the appropriate program. Then select to pin to the application. That's it! From the jump list created for a particular application, you only need to click on the link to access the file. To view thumbnails of your active files in an application or just visited websites, just hover your mouse over the program's icon in the taskbar to see thumbnail previews of any open windows within that application.

Note: As Mac computers have widgets for mini programs, Windows 7 had "gadgets," which are no longer provided due to security issues. Windows 8 uses app tiles that are built in securely into the system.

Here you will pin the Internet Explorer program and another to the taskbar. Be wary that if you are on a network, secure settings may not allow you to perform this exercise.

1. With Windows 7 on, click on the Start Menu button, and then right-click on the Internet Explorer icon (Figure 1-39).

2. Click on the Pin to Taskbar link and you'll see the icon displayed on the taskbar.

3. Go ahead onto the Internet; type www.microsoft.com to access the Microsoft site.

4. Go to a few other sites and then hover your mouse over the Explorer icon in the taskbar to see a list or thumbnail previews of the sites you just visited.

5. If you drag the Internet Explorer icon to the desktop, you may find a jump list of frequent sites and tasks.

6. Click the Start Menu button and click the All Programs link on the bottom to find Microsoft Word, or any application you would like to pin to the taskbar.

7. Right-click on the icon and select to Pin to Taskbar as was done with Internet Explorer. You'll see again the icon is now on the taskbar for quick access. You can then create a document and save to the desktop, then drag to the icon to pin to the application.

Windows 7 features for desktop organization include pinning applications to taskbar, jump lists of recent documents, or websites, and peek function to toggle desktop view.

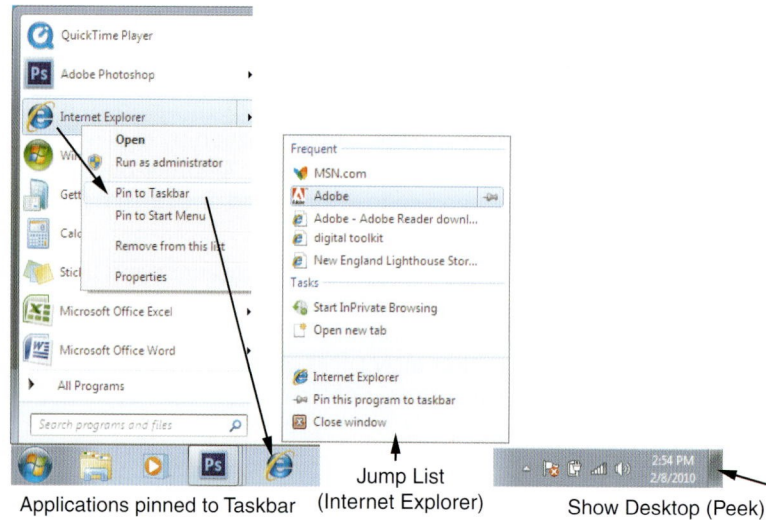

Applications pinned to Taskbar   Jump List (Internet Explorer)   Show Desktop (Peek)

USING THE WINDOWS 8 TASKBAR AND PINNING APPLICATIONS

The Desktop on Windows 8 looks much the same as on Windows 7, without the Start menu button. Windows 8 (and 7) has a feature called pinning, which allows you to pin your favorite programs on the Start Screen as application tiles, or on the Desktop taskbar. Remember, you can access the Desktop by clicking the Desktop tile, by toggling the Start Screen Windows icon on the bottom left of the screen, or by pressing the Windows icon on your keyboard.

By default, the Start Screen doesn't show all of the apps on your computer. You can display all your apps by clicking the arrow displayed on the background, by swiping downward, or by right-clicking on the background to display the Control bar (sometimes referred to as the Tile Control bar) on the bottom of the screen, and select the All apps icon. However, it's easy to pin your favorite apps to the Start Screen so that you can open them quickly. The Control bar displays at the bottom of your screen, when you right-click on the application tile to make the desired change. The Control bar provides commands that also include removing or uninstalling a program. Sometimes you may want to resize an app tile on the Start Screen to help organize your displayed tiles, or to uninstall the application altogether. You can also perform these functions on the Control bar.

To Pin and Unpin an App to the Start Screen

Here you will select a favorite app to the Start Screen. You will also unpin an application tile from the Start Screen, and resize an app tile.

1. Hover your mouse near the bottom left side of the Start Screen under the last row of tiles and you'll find an arrow displayed pointing downward. This will display all the applications on your computer. Select or tap and a screen of

icons will display of all apps (sometimes if you right-click the blank portion of the background, an All apps button will appear for the same function). For touch screens, just swipe downward.

2. Locate and right-click on the desired app icon you want to pin to the Start Screen (don't click on it to launch it), let's say Adobe Reader, to open and read PDF files, or Photoshop, which will be covered in Chapter 3. *Note: If an application opens, one way to close it is to drag from the very top of the screen (displays as hand cursor) to the bottom.*

3. On the Control bar at the bottom of the screen, click Pin to Start, to place it as a tile on the Start Screen (Figure 1-40). *Note: If you choose Pin to taskbar, it will be placed as a minimized icon on the desktop's taskbar.*

▷ FIGURE 1-40

Pinning apps to the Start Screen or Desktop Taskbar.

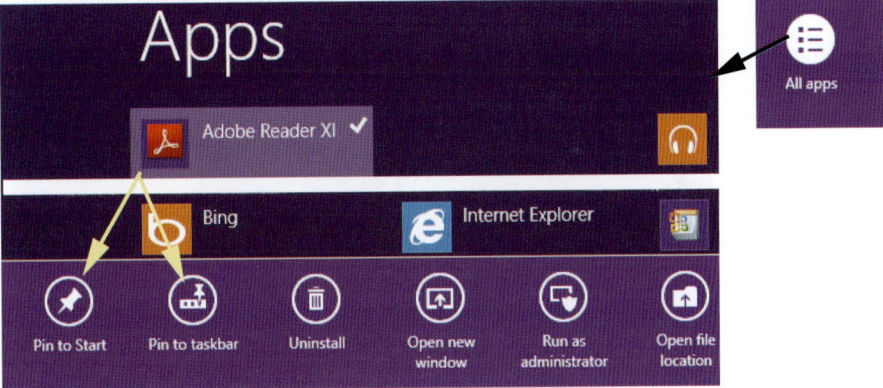

4. Click the lower left corner on the Start Screen icon to return to the Start Screen. Your app will now appear on the Start Screen, but it will pin on the far right side and you may have to swipe sideways, or click on the bottom right arrow to move the screen to the left to view the app's tile.

5. To move the tile, just click or tap, and drag to where you want it to display. A selected tile displays a check mark on the upper right corner of the tile.

6. To unpin the app, from the Start Screen, right-click the desired app tile, or an app you would like to remove from the Start Screen. *Note: This may not be allowed on your network's security.*

7. At the bottom of the screen, click Unpin from Start. The app will disappear from the Start Screen (Figure 1-41), but does nothing to the actual application itself.

▷ FIGURE 1-41

From Start Screen control options provided when right-clicking the selected app, choose to Unpin from Start to remove tile from screen.

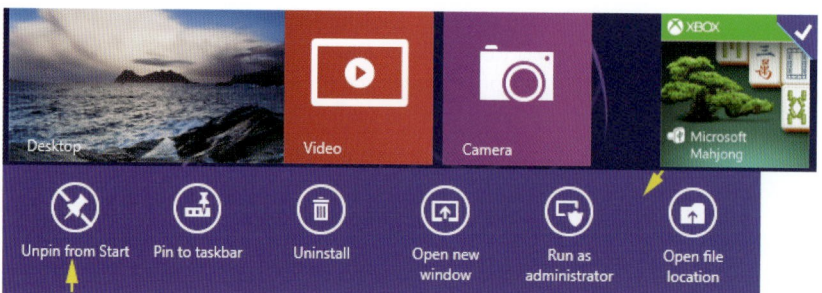

8. You can also choose to make the tile smaller, turn it off, or uninstall it (Figure 1-42). When you right-click on the app tile, choose the Resize icon on the Control bar and change the size of our tile.

9. To create a group of tiles, just click and hold, or right-click the tiles you want to group together, then drag the tiles to a space between other tiles that displays a gray bar and release. This creates a new group.

10. To name a group, just click or tap on the Name group box above the tiles and type in a new name.

▷ FIGURE 1-42

Start Screen control options to remove, resize, or uninstall selected app tile.

To Pin Apps and Folders from the Desktop to the Taskbar

Just as applications and active files can be pinned as tiles on the Start Screen, Windows uses the taskbar on the Desktop Screen to display minimized active files and applications, similar to how the Dock operates on the Mac. Applications can also be pinned to the Desktop taskbar so that when the computer starts up again, the applications can remain on the taskbar for quick access. To launch an application pinned on the taskbar, or restore an active application to its original size, click on its minimized taskbar icon. Files can be dragged from the Desktop or drive onto the application on the taskbar to be pinned for future access. To have quick access to folders, drag a folder of contents onto the taskbar, or on the File explorer icon itself to pin it into File Explorer, then just right-click on File Explorer to display the context sensitive menu.

Here, using the Desktop Screen, you will pin an application to the taskbar, and pin a folder to File Explorer.

1. On the Desktop Screen, click the application you want to open and you will see its thumbnail on the taskbar.

2. Right-click the thumbnail icon and select Pin this program to taskbar from the context sensitive menu. You may also be able to select to Pin to Start to also place it as a tile on the Start Screen as well.

3. In the Desktop Screen, drag a folder, say the *Toolkit* folder or *Goodies* folder you created earlier, or another folder to the taskbar, and you'll find it will display as Pin to File Explorer (Figure 1-43).

▷ FIGURE 1-43

To pin onto the taskbar, right-click on an application, and select Pin this program to taskbar. You can also drag folders to pin in File Explorer.

Pinning iTunes App

Pinning Folder to File Explorer

4. Release the folder onto the taskbar and right-click on the File Explorer icon, where you'll find it added to the "Pinned" list for quick access.

5. To take the icon off the taskbar, just select Unpin this program from taskbar.

Windows 8 Jump Lists

A Jump List is like a mini-menu that you can open from the taskbar of your Desktop Screen. It allows quick access to recent files, frequently viewed items, performance tasks, pinned files and folders, and more. To access a jump list, right-click on the app icon on the taskbar. You may also hover your mouse over a recent document, and right-click to pin your favorite documents, files, or recently accessed websites to the jump list.

Here you'll take a look at the power of using jump lists by right-clicking on File Explorer and an application to display the recent files and folders visited.

1. In the Desktop Screen, right-click on the File Explorer icon on the taskbar to access previous libraries, drives, and folders visited in the Recent section.

2. Click on one of the previous folders to access your contents (Figure 1-44). The contents should display for quick access.

3. In an application that you have pinned to the taskbar, which you are comfortable with, open a series of files and then save and close them on the desktop. If you want to use Word for instance, you can create three documents and save as Test 1, Test 2, and Test 3.

4. Right-click on the application (Word) to display the "recent" files you opened and click on one of the files to open in that application. Close when opened.

5. To pin one of your recent documents to the application list, right-click on the file of folder in the jump list and select Pin to this list for it to remain permanently in the "Pinned" section until you choose to remove it from the list.

▷ FIGURE 1-44

Using Windows jump Lists.

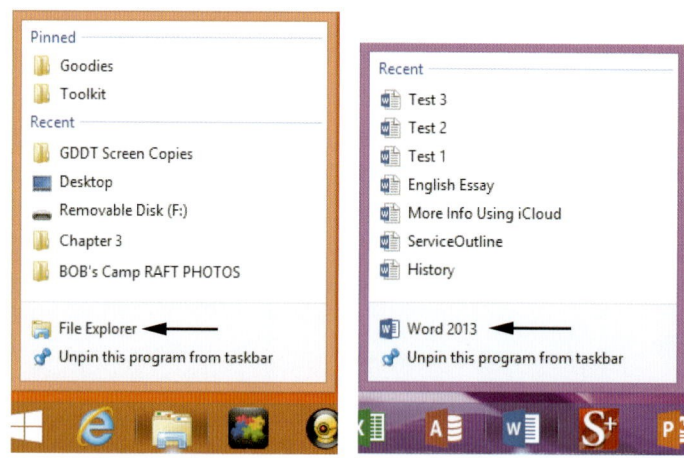

File Explorer Jump List   Application (Word) Jump List

ADVANCED USERS: Creating Electronic Slide Shows of Images

A designer or photographer may need to send their images to a potential client electronically. Mac OS X, Windows 7, and Windows 8 operating systems provide additional applications that allow the designer or photographer to work with different media. In Mac OS X they are Quick Look and Preview; and in Windows 7, you can select between the Pictures category or link, Windows Photo Viewer, or Windows Media Center. Windows 8 uses the Photos application tile on the Start Screen, and Windows Media Player. Both Mac OS X and Windows have a storage folder on the computer's hard drive that you can access through the Pictures link. Windows 7 and 8 allow you to create an instant slide show from this link. In this exercise, you will learn to create slide shows of selected images using Quick Look and Preview applications on the Mac; on Windows 7 using the Pictures link, Windows Photo Viewer, and Windows Media Center; and on Windows 8 using the Photos application tile, Pictures library, and Windows Media Player.

TOOLKIT TIP When downloading images from the Internet, usually the image that you see is full size. Make sure you have an image large enough so that it will display adequately on your screen. Be aware also that when you create a full screen slide show the application may create larger images than the original, which may cause the original sharp image to have a soft or blurry look.

RETRIEVING IMAGES OFF THE INTERNET

Here you learn the most common method of saving images from the Internet to your computer drive (see Figure 1-45), but be wary of copyright laws when copying photos. In this case, you may download images for fair use for educational purposes, but not for marketing or for sale, unless you have direct permission from the originator on a release form. Make sure any images you download appear large enough on the screen you are downloading from.

▷ FIGURE 1-45

Saving images from the Internet on your drive.

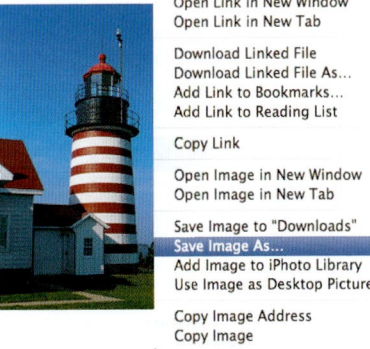

Saving Internet Images on a Mac

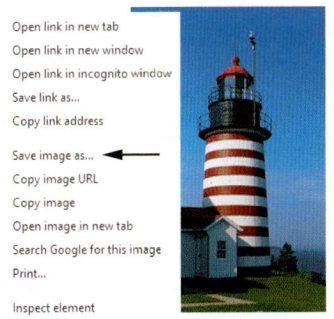

Saving Internet Images in Windows

Macintosh OS X

1. For this exercise, create a folder on the desktop and name it *Images*.

2. Connect to the Internet and find websites that contain images you would like to use for this exercise.

3. Using the Mac, press the Control key and then click the image to get the menu; when a display menu comes up, select the option Save Image As.., locate your *Images* folder, and save the file with its default name, or use your own. If, when you CTRL + click on the image, the menu is not displayed, it is specially protected and cannot be copied. Find another set of images.

4. Locate the *Images* folder you created on the desktop to store the images, and select Save. Your image will download to that folder.

5. Repeat until you have enough images to use in your electronic slide show. Try to keep your images the same size: it makes a better slide presentation.

Windows 7 and 8

1. For this exercise, you can also just create a folder on the desktop and name it *Images*.

2. Connect to the Internet and select websites that contain images you would like to use for this exercise.

3. Using Windows, right-click the image you have selected, and select Save Picture As. If, when you right-click on the image, the menu is not displayed, it is specially protected and cannot be copied. Find another set of images.

4. Locate the *Images* folder you created on the desktop, and select Save. Your image will download to that folder.

5. Repeat until you have enough images to use in your electronic slide show. Try to keep your images the same size: it makes a better slide presentation.

GATHERING FILE INFO AND PREVIEWING IMAGES

Once images are stored, it is a good idea to preview them before adding them to your slide show. Previewing helps you see if the image is too small, because they usually display at full size. It also helps to know what type of file you are using. It is important whenever working with electronic files to keep the file size as small as possible, while still maintaining image quality. Photographic files for electronic media should contain a universal extension, like .JPG, which indicates a compressed file format to keep the file size small. Or they may be saved with a .GIF extension for graphics. We will cover these aspects more in depth in later chapters.

- To see information about a file on the Mac, locate the photos in your *Images* folder, then click the image and select File > Get Info.

- To see what file extension is used in Windows, right-click on the image, then select Properties. Select the Details tab to see the file data.

- Most of the time, images will be either a JPEG of GIF file, such as photoname.jpg, which is fine for this exercise. Make sure your images have JPEG extensions for our purposes here. Other types will be discussed later. Also look for images with a range of a width of between 200 and 800 pixels for your slide show.

- To quickly view your images in Mac OS X, use Cover Flow View.

- To quickly view your images in Windows, use the Computer function to select the folder, and change the view to Extra Large icons to view good sized thumbnails.

- Note: If you double-click on an image and it opens up an application like Photoshop as the default application, check to see if the image is displayed at 100% in the toolbar. That way, you will know it will display on screen full size at 72 DPI, as if it were going to be used for the web. If not, use the View menu and select other options. More on that in Chapter 3.

MAC OS X: CREATING A MANUAL SLIDE SHOW USING QUICK LOOK

The Mac OS X has a Quick Look function that looks like an eye icon to create quick slide shows. This program works great when you need a simple slide show of selected files that can even be displayed full screen. In Mac OS X, you'll find some windows have a double arrow on the upper right you can click for a full screen preview. Quick Look is also coordinated with the Preview application for additional editing, display characteristics, and to display an automatic slide show, or may default to other designated applications, based upon the file's extension.

Check out your images using Quick Look.

1. Locate your folder *Images* you just created.

2. Select the images you want to have in the slide show; make sure you select the image files, not just the folder (Figure 1-46).

3. Click the Quick Look (eye) button on the Tools menu bar, or press the Space bar.

4. A Quick Look window opens with the first selected image displayed.

▷ FIGURE 1-46

The Quick Look function is a fast, easy way to view your images, and play a slide show.

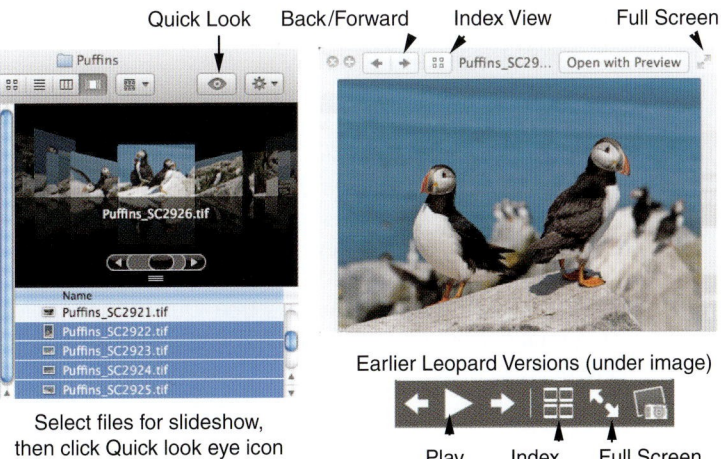

Quick Look   Back/Forward   Index View   Full Screen

Puffins_SC2926.tif

Name
Puffins_SC2921.tif
Puffins_SC2922.tif
Puffins_SC2923.tif
Puffins_SC2924.tif
Puffins_SC2925.tif

Select files for slideshow, then click Quick look eye icon

Puffins_SC29...   Open with Preview

Earlier Leopard Versions (under image)

Play   Index   Full Screen

5. Use the back and forward arrow buttons along the top (bottom in earlier versions), to move from slide to slide or switch to full screen view, or click on the index view to see thumbnails of your selected images.

6. Quick Look allows you to manually scroll through your images. To play a slide show, you can hold down the *Alt/Option* key, which changes the eye icon into an arrow-like play icon. You can also select the "Open with Preview" button, which opens the more robust Preview program, which we'll discuss next.

7. Select ESC key when done. Quick Look can also be used for all kinds of documents and files as well.

MAC OS X: CREATING A SLIDE SHOW USING PREVIEW

The Preview application is used not only for slide shows; you can also perform basic editing operations where you can resize and make adjustments to images and you can view all kinds of documents, as well as images. You can display a slide show of all the images in a window, even at full screen, and controls at the bottom of the screen let you move from image to image or end the slide show. You can also make annotated notes on files with Preview.

In this exercise, you will use the Preview application to view a full screen slide show of your *Images* folder.

1. If you still have the Quick Look program open, select "Open with Preview" to open the application. Or, from the Applications menu in Finder, select Go > Applications > Preview and launch the Preview application.

2. Select File > Open and locate your *Images* folder you created.

3. You do not have to select the individual images, just the folder, and all images will display in the Preview display. Preview not only provides full screen slide shows, but also allows you to resize images, view all kinds of electronic documents, and make annotated comments.

4. Notice you have various options for what you can do with your images, including what view they can be displayed.

5. To view a full screen slide show, select View > Slideshow. If it is grayed out, select the image files first (Figure 1-47).

6. Press the ESC key when you have finished.

On the sidebar, you may find a Pictures Library, which you can use to store your images, or create your own folder of images on the side bar. By double-clicking the Pictures folder, or any special folder you created in the sidebar, it opens up in Preview where you can view the contents and play a slide show. There are other applications that come with MAC OS X that, among other media uses, will also play image slide shows. Apple's free QuickTime application is one, which plays one image at a time, while predominantly playing downloaded movies from the Internet.

▷ FIGURE 1-47

Preview not only provides full screen slide shows, but also allows you to resize images, view all kinds of electronic documents, and make annotated comments.

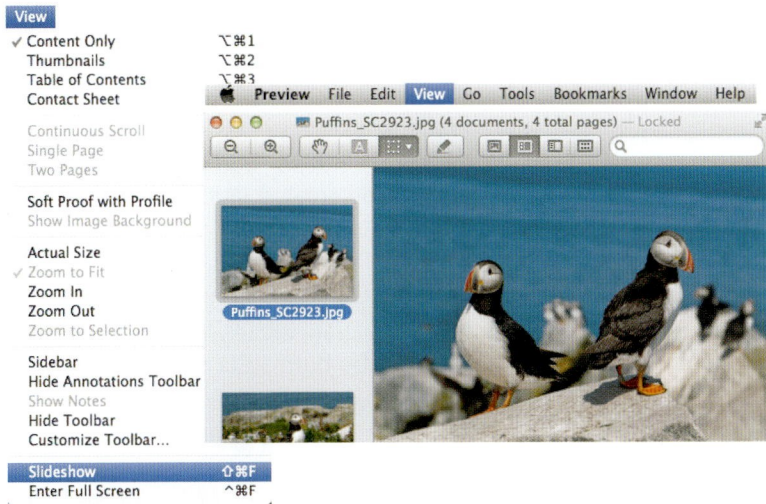

WINDOWS 7: CREATING AN ELECTRONIC SLIDE SHOW FROM THE PICTURES LIBRARY

Storing your images in the Pictures library section on your computer's hard drive allows quick access to folders of images when you select the Pictures link. By creating a folder of your images in Pictures, it allows you to make choices about what you want to do with the images, including displaying a slide show of a folder's contents (see Figure 1-48). Windows 7 users will find that the operating system prefers the user to place images in its Pictures library, which allows you to use the applications discussed here. If you have folders of images in the Pictures library, you can also use Windows Media Player, which not only is used for playing music but can also play slide shows of images, and burn CDs of your work. You can also select image files, create tags, and rate each image. Note: If you are on a secure network, you may not be able to perform this exercise.

▷ FIGURE 1-48

From the Windows Pictures library, select folder of images, then click the Slide Show button. Windows Media Player can also create professional slide shows.

1. If you are using a flash drive, you can use the Computer function to locate the *Images* folder you created, then select to "Include in library" and copy the folder into the Pictures library. If you are using your computer's hard drive, select Start > Pictures, or locate the Pictures library with the Windows Explorer icon, and locate the folder *Images* you created.

2. On the left sidebar, you will find libraries, including Pictures. Select the folder *Images* you created, and click on the *Slide Show* tab button below the Tools menu bar (you will notice there are other choices besides the slide show). View your images.

3. Press the ESC key on your keyboard to stop the slide show.

4. Other selections allow you to email, print, or publish your images to a website. You can also burn a CD of your images from here.

5. If you have folders of images in the Pictures library, you can also use Windows Media Player. Select Start > Windows Media Player or select the icon if it is pinned to the taskbar.

6. Select the *Images* folder to open, and select the Play button to play a professional looking slide show. Press ESC when finished.

7. Extra: To rate images and create captions, select the *Images* folder you created earlier inside the Pictures library. Then select individual images and rate them using stars by selecting the number of stars for each image on the right side. You can also create tags or captions by typing in your tag and selecting Add Caption (Figure 1-48).

WINDOWS 7: CREATING AN ELECTRONIC SLIDE SHOW USING WINDOWS PHOTO VIEWER

The Windows Photo Viewer allows quick access to view, organize, edit, and print digital pictures (see Figure 1-49). When you plug a memory card from your digital camera or images from your flash drive into your computer, a dialog box opens to provide choices to transfer your images to the Pictures library, which is located on your hard drive. You can choose what you want to do with the images, including importing them or displaying a slide show of a folder's contents. You need to

▷ FIGURE 1-49

In Windows 7 Photo Viewer, press the slide show button to view images in folder.

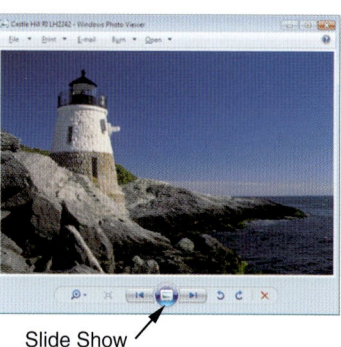

Slide Show

add images to the viewer first before you choose to edit or make changes. If you want to display images in a folder you already have created, select the folder, then right-click the first image and select to Open With > Windows Photo Viewer.

1. Locate the *Images* folder you created and double-click the folder to open it displaying the image files.

2. Right-click on the first image and when the dialog box displays, select Open With > Windows Photo Viewer. Note: Usually you can also double-click the image itself and it may default to open in Windows Photo Viewer.

3. When Windows Photo Viewer opens, view your images as a full screen slide show by selecting the Slide Show button at the bottom middle of the display.

4. Press the ESC key on your keyboard to stop the show.

5. Extra: Other selections on the toolbar allow you to print, email, or publish your images to a website. You can also burn a CD of your images from here.

WINDOWS 7: DISPLAYING AN ELECTRONIC SLIDE SHOW USING WINDOWS MEDIA CENTER

The Windows Media Center allows you to view photos, movies, and all kinds of visual media full-screen on your computer or on your TV (see Figure 1-50). Photos display a very nice professional zoom technique to wow your audience. Simply import images first to the Pictures library on your hard drive, or create a folder to import your images in, right-click on the folder and select Include in library, then select Picture Library; locate the folder you want to display in Windows Media Center, and simply select Play Slide Show.

1. Select Start > All Programs > Windows Media Center.

2. When the program opens, select the Picture Library option from Pictures and Videos.

3. Option A: In the Picture Library, locate the folder *Images* you created (Computer > C:\ or Network drive, then locate your folder).

4. Option B: Previously, if you were using a media card from a digital camera, card reader, or flash drive, when you inserted the media, the dialog box would

▷ FIGURE 1-50

Using Windows Media Center to display slide shows, videos, and play music.

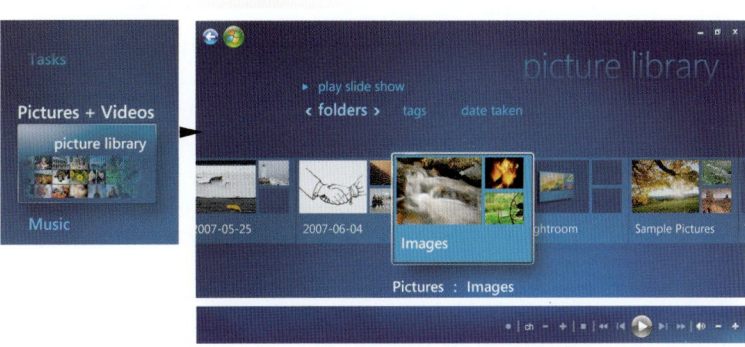

Windows Media Center

have displayed to allow you to Import images; select this option first to place images in the Pictures section. When images are imported, they are usually sorted automatically by date created; then, you can create folders to drag or copy the files into.

5. To enlarge images a little to see details before playing the slide show, let the mouse hover over the image and it will expand.

6. Select Play Slide Show to view your images. It will display images using appealing zoom techniques. Very cool!

7. To stop the show, select the Start Menu Windows icon (top left) to go back, or select the X (top right) to close the application.

Windows Media Center is also used for not only photos and music, but also for recording live TV and free Internet TV. Another application that can be used for looking at your images is Picture Viewer, which is a component of the QuickTime movie application that also allows you to watch videos off the Internet.

WINDOWS 8 SLIDE SHOWS FROM THE DESKTOP SCREEN: USING EITHER THE PICTURES LIBRARY OR WINDOWS MEDIA PLAYER

The easiest way to play your images is to have them in folders in your Pictures library. This way you can play slide shows using Windows Media Player or, using Windows 8, you can select the folder of images and use the Picture Tools ribbon to create a slide show from the Manage Tab. Storing your images in the Pictures library section on your computer's hard drive allows quick access to folders of images when you select the Pictures link. By creating a folder of your images in Pictures, you can make choices about what you want to do with the images, including displaying a slide show of a folder's contents (see Figure 1-51). If you have folders of images in the Pictures library, you can also use Windows Media Player, which not only is used for playing music but can also play slide shows of images, and burn CDs of your work. Note: If you are on a secure network, you may not be able to perform this exercise.

Here, you will create slide shows from the Picture Tools ribbon, and Windows Media Player.

1. With the Windows 8 Desktop Screen open, insert a flash drive with a folder of images you want to try, or create a folder of images on your desktop, as was done in the previous exercise. When inserting a flash drive, the Drive Tools ribbon opens to display your folders, or you can use File Explorer to locate your folder of images (Figure 1-51).

2. To place the folder of images in your Pictures library, you can drag the folder between windows, or right-click the folder, and select Include in library > Pictures.

3. With your folder in the Pictures library you now have options. You can select the folder in the Pictures library, or on the Pictures link under My PC.

▷ **FIGURE 1-51**

Creating slide shows in Windows 8 using the Picture Tools ribbon, and Windows Media Player.

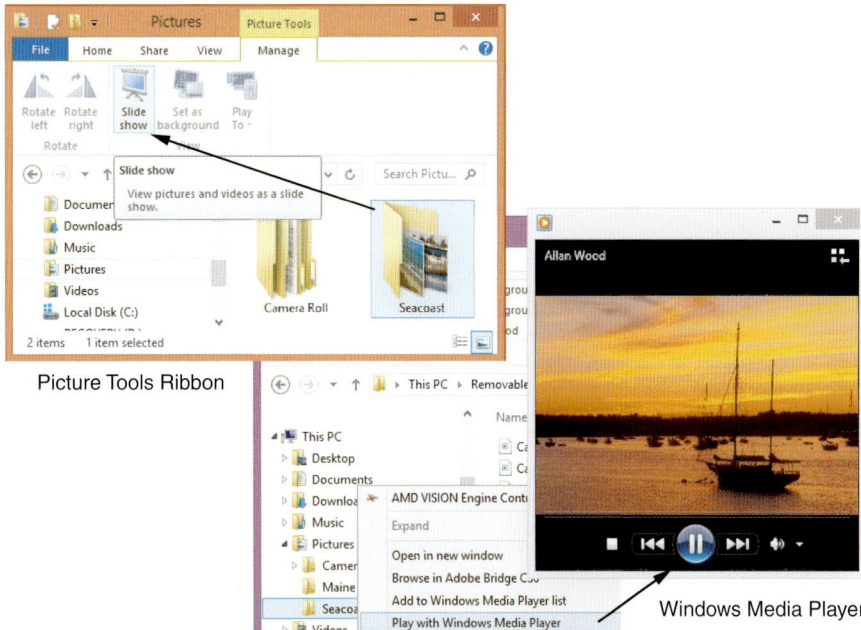

Picture Tools Ribbon

Windows Media Player

4. Click on the folder of images, and in the Picture Tools ribbon, which automatically displays, select Manage > Slide Show to play a full screen slide show. Press the ESC key on your keyboard to quit the slideshow when done. If the Slide Show icon doesn't display, make sure you are under the Picture Tools ribbon.

5. You can right-click on the folder of images and select Play with Windows Media Player to bring up this simple and useful application. You can use this to resize how big you want your slide show to display.

6. Press the Play button to play your slide show, and then press ESC to quit.

7. You can use Windows Media Player without having to place your images in the Pictures library. Just right-click on your folder of images (videos and music too) from wherever it is located, and select Play with Windows Media Player. That's it!

WINDOWS 8 SLIDE SHOWS FROM THE START SCREEN USING PHOTOS APP

The Start Screen on Windows 8 has a **Photos app** tile; when you select the tile, it brings up folders placed in the Pictures library, and a Control bar below with ways to play selected images. Here you can select Slide show on the Control bar to play your selected images.

Here is how to use the Photos app tile on the Start Screen.

1. Make sure your images are in a folder in the Pictures library as described in the previous exercise.

2. Press the Windows icon on the keyboard to toggle to the Start Screen if it isn't already displayed.

3. Click on the Photos app. The screen will display any folders in the Pictures library, on the left side. Click on your folder to display images.

4. Select which ones you want to display by right-clicking on each image. Selected images will show a check mark in the upper right corner of the thumbnail.

5. Select Slide Show on the bottom right side of the Control bar to display your images full screen (Figure 1-52). Here you can also import images from a memory card or your camera.

6. Press the ESC key on your keyboard when done to quit. Go ahead and play with other options available on the Control bar.

7. To close the application, drag from the top down to the bottom of the screen.

▷ FIGURE 1-52

Using the Photos tile app on the Windows 8 Start Screen to create a slide show.

DIGITAL TOOLKIT EXTRA: Burning Music, Photo, and Data CDs

Both Mac OS X and Windows allow you to write or burn documents, images, video, and music onto recordable CDs or DVDs as long as you have a CD or DVD recorder drive. It is a good habit to backup important files and folders to a recordable medium, such as CDs, DVDs, USB flash drives, and portable hard drives. Here you will learn how to burn the *Toolkit* folder on a backup CD and how to burn your favorite music CDs on either platform. You will find there are different applications for burning CDs and DVDs, iTunes becoming one of the most popular.

MAC OS X: CREATING A DATA OR PHOTO CD

When you place a blank recordable CD or DVD in your Mac, a dialog box pops up asking what action you want to take. To burn data CDs of your important folders and files, and of your favorite images and music, you can use the Finder application (see Figure 1-53). Select the files you want to copy, hold down the Option key, and drag them onto the CD icon on the desktop. Then drag the CD icon into the Trash to burn the CD. Mac OS X burns discs that can also be used on Windows computers and other types of computers. You can also burn discs using applications such as Disk Utility, iTunes, or iDVD. If you frequently burn the same items to disc, create a burn folder by choosing File > New Burn Folder, and copy those items to it. Then, to create a disc with those items, open the burn folder and click Burn. If you want to burn items to a disc in more than one session until the disc is full, open Disk Utility in Applications/Utilities from the Finder desktop and follow the help instructions.

Here you will learn how to create a CD backup of your *Toolkit* folder from your hard drive.

1. Place a blank recordable CD or DVD in the DVD recordable drive.

2. Choose Open Finder to use the Finder application from the dialog box menu; click OK and name the disk *Toolkit* (the iTunes application choice is best to burn audio files).

▷ FIGURE 1-53

Select the Finder application to copy data files and folders to a blank CD or DVD. Drag the files onto the CD or DVD icon on the desktop, then use the Trash icon to burn the CD or DVD; or create a burn folder to drag files into, then select File > Burn Disc.

3. Double-click the hard drive icon and locate the *Toolkit* folder you created.

4. Select the *Toolkit* folder and hold down the Option key as you drag it to the CD disc icon on the desktop. Feel free to drag other files and folders onto the blank CD from a USB flash drive or other source.

5. When you have all the files you want to copy, drag the CD disc icon into the Trash icon on the Dock: It acts as a CD burning application.

6. Extra: If you are thinking about making multiple copies of the same contents, you can create a Burn Folder, like a suitcase to put your files in. To create a burn folder, select File > New Burn Folder from the Finder menu, then simply drag files and folders to the burn folder; it creates aliases temporarily until you are ready to copy or burn the original contents onto the blank CD. Then it locates the files chosen and helps to burn them onto a CD. When you are ready to burn the folder's contents to a disc, double-click it and then click Burn.

7. It will ask you to insert a blank disc: just follow the instructions.

 PROBLEM If the Finder cannot find the original file for an alias shortcut while burning, it asks whether to cancel burning or to continue without that item. If you cancel, the disc remains empty. Another popular application you can purchase for easy disc burning is Toast, for Mac computers.

MAC OS X AND WINDOWS: CREATING MUSIC CDS USING ITUNES

The application iTunes lets you create your own personal digital music library, tune into Internet radio stations, download movies, download podcasts for an iPod, watch television shows, and burn your own audio CDs (see Figure 1-54). Before copying music tracks onto a blank CD, it is a good idea to import selected tracks from your music CD onto the iTunes music library first, or download paid songs from the iTunes music site. It converts them into compressed MP3 files to save space on your hard drive. Then create a Playlist and drag the music files you want to burn from your Library. Select your new Playlist, and burn the music CD using the Burn button at the bottom right of the iTunes window. This feature is also available for Windows platforms.

 TOOLKIT TIP You can also automatically add music files to the iTunes Library by creating a folder of songs on the desktop and selecting File > Add to Library. The newer versions of iTunes allow you to have playlists created for you using the Genius feature. The iTunes DJ will shuffle your songs for variety in playback.

Here you will learn how to import music files into the Library, how to create a Playlist, and how to burn your Playlist onto a blank CD.

1. Insert your music CD in your computer, and answer "Yes" in the dialog box to import your CD tracks into the iTunes library.

2. When the iTunes window opens up with the list of your tracks, check only the ones you want to burn.

3. If songs do not start to import, select File > Add to Library to add the selected songs to the library. Once imported into the Library, they are compressed into MP3 files and are stored in the Music folder on the hard drive.

4. To eject the music CD, select Controls > Eject Disc, or press the Media Eject key (Mac).

5. To create a Playlist of the files you want to link to on your hard drive, select File > New > Playlist.

▷ FIGURE 1-54

The Macintosh iTunes program (also on Windows) allows you to create MP3 CDs of your favorite songs to be played on any computer or device that will play MP3 compressed files.

Select tracks, import to Library, then create Playlist.
You can then drag selected songs to your playlist.

Playlist name

To create MP3 music CD, insert blank CD, select favorite playlists to burn, then select Burn Playlist to Disc.

6. Type a name for the Playlist, then drag the songs you want into the Playlist you created. This would also be the same procedure if you wanted to burn songs downloaded from the iTunes store.

7. You can create regular audio CDs (WAV files) that can be played on any stereo or create compressed MP3 CDs that can be played on any computer or most current CD players.

8. Insert a blank recordable CD or DVD, select iTunes as the application, select the Playlist or group of playlists you want to burn to the CD. You can also select File > Burn Playlist to Disc, or right-click the playlist you want to include, and select Burn Playlist to Disc.

9. A dialog box will open to format the disc as an audio CD (WAV files) on which you can place about 70 minutes of music, an MP3 CD for compressed MP3 files for lots of songs (won't work with DVDs), or a Data CD or DVD which will take DVDs and play music, but may not work with some players. Choose MP3 CD, then select the Burn button to start the process. It will indicate when the CD burning is completed.

TOOLKIT TIP If you are importing music copies and they appear as "track numbers," you can rename your files by selecting File > Get Info. When the song dialog box opens up, select Info and put in the song title, artist, and any other info. Select OK when done and the new title will be displayed in the music Library.

MAC OS X AND WINDOWS: USING ICLOUD TO SYNC WITH YOUR MOBILE "I" DEVICES

One of the more recent developments involves the use of a free application called iCloud. This is where you can have your content, including images, documents, and music, stored on the Internet, and have it synced with your computer, iPhone, iPod, or iPad.

To set up iCloud on your Mac OS X computer, or your PC, go to Apple's website at www.apple.com/icloud/setup. You can set up iTunes from the Apple site as well.

After setting up the cloud feature on your computer and devices using the Apple website, to use the iCloud feature in iTunes, here is the procedure:

1. Open iTunes, and activate or authorize for your computer (Store > Authorize Computer), or mobile device.

2. On the left side, under Store category, select Purchased, and scroll to the bottom of the window. There you'll find "Configure Automatic Downloads" and "Download Previous Purchases" links.

3. Click the arrow on "Configure Automatic Downloads" and select the categories you want to enable for you devices (Figure 1-55).

4. To be selective for specific purchases, click on the "Download Previous Purchases" arrow and sign in with your free Apple ID and Password. This is very simple to set up using your email address if you haven't already set it up.

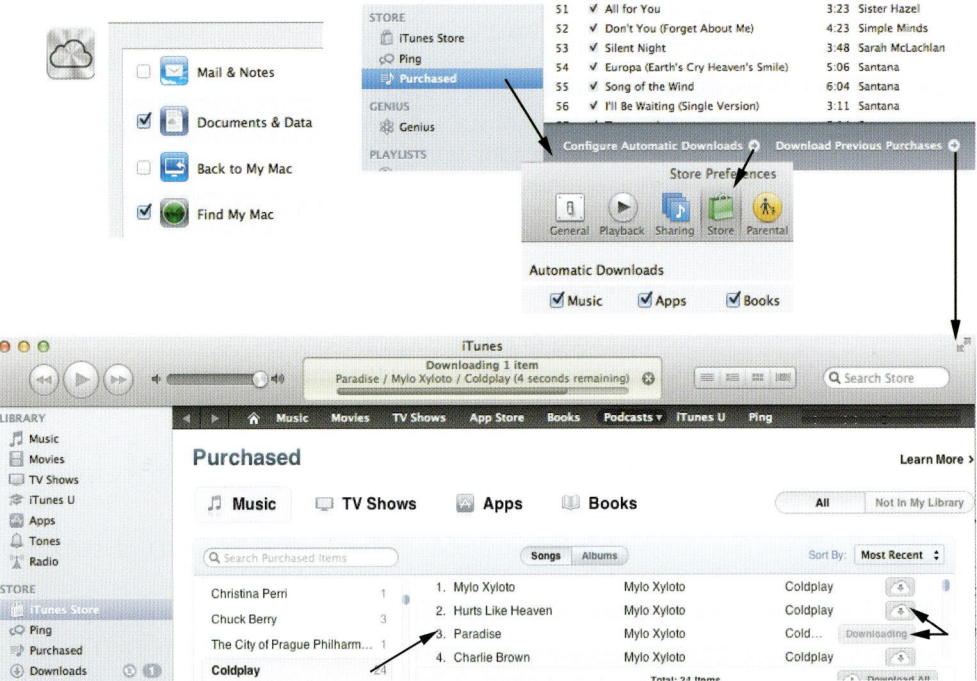

▷ FIGURE 1-55

Using iCloud to sync iTunes purchases to multiple devices and computers.

5. When you click on recent purchases, you'll find a list with cloud icons on the right side. To be selective, just click on the clouds next to the only songs, movies, TV shows, podcasts, etc., that you want to put on your device (my preference).

Here's how to set up iCloud on your mobile iPad, iPhone, or iPod Touch device, if you have one:

1. If you don't have the iTunes application, go to the Apple store at www.apple.com and follow the instructions to download this free app. Open iTunes on your computer, or your iPad, iPhone (3GS or later), or iPod Touch (at least third generation) device to your computer and follow the on screen instructions in iTunes.

2. Using your mobile device Home screen, tap the Settings icon and select iCloud, then just tap the On/Off switches to enable iCloud services. My suggestion would at this point to select only the categories "Documents" and Find My iPhone.

3. You can enable automatic downloads for music, apps, and books. Tap the Settings icon on the Home screen of your mobile device and select Store. When you make a purchase on one of your devices or other computers, the purchased item downloads to your computer at the same time that it downloads to your device.

Using iTunes iCloud automatically updates your documents, images, contacts, email, Safari bookmarks, and music across all your devices as long as you can access the Internet. There is also a setting to locate your Mac (Find My iPhone) or mobile device in case it is lost or stolen, or need to contract it remotely. You are allowed free 5 MB of storage, not including music or documents, which provides the service for no additional space for free. Note: If you turn storage and backup off in your settings, you should be able to keep the 5 MB of storage without needing to purchase any additional storage.

WINDOWS 7 AND 8: CREATING DATA AND PHOTO CDS

When you need to create data CDs, photo CDs, or backup applications, Windows allows you to copy files and folders onto a recordable (blank) CD or DVD, as long as you have a CD or DVD recorder drive.

Here you will learn how to create a copy of the *Toolkit* folder you just created. You can also use this technique to backup your important documents or your favorite digital images.

1. Insert a blank, writable CD or DVD in your CD or DVD drive recorder on your computer. In Windows 8, just tap as asked.

2. When the Blank CD options dialog box displays, click on the Burn files to disc link. The drive will then format or set up the CD or DVD to be able to burn files and folders (Figure 1-56). You'll be given a choice in the display "Like a USB flash" device, which allows you to delete files later as you would a regular flash drive, or the option "With a CD/DVD player," which allows you to burn a large collection of files. For this exercise select the CD/DVD option and label it *Toolkit*.

▷ FIGURE 1-56

Once a blank CD/ DVD is formatted, select files and folders and drag them onto CD/DVD window to copy contents; the disc will be burned for use on any computer.

To burn data files or graphics files, select Burn files to disc, then choose CD/DVD or USB flash drive. Drag folder to the CD/DVD display window to the right side, then select Burn to disc.

3. Locate the *Toolkit* folder you created on your hard drive, or locate files you want to burn.

4. With a window open displaying files you want to drag and burn, and the CD window of files and folders you want to drag contents to also open, resize both window displays and click and drag files and folders into the CD window. You will notice a copy files window to burn the selected contents onto your formatted CD or DVD (Figure 1-56).

5. Select the *Toolkit* folder, then select the Burn button in the Toolbar (Windows 7) or select Share > Burn to disc from the Ribbon in Windows 8. Leave the default settings as the CD is being burnt.

6. To view the contents of your new CD, insert the CD or DVD; when the dialog window displays, select "Open folder to view files."

WINDOWS 7 AND 8: CREATING MUSIC CDS USING WINDOWS MEDIA PLAYER

Windows 7 and 8 have an application called **Windows Media Player**, which lets you create or burn your own audio and video CDs from files that you can drag over from folders on the computer or in the library of the Media Player itself.

Before copying music tracks to be burned on a recordable CD, they need to be placed in either a folder on the computer or in the Music library. Here you will copy or **rip** audio tracks from a music CD to the Music library, then copy the selected tracks from a Playlist to a blank recordable CD. **Ripping** involves converting audio music from store bought CDs (or those that have not been compressed or converted to MP3 format) to be used on the computer as MP3 compressed format (see Figure 1-57). If you are copying music that has simply been downloaded or already in MP3 compressed format, you won't need to rip your selected tracks. Skip those beginning steps.

1. Insert a music CD into the CD drive; it will usually default to open Windows Media Player, and a Now Playing tab will be selected. If you insert a music CD and the CD dialog window displays, select Play Audio CD. You can also open the Media Player by choosing Start > Windows Media Player (Windows 7), or select Windows Media Player from the "App list" in the Windows 8 Start screen.

2. To prepare to burn to a blank CD or DVD, when Windows Media Player opens up, select the Rip tab (Windows 7) or Burn tab (Windows 8). Set any other preferences and leave only the tracks you want to copy checked, and uncheck the rest.

3. With the tracks selected, click on the Start Rip (Windows 7) or the Rip CD (Windows 8) button. Each track will be copied to the library, which will hold all your music (Figure 1-57).

4. Select the Library tab menu to display the tracks added to the library; select Create Playlist, then name the Playlist (Figure 1-57). Remove the music CD and put in a blank CD or DVD.

5. Drag the selected tracks from the Recently Added section on the left or from your CD tracks to your new Playlist on the right side. It will display how much is left: usually 10 megabytes (MB) equals one minute of audio play.

▷   FIGURE 1-57

To copy music CDs, use Windows Media Player to convert, or rip, music tracks to the Music Library; then create a playlist using Windows Media Player by dragging selected tracks.

6. Select whatever Playlist you want copied, and click check boxes for tracks that you want to copy. To add additional albums or tracks from the library, drag from the Details Pane display on the left side to the List Pane with the CD icon on the right. You can also right-click the album icon of tracks in the library, and select Add to Burn List.

7. With enough tracks in the Playlist, drag the tracks around for a specific order, then select Start Burn.

8. To burn the selected tracks from the Playlist to a recordable CD, select the Burn tab; click the Start Burn link (Figure 1-58).

9. Remove the music CD and insert a blank recordable disc. The CD or DVD will start burning the selected tracks. The rest of the process is automatic, and the CD will eject when the CD copying is completed. That's it!

To rip tracks to MP3 format, select tracks then select Burn. When finished, select Create playlist, and name the new playlist.

Ripping Using Windows Media Player

With a playlist created, drag tracks to playlist window to add, then save.

TOOLKIT TIP Do not copy more files than the CD can handle (650 to 800 MB depending on the CD) or you will receive a *What to do?* display or a *Will not fit* warning. You cannot burn additional tracks to the CD after copying is completed. If your computer has the capability to write to a DVD, then you have at least 4 gigabytes (GB) to play with.

▷ FIGURE 1-58

With a Playlist created, a blank CD can be turned into a favorite music CD.

Select Burn tab, insert blank CD, drag the select tracks, and select Start burn to create music CD.

CHAPTER SUMMARY

As a designer or photographer, it is important to have a basic understanding of Windows 7, Windows 8, and Mac OS X operating systems when working with files from various clients. In this chapter, you were able to learn the basics of Windows 7 and 8, and Mac OS X operating systems, their similarities and differences, and how to use files on both systems when possible. You also had an opportunity to navigate around each system. You got a taste of similarities in terms of various functions and keystrokes with different names applied. Folders were created to copy the text exercise files and create a manageable work environment. You played with various techniques and functions to keep your desktop organized, and to find your recently used applications and files quickly. In the Advanced Users section you created electronic slide shows using various applications that come with Mac OS X and Windows operating systems. In the Digital Toolkit Extra section, you learned to burn music, photo, and data CDs or DVDs.

REVIEW QUESTIONS

1. Explain why Macintosh computers are preferred over Windows in most graphic environments.

2. Explain eight different functions and keys that have the same result on either Mac or Windows operating system.

3. Why do files need to have extensions?

4. What is the purpose of file management to the designer or photographer?

5. Name some of the applications used within Mac OS X and Windows 7 or 8 operating systems to create slide shows and burn music and photo CDs.

▷ FIGURE 1-59

File management projects, and desktop fun using Macintosh OS X (top) and Windows 7 (bottom) operating systems.

Macintosh OS X Mavericks desktop

Windows 7 desktop

▷ FIGURE 1-60

File management projects and desktop fun using the Windows 8 operating system using the Start Screen and Desktop Screen.

Windows 8 Start Screen

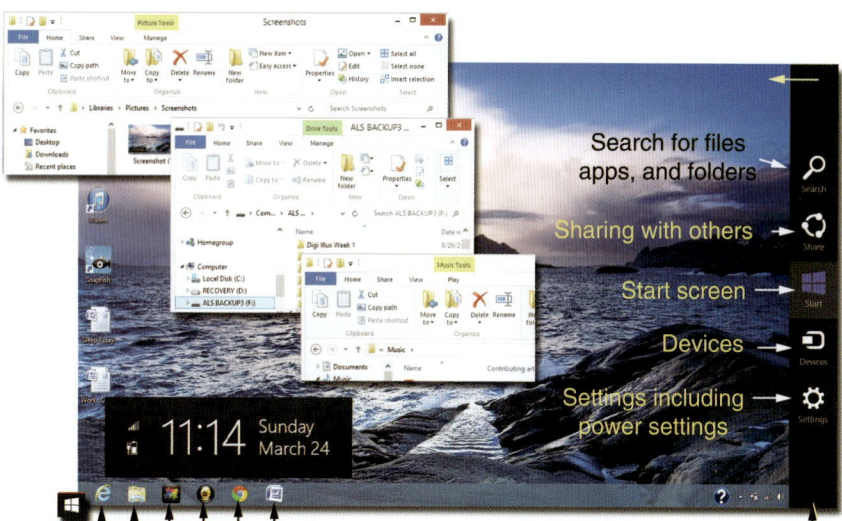

Windows 8 Desktop Screen

▷ FIGURE 1-61

CHAPTER 1 ADVANCED

Applications included in Mac OS X and Windows 7 used in creating electronic slide shows.

▷ FIGURE 1-62

CHAPTER 1: ADVANCED

**Applications in
Windows 8 used in
creating slide shows.**

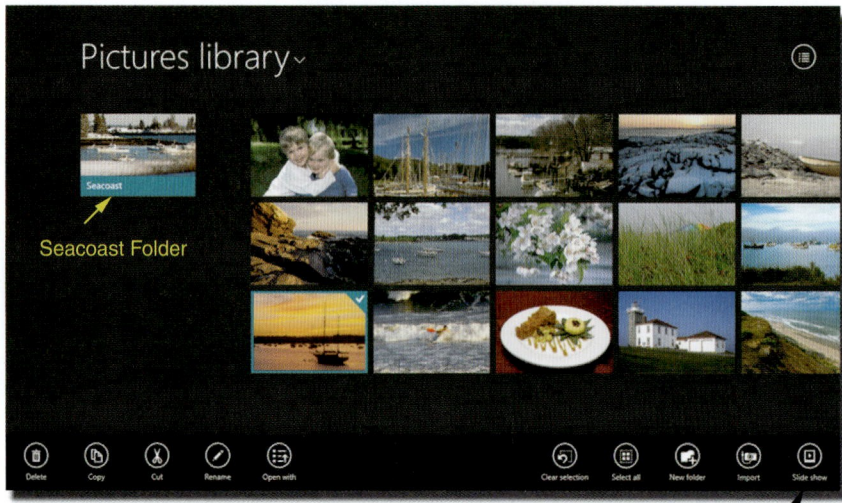

Seacoast Folder

Photos App on the Start Screen Displays Images from Pictures Library   Slide Show

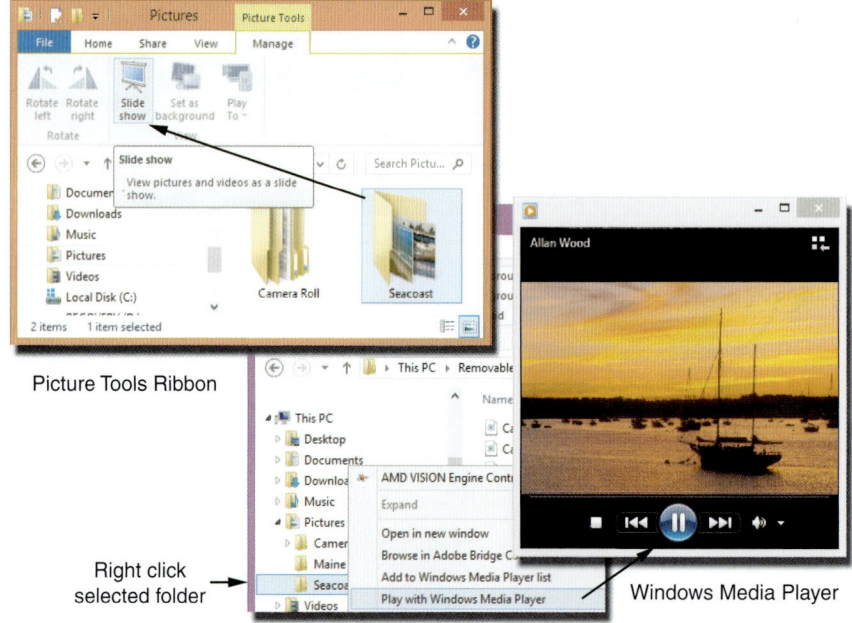

Picture Tools Ribbon

Right click
selected folder

Windows Media Player

▷ FIGURE 1-63

CHAPTER 1: EXTRA

Creating music Playlists in libraries to burn music CDs using iTunes (top) and Windows Media Player (bottom).

Select tracks, import to Library, then create Playlist. You can then drag the selected songs to your playlist.

Drag tracks from Playlist to burn window

CHAPTER

2

Designing for the Client

CHAPTER OBJECTIVES: To understand the importance of design in creating the appropriate message for the intended audience, in this chapter you will:

▷ Learn the elements and principles of design.

▷ Learn the importance of using visual imagery, color, and typography to convey a message.

▷ Learn the design process, from working with a client to developing a concept to creating final proofs.

▷ Create thumbnail sketches and a final rough for client approval.

▷ ADVANCED USERS: Identify design elements and principles used in various ads for various media.

▷ DIGITAL TOOLKIT EXTRA: Use Internet resources to research tutorials and locate application information.

It is great to have talent, because this will get you in the door to meet with a potential client. However, discipline and responsibility go a long way toward developing a profitable and rewarding career in graphics. Issues such as keeping deadlines, being a good communicator with a client, and establishing good relations will help ensure continued success and provide a network for new clientele. Always remember: you are not creating for your enjoyment; you are creating for your clients. In the final analysis, they determine what they like, whether you agree or not. This chapter will take you through the basic design principles and elements, the importance of typography and visual imagery, and the design processes involving the client.

ELEMENTS OF DESIGN

The placement of elements within a design, page, or website will have much influence on what kind of message is perceived by what kind of market. Formal design elements that are the basic building blocks of design are *line, shape, color, texture, value,* and *format.* Designers also use illusions of depth and motion to help create a 3-D effect on a 2-D surface. For every design, you are trying to communicate something. These physical elements of design are your communication tools; knowing when and how to use these elements is essential to building a successful design. All these formal elements are interdependent, and they interact to complement one another and function as a team.

LINES AND SHAPES

The way a line moves determines the type of line it is. **Lines** can be straight, angular, or curved, and they may be drawn in horizontal, vertical, or diagonal directions. A line's visual quality is determined by how the line is drawn, whether thick or thin, broken or smooth. **Shapes** are usually considered closed forms or outlines. How a shape is drawn, like a curved shape or an angular shape, gives it a specific quality. A designer uses lines as outlines or edges to create shapes, like a pyramid or a circle (Figure 2-1). Color can also define a shape without lines. If the color creates an edge, it also defines the shape.

Strength   **Peaceful**   **Graceful**   **Shape**
(defined by lines)   **Shape**
(defined by color)

▷ FIGURE 2-1

The manner in which lines and shapes are drawn define various forms within a design piece.

TEXTURE

Texture describes surface quality, like rust, velvet, or sandpaper. The two categories of texture in the artistic sense are *tactile* and *visual.* **Tactile texture** involves the actual feeling of a surface texture like a sculpture. Designers and artists use **visual texture** to create the illusion of texture in artwork, using varying line qualities, patterns, or adjusting the value and colors of an element. Computers can create digital textures through various filters and effects within software programs (Figure 2-2).

▷ FIGURE 2-2

Value and texture help to determine the viewer's emotional response.

Logos displaying value and texture

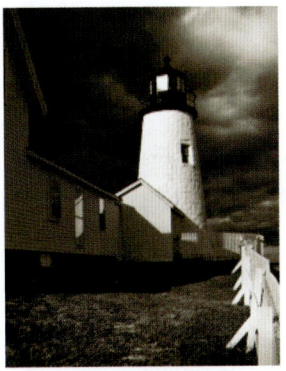

High-contrast images evoke a different response than low-contrast images

VALUE

Value determines depth and dimension by the range of lightness or darkness of an element. Value is the shading, tonality, and tint of a color (light blue and dark blue). The use of shading can help provide a three-dimensional value to an image. Value creates a focal point or center of attention. **Value contrast** is the relationship between black and white or lightness and darkness of an image, and it is a result of the relationship between different elements; it produces both visual and emotional effects. As the viewer observes an image and interprets its value, the eye is drawn to light areas first, which the designer or artist can use to provide contrast and balance in an image.

Values in color and contrast can provoke a variety of emotional responses. Low contrast or closely related values can evoke a sense of calmness or tranquility, while high-contrast images or sharp-value images can create a sense of excitement, drama, or conflict between elements. An overall darker image can promote a sense of mystery or even sadness, while an overall lighter image invites the viewer with an uplifting tone or feeling of relaxation.

DEPTH PERCEPTION

In the two-dimensional world of drawings, photographs, paintings, and prints, designers often need to convey a feeling of space or depth perception. Some of the elements that convey these characteristics are the sizes of objects and their relationship to one another, the overall blending of colors and shapes by adjusting tonal values, and the point of view or depth perspective. By varying the size of similar shapes—for example, rectangles—the illusion is more pronounced than with differing shapes. Spatial depth is more pronounced if shapes become smaller as they overlap, creating the illusion of objects receding (Figure 2-3). This is a form of **spatial recession**. By combining elements and blending the tonal values to match the background, the illusion of receding into the background creates an even more pronounced sense of depth. Converging lines may also create this effect. **Tonal value** involves the lightness and darkness of an image by varying its tone or value to the surrounding background. In landscape, objects are placed in the foreground to give a feeling of depth; or **framing techniques** are employed in which another subject surrounds the main subject for emphasis. Using tree branches in the foreground, for instance, provides emphasis to a distant subject.

▷ FIGURE 2-3

One way of creating the illusion of spatial depth is made by the appearance of making similar shapes smaller, to recede into the background, or using converging lines.

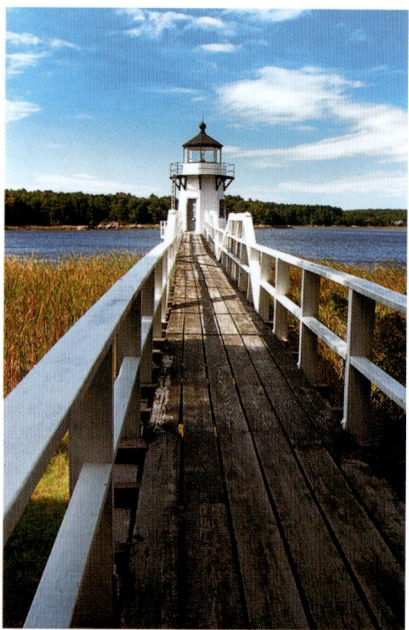

PERSPECTIVE AND ANGLE OF VIEW

Artists and photographers create images that show a higher or lower point of view that can enhance the feeling of depth in an image. One technique involves the use of **linear perspective**. This is where a horizon line is placed to approximate the eye level of the artist. From this line, invisible lines or edges—called *vanishing points*—are directed to lead the viewer into the image. **One-point perspective** involves using converging lines to lead the eye to a subject or point along a horizontal line to provide depth in perspective within the image. **Two-point perspective** involves a more natural approach, similar to how we view the world around us, at an angle with two edge points along the horizon line. In this view, vanishing points recede at either end of a horizontal line. Vertical lines would be parallel to the edges of the picture. An example would be if the viewer were standing on a city street corner, taking a photo of the buildings; there would be little or no vertical convergence, but rather parallel alignment of the sides of the buildings. It is not as dramatic an approach as using converging lines, and it permits the viewer to scan an image from one edge to the other.

Artists can also use fences, roads, stairways, and other techniques in compositions involving **leading lines** to create the effect of depth perception. **Aerial perspective** uses the lighter background contrast of the atmosphere with darker subjects that are closer to the viewer in landscapes to show a sense of depth. The background recedes to the lighter contrast from the darker foreground subject. To add drama to an image, artists and photographers constantly create images from lower and higher angles than a viewer's normal eye level (Figure 2-4).

▷ FIGURE 2-4

Linear perspective uses vanishing points along a horizontal plane. Changing the angle of view (above or below the subject) can add drama to images.

USING MOTION

Creating the illusion of motion can suggest an anticipation of movement either in slow motion or in what is termed as **stop action** (Figure 2-5). Artists use these techniques to trigger memories or record events, or with special effects like blurring water to give an image an ethereal quality. The feeling of movement can also be heightened by contrast, showing activity. Repeating figures or multi-exposed images have also been used to create the illusion of motion.

Using images that employ a sense of motion is a technique that enhances anticipation.

COLOR

Color is one of the most powerful design elements. A designer needs to understand which colors are appropriate to complement the message. Color is based on wavelengths of light and contains a wide range of visual differences and contrasts. Color is divided into three categories: *hue, value,* and *saturation.* **Hue** is the name of the color (red, green, and blue). **Value** is the shading, tonality, or tint of a color (light and dark blue). **Saturation** is the intensity of color (bright red or dull red).

In design, a color wheel that displays basic colors and their **complementary colors**, or opposite colors, is used as a guideline. Most color wheels use 12 color hues as the basis for all color mixtures. With pigment colors that are used for painting or traditional artwork, the **traditional primary colors** are *red, yellow,* and *blue.* These are the main colors that create all others. For instance, combining red and yellow creates orange. The **secondary colors** are *orange, green,* and *purple,* and they can be further mixed for many color variations. The six **tertiary colors** are created by mixing one primary and one secondary color. They consist of *yellow orange, red orange, red violet, blue violet, blue green,* and *yellow green* (Figure 2-6).

Color intensity or saturation is the brightness of a color. To lower a color's intensity without changing its value, a designer can add gray or combine the color with its complementary color, which is the color across from it on the color wheel. When complementary colors are placed next to each other, their brightness is intensified. For example, the opposite of orange is blue; a designer might package oranges using blue lettering to highlight the fruit, thus making it look fresher. When various colors are coordinated together in the color scheme of an image, warm colors like reds, yellows, and oranges generally seem to come forward, while cool colors like blues, greens, and purples appear to fade to the back. High-contrast colors appear to come forward visually, while low-contrast colors appear to recede. Low-intensity versions of a color are generally considered the *tones* of a color. Colors mixed with neutral grays can result in different **tones** of color.

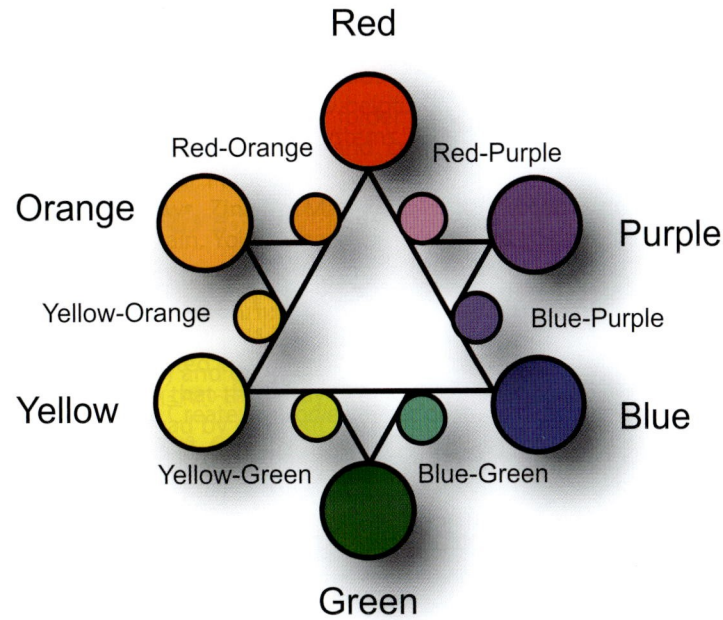

▷ FIGURE 2-6

A color wheel displays complementary, or opposite, colors used in the creation of all colors.

Colors created on the computer are made by adding the primary colors of light, *red, green,* and *blue* (*RGB*), which act differently than pigment but are fine for electronic document design such as web pages. The colors *cyan, magenta, yellow,* and *black* (*CMYK*) are used for commercial printing. Color plates used in commercial printing use the colors *cyan, magenta,* and *yellow* (*CMY*) as the basis for creating all other colors for print. *Black* (*K*) is then added for purity and contrast.

FORMATS, GUIDELINES, AND GRIDS

Brochures, CD covers, business cards, and posters are some of the **formats** designers use for their clients. The project the client brings to you will determine the format. Your design should work well within the given format. Formats have advantages and limitations that need to be considered in creating a particular design. For instance, will the final layout be a vertical or **portrait orientation**, or a horizontal display of elements, called a **landscape orientation**? What size paper and shape will it be? How will it be used, and where will it be seen? These are all considerations as you work with a particular format.

Most graphic computer applications have a set of rulers, or ruler guides, displayed along the top and left side of the document that a designer can use for measuring. A designer can click and drag from one of the ruler guides onto the document, creating what are called **guidelines**. These nonprintable guidelines are used for exact placement of specific sized text and graphics boxes on brochures, flyers, web pages, and so on. They also can be used to create **margin guides,** usually purple or blue in color, for outer margins and for spacing between text and graphic boxes for folding procedures and alignment (Figure 2-7).

DESIGN TIP

Theoretically, the three primary colors used for printing (CMY) would combine to produce black; however, this may result in a more muddy color due to impurities in the ink pigments. Black ink is added as a fourth color to create true black and add contrast to images.

▷ FIGURE 2-7

Grids, which are made up of a network or intersecting horizontal and vertical lines, provide the framework to unify placement of type and graphics.

Grids are developed from a network of intersecting horizontal and vertical guidelines. Designers use grids for consistent placement and spacing of text and graphic elements within a unified theme on successive pages to create catalogs, books, newsletters, pamphlets, magazines, and so forth.

DESIGN PRINCIPLES

A designer must be careful to understand the client's needs. By researching what the client wants to convey to the target market, the designer will be able to create the appropriate message. Principles in design are followed to combine individual elements into one harmonious piece. This involves taking various elements and providing proper balance, adding selective emphasis to create a focal point, using rhythm to set the mood, and establishing unity.

BALANCE

The concept of balance is to arrange elements within an area so that these elements promote a harmonious response. Visual balance is determined by the weight, position, and arrangement of elements (Figure 2-8). Balance can be formal, informal, or radial. **Formal balance**, also referred to as **symmetrical balance**, places elements with equal distribution to convey trustworthiness and integrity, as used by financial institutions or insurance companies. **Informal balance**, also referred to as *asymmetrical balance,* uses elements that counterbalance one another instead to create a harmonious composition. This type of balance gives the appearance of being casual, energetic, or trendy usually found in retail and lifestyle organizations. **Radial balance** arranges elements around a central point and is used to promote unity or teamwork, which may be found in non-profit organizations, or children's ads.

Balance is the arrangement of various elements and their visual weights within the composition.

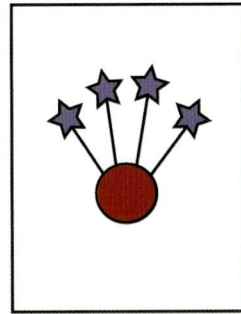

Formal Balance
(centered)

Informal Balance
(off-centered)

Radial Balance
(equal value)

USE OF NEGATIVE AND POSITIVE SPACE

Using empty or **negative space**, absent of visual elements, is a visual element in itself that actually does more to promote luxury or elegance, and sometimes a sense of mystery, than most other effects. This may utilize the "less is more" concept in design. **Positive space** uses content to fill up space to identify or explain something in a particular page. In an ad using empty space, a line of black type on a white background, or a line of white type on a black background, can change perception of the content of the page (Figure 2-9). Reversing colors sometimes makes an ad stand out in a crowd of ads. Care needs to be taken in the use of empty space over positive space, including type size in relation to the graphic.

Positive space fills the frame with descriptive imagery and/or text. Negative space promotes elegance or mystery. Which message caught your eye first?

Create projects designers may encounter using Photoshop, Illustrator, and InDesign.

Learn what you need to know.

Come play...

tv.adobe.com

Learn...
What you need to know

tv.adobe.com

EMPHASIS

Emphasis provides direction to various elements in a given design, promoting the concept that some things are more important than others. To find and decide what is most important, the reader searches for a focal point in a design. A primary focal point can be established with accents that lead the viewer to it. A **focal point** can be determined by an element's size, shape, color, texture, or position in the layout. Emphasis can be created by contrast, where one element differs from the surrounding elements, and by isolation, where an element is removed or isolated from the surrounding elements. Use of color or an element that is lighter than its surroundings draws attention to that subject. Reds and yellows are great eye catchers.

Placement is another useful technique to emphasize the subject. In many cases, an artist may visibly divide an image into thirds for placement of elements within the composition. This technique is called the **Rule of Thirds** (Figure 2-10). Placing the subject in a noncentered position or off balance draws attention and keeps the elements of the composition from appearing static.

▷ FIGURE 2-10

Emphasis provides direction and focal point for elements in a composition.

  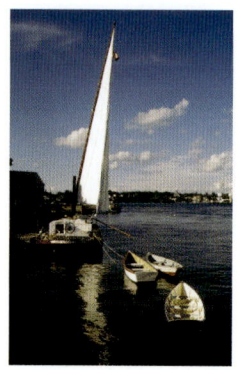

Courtesy of Shelly Britton.

RHYTHM

Rhythm is a visual pattern of repeating elements that creates a sense of movement (Figure 2-11). It is constantly used in printed media as well as in architecture. Variation in rhythm can be adjusted by changing the shape, size, color, spacing, and position of elements in a design. This change in arrangement helps to promote the mood of the design. The viewer looks at certain elements before others.

▷ FIGURE 2-11

Rhythm is a visual pattern of repeating elements in a design.

 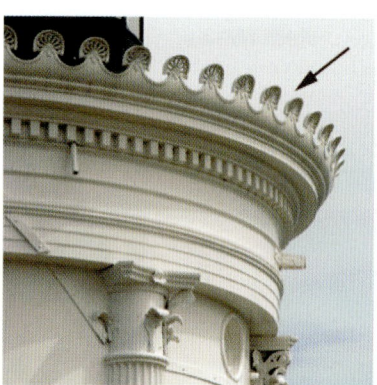

Those elements that are larger, darker, or have a more unusual shape than their surrounding counterparts are used to draw the viewer's eyes into the composition. You probably have seen examples in the use of this pattern along the edges of a design like greeting cards, flyers, or in architecture.

HARMONY (UNITY)

Harmony (sometimes referred to as **Unity**) is the organization of elements in a design as though they belong together (Figure 2-12). It allows the designer to view individual components as one integrated whole. Harmony, or unity, establishes continuity with a variety of elements and promotes consistency within the piece, and it combines balance, rhythm, type, imagery, and tone to evoke a particular emotion from the viewer.

▷ FIGURE 2-12

Unity is the organization of visual elements as part of an integrated whole.

  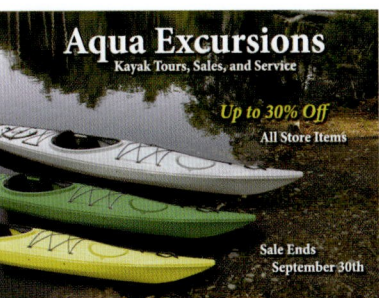

Original Image ⟶ Imagery created and text added for completed advertisement

DESIGN STAGES: FROM CONCEPT TO COMPLETION

A design solution's "personality" is created when the formal elements of color, line, shape, texture, format, and value are put together using the principles of graphic design in spatial relationships, balance, rhythm, emphasis, and unity. These elements collaborate to elicit the kind of audience reaction the client desires.

WORKING WITH THE CLIENT

The whole idea behind designing is being able to solve problems visually that help the client best communicate his or her message. Before you start designing, talk to your client and listen; then keep your client involved in the process (Figure 2-13).

- Listen to the client to understand the design challenge. Make the client feel involved. Try to assist gently when suggesting changes you feel would create a better product, but do not make the client feel incompetent. You need to fully understand the client's project in order to help.

- You need to know the market the design is intended for and what the client's design specifications are. Is this design going to be used for print and electronic media?

▷   FIGURE 2-13

Listen to the clients' needs and keep them involved in the design process.

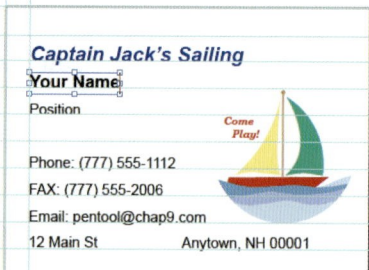

Illustration courtesy of Carla Clancy.

If so, then understanding different ways images and text are going to be presented for each medium is crucial to the success of the project.

- What materials are needed for the project, and what is your experience with these materials? What software or hardware are you comfortable with, and which ones will require that you rely on others for expertise?

- Know your budget and guidelines. Complete as much research as possible so you will be able to stay within your estimate. Set a time frame for completion of various components of the project.

THE DESIGNING PROCESS

Graphic design begins with a visual concept—the main idea behind creating the design piece. Before coming up with a concept, you need to plan a strategy and set design objectives that meet your client's needs. Then research information, material, and visuals about your subject, and start writing down your ideas. Make changes and decisions on those ideas with the client, and then generate final comps for the intended media.

Thumbnails

Thumbnails are sketched variations of an idea (Figure 2-14). Once you have your design idea, thumbnails help create different possibilities for that idea. Create a dozen or more thumbnails, and then narrow them down to about six to ten per concept to show the client. For consistency, make thumbnails the same proportion as the final piece.

▷   FIGURE 2-14

Thumbnails are sketched variations of an idea. Roughs are full-sized representations from ideas.

Roughs

Roughs are created as a result of combining specific elements from each thumbnail, or they may be the result of one good thumbnail (Figure 2-15). A rough is a full-size rendition of your design, including the layout of images and text and overall compositional elements that you show to the client. This version can be created while still at the drawing stage, or it can be done on the computer. The final rough usually must be created on the computer. Generating three to six roughs gives the client a good idea of what the final design will look like.

▷ FIGURE 2-15

Roughs can provide variations of a design theme for the client, with the final roughs completed on computer.

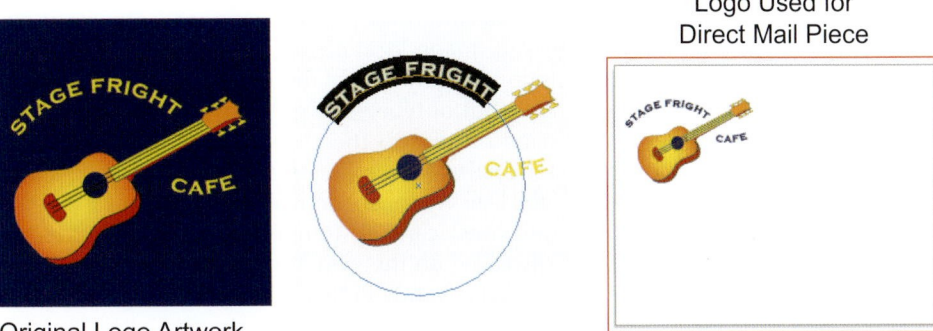

Logo Used for
Direct Mail Piece

Original Logo Artwork

Comps

Comps show exactly what the final design will look like when printed. The designer must take painstaking efforts to make sure everything is exactly what the client had agreed to in the final rough. This is where all text, color, imagery, and compositional elements need to come together for the final client approval before going to press, electronic media, or both (Figure 2-16).

▷ FIGURE 2-16

Comps show the client exactly what the final designs will look like when printed.

CD Cover

Direct Mail

Business Card

3D Mug and 2D Logo

Final Proofs for Press

The client should have the proof that provides instructions for the press and finishing operators. The **print proof** should show indications for folding, cutting, bleeding, trapping, registration, and any special requirements (this will be covered in depth in later chapters). Keep in mind that most ink-jet proofs will not show exact color but may be close enough for client approval, as long as the client understands before going to press that there may be a slight difference in some colors in the final product. Another final proof will be generated at the print site, provided for and to be approved by the client, so he or she knows precisely what all the elements will look like. The designer should also furnish a disc to the client with fonts and images used, along with any other specific information needed.

Final Electronic Proofs for Electronic Media

For website designers or multimedia designers, the **electronic media proof** should show indications for pixel dimensions, software used, resolution requirements, text and image locations, and information, if needed, for publishing to the web, along with any special requirements. A *final printed proof* is also needed for checking layout of type, imagery, and all elements used, along with the final layout supplied on disc to the client. The client should have the disc contents checked on a calibrated monitor to see as closely as possible what the web page or site will look like. When working with a limited color palette for web design, the client needs to check carefully to make sure that the colors are as accurate as possible to be displayed on the web. It must also be noted that colors on a Mac and colors on a PC vary slightly in their display.

TYPOGRAPHY

Typography is the study and use of text in a document. A designer uses type in titles or headlines and in the body of the document to enhance an ad; it helps to establish a mood or theme in the design or document (Figure 2-17). A **type family**, sometimes referred to as a **typeface**, is a group of fonts that share a basic character construction, like the Arial family, which includes Arial Black, Arial Narrow, Arial Alternative, and so on, similar to having your family of uncles, aunts, cousins, and grandparents. A **font** is a set of characters such as Arial, Times New Roman, Verdana, or Wingdings by themselves, like your immediate family. A **font size** is measured in **points** instead of inches (1 pt = 1/72 inch). When you open a document, the default size is usually 12 pt. When you need to bold, underline, or italicize type, you are creating a change to that type by applying a **font style**.

CHARACTER AND LINE SPACING

The spacing between characters and lines of text also determines how that type looks on your document. **Tracking** adjusts the spacing between characters and words. Adjusting the tracking of words too tightly in a paragraph can make it difficult to read, whereas adjusting too loosely can create "rivers" of white spacing in a paragraph, especially when type is either left or right justified. Sometimes a designer will create a loose tracking effect on a single word, or a few words, in the title of an ad or magazine cover as an attention getter. **Kerning** is a technique used for pairs of characters in titles or headlines that may need to be

DESIGN TIP

Typography should enhance a message, not detract from it, by using typefaces that are appropriate to the message. Color of type should also play a vital role in enhancing the visual expression but should not hinder readability. Because our eyes tend to read the largest elements first, such as headlines or titles, create a visual hierarchy for your text.

brought closer together for a more consistent look. **Leading** refers to the spacing between lines of text. Usually the default leading is 120 percent of the letter size for most documents.

▷ FIGURE 2-17
Typography consists of typeface families, measured in points with styles sometimes applied.

This is a 12-pt "Arial Regular" Font
This is a 12-pt "Arial Regular" font with an Italicized style.
This is a 12-pt "Arial Black" font in the Arial family
This is an18-pt size "Arial Regular" Font

DESIGN TIP

Word and line spacing creates the specific rhythm or pace at which the viewer reads the message. Alignment or arrangement of type should enhance readability.

In long articles or newsletters, less space between lines of text tends to darken the document, whereas more space will lighten it up. The message or mood you want to convey will determine how you will set up your text and what fonts you will need. The style or arrangement of setting type is called **type alignment**. Left aligned flushes the type to the left and is easy to read; we associate right aligned with professional return addresses on letters. Centered lines of type are used in some headlines or titles, while **justified alignment** places text equally on left and right sides in a column (Figure 2-18). This technique is found in multi-column documents like newspapers and magazine articles.

▷ FIGURE 2-18
Character and line spacing, along with the alignment of type, help set a particular mood or message.

CATEGORIES OF TYPE

Two main categories of type are *serif type* and *sans-serif type.* **Serif type** characters contain what look like "feet," or extended strokes, on the tops and bottoms; these are used to convey a conservative look and make it easier to read long articles or bodies of text. **Sans-serif type** has characters without these strokes, and it is more legible for labeling illustrations, headlines, and titles. **ASCII type** is the American standard of type: it is plain text and unformatted and can be read by any application or computer. It uses the extension .TXT. Other type categories include script type, decorative type, and symbol type (Figure 2-19). **Script fonts** are typically used in announcements or invitations and convey the appearance of being created with a pen or brush. **Decorative type** is sometimes used in headlines to create a specific meaning, and **symbol type** is a collection of related symbols, often called *dingbats,* that can be used for bullets, map symbols, or logos. The type you select should be appropriate and must complement your design.

▷ FIGURE 2-19

**The five main cat-
egories of type are**
*serif, sans serif, script,
decorative,* **and**
symbol type.

Times New Roman is a serif type with extensions.
Arial is a sans serif type withouth extensions.
Brush Script is a script type used in invitations.
Papyrus is used as decorative type.
  Symbol type (Webdings) for bullets, etc.

DESIGN TIP

A designer needs
to be very careful
when combining
different fonts;
look at whether
they enhance
the message
appropriately, use
contrast and weight,
and provide a visual
hierarchy. Fonts
need to be similar
to carry a consistent
message, so try
using fonts within
the same type family.

USING TYPE IN PRINT MEDIA

Here are a few design guidelines for starters when creating text documents to be printed:

- Use the same fonts and sizes for various headings in the same document. If you have to use different fonts, stick with the same type family for consistency.

- Use 10-pt or 12-pt size serif type minimum for the body of text for easier reading on printed material.

- Use italics sparingly and infrequently, for emphasis only.

- When using text type, do not use type in all upper case and do not allow too much or too little spacing between lines of type. Use the default leading on your word processor as a guide.

TOOLKIT TIP To create universal text document files that can be read by older Mac and Windows systems, save with .RTF extensions for text that contains formatting commands like bold or italic, or use .TXT extensions for plain text. If you do not have Microsoft Word applications, both operating systems have basic ASCII word processors. You can open WordPad in Windows (Start > All Programs > Accessories > WordPad), or use TextEdit in Macintosh OS X (Go > Applications > TextEdit). Microsoft Office Word works well between Macs and PCs.

▷ FIGURE 2-20

To install the fonts downloaded from the website *www.CengageBrain.com,* **use the Font Book utility to install your fonts into the** *Fonts* **folder.**

USING TYPE FOR ELECTRONIC MEDIA

Here are a few design guidelines when creating electronic documents:

- Try using sans-serif fonts especially for light-colored text against a dark or black background for easier reading. Bolder fonts also work better when reversing type out of a solid or textured background.
- Use a minimum 12-pt size for body text, because text is displayed electronically and can be tiring on the eyes over periods of time.
- Use color for emphasis of graphic statements. Electronic media is a great means for entertaining visual stimulation.
- Usually it helps to keep sentences short and use small paragraphs to hold the reader's interest.

INSTALLING FONTS FOR TEXT ASSIGNMENTS (OPTIONAL)

Whether you are designing ads or creating multipage newsletters, text is one of the most important elements of any design. The fonts that can be used on Macs can be found at *www.CengageBrain.com* in a Fonts folder, because fonts in Windows may not exactly match the same fonts in Mac OS X. You will copy the fonts from *www .CengageBrain.com* to the *Fonts* folder, which resides inside the *Library* folder on the Mac hard drive, using Macintosh's Font Book utility (Figure 2-20). For any of the exercises you may always use your own standard fonts, although you may find issues in terms of spacing with those documents that use a lot of text. There is no Fonts folder for PCs online, but you can either download fonts from the Microsoft site or Google for "type foundry" sites and download to your flash drive. These exercises installing fonts are best for a home computer without network security.

Macintosh OS X

On your Mac, the *Fonts* folder is located inside the *Library* folder on the computer's hard drive. You will need to download the contents of the fonts link from the website *www.CengageBrain.com*, then you can use the Font Book utility to add these fonts to your computer's list of current fonts. You can use the Font Book's File menu to add and remove fonts, and you can quickly view fonts and their shapes.

1. Make sure you have downloaded the fonts link at the *www.CengageBrain.com* website as described in Chapter 1, and unzipped the file to display the contents of the *MACFonts* folder inside the *Fonts* folder. If you want to do this on a home computer, feel free to download fonts from other sources.

2. To locate the *Library* folder on your hard drive, double-click the hard drive icon on your desktop, then select Library > Fonts to locate the fonts already installed on the computer.

3. Double-click any one of the fonts displayed in the *Fonts* folder to open the Font Book window. Select File > Add Fonts..., then locate your *MACFonts* folder, and select Open. Your fonts will install automatically. If there is an issue, it will provide a checklist and flag if something is wrong, say the font being installed is a duplicate. Installing these fonts will not hurt your computer (Figure 2-20).

4. If you have a downloaded fonts from another source, you can also double-click the font name and a dialog box will open with a simple button that reads Install Font. Select the button, and if there is an issue, it will also provide a checklist and warn if it is a duplicate file.

5. A third method involves dragging font files between windows. Resize and position both windows next to one another, then click and drag the font files from the downloaded *MACFonts* folder into the *Fonts* folder (Figure 2-21).

▷ FIGURE 2-21

Another method to install fonts is to select and drag fonts into the *Fonts* folder.

Windows 7 and 8

In Windows, you would open the *Fonts* folder in the Appearance and Personalization command in the Control Panel; then from the source window just drag the icon into the fonts folder and it will automatically install (Figure 2-22).

1. To install your fonts in Windows, select the Start button, then select the Control Panel.

DESIGN TIP

Try not to switch back and forth between Mac and PC with the same project, because the fonts are not exactly the same on either computer. If you have to switch, try to use fonts with the same name.

2. Select the Appearance and Personalization link, not the links underneath, then locate the Fonts icon.

3. Click on the Fonts link to open the Fonts folder displaying the fonts on your computer and resize the window to half screen or less.

4. If you download a particular font you like, just drag the icon or the folder onto the desktop. Resize the window display, then all you need to do is drag the new font icon into the display of Fonts folder. It will automatically install.

5. To delete a font, click on the icon and press delete from the toolbar, or right-click the icon and select Delete. Be careful when deleting as it cannot be undone.

6. Close the dialog boxes to get back to the desktop. Your fonts are added to your computer and ready for the text exercises.

▷ FIGURE 2-22

Installing Fonts in Windows 7 and Windows 8.

To add font, drag font icon from source to *Fonts* folder of icons.
To delete a font, select font icon and choose to delete.

TOOLKIT TIP ClearType is a software technology developed by Microsoft that improves the readability of text on existing LCDs, such as laptop screens, Pocket PC screens, and flat panel monitors. With ClearType font technology, the words on your computer screen are more sharpened and clear. With your home computer, you can turn on and adjust the screen for best readability using ClearType technology. To adjust, select Start Menu > Control Panel > Appearance and Personalization > Fonts > Adjust ClearType text. Then just follow the instructions.

IMAGERY

Images are needed to explain ideas, provide further illustration to text in long articles, and strengthen the mood or idea the designer is trying to convey. We are basically visual learners of our environment. When designing with computer imagery, graphics can be categorized as either *vector images* or *bitmap images* (Figure 2-23). **Vector images** are illustrations, logos, drawings, or clip art that can be enlarged to any size without affecting the quality of the original image. **Bitmap images,** or **raster images,** are photographs, paintings, or complex designs that use millions of colors to record subtle gradations of tone in the image. They are not capable of being scaled larger than the original size without deteriorating the quality.

Vector Image

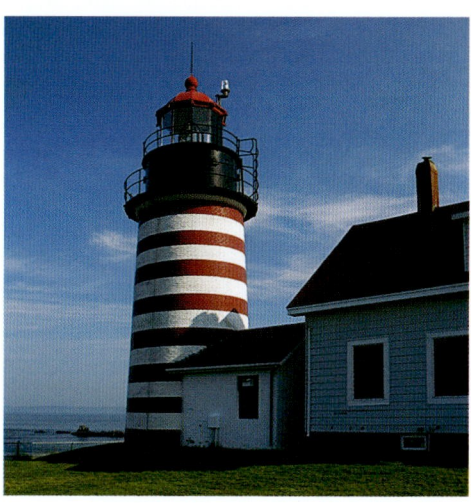

Bitmap (raster) Image

▷ FIGURE 2-23

Computer images are either categorized as vector or bitmap (raster) images.

SAVING GRAPHIC FILE FORMATS

Graphic applications allow the designer to save files in specific universal formats for an intended purpose. The file extension determines the type of graphic format saved and how a file may be used. Saving graphic files in these universal formats—extensions such as .EPS, .TIF, .JPG, .GIF, .PNG, or .PDF—gives them the flexibility to be used with other graphics programs for specific purposes. Specific graphic formats will be discussed in detail throughout this text.

TOOLKIT TIP The Save As command is used when changing a file's extension the first time a document is saved and when saving it with a different name or to a different drive or location. Using the Save command saves a file with the same name, in the same directory or location, or in the same drive.

The table below gives an overview of file formats.

FORMAT	ADVANTAGES	CONSIDERATIONS
.PNG	Records transparencies in bitmap and vector images. Compresses files without losing data. Web use.	Cannot be read by older browsers. Larger size files but can still be used for the web. Cannot be enlarged.
.GIF	Used for vector graphics and animation. Used on the web. Keeps transparencies.	GIF files have only 256 colors. Scalable.
.JPG	Compressed format used in photographic images. Keeps file sizes small. Used for web and ink-jet proof printing.	Data is thrown out each time the image is saved, gradually deteriorating quality. No transparencies. Not for commercial press. Cannot be enlarged.
.TIF	Most accurate recording of detail in photographs. Quality maintains as original regardless of changes. Can be used for commercial printing of photographs.	Largest file size. Not used for the web. Cannot be enlarged.
.PDF	Compresses text and graphics in documents without losing data for electronic distribution and the web. Works best with many documents. Can also be used for soft proofs and commercial printing.	Can also be read in free Adobe Reader program.
.EPS	Preferred method when combining graphics and type. Vector graphics can be scalable. Used extensively for commercial printing.	Large file size. Not for the web.

UNDERSTANDING THE IMPORTANCE OF COLOR

Creating a design with appropriate colors is a major factor in client approval. Research on the designer's part is critical to the success of the design. Some colors work better in small quantities than others. A designer must also be wary of design components using dark or light tones in specific quantities that may symbolize positive or negative aspects (Figure 2-24). Complementary background colors or lettering may be used with products extensively in package design. A bag of apples might have green lettering on the package as its complement to highlight the red color of the produce, giving a fresher appearance. When working with advertising agencies, whether on a local or global scale, color is used differently within various cultures. Designers need to be aware of the intended market. For instance, the color of royalty is purple in America and in Europe, but in China it is yellow. We in America look at white as symbolizing purity, and we associate it with weddings, whereas in China red is the usual bridal color.

▷ FIGURE 2-24

The lightness and darkness of tone in a design generate different emotional appeal. Understand the message you want to convey before designing for a particular market.

Inside Fold   Back   Front

3-Way Folding Brochure (outside page)

DESIGN TIP

When you specify a color for a design, consider how the final product will be used. Be wary of various themes with specific colors and their tonalities. Darker tones may have a contrary or more adverse impact than lighter tones. Be selective and keep color combinations simple and pertinent to the overall design.

Depending on the intended message, colors can have contrary effects. Here are some general concepts regarding the use of color in our American culture:

- White will usually stand for purity, but can also be utilized to generate a feeling of emptiness. Websites sometimes use white backgrounds as a neutral setting for images and for easier readability of text.

- Black can show value in terms of elegance, such as in tuxedos and gowns. Black can be used as an attention getter as a background with white, or *reversed,* type. Black can also suggest danger or something negative. It is also used as a neutral background in designing web pages that have many photographs.

- Gray (if a very light gray is used) can provide a subtle background on electronic media, lending a neutral balance for images and colored type. On printed media, it is used very sparingly. Gray can also have powerful negative symbolism, such as stormy weather.

- Red can make the boldest of statements and may draw the viewer's eye more than any other color. Red can be used in small amounts for emphasis. Red can symbolize love (bright or medium red), strength (middle or true red), or anger (dark red) depending on the tone.

- Pink is a color used often in the bakery industry. Pink can also suggest high value in packaged goods and is a feminine color.

- Violet is another color that is generally used in small quantities. Dark violet, for instance, may suggest royalty.

- Blue, as one of the most widely used colors, has different effects. Lighter shades of blue may signify dream-like fantasies. Medium and dark blues may be used to signify honesty, professionalism, and sometimes spirituality. However, in some instances, blue used as the dominant color can adversely signify depression, dreariness, or isolation.

- Green signifies nature and can be used for produce, products related to healing, or for environmental issues. Green is also used to represent wealth, perhaps for banking institutions. Contrarily, green can imply jealousy or greed.

- Yellow can produce feelings of warmth and may be used to signify fast service (taxis, fast food). In contrast, yellow can also suggest danger or caution.

CREATING COLORS ON THE COMPUTER

Millions of light-emitted colors can be created on the computer by mixing the electronic primary colors: red, green, and blue. These **RGB mode** colors are used for electronic display such as web pages. Computers use an additive process to create color from the primary colors. The computer's secondary colors are magenta, cyan, and yellow, or **CMYK mode** (K stands for black, which is used to increase contrast). Mix red and blue and you get magenta. White is theoretically created by mixing red, green, and blue at their full intensity (Figure 2-25). Using computer software, you can convert files from RGB mode to CMYK mode to create colors that will closely match pigment colors used in commercial printing.

DESIGN TIP

When designing for a client, avoid symbols that are recognizable (road signs, hearts, icons) that may be used as clichés for a product. They can become ineffective if used too often.

▷ FIGURE 2-25

A computer's primary colors are red, green, and blue. Adding these colors creates the secondary colors: cyan, magenta, and yellow. White is created by adding red, green, and blue at full intensity.

TOOLKIT TIP When designing in color on a computer, keep in mind that you are mixing light and that the colors may print differently on a reflective surface such as paper. RGB mode colors are the best colors to use for electronic display and for soft proof printouts from ink-jet printers.

CLIENT ASSIGNMENT: Designing in Color or Black and White Contrasts

Here is an assignment that will allow you to design a layout that would be used in this book as a two-page spread to make the section "Understanding the Importance of Color" look more appealing by using imagery to complement the text descriptions. In this section, colors are described as having certain effects on a design when used in different tones, shades, or quantity. As part of this layout, with each color description, you are going to include two-color (or you can challenge yourself to use only black-and-white images) contrasting images for emphasis. You need to think how best to portray the colors mentioned. Create a series of three or more sketches to show peers or your instructor—as your clients—the proposed layout of images with text. Using their input, create a final rough at full scale, using your word processor to print out images to be pasted, or create fine detailed drawings as if for final approval before setting up a comp. Have fun!

ACTION ITEMS OVERVIEW

Here is a breakdown of what you need to do:

- Determine the layout of images and text, including spacing and margins, for the final size.
- Research what images will be used and what fonts, styles, and sizes will be used.
- Create three or more thumbnail sketches of how the images will be laid out with the text descriptions (normally, you would create more sketches, but this will do for this exercise).
- Present your thumbnail sketches to your instructor or peers to get their input.
- With the sketches narrowed down, create the final, full-size rough combining elements from various sketches. Then show them to your clients for approval.
- ADVANCED USERS: Identify design elements and principles in various ads.

DESIGN TIP

It is always best to create in the computer's RGB mode first; then, create a duplicate file and convert it to CMYK mode.

CONSIDERATIONS IN THE DESIGN PROCESS

In the following chapters, you will be guided through the designing process to create and complete the assignments using various graphic applications. Here, we will help you work through the process of creating a two-page color (or black-and-white) spread describing color (Figure 2-26).

▷ FIGURE 2-26

Create a two-page spread with space for margins, text, and images.

DESIGN TIP

Although you need not be concerned with trimming at this point, just as an FYI, when looking at determining size, it is a good idea to add an extra eighth inch horizontally and vertically for final trimming purposes if a commercial printer will be used. For instance, a final page dimension of 9 3/4 × 7 3/4 inches would actually be set up as printing on a 10-by-8-inch sheet.

Here are some considerations.

1. First, as a designer you have to think of portraying color in this book with recognizable images that will be printed in color (or black and white or shades of gray, if you are up to the challenge).

2. Consider one table or column for each page; obviously you would not want text across both pages. Create two separate pages for our purposes.

3. Determine the layout for incorporating text and images, as if it would be used as a two-page spread within this text. Use this book as a guide for measurements (Figure 2-26).

4. Locate the *Color* file in the *Chapter 2* folder (Client > Chapter 2 > Color) on your hard drive, or locate it online at *www.CengageBrain.com*. It contains the text you need, so you do not have to type it over again and can concentrate on designing instead.

5. Open the *Color* file in your word processing program, such as Microsoft Word.

6. Determine what fonts will be used for the title and body of the text. Consider using a sans-serif font, such as Arial or Helvetica, for the title and headlines. Try a serif font for the body of the text. Times Roman, Georgia, or Century Schoolbook fonts provide a good starting point.

7. Highlight the text and make printouts with your chosen fonts at 10- and 12-pt sizes to start.

8. Observe the text and its relationship to the rest of the document. Determine the sizes of the title, headlines, and the body text. Leave enough extra blank space for margins all around and between the images and text so they do not appear to run into one another. Try inch-wide margins along the outside to start.

9. Determine what type of images will be used. Will they be photographs, clip art, or your own drawings? Your images may be fairly small, so keep the images simple and basic. Stay consistent when you decide what type of images to use.

10. Research what images you need to best complement each color description. You can use not only images from your word processing program, such as Microsoft Word (Insert > Picture > Clip Art), but you can also cull graphics from the Internet; find websites where you can download free images (see Chapter 1).

TOOLKIT TIP At *www.CengageBrain.com*, there is an *Extras & Goodies* folder with additional tutorials. There you'll find, in the Chapter 2 folder, a text file named Download that describes how to download images off the Internet if needed. Be careful not to use images that are copyrighted (©) or have a visible watermark on the image.

11. Create a series of two or more proportional thumbnail sketches of possible layouts that show where to place contrasting images alongside each description. Include printed images or image descriptions alongside the text description in each sketch. Figure 2-27 gives you a few ideas for layouts.

▷ FIGURE 2-27

Here are some layout ideas to position your text and images (lines are text, squares are images).

12. Get feedback from your peers or instructor as to which layout, images, and text would best suit this assignment; then create the final rough.

13. Use your word processor to help position text and possible images or, if you are not comfortable with positioning elements using the computer yet, cut out, arrange, and paste the elements to create a full-size rough. You can also create a detailed, full-size drawing if you want. Draw guidelines, if needed, to help with placement.

DESIGN TIP

Professional presentations may involve spray mounting your designs onto gray or black matte (illustration or foam-core) board with appropriate margins for a nice, clean look.

TOOLKIT TIP In the *Chapter 2* folder, you will find a file *PlaceIMG* that describes how to insert images into a word processor document. Open this file in your word processor.

14. Go back to your "clients" to get final approval or input on your rough for any last-minute changes. Ask them how they would like the final rough presented, and then present it to your clients neatly.

15. Remember: Presentation is an important component in design. It shows professionalism to a client. Designers can present labeled roughs and comps mounted on illustration board for stability, inside a binder encased in transparent sheeting, or by any other method that makes the presentation look clean and neat.

16. Welcome to the world of design!

ADVANCED USERS: Identifying Design Elements and Principles in Various Ads

Here is a little exercise to help you think about design principles and elements. Formal design elements that make up the basic building blocks of design are *line, shape, color, texture, value,* and *format.* You are trying to communicate something in each design you create, and these physical elements of design are your tools for communication; knowing when and how to use them is essential to design building. Here, you will identify design elements used in various ads and media and the design principles they employed.

1. Locate four good magazine ads, either half or full page, with graphic imagery and text.

2. Locate two CD covers either from iTunes or from your own collection that you find very pleasing.

3. Find a book cover that looks appealing.

4. Find your favorite website.

5. Define the design elements used in each and the design principles established.

6. Identify the typography used (serif or sans serif, alignment, etc.).

7. Explain how color was used for emotional appeal.

8. Pick one of the pieces and try to design it a little differently, creating three sketches, or roughs, if time allows.

9. Explain to your client, peer, or instructor why you would make these changes.

DIGITAL TOOLKIT EXTRA: Internet Resources

One of the best resources for locating current technologies, tutorials, information, or design concepts is on the Internet. There is a wealth of information that you can print or save as a bookmark. To learn how to create bookmarks of your favorite sites in Internet Explorer, open the file Bookmark in the Chapter 2 folder. We have included a list below for you to access information and download trial versions of the software, to find special applications, and to search for tutorials about each application we are using in this book. You will find these and additional lists of resources in a file called Research in the Chapter 2 folder. Just click on any underlined text links in the document, and it will take you to these websites. Feel free to check out the *Extras & Goodies* folder for each chapter online at *www.CengageBrain.com*.

INTERNET RESOURCES

To access information, tutorials, software and hardware updates, and to try versions of the applications used in this book, visit these websites:

- To access information regarding Microsoft products:
  http://www.microsoft.com

- To access information about using Microsoft's Office Suite products on a Mac (OfficeMac) check out the Microsoft Office for Mac site:
  http://www.microsoft.com/mac/default.mspx

- If you are a student or educator, check out these two sites that will give you great discounts on software and hardware:
  http://www.academicsuperstore.com
  http://www.journeyed.com

- For information on Macintosh OS X and software utilities you can download, including iTunes and QuickTime (for movies): **http://www.apple.com**

- For digital imaging (Photoshop), digital desktop publishing (InDesign), and digital illustration (Illustrator):
  http://www.adobe.com

You can also download the free Adobe Reader application to view any portable document files (PDFs) created electronically, and you can download a free Flash Player and Shockwave to view animations. We will get into these next in the Unit 1 Review. Also, you can check out their library of video tutorials on many Adobe products at **http://tv.adobe.com**

- To get information and ideas in design:
  http://www.graphicdesign.about.com

- For information in all areas of desktop publishing, web design, digital imaging, and illustration, use the About website. It is a great place to start!
  http://www.about.com

- So, you want to download and watch Photoshop TV on your iPod or on the big screen to learn all kinds of great tricks and tips?
  http://www.photoshopusertv.com

CHAPTER SUMMARY

This chapter introduced lots of information to get you prepared to work in the upcoming chapters. You learned about incorporating various design elements and principles to create effective layouts. You were exposed to typography basics and the importance of using the right fonts and spacing for your design. You installed fonts for the text exercises, and you learned how color can affect the message or mood of a piece. In your assignment, you learned to research and use color symbols—and you could attempt this assignment in black and white—to complement the text descriptions. You learned the design process with client input. Do not forget to check out the *Extras & Goodies* link for more tutorials after the *Student Data files* link on *www.CengageBrain.com* for more projects and ideas in each chapter.

REVIEW QUESTIONS

1. Explain the design elements used in graphic design.

2. Explain the principles of graphic design.

3. Describe font, type family, font size, tracking, leading, and four kinds of type alignment.

4. Explain in general terms contrasting symbolism or emphasis for the colors white, black, red, blue, green, and yellow, or when a different shade of a particular color is used.

5. Explain the design process from concept to completion when working with a client.

▷ FIGURE 2-28

Excerpts: Design Elements and Principles, Design Process, Typography, Imagery, and Color. Chapter project involves using design components to lay out contrary color images to match descriptions to be used in a color (or black-and-white) spread.

Design Elements:
Line, Shape, Value, Texture, Contrast, Depth Perception, Motion, Color, and Format

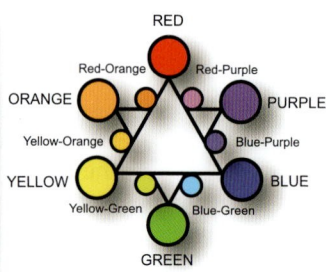

Design Principles:
Balance, Rythym, Space, Emphasis, and Harmony

Color and Typography

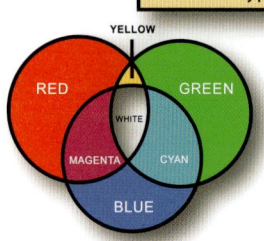

Book Antiqua (serif type)
Arial **Bold (sans-serif type)**
Papyrus (decorative type)
Brush Script Italic (script type)
🚌 🚲 🛥 **?** (symbol type)

Designing for the Client

Getting Ready for Production

This review encompasses some of the topics covered in the first two chapters to get you, as a designer, ready for production. You will install the free Adobe Reader application from the Adobe website that is used to read universal portable document formats (PDFs). You can also use this application to look at and print additional resources and projects in the *Extras & Goodies* folder downloaded from Cengage Learning's website, *www.cengagebrain.com.* To prepare you for the next unit in Photoshop, you will check for the size and memory space needed on your computer, then go through the process of downloading and installing the trial software, which you can download from the Adobe site at *http://www.adobe.com,* using the Creative Cloud subscription service utilized by Adobe, or see your instructor. You will also sketch and explain how you would improve a particular design and review some basic design techniques to use throughout this book.

CLIENT ASSIGNMENT: Installing Adobe Reader, Photoshop Trial Software, and Improving a Design

You will install the free application (not a trial version) Adobe Reader from the Adobe site, which is used to read universal electronic portable document format (PDF) files. You will find additional assignments, resources, and other information in the *Extras & Goodies* folder, which you can download from the publisher's website. Many of these will be in PDF format. Trial versions of software work just like the real application and are useful for a set number of days. To get ready for the next unit about Photoshop, you can go through the process to install the trial version of Photoshop from the Adobe website *(http://www.adobe.com)* on your computer, or see your instructor to go through the process on your network drive. It is important to first find out if you have the needed system requirements to use the software, such as having enough RAM memory, before installing a large program. You will see where you can find this information on your computer. We will also review some important design points to consider as you go through the exercises in this book.

ACTION ITEMS OVERVIEW

- Install Adobe Reader to be able to read and print portable documents that you can find in the *Extras & Goodies* folder on the publisher's website where you downloaded the text exercise files.

- Find information about your computer's memory and system requirements before you install an application.

- Go through the process of installing the Photoshop trial demo onto your computer. You can also install it to use in the next unit if you do not have the current version installed.

- Review techniques in design and create a sketch of an improved design.

DOWNLOADING AND INSTALLING ADOBE READER

Macintosh OS X and Windows operating systems contain many programs or applications that allow the user to perform all kinds of operations. They become the coordinators or managers of the applications running within them. There are some free application utilities that can be useful to help you become more productive. One of them is Adobe Reader, which can be found at the Adobe website (*http://www.adobe.com*). As a cross-platform application, this free application allows both Mac and Windows users to read each other's PDFs, and make comments to communicate with one another, as long as document rights are allowed. Many manuals, support information, and other documentation, including illustrations, are created in PDF form. With the Adobe Reader, you can e-mail PDF documents. because they are small in file size, and they can be printed. We will be covering PDFs in more detail later. In the *Extras & Goodies* link, near the *Student Data Files* link on the publisher's website, *www.cengagebrain.com*, you will find additional resources and assignments. Much of the documentation is in PDF form. You will also be using the Address bar to not only locate and display folders on your drive, but also to type in the **URL** or website address.

In this exercise you will be downloading Adobe Reader and installing it on your desktop. You will then locate the *Goodies* folder you created in Chapter 1 on your desktop or flash drive, which contains additional assignments and info that you downloaded in Chapter 1, and use the Adobe Reader to display the file. This is one of those applications that is a must for every computer and is safe to install. Note: If you haven't already done so, follow the instructions on the inside back cover of your book, or from the previous exercise "Downloading the Student Data Files" in Chapter 1 and download the chapters in the *Extras & Goodies* section from the book website where you downloaded the student data files onto your desktop.

Macintosh OS X

1. Make sure you are connected to the Internet and type in the address bar the site *http://www.adobe.com.*

2. At the first page of the site, or Home page, you will find the Downloads tab for the Adobe Reader application. If not, select the Menu link, and then select Downloads.

3. Click the Downloads tab, then click on the Adobe Reader button or link. You'll notice it will display steps to go through.

4. When the Download Adobe Reader window comes up, select the type of computer platform (if asked), version, and language you want to download. Select Install now to start the download process onto your computer. Adobe will provide further instructions if needed for you to follow.

5. The application installer will have a ".dmg" extension, or something similar depending on the country and language, and will download to the desktop (Figure UR 1-1).

▷ FIGURE UR 1-1

Downloading and installing Adobe Reader on Mac OS X.

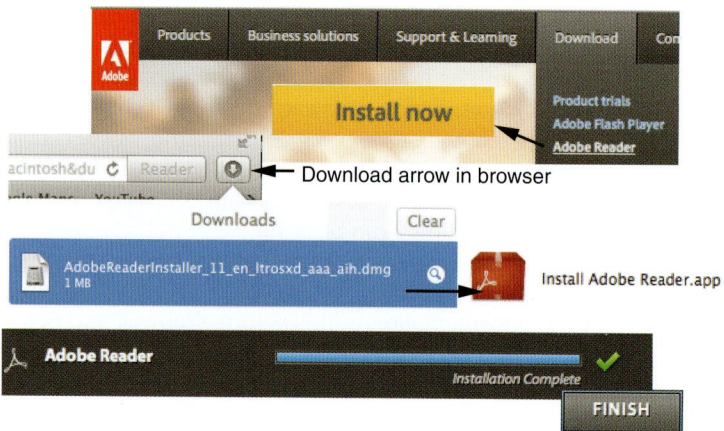

6. When the downloaded compressed file is completed, an icon named the Adobe Reader installer will be displayed on the desktop, or use the download icon to locate the installer on the top right side of your browser window. Click on the icon and the application will start to automatically install.

7. Follow the instructions to install the application, and agree to the installation. Click the Finish button when the installation is completed.

8. To check to see if it installed correctly, click on the desktop, and using Finder, select Go > Applications. You will find the Adobe Reader application among the list of applications.

9. If possible, make an alias of the application by selecting the application, then selecting File > Make Alias, and when the Adobe Reader Alias appears, drag it to the desktop.

10. Launch Adobe Reader, then open the *Goodies* folder you created on your desktop or drive, where you will find additional info in each chapter. Open the *Chapter 2* folder and select the *Info* folder, then, in the *View as PDFs* folder, select *Color Wheel.pdf.* Note: With Adobe Reader installed you can simply double-click the file *Color Wheel.pdf*, which will automatically launch the Adobe Reader application and display the file contents.

11. The Adobe Reader application should display the Color Wheel illustration.

12. When finished, select File > Close to close the file and feel free to look at other documents and information in the folder.

Windows 7 and 8

1. Make sure you are connected to the Internet, and type in the Address bar the site http://www.adobe.com.

2. At the first page of the Adobe website, or Home page, you will find the Downloads tab (Figure UR 1-2). If not, select the Menu link, and then select Downloads.

▷ FIGURE UR 1-2

Downloading and installing Adobe Reader in Windows 7 and 8.

3. Click the Downloads tab, then click the Adobe Reader button or link; When the Download Adobe Reader window comes up, select the type of computer platform and a language if asked, then select the Install now button.

4. The "installer" file will download with an ".exe" extension and will display on the bottom left of your screen. Click on the executable (exe) file when completed to open up the installer.

5. If a security dialog box appears, select Run for our purposes, when given a choice to either Run or Save the application. You can also save it on your home computer as well. Select Yes to the dialog box asking to make changes to your computer, and the installer will continue to install Adobe Reader. Click Finish when done.

6. To check to see if it installed correctly, click Start > All Programs (Windows 7), or check the applications in your Start Screen on Windows 8, and see if it is displayed among the list of programs or applications.

7. If possible, make a shortcut of the application by locating the Adobe Reader application in the Programs list; then right-click once to display a menu.

8. Select Send To > Desktop to place a shortcut on the desktop.

9. Launch Adobe Reader, then open the *Goodies* folder you created on your desktop or drive in Chapter 1, in which you will find additional information for each chapter. Open the *Chapter 2* folder and select the *Info* folder, then, in the *View as PDFs* folder, select *Color Wheel.pdf.* Note: With Adobe Reader installed you can also simply double-click the file *Color Wheel.pdf,* which will automatically launch the Adobe Reader application and display the file contents.

10. When finished, select File > Close to close the file and feel free to look at other documents in the *Goodies* folder.

TOOLKIT TIP There are a couple ways to install applications in Windows if they do not start automatically. If the file has an .exe extension, it is a compressed file, and you can simply double-click it and it will guide you through a set of screen instructions. The Add and Remove Programs command in the Control panel works well with all applications safely to install or remove programs. With Windows, it's a good idea to create a Download folder in order to keep track of files downloaded from the Internet in case you may need to reinstall them at a later date. In the right side of the title bar or near the Search box of many a browser's window there will usually be a download arrow that you can click on to locate downloaded files and applications.

DOWNLOADING AND INSTALLING PHOTOSHOP CREATIVE CLOUD (CC) TRIAL SOFTWARE

You can download trial or demo versions of the applications used in this text; download Photoshop, InDesign, and Illustrator software from *http://www.adobe .com,* or see your instructor. You may install these when you are ready to work on your chapter assignments, if you do not already have the application on your computer. Here you will learn to install a trial version of Photoshop for the next unit. This trial version will work as a regular application for 30 days—enough time to complete Digital Imaging (Photoshop), the next unit. Note: CD/DVDs of applications are no longer available from Adobe, as they have all gone to a subscription service. When downloading a trial version of Adobe software, you can choose to purchase a monthly or annual subscription after your trial period.

ADOBE'S CREATIVE CLOUD VERSION SOFTWARE

Creative Cloud (CC) is Adobe's current version of its suite of applications, three of which you'll be working on in this text: Photoshop (digital imaging), Illustrator (illustration), and InDesign (desktop publishing). It is comprised of a new subscription/membership based service where students, faculty, and professionals pay a periodic monthly fee to use one, some, or all its suite of applications for basically the same price. This is going to become the new trend in the industry for designers and photographers who don't want to try to budget large sums of money for purchases of one or more of Adobe's products, but to plan with a simple monthly or yearly fee, and use on multiple devices. Cloud storage and file syncing capabilities allow designers to reliably access their files wherever they are, even on a mobile device, and can share concepts with clients or colleagues more easily than ever. **Cloud-based services** let designers build and publish websites, mobile apps, iPad publications, and content for any medium or device.

Although not recommended if you are planning only to download and use the trial versions in the following exercises, if you decide to take advantage of the subscription membership service, when you download the Creative Cloud application, it becomes a manager of all Adobe applications you download and helps provide instant updates. The process is much the same for downloading the actual software as for downloading the trial versions described in the next exercises.

TOOLKIT TIP If you already have Photoshop installed, you can still go through the process of installing the trial version and then canceling, which we will show you in the steps below. If you do not wish to install this trial software, you will find that most of the main exercises will work with earlier versions of Photoshop.

TOOLKIT TIP Most school systems have security settings that may allow you to install an application but will not hurt the computer, because the computer automatically resets to its original set state when shut down. This protection avoids any tampering with lab computers to keep a safe environment. Check with your instructor.

Macintosh OS X

Here you will check information about the computer's memory using the Apple Menu, then go through the process to download the Photoshop Trial version on your Mac OS X computer, which you can use for the next unit for 30 days. To do this exercise, you need a DSL or cable connection, *not* dial up. The file size is very large, over 2.2 gigabytes for Mac. Adobe also routinely changes their website, so the following steps may not be exactly what you may find, but they will be quite close, and you should have no problem following along.

▷ FIGURE UR 1-3

Finding out info on your Mac, and downloading Photoshop trial software.

▷ FIGURE UR 1-3

Finding out info on your Mac, and downloading Photoshop trial software.

1. Mac OS X: To find how much memory you have on your Mac computer, select the Apple menu in the corner, and then select About This Mac from the drop-down list. The display will tell you what version you are working in, how much memory you have, and so on. You should have at least 2 gigabytes (2000 MB) of RAM memory, and a 1 GHz processor to continue.

2. Connect to the Internet and in your browser address bar type *http://www.adobe.com.* When the site opens, select Menu > Download > Product trials, then select Photoshop CC icon, and click the Try link (Figure UR 1-3).

3. You may be asked to register to create an Adobe ID free account and password that does not share any personal info but allows you to download future trials, updates, and so forth.

4. After posting the information, you will need to select a language and platform (Windows or Macintosh) to download, then click Continue to accept the software policy that you will use it yourself.

5. The installer will automatically download with the application and will be placed on the desktop. If you already have Photoshop CC on your computer, then do not install it; drag the icon to the trash to delete the file.

6. If you wish to install the trial version, locate and double-click the *Photoshop* folder on your desktop, then double-click the Install Adobe Photoshop icon. When the dialog box pops up, select Continue, then Accept the agreement, if posted, if you want to install. Follow any instructions and you are ready!

TOOLKIT TIP If you are not sure about the size of the file or the amount of memory you need before installing a large application on your Mac, select the file, and then select File > Get Info to get the information you need. This is a good, safe habit to get into.

Windows 7 and 8

Here, you will use the Control Panel to find information about your computer and then install a Photoshop trial version that you can use for the next 30 days. To do this exercise, you need a DSL or cable connection, *not* dial up. The file size is very

▷ FIGURE UR 1-4

Checking PC (Windows) system and downloading Photoshop trial version of software.

large: over 2 gigabytes (2000 MB). Adobe also routinely changes their website, so the following steps may not be exactly what you may find, but they will be quite close and you should have no problem following along.

1. With Windows 7, to find information about your PC, select Start Menu > Control Panel > System and Security > System. When you select the System link, you will find the information you need about your computer. With Windows 8, use File Explorer on your Desktop Screen, select the Computer Tab on the This PC ribbon, and then select System Properties (Figure UR1-4). You should have at least 2 gigabytes (2000 MB) of RAM memory, and a 1 GHz processor to continue. More is better.

2. Connect to the Internet and in your browser address bar type *http://www .adobe.com*. When the site opens, select Menu > Downloads > Product trials, then select Photoshop CC icon, and click the Try link.

3. You may be asked to register to create an Adobe ID free account and password that does not share any personal info but allows you to download future trials, updates, and so forth.

4. You may find another dialog box open, select Launch Application as the default response, then the Application Manager will download and update. If a security dialog box comes up about running on your computer, select Yes.

5. If a dialog box asks whether you want to Open or Save the file, you can choose Open if you want the application to install at some default location on your hard drive. This will work if you are downloading to a home computer.

6. If you choose Open, the application will automatically open and install the application. If you have saved the file to another location, and you wish to install, double-click to open the file and the application will install. Just follow any additional instructions if given.

TOOLKIT TIP In Windows, you can find information about a file by selecting the file and selecting the Properties command (File > Properties).

DESIGN TECHNIQUES

1. Try to find a CD cover, web home page, book cover, magazine front cover, or magazine ad design that you would like to make better.

2. Sketch in the changes and identify design elements used and design principles emphasized.

Here are some helpful hints in design techniques to watch for as you go through the text chapters:

- Listen to your client. Research, research, research. Determine your market.

- Use file management techniques to keep your work organized.

- Stay focused on the theme or message. Strive for simplicity.

- Provide a hierarchy of content to lead the viewer through your composition.

- Maintain consistency in fonts, font sizes, and spacing throughout.

- Choose the appropriate font to complement the imagery in the design.

- Typography should enhance a message, not detract from it. Use typefaces that are appropriate to the message. Color of type should also play a vital role in enhancing the visual expression, but should not hinder readability.

- Be wary of various themes with specific colors and their tonalities. Darker tones may have a more negative impact than lighter tones. Be selective and keep color combinations simple and pertinent to the overall design.

- Avoid using recognizable, clichéd symbols (road signs, hearts, or trite icons) for a product.

- Develop a sense of consistency, using the same margins and column layouts on every page; provide consistency in typeface, line spacing, and alignment.

- Always present your designs neatly, professionally, and on time.

UNIT

2

CHAPTER

3

Adjusting Images in Photoshop

CHAPTER OBJECTIVES: To understand the importance of Photoshop's function as an image-editing program to adjust and enhance images, in this chapter you will:

▷ Learn Photoshop's desktop components and how they interact with one another.

▷ Navigate around an image using the Navigator panel, Zoom, and Hand tools.

▷ Use the Image menu to perform global adjustments or enhancements to an image.

▷ Use the Color Balance and Auto Color commands to remove color casts, and the Auto Tone, Brightness/Contrast, and Auto Contrast commands to maintain detail in highlight and shadow areas.

▷ Use the Shadows/Highlights command for correcting poorly exposed or flat contrast images.

▷ Learn the importance of file management techniques by saving to specific file formats, and creating images for print and web media.

▷ Adjust image size, resolution, and determine color modes for print and web media.

▷ ADVANCED USERS: Image precision adjustments using histograms, the Histogram panel, and using the Levels adjustment and Curves adjustment. Using Crop and Perspective tools to straighten and adjust an image's perspective.

▷ DIGITAL TOOLKIT EXTRA: Using Adobe Creative Cloud and Adobe Bridge for Managing Image Files.

Digital imaging involves the process of scanning or importing images—photographs, paintings, illustrations, and so on—from scanners, digital cameras, drives, or other digital devices into the computer so the software can convert them into editable digital images for enhancing, retouching, digital artwork, and restoration. Using Adobe Photoshop a designer or photographer can edit, manipulate, enhance, or apply effects to selected parts of an image or to the entire image. Images can also be combined as composites. Photoshop CC version, the CC stands for Creative Cloud, provides tools not only to create images that can be integrated with other Adobe Creative Cloud products, which we will explore later in this text, but to create publishable images for both print and web media that can be shared on multiple devices at various locations with access to the Internet, and among peers. In this chapter, you will perform basic image enhancements while exploring some of Photoshop's tools and functions. You will also create images for both print and web media. Note: If you need to download the files for this for any of the chapters in this book, they are at *www.CengageBrain.com.*

THE PHOTOSHOP ENVIRONMENT

When an existing or new file is opened within Photoshop, the Photoshop desktop contains the Title bar, which displays the file title, Menu bar, Tools panel, Tool Options bar, and other panels (Figure 3-1). The Menu bar provides commands to perform almost any type of editing your creative mind can come up with. The Tools panel contains the tools you need to edit your image, with different options for each tool available in the Tool Options bar.

Panels provide commands and functions to help you modify and monitor your images. They can be collapsed into icons, or small pictures, to conserve space on your desktop. The Window menu on the Menu bar allows you to display panels, the Tools panel, the Application Frame which allows you to group everything together in one window, preset workspaces, and the Tool Options bar. By clicking on the list, you choose which items you want to display. You will find that Photoshop's active features change when you open an existing image, or when you are editing the current image. The Window menu also has an Arrange command where you can select to display your image files as separate windows or as a tabbed display. In working with various Adobe programs, you'll find the interface similar between all applications so that once you learn to navigate around one application, the others will feel quite familiar.

 TOOLKIT TIP The default color of the CC interface is dark gray or black, as opposed to light gray in previous versions. To change the color of the interface, choose Photoshop > Preferences > Interface > Color Theme, if you are using a Mac, or Edit > Preferences > Interface > Color Theme, for Windows users.

WORKING WITH BITMAP (RASTER) IMAGES

On your computer's monitor, individually colored square dots, or **pixels**, are displayed and are the smallest picture elements on your computer screen. Images created in Photoshop or imported from cameras or other devices into Photoshop are converted into bitmap, or raster images. Bitmap images are the most accurate for recording details in photographic images or paintings and use may millions or even billions of individually colored pixels that determine the details in shading and tonality of the image. These images are *nonscalable*, so a designer or photographer should not add pixels to make the final image larger than the original image size without understanding that he or she may be sacrificing detail. The **resolution** determines the amount of detail in an image. An image's resolution, measured as **dpi** (dots per inch), is used for printing documents; 300 dpi is the norm for high-resolution, quality images for press or photographic output. Images measured as **ppi** (pixels per inch) refer to the screen resolution that you see on your computer monitor. The standard for creating web pages is 72 ppi; the higher the resolution, the more detail there will be in shading, highlights, and tonality—and the larger the file size.

TOOLKIT TIP In Photoshop, when you choose File > New to create a new file, you have a predefined set of document size choices for print, web publishing, mobile devices, and for video, with the resolution already built in. Use this option if you already know the image size or resolution that you will need.

PHOTOSHOP TOOLS PANEL

The **Photoshop tools panel** provides the tools to select, edit, manage, and manipulate image pixels and to draw or add type to images. On some of the tools, you will notice a small triangle at the bottom right of the tool to indicate there are more related tools that will be displayed when you select the tool and hold the mouse down. The corresponding keystroke to access that tool is also displayed. We will be using the most common tools in the chapters that follow. You can change the shape of the Tools panel from two columns to one column wide to help conserve desktop space by clicking on the double arrows at the top of the Tools panel (Figure 3-2).

Here is Photoshop's tools panel broken down into various categories of tools with a brief description of each, including the corresponding keystroke in parentheses for each tool group:

- **Navigation** in an image can be done with the Zoom Tool (Z) or Hand Tool (H). The Rotate View Tool provides a different perspective.

- **Selection tools** select and isolate image areas. Marquee tools (M) select rectangular or elliptical selections, while Lasso tools (L) allow you to make freehand selections. The Magic Wand Tool (W) and the Quick Selection Tool select by similar color. The Move Tool (V) technically does not generate a selection, but moves selections onto or within an image. The Crop and Perspective Crop tools (C) draw rectangular or four-sided selections inside the image area that trim away what is outside the selection area. The Slice tools (C) are used to cut up portions of an image, for web use.

- **Painting and drawing tools** allow you to apply brush or shape effects. The Shape tools (U) are used to create various shapes that help with selections. Brush, Mixer Brush, and Pencil tools (B) are used for painting. The Color Replacement Tool (B) replaces colors under the brush with the foreground color while retaining the detail and shading in the image. History and Art History brushes (Y) allow you to go back in time to a previously used brush

Photoshop Tools panel

Photoshop Tools panel contains the essential tools for image editing. Other tools also display whenever any tool button with a triangle is clicked on.

or apply an effect. Pen tools (P) create paths using anchor points for precise selections. Path and Direct Selection tools (A) are used to select paths created by the Pen Tool.

- **Editing and retouching tools** help to improve or enhance an image. The Healing Brush, Red Eye, Content-Aware Move, and Patch tools (J) blend in lighting and shading of the sampled area to be copied for more detailed precision. The Crop and Perspective Crop tools (C) trim a rectangular or four-sided area and can change perspective of an image. The Slice tools (C) delineate and select image components to use for the web, which allow faster downloading. The Eraser tools (E) remove selected pixels or background colors or make the background transparent. The Gradient Tool (G) creates a shaded fill from one color to another, the Paint Bucket Tool (G) fills in solid colors, while the 3D Material Drop Tool (G) applies textures. The Blur, Sharpen, and Smudge tools, and the Burn, Dodge, and Sponge tools (O) let you soften, sharpen, lighten, or darken parts of an image. The Clone and Pattern Stamp tools (S) copy over sampled image areas.

- **Type tools** (T) bring text into your images with various type orientations and type masks. They create vector type that can be scaled to any size and still remain sharp. The Type Mask tools create a selection in the shape of type.

- The **Note Tool** (N) allows you to leave electronic notes to yourself or other members of your team that can be attached to an image.

- **Color tools**, like the Eyedropper, 3D Material Eyedropper, and Color Sampler tools (I) are used to sample any color or texture on any image to make a new foreground color by default and provide color information. Below the tools, you will find the Color Picker area, which displays the foreground color for use by color, painting, and retouching tools and the background color used by the Eraser and Gradient tools. You can select and switch between colors (X) and also default to black and white (D).

- **Measuring tools**, involve the Measure Tool (I), which checks distances and dimensions, whereas the Count Tool (I) counts objects in an image.

THE TOOL OPTIONS BAR

In Photoshop, when you select a tool in the Tools panel, the **Tool Options bar** displays options for that particular tool (Figure 3-3). If the Tool Options bar is not displayed, open it from the Window menu. On the left side there is also a Tool Preset Picker displaying preset tool functions of the current tool or for all tools, which you can create and add your own settings at any time. The Tool Presets are also displayed as a panel; this allows you to create preferred settings for your tools to increase your productivity. On the Mac OS, you can also work within an Application frame from the Window menu, which keeps all Photoshop's windows and panels together within the single display frame.

TOOLKIT TIP Any changes you make to most of the options on the Tool Options bar will remain in place even after you close Photoshop. Any tool presets you create are saved, so you can have your own group of preset tools for future use until you change them.

PANELS

Panels display many options, and they help modify and control information about your image. Some panels provide thumbnail representations of the image to help with your editing. On the top right side of each panel, you will notice

▷ FIGURE 3-3

The Tool Options bar allows you to create and store tool presets, add additional presets by category, and set tool options.

Tool Options bar (Crop Tool)

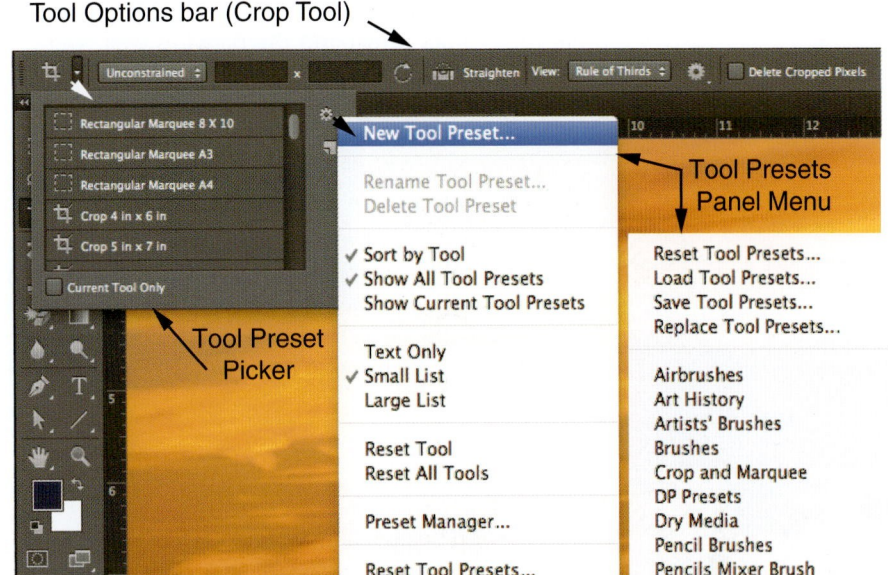

Tool Presets Panel Menu

Tool Preset Picker

Append additional tool presets (various categories)

▷ FIGURE 3-4

Click on the top right corner (three lines) to display each panels' individual menu. To expand, click on the panel icon; to expand or collapse a panel, click on the double arrow at top right, or the tab itself.

three lines (Figure 3-4). This is the **Panel Menu button**, which displays commands used for each particular panel. Most of these same commands may be located on the Menu bar as well. To display a panel, you can select it from the Window menu. Panels can be grouped together for easy access by clicking and dragging the panels tab in the top of the display and releasing it on top of the target group. They can also be dragged to the right of the desktop to become

Double-click tab to toggle to close or expand panel

Click to expand and collapse Panel Menu

Color panel

3D panel

Click right arrows to expand all panels in column

Click individual icons to expand that panel

Click left arrows to collapse to icon

Color Panel Menu

Collapsed icons of most used panels

Expanded Layers panel

collapsible icons that you simply click on to expand; you can click on the panel top bar to contract or expand the panel as well. You can dock or organize your panels to have the ones you use most go in the left column as icons; others could go to the rightmost column displaying the panel name. You can also dock panels on the left side.

TOOLKIT TIP If you are using specific panels for a particular project you are working on, you can save the panels and their arrangement on your workspace when you edit the file in the future by selecting Window > Workspace > New Workspace, then give it a name so it can be used for similar work.

TOOLKIT TIP Panels and Tools panel looking too cluttered around your image? Press the Tab key and they disappear; press it again and they reappear. To keep just the Tools panel visible and hide the panels, press the Shift and Tab keys together.

USING PHOTOSHOP HELP

▷ FIGURE 3-5

The Photoshop Help menu displays popular tasks and tutorials, updates, and online access. It also allows the designer to search by keywords, or online at the support center.

Photoshop's Help menu allows the designer or photographer access to any information about tools, application features, updates, tasks, and terminology (Figure 3-5). In the Help menu, special wizards walk you through certain popular tasks, like resizing an image for web media or transferring your software activation to another computer. The Photoshop Help menu also displays a list of popular "How To" tutorials for many tasks, and you can create your own tutorial. You can look for topics by searching for keywords, or simply jumping from one topic to another by selecting from a list of text links. The online Adobe Help and

Photoshop Help menu   Type in your topic

Photoshop Help center

Adobe Topic Search   Photoshop Online Support

Support Center lets you seek help among Photoshop and other Adobe applications in a weblike format, and it provides additional links to resources, documentation, and community support from peers, including video tutorials you can view and get expert product support. Online Help, titled Photoshop Help and Support, can be accessed by selecting Help > Photoshop Help, or Photoshop Online in the Help menu. You can also download Help PDFs of tutorials and print them for later use. If you are looking for a specific function or technique, type it in the Search box, and Photoshop will display where it is located using floating arrows.

CLIENT ASSIGNMENT: Basic Image Correction: Saving to Specific File Formats

Your client, Chris Winston, was given three images, two images for a local newsletter story and for a website on lighthouse restoration by a local resident, and one color image of an antique car behind a barn that needs to be converted to a B&W image for a local gallery advertisement in the newspaper. One of the lighthouse images is a low-contrast image and the other is an image that is off color. The car image is fine in color but needs to be converted and adjusted as a quality B&W image. He needs to have all images scanned, enhanced, and resized to be used for both commercial print use and a website. Looking at the images, you notice that both lighthouse images need overall color corrections, and the car image is a good candidate to create a quality B&W toned image. You know all these adjustments can be made by using the Image menu in Photoshop (Figure 3-6). You tell Chris to come around 5 o'clock and pick up his images.

ACTION ITEMS OVERVIEW

As a designer or photographer, you will be taking flat contrast and off-color images and correcting them for the best color and definition for your client. You will also be taking a properly exposed color image and converting into a well-toned B&W image. This assignment will also walk you through adjusting image sizes for print and web media output, along with using special automated commands and techniques in color correction. In your career, your judgment in creating good quality color images and your knowledge of managing those images for various print and web media are essential to providing the right information and files for your client. You will save the images with the proper file extensions for use in printing and the web. For images used for the press, you will convert the default RGB color mode to CMYK color mode. This will help you understand the purpose of using various graphic file-format extensions. If you need to download the files for this chapter, they are at the Student Data Files link at *www.CengageBrain.com* (see Chapter 1).

Originals

Adjusting,
contrast, shadows,
and highlights

Converting colors for accurate
B&W tones

Adjusting color balance

▷ FIGURE 3-6

**Correcting images
using special com-
mands in the Image
menu.**

Here is what you will need to do:

- Duplicate the images for print and web use, keeping the originals as backups.
- Adjust the tone (Auto Tone) on the low-contrast lighthouse image, compare the results, then adjust the original image again using the Shadows/Highlights command and compare with Auto Contrast for best accuracy of tones and color.
- Apply the Auto Color command to the lighthouse image with a magenta cast to correct it. You will then apply techniques using the Color Balance command and compare the results.
- Convert the car behind barn color image to an accurately toned B&W image.
- Convert all three high-resolution RGB images for print to CMYK mode.
- Save the files used for print with .TIF extensions.
- Decrease the resolution of the two duplicated images to 72 dpi for monitor display on the web by using Photoshop's Image > Image Size command.
- Save the files for web media with .JPG extensions.

- The final nine files will be named for specific purposes: *FIXLight1.tif* and *FIXLight2.tif*, and *B&WCarbarn.tif* for editing and printing; *CMYKLight1.tif, CMYKLight2.tif,* and *CMYKCarbarn.tif* for use in commercial printing; and *WEBLight1.jpg, WEBLight2.jpg,* and *WEBCarbarn.jpg* for electronic use. There is also an additional option to save images in native PSD format.
- Zip files in one folder ready to send to a potential client.

CORRECTING IMAGES FOR PRINT

Digital cameras, flash and portable hard drives, and scanned images are still the most popular formats to get an image into your computer. Once images are converted into digital files, Photoshop or any image-editing program can enhance, manipulate, or combine them with other images.

A WORD ABOUT SCANNING AND RESOLUTION

As a designer or photographer, if you are scanning an image print, you need to determine the image's use. You need to determine whether it will be a high- or low-resolution image, which will dictate the amount of detail required in the image. Scan at a resolution of 300 dpi if you want to print an image ready for commercial press. For the web or email only, scan at 72 dpi, because this is all your monitor needs to keep the file size small for quick downloading. Scanning an image larger than the **optical resolution** (scanner's default settings) may add pixels between the actual pixels. This is known as **interpolation,** and it deteriorates the image sharpness and quality (to learn more about scanning, check out the exercise in the *Extras & Goodies > Chapter 3* folder online at *www.CengageBrain.com*). Always scan at the highest resolution you think you will need first.

TOOLKIT TIP Scanning software allows some basic editing during the preview scan before you do the final scan into Photoshop. Always preview the image first, make adjustments, and then perform the final scan.

NAVIGATING AROUND THE IMAGE

The **Zoom Tool** allows you to get in close and then zoom out to observe the whole image. Selecting the plus sign on the Tool Options bar zooms in on an image, while selecting the minus sign allows you to zoom out and observe your work. You can check the **Scrubby Zoom** option in the Tool Options bar to allow you to click and drag to zoom in and out of the image. If the Tool Options bar is not displayed, select it from the Window menu. Using the **Hand Tool** is like moving a document with your own hands; it is great for quick positioning (Figure 3-7). The **Navigator panel** helps you see what portion of the image you have zoomed into. There is also the **Rotate View Tool** (by the Hand Tool) to rotate the image view nondestructively.

▷ FIGURE 3-7

**Use the Zoom and
Hand tools and the
Navigator panel
to find your way
around the image.**

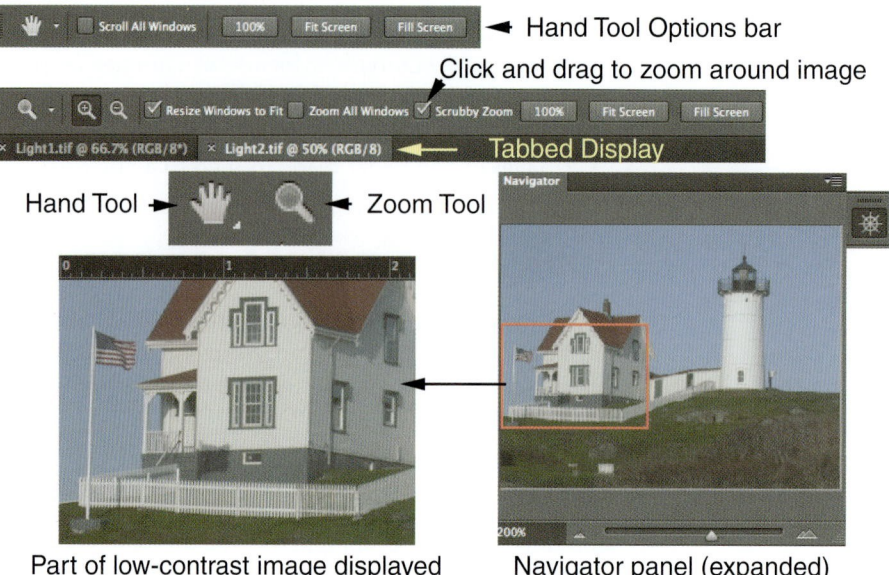

Part of low-contrast image displayed   Navigator panel (expanded)

TOOLKIT TIP To quickly zoom out of an image when the Zoom Tool is selected, press the Option (Mac) or ALT (PC) key. You can also use the View > Zoom In or View > Zoom Out functions or type in the percentage at the bottom left of the window to display different percentage amounts. Double-clicking on the Zoom Tool goes to 100%, while double-clicking on the Hand Tool fits the image in the window.

You will open the original, poorly exposed Light1 and Light2 images in your *Chapter 3* folder, and then you will use the Zoom and Hand tools to navigate your way around the images.

1. Launch Photoshop and open (File > Open) the two files *Light1.tif* and *Light2.tif* in your *Chapter 3* folder inside the *Photoshop* folder you created in Chapter 1; or open the files located online at *www.CengageBrain.com* (if a dialog box displays about ignoring file info data, click OK).

2. If the images are not displayed as tabbed (see Figure 3-7), select Window > Arrange > Consolidate All to Tabs. This makes it easier to work with multiple images together, as opposed to all separate windows.

3. Select the View menu and make sure Rulers is checked to display the rulers. Select the Zoom Tool, then select the *Light1* image and click until the image is at 100% (shown on the Title bar). Using the Navigator panel (Window > Navigator), note where you are on the image by observing the red rectangle around the view area.

4. Use the scroll bars to move around and to observe that any changes you make will show up in the Navigator panel. You can also drag the slider on the Navigator panel to zoom around the image.

5. Select the minus sign on the Tool Options bar and zoom out until the entire image shows on the screen. You can also hold down the Option/ALT key to zoom back out. Remember this is a poor quality image.

6. Make sure the Scrubby Zoom option is checked in the toolbar, then click on the image and drag with your mouse to zoom in and out of the image. Note: If the Scrubby Zoom option is grayed out, your computer and Photoshop is set for older 32-bit computers, and must be set for 64-bit.

7. Leave both files open for the next exercise.

TOOLKIT TIP If you have a Mac computer that utilizes the tight screen resolution called Retina, they can easily jump to 200% zoom. This is also useful for checking your image for dust spots or imperfections. In Photoshop CC you have options where you can: (1) select 200% zoom which is available in the View menu, or (2) hold down the Command key and then double-click the Zoom Tool to zoom the current document to 200%, or (3) if you Command/right-click on the canvas when the Hand or Zoom Tool is active, you'll see that 200% is available.

TOOLKIT TIP Now, it is time for your math quiz. In Photoshop, if the images that you are viewing with the Zoom and Hand tools are high resolution of 300 dpi, why would they display very large on your monitor? Your monitor only displays at 72 dpi! How much bigger is the 300 dpi image going to be on your 72 dpi monitor at full size? Yep, about four times the size, which is why the image may appear much larger full size (the title bar will read 100%) on the monitor. This is important if you are using images for the web, they always display at 100%. To see the actual size, choose View > Print Size.

USING THE IMAGE MENU

The **Image menu** in Photoshop contains commands for all kinds of image enhancements and modifications (Figure 3-8). Some of the commands you will be using are the Mode, Duplicate, Adjustments, and Image Size commands. The **Duplicate command** creates an exact image copy. The **Adjustments command** in the Image menu (Image > Adjustments) gives you the ability to make a variety of color adjustments and editing changes to an image or to selected portions of an image. The **Image Size command** allows you to adjust an image's size while the **Mode command** assigns different color modes and profiles for various media.

Image		
Mode	▶	Assign color modes and profiles
Adjustments	▶	Enhancing and modifying the image
Auto Tone	⇧⌘L	Adjusts tonal balance of colors for detail in highlights and shadows
Auto Contrast	⌥⇧⌘L	Readjusts an image's washed out highlights or blocked shadows
Auto Color	⇧⌘B	Adjusts color imbalances by looking for black or white areas
Image Size...	⌥⌘I	Adjusts the document and screen size of the image
Canvas Size...	⌥⌘C	Placement of the image within the canvas or page
Image Rotation	▶	Rotation of the entire document (including all layers)
Crop		Removes the background outside of the image selection
Trim...		Precise removal of background pixels and image edges
Reveal All		Reveals position of layer images outside of the page area
Duplicate...		Creates an exact image copy
Apply Image...		Blend one layer onto another image
Calculations...		Blend from multiple sources with varying opacities
Variables	▶	Used to define which elements in a template change
Apply Data Set...		Apply a data set's contents to the base image
Trap...		Setting used in printing to prevent gaps between overlapping images
Analysis	▶	Analyzing measurements and scaling

DUPLICATING IMAGES

When you have an image that you want to make changes to, it is a good idea to always make a copy of the original image in case something goes wrong (Figure 3-9). You should always duplicate the original image before applying any changes, because once changes are saved, they may not be able to be undone. The copy serves as a backup. Duplicating an image only makes a duplicate of the displayed image within Photoshop; it does not automatically save the duplicate copy to the hard drive.

In this exercise, you will duplicate the *Light1* and *Light2* files for the next exercises.

1. Select the *Light1* image on the Photoshop desktop.

2. Select Image > Duplicate to create an image copy before making any adjustments; name the copy *FIXLight1*, then select OK.

3. Select the file *Light2* you opened in Photoshop.

4. Select Image > Duplicate to create an image copy before making any adjustments; name the copy *FIXLight2*, then select OK.

5. Close both the original *Light1* and *Light2* TIF files—do not save any changes—to serve as backup copies; leave the *FIXLight1* and *FIXLight2* files open for the next exercise.

COMPARING IMAGES USING AUTO TONE AND BRIGHTNESS/CONTRAST

You can adjust an image's contrast or its highlights and shadows by using Auto Tone and Brightness/Contrast from the Image menu (Figure 3-10). **Auto Tone** adjusts the tonal balance of colors to show detail in highlights and shadows, which works well by rearranging an image's tones slightly to provide detail in all areas. The **Brightness/Contrast** command lets you make simple adjustments to the tonal range of an image. There is an Auto adjustment that balances the tones before you make adjustments. It works well with poor contrast images, and also those that are properly exposed. **Auto Contrast** works with images that need some lightening and darkening in highlights and/or shadows. It does not improve flat, faint, or underexposed images. There are different ways to observe the changes before and after you have applied the effect. You can use the Edit > Undo/Redo commands, or Undo State Change (or Undo "effect name"), or you can toggle the Command/ CTRL + Z keys on your keyboard. The **Fade command** in the Edit menu allows you to adjust the amount of the effect you are applying and blending modes.

TOOLKIT TIP To toggle the changes and see the results before and after the applied effect, hold down the Command (Apple) key on the Mac, or CTRL key on the PC, and press the Z key, which when pressed again, toggles the before and after effects. These are great hot-key combos for quick observations.

Here, you will use the Auto Tone and Brightness/Contrast commands to enhance a dull image to compare which looks best. To observe the changes, you can use the Undo/Redo or Step Backward/Step Forward commands, in the Edit menu, and the toggle keys Command + Z (Mac)/CTRL + Z (PC).

1. Select the *FIXLight1* image of the low-contrast lighthouse on the Photoshop desktop. Use the Zoom Tool to view the entire image, or press Command/CTRL 0.

2. Select Image > Auto Tone to adjust the tonal balance. Select Edit > Fade Auto Tone and adjust the amount of the effect for best overall image tone.

3. Select Edit > Undo Fade Auto Tone to see the previous image, then Edit > Redo Fade Auto Tone (or Undo State Change if it displays), to toggle back to the corrected image. You will notice that it makes fairly good color and tonal corrections. Use the Edit menu to Step Backward (twice) to the original low-contrast image.

 FIGURE 3-10

Photoshop provides the Auto Tone commands to adjust poorly exposed or flat images. You can step through your changes or Fade in your effect in the Edit menu.

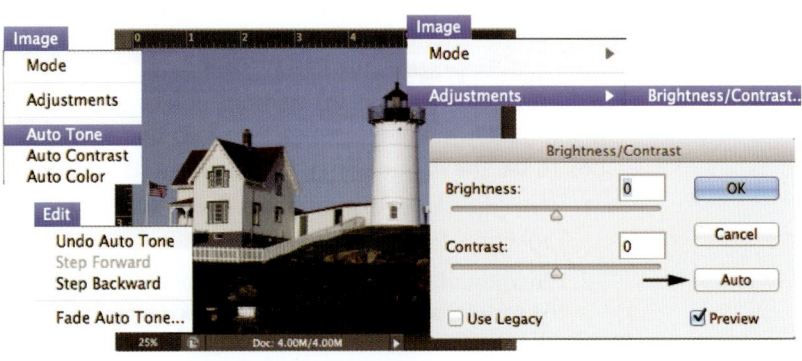

4. Select Image > Adjustments > Brightness/Contrast. Click the Auto button for a great starting point. Drag the sliders to tweak.

5. Click OK, then select Edit > Fade Brightness/Contrast and make adjustments, then click OK again. As you can see, this command gives you more control over correcting your image.

6. To step through your adjustments, select Edit > Step Forward or Step Backward. Go back to the original low-contrast image when you are done.

7. If you want to see how Auto Contrast works, select Image > Auto Contrast. You can see that it does not work well with poorly exposed or faint images, very contrasty.

8. Toggle the keys Command + Z (Mac) or CTRL + Z (Windows) to observe the before and after effects. Go back to the original low-contrast image when you are done.

USING THE SHADOWS/HIGHLIGHTS COMMAND

The Shadows/Highlights command (Image > Adjustments > Shadows/Highlights) is used for carefully correcting poorly exposed (overexposed: too light; underexposed: too dark) areas in photographic images—it has a dialog box that allows you to adjust highlights and shadows in an image (Figure 3-11). When Show More Options is checked, it provides a series of sliders for more advanced detailed adjustments in highlights, shadows, and color correction by adjusting Tonal Width, Pixel Radius, and Midtones. Here, you can use the Fade command to adjust the amount of the effect applied. The dialog box here, used with many commands, has a Preview check box to toggle between viewing your changes.

▷ FIGURE 3-11

The Shadows/ Highlights command corrects underexposed and overexposed images and flat images more accurately than other methods by precisely fine-tuning highlights, shadows, midtones, and color.

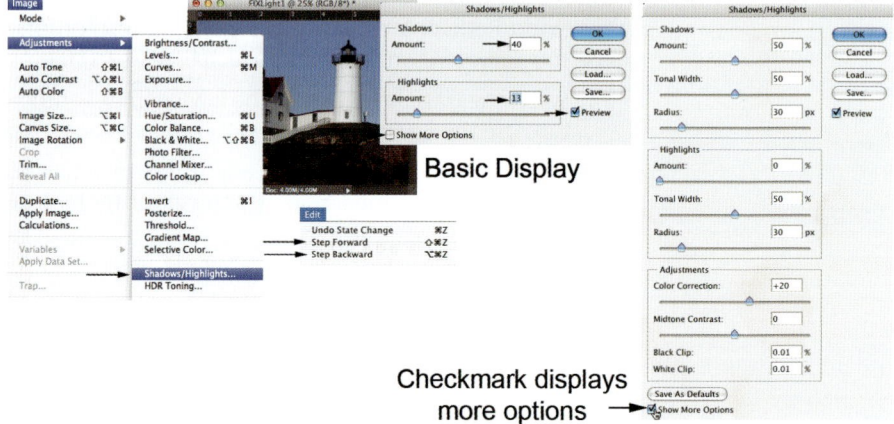

Here, you will make adjustments to the image using the Shadows/Highlights command until it is visibly accurate to your eye; then, you will use the Preview check box to see the image before and after effects are applied.

1. With the *FIXLight1* image displayed, select Image > Adjustments > Shadows/Highlights to adjust the tonal balance.

2. When the dialog box comes up, make sure the Preview box is checked to view the results, and drag the dialog box alongside the image.

3. Start with 40% in the Shadows area to lighten it up and 15% in the Highlights area. You can either move the sliders, or to be more accurate, type the amounts in the appropriate boxes.

4. Adjust the sliders to make the picture look better, then click on the Show More Options check box to display more adjustments.

5. Feel free to make slight adjustments with these effects until the image shows details in the shadows and highlights, and visibly accurate color of the white lighthouse set in green grass against the blue sky. Check, then uncheck the Preview button to also view before and after effects. Click OK.

6. Notice that you have much better accurate control with the Shadows/Highlights effect than in the previous exercise with Auto Tone and Auto Contrast.

7. Leave the *FIXLight1* image open for the later exercise in saving as a .TIF file.

CORRECTING COLOR CASTS WITH COLOR BALANCE AND AUTO COLOR

Sometimes designers may receive images from a client that may have an overall cyan or magenta cast. Causes may be from scanning older digital images, improper digital camera white balance settings, or from an inaccurate monitor. There are two methods to correct this issue. One involves the **Auto Color** command (Image > Auto Color), which searches for blacks and whites in an image to rearrange color tones. The other involves the **Color Balance** command (Image > Adjustments > Color Balance) to allow you to replace colors that are opposite the color cast in your image using sliders for shadows, midtones, and highlight tones for more accurate precision, along with an image's **luminosity**, or quality of light in an image. The Color Balance command can also be used to add warmth or coolness to image tones as well. To adjust the amount of correction applied in either of the two commands, adjust the "Fade" option in the Edit menu.

In this exercise, you will try and compare using the Auto Color command and the Color Balance command to remove a red color cast.

1. Select the file *FIXLight2*, which has a red color cast.

2. Choose Image > Auto Color to see the changes in the image. You'll find it makes the image too green for this case. Try adjusting the Fade Auto Color in the Edit menu to tweak to about 70%. Toggle the Preview check box to see before and after changes, which are very subtle, then press OK.

3. Select Edit > Step Backward (or Undo State Change if it displays) to see the previous image; then Edit > Step Forward to toggle between the corrected image and the original off-color image. Return to the original magenta cast image.

4. Now select the Color Balance command (Image > Adjustments > Color Balance), and adjust the Cyan – Magenta slider for midtones only, and add a little yellow for warmth. Use the settings in Figure 3-12 in the previous page as a starting point. Feel free to make your own visual adjustments. Use the Preview button as a toggle to see your changes quickly.

DESIGN TIP

The Color Balance command provides more accurate precision for toning and adjusting color of individual images. The Auto Color command is used to correct many color cast images quickly, but may not be as accurate, but can be used as a starting point for further color correction.

▷ FIGURE 3-12

The Color Balance and Auto Color commands are used to remove unwanted color casts in an image.

5. Try Edit > Fade Color Balance and adjust the Opacity setting to tweak the changes in color. Toggle between states until you feel the best color displays; leave the mode set to Normal for now.

6. Leave this file open with the new changes applied. We will save both adjusted images in the next exercise.

SAVING FILES WITH THE .TIF EXTENSION

Files saved with a .TIF extension can be edited repeatedly and still be as accurate as the original image. They can be edited and saved in Photoshop or any graphic application without losing quality, because they are saved in a **universal format** that can be read by any graphic application (Figure 3-13). Graphic files saved with a .TIF extension are preferred in the commercial printing industry; they also generate the largest file sizes, so be aware of the space needed to store these files.

▷ FIGURE 3-13

Save both adjusted images as .TIF extension files for a universal format that can be read by any graphics application.

Here, you will save the two adjusted *FIXLight* files as .TIF files for commercial printing.

1. Select the *FIXLight1* tab and Save As *FIXlight1.tif* in the *Chapter 3* folder on your drive (File > Save As, and keep default settings).

2. When the .TIF Options window displays, select an Image Compression of NONE for best accuracy, then in the Byte Order section, select your computer (IBM PC or Macintosh).

3. Select OK and leave the file open for the next exercise.

4. Repeat the same process with the *FIXLight2* image and Save As *FIXLight2.tif* in the *Chapter 3* folder. Select OK after you have entered all settings and, again, leave the file open.

SAVING IN PHOTOSHOP'S NATIVE PSD FORMAT (OPTIONAL)

It is sometimes a good idea to save an image in the application's native format to use as a backup copy. In the case of Photoshop, the extension is **.PSD** (Photoshop document). As a native file, it can be read by other Adobe products or other Photoshop users and edited with ease without losing quality; but some other graphic applications may not be able to read it. It does provide an accurate backup copy of the original image for future use. To save in a different identifiable format extension, in a different location, or as a different file name, you would use the Save As command. Whether you save a file as a .TIF extension or its native extension, .PSD, the quality on both is the same. As you save to a new format, PSD for instance, the newly saved format remains open and the previous format (TIF) closes.

 TOOLKIT TIP In Windows, you may notice that no other files are displayed in the *Chapter 3* folder when you are saving in .PSD format. That is because only files with the same format extension are displayed, and since there are no other .PSD files in the folder, it appears blank.

Here you will save the corrected images in Photoshop's native .PSD format on your hard drive. You will also display the images with rulers on the top and left sides.

1. Select the *FIXLight1.tif* file. For Mac users, select File > Save As > *FIXLight1 .psd*. In the Format drop-down box, select the Photoshop (or PSD in other versions) format to save in Photoshop's native format in the *Chapter 3* folder on your drive. For Windows users, select File > Save As > File name > *FIXLight1 .psd*. Select Photoshop as the format and save in the *Chapter 3* folder. Leave all other default settings as they are.

2. Select the other *FIXLight2.tif* and Save As *FIXLight2.psd* in the *Chapter 3* folder, as mentioned in Step 1. Leave all other default settings as they are.

3. For future editing, and to get an idea of the image sizes, select View and make sure Rulers (View > Rulers) is checked to display the rulers.

4. Close the .PSD files to be used as backups, and reopen your TIF files, *FIXLight1* and *FIXlight2*, in your *Chapter 3* folder for the exercise after the following exercise in creating a B&W image; they should display as tabbed (if not, select, Window > Arrange > Consolidate All to Tabs).

CONVERTING A COLOR IMAGE TO BLACK AND WHITE

The Image menu also provides a designer or photographer the ability to make special changes to the pixels in an image. The Adjustments menu (Image > Adjustments) provides a series of commands to modify, enhance, or adjust an image's pixels. The Black and White command inside the Adjustments menu provides a series of color-based adjustments to create a well-toned B&W image from the original color image. The colors act as filters much as are sometimes used by photographers in front of their cameras or in the chemical darkroom. As a guide, increasing the color lightens that B&W tone in the image, and decreasing the color darkens that B&W tone in the image. You can also use a series of preset settings and create your own customized settings, including various color tints for special effect.

This exercise will serve also as a review of what has been covered so far. You will be converting the car behind the barn color image to an image that displays a wide range of B&W tones.

1. Open the file *Carbarn.tif* in your *Chapter 3* folder inside the Photoshop folder you created in Chapter 1; or open the file located online at *www.CengageBrain.com*. Make sure the whole image displays 100%.

2. Select Image > Duplicate to create an image copy before making any adjustments; name the copy *B&WCarbarn.tif*, then select OK.

3. Close the original *Carbarn.tif* file you just made a copy of to serve as the original backup copy; leave the *B&WCarbarn.tif* file open.

4. Select Image > Adjustments > Black & White. Use Figure 3-14 in the previous page as a starting point for your adjustments. Use the Zoom Tool and Navigation panel to look at details of your adjustments. Use the Edit menu to move backward and forward for any adjustments.

5. Make note of your favorite settings, then click on the Presets selections to see other B&W options for the image, or create your own and Save as a Preset. Adjust for the best range of B&W tones. Pretty nice, huh?

6. Select File > Save > *B&WCarbarn.tif* and keep the default settings.

7. When the .TIF Options window displays, select an Image Compression of NONE for best accuracy, then in the Byte Order section, select your computer (IBM PC or Macintosh). Save the file in the *Chapter 3* folder you created. Optional: Feel free to save an additional file in the native PSD extension as shown earlier.

8. Select OK. If a dialog box appears regarding layers and file size issues, select OK, and leave the file open for the next exercise.

Use special presets or create your own

▷ FIGURE 3-14

The Black and White command provides all the adjustments needed to convert color images into well-toned B&W images.

SETTING RESOLUTION AND IMAGE SIZE IN PHOTOSHOP

Increasing or decreasing an image's size or resolution, either for print or for the web, is called *resampling*. You can use the Image Size command under the Image menu to do this by changing Pixel Dimensions for electronic media or Document Size for print output. In Photoshop CC the Image Size dialog has been refined to include a more intuitive Fit To options list. This list provides preset options for dimensions of the most popular sizes and resolutions for print and web media, and you can also create your own custom dimensions which can be saved as a preset. By keeping a check mark in the **Resample** box in the Image Size dialog box, you can change the resolution or the image size, which automatically changes the number of pixels and adjusts the file size. When you make changes to the pixels or the document size, Photoshop adjusts the rest proportionately (Figure 3-15). Interpolation, mentioned earlier, is the action of adding pixels in between pixels to enlarge an image; this seriously deteriorates image quality. You will almost always resample or resize down in an original image to maintain quality—rarely up. Now we need to adjust the image sizes for print. The resolution is already set in this example for a newspaper submission.

▷   FIGURE 3-15

By keeping the Resample box checked, you can resize an image's dimensions proportionately.

TOOLKIT TIP If you are using earlier Photoshop versions, keeping a check mark in the **Constrain Proportions** box allows you to increase or reduce the image size proportionately to avoid distortion. Another box to keep checked is the **Scale Styles** box, especially if you applied any effects on your image (Figure 3-15).

TOOLKIT TIP When resizing a corrected image, you could again create a duplicate, rename it, and save it as a copy of the original corrected file. Also when resizing an image, always set the highest resolution first, then adjust the size.

Now you will resize the corrected images so they will be ready for print.

1. Select the *FIXLight1* tab and choose Image > Image Size in the Menu bar.

2. Make sure Resample (in earlier versions Scale Styles, Constrain Proportions, and Resample Image) is checked. The resolution is already set previously for a newspaper, and you can leave the Resample option at Automatic.

3. Type a "4" in the Width of the Document Size area and Photoshop adjusts the rest—make sure the units are set to Inches. Click OK.

4. Select the *FIXLight2* tab and choose Image > Image Size, entering a 4-inch Width, as shown in Figure 3-15. Repeat the same process with the *B&WCarbarn* file. Do not adjust the resolution.

5. You will notice in all three images that the pixel dimensions decreased, which in turn decreased the file size. Actual numbers may be slightly different than shown.

6. Save all three files in your *Chapter 3* folder with their default names, and leave open for the next exercise.

INTELLIGENT UPSAMPLING USING PHOTOSHOP CREATIVE CLOUD (CC)

Previously if you created a low-resolution image, say, from an incorrect setting on your camera and needed decent prints made, it was very difficult to achieve adequate quality. In the previous exercises we have discussed the importance of avoiding having to "upsample" or add pixels (interpolate) in an image. Photoshop Creative Cloud (CC) provides new technologies in the Image Size dialog box that preserve detail in allowing you to interpolate sharp low-resolution images without introducing too much noise or pixelation issues. It should be used as a last resort.

In Photoshop CC, there are choices in the Resample options box to maintain image quality. One of these is called **Intelligent Upsampling**. In a case where upsampling is needed, say in creating a printable image, you can select Preserve Details (enlargement) in the Resample options box to get good quality printable images from an original low-resolution image, or larger printable images from smaller high-resolution images. As mentioned previously, always start off with the largest image first to minimize having to add additional pixels to your image.

In this exercise, you are going to increase pixels to the *B&WCarbarn.tif* file as if your client decided to use it in a magazine and needed the same size at 300 dpi. This is not a perfect example, but you can see how this new technology allows you to make this acceptable change. If you are not using Photoshop CC, skip this exercise.

▷ FIGURE 3-16

In Photoshop CC, you can upsample images using the Preserve Details (enlargement) setting in the Resample options box.

1. With the *B&WCarbarn.tif* file in Photoshop, if possible, print out the image at its current size and 200 dpi resolution. You'll use this to compare.

2. Select Image > Image Size and make sure to check the Resample box. Select Preserve Details (enlargement) in the Resample option box (Figure 3-16). Reduce the noise to 20% and click OK.

3. In earlier versions the image would appear fuzzy from adding so many pixels, but with CC you should see little change between the image at 200 dpi, and the new image at 300 dpi resolution.

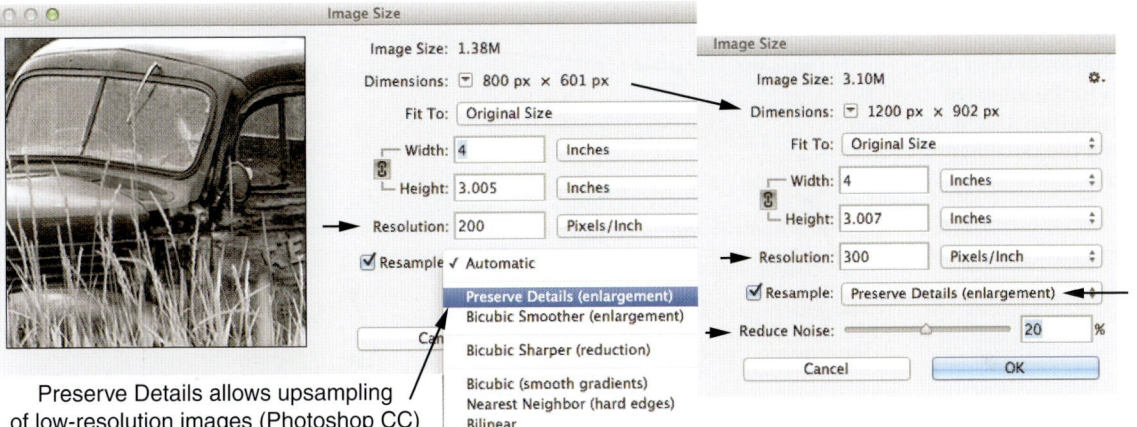

Preserve Details allows upsampling
of low-resolution images (Photoshop CC)

4. If possible, print out the new adjusted image at 300 dpi and compare both images, looking at edges of the car and barn. With the new technology there should be little observable change. Again, mistakes happen, and sometimes demand for high-resolution work comes without prior notice where larger file sizes are needed, but this should only be used infrequently.

ENLARGING AN IMAGE WITHOUT INTERPOLATION

For good quality prints to be used for commercial press work, you rarely need more than 300 dpi resolution. However, if you need to enlarge the original image's size and avoid interpolation, you can scan the image or document at a higher dpi—like 600 dpi, to double the size of the original image—and then resample the resolution in Photoshop to 300 dpi without adding any pixels.

You can do this by removing the check mark in the Resample Image box and leaving the Constrain Proportions box checked to adjust the file size in conjunction with the resolution proportionately; while maintaining the same number of pixels, it merely redistributes the pixels within the image. Figure 3-17 shows you how it is done; no exercises are necessary. Always remember to adjust the image resolution before resizing the dimensions.

 TOOLKIT TIP In Photoshop, with the Image Size dialog box, you will see choices beside Resample. Try Bicubic Smoother, which works nicely in creating enlargements; Automatic is always the default when in doubt. In Photoshop CC, you can select Preserve Details (enlargement) in the Resample option box to get good quality printable images.

▷ FIGURE 3-17

Unchecking Resample box rearranges the same amount of pixels to the adjusted resolution, changing only the document size.

Number of pixels and file size remains the same

Resample checked adjusts dimensions

Resample unchecked rearranges but does not add or remove pixels

USING RGB AND CMYK COLOR MODES

When working with images in Photoshop, it defaults to the RGB color mode; this is because red, green, and blue, when added in different combinations, create all other colors electronically. This is the working color space you normally use with your computer's monitor, because RGB images contain the original image data. Use RGB mode for all initial setup and editing, which we have done in the exercises in this chapter. This mode works fine for designing images for electronic displays, like web pages, computer monitors, email, and for local printing to an ink-jet printer or laser printer. This is good for showing a client proofs of what the final design and layout will look like. Since image files *FIXLight1, B&WCarbarn,* and *FIXLight2* will be printed on commercial press for a newspaper, you should convert the images to CMYK to closely match the ink pigments on the press. The colors cyan (C), magenta (M), and yellow (Y) are used as part of a subtractive process by creating all ink colors as a percentage of these three colors. Black (K) is automatically added for details in the shadows and to provide contrast in ink colors. Commercial printers only use CMYK color, and it is important for you, the designer or photographer, to send them the final images as CMYK (Figure 3-18).

▷ FIGURE 3-18

Images used for commercial printing need to be converted to CMYK color mode. Tiling document windows allows you to view image effects side by side.

Convert to CMYK for printer

Arrange image windows

Arrange command provides options to tile, float, or consolidate image windows

Saving images in CMYK mode before going to the printer helps the designer or photographer visualize any possible changes that may occur in color from RGB mode. Remember, you will still be seeing it on an RGB monitor, but you will have a better idea of how colors will be affected. It is a good habit always to save the original document in RGB mode for future editing and keep a duplicate document in CMYK mode for press. The Window menu provides an Arrange command for you to decide whether you want multiple images displayed as separate floating, tiled alongside one another, or consolidated together in a tabbed display.

Here you will convert and save the three adjusted images as CMYK files in preparation for use by a commercial printer, then look for any color shifts.

1. With the *B&WCarbarn.tif, FIXLight1.tif, and FIXLight2.tif* images open on the Photoshop desktop, select each image and select Image > Duplicate, leaving the default name as a copy. Select the *FIXLight1 copy* image and then choose Image > Mode > CMYK Color. When a display box opens warning about choosing CMYK, select OK to continue, because you made a duplicate of the *FIXLight1* file. Save the file in your *Chapter 3* folder as *CMYKLight1.tif* so that *FIXLight1* remains as the backup RGB file for any future editing. You always want the original edit in RGB mode.

2. Repeat the same process for the *FIXLight2.tif* and the *B&WCarbarn.tif* files. To display all the images next to each other to compare for any color changes, select Window > Arrange >Tile All Vertically; look carefully: the change may be slight. Close the CMYK files you just created after they have been saved.

3. When finished, select Window > Arrange > Consolidate All to Tabs to display image windows as tabbed displays. Your CMYK files are ready for press. Note: These images are a lower resolution for educational purposes and thus are not the high-resolution 300 dpi images you would normally need for preparing for press.

PREPARING IMAGES FOR WEB MEDIA

With the three images adjusted for commercial print output, you can duplicate the corrected images you created earlier in the default RGB format, and saved as "FIX" files, change the resolution settings, and save the file in a compressed format for much smaller file sizes appropriate for web display (Figure 3-19).

▷ FIGURE 3-19

**Duplicating the
adjusted images for
web media.**

DUPLICATING AND RENAMING CORRECTED IMAGES

With the three images corrected, you can now make duplicates and rename them so they can be adjusted for web media. The corrections will remain intact in the copies.

In the next exercise, you will duplicate the new enhanced images so they can be adjusted for use on the web.

1. Select the *FIXLight1.tif* image on the Photoshop desktop.

2. Choose Image > Duplicate to make a copy of the image.

3. When the dialog box appears, name the copy *WEBLight1*. Click OK and leave the file open. Close the *FIXLight1.tif* file.

4. Repeat the same process with the *FIXLight2.tif* and *B&WCarbarn.tif* files, leaving the WEB files open and closing both *FIXLight* files and the *B&WCarbarn.tif* file.

ADJUSTING IMAGE SIZE FOR WEB MEDIA

To get the images ready for the web, they need to be resampled down to a resolution of 72 ppi in order to display correctly on a monitor and keep the file size to a minimum (Figure 3-20). When adjusting or measuring images for electronic display, use the Pixel Dimensions area in the Image Size dialog box for adjustments; change the resolution to 72 ppi as the standard size. Remember, always adjust the resolution first, then the image size.

In this exercise, you will take the web-labeled images and resample them down to 72 ppi for use on the web.

1. Select the file *WEBLight1* on your desktop.

2. Select Image > Image Size to display the dialog box.

3. You will notice the resolution is set at 200 dpi for newspaper print media (for high-quality commercial prints, you would normally use 300 dpi).

4. Make sure the Resample box is checked, and in earlier versions the Scale Styles, Constrain Proportions, and Resample Image boxes are all checked.

5. Try choosing Bicubic Sharper (reduction), in the Resample options box, when reducing image sizes to maintain image clarity. When in doubt, keep the default Automatic setting (Figure 3-20).

6. Enter 72 in the Resolution box; the pixel dimensions will change automatically, decreasing the file size for the web (Figure 3-20 shows settings for *WEBLight1*).

7. Leave the document size the same and select OK.

8. Zoom the image to 100% (displays in Title bar).

9. Repeat the same process with the *WEBLight2* and *WEBB&WCarbarn* files. Leave the three files open to save as JPEGs in the next exercise.

> **TOOLKIT TIP** The safest method to see the maximum size under the resolution you have chosen is to *uncheck* Resample. Type in the Resolution (highest first), then go back and type in the size. The resolution will not change and the pixels will either be redistributed so you can see the maximum size allowed, or the pixels will be removed, maintaining maximum image quality.

SAVING IMAGES AS JPEG FILES

Images saved with a .JPG extension generate smaller compressed files and are used primarily for the web or when smaller file sizes are needed. This is a universal format, which can be read by most graphic applications. Images that are saved as JPEGs, however, lose data each time they are compressed and saved. When JPEG images are edited and resaved a number of times, they will start to deteriorate—without necessarily reducing the file size. You can set the quality of the compressed, saved image at the maximum number (12), resulting in the highest quality or accuracy and a larger file size. The lower the number, the lower the quality; however, electronic display of images is pretty forgiving because of the limited number of colors monitors can display.

DESIGN TIP

When creating duplicate images that will be used for different media, always start off enhancing the highest resolution image first; then make a copy for other media, such as the web, that can be adjusted in Photoshop. The duplicate will retain the changes used in the original enhanced image.

DESIGN TIP

Always scan at your highest resolution size needed first (i.e., 300 dpi for print), and then make adjustments for lower resolution or smaller size images later. When you resize or modify an image in Photoshop to be used for the web, display the image at full size while making changes. When preparing images for the web, make sure they are at the exact dimensions needed; they will always display at full size.

Image file size changes with Resample checked and resolution adjusted

▷   FIGURE 3-20

To set up for web media, with check marks as shown, type in a resolution of 72 ppi. You can then subtract further pixels as desired.

DESIGN TIP

Remember, you can safely resample down or remove pixels, but enlarging by adding more pixels than those contained in the original image will cause interpolation and could seriously deteriorate the image quality.

TOOLKIT TIP TIF and JPEG images can both be used for local print media like ink-jet printers, although TIF images are required when photographs are used in commercial printing because of the accuracy they produce. JPEG four-sided images are used exclusively for most photographic work on the web that does not require background transparency (Figure 3-21), otherwise the background turns white, say from an older oval image.

Here, you will save the new web images as JPEGs to keep the file size down.

1. Select and Save the image *WEBLight1.tif* as *WEBLight1.jpg* in your *Chapter 3* folder (File > Save As > *WEBLight1.jpg*, making sure you select the JPEG format), leaving any default settings (Figure 3-21).

2. Select the High setting of 8 in Image Options for an image that will display nicely on a web page while keeping the file size small for faster downloading.

3. Select and save the images *WEBLight2.tif* as *WEBLight2.jpg*, and *WEBB&WCarbarn .tif* as *WEBCarbarn.jpg*, with the High setting of 8, in your *Chapter 3* folder. Leave any default settings.

4. You now have three enhanced images for web display, along with the high-resolution images you created earlier for commercial print media. Close all files except for the *WEBLight2.jpg* file for the next exercise.

SAVE FOR WEB COMMAND IN PHOTOSHOP

To save images that will be used on the web, Photoshop also has a Save for Web command (File > Save for Web). Before using this command, a designer or photographer should have the image dimensions already established for the web to display it at actual size (100%). When working with images for the web in Photoshop, always make sure the image is displayed at 100% and is the final size decided upon for display. If the image is too large to be displayed at 100%, and you find

▷   FIGURE 3-21

Saving files in JPEG format helps compress the file size for use in electronic display or the web.

DESIGN TIP

For web images, you usually would not need to save a JPEG with the maximum setting, unless you are planning on further editing. A high-quality setting for a large screen image provides all the needed details and keeps the file size smaller for faster download times. Lower quality settings may be useful for smaller image sizes or thumbnails on a web page.

yourself scrolling around the display, go into the Image menu (Image > Image Size) and adjust the pixel size at 72 dpi resolution, unless the image is to be used as a background image to fill the screen. With the Save for Web command, a designer or photographer can choose up to four methods of output display in quality (Original, .GIF, .JPG, and .PNG formats) and an approximate download time to observe what works best for the intended purpose (Figure 3-22).

To use the Save for Web command (covered in depth in Chapter 10), you'll open up the *WEBLight2.jpg* file, resize it again, and then open it using the Save for Web command. There you will compare the display at various file extensions, adjust download time, and save again.

1. Make sure your *WebLight2.jpg* file is displayed from your *Chapter 3* folder.

2. Select Image > Image Size and enter 400 pixels width, leaving all other settings as is. Select OK.

3. Select File > Save for Web to open the display.

4. Click on the 4-up tab to display the image four times. Use the Zoom Tool on the display to make sure the image is displayed at 100%, as if preparing for the web. You'll find that the image is larger than the window. Use the Hand Tool to move around the "original display," which, in turn, will move all the displays together, until the top portion of the lighthouse is shown (Figure 3-22).

5. Leave the first box as the original for comparison, then select each of the other boxes and click a JPG high quality (60), GIF, and PNG-24 file type. Compare images at 100%, what would actually show on a web page, and you'll find that there may be very little difference among your displays here.

6. Zoom in a little more to 200% and compare. You may notice the GIF display may look a little spotty. You could probably even change the JPG quality to medium to compare. Zoom back out to 100%.

7. Now select Cable/DSL or another download time to compare how much time it may take to download the image from a web page. This can be very important, especially if customers are located in rural areas. Compare the download times where this is a rather large web image.

Select image frame, choose file format
to view, select download time, then save

8. With the JPG High (60 quality) image box selected, leave all other settings at defaults, and select Save.

9. When the next dialog box opens up, keep the same file name (*WEBLight2 .jpg*), find your *Chapter 3* folder, select Format: Images Only, Settings: Default Settings (Figure 3-23).

10. Click Save, and your file will be placed in the *Chapter 3* folder (Figure 3-23). You can see how helpful this could be for preparing images for web use.

In addition to the original files (which you downloaded from the publisher's website at *www.CengageBrain.com*), *LIght1.tif*, *Light2.tif*, and *Carbarn.tif*, after completing the exercises in this chapter, you should have the following files completed and saved in your *Chapter 3* folder. These files would be used for specific purposes and labeled accordingly for quick access: *FIXLight1.tif*, *FIXlight2.tif*, and *B&WCarbarn.tif* for initial editing and printing; *CMYKLight1.tif*, *CMYKLight2.tif*, and *CMYKCarbarn.tif* for use in commercial printing; and *WEBLight1.jpg*, *WEBLight2.jpg*, and *WEBCarbarn.jpg* for electronic use (12 files total). If you also completed the optional exercise of saving the files in Photoshop's native PSD format, which could be used as a backup, you would also have the files labeled as *FIXLight1.psd* and *FIXlight2.psd*, and possibly *B&WCarbarn.psd*. It is important to understand the relevance of organizing your files and work, and labeling for intended use. It helps to save time and coordinate your workflow as a designer. Place your *Chapter 3* folder on your desktop for the next exercise where you'll zip all your files together.

ZIPPING MULTIPLE FILES FOR A POTENTIAL CLIENT

Now that you have many files completed and labeled for specific purposes, some of these files may be needed for your potential client. You could clog up their email and send all as separate attachments, running the risk of the client losing one of these files, or you could zip up all your files into one folder and send as one file attachment. This helps to avoid confusion and keeps all your files in one place. When a folder of files is **zipped**, it is making a compressed copy and becomes one "file" that can be sent electronically.

Here you will zip all your files created in this chapter as if ready to send to your client (or instructor).

1. Place your *Chapter 3* folder on your desktop (Windows 8 Desktop Screen).

2. Make another folder on the desktop labeled *ZIP CH3* and drag all your image files previously mentioned that were created and used for the exercises in this chapter (12 files with originals, 14 files with optional PSD exercise).

3. For Mac users, CTRL-click on the *ZIP CH3* folder, and select Compress "ZIP CH3." A copy with a ZIP is created that can now be sent as a file attachment. For Windows 7 and 8 users, right-click on the *ZIP CH3* folder, and select Send To > Compressed (zipped) folder (Figure 3-24).

▷ FIGURE 3-24

Creating a compressed zipped folder of files from Chapter 3 exercises.

Creating zipped folder of files using Windows

Creating zipped folder of files using Mac OS X

4. On Mac OS X and Windows, the zipped files will have a ".zip" extension to identify them as zipped files. Feel free to rename the new zipped folder as *ZIPPED CH3*, to avoid confusion. The folder is now ready to be sent to your client where their computer will have a program to unzip the files for viewing.

FILE FORMATS REVIEW

Here is a table to give you an idea of some graphic file extension formats. We have covered in depth TIF and JPEG, and introduced Photoshop's native PSD format so far. The rest we'll be covering in future chapters. When you are creating images for a client, it is crucial to understand how the graphic files will be used.

FORMAT	ADVANTAGES	CONSIDERATIONS
PNG	Records transparencies in bitmap and vector images. Compresses files without losing data. Web use.	Cannot be read by older browsers. Larger size files but can still be used for the web. Cannot be enlarged.
GIF	Used for vector graphics and animation. Used on the web. Keeps transparencies.	GIF files have only 256 colors.
JPEG	Compressed format used in photographic images. Keeps file sizes small. Used for web and ink-jet proof printing.	Data is thrown out each time the image is saved, gradually deteriorating quality. No transparencies. Not for commercial press. Cannot be enlarged.
TIF	Most accurate recording of detail in photographs. Quality maintains as original regardless of saved changes. Can be used for commercial printing of photographs.	Largest file size. Not used for the web. Cannot be enlarged.
PSD	Photoshop's native format. Extremely accurate in maintaining quality, regardless of saved changes. Used for backups.	Some graphics programs may not be able to read this format.
PDF	Compresses text and graphics in documents without losing data for electronic distribution and the web. Works best with many documents. Can also be used for soft proofs and commercial printing. Editable in Photoshop and Illustrator.	Can also be read in free Adobe Reader program.
EPS	Preferred method when combining graphics and type. Vector graphics can be scalable. Used extensively for commercial printing.	Large file size. Not for the web.

ADVANCED USERS: Precision Image Adjustments Using Histograms, Levels, Curves, and Crop tools

There are a lot of manual adjustments you can make on your own to enhance an image. One of these, the Shadows/Highlights command used earlier, adjusted poorly exposed images. Another of these is the **Levels command** in the Image menu. This provides more subtlety and precision by making adjustments to details in the highlights and shadows of an image. The Levels dialog box displays what is called a **histogram**, which is a graph that shows the highlight, shadow, and midtone properties of an image. By adjusting the histogram, you can control the amount of detail in the highlights and shadows by redistributing pixels to generate the full range of tones. In Photoshop, there is a **Histogram panel** (Window > Histogram) that displays the before (gray) and after (white–black in earlier versions) histograms to see the changes made in an image (Figure 3-25). Adjusting the levels of an image brings back hidden details. Many digital cameras can display a histogram in the LCD display, so the photographer can check for proper exposure. When the image is opened in Photoshop, this same histogram is displayed as the image's digital fingerprint when accessed through the Levels dialog box and the Histogram panel. Histograms can be edited in whatever color mode is selected or in the individual channels, R, G, or B or C, M, Y, and K. The Histogram panel allows you to view individual color channels. Photoshop also has a **Curves** adjustment,

▷ FIGURE 3-25

Use the Levels command to bring out details in highlights, shadows, and midtones in an image. Use the Histogram panel to observe levels before and after adjustments are applied.

Levels Histogram on poor image before adjustments

Histogram panel displaying properly exposed image

Histogram panel menu Show Channels in Color (good exposed image)

Adjusting Level on poor image (Image > Adjustments > Levels)

Histogram panel (RGB) displays before (gray) and after (white) of poor contrast image which allows the designer or photographer more precision in adjusting for toning in highlights, midtones, and shadow details using a system of plotting points in those areas that need adjustments. The Crop Tool has a feature besides trimming that can precisely rotate an image, and the Perspective Crop Tool corrects an image's perspective.

TOOLKIT TIP Many well-exposed image histograms with details in shadows, midtones, and highlights display a graph across all tones with peaks and valleys. Adjusting on either side of the start and end of a graph "mountain" increases details to recreate the actual image. Histograms can also give the designer an indication whether the image is properly exposed. Images that are too dark (underexposed) will show the histogram graph curving up, cutting off at the shadow side while washed out images (overexposed) will have the graph curve up and cut off on the right side. For advanced users, the Histogram panel can also display changes in individual color channels, such as RGB or CMYK, by selecting the All Channels View from the panel submenu and then Show Channels in Color from the panel submenu.

USING LEVELS AND HISTOGRAMS

In this exercise, you will open the *Schooner.tif* image and use the Levels commands and Histogram to create a better enhanced image.

DESIGN TIP

This technique of using Levels to make sure the shadows and highlights adjustment arrows are dragged to the start and ending points of your histogram ensures all tones are accurately displayed.

1. Open the file *Schooner.tif* in your *Chapter 3* folder.

2. If a Profile Mismatch dialog box appears, select OK.

3. Duplicate the image so you will be able to see the differences between the original and your altered version, and rename it *SchoonerLVL*. Select Arrange from the Window menu, then select the "Float All in Windows" option.

4. To display the Histogram panel, select Window > Histogram.

5. Select Image > Adjustments > Levels. The Levels dialog box displays with the image's histogram. Make sure the Preview box is checked to observe the changes and drag the *SchoonerLVL* image window next to the Histogram panel, which shows what you see in the levels display as a gray mountain.

6. In the Levels dialog box from the Image menu, the default channel displayed is RGB that combines all the colors together, and there are three triangle sliders under the histogram graph. The left is for the shadows, the right is for the highlights, and the one in the middle is for the midtones. You will notice they are positioned below the graph with flat areas on both sides. What you want to do is to drag these sliders to the start and ending points of the "graph mountain."

7. Drag the shadow and highlight triangles on either side to the start and end of the graph in the Levels dialog box (see Figure 3-26). The middle triangle will adjust automatically, but you can also adjust that slider separately to adjust the midtones. Notice the difference between the adjusted image and the original image, by clicking the Preview button. All the tones are rearranged for a clearer, more accurate color image. You can use the Shadows/Highlights

▷ FIGURE 3-26

By dragging the highlights and shadows arrows to the beginning of their peaks all details are remapped for a well-toned image.

Image histogram before adjustments

Drag shadows and highlights arrows to start and end of graph

Final image has details in highlights and shadows

command in Image > Adjustments afterwards to further tweak for details in your images as done in the earlier exercise in this chapter.

8. Notice the before and after effects in the Histogram panel: the before image is gray, while the after image is white, or black in earlier versions. Also, in the Levels dialog box, you can make more precise color levels adjustments by selecting and adjusting the individual red, green, and blue channels to further tweak the levels in the image; use the Channel pop-up menu to select each in turn.

9. Save the file as *SchoonerLVL.tif* in your *Chapter 3* folder. Click the original *Schooner.tif* image to see the difference in the histograms.

10. In the Levels dialog box there is also a Preset menu containing preset adjustments. Try this with any image.

USING CURVES FOR PRECISION TONING

When you open an image and choose to adjust it using Curves, the display will have a slanted line with a faint histogram display in the background, which provides a handy guide to maintain proper highlight and shadow detail. The upper portion of the slanted line represents the highlight areas while the bottom left portion of the line represents shadow details, with the middle area for midtones. With Curves you can make incremental adjustments by clicking on the line graph to create a point, then dragging the active point using your mouse very carefully, or you can simply use the arrow keys on your keyboard. This is used for precision adjustments, so a slight adjustment may go a long way in making changes to your image. Only one plotted point is active at any given time. To switch from one point to another existing point, simply re-click on it. To remove a point, simply drag it off the graph and it will go away.

TOOLKIT TIP You'll find when you adjust the levels to start and end on the histogram graphic, your remapped images will display more depth and tonality. This works nicely for most any digital image, even flat contrast images like the Light1 image in your *Chapter 3* folder. Feel free to open the file, and adjust to compare.

1. Open the original file *Patriot.tif* in your *Chapter 3* folder.

2. Duplicate the image so you will be able to see the differences between the original and your altered version, and rename it *PatriotCRV*. Select the "Float All in Windows" option from the Arrange Documents icon on the Application bar.

3. Select Image > Adjustments > Curves. The Curves dialog box displays as a slanted line graph with the image's histogram in the background. Make sure the Preview box is checked to observe the differences (Figure 3-27).

4. Click on three places on the line graph as shown in Figure 3-27: in the middle, then on the top right corner of the bottom left square (shadows), then the bottom left corner of the top right square (highlights). This will allow you to make slight adjustments in the highlights and shadow areas. Having less plotted points is always better than having too many.

5. You're going to darken the shadows of the image a little to provide a little more "punch," then we'll increase the highlights slightly to provide good contrast with the flag. Hover your mouse over the highlight point, and when you see the cursor change to a black cross with little arrows, click on the middle point. Use your arrow keys and press a few times to bring the graph downwards a little to darken the midtones slightly.

6. Do the same procedure with the bottom point to darken the shadows, then click on the upper point and increase the highlight area slightly.

DESIGN TIP

Using Curves adjustments provides precision toning and contrast with subtle adjustments. It is best used with properly exposed images.

 FIGURE 3-27

Using Curves adjustments for subtly toning highlights, midtones, and shadows.

7. Click on the Preview button, then click again to see before and after results. You can also use the original *Patriot.tif* image to see the differences.

8. Use Figure 3-27 as a starting point and make slight adjustments to suit your tastes. Be careful, in that a little adjustment goes a long way. You can plot points anywhere on the line. Again less is better. If you need to delete a point, simply drag it off the graph and it will go away.

9. As with Levels, you can also experiment with customized presets, or create and save your own presets for future projects.

10. Save the file *as PatriotCRV.tif* in your *Chapter 3* folder when done.

PHOTOSHOP'S CROP AND PERSPECTIVE CROP TOOLS

One of the most useful tools in working with images is the ability to crop when needed as either a correction feature or an enhancement feature. The Crop Tool (C) allows you to not only trim an image (discussed in Chapter 6), but you can use it to straighten out a misaligned image along a horizontal or vertical plane. The Perspective Crop Tool can correct issues regarding perspective in an image. It's a simple method of dragging either corner or side points and crop to "straighten out" an angle of view.

In this exercise, you'll straighten out an image, using the Crop Tool, which seems to be leaning slightly to one side. You will then use the Perspective Crop Tool to correct the image's perspective view, due to the camera being pointed slightly upward, which created slightly converging lines.

1. In Photoshop, open up the *Tree.tif* image in your *Chapter 3* folder.

2. Zoom in to about 200% using the Zoom Tool and select the Crop Tool.

3. Click on the Straighten button, and drag carefully along one of the windows (Figure 3-28). You'll notice when you let go the image will rotate slightly.

4. To complete the operation, you need to click on the Crop Tool again and when the display open up select the Crop button.

5. Zoom back out until the entire image displays for the next part of this exercise.

6. Hold down the Crop Tool on the Tools panel and select Perspective Crop Tool from the list of tools.

7. Select the entire image with the Perspective Crop Tool, and you'll notice a grid displays over the image (Figure 3-28).

8. Observe on both sides the converging lines between the edge of the image and the brick wall. Select the top corner point on both sides and drag inward until the crop lines are parallel with the brick lines along the wall in the image.

9. When you are ready, click on the Perspective Crop Tool again, and when the dialog box displays, select Crop as you did with the Crop Tool previously.

▷ FIGURE 3-28

The Crop Tool allows you to straighten out an image along with trimming. There is also a Perspective Crop Tool to correct perspective in an image.

Crop Tool

Perspective
Crop Tool

10. You should see the image "straighten out" for you. You can see how this tool can be used to adjust any alignment issue in an image. It may take a couple of tries until you feel it is corrected accurately. Keep in mind when you crop, you remove part of the image.

11. Save the corrected image as *FIXTree.tif*, at highest quality with default settings in your *Chapter 3* folder.

DIGITAL TOOLKIT EXTRA: Using Adobe Creative Cloud and Adobe Bridge for Managing Image Files

Photoshop Creative Cloud (CC) version provides designers and photographers the ability to submit, access, sync, share, and manage image files with various extensions, which include PSD, AI, INDD, JPG, PDF, GIF, and PNG files, remotely with access from most any computer or device. With Creative Cloud, designers and photographers have access to all Adobe applications, with instant updates, even for those who may still have CS6 versions of software.

Where Adobe Creative Cloud helps to manage image files remotely, Adobe Bridge provides tools and techniques to import images from your computer or devices, manage, edit, and can play slide shows for quick viewing with a client. Adobe Bridge is an application within each of the Adobe applications, or it can be launched as a standalone application. Designers and Photographers use it to manage not only Adobe image files, but Microsoft Office files as well. You can search by keywords, image metadata, file types, and various folders, create contact sheets, and send images to online printing services.

SUBMITTING AND ACCESSING YOUR IMAGES USING CREATIVE CLOUD

Now that you've had a taste of the power of Photoshop, you can also enjoy the benefits of utilizing cloud technology in setting up Adobe's Creative Cloud to submit and retrieve your files from any computer or device. Whether you download a free 30-day trial version of Photoshop (or any Adobe application), or have decided to pay for the monthly subscription service, you can install and launch Creative Cloud to upload your files to the Creative Cloud remote server for storage. You can also access your files from any other computer or device for future editing or to display to coworkers and friends. The process involves simply creating a basic free Adobe ID. With Creative Cloud installed, you can upload, access, and download your image files for future editing, and sync your files so that you are always using the current version. This saves a lot of time when working with files between home and work, or for submitting assignments in school. We'll cover submitting and accessing your image files in this set of exercises.

INSTALLING CREATIVE CLOUD

Creative Cloud can be installed for a 30-day free trial or as part of your paid subscription service. The benefits of using Creative Cloud is the ability to submit, store, and access your files for most any computer or device. This can be quite helpful to the student working on assignments, or the designer working on a team or individual project.

Here you will install Creative Cloud to submit and access your files remotely.

1. To install Creative Cloud on your computer or device, go to Adobe's website at *www.adobe.com*.

2. Select Download > Product trials as discussed in the Unit 1 Review. You'll find a page listing "Featured free trial downloads." Select the link, Start for Free (to use the trial version), or select Join to pay by monthly subscription, under the Creative Cloud icon (Figure 3-29).

3. You'll need to create a free Adobe ID, which involves creating a valid email, placing in your password, and your date of birth for security purposes. With your information entered, select Create, follow instructions and you are ready to submit your files for remote access. You can also download Creative Cloud on your tablet. To use Creative Cloud on your smartphone, you'll need to purchase the inexpensive Photoshop Touch App.

▷ FIGURE 3-29

Setting up Adobe ID to use Creative Cloud and download applications.

This is where you set up your free Adobe ID

SUBMITTING AND RETRIEVING IMAGES

One of the main functions in Creative Cloud is the ability to submit files to this remote server (hard drive) for storage, and to be able to access image files from most any computer. If you have the 30-day free trial you can store up to 2 GB of images, with those with paid subscriptions, up to 20 GB of images can be stored. The real purpose of using this is not so much for permanent storage, but for use as part of your intended workflow. You can upload additional images with thumbnails displayed, and download your image(s) from Creative Cloud with the image expanded.

In this exercise, you'll use Creative Cloud to submit files, and then access those files and download to your computer.

1. On your computer, if it isn't already active, launch Creative Cloud as you would any other application from your Applications (Mac) or Programs (Windows) folder. (In Windows 8 you can also type in "Creative Cloud" from the Start Screen.)

2. With Creative Cloud active, click on the icon and select the Files tab to display the folder icon (Figure 3-30).

3. Click Open Folder and drag an image file you created in Photoshop from one of the earlier exercises in Chapter 3 into the open folder, which may read Creative Cloud Files in the title bar.

4. To access your files on the Creative Cloud server, locate the Creative Cloud website at *https://creative.adobe.com* and log in with your Adobe ID, which will direct you to the Creative Cloud website.

5. From the Creative Cloud website, select the Files tab. Your image file should display as a thumbnail. Click on the thumbnail to expand the screen view.

▷ FIGURE 3-30

Submitting and accessing image files in Creative Cloud.

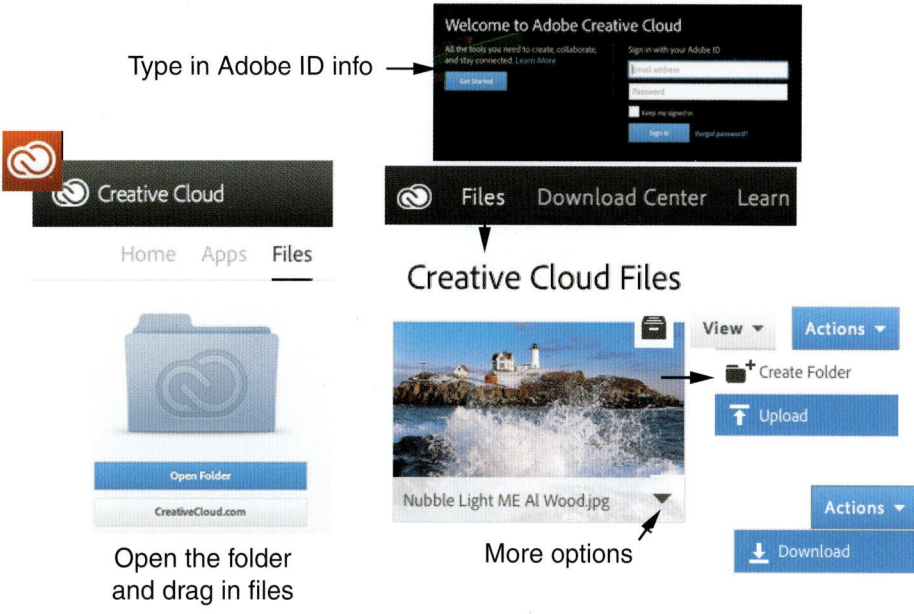

Type in Adobe ID info →

Creative Cloud Files

Open the folder and drag in files

More options

Creative Cloud on computer   Creative Cloud website

6. In the Actions panel, with the image expanded, select Download and your expanded image will be downloaded onto your computer, even if Creative Cloud is not installed on that computer. As long as you have an Adobe ID you can access your image file on the Creative Cloud suite and download your image file to most any computer or device. Note: If you have Create Cloud installed on multiple computers, you can access your image file, edit it, and then send it back up to the Creative Cloud, where it will replace the older version. That way your image version stays current.

7. Select the Creative Cloud Files link above the expanded screen size of your expanded image to minimize to the original thumbnail.

8. You can also upload your image files from your computer to the Creative Cloud site. To upload files, with the image thumbnail(s) displayed, select Actions > Upload and load up another image file of your own or one of the images from the earlier exercises in Chapter 3 into the Cloud (Figure 3-30). You can also drag an image from the desktop into the Files tab window in Creative Cloud.

9. When you select the arrow under the image thumbnail, or in the actions panel, you'll find lots of other actions you can accomplish like sharing and syncing files, and syncing application settings in Creative Cloud. We'll cover these in much more detail in Chapter 6 Advanced Users section.

10. Log out of the website when done.

TOOLKIT TIP One of quick benefits of Creative Cloud is that you can have your application updated automatically, even those from the earlier CS6 version, like Photoshop CS6. This will occur even if you have the free 30-day trial version.

USING ADOBE BRIDGE AND MINI BRIDGE FOR RETRIEVING AND MANAGING IMAGES

▷ FIGURE 3-31

Use Adobe Bridge to observe, manage, and retrieve all types of graphic files.

Adobe Bridge is an additional application within Photoshop and other Adobe applications that "bridges" the other Creative Cloud applications (Figure 3-31). The Adobe Creative Cloud consists of Adobe products for all types of media; Photoshop, Illustrator, InDesign, Acrobat, and Dreamweaver to name a few, and all work together with various types of files. Adobe Bridge is the hub for retrieving and editing files and their information to help with file management and automation between files, various pieces of artwork, and between applications within the Adobe Creative Cloud. Bridge can be opened within an application's File

Get Photos From Camera

Display Views

Key Word Search

Compact Mode

Filter Categories Search
Click on list inside Filter category to display matching images

Thumbnail View

menu, or as a stand-alone application, and there is also a version in each application called Mini Bridge. You can open Bridge in Photoshop. To do so, select File > Browse in Bridge; or select File > Close and Go to Bridge if you need to close Photoshop. You can also access Bridge as a stand-alone application through Windows or Mac OS X. The vast amount of information that can be obtained from digital files, especially from cameras and other devices, is all recorded and can be retrieved using Adobe Bridge. Here is a brief list to show you some of Adobe Bridge's features:

- It provides thumbnail previews of multiple image files from which you can select various sizes of displays. You can select how you want the images and information displayed from four workspace view buttons at the top (bottom in earlier versions) of the display [Essentials (Default), Filmstrip (Slide), and Metadata]. There is an Output button to choose a specific workspace, display. Click and drag the edges of the panels to enlarge thumbnails to check out details.

- Bridge generates and displays data in the Metadata pane about your file: file properties information, camera and exposure data, camera RAW data, GPS information, and editing history. You can also add information and instructions—including copyright, author, source, and creation information—and you can edit the information on multiple files simultaneously.

- Use the Filter panel, where images can be sorted by various file properties and data information; you can flag important files, color code, and rate them. Images can also be rotated, deleted, and automatically batch processed to a set standard, size, color mode, and so on with renaming of multiple files starting with a specified number.

- You can search for, or apply keywords to, one or more files. This is useful for image file management.

- In the Tools menu (Tools > Photoshop > Batch), you can batch process many images, create contact sheets of your images, and send digital images directly to online services for ordering prints, books, and so on. You can also create your own picture package with various combinations of sizes of your images.

- Image previews can be moved around as if they were slides on a light table.

- Use the Compact Mode icon at the top right to create a smaller window display from which you can drag thumbnails into an open Adobe application, such as Photoshop. Double-clicking a thumbnail will open the image in the application in which it was created.

In this exercise, you will locate and observe the files you created in this chapter using Adobe Bridge.

1. There are different ways to launch the Bridge application. From the Photoshop File Menu, you can select to browse within Photoshop by selecting File > Browse in Bridge, or you can close Photoshop and open up Bridge on its own by selecting File > Close and Go to Bridge. To select it as an application on its own, from the Mac desktop, select Go > Applications >

Adobe Bridge CC; from the Windows desktop, select Start > Programs > Adobe Bridge CC.

2. Select the Folders panel and locate the images in your *Chapter 3* folder to display the contents (double-click folders to open them). You can also try to use the Favorites panel to locate the files.

3. Select the *WEBLight1.jpg* image; you will notice thumbnail images and a lot of file information in the Metadata pane. Notice the file size. Select the *FIXLight1 .tif* image and notice the difference in the data. If the files were not properly named, this method of searching through Bridge can help you to locate files by data. You can also color code the images so that, say, all low-resolution images for the web may be color coded blue, which would then allow you to use the Filter panel locate them (Figure 3-31).

4. Select the other images in the *Chapter 3* folder and notice differences in file size and other properties information in the Metadata pane. You can also try to look for images you may have of your own in another folder.

5. In the Menu bar, observe the many features available. Click the Compact Mode icon to view the Window display option, then bring it back to the original size. Leave Bridge open for the next exercise.

CREATING SLIDE SHOWS USING BRIDGE

Adobe Bridge allows a designer or photographer to create a slide show to display their artwork from any combination of applications they are using. This is a great tool you can use to show your work to a client. You can choose how you want your artwork to display, how long the images are displayed, etc. Before you create a slide show you should have a folder of artwork or images ready.

Here you'll open a folder of images and create a quick slide show of your images.

1. Create a folder for your images and drag your favorite images into that folder, or, you can use your *Images* folder that you created in Chapter 1 Advanced section of Internet images, or, open your *Chapter 3* folder of images you saved; although there will be much repetition, you can still get the idea.

2. Launch the Bridge application by selecting File > Browse in Bridge in Photoshop, or from any of the other methods described in the previous exercise.

3. Select File > Open and locate the folder of images you want to make into a slide show. In Figure 3-32, you'll notice I went to locate a folder called *Favorites*; a directory structure is displayed at the top. Thumbnails of your images will then be displayed.

4. To set up your slide show settings, select View > Slideshow Options. Use the settings shown in Figure 3-32 as a starting point, then select Play to test the slideshow. That's it!

5. Press the ESC key on your keyboard to get out of the slide show, and you can use the arrow keys on your keyboard to view at your own pace. The settings will remain until you change them another time.

▷ FIGURE 3-32

Using Adobe Bridge to create an instant slide show for your artwork.

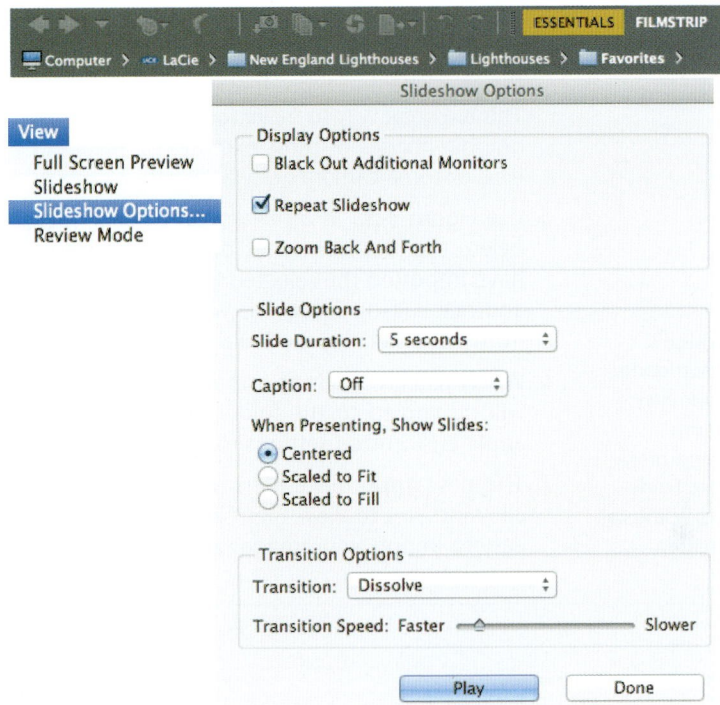

USING BRIDGE TO IMPORT IMAGES FROM YOUR DIGITAL CAMERA

Bridge comes with a built-in application called Photo Downloader, which can download images automatically from your digital camera. To help with production, it's easier to use Adobe Bridge to view multiple images before opening them in Photoshop or an other application. Adobe Bridge is also useful in renaming files and images, and as a file management system.

If you have images from a digital camera, it doesn't matter what type, you can use Adobe Bridge's Photo Downloader to manage your images. Try the following steps.

1. Create a folder to place your images, either on your hard drive or on the desktop. Name the folder *Gallery*, or *Family*, or whatever you like.

2. In Adobe Bridge, select File > Get Photos from Camera, or click on the camera icon. If the program asks whether to use Photo Downloader, select to make it the default for this exercise.

3. Plug your card reader or your camera's USB connection into your computer. When the Adobe Bridge Photo Downloader display box opens, you have some choices to make. You can batch rename as one name with sequential numbers, have subfolders created that are separated by the shooting dates, etc. This helps in later identifying what event was photographed within a certain date, and keeps images better organized, making it easier to find your images.

4. You can use the default Standard Dialog display window if you want to import *all* the images on your card. Alternatively, you can use the Advanced Dialog display if you want to be able to select the images you want to import; simply remove the check next to those that you don't want to import, as shown in Figure 3-33. This is a great way to make some quick edits on lots of images. Bridge will display graphic images of most extensions, including what are called "Camera RAW" files, or some camera's digital negatives, which will be covered in Chapter 4.

5. Use Figure 3-33 as an example for your settings. One good habit is never to delete the files from your original memory card until you are confident you have imported the selected files. You can also check Save copies to:, choosing another backup folder for your work that makes backup copies of your files from your memory card without renaming.

6. When you are ready to import your images, select Get Media and the images will be copied to the folder you designate. You can also rename them and apply customized settings for easy access for future projects you created.

7. The new imported folders and selected images will then display in Bridge, allowing you to view them in more detail for further editing. Bridge makes it easy to import your images and manage your files for faster production.

▷ FIGURE 3-33

Adobe Bridge's Photo Downloader provides an easy way to import, rename, and manage images from your digital camera or card reader.

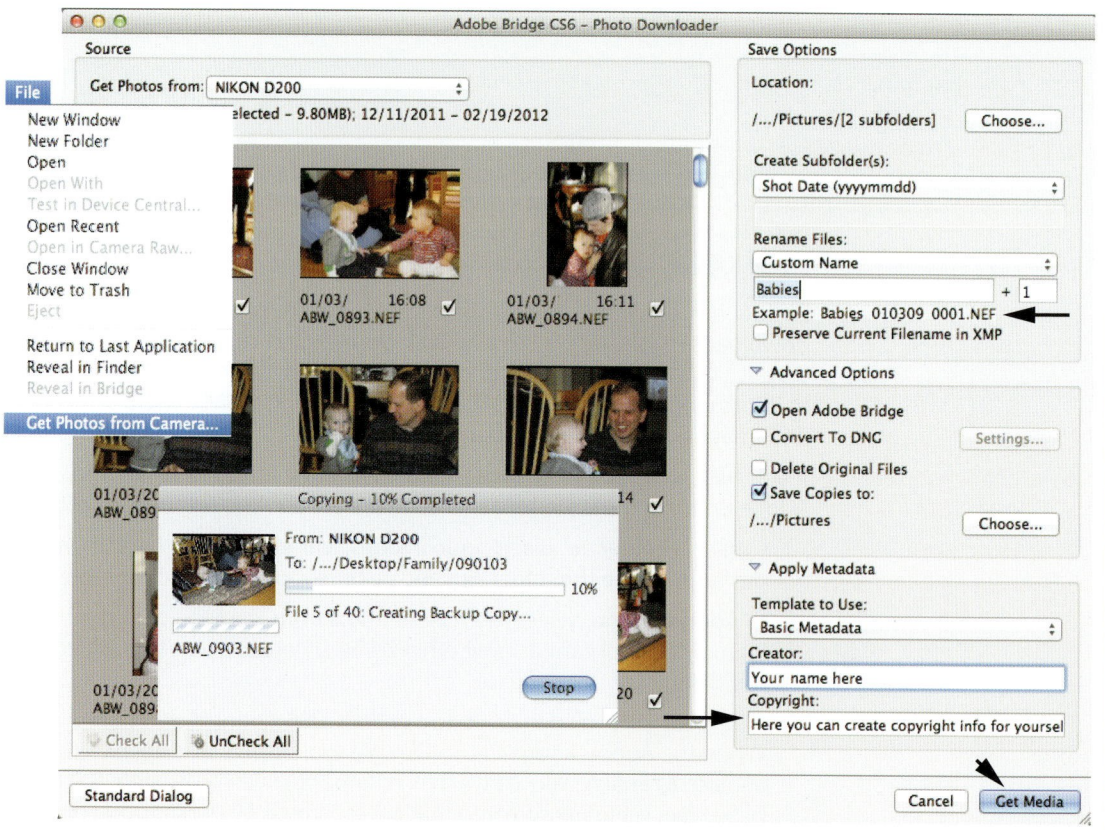

Advanced Dialog display is shown here.

USING MINI BRIDGE

Mini Bridge is an extension within an Adobe application, like Photoshop. It allows you to work using many of the Adobe Bridge features, especially if you may need to work between different applications using various types of files or documents. You can search for, sort, display thumbnails, batch process for multiple tasks, and also create slide shows from Mini Bridge's panel when you launch the application. Mini Bridge also communicates with the parent Adobe Bridge to create thumbnails, keep files organized and synched, among other tasks.

Here you will use Mini Bridge to look at files.

1. In Photoshop, select File > Browse in Mini Bridge, or choose Window > Extensions > Mini Bridge.

2. Click the Launch Bridge button at the bottom of the screen to launch Mini Bridge; the Mini Bridge panel will open with a Path bar, and Navigation Pod and Content Pod inside. Use the Path bar (Figure 3-34) to locate a folder of images you may have from another location.

3. Scroll through the thumbnails in the Content Pod to view your images.

4. Click on the View > Slideshow to display a slideshow of images. Press the ESC key when done.

5. To locate one file, click on the magnifying glass icon to search for one of the files by typing its name (*B&WCarbarn.jpg* for instance). It should then display as a thumbnail.

6. To open a file to display in Photoshop using Mini Bridge, double-click it in the Content Pod, or drag it onto the Photoshop screen.

▷ FIGURE 3-34

Mini Bridge provides the power of the parent Adobe Bridge locally within the Photoshop application for searching, filtering, and displaying files.

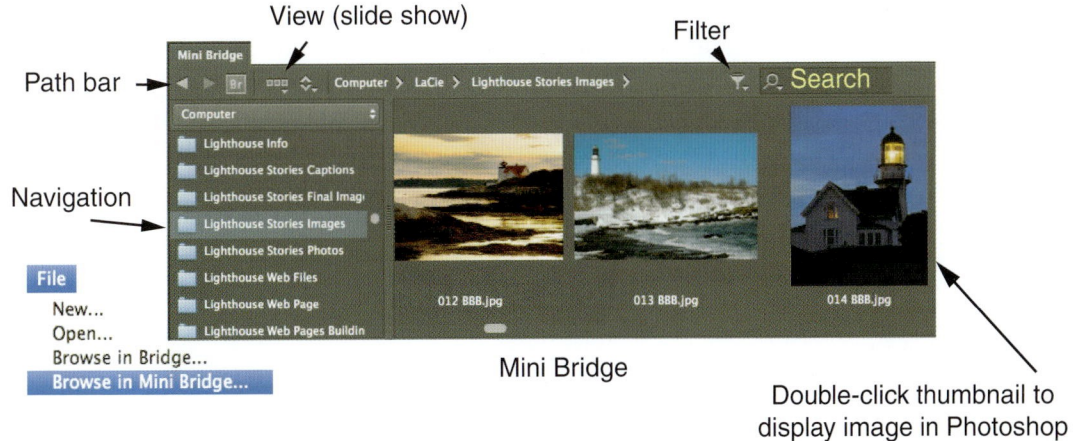

CHAPTER SUMMARY

In this chapter, you were introduced to Photoshop and some of its basic functions and components in making global adjustments to your images. You learned about the importance of determining the appropriate resolution of your image for different media. You saved files in .PSD, .TIF, and .JPG formats for specific uses. You learned the purpose of RGB color mode for electronic media and desktop printing and CMYK color mode for commercial press. The Image menu contains commands for enhancing, duplicating, resizing, trimming, and rotating an image. The Edit menu helps you to go back and compare before and after effects when applying a command or effect. For Advanced Users, you worked with image toning using curves and levels adjustments. You also used the Crop and Perspective Crop tools to straighten and adjust image perspective. In the Digital Toolkit Extra section, you used Creative Cloud to submit and access images files remotely, and you learned that Adobe Bridge helps you to search, view thumbnails, identify, sort your images, create slide shows, and import images from your digital camera. Do not forget to check out the *Extras & Goodies* folder on *www.CengageBrain.com* for more projects and ideas.

REVIEW QUESTIONS

1. Explain the use of the Tool Options bar and its components.

2. Explain the purposes of using 72 dpi and 300 dpi resolutions.

3. Explain the differences when saving images in .PSD, .TIF, and .JPG formats.

4. Why does a 300 dpi image appear larger on the monitor when viewed at full size than when it is printed?

5. Explain RGB and CMYK color modes, Auto Color command, Shadows/Highlights command, Color Balance command, and Auto Tone command.

6. What is a histogram? What is the purpose of the Histogram panel?

Originals

Adjusting contrast, shadows, and highlights

Converting colors for accurate B&W tones

CHAPTER 3
Corrected images using special commands in Photoshop's Image menu

Adjusting color balance

Crop Tool

Perspective Crop Tool

CHAPTER 3 ADVANCED
Using histograms, levels, and curves adjustments in Photoshop to adjust shadows, midtones, and highlights for quality images. Using Crop tools to adjust images.

▷ FIGURE 3-35

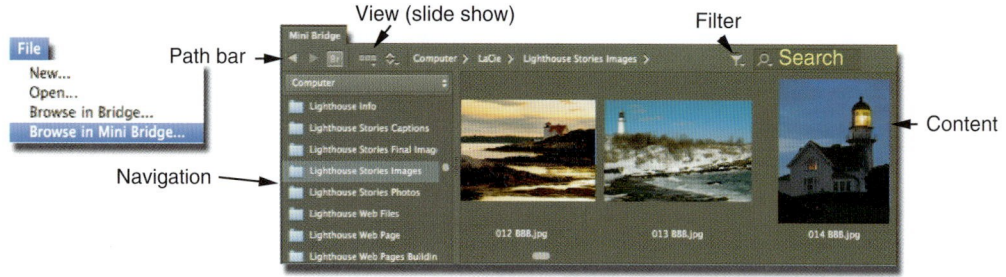

Get Photos
From Camera

Display Views

Key Word Search

Compact
Mode

Adobe Bridge interface

View (slide show)

Filter

Path bar

File
New...
Open...
Browse in Bridge...
Browse in Mini Bridge...

Navigation

Content

Mini Bridge

CHAPTER 3 EXTRA

Using Creative Cloud to submit and access image files. Adobe Bridge and Mini Bridge, which is inside each Adobe application like Photoshop, allows you to import, retrieve, display, manage, and edit files.

▷ FIGURE 3-36

Working with Selections and Channels

CHAPTER OBJECTIVES: To understand the importance of using selection tools and techniques in Photoshop, in this chapter you will:

▷ Use the Marquee, Magic Wand, Quick Selection, Move, and Lasso tools for specific selections.

▷ Learn to add, subtract, and combine selection tools to create complex selections.

▷ Create selections that can be saved permanently as channels in the Channels panel.

▷ Modify and edit selections using the Select menu.

▷ Use the Hue/Saturation command to adjust color while retaining the image's shadows and highlights.

▷ ADVANCED USERS: Make detailed selections using Quick Mask. Select part of an image by Color Range and use Paste Into to combine images. Adjust perspective and vantage points in 3D space using Perspective Warp.

▷ DIGITAL TOOLKIT EXTRA: Preparing Camera RAW files, the new digital negative for accurate toning.

When making changes within areas of an image, a designer or photographer usually needs to isolate certain portions of that image, like in case a client decides to change the color of a model's shirt or dress in an advertisement, for instance. Creating selections gives the designer or photographer a variety of ways to isolate those portions of the image that need to be modified, duplicated, or deleted. Photoshop provides tools and techniques for just about any type of selection needed. You can make changes to the selected portion of the image without affecting any areas outside that selection and then save it for later use. In this chapter, we will examine how to create and save selections using some of Photoshop's tools and techniques.

PHOTOSHOP'S SELECTION TOOLS

Much of Photoshop's image editing involves making selections within an image area and making changes. Photoshop provides a variety of selection tools and techniques with special purposes to aid the designer or photographer in creating virtually any type of selection needed (Figure 4-1). When you make a selection, you will notice a moving line or dashes ("marching ants") called a *marquee*. Selections use marquees to display the selected areas. When a selection is active, the area inside that selection can be edited; anything outside the selected area cannot be changed, unless the selection is reversed using the Select menu. Photoshop's selection tools are the Marquee (M), Lasso (L), the Magic Wand (W), and Quick Selection (W). The Move Tool (V) is also in the category of selection tools, although technically, it does not generate a selection but moves or cuts a selected area. Note: Crop Tool (C) and Slice Tool (C) are technically not selection tools, although they create initial selections before cutting or trimming parts of an image. You can access these tools by typing in their specific shortcut keys, or by holding down the mouse and selecting the tool you need. The Marquee, Lasso, Magic Wand, and Quick Selection tools have a black triangle at the bottom of the tool to indicate there are more tools in the same category. You can access these tools using the mouse, or you can navigate between each group of tools by holding down Shift and pressing the appropriate letter key.

▷ FIGURE 4-1

Photoshop selection tools.

MARQUEE TOOLS

Marquee tools select rectangular boxes, elliptical areas, and single pixel row or column selections. The Rectangular and Elliptical Marquee tools (M) can help the designer or photographer select images that need to be modified, cropped, or resized to a specific dimension. The Single Row and Single Column Marquees are used as temporary pixel-wide guidelines for aligning images and text.

TOOLKIT TIP To make perfect square and perfect circle selections with the Rectangular or Elliptical (circles) Marquee tools, hold down the Shift key as you drag diagonally with the mouse.

EDITING SELECTIONS WITH THE TOOL OPTIONS BAR

The Tool Options bar provides options for each selection tool. The Marquee and Lasso tools in Photoshop have buttons on the Tool Options bar that indicate each new selection you are making (default) and allow you to add, subtract, and intersect with other selections. You can also create specific basic shape selections by using combinations of these selection buttons, as shown in Figure 4-2. The Crop and Move tools, for instance, will have different options to enter than the Marquee and Lasso tools. You will also notice a **Refine Edge** button on a selection tool's Tool Options bar. This allows you to soften or enhance a selections edge and to preview the results on different backgrounds to see the effect created.

LASSO TOOLS

The **Lasso tools** (L) work well with selections that are needed as either freeform or complex selections (Figure 4-3). When using any Lasso Tool, the cursor will display a circle "o" when brought back to the original point. Click and the selection will be completed. You can also double-click the mouse, and the selection will be completed with a line back to the original point.

New
selection

Softens edge
selection

Type of
selection

Smoothes or Refines
selection edges

Rectangular
Marquee Tool

Add to
selection

Subtract
selection

Intersect
with selection

▷ FIGURE 4-2

In the Tool Options bar for selection tools, there are options specific to these tools, including the ability to add, subtract, and intersect selections, as well as to soften or refine the edges.

- The *Lasso* Tool itself works as a freehand tool; you simply click for a starting point and drag the cursor around any area you choose. It is a useful tool as a starting point for the designer or photographer who needs to make general selections on a large area, as a tool for cleaning up or fine-tuning selections, or when making a selection in a small area of an image that is zoomed in close.

- The *Polygonal Lasso* Tool is a great tool to make straight-line selections on images such as buildings or products. Every time you click with the Polygonal Lasso Tool, a straight line is created from one point to the next.

- The *Magnetic Lasso* Tool is useful for image areas that have edges with good contrast. It snaps to the edge of an area, which is helpful when making a detailed selection of images of people, cars, products, or wherever there is good edge contrast.

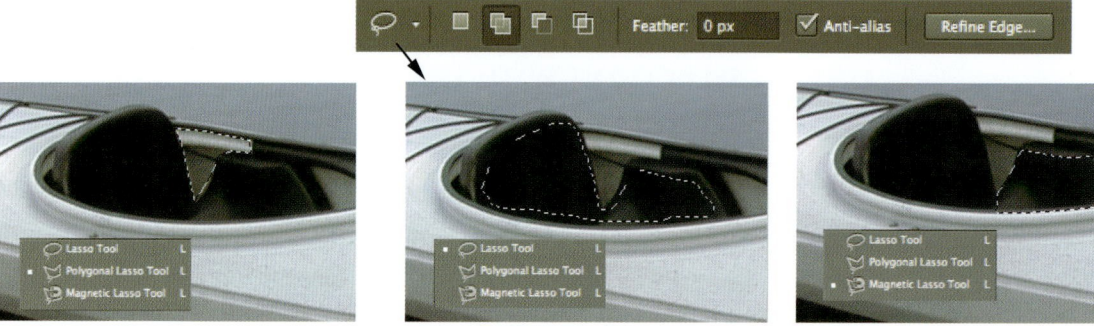

▷ FIGURE 4-3

Lasso tools.

THE MAGIC WAND TOOL

The **Magic Wand Tool** (W) selects parts of an image based on similar tints or shadings of colors (Figure 4-4). This tool is used for areas with difficult outlines or soft edges that cannot be traced easily with the Lasso tools. It helps the designer or photographer who needs to make selections based on color. The **Tolerance** setting for the Magic Wand in the Tool Options bar is important, because it determines the amount of similar colors selected; the lower the tolerance, the fewer similar colors are selected. The **Point Sample** reads the average color values of a pixel or a pixel area.

Magic Wand Tool — Samples point value of pixel or pixel area — Determines the amount of similar colors selected — Precise refinement of selection edges

▷ FIGURE 4-4

The Magic Wand Tool creates selections based on similar colors.

TOOLKIT TIP Deselect selections created by the Marquee, Lasso, Quick Selection, and Magic Wand tools by selecting Command/CTRL + D on the keyboard or by selecting another tool on the Tools panel and then clicking outside the selected area.

THE QUICK SELECTION TOOL

The **Quick Selection Tool** (W), like the Magic Wand Tool, selects similar colors, tints, or shadings of color. It allows you to "paint" a selection of a predefined brush width you set in the Tool options bar, then looks for similar adjacent colors and defined edges and shapes as you paint (Figure 4-5). It works well with edges with good contrast, and can save time in creating complicated selections.

▷ FIGURE 4-5

The Quick Selection Tool allows you to paint in a selection, following defined edges and shapes.

Quick Selection Tool

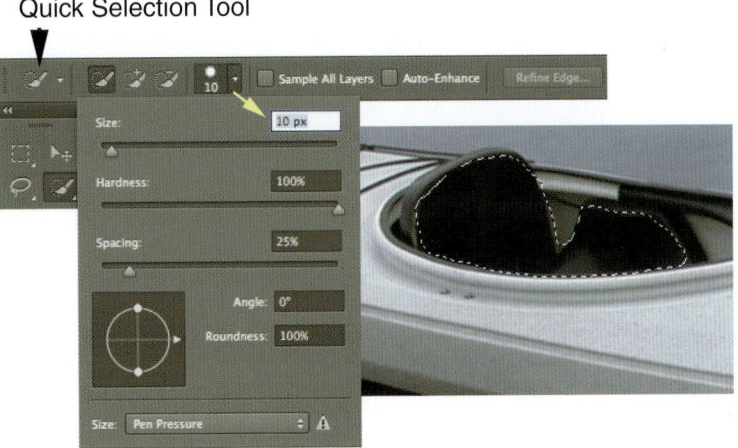

THE CHANNELS PANEL

Photoshop uses the **Channels panel** to store selections permanently. A designer or photographer can create a variety of complex selections, and then name and save them as **channels** in the Channels panel for later use. These channels are saved with the document and can be used or edited at any time. Channels also store an image's color mode information in separate color channels (Figure 4-6). For instance, an RGB image will have red, green, and blue channels, which can be edited individually.

▷ FIGURE 4-6

The Channels panel saves selections and an image's color mode information.

Color channels (RGB)

Saved selections (alpha channels)

CLIENT ASSIGNMENT: Replacing Color on a Sports Car

Steve Lyons is a local car dealer and enjoys sports cars. His brother Bryan owns a local auto body shop. Steve has a favorite black sports car that is close to having a 25th year anniversary of the car's model in business. He'd like to have his brother paint his car in gold to celebrate the anniversary and also use it to help promote his brother's business. He comes to you with a digital photo of the car and asks you to create a gold color so he can show to his brother what he is looking for. You know this will involve using selections to remove the background and to change the color of the car. You tell him it will be ready the following day.

ACTION ITEMS OVERVIEW

This project shows how a designer or photographer can use selections to create a totally realistic different colored object from the same selected object (Figure 4-7). Designers or photographers constantly use these techniques with different colored products: clothing, packaging products, and the like. Selections are like building the foundation of a house: they need to be created in accurate detail, and they are essential for the successful completion of the final project. As a designer or photographer, your goal is to create a detailed selection of the car that can

Original image

Completed recolored image

▷ FIGURE 4-7

Accurate selections of just the areas of the car to be "painted" provided a realistic effect in changing its color while maintaining tones.

be saved permanently with only those portions that should be used for painting, minus the lights, windshield, and hardware. Be wary—this is a complicated project and may take a number of attempts to create an accurate selection. Provide ample time for corrections. If you need to download the files for this chapter, they are at *www.CengageBrain.com.*

To create accurate selections of this project, here is what you need to do:

- Create a duplicate copy of the original image to serve as a backup copy.
- Crop the image to remove part of the background to emphasize the car using the Rectangular Marquee Tool.
- Create the initial selection for changing the color by using the Magic Wand, Quick Selection, and Lasso selection tools. Only the areas of the car that are to be changed must be selected; all hardware, lights, windshield, tires, etc., and background must be isolated.
- Use the Tool Options bar, Select menu, and Edit menu to help with editing selections.
- Make the selection permanent by saving it as a channel in the Channels panel for reuse and future editing.
- Create a new color using the Hue/Saturation command.
- ADVANCED USERS: Create a Quick Mask for final detail work on the selections and then save the masked selections permanently in the Channels panel. Create complex selections using Color Range, and combine images using the Paste Into command. Use Perspective Warp to adjust perspective and vantage points in 3D space.

DUPLICATING AND SAVING THE FILE

It is always a good habit to make duplicates of any file you are working on and save as often as possible. Save your images throughout the chapters here with a .TIF extension (File > Save As > *SportscarGOLD.tif*) as a default setting on your computer, so you can edit your image as many times as needed, and the quality will always remain the same (Figure 4-8). You can save Photoshop files in either .PSD or .TIF formats, and you will be able to edit either one and still maintain the

▷ FIGURE 4-8

Before editing the image, make a duplicate of the image and save it as a .TIF extension to maintain accuracy.

original quality. Photoshop's native .PSD format can primarily be read by Adobe applications, whereas **TIF format files** are universally read. In this chapter, you will save and work with this file as a .TIF. If you have room, create a backup .PSD file in your *Chapter 4* folder for practice.

TOOLKIT TIP Most images carry a color identity profile or what is called an **ICC profile** that defines colors and embeds the color information with the file. If you open a file, and a Profile Mismatch dialog box appears, select Use the Embedded Profile and Photoshop will automatically make a slight adjustment to match the colors of that image for consistency. If you choose to open it in the default working space, or if you convert to the current color space on your computer, it will adjust the colors slightly in your default working space. You will notice little if any visual difference, and it will not cause any problems with your computer.

You will check to make sure you have access to panels using the Window menu; then you will create a duplicate copy of the original *Sportscar* file and save it with a new name and a .TIF extension.

1. Make sure to locate the Navigator and Channels panels on the desktop to assist you in creating the ad for this chapter. If they are not open, use the Window menu to select the panel you need; it will put a check mark beside all those panels expanded on the desktop. If the Tool Options bar or Tools panel is not displayed, select Options, or Tools, from the Window menu to open them.

2. To bring in the *Sportscar.tif* image, choose File > Open and select the *Sportscar.tif* image located in the *Chapter 4* folder on your drive. If a dialog box opens up regarding reading info or profile matching, just click OK and continue.

3. Create a duplicate image by selecting Image > Duplicate.

4. Name the new copy *SportscarGOLD* and Save As *SportscarGOLD.tif* to your *Chapter 4* folder on your drive with the default settings. The new *SportscarGOLD.tif* file is what you will be working with.

5. Close the original *Sportscar.tif* file.

TOOLKIT TIP When you get familiar with certain panels you prefer to have open on your workspace, you can save it as a customized workspace (Window > Workspace > New Workspace). You can name it and assign a hot key combination to it.

SELECTING THE SPORTS CAR TO CHANGE COLOR

This selection will be used for changing the car's black painted color to the gold color specified by the client. Here, only the black painted colors of the original sports car are going to be selected; all hardware, lights, tires, windshield, and background must be isolated so they will not change color. Make sure you have enough time to complete this series of exercises so that you can save your selections permanently at the end.

USING THE RECTANGULAR MARQUEE SELECTION TOOL FOR CROPPING

The Rectangular Marquee Tool can be used to make specific square or rectangular selections on an image. These selections can be used to provide an emphasis to an image in creating borders, vignettes, or for cropping a busy looking image. Many times, as you can see with the Sportscar photo, a client will hand a designer a snapshot image to help explain what they are looking for. The Rectangular Marquee Tool can create specific or freehand dimensions using the Style button on the Tool Options bar. A Fixed Size dimension can be entered in the Width and Height boxes as a specific pixel (px) or inches (in) amount. A Fixed Ratio option can be entered to meet a specific format indicated by the client. The default Normal Style provides a freehand dimension to be used to isolate outer components of an image, which is what is needed for this image, without worrying about specific dimensions, as the final image will be used as a guide. The Rectangular Marquee Tool can also be used to crop an image along with the Image menu (Image > Crop). Note: The Crop Tool can also be used for more precise image cropping.

In order to focus on the car, you will crop some of the outside cars to be able to keep your attention in working with this car.

1. With the *SportscarGOLD* image displayed, select the Rectangular Marquee Tool, and on the Tool Options bar, select Normal on the Style button (Figure 4-9).

▷ FIGURE 4-9

The Rectangular Marquee Tool can be used to draw freehand, or specific four-corner selections on an image for cropping and emphasizing selected components.

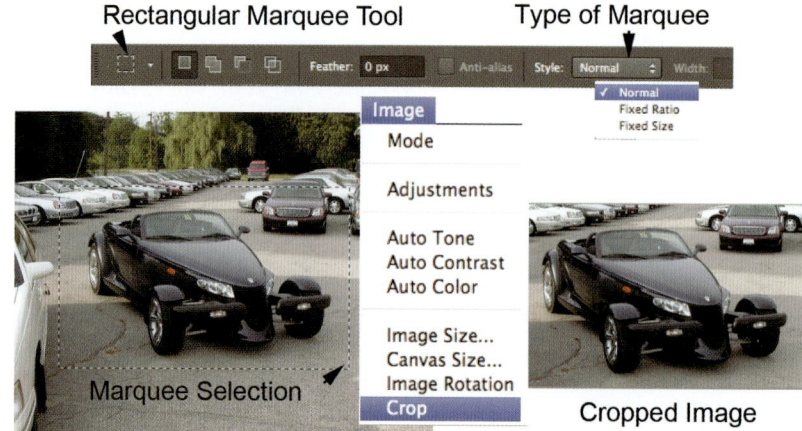

Rectangular Marquee Tool   Type of Marquee

Marquee Selection   Cropped Image

2. Drag diagonally from the top left to the bottom right, leaving enough room to work on the car, but removing the white car on the left side and upper background. To redo a selection, click outside the selection and try again.

3. Use the arrow keys on the keyboard to move your selection around accurately.

4. When you are happy with your selection, select Image > Crop to crop your image, removing some of the unwanted background.

5. Save the file in your *Chapter 4* folder and leave open for the next exercise.

USING THE MAGIC WAND TOOL

Since the car is a basic black color, you will use the Magic Wand Tool. This tool works well for selecting an image using similar adjacent colors as determined by the Tolerance setting, and the sampling of pixel values on the Tool Options bar. Make sure the Anti-alias setting is checked on the Tool Options bar to keep the pixel edges from looking jagged by softening the transition between colors.

Here, you are going to set the options for the Magic Wand Tool and start selecting the black painted areas of the car.

1. Zoom in to about 100% with the Zoom Tool to get a good, detailed view. Click on the Actual Pixels button, or try using the Scrubby Zoom option on the Tool Options bar to click and zoom to get the full view of the car. The percentage the window displays will show on the title bar of the image window.

2. Select the Magic Wand Tool.

3. Set the Tolerance to 20 pixels on the Tool Options bar to indicate how many pixels of relatively the same shade of black color should be selected.

4. Place a check in the Anti-alias box in the Tool Options bar by clicking on the box. This setting helps to gradually smooth out square pixels so they will not appear as jagged edges. Finally, check in the Contiguous box to be able to select colors next to one another as shown in Figure 4-10.

5. Select the front hood area of the car. A marquee selection will show on your image.

DESIGN TIP

It is a good habit to zoom in with the Zoom Tool and work on a small area at a time, and then to zoom out and observe results in the bigger picture, much like an artist would when working on a painting or sketch.

New selection

Add to selection

Subtract from selection

Samples point value
of pixel or pixel area

Determines range
of colors to select

Sample Size: 3 by 3 Average | Tolerance: 20

Magic Wand
Tool

Intersect with selection

Select colors next
to one another

Improves the quality of a selection's edges
by testing against different backgrounds

Softens pixel edges
(less jagged edges)

✓ Anti-alias ✓ Contiguous ☐ Sample All Layers Refine Edge...

Sample colors only
on current layer
(leave unchecked for now)

▷ FIGURE 4-10

**Magic Wand Tool
Options bar.**

ADDING AND SUBTRACTING SELECTIONS

The selection tools have buttons on the Tool Options bar that allow you to add, subtract, and intersect with previous selections (Figure 4-10). When you add to or subtract from a selection, you will notice a plus or minus sign under the tool cursor. When the intersect selection button is chosen, an "x" is displayed under the cursor. Use these buttons carefully each time you want to edit your selection.

TOOLKIT TIP If you like keystrokes instead of the buttons on the Tool Options bar, holding down the Option/ALT key will subtract from your selection, and holding down the Shift key will add to your selection.

Follow the steps below using the buttons on the Tool Options bar to add to and subtract from the selection you are making.

1. While your marquee is still showing, and the Magic Wand Tool is selected, set the Tolerance to between 10 and 15 pixels.

2. Use the Tool Options bar buttons, or the keystroke shortcuts, to add to and subtract from your selection until you have part of the front hood and side selected, excluding any hardware or background (Figure 4-10). Do not select the background, front radiator area, tires, or windshield area. If you select too much, select Command/CTRL + Z to undo the selection. Use the Option/ALT key to minus the selection.

3. Work on selecting the front hood and side of the car for now. Adjust the Tolerance to 10 and 5 pixels. Don't worry about stray selections; you'll be cleaning them up later.

4. Keep the selection active, and save your file, but do not close it.

> **(X) PROBLEM** A selection is automatically removed if you have the New Selection button on the Tool Options bar set when making another selection. To remove all selections on the image, choose Select > Deselect. If you make a mistake, choose Select > Reselect. To go back to the last action, choose Edit > Undo State Change, or toggle Command/CTRL Z.

FINE-TUNING WITH THE QUICK SELECTION TOOL

The **Quick Selection Tool** can help to paint or add to the selection of the black painted areas of the car, or to delete parts of the selection that may have gone outside the sports car itself (Figure 4-11). Zoom in closer and keep the paintbrush at 10 pixels wide or less to start, using the Add To Selection and Subtract From Selection icons on the Tool Options bar to fine-tune your selection.

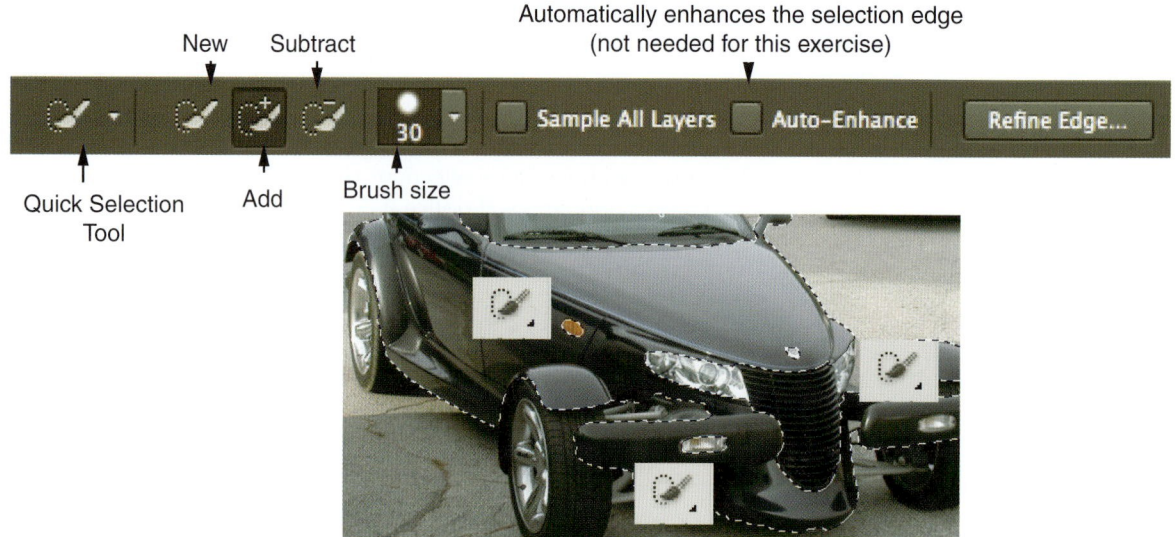

> ▷ FIGURE 4-11
>
> **Add to the selection by painting it in using the Quick Selection Tool.**

> **TOOLKIT TIP** You can quickly adjust the brush size of this tool or any painting tool by pressing the bracket keys on your keyboard. The left bracket ([) makes the size smaller and the right bracket (]) increases the size. To save time, you can also use the spacebar instead of the Hand Tool to scroll around the image as you work.

1. Zoom in to 100% or closer to observe the detail in the selection area. Use the Hand Tool and Navigator panel to move around the image.

2. To select the Quick Selection Tool, click on the Magic Wand Tool's lower right triangle on the Tools panel to display the Quick Selection Tool. Select this tool to make it active. With the Quick Selection Tool displayed in the Tools panel, set the brush size to 5 pixels wide or less to start. Zoom in close to click and drag selections; you'll notice it cleans up stray pixels as well. For details, zoom to 200% or more and set pixel size to 1 or 2 pixels to select minute edges. Do the front fender areas last at 1 pixel as they will blend into the color of the tires easily.

3. Now click and drag to paint or to add or subtract from the selection area. Use the Tool Options bar icons to add to and subtract from your selection until you have most of the car's black painted color selected, excluding any hardware or background (Figure 4-11). Understand that being detailed in your work is what it is all about. You will finish fine-tuning this selection in the next exercise.

4. Select the Zoom Tool, click on the Scrubby Zoom option in the Tool Options bar, then click on the image and drag to quickly zoom in and out of the image to observe your work, or select the zoom in and zoom out icons. You can also select the Fit screen button to have the image fill your screen. Make any additional adjustments as necessary. Keep the selection active and save it, but do not close the file.

CLEANING UP WITH THE LASSO TOOLS

The Lasso tools can be used to help clean up stray areas not yet selected by the Magic Wand or Quick Selection tools. You can use them to combine with and subtract from selected areas and for straight edge selections. After general selections are made, you can zoom in close and work on detailed areas with the Lasso Tool (Figure 4-12).

▷ FIGURE 4-12

Using the Lasso Tool for free-hand selections.

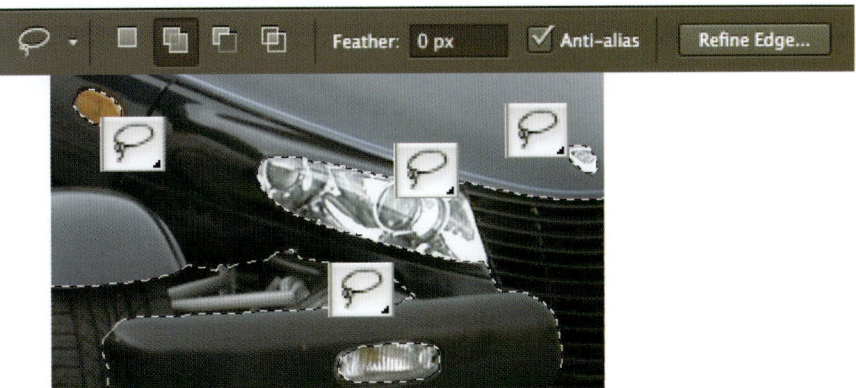

In this exercise, you will use the Lasso tools for editing your selections in detail.

1. Using the Zoom Tool (Z), zoom to about 200% (or use Command/CTRL + 0), or select the Fit Screen button on the Tool Options bar.

2. Select the regular Lasso Tool (L) to make freehand selections on the car's black painted color.

3. Use the buttons on the Tool Options bar for adding to the previous selection made by the Magic Wand and Quick Selection tools (W), and then subtract any part of the selection that included hardware or the background.

4. When you return to the starting point of your selection, indicated by a small circle underneath the cursor, let go of your mouse to close the path. Since you can add to or subtract from a selection at will, it is okay to select or deselect small areas to remain precise.

5. Zoom in to about 200% or closer to start editing the selection near the hardware and alongside the edges of the car. Remember: only the black painted color areas are to be selected. Do not drink any coffee before doing this!

6. Save the file and leave the file open with the selection active.

THE SELECT MENU

The Select menu contains commands to edit selections (Figure 4-13). You still may need to work on selecting small areas of black on the car. The Select menu is a helpful tool for making slight changes in selections and for saving and reusing selections. Using the Select menu, you can increase a selection of similar adjacent colors by choosing Select > Grow, or by selecting similar colors throughout the image by choosing Select > Similar. To clean up stray pixels, the Smooth command (Select > Modify > Smooth) works nicely. You can also choose to select and deselect all layers within a document, or select layers of the same type, such as selecting all layers that contain text.

▷   FIGURE 4-13

The Select menu.

Select		
All	⌘A	◀— Selects everything on page
Deselect	⌘D	◀— Deselects all selections made
Reselect	⇧⌘D	◀— Restores selection action
Inverse	⇧⌘I	◀— Reverses selected area from inside to outside of selection
All Layers	⌥⌘A	◀— Selects all layers in document
Deselect Layers		◀— Deselects all selected layers in a document
Find Layers	⌥⇧⌘F	◀— Finds selected layers by type
Isolate Layers		◀— Isolates selected layers of similar type
Color Range...		◀— Creates selections based on color range
Focus Area...		◀— Generates a selection based on sharp focus
Refine Edge...	⌥⌘R	◀— Softens the edge of the selection
Modify	▶	◀— Modifies selection size and smoothes out selections
Grow		◀— Expands selection of adjacent pixels in color range
Similar		◀— Expands selection of non-adjacent pixels in color range
Transform Selection		◀— Changes size, position, angle, and shape of a selection
Edit in Quick Mask Mode		◀— Paint in a mask that can be converted to a selection
Load Selection...		◀— Loads selection saved in the Channels palette for editing
Save Selection...		◀— Saves selection permanently in the Channels palette
New 3D Extrusion		◀— Creates 3D shape based on selection

In this exercise, if needed, you will adjust the selections slightly and smooth out any stray areas that need to be included as part of the selection.

1. If you have large places that still need to be selected, select the Magic Wand Tool (W), and set the Tolerance to 5 pixels on the Tool Options bar to keep the selection confined to a small amount of black tones of the car.

2. To add to the selection, choose Select > Grow for adjacent pixels or Select > Similar for nonadjacent pixels of similar colors.

3. To fill in stray areas that are not selected, choose Select > Modify > Smooth. Choose a 1- or 2-pixel sample radius; make sure the hardware and the background are *not* selected—the key is making sure all black painted areas have been selected, and no hardware or background is selected, much like a body shop would mask off areas that are not to be painted.

4. Save your file and leave it open with the selections active. It is time to fine-tune the edges of your selection. Do not deselect your work.

SAVING SELECTIONS PERMANENTLY USING CHANNELS

Photoshop uses channels in its Channels panel to save and store selections of an image area permanently called **alpha channels**, so they can be used again. These channels can also be edited at any time. Channels also store an image's color mode information in separate channels like the colors red, green, and blue for RGB color mode. You will notice these are displayed individually on the Channels panel. The Select menu allows you to save a selection to the Channels panel, so you will not lose all that hard work. Choose Select > Save Selection and name a new channel to save your selection. To load a selection already created from the Channels panel, choose Select > Load Selection.

You are going to create a permanent channel in this exercise to save the selection. You will name the selection and save the file.

1. Make sure the Channels panel is displayed by selecting Channels from the Window menu; if it is already on your desktop, click the icon to expand it.

2. Click on Select > Save Selection from the Menu bar; when the Save Selection dialog box comes up, select New Channel and name it *Color* (Figure 4-14). Click OK.

▷ FIGURE 4-14

Save the selection as Color in a channel.

3. Select the Channels panel, and you will notice that a new channel titled *Color* has been created that actually shows a black and white thumbnail of what is selected. Notice that the separate RGB color channels are displayed, as well (Figure 4-15).

▷ FIGURE 4-15

The Channels panel.

4. The *Color* channel is the new permanent alpha channel you just created. If the eye icon is hidden (not displayed), you will see the image in its normal (RGB) view.

5. In the Channels panel, when you click the box to show the eye icon, a red overlay mask shows the areas that are not to be changed. The normal image areas *without* the red overlay are the selected areas you created earlier that are going to be used to change the sports car's color.

6. Hide the eye icon by clicking the box again next to the *Color* channel to display the color channel's eye icons (RGB). The normal image will display.

7. Save the file again as *SportscarGOLD* again in your *Chapter 4* folder, making sure that the Alpha Channels box is checked for permanent selections. If a dialog box displays asking to replace the file, choose to replace it. Close the file; your selection is now permanent with the image.

EDITING CHANNELS

You can repeatedly modify and save the changes to your selection by choosing Selection > Save Selection and select Replace Channel in the Channel drop-down menu as the operation. This replaces the old selection with the new, edited selection. If you want to save multiple selections at various stages, choose Select > Save Selection and provide different names to describe different channels.

Here, you will make final changes to the selection and save them in the *Color* channel you created earlier.

1. To check your selection, open the file *SportscarGOLD* in your *Chapter 4* folder (if a dialog box displays about the file, click OK), then choose Select > Load Selection. When the dialog box opens, you will see the *Color* channel. Since it is the only alpha channel you created, it is the only one available to load.

2. Select OK. The selection you saved displays on the image showing with a marquee. You can now edit your selection.

3. Go back and use the Lasso Tool, Quick Selection Tool, or Select menu to complete the selection so that only black painted areas are selected. Zoom in to 200% to check any details.

4. To replace the permanent channel selection with the most recent version, choose Select > Save Selection (Figure 4-16).

5. Locate the *Color* channel on the drop-down display and select Replace Channel. This replaces the old selection with the new edited selection. Select OK.

6. Continue until you are confident you have all the areas for recoloring the sports car selected.

7. Save the file in your *Chapter 4* folder on your hard drive.

▷ FIGURE 4-16

Loading, saving, and replacing a selection.

Load the selection first, then add to the selection, save it by replacing the channel with new selection.

REFINING THE EDGES OF THE SPORTS CAR COLOR SELECTION

With any of the selection tools used, you will notice a **Refine Edge** button in the Tool Options bar. This provides the designer or photographer the opportunity to soften, increase the contrast of, or expand the selection edges, and to test them against various backgrounds for accuracy (Figure 4-17). Pixels are not round: they are square and create jagged edges for selections along curved areas. The Refine Edge feature provides additional minute adjustments to soften selection edges. You can observe various masks and views that show your selection, and adjust the sliders so the selection will make a smooth, softened transition within its surroundings for true realism in your final image. This function can also be used to accurately remove an object from its surroundings. Keep in mind that adjusting the selection edges to soften should be done when you have your final selections completed as accurately as possible.

▷ FIGURE 4-17

The Refine Edge button provides softening or enhancing adjustments of selections that can be viewed on various backgrounds or masks.

Now that you have finalized your detailed selection for changing the color of the sports car, you will use the Refine Edge command to soften the edges for the car to blend into the background area of the image, which will make the transition more believable. You will also check the selection against various background masks.

1. With the sports car selection still active, zoom out the car to at least 100% to show the front area, and then select one of the selection tools. Click the Refine Edge button on the Tool Options bar.

2. As a starting point, select the Overlay View in the Refine Edge dialog box to display a red mask around those areas NOT to be painted, and make subtle adjustments using the sliders, starting with those displayed in Figure 4-17.

3. If you find that there are any stray areas that were not selected, or any place over selected (background areas), then you may need to go back and use the selection tools to correct the problem areas. Refine Edge can also help as a guide to check selections closely for accuracy.

4. To continue to check, you can press "P" to toggle the preview of the edge refinements, press "F" to cycle through the various preview modes or masks, or press "X" to disable all views, allowing you to view the original image again. Select the Marching Ants (M) View to see your new selection.

5. When the edges seem smooth enough, click OK. Subtlety in making changes is important here. It is easier to come back and add to soften the edges than it is to remove them sometimes.

6. To save your new selection, change to replace the existing channel, choose Select > Save Selection > Color Channel > Replace Channel > OK. You are now ready to change the car's color but first you want to duplicate the file to use the selections for future use.

7. Select Image > Duplicate and name the copy *Car_Selections*. Save the duplicate as *Sportscar_Selections.tif* in your *Chapter 4* folder, then close the file. This way you have your selections for future editing BEFORE applying color. This file can also be used in the Advanced Users section on using Quick Mask.

8. Leave *SportscarGOLD.tif* open for the next exercise to apply color.

TOOLKIT TIP Inversing a selection: Sometimes it is easier to select what you do not want at first, because it is easier to select areas that are not as complex; then you can inverse the selection to include the area you actually want to edit. For instance, you have a landscape image with a blue sky, but you want to adjust the tones in the image except for the blue sky. Instead of selecting the landscape area you want to adjust, select the blue sky then choose Select > Inverse from the Select menu to change the selection to surround the landscape—what you really want to edit. You can then save the inverted selection permanently as a channel.

DESIGN TIP

If you were to try to "paint" the car with a brush, even at a low opacity, the shadow areas in particular would appear "filled in" and unrealistic looking. Painting is best done in small areas of an image. Using the Hue/ Saturation command works best with large areas or images with varying shadows and highlights.

ADJUSTING COLOR USING THE HUE/ SATURATION COMMAND

We are now ready to change the color of the sports car using the Hue/Saturation command in the Image menu. The **Hue/Saturation command** lets you adjust the hue, saturation, and lightness of an image or selected areas of an image. It works well with large items that have varying shadow and highlight detail. This technique works wonderfully when changing the color of a car, for instance. You can use the Hue slider to select new colors and the Saturation and Lightness sliders for color purity and intensity. You also have the option to try out various preset settings in the Hue/Saturation panel, or create your own customized preset settings that you can save and access for future projects.

In this exercise, you are going to accurately color the sports car. You will load the completed *Color* channel selection you created, and then you will use the Hue/ Saturation command to get the color you want.

DESIGN TIP

When scanning images or photograph documents, sometimes an image may appear overly saturated in color, especially in skin tones. You can use the Hue/Saturation command to help to bring back the original colors by decreasing the image's saturation.

1. With your *SportscarGOLD.tif* file open, to retrieve your selection, choose Select > Load Selection > Color > OK. This is the alpha selection channel you created for only those areas of the car that are going to be colored.

2. Select Image > Adjustments > Hue/Saturation and make sure the Colorize and Preview option boxes are checked.

3. Move the dialog box alongside the image so you can see the effects.

4. To change the color of the sports car to gold, start with these settings and adjust the sliders until you have a nice golden color.
   Hue: 40, Saturation: 55, Lightness: –5 (minus 5). See Figure 4-18 for settings. To save your color settings, click the Preset Options menu, and choose Save Preset.

▷ FIGURE 4-18

The Hue/Saturation command blends in colors with tones for a more realistic look on your image.

5. Name the preset *Gold* in the Hue/Saturation panel. It will be saved as a custom preset.

6. Save your file.

7. Optional: Feel free to duplicate your *SportscarGOLD* file and make your own colors; the selection will still be saved as a channel. Try candy apple red, turquoise green, or purple as color ideas. Simply adjust the Hue/Saturation sliders to taste.

 PROBLEM If you are not getting close to the color you want, make sure the Colorize box is checked in the Hue/Saturation dialog box.

 TOOLKIT TIP In Photoshop CC, there is a special selection function in the Select menu named **Focus Area...**, which generates selections based on areas of a digital image that are in the clearest focus. This type of selection will work nicely when the background is blurred and you may want to remove your subject, as in portraiture or product work. It would not have worked in the car example as everything was sharp.

 TOOLKIT TIP If you are using the current Mac OS X Mavericks version, when you select File > Save As, you will find you can also assign your document or image file to a color tag or text tag (see Chapter 1) that you may have previously created, or you can start a new tag, for quick access in the future. These tags can be created for any Adobe or Microsoft files.

ADVANCED USERS: Selection Techniques Using Masking and by Color Range, Making Adjustments in 3D Space with Perspective Warp

Selections are the main building blocks in creative image development with adjustments, composites, and retouching of images in Photoshop. For complex selections, painting in selections using the **Quick Mask** technique provides precision in making sure only those areas to be painted or adjusted are selected. Selecting by **color range** applies selections to areas of similar color and color tones over the entire image, which can be very useful with non-adjacent color selections. **Paste Into** is a technique in which two selected components are combined together as one image. One selection creates a "window" for the other selection to be pasted into place.

Although a different aspect of the selection process, in Photoshop Creative Cloud (CC) version, there is a function called **Perspective Warp**. This feature allows designers to create and work in a three-dimensional space to slightly move things around or adjust perspective, by setting up a three-dimensional plane and moving points. This works well in architectural photographic images.

USING QUICK MASK FOR MASKING SELECTIONS

Using a **Quick Mask** and saving it as a selection is another method to further edit your selections for more advanced detail work. As you noticed using the Refine Edge function, you observed different masks of the selection you had made of the sports car as a way to check your accuracy, and to soften the edge selections. Using the Quick Mask method allows you to create a detailed selection using the brush or pencils tools based on observing the mask as a guide. You may find this a more preferred alternative than using the selection tools covered.

In Photoshop, located at the bottom of the Tools panel, you will find your image that you are working on, by default, is in normal Standard Mode [bottom (left) icon]. You are going to work in Quick Mask mode by simply pressing the same button, which acts as a toggle (Figure 4-19), and paint to add or remove part of the selection. You would paint with white to remove areas of the mask or SUBTRACT from the selection. Painting with black would ADD to the mask or selection (as far as the image goes, remember, painting with white reveals, painting with black conceals). Quick masks, however, are not permanent; after you have set up your selection mask and checked it, you will need to make a permanent selection channel again as done earlier.

As for the Brush and Pencil tools, when you select either tool, you can click on the brush size icon to bring up the tool's Preset Picker of customized tools. You can also use the sliders to determine the size and edge hardness of the tools and create your own preset tool.

▷ **Masks** are used to protect parts of an image from being changed the same way an auto body shop masks off parts of an auto not to be painted.

Pencil Tool

Brush Tool

Paint with black adds to mask

Switch Foreground and Background colors

Toggle Black and White foreground

Paint with white removes mask

Change Screen Mode

Brush Preset Picker

Toggle Standard Mode and Quick Mask Mode

▷ FIGURE 4-19

You can add or subtract from a selection mask by painting with the Pencil Tool or Brush Tool in Quick Mask mode.

▷ Masks are great for working in minute detail, maintaining accuracy and providing another way to save a selection.

▷ Using a mask covers areas outside the selected area with a red colored overlay. You noticed a red mask was one of the options when you chose the Refine Edge function.

▷ All exposed areas (unmasked or not red) are part of the selection you made for making changes. Here, you should use the Brush Tool for soft edges and the Pencil Tool for sharp contrast edges; you will also find that Lasso tools and the Eraser Tool work in Quick Mask mode as well.

DESIGN TIP

Here is where a designer can really get into accurate details with a very small brush size. Painting with masks allows you to edit minute details within an image, so there is little room left for mistakes; this attention to detail provides quality workmanship that pays back with customer satisfaction and loyalty.

TOOLKIT TIP You can quickly adjust the brush size of any painting tool by pressing the bracket keys on your keyboard. The left bracket ([) decreases the brush size; the right bracket (]) increases it.

TOOLKIT TIP You can switch back and forth between adding to the mask with black and subtracting from the mask with white foreground colors by pressing the X key on your keyboard. Remember, white removes the mask, black will add to the mask. If you use the Eraser, make sure the background color is set to white to delete parts of the mask.

TOOLKIT TIP When you adjust selections using Quick Mask the color you created in your *SportscarGOLD* file doesn't normally spread or adjust to the new selection, and you would need to re-apply color to the entire new selection. If using Quick Mask, it works better BEFORE color is applied as you would only be adjusting the overall selection, not changing the color, which would be the final step.

Now you will paint with the Brush and Pencil tools to add to or subtract from the mask using either black or white to reveal or conceal portions of the mask.

1. Starting from the beginning, open the original *Sportscar.tif* file or your own image, and make basic selections on some areas you want to color. Save the selection using Select > Save Selection > New Channel and name the channel *Color*. To start with selections already made earlier, select the *SportscarSelections.tif* file in your *Chapter 4* folder. It will have the selections you had saved as channels.

2. Click by the bottom left icon on the Tools panel to toggle from the default Standard Mode (Q) to Quick Mask Mode (Q) (Figure 4-19). You will observe a red overlay on the image indicating what has been masked out. You can also select Edit in Quick Mask Mode in the Select menu.

3. Zoom in to around 200% to 300% to observe what needs editing.

4. Masking and unmasking, use the foreground and background colors in the Tools panel and either the Brush for larger areas or Pencil Tool for smaller areas as starting points to paint. White removes the mask; black will add to the mask.

5. Select either a harder edge brush or try the Pencil Tool and enter 5 pixels or less brush size to start in the Tool Options bar. You are working with detail here, so a smaller brush size will be easier to work with.

6. On the Tool Options bar, set Mode to Normal and the Opacity settings to 100%.

▷ FIGURE 4-20

Completing the mask to make a very accurate selection.

7. Select the Foreground color as white by clicking the bent arrow above the Foreground/Background color icons so that white displays as the Foreground color (or simply press "X" on the keyboard to switch them). Paint with white to remove areas of the mask to expose any missed black areas of the car (Figure 4-20).

Black adds to selection mask

Toggle Black and White foreground

White removes selection mask

Toggle Standard Mode and Quick Mask Mode

Quick Mask

Pencil Tool

Brush Tool

8. Select the bent arrow again—it acts as a toggle—to change the Foreground color to black. Use this to add to the mask. Change brush sizes depending on the size of the area.

9. Work on small details around the lights, tires, background, and seat of the car to edit the mask. Remember, you want to isolate the hardware and background completely from the black area of the car.

10. Click the mask icon to toggle between Standard Mode and Quick Mask Mode on the Tools panel to see your new edited selection.

11. Select the Brush Tool for painting along the outer edges of the car.

12. When you have everything selected as accurately as possible, select one of the selection tools, then select Refine Edge on the Tool Options bar to check your work. If everything looks great, go ahead and soften the edge selection. Select OK when finished.

13. To replace the alpha channel with the most recent selection, click on the left icon at the bottom of the Tools panel to toggle back to Standard mode to view the selected car, then choose Select > Save Selection (Figure 4-20).

14. Locate the *Color* channel on the drop-down display and select Replace Channel. This replaces the old selection with the new edited selection.

15. When your selection is complete, make sure your selection is active on the image (Select > Load Selection > Channel: Color), then select Image > Adjustments > Hue/Saturation (make sure Colorize and Preview boxes are checked), adjust for your new color, Save as *CarColor.tif,* and close the file in the *Chapter 4* folder.

SELECTING BY COLOR RANGE AND COMBINING IMAGES USING THE PASTE INTO COMMAND

Here is a way to change a blue sky to enhance your image by adding clouds from another image. The idea is to Paste the new improved sky into a selection made from the plain sky using the **Paste Into command** (Figure 4-21). To replace the blue sky with the image of the clouds, a selection of the blue sky needs to be made and then a selection of the entire clouds image. The blue sky selection becomes a cutout, or window, into which you place the clouds image. You can create all kinds of different image combinations with this technique.

CROPPING A FIXED SELECTION SIZE

The Marquee Tool can create selections based on a fixed width and height set in the Tool Options bar. The area outside the selection can be removed by choosing Image > Crop to make the image a specific size. Of the Marquee tools, cropping a fixed image selection is best done with the Rectangular Marquee Tool, which will create a rectangular crop. Since the lighthouse image is slightly larger than the clouds image, you will crop the lighthouse image to size. Both images are the same resolution, so there will be no distortion.

Original images   Final image with clouds inserted

▷ FIGURE 4-21

Using the Paste Into command lets you combine images for dramatic effects.

TOOLKIT TIP Before you combine images, make sure that the resolution ppi is the same for both images by choosing Image > Image Size and checking the Resolution setting.

Here you will crop the lighthouse image size to match the size of the image of the clouds.

1. Open the *Litehous.tif* file from the *Chapter 4* folder on your drive.

2. Select the Rectangular Marquee Tool. In the Tool Options bar, select Fixed Size for Style and enter "7 in" for Width and "5 in" for Height. This creates a fixed, 7-inch by 5-inch selection.

3. Click on the image once to place the marquee, and then use the arrow keys to position the selection so the tank on the left side of the picture is eliminated (Figure 4-22).

4. To remove the area outside of the selection, choose Image > Crop, then remove the selection (Select > Deselect). Leave the image open. Note: Cropping an image to a specified size can also be done using the Crop Tool (covered in Chapter 6).

Rectangular Marquee Tool   Fixed Size Style

▷ FIGURE 4-22

Enter a fixed size of 7 by 5 inches, then crop the image using the Rectangular Marquee Tool.

SELECTING BY COLOR RANGE

Another more complicated method of selection involves selecting same areas of color and color tones using the **Color Range command** from the Select menu. This works best with either solid colors, or same color tones in same area, such as a bowl of fruit like strawberries that may need to have their color enhanced. You'll find that using the Color Range as a mode of selection helps when you have tiny areas you want to keep away from the selection, like the lighthouse antennae here. This is a little more advanced, but more accurate approach.

TOOLKIT TIP In CS6 and Creative Cloud (CC), you also have the option of selecting colors by skin tone, using the Detect Faces feature. It provides an excellent way to enhance skin tones, and adjust portrait subjects in various lighting conditions. For instance, you can select and warm up skin tones in shadow areas.

Here you are going to use the Color Range function in the Select menu to select the blue sky and save as a selection channel.

1. Zoom in to 100% or closer to view details of the low-resolution lighthouse image. Choose Select > Color Range.

2. When the dialog box opens, check Localized Color Clusters to keep all selection areas adjacent to one another. This keeps the chosen colors from spilling to other unwanted areas of the image.

3. Keep the Fuzziness setting to around 20 or less to keep the color selection area relatively small, since we only want the blue-sky area.

4. Select the eyedropper with a plus sign to click, hold down, and drag to add each selection and carefully paint, the sky in the image first along the sky area, close to the lighthouse. Use the minus eyedropper if you selected areas other than just the sky. You will see the black and white thumbnail will display the lighthouse as black and the selected blue sky area as white (Figure 4-23). You can also use the same eyedropper tool to click and drag on the thumbnail itself as well. Usually starting on the image first provides a more accurate selection. Be careful: the lighthouse and ground is not included in the color range selection.

▷ FIGURE 4-23

The Color Range samples colors and their tones to create color-based selections.

5. On the Color Range display, choose Black Matte from the Selection Preview list to get an idea of your selected area; take a look at the other types of previews, and then select the default None when you are ready.

6. Select OK to display the new selection areas you just made on the original lighthouse image; use the Lasso tools (subtract selection) to remove or clean up any stray areas of pixels, or choose Select > Grow for any pixels left in the sky.

7. Choose Select > Save Selection and name the new channel Blue Sky. Leave the selected blue sky open.

8. Click on one of the selection tools and select Refine Edge on the Tool Options bar to soften the edge selections. Adjust as needed.

9. You have now created a window to put the clouds image in without affecting any other part of the lighthouse image. Select the Black & White View mask as a guide. Click the zoom icon on the Refine Edge display to 200% to get close and adjust as needed. Leave the sky selected.

10. Open the *Clouds.tif* file from your *Chapter 4* folder.

11. Choose Select > All (or Command/CTRL + A) to select everything in the image. Both images will maintain their selections for the next exercise.

COMBINING IMAGES USING PASTE INTO

▷ **FIGURE 4-24**

The Paste Into command pastes a copy of the clouds into the selected blue sky window you created. Adjust with the Move Tool.

With selections made for both images, you will use the Paste Into command to paste the new cloud selection into the selection you made in the lighthouse image. The selection in the lighthouse image becomes a cutout or window that hides the blue sky, so you can paste the clouds image into the window. The Move Tool will then help to position the clouds in place (Figure 4-24). The **Move Tool** allows you to move a selection or an entire image onto another image or another area of the same image. When moving a selected area to another place within an image, you can use the mouse for basic positioning and the arrow keys on the keyboard for more accurate positioning.

Using the Move Tool to adjust the position of the pasted clouds

Completed image with clouds added

DESIGN TIP

One advantage to using the Paste Into command is that it allows the designer to move the image around within the original selection "window" to get the best possible look.

1. With the *Clouds* image active (click on the title bar), choose Edit > Copy to copy the selection to memory in the Clipboard, which is a storage area on your computer's memory. Although you cannot see any changes, the new cloud image is ready to be pasted into the old sky portion of the *Litehous.tif* image.

2. Close the Clouds file without saving it, leaving the *Litehous* file still open. When you click the *Litehous* image, the previous selection of the blue sky on the lighthouse will be displayed.

3. With the sky still selected in the *Litehous* file, select Edit > Paste Special > Paste Into (earlier versions: Edit > Paste Into). Paste Into will paste your new clouds into the blue sky selection covering the original blue sky.

4. Select the Move Tool and drag the image to where you want it.

5. Save the file as *NewSKY.tif* using the default settings in your *Chapter 4* folder.

6. To give a slight introduction to layers which we will cover in Chapter 5, select the Layers panel (Window > Layers) and you'll notice the original lighthouse image on the bottom layer, and then another layer on top of it that shows the image of the clouds with a layer "mask" next to it, black to hide the lighthouse, and to white to show the sky "window." Whenever you paste or move an image onto another it creates another layer. Try this technique with your own images.

PROBLEM If you cannot move the clouds, make sure the clouds *Layer 1* is high-lighted in the Layers panel (Window > Layers). The layer will be shaded blue. If not, click the layer with your mouse to select it. We will be using layers in the next chapter.

USING PERSPECTIVE WARP FOR ADJUSTMENTS IN 3D SPACE

▷ FIGURE 4-25

Perspective Warp can not only adjust perspective, it allows the designer to move around in three-dimensional space for additional vantage points of an architectural structure.

Photoshop Creative Cloud (CC) has a function called **Perspective Warp**, located in the Edit menu. It creates a three-dimensional space to slightly move things around or adjust perspective, by setting up a three-dimensional plane and moving points. This works well especially in architecture within a two-dimensional pho-tograph. Where the Perspective Crop adjusts converging lines from angles cre-ated by camera lenses, the Perspective Warp command can provide this feature, and allow you to "move" your building along a vertical axis or reference line in 3D space, as if you are walking around a few more feet for a better composition (Figure 4-25). This technique provides the ability to give an image a little extra room for aesthetic purposes, change perspective, or adjust vantage points. Be wary that this technique will involve cropping your image.

One method of cropping an image is using the Marquee Tool and setting a Fixed Ratio Style. This allows a designer to enter a ratio format to fit a particular required size and draw a rectangular selection based upon that ratio.

Original image

With Perspective Warp applied

In this exercise, you will adjust perspective of the *Mansion.tif* image, then move the left side of the building for a slightly better view of the architecture. You'll then use the Marquee Tool with a Fixed Ratio Style to crop a predetermined proportion.

1. Make sure that rulers display in Photoshop (View > Rulers) and measuring is set to inches (Photoshop > Preferences > Units and Rulers > Rulers: Inches).

2. Open the *Mansion.tif* image in your *Chapter 4* folder. You'll notice because of the wide-angle lens used, the sides converge, but also we would like to enhance more of the left side archway.

3. Create a duplicate image by selecting Image > Duplicate, and name the duplicate FIX Mansion. Close the original *Mansion.tif* file.

4. Select Edit > Perspective Warp, then carefully click and drag a grid aligned with the corner of the building, facing along the right side as shown in Figure 4-26. You can click and drag any corner point to align with the sides so that perspective can be adjusted. It's very important to make sure gridlines align accurately. You may need to extend your grid outside the picture frame. Make sure your grid is placed above the chimneys to include these in the change.

TOOLKIT TIP If, when you look in the Edit menu, you see that Perspective Warp is grayed out, you need to enable your graphics processor to handle your computer's computations. On a Mac, select Photoshop Preferences > Performance, make sure you have "Use Graphics Processor" checked. Then click the "Advanced Settings" box and in the next dialog box, check the box for "Use Graphics Processor to Accelerate Computation." If using Windows, in Photoshop, select Edit > Preferences > GPU support > Performance > Advanced > Use for computations.

▷ FIGURE 4-26

Setting up two grids to snap together along designated vertical axis for adjustments.

5. With the first grid plane created, click and drag to start creating another grid that aligns with the left side of the building. When you drag your line next to the building corner, both lines highlight as blue lines and snap together. This is your line of reference. You'll find you'll need to create the grid beyond the image. Note: To rotate on one plane, hold down the Shift key and select the line, now you have an axis to spin on. You can also use the Shift key to lengthen the vanishing point proportionately as far as needed.

Align the first grid to all slanted sides

Align the left side grid to snap with main vertical axis and align carefully. Continue to drag points to match total alignment.

6. This will take some time as you carefully try to align all planes to match your lines on both sides of your building. Use Figure 4-26 as a guide.

7. With the two grids carefully aligned, click on the Warp button on the Tool Options bar. Now comes the delicate part where you can carefully drag any point in any direction. First, click and drag the two vertical points that snapped the two grids together on the corner of the building. Drag these points to the right, as you want to expose more of the left side architecture.

8. Take your time and drag all points to make the image as realistic as possible. Be careful to drag the bottom points to make the fence also realistic. This will take a steady hand and constantly viewing your work and what happens when points are dragged. Use Figure 4-27 above as a guide.

▷ FIGURE 4-27

Warping image along a vertical axis between two grids to adjust perspective and vantage points.

Perspective Warp Tool Options bar

9. The Perspective Warp Tool Options bar allows you to undo if you went too far with an arrow facing to the left, to completely start again by select the circle with a line through it, and to accept the changes by pressing the check mark button. If you are satisfied with your efforts, select the check mark button to observe the change. You'll notice lots of blank (checkered) space that needs to be cropped out (Figure 4-27).

10. To crop your image proportionately, select the Rectangular Marquee Tool (M), choose a Style of Fixed Ratio, and then type in "6" Width and "4" Height. This creates your image to a particular sized fixed ratio. Very useful for standard sizes.

▷ FIGURE 4-28

Cropping proportionately using the Rectangular Marquee Tool's Fixed Ratio Style.

11. Drag a rectangle around the displayed area of the image. Avoid hitting the blank space, and try to avoid cropping the chimneys. Use the arrow keys for fine tune adjusting (Figure 4-28).

12. When you are ready to crop select Image > Crop. Save the image in your *Chapter 4* folder as *FIXMansion.tif* with default settings. Compare the original image with your new image to see the power of this new tool. It takes lots of practice to get it perfect.

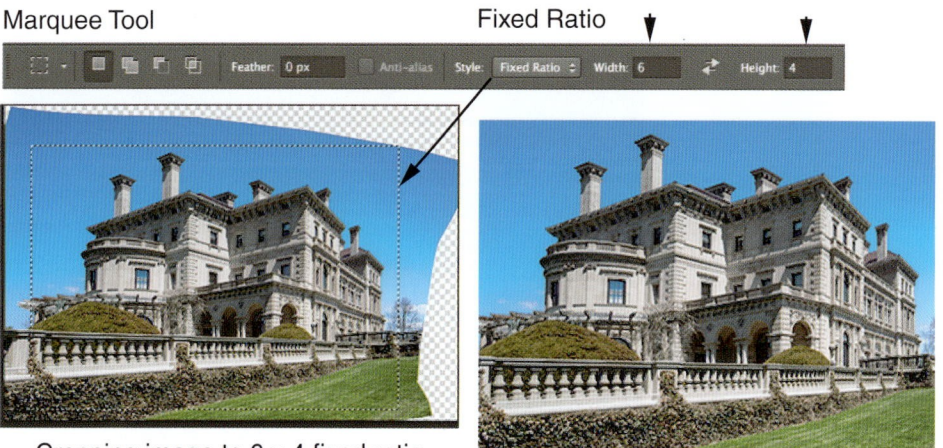

Cropping image to 6 x 4 fixed ratio

Completed image

DIGITAL TOOLKIT EXTRA: Preparing Camera Raw Files: The Digital Negative

Most digital images created in moderately priced and professional digital cameras are either set to process the images automatically or to create images as **Camera Raw files,** which lets photographers and designers interpret the image data themselves, rather than letting the camera make adjustments and conversions (Figure 4-29). Here are some options and information regarding these files:

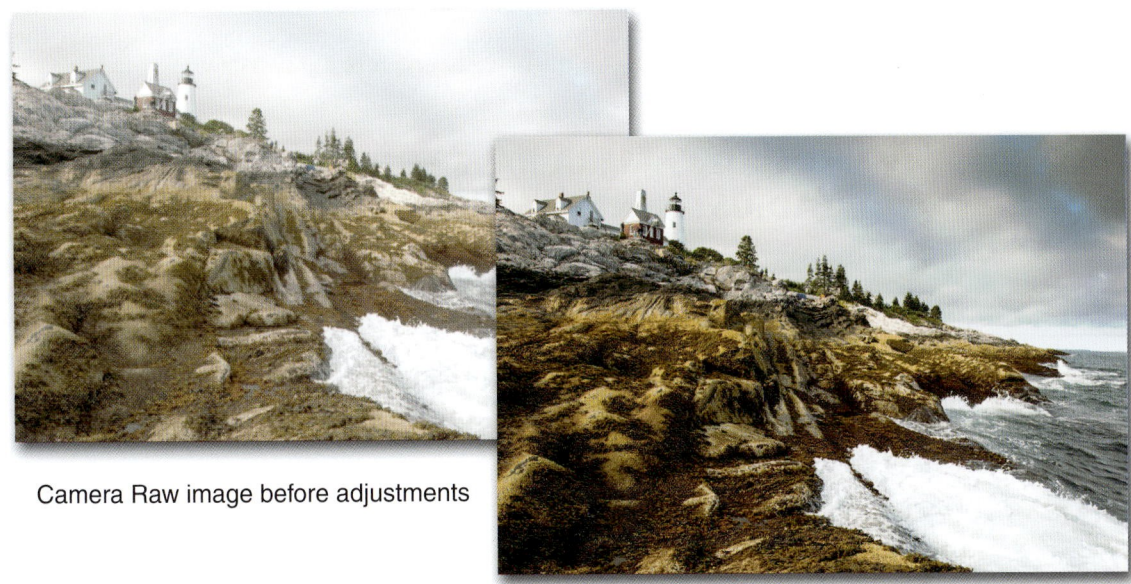

Camera Raw image before adjustments

Camera Raw image after adjustments

▷ FIGURE 4-29

Camera Raw images before and after adjustments: the digital negative.

- A Camera Raw file contains unprocessed picture data from a digital camera's image sensor.
- Only Camera Raw image files contain the actual data captured by the sensor without any in-camera processing.
- Working with Camera Raw files still lets you set the white balance that reflects the lighting conditions under which the photo was taken, tonal range, contrast, color saturation, and sharpening, or you can shoot automatically and adjust those aspects later. The original RAW file is never adjusted permanently; always a copy is saved after adjustments. You can easily default back to the original settings and start over.
- Think of Camera Raw files as your photo negative. You can go back and reprocess the file to achieve the results you want. Camera Raw files always remain pure recordings, like a film negative or transparency.
- Your camera saves files in its own raw file format. When you download the files from the camera, they will have file extensions such as .NEF (Nikon), or .CRW (Canon) to identify their own raw format.

- You can save various versions of these files with special adjustments, the same as you would save different prints or experiment with different exposures. You can save to Adobe's universal digital negative (DNG) version, especially if you are downloading raw files using different cameras on the same computer. You can also save to Photoshop's PSD format, JPEG, and TIF formats after you have made your adjustments. Camera Raw files always remain pure: you open up your image and save it to a file format after you make changes, and the Camera Raw application makes a digital copy of the edited image. You can always default back to the original settings.

- Camera Raw is a free application included inside Photoshop that is automatically installed for you. If you purchase a new camera, you should check the Adobe website for the newest version of Camera Raw.

USING CAMERA RAW TOOLS FOR PROFESSIONAL ADJUSTMENTS AND EFFECTS

When you open a raw file, it will open in the Camera Raw application within Photoshop. Even though your image may look flat or off color, it contains all unprocessed information, just like a digital negative. Use this application as your new digital darkroom with no chemicals. You will find in the Camera Raw dialog box, in addition to other controls, White Balance, which sets the color balance for various lighting conditions; the Temperature control, which controls the color temperature; and Tint to compensate for green or magenta tints in photos. Moving the temperature slider to the left, for instance, makes the color a cooler, bluer tone; moving the slider to the right warms the image. You also notice plenty of additional tools and controls you can play with to achieve the best image (Figure 4-30).

Next, we will open a Camera Raw lighthouse image I photographed in Maine, and use some functions to make adjustments and effects for dramatic impact.

1. Launch Photoshop and open the *ABW0880.NEF* file in your *Chapter 4* folder.

2. When you open the image, you will notice the Camera Raw dialog box (Figure 4-30). This is a raw image made on a very overcast day with very flat lighting; it has been saved in a NEF format with a Nikon camera.

3. This dialog box is your digital darkroom, where you can experiment with your digital negative. You will notice the White Balance settings are As Shot, which uses the camera's settings, the same as the auto setting that many people use on their cameras. Select other White Balance options to see some interesting color adjustments, then go back to As Shot. Notice the color temperature changes as you select various White Balance settings.

4. Adjust the Temperature slider to see the effects. Try increasing the saturation and other options, until you have an image representing what the scene might look like to show more vibrant colors. Use the settings in Figure 4-30 as a starting point. Observe the histogram graph, and if shadows start to become clipped, or highlights, you can click on the side arrow to see if the details lost are in an important area. Press Command/CTRL + Z to undo.

DESIGN TIP

In digital images always try to avoid clipping highlight details as they cannot be retrieved. Shadow details that are clipped, however, may be retrievable.

Zoom (reset)
White Balance
Hand
Color Sampler

Straighten
Remove Red Eye
Prefs
Rotate CCW
Crop
Retouch
Adj Brush
Rotate CW

Basic (default)
Detail (sharpen)
Split Toning
Camera Calibration
Effects
Snapshots
Tone Curve
HSL (Grayscale)
Lens Correction
Presets

Targeted Adjustment Tool
Graduated Filter
Radial Filter
Toggle for Full Screen (F)
Click to display shadow details clipped

Basic

R: ---
G: ---
B: ---
f/16 1/125 s
ISO 400 24–120@31 mm

Basic

White Balance: As Shot

Temperature 5700

Tint −8

Auto Default

Exposure 0.00

Contrast +8

Highlights +5

Shadows +10

Whites +9

Blacks −4

Clarity +11

Vibrance +8

Saturation +10

16.4% ABW_0880.NEF

Save Image...
Adobe RGB (1998); 8 bit; 4256 by 2832 (12.1MP); 300 ppi
Open Image Cancel Done

Save your new adjusted image in a variety of formats
File Info
Open into Photoshop
Apply changes without opening image

▷ FIGURE 4-30

Camera Raw dialog box tools for adjusting minute details.

5. You will notice that when you select the icons alongside the Basic icon, you'll find various icons or buttons for more accurate adjustments. Any adjustments made do not affect the original Camera Raw image. For our purposes, select the Tone Curve icon and adjust as shown in Figure 4-31 as a starting point (Note: For both toning and histogram adjustments, refer back to Chapter 3 Advanced Users section). When you are happy with the results, click back on the Basic icon, and readjust if necessary.

TOOLKIT TIP With your changes made for the image, you can choose to select Save Image, Open Image, or Done. If you select Open Image, wherever you are in applying adjustments or effects, or if you want to bring it into Photoshop's desktop without any changes applied, it opens into Photoshop still as a Camera Raw extension file. If you select Done, it keeps any adjustments or effects you have applied as a starting point, leaving the image in its original location without opening it up into Photoshop. An additional text file is created with an XMP extension file with directions to your computer as to applying the changes when you open the file in Camera Raw again. This comes in handy when you're not done with your adjustments and want to come back to where you left off. The Save Image function allows you to make a copy of your Camera Raw image with all adjustments and effects applied, to be saved as a regular file with JPEG, TIF, and PSD extensions in Photoshop.

▷ FIGURE 4-31

Using the Tone Curve function to create impact in highlights and shadows.

6. Let's darken the clouds a bit for impact. Select the Graduated Filter icon on the right side. This provides a gradual effect according to the settings you provide. Set the adjustments as indicated in Figure 4-32 as a starting point. Drag from the top downward along the diagonal coastal rock line. You'll notice the skies darken. You can adjust the direction line, and settings on the fly. To undo the action if needed, press Command/CTRL + Z to undo, or to reset, press Cancel. Adjust for good quality, and then select the Zoom Tool icon to bring you back to the default Basic menu.

7. With the image toned and adjusted for realism, select the Save Image button in the Camera Raw display. Save the final image as *Lighthouse Fixed.tif*. When you save your image, choose to Save in New Location and locate your *Chapter 4* folder (Figure 4-33). Leave default settings. Remember, the image is always saved as a copy of the original Camera Raw file.

Click the Zoom Tool to return to the default Basic menu, after effects and adjustments are applied.

▷ FIGURE 4-32

Using the Graduated Filter function to darken the skies.

8. Leave the file open for the next exercise. Note: As your original Camera Raw file is never ruined, if you make a mistake, you can always restore it to its default Camera Raw setting in your camera before your applied effects. To remove all adjustments, or return to the original setting, choose Camera Raw Defaults from the top right panel menu in the Basic menu (Figure 4-33).

TOOLKIT TIP Along the top of this window, next to the Hand Tool, you will notice the **White Balance Tool** (I) which you can use if you have a very tinted image. This only works well when you have an image that contains a neutral gray or neutral white color. To balance the color, try using pavement, rocks, and other neutral gray tones, if they are in your image. When making edits, keep an eye on your histogram to make sure that both sides for shadows and highlights of the histogram show the bottom or start and end of the peak to avoid what is called *clipping* of highlight and shadows.

▷ FIGURE 4-33

Choosing Save Image to save the completed Camera Raw file. To reset to original settings, select Camera Raw Defaults from the Basic panel menu.

USING SMART SHARPEN FOR YOUR IMAGES

Photoshop's Filter menu provides a wide assortment of adjustments along with special effects you can create on your images. In working with digital images, in many cases, the final images will need to be sharpened, but not so much as to display "halos" around the image. The **Smart Sharpen filter** takes out a lot of the guesswork and creates distinct sharp images without adding noise.

With the image saved, you will use the Smart Sharpen filter to apply enough sharpening to make the image look professionally done.

1. If not displayed, open your *Lighthouse Fixed.tif* image in your *Chapter 4* folder, saved from the previous exercise, and select Filter > Sharpen > Smart Sharpen.

2. Use the settings in Figure 4-34 as a starting point for users of Creative Cloud. These are pretty much set as defaults here, as applying less of an adjustment or effect is sometimes better. As you can see, in Photoshop Creative Cloud (CC), you can also make slight adjustments to remove noise, decide the radius of pixels affected, and more advanced adjustments in the Shadows/Highlights menu. It's always easier to add to the effects or settings later, than to put too much of an initial adjustment and try to remove it. Usually applying less than "100" for Amount is a good starting point (earlier versions, try less than 75) for medium to high-resolution images.

DESIGN TIP

After all effects and adjustments have been made, the image should be sharpened as a final step. Avoid over sharpening, less is better.

3. With Preview checked, you can click on the image to see the before and after adjustments on the image as they are applied.

4. Save the file again as *Lighthouse Fixed.tif* in your *Chapter 4* folder.

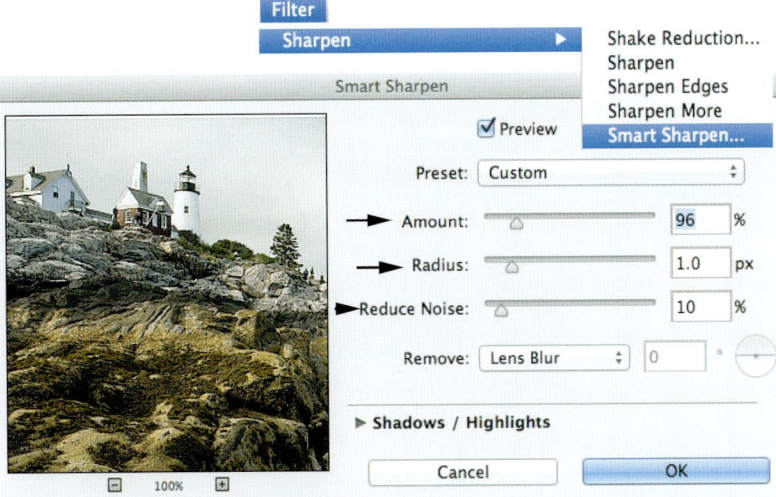

▷ FIGURE 4-34

Sharpening digital adjusted images with precision using the Smart Sharpen filter.

PHOTOSHOP CREATIVE CLOUD (CC) CAMERA RAW FILTER

In the current Creative Cloud (CC) version there are a couple of new tools you can play with in the Camera Raw dialog box. Although a little advanced, you will find a Radial Filter (J), which allows a user to select and apply various color and sharpening options by dragging inward or outward along a spherical plane, and a Lens Corrections function that provides the ability to adjust lens perspective or correct lens distortions (see Figures 4-30 and 4-35).

In Creative Cloud (CC) versions, Camera Raw is also available as a standard Photoshop filter, called **Camera Raw Filter**, (Filter > Camera Raw Filter...). This filter allows you to use most of the Camera Raw tools and settings with not only Camera Raw files, but also files saved as JPGs, TIFs, and PSDs. Note: Although beyond the scope of this book, you'll find plenty of special functions in Photoshop's Filter menu.

In this exercise, you'll open a JPEG file in Photoshop Creative Cloud, select the new Camera Raw Filter from the Filter menu to make basic adjustments, and use the new Lens Correction function for subtle adjustments in correcting vertical and horizontal perspective.

1. Open the *Annisquam Light.JPG* image from your *Chapter 4* folder in Photoshop Creative Cloud (CC).

2. Select Filter > Camera Raw Filter..., and in the default Basic menu, make corrections to add impact. Use whatever tools you want to make a good quality image in terms of color and tonality.

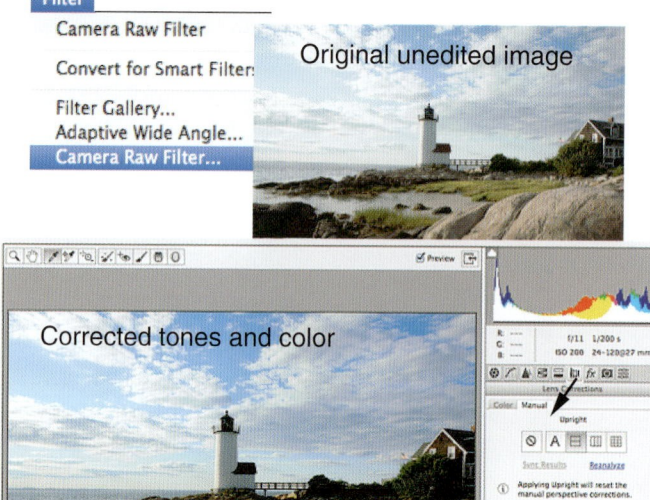

▷ FIGURE 4-35

Camera Raw Filter functions can be used on all types of image files. The Lens Correction function adjusts lens distortion and perspective.

3. Notice the ocean horizon line aims upward and there are some very subtle distortions around the buildings. Click on the Lens Corrections icon near the Basic menu. Click on the Manual tab and you'll find automatic corrections in the top area labeled Upright, and manual corrections in the Transform area.

4. Try the various automatic functions first in terms of horizontal and vertical adjustments; you'll notice you can align along vertical and horizontal planes, and combinations of both, and sometimes they go too far. Press Command/CTRL + Z to undo, or press the circle icon with a line through it. We'll try manual adjustments next for more precision.

5. Use the settings in Figure 4-35 as a guide for starters. You'll find you have a lot of flexibility in making very subtle adjustments.

6. When you have the image adjusted without any visible distortions, select OK, then save the new image in your *Chapter 4* folder as *Annisquam Fixed.tif.*

7. As shown in the previous exercise, if you want to sharpen the image a little more, select Filter > Smart Sharpen and apply the same settings shown in Figure 4-34 as a starting point, clicking OK when done.

8. Save the image again in your *Chapter 4* folder. Feel free to open your favorite images and play with this powerful filter.

TOOLKIT TIP In Photoshop Creative Cloud (CC), you can apply Camera Raw adjustments and edits not only to overall files, but individual layers that may be created in those image files. We'll be covering layers in the next chapter. The default color of the current interface is dark gray or black, as opposed to light gray in previous versions. To change the color of the interface, choose Photoshop > Preferences > Interface > Color Theme if you are using a Mac, or Edit > Preferences > Interface > Color Theme for Windows users.

CHAPTER SUMMARY

You have now created an accurate complex selection using the Magic Wand Tool and Quick Selection Tool for similar colors and then the Lasso tools for additional editing. The Tool Options bar and its settings for each tool were used to edit the selections until they were perfect. You have created, named, and saved a permanent selection for changing the sports car's color, and then created a new color using the Hue/Saturation to accurately blend in tones for a realistic effect. Advanced users created masks with Quick Mask mode using the Brush and Pencil tools to make more accurate selections, and combined images using the Paste Into command. For Advanced Users with Photoshop CC, you have ability to use the Perspective Warp command to make adjustments, especially in architectural imagery, in adjusting perspective in 3D space. In the Digital Toolkit Extra section the Camera Raw application allowed you to make adjustments in digital raw formats from digital cameras. In Photoshop CC, there is a Camera Raw Filter where you can apply many of the same effects, but with JPG and TIF image extensions as well. Do not forget to check out the *Extras & Goodies* link on *www.CengageBrain.com* for more projects and ideas.

REVIEW QUESTIONS

1. Explain some of the differences and similarities between the Lasso, Marquee, Move, Quick Selection, and Magic Wand tools.

2. Why should you save images as .TIF files for editing instead of saving them as JPEGs?

3. Why is the Tolerance setting important for the Magic Wand Tool?

4. Explain how to create perfect circles and squares with the Marquee tools.

5. Explain the purposes of channels and the differences between color and alpha channels.

6. What are some of the uses of the Select menu?

7. How do you save a channel that has been edited?

8. What are Quick Masks and how do they work?

9. What color would you paint to remove part of a mask? To add to the mask?

10. What is the purpose of the Paste Into command in the Edit menu?

Completed recolored image

Original image,
then selected image

CHAPTER 4
Using selection tools and techniques to change
a sports car's color while maintaining tonality.

CHAPTER 4 ADVANCED
Adding and subtracting selections
with precision using Quick Mask function,
Brush and Pencil tools.

Toggle Quick Mask
and Standard modes

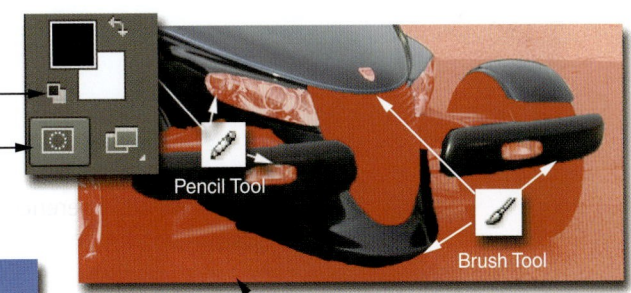

Pencil Tool

Brush Tool

Quick Mask

CHAPTER 4 ADVANCED
Combining images for dramatic effects, selecting by Color Range,
then using the Paste Into command.

▷ FIGURE 4-36

Original image

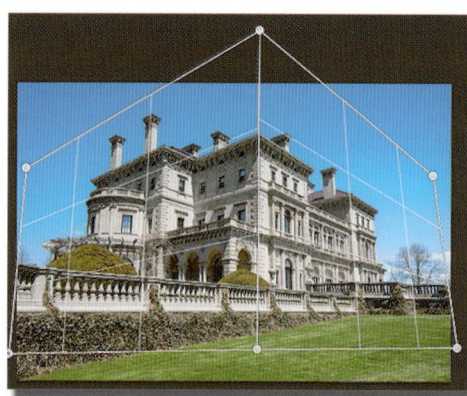

Align grids along corner axis

Warping to adjust perspective and vantage point

With Perspective Warp applied

CHAPTER 4 ADVANCED
Using the Perspective Warp function to adjust
three-dimensional perspective and vantage points

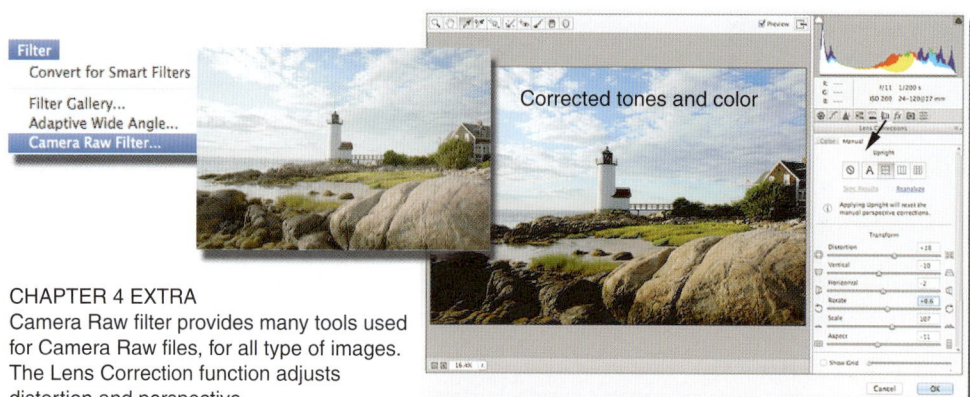

CHAPTER 4 EXTRA
Camera Raw filter provides many tools used
for Camera Raw files, for all type of images.
The Lens Correction function adjusts
distortion and perspective.

▷ FIGURE 4-37

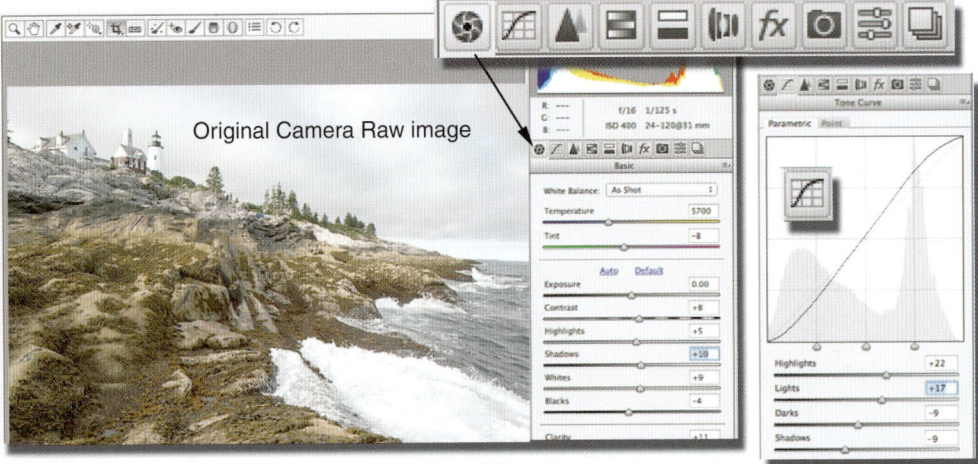

Basic and Tone Curve adjustments

Graduated Filter adjustments

CHAPTER 4 EXTRA
Taking a flat Camera Raw file from a digital camera and making precise adjustments using the Camera Raw functions and tools in Photoshop. The new digital darkroom.

Final adjusted Camera Raw image

▷ FIGURE 4-38

CHAPTER

5

Using Layers

CHAPTER OBJECTIVES: To understand the importance of using layers in Photoshop, in this chapter you will:

▷ Rename, duplicate, and move layers.

▷ Create two permanent selections to duplicate graphics for replication with a variety of realistic colors.

▷ Use the Hue/Saturation command to adjust color while retaining shadows and highlights within an image.

▷ Use layer styles to create drop shadows and specialized effects.

▷ Create type layers and make adjustments.

▷ Record states of layers in various stages of development with Layer Comps.

▷ Merge layers and prepare files for commercial printing and for electronic distribution.

▷ ADVANCED USERS: Special Creations Using Adjustment Layers and Layer Masks. Creating a Figure Diagram Using Custom Shapes.

▷ DIGITAL TOOLKIT EXTRA: Image Transformations using Content-Aware Fill, Move, and Scale to remove unwanted background elements, move components, and resize images. Using the Color Replacement Tool in changing product colors, and as a corrective tool.

Every Photoshop file contains one or more layers. *Layers* are like stacks of transparent sheets with parts of an image laid one on top of another. Layers are used to modify selected portions of an image and to combine different images, or selected areas, together. Special effects can also be added to each layer, so layers provide the designer or photographer the flexibility to make changes to any precise area of an image to achieve whatever effect is needed. In this chapter, we will explore using layers for duplicating and coloring images, creating special effects, and for adding lines of text.

PHOTOSHOP'S LAYERS

Layers can be used by the designer or photographer for a variety of purposes and can be arranged for a variety of effects. When areas of an image are selected, layers can be created to isolate those areas for modification. Layers can also be used to combine images, duplicate selected areas, and create special effects on selected areas. The Layers panel provides thumbnails of layers stacked on top of one another. An effect on one layer may or may not have an effect on the layers below it, depending on the Opacity setting and Blending Mode options chosen. For example, a Normal Mode (default) setting at 100% opacity allows you to make changes to an active layer without affecting any layers below it.

DISPLAYING AND HIDING LAYERS

When a layer is selected, the active layer is highlighted and shaded in blue. The **eye icon** displayed indicates that the layer is visible. You can hide or show a layer by clicking the eye icon. Layers are part of the new collapsible workspace, where layer panels can be minimized or docked to an icon image to allow more work space (Figure 5-1). By clicking on the icon, panels can be expanded for instant display. You can click on the top tab of any panel to collapse it to an icon display. You can also filter layers in your project by various kinds of layers. This is quite efficient for a designer who has created many layers and needs to locate certain types all together.

Expand/Contract panel

Filtering options for types of layers

Blending mode (default is normal)

"T" Indicates type layer

Indicates effect visibility (eye icons)

Indicates layer visibility (eye icon)

Copy/Paste selection creates transparent background

Indicates active layer (shaded blue)

Linking Layers

Layer Style

Layer Mask

Layer Set

Panel menu (click here)

Adjust amount of effect on layers underneath selected layers

Layer effects icon (expand/collapse list)

Text layer style drop shadow effect

Image layer style drop shadow effect

Locked layer

Background Layer (renamed as Gray Kayak Layer)

Delete Layer

Create New Layer

Adjustment Layer

▷ FIGURE 5-1

Layers panel with options.

LAYERS PANEL AND LAYER MENU

You can use either the **Layers panel** or **Layer menu** to display, modify, edit, copy, group, or delete layers, along with other various commands and options for layers and layer effects. The Layers panel allows you to view thumbnails of the content contained in each layer, and you can move layers above or below others for specific effects (Figure 5-2). Selecting the Layers panel submenu or the icons at the bottom of the Layers panel will give you many of the same commands found in the Layer menu. The Layer menu contains additional commands for editing individual layers and effects between selected layers. An arrow pointing to the right at the end of the command indicates that there are more functions from which to choose from.

THE BACKGROUND LAYER

Every time you open an image or create a new image or blank document, there will always be one special layer to start called the *Background,* which contains the original image or blank canvas. The Background remains locked at the bottom until you double-click the Background layer's name and rename it. It then behaves as a normal layer and can be moved around between other layers.

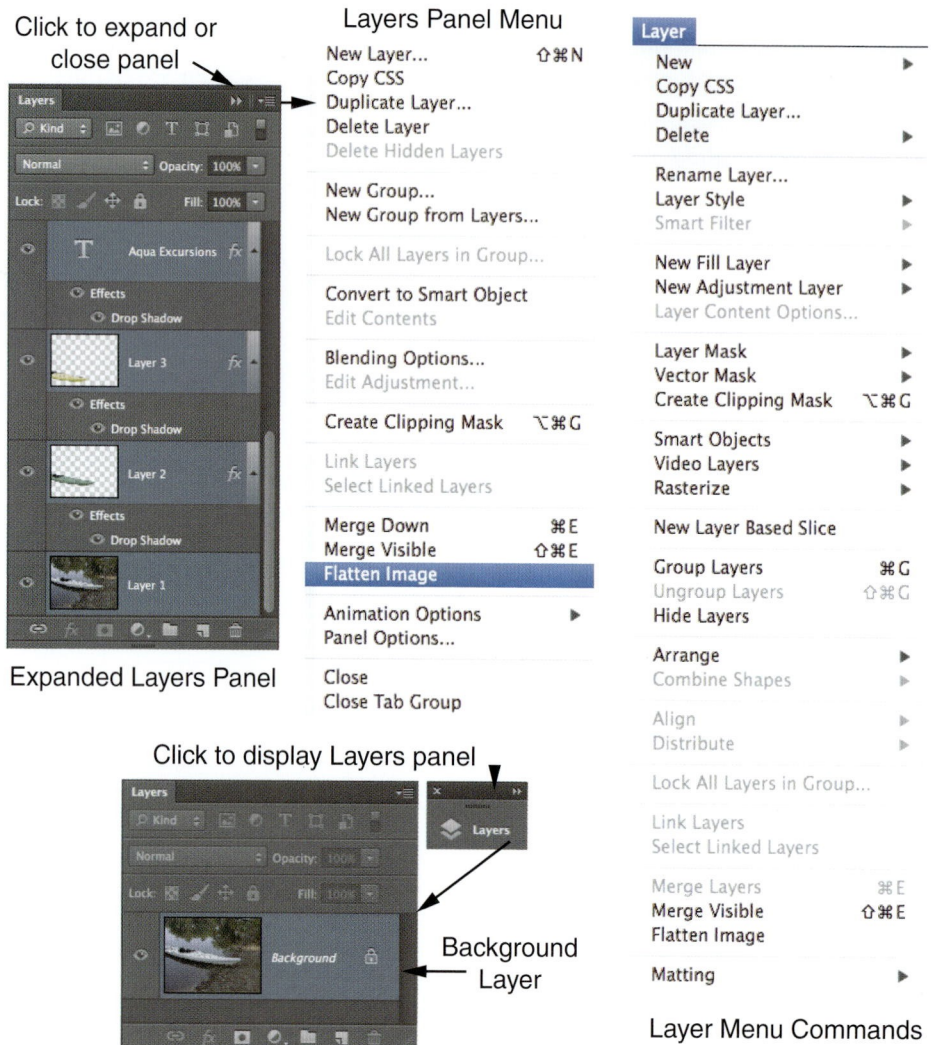

Click to expand or close panel

Layers Panel Menu

Expanded Layers Panel

Click to display Layers panel

Background Layer

Layer Menu Commands

Layers panel, Panel menu, and Layer menu.

THE MOVE TOOL

The Move Tool (V) is used to drag selected areas within the image to create additional layers, or to drag selections created from other images onto the image, which automatically creates a new layer. For precision positioning of selections within an image, select the Move Tool and use the arrow keys on the keyboard for precise placement of artwork (Figure 5-3).

▷ FIGURE 5-3

Use the Move Tool to move selected areas within an image, or move selected images between image windows.

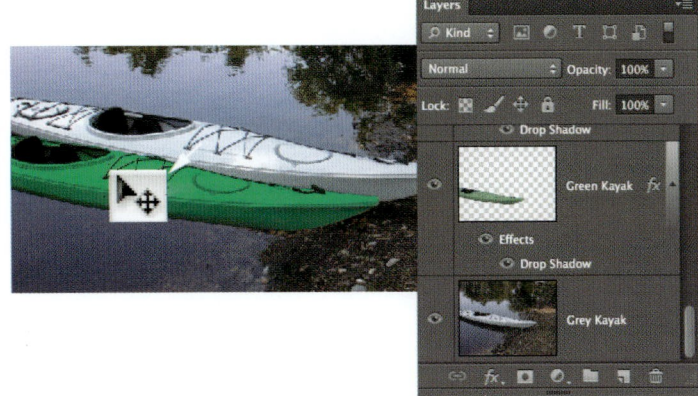

SAVING IMAGES WITH LAYERS

To keep your layers editable, make sure you save the file with Photoshop's native extension, .PSD, or as a .TIF file. Files saved in TIF or PSD formats maintain the original quality no matter how many times you make changes. If you save the file in a **JPEG format,** you should make sure all layers are combined as one, although data will be discarded each time the file is edited and saved, gradually deteriorating image quality. JPEG files cannot be changed later either. If you need to decrease the file size to distribute it electronically for a client, make a back-up copy of the TIF file, then combine the layers and save the file with a .JPG extension. Most applications use the universal form of PDF files to communicate; in Photoshop you can save your layered files in the Photoshop PDF format, and anyone can view the image with the free Adobe Reader you downloaded in Chapter 1. PDF files retain all the formatting used in the document; and you can also use this method to create "flattened" PDF files for electronic distribution or high-resolution files that can be used for commercial printing.

CLIENT ASSIGNMENT: Creating a Multicolor Product Advertisement

Your client, Alyce Powell, who owns a kayak sales and touring service called Aqua Excursions, wants to have a direct mail advertisement created for her customers. The purpose of the ad is to move her current inventory to make room for next year's models and supplies by having a sale for her customers in September. She gives you a call to help her create the ad. When you meet, she informs you that she has a photograph of one gray kayak and wants you to create two other kayaks of different colors. You both decide that, in addition to the gray kayak, a hunter green and yellow kayak will also be created. The green and gray kayaks will be marketed to the outdoor enthusiast, while the yellow kayak will cater more to the recreational user. With a lake shoreline as the background, the ad will display the three different colored kayaks (gray, dark green, and yellow) placed diagonally with drop shadows for added realism and depth. The white business title and ad text will be placed in the dark areas of the image, and for emphasis, a yellow text line describes the sale. Alyce leaves excited to see the final layout.

Original Image

Completed Kayak Advertisement

Portion of
layers used

▷ FIGURE 5-4

**Completed adver-
tisement and some
of the types of
layers created in
this chapter.**

DESIGN TIP

The completed
image will display
angles in text lines
and alignment of
the kayaks, promot-
ing an informal
balance in the final
composition. This
type of layout wel-
comes the reader
and is used in many
retail, tourism, and
service industries.

ACTION ITEMS

This assignment also provides a review of selection tools and techniques from Chapter 4. It shows how a designer or photographer can use selections to create mul-tiple colored objects from the same selected object for an advertisement. Selections are essential for the successful completion of the ad. As a designer or photographer, your goal is to create two detailed selections of the original gray kayak that can be saved permanently. One selection will be used to recolor the kayak, without includ-ing hardware, straps, or seat. The other selection will be used to include the kayak with all hardware so you can duplicate it to create multiple images. These selections will be used to make layers that allow you to duplicate the kayak image, color it, and position it in the ad. You will then create text layers for each line of type in the ad. Drop shadow layer effects for the type and images will make the text stand out and match the gray kayak's shadow. Finally, you will organize the text layers under one layer set and prepare the file for electronic distribution and commercial printing (Figure 5-4). If you haven't downloaded the files for the exercises in this chapter, you can download them at *www.CengageBrain.com.*

To create the additional images and text for this assignment, here is what you need to do:

• Create the first selection for changing the color by using the Magic Wand, Quick Selection, and Lasso selection tools. Only the gray areas of the kayak must be selected; all hardware, seat, cords, and background must be isolated.

• Create a second selection, which will be used for duplicating the entire kayak by *including* hardware, seat, and cords in the selection.

• Make the two selections permanent by saving them as channels in the Channels panel for reuse and future editing.

• Load the channel selection (*KayakALL*) for the whole kayak; copy and paste the selection to create a new layer.

• Load the channel selection (*Kayak Color*) for changing the color of the new kayak.

- Create new color (Hunter Green) using the Hue/Saturation command as part of an adjustment layer.
- Load the *KayakALL* channel selection again to select the entire kayak, duplicate it, and drag it into position using the Move Tool.
- Repeat the same process to create and position the yellow kayak.
- Apply drop shadows using the layer styles for the green and yellow kayaks to match the gray kayak shadow angle and color. Apply shadows for the text layers.
- Create Layer Comps to record various layer stages in development and to provide variations within the project.
- Decrease the file size by using layer groups, merging layers, and flattening layers to prepare the ad for press.
- Advanced Users: Special Creations Using Adjustment Layers and Layer Masks. Creating a basic figure illustration using Shape tools.

DESIGN TIP

It is a good habit to zoom in with the Zoom Tool and work on a small area at a time, and then to zoom out and observe results in the bigger picture, much like an artist would when working on a painting or sketch.

CREATING THE KAYAK SELECTIONS FOR COLOR AND DUPLICATION

Selections are essential for the successful completion of the ad. As a designer or photographer, your goal is to create two detailed selections of the original gray kayak that can be saved permanently. You will use those selections to make layers that allow you to color the kayak image, duplicate it, position it, and create realistic drop shadows in the ad.

FIRST SELECTION OF THE KAYAK FOR COLOR CHANGE

This important selection will be used for changing the kayak's gray color to the other colors specified by the client. Here, only the gray colors of the original kayak are going to be selected; all hardware, seats, and background must be isolated so they will not change color, much as a body shop would mask off all areas except those that are to be painted. Make sure you have enough time to complete this series of exercises so that you can save your selections permanently using channels.

TOOLKIT TIP If you like keystrokes instead of the buttons on the Tool Options bar, holding down the Option/ALT key will subtract from your selection, and holding down the Shift key will add to your selection. You can quickly adjust the brush size of this tool or any painting tool by pressing the bracket keys on your keyboard. The left bracket ([) makes the size smaller and the right bracket (]) increases the size. To save time, you can also use the spacebar instead of the Hand Tool to scroll around the image as you work.

New   Subtract

Quick Selection
Tool

Add   Brush Size

Add to selection

New selection | Subtract from selection   Sample pixel area

Determines range of colors to select

Magic Wand
Tool

Intersect with selection

Softens pixel edges →
(less jagged edges)

Anti-alias   Contiguous

Select colors next
to one another

▷ FIGURE 5-5

**Add/Subtract
selections by using
the Quick Selection
and Magic
Wand tools.**

Here, you are going to set the options for your selection tools and start selecting the gray areas of the kayak to be recolored.

1. Launch Photoshop and open the *Kayak.tif* file in your *Chapter 5* folder. Zoom in to about 100% with the Zoom Tool (Z) to get a good, detailed view.

2. Select the Quick Selection Tool (W) and set the Brush Picker box to 5 pixels, and then select the Add to selection icon on the Tool Options bar (Figure 5-5).

3. Select the front gray area of the kayak. Use the Tool Options bar buttons, or the keystroke shortcuts (try pressing the bracket keys on your keyboard to increase or decrease the brush size), to add to and subtract from your selection until you have a lot of the kayak's gray color selected, excluding the seat, any hardware, or background (Figure 5-5). Decrease the Brush Size setting to 3 pixels to gradually build on your selection.

4. Zoom in to 100% or closer to observe the detail in the selection area. Use the Scrubby Zoom on the Tool Options bar for quick observation. Make any additional adjustments as necessary. Use the Hand Tool (H) and Navigator panel to move around the image.

5. If needed, select the Magic Wand Tool and set the Tolerance to 5 pixels wide or less to start, making sure the Anti-alias and Contiguous boxes are checked, to indicate how many pixels of relatively the same shade of gray color should be selected and added (Figure 5-5). Now click and drag to paint or to add or subtract from the selection area, especially around the straps. Use the Tool Options bar icons to add to and subtract from your selection until you have most of the kayak's gray color selected, excluding any hardware or background.

6. Save the File as *KayakAD.tif* in your *Chapter 5* folder.

PROBLEM A selection is automatically removed if you have the New Selection button on the Tool Options bar set when making another selection. To remove all selections on the image, choose Select > Deselect. If you make a mistake, choose Select > Reselect. To go back to the last action, choose Edit > Undo State Change, or toggle Command/CTRL Z.

CLEANING UP WITH THE LASSO TOOLS AND SELECT MENU

The Lasso tools can be used to help clean up stray areas not yet selected by the Magic Wand or Quick Selection tools. You can use them to combine with and subtract from selected areas and for straight edge selections. The Select menu allows you to expand, contract, and fill in stray selected areas.

In this exercise, you will adjust the selections slightly and smooth out any stray areas that need to be included as part of the selection.

1. Select the regular Lasso Tool (L) to make freehand selections on the kayak's gray color (Figure 5-6). Use the buttons on the Tool Options bar for adding to the previous selection made by the Magic Wand and Quick Selection tools (W), and then subtract any part of the selection that included hardware or the background.

▷ FIGURE 5-6

Using the Lasso Tool for freehand selections, and Select menu to enhance the selection areas.

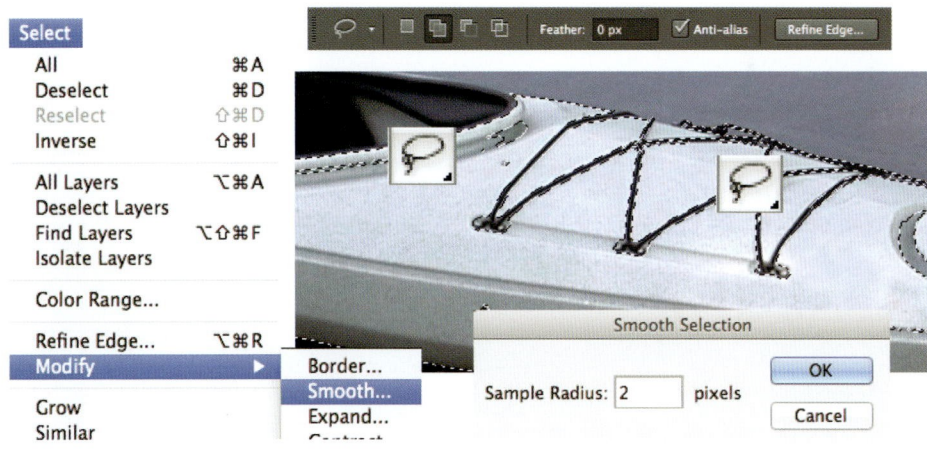

2. Zoom in to about 200% or closer to start editing the selection alongside the edges of the kayak. Remember: only the gray painted areas are to be selected, much like a body shop would mask off areas that are not to be painted. Leave the file open with the selection active.

3. To fill in stray areas that are not selected, choose Select > Modify > Smooth, then choose a 1- or 2-pixel sample radius. To add to the selection, choose Select > Grow for adjacent pixels.

4. Save your file and leave it open with the selection active.

Ⓧ **PROBLEM** If you have problems with straight edges, try using the Polygonal Lasso Tool (L). You can use this tool for selecting the cords, clicking along the straight edges between points. Select either the Add or Subtract button on the Tool Options bar to edit your selection. With this tool, it is important to make sure you click as a closed selection path. Return to the place you started, when the cursor underneath displays a circle click to close the path.

SAVING AND EDITING SELECTIONS AS PERMANENT CHANNELS

▷ FIGURE 5-7

Saving and replacing a channel selection.

When you save your selections as channels, they remain permanent so they can be used for editing in the future. You can create channels using the Select menu, or by clicking the icons at the bottom of the Channels panel. You can repeatedly modify and save the changes. The best way to edit channels is to save the selection and choose to "Replace" the channel. You can view your selection as a selection mask in the Channels panel. A **selection mask** displays areas that are exposed or selected (white); areas that are hidden (not selected) are displayed in black Figure 5-7).

Channel Selection Mask

You are going to create, name, and save a permanent channel in this exercise.

1. With your selection still active, choose Select > Save Selection from the Menu bar; when the Save Selection dialog box comes up, select New Channel and name it *Kayak Color* (Figure 5-7). Click OK.

2. Select the Channels panel, and you will notice that a new permanent selection channel entitled *Kayak Color* has been created. This same selection will display as a mask on the Channels panel (Window > Channels).

3. If you find areas that you have missed, go back using the selection tools to make the final selection as accurate as possible. If you need to take a break, with the selection permanent, you can close the file, then reopen it later; choose Select > Load Selection > *Kayak Color* to get your saved selection to edit.

4. To replace the permanent channel selection with the most recent version, choose Select > Save Selection.

5. Locate the *Kayak Color* channel on the drop-down display and select Replace Channel. Select OK. You can also use the icons in the Channels panel to create, save, and edit selection channels (Figure 5-8).

6. Save the file.

▷ FIGURE 5-8

The Channels panel.

Color channels

Load channel as selection

Create new channel

New Selection Channel

Save selection as channel

Delete channel

USING QUICK MASK FOR DETAILED SELECTIONS

As was shown in the Advanced section of Chapter 4, you can use the Quick Mask option to mask any minute areas of the background, cords, and seat of the kayak that are not the gray color and replace the *Kayak Color* channel selection with the new edited selection from the mask. This is a great project to try this technique.

Now you will paint with the Brush and Pencil tools to add to or subtract from the mask. You will then replace the old selections with the new, edited selections by saving the new selections in the *Kayak Color* channel.

Pencil Tool Brush Size

Brush Tool

Paint with black adds mask

Toggle black and white foreground

Paint with white removes mask

Quick Mask

Pencil Tool

Brush Tool

Toggle Standard Mode and Quick Mask Mode

▷ FIGURE 5-9

Using Quick Mask for very detailed selections.

1. If your selection is not active, choose Select > Load Selection and select the *Kayak Color* channel.

2. Click the icon near the bottom of the Tools panel to toggle to Quick Mask mode (Figure 5-9). You will notice a red overlay indicating what has been masked out. Note: You can also select Edit in Quick Mask Mode in the Select menu.

3. Zoom in to around 200% to 300% to observe what needs editing, masking, and unmasking; use the foreground and background colors in the Tools panel and either the Brush or Pencil Tool (B) to paint. White removes the mask; black will add to the mask, or selection.

4. Select either a harder edge brush or try the Pencil Tool (B) and enter 3 pixels or less brush size to start in the Tool Options bar. You are working with detail here, so a smaller brush size will be easier to work with.

5. On the Tool Options bar, set Mode to Normal and the Opacity settings to 100%.

6. Select the Foreground color as white by clicking the bent arrow above the Foreground/Background color icons so that white displays as the Foreground color (or simply press "X" on the keyboard to switch them). Paint with white to remove areas of the mask to expose any missed gray areas of the kayak (Figure 5-9).

7. Select the bent arrow again—it acts as a toggle—to change the Foreground color to black. Use this to add to the mask. Change brush sizes depending on the size of the area. You can quickly adjust the brush size of either tool by pressing the bracket keys on your keyboard. The left bracket ([) makes the size smaller and the right bracket (]) increases the size.

8. Work on small details around the straps, cords, and seat of the kayak to edit the mask. Remember, you want to isolate the hardware and background completely from the gray area of the kayak.

9. Toggle between Standard Mode and Quick Mask Mode on the Tools panel to see your new edited selection.

10. To replace the *Kayak Color* selection channel with the most recent selection, toggle back to Standard mode to view the selected kayak, then choose Select > Save Selection.

11. Locate the *Kayak Color* channel on the drop-down display, and then select Replace Channel.

12. You can also use this same procedure to remove minute areas of the mask from around any parts of the hardware or the kayak itself in the *KayakALL* selection channel you'll be creating.

13. When you are all set, save the file *KayakAD.tif* in the *Chapter 5* folder. Leave open for the next exercise.

ENHANCING SELECTION EDGES USING REFINE EDGE

Now that you have finalized your detailed selection for changing the color of the kayak, you will use the Refine Edge command to soften the edges for the kayak to blend into the background area of the image, which will make the transition more believable. You will also check the selection against various background masks.

DESIGN TIP

Since the kayak is being duplicated, with drop shadow effects to be applied later, the selection's edges should be softened, so the transition between the change in colors will make the kayak look more realistic next to the background, avoiding a cut-out effect.

TOOLKIT TIP The Refine Edge dialog box contains an Edge Detection function using Smart Radius. This feature helps to make highly precise selections of complex subjects easily, enabling faster, more accurate combinations of multiple images. You can then use the extra view modes to assist you in previewing the quality of your selections. You can also have any residual background color removed from around your selections using the color decontamination settings.

Here you will slightly soften the edges for a smoother transition to the background.

1. With the kayak selection still active, select one of the selection tools then click the Refine Edge button on the Tool Options bar.

2. Click on the Black & White or Overlay (red) mask view to see if there are any stray areas that were not selected or any place overselected that you may have to go back and fix. If more work is needed, select Cancel.

3. Continue making adjustments with selection tools until you are confident you have all the areas for recoloring the kayak selected. Zoom in to 200% to check any details.

4. When you have all adjustments complete, choose one of the selection tools again, select Refine Edge, then choose one of the views (try Black & White or Overlay) and make slight adjustments. Start with 1 pixel Edge Detection, and 3 for Smooth, 3 for Contrast (Figure 5-10) to slightly soften the edges. Do not click to Decontaminate Colors. Click OK when ready.

5. Click on the Marching Ants view and zoom in to see your results.

6. To save your new selection change, choose Select > Save Selection > *Kayak Color* > Replace Channel > OK. Save the file.

▷   FIGURE 5-10

Using Refine Edge to check for selection details and soften edges.

SECOND SELECTION: THE ENTIRE KAYAK FOR DUPLICATING

The second selection is for duplicating the entire kayak image. You have already done the hard part with the initial *Kayak Color* selection. Now all that is needed is to include all the hardware on the kayak by *adding* to the selection so that it outlines the entire kayak. The new selection will be saved as another permanent selection channel named *KayakALL*. You do not have to start this second selection from scratch. By saving the first selection, *Kayak Color*, again with a new name (*KayakALL*), you can easily build upon that first selection. This *KayakALL* selection will be used to make multiple copies of the original kayak for the advertisement.

In this exercise, you are going to create a new channel *KayakALL* from the first selection *Kayak Color*, where you will name the new channel, and save it. You can then edit this new channel to include all the hardware and then save the new edited selection.

1. Click Select > Load Selection. When the dialog box opens, you will see the *Kayak Color* channel. Click OK.

2. Choose Select > Save Selection > New Channel. Name the new channel *KayakALL*. This will be the second permanent selection (alpha) channel that you will edit for duplicating the entire kayak. Select OK.

3. Zoom in to around 200% with the Zoom Tool (Z) to search the areas that need to be selected.

4. Use the Lasso tools and the Quick Selection Tool (W), and add to the selection to *include* all the hardware and the seat of the kayak this time. Take your time; again, you need to be very detailed in creating this selection for the final advertisement to look professional.

5. Continue until you are confident you have the entire kayak selected (feel free to try the Quick Mask option mentioned earlier).

6. Select Refine Edge to create a slightly soft edge on the outside of the kayak to make a smooth transition of colors between the kayak and the background. Start with 1 pixel Edge Detection, and 3 for Smooth. Do not choose to Decontaminate Colors for this exercise.

7. Use one of the View Masks as your guide.

8. To replace the channel selection *KayakALL* with your selection involving the entire kayak, choose Select > Save Selection. Locate the *KayakALL* channel in the drop-down display and select Replace Channel (Figure 5-11).

9. Save the file again in your *Chapter 5* folder on your drive.

▷ FIGURE 5-11

Saving the second selection of the entire kayak with hardware, as *KayakALL*.

CREATING THE THREE KAYAK IMAGE LAYERS

Now that you have the selections created for duplicating the entire kayak image and for changing the *kayak color*, you will see how to put it all together. In the next exercises, you are going to duplicate and change the color of the original kayak to create the green and yellow kayaks, creating a separate layer for each one. Drop shadows will be created on the new kayaks to match the original kayak.

CONVERTING THE BACKGROUND LAYER TO A NORMAL LAYER

The first layer in any document is the **Background layer.** It always displays on the bottom of the Layers panel. As a Background layer, it cannot be moved among other layers. Additional layers, when they are first created, are placed above the selected layer in the Layers panel and can easily be moved around between any other layers for various effects. If a Background layer is converted to a normal layer, it can then be moved between other layers and can also be renamed. Naming your layers helps to keep track of each layer for making further changes. You will rename the Background layer as *Gray Kayak,* allowing it to become a normal layer and identifying it as the gray kayak image.

Now you will rename the Background layer *Gray Kayak.*

1. With the *KayakAD.tif* image open, display the Channels, Navigator, Color, and Layers panels. If not displayed, open them by selecting them from the Window menu, or click on their icons to expand each panel.

2. In the Layers panel, double-click on the Background layer to bring up the New Layer display box. You can double-click anywhere in the Background layer to open the New Layer dialog box (Figure 5-12).

3. In the Layer Name field, type *Gray Kayak;* leave the other settings at their defaults.

4. Click OK and you will notice the layer name has been changed to *Gray Kayak* (Figure 5-12). It is now a normal layer that can be moved if needed.

Double-click on the layer, not the text

▷ FIGURE 5-12

Changing the Background layer to a normal layer for editing and renaming the layer as *Gray Kayak.*

PASTING A SELECTION CREATES A NEW LAYER

Each layer is like a clear sheet with all or part of an image on it. When you copy and paste a selection, a new layer is created with those areas that were selected on the image. This displays a new layer, showing all areas that were *not* selected as transparent. These transparent areas display as a checkerboard on the layer thumbnail. To color and duplicate the kayak without the background, additional layers need to be created for each kayak with the background left transparent. Pasting a selection on its own layer gives the designer the flexibility of editing certain areas of an image without affecting other areas or other layers; that is, unless a particular Blending Mode or Opacity level is chosen on the Layers panel.

It is time to use the alpha (selection) channel (*KayakALL*) of the entire kayak you created in the last chapter. In this exercise, we're going to make an additional layer of the original kayak image, removing the background (Figure 5-13).

▷ FIGURE 5-13

Duplicating the kayak image to create a new layer.

1. Click the *Gray Kayak* layer in the Layers panel to highlight it.

2. Choose Select > Load Selection > *KayakALL* > OK. This is the alpha channel you created for the whole kayak by saving your selection. Notice the marquee is displayed along the outer edges of the kayak.

3. Choose Edit > Copy, then choose Edit > Paste. Although you will not notice any change on the original kayak image, you have actually pasted a copy directly on top of the original kayak. When you have pasted an image, it creates a new layer—*Layer 1*—on top of the *Gray Kayak* layer in the Layers panel. You will notice the additional *Layer1* containing the kayak and a transparent background.

4. Now we will rename it. Double-click the text *Layer 1* in the Layers panel and rename it *Green Kayak* (Figure 5-13). If you accidentally double-click the layer, you will be presented with a Layer Style dialog box; if this happens, just click Cancel and try again.

5. Press the Return/Enter key to accept the change. If you want to see larger thumbnails of your work, click the Layers Panel Menu > Panel Options and click on the large thumbnail.

6. Save the file again (including layers) as *KayakAD.tif* in your *Chapter 5* folder.

TOOLKIT TIP You can save Photoshop files in either PSD or TIF formats, and you will be able to edit either one with layers while maintaining the original quality. Photoshop's native PSD format can only be read by Adobe applications, whereas TIF files are universally read. In this chapter, you will save and work with the file as a TIF; remember to leave "Layers" checked in the Save As dialog box. As a good practice, if you have room, create a back-up PSD file in your *Chapter 5* folder.

ADJUSTING COLOR USING THE HUE/SATURATION COMMAND

We are now ready to change the color of the kayak using the Hue/Saturation command in the Image menu. The **Hue/Saturation command** lets you adjust the hue, saturation, and lightness of an image or selected areas of an image. It works well with large items that have varying shadow and highlight detail. This technique works wonderfully when changing the color of a product, when you need to retain all highlight and shadow tonal details. You can use the Hue slider to select new colors and the Saturation and Lightness sliders for color purity and intensity. You have the option to try out various preset settings in the Hue/Saturation panel, or create your own customized preset settings that you can save and access for future projects.

In this exercise, you are going to color the new pasted kayak. You need to use the *Kayak Color* channel selection you created earlier to select only those areas that need to be colored, much like an auto body shop would paint on unmasked areas, and then you will use the Hue/Saturation command to get the color you want (Figure 5-14).

▷ FIGURE 5-14

Creating the green color for the new kayak with the Hue/Saturation command.

1. In the Tools panel, set the foreground color to the default black. If black is not the foreground color, select the two small squares underneath to toggle to the black foreground.

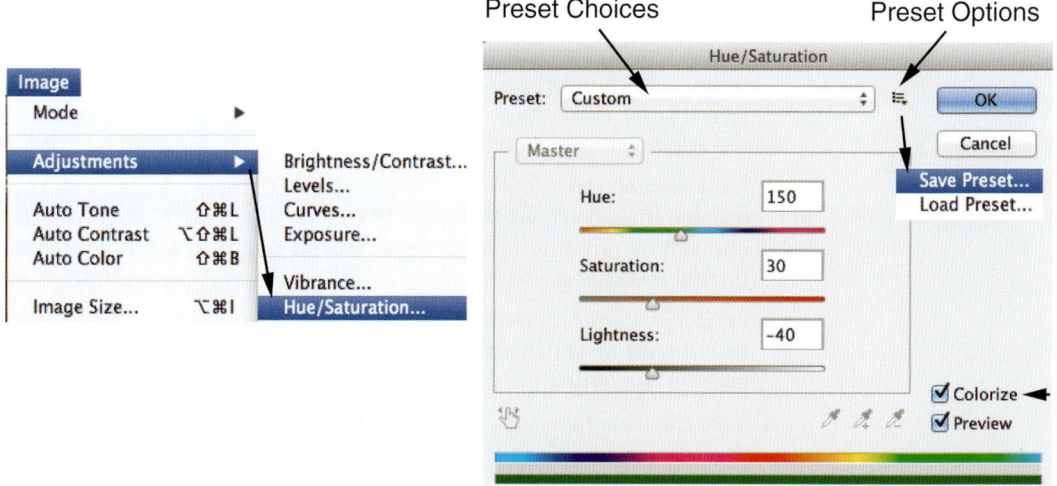

Suggested green color with Colorize button checked

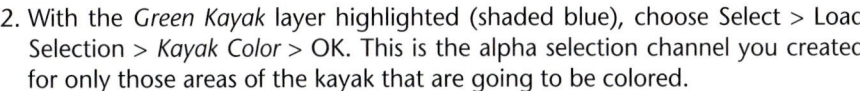

2. With the *Green Kayak* layer highlighted (shaded blue), choose Select > Load Selection > *Kayak Color* > OK. This is the alpha selection channel you created for only those areas of the kayak that are going to be colored.

3. Select Image > Adjustments > Hue/Saturation and make sure the Colorize and Preview option boxes are checked.

4. Move the dialog box alongside the image so you can see the effects.

5. To change the color of the gray kayak to hunter green, start with these settings and adjust the sliders until you have a dark green. Hue: 150, Saturation: 30, Lightness: –40 (minus 40). See Figure 5-14 for settings. To save your color settings, click the Preset Options menu, and choose Save Preset. Name the preset *Hunter Green*, and then select Save again to save the new preset to Photoshop's default location on your computer. Click OK. It will be saved as a custom preset.

6. Save your file.

DESIGN TIP

If you were to try to "paint" the kayak with a brush, even at a low opacity, the shadow areas in particular would appear "filled in" and unrealistic looking. Painting is best done in small areas of an image. Using the Hue/Saturation command works best with large areas or images with varying shadows and highlights.

 PROBLEM If you are not getting close to the color you want, make sure the Colorize box is checked in the Hue/Saturation dialog box.

POSITIONING LAYERS WITH THE MOVE TOOL

The Move Tool (V) allows you to move a selection within an image or onto another image file. When you use the Move Tool (V) to readjust or position a selection, the new position of the image you are moving will be updated in the layer thumbnail on the Layers panel.

You are now going to select the entire kayak and move the duplicate away from the original and position it.

1. With the *Green Kayak* layer highlighted, choose Select > Load Selection > *KayakALL* > OK to select the entire kayak to be moved.

2. Select the Move Tool (V) and click and drag the green kayak image to move it away from the original. Place it under the original kayak, as shown in Figure 5-15 on the next page. You will notice as you move the green kayak away, the gray kayak will show underneath.

3. Choose Select > Deselect. Save the file in your *Chapter 5* folder.

DESIGN TIP

When scanning images, sometimes an image may appear overly saturated in color, especially in skin tones. You can use the Hue/Saturation command to help to bring back the original colors by decreasing the image's saturation.

 PROBLEM If you have the *Gray Kayak* layer selected by mistake, you will end up moving the gray kayak along with the background. Make sure the *Green Kayak* layer is highlighted.

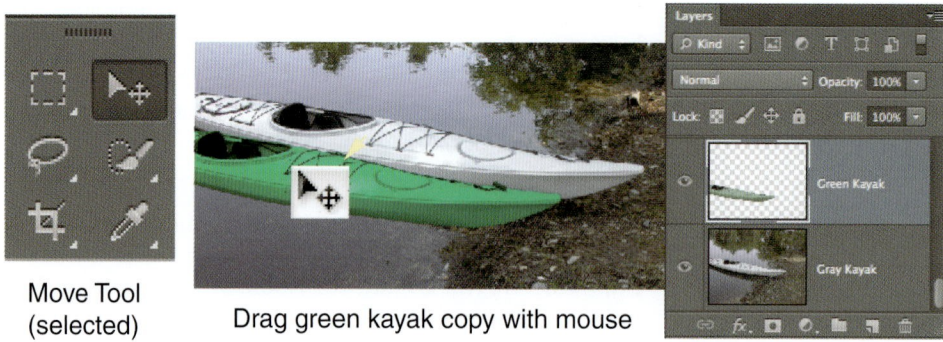

Move Tool
(selected)

Drag green kayak copy with mouse

▷ FIGURE 5-15

Use the Move Tool to drag the newly created green kayak into position.

CREATING THE YELLOW KAYAK LAYER

It is time to duplicate the third kayak in the ad and color it yellow. Then you will rename the layer and put a drop shadow effect on the yellow and green kayaks to approximate the original gray kayak's shadow.

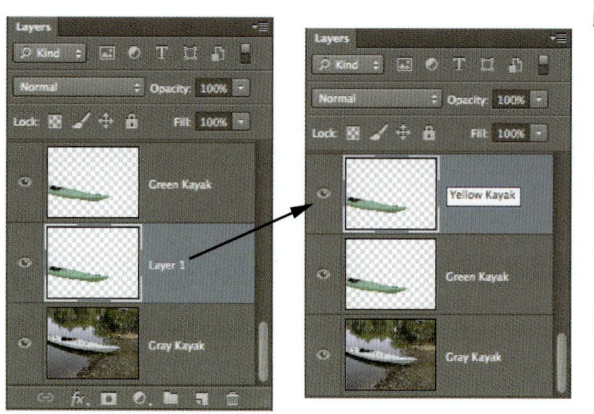

Copying, pasting, and renaming selected layer

Suggested settings for yellow kayak

▷ FIGURE 5-16

Creating another layer for the yellow kayak and applying color change with the Hue/Saturation command.

In this exercise, you will duplicate the gray kayak again and color it yellow (Figure 5-16).

1. Make sure the original *Gray Kayak* layer is selected (shaded in blue).

2. Choose Select > Load Selection > *KayakALL* > OK. This selection will be used for duplicating the whole kayak.

3. Choose Edit > Copy, then choose Edit > Paste to copy the selection in a new layer above the original kayak. Again the new kayak is pasted directly on top of the original.

PROBLEM If you receive an error box displaying Unable to Copy Contents, make sure the *Gray Kayak* layer is selected and not any other layer.

4. Notice a third layer named *Layer 1* is placed between the other two. Photoshop places new layers above the selected one.

5. Select and drag the new *Layer 1* above the *Green Kayak* layer. A black line appears at the top of the Layers panel to show you the position of the layer you are dragging.

6. Double-click the *Layer 1* text name and rename it *Yellow Kayak* (Figure 5-16), then press the Return/Enter key to accept the change.

7. To get the channel selection for just the *kayak color*, make sure the Yellow Kayak layer is still highlighted, choose Select > Load Selection > *Kayak Color* > OK.

8. To create the yellow color, choose Image > Adjustments > Hue/Saturation again. Drag (or type in) the settings to Hue: 60, Saturation: 60, Lightness: –10 (minus 10) as a starting point. Make sure the Colorize box is checked. Use Figure 5-16 as a guide. To save your color settings, click the Preset Options menu, and choose Save Preset. Name the preset Yellow Kayak, and then select Save again to save the new preset to Photoshop's default location on your computer. Click OK. It will be saved as a custom preset.

9. To select the whole kayak again to be moved into position, choose Select > Load Selection > *KayakAll* > OK. A marquee will display around the kayak's outer edges. This step is very important.

10. With the *Yellow Kayak* layer selected, use the Move Tool (V) to drag the pasted yellow kayak below the green one (Figure 5-17).

▷ FIGURE 5-17

Three different colored kayaks.

EDITING INDIVIDUAL PASTED LAYERS

The alpha selection channels you created were based on the original *Gray Kayak* layer. When you paste a copied selection on its own layer and you want to make changes, like adjusting the color on one of the kayak layers, you need to create a selection on that layer. With pasted layers from these exercises, you can:

• Select the *Green Kayak* or *Yellow Kayak* layer

• Select only the hardware and seat

- Invert the selection by choosing Select > Inverse, which would have no effect on the transparent background but will cover only those areas that are to be colored or edited

- Save the selection as a channel that can be called upon anytime on that layer

With individual layers you can make adjustments that only affect that layer, unless you choose to change blending modes or opacity settings that affect layers underneath. With the channel selection created on one of the pasted layers to color the kayak, you can edit the color on that layer whenever the client wants without having to redo the image again.

LAYER STYLE EFFECT: DROP SHADOWS

When you double-click on a thumbnail image in the Layers panel or select the Layer Style icon (it looks like "Fx" in a circle) at the bottom of the Layers panel, a Layer Style dialog box opens up. Layer styles allow you to create shadows, embossing, bevels, overlays, glow, and stroke effects on selected portions of an image or text. You can create a realistic drop shadow effect by adjusting the distance, size, and angle settings to match the original shadow. Make sure the **Use Global Light** option is checked to cast all the shadows at the same angle so that all shadows in future layers will look like they have the same light source for visual accuracy.

In this exercise you will create a drop shadow on the new kayak layers to add a sense of realism consistent with the original kayak (Figure 5-18).

1. Double-click the *Green Kayak* thumbnail image you created on the Layers panel, or select the Add a layer style icon at the bottom of the Layers panel. Do not double-click on the text.

DESIGN TIP

To create a sense of realism, especially when duplicating an image, always place a check in the Use Global Light box in the Drop Shadows dialog box for consistent placement and angle of shadows in line with the original image.

▷   FIGURE 5-18

Applying drop shadow layer style effect to new kayaks to match the original kayak shadow.

2. The Layer Style dialog box will open. Position the display alongside the image to preview the effect.

3. Click the Drop Shadow name under Styles in the dialog box to access the Drop Shadow dialog box.

4. To duplicate the original gray kayak's shadow, set the Angle to 30 degrees, Blend Mode at Normal with Opacity at 75%, and Distance of 100 pixels with a shadow Size of 60 pixels for a soft shadow effect (Figure 5-18).

5. Make sure Anti-aliased, Use Global Light, and Preview are all checked. Click OK to apply the effect. You will find a nice shadow set beneath the green kayak.

6. Notice on the Layers panel, the layer style effect is placed under the *Green Kayak* layer. You can double-click any layer effects for future adjustments. If you do not see the effects, click on the triangle next to the "Fx" at the right end of the layer.

7. To make a drop shadow of the yellow kayak image with the same setting as the green kayak, make sure the *Yellow Kayak* layer is highlighted.

8. Select the Add a layer style icon at the bottom of the Layers panel, then select Drop Shadow from the menu. The Layer Style dialog box opens up.

9. Position the display alongside the image to preview the effect.

10. Set the Angle to 30 degrees, Blend Mode at Normal with Opacity at 75%, and Distance of 100 pixels with a shadow Size of 60 pixels.

11. Make sure Anti-aliased, Use Global Light, and Preview are all checked, and then select OK to apply the effect (Figure 5-19).

12. Save the file in your *Chapter 5* folder.

DESIGN TIP

Placement of light and dark colors helps achieve balance within an image. With the shadow reflections on the water dominating the upper portion of the kayak image, placing the bright yellow kayak near the bottom and having the dark green kayak in between the light gray and yellow kayaks provide that balance.

▷ FIGURE 5-19

Kayaks with drop shadow effects applied to realism.

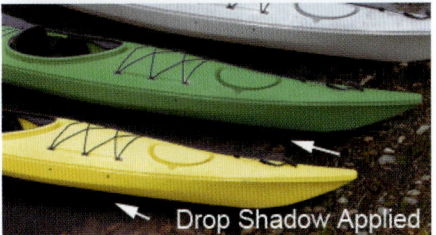

PROBLEM If any of the menu commands are grayed out so they cannot be selected, chances are the wrong layer is selected. Select the layer you need to work on, and the commands should display.

TOOLKIT TIP You can copy Layer Style effects created in one layer to another layer by selecting the effects created in one layer, holding down the Option/Alt key, and dragging to copy the effects to the next layer. Release the mouse first when copying, then the key.

RECORDING STATES OF PROJECT DEVELOPMENT USING THE LAYER COMPS PANEL

The **Layer Comps panel** allows the designer or photographer to capture the various stages or states of development of a document by recording existing settings for the visibility or opacity of layers and their effects on the previous layers, their position in the document, and various blending options. Record various states of development using the New Layer Comp button, which gives you the flexibility to hide or display layers and to show before and after views when applying effects or making changes. This provides the ability to experiment, and you can show variations of the project to your client, then cycle back through previously recorded stages. You can also include comments to describe the recorded state; states recorded in the Layer Comps panel are permanent for future reference or editing. The Layer Comps panel can be opened using the Window menu.

You will record the state of the three colored kayaks at present in the Layer Comps panel.

▷ FIGURE 5-20

Using Layer Comps to record a layer's state or variations of a project.

1. With all three kayaks in position, make sure all eye icons are displayed in the Layers panel.

2. Select the Layer Comps panel or open it from the Window menu (Window > Layer Comps); select the Create New Layer Comp icon on the panel bottom or from the Panel menu (Figure 5-20).

Kayaks with drop shadows

Create New Layer Comp

3. When the New Layer Comp dialog box displays, name the layer state *Kayaks with Drop Shadows*.

4. In the Apply to Layers section, check the boxes for Visibility, Position, and Appearance (Layer Style) settings to record everything thus far.

5. In the Comment section, type "Kayaks duplicated, recolored, and positioned with drop shadows applied," then select OK. The Layer Comp title and description are displayed in the Layer Comps panel.

LAYER COMPS RECORD BEFORE AND AFTER EFFECTS

With the Layer Comps panel, a designer or photographer can create various layer configurations to observe before and after effects by selecting the eye icons to display or hide effects. Layer Comps also provide the opportunity to experiment with different layer combinations to observe their effects by simply turning on and off layers and their effects. If you click once on the Effects eye in the Layers panel, all effects are hidden in that layer. Select the eye again and it toggles to display the effects. If you click on the eye icon next to just the individual effect—for instance, the eye icon where you created drop shadow effects in the last exercise—only that effect is hidden or displayed. Recorded states in Layer Comps are permanent so that when you close and save a file, the Layer Comps you created are saved with the image. To observe the various states you saved, click on the box at the left of the layer comp to make it active.

Next, you will create a Layer Comp of the kayaks without the shadow effects applied earlier to observe the before and after effects of applying drop shadows.

1. In the Layers panel, click on the eye icons beside Drop Shadow to hide the Layer Style drop shadows in the *Green Kayak* layer and the *Yellow Kayak* layer. The eye icon will disappear. Leave the Green, Yellow, and Gray kayak layers displayed (Figure 5-21).

▷ FIGURE 5-21

You can also create different Layer Comp configurations and choose between states to experiment.

Active state

Kayak layers without drop shadows are displayed
(click eye icon to remove drop shadow effect)

2. Click on the Layer Comps tab to display the Layer Comps panel.

3. Select the New Layer Comp icon on the panel bottom or from the Panel submenu.

4. When the New Layer Comp dialog box displays, name the layer state *Kayaks Before Shadows.*

5. In the Apply to Layers section, check the boxes for Visibility and Position. There are no layer styles to affect the Appearance setting.

6. In the Comment section, type "Kayaks before Drop Shadows," and then select OK.

7. In the Layer Comps panel, select the boxes to the left of the Layer Comp boxes *Kayak before Shadows* and *Kayaks with Drop Shadows* to make them active individually. Observe the before and after effects of applying the drop shadows. (See Figure 5-21.)

8. Select and leave the original Layer Comp state, *Kayaks with Drop Shadows,* with all eye icons displayed in the Layers panel to show the three kayaks and drop shadows.

9. Save the file in your *Chapter 5* folder and leave it open.

TOOLKIT TIP In Photoshop CC you can change the visibility, position, or appearance of one layer in a Layer Comp, then sync the adjustments made to see how they appear in all the other Layer Comps. You can choose various update options in the Layer Comps panel menu to view the changes.

LOCKING LAYERS

To prevent inadvertent edits, you can lock layers by selecting the layer to be locked and clicking one of the locking icons near the top of the Layers panel, usually the one that looks like a padlock (Lock all). The lock icon is then displayed on the active layer. This locks all sublayers, like Layer Style effects, under the main layer. To remove a lock, select the lock icon again. It acts as a toggle (Figure 5-22).

Now that you have all three kayaks positioned, colored, and shaded, you will lock them so they cannot be accidentally edited.

1. Select the *Gray Kayak* layer and then select the Lock all icon. You will notice it looks like a padlock on the right side of the layer (Figure 5-22).

2. Repeat the same procedure for the *Green Kayak* and *Yellow Kayak* layers. This will also lock the Layer Style shadow effects with each new kayak layer. (To hide effects in sublayers, click on that effect's eye icon first before locking.)

3. Save the file.

▷ FIGURE 5-22

Locking layers prevents inadvertent editing.

Locks all sublayers within a layer

CREATING TYPE LAYERS

When you use the Type Tool (T), a text layer is created specifically for the text. Wherever you click, you can type on a path. To reposition the text, just use the Move Tool (V). Sometimes it helps to have each text line as a different text layer, so they can be moved individually or linked to move together. To start another new text layer, select another tool in the Tools panel, such as the Move Tool (V), then click on the Type Tool (T) again. The Type Tool Options bar contains many formatting options for editing type. Photoshop's Character panel can also provide many of the same options and any changes made are reflected in the Tool Options bar.

FORMATTING TYPE IN THE TOOL OPTIONS BAR

In the Tool Options bar for the Type Tool (T), you can change font, color, size, anti-alias method, alignment, and text warp effects. You can change the text orientation (vertical or horizontal) and create special Type Tool (T) presets. You can observe what the various fonts look like for making quick decisions on what type to use on a given project. Photoshop Creative Cloud (CC) uses font search, so when you type in the name of a font, all fonts and styles that match the criteria will display in a drop-down list. You can also hover your mouse over fonts to preview how they look. Always start off text with the anti-alias setting turned on as the default. Using the Anti-alias setting helps smooth the transition between different colored pixel edges, keeping them from getting the jaggies.

DESIGN TIP

In the Tool Options bar, a good starting point for Anti-alias settings for type is to use a Strong or Sharp setting for text that will be printed, and a Crisp setting for text that will only be displayed electronically, like on the Web. Settings may also vary depending on the font and point size.

TOOLKIT TIP Use the Move Tool (V) to position text. If you need to make any changes to text, select the Type Tool (T) again, then select the text layer you want to edit; highlight the text with your cursor to make any changes.

In this exercise, you will format type for the *Aqua Excursions* company.

1. Select/highlight the *Yellow Kayak* layer.

2. Select the Horizontal Type Tool (T).

3. In the Tool Options bar, type "Minion" in the font family drop box to display all choices in Photoshop CC. Select Minion Pro Bold and set the type at 48-pt with a Strong Anti-alias (feel free to substitute another wide serif font by selecting it from the drop-down menu under the Font Face field in the Tool Options bar).

4. Set white as your foreground color. You can click the top left corner within the color box, or you can switch the Foreground/Background color box on the Tools panel for a white foreground (press the X key).

5. Type "Aqua Excursions" near the top left corner of the image.

6. Select the Move Tool (V) to center the text between the left and right edges, about one-quarter inch away from the top edge.

7. You will notice a "T" (type) layer is created displaying the text you have typed in the Layers panel (Figure 5-23).

8. Make sure the type layer is located at the top of the Layers panel.

9. Save the file in your *Chapter 5* folder.

▷ FIGURE 5-23

Select options for Type tools using the Tool Options bar or the Character panel. Type uses its own layer for editing.

PROBLEM If you do not see any text while typing, make sure the text layer is on top of the other *Gray Kayak* layer. If not, simply click the text layer and drag it to the top.

USING THE CHARACTER PANEL

Photoshop's Character panel contains additional commands for formatting text. Any changes made in the Character panel are reflected in the Tool Options bar and vice versa. Create a new text layer first before making any formatting changes. You can access the Character panel on the Type Tool Options bar using the Character/Paragraph panel button, or from the Window menu. There is also a Paragraph panel in Photoshop for formatting blocks of text, usually as a tab next to the Character panel. In Photoshop CC, you'll also find the font search technique in the Character panel.

 TOOLKIT TIP After typing a line of text, selecting another tool like the Move Tool (V) then selecting the Type Tool (T) again will automatically create a new type layer.

You will now format the type in the second line of the ad using the Character panel.

1. Select the Move Tool (V) to exit the previous type layer, and then select the Horizontal Type Tool (T) again to create the next line of type.

2. Click under the *u* in *Aqua* to create a new text layer (Figure 5-24). A new layer needs to be created *before* you make any changes to the text formatting, otherwise the changes occur on the previous type layer.

▷ FIGURE 5-24

Format type using the Tool Options bar for the first line, then try using the Character panel for the second line of type.

Click for Character Panel

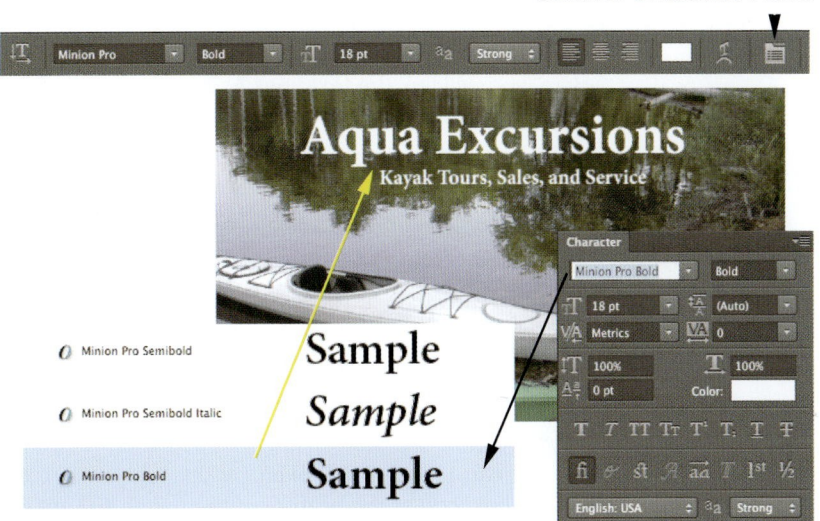

3. Make sure the Character panel is displayed (Window > Character or select the Character/Paragraph button on the Tool Options bar).

4. In the Character panel, change the text size to 18-pt, white color, Minion Pro Bold font to make it stand out in the dark portion of the image.

5. Notice the changes made in the Character panel display in the Tool Options bar.

6. Type "Kayak Tours, Sales, and Service."

7. Position the text with the Move Tool (V) as shown in Figure 5-24, aligning the top of the line with the bottom of the *q* extension.

8. Save the file in your *Chapter 5* folder.

SELECTING AND LINKING LAYERS

Linking layers allows you to move several layers together for accurate positioning. Layers that are linked can be moved and transformed simultaneously, keeping the alignment and composite layering intact. Once layers are linked, if any minor adjustments need to be made, they will be moved together. You can link any normal unlocked layer to another layer or layers. The Link Layers icon is located at the bottom of the Layers panel. The Select menu also contains commands to select to Find Layers, Deselect Layers, and Select All Layers. You can select a group of similar layers, such as type layers, using the Select > Similar layers command and then click the Linking Layers icon to connect them together for easy moving and alignment.

 TOOLKIT TIP To select adjacent layers, hold down the Shift key and select both layers, then click the Link Layers icon at the bottom of the Layers panel. To select nonadjacent layers, use the Command (Mac) or CTRL key (Windows).

Here, you will link the text lines *Aqua Excursions* and *Kayak Tours, Sales, and Service* together. This will keep both layers together for final positioning.

1. Once both lines are in position, click on the *Kayak Tours, Sales, and Service* layer to highlight it.

2. Hold down the Shift key, and click both type layers. Click the Link layers icon at the bottom of the Layers panel.

3. Now the *Aqua Excursions* text line is linked to the *Kayak Tours, Sales, and Service* text line. You will notice a link icon is displayed at the right of each layer affected in the Layers panel (Figure 5-25 on previous page).

4. Select the Move Tool (V) and position the two text lines accurately. Use the arrow keys to make small adjustments.

5. You can toggle the link off by selecting one of the linked layers and clicking the link icon at the bottom of the panel. To turn it back on, highlight both layers and click again.

▷ FIGURE 5-25

Link type layers to make any adjustments together.

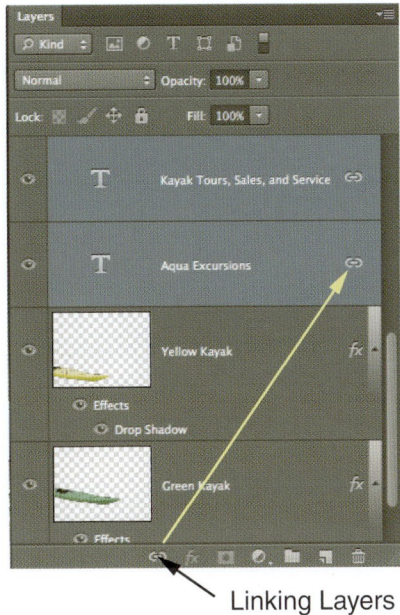

Linking Layers

ADDING TYPE USING SEPARATE TYPE LAYERS

To start each line of type on its own layer, click on the Move Tool (V), then select the Type Tool (T), and click in the document image before making any text formatting changes. This allows you to change the text without affecting the existing text. This also makes it easier to move each line into exact position without affecting the other lines.

In this exercise, you will create the final three lines of text, creating a layer for each.

1. Select the Move Tool, then the Type Tool (T), and click on the document to create a new type layer.

2. Use either the Tool Options bar or the Character panel to select the white Minion Pro Bold Italic font, and change the font size to 18-pt.

3. Click and type "Up to 30% Off" using Figure 5-26 on the next page as a guide.

4. Select the Move Tool (V), then reselect the Type Tool (T), and type in the remaining lines of the ad: "All Store Items" and "Sale Ends September 30th" to create two more type layers. After the words "Sale Ends," press the Return/Enter key to put "September 30th" beneath it. Press the space bar a few times to move it under the *I* in *Sale.*

5. Select each individual text layer in the Layers panel; use the Move Tool to position each line as shown in Figure 5-26.

6. Save the file in your *Chapter 5* folder.

DESIGN TIP

When presenting a line of sale information, it is important to make that line of text stand out by increasing the type size, using a different font, or applying a different color. Yellow or red is a great attention-getting color.

▷ FIGURE 5-26

Create separate type layers for each line of text.

USING THE COLOR PICKER TO SAMPLE COLORS

Use the Tool Options bar to make changes to type. Simply highlight the text and make the changes. Here, we will make the line "Up to 30% Off" stand out by making it italic for emphasis, increasing the size slightly, and changing the color to match the color of the yellow kayak. With the Color Picker display window open, you can either select colors in the Picker itself, type in the values if you know them, or simply use the cursor and click on any part of the color box to select a color. In this case, we will use the Color Picker to select the yellow color from the kayak.

TOOLKIT TIP You can select multiple type layers and apply changes that affect all type layers at once, like changing fonts, sizes, styles, color, and so on. Use special effects on type sparingly to create more drama.

Next, you will change "Up to 30% Off" to make it stand out as the sale line.

1. Select the Type Tool, and click the "Up to 30% Off" layer in the Layers panel to make it active.

2. Highlight the type by clicking and dragging through it with the Type Tool (T).

3. Change the font to Minion Pro Bold Italic (or use an italic style with your selected font); select a 24-pt size.

4. Click the Set the text color box in the Tool Options bar to open up the Set text color display, and then move the window above the kayak image (Figure 5-27).

Double-click to open the Color Picker and sample the yellow kayak

▷ FIGURE 5-27

Using the Color Picker to sample the yellow kayak for the text sale line.

▷ FIGURE 5-28

Drop shadow layer style settings for type lines.

5. Position the eyedropper cursor over the darker yellow area of the kayak and click; the eyedropper acts as a color selector, and changes the type line to the color you selected. Your setting may be a little different from the one on Figure 5-27. Click OK to close the Color Picker.

6. To see the new color, deselect the type by selecting the Move Tool (V). With the type layer for the sale selected, position the type as indicated in the layout (refer to Figure 5-28).

7. Change the foreground color on the Tools panel back to black as the default color.

8. Save the file.

TOOLKIT TIP You can also use the Eyedropper Tool (I) in the Tools panel to select the color on the darker side of the yellow kayak.

 TOOLKIT TIP If you are using a Color Picker, and a cube displays next to the color you have chosen, it indicates that the color you picked may not display precisely when viewed on the Web. If this happens, and you want to send the color for print, it will be fine. If you observe a yellow triangle with an exclamation point inside, the color will not print on commercial press precisely, but will display on the Web properly. If any of these cautions are displayed, you can click on the cube or triangle icon and Photoshop will display the nearest available color.

TYPE LAYER STYLES AND BLENDING MODES

Type layer style effects can be applied the same way as image effects. Type layer styles help to create special effects to accent type against photographic images and backgrounds or to add special emphasis to text in an image. Another feature in the Layers panel is the use of various blending modes that allow the designer or photographer to determine how pixels in one layer blend with pixels in the underlying layers. Different blending modes produce different results between layers, and these allow you to create a variety of special effects. The default blending mode is Normal. Use the Color Burn mode to darken or burn the text shadows.

In this exercise, to help accent the light-colored text against the dark background, you are going to create a drop shadow on all the text and use a Color Burn blending mode. While this is not something you would want to do all the time, it is important to learn how to do it, so you can apply the effect in special cases.

1. If the Add a layer style icon (looks like "Fx") is grayed out, click on the Link layers icon to remove the link between two text layers. Click on the *Aqua Excursions* type layer in the Layers panel to make it active. This will be the first type layer we will work on.

2. Click and hold the Add a layer style icon at the bottom of the Layers panel.

3. Select Drop Shadow from the drop-down menu to open up the Drop Shadow Layer Style dialog box.

4. Enter the settings as shown in Figure 5-28. Make sure Use Global Light, Preview, and Anti-aliased are checked.

5. Set the Blend Mode to Color Burn. Color Burn mode creates a very dark shadow under the type. Select OK to create the shadow effect.

6. Select each type layer in the Layers panel and repeat the same procedure to create a shadow for each line of text.

7. Save the file in your *Chapter 5* folder.

LAYER COMPS FOR TYPE AND SPECIAL COMBINATIONS

As was done earlier with the kayak layers, you can also create a Layer Comp that includes Type layers. Layer Comps help when you want to document the stages of your layers in developing your image. They also provide a means to experiment with different layer combinations to display various effects. To hide all layers and sublayers, such as Layer Style effects, click on the eye icon on the main layer, and the sublayers will be dimmed out. To hide just layer effects, click the eye icon next to the Effects sublayer.

Now you will create a Layer Comp of all the layers in your layout, including type layers; observe all states recorded.

1. Make sure all layers are displayed at this point by having the eye icon on in the Layers panel.

2. Click on the Layer Comps icon to display the panel, or select Window > Layer Comps. In earlier versions it appears on the right side of the Tool Options bar.

3. Select the New Layer Comp icon at the bottom of the panel or from the panel submenu.

4. When the New Layer Comp dialog box displays, name the layer state *Kayaks and Text* (Figure 5-29).

5. In the Apply to Layers section, check the boxes for Visibility, Position, and Appearance (Layer Style) settings to record everything thus far.

6. In the Comment section, type "Kayaks and text with layer style shadows applied," and then select OK.

7. Hide the yellow and green kayak eye icons in the Layers panel and make sure the eye icons are displayed in the *Gray Kayak* layer and all the Text Layers with effects.

▷ FIGURE 5-29

Creating Layer Comps combining various layers with type.

8. Select the Layer Comps tab, and then select the New Layer Comp icon on the Layer Comp panel.

9. Name the layer state *Text and Gray Kayak* and in the Apply to Layers section, check the boxes for Visibility, Position, and Appearance (Layer Style) settings.

10. Leave the Comment section blank, then click OK.

11. Click on the box next to each Layer Comp to display the different states you created in the Layer Comps panel. Observe how each is recorded with certain layers displayed and hidden (Figure 5-29).

12. Select the Layer Comp state Kayaks and Text with all eye icons displayed on the Layers panel to show the three kayaks and the type, along with the Layer Style effects.

13. Save the file as *KayakAD.tif* again in your *Chapter 5* folder.

ORGANIZING LAYERS AND PREPARING THE AD FOR PRESS

When you are finished with your project, or perhaps during various stages of development, you may find the need to streamline your layers to increase productivity and decrease file size. Creating layer groups allows you to assemble several layers within a folder. Merging layers combines layers permanently, while **flattening** layers combines all layers into one without losing any detail. Providing a client with an image flattened into one layer creates the smallest file size for easier portability. Use Adobe Bridge to compare file properties, like file sizes, to determine which file fits your client's needs.

LAYER FILTERING

A recent addition to the layers panel involves the use of layer filtering. As you can imagine some projects could involve many layers, and trying to find specific types of layers can be a daunting task. With layer filtering, you can find all kinds or types of layers quickly and efficiently. The filter icons are merely toggles where you can turn on or off what you want to filter.

TOOLKIT TIP In Photoshop CC, there is a layer filtering option called Isolation Mode that allows you to filter any active selected layers you choose in a document to focus on certain aspects of your work. To select Isolation Mode, you can either set the layer filtering option in the Layers panel to Selected, or select the Isolate Layers option in the Select menu. To exit, just choose the Isolate Layers option in the Select menu again to toggle the check mark as off.

In this exercise, you'll use layer filtering to find all the text layers in your project.

1. On the Layers panel, click the Filter for type layers ("T") icon to filter only the type layers. Leave the default filter type as Kind, and the icon on the far right, labeled as Turn layer filtering on/off, should display with an orange button to indicate it is turned on (Figure 5-30).

2. The kayak layers will disappear and only the type layers will display.

3. You can see how useful layer filters can be to a designer whose project involves many types of layers.

4. Turn the filter off for the next exercise by clicking the far right icon again with the orange square. This time the icon is dimmed and does not display an orange button. You should find all layers displayed now.

All Type Layers Filtered

▷ FIGURE 5-30

Filtering type layers.

LAYER GROUPS

Here is a great tool to organize your layers: *layer groups.* Earlier versions of Photoshop called these *layer sets.* A **layer group** allows you to place several layers within one folder. The layer group folder is created above the active layer and can display just the name of the layer group on the layers panel, or, by clicking on the triangle next to the folder, display all the layers within that group. Click the triangle, which flips down or up, to hide or show the layers included.

TOOLKIT TIP To select all the Type layers, you Select > Similar Layers. To move a layer out of its group, just drag the layer above or below the layer group folder. You can also drag a layer within a group over to another layer group folder.

In the next exercise, you will create a layer group to group all the type layers.

1. If it is not open already, open the *KayakAD.tif* file and highlight the topmost type layer in the Layers panel.

2. Select the Create a new group folder icon at the bottom of the Layers panel. A new layer with the default name of *Group 1* and a folder icon will display.

3. Double-click on the *Group 1* name, and rename the layer set *Text*. Press the Return/Enter key to accept the change. Note: If you don't see the Text group folder displayed, make sure the layer filtering icon is off.

4. Click each type layer and drag it into the *Text* folder.

5. When the folder arrow is clicked to display the contents, the newly positioned type layer inside the *Text* layer group will display as an indented thumbnail beneath the layer group folder (Figure 5-31).

6. When all the type layers are in the *Text* folder, click the triangle to hide the list, displaying only the *Text* folder.

7. Using the default settings, save the file as *KayakAD.tif* in your *Chapter 5* folder. Your file will keep all the layers intact as long as you keep RLE (faster saves, bigger files) selected in the TIF options dialog box.

Folder contents displayed

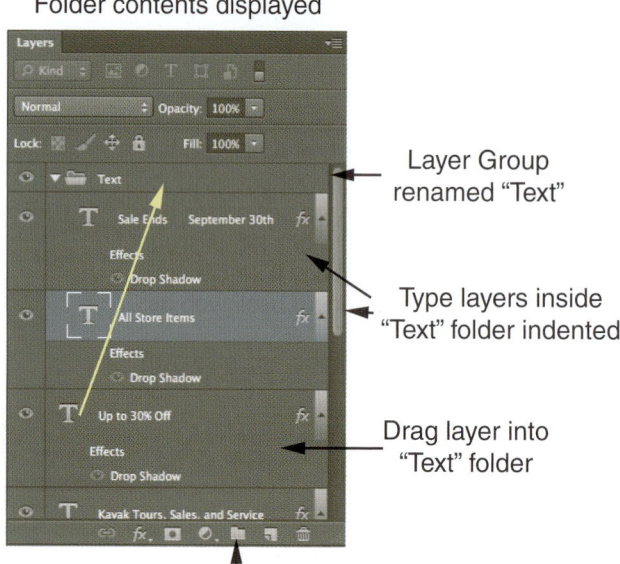

Layer Group renamed "Text"

Type layers inside "Text" folder indented

Drag layer into "Text" folder

Create a New Layer Group

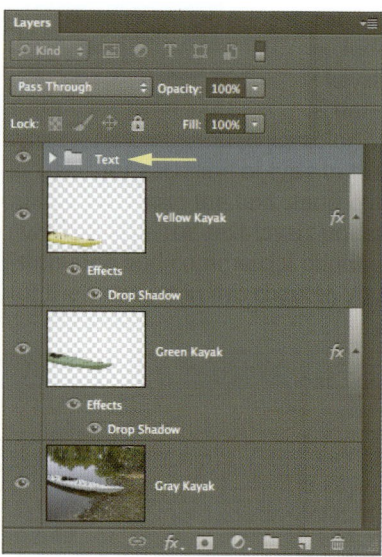

Layer Group "Text" (contains all type layers)

▷ FIGURE 5-31

Grouping all type layers in a Layer Group folder.

TOOLKIT TIP Warning! When you change how layers are displayed, if you open the Layer Comps panel, you will notice warnings in the various states, because they have been altered. It is a good habit to duplicate a file before making any permanent changes.

MERGING LAYERS

When you have finished a series of layers, and you are ready to combine several layers into one, you can merge them. This helps to decrease the file size, since every time you add layers to your document, you increase its file size. **Merging layers** still maintains the image quality and allows you to group any combination of layers together. The Merge Layers function merges only highlighted layers and is one of the safer commands for merging. There are many merge commands, like the **Merge Visible command**, in which only layers that display the eye icon are merged. After merging layers, they take on the name of the bottom layer in the merged group, which you can rename afterwards. Be careful using the various Merge commands because most are final once you save the file and cannot be edited later.

In this exercise, you will merge the three visible kayak images and remove the alpha (selection) channels you created since you will not need them anymore.

1. With the *KayakAD.tif* file open, make sure the eye icons are visible on all the kayak image layers, along with their drop shadow effects. Even though they are locked, they can be combined as one image.

2. Duplicate the *KayakAD* file (Image > Duplicate), and name the copy *KayakMERGE*. This leaves the *KayakAD* original with all its separate layers in case any future editing may be needed. Close the *KayakAD* file.

3. Click the eye icon by the *Text* layer group to hide all type layers (Figure 5-32). The eye icon will disappear, along with the text.

4. Select the *Gray Kayak* layer to make it active; this will become the name of the layer of the combined kayak images. You will rename the layer later.

▷ FIGURE 5-32

Merging all kayak layers into one.

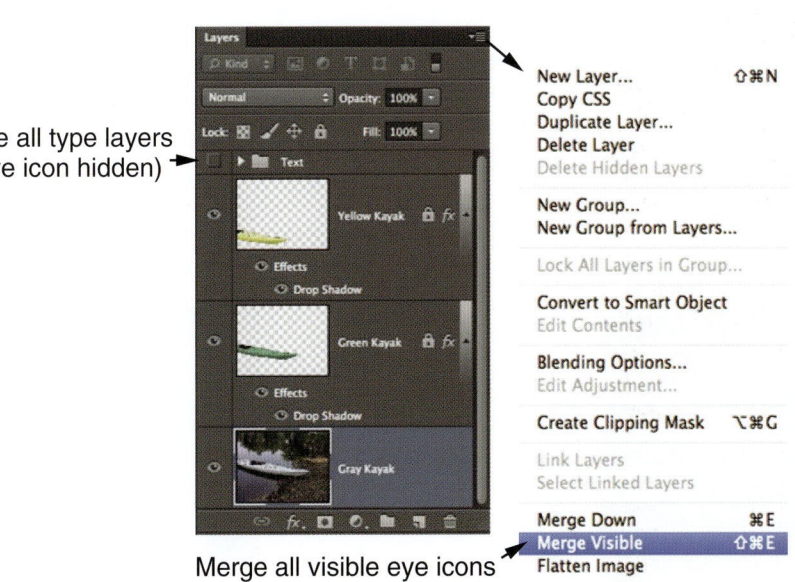

Hide all type layers (eye icon hidden) ▶

Merge all visible eye icons

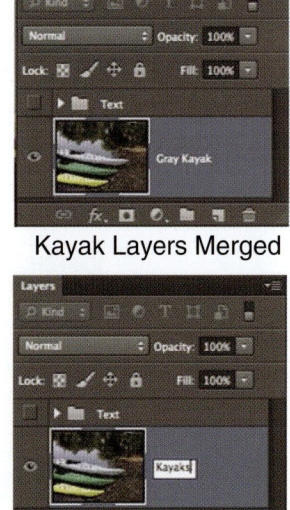

Kayak Layers Merged

Renamed to Kayaks

5. Select Merge Visible from the Layers panel submenu or from the Layer menu to merge all the displayed kayak layers and their effects together. The type layers are unaffected, because they were hidden when Merge Visible was selected.

6. Double-click the *Gray Kayak* layer and rename it *Kayaks*. Press the Return/Enter key to accept the change. All the kayaks are now on one layer.

7. To display the text again, click the leftmost box to display the eye icon next to the *Text* layer group folder.

8. Select the Channels panel, and drag the *KayakALL* and *Kayak Color* alpha (selection) channels into the trash; they are no longer needed.

9. Use the Save As command (File > Save As) and save the file in your *Chapter 5* folder as *KayakMERGE.tif* using the default settings. This will provide a thumbnail visual of all three kayak images together on one layer. Leave open for the next exercise.

FLATTENING THE FILE FOR ELECTRONIC DISTRIBUTION

Some applications may not be able to read multilayer images, so it is important to duplicate a completed image with layers, flatten it, and save it to show the work to a client. Merging all the layers in a document into a single layer is called *flattening* the image. Although saving a file as a JPEG automatically compresses it significantly into one layer and deletes some data, it is useful for showing the client the final project electronically. Since flattened files are permanent, keep an original image with all layers as a backup in case the client may need changes.

To make sure your file is compatible with any graphic application that your client may be using, you will need to flatten the file and rename it (Figure 5-33). Since we do not need the alpha channels we used for selections, we will delete them here. Then compare file sizes. Be aware that when you flatten a file with type, it rasterizes the type into a bitmap; this is not good quality for print, only for electronic distribution or for a rough proof on a local printer.

Completed ad flattened to one layer for electronic distribution

1. Open the *KayakMERGE.tif* file and click the eye icon of the *Text* layer group to make sure it is visible, then duplicate the file (Image > Duplicate); give it the name *KayakFLAT.tif* (Image > Duplicate > As KayakFLAT). Close the *KayakAD* file.

2. Select the Channels panel, and if they are not already deleted, drag the *KayakALL* and *Kayak Color* alpha (selection) channels into the trash.

3. To flatten the entire file, select Layer > Flatten Image from the Layer menu, or select Flatten Image from the Layers panel menu. If you get a dialog box asking to discard hidden layers, select OK (Figure 5-33).

4. To save the file for electronic distribution, use File > Save As to save the file again as *KayakFLAT.jpg* with maximum quality settings (if a warning displays, select to save it anyway, which will save it as a copy) in your *Chapter 5* folder. Files that are flattened and saved as either JPEG or TIF files can be read by most any graphic application universally.

5. Close the *KayakFLAT* file.

TOOLKIT TIP Although the final file here is still in RGB color space mode, you can print JPEG and TIF files locally to your ink jet printer for a "soft" proof of your work to check for composition and relative color or to give the client an idea of the completed product. You can also send your JPEG file (still in the computer's default RGB color space mode) to a client electronically. If you are sending files electronically, keep the file sizes under 3 MB to minimize download time; less is better. Understand that the client's computer setup, or the network the client is on, may have a low tolerance for downloading files over 3 MB, unless you can FTP to a provider's server.

PREPARING THE AD FOR PRESS

As a last step, since all editing has been done while in RGB color mode, and the completed ad will be sent to a commercial printer, a duplicate file needs to be created of the *KayakMERGE.tif* file, and it needs to be converted to CMYK color mode. In most instances, a commercial printer will need an image converted to CMYK color, but always keep the RGB image as back-up or for future editing. The printer may need all image layers merged or combined into one layer for production purposes (always check with them regarding their preferences). To send images to press, only send TIF or EPS files, or high-resolution PDF files.

TOOLKIT TIP For high-resolution, high-quality commercial printing, better text quality for combining text and graphics images is accomplished by opening or "placing" your image file in Illustrator, and using Illustrator's vector text, then outputting to EPS format. We'll cover this in detail later in Unit 3 Digital Illustration.

Next, you will learn the procedure to prepare a CMYK file with a TIF extension.

1. Open the *KayakMERGE.tif* file, then select Image > Duplicate, and name the file *KayakCMYK;* select OK. The image layers should already be combined and the text layers grouped, but not merged together. Close the *KayakMERGE.tif* file.

2. With the *KayakCMYK* copy displayed, select Image > Mode > CMYK Color to prepare the file for press. If a dialog box displays regarding merging layers, choose to Merge for our purposes here. If another displays regarding your profile, choose to keep the current profile you have on your computer.

3. Save the duplicate file as *KayakCMYK.tif* using the default settings in the *Chapter 5* folder (Figure 5-34). You'll notice the CMYK mode will also be displayed in the title bar.

▷   FIGURE 5-34

After all editing is complete, convert to CMYK color mode for press.

4. Now the ad is ready for press and the RGB file remains as a backup.

5. Although this may seem a little redundant, having back-up copies for specific applications helps to keep you organized. If you performed all the exercises up to this point, you should have these files in your *Chapter 5* folder: *KayakAD.tif, KayakFLAT.jpg, KayakMERGE.tif,* and *KayakCMYK.tif.* Note: Many service providers prefer files that contain both images and text to be saved as EPS. Photoshop has this capability (Save As > Photoshop EPS, leave defaults, click OK) so feel free to add this optional format, although these EPS files are still bitmaps. True EPS files for crisp vector text are best created and saved using Illustrator.

6. Feel free to use Adobe Bridge to compare properties and determine which files would suit your needs for specific purposes.

OPTIONAL: SOFT PROOF PRINTING TO YOUR LOCAL COLOR PRINTER

When printing graphic files to your ink-jet printer, you are printing what is called a *soft proof* that hopefully matches your accurate monitor's screen. This is usually a three-step process. When you select File > Print, a display opens that provides a variety settings for your image and to the printer you are using. In the Print Settings section, you determine the page size, which printer to use, and the format (portrait or landscape); then, in the Color Management section, you set up how the color will match the final proof; you can then find and select other options before sending to your local printer. It is a good idea to create a soft proof in CMYK mode, as you find slight color variations from RGB monitor mode, especially in greens and blues; then, you may need to correct these hues. This exercise is optional if you have access to a local printer; otherwise, feel free to continue to the next exercise.

These steps will give you some ideas in setting up your printer to use as a soft proof device of your design. Some of these descriptions are not shown in earlier versions.

1. Open your *KayakCMYK.tif* file if it is not displayed and select File > Print to open the printer settings dialog box.

2. When the Print Settings dialog box displays, in the Printer Setup section, locate your local printer; leave the Layout at Portrait orientation. Leave the Print Settings button with its default settings (Figure 5-35).

3. In the Position and Size section, place a check in the Center box to keep the image centered in the page for our purposes here. If this is left unchecked, you can move the image around with your mouse.

4. Your desktop printer will already have special paper profiles already installed for the type of paper you are using. You can also find special paper setting information with the type of special paper you have purchased. In the Color Management section, use the Printer Manages Colors setting, as it is usually the most accurate for your intended printer.

▷ FIGURE 5-35

Print settings in the Print dialog box.

5. Also, you want to keep the Rendering Intent to the default Relative Colorimetric for images with text. This helps to preserve more of the original colors for your graphics work.

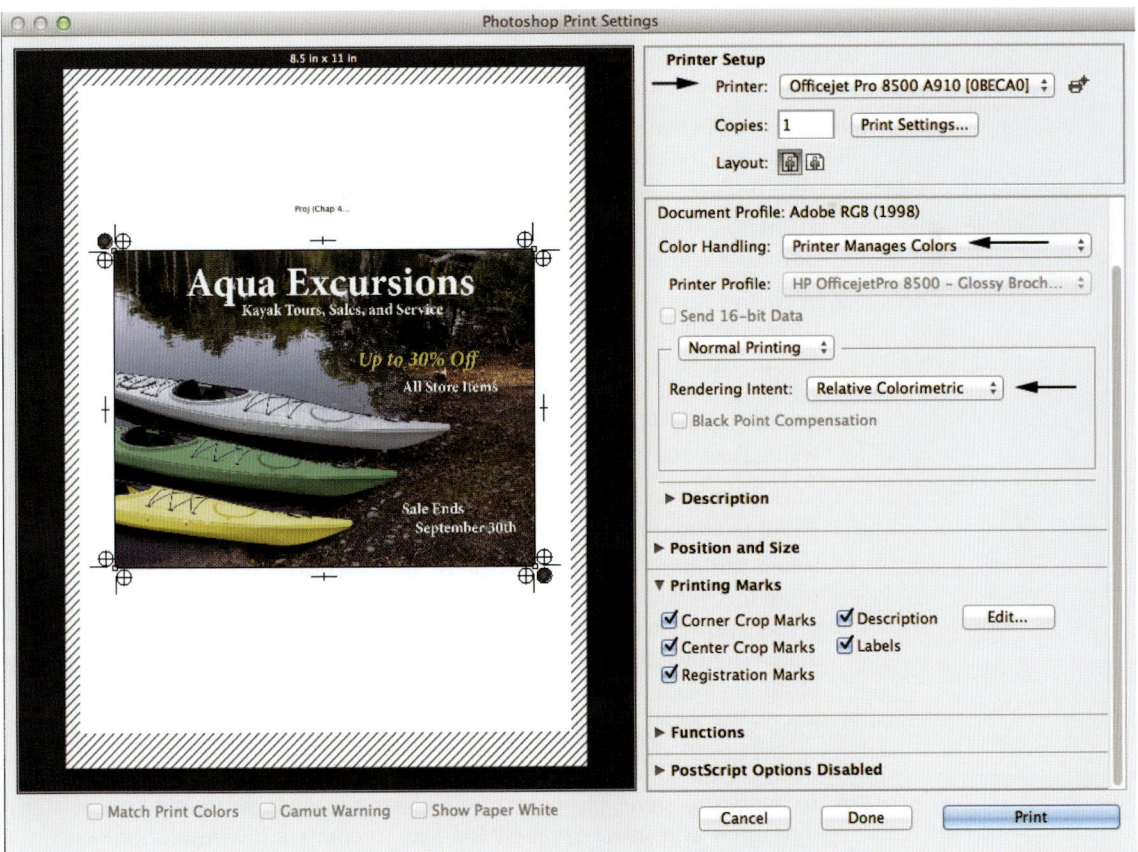

6. To give you an idea of various printer's marks you can place for your service provider to use as a reference, you can click on all boxes in the Printing Marks section. In our example, there is not a provision made for trimming (called bleeds, which we'll cover later), which is helpful when using these marks, but this will provide an insight to what a printer service may ask for you to provide.

7. With all your settings made, select Print on the dialog box. Leave the file open for the next exercise.

CREATING PDF FILES FOR PRESS AND FOR CLIENT COMMUNICATION

Most applications use the universal form of Portable Document Format (PDF) files to communicate. Most commercial press establishments and clients prefer communicating in this format, because anyone can open and see your exact layout, including images and fonts. In Photoshop you can save layered files in the Photoshop PDF format, and anyone can view them with the free Adobe Reader you downloaded in Chapter 1 without having to use any graphic applications. PDF files retain all formatting used in the document, and you can also use this method to create flattened PDF files for electronic distribution and as a high-resolution CMYK file that can be used for commercial printing. You can save a PDF file as a CMYK copy without having to worry about going through the Image menu to convert it; and it will automatically produce a CMYK version that can be printed or distributed electronically. We will cover more on PDF files in Chapter 10.

Next, you will create a PDF document in Photoshop for electronic distribution to the client and make a high-resolution copy for the commercial press.

1. Open the *KayakCMYK.tif* file, then select Image > Duplicate, and name the file *KayakPDF*, then select OK. The image layers should already be flattened into one layer. Close the *KayakCMYK* file.

2. With the *KayakPDF* copy displayed, select File > Save As >Photoshop PDF. When the display box opens, make sure you check Save As a Copy, Use Proof Setup: Working CMYK, and Embed Color profile U.S. Web coated (SWOP) to create a CMYK copy ready for press (Figure 5-36). By selecting to embed a CMYK profile, Photoshop will automatically open a display box indicating it will make a copy. This helps to preserve the previous file.

3. Click Save to save in your *Chapter 5* folder. If you get a warning dialog box about overriding current settings, just click OK to continue.

4. When the Preset dialog box opens, select to save as Press Quality if you are sending the file to a commercial printer, and uncheck where it asks about preserving Photoshop's editing capabilities, which will prevent someone from inadvertently editing it. It will save so that someone who has an earlier version of Adobe Reader (version 5) will be able to read it.

5. Click Save PDF to convert the file. Go ahead and locate the file and double-click it to open the Adobe Reader application and take a look at it.

6. To send the same file to a client electronically, you would repeat steps 1 through 4 and select Smallest File Size to create a low-resolution version. Go ahead give it a shot, and save it as *KayakPDF2*.

Saving for Press Quality preset when ready for commercial press

▷ FIGURE 5-36

Saving final files as press quality PDFs for commercial press.

7. Prepare to zip all your files into one folder. Make a folder on the desktop labeled *ZIP CH5* and drag all your completed image files from your *Chapter 5* folder. If you performed all the exercises in this chapter, you should have these files in your *Chapter 5* folder: *KayakAD.tif, KayakFLAT.jpg, KayakMERGE.tif, KayakCMYK.tif,* and *KayakPDF.pdf.,* to show you the importance of proper labeling to help you in organizing your workflow.

8. For Mac users, Ctrl-click on the *ZIP CH5* folder, and select Compress "ZIP CH5." A copy with a ZIP icon is created that can now be sent as a file attachment. For Windows users, right-click on the *ZIP CH5* folder, and select Send To > Compressed (zipped) Folder. The folder is now ready to be sent to your client.

TOOLKIT TIP If you download the latest free version of Adobe Reader, you have several options. You can add comments to documents, upload the file to be printed and sent through FedEx/Kinkos, and much more.

ADVANCED USERS: Special Layering Creations Using Adjustment Layers, Layer Masks, and Custom Shapes

When making special changes or creations to original images, most designers want the ability to be able make those changes while keeping the original image intact. Using layer masks and adjustment layers in Photoshop allows designers to evaluate different effects, which will have no impact on the original layer. Although Photoshop is used primarily in the creation of bitmap images, it also provides designers the availability of vector shapes, which can also be set up on their own individual layers, like text and image layers.

EDITING WITH NON-DESTRUCTIBLE LAYER MASKS AND ADJUSTMENT LAYERS

▷ FIGURE 5-37

Using adjustment layers and masks to create special compositions.

Here is a project that uses the concept of **layer masks**, which allow parts of an edited image to display (white area of mask), and block portions of an edited image from displaying (black area of mask) with various layers. This project also involves the use of adjustment Layers, using the Adjustments panel to create layers of special adjustments without editing any pixels on the original layers. Using adjustment layers allows you to experiment with various effects without harming the original image. A designer or photographer would then create various layer masks to isolate the effects on certain selected areas of an image. In this project you are going to select the flag, increase the vibrancy of the colors, save the selection, then invert the selection to convert the background into an accurately B&W toned image, to emphasize the colors of the flag (Figure 5-37).

ISOLATING FLAG USING SELECTION TOOLS OR PAINTING QUICK MASK

Here you'll create a selection of the flag area using selection tools or try painting a mask using the Quick Mask Tool on the Tools panel.

1. Launch Photoshop and open the *Patriot.tif* file from your *Chapter 5* folder. Make sure the Adjustments, Properties (Masks panel in earlier versions), and Layers panels are displayed.

2. Create a duplicate of the file and name it *PatriotADJ.tif*. Save in the *Chapter 5* folder.

3. Zoom in at 200%. Use either the Quick Select, Magic Wand, and Lasso tools to start selecting the flag.

4. Create an alpha selection channel (Select > Save Selection > Channel) of the selected flag and name it *Flag*.

5. To continue on the fine details of your selection, make sure the flag is still selected, then go ahead and select the Quick Mask at the bottom of the Tools panel (Figure 5-38), select a Brush at 100% Opacity to paint Black as the foreground color to "add to" (red overlay mask) the selection of the flag, and White to remove areas that should not be part of the selection.

6. Use the bracket keys on your keyboard for selecting quick brush sizes. Remember painting with white reveals, and painting with black conceals or masks the effect.

7. In using the Quick Mask option, to display the selection, just toggle the button to get back to Standard mode, watch for the red mask and the red portion of the flag.

▷ FIGURE 5-38

Use the selection tools, or Quick Mask as shown, to paint in the flag selection.

 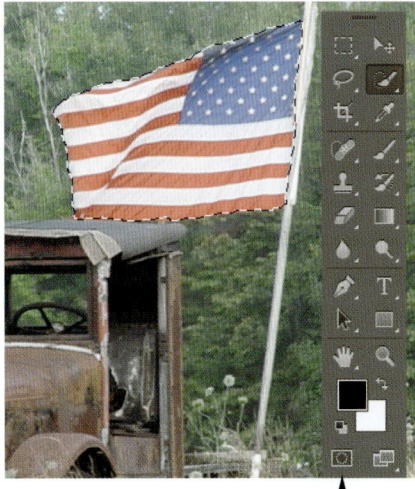

Quick Mask Mode Standard Mode

8. When all areas of the flag are selected accurately, save the selection again as *Flag* (Select > Save Selection) and choose the Flag channel you just created, making sure Replace Channel is selected to replace the previous Flag selection channel.

9. Toggle the Quick Mask button to display the Standard mode, with the flag showing the selection marquee (Figure 5-38).

▷ FIGURE 5-39

Saving the selection as a channel and adjusting the edge of the mask of the flag outline.

10. Select one of the selection tools and click on the Refine Edge button on the Tool Options bar. Choose the On Black View mask and create a fairly sharp edge for the contrast between the color flag and the new B&W background you are going to create. Use the settings as a guide, tabbing between settings (Figure 5-39). Click OK.

CREATING ADJUSTMENT LAYERS AND LAYER MASKS WITH THE PROPERTIES AND ADJUSTMENTS PANELS

Using **adjustment layers** within an image allows a designer to create a series of layered effects over the original image that are non-destructible, so that the pixels in the original image are not manipulated. Adjustment layers have their effects on their own individual layers and can easily be edited. The **layer mask** provides a window for these effects as they trickle down through the layers, giving total control to the user. The **Adjustments panel** works alongside the Properties panel in that the Adjustments panel creates adjustment layers of a selected area, which displays as the white area, and as a part of a layer mask on the Properties panel. Both adjustment layer and layer mask of the selected area are displayed in their own layer on the Layers panel. As you hover your mouse over various icons on the Adjustments panel, their title functions are displayed. They provide a quick and easy way to create the most widely used Adjustment layers. You can also create fill and adjustment layers from the adjustment layer icon at the bottom of the Layers panel (icon looks like a half moon). As you create multiple adjustment layers on your Layers panel, just click on each individually and they will display in the Properties panel for their own particular color adjustments and mask selection adjustments in one place. The **Properties panel** provides a one-stop place to change selection properties of layer masks and color toning properties of adjustment layers. It shows the layer vector mask on the highlighted or selected layer. It can select by color range too so that a designer can adjust the same color tones in an image. The Properties panel can invert or reverse a selection, and it defines the selection edges using the Mask Edge function.

The **Vibrance command** adjusts color saturation on selected portions of an image. Vibrance controls the intensity of saturated colors. It adjusts the saturation so that clipping is minimized as colors approach full saturation. There is also a Vibrance command in the Adjustments menu (Image > Adjustments > Vibrance).

TOOLKIT TIP The Layers panel has adjustment layers and masks you can create by selecting the appropriate icon at the bottom of the panel. The process is relatively the same as discussed in these exercises using the Adjustments and Properties panels; in earlier versions new panels just make the workflow much easier than was done previously using the Layers panel. If you are using an earlier version of Photoshop, you can still perform the exercises below using the Masks panel when the Properties panel is addressed.

Here you will increase the saturation and vibrancy of the selected flag image.

1. Make sure the flag is selected. Select > Load Selection > Flag.

2. Select the Adjustments panel, and then select the Vibrance icon (looks like an inverted triangle) that reads Create a new Vibrance adjustment layer. You'll notice a new adjustment layer is created with a layer mask of the flag next to the thumbnail image of the Vibrance icon on the Layers panel.

3. Notice also, in the new Properties panel, that the settings display for the Vibrance adjustment layer, and the Masks icon displays, allowing you to make adjustments for color and selection on the fly.

4. In the Properties panel, select the Vibrance icon and increase the saturation and vibrancy of the colors (Figure 5-40). The background outside the selection layer mask is not affected.

5. Since both the Vibrance adjustment layer and the layer mask are on the same layer in the Layers panel, and are coordinated with the Properties panel, you

Adjustments Panel

Vibrance adjustment layer
in Layers Panel

Layer mask with selection
settings in Properties Panel

Vibrance settings in
Properties Panel

Adjusment layer (half moon icon)
at bottom of Layers Panel

▷ FIGURE 5-40

**Creating a
Vibrance adjust-
ment layer on a
selection layer
mask using the
Adjustments
panel in coordi-
nation with the
Properties panel.**

can click on the Vibrance icon to further edit the effect using the Properties panel. When you have your selected portion of your image displayed, and you click on the layer mask on the Layers panel, the Properties panel displays settings you can use to tweak your selection, including selecting by Color Range.

6. Deselect the selection on the image when done. Notice the Layer mask still displays on the Layers and Properties panels. They remain as permanent layers.

USING THE ADJUSTMENT PANEL'S "HAND TOOL" FOR PRECISE TONING

You can add many different adjustment layers as needed for various effects on the Layers panel. The Properties panel, in addition to providing many different effects to choose from, also provides preset settings of each selected adjustment layer, which gives you the ability to customize your own presets on many of these effects. The Properties panel's individual adjustment layer settings may have a special "hand" tool on some of its display boxes that when following the indicated arrows, lets you make tonal adjustments over a small area that you drag over in the direction of the arrows. This allows you to make quick accurate adjustments on the fly with little effort. You can call this the "Adjustment Hand Tool" if you like. The Properties panel also allows you to invert or reverse a selection area or mask (Figure 5-41). Note: The adjustments using this "Hand Tool" can be found in earlier versions on the Adjustments panel.

Select Black and White

Selection of flag before invert

Invert the flag selection to
display b&w background

Adjustment layers and layer masks
created over original layer image

▷ FIGURE 5-41

**Black and White
adjustment layer,
and inverting flag
selection using
Properties Panel.
Adjustment layers and
layer masks on indi-
vidual layers to con-
trol desired effects.**

In this exercise, you are going to invert the selection using the Properties panel,
and create a well-toned B&W background using the panel's hand tool.

1. With the image open, load the Flag selection you created earlier (Select > Load
   Selection > Channel - Flag > OK).

2. Select the Black & White adjustment layer icon from the Adjustments panel.
   Don't worry if the flag is black; we're going to invert the selection.

3. With the Black and White adjustment layer created and highlighted on the
   Layers panel, select the Masks icon on the Properties panel to display the layer
   mask. Select the Invert button to inverse the flag selection, which will become
   the new background selection (Figure 5-41).

4. The background should be B&W and the colors of the flag should remain.

5. Click the Black and White Icon (top left) in the Properties panel to display the
   Black and White Adjustments panel. You can choose one of the B&W presets
   on the Properties panel, or find the "Hand Tool" in the corresponding Black
   and White adjustments panel (not the Tools panel). Select on a small area and
   drag sideways as indicated by the arrows, and create your own visual B&W
   toning. As you drag the sliders over different areas of the image, the hand tool
   senses color tones in that particular area and will lighten and darken those
   tones and cover all selected tones in the image (Figure 5-42). Very cool!

6. Save the completed image as *PatriotADJ.tif* with its layers in your *Chapter 5* folder.

7. With the adjustment layers and layer masks saved, you can come back to the
   image at any time and edit the adjustment icon by clicking on it, or the mask
   itself by clicking on it.

Drag sideways

"Adjustment
Tool"

Black and White Adjustments Panel

▷ FIGURE 5-42

Creating a well-toned black and white background using the Black & White Properties panel's hand "Adjustment Tool."

TOOLKIT TIP Just as was done years ago in a chemical darkroom, slightly lightening and darkening on selected parts of an image can be done digitally using the Dodge, Burn, or Sponge tools. Photoshop has greatly enhanced these tools to provide accurate lightening, saturating, and darkening of the tones of an image. Go ahead and try these tools on either the new *PatriotADJ* file you just created, on the original color *Patriot* file, or on your own work to see how you can carefully and precisely tone an image using these improved tools!

CREATING A FIGURE ILLUSTRATION

Creating figure illustrations, or diagrams, like those used in this book may involve using various screen copies, text layers, and shape tools, and combining them into one composite of multiple layers that can be moved around with the Move Tool. **Shape tools** are paths created as vector shapes that can be resized without losing any edge sharpness and can also be selected, moved, and adjusted with the **Path Selection Tool (A)**. There's also a **Custom Shape Tool (U)** with a preset display panel toolbox of premade custom shapes. In Photoshop Creative Cloud (CC), designers can resize each corner of a rounded rectangle, and align shapes, images, and text using **Smart Guides**. These guides will display when you are using the Move Tool (V) or the Path Selection Tool (A). Here you will create a basic figure diagram on the shape tools we are discussing involving composite layers of screen copy images, custom shapes, and basic labeling (Figure 5-43). This will serve as a precursor for working with vector shapes, which we will cover in more detail in the Adobe Illustrator chapters.

▷ FIGURE 5-43

Using smart guides for accurate placement of images, creating separate image layers.

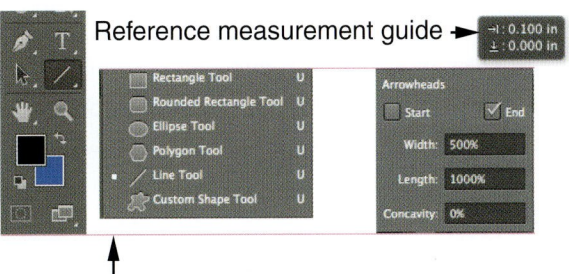

Reference measurement guide

Smart Guides for alignment

CREATING SEPARATE IMAGE LAYERS

You can take various screen copy images, or parts of images, and drag onto a new document using the Move Tool (V). This allows each image to have its own layer, so you can adjust each image individually or link with other layers as we demonstrated in Chapter 5 with the kayaks. Image screen copies are supplied here, but you can always create your own.

In this exercise, you are going to drag in images of various screen copies of dialog boxes and the Tools panel to create separate layers, and align using Smart Guides.

1. First, launch Photoshop and create a new document into which you'll move all the screen copy images. Select File > New > Preset Size of U.S. Paper: Letter (8.5x11 inches) > Resolution 150 dpi > White Background. Normally for print you would create at least a 150 dpi document. Name the file *Shapes*.

2. Make sure rulers are displayed around the image or select View > Rulers. These can be helpful to keep you oriented. Use the Window menu to activate the Layers, History, and Properties panels. Use the Window > Arrange > Consolidate All to Tabs option to keep all documents in one place for easier moving.

3. Open the files *Tools Panel.tif*, *Arrowhead.tif*, and *Shape Tools.tif*, from the *Screen Copies* folder inside your *Chapter 5 folder*.

4. Use the Move Tool (V) to select the *Tools Panel.tif* image and drag onto the *Shapes* document about 2 inches below the top of the document, then drag the *Shape Tools.tif* image onto the same document about a quarter inch alongside the Line Tool displayed on the Tools panel.

5. To see how the Smart Guides feature works (View > Show > Smart Guides), in Photoshop CC, drag the *Arrowhead.tif* image onto the Shapes document so that the bottom of the image aligns with the bottom of the Tools Panel. As you hold down your mouse and drag, a little measurement display box with reference measurement guides will display, release when the vertical distance reaches 1.0, and horizontal line reads as 0.0. You can see how this new feature can help with precise alignment (Figure 5-43).

6. Close the files *Tools Panel.tif*, *Arrowhead.tif*, and *Shape Tools.tif*, leaving the new *Shapes* document open with all the images as separate layers. As you add images or files into a new document, Photoshop creates a new layer for each image.

7. Rename these new layers *Tools Panel*, *Arrowhead*, *Shape Tools*, in the Layers panel.

8. Save the file as *Shapes.tif* in your *Chapter 5* folder.

CREATING CUSTOM SHAPES AND SHAPE LAYERS

Like type lines, shapes can also be placed on separate layers. In Photoshop Creative Cloud (CC), rounded rectangle shapes can have individual corners adjusted. Not only can you fill in shapes with color, you can adjust the outline on the shape, or its stroke color using either the Shape Tool Options bar of the selected shape, the Path Selection Tool (A) to select the outlining edges of the shape, or the Properties panel. You can select a Shape Tool (U), and decide to click and drag and make adjustments afterwards, or just click on the document and type in measurements.

Creating a Custom Rounded Rectangle Shape

Photoshop Creative Cloud (CC) lets you create rounded rectangles with precision; you can adjust each corner independently, and Smart Guides help in aligning your images and vector objects. To outline the edge of the shape, you can apply a stroke color from the Shape Tool Options bar, or from the Properties panel.

In this exercise, you will use the Rounded Rectangle Tool (U) to create different corner sizes (Photoshop CC), and create a stroke to outline the shape. You'll then create a subtle layer style drop shadow on your shape and screen copy images.

1. Select a yellow or light color fill in the Tools panel. Click on the Shape Tool displayed (under the Type Tool) and select the Rounded Rectangle Tool (U).

2. Click once on the document to bring up the shape's dialog box. Type in the Width and Height at 200 px (pixels), and adjust the top corners to "32 px," and bottom corners to "10 px," or you can also drag sideways (hand adjustment icon) to make the number as well. (In earlier versions, just create a rounded rectangle.) Click OK.

3. The new shape will display on your document. In the Tool Options bar (or Properties panel), choose a deep blue or dark color to outline your custom shape in the Stroke box and make the size 1 pt. The shape is displayed on its own layer (Figure 5-44). You can also select your shape with the Path Selection Tool (A) for any future editing.

4. You can move shapes with the Move Tool (V) or the Path Selection Tool (A). Drag your new custom shape until the top aligns using the Smart Guides with the top of the Tools panel.

5. To practice using layer styles again, using the Layers panel, select the Layer Styles icon and create a drop shadow layer style effect for each screen copy layer and your custom shape layer, to help outline the individual boxes a little. Use the settings of a Normal Blend, 130-degree Angle, using Global Light, 75% Opacity, with the Distance, Speed, and Size set at 5 for each.

▷ FIGURE 5-44

Creating special sized corners and a stroke outline in custom rounded rectangle shape.

6. Once you create the effect for one layer, just hold down the Option\Alt key, click on the Effects sublayer, and drag to "copy" the effect from one layer to the next. Make sure you only select the Effects sublayer and drag, and not the entire layer.

7. Save the file in your *Chapter 5* folder.

TOOLKIT TIP Smart Guides can provide smart spacing to space multiple shapes equidistant from one another. With one layer selected, if you press the Command/Ctrl key while hovering over another layer, the Reference Measurement Guides will display. If you hold down the Option/Alt key while dragging a layer, the Reference Measurement Guides will display the distance between the duplicate layer and the original layer.

Using Preset Custom Shapes

There are premade custom shapes you can pick from when you select the Custom Shapes Tool (U), and then select the down arrow next to Shape: to display the custom shapes panel in the Tool Options bar. You'll also find more examples if you click on the gear icon in the custom shapes display panel. You can also place one shape layer over another and stack them to rearrange as needed.

Here you will place a premade custom shape over the Rounded Rectangle shape you created in the previous exercise.

1. Select the Move Tool (V) to start a new layer, select the Custom Shape Tool (U) and in the Tool Options bar, then click the downward arrow next to Shape: to view your choices in the custom shapes display panel. We chose Fleur-De-Lis for our example (Figure 5-45).

Using the Custom Shape Tool (U) to select premade custom shape and place over other shape.

Custom Shape Tool

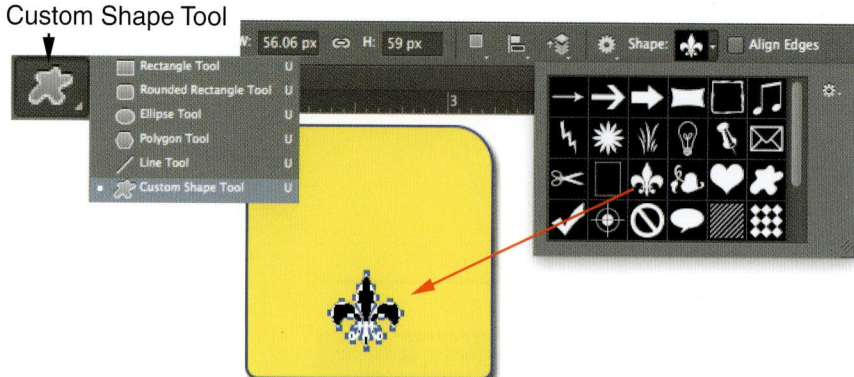

2. Select one, hold the Shift key down to constrain proportions, then click and drag near the lower portion of your rounded rectangle shape. Use the smart guides to help you find the centerline and release. Select and adjust color if needed.

3. Save the file in your *Chapter 5* folder.

TOOLKIT TIP If you make a mistake, you can drag the layer into the Trash or you can select the Path Selection Tool on the Tools panel, select the shape to be removed, and press the Delete key.

Creating Custom Arrowheads

We're going to make some arrows pointing to lead the viewer's eye to different components of the figure—something you find quite often in any labeling diagram. You use the Line Tool (U) and then select the gear icon on the Tool Options bar, where you can set up how it will display. Use the Shift key while you drag to create straight arrows. Holding the Shift key down gives straight horizontal, vertical, and 45-degree angle lines.

Here you will create arrows to help in identifying what shape tools are being used in this figure.

1. To create an arrowhead, select the Move Tool (V) to prepare to create another layer. Select the Line Tool (U) from the Shape Tools panel. Change the Fill color to Black or a dark color, and the Stroke to None (red line through box) in the Tool Options bar, use a weight of 2 pixels.

2. Select the gear icon on the Tool Options bar, making sure the End arrowhead is checked so that you can drag toward where you want the arrowhead to aim (Figure 5-46). The Concavity is the curvature of the bottom of the arrowhead, which we left at "0."

3. To make the arrow, hold the Shift key down, click on the Shape Tools image, and drag from the Line Tool description toward the Arrowheads dialog box on the document. Release the mouse before releasing the Shift key. If none or only part of your arrow displays, just drag the layer to the top. Feel free to experiment with different arrowhead settings.

▷ FIGURE 5-46

Using the Line Shape Tool to create vector arrows to identify processes and locations for labeling.

Line Tool

Arrowhead Settings

Position of arrows

4. To create another arrow to identify the rounded rectangle shape, first, select the Move Tool (V) again to place on a separate layer. Otherwise both arrow shapes will share the same layer. Drag from the Rounded Rectangle Tool description to the shape you created (freehand). If you need to select the arrowhead shape, select the layer with the Path Selection Tool (A) and adjust position. You could also use the Move Tool (V) or the arrow keys on your keyboard to adjust position.

5. The third arrow you will draw towards the custom shape you just placed in your rounded rectangle shape. Select the Move Tool (V) to create a separate layer, and then hold down the Shift key and drag outside the rounded rectangle shape towards the custom shape.

6. Save the file in your *Chapter 5* folder.

LABELING YOUR FIGURE ILLUSTRATION

With all shapes created and adjusted, it's time to label. You can create text lines inside shapes as well. Use the Smart Guides (Photoshop CC) to help with alignment of text. When creating any figure for publication, you also need to have a figure description or caption to accompany your illustration.

Here you will label the important components of your figure diagram to help your viewer understand the process, and a figure description underneath.

1. To make a quick statement inside the custom rectangle shape you created, select the Type Tool (T) with a black or dark color 14-pt Trebuchet font, bold, center aligned, with a sharp anti-alias on the Tool Options bar (or choose your own font, if you want).

2. Press the Return/Enter key once, type the line "*It's the,*" hit the Return/Enter key, and type "*Shape Tools!*" Use the Move Tool to position the type inside the custom shape (Figure 5-47). Make sure the type layer is above the *Shape 1* layer on the Layers panel or the text will not display. You can also link the shape layer and its type layer to move both together for further alignment.

DESIGN TIP

When you have a light color, don't use light type inside it (and vice versa); use a dark colored sans-serif type or opposite tone for contrast. Sans serif text is easier to read, especially in labeling. When creating figure illustrations, provide just enough information for the user to understand the message you are conveying. Sometimes less is more.

▷ FIGURE 5-47

Completed figure illustration diagram using custom shapes and composite layering techniques.

3. To label the Shape Tools panel, select the Type Tool (T) with a black 10-pt Arial regular font, center aligned, and a sharp anti-alias. Type the label "*Shape Tools*" under the image, then select the Move Tool (V) and position the text line to start another text layer.

4. To label the Arrowheads image from the Line Tool, type the label "*Arrowhead Settings*," hit the Return/Enter key, and type "(*Line Tool*)" under the arrowhead settings image. Select the Move Tool (V) and position the text line.

5. To label the Custom Shape, type in front of the arrow "*Custom Shape Tool*," then use the Move Tool (V) to position.

6. Finally to write a figure description or caption, left-align the text and type the first line "*Figure 5-XX*," hit the Return/Enter key, and type the second line underneath, "*Photoshop shape tools create custom vector shapes.*"

7. Save your completed *Shapes.tif* file in your *Chapter 5* folder. To save an EPS copy in your *Chapter 5* folder, as if submitting for a high-quality print run, keep the file name as *Shapes* and choose File > Save As > Photoshop EPS. Leave at defaults and press OK. The new EPS file (*Shapes.eps*) should not be opened in Photoshop, but in a vector program like Illustrator.

Saving in Photoshop EPS Format

For figure illustrations that contain large shapes and small amounts of text for labeling, as in in this tutorial, saving your file as a TIF extension should be fine for most applications. Although this topic will be covered more in the next unit in Digital Illustration using Illustrator, usually when combining text and graphics, most commercial printers, for high quality or a large quantity of work, prefer files to be saved in EPS (or PDF) format. Photoshop has a Photoshop EPS format, although the text is still rasterized and treated as a bitmap if opened in Photoshop, but can be opened in Illustrator with better clarity. Placing the Photoshop image in Adobe Illustrator, creating vector text in Illustrator and saving as EPS, best accomplishes sharpest text. To compare the two types of files, print the *Shapes.tif* file in Photoshop, and then open the *Shapes.eps* file in Illustrator and print. You may find a slight difference in clarity. Do not open the *Shapes.eps* file in Photoshop as it will rasterize the text and shapes as a bitmap and may make the text and shapes appear fuzzy.

TOOLKIT TIP When labeling diagrams or figures, keep the weight of the line or arrow to no less than 1 pixel for publishing. Labels are usually 10-pt black type fonts that may have capitalization of the first letter in each word if it is a particular named item like a tool. When providing a description or figure caption, type as a regular sentence. Having a Sharp Anti-alias setting helps to keep most type easily readable for most uses, however when working with vector illustrations or text, Illustrator is preferred for high-quality work. When providing a figure description or caption, have the figure with the chapter number and the sequential number (Figure 5-10), where the "5" is the chapter number and "10" is the tenth figure in the chapter.

DIGITAL TOOLKIT EXTRA: Image Transformations Using Content-Aware Fill, Content-Aware Scale, Content-Aware Move, and the Color Replacement Tool

Sometimes you need to make radical changes to your image to make it stand out. You may find parts of the image may be distracting and need to be removed. You may have need for the image to fit a client's specific dimension, which may involve accurately stretching or shrinking the image without ruining the original components. Sometimes slightly rearranging subjects in a photograph can create a whole new concept within the image. Photoshop has Content-Aware tools and techniques to sense surrounding pixels to blend in elements of an image. In previous exercises you replaced colors on reflective projects using the Hue/Saturation command. There is also the Color Replacement Tool (B), which when used in conjunction with the Eyedropper Tool (I), can accurately replace color in fabric products and can be used as a corrective tool in removing rust or stains in an outdoor structure.

USING CONTENT-AWARE FILL IN REMOVING BACKGROUND DISTRACTIONS

▷ FIGURE 5-48

The Content-Aware Fill technique used with the Spot Healing Brush removes elements and fills in with surrounding background elements.

The **Content-Aware Fill** command has the ability to remove an image element and replace it with details that blend in closely to match the lighting, tone, and image elements of the surrounding area. It is used when you decide to select the area you want to remove, press the delete key, and choose the Content-Aware Fill option in the dialog box. This technique works best with cluttered or open backgrounds that don't have a pattern, such as background trees, or sky area. You can use Content-Aware Fill in conjunction with the Spot Healing Brush for optimum results. The **Spot Healing Brush** analyzes the parts of the image and blends into surrounding pixels. This tool will be covered in depth in the next chapter. You can see its usefulness and its limitation with this exercise. In many cases, it is best to have all color adjustments and toning already done before removing.

Here you have a rather complex photo that needs a lot of removal of distracting components. You will select certain areas, and use the Content-Aware Fill option to remove most of these problems. Be aware that the final results will not be perfect.

1. Open the file *Badbridge.tif* from your *Chapter 5* folder. You will notice lots of distractions. Duplicate the image (Image > Duplicate) and save the file as *BadbridgeFILL.tif* in your *Chapter 5* folder. Close the original *Badbridge* file.

2. Using your Lasso Tool, make a close selection around the left top sign as shown in Figure 5-48 in the previous page. Less is better when using this technique.

3. Press the Delete key on your keyboard, and when the Fill dialog box comes up, choose Content-Aware, then click OK. You will find the sign replaced with the surrounding trees. Deselect when done. It is not perfect, but shows what can be done. If you press the Delete key and the Fill dialog box <u>does not</u> come up, choose Edit > Fill, and you can select the Content-Aware menu item from there.

4. Select the second sign down and repeat the process. You may find that you may want to undo (Cmnd/CTRL+Z, or Edit > Step Backward) a few times to try practicing to get this technique more accurate. Deselect when done. The sign in front of the fence will not work well because it is a pattern that Content-Aware Fill will not adjust to accurately so it will have to stay.

5. Select the Spot Healing Brush, with a 15 pixel brush for starters, and simply click inside or around the outside area that was filled and you will find it starts to help to blend in nicely. You may find again that it will take frequent attempts to get it realistic looking (love the undo functions!). Avoid having repetitive patterns from the brush and try to keep the background blending in nicely.

6. You can use the Spot Healing Brush (J) to delicately cover the bottom portion of the left sign with copied flowers, and hide a portion of the left side house behind the bridge. Be careful you don't copy the bridge edge, or just undo and try again.

7. You can use the Content-Aware Fill feature to initially remove selected telephone wires, the house on the right side and the sign (remember to select individual elements to remove), then use the Spot Healing Brush Tool (J) to fill in the edges. You can see the right side is much easier and looks probably more realistic initially (Figure 5-49). Deselect when done.

8. This technique takes a lot of patience and practice but can help to make a better image. In Chapter 6, you'll learn other methods of retouching images where you can come back and use to tweak this image. When you feel confident with your image here, save and close the file.

Original Image   Image with Corrections Applied

USING CONTENT-AWARE SCALE FOR IMAGE RESIZING

Where normal scaling affects all pixels uniformly, the Content-Aware Scale function allows you to resize an image without changing the important elements like people, buildings, animals, etc., by affecting pixels in areas that aren't visually important. This handy tool may help you get out of a jam with a client if the image needs to be a slightly reduced dimension, say from an 8×12 inch full size to 8×10 inch standard size image. You can also create a canvas larger than the original image, move your image onto the larger canvas, and stretch your image to a specific size, say for a panoramic size print. Content-Aware Scale allows you to drag the vertical handle of a selected image and the image's horizontal pixels are blended in without affecting the vertical elements of an image. The opposite holds when dragging the horizontal handle, only the vertical elements are blended. Content-Aware Scale works on layers and selections. As with the Content-Aware Fill function mentioned earlier, the success of this technique depends on the type of image you want to use. Images with simple backgrounds work best.

For this exercise, you will adjust an original image that is roughly 4×6.5 inches, to an image that is 4×5 inch format using the Content-Aware Scale command (Figure 5-50).

1. Open the file *Ship.tif* from your *Chapter 5* folder, duplicate the image (Image > Duplicate), and save the copy as *SCALEShip.tif* in your *Chapter 5* folder. Close the original *Ship* file.

2. Make sure Rulers are displayed; View > Rulers.

3. To scale your image, use the Rectangular Marquee Tool (M) and select the entire image or choose Select > Select All (or Cmnd/CTRL+A).

4. With the entire image selected, choose Edit > Content-Aware Scale and you will find the selection with handles in the corners and middle of each side.

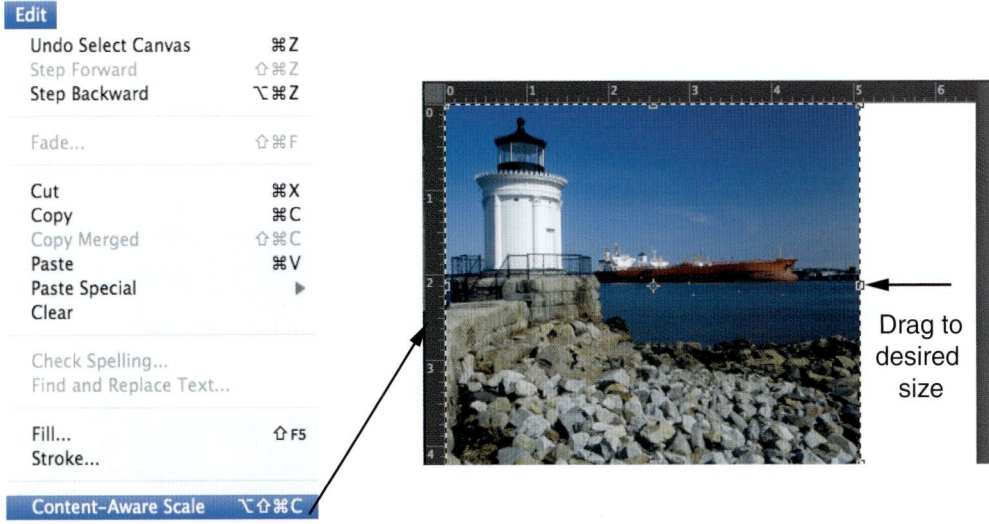

Drag to desired size

▷ FIGURE 5-50

You can use Content-Aware Scale to make resizing adjustments to simple images while maintaining accuracy.

5. Click on the middle vertical handle on the right side and drag inward until you reach the 5-inch mark on the ruler guide (Figure 5-50). Notice the pixels in the horizontal red ship and sky adjust to the change but the vertical lighthouse remains accurately displayed, although it too has been slightly adjusted.

6. Press the Return/Enter key to accept the change. Deselect the selection.

7. Select the Rectangular Marquee Tool (M), select the Style of Normal in the Tool Options bar, and drag over the image, to crop as 4×5. Select Image > Crop to trim the image.

8. Save the file in your *Chapter 5* folder.

To create a panoramic 4×8 inch image, or one that is longer than the original image, you'll need to create an image canvas to the size, then move your original image as a separate layer, and then stretch it.

1. Create a new custom document, which will be at Web resolution for our purposes here (File > New > Preset Custom, Width 8 inches, Height 4 inches, Resolution 200 pixels). Click OK to get your blank document (Figure 5-51).

2. Open the file *Ship.tif* from your *Chapter 5* folder, duplicate the image (Image > Duplicate), and save the copy as *SCALEShip2.tif* in your *Chapter 5* folder. Close the original *Ship.tif* file.

3. Resize both windows of both documents next to one another, select the Move Tool, and drag the *SCALEShip2* image onto the blank canvas aligning it along the left side edge (Figure 5-51). Use the keyboard arrow keys if needed.

4. You'll notice two layers displayed on the Layers panel. Make sure the "Layer 1" is active, then choose Select > Select All (or Cmnd/CTRL+A).

5. With the entire image selected, choose Edit > Content-Aware Scale.

▷ FIGURE 5-51

**You can use
Content-Aware
Scale to create
images larger
than the original
by creating a new
document canvas
to move the image
onto, then stretch
to taste.**

6. If it does not automatically fit into the new dimensions, click on the middle of the vertical handle on the right side and drag outward until you reach the 8-inch mark on the ruler guide (Figure 5-51). Notice again, the pixels in the horizontal red ship and sky adjust to the change but the vertical lighthouse remains accurately displayed, although it too has been slightly adjusted.

7. Press the Return/Enter key to accept the change.

8. When you are ready, flatten the layers (Layer > Flatten Image), and then save the file *SCALEship2.tif* in your *Chapter 5* folder and close the file.

TOOLKIT TIP   When using Content-Aware Fill command, if you press the Delete key and the Fill dialog box <u>does not</u> come up, choose Edit > Fill and you can select the Content-Aware menu item from there. Sometimes this problem occurs when working with multiple layers, where pressing the Delete key on a selected area in a particular layer clears the selected area.

USING THE CONTENT-AWARE MOVE TOOL FOR SUBJECT REPOSITIONING

Using content-aware technology, you now have the ability to select an object and move it into another position in your image without having to use layering techniques. When you move the selected subject with the **Content-Aware Move Tool** (J), the technology senses the surrounding pixels and helps to blend in the subject to the newly adjusted background. You can adjust the adaptation from very strict to very loose to choose how much blending you'd like. You can also choose to have the original location deleted when you move your subject to its new location using Move Mode, or to create a duplicate using Extend Mode. Using Move Mode allows the content-aware technology to sense where the original selected subject is removed from, and it fills in the background there as well. This special effect technique works best with a simple background for the area around the subject to blend in nicely.

In this exercise, you'll move one of New England's rare seacoast birds, a puffin, a little closer to its friends. The trick is to carefully place this bird in its new location so it looks realistic.

1. Open the *Maine Puffins.jpg* file from your *Chapter 5* folder. Zoom to 100%.

▷ FIGURE 5-52

Selecting the Content-Aware Move Tool and repositioning the bird.

2. Using the Lasso Tool (L), make a careful selection around the outside area of the bird on the rightmost part of the image. Do not select the edge of the bird; make the selection on the background surrounding close to the bird. Leave enough room to blend in the background once it's moved.

3. In the Tools panel, where you will find the Spot Healing Brush, select the Content-Aware Move Tool (J). See Figure 5-52 as a guide.

4. In the Tool Options bar, choose a Mode of Move to remove the original image location to blend into the background once the selected image has been placed in its new location, and then choose an Adaptation of Strict to carefully blend in the pixels for a close match (Figure 5-52). Note: A Mode of Extend would allow you to create an exact duplicate and blend the selection into the background.

5. Click the selected bird, and carefully move it along the rock closer to its friends, aligning its foot along the rock edge, and let go. At first, it will appear like you are duplicating the selected image. You'll notice the new location with the bird fills in with the background, and the area where the puffin was moved from is also filled in. This may take a couple of tries until the bird matches perfectly along the rock edge.

6. When you have the bird placed exactly as you want, choose Select > Deselect or Command/CTRL+D to deselect the selection (Figure 5-53).

7. If the blue background displays as a halo around the new bird image, use the Spot Healing Brush with a 10-pixel brush and blend in the edges. In other cases, you might create a layer mask as demonstrated in the Advanced Users section before, and paint out the surrounding background.

8. Save the file as *Moved_Puffin.jpg* in your *Chapter 5* folder.

▷ FIGURE 5-53

Using Content-Aware Move Tool to reposition selected subjects.

Original Image

Content-Aware Move to Reposition Subject

REPLACING COLOR WITH THE EYEDROPPER TOOL AND COLOR REPLACEMENT TOOL

The **Color Replacement Tool** (B) is used in conjunction with the **Eyedropper Tool** (I) to replace color in a selected area, by simply painting where you want to make the change. This tool works best with fabric-textured products, on small areas of a product, or as a retouching tool (Figure 5-54). The first step in replacing color is to select an area of color to be replaced, then use the Eyedropper Tool to sample color from either the Swatches panel or Color panel, or from a part of an another image. The **Swatches panel** is a selection of predefined colors from

▷ FIGURE 5-54

Using the Eyedropper and Color Replacement tools to replace colors in products and for corrective measures.

which you can select a color and paint. The **Color panel** is a blend of colors or hues of color you can also select from. These panels will be covered more in depth in the next chapter. When you sample a color with the Eyedropper Tool, it displays in the Fill box of the Tools panel. To paint the new color, select the Color Replacement Tool (B), which can be found inside the Brush tool area of the Tools panel, and simply brush over the selected area. The color maintains the selected area's tonality with highlights and shadows for accurate reproduction.

Replacing Color on Fabric

Replacing Color as a Corrective Method

REPLACING COLOR ON A PRODUCT

Here you'll see how to use the Eyedropper Tool (I) to select a color from the Swatches panel, and then use the Color Replacement Tool (B) to change the color on a product fabric.

▷ FIGURE 5-55

Select area to be covered with combination of selection tools, then select Refine Edge to soften edge pixels.

Quick Selection Tool
Eyedropper Tool
Color Replacement Tool

1. Open the image *Backpack.tif* in your *Chapter 5* folder. Duplicate the file (Image > Duplicate) and name the duplicate *BackpackCOLOR*. Close the original *Backpack.tif* file.

2. Start selections using the Quick Selection Tool (W), or Magic Wand Tool (W), for starters. Then zoom in close and use one of the Lasso (L) selection tools to complete the selected area of color you want to change. You can even choose the Quick Mask method. In the example of Figure 5-55, we chose to select the gray areas of fabric.

3. Use the Refine Edge button in the Tool Options bar from any selection tool to soften your selection edges. Start off with one of the masks, possibly the white background, a Smart Radius of 2 pixels, and slightly adjust settings to soften the edges, then select OK when done.

4. To save the selection as a channel, choose Select > Save Selection, name the channel as *ColorA*, and select OK when done. Zoom back out to view the full image.

5. Select the Swatches panel (Window > Swatches). Then, in the Tools panel, select the Eyedropper Tool (I) underneath the Quick Selection or Magic Wand Tool. Select Sample Size of 3x3. Average, and choose a complimentary color, or a color you'd like to try. We chose a light yellow color here. You'll notice the chosen color will display in the Foreground Color in the Tools panel (Figure 5-55).

6. Select the Color Replacement Tool (B) with a large enough brush size to paint once over the selected area. Leave settings as Mode of Color and Tolerance of 100 for starters. The lower the Tolerance the more of the original color will bleed through, which works if you want to blend between the original and the new color. For our purposes here, we want to completely replace it.

▷ FIGURE 5-56

Sample color using the Eyedropper Tool, then select the Color Replacement Tool and paint inside selected area.

7. Paint over the selected area and you'll find the color is replaced by the color you've chosen. Deselect the selection when done (Select > Deselect). Feel free to continue to experiment, then when finished, save the file as *BackpackCOLOR .tif* in your *Chapter 5* folder (Figure 5-56).

▷ FIGURE 5-57

Select area with Polygon Lasso Tool, sample clean area with Eyedropper Tool, then paint over area to be replaced with the Color Replacement Tool.

USING THE POLYGON LASSO TOOL AND REPLACING COLOR AS A CORRECTIVE METHOD

The combination of sampling color with the Eyedropper Tool (I) and replacing a sampled color with the Color Replacement Tool (B) can also be used for retouching images, especially in architecture. You can use these tools to get rid of rust or watermarks for a more clean look. Another type of selection is the **Polygon Lasso Tool** (L). This tool allows you to select along straight edges by simply clicking between points, making a straight edge selection.

Select image with stains

Sample and paint

Stains removed

In this exercise, you'll create a straight edge selection using the Polygon Lasso Tool (L). You'll then use the Eyedropper Tool (I) to sample a clean area, and use the Color Replacement Tool (B) to paint out a weathered stain on a lighthouse. It is basically the same procedure as previously done.

1. Open the file *CT Light.tif* in your *Chapter 5* folder, and Zoom in to about 200%. You'll notice the large stain on the structure.

2. Select the Polygon Lasso Tool (L) in the Lasso Tool area, and click a couple of points to align the selection to the edge of the sunlit areas of the structure. Click carefully in straight lines around the area you want to include. As you hover over the first selection point you made, a circle displays under the cursor indicating the selection is ready to be closed. Make sure this circle displays or the selection will follow your mouse.

3. Use the Refine Edge button in the Tool Options bar to soften the edges of your selection for a smooth transition between pixels.

4. Select the Eyedropper Tool (I) and sample one of the clean areas outside the selection.

5. Select the Color Replacement Tool (B) and adjust the brush size to paint over the stain. If it is off color, just sample another area with the Eyedropper Tool (I) and try again (Figure 5-57).

6. Select the shadow area and repeat the same procedure, sampling a good area with the Eyedropper Tool (I), then painting over with the Color Replacement Tool (B).

7. The stain is gone, but the peeling paint is still there. Oh well, can't fix everything here. Save the file as *CT LightFIX.tif* in your *Chapter 5* folder.

CHAPTER SUMMARY

In this chapter, you completed a rather complex project that gave you quite an overview of Photoshop's use of selections, layers, and text. With the selections created, the original kayak was duplicated and pasted into separate layers, which allowed you to change the colors on the kayaks separately using the Hue/Saturation command; then the kayaks were moved into position. You were able to rename layers, move layers, duplicate layers, and use layer styles to create realistic drop shadows for the kayaks and to the text for added dimension. The final image was saved as a TIF file with all layers intact for future editing. You created a layer group (set) to combine all the type layers, then you merged the kayak images together onto a single layer. The ad was then duplicated and flattened to one layer, decreasing the file size and allowing you to send an electronic proof to the client. The advertisement was then converted to CMYK color mode, ready for press. In the advanced section you got a taste of working with layer masks and adjustment layers. You explored syncing and sharing your files between computers and other devices using Creative Cloud, and the ability to also sync settings in Photoshop between computers. In the Digital Toolkit Extra section, you worked with the Content-Aware Fill, Scale, and Move tools to shrink and expand an image's dimensions while keeping the main subject proportionate, removing distractions, and adjusting a subject's position in the image. You also had an opportunity to use the Color Replacement Tool to replace a product's color, and explore its versatility as a corrective tool. Do not forget to check out the *Extras & Goodies* folder on *www.CengageBrain.com* for more projects and ideas.

REVIEW QUESTIONS

1. Explain the procedure used to duplicate and recolor the kayaks.

2. Explain how using the Hue/Saturation command is helpful for changing color on large-scale products.

3. Explain Anti-alias settings, Layer Style effects, and layer groups.

4. Explain how to use Layer Comps.

5. Explain the differences between flattening an image using Photoshop's Layers panel and saving a file as a JPEG, which automatically flattens an image's layers.

6. What is the purpose of using the Properties panel?

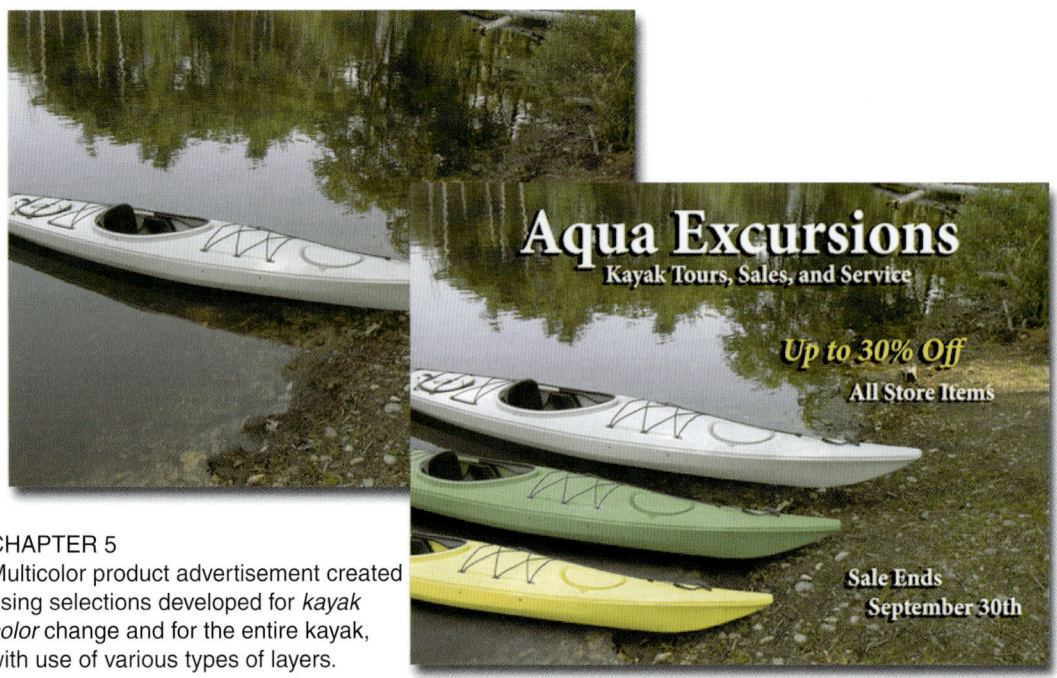

CHAPTER 5
Multicolor product advertisement created using selections developed for *kayak color* change and for the entire kayak, with use of various types of layers.

CHAPTER 5 ADVANCED
Using adjustment layers and layer masks to create special compositions. Creating a figure illustration using custom shapes.

CHAPTER 5 EXTRA

Using the Content-Aware Fill and Spot Healing Brush to remove unwanted distractions in an image (bridge).

Using Content-Aware Scale to resize unimportant image elements with accuracy (lighthouse and red ship).

Using Content-Aware Move to reposition subject (birds).

Using the Eyedropper and Color Replacement tools to replace color in products and as a corrective technique (back packs and stained lighthouse below).

▷ FIGURE 5-59

CHAPTER 6

Restoring and Coloring a Black and White Photograph

CHAPTER OBJECTIVES: To understand Photoshop's tools and techniques for image restoration and retouching, in this chapter you will:

▷ Use the Dust & Scratches and Gaussian Blur filters and the Blur Tool to smooth out or replace imperfections.

▷ Use the Clone Stamp, Patch, Healing Brush, and Spot Healing Brush tools to repair parts of an image.

▷ Use the History panel to avoid mishaps and create snapshots at certain points in the editing progress and save them.

▷ Use the painting tools and color panels to select, sample, and paint realistic colors on a black-and-white image.

▷ Learn the importance of RGB, CMYK, and Grayscale color modes.

▷ ADVANCED USERS: Color cast correction by neutralizing shadow and highlight areas using the Threshold feature, Levels sample points, and Info panel. Syncing files and Photoshop settings using Creative Cloud.

▷ DIGITAL TOOLKIT EXTRA: Creating actions for special effects and repetitive tasks. Batch processing multiple images to apply actions. Creating 3D Objects.

CREATIVE CLOUD EDITION

One of the things that Photoshop is best known for is its arsenal of **editing and retouching tools** that can help repair and reconstruct images. As a designer or professional photographer, whenever you receive an image, you will need to examine it thoroughly for imperfections, defects, or color problems, and then retouch the image to make it publishable. In your profession, you may find yourself involved with a lot of minor and major retouching (and painting) projects for clients. In this chapter, you will get a taste of some of the tools and special panels that provide you the necessary equipment to take on most retouching tasks.

TOOLS AND PANELS FOR EDITING

Retouching tools can be used for all kinds of restoration and image enhancement projects, which may involve replacing image components, editing selected areas, and trimming outside portions of an image. Painting tools and special panels allow you to sample and apply color from images, store colors, create new tool settings and brushes, or paint back to a previous state in a document.

TOOLKIT TIP Getting to know the appropriate shortcut or "hot key" for most used tools will make a designer or photographer more productive by saving time.

RETOUCHING TOOLS

Retouching tools are the most widely used tools for restoration and retouching projects (Figure 6-1); their shortcut keys follow the tool name in parentheses.

- Healing Brush, Spot Healing Brush, Red Eye, Content-Aware Move, and Patch tools (J) restore damaged sections of an image by sampling pixels from a good area and then blending in lighting and shading; they are great for working on portrait restorations and old photos, or removing distractions.
- The Color Replacement Tool (B) replaces the color underneath the brush cursor with the foreground color.
- The Clone Stamp and Pattern Stamp tools (S) copy sampled image areas, replacing the target area with the same pixel information.

- The Crop Tool trims a rectangular area, the Perspective Crop Tool adjusts an image's perspective, while the Slice tools split an image into many components of a web page for links and rollovers (C).
- The Eraser tools (E) consist of the Eraser, Background Eraser, and Magic Eraser; these remove selected pixels, background colors, or make the background transparent.
- The Gradient Tool (G) creates a shaded fill from one color to another, while the Paint Bucket Tool (G) fills in solid colors, and the 3D Material Drop Tool (G) creates various textures.
- The Blur, Sharpen, and Smudge tools (R) let you soften or sharpen selected parts of an image. The Burn, Sponge, and Dodge tools (O) lighten, darken, or saturate the tones of color in an image.

▷ FIGURE 6-1

Photoshop retouching tools.

PAINTING TOOLS, SPECIAL TOOLS, AND PANELS

Painting tools allow you to apply selected colors and effects. The Tool Presets panel is where you can create custom tools with specific options and save them for later use.

- Brush, Color Replacement, Mixer Brush, and Pencil tools (B) are used for painting. The Brushes panel allows you to select from an array of regular and custom brushes of varying sizes and shapes.
- The Shape tools (U) are used to create various shapes that help with selections.
- The Pen tools (P) create paths using anchor points for precise selections.
- The Path Selection and Direct Selection tools (A) are used to select paths created by the Pen tools (Figure 6-2). Slice tools (C) divide an image into smaller images that can then be reassembled on a web page.
- The History Brush and Art History Brush (Y) tools allow you to go back in time to a previous brush used or to apply an effect. The History panel records all actions as states and snapshots. It allows the user to easily revert to previous states.

▷ FIGURE 6-2

**Painting tools,
special tools,
and panels.**

▷ FIGURE 6-2

Painting tools, special tools, and panels.

Various Tool Presets

Crop and Slice tools

Shape tools

History panel

Pen tools

History, Art History, and Path Selection tools

COLOR TOOLS, SWATCHES, AND COLOR PANELS

Color tools like the Eyedropper and **Color Sampler Tool** (I) are used to sample any color in an image and provide color information (Figure 6-3). The 3D Material Eyedropper Tool (I) is used to sample 3D textures and shading. You will also find within the same tool area Ruler and Count tools for measuring with precision for more complex projects. You can select colors or sample colors with the **Color panel** and create or use preset colors in the Swatches panel. Below the tool buttons, you will find the **Color Picker** icons, where you can select and switch between foreground and background colors (X), and also default to black and white (D).

SPECIAL FILTERS

Photoshop has an arsenal of filters, most in the Filter menu, to enhance or apply special effects to selected portions of an image like applying special artistic effects, or create special distortions and lighting effects. Some additional filters can be provided by third-party developers and are available as plug-ins. Photoshop

▷ FIGURE 6-3

**Color and measure-
ment tools, Color
panel, Swatches
panel, and
Color Picker.**

also has special filters to help with the retouching and the enhancing process
(Figure 6-4). To get rid of dust and scratches or clean up solid color areas, like the
blue sky in an image, use the **Dust & Scratches filter** or the **Median filter**.
To soften a portrait image or a scanned image that was printed on a matte surface, use the **Gaussian Blur filter**. For precision in sharpening images or their
components, the **Unsharp Mask filter** is a designer's special digital tool. The
Smart Sharpen filter precisely locates areas that need to be sharpened. There is
also the **Filter Gallery** under the Filter menu to preview and apply various filter
effects on an image. There is also the Photo Filter function under the Image menu
(Image > Adjustments) to simulate the effect of standard photographic lens filters.
You can control the amount of effect by adjusting the density.

▷ FIGURE 6-4

**Special retouch-
ing filters: Smart
Sharpen, Gaussian
Blur, and Photo
filters.**

CLIENT ASSIGNMENT: Retouching and Coloring a Black and White Photograph

Your client, Elizabeth Roberts, has an old black-and-white photo of her father in the service that has been damaged over the years. She wants to have the image restored and an additional copy colorized to give to family members at their family reunion. When you discuss possible colors, she mentions her father's army uniform was a standard very deep green, and the background was a light blue. You tell her you will also try to match the flesh tones by using another photo of children with the same basic skin tones. She is excited about the project, and you tell her you will have it done by the end of the week.

ACTION ITEMS OVERVIEW

This job requires two important phases: First, to maintain the image quality, you need to restore the black-and-white image as close to its original state as possible before applying any effects or colors. The second phase is to make a realistic color painting using color from the Swatches and Color panels and to apply the colors using painting tools with a low opacity brush. The Color Sampler Tool (I) will also be used in sampling skin color tones to apply to the B&W image. Because painting will involve a special brush, a custom brush will be created for more accurate work on the image (Figure 6-5). If you haven't downloaded the image files for this chapter you can find them at *www.CengageBrain.com*.

▷ FIGURE 6-5

Before and after restoration.

Photo courtesy of Carla Clancy.

Here are some things you will learn to do in this chapter:

- Duplicate the image, one for restored black and white and another for color.
- Soften and replace background imperfections using the Dust & Scratches filter.
- Use the Clone, Patch, Healing Brush, and Spot Healing Brush tools to remove the cracks and defects in the photo.
- Use the History panel for multiple undos and to save previous editing changes.
- Soften the matte surface of the image slightly using the Gaussian Blur Tool.
- Change the Grayscale color mode to RGB to add color.
- Create a new brush in the Tool Presets panel for carefully painting the image.
- Create a custom color for the Swatches panel to paint the clothing background using a low opacity setting with the **Brush Tool (B)**.
- Sample skin tone color from a color image using the Color Sampler Tool (I) and paint with a low opacity setting to make realistic flesh tones.
- ADVANCED USERS: Correct colors casts using the Threshold Adjustment Layer, Levels sample points, and the Info panel. Syncing files and Photoshop settings using Creative Cloud.

RESTORING THE IMAGE

Before adding color to a black-and-white photo, it has to be restored to the best quality possible. This is done by selecting the areas that will be adjusted, then editing with special retouching tools and the Dust & Scratches filter to help remove and replace any imperfections, cracks, and dust spots. This part of the process involves a lot of trial and error to create an accurately restored image. Using the **History panel** helps to avoid problems by providing multiple undos and saving recorded actions or states during the editing process, which are called snapshots.

DUPLICATING AND SAVING THE IMAGE FILE

It is always a good habit to make duplicates of any file you are working on and to save your work frequently. Save your images throughout this chapter with a .TIF extension (File > Save As > *ADJSoldier.tif*) so you can edit your image as many times as needed without compromising the quality.

You will create a duplicate of the original file *Soldier.tif* and save it with a new name.

1. Choose File > Open and select the *Soldier.tif* image located in the *Chapter 6* folder.

2. Make sure the Navigator, History, Color, and Swatches panels are displayed on the desktop to assist you. If not, use the Window menu to access the panels you need.

3. Create a duplicate image by selecting Image > Duplicate.

4. Name the new copy *ADJSoldier* and save it as a TIF file using the default settings in your *Chapter 6* folder. Now you have a back-up copy. Leave the *ADJSoldier* file open and close the *Soldier* file.

DESIGN TIP

The Dust & Scratches filter is a great tool when a designer is given dirty or grainy slides and negatives with blue skies or solid background colors. Try also using the Median filter, another pixel-softening filter that works nicely, especially with single color blue skies. Applying these filters softens the details in selected areas without losing sharpness in the rest of the image.

5. To remove the white border along the outside of the portrait, select the Rectangular Marquee Tool (M) and with a Normal Style setting on the Tool Options bar, drag diagonally across the image to make sure the selection does not include the white border.

6. Select Image > Crop, to remove the border.

7. With the image cropped, to remove the selection, choose Select > Deselect.

MAKING SELECTIONS AND APPLYING THE DUST & SCRATCHES FILTER

With any image or image selection, such as a solid color background or blue sky with slight imperfections or dust spots, the Dust & Scratches filter in the Filter menu can help to smooth out pixels to blend them in and remove small dust spots. This will provide a nice review of using selections.

In this exercise, you will select the background area of the image with the Quick Selection Tool (W) and Lasso tools and blur the pixels to smooth out the stray selections; then remove dust marks and imperfections using the Dust & Scratches filter or the Median filter.

1. Select the Quick Selection Tool (W) and set the Brush size to 4 pixels in the Tool Options bar. Click on the Add to selection button, and then select the background, making sure the man's ears are not selected.

2. Use the Lasso Tool (L) for editing the selection if needed. Use the Tool Options bar buttons to add to and subtract from selections. Feel free to click the Quick Mask icon in the bottom of the Tools panel for fine-tuning.

3. If you need to eliminate any stray pixels from inside your selection, choose Select > Modify > Smooth > 2 pixels. Click OK.

4. Save the selection as an alpha selection channel using Select > Save Selection. Name the channel *Background*. Now you will be able to edit this saved selection if needed.

5. With the background selected, choose Filter > Noise > Dust & Scratches. Click and drag the image in the dialog box to show part of the selected background. If you inadvertently deselect the background, use Select > Load Selection and choose your *Background* selection channel (Figure 6-6).

6. Drag the Dust & Scratches window next to the image and enter these settings: Radius at 20 pixels, a Threshold of 1 level, and check the Preview box.

7. You will find most of the cracks and pits are softened if not completely blurred out. You may notice the matted surface of the scanned image when you zoom in on the image. Not to worry; we will adjust that later.

8. Click and hold inside the preview image to see the original; let go to see the revision. Click OK when you are satisfied.

9. Click on the background to select it, then click the Refine Edge button on the Tool Options bar and select the Black & White View Mask icon to smooth out the edge pixels. Try the settings shown in Figure 6-7 for starters, including placing a check in Smart Radius for increased accuracy, and click OK when done. To see the edge effects, click on the Show Original Preview button.

DESIGN TIP

The key to removing cracks and imperfections accurately is to zoom in very close and start working with a brush size just a little larger than the defect size; gradually increase the brush size to smooth out details.

Photo courtesy of Carla Clancy.

▷ FIGURE 6-6

Use the selection tools and the Dust & Scratches filter to smooth out background imperfections.

10. Save the Background selection again to update it. Select > Save Selection > Channel Background > Replace Channel > OK.

11. Save the file and leave it open. You may see some evidence still of visual cracks that are very blurred out. We'll fix these later.

TOOLKIT TIP The Refine Edge dialog box contains an Edge Detection function using Smart Radius. This feature helps to make highly precise selections of complex subjects easily, enabling faster, more accurate combinations of multiple images. You can then use the extra view modes to assist you in previewing the quality of your selections.

▷ FIGURE 6-7

Use the Refine Edge command to soften the selection edges.

THE HISTORY PANEL

Say you started working on an image, but went too far and feel you may have to start over. With the History panel, your previous actions are recorded in what are called **states,** so you can go backward in a series of steps, as if going through multiple undos. You can click on a previous state or drag the most recent states into the Trash. You can save a state as a **snapshot** for later editing as long as the document remains open. You can create a new document from a snapshot and save it for later use. A snapshot allows you to record an image's state at a particular time in the editing process, and you can go back to that snapshot at any time as you experiment. Warning! As soon as you close a file, all those history states are removed, because they are not permanently saved. The amount of states displayed is limited, so it is a good habit to create a snapshot when an area is completed.

 TOOLKIT TIP The History panel is your quickest way to get out of potential trouble by dragging mistakes into the Trash or by selecting and saving a previous state layer. If you know you have just made a mistake, use the Command/CTRL Z undo, or you can use the Edit > Step Forward and Step Backward commands.

The History panel allows you to go back and observe previous actions.

1. Select a previous state on the History panel to see some of the earlier actions you took. Notice that the more recent actions are undone (Figure 6-8).

2. To create a snapshot of the Dust & Scratches technique in removing the background cracks, select the "Create new snapshot" icon (camera icon) at the bottom of the panel. The snapshot thumbnail will appear on the top panel area under the original image, and it will be named *Snapshot 1*.

3. Double-click the *Snapshot 1* text line and renamed it Dust & Scratches, or whatever you chose as a state to return to. You now have a new snapshot you can go back to when needed.

▷ FIGURE 6-8

The History panel allows you to select previous commands and to create snapshots at specific points in the most recent development of your work.

Create new snapshot

Renamed snapshot (active snapshot)

4. Go back to your last action in the History panel. Note that the panel only records back a certain amount of actions depending on the default settings in Photoshop.

5. Save the file when you are finished, leaving it open for the next exercise.

THE CLONE STAMP TOOL

The **Clone Stamp Tool (S)** allows you to sample a group of pixels from a source area and transfer or clone those pixels to another area. This tool works great for replacing difficult spots and scratches in an image. To use the Clone Stamp Tool (S) successfully, hold down the Option (Mac)/ALT (Windows) key and click a clean area to sample from. This becomes your reference point. Click within the area to be replaced, making a short stroke with the mouse, and the sampled pixels replace the defective parts of the image. You need to continually sample and set different reference points to provide a final realistic effect.

TOOLKIT TIP Making realistic restorations with the Clone Stamp Tool (S) is accomplished by holding down the Option (Mac)/ALT (Windows) key and clicking on good areas and then applying those over the defective area by dragging the mouse in short movements. If you know you have just made a mistake, use the Command/CTRL Z undo, or you can use the Edit > Step Forward and Step Backward commands.

Here, you will inverse the Background selection to include only the soldier and create a new selection channel. You will then use the Clone Stamp Tool (S) to sample the source pixels and clone those pixels to the cracks in the uniform cap, and—when you feel ready to get a little more precise—the cracks that appear in the man's uniform.

1. To be able to work only on the uniform and cap, inverse the background selection (Select > Inverse). With the selection of only the soldier now, choose Select > Save Selection, name the new channel *Soldier* and click OK.

2. Zoom in to show just the uniform cap, then select the Clone Stamp Tool (S) and enter a brush size of 40 pixels in the Tool Options bar.

3. Hold down the Option (Mac)/ALT (Windows) key and click on a good spot to use as a reference. It also works better to sample an area close to the piece you want to correct so the patterns and cloth weaving may match (Figure 6-9).

4. Drag a short stroke with the mouse on the area you want to replace, and you will notice a tiny brush thumbnail cursor that shows the area you referenced, along with your brush icon as you replace the defective area with the pixels you sampled.

5. Continue Option/ALT-clicking for new reference spots to replace the dust spots and general defects in the uniform cap.

6. To undo or redo previous actions, select Edit > Step Forward and Step Backward.

7. Zoom the picture back to see the effects. When you are satisfied and feel comfortable working with the Clone Stamp Tool on the cap, zoom in close on the left side of the uniform jacket (as you are facing the image); you will notice more cracks in the image (Figure 6-9).

Use the Clone Stamp Tool to replace
damaged pixels with good pixels

**Clone Stamp
Tool**

Option/ALT-click a good area
as reference to clone from

Photo courtesy of Carla Clancy.

▷   FIGURE 6-9

**Use the Clone Tool
to replace imperfec-
tions in the cap and
uniform. Don't use on
the skin.**

8. Start the Clone Stamp Tool (S) brush size at 40 pixels, adjust as needed, and continue Option (Mac)/ALT (Windows) clicking periodically to consistently reference the sampled area, and replace the cracks on the man's uniform. When working around the collar area, be careful to align the edge of the collar when Option/ALT-clicking to keep a straight line.

9. Be careful to constantly resample and use short strokes to maintain a realistic look.

10. Zoom out when completed to see your work. Do not work on the other side of the uniform or on any skin areas yet; you will use the Healing Brushes and Patch Tool for that.

11. Save the file and leave it open.

(X) PROBLEM If the Clone Stamp Tool (S) does not seem to work, or you get a dialog box that indicates no pixels were selected, make sure you Option (Mac)/ALT (Windows) click the reference area first.

THE PATCH TOOL

The **Patch Tool (J)** samples patterns and textures in an image. It analyzes the texture and lighting and matches the source pixels to blend in with a destination area. You drag around a selection the size of the area you want to replace, or a little smaller, click and drag it over to the defective area, and watch the source area blend into the defective area with the corrected texture, lighting, and color. Very cool! You can also choose and load preset patterns using the Tool Options bar for special effects.

In this exercise, you will use the Patch Tool (J) to replace the cracked area of the soldier's cheeks; you will notice the lighting and texture will blend right in.

1. Select the Patch Tool (J) (it is underneath the Healing Brush if that tool is displayed) and choose the Destination setting on the Tool Options bar. This will allow you to select a good sample area and replace the defective destination area. Make sure transparent is *not* checked.

2. Zoom in to the left side cheek area (as you are facing the image) where you will notice cracks.

3. Make a freehand selection, much like you would with the Lasso Tool, of an area near the defective area (Figure 6-10).

4. Click and drag the selection over the cracked area and the crack is gone! Create another Patch Tool selection to replace other areas of the cracks until you reach just under the nose area. To deselect the Patch Tool, choose Select > Deselect.

5. Repeat the same process creating selections on the right side cheek. Be very careful not to include the background.

6. Use the History panel to return to previous actions if needed.

7. When you have completed the large areas on the face with the Patch Tool, choose Select > Load Selection and bring up the Soldier Channel to select only the soldier. Leave the file open for the next exercise.

▷ FIGURE 6-10

Using the Patch Tool, create a freehand selection on the source to be sampled, then drag over the defective area to blend in the pixels.

Patch Tool

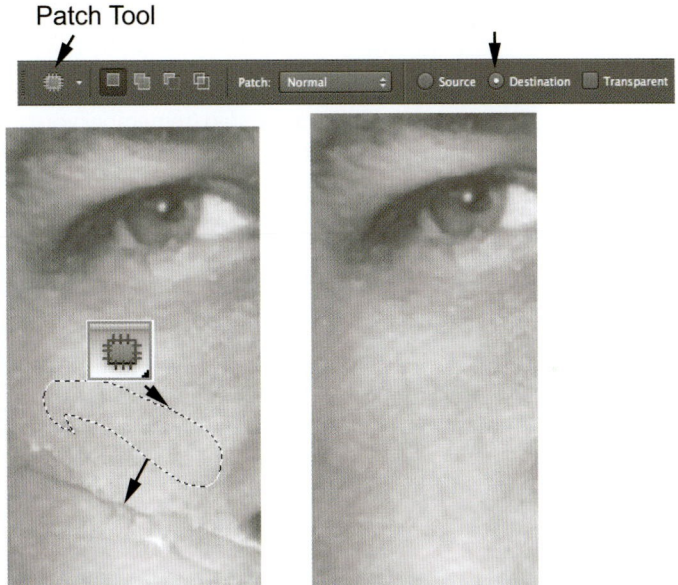

Create selection to sample and drag over area to patch

Crack replaced

Photo courtesy of Carla Clancy.

THE HEALING BRUSH AND SPOT HEALING BRUSH

The **Healing Brush Tool (J)** works the same way as the Clone Stamp Tool (S): by selecting a reference area using the Option/ALT key to establish a source, then clicking and dragging the mouse using a short stroke over the area you want to replace. The Healing Brush also works like the Patch Tool (J): it analyzes the texture, lighting, and color and blends them in. These tools are wonderful for restoring portrait images. The **Spot Healing Brush Tool (J)** allows you to simply click on smaller areas that need to be replaced without having to use the Option/ALT key to set a sampled area. It makes the change automatically.

TOOLKIT TIP You'll find a Content-Aware button on the Tool Options bar that allows you to select an area to be replaced with the Spot Healing Brush and then, when removed, can be filled in with the (content-aware) surrounding background.

In this exercise, you will use the Healing Brush to replace the cracks on the soldier's face.

1. Use the Zoom Tool (Z) to get in close to the soldier's face.

2. Select the Healing Brush with a brush size of 20 pixels to start. Leave the default settings in the Brush panel.

3. Option/ALT-click a good reference area on an area of the man's ear and apply the Healing Brush effect with short strokes (Figure 6-11).

4. Zoom out to view the image, then zoom in to work on small areas. You can also use the Command/CTRL followed by the plus sign or dash key to zoom in or out quickly.

5. Change the brush size as needed (remember you can use the bracket keys to do this quickly) and continue Option/ALT-clicking different reference areas and applying the Healing Brush, watching how the texture and shading blend in nicely.

6. Use the History panel to help with any problems or save snapshots for reference.

7. Continue on areas that may display small cracks on the right side of the soldier's uniform, and you may find going over the cap area will also help to maintain consistent texture.

8. To take care of minute areas under the nose, face, and uniform, select the Spot Healing Brush Tool (J), and with a brush size of about 9 pixels, select the Content-Aware button on the Tool Options bar, then just click on those areas of small cracks and spots that need repair. There is no need to Option/ALT-click first with this tool.

DESIGN TIP

Inverting a selection comes in quite handy when you cannot select a complex image too well. Select a same color area instead, then invert the selection to apply your effect. The Gaussian Blur filter is also a great tool for softening skin pores and blemishes in portrait images.

▷   FIGURE 6-11

The Healing Brush and Spot Healing Brush analyze and correct shading and textures to blend in pixels.

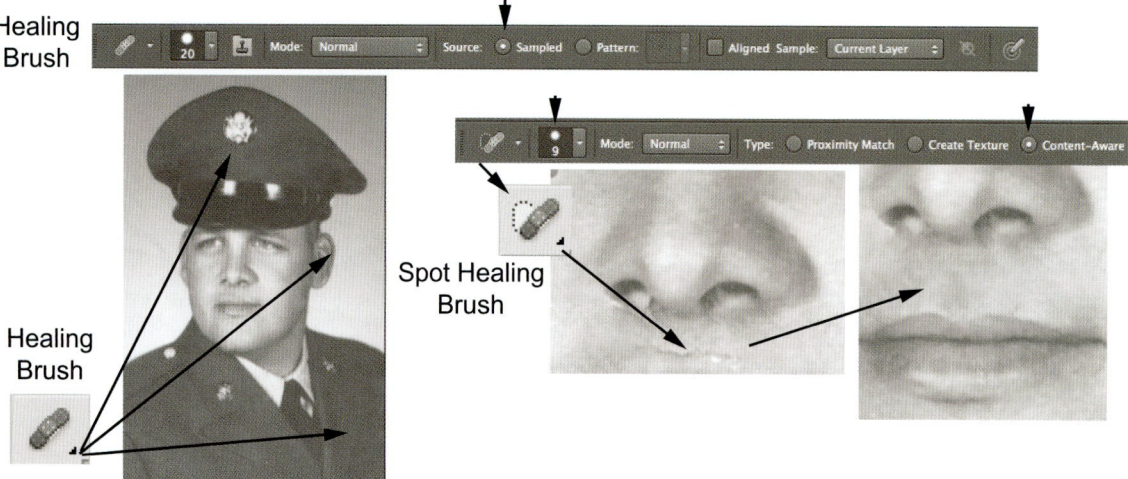

Photo courtesy of Carla Clancy.

9. To remove the softened background cracks, choose Select > Inverse to invert the selection from the portrait to the background and paint over the cracks with the Spot Healing Brush. After the background is completed, invert the selection again (Select > Inverse) to select the portrait again.

10. When you have completed the restoration, zoom out to see your work. Save the file again as *ADJSoldier.tif* in your *Chapter 6* folder.

TOOLKIT TIP You can use the Clone Source panel (Window > Clone Source) with the Clone Tool or Healing Brush tools to set cloning from five different sources. There is an Overlay option that allows you to precisely position, rotate, and transform the destination brush stroke. This can also be used in working with video and animation projects.

SOFTENING A SCANNED MATTE SURFACE WITH GAUSSIAN BLUR AND THE BLUR TOOL

With the restoration complete, you will notice that the image of the soldier shows the matte surface of the scanned image. To soften this matte surface, you can apply a **Gaussian Blur filter**. To help soften the edges so that he does not look like a cutout, use the **Blur Tool** on the edges with a 20-pixel brush and 50% strength (Figure 6-12). Photoshop has an arsenal of filters to enhance, distort, or create special effects on selected portions of images.

TOOLKIT TIP If you want to invert any selection, you can choose Select > Inverse.

▷ FIGURE 6-12

Softening the matte surface of the scanned image by applying a Gaussian Blur effect. You can also soften selection edges using the Blur Tool to avoid a cutout effect.

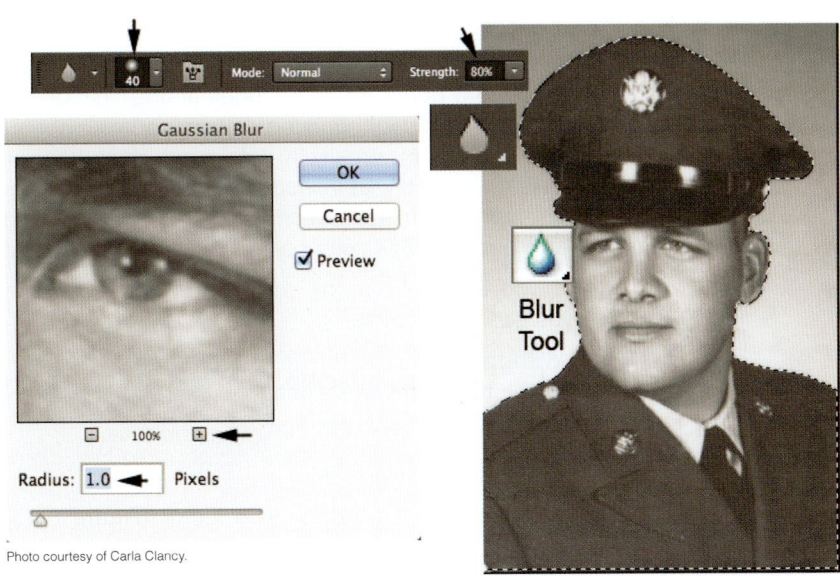

Photo courtesy of Carla Clancy.

Now you will select the soldier and soften the matte surface.

1. With the *ADJSoldier.tif* file open, if the portrait is not selected, choose Select > Load Selection and select the *Soldier* selection channel you created earlier. Zoom in close to see the effect.

2. With the portrait selected, select Filter > Blur > Gaussian Blur.

3. In the dialog box, select 1.0 Radius for affected pixels; click the zoom on the dialog box till it reaches 100%, then click and drag to display the soldier's eye as a guide.

4. By applying a slight amount of blur, the image remains relatively sharp and the indentations of the old matte surface are significantly reduced. To view the before and after effects on the preview image, click and hold, then let go, or toggle the Preview button. Select OK. Zoom back out when done.

5. With the soldier still selected, use the Blur Tool on the edges with a 40-pixel brush and 80% strength to start softening the edges to avoid the cut-out look. It will show slightly when you paint later. You've completed retouching the image.

6. Save the file and leave open for the next exercise.

COLORING THE BLACK-AND-WHITE IMAGE

The second part of this chapter deals with using color tools and panels to apply color to your black-and-white image. This involves converting the image color mode from Grayscale to RGB color, then selecting areas to be painted. You can create your own custom brush sizes and options in the Tool Presets panel, and you can select colors from the Swatches and Color panels.

COLOR MODES

Any image you are working with has a color mode. Images that are shades of gray are set in Grayscale mode, which is the color mode of your original restoration image. When you need to apply RGB colors to a Grayscale image, all you have to do is create a duplicate of the original and change the mode from Grayscale to RGB color. The default working color mode you would use initially while working on your computer is usually RGB color, which is also used as the default color mode for electronic display, as in web design, and for printing on desktop printers. If you were sending an image to a printing press, you would convert the RGB (red, green, blue) image to CMYK color (cyan, magenta, yellow, and black) for reproduction.

Here, you will duplicate the image and convert the Grayscale image to RGB color, so you can apply colors.

1. With the *ADJSoldier* image restored, select Image > Duplicate to make a copy of the black-and-white image.

2. Name the file copy *COLORSoldier* and save it.

3. Close the *ADJSoldier* file.

4. Select Image > Mode > RGB Color (Figure 6-13). Now you are ready to apply colors.

▷ FIGURE 6-13

Changing the color mode from Grayscale to RGB to color the black-and-white image.

DESIGN TIP

When a designer colors a Grayscale image, a low-opacity setting of around 20% or less allows the color to be applied gradually, providing more control over the entire process. Use a soft edge brush to allow the color edges to blend nicely together.

TOOLKIT TIP If you want to create an overall color cast in an image, try using one of the Photo Filter options (Image > Adjustments > Photo Filter). To create an old-fashioned sepia tone of the black-and-white image of the soldier, duplicate the *ADJSoldier* image again, change the mode from Grayscale to RGB color mode, then select Sepia from the Photo Filter options (see Figure 6-4). Adjust the Density setting to the desired effect. These filters can be used on individual layers as well for special effects.

PAINTING COLORS USING THE SWATCHES PANEL

The **Swatches panel** is a selection of predefined colors from which you can select a color and paint. When selecting a color from the Swatches panel, the Color Picker's foreground color on the Tools panel changes to that color. The Color panel will display the color mode settings for that color. You can also create your own color and add it to the Swatches panel. The key to painting is to use a sweeping motion with the Brush Tool (B) at a low opacity setting (Figure 6-14).

▷ FIGURE 6-14

To paint the background, select a large brush with low opacity and gently sweep across the selected area.

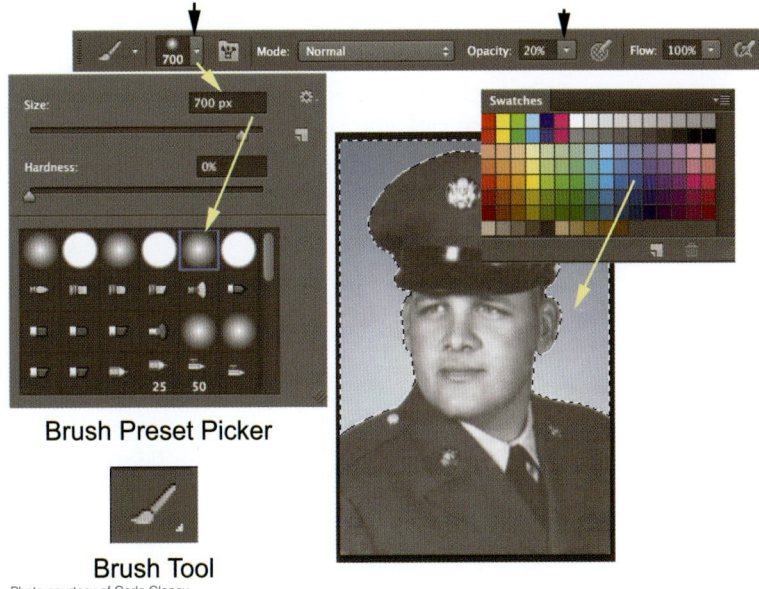

Brush Preset Picker

Brush Tool

Photo courtesy of Carla Clancy.

Here you will use the Swatches panel to select a light opacity pure blue color for the background, and you will paint using a large brush with sweeping strokes.

DESIGN TIP

When applying color over an area, make sure the brush size is large enough to cover a majority of the selected area in the first sweeps to avoid overlapping paint lines. Try to cover the entire area without letting up on the mouse.

1. Make sure the file *COLORSoldier* is displayed in Photoshop, if it is not open.

2. Choose Select > Load Selection > Channel Background > OK to load the Background selection channel.

3. Choose a pure blue (it displays the name when your mouse hovers over it) color from the Swatches panel (see Row 5, Column 11).

4. Select the Brush Tool (B) and select a soft-edge brush size of 700 pixels at 20% opacity for a much larger sweep (Figure 6-14). Make only one or two across the background, until the background is a light blue (Figure 6-14). Use the History panel to track your progress.

5. Save the file in your *Chapter 6* folder when you feel comfortable with the image.

CREATING A CUSTOM SWATCH

Besides choosing from various swatches, or preset colors, you can create your own custom swatch as a permanent addition to your Swatches panel. For this exercise you would need to create a deep green color of the uniform from that period. You can use the Color picker to find colors by various methods, including sampling an image color using the Eyedropper Tool, and finding a 6-digit hexadecimal color number. An image was sampled previously using the Eyedropper Tool, creating a 6-digit number from the Color Picker. You will use the number to create a new swatch color that will be used to color the uniform.

To create the custom swatch, you'll type in the 6-digit number in the Set the foreground swatch of the Color Picker, and add it to the Swatches panel.

1. Make sure the Swatches panel is displayed, and double-click the foreground color swatch on the Tools panel to open up the Color Picker.

2. In the Color Picker display, at the bottom by the pound (#) sign, type 53785D for the uniform color (Figure 6-15).

3. Click Add to Swatches. When the display box opens, name the new swatch *Army*, then click OK.

4. The new swatch will be added at the bottom of the Swatches panel. Click OK to close the Color Picker.

CREATING A CUSTOM BRUSH IN THE TOOL PRESETS PANEL

Another panel in Photoshop is the Tool Presets panel. You can create a custom brush with special options, which you specify in the Tool Options bar. You can then save the customized brush for future images. Once you create your special tool, you can select it from either the Brush panel or the Brush Tool's Preset Picker in the Tool Options bar. When you create a tool in the Tool Presets panel, give it a name that describes the settings or options for that tool.

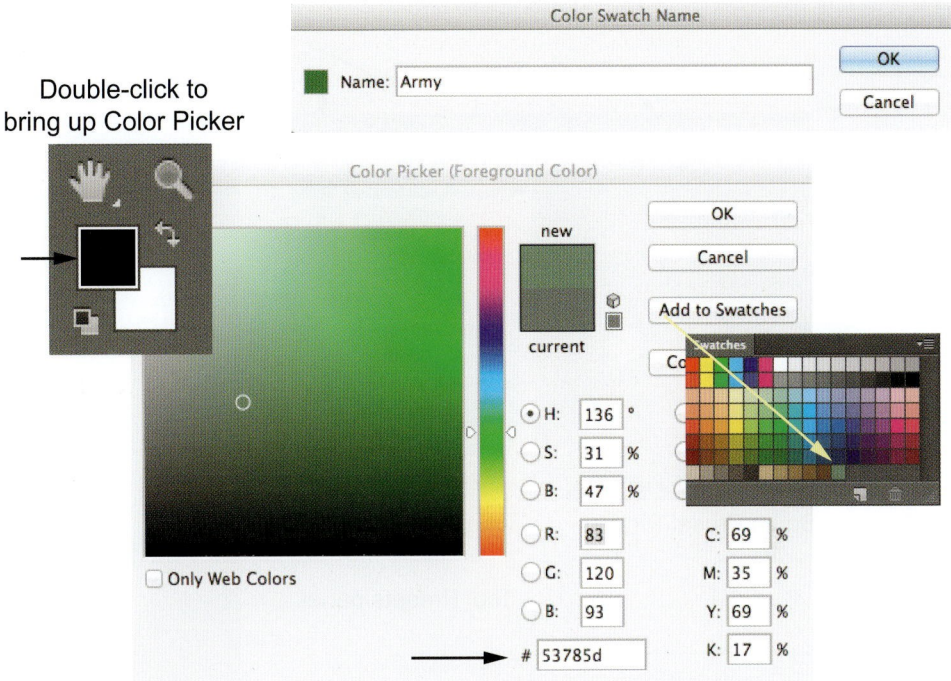

Double-click to bring up Color Picker

▷ FIGURE 6-15

Create custom swatch by typing in 6-digit character.

Here, you will create a large custom brush to paint with a low opacity using the Tool Presets panel.

1. Select the Brush Tool (B) and enter a Brush Size of 200 pixels with an Opacity setting of 15% in the Tool Options bar (Figure 6-16).

2. Click the arrow in the Brush pixel box to open the Brush Presets Picker. Select a soft edge brush and click on the panel menu to display the Tool Presets menu, then select New Brush Preset.

3. Name the tool *Soft Brush Round 200 px 15 Opacity* and click OK. You now have a new custom brush that will be displayed in the Brush Presets Picker, and when you click on the Brush panel icon in the Tool Options bar, you'll find it is added to the Brush panel, and the Brush Presets panel.

PREPARING TO PAINT THE UNIFORM: USING MASK SELECTION TECHNIQUE

The benefit of creating channel selections is you can create other selections from these initial permanent selections. The easiest and most convenient way of making complex selections is by painting using the Quick Mask Mode (Q). You want to apply the red mask on those areas NOT to be painted the color of the uniform, like the soldier's face, cap visor, shirt, tie, insignias, and buttons.

Toggle Brush panel

Brush Preset Picker

Tool Presets panel

Brush Name

Name: Soft Brush Round 200 px 15 Opacity

☑ Capture Brush Size in Preset

200

Brushes panel with preset brushes
(also displays in Brush Preset Picker)

▷ FIGURE 6-16

The Tool Presets panel allows you to create and save your own custom brushes and other settings for tools.

This will help to serve as another review of using Quick Mask for complex selections. Here you will use the Quick Mask function to add to the mask by painting in black those areas that are not part of the uniform to be colored. You will then save the selection as another permanent channel selection.

1. To inverse the Background selection, which you painted earlier, you can choose Select > Inverse, or choose Select > Load Selection, and select the *Soldier* selection channel.

2. You'll need to make sure that the face, cap visor, buttons, and insignias are removed from the selection by using the Quick Mask Mode (Q) function near the bottom of the Tools panel. Select a brush at about 100 pixels for starters, with an Opacity of 100%, and then click the Quick Mask icon near the bottom of the Tools panel.

3. Using black for the foreground color, paint in those areas NOT to be colored (Figure 6-17).

4. Remember black adds to the mask, or what is NOT to be painted in color later, and white adds to the painting selection what IS to be colored. Use the bracket keys to change your brush sizes.

5. Toggle the Quick Mask back to a regular selection to view your work, then toggle the mask to paint until you are satisfied with your selection.

6. You can also use the Lasso Tool (L) to fine-tune the selections by drawing closely and adding and subtracting edges to generate an accurate selection.

▷ FIGURE 6-17

Painting selection mask using Quick Mask Mode to exclude everything except uniform to be colored.

Toggle Quick
Mask Mode (Q)

Painting with black adds to the mask, those areas NOT to be painted.
Painting with white adds to the selection, those to be painted.

Photo courtesy of Carla Clancy.

7. When completed, save the selection as a new channel named *Uniform* (Select > Save Selection > New Channel > Uniform > OK).

8. Leave the image with selection active to paint the uniform in the next exercise.

PAINTING WITH A CUSTOM BRUSH

After creating a custom brush that includes brush size and opacity settings, and creating a mask so that only the uniform is painted, you can apply colors with these brush settings to any selected area. To color the soldier's uniform, you will select the custom color you created, and paint using sweeping strokes.

TOOLKIT TIP Only color over an area a few times; otherwise, it will start to fill in too much and may look flat and unrealistic. Use the History panel to track and edit your progress.

Now you will paint with the custom color and brush you created.

1. Make sure the Uniform channel selection is active (Select > Load Selection > Channel Uniform).

2. Select the custom dark green color you created from the Swatches panel named *Army* (hover mouse over to see name displayed, bottom row, last color).

3. Select the Brush Tool (B), and from the Brush Preset Picker in the Options bar, select the *Soft Brush Round 200 px 15 Opacity* brush you just created (Figure 6-18). If you find it easier to find your brush using the text description, select "Text Only" from the panel submenu to provide that option. It should be at the bottom of the list in the panel.

▷ FIGURE 6-18

To colorize a gray-scale image, select the area to be painted, then select the new brush preset with low opacity. Choose the color from the Swatches panel, and apply a sweeping stroke over the selected area.

Photo courtesy of Carla Clancy.

4. Sweep over the selected area of the uniform with the mouse a few times.

5. If the selected painted uniform looks too bright, select Image > Adjustment > Brightness/Contrast and increase the contrast to darken the uniform.

6. Save the file and leave open for the next exercise.

UNMASKING THE FACE: PREPARING TO APPLY COLOR

This exercise is a continuation of your masking techniques applied using the Quick Mask Mode (Q) method earlier in preparing the uniform. Here, you'll unmask the face to prepare for applying skin tones. It's important here to make sure the eyes and mouth are also masked along with the uniform and shirt.

The easiest way to prepare to color the face is to select the *Soldier* channel created earlier, and then mask outside the face. You will then save it as another permanent channel selection named *Face*.

1. With the *COLORSoldier* file open, you want to select the *Soldier* selection channel you created earlier to highlight the portrait only. Choose Select > Load Selection, and then select the Soldier selection channel.

2. Using the Quick Mask Mode (Q) function near the bottom of the Tools panel, select a hard round brush at about 100 pixels for starters, with an Opacity of 100%, and then click the Quick Mask Mode (Q) icon near the bottom of the Tools panel.

3. Using black for the foreground color, paint in those areas NOT to be skin color, or those areas surrounding the face like the cap visor, shirt, and uniform. Also, decrease the brush size and mask the eyes and mouth (Figure 6-19).

4. Remember black adds to the mask, or what is NOT to be painted in color later, and white adds to the painting selection what IS to be colored. Use the bracket keys to change your brush sizes.

5. Toggle the Quick Mask back to a regular selection to view your work, then toggle the mask to paint until you are satisfied with your selection.

▷   FIGURE 6-19

Unmasking the face to apply color; masking eyes, mouth, and surrounding uniform.

Black (foreground) adds to mask

Toggle Quick
Mask Mode (Q)

Photo courtesy of Carla Clancy.

6. You can also use the Lasso Tool (L) to fine-tune the selections by drawing closely and adding and subtracting edges to generate an accurate selection.

7. Use the Refine Edge (select any selection tool and it will appear in the Tool Options bar) to soften the selection edges; use Black and White View.

8. When finished, save the selection as a new channel named *Face* (Select > Save Selection > New Channel > Face > OK).

9. Leave the image with selection active to paint the face in the next exercise.

SAMPLING AND APPLYING SKIN TONES

Sampling for skin tones and painting them on a black-and-white image is a little tricky, because you are still trying to create a realistic effect. To do this, you need to select only the skin areas first, not the eyes or mouth, on the black-and-white image. You can then use the Eyedropper Tool (I) to sample a closely matching skin tone color from another color image. The color must be applied carefully in a few sweeps with a large brush size and low opacity setting to avoid overlapping the color stroke lines. The Brush tools (B) have a Paint Mode setting in the Tool Options bar that allows a designer to use various modes of blending in colors. The default setting is Normal. Overlay Paint Mode works nicely with skin tones as it helps to retain shadows and toning as the color is applied.

SAMPLING AND PLACING COLOR WITH THE EYEDROPPER TOOL

The **Eyedropper Tool (I)** is used to sample and place a color in the Color Picker. It can sample color from a current image or another image. The sample will show its color mode information in the Color panel, if you need to record it. Once you have a sample color displayed in the Color Picker, you can add that color to the Swatches panel for later use by selecting the Create new swatch of foreground color icon at the bottom of the Swatches panel.

In this exercise, you will sample a skin tone and save the color in the Swatches panel, then use the color on the selected skin areas of the soldier. You'll then paint in the mouth and eyes.

1. With the Face selection active on the *COLORSoldier* image, now open the file *Myboys.tif* in the *Chapter 6* folder.

2. Select the Eyedropper Tool (I) and click on the cheek or hand of one of the boys. You will notice that the color is displayed as the foreground color in the Color Picker.

3. Select the Swatches panel and click the icon button Create new swatch of foreground color (Figure 6-20), then save the color as Skin Tone. Note: You can also click on the Color Picker, and when the display opens, select Add to Swatches button. The skin tone color will remain permanently on the Swatches panel. You can just click in the Swatches panel to add the color. Clicking inside the panel also lets you name your swatch.

Photo of soldier courtesy of Carla Clancy.

▷ FIGURE 6-20

Sample skin tones from other images with the Eyedropper Tool (I), then apply a wide brush over the selected areas of the image. You can then add the color sample as a swatch in the Swatches panel.

4. Close the *Myboys* file; it was needed just to sample colors here.

5. Select the Brush Tool (B), change the Paint Mode in the Tool Options bar to Overlay, then set to 25% opacity as a starting point, and use a large, soft-edge brush size of about 700 pixels to sweep the skin tone color across the selected areas.

6. Use the History panel to keep track and redo the brush with a different Opacity setting if necessary. The trick is to add just enough color, but not to overpaint. This may take a number of attempts.

7. Now it's time to paint in the eyes and mouth. Inverse your selection (Select > Inverse) and zoom in close to work on these details.

8. For the mouth, decrease the brush size to 200 pixels, change the Paint Mode to Normal, and set at 10% Opacity. Click the color Darker Magenta Red on the Swatches panel (Row 7, Column 16). Paint over only once or twice for a very subtle color.

9. For the eyes, which are blue, decrease the brush size to 30 pixels, keep Paint Mode to Normal, then set Opacity to 20%. Select the Darker Blue color in the Swatches panel (Row 7, Column 12), then paint in the eyes.

10. Save the file as *COLORSoldier.tif* in your *Chapter 6* folder. You now have a nicely restored black-and-white image that has also been colored for a realistic effect (Figure 6-21). Feel free to make slight adjustments in increasing the saturation of color, or bumping up the contrast slightly if needed for the final effect.

Photo courtesy of Carla Clancy.

Completed Image   Original Image

▷ FIGURE 6-21

Color including skin tones, eyes, and mouth applied to restored B&W image

TOOLKIT TIP Another tool for retouching is called the Mixer Brush. Let's say you completed painting in your predetermined colors using a regular brush as is being done in these exercises. For a painterly effect to your image, you can use the Mixer Brush to provide extensive control over a brush's wetness, define multiple colors on a single tip, mixing and blending to taste on your image, and select choices as to whether to clean or refill your brush, much as an artist would approach their painting. Photoshop's painting tools have Bristle Tips and Bristle Qualities incorporated to give you more control when painting. Go ahead and play with this tool when you have a chance.

ADVANCED USERS: Color Cast Correction by Neutralizing Shadow and Highlight Areas, and Syncing Settings and Files between Computers.

Graphic designers or photographers presented with digital images that are off color, or poor quality, or have flat contrast are quite common in the industry today. Whether images are found with an incorrect digital camera white balance or exposure, or non-calibrated monitor display, or even from an aged photo, Photoshop provides special techniques to find the correct color tones in an image. It usually involves finding a white, gray, or black within the image and correcting from there.

In Photoshop Creative Cloud (CC) and in all Adobe products, subscribers can manage their work remotely in the Creative Cloud. Now, images are synced from one computer to a remote secure server Adobe maintains, and are able to be accessed and downloaded to other computers or even devices, like tablets and smart phones from another area. One of the other benefits of this new service in utilizing today's cloud technology is the ability for designers to sync their settings from their Adobe application, like Photoshop, to another computer, say from the workplace to their home computer. This saves time in managing their workflow, and in keeping the current version of their work always available.

FINDING HIGHLIGHT AND SHADOW DETAILS USING LEVELS

Many images may have a color cast to them, whether from old age, or from incorrect color exposure or white balance with a digital camera. There are a variety of ways to correct this issue. One way is to find the darkest shadow black parts of the image and a highlight area with detail and remap the pixels using the black and white components as a guide to accurately bring all colors in the image. This same technique can also be used for old images that have a color cast. The file provided is a digital image of flowers that had the wrong white balance setting. It was mistakenly set to incandescent light that would normally be used to photograph indoors with normal tungsten lights without a flash (would normally make images have an orange cast); however, the same setting used outdoors makes the image a blue cast. This problem happens quite often when people forget to adjust their digital camera settings.

This technique again uses the Levels command described in the "Advanced Users" section in Chapter 3, but takes it a step further in that you can sample the highlight and shadow areas by setting their point as black and white, which adjust all the pixels to those samples. This technique involves trial and error; if you find it bounces way off in tones, then cancel and try another area. The key is to first locate a shadow of darkest color areas with slight detail, then locate a highlight area with detail. In working with digital images, be careful when selecting highlight detail that it is not a pure white without detail. Otherwise your image may appear very washed out. In digital always look for highlight detail, as pure white cannot be corrected (Figure 6-22).

Original Color Cast Image

Corrected Image

▷ FIGURE 6-22

Neutralizing shadow and high-lights to correct color cast image.

TOOLKIT TIP To neutralize shadow and highlight areas, the key is to have the RGB channels the same number, the lowest for the shadow, and the highest for the high-light. When using highlight or the whitest area, decide if you need to use an area that may have specular highlights or pure white, or highlights that need to have detail in the brightest areas. Works best with old photos, food, and product photography.

THE INFO PANEL

The Info panel is useful in looking at color from a numerical standpoint. You can move the eyedropper over an area and the RGB (or CMYK) values are displayed. The lower the numbers the more towards shadow detail, the highest numbers represent the highlight detail. The numbers range from pure black at "0" to pure white at "255" with mid-tones in between (120–140). An image with proper color balance will have the RGB numerical values close together in both the shadow and highlight areas. An image with a color cast as in the *Bluecast* image you will be working on will obviously show an abundance of blue and green in the RGB values since the white balance setting was set incorrectly. Use the Info panel as a guide with the Levels eyedropper samplers to find the shadow and highlight areas that can be neutralized.

TOOLKIT TIP Sometimes it's a good practice to neutralize the shadow areas first, taking care to watch for blocked up or black shadows in areas where there should be some slight detail, then neutralize the highlight detail, making sure glare or light refractions are not chosen. There needs to be some detail in the highlights, especially with digital images. When shooting images with a digital camera, always expose for the highlights first for detail; shadows are easier to readjust.

Here you will neutralize the shadow detail area first on the image.

1. Launch Photoshop, then open the file *Bluecast.tif*, duplicate the image (Image > Duplicate) and save in your *Chapter 6* folder as *BluecastADJ.tif*. Close the original *Bluecast* file and display the new *BluecastADJ* file at 100%.

2. Select the Info panel ("i" in circle icon) to display, or select Window > Info.

3. Select Image > Adjustments > Levels and move the display next to the image.

4. Select the black eyedropper on the Levels display that indicates "Sample in image to set black point" and hover over the image observing the RGB values on the Info panel. You will notice most values display with an abundance of blue and green values, which you can easily see in the image itself (Figure 6-23).

▷ FIGURE 6-23

Using the Info panel to find RGB values.

Set black point eyedropper

Shadow areas of image display overall blue-green cast [Green (G) and Blue (B) have highest numbers]

5. Locate a shadow area under one of the flowers or leaves, or on the branch behind the leaves. Notice no values display a pure black "0" which is good; always look for shadow details that display in the "teens" for numerical values.

6. When you think you have pretty much the lowest number, click the spot to remap the RGB pixel values close to the lowest number so that shadow details are not "clipped" away and are neutralized or spread out. Now this lowest number doesn't mean all your shadows are a pure black; the details are simply pulled out and remapped so that now the lowest number still indicates shadow detail (Figure 6-24).

7. If everything looks too dark or black, hit CMD+Z or your Mac, or CTRL+Z on your Windows to undo and try again.

8. Select the white eyedropper on the Levels display that indicates "Sample in image to set white point" and hover over the image observing the RGB values on the Info panel (Figure 6-25).

9. To set the highlight detail, find a white lower area that shows detail in the highlights. Use the Info panel to spot a white area closest to 255 here, which you'll probably find in the blue channel because of the color cast.

▷ FIGURE 6-24

Locating and neutralizing the shadow detail areas of the image.

▷ FIGURE 6-25

Setting the highlight or white point to readjust the color cast to its correct colors.

10. Click on the bright white area of one of the flowers. You'll notice the RGB colors will be remapped to "255" each or close to that number (Figure 6-25).

11. If everything looks too bright, hit CMD+Z or your Mac or CTRL+Z on your Windows to undo and try again. Select the highlight sample tool and try again; you can use the Preview button to observe the before and after effects.

12. When you look at the histogram on the Levels dialog box, you want the least clipping on both the highlight (far right) and shadow areas (far left) to show. You want as close to the entire "mountain" histogram as possible to show with little if anything cut off.

13. The final corrected image should not show any blown out highlights. Save the image in your *Chapter 6* folder. Feel free to open up the original *Bluecast* image to make comparisons. This technique also works great with old color cast images as well.

NEUTRALIZING SHADOW AND HIGHLIGHT AREAS USING THE THRESHOLD COMMAND

Sometimes our eyes adjust very quickly to subtle changes in color, or as designers you may have received an image from a client who may not have as well-calibrated a monitor as you may have, or perhaps your own monitor may not be adequately calibrated. You can use the Info panel to see if there is any slight color cast, and neutralize shadows and highlights by finding an image's black and white points to sample and remap the pixels. One feature that has been around in Photoshop for a while is called Threshold, which can be used to find true black and white areas with no guessing. It is found in the Adjustments section (Image > Adjustments > Threshold) or as an adjustment layer in the Layers panel. You may find this technique used by perfectionists working in the commercial or advertising industries where color is critical. Again the trick is finding black and white points, and all other colors will remap to those colors. You can make all adjustments to adjustment layers using the Properties panel as was shown in Chapter 5. The benefit of using Adjustment layers is that all adjustments or corrections aren't made directly on the original image.

▷ FIGURE 6-26

Precision in neutralizing color casts using the Threshold command, Color Sampler Tool, and Levels command.

THE THRESHOLD COMMAND AND THE COLOR SAMPLER TOOL

The **Threshold command** works in conjunction with the Color Sampler Tool (I). You use the Threshold command to find the darkest blacks and whitest whites, while **the Color Sampler Tool (I)**, although used to sample colors, can also be

Before

After

used to create reference points for the black and white areas of an image that are transferred onto the Info panel. You can sample a series of adjacent sample areas too. After creating the reference points for optimum shadow and highlight areas, you then use the Levels command black and white sampler eyedropper to click on the reference points to remap the shadows, highlights, and accurate color tones.

Here you'll use the Threshold command and the Color Sampler Tool to sample the correct shadow and highlight areas. Make sure the Info panel is displayed. You'll find the shadow area first (Figure 6-26).

1. Launch Photoshop and open the *Plate.jpg* image. Make a duplicate image (Image > Duplicate) and save as *PlateADJ.jpg* in your *Chapter 6* folder.

2. Zoom in and use the Hand Tool (H) to position the image area to the front side of the plate. Make sure the Properties panel is displayed (Window > Properties).

3. Select the Color Sampler Tool (I). The Color Sampler Tool (I) is the eyedropper icon with a bullseye on it (Figure 6-27). It may be located where you may just see an eyedropper on the Tools panel.

▷ FIGURE 6-27

Using the Threshold command to find accurate shadow areas of the image. The Color Sampler Tool is used to create point samples for reference.

4. In the Tools Option bar, select a 3x3 Average pixel Sample Size from the drop-down menu for sampling adjacent colors. This is a good starting point so you don't select a stray off-color pixel.

5. At the bottom of the Layers panel, click the icon that reads "Create new fill or adjustment layer" (looks like a half moon); then click on the Threshold command. The Threshold adjustment layer thumbnail will appear black and white above the Background layer.

6. In the Properties panel, you'll notice a histogram with a sliding arrow underneath in the middle. If you slide the arrow icon to the left, it will display only darkest shadow areas; slide it to the right and it will display the highlight areas of the image.

7. To find the darkest shadow area, which will appear under the plate, drag the arrow slider from the default middle area to the left (Figure 6-27).

8. Shift-Click in the shadow area to set the color sample point #1 on that portion of the image area. It will display in the Info panel as #1 before and after number values with RGB color channels.

9. In the Threshold panel, drag the slider to the right to find the highlight with detail that does not display bright light reflections as at the plate edges. Select the white area near the icing of the food and Shift-Click to set the color sample point on that portion of the image area. It will display in the Info panel as #2 for highlight RGB color channels (Figure 6-28).

For highlights,
drag to the right

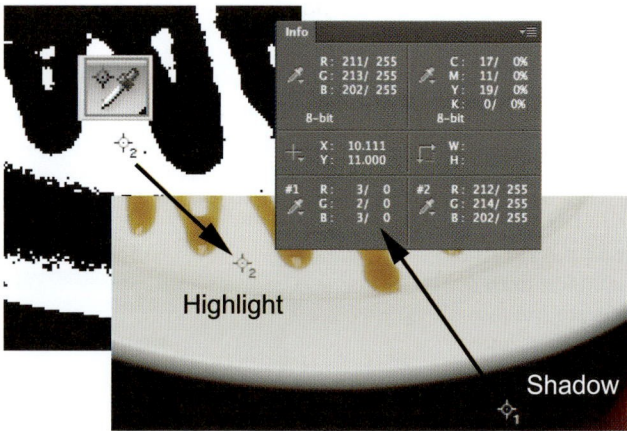

Highlight

Shadow

Shift click to create reference
point with Color Sampler Tool

10. Click the eye icon in the Layers panel next to the Threshold 1 copy thumbnail to see the #1 and #2 reference points on the image.

11. If you need to move either of the sample reference points you just made, move the cursor over the point (or Shift-click in earlier versions), the cursor turns into an arrowhead, and drag the point spot to move into place.

12. When you feel comfortable with reference points made, move the Threshold adjustment layer into the Trash. The non-printable reference points will still display on the image.

NEUTRALIZING COLORS WITH LEVELS SAMPLE POINTS

With the extra steps you just made creating the shadow and highlight reference points, all you need to do is use the eyedropper point samplers in the Levels display box to Shift-Click on the points you created and Photoshop will remap highlights and shadows and all color toners to the black and white reference points with precision.

1. To neutralize the colors using Levels, still zoom in on the image about 200%, and select Image > Adjustment > Levels.

2. Select the "Sample in image to set black point" to select black point eyedropper icon and click over the #1 sample point (shadow).

3. Select the "Sample in image to select white point" to set white point eyedropper icon and click over the #2 sample point (highlight). You'll notice a major change here.

4. The color should be neutralized. Click the Preview button to see your before and after work. Click OK when satisfied. Notice how the adjusted white of the plate makes the food stand out better (Figure 6-29).

5. You may also notice on the histogram that the highlights show clipping or are cropped at the end; this represents the area of pure white on the plate from bright light reflections, and as long as the rest of the plate isn't "glowing," you have accurately remapped your image for best tonal representation.

6. To remove the reference points, drag the points as the mouse becomes an arrowhead out from the edge of the image. The point references will also be removed from the Info panel.

7. Save the file in your *Chapter 6* folder.

▷ **FIGURE 6-29**

Using the Levels command black and white sampler icons to click on reference points and accurately remap all tones and colors.

Shadow (#1) Highlight (#2)

SYNCING IMAGES AND SETTINGS BETWEEN COMPUTERS USING CREATIVE CLOUD

The Creative Cloud (CC) subscription-based version of Adobe products allows designers access to all of Adobe's products, and the ability to automatically sync their fonts, custom tools and brushes, actions, colors and settings between applications and multiple devices, no matter whether they are on a Mac or Windows. Creative Cloud members automatically are given online cloud storage (storage space on a remote drive or server) and the ability to sync to any device, so that files are easily accessible from any location. These exercises are set up for those who are members of Adobe's subscription service, and who may have Photoshop and Creative Cloud on multiple devices. You will need to have created a free Adobe ID, which is usually an email with a password afterwards. This is included in this book as a valid reference as this is the direction the industry is going in utilizing cloud technologies in submitting and sharing work over the Internet.

TOOLKIT TIP To install Creative Cloud on your computer or device, go to Adobe's website at *www.adobe.com*, select Download > Product trials as discussed in the Unit 1 Review. You'll find a page listing "Featured free trial downloads" and select the link, Start for Free, under the Creative Cloud icon. You'll need to create a free Adobe ID, which involves creating a valid email, placing in your password, and a little personal secure information. Select Create, follow instructions, and you're ready. To use Creative Cloud on your smartphone, you'll need to purchase an inexpensive Photoshop Touch App.

MANAGING YOUR IMAGES AND SHARING YOUR WORK

With Creative Cloud on your computer, you can not only download Adobe applications which automatically update, but you can also place files in a Creative Cloud folder so that they are stored online, and then can be accessed from another computer with Creative Cloud installed. Any additions, modifications, or deletions are reflected on all connected computers and devices. For example, if you upload a Photoshop file using the Creative Cloud Files page, it is automatically downloaded on all connected computers, or can be downloaded onto any device when you sign on with your Adobe ID. You can preview many creative file types directly in a web browser on your computer, tablet, or smartphone. These file types include: PSD, AI, INDD, JPG, PDF, GIF, PNG, Photoshop Touch, Ideas, and others. No more having to worry about whether you are using the most current version, as all your files are updated through the Creative Cloud.

In this exercise, if you have the free Creative Cloud application installed on your computer as part of your subscription, you'll take a file and submit it to be stored in the cloud and then retrieve it on another computer with Creative Cloud.

1. With Creative Cloud active, click on the icon and select the Files tab to display the folder icon.

2. Click Open Folder and drag an image file you created in Photoshop from the earlier exercise, or any Adobe file, into the open folder. This file is also set up inside a Creative Cloud Files directory folder on your computer (Home or Users > Creative Cloud Files). When you drag the file into the folder, it may display as Syncing. Within Photoshop or any application, you can also choose File > Save As, and navigate to the Creative Cloud Files directory on your computer.

3. When completed, it may read, "All files up to date." It has pushed the file(s) on your computer to the Creative Cloud online server

4. You can now go over to another computer, which we'll call Computer B, click on the Creative Cloud icon, then the Files tab and wait until syncing is completed.

5. Open the Creative Cloud folder and you'll find the updated file. All files that are synced and up to date will display a green checkmark.

6. If you click on the thumbnail, it will expand to fill the screen, click on the Creative Cloud Files link above the image to minimize to a thumbnail again.

7. To see how the syncing works when you make a change, open the same file in Photoshop in Computer B, create a title across the image and resave, then make sure it is still in the Creative Cloud folder (or Creative Cloud Files directory).

8. Go back to your initial computer, and open the file from Creative Cloud, it may display as syncing, and you'll find it updates to display the title on your image you created in Computer B. This works nicely if you are working between computers, say between work and home, or school and home.

▷ FIGURE 6-30

Use Creative Cloud to sync files saved from any application, or dragged into the Creative Cloud folder. Files are then updated for access from another device.

9. You can also use the Actions button (gear icon) on Creative Cloud on your computer to find information regarding your files on the Creative Cloud website.

10. You can also sign in using your tablet, smartphone, or computer with your Adobe ID to locate your files stored in Creative Cloud at *creative.adobe.com*. From the Creative Cloud website, you can also upload files directly to the Creative Cloud Files page where you can create folders, and share your work using the website Actions button (Figure 6-30). Check it out! This provides quick access when you need to show your work using your tablet or smartphone.

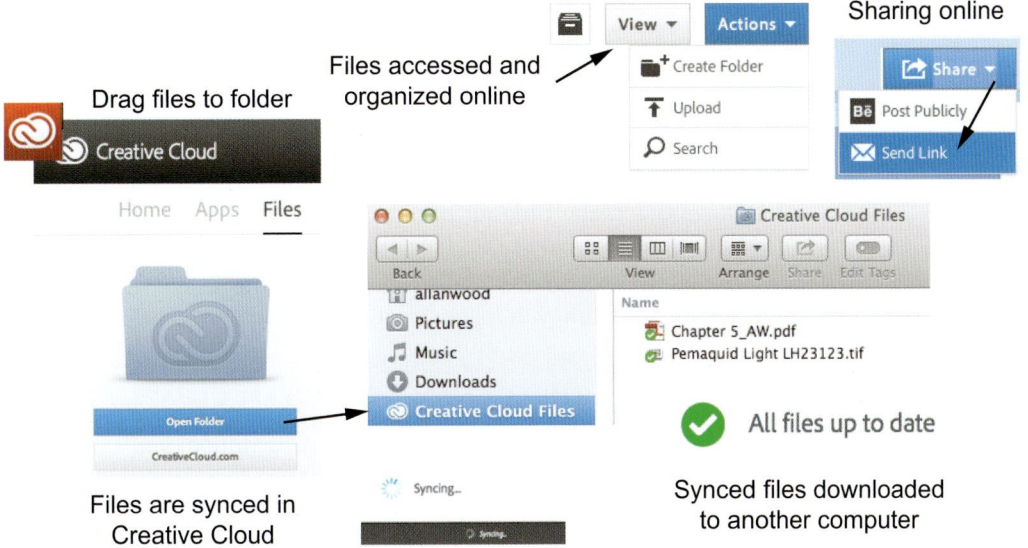

Drag files to folder

Files accessed and organized online

Sharing online

Files are synced in Creative Cloud

Synced files downloaded to another computer

Sharing Work Using Creative Cloud

You can share files with others from the Creative Cloud Files page as well. This opens up a world of opportunity in distributing your work to potential employers or clients, getting feedback from other professionals, or in working on a project as part of a team.

1. Go to the website *https://creative.adobe.com* and log in using your Adobe ID.

2. On the Creative Cloud Files page, navigate to the file you want to share and click to open it onto the screen. To display the image full screen click the cross arrows under the image, click again to bring you back.

3. From the Share menu, choose Send Link. When the dialog box displays, and you want to make it public instead of keeping it private for yourself, click Make Public (Figure 6-31). The file is ready to be shared and a short URL is created. Note: You can also choose Post Publicly through Behance, which is an online service used by many designers and photographers.

▷ FIGURE 6-31

Sharing your files from Creative Cloud.

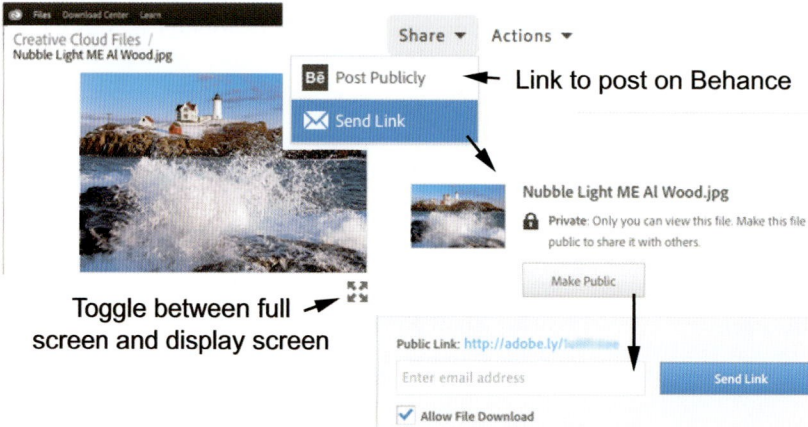

4. Enter the email addresses to send this link to. Optionally, enable Allow File Download.

5. Click Send Link and your image will be distributed to your contacts. If you want to have the image brought back to its original thumbnail display position, click the Creative Cloud Files link above your image name on the left.

6. Log out when done. You can see how important this useful feature can be when sharing your work with follow creators, friends, or as part of a team.

SYNCING PHOTOSHOP SETTINGS BETWEEN COMPUTERS

As mentioned in the previous exercise, with a paid subscription, you can save any image file, say from Photoshop, to be synced for access from another computer by saving to the Creative Cloud Files directory, or save to any designated location on your initial computer, then drag or copy the file into the open Creative Cloud folder in Creative Cloud.

Adobe applications also come with a Sync Settings feature, which enables you to sync preferences and custom settings, brushes, actions, tool presets, and so forth. This makes it easy for you to keep those settings synchronized across multiple computers. In Photoshop, you can sync settings through the Photoshop (Mac) or Edit (Windows) menus, or right from the image itself when opened, along with the option to share your file on a public website called Behance. You need to initiate the sync manually; it does not happen automatically and it cannot be scheduled. Sync your custom settings from within the application, say in Photoshop, and at home, usually not on a secure network. Make sure you are signed in with your free Adobe ID so it will display when you select the Photoshop (Mac) or Edit (Windows) menu.

(X) PROBLEM When ready to sync your settings to the Creative Cloud, if you cannot find your Adobe ID displayed in the Photoshop (Mac) or Edit (Windows) menu, you'll need to sign out of Photoshop, and then sign back in again. Go to Help > Sign Out... to sign out. Choose Help > Sign-in... to sign in again. Quit Photoshop, and then launch Photoshop again. Sync Settings should then be enabled.

Let's say you created a custom brush or special tool presets as done in the Chapter 6 exercise, and you want to sync it/them to another computer. Here, you'll sync those settings between two computers using Photoshop's menu to Sync Settings.

▷ FIGURE 6-32

Settings selections available in Photoshop for syncing to another computer.

1. Make a tool change in the brush size and other changes and take note of the changes being made. You can even change Tool Presets, Workspaces (same platform or OS), Custom Shapes, Swatches, and others (see what settings you can sync in Figure 6-32).

2. Select Photoshop (Mac) or Edit (Windows) and make sure your Adobe ID (email) is displayed. Note: If your Adobe ID doesn't display, follow directions in the Problem section above.

3. After closing any open documents or files in Photoshop, select Upload Settings in the Photoshop (Mac) or Edit (Windows) menu. It will automatically send all your settings to the Creative Cloud.

4. Open your other computer (computer B), making sure you are logged in with your Adobe ID again. After closing all documents, choose Download Settings.

5. If a dialog box displays as Updated settings are ready, select Apply Now to bring the settings from the Creative Cloud onto your other computer. Your new settings synced from Photoshop on your initial computer will display on the second computer. Very handy!

TOOLKIT TIP For more control of what settings you would like to sync, if you choose Preferences > Sync Settings, you can choose to Sync, Everything (the default), Custom to turn off specific types of settings you don't want to sync, or Nothing for the particular computer you are working on (Figure 6-32). Make selections then select Upload (or Download if downloading from the Cloud server) to start the process. It will also display a log of what is being completed. Click OK when done.

Icons on Each Image to Sync Settings and Share Your Work

In Creative Cloud (CC), when an image is displayed, let's say in Photoshop, there may be two additional icon options on the bottom left of the document. One, which looks like a gear icon, is labeled Sync settings to Creative Cloud (if settings have not been synced recently). This allows a designer to click with the image open to sync the current settings directly into the Creative Cloud. When you click on the icon, your Adobe ID will display and a button will display as Sync Settings Now (Figure 6-33). By clicking the button you push your settings into the Creative Cloud to be downloaded to another computer.

The other icon, which looks like a right facing arrow, is called Share on Behance. This provides the option to share your images as a public portfolio, with others as part of a team, or on social networks, and receive feedback from your design community. You can also access Behance by selecting File > Share on Behance. When prompted to log in to Behance, use your Adobe ID. It's a free service for Adobe Creative Cloud subscribers and allows you to share your work with others.

▷ FIGURE 6-33

Icons underneath each open image to set current settings into Creative Cloud or share displayed files on public website Behance.

DIGITAL TOOLKIT EXTRA: Developing Special Effects Using Photoshop's Actions and Creating 3D Objects

Actions are little scripts or mini programs you can create for applying special effects; minimize repetitive tasks, and other creative methods of enhancing your workflow, so you can play. You can use your actions on individual images or groups of images. The Actions panel has prescribed actions and you can add customized actions as we are doing here. Once an action is created on a test image, and works correctly, the action is automatically saved permanently for future edits. You can even turn on and off action "layers" for editing tasks, much like you can do with the Layers panel.

Creating objects in 3D space is becoming quite popular and useful in today's design industry as the availability of 3D evolves into our main stream culture. Photoshop provides the tools for designers to work in developing 3D objects for print and electronic media. Designers can also output to 3D printers, or to an online 3D printing service.

CREATING AN ACTION THAT BOOSTS THE COLOR AND TONE OF YOUR IMAGES

The action you will create for this exercise creates two adjustment layers so your original image is not altered. The first adjustment layer adds a little saturation of color, and the second applies a curves adjustment to bump up the contrast and give your image a little boost to make it stand out (Figure 6-34).

SETTING UP AN ACTION

You can name your action so it's easy find, have a special color assigned to it, create it as part of a group of similar actions called a **set**, and you can even assign combinations of keyboard function keys and other keys on your keyboard. Once you set up your action, you're ready to start recording. It's a good idea to have a test image ready as well. Always create a duplicate; you never want to test on the original image.

Here you'll need to set up your action before recording any procedures, which includes using a test image.

1. Open the file *Chairs.tif* in your *Chapter 6* folder, and make sure the Layers and Properties panels are displayed. The image is an early morning photograph.

2. Duplicate the Image and name it as *ADJChairs.*

3. Make sure the Actions panel is displayed (Window > Actions). You'll notice there are already actions Photoshop has included in the Default set group. For our purposes here, we will create our action in the Default group as well.

4. Click on the "Create new action" icon at the bottom of the Actions panel.

Action created for adding
two adjustment layers with settings

Image after action applied
(contrast boost, and slight saturation)

Image before action applied

▷ FIGURE 6-34

Creating an action for subtle effects in boosting contrast and color saturation.

5. When the New Action display box opens, name the action *Curves and Saturation*, and create a blue color to make it stand out from the other actions. Leave everything else in the Default set (Figure 6-35).

6. Click on the Record button and you'll notice the record circular icon in the Actions panel displays as red when active. It will record various commands and functions you apply to your image, and you have the option to stop recording anytime and resume when ready.

RECORDING THE CREATION OF TWO ADJUSTMENT LAYERS

Now that you have set up the action, you are going to create two adjustment layers on your image. One will be used for increasing the saturation of color, and the other will bump up the shadows and highlights using a Curves adjustment layer. The benefit of having these two adjustment layers is, when you apply them using your action, you can also further tweak each adjustment layer to your liking for that particular image, without damaging the original image.

In this exercise, while the action is recording you will create two adjustment layers.

Stop playing/recording

Play

Delete

Begin recording (active)

Create new action

Create new set

▷ FIGURE 6-35

Creating a new action.

1. With the action recording in active mode (red button) in the Actions panel, at the bottom of the Layers panel, click the "Create new fill or adjustment layer" icon (half moon).

2. From the list, select the Curves… adjustment layer. It will display on its own separate layer above the original image and will display in the Properties panel.

3. Click to create a point and slightly drag the shadows (bottom portion of the diagonal line) downward.

▷ FIGURE 6-36

Recording action to create Curves and Hue/Saturation adjustment layers.

4. Click, and drag slightly the highlight (upper portion of the curves diagonal line) upward as shown in Figure 6-36. This provides a little "snap" in contrast to the image. You'll also notice the action is recorded in the Actions panel.

Curves adjustment layer

Create new fill or adjustment layer

5. Click the "Create new fill or adjustment layer" icon again, and select the Hue/Saturation adjustment layer. When it displays in the Properties panel, increase the Saturation by 10 pt. This will provide some additional color saturation in the image. Again, the action is recorded, and the adjustment layer displays above the Curves adjustment layer.

6. To stop the action recording anything further, click the "Stop playing/recording" square icon on the bottom of the Actions panel.

7. You'll notice, under your title action "Curves and Saturation," other arrows next to each component that, that when clicked, will display the settings you created for each adjustment layer. You can go in and change these components of your action if you need to, and with a check mark displayed next to each component, that part of the action will be played. By default, all parts will work when the action is played, but you can also choose to only have certain components of the action to play (Figure 6-37).

8. Click the arrows again to toggle them to close, leaving just the action title displayed. Now you're ready to test your action.

▷ FIGURE 6-37

Stopping your action recording and observing your action settings.

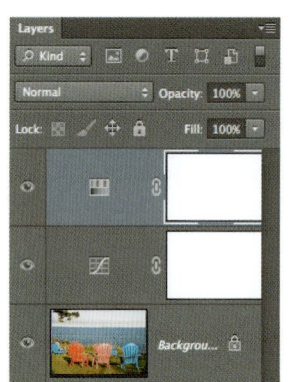

Curves and Hue/Saturation
adjustment layers

Stop playing/recording

Action component
ready to play

Click arrows to see settings
of action components

TESTING THE ACTION

Now that you have created an action and it is now turned off, it's time to test it. All you have to do is select the "Play" icon, which looks like an arrow, and see your results. Again, in our case in creating adjustment layers, after playing the action to get the initial settings, you can simply double-click on the layer adjustment thumbnail and further tweak the settings for the image you're working on. If the effect doesn't work for your image, and in some cases it may not, just drag the adjustment layers into the Delete trash icon at the bottom of the Layers panel. This particular action you have created provides a subtle starting point to give your image a little boost in color and tone as an effect.

Let's test our action. We'll use our same test image, but we will duplicate it again.

1. Close the *ADJChairs* image WITHOUT saving so we have the original *ADJChairs. tif* image displayed.

2. Duplicate the *Chairs.tif* image again and name it *ADJChairs* so we can try on the same image. Now comes the fun part! With the Actions panel displayed, select the Curves and Saturation action you just created.

3. Click on the Play icon at the bottom of the Actions panel and watch the adjustment layers be added to your Layers panel, then the change in your image. If something doesn't look right or doesn't work, simply recreate your action, in the previous exercise (Figure 6-38).

4. To make further adjustments, you can double-click on the adjustment layer thumbnail, not the mask (that's where you paint in or mask out parts of the effect on the image) and adjust using the Properties panel.

5. You can see how this can be a lot of fun, and free you of repetitive tasks as well. Save the file as *ADJChairs.tif* in your *Chapter 6* folder.

6. You can also add to your action by simply selecting the action layer before the new component you want to add, start recording, perform the additional function (like maybe you want to duplicate the image first before adding adjustment layers), then turn off the new action component when done, and test. You can also delete a component by dragging into the Delete icon at the bottom of the panel.

▷ FIGURE 6-38

Testing the action to see applied effects.

7. Feel free to try this action on your own images.

Original   Play   Action Applied

BATCH PROCESSING IMAGES WITH ACTIONS

After you have created an action, you can create a "factory" or assembly line where you take many images from one folder, apply the action, and place the "processed" images in another folder. This process is known as **batch processing**. One of the main batch processing actions I do is to make sure all my imagery and designs are copyrighted, as any designer or photographer should do. This would be a very repetitive and somewhat daunting task to have to apply this action one image at a time. This is where batch processing comes in, to handle repetitive tasks quickly and efficiently. This will also introduce you to the File Info panel in Photoshop, and the Automate command, which contains other preset actions you can play with. As mentioned before, the action must be created first.

SETTING UP THE ACTION FIRST

Again you're going to create the action script first, in this case to have the image copyrighted. Here you should use one of your own images or designs. If you don't have one on hand, open up the *Myboys.tif* image of, yep, my kids. It's an old photo and I'm not too worried if you want to call the image your own, but it hasn't been copyrighted yet and would work fine for our purposes here. Whenever you create initial actions, always use a duplicated image, never the original.

Here, this exercise will show you how to create an action to copyright your images. Then we'll process them in the following exercise.

1. Again you're going to create the action script first. Open up a test image of your own work (it should be a duplicate so there won't be a possible problem with the original). If you don't have one, open up the *Myboys.tif* image, which hasn't been copyrighted yet, and duplicate it. It will work fine for our purposes here. You have my permission to use it.

2. In the Actions panel, select "Create new action" to open up the New Action display panel. Name the action *Copyright*, set the color reference to Red if you want, and leave all other defaults (Figure 6-39).

▷ FIGURE 6-39

Setting up new action named Copyright.

3. Click Record and the Begin recording icon will turn red to display that it is ready to record.

Create new action

Begin recording

CREATING THE COPYRIGHT ACTION USING THE FILE INFO COMMAND

In Photoshop's File menu, you will find a File Info command that is a great resource for information relating to your photograph or design. You can also perform all kinds of edits for your image by providing additional information. For our purposes here we will concentrate on the Description panel where we will place in related Copyright information as part of our action script.

1. With the Actions panel recording, select File > File Info to bring up the display panel of your file. Click on the Description tab.

2. As this is going to be applied to many images, you only want to put general information, like your name and title, near the top.

3. Partway down you will find a copyright status button. Select Copyrighted. Even though you may not have copyrighted your images with the government, this is a great starting point in identifying that you are the author of your work. Again, it is most important to start here with a piece of your own work, but I am giving you permission to use the *Myboys* file for educational purposes so it is legal for you to use this if you need to practice.

4. Next you will find, by Copyright notice, where you would type in "Copyright (your name). All rights reserved. Do not use without direct permission from the author." You can also put in general contact info but be careful; it's better to provide only general info. If they want to use your image, they must find a way to contact you. This just helps to protect against those who may want to use or copy your image.

5. That's all you need; use my example on Figure 6-40 as a guide. Click OK, then click to stop recording on the Actions panel. Make sure the action has a check mark next to it. You should find a copyright symbol in the title of your file.

6. To test, close the duplicate without saving, create another duplicate of the image, and play the action. You should find the copyright symbol in the image title, and the info you put in, when you selected the File Info command again.

7. If it works, it's time to create a batch process.

▷ FIGURE 6-40

Using File Info command to place copyright information on your image.

CREATING A BATCH PROCESS OF YOUR ACTION: THE AUTOMATE FUNCTION

You can use the Automate command in Photoshop's File menu to perform various special automations, and it is here you also assign actions. Once you have a group of images or artwork you need performed on, set in a CD, or duplicated in a folder, you can then create another folder where you want the processed images to be placed. This is a little tricky, and as always, you want to use this on duplicated files first to make sure the batch process works exactly as you have intended. For this to be effective for your own purpose, you will need to gather duplicates of your imagery or artwork and place in a folder where the action will perform the process.

Now you'll see if the action performs on a group of your own images or artwork.

1. Create a folder on your desktop called *Original*, or whatever you feel works, and drag a group of duplicated images into the folder. You can also insert a CD of your images and use this as the place to take the images from instead if you prefer. For this test, it's a good idea to just try on a half dozen images or so to make sure the process works.

2. You the need to create a folder on your desktop named as *Copyrighted* to process the copyrighted images to.

3. Select File > Automate. Here you'll find scripts or programs that automate tasks you can try later. Select Batch to open the Batch dialog box.

4. In the Action line, select Copyright to set up the Copyright action you just created.

5. Your Source should be set at Folder, then select the Choose button to locate the folder where your images are that you want to have copyrighted. Leave the rest at default as shown in Figure 6-41 on the previous page.

6. For the Destination, select Folder again, and Choose the location of your *Copyrighted* folder.

7. Leave everything else at defaults, unchecked as shown in Figure 6-41 for our purposes here, except click all operating systems displayed for Compatibility.

8. When you are absolutely sure you have everything set up correctly, press OK. Like a factory you'll see your image opened up, the action quickly applied, and placed in your *Copyrighted* folder; then the next image is opened up. Hopefully all the processed images should end up in your *Copyrighted* folder, correctly as you had planned.

9. Check to make sure it is correct, as you had intended. Then, if all is correct, you can perform the operation on many more images.

10. Go ahead and create a batch process of the initial action you created in the beginning, in creating adjustment layers for boosting the tone and color of your images. Check out some of the other operations in the Automate command area. Go ahead and play!

▷ FIGURE 6-41

Using Batch Process to place copyright info on folder of files.

USING PHOTOSHOP TO CREATE 3D OBJECTS

Available in Photoshop Creative Cloud (CC) is the ability to create 3D objects, with all kinds of effects and lighting applied. **3D objects** are usually converted from 2D text, preset shapes, a selection on an image, or a layer mask. The **3D application** within Photoshop provides designers the opportunity to create complex 3D objects for both print and web media. The 3D workspace contains a 3D menu within Photoshop and a corresponding 3D panel to allow you to select scenes, camera views, and various surfaces of a selected 3D object, and apply various materials and color effects, and any 3D objects can also be painted on.

The **Properties panel** provides the designer the ability to shape, distort, move, and scale objects. You can also apply various types of material textures to your 3D object, and control the lighting direction. Movements on 3D objects involve using the Move Tool (V) and the 3D axis widgets. When the Move Tool (V) is selected, a grid is displayed as a reference plane with a **Camera View widget** that you can click and drag around to adjust how you want the 3D objects to be viewed (Figure 6-42).

▷ FIGURE 6-42

The Photoshop 3D Workspace.

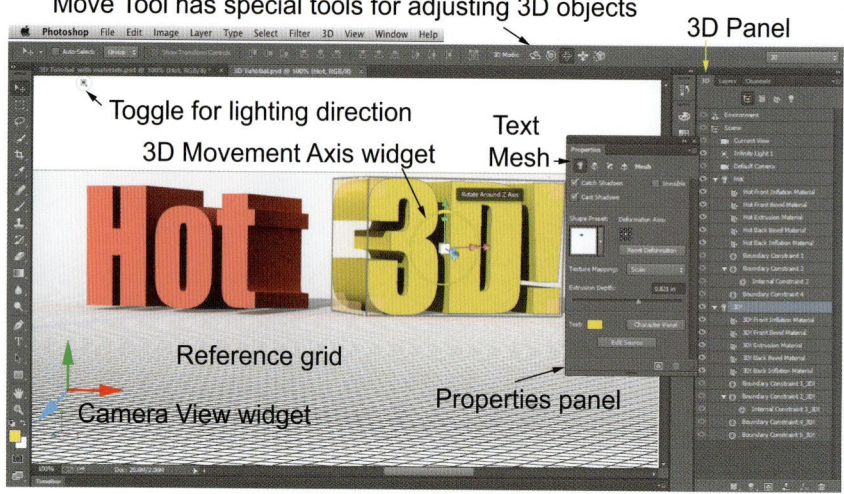

Move Tool has special tools for adjusting 3D objects

3D Panel

Toggle for lighting direction

3D Movement Axis widget

Text Mesh→

Reference grid

Camera View widget

Properties panel

Objects can be rotated and moved along the grid from 3D Mode buttons on the Move Tool's Options bar. There is also the 3D Movement Axis widget and the Screen Axis widget to assist designers in positioning and adjusting 3D objects in 3D workspace. After the scene is positioned with effects and lighting direction applied, the 3D objects are placed through a process called **rendering** or **ray tracing** where all effects and changes are identified and accurately reproduced.

PROBLEM The 3D engine in Photoshop CC requires a minimum of 512MB of Video RAM (VRAM) on the computer's graphics card to operate. If you select Photoshop's 3D menu and all is grayed out, you may not have the required video RAM memory needed. To check, select About This Mac > More Info (Mac), or, right-click the desktop > Personalize > Change Display Settings> Advanced Settings > Adapter (Windows). If you have enough video RAM, you must also have Open GL enabled, go to Photoshop > Preferences > Performances > Advanced Settings (Mac), or, Edit > Preferences > Performance (Windows).

CREATING TYPE 3D OBJECTS

A good starting in point in learning to work in 3D space is to be able to convert 2D text into 3D text objects and have lighting and materials effects applied. A **mesh**, sometimes referred to as a wireframe or polygonal model, is the structural part of an object or character 3D displayed as a low-resolution color image before rendering is applied to create an accurate representation of the 3D object. The mesh is a collection of faces, or surfaces, vertices, and edges, which define the shape of the 3D object. **Extruding** is a process that extends a 2D object along the object's Z-axis to add depth to the object. For example, if you extrude a 2D ellipse or

▷ FIGURE 6-43

Completed 3D objects.

circle, it becomes a cylinder. This series of exercises will provide some exposure to some of the many tools, techniques, and effects you can use in creating 3D objects (Figure 6-43).

In Photoshop, you're going to create a 3D text to be set up as part of a print design. You have preset dimensions in Photoshop for print and electronic media.

1. In Photoshop, select File > New > and then select the Preset: Photo with Size: Landscape 8x10 inches at 300 dpi resolution. Click OK. This will provide space for zooming in to view your work.

2. You'll need to create two lines of text, or two separate type layers for the Layers panel. Use Impact for a font, or some font with wide characters at 72 pt.

3. For the first line, select the Type Tool (T) and type "Hot," and set up whatever colors you like using the Swatches or Color panel, we chose a red Fill for the *Hot* text line. Select the Move Tool (V) to reset and create another separate layer.

4. Type another text line "3D!" alongside the first line "Hot," which will display as a separate layer on the Layers panel. Use the same font, and have both type lines in your window aligned along the same bottom or base line. Set up a bright color, like yellow for the *3D!* text line.

5. Select the *Hot* text line with the Type Tool (T) and you'll notice a 3D button on the far right side of the Tool Options bar, make sure the *Hot* text line is highlighted as well on the Layers panel. Click on the 3D button, and if a dialog displays "You are about to create a 3D layer. Would you like to switch to the 3D workspace?" select Yes to make the transition. A 3D grid displays with your new 3D object (Figure 6-44). In most cases a 2D view is displayed on the left for orientation, which you can close if you want.

2D Top View ►

▷ FIGURE 6-44

Set up the document with high resolution for easier viewing, create two text lines, and select 3D to convert.

6. Repeat the same for the *3D!* text line, select the *3D!* text line in your window, and make sure the line *3D!* in the Layers panel is highlighted as well before selecting 3D in the Tool Options bar. On either line you now no longer have text but converted shapes called objects.

7. You'll notice you have a 3D panel with many sublayers, which correspond to various surfaces on your 3D object. These provide choices in making adjustments. There is also the Properties panel with related choices in determining what materials to use for texture, and the Layers panel, which now displays the converted text as 3D objects.

8. Select the Move Tool (V), and you'll notice a grid displays to display vantage points and orientation along a reference plane. It controls the positioning of your 3D text object. Note: To get out of the grid, just click on another tool in the Tools panel. To work again in 3D with the grid, click the Move Tool (V) again.

9. On the bottom left of your screen, you'll find a Camera View widget, so as you click and drag, the grid adjusts along that reference plane. Make adjustments to suit your taste. Note: You can also select the Default Camera layer in the 3D panel and use that as a starting point to adjust camera view angles.

10. You're going to position both of your new 3D objects first. Select the Layers panel and make sure the *Hot* layer is highlighted; we'll work on that first.

POSITIONING YOUR TEXT 3D OBJECTS

When the Move Tool (V) is selected, a grid is displayed as a reference plane with a **Camera View widget** that you can click and drag around to adjust how you want the 3D objects to be viewed. Objects can be rotated and moved along the grid from 3D Mode buttons on the Move Tool's Options bar.

Clicking once on any surface of a 3D object surrounds the object in what is called a **cage** to make changes, and displays the **3D Axis Movement widget**, which allows the object to be moved along the X-axis (width), Y-axis (height), and Z-axis (depth), and provides icons to rotate and scale objects along these axes. The 3D axis movement widget has 3 arrows; each arrow corresponds to a direction of movement and will move the object in the direction it is pointing. The second element under the arrow will rotate the object across its axis, and the third square element (rectangle) will scale the object along this axis. At the base of the widget is a white square, which allows you to scale the object proportionately.

Here you will position your text objects along the grid using the 3D Axis Movement widget, and the Move Tool Options bar.

1. Make sure the "Hot" layer in the Layers panel is selected, and then select the Move Tool (V). You'll work with Move Tool 3D options in the Tool Options bar first.

2. In the Move Tool Options bar you'll find various 3D controls in the 3D Mode area on the right. Select the Rotate the 3D object icon in the Move Tool's Tool Options bar. You may notice the 3D axis ground plane of lines on the bottom left of the screen.

3. Click on the *Hot* text object, and you'll find a box surrounding it called a cage. The cage houses the controls you have on your 3D object. Drag to the left carefully, you'll notice a grid will display.

4. You may also notice a 3D Axis Movement widget will display, and as you hover your mouse over various sections of the icon, it displays to rotate, move, and scale along X (width), Y (height), or Z (depth) axes (see Figure 6-45), and shades areas of your object that may be affected when you drag. Try to move the object along the X-Axis to turn the "H" towards the background.

▷ FIGURE 6-45

The Move Tool uses the 3D Mode area in its Tool Options bar to scale and position objects. The 3D Movement Axis widget provides precise adjustments.

3D Mode for Positioning 3D Objects

3D Movement Axis Widget

5. Select the Drag the 3D Object icon in the 3D Mode area on the Move Tool Options bar and move the *Hot* text object a short distance away to the left of your *3D!* text object to provide spacing if needed.

6. You're going to make the *Hot* text object a little smaller than the *3D!* text object. Click on the Zoom the 3D Camera icon in the 3D Mode section of the Move Tool Options bar, and drag downward to scale the text smaller. To align the smaller *Hot* text object on the same bottom line as the *3D!* object, select the Pan the 3D Camera icon in the 3D Mode section and drag to move the object so that it is aligned with the bottom of the *3D!* text object.

7. Let's adjust the *3D!* text object. Select the *3D!* text layer in the Layers panel. Select the Rotate the 3D object icon in the Move Tool Options bar, and adjust by dragging to the right (Figure 6-46).

8. Zoom in a little closer with the Zoom Tool (Z), and then click on the Move Tool (V) again.

9. Click on the *3D!* text object, to display the 3D Movement Axis widget on your object, which allows you to move, scale, and rotate your new object. Adjust so the "!" of your *3D!* text object points slightly towards the background as shown. Play with the other 3D Movement Axis widget controls to perfect your adjustments, remember slight adjustments work best here (Figure 6-46).

10. You can also select and move the entire text object (just like 2D clip art or illustrations) as if in 2D space by selecting to display the cage around the object, then hover your mouse near the top of the cage outline until a 4-arrow icon displays, then just click and drag the object.

11. Save the file as *3D Text.tif* in your *Chapter 6* folder and leave open for the next exercise.

▷ FIGURE 6-46

Use the 3D Mode area in the Move Tool Options bar for general adjustments. Click on the text object to display the 3D Movement Axis widget for precise adjustments.

3D Movement Axis widget

Scale the 3D Object

Drag the 3D Object

Rotate the 3D Object

3D Mode:

Camera View Axis widget displayed at bottom of screen

CONTROLLING LIGHTING DIRECTION ON 3D OBJECTS

The **3D panel** controls layer selections of camera view, the lighting, the 3D workspace environment and current scene, and each surface or face of your object. The 3D menu in Photoshop's menu bar provides many of the same and additional commands in adjusting and controlling your 3D objects. The Properties panel provides further adjustments to the surface and shadow of your 3D object. Ideally multiple 3D text objects should be in the same 3D layer in the Layers panel. By merging them together in the Layers panel it enables the 3D objects to interact with each other, share lights, etc. When 3D objects are merged in the Layers panel, they will still display separately in the 3D panel.

Photoshop 3D objects have light source that will be used to illuminate the scene, as well as cast shadows (if needed). Creating an object in Photoshop 3D will, by default, create an infinite light that can be toggled on and off by the white light icon at the top of the screen. Toggling the light source on (default), displays a **Lighting Direction widget** where you can position the direction of your lighting by dragging the small ball in front. This will re-position the light source and move the shadows. The Infinite Light layer displays in the 3D panel where you can also add additional lighting for complex 3D objects by clicking the light bulb icon at the bottom of the panel. The shadows can also be moved into position without using the Lighting Direction widget, by holding the SHIFT key and dragging within the scene (the pointer will turn into a cross hair).

In this exercise, you will merge the text objects together in the Layers panel, observe that they will still display separately for adjustments in the 3D panel, and adjust the lighting direction.

1. You are going to merge the two text layers together in the Layers panel so they can share the same lighting and characteristics, and this way they can interact with one another. Note: This could also have been done previously after the two type layers were created. Select both layers in the Layers panel, and then select the 3D menu in Photoshop's menu bar, then select Merge 3D Layers.

2. Select the 3D panel (Window > 3D), you'll find both objects are still displayed with separate properties you can adjust. Select Infinite Light on the 3D panel, which turns on light direction.

3. Click and drag to create the shadows to accent your objects. You'll notice with the objects merged together they share the same lighting direction. In this example we used light from a high 45-degree angle, but feel free to experiment.

4. To turn off the light, click the small Infinite Light icon above the image which acts as a toggle, or select the Current View in the 3D panel to get back to the original position and view of your objects with the new lighting you've chosen (Figure 6-47).

5. You can still select the objects individually in the 3D panel to make last minute adjustments.

6. Make any final adjustments and save the file as *3D Text.tif* in your *Chapter 6* folder. This can be used as a backup for future editing so that you can change the text even with 3D effects applied by selecting the Edit Source button in the Properties panel.

Adjusting the lighting direction on the text objects.

← Infinite Light toggle to turn on/off lighting

Lighting Direction widget

Adjust direction of Infinite Light

Add new Light to Scene

7. Make a duplicate image (Image > Duplicate) of your *3D Text.tif* file and save that file as *3D Text ADJ.tif* in your *Chapter 6* folder. Close the original *3D Text.tif* file and leave open the *3D Text ADJ.tif* file for the next exercise in applying 3D materials.

TOOLKIT TIP In the default **Mesh mode** in the Properties panel, you can change the text even with 3D effects applied by selecting the Edit Source button. The text will open in a different window, where you can make your changes and save as the default large document PSB file in its default location. When you open select the document with your 3D effects, you'll find the text changes made, and the 3D effects applied to the new text as well.

APPLYING MATERIALS EFFECTS USING THE PROPERTIES PANEL

An object's material can be changed in the Properties panel by clicking on the object twice (once to select the cage, the second time to select part of the object; any surface that is visible can be selected, or you can select a surface in the 3D panel). To select the front face, click on the front of the object twice, Photoshop CC will select the front extrusion, selecting the appropriate part of the object in this panel, will also select it's properties. You can also use the Properties panel to adjust the object's extrusion, which is usually its thickness of depth.

The material currently selected is shown as a thumbnail image in the small square box in the Properties panel. Clicking on the down arrow next to the thumbnail image will show thumbnail images of other materials that can be applied to the selected part of the object. You can hover your mouse over each material to display its name or texture.

In this exercise, you'll select surfaces of your 3D text objects, and apply special materials with adjustments from the Properties panel.

1. Make sure both the Properties panel (Window > Properties) and 3D panel (Window > 3D) are still displayed.

2. You can control the "thickness" of your text using the Properties panel. This is usually referred to as its **extrusion depth**. By clicking once on the front surface of your *Hot* text object, drag the Extrusion slider as shown on the Properties panel until the thickness is half that of the *3D!* text object. We extruded the thickness to 0.125 in (Figure 6-48). This will also display on the 3D panel as "Hot Front Inflation Material," so you know which surface you are working with ("Hot" is the default text object name).

3. Click once more on the front surface of the *Hot* text object to bring up the choice of materials to apply on the Properties panel. If it doesn't display, click on the front surface one more time. When the Materials section displays, click the down arrow next to the default material for your available choices. Hovering your mouse will provide a description of each material.

4. Pick a Material you'd like to try by clicking on the icon. We chose Wood Ash as we are looking for a more "burnt look" of the text. You'll notice the color changed in the text object as well which we'll adjust in the next exercise. You can always undo (Command/CTRL+Z) if you don't like your choice.

5. The Properties panel now will display a series of surface sliders to make adjustments. Feel free to use the settings in Figure 6-48 as a starting point or create your own.

▷ FIGURE 6-48

Extruding thickness of 3D object and applying Wood Ash material from the Properties panel.

Adjust extrusion depth to 0.125 inch

Click twice on 3D object surface to bring up Materials

Wood Ash material selected and applied

Click 3D surface twice to bring up the Materials display in the Properties panel

6. If you also want to apply the same effect to the sides that you just extruded as we have done, just click to display the side, or select Hot Extrusion Material on the 3D panel to highlight the designated side, and select the icon in the Materials area of the Properties panel as just previously completed for the front side. You can also choose different materials for various sides.

7. For the *3D*! text object we are going to create a Metal Gold material effect as a contrast from the burnt wood effect of the *Hot* text object. Click twice on the Front surface of the *3D*! text object and in the Properties panel, select the Metal Gold material or select your own choice. Adjust to suit your taste or use the sliders in Figure 6-49 as a starting point.

8. Click the left side (or you can select the side by clicking on the 3D! Extrusion Material layer on the 3D panel) and also apply the Metal Gold material effect, adjusting to provide a contrast to suit your taste.

9. Save the file as *3D Text ADJ.tif* in your *Chapter 6* folder.

▷ FIGURE 6-49

Using the Properties panel and applying Metal Gold material to the selected *3D*! text object.

CHANGING COLOR AND TEXTURE OF 3D MATERIALS

Changing the color of your materials involves making adjustments in the Diffuse color box of the Properties panel. In most cases to apply the new color or special material, you choose the color so it displays in the Diffuse color box, and then apply the change. If it doesn't work, then you'll need to remove the original texture displayed in the thumbnail. The new color material will then replace the material you removed. Remember, to bring up the Materials display in the Properties panel, you need to click the 3D object surface twice.

Here you'll change the color of your chosen material of the *Hot* text object.

1. Click the front surface of the *Hot* text object twice if needed to bring up the Materials display section in the Properties panel.

2. After making adjustments on your material, click the "Set the Diffuse Color" box to the right of Diffuse, and select your color when the Color Picker displays. Click OK and the color should display in the Diffuse color box.

3. To apply the change of material color you may need to remove the original texture. Next to the Diffuse color box, click the folder icon to the right and select Remove Texture from the menu. The color on the material will be replaced with the new color you chose, and also automatically be applied to your selected *Hot* text object on the front surface (Figure 6-50).

4. Try this with the extrusion portion (thickness) of your *Hot* text object by clicking on the surface (or, in the 3D panel, select Hot Extrusion Material). To apply other colors, in most cases, with the original material texture removed, you may not need to repeat Step 2 previously in removing texture. Just select the object surface you want to change, click the Diffuse color box, change to the new color, and click OK. The new color should automatically replace the previous color displayed.

5. To apply colors to other surfaces, just select each defined surface in the 3D panel, or click on the surface itself of your object. You can also select colors with the Color Picker open and use the eyedropper to sample color on another part of the image outside the window. For the *Hot* 3D text object, we chose to make the extrusion surface a dark color to contrast with the deep red front surface. Feel free to apply another color in the extrusion portion of the object.

6. Save the file as *3D Text ADJ.tif* in your *Chapter 6* folder and leave open for the next exercise.

▷ FIGURE 6-50

Replacing color in the Diffuse color box, and removing texture to apply new material texture and color.

Click surface twice to bring up Materials display in the Properties panel

SPLITTING YOUR "HOT" TEXT OBJECT INTO SEPARATE LETTER OBJECTS

You can split your text object into individual objects using the Split Extrusion command in the 3D menu in Photoshop's menu bar. This way, your Hot 3D text object will display as separate 3D object text letters on the 3D panel where you can position as needed. Because it is still part of the original merged layer in the Layers panel, the lighting and shadows are still consistent.

TOOLKIT TIP You can still select and move the entire text object by itself by selecting to display the cage around the object, hover your mouse near the top of the outline of the cage until a 4-arrow icon displays, and then just click and drag the object.

Here you will split the *Hot* 3D text object into separate 3D object letters and adjust each letter.

1. Select the *Hot* text object, if needed, so just the cage displays around the object.

2. In Photoshop's 3D menu, select Split Extrusion. If a dialog box displays warning about losing animation, click OK.

3. On the 3D panel, you'll notice all three letters display separately under the main Hot 3D object layer, with sublayers of each surface so you can make changes in each individual 3D text object (Figure 6-51).

▷   FIGURE 6-51

Using Split Extrusion in the 3D menu to create separate 3D text objects.

4. Click on the "H" 3D text object, and then hover your mouse on the upper portion of the cage until your cursor turns into a 4-arrow cross. Click and drag the entire object to the left to provide some spacing between the letters.

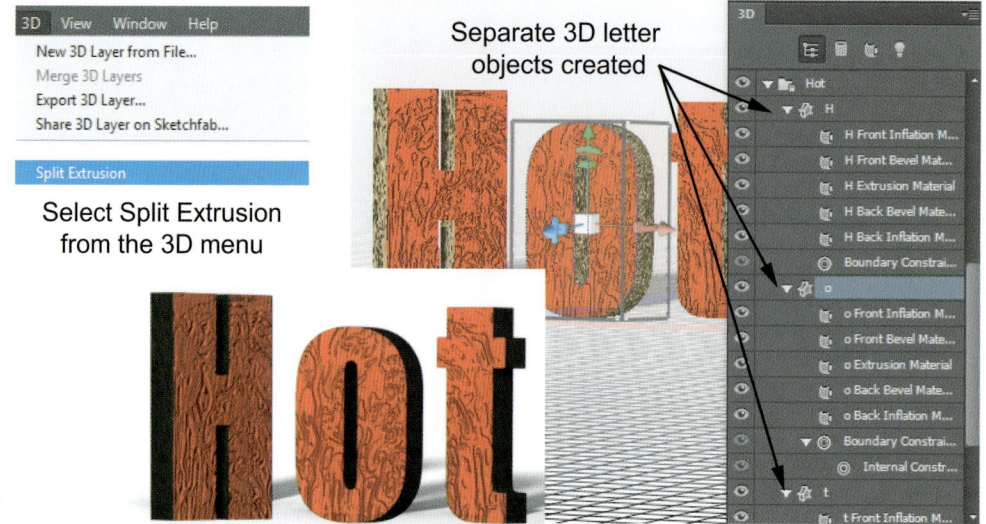

Select Split Extrusion from the 3D menu

Separate 3D letter objects created

5. To move the right side of the letter to face inward, with the Move Tool selected, select the Rotate the 3D object setting in the 3D Mode area of the Tool Options bar. Rotate the "H" 3D text object as needed.

6. Select the "T" 3D text object and use the process just mentioned to rotate the letter so the left side is turned away towards the background. This way, if looking from the top view, the letters would appear in a curved configuration. Adjust the three letters as shown in Figure 6-51.

7. Notice the lighting stays the same. Save the file as *3D Text ADJ.tif* in your *Chapter 6* folder and leave open for the next exercise.

ADJUSTING BEVEL AND INFLATION OF YOUR 3D TEXT OBJECT

The physical appearance of the 3D model can be changed. Clicking on the object once will show the 3D Movement Axis widget, which we used earlier. There is also a **Screen Axis widget**, which has 3 modes to adjust your 3D Objects in positioning, extruding, beveling, and inflating your selected 3D objects and can be accessed by pressing the 'V' key multiple times. You can also find these functions as icons just below the word "Properties" in the Properties panel when the cage is selected (Figure 6-52). Press the 'V' on your keyboard until you find the **Bevel and Inflate widget** (looks like two half circles with rectangles inside). The left hand side of the widget will increase the bevel edge of the object (its strength is controlled by the outer widget). The bevel is modified on the right hand side widget (its strength is also controlled by its corresponding widget). You'll also find other adjustments displayed in the Properties panel.

In this exercise, you will create the forged effect for your gold *3D!* text 3D object.

1. Select the *3D!* text object to display the cage around the object. You'll probably see the 3D Movement Axis widget displayed. As the 3D object has been

▷ FIGURE 6-52

Using the Bevel and Inflate widget (select Cap on the Properties panel) to apply a forged effect for the *3D!* text object.

Mesh Mode (default)
Deform Coordinates
Cap

Select Cap or Press "V" key adjust settings shown

Bevel and Inflate widget

created using gold metal material from the Properties panel, we want to make it look as if cast in a mold.

2. Select the "V" key on your keyboard twice (or select the Cap icon in the Properties panel) to display the widget for adjusting bevel and inflation (Figure 6-52). In our example, we are inflating the letters so you can drag upward to inflate the letters. You can also drag around the widget circle to adjust the angle of the inflation. Drag upward and around until you have an inflated area as in Figure 6-52.

3. There are other settings like changing the contour to provide an edge, as done with many metallic products, among more subtle adjustments you can make using the Properties panel. Use the settings in the Properties panel and adjust using Figure 6-52 as a guide, including adjusting the Contour.

4. Adjust lighting and any final positioning and adjustments. Use the Properties panel to adjust the intensity of your shadows and lighting to taste.

5. Save the file as *3D Text ADJ.tif* in your *Chapter 6* folder and leave open for the next exercise. It's time to create the rendering process of your 3D objects.

RENDERING OR RAY TRACING YOUR ADJUSTED 3D OBJECTS

After the scene is positioned with effects and lighting direction applied, the 3D objects are placed through a process called **rendering** or **ray tracing** where all effects and changes are identified and accurately reproduced. The ray tracing or rendering process will apply light to the scene, the ray-tracer will render the materials, illumination, texture, and shadows, to create the final 3D object. Be wary, this process may take some time (over an hour) so if you simply create a selection of the objects with the Rectangular Marquee Tool (M), the process will only involve the area inside the selection area and will take much less time. Note: For the purposes of this tutorial, you only need to render long enough to be comfortable as to how your completed 3D text objects display on the monitor, as you won't be printing these.

It's time for the final process of rendering until you are comfortable with the look of your 3D objects, then just press ESC to finish at that stage and save your file.

1. With your objects positioned, effects and lighting applied, you are ready to render the screen. First, select the Rectangular Marquee Tool (M) and drag a selection that encompasses the 3D text objects and the shadows created (Figure 6-53). This will focus the process only inside the selection.

2. Select the 3D menu from the Photoshop menu bar, and then select Render to start the process (3D > Render). You can also select the Render icon at the bottom of the Properties panel.

3. The time to process will be displayed. You can allow the time to complete the process so your final images are crisp and display accurate effects. To cancel, you can just press the ESC key on your keyboard. Partial rendering is used often to give designers a quick overview of what the final project will look like.

4. When completed, or if you even had to cancel due to time constraints, you can still save it as *3D Text ADJ.tif* as before in your *Chapter 6* folder. You can open and edit it in the future.

Render →

▷ FIGURE 6-53

Before final rendering, drag a rectangular selection only around the 3D object area to save time.

CREATING 3D SHAPE OBJECTS

In the Photoshop Creative Cloud (CC) 3D panel you can add, delete, duplicate, and even bake 3D objects. The process of baking creates a more realistic appearance, like a specific texture on the selected 3D object. You can also create a clone of an existing object called an **instance**. This way when you make a change to the original (parent) object, the change will be applied to all instances of that object. If you have 3D objects on different layers, in Photoshop Creative Cloud (CC) you can group and reverse the stacking order, and you can merge them together into one layer. This allows you the flexibility to manipulate the 3D objects individually or together. Photoshop's 3D menu also provides a command to access a selection of premade custom shapes you can use for starting points in your work called New Mesh from Layer.

Here, you will open a preset shape and create an instance, and a duplicate 3D object, to compare.

1. Create a new document (File > New Document), the choose Preset: Web, then select the 1024 x 768 pixel size. Name the document *Soda* and click OK.

2. To generate a 3D premade shape of a soda can, select in Photoshop's menu, 3D > New Mesh from Layer > Mesh Preset > Soda (Figure 6-54). You could also choose the same in the 3D panel.

3. Click once to display the 3D Movement Axis Widget, and feel free to rotate and scale the soda can smaller. Click on the universal scale (white block) on the bottom of the widget to scale everything smaller proportionately. You can also select the Move Tool (V) and use the 3D Mode options on the Tool Options bar.

4. Open the Swatches panel and click once more on the front surface of the can to display the Materials to choose from in the Properties panel. We're going to change the material next.

▷ FIGURE 6-54

Creating a soda can custom shape and changing the color texture in the Diffuse color box.

5. Click the color box by Diffuse to open the Color Picker (Figure 6-54). As you hover your mouse over the Swatches panel the cursor will display as an eye-dropper. Click on a light tan color on the Swatches panel. The color will display on the Color Picker. Click OK.

6. To apply the color to the can surface, click the folder icon next to the Diffuse color box and select Remove Texture. The color will display on the can (Figure 6-54). Select the new soda can.

7. To create an instance of the new colored can, select from the 3D panel menu in the top right corner, Instance Object (Figure 6-55). A copy will be created over the original can (if Instance Object is grayed out, you need to make sure the original soda can is selected).

8. Select the Move Tool (V) to move the new instance and use the 3D Movement Axis widget to move and scale. Hint: When the cursor displays as a Y-like illustration with three arrows that is the scaling cursor. Click and drag to enlarge or make smaller.

9. Now you're going to duplicate the original can. From the first original can displayed, select it and choose from the 3D panel menu (top right), Duplicate Object (Figure 6-55). Use the Move Tool (V) to move the duplicate off the second can (if Duplicate Object is grayed out, make sure you have selected the first can before duplicating). Feel free to scale and rotate.

10. You now have three cans as 3D objects of the same color. If you look in the 3D panel you will notice the three soda cans as displayed as 3 separate 3d objects (Soda, Soda 1, Soda 2). Leave open for the next exercise.

Original   Instance

Instance   Duplicate

▷ FIGURE 6-55

From the 3D panel menu create an Instance Object, and a Duplicate Object for the next exercise.

COMPARING 3D OBJECT INSTANCES AND DUPLICATES

You can also create various textures of surface that can include images, text, etc. You can load them as textures (Load Texture command) and they are instantly applied to the shape. You can apply any 2D image onto the surface of an object. Usually it helps to pre-size ahead of time before applying the final effect.

Here you will see what occurs when you change instances, and duplicates of 3D objects.

1. To apply a different texture, and to demonstrate the difference between creating a linked instance and a duplicate, select the Move Tool (V), then click on the first original can until you see displayed the Materials display section on the Properties panel.

2. Click the folder icon next to the Diffuse color box, and select Load Texture. Locate the file *Rocky.tif* from your *Chapter 6* folder, select it, and click Open. If a font error occurs, open the file in Photoshop and try using a different font. For PCs we used Elephant, for Macs, we used Campbell font type.

3. Instantly the new texture with a warped type text logo, graphic shape, and different background color will display over the original can and the second can that was created as an instance, but the third can, the duplicate, remains the same (Figure 6-56).

4. Select the third can that was duplicated until the Materials section displays in the Properties panel. Click on the Diffuse color box in the Materials section to bring up the Color Picker and select either a different color there or from the open Swatches panel, then select OK in the Color Picker to apply the color.

▷ FIGURE 6-56

When applying material changes to the original, the instance displays, but does not apply to the duplicate.

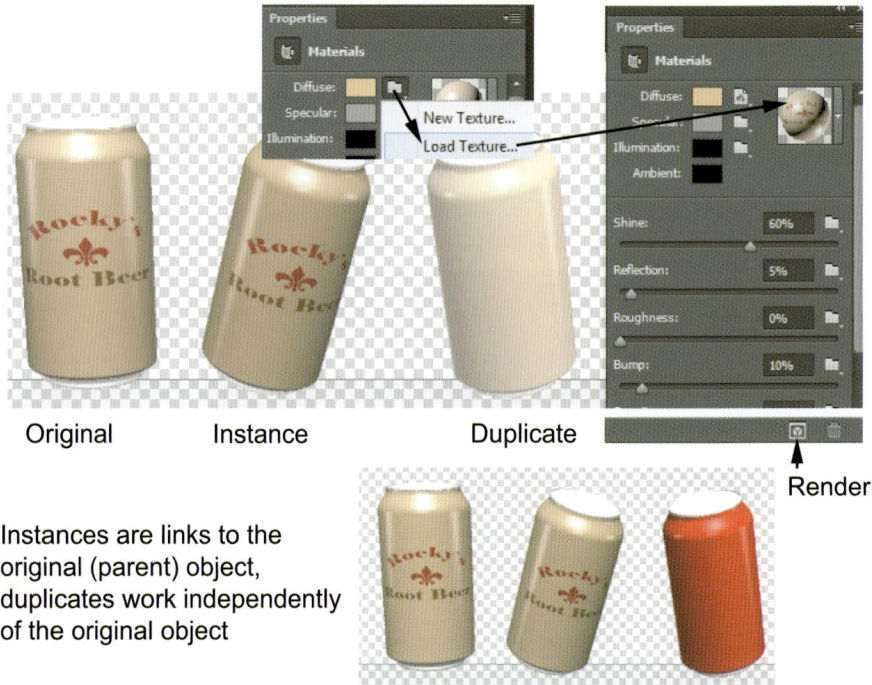

Original   Instance   Duplicate

Render

Instances are links to the original (parent) object, duplicates work independently of the original object

5. The color automatically displays on the can that was duplicated but not on the other two cans (Figure 6-56). A duplicated object works independently of the original, and a copy that has been created as an instance, is a direct link to the original (parent) object and will display changes made from the original.

6. Select the 3D menu, and then select Render to start the process. When the cans are accurately observed, you can just press the ESC key on your keyboard to stop when ready to be saved. You can open and edit it in the future.

7. Save the file as *3Sodas.tif* in your *Chapter 6* folder.

TOOLKIT TIP The simple background texture from the *Rocky.tif* file was made by using the Type Tool (T) and selecting the Create Warped Text icon in the Tool Options bar, or select Type > Warp Text. Creating an adjustment layer and applying a Solid Color Fill completed the background "texture" applied on the 3D object. Try to create your own. For Windows computers, try Elephant font type, for Macs, try Campbell font type, or find a wide character font. Have the resolution and dimensions of the document the same as what you are using for the 3D objects and link the layers in your new texture background before applying the 3D materials effect.

Printing to 3D Printers in Photoshop Creative Cloud (CC)

In Photoshop Creative Cloud (CC), this feature allows designers to use Photoshop to clean up, preview, and prep their 3D designs, as would normally be done with a normal paper printer. It makes 3D printing easy, and what users see on the screen is what they'll get. Photoshop also supports file formats from other 3D programs as well. 3D printing will soon become part of a designer's mainstream workflow as prices become more competitive.

If you don't have access to a 3D printer or you want your models created in a variety of materials and finishes, Adobe is partnering with Shapeways as well. From Photoshop you can have your project sent to this online 3D printing service to have your project printed with support for nearly 40 materials.

To access the print panel, you can click on the icon at the bottom of the 3D panel (Start Print) or near the top of the Properties panel (3D Print settings). If you don't have a 3D printer you can select Shapeways, create an account, and send your work to this online service (Figure 6-57). Welcome to this great feature of the design industry!

▷ FIGURE 6-57

Enabling use of 3D printer settings in Photoshop CC.

 TOOLKIT TIP You can also paint your 3D object, and in Photoshop CC, you can paint on separate selected surfaces, on a 2D wireframe overlay instead, which will also display on your 3D object (UV Overlays checkbox in the Properties panel), and observe your painting with a live cursor preview. In the Properties panel, click the 3D Paint button, make a choice to either Paint On which selects the type of texture the paint will end up, Paint Falloff to control how much paint is applied using Min and Max angles, or Select Paintable Area which will auto-select areas to paint for you. Have fun!

CHAPTER SUMMARY

Well, you have completed the restoration and retouching of an image in Photoshop. With so many tools available, you have almost limitless abilities to perform any restoration or editing procedure with confidence. You learned to repair cracks and defects with the Clone Stamp Tool, the Patch, and various Healing Brush tools. You sampled colors and saved them in the Swatches panel, created a custom swatch color and brush to add color to a black-and-white image, and created previous states using the History panel. You also sampled skin tone colors from a color image and applied them to a black-and-white portrait. In the Advanced section you learned how to neutralize shadows and highlights to correct color casts, using the Threshold command, Levels command, and Color Sampler Tool. You explored syncing capabilities (for subscribers to Adobe products) using Creative Cloud in managing your images and your application settings between computers and devices. In the Extra section, you learned how to create an action to apply adjustment layer effects on image, and to batch process an action to perform the action on many files in a folder to save time in doing repetitive tasks. You explored how to create 3D objects, a growing popular design format in today's industry.

REVIEW QUESTIONS

1. Explain the difference between the Healing Brush Tool (J) and the Clone Stamp Tool.

2. Explain the process of cloning a crack in an image.

3. Explain Grayscale, RGB, and CMYK color modes.

4. Explain how to create a custom brush in the new Tool Presets panel.

5. Explain how to create a state to be able to go back to a previous place in development with the History panel.

CHAPTER 6
Restored and retouched photograph using
Photoshop's restoration tools and techniques.

Apply custom colors to black-and-white
image. Sample skin tones from
another color image to apply to skin
tones in final B&W restored image.

Photo courtesy of Carla Clancy.

▷ FIGURE 6-58

Original Color Cast Image

Corrected Image

Before

After

Creative Cloud Settings

CHAPTER 6 ADVANCED

Neutralizing shadows and highlights to correct color cast images.
Using Creative Cloud to sync application settings and images between computers.

Play

Original Image   Action Applied

CHAPTER 6 EXTRA

Creating an action to place adjustment
layers on images for color and tone effects.
Batch processing action on multiple files.
Creating and working with 3D objects.

Digital Image Editing: Adobe Photoshop CC

CREATIV
CLOUD
EDITION

Ever wonder how to put together a CD cover? Photoshop is the cornerstone of the digital editing industry, and you will use a lot of the tools, techniques, and functions that you learned in the preceding chapters in the making of this CD cover. You will also use a few new tools and techniques that will be introduced in this project to further your learning. You will be working with multiple images to create final composite CD cover images, and getting comfortable with managing display windows and images on your desktop to avoid too much clutter. Have fun!

CLIENT ASSIGNMENT: Creating a Music CD Cover

An alternative rock band called the Pundits is recording an album of good old rockabilly and rhythm and blues in their own style, titled *Back to Rock*. They schedule a meeting with you to discuss some ideas they have for their album covers. They want to provide old style CDs for their traditional fans from their concerts, and also use the front cover image to display on their website for those who want to download tracks or order the CD directly. After running through a series of thumbnail sketches, a final concept has been decided upon. The main cover image of a tunnel carved out of rock with a paved road going through it will be provided by the guitarist. The front cover will have an older car coming out from the tunnel, with the *Back to Rock* title engraved above the tunnel entrance, in the same basic curve pattern as the tunnel. The back cover will have the tunnel image and CD title flipped, with a sports car parked facing toward the tunnel. The song titles on the back cover will be left aligned. The band members decide on a photo of a friend of theirs in his old '64 rambler and another photo the drummer has of his favorite sports car. You tell the excited band that by using these photos, you will be able to bring all the images and effects together and make the final image look realistic.

Front Cover

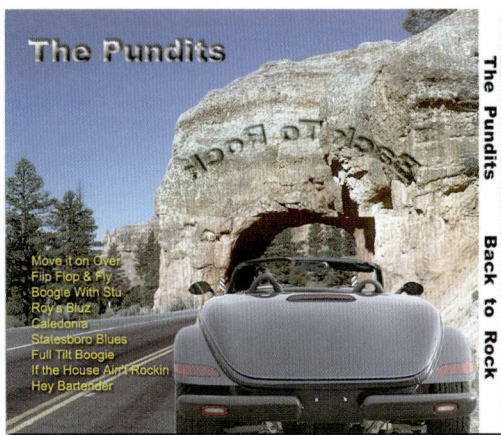

Back Cover

ACTION ITEMS OVERVIEW

Before putting all the elements together, this project is going to involve some detail work on the images. The image of the rock tunnel is old and needs some basic retouching, and it will also be cropped on the left side for the CD format. The cars need to be selected carefully and taken out of their backgrounds to be moved into the rock tunnel image later. The windshields of the cars need to be "clear" to show the road and background of the tunnel image they are being put into. The images will then be placed together and the text for the title of the band and CD name will be placed on the image.

For this project using Photoshop, here is what you need to accomplish:

- Create duplicates of the original images.
- Use the Crop Tool (C) to trim the tunnel image for the CD format.
- Clean the sky in the tunnel image with the Dust and Scratches filter, and replace the oil mark on the road with the Clone Stamp, Patch Tool, and Brush tools.
- Use the selection tools to select and remove the cars from their backgrounds.
- "Clear" the glass in the windshields of the old Rambler and the sports car using the Eraser tools, so the background image shows through.
- Create the text for the CD title and the band name using Layer Style effects, and then create a duplicate image for the back cover and reverse the image.
- Place the car images on the front and back CD covers.
- On the back cover, place the song titles to the side of the sports car, and rotate the text line for the CD spine with the band's name and the title of the CD.
- Use the Smart Sharpen filter to sharpen the final image.

DUPLICATING AND SAVING THE FILES

To make sure the original images are kept for backup copies, you need to make duplicate files of all three images that are going to be used in this project. Since there will be a lot of edits, save each file with a TIF extension to ensure image quality through all the changes you are going to make.

In this first exercise, you will open all three images, make duplicates, and save the new files. You will then close the original files for safekeeping.

1. In Photoshop, open the files *Tunnel.tif*, *Oldcar.tif*, and *Newcar.tif* in your *Unit 2 Review* folder.

2. Duplicate each image (Image > Duplicate) and name the new images *TunnelCD*, *OldcarCD*, and *NewcarCD*, respectively.

3. Save each image with a TIF extension with default settings for your computer in the *Unit 2 Review* folder.

4. Close the original *Tunnel.tif*, *Oldcar.tif*, and *Newcar.tif* files, leaving the new files open.

5. Select the *TunnelCD.tif* tab to work on first.

PREPARING THE TUNNEL IMAGE

To make the *TunnelCD.tif* image ready, it needs to be cropped to CD size, sky areas must be cleaned, the oil mark on the road removed, and the pavement restored, so as not to detract from the final image.

CROPPING AND ADJUSTING THE IMAGE COLOR

The *TunnelCD.tif* image needs to be cleaned and adjusted for color and then cropped to size for the back cover first, since it is larger than the front cover size. You will use the Rectangular Marquee Tool (M) and place a fixed-size selection on the image and crop it using the Image menu. The edited image will then be duplicated and cropped later for the front cover size. You'll use the Magic Wand Tool (W), which works much the same way as the Quick Selection Tool (W), located in the same area in the Tools panel. It uses a Tolerance setting that determines the range of similar colors.

In this exercise, you will select the sky with the Magic Wand Tool (W) and use the Dust and Scratches filter to clean it. Here are some options to try also.

1. Make sure the *TunnelCD.tif* image is open.

2. To adjust the colors, because there is slight magenta color cast, try Image > Adjustments > Color Balance, and add 5 pt of green and 5 pt of blue to begin with.

3. Use the Levels function (Image > Adjustments > Levels) and set only the white eyedropper to click on the white stripe on the pavement.

4. Select the Magic Wand Tool (W), set the Tolerance to 30 pixels, and select the sky; then use the Lasso Tool (L) to add to the selection any stray areas. Use the Refine Edge function to soften the transition edges a little, setting the Smart Radius at .5 pixels, and Smooth at 1 pixel. Click OK.

5. To smooth out and remove the graininess in the sky, select Filter > Noise > Dust and Scratches with a setting of 5 pixels Radius and 3 levels Threshold. Save the selection as SKY (Select > Save Selection > New Channel > SKY). Deselect the selection.

6. To crop the image, select the Rectangular Marquee Tool (M) and enter a Fixed Size Style with a Width of 5.75 inches (5.75 in) to be able to wrap around the CD spine for the album title, and Height of 4.75 inches (4.75 in) in the Tool Options bar (Figure UR 2-2).

▷ FIGURE UR 2-2

Marquee fixed-size settings to crop for CD back cover.

7. Click to display the selection on the right side of the image and move into place using the arrow keys on your keyboard. Use Figure UR 2-1 as a guide.

8. Select Image > Crop, and Save the file as *TunnelCD.tif.* Click Select > Deselect.

FIXING THE ROAD WITH PATCH, BRUSH, AND CLONE TOOLS

When given an image, it is important for the designer to carefully observe and repair any defects and remove distractions that may draw a viewer's attention away from the intended message of the final image. In this section, you will remove the distracting oil stain on the pavement and finish painting in the white stripe using the Patch, Clone Stamp, and Brush tools. The Patch Tool (J) is located with the Healing Brush tools as one of the retouching tools.

Next, you will use the Patch, Clone Stamp, and Brush tools to remove the oil slick and paint in the white line on the road.

1. To remove the oil mark on the road on the left side of the image, zoom in to about 200% with the Zoom Tool (Z) (click and drag around the area you want to work on).

2. Select the Patch Tool (J) with Destination checked in the Tool Options bar to make a freehand selection of a good portion of the pavement (Figure UR 2-3). Do not select the white stripe yet.

▷ FIGURE UR 2-3

Use the Patch Tool to replace the oil mark, the Clone Stamp Tool to replace smaller detail areas, and then paint in the white stripe with the Brush tool.

3. Drag the selection over the stain and watch the new pixels blend in nicely. Deselect the selection when done (Select > Deselect). Repeat this process until the road looks natural to its surroundings.

4. Use the Clone Stamp Tool (S) with a brush size of 10 pixels to replace the rest of the pavement next to the white stripe. Option/ALT-click frequently to sample new pixels of the pavement on both sides of the white stripe without selecting the stripe itself. If it still looks a little unnatural, use the Patch Tool (J) again to blend in.

5. Use the History panel to undo and redo your work and save snapshots if needed.

6. Zoom in to 300% to paint in the white stripe, then sample the color of the white stripe by clicking on it using the Eyedropper Tool (I).

7. Select the Brush Tool (B) and enter a brush size of 10 pixels with 90% Opacity. Paint in the white stripe with the white, sampled foreground color to match the rest of the road.

8. When you feel comfortable with the road repair, zoom out to full view again.

9. Save the *TunnelCD.tif* file in TIF format with the default settings in your *Unit 2 Review* folder.

USING SMART SHARPEN

Smart Sharpen pinpoints those fuzzy areas that need to be brought back into sharp focus. You will notice that the tunnel entrance is a little soft due to the scanning of an old slide film image that may have been slightly curved. This is where a designer would look at details from scanned images for anything that may need further adjustments or enhancements.

You will select this area and use Smart Sharpen to sharpen that area.

1. Select the Quick Selection Tool (W) and, with a 5 pixel brush size, drag around the soft roof area of the tunnel.

▷ FIGURE UR 2-4

Use Smart Sharpen to sharpen those soft areas of an image.

2. Select Filter > Sharpen > Smart Sharpen, and use the settings in Figure UR 2-4 as a guide if using Photoshop CC, for earlier versions start at 70% amount. You don't want to oversharpen, but to sharpen enough so it matches the surrounding rock. Click OK when done.

3. Deselect the selected rock and save the file.

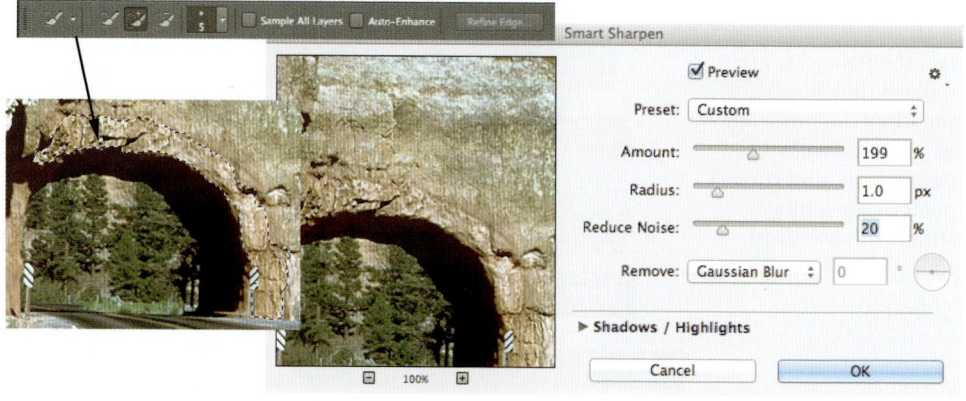

PREPARING THE CAR IMAGES: SELECTION AND REMOVING BACKGROUNDS

The car images need to be completely removed from their backgrounds, and the windshield glass "cleared" so they look realistic in front of the tunnel. You will use the various selection tools and eraser tools to prepare the images, and save each car selection as a channel.

SELECTING THE VEHICLES

As with selecting the kayaks earlier, use the selection tools to remove the two car images from their backgrounds and permanently save the selections as channels. You can select the cars using the Quick Selection Tool (W), the Magic Wand Tool (W), and the Lasso Tool (L) for these complex selections. The Quick Selection Tool (W) selects a range of colors determined by the amount of pixels. The Magic Wand Tool (W) uses a Tolerance setting that determines the range of similar colors.

TOOLKIT TIP Try clicking on the toggle icon to display Quick Mask mode at the bottom of your Tools panel; you normally work in Standard mode. Zoom in to about 200% to look for details of any part not selected. Using mostly the Pencil Tool (N) with a 5-pixel brush size or smaller, paint with white to remove the mask in any areas within the car. Paint with black to add to the mask in the background. Select Standard mode to see the original image.

▷ FIGURE UR 2-5

Saving the selections of both the new and old car images as permanent channel selections.

Here you will select the cars and save the selections as channels (Figure UR 2-5).

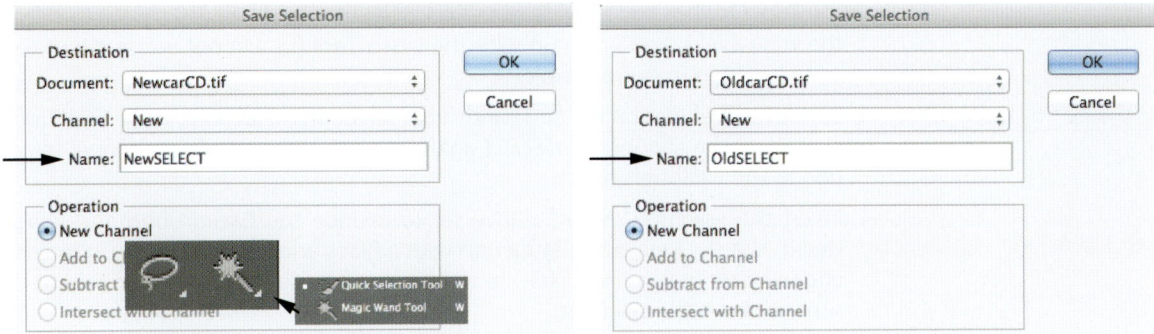

1. Select the *NewcarCD.tif* tab.

2. Use the Lasso tools to select most of the car (try using the Polygonal Lasso Tool (L) to select straight edges), then zoom in and use the Magic Wand or Quick Selection Tool (W) with a small brush setting to add to or subtract from the selection until the entire car is selected.

3. Use the History panel to help with your editing.

4. Save the selection as a channel with the name *NewSELECT* (Select > Save Selection > NewSELECT), then click OK.

5. Zoom in to make sure the entire car is completely selected, no shadows. Use the Refine Edge command from one of the selection tools in the Tool Options bar to soften the selection edges. Continue resaving the selection in the *NewSELECT* channel until completed.

6. Save the file as *NewcarCD.tif* in your *Unit 2 Review* folder.

7. Select the *OldcarCD.tif* tab to work on the classic Rambler.

8. Repeat the same procedure, use the Refine Edge command to soften the edge selections, and save the selection as a channel named *OldSELECT*. Remember: you are only saving the selection.

9. Save the file as *OldcarCD*.tif in your *Unit 2 Review* folder and leave it open.

CLEARING THE WINDSHIELDS

In order to bring in the car image and have it look realistic, the windshield needs to be "clear" to show the background of the image it is being moved into. You need to subtract from your selection to delete the windshield area. To remove background area behind the windshield, you will need to delete the windshield from the car selection, then invert the selection to include the background and windshield. This requires attention to detail.

In this exercise, you will use the selection tools again to select the windshield area and add to the channel selections on both images.

1. Make sure that the background color on the Tools panel Color Picker is set to white and the car is still selected. If it is not, use Select > Load Selection and use the *OldSELECT* channel to make it active again.

2. With the file *OldcarCD.tif* open, select Subtract from the Selection button on the Tool Options bar and use the Quick Selection Tool (W) (10 pixels) to select the windshield, and finish up with the Lasso Tool (L). Do not worry about the vent windows in our example.

3. Save the combination car and windshield selection (Selection > Save Selection) and select the channel *OldSELECT* again, replacing the previous channel selection in the Channels panel.

4. Invert the selection (Select > Inverse) to include the background and windshield. Use the Refine Edge function with a Black and White mask to soften the edges by roughly a few pixels, to determine if you need to paint to add to or subtract from the selection.

5. Press the Delete key to remove the background and windshield; the background and windshield should appear white; if the Fill dialog box appears, choose Background color (white). Make sure no areas of the car are removed when you delete the background (Figure UR 2-6). If there are, undo the action (use the History panel to go back to a previous state, or Command/ Ctrl Z) and keep editing and saving the selection. Deselect the selection when done.

▷ FIGURE UR 2-6

Selecting the windshield and removing the background to make the image composite look realistic.

6. Save the file in your *Unit 2 Review* folder when the selection is complete.

7. Repeat the same process with the *NewcarCD.tif* file (Figure UR 2-7).

8. Save the file in your *Unit 2 Review* folder. Leave both images open.

▷ FIGURE UR 2-7

Background removed and windshield cleared using various selection tools, the History Brush tool, and the Magic Eraser.

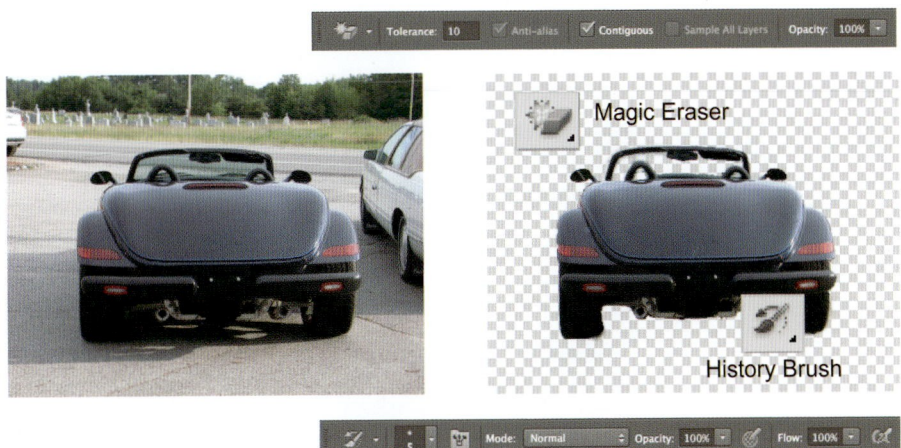

THE MAGIC ERASER TOOL AND THE HISTORY BRUSH

One of the retouching tools is the **Magic Eraser Tool (E).** It simply erases a single color background on the image to make it transparent. Use this tool when you want to bring different images together without any backgrounds. This way, when you bring the images into the tunnel image, the road of the tunnel image will display through the windshields. The **History Brush (Y)** is used in conjunction with the Eraser tools and other retouching tools, and is useful for painting back original areas that have been mistakenly erased by one of these tools.

Here, you will use the Magic Eraser Tool (E) and History Brush Tool (Y) to make both the background of the cars and the windshields transparent.

1. Select the *NewcarCD.tif* file and double-click the background layer to make it a normal layer with a transparent background. If it does not show, name the new layer *Background*.

2. Zoom in 200%. Select the Magic Eraser Tool (E) with a Tolerance of 10 pixels to make the rear windshield of the car and background transparent; it should look like a checkerboard. (See Figure UR 2-7.)

3. Click on the white background areas until all areas outside of the selection are transparent. Use the History Brush (Y) to carefully paint back any parts of the original image if needed, starting with a 5 pixel brush.

4. Repeat the same process for the *OldcarCD.tif* file (Figure UR 2-8). Crop the image to just show the top portion of the car, beginning at the top of the bumper (Figure UR 2-8).

5. Save both files.

6. Leave open the *NewcarCD.tif* and *OldcarCD.tif* images in their tabs. You will be bringing the cars into the tunnel image soon. Select *TunnelCD.tif* tab for the next exercise.

▷ FIGURE UR 2-8

Using the Selection and Magic Eraser tools to remove the background and windshield area.

CREATING THE TITLES AND CROPPING THE COVERS

Here you will create the CD title *Back To Rock* and make it look like it is chiseled into the rock of the tunnel using a combination of Layer Style effects, the Create Warped Text function, and the Screen blending mode. Blending modes affect the way layers blend with one another. The Screen blending mode on the Layers panel screens or lightens the colors of the layers above—in this case, the lettering will blend with the background layer to make them appear chiseled in the rock. The band's name, The Pundits, will be placed in the sky area of both the front and back covers with Layer Style effects. Then the *TunnelCD.tif* file will be duplicated, cropped to size, and reversed with "Back To Rock" backwards for the back cover, but the band's name will read correctly. The spine where the band and CD titles are placed will use horizontal type rotated 90 degrees.

CHISELING EFFECT USING WARPED TEXT, LAYER STYLES, AND SCREEN BLENDING MODE

The type tools have a warped text function to bend or curve type lines to a specific shape. In this exercise, you will use the warped text feature to match the curvature of the tunnel and apply the special Layer Style effects, Bevel and Emboss, and use a Drop Shadow to make it look like it is chiseled. **Blending modes** in the Layers panel dictate how one layer blends onto the layer below it, by contrast, tonality, or color for all kinds of special effects. In this exercise you will apply a Screen Blending mode to make the lettering take on the color of the rocks and appear to blend into the rock.

Here is how to create the effects.

1. With the *TunnelCD.tif* file open and zoomed to 100%, select the Horizontal Type Tool (T) and set the font to 24-pt Arial Black Regular with a Strong Anti-alias in the Tool Options bar. Make sure the Foreground text color is set to black.

2. Click above the tunnel and type "Back to Rock," then highlight the text.

3. Select the Create warped text button on the Tool Options bar to bring up the dialog box (Figure UR 2-9).

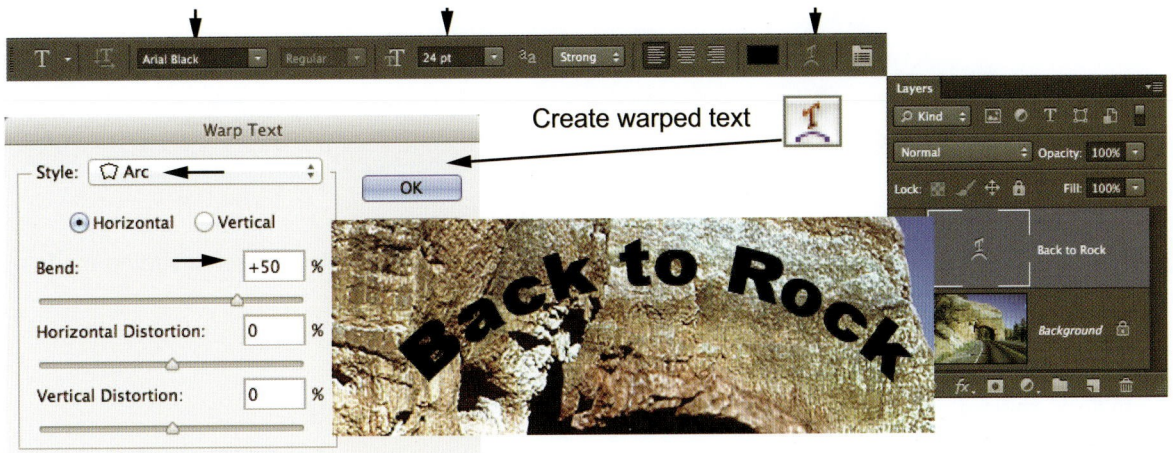

▷ FIGURE UR 2-9

Using the Create Warped Text command to bend the type line.

4. Choose the Horizontal Arc Style with a 50% Bend, then select OK.

5. Select the Move Tool (V) and drag the type line into place above the tunnel entrance.

6. Click the Add a layer style icon at the bottom of the Layers panel ("Fx" icon) to apply a Drop Shadow effect as shown in Figure UR 2-10, including entering the angle of *minus* 126 degrees and other settings shown.

7. Make sure Layer Knocks Out Drop Shadow is also checked in the middle of the display. After creating the drop shadow layer style settings, place a check in the Bevel and Emboss style *before* you create the next layer style.

8. Without exiting the layer style dialog box, double-click the Bevel and Emboss option and match the settings in Figure UR 2-10 to create a chiseled look in the rock. Click OK when you have finished.

▷ FIGURE UR 2-10

Layer Style settings and using the Screen Blending mode for the "Back to Rock" chiseled effect in the CD title.

9. To make the effect of chiseling into the rock, select Screen blending mode in the Layers panel.

10. Save the file.

CREATING THE BACK COVER AND SPINE

Now that all the editing has been done to the tunnel image, the image needs to be duplicated to be used as the back cover with a spine added for the band's name and CD title and for the front cover. The back cover image will also be flipped so the CD title reads backwards. Flipping or rotating an image is done in the Image menu. To type the title of the CD and band's name vertically on the spine of the back cover image, you will use the Horizontal Type Tool, then rotate the text line using the Transform command. The **Transform command** in the Edit menu allows you to move, rotate, reflect, scale, skew, and flip an image or text in specified degrees or amounts.

It is time to duplicate and flip the tunnel image, reverse it for the back cover, and create the type for the band's name and CD title on the spine.

1. Select Image > Duplicate to copy the *TunnelCD.tif* file. Name the copy *Backcover*.

2. Make sure the *TunnelCD.tif* image remains active; you will use it for the front cover later.

3. Make sure the *Backcover* image is displayed.

4. Select Image > Image Rotation > Flip Canvas Horizontal to reverse the image. The chiseled "Back To Rock" line will also appear reversed. Yep, the client wants this effect as if going through a time warp.

5. To create a space for the spine, select the Rectangular Marquee Tool (M) and select the Fixed Size Style in the Tool Options bar. Type in a fixed size of ".25" in Width and "4.75" in Height and use the arrow keys to position the selection to the rightmost edge of the image. Don't go beyond the image area.

6. Select the *Background* layer on the Layers panel and press the Delete key to remove the background. If the Fill dialog box displays, select Background Color (white).

7. To make the vertical text spine for the CD back cover, select the Horizontal Type Tool (T), using 14-pt Arial Black in the Tool Options bar. Select black for the color and click on the Center Text icon on the Tool Options bar. Leave Strong for the anti-alias (Figure UR 2-11).

▷ FIGURE UR 2-11

Rotating text to create the CD spine.

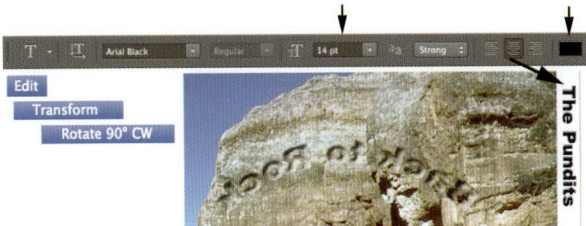

8. Type in "THE" (space bar twice) "PUNDITS" on the sky area; then hit the space bar nine times and type "Back To Rock" placing two spaces between words. Select Edit > Transform > Rotate 90 degrees CW to make the text line vertical. Use the Move Tool (V) and arrow keys to position the vertical text line centered in the white area at the right.

9. Save the file as *Backcover.tif* in your *Unit 2 Review* folder using the default settings. Click on the Move Tool (V) to deselect the text.

CROPPING FOR THE CD FRONT COVER

The front cover is narrower than the back cover and needs to be cropped to fit the front cover case. You can use either the Rectangular Marquee Tool (M) or the Crop Tool (C) to trim the TunnelCD image to size. Here, you will use the Crop Tool (C) as an alternative. The Crop Tool (C) is most useful in many types of trimming functions. You can type in the size to be cropped or trimmed and choose various ways of displaying a grid and other crop options. When you set the area to crop, the area is shaded (known as the Crop Shield). You can drag along a straight line to straighten a slightly crooked image and crop to preset ratios.

Here is where you will crop the *TunnelCD.tif* to size for the front cover (Figure UR 2-12).

1. To crop for the CD front cover size, select the *TunnelCD.tif* file.

2. Select the Crop Tool (C), entering the Width to 4.75 inches and Height to 4.75 inches in the Options bar to allow a little room to be able to close the case. The crop outline should display. Select the gear-like icon "Set additional Crop options" to Use Classic Mode to drag corner points and sides if needed (Figure UR 2-12).

▷ FIGURE UR 2-12

Cropping the image for the front cover.

3. Use the arrow keys to move the marquee to the top and right side of the image.

4. Click on the Crop Tool (C) again and click Crop. If you have problems with the Crop Tool, click the Move Tool (V) to deselect it.

5. Save the *TunnelCD.tif* file. This will now be your front cover.

CREATING THE BAND NAME

It is time to create the type for the band's name and apply Layer Styles on both the *Backcover.tif* and *TunnelCD.tif* files.

▷ FIGURE UR 2-13

Layer Style settings for the band name, The Pundits.

1. Maximize the *Backcover.tif* file and select the Horizontal Type Tool (T). Use 24-pt Arial Black Regular with a Strong Anti-alias in the Tool Options bar.

2. Type "The Pundits" in the sky area (Figure UR 2-13). Keep the Type layer highlighted on the Layers panel.

3. Click the Add a layer style icon (Fx) at the bottom of the Layers panel to apply the effects and settings as shown in Figure UR 2-13. Start by selecting the Drop Shadow Layer Style, determine your settings, and then double-click on the Bevel and Emboss option to establish those settings. Then just add a check in Gradient Overlay to complete the effect. Go ahead and experiment if you want, creating your own type style.

4. Position the type with the Move Tool (V) and Save the file. Minimize the *Back-cover* window.

5. Select the *TunnelCD.tif* (front CD cover) and repeat steps 1 through 4.

6. Save the *TunnelCD.tif* file. Leave the file open for the next exercise.

COMBINING IMAGES AND ADDING SONG TITLES

Now that you have done the hard part, it is time to put these images together. The front cover will have the old car and the back cover will be reversed, showing the sports car. In the final exercise, you will add the song titles, and then you will be done!

In this exercise, you will position the cars for the CD covers as shown in Figure UR 2-14 and sharpen the final image with the Smart Sharpen filter. The Smart Sharpen filter looks at your image and determines how much sharpening to apply based upon your initial settings.

▷ FIGURE UR 2-14

Placing the car images into the CD covers and adding song titles.

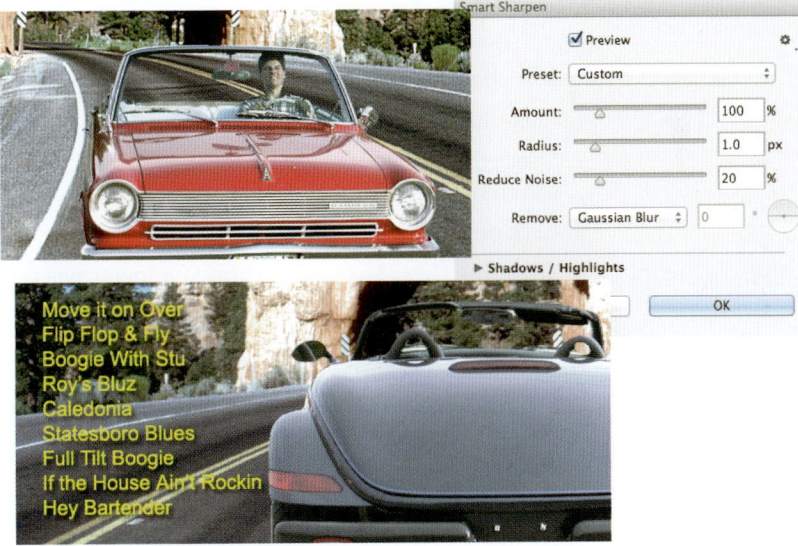

1. Open the image *TunnelCD.tif* and maximize the *OldcarCD.tif* window. Resize and position the windows next to each other.

2. Select the Move Tool (V) and drag the *OldcarCD* image onto the front cover *TunnelCD* image, positioning it as shown in Figure UR 2-14. Do not show the tires. The old car will automatically be placed on its own layer. Rename the layer *Old car.*

3. To sharpen the tunnel image, select one of the image layers at a time, then select Filter > Sharpen > Smart Sharpen and enter settings shown in Figure UR 2-14 for starters. Judge how you want it to look: not to make it too sharpened it that it looks obvious. Check the Preview button and click on the image to see the change applied, when you are satisfied, click OK.

4. Save the *TunnelCD.tif* in TIF format in your *Unit 2 Review* folder.

5. Close both the *TunnelCD.tif* and *OldcarCD.tif* files. The front cover is finished.

6. Maximize the *Backcover* image window and open the *NewcarCD.tif* image.

7. Select the Move Tool (V) and drag the *NewcarCD.tif* image into the *Backcover .tif* image, positioning it to the right of the image as shown in Figure UR 2-14; do not show the tires.

8. Close the *NewcarCD.tif* file and leave the *Backcover* file open.

TOOLKIT TIP Create layer comps that show "Back To Rock" placed on the tunnel, the tunnel image with the car, and the tunnel image by itself. This will help you understand the process. The Dodge, Burn, and Sponge tools have been greatly enhanced so a designer can apply slight variations of toning in lightening, darkening, or saturating parts of an image using these tools as brushes without having to select first. Try these tools on your own images. Welcome to the digital darkroom!

ADDING SONG TITLES

In this exercise, you will enter the song titles on the back cover and create a drop shadow effect.

1. Make sure the *Backcover.tif* file is open.

2. Select the Horizontal Type Tool (T) and use 10-pt Arial text. Select white for the color, then select Left Align in the Options bar.

3. Click on the left side and type "Move it on Over."

4. Select the Layer Style effect Drop Shadow (Layer > Layer Style > Drop Shadow) and use its default settings or create your own. If this is affecting other layers, make sure the layers aren't "linked" together.

5. Continue typing the following songs and the drop shadows will automatically be created: "Flip Flop and Fly," "Boogie with Stu," "Roy's Bluz," "Caledonia," "Statesboro Blues," "Full Tilt Boogie," "If the House Ain't Rockin," and "Hey Bartender" (Figure UR 2-14). If drop shadows are not created automatically, Option/ALT-copy the effects from one line to the next.

6. The back cover is done. Save the *Backcover.tif* file in your *Unit 2 Review* folder.

TOOLKIT TIP To experiment with the car images, feel free to use the Adjustments panel to add "Vibrance" to the red car image, or try making the new car image a "Black and White" image, or select the color as done in Chapters 4 and 5 and paint a candy apple red color. Try making your own image composites for a CD cover. You can also create custom sizes for CDs (File > New > Custom > Save Preset). You'll find more Photoshop tutorials and info in the Extras & Goodies folder found online.

Front Cover

Back Cover

Images used for CD covers

UNIT II REVIEW
Creating CD covers (front and back)
from multiple images using Photoshop.

▷ FIGURE UR 2-15

Creating Shapes with Illustrator

CHAPTER OBJECTIVES: To understand Illustrator's basic functions in digital illustration, in this chapter you will:

▷ Learn Illustrator's desktop components and how they interact with one another.

▷ Switch between Preview and Outline views to observe and evaluate precision work with paths and the entire image with colors.

▷ Apply and edit stroke and fill colors.

▷ Learn to create, color, combine, transform, and align basic shapes precisely.

▷ Explore Illustrator's Color, Swatches, and Color Guide panels in finding harmonious colors.

▷ ADVANCED USERS: Build a lighthouse from complex shapes with precision adjustments and alignments. Create a complex figure illustration introducing Illustrator's Live Corners feature and saving in EPS format.

▷ DIGITAL TOOLKIT EXTRA: Create playing cards by making custom shapes using shape and selection tools, and the Shape Builder Tool.

CREATIVE CLOUD EDITION

Illustrator is the premiere application for creating and editing vector-based digital illustrations. Artwork drawn on paper can be scanned into the computer through Photoshop and placed into Illustrator to be "traced over" and scaled up or down without compromising image quality. Digital artwork can also be created on the computer using Illustrator's tools, which allow for precise placement of individual objects, application of colors, transformations, and so on. Complex illustrations can be created by applying various layers on top of one another. Artwork from other drawings created in other applications can have individual components modified in order to create a new composite image. Adobe Illustrator Creative Cloud (CC) provides tools design professionals need not only to create scalable images and type that can be integrated into other Adobe products, like Photoshop and InDesign, but to create images for print, web, mobile devices, and other media. In this chapter, you will learn to work with basic shapes and coloring and to understand the importance of accurate placement and alignment.

THE ILLUSTRATOR ENVIRONMENT

The Illustrator desktop shares many similarities with Photoshop's tools, panels, and menus, including the default darker interface. When you work on your **artwork,** or illustration, created in Illustrator using shapes, tools, paths, and panels, you will notice that there is a rectangle on the document. The area inside the rectangle is called the **artboard,** which is where you will create and modify all your illustrations. Illustrator provides designers the ability to work with multiple artboards for creating a variety of things such as multiple-page PDFs, printed pages with different sizes or different elements, etc. The area outside the artboard area is called the **scratch** area. This is a nonprintable area that you can use to store artwork components in case you need them; place elements you might want to use again here, rather than deleting them. The panels are used to monitor, arrange, and make changes to your artwork. The **Tools panel** contains all the tools to select, create, and manipulate objects. Various selection tools are used to select colors, shapes, and paths. The **Control panel** in Illustrator, like the Tool Options bar in Photoshop, provides options related to a selected tool, and information regarding object dimensions and location, fill and stroke colors, opacity, and selecting the Bridge application. A **bounding box** is made when selecting objects to move or resize, which can also be toggled to be hidden in the View menu. The Illustrator Creative Cloud (CC) workspace is shown in Figure 7-1.

▷ FIGURE 7-1
Illustrator CC workspace.

WORKING WITH VECTOR IMAGES

Illustrator creates vector images used for illustrations, drawings, CAD images, video, and clip art. In Illustrator, vector images are created as **objects** or **paths** that have starting and ending points and determine the shape of an image. These paths can be closed like circles or open like lines. Paths contain nonprinting **anchor points** that define where line segments begin and end. **Segments** are curved or straight lines between anchor points (Figure 7-2). All vector images can be scaled to any size the designer needs, because they use mathematical formulas to calculate distances between points as they are resized, rather than inventing pixels as in raster or bitmap images. The quality stays the same, with smooth crisp edges no matter what size is used. Illustrations have a lower **color depth,** because they usually use fewer total variations of color, and therefore the file sizes of vector images are small.

▷ FIGURE 7-2

Vector images consists of open and closed paths using anchor points between path segments.

Open Path   Closed Path

ILLUSTRATOR VIEWS

Illustrator provides different ways to view your artwork. When you open a file, it first displays the artwork in full color **Preview view**, showing all the colors and how it will look when printed. Otherwise, choose View > Preview to see all the artwork. You can also choose to display just the outlines of shapes as **Outline view** by selecting View > Outline (Figure 7-3). There are other views available, and you can save views to help with your work production.

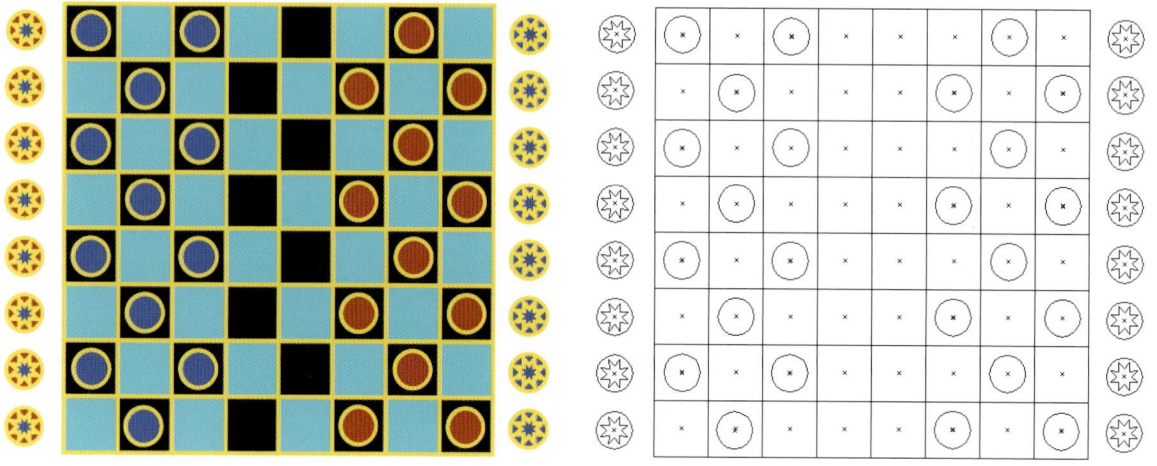

Preview View   Outline View

▷ FIGURE 7-3

Preview and Outline views.

THE ILLUSTRATOR TOOLS PANEL AND CONTROL PANEL

The Tools panel in Illustrator contains all the tools you need to create and modify objects and their individual components. It contains selection tools, drawing and painting tools, shape and liquefy tools, gradient tools, editing and viewing tools, transformation tools, and the Fill and Stroke color selection boxes. Many of the tools in Illustrator create paths or shapes like the Pen tools, Line Segment tools, Shape and Liquefy tools, Brush and Pencil tools, and Symbolism tools. Like the tools in Photoshop, any tool that displays a triangle will show other tools hidden underneath, when you click and hold the mouse on the tool icon. If the mouse hovers over the tool icon, the name of the tool and the corresponding keystroke are displayed. For tool buttons that have hidden tools, you can isolate the tools from the Tools panel by clicking and dragging the tear off bar on the right side to make it a separate toolbar panel. To access options on several of the tools, select the tool first; then, click on the artwork area, and a dialog box will be displayed to enter settings.

▷ FIGURE 7-4

Illustrator CC Tools panel and Control panel.

The Control panel, located below the Menu bar, is displayed to provide options pertaining to a selected object or tool, including color stroke and fill information; it provides information regarding object size and location. The Control panel is used to combine some of the most used functions of some of the more popular panels to minimize workspace. It contains a panel menu on the far right that allows toggling to display commands and to dock the panel either on the top or bottom of the screen (Figure 7-4).

FILL AND STROKE BOXES AND PANELS

On the Tools panel, below the small tool icons, you will find the larger Color Picker, which contains the Fill and Stroke boxes. You can sample colors in the Color panel or use preset colors and save new ones in the Swatches panel. The Swatches panel in Illustrator has a feature that allows you to save a set of colors as a group, view the grouping structure, and take out those colors used in a selected piece of artwork as a group. The **Fill box** in the Color Picker is used to fill color inside an object, whereas the **Stroke box** is used to define the outline or edge of the object. The stroke thickness is determined by entering the stroke weight in the **Stroke panel**, which is also used to determine how stroke lines are joined, capped, or changed to dashed strokes, or in the Control panel. You can also use the Stroke panel to create variable width strokes and custom arrowheads. A Fill or Stroke box with a red line through it indicates no color or transparency. **Color modes** below the Fill and Stroke boxes determine how color is applied to either the fill or stroke of an object or path. You can create and use a gradient or blend of colors in a stroke (Figure 7-5). They are the *Color* (default), *Gradient,* and *None* (red line) modes. As in Photoshop, you can minimize or expand your panels by clicking on the double arrows on the panel name tab, the icon if it is docked on the side, or by using the Window Menu.

▷ FIGURE 7-5

Stroke characteristics are defined in the Stroke panel. Select Stroke and Fill colors for objects through the Tools, Color, or Swatches panels.

Switch between
Stroke and Fill colors

Fill box

Default B&W

Color mode

Stroke box

None

Gradient

Color panel allows you
to select any color

Stroke panel determines how the
outline or stroke of an illustration displays

Swatches panel contains preset
individual colors and groups of colors

TOOLKIT TIP To switch between fill and stroke colors, press the X key on your keyboard; to switch to the default black stroke with white fill, click to toggle the default icon or press the D key. These are the same keystroke shortcuts used in Photoshop.

USING ADOBE ILLUSTRATOR HELP

Illustrator's Help menu allows the designer access to any information about tools, application features, updates, tasks, and terminology, along with information about transferring your software activation to another computer and access to the **Adobe Help and Support Center** on the web by selecting the Illustrator Help link. The Help and Support Center displays tasks, index help, and bookmarks of previously visited help areas. You can look for topics by searching for keywords, using the alphabetized index, looking through a table of contents, or simply jumping from one topic to another by selecting underlined text links (Figure 7-6). The online Adobe Help and Support Center also lets you seek help from other Adobe applications in a weblike format and provides additional links to resources and support, and video tutorials. If you are looking for a specific function or technique, type it in the Help > Search box, and Illustrator will display where it is located using floating arrows. In Illustrator Help, there is also a What's New link to keep you up to date with each new set of improvements and additions to illustrator Creative Cloud (CC).

Here you will search the Help and Support Center, then search for the Color Guide function.

1. Launch Illustrator and select Help > Illustrator Help from the Menu bar. It will then take you into the Adobe Help and Support Center on Adobe's website.

2. At the website, navigate around the various links, including any new features in Creative Cloud (CC). You can also select the link What's New in the Help menu.

▷ FIGURE 7-6

Using Illustrator Help to find information about the Color Guide feature.

3. In the Help and Support box, type in Color Guide, a feature regarding matching colors, and choose from a list a tutorials and videos. Navigate around, then close when done.

4. In the Help menu again, type Color Guide in the Search box, and you'll find a floating arrow pointing to its location in the Window menu (Figure 7-6).

LIVE COLOR IN ILLUSTRATOR

One great feature in Illustrator is the ability to look at color groups and assign new colors to selected artwork on the fly, called Live Color, along with a new Color Guide panel. The Kuler panel as part of Live Color is used by designers to find colors that complement one another or to experiment with colors in their artwork and then create custom groupings of colors. You can create and reuse groups of colors to help enhance your productivity and work flow. The **Color Guide panel** provides quick access to color groups. The Swatches panel in Illustrator allows a designer to save a set of colors as a group, view the grouping structure, and save those colors used in the artwork as a group. Finally, there is a Recolor Artwork dialog box that helps the designer edit or rearrange various color combinations using preset color groups, individual colors, or by using an interactive color wheel to define and save those custom color groups (Figure 7-7). It also helps to constrain your selections within specific color spaces, such as web colors or Pantone print colors.

Color Guide panel

Color Group selections

Edit or apply colors

Recolor Artwork to edit and assign color groups

CLIENT ASSIGNMENT: Creating an Electronic Checkerboard Game for Email

A good friend of yours, Thomas Mate, wants to be able to play checkers through email with a friend who has moved away. He comes to you and wants you to create a checkerboard and pieces that can be sent back and forth through email. After discussing colors, you both decide to use black and light blue colors for the checkerboard, with deep blue and deep red colors for the checkers, to be more distinctive. You know this project should be created in Illustrator since it involves creating basic shapes and using the selection tools to move the pieces (Figure 7-8). You find out that both Thomas and his friend have Illustrator on their computers and can easily play the games that way. You tell him you will have it ready the next day.

ACTION ITEMS OVERVIEW

As a designer using Illustrator, you need to have a basic understanding of the importance of creating shapes and the alignment or placement of objects precisely. First, the checkerboard itself is created by copying, combining, and accurately aligning squares to make the board (Figure 7-8). Next, the colored checker vpieces are constructed for both players. Note: No files needed for this tutorial.

▷ FIGURE 7-8

Completed checkerboard.

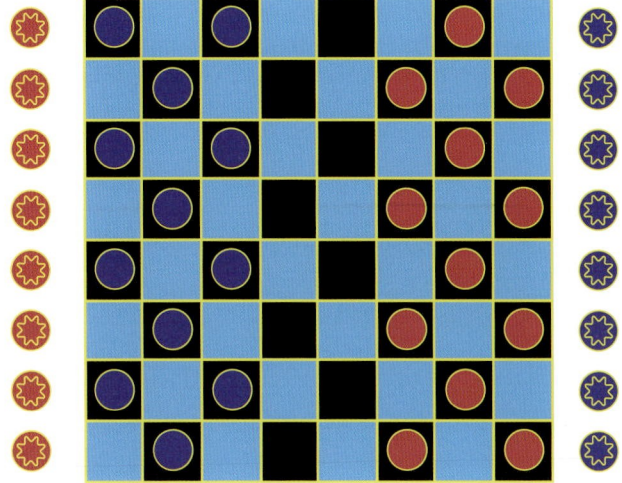

Here is what you need to do:

- For the checkerboard, create two different colored squares with a yellow stroke (RGB Color mode).

- Group the two squares and align them, and then copy the squares and align to make rows, and then copy and align again until the checkerboard is completed.

- For the checkers, create blue and deep red perfect circles with a yellow stroke.

- Copy to make 12 pieces for the board and place these centered in the appropriate playing squares to begin the game.

- Use the Color Guide panel to find harmonious color combinations to change colors on the board.

- Combine and transform shapes to make the crown pieces.

- Advanced Users: Create complex shapes together in building a lighthouse. Creating a complex figure illustration.

CREATING CHECKERBOARD SQUARES

Creating illustrations can start with building upon basic shapes and then editing them or modifying them to create other shapes. In this phase, you will be creating the checkerboard by creating, copying, and aligning the two different-colored squares into a checkerboard that is eight rows by eight columns. A document can be set up as either a vertical portrait orientation (default) for normal documents or as a landscape orientation, displaying the document lengthwise horizontally. This document will be created in landscape orientation.

CREATING A NEW DOCUMENT

In Illustrator you can always create a new document, open an existing document, or open a template. When you set up a new document, you need to determine its dimensions, orientation (portrait or landscape), and color mode (RGB or CMYK). Illustrator's default color mode is in CMYK. If you use the Welcome window, if it is enabled, you can start a new document there as well. For new documents created using the Web document profile, use the option Align New Objects to Pixel Grid. This feature, when enabled, allows an object to have its vertical and horizontal paths aligned to the pixel grid, which remains with the object even when it is later modified. It helps maintain a crisp appearance of pixel-aligned strokes for all web documents.

TOOLKIT TIP If you need to change your existing color mode to a different mode, go to File > Document Color Mode. You can also create a new document as always using the File > New command, and you will get the same New Document dialog box.

Next, you will set up a new electronic document for the checkerboard.

1. Launch Illustrator, and select File > New.

2. Create a new web document by selecting Profile: Web from the down arrow. Choose Landscape Orientation using 1024 × 768 px size with settings shown, since it will be used for electronic display (Figure 7-9). Click on the Advanced arrow to make sure Color Mode is set to RGB Color. The new document should automatically be set up in RGB color mode. Place a check in the Align New Objects to Pixel Grid box.

▷ FIGURE 7-9

Setting up a new electronic document.

3. Name the document *Chkrbrd*, then select OK. The new blank document will display. You'll notice in the Control panel that you can select more settings in the Document Setup and Preferences buttons, if needed.

TOOLKIT TIP The default color of the Illustrator interface is a dark gray. To change the color of the interface, choose Illustrator > Preferences > Interface > then change the Brightness setting. Screen displays measure 72 px per inch. In this project, pixels will be the unit of measurement.

USING FILL AND STROKE COLORS WITH SHAPES

DESIGN TIP

Illustrator works in CMYK as the default color mode, which is used for images that are going to press. For creating artwork with colors that will be used primarily for electronic display like the web or email, a designer should create the project with RGB Color.

When working with basic shapes, the Shape tools provide an initial starting point from which to build upon. There are different methods in Illustrator for selecting fill and stroke color and weight. The **Fill** is the color selected to fill the inside of an object. The **stroke** is the outline of the object, and the **stroke weight** determines its thickness. The outline of the shape, or stroke, is determined by selecting the Stroke box in the Tools panel or Color panel, selecting the color, and then determining the stroke weight in the Stroke panel. You can also create strokes of variable widths, and strokes can also include gradients. You can also find these options in the Control panel. The fill color of the shape is determined by selecting swatches from the Control panel, or by selecting the Fill box on the Tools panel, then choosing a color from either the Swatches panel, which contains preset colors, or the Color panel, where colors are sampled or mixed. For black and white colors, you can select preset squares from the Control panel's Fill and Stroke swatches, or from the Swatches panel or Color panel.

TOOLKIT TIP Before creating shapes or selecting a drawing tool, set up the Fill and Stroke colors in the Color Picker or the Control panel first. The Control panel is most useful in editing selected objects that are already created.

There are several different ways to select fill and stroke colors in Illustrator. In this exercise, you will create the initial black square with the Rectangular Tool (M), with a yellow stroke outlining the square. If you want, try using the Control panel. Select the object first, then select the fill and stroke color you want.

1. First, make sure the Control, Stroke, Color, Align, and Swatches panels on your desktop are displayed; you can also select them using the Window menu. Click on the Shape tools box in the Tools panel.

2. To make the black square of the checkerboard, select the Fill button on the Control panel, or select the Fill box in the Tools panel to bring it forward in the Color Picker.

3. Select the black color from either the swatches displayed in the Control panel or from the Swatches panel to make the fill color black, or you can select the black rectangle in the Color panel (Figure 7-10).

Black

Fill Color →

Fill Color with
Yellow Stroke

No Fill →
Stroke Color →

RGB Yellow

Yellow Stroke Color
No Fill

Control panel →

Many of the Fill and Stroke options
can also be applied using the Control panel

▷ FIGURE 7-10

Stroke and Fill settings for the black color and yellow outline of the checkerboard.

4. Select the Stroke button on the Control panel, or the Stroke color box on the Tools panel, and select a yellow color from the displayed Swatches panel.

5. Enter 4 pt Weight in the Control panel, or use the Stroke panel to enter 4 pt Weight (Figure 7-10).

6. Select the Rectangle Tool (M) and click—do not drag—in the upper-left area of the artboard to display the dialog box (Figure 7-11).

7. Enter "75 px" for both Width and Height. Select OK. Notice how this information displays in the Control panel. You have a 75 px × 75 px black square with a yellow 4-pt stroke weight. Note: When you press the Return/Enter key to place the square, in Illustrator CC, you may see four circles inside the square which are widgets for rounding corners.

8. Leave open for the next exercise.

TOOLKIT TIP Dragging a shape tool diagonally while holding down the Shift key also creates proportional objects, such as perfect circles and squares (Figure 7-11). Holding down the Shift key while dragging a corner point from a selected object scales the size proportionately. You can also click the Constrain Width and Height Proportions icon in the display box to keep the same size proportions. In Illustrator CC, you will see circles inside a selected four-sided shape that are corner widgets for rounding corners.

▷ FIGURE 7-11

Creating a perfect square with the Rectangle Tool.

ILLUSTRATOR SELECTION TOOLS

Selection tools allow the designer to select a specific path, its segments, or an entire object (Figure 7-12). The **Selection Tool (V)** selects objects, creating a bounding box around them; use the View menu to hide or display the bounding box, if needed. A bounding box around a selected object has handles in its corners and can be used to reshape, copy, or rotate that object. In Illustrator CC, selected shapes with the Direct Selection Tool (A) with corners may display circles in each corner. These are corner widgets that can adjust the radius of corners and are also used for rotating the selected object. The **Group Selection Tool** (with a plus sign) selects paths in a group. The **Direct Selection Tool (A)** selects anchor points and segments on a path, whereas the **Magic Wand Tool (Y)** selects objects with similar attributes, such as color, and the **Lasso Tool (Q)** selects path components. The Selection Tool (V) and Direct Selection Tool (A) are the most widely used selection tools.

▷ FIGURE 7-12

Illustrator's selection tools.

 TOOLKIT TIP Holding down the Option/ALT key while an object is selected makes a copy of the image. Make sure to release the mouse first and then the Option/ALT key. Holding down the Shift key and the Option/ALT key moves the copy in alignment with the original.

COPYING SELECTIONS USING THE OPTION/ALT KEY

Copying an object is done by first selecting the object with the Selection Tool, then holding down the Option/ALT key while clicking and dragging the selected object. You can also select an object and move it using the Selection Tool.

In this exercise, you will use the Selection Tool (V) to select the square, copy it by holding down the Option/ALT key, change the fill color, and then select both squares to create a bounding box that will be used to make multiple copies.

1. To duplicate the black checker box you just created, choose the Selection Tool (V), then select the box and hold down the Option/ALT key while dragging to the right to make a copy. If you want, try also to use the Shift key with the Option/ALT key to keep the boxes aligned (Figure 7-13).

DESIGN TIP

One method to accurately place one object within another is to use the handles on the bounding box created by the Selection Tool (V) as a guide for centering and positioning.

Select a medium red color

Option/ALT Copy Square

Shift-select both squares
to create bounding box

▷ FIGURE 7-13

With the Selection Tool, Option/ALT-click and drag to make a copy of the selected square, change color to red using the Swatches panel.

2. With the copy still selected, click the Fill box in the Tools panel so that it appears in front of the Stroke box, and then select one of the red colors—something easy on the eyes—from the Swatches panel. Leave the stroke the same yellow color. You now have the two colored squares for the checkerboard.

3. Hold down the Shift key; with the Selection Tool (V), either click on each square or drag across them both to select them. This will create a bounding box for the next exercise. If you don't get a bounding box, go to View > Show Bounding Box and click it if it is displayed.

THE ALIGN PANEL AND SMART GUIDES

The **Align panel** is used to align multiple selected items along a horizontal or vertical axis. The Align panel can also be used to evenly space the distance between multiple objects. The Align panel can be used to align to a selection, an artboard from its multiple artboards feature, or a key object as one specific object in a selection of multiple objects. Illustrator also uses **smart guides**, which are guides that display when the centers of two or more objects are properly aligned or intersected for visual reference.

TOOLKIT TIP To select multiple objects easily with the Selection Tool (V), click and drag diagonally over the objects you want to include.

Now you will use the Align panel and arrow keys to position the first two squares. Then, using the Selection Tool (V) and the arrow keys on your keyboard, you will copy and align three more pairs and position them precisely to make the first row of the checkerboard.

DESIGN TIP

Using the arrow keys with any object selected will move it one pixel at a time (default) for precise alignment. Changing the image to Outline View in the View menu helps with alignment of lines.

1. With both squares selected and the bounding box visible, make sure the Align panel is displayed (Window > Align is checked). To enable smart guides, select View > Smart Guides, then zoom in to 200%.

2. Select the Vertical Align Top icon on the Align panel to put both squares on the same X axis.

3. Zoom in to 200%–300%, then with the Selection Tool (V), click outside the squares to deselect them, then select only the red square on the right. Use the arrow keys on the keyboard to move it, so the yellow strokes overlap by 4 keystrokes to keep the stroke the same width (Figure 7-14). You can check also by using Outline View (View > Outline) and then check back to Preview View.

Selected Checker Squares

Aligned Squares

Use arrow keys to position overlapping squares

▷ FIGURE 7-14

Use the Align panel to align the squares, then use the arrow keys on your keyboard for precise placement of squares.

4. To copy the squares, zoom back out to 100%, then select both black and red squares with the Shift key, then hold down the Option/ALT key while dragging the selected boxes to the right. You will notice the smart guides will display that align with the center of each group of squares to visually help keep your squares aligned vertically.

▷ FIGURE 7-15

**Creating the first
row of squares for
the checkerboard.**

Smart guides for visual center alignment

Shift-select each pair and use the arrow keys on the keyboard
for precise placement to make sure the stroke is equal throughout

First row of eight squares completed

5. Repeat twice more so that you have a total of eight squares showing (Figure 7-15). Select all squares using the Selection Tool (V).

6. Select the Align panel, then select the Vertical Align Top icon again to align the squares into a row.

7. Use the Navigation panel (Window > Navigation) or Zoom Tool (Z) to move in close—200% to 300%—to check placement.

8. To combine all the pairs of squares together, select pairs and use the arrow keys for precise placement, overlapping the edges by 4 px to create the same yellow stroke throughout. Zoom out when done. Drag over each pair and using the smart guides, when you start to overlap, you'll see "intersect" display. Release the mouse when this displays and the overlap should be equal.

USING OUTLINE VIEW TO CHECK ARTWORK

One of the best ways to check for precise placement of shapes is the Outline view option. Look for overlapping, misshapen, broken, or missing lines.

1. To check whether all the boxes are properly aligned, select View > Outline.

2. Make sure that all squares meet together as single lines, as shown in Figure 7-16.

▷ FIGURE 7-16

**Preview view and
Outline view to
check accuracy of
alignment.**

Preview
View

Outline
View

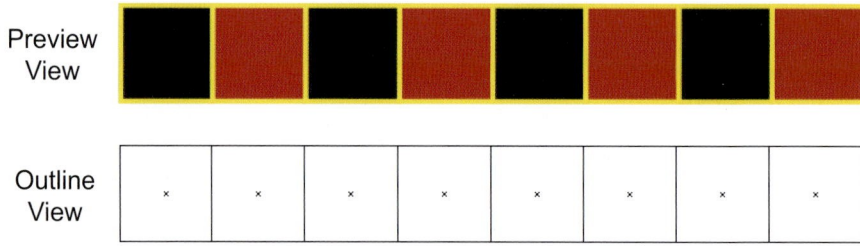

3. If not, realign the squares using the Selection Tool (V) and left and right arrow keys on your keyboard or the smart guides. Zoom in for more precision.

4. When all squares are aligned perfectly, switch back to the artwork by selecting View > Preview.

SAVING ILLUSTRATOR IMAGES

Illustrator images can be saved in a variety of formats, and Illustrator can read many graphic file formats. Graphic file formats are determined by the particular ways they represent graphic information.

- Illustrations saved with **Encapsulated PostScript (EPS)** extensions are used in page-layout programs for print, especially when graphics and text are combined.

- The **Portable Document Format (PDF)**, which in Illustrator is labeled as Adobe PDF (pdf), is used for electronic publishing that can be read by Adobe Acrobat, Adobe Reader, or other Adobe applications. The PDF format is universally accepted for commercial printing, as a proofing mechanism for layout of imagery and type, and can also be viewed in other graphics applications. It can also be used as the final proof in commercial printing establishments.

- **Save Selected Slices** in Illustrator uses slices of parts of an image to define the boundaries of different web elements in your artwork.

- **Scalable Vector Graphic, or SVG**, is a vector format that describes images as shapes, paths, text, and filter effects. The resulting files are compact and provide high-quality graphics that are used in the development of web pages.

- Artwork can be converted for web use by using **Save for Web**. This process will flatten any layers on your artwork.

- The **Save as Template** option allows you to save documents as templates for future projects. It has an **.ait** extension. For duplication, use the **Save a Copy** feature.

- When saving illustrations within Adobe applications, you can use the application's native format; in the case of Illustrator, this is an **.AI extension**. Saving a document in Illustrator's native format provides a good back-up file for future editing.

- You can save files with *backwards compatibility,* so someone who may not be using the same version as you can open and work on it. Be aware that when you save to earlier versions, Illustrator warns you that some operations or functions may not be backwards compatible.

 TOOLKIT TIP For the purposes of this assignment, you will save artwork in Illustrator's native format (Figure 7-17) and later as a GIF document for web use. You can also save the checkerboard file as a PDF or SVG file (be sure to embed all elements) and still be able to move the checkers with the Selection Tool (V). Saving as a PDF is the most universal method and allows you to use the file in other graphic applications or use the free Adobe Reader from the Adobe website.

▷ FIGURE 7-17

Saving Illustrator artwork in its native format.

In this exercise, you will save the file in Illustrator's native file extension.

1. Save the file as *Checkerboard.ai* (File > Save As > Adobe Illustrator), using the default settings, in your *Chapter 7* folder.

2. Leave the file open to continue creating the checkerboard.

THE OBJECT MENU

The **Object menu** is used for editing, combining, and transforming objects. With the first row of the checkerboard created accurately, the squares will be grouped together; then a copy will be rotated 180 degrees so the red squares are below the black squares, creating the pattern for the rest of the checkerboard.

DESIGN TIP

In Illustrator accuracy and the alignment of objects is important. Use Outline View frequently to check your work. Lines or paths that are overlapping, as in the case of the checkerboard, need to be viewed as a single line in Outline View for precise measurment.

TOOLKIT TIP By grouping the squares together, you can use the Selection Tool to select the whole group at once. To select each square individually, use the Direct Selection Tool. For accuracy, when lines are overlapping, make sure they appear as one line in Outline View. Sometimes it is easier to adjust objects in Outline View. You can flip back and forth between Outline View and Preview View using Command/ CTRL Y.

In this exercise, you will use the Object menu to group and rotate squares for two rows.

1. Select the eight squares by dragging diagonally over all squares with the Selection Tool (V), which will create a bounding box.

2. Select Object > Group to combine all eight squares together.

▷ FIGURE 7-18

Use the Object menu to group and rotate objects. Control panel can help with alignment.

3. With the squares still selected, use the Selection Tool (V) and hold down the Option/ALT key to make a copy of the row, and drag it below the first row. Use the arrow keys on the keyboard to position it accurately.

4. Using the Control panel's Align icons, or the Align panel, with both rows of squares selected, click the Horizontal Align Left to align the rows. Use Outline View (View > Outline View) to check for accuracy and adjust the rows as needed. In Outline View, all lines should be single lines (Figure 7-18).

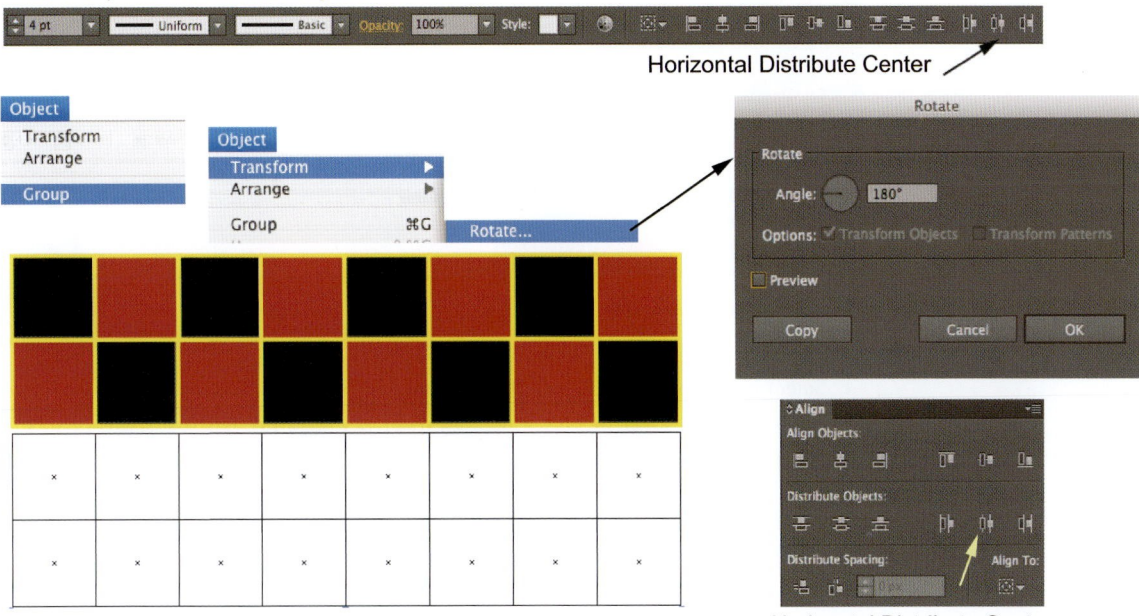

5. To rotate only the bottom row 180 degrees, so that the red squares are under the black squares and vice versa, select the bottom row with the Selection Tool (V), then choose Object > Transform > Rotate > 180 degrees. Click OK. Move the two rows to overlap equally using the Selection Tool. Watch for the "intersect" reading at the center of the grouped objects before releasing the mouse. You can also use the arrow keys on your keyboard.

6. To group the two rows together, select both rows with the Selection Tool (V) and choose Object > Group.

7. You now have the basic pattern for the rest of the board.

TOOLKIT TIP In all versions of Illustrator, you can also rotate the squares using the bounding box made by the Selection Tool (V); this is done by moving the cursor to the corner until it becomes a bent arrow and then dragging while holding the Shift key to adjust every 45 degrees.

DUPLICATING AND ALIGNING THE REMAINING ROWS

With the two rows created and aligned perfectly, all that remains is to copy the two rows three more times, align them, and place them snugly together to make the checkerboard of eight rows by eight columns (Figure 7-19).

▷ FIGURE 7-19

Final checkerboard.

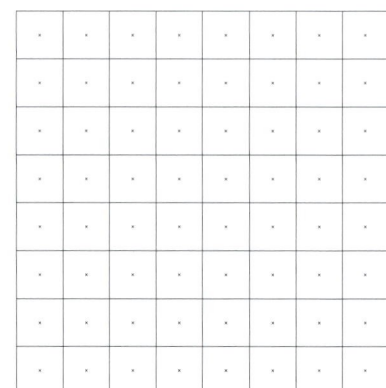

Preview View   Outline View

1. Select the two rows you just created with the Selection Tool (V), then hold down the Option/ALT key to click and drag a copy, placing it below the selected rows.

2. Use the arrow keys to position these new rows precisely. Use Outline View to check for final accuracy, then make additional adjustments as needed. When you have all four rows aligned precisely, select them all with the Selection Tool and group them using the Object menu.

3. With the Selection Tool (V), select the four rows you just created, then hold down the Option/ALT key to click and drag a final copy below the four selected rows.

4. Zoom in and use the smart guides to help with positioning, or use the arrow keys and the Selection Tool (V) to ensure precise positioning. To check your work to make sure all the boxes are aligned, select View > Outline and zoom in; all lines must be displayed as single lines for accuracy.

5. When everything is aligned perfectly, switch back to the artwork by selecting View > Preview.

6. Select Object > Group to group all rows into one checkerboard. Move the entire checkerboard with the Selection Tool so that it is centered on the document.

7. Save the file as *Checkerboard.ai* inside the *Chapter 7* folder.

DUPLICATING AND LOCKING LAYERS

The Layers panel in Illustrator works much the same way as in Photoshop. Layers can be renamed, duplicated, moved, and locked (Figure 7-20). To keep the checkerboard from being moved or edited by mistake, the layer can be

▷ FIGURE 7-20

Renaming and locking layers.

duplicated for placing the checker pieces and recoloring, and then the original layer can be locked for prevention.

With the squares on the checkerboard aligned precisely, you will duplicate the layer in the Layers panel and then lock the original layer. The layers will be renamed to identify them.

1. Make sure the Layers panel is displayed (Window > Layers) or click on the icon in the dock.

2. Double-click the icon next to the Layer 1 text; when the Layer Options dialog box displays, enter "Checkerboard" in the Name area and then check the Lock option as shown (Figure 7-20).

3. Click OK.

4. Select the Layers panel menu and click on Duplicate "Checkerboard."

5. Double-click the new layer and rename it *Checkers*, making sure that Lock is unchecked in the Layer Options box to add the checkers. To lock any layer on the Layers panel, just click on the blank box next to the eye icon. To unlock, click on the lock to toggle off.

6. Save the file as *Checkerboard.ai* in your *Chapter 7* folder.

DESIGN TIP

There is a preset limited color selection with the Swatches panel; but with the Color panel, there is much more freedom to select or create a color. Double-clicking on the Stroke or Fill box in the Tools panel will display the Color Picker for plenty of experimentation.

CREATING THE CHECKERS

With the checkerboard completed, it is time to make the light and deep blue checker pieces, using the Color panel. The checkers are going to be created with the Ellipse Tool (L), colored, copied, and centered on all the playing squares of the checkerboard.

ELLIPSE TOOL AND COLOR PANEL

Any oval or circle can be created by selecting the Ellipse Tool (L) in the Shape tools area of the Tools panel; click once on the artboard and enter the options in the dialog box by clicking and dragging diagonally or by drawing outward from the center while holding down the Option/ALT key. Holding down the Shift key will create a perfect circle as you drag. The Color panel provides the designer with plenty of color choices to experiment with. Colors can be either selected randomly, or in their 6-digit hexadecimal values, used for printing purposes, can be typed in. All colors in RGB mode are combinations of red, green, and blue, with values that range from 0 to 255 for each, which can also be typed in.

To make the checkers, you will use the Ellipse Tool (L) to create the circles with a yellow color stroke, and then select the two different blue colors from the Color panel by entering the appropriate RGB settings (Figure 7-21).

▷ FIGURE 7-21

Creating the checker pieces.

Ellipse Tool

Precise dimensions using the Ellipse Tool

Deep Blue Checker

Light Blue Checker

1. To make the deep blue checker for the board, first select the *Checkers* layer in the Layers panel, then select the Ellipse Tool (L) and click—do not drag—on the artboard to display the dialog box.

2. Enter 50 px Width and 50 px Height for the circle and select OK.

3. With the circle still selected, use the Stroke box in the Swatches panel and choose a yellow color (yellow may still be selected from before, when we created the squares).

4. Open the Stroke panel and enter 2 points (2 pt) for the stroke weight.

5. Select the Fill box within the Color Picker to change the fill color.

6. Select the Color panel or double-click on the Fill box to access the Color Picker and enter the settings R=51, G=51, and B=153 to make the fill color a deep blue. You can use the Tab key to move from one field to the next.

7. To make the second checker piece, choose the Selection Tool (V), then select the circle and hold down the Option/ALT key and drag to make a copy. Always release the mouse first before the Option/ALT key.

8. Select the Fill box in the Tools panel and select the Color panel. Enter the settings R=102, G=153, and B=204 to make a light blue color. You now have two checker pieces for the checkerboard. If RGB values do not appear, click the double vertical arrow on the upper portion of the Color panel to expand.

9. Use the Selection Tool (V) to move both pieces outside the checkerboard.

 PROBLEM If the Color panel doesn't display RGB colors, select the Color panel menu and choose RGB.

PLACING THE PIECES ON THE BOARD

With the two colored checker pieces created, each piece now needs to be copied and centered on the black squares. This will give you a little review of using the Selection Tool, copying the circles by holding down the Option/ALT key, and then placing the circles aligned precisely in the black squares. Another option for alignment is using smart guides again.

Next, you will duplicate the checker pieces and center them accurately inside the squares.

1. Select the light blue checker with the Selection Tool (V) and drag copies to the first three columns of black squares on the board's left side using the Option/ ALT key.

2. Continue until all 12 pieces are copied onto the squares as shown (Figure 7-22).

▷ FIGURE 7-22

Checkerboard before adjusting colors.

3. Select each circle piece and position it exactly in the center with the arrow keys. You can also be precise by matching the centers of the circles with the centers of the squares in Outline View, or you can turn on smart guides (View > Smart Guides) and move the piece until it reads "Intersects" which indicates the center of the square intersecting with the center of the circle.

4. Repeat the same process with the deep blue checkers for the right side of the board.

5. Save the file as *Checkerboard.ai* in your *Chapter 7* folder.

CHANGING COLORS OF THE CHECKERBOARD AND CHECKERS

▷   FIGURE 7-23

The cube indicates a color that is not web safe, the triangle indicates a color that is not print safe. Clicking the cube or triangle allows Illustrator to choose the correct colors for that media.

Just as was done in Photoshop, you can select similar colors to make changes using the Magic Wand Tool (Y) in Illustrator. With the duplicate layer created you can experiment all you want and the original (locked) layer is not affected by any changes. There are different time-saving ways to access color, and to find colors that match. The Color panel allows you to discretely select various hues of color in whatever color mode you have set up. In our checkerboard, we are using RGB mode. If a color is chosen that doesn't match web safe colors, a small cube displays. Just click on the cube and the nearest color is chosen for you. If you find a triangle displays with an explanation point inside, it indicates the color you have chosen won't print correctly. Again, just click on the icon to find the nearest color. Any color you choose can be selected and dragged into the Swatches panel for your own set of custom colors, or you can choose colors from special premade libraries. For finding harmonious colors, you can use the Color Guide panel, Illustrator's Live Color, or find colors used by designers on the web using the Kuler panel.

CHOOSING WEB SAFE (AND PRINT SAFE) COLORS

Time to play with the colors! When selecting a color and a small cube appears, it is a warning that the color you have chosen may not display correctly on the web. Click on the cube to display web-safe colors (Figure 7-23). If a triangle with an explanation point appears, it indicates that the color will not print accurately, which you would also click to find the nearest matching color. In our project, as we are going to work with web safe colors (although with today's monitor displays, it is not a real concern), so the print warning wouldn't matter here. Go ahead, break the traditional-color barrier!

Click on cube to make it RGB web safe

Click on triangle to make it print safe

Color is accurate for web (and print) use

ILLUSTRATOR CC SWATCHES PANEL

▷ FIGURE 7-24

The Illustrator Swatches panel helps to manage colors that you create or retrieve from preset libraries.

Swatches are named colors, tints, gradients, and patterns. Swatches can appear individually or in groups, and in Illustrator CC, they can displayed as visual thumbnails, or can be displayed as a named list of colors and their mixed settings. You can create or select any color or group of colors (color groups) from any source like the Color panel or Color Guide panel, or you can use the web-based Kuler panel to share and drag them into the Swatches panel for future editing. Creating a group of colors in your documents is as simple as selecting your artwork, and selecting New Color Group to have the associated colors displayed together. You also search for colors or percentages of colors ("red" or C=20) or color numbers, say Pantone 3 types (P 3), by enabling the Show Find Field function on the Swatches panel menu. There are plenty of libraries of preset colors under various themes to choose as well, which also include ink libraries (Pantone, Trumatch, HKS, etc.) for printing. Any selected libraries display in their own separate panels.

Let's explore the Swatches panel.

1. With the Swatches panel displayed (Window > Swatches) you should see some color swatches displayed as thumbnail views, and as you hover your mouse over their descriptions will appear. You should be in RGB mode so you would see color with RGB descriptions (numbers) displayed.

2. Click on the Color panel, select a color, and drag the swatch into the Swatches panel. When you see a plus sign displayed to add the swatch, release the mouse to add the swatch into the Swatches panel.

3. Notice, in Illustrator CC the Swatches panel displays Fill and Stroke colors that match the Color Picker at the bottom of the Tools panel. Make a change in color in the Color Picker panel, and the change is displayed in the Swatches panel.

4. To look in preset libraries, click either the Swatch Libraries menu on the bottom of the panel, or select Open Swatch Library from the Swatches panel menu. Select some colors for your checkerboard and drag them onto the Swatches panel.

5. When you have some colors, select Show Find Field from the Swatches panel menu and type in *red* to see if you end up with anything with the word red in it. Try a few other searches to see if you can find anything related. This actually works best when you have a lot of colors displayed, or you know the color you are searching for.

6. In Illustrator CC, to display the list of your colors, click the Show List View icon to see your colors listed with RGB number descriptions. Click the Show Thumbnail View icon when done to return to this view.

7. To create a color group of the current colors in your checkerboard, use the Selection Tool and highlight your checkerboard and checkers by dragging around all your artwork. Click the New Color Group icon on the bottom of the panel.

8. In the New Color Group display name the group *Checkerboard1*, select the Create From Selected Artwork button, then click OK. Your group with its related colors will display in the Swatches panel. You can also create a Color Group first and then drag swatches alongside the color group.

9. Save the file as *Checkerboard.ai* in your *Chapter 7* folder and leave open for the next exercise.

SELECTING WITH THE MAGIC WAND TOOL

▷ FIGURE 7-25

The Magic Wand Tool selects all the same colors in the image when the Fill Color box is selected.

The Illustrator Magic Wand Tool (Y) allows you to select similar attributes, like fill colors, stroke colors and weights, blending modes, and opacities. Adjust the Tolerance in the **Magic Wand panel** to determine the amount of similar color that will be selected, much like setting the Magic Wand Tolerance in Photoshop. Use the Magic Wand Tool (Y) to select a color area by just clicking on the color. All colors on the checkerboard that are the same will be selected as long as the Fill Color box is checked in the Magic Wand panel (Figure 7-25). To access the panel, double-click on the Magic Wand Tool (Y), or select Window > Magic Wand.

Magic Wand Tool

It is time to select all the checkers and checkerboard squares to apply a different color.

1. Double-click the Magic Wand Tool (Y) to display the Magic Wand panel (or select Window > Magic Wand). If the display does not show as in Figure 7-25, click the double arrows left of "Magic" on the panel. Make sure the Checkers layer is selected and unlocked on the Layers panel.

2. Make sure the Fill Color box is checked in the Magic Wand panel to select all similar colors on the document. Enter 5 px for Tolerance and leave all the other defaults as is (Figure 7-25). You can leave this panel open.

3. Select the Fill box in the Tools panel, then select one of the light blue checker circles on the checkerboard. By clicking on one circle, they all should become selected.

4. Use your cursor to select another color from either the Swatches panel or the Color panel; the selected objects' colors will all change. Go ahead and try using other colors, then select the checker squares and change colors to suit your preference. Checker squares with the Magic Wand Tool (Y).

FINDING HARMONIOUS COLORS USING THE COLOR GUIDE

A nice feature in Illustrator is **Live Color,** along with the Color Guide panel. Designers can use this feature to find colors that complement one another and experiment with colors. Along with this comes the option to create custom groupings of colors as you completed using the Swatches panel. The **Color Guide panel** provides quick access to finding color groups. Use the Color Guide panel (Window > Color Guide) as a use for color inspiration while you create your artwork. The Color Guide panel suggests harmonious categories of colors based on the current color in the Tools panel. You can use these to color artwork or you can save them as swatches. On the Control panel, you will also find an icon to edit colors within artwork (or select Edit > Edit Color > Recolor Artwork).

To find colors that may be appealing for your checkerboard and its checkers, you will use the Color panel to select various combinations of colors that go together.

1. To keep the new color choices you just made, duplicate the *Checkers* layer in the Layers panel menu (Duplicate "Checkers"). This way you can create another set of colors separate from the original locked *Checkerboard* layer and the *Checkers* layer. Name the new layer *Checkers2.*

2. Open the Color Guide panel (Window > Color Guide) and select the one of the checkers of your choice.

3. Click on the color icon at the top left of the Color Guide panel to create a set of colors (set base color to the current color) based on the color you have selected (Figure 7-26).

Kuler panel

Shades   Tints

Harmony Rules

Swatch libraries

Save color group to Swatches panel

Colors that match the base color selected

Swatches

Display as labeled list or thumbnails

Color group created

Saving a Color Group in the Swatches panel

Selected color change using Color Guide panel

▷ FIGURE 7-26

Using the Color Guide panel to create colors that work well together in an illustration.

4. Select the drop-down arrow next to the color field to see other combinations of colors that work with the color you selected. Select the Pentagram combination at the bottom of the list (you may have to scroll down—there are many options).

5. Use the Magic Wand panel again, with Fill Color selected and a tolerance of 5 px, and use the Magic Wand Tool (Y) to select all checkers of the same color.

6. Click the swatch box in the Color Guide panel to see a set of colors that work with the selected checkers or checkerboard. Go through and select combinations of both checkerboard squares and checkers that match the color scheme

of Pentagram, or try another group of colors from the list to see what works for you. Check out the "Swatches Library" for themes color choices on the Color panel, or the Kuler panel (Window > Extensions > Kuler), an online group of colors and themes from professional designers.

7. When you have made your color choices, save the file as *Checkerboard.ai* and look at the other color combinations from the other two checkerboard layers you created by toggling the eye icons. Highlight the *Checkers2* layer for the next exercise.

8. To save the color group from the *Checkers2* layer, click the Save color group to Swatch panel at the bottom of the Color Guide panel (it looks like a folder). It will then be displayed as a group of colors in the Swatches panel for future projects.

9. Save the *Checkerboard.ai* file in your *Chapter 7* folder and leave open for the next exercise.

TOOLKIT TIP Illustrator has a Kuler panel (Window > Extensions > Kuler) that provides more color groups or themes created by a community of designers accessible online.

COMBINING COMPLEX SHAPES: CROWNED CHECKERS

Illustrator's Shape tools can be modified for all kinds of purposes. You can reshape, combine, or remove portions of objects to create new objects. You can also create complex artwork by laying paths on top of one another. As a continuation of the checkerboard project, you will see how to combine shapes to create other objects, creating crowns for the checkers by combining shapes. You will also be introduced to the Live Corners feature in Illustrator CC which creates special curved corners using widgets. You will use the Transform command in the Object menu to scale shapes to size.

USING THE STAR TOOL

The **Star Tool** will be used to create a pointed star shape for the crown pieces that will be used when a player reaches the end zone. To determine the star shape, you enter an outside radius, an inner radius, and the number of points for the star.

Here, you will create the crown shape with the Star Tool.

1. With the *Checkerboard.ai* file open, make sure the *Checkers2* layer is selected in the Layers panel. In the Tools panel, set a Fill of None and a Stroke of Black. Set the stroke to 1 pt in the Stroke panel if necessary. Select the Star Tool, then click (don't drag) inside the artboard to access the dialog box.

2. Enter a Radius 1, the outside radius, of 150 px. Enter a Radius 2, the inside radius, of 75 px. Then, adjust the number of Points to 8 (Figure 7-27); you will resize it later. Note: Radii 1 and 2 are interchangeable—the larger number is automatically set as the outer radius, and the smaller number is automatically set as the inner radius.

▷ FIGURE 7-27

Create an eight-point star for the crown checker piece.

3. Use the Selection Tool (Y) to click on the star to display the bounding box.

4. Move the cursor to the lower-right corner until a bent arrow displays, then rotate until 2 pt are standing vertically (Figure 7-27).

USING LIVE CORNERS TO CURVE SHAPE POINTS

In Illustrator Creative Cloud (CC) there is a feature that allows designers to adjust or reshape corners of closed paths, called **Live Corners**. This feature uses corner and scaling widgets that display as small circles. When enabled (View > Show Corner Widget), the widget provides flexibility in rounding or reshaping corners collectively or individually on objects selected by the Direct Selection Tool. With most shape objects, when they are selected with the Direct Selection Tool, a Corners link displays in the associated Tool Options bar for more precise work. Using Live Corners will be covered more in depth in the Advanced Users section of this chapter.

Here, you'll round off the edges of your star shape. If you are using earlier versions of Illustrator skip this exercise in making corners.

1. With the Direct Selection Tool (white arrow), select the star shape and you'll find blue circle corner widgets display at each anchor point (Figure 7-28). You can drag these widgets and all points will be rounded off. When you hover your mouse over the widget, the type of effect is displayed under the Direct Selection Tool (A) cursor, like a curve, which would provide a round corner effect. There are also 3 different types of widgets, which if you select the Corners link in the Tool Options panel will display. You want the Round corner (default).

Select shape with
Direct Selection Tool

Select "Round" Corner
Radius 15 px

Result of shape
with rounded edges

▷ FIGURE 7-28

Using the Direct Selection Tool and Live Corners to change the star shape.

2. Select the Corners link and adjust the Round corner widgets to 15 px or less, and the result will display on the selected star shape. Before this feature, it would take much longer to create this shape. Feel free to experiment and create your own shape using the eight-point star.

3. Save the file. It's time to combine and scale your checkers.

THE TRANSFORM COMMAND

The **Transform command** under the Object menu allows you to move, rotate, reflect, scale, or shear an object in specified degrees or amounts. Since the star shape will be very small, the stroke color will be changed to yellow, and the width will be adjusted to 2 pt. The fill color will be set to None to make the inside of the star transparent.

To create the crowned checker, you will scale the star shape to fit inside the checker piece, then make aligned copies placed outside of the checkerboard (Figure 7-29).

1. Option/ALT-copy one checker from each side of the checkerboard; drag them to the pasteboard and deselect them by clicking in a blank area of the artboard.

2. With the eight-point star selected, set the Fill to none. Make sure the Stroke box in the Tools panel is set with a yellow stroke at 2 pt on the Stroke panel.

3. To scale down the star, choose Object > Transform > Scale and enter 15%. Click OK. If thicker lines are preferred adjust the stroke width.

4. Use the Selection Tool (Y) to drag the star inside one of the checkers. If it does not fit inside the checker, undo (Edit > Undo or Command/CTRL Z) and try scaling it again in increments of 5%. Use smart guides to wait for the intersect to display indicating the the star is inside the circle.

▷ FIGURE 7-29

Scaling and placing crowns inside the checker pieces.

5. With the Selection Tool (Y), use Option/ALT to copy the star and drag it to the opponents' checkers.

6. When both crown pieces are complete, group each individually by selecting the checker and the star and choosing Object > Group.

7. Use the Selection Tool (Y) while pressing the Option/ALT key to copy each opponent's crowned checker seven more times; place them along the opponent's side of the board, outside the checkerboard area. Do not worry about aligning them perfectly yet—we will cover that next.

HORIZONTAL AND VERTICAL ALIGNMENT

The Align panel allows you to align objects in either a horizontal or vertical fashion. You can also align objects so that they are distributed evenly along an axis.

To complete the checkers, you will align them evenly along the outsides of the checkerboard (Figure 7-30).

▷ FIGURE 7-30

Use settings on the Align panel to align and evenly distribute crowned pieces.

Horizontal Align Right

Vertical Distribute Center

1. For more precise placement, use the Selection Tool (Y) and Shift-select all the crowned pieces on one side of the checkerboard to display a bounding box.

2. Open the Align panel and click the Horizontal Align Right icon to align the pieces along the vertical side of the bounding box, then select the Vertical Distribute Center icon to evenly distribute the pieces. You can also use smart guides to align your crowned checkers as well.

3. Repeat the same process for the opponent's crowned checkers.

4. Save the file as *Checkerboard.ai* in your *Chapter 7* folder. Also, save as an Adobe PDF file (File > Save As > Adobe PDF). When the Save Adobe PDF dialog box comes up, choose Adobe PDF Preset: Smallest File Size. Leave the rest at their default settings. Save as *Checkerboard.pdf* in your *Chapter 7* folder.

5. Now, using Illustrator and the Selection Tool (Y) you can move the pieces to play the game in either Illustrator's native (ai) format or in the universal PDF format for those that don't have Illustrator, but can download the free Adobe Reader (Figure 7-31). Have fun! Close file when you are done. Note: you can also save the file as an SVG leaving all settings at defaults and move the checkers as well.

▷ FIGURE 7-31

Completed checkerboard, checkers, and crowned checkers. Your colors will differ.

SAVE FOR WEB

To use Save for Web, choosing File > Save for Web provides quick formatting options for electronic media (Figure 7-32). You can choose to format a file as simply optimized, if you know exactly what you want to use for a file extension; or you can select various format options and see up to multiple variations of your artwork. Each file version includes information as to what your image will look like using those formats, and the file size. One method of choosing a file extension for artwork is to save the artwork as a **GIF** file: it does not use more than 256 colors and artwork can contain no applied gradients, but it allows transparency within the artwork and creates a small file size compared to a JPEG format. You can use Save for Web to see if your artwork displays properly as a GIF file. GIF files are also the base files used in some animations. You also have a Preview button that allows you to see how your artwork will display on the web using a particular browser.

Here you will use the Save for Web command to view the checkerboard and optimize it to be saved as a GIF to keep the file size small.

1. Open your *Checkerboard.ai* file. Select File > Save for Web and choose the Optimized tab at the top left of this window to display just the artwork.

2. Select the GIF preset settings; observe that it does not alter the quality of the image. Click the Preview button, and select from the list of Browsers to see what your artwork would look like as a web document. Close the preview window when done.

▷ FIGURE 7-32

Using Save for Web to optimize the artwork for web and electronic (email) use.

Saving the Illustration as a GIF extension file

DESIGN TIP

Color has a way of stimulating us and can provide pleasing and not so pleasing combinations. Using the Color Guide can help you in the creative process to find colors that work together. Look at the various combinations available based on a color you choose from the Swatches panel.

3. Click Save to save the file as a GIF in your *Chapter 7* folder. Because it has a different extension, the other files in Illustrator's native format will not be affected. Observe the slight differences in file sizes and quality. Note: Because it is saving for web use, any layers are flattened, which would not work for purposes of moving checkers here. The purpose would be to show a client artwork on a flattened file.

4. You should have the files *Checkerboard.ai, Checkerboard.pdf,* and *Checkerboard .gif* in your *Chapter 7* folder. Zip these up in a *Checkerboard* folder and you're done.

TOOLKIT TIP As you look at the Save for Web dialog box, you will also notice the option for a PNG extension. PNG files are sometimes used on the web in place of JPEGs, because they can handle millions of colors, and they can handle transparencies. JPEGs cannot display graphics with transparencies. The drawback depends on your market: the files can be larger, which slows download time; and older browsers, such as Internet Explorer 4.0 or earlier, cannot read these files.

ADVANCED USERS: Working with Complex Shapes in Creating Artwork and Illustrations

These tutorials will provide an insight into combining shapes to create composite illustrative artwork using various shape tools, and using Illustrator's Live Corners feature. You'll explore the benefits of not only using guidelines and smart guides for proper alignment and placement of objects, but also when to use the Selection and Direct Selection tools to adjust, move, and modify your shape objects. You'll also compare, in creating a complex figure illustration, the differences when working with bitmaps, vector shapes, and text between Photoshop and Illustrator. You'll be introduced to Illustrator's Place command and saving objects in the preferred EPS format when working with text and graphics, which will be covered in more detail in later chapters.

BUILDING A LIGHTHOUSE WITH COMPLEX SHAPES

Here are some more advanced methods for making complex shapes using the Direct Selection Tool (V) and positioning selected anchor points precisely with the arrow keys on the keyboard. This graphic will be used as a symbol in the next chapter as part of a map. You can create images or shapes that are composites of multiple shapes and group them using the Object menu. Using guides helps to create perfectly symmetrical shapes. You can use the Color panel or Swatches panel to sample colors, including pure black and white colors (Figure 7-33). You will also scale the lighthouse using the Transform command.

TOOLKIT TIP When rulers are visible on the sides of your document, you will notice the position of the cursor always displays as a dotted line on each ruler. This helps with measuring distances and positioning objects.

▷ FIGURE 7-33

Selecting pure white or black is easy using the Color panel.

Pure Black (Print)
(C=0, M=0, Y=0, K=100)

Pure White
(C=0, M=0, Y=0, K=0)

DESIGN TIP

One method used to center objects on top of one another is to use the center point of the selected object's bounding box. You can also use the vertical and horizontal alignment options in the Align panel.

SHAPING THE LIGHTHOUSE TOP

The upper portion of the lighthouse is made by combining various shapes created by the Rounded Rectangle Tool, the Ellipse Tool (L), and the Polygon Tool; this will help you understand how to combine basic shapes into complex artwork. Creating shapes on top of one another is like having each shape on its own clear sheet of acetate; you can rearrange the position of these shapes behind or in front of one another using the Arrange command, use smart guides to help with alignment, then group them together as one object using the Group command.

TOOLKIT TIP Before selecting another shape with a different fill and stroke, always deselect the previously selected object. To do this, either select the Selection Tool (Y) and then click an empty area on the artboard, or choose Select > Deselect from the Select menu.

Next, you will create and position objects with various shapes to make the lighthouse top.

1. Use File > New to create a new, letter size Print file with portrait orientation and CMYK color. Select Profile > Print, then set measurement Units to inches. Leave Align New Objects to Pixel Grid unchecked for this assignment.

2. Name the file *Light* and click OK.

3. Make sure to display the ruler guides (select View > Rulers > Show Rulers) and smart guides (View > Smart Guides).

4. For the lighthouse roof, select a Fill of red from the Swatches panel (or try C=0, M=100, Y=100. K=0 in the Color panel), and a 2-pt Stroke of black. Use the Control panel to set the color and width of the Stroke.

▷ FIGURE 7-34

Creating the lighthouse top using some of the Shape tools.

5. Select the Polygon Tool, then click on the artboard to access the dialog box. Enter a radius 0.75 inch and 3 Sides. Click OK. You will build the lighthouse from the top down to the base (Figure 7-34).

6. Deselect the roof shape before continuing (Select > Deselect).

7. To make the lantern room, select a Fill of None and a black Stroke of 2 pt.

8. Select the Rounded Rectangle Tool, then click once on the artboard.

9. Enter a 1 inch Width and a 0.75 inch Height. Leave the Corner Radius at its default, and click OK.

10. Using the arrow keys on the keyboard, center the shape below the triangle roof. Deselect the shape.

11. For the light, select a Stroke of None and a Fill of yellow or orange.

12. Select the Ellipse Tool (L), then click on the artboard and enter 0.75 inch for both Width and Height. Click OK.

13. Center the light inside the rectangle with the arrow keys, then select Object > Arrange > Send to Back to position the light behind the rectangle. Deselect the shape. (If the shape disappears, it means the rounded rectangle did not have a Fill color of None. Select it and correct the Fill color using the Options panel.)

14. To make the walkway, set the Fill to black and use a 2-pt black Stroke.

15. Select the Rounded Rectangle Tool again, and click once on the artboard area.

16. Enter a 1.5 inch Width and a 0.75 inch Height with the Corner Radius at its default. Click OK. Center it under the lamp.

17. Using the Selection Tool (V), select all the shapes by dragging diagonally over them to display a bounding box.

18. Select Object > Group, and then Save the file as *Light.ai* in your *Chapter 7* folder, using the default settings.

TOOLKIT TIP The CMYK color mode for printing is a **subtractive process** using percentages of ink: cyan (C), magenta (M), yellow (Y), and black (K). When you are creating pure white or pure black colors using the Color panel or Swatches panel, a pure black would be C=0, M=0, Y=0, and K=100 (most designers and illustrators actually add 50% cyan to create a "rich" black). A pure white in printing would be the absence of color or C=0, M=0, Y=0, and K=0. RGB—which stands for red, green, blue—is an additive process with 255 as the highest number for each color. For pure black, all RGB colors would be set at 0; for pure white, they would be set at 255.

GUIDING THE LIGHTHOUSE

When creating custom shapes, it helps to use nonprintable guidelines created from ruler guides to position anchor points and path segments with accuracy. Guides can be created by clicking and dragging them into position from either the horizontal or vertical rulers.

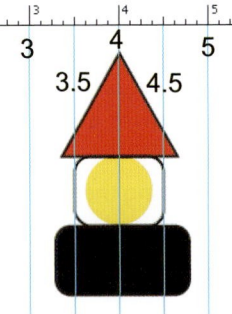

Here, you will draw guidelines for making accurate angles for the base.

1. Make sure the rulers are visible (View > Rulers > Show Rulers).

2. Drag a guide from the left Vertical ruler, and drag it to the 4 inch mark on the Horizontal Ruler; this will be the center of the lighthouse.

3. Use the Selection Tool (V) to select the grouped shapes you created. You can also try using smart guides to help with alignment of your individual object pieces. With the arrow keys, move them so they are centered on the guide. Use the center resizing handle of the bounding box as a guide. Deselect it when it is in position.

4. To make guidelines for the base, drag vertical guidelines to the 3.0, 3.5, 4.5, and 5.0 inch positions (Figure 7-35). Now you are ready to create an angle base.

▷ FIGURE 7-35

Setting the guides for placement of the lighthouse base and additional adjustments.

SHAPING THE LIGHTHOUSE BASE

You can adjust the shape of any object by moving its anchor points. The **Direct Selection Tool (A)** allows you to select and move individual anchor points or path segments. After creating the basic shape for the lighthouse base, you will use the Direct Selection Tool (A) to select anchor points and move them into position using the arrow keys on the keyboard to make fine adjustments (Figure 7-36).

▷ FIGURE 7-36

Use guides to lay out custom angles, the Direct Selection Tool to select individual anchor points, and the arrow keys on your keyboard for positioning.

Select anchor point with Direct Selection Tool

Direct Selection Tool (A)

Position with arrow keys on keyboard

When the Direct Selection Tool (A) is hovering over an anchor point, the anchor point will enlarge so you can select it easily.

It is time to adjust the roof and create the angled base using the Direct Selection Tool (A) and arrow keys.

DESIGN TIP

When guides are unlocked, you can use the Options panel to type in an exact position.

1. To adjust the lighthouse roof, select the Direct Selection Tool (A) and click on the artboard. Click the top anchor point of the roof. A large square displays under the cursor; once the anchor point is selected, the anchor point will turn solid, but the rest will remain white.

2. Tap the Down arrow key 20 times to minimize the roof angle. Deselect the roof. (You can also hold the Shift key down and press the arrow key twice instead. Holding the Shift key while using the arrow keys moves a selected point or path 10 times the normal increment.)

3. For the base, set a Fill of White and a black Stroke of 1 pt; try typing the letter D, which resets the colors to this default.

4. Select the Rectangle Tool (M), click once on the artboard, and enter a Width of 2 inches and a Height of 3 inches. Click OK.

5. Center the box below the upper portion of the lighthouse, between the outer guidelines, using either the Selection Tool or the arrow keys.

TOOLKIT TIP When using the Direct Selection Tool (A), always click on the artboard first before selecting the anchor point or path segment you want to edit.

DESIGN TIP

For the most accurate positioning of anchor points, select individual anchor points with the Direct Selection Tool, and then use the arrow keys to move around.

6. Select the Direct Selection Tool (A) and click on the artboard to deselect the rectangle, then click the upper-left anchor point of the rectangle to select it.

7. Use the right arrow key to move the anchor point to the 3.5-inch guide. (You can also enter 3.5 in the *X* value in the Control panel instead.)

8. Click on the artboard again, and select the upper-right anchor point.

9. Use the right arrow key to move the anchor point to the 4.5-inch guide.

10. The base outline is completed; now it is time to add the stripes (Figure 7-37).

MAKING THE LIGHTHOUSE STRIPES

To further your skills in making angled shapes (trapezoids) using the Direct Selection Tool (A) and the arrow keys, you will create three stripes on the lighthouse base. When creating angled shapes for precise placement on top of other objects, it is easier to work in Outline view.

Here you will create three stripes at angles to match the lighthouse base.

1. First, click on the red roof, then click on the artboard to deselect it. Doing this will reset your stroke and fill colors to match the roof, so the stripes will also be red with a 1-pt black stroke.

2. Select the Rectangle Tool (M), then click on the artboard once.

Position Square (Preview View)

Select anchor point with Direct Selection Tool, position with arrow keys

Outline View

Complete with corner points

Completed Graphic

▷ FIGURE 7-37

Sometimes positioning accurate points is best done in Outline view. Select anchor points with the Direct Selection Tool, and position precisely with the arrow keys.

3. Enter a 2-inch Width and 0.5-inch Height in the display box. Select OK

4. Move the first red rectangle at the top of the base with the Selection Tool (V).

5. Use the Selection Tool (V) and Option/ALT drag down to make two more copies of the red stripe. Make sure the bottom rectangle is placed at the bottom of the lighthouse base. Select all three stripes (Shift and click each one) and use the Align panel to distribute them evenly if needed, or use smart guides (Figure 7-37).

6. To ensure precision, switch to Outline view (View > Outline).

7. Select the Direct Selection Tool (A) and click on the artboard before selecting a corner anchor point. This will avoid moving the whole object.

8. Use the arrow keys to move each corner point alongside the angled base until they are all aligned with it (Figure 7-37). You want the blended lines to display as one to avoid incorrect overlapping.

9. Drag the second rectangle down a half inch under the top stripe, and use the Direct Selection Tool (A) and arrow keys to select and drag the corner points in as before.

10. Repeat this process for the middle and bottom rectangles.

11. To group all the elements together, choose the Selection Tool (V) and drag a box diagonally over the entire lighthouse.

12. Select Object > Group. The lighthouse is now one object.

13. Scale the lighthouse to size for the next chapter using Object > Transform > Scale > 10%. Place a check in Scale Strokes and Effects, then click OK.

14. Save the file as *Light.ai* in your *Chapter 7* folder.

15. Feel free to experiment with color choices using the Color Guide (Window > Color Guide) panel or the Kuler panel (Window > Extensions > Kuler). Enjoy!

CREATING A COMPLEX FIGURE DIAGRAM TO ILLUSTRATE LIVE CORNERS

In Illustrator Creative Cloud (CC), designers can use various corner widgets in the Live Corners feature to adjust radii, scaling, and attributes of corner components in images selected with the Direct Selection Tool. This provides precision and flexibility in making overall shape adjustments. To provide a visual reference, you will create a more complex figure illustration involving positioning of many elements, and labeling to learn about Illustrator's Live Corners feature. When the illustration is complete, to keep all shape objects and text sharp as if ready for a large commercial print run, you can save in Illustrator's EPS format, which is the preferred method when combining text and graphic elements together. This tutorial will also help you to compare working with images and vector graphics between Photoshop and Illustrator. Images for this tutorial are found at *www.CengageBrain.com*.

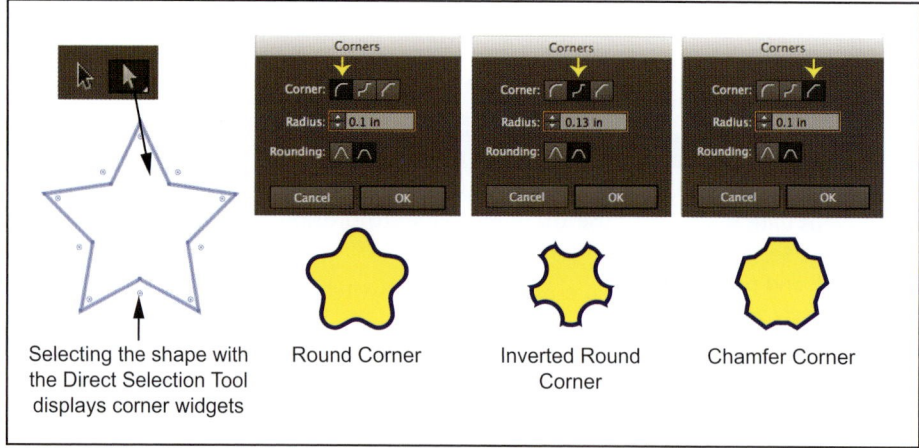

Selecting the shape with the Direct Selection Tool displays corner widgets

Round Corner

Inverted Round Corner

Chamfer Corner

Figure 7-XX
Double-clicking corner widgets with the Direct Selection Tool allows designers to create three types of Live Corners.

▷ FIGURE 7-38

Completed complex figure illustration introducing Illustrator's Live Corners feature.

PLACING BITMAP IMAGES IN ILLUSTRATOR

Beforehand you created a very basic figure diagram with only a couple of text lines in Photoshop. Complex figure artwork sometimes involves using the "Place" command to bring in bitmap Photoshop images into an Illustrator document. Objects placed into Illustrator are usually linked so that any last minute changes that need to be made in Photoshop will automatically make the change in your linked image in Illustrator. When our figure illustration is completed, it will be embedded or pasted into the document at the end. As Illustrator defaults to CMYK mode for commercial printing, when bringing in images from Photoshop's RGB color mode, they should be converted to CMYK mode (duplicates) before bringing them into Illustrator. If not, when saving say to EPS format, a warning may appear indicating there may be a change in color, which in most cases you would accept and the change would be applied.

In this exercise, you are going to place screen copy images on your document. They have already been converted to Illustrator's CMYK format.

1. First, launch Illustrator and create a new document with Profile: Print into which you'll bring in screen copy images, and Units of Inches to help in measurement. Leave the default CMYK color mode settings as this would be going to a commercial printer. Name the file *Live Corners*, and save the file as *Live Corners.ai* in Illustrator's native file format with default settings in your *Chapter 7* folder.

2. To set up your workspace, make sure rulers are displayed around the image (View > Rulers > Show Rulers). Drag guidelines from the one-inch marks to create a margin. Use the Window menu to activate the Layers, Swatches, and Stroke panels if they aren't already displayed. Zoom into the document to about 200%.

3. Select File > Place and click on the *Direct Selection.tif* file within your *Chapter 7* folder to bring in an image of the Selection and Direct Selection tools. As you hover the cursor over the document a thumbnail icon displays. Click the document where the guidelines intersect at the one-inch mark to place the selected image, and use the Selection Tool, if needed, to locate the image edge on the one-inch border. When you click on a blank area of the document the image is no longer selected.

4. The second image is one with the widgets displayed, which had to be accessed and created using the screen copy application Grab (Mac). Although it is a bit-map of a vector image it will work here by reducing the image size. Select File > Place, and choose the *Widgets.tif* file inside your *Chapter 7* folder.

5. Click on the document to place the image, and you will notice the image will display rather large so we need to reduce it. Hold down the Shift key (to keep all proportions equal) and drag from one of the corner anchor points inward until the image is about 1.5 inches in size. The quality will remain crisp here. Drag under the Direct Selection image as shown in Figure 7-39.

6. There are three corner types so you will place these horizontally aligned so that you can show the differences in the next exercise. Select File > Place

▷ FIGURE 7-39

Setting up the Illustrator document and placing the tools and widgets images.

and locate the Round *Corner.tif* file first, and align with the top of the selection tools image and vertically along the 2.5 or 2.75-inch horizontal ruler mark. Hold down the Shift key and drag from one of the corner anchor points inward to shrink the image to about 1.5 inches in width so it is still easily readable. Use the smart guides to align (Figure 7-40).

7. Place the *Inverted Round Corner.tif* file next alongside the Round Corner image, shrinking to the same size using the smart guides to help align and position the image about one-eighth of an inch away.

8. Place the *Chamfer Corner.tif* image and resize to equal the other two images as shown in Figure 7-40.

▷ FIGURE 7-40

Positioning of placed images using smart guides.

Use smart guides to help with positioning of placed images

Images positioned equidistant from one another

TOOLKIT TIP When bringing in screen copies, or images from Photoshop, all editing should be done using Photoshop first before they are brought into Illustrator. If there is an image with certain parts of the background to be removed (Magic Eraser Tool), which creates an irregular-sided image, it should be completed in Photoshop and saved as either a PNG or GIF file to maintain the transparent background to bring into Illustrator. As in Photoshop, use the smart guides feature (View > Smart Guides) to help with positioning. Regular four-sided images can be saved as TIFs or JPGs as there is no worry about a transparent background.

LAYERS AND LAYERING IN ILLUSTRATOR

Illustrator uses layers like Photoshop, but the main difference is that in Illustrator, there is a main layer, then there are sublayers underneath that correspond to different bitmap images brought in, Illustrator objects and individual paths created, text, and even guidelines. The benefit to this type of layering is you can create layer "categories" of each type of artwork for quick access. Layers and sublayers in Illustrator, like Photoshop layers, can be moved around for different effects and displays. The images you brought in have been placed on separate sublayers under the main layer and can still be moved around. When you select any object, the layer—and its associated sublayer—is highlighted with a bright colored square icon on the right side for quick access. When you select multiple objects, all related layers and sublayers are highlighted. There are also eye icons to turn on and off layers and sublayers.

In this exercise, you will explore the Layers panel and create three categories of layers to keep organized for your images you just brought in, vector image shapes, and text labels.

1. With the Layers panel open, you should find a *Layer 1* layer. Click on the arrow next to Layer 1 to display all objects brought into your document, even the guides. Click on the widgets image and the *Layer1* layer is highlighted with the sublayer "*Widgets*" highlighted as well with a colored box (Figure 7-41). Drag the Selection Tool over the three corner images and you'll notice all layers are highlighted that are related to the images you just selected.

Selected object displayed
as highlighted sublayer

Create New Layer   Renamed Layers

▷ FIGURE 7-41

Observing highlighted layers and renaming layers.

2. Let's create the categories of layers. Double-click on the *Layer 1* text and rename as *Images*.

3. To create two more main layers, select the Create New Layer icon at the bottom of the Layers panel twice, which will display as *Layer 2* and *Layer 3*.

4. Rename *Layer 2* as *Corner Shapes* and *Layer 3* as *Text*. This will help to keep your document work organized (Figure 7-41).

5. Save the document in Illustrator's native format as *Live Corners.ai* in your *Chapter 7* folder. Leave all settings at their default.

TOOLKIT TIP If your bitmap images in your Illustrator document don't appear to be as "sharp" as you'd expect, in most cases they are usually displayed as low-resolution previews in Illustrator when using the Place command as they probably are linked to the high resolution original. When you print to your local printer or when your service provider will print, the low-resolution preview is automatically replaced with high resolution graphic for a sharp print. Try printing on your local printer to see the difference between your monitor display and the actual print. You can also go into Preferences > File Handling and Clipboard and make sure Display Bitmaps as Anti-Aliased Images in Pixel Preview is checked.

CREATING THE THREE CORNER TYPES (ROUND, INVERTED ROUND, CHAMFER)

There are three corner types that can be created. They are round, inverted round, and chamfer. When enabled (View > Show Corner Widget) the widget provides flexibility in rounding or reshaping corners collectively or individually on objects selected by the Direct Selection Tool. To bring up the Corners display, you can double-click on any corner widget with the Direct Selection Tool or select the Corners link on the Control panel of the selected shape. The larger the shape the more precision you have in creating adjustments, with smaller shapes you are more limited.

Here you will create a star image and apply the three different types of corners as three different shapes using Live Corners to serve as a visual preview.

1. Select the *Corner Shapes* layer in the Layers panel and have your *Live Corners* document zoomed in at 200%.

2. In the Color Picker in the Tools panel, select colors for Fill and Stroke from the Swatches or Color panel. We chose a yellow Fill and a deep blue 2-pt Stroke, but feel free to choose your own colors. The key is to choose colors that will accent the shapes for comparison.

▷ FIGURE 7-42

Selecting Corners link from Control panel and creating round corners on star shape.

3. Click the Shapes tools below the Type Tool and select the Star Tool. Click on the document to bring up the dialog box and enter *Radius 1: 0.5 in, Radius 2: 2.5 in,* and *Points: 5*. Due to the small image sizes for your diagram, the settings will be limited (Figure 7-42).

Star shape settings   Select Corners link and create Round radius   New shape generated

4. When the object displays on your document, click the Direct Selection Tool (A) on your Tools panel to bring up the widgets that display as small circles around your star shape. You'll also find the Corners link displayed on your Control panel (if the widgets don't display, select View > Show Corner Widget).

5. Select the Corners link to show the Corners display box. Select the Round corner and use the arrows to display a radius of "0.1 in" as shown in your image on your document. You'll notice the shape changes as you adjusted the arrows. Click OK to apply the change. When the radius is displayed as 0, your shape returns to its original form.

6. Use the Selection Tool (V) and Option/ALT key and copy another star image, or select the star tool again and use the same settings as before so that the completed images will fit under the Corners images on your illustration. You'll need to create two copies of the star shape.

 TOOLKIT TIP With the widgets displayed on your shape when the Direct Selection Tool is selected, if you Option/ALT-click on any corner widget, the widget cycles through all three corner styles showing the icons under your Direct Selection Tool cursor.

7. Select the second star image and select the Direct Selection Tool (A) to bring up the widgets. You can use the Corners link again in the Control panel, or double-click any widget to bring up the Corners display box. Select the Inverted Round icon and adjust the radius to the settings shown on the image on your document. Click OK to apply.

8. Repeat the same for the third image, creating a Chamfer corner shape using the settings on your document as a guide and center each changed shape under each related image. Use Figure 7-43 as a guide.

9. These small images you just created are used to represent changes when playing with corner effects. Feel free to use larger images for more precise adjustment. When done remove and leave the images you created in this excise properly aligned as shown in Figure 7-43.

10. Save the document in Illustrator's native format as *Live Corners.ai* in your *Chapter 7* folder. Leave all settings at their default.

▷ FIGURE 7-43

Star shape corners adjusted for round, inverted round, and chamfer using Corners display as a guide.

 TOOLKIT TIP To change only one corner or a shape, deselect the object shape, and then use the Direct Selection Tool (A) to select one anchor point. Double-click the associated widget that displays to bring up the Corners dialog box and make the changes that will only affect that corner.

CREATING ARROWHEADS IN ILLUSTRATOR

Arrowheads help to lead the viewer to certain important areas of your illustration. Illustrator provides more arrowhead options than Photoshop. Most settings and adjustments can be made in the Stroke panel. You start by using the Line Segment Tool (\), and then use the Stroke panel to choose various arrowhead designs to add to your line. It's a good habit to make sure the line of your arrowhead is not less than 1 pt in width, otherwise it may not display properly in print.

You will create arrowheads to help the viewer follow what you are trying to emphasize before labeling the diagram.

1. Make sure the *Corner Shapes* layer is selected. You'll notice that all the shapes you created in the previous exercise are displayed in sublayers under the *Corner Shapes* layer. Have the Stroke panel displayed with a Black Stroke and no Fill color in the Tools panel.

2. Select the Line Segment Tool (\) in the Tools panel, and drag down from the image of the selection tools (Direct Selection Tool) inside the star image with widgets displayed. In the Stroke panel choose a 1-pt Stroke, and select the type of end arrowhead on the right side. We chose Arrow 9 from the drop-down list but feel free to choose your own. Also, reduce the selection tools image dragging inward from a corner with the Selection Tool (V) to balance it with the arrow and widgets image.

▷ FIGURE 7-44

Creating arrow-heads using the Line Segment Tool and Stroke panel.

3. Create another line segment from underneath the star image towards the center widget. Hold down the Shift key while dragging to keep the arrow vertical. Apply the same arrowhead in the Stroke panel (Figure 7-44).

Line Segment Tool

Arrowhead Selection   Inserting Black Arrows

DESIGN TIP

Consistency is important. Although there are two different styles of arrows and two different colors, they are far enough away from one another, and are located at different segments of the illustration, that one doesn't overpower the other, or cause confusion with your viewer.

4. The next set of arrows will point to each type of corner being used in the three corners images. These are going to be small arrows and you'll need to change the Stroke color to yellow or a very light color for them to stand out over the dark image. Select the Selection Tool (V) to create the new color and click on a blank area of your document. Change the Stroke color to yellow and leave the width at 1 pt in the Stroke panel.

5. Select the Line Segment Tool (\) and hold down the Shift key to create vertical light colored lines over each type of highlighted corner. Make sure the lines are centered using the Selection Tool (V) to move.

6. Each line has to be selected before applying the arrowhead. For these three arrows we used the Arrow 4 type so there is distinction between the line and the arrowhead (Figure 7-45). Choose what looks best and still makes the arrow stand out.

7. Use the Selection Tool (V) to make any final adjustments; it's time for labeling your illustration.

TEXT LABELING YOUR ILLUSTRATION

Labeling your illustration is a very important aspect in any figure illustration artwork. The purpose is to identify for your viewer the components of your illustration in coordination with your arrows so the message is clearly and quickly understood. Labels that have a couple of words to identify something may have the words capitalized, whereas a description of more than a few words of a process or technique usually involves capitalization of the first word only. Tools in an application are capitalized. Usually 10 pt sans serif fonts like Arial Regular provide easy reading for the viewer. Figure captions or callouts are placed underneath as the figure is referenced in the text (chapter number then figure number in the chapter like "Figure 7-10") and a description of the illustration is provided. Illustrator CC has a Font Search feature in the Control panel and Character panel. There, you can start to type the font or font area (or even font style) you're looking for, and the choices will be filtered to display fonts that match the criteria you type in along with associated samples.

It's time to label your artwork to put the finishing touches.

1. Make sure you have the *Text* layer selected in the Layers panel, as this will be where you will have all your labeling.

2. Select the Type Tool (T) and in the Control panel in front of the Character link type "A." You'll notice all fonts that start with that letter will be filtered to display. We chose a sans serif font like Arial Regular at 10 pt with Align Center selected from the Type Control panel. Use a Fill color of Black or a dark color and a Stroke of None in the Tools panel.

3. Under the star image with the widgets displayed by the vertical arrow, type "Selecting the shape with," press Return/Enter for the next line and type "the Direct Selection Tool," then press Return/Enter for the third line and type "displays corner widgets." Where this is a statement of description only the first word is capitalized (Figure 7-46).

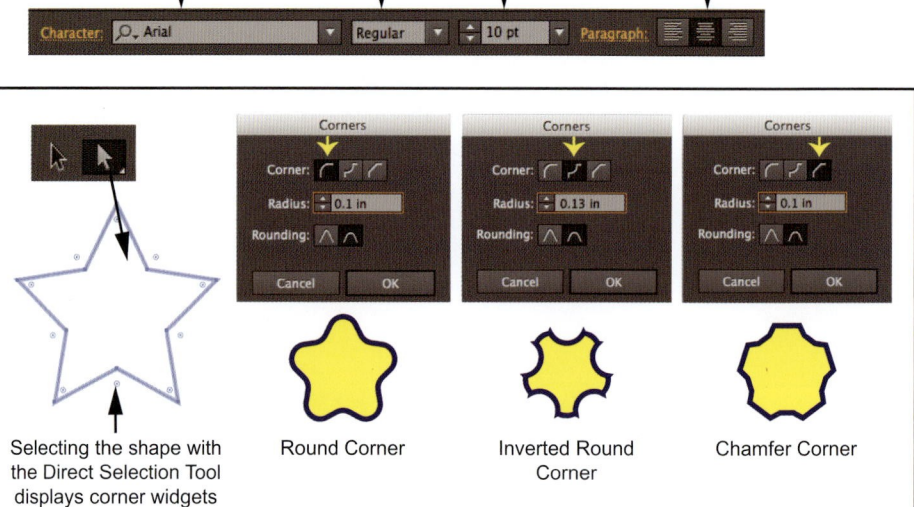

Selecting the shape with the Direct Selection Tool displays corner widgets

Round Corner

Inverted Round Corner

Chamfer Corner

▷ FIGURE 7-46

Completed illustration on three types of live corners.

4. Now to label the shapes underneath. Click on the Selection Tool (V) to create a new line of type, and then select the Type Tool (T) again. Under the first shape, type "Round Corner," then click the Selection Tool (V) and use the smart guides to center the type line under the image.

5. Select the Type Tool (T) again and under the middle shape type "Inverted Round," then press Return/Enter and type "Corner." Use the Selection Tool to reposition as centered.

6. Select the Type Tool (T) again and type "Chamfer Corner," then use the Selection Tool to reposition the text line. Make sure the three type lines are centered under each image shape and the first line of each is on the same smart guideline (Figure 7-46).

7. To remove the guides created in the beginning choose View > Guides > Clear Guides.

8. To set up the figure callout, select the Type Tool (T) and then change the alignment to Left Align on the Control panel. Keep the same font you used for labeling.

9. Type "Figure 7-XX" then press the Return/Enter key. Type "Double-clicking corner widgets with the Direct Selection Tool," press Return/Enter, and type "allows designers to create three types of Live Corners."

10. Optional: Sometimes, although not necessary here, to tie different components together a 1-pt stroke border may be created around the illustration (not the callout). The trick is to make sure the border surrounds the artwork equally on all sides (Figure 7-46). We created one to show you what it would look like. Feel free to create one.

11. Save the file as *Live Corners.ai* in Illustrator's native format as your backup in your *Chapter 7* folder. We'll save the image in EPS format for the service provider next.

EMBEDDING IMAGES IN ILLUSTRATOR'S EPS FORMAT

As always it's best to save in the application's native format, in this case in Illustrator's native AI format. This works fine as a backup copy and is also accepted by many service providers. As mentioned earlier, where we are using multiple vector shapes, bitmap images, and text that will be used to label the figure illustration, EPS is a general universally accepted format when combining text and graphics artwork on one document. PDFs are also acceptable in many instances, which we'll cover more in depth later. Although when a graphic is "placed" in an Illustrator document, it is still linked to the original file and its location, which comes in handy for any last minute changes that need to be done with the original, the change is also made on the linked image in your document. For this illustration, you no longer need to include any relation linking to the original images so you want to "embed" or paste permanently your images here.

Here you will save your figure illustration in EPS format without links so the images are embedded in the document.

1. Save your file as *Live Corners.eps* in your *Chapter 7* folder. When the dialog box displays leave the current version of Illustrator you are using, and default settings for CMYK, but make sure *Include Linked* Files is unchecked. Click OK.

2. A warning dialog box will display indicating that files will be no longer be linked but embedded to keep the document as self-contained (Figure 7-47). Click on the Embed Files button to paste all images and info onto the document.

3. The image will not need any outside original images and is saved ready for press. We'll cover more in depth about using linked and placed images in later chapters.

▷ FIGURE 7-47

Saving the document in EPS format and embedding the files.

DIGITAL TOOLKIT EXTRA: Custom Shapes to Create Playing Cards

This assignment involves using the Shape Builder Tool (Shift+M) to create complex shapes out of a series of separate shapes. In creating the Ace playing cards, you'll use various shape tools, then combine with the Shape Builder Tool (Shift+M) to create a diamond, club, spade, and heart shape (Figure 7-48). You will also learn to use the Direct Selection Tool (A) again, which allows you to select parts of either an object's anchor points or path lines to accurately adjust using the arrow keys on your keyboard. You will get familiar with the Ellipse, Polygon, Rounded Rectangle, and Rectangle shape tools for your cards. The Transform command is also used here to reflect, rotate, and scale shapes and adjust the "Ace" font character.

▷ FIGURE 7-48

Creating playing cards using custom shapes, Transform command, and the Shape Builder Tool.

CREATING THE CARD OUTLINE WITH THE ROUNDED RECTANGLE TOOL

The Rounded Rectangle Tool does exactly what its name implies: rounds the corners of a square or rectangle. Professional playing cards have rounded corners, which is what you will create for this exercise. You will also set your document for printing and use the Control panel to create the stroke outline for the cards.

You will set up the document as a print document, measuring in inches, and create the card outline.

1. In Illustrator, create a new Print document by selecting File > New > Profile – Print.

2. Change the Units measurement to Inches instead of points and change the orientation to Landscape, 11 inches Width by 8.5 inches Height. Keep all other default settings (Figure 7-49). Name the document *Cards* and click OK.

Control panel

▷ FIGURE 7-49

Creating the playing cards outline using the Rounded Rectangle Tool.

3. Select the Rounded Rectangular Tool and click on the artboard to bring up the dialog box. Create a size 2.5 inches Width by 3.5 inches Height, by 0.2 Rounded Corners. Click OK.

4. With the selected shape on the document, use the Control panel to make sure the Stroke is black with a 2-pt thickness and the Foreground is white.

5. Make sure Smart Guides, Snap to Point, and Rulers are checked in the View menu.

USING TYPE IN ILLUSTRATOR

As you learned in Photoshop, Illustrator also has a Type Tool (T) and a Type menu to select from a font list. The list displays the fonts as thumbnail representations of what the font will look like to help you in your selection. You can also use the Control panel once the Type Tool (T) is selected to also make selections. In Illustrator you can use the Type Tool (T) to click anywhere on the artboard and begin typing normally. You then use the Selection Tool (V) (black arrow tool) to position the type character(s) the same way you would with any shape object. This will be covered more in depth in the next chapter.

In this exercise you will select a serif font, type and position it, then make a copy and flip it using the Transform command.

1. To choose a regular font in Illustrator, select Type > Font > and select from the list of fonts displayed. Choose a slender serif font like Georgia, Garamond, or Times New Roman. For this example we are using Cambria (Regular). Official playing cards use their own custom font, so we will improvise here.

2. Select Type > Size and choose a 36-pt size, then set the Foreground color to black. You will also notice you can also make these settings using the Control panel as well.

DESIGN TIP

In most cases, especially in traditional design, you want to allow ample space between type and the edge of the document, and, in the case of creating these playing cards, between the type and the shapes you are creating.

3. Select the Type Tool (T) and type an uppercase "A" in the upper-right corner of the card, allowing about a one-eight inch space from the right edge and a quarter inch space from the top. Use the Selection Tool (V) or arrow keys to position your letter.

4. Select the character and copy it by holding down the Option/ALT key and dragging it to the bottom left of the card with the same spacing from the edge as you made in the upper-right corner.

5. You need to flip the character in the bottom left by selecting the character, then select Object > Transform > Reflect. When the Reflect dialog box displays, select Axis > Horizontal. Click OK. Reposition your character.

6. Now that you have one card outline completed, use the Selection Tool (V) and drag diagonally to select the card outline and contents, and either use the Edit menu to copy and paste three more cards, or use the Option/ALT key and drag three times to make three copies.

▷ FIGURE 7-50

Using the Type menu and Type Tool to make the character for the playing cards.

7. Position the cards apart from one another on the left side of the artboard, two on top, two on bottom, using the smart guides as practice for even alignment. The right side of the artboard will be used as a work area for creating your shapes (Figure 7-50).

8. Select the "A" character on the top left card, and choose a red color from the Swatches panel. Change the color of the other characters on the two top cards to the same red color.

9. Save the file in Illustrator's native format as *Cards.ai* in your *Chapter 7* folder.

CREATING THE DIAMOND SHAPE USING THE DIRECT SELECTION TOOL

In the previous exercises, you have been using the Selection Tool (V), which is the black arrow icon to move entire objects or shapes. Next to the Selection Tool (V) is the **Direct Selection Tool (A)**, which is displayed as a white arrow icon. This tool is used to select parts of a path, or an object's anchor point described in the beginning of this chapter, and move or adjust only that component. In creating the diamond shape, a square will be created, rotated, and then adjusted using the Direct Selection Tool (A). Again this tool will be used more in depth in the next chapters. You can also choose to have a Stroke color of None displayed by choosing the Stroke color icon in the Tools panel, then either selecting the None icon, which displays as a box with a red line through it below, or through the color or Swatches panels.

Here you will use the familiar Rectangle Tool used in the checkerboard assignment to make the square, and then rotate it 45 degrees using the Transform command. The sides will be adjusted using the Direct Selection Tool (A).

1. On the Tools panel, select the red Foreground color from the Swatches panel, and select the None icon (red line through square) for the Stroke color. You can also do this using the Swatches panel. Make sure Rulers is still checked (View Rulers).

2. Select the Rectangle Tool and click on the black space on the right side of the artboard. Enter a 1-inch Width and Height. Click OK.

3. To rotate, select Object > Transform > Rotate. Enter 45 degrees, in the display box and then click OK.

4. Click on the artboard to deselect the object. Click on the Direct Selection Tool (A) and click on the left point of the diamond object to access the anchor point. When you have an anchor point selected, or when the cursor hovers over an anchor point, the white arrow displays a white square underneath.

5. Press the right arrow key on your keyboard 15 times, then select the anchor point on the right side and press the left arrow key 15 times. This will slender down the diamond shape accurately.

6. Click on the artboard to deselect the diamond from the Direct Selection Tool (A), then select the Selection Tool (black arrow) and select the shape again. Using the smart guides to assist you, position the shape in the center of the top left card when you see the intersection lines appear.

7. To create the little diamond shapes that will appear underneath the "A" character you created, with the diamond selected, hold down the Option/ALT key and drag twice to create two copies (or you can use the Edit command to copy and paste the object twice).

8. For each, select Object > Transform > Scale > and enter "25" in the display dialog box (Figure 7-51) to scale down one-quarter the original size.

9. Use the Selection Tool (V) and move each under the "A" character centered with some space. A good rule of thumb is to use the space of an anchor point from the bounding box to the bottom of the character.

▷ FIGURE 7-51

Creating the diamond shape using Direct Selection Tool and Transform command.

10. To flip the bottom left diamond shape (although it wouldn't be noticeable for this shape), select it and choose Object > Transform > Reflect > Horizontal.

11. Your first card, the Ace of Diamonds, is finished.

12. Save the file in your *Chapter 7* folder.

 TOOLKIT TIP You can also rotate an object at 45-degree increments by selecting the object using the Selection Tool (V), and hover the cursor over the bottom right corner until a bent arrow appears as a cursor. Hold down the Shift key and drag to the left or right and the object will turn in 45-degree increments. Release the mouse when you are done.

CREATING THE HEART SHAPE USING SHAPE TOOLS AND SHAPE BUILDER TOOL

The **Shape Builder Tool** (Shift+M) allows you to create one complex shape out of a group of selected shapes. The default setting for this tool is to merge shapes together. It can also be used to help fill in gaps with color. To change or adjust settings, you can double-click on the tool and make your changes, but we will keep the default settings for this exercise. You can also use the Direct Selection Tool (A) to select not only anchor points, but path lines as well, and then adjust using the arrow keys.

Here you will use the Ellipse and Polygon shape tools, and the Shape Builder Tool, to create the heart shape for the next playing card.

1. To create the top of the heart shape, make sure the Foreground color is red with a Stroke of none. Select the Ellipse Tool (L), click on the blank right side of the artboard, and enter a 0.5-inch Height and Width.

2. Use the Option/ALT key and hold down the selected shape, creating another copy to move to the right of the first circle with the inside edges touching.

3. To create the point area, select the Polygon Tool, click on the artboard, and create a 3-sided object at 0.5 Radius.

4. To flip the triangle, select it and choose Object > Transform > Reflect > Horizontal.

5. With the triangle object selected, use the Selection Tool (V) and drag underneath until the two circle edges blend visually with the side as accurately as possible (Figure 7-52). You will notice a gap is between the three shapes.

6. Select all three shapes with the Selection Tool (V), and then select the Shape Builder Tool (Shift + M). Shapes must always be selected first.

▷ FIGURE 7-52

Creating the heart shape using Ellipse, Polygon, and Shape Builder tools.

7. Click on the left circle shape and drag across diagonally to blend in the other shapes. You will notice the highlighted shapes have a cross mesh displayed. When you let go the shapes start to merge together and the gap between the shapes will also be filled in.

8. Continue until the heart shape is blended together as one shape.

9. OPTIONAL: The shape will probably not be perfect at this stage of your learn-ing, but you can use it for the rest of the exercises. There are many more advanced ways to make adjustments, which you'll learn later. One way, if you want to attempt it, is to zoom at 300% and use the Direct Selection Tool (A) and click on the path line, or the anchor point, near the left edge of the circle and then click the right arrow key only once or twice to adjust the shape to make it more accurate (Figure 7-52), then try on the other side. If it doesn't work you can always undo the action (Edit > Undo).

10. Click on the artboard to deselect the heart shape, and then select the Selection Tool (black arrow) to select the shape again. Using the smart guides to assist you, position the shape in the center when you see the intersection lines appear.

11. To create the little heart shapes that will appear underneath the "A" character you created, select the heart shape, then hold down the Option/ALT key and drag to create a copy.

12. Select and choose Object > Transform > Scale > and enter "25" in the display dialog box to scale down one-quarter the original size.

13. Use the Selection Tool (V) and move each under the top right "A" character centered with some space, using the smart guides for proper alignment with the previous card. A good rule of thumb is to use the space of a square anchor point from the bounding box to the bottom of the character.

14. With the little heart selected, hold down the Option/ALT key to create a dupli-cate and drag to the bottom left under the upside down "A."

15. To flip the bottom left heart shape, select it and choose Object > Transform > Reflect > Horizontal. Reposition if needed using the smart guides.

16. Your second card, the Ace of Hearts, is finished.

17. Save the file in your *Chapter 7* folder.

TOOLKIT TIP Although a little advanced for now, you can use the Direct Selec-tion Tool (A) to select the path line, not the anchor point, and slightly curve inward the heart shape (and the previous diamond shape as well), as would be done in professional playing card shapes. You will find little lines coming out of the anchor point, which are called directional lines and can also be used to more accurately change the shape of the curve as well. The trick is to make sure they are both ac-curate on both sides. This will be covered more in depth in Chapter 9.

COMBINING SHAPES TO CREATE THE SPADE SHAPE

To create the spade shape, you can flip the heart shape you just created, and then add a triangle underneath, and adjust using the Direct Selection Tool (A). This allows you to then use the Shape Builder Tool (Shift + M) to create another custom shape.

Here you will create the spade shape built upon the heart shape you just created.

1. Using the Selection Tool (V), select the heart shape; create a duplicate copy by holding down the Option/ALT key and dragging to a blank workspace on the artboard.

2. Change the Foreground color to black with a Stroke of none, using the Swatches or Color panel. The new color will display on the Tools panel.

3. To flip the heart shape upside down, select it and choose Object > Transform > Reflect > Horizontal.

4. To create the bottom portion of the spade, select the Polygon Tool, click on the artboard, and create a 3-sided object at 0.5 Radius.

5. With the triangle object selected, use the Selection Tool (V) and drag underneath the center of the upside down shape about a third of the shape overlapping, as shown in Figure 7-53.

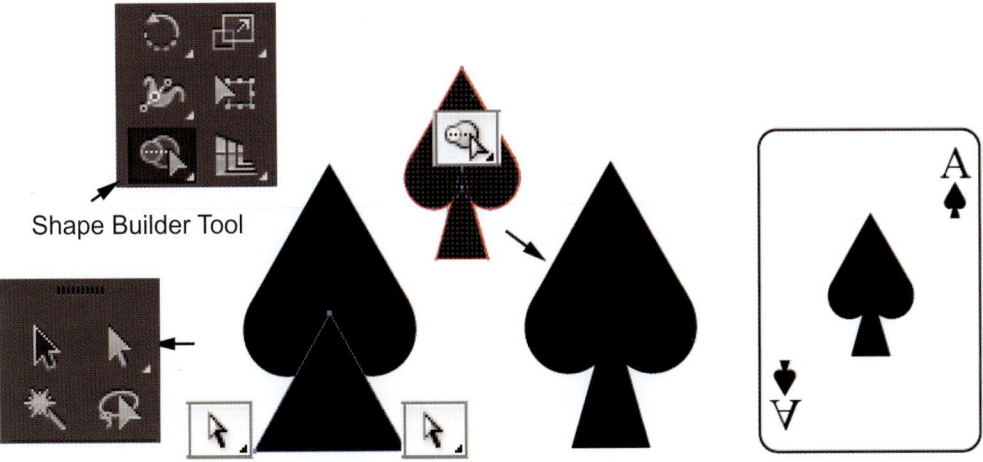

Shape Builder Tool

▷   FIGURE 7-53

Creating the spade shape using the Shape Builder Tool. Making adjustments with the Direct Selection Tool.

6. Select the Direct Selection Tool (A) and click on the left bottom anchor point and click the right arrow key 15 times to slender the shape size. Do the same with the right side anchor point using the left arrow key.

7. Select both shapes with the Selection Tool (V), and then select the Shape Builder Tool (Shift + M). Shapes must always be selected first.

8. Click on the upside down heart shape and drag downward to blend in the two shapes. You will notice the highlighted shapes have a cross mesh displayed. When you let go, the shapes start to merge together.

9. Click on the artboard to deselect the spade shape, and then select the Selection Tool (V) (black arrow) to select the shape again. Using the smart guides to assist you, position the new spade shape in the center of the bottom left card when you see the intersection lines appear.

10. To create the little spade shape that will appear underneath the "A" character you created, with the spade object selected, hold down the Option/ALT key and drag to create a copy.

11. Select and choose Object > Transform > Scale > and enter "25" in the display dialog box to scale down one-quarter the original size.

12. Use the Selection Tool (V) and move under the top right "A" character centered with some space, using the smart guides for proper alignment with the previous card. Use the space of a square anchor point from the bounding box to the bottom of the "A" character.

13. With the little spade object selected, hold down the Option/ALT key to create a duplicate and drag to the bottom left under the upside down "A."

14. To flip the bottom left heart shape, select it and choose Object > Transform > Reflect > Horizontal. Reposition if needed using the smart guides.

15. Your third card, the Ace of Spades, is finished.

16. Save the file in your *Chapter 7* folder.

CREATING THE CLUB SHAPE USING THE SHAPE BUILDER TOOL

The final shape, the club, provides a nice review of some of the shape tools, and in using the Shape Builder Tool (Shift+M) again. This time, with the shapes a bit further away from one another, you will hold down the Shift key with the Shape Builder Tool (Shift + M) to make this custom shape. When all four cards are completed, you can save the document as a template for creating future cards. Templates have an "ait" extension.

Here you will complete the last card, the Ace of Clubs.

1. Set the Foreground at a black color and Stroke of none.

2. Select the Ellipse Tool (L) and click on the artboard. Enter a Height and Width of 0.5 inches to make a circle.

▷   FIGURE 7-54

Creating the Ace of Clubs using the shape tools and Direct Selection Tool.

3. Hold down the Option/ALT key and copy two more circles, placing them with the Selection Tool (V) to the bottom left and right and touching the original circle, using the smart guides for proper alignment.

4. Create another smaller circle with the Ellipse Tool (L) at 0.25×0.25 inches, and then using the Selection Tool (V), place the circle in the center underneath the three larger circles (Figure 7-54).

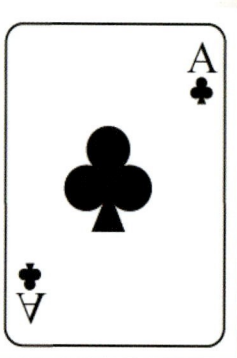

5. Select the Polygon Tool, then click on the artboard, and create a 3-sided object at 0.3 Radius.

6. With the triangle object selected, use the Selection Tool (V) and drag underneath the center of the upside down shape, overlapping slightly.

7. Select the Direct Selection Tool (V) and click on the left bottom anchor point and click the right arrow key 5 times to slender the shape size. Do the same with the right side anchor point using the left arrow key.

8. Select all five shapes with the Selection Tool (V), and then select the Shape Builder Tool (Shift+M). Shapes must always be selected first.

9. Since this is a rather complex shape with components further away, hold down the Shift key and drag from the middle circle to the other shapes to include all shapes. When you let go, the shapes start to merge together. Repeat if necessary.

10. Click on the artboard to deselect the new club shape, and then select the Selection Tool (black arrow) to select the shape again. Using the smart guides to assist you, position the shape in the center of the bottom right card when you see the intersection lines appear.

11. To create the little club shape that will appear underneath the "A" character you created, with the club object selected, hold down the Option/ALT key and drag to create a copy.

12. Select and choose Object > Transform > Scale > and enter "25" in the display dialog box to scale down one-quarter the original size.

13. With the little spade object selected, hold down the Option/ALT key to create a duplicate and drag to the bottom left under the upside down "A."

14. Use the Selection Tool (V) and move under the top right "A" character centered with some space, using the smart guides for proper alignment with the previous card, and the space of a square anchor point from the bounding box to the bottom of the "A" character.

15. To flip the bottom left club shape, select it and choose Object > Transform > Reflect > Horizontal. Reposition if needed using the smart guides.

16. Your fourth card, the Ace of Clubs, is finished. Remove the excess shapes in the workspace area you created by selecting with the Selection Tool (V), then pressing the delete key.

17. Save as a template file for future cards by selecting File > Save as Template in your *Chapter 7* folder. It will have an "ait" extension.

18. Save the file again as the normal Illustrator file *Cards.ai* in your *Chapter 7* folder.

POSITIONING THE PLAYING CARDS USING THE OBJECT MENU AND SELECTION TOOL

In this final exercise, you'll use the Object menu to group each individual card's components as one unit, and then arrange the cards. The Object menu allows you to take selected objects or groups of objects and place them in front of or behind one another. You will then use the Selection Tool (V) to move the selected cards at angles to one another so they appear as a hand of cards.

Here you will use the Object menu to place the cards overlapping one another, then use the Selection Tool (V) and arrow keys to move the card corners.

1. Before moving the cards, you will need to make them as individual groups. To make sure each card's components are grouped together, use the Selection Tool (V) and select the first Ace of Diamonds card, then select Object > Group.

2. Repeat the same with the other three cards individually. You can now move around each individual card with all its objects as one using the Selection Tool.

3. Move the cards around so they overlap one another by about half a card.

4. Select the cards where needed, and select Object > Arrange >Send to Back, or Send to Front so they appear in order shown in Figure 7-55.

5. Select the Ace of Diamonds card, and then hover the cursor over the bottom right corner until a bent arrow appears, then click and drag to move the card at an angle. Use the arrow keys for further positioning.

6. Repeat the same process with the other cards as needed.

7. Save the file again as *Cards.ai* in your *Chapter 7* folder.

8. Go ahead and create some other cards using the template you just created with all the shapes completed. Enjoy!

▷ FIGURE 7-55

Creating a four aces hand.

Select card, and when bent arrow appears at corner, drag to angle card

Four Aces Hand

CHAPTER SUMMARY

Illustrator is a digital illustration program that creates scalable vector images. In this chapter, you learned the importance of precise alignment, creating and modifying basic shapes, and grouping shapes together to create more complex objects. You used the Selection Tool (V) combined with Option/ALT and Shift keys to select multiple objects and to copy objects. You found using the Direct Selection Tool (A) helpful in editing path segments or anchor points. You learned how to select fill and stroke colors using the Swatches, Color Guide, and Color panels and find harmonious colors. In the Advanced Users section you created complex graphics by combining shapes and created a complex figure illustration to showcase Illustrator CC's Live Corners feature. You explored using the Shape Builder Tool to combine graphic elements into complex shapes in the Extra section. Do not forget to check out the *Extras & Goodies* folder on *www.CengageBrain.com* for more projects and ideas.

REVIEW QUESTIONS

1. Define objects or paths, anchor points, path segments, and the artboard area.

2. Explain the characteristics of vector images.

3. Explain how to copy an object.

4. Explain the purpose of Preview view and Outline view.

5. Explain the difference between the Swatches, Color, and Color Guide panels.

6. Explain four graphic file formats or extensions in which Illustrator files can be saved.

CHAPTER 7
Electronic checkerboard created in Illustrator using shapes.

CHAPTER 7 ADVANCED
Building a lighthouse by creating and combining custom shapes. Creating a complex figure illustration to showcase Illustrator's Live Corners feature.

CHAPTER 7 EXTRA
Creating playing cards using custom shapes, Shape Builder Tool, and Object menu.

▷ FIGURE 7-56

CHAPTER

8

Working with Brushes, Symbols, and Layers

CHAPTER OBJECTIVES: To understand the importance of using Illustrator to create images from basic sketches, in this chapter you will:

▷ Use a sketch or line art in Illustrator as a template to make artwork scalable and sharp with Illustrator's drawing tools.

▷ Learn to trace an image accurately using Illustrator's drawing tools and the Image Trace Tool.

▷ Create and apply brushes, place symbols, and format text by applying styles.

▷ Create symbols to add to the Symbols panel.

▷ Work with Symbolism tools and symbol libraries.

▷ Package artwork for commercial press.

▷ Sync artwork and Illustrator settings between computers.

▷ ADVANCED USERS: Place a logo created by the Blob Brush Tool onto multiple artboards.

▷ DIGITAL TOOLKIT EXTRA: Create 3D objects and map labels using various types of brushes.

A digital illustration can be started from scratch or by tracing an image drawn on paper and scanning that image into the computer. A template is then made from that graphic that can be traced and modified with a variety of drawing tools and functions. As in Photoshop, using layers for various parts of the image allows the designer to work on one area at a time without affecting the other layers. Layers can be moved around for a variety of effects. Brushes and symbols in Illustrator allow the designer to apply all kinds of strokes, artwork, and other effects with ease. In this chapter, you will learn how to trace images and create and apply brushes and symbols. You will be creating a simple map to demonstrate some of the basic skills a cartographer, a map illustrator, would use.

MAKING DIGITAL ILLUSTRATIONS FROM DRAWINGS

When drawings are scanned in a digital imaging application, like Photoshop, and then traced and recreated in Illustrator, they can be scaled to any size and edited without losing their sharp edges. A nonprintable template can be created from a scanned image, traced, and edited using many of Illustrator's drawing tools, such as the Pen, Pencil, Smooth, Eraser, Direct Selection, and Blob Brush tools. Any graphic can also be saved as a symbol for later use on a document, and brushes can be applied to any path created. Illustrator also uses type, which can be formatted with various commands or style panels.

CREATING TEMPLATES IN ILLUSTRATOR

One of the nice features of illustration programs like Illustrator is that you can trace any image or drawing very accurately by creating a nonprintable **template**. A template is a faded version of the original image that acts as a guide for recreating it (Figure 8-1). A new working layer for using these drawing tools is created on top of the template layer. A new vector drawing is made using the template, which can be modified and resized while retaining its image clarity.

▷ FIGURE 8-1

Tracing over a template.

Sketched map of Cape Cod, Massachusetts

Tracing with the Pencil Tool

Template Lines

THE PENCIL, SMOOTH, BLOB BRUSH, AND PATH ERASER TOOLS

The **Pencil Tool (N)** allows the designer to draw freely, or trace from a template, any drawing or image. As a line is drawn, a path is automatically created with anchor points when the mouse is released. One of the benefits of the Pencil Tool (N) is that you can create joining open paths, allowing you to stop and start again along the way. As long as you start on the ending anchor point, the paths should join together. In Illustrator CC, the Pencil Tool has been reconstructed for more precise curved paths and you can apply straight line segments. The **Smooth Tool** moves and deletes anchor points to smooth out crooked freehand path segments created by the Pencil Tool (N). The **Eraser Tool (Shift + E)** removes anchor points and path segments (Figure 8-2). The Blob Brush Tool (Shift + B) creates clean vector paths and shapes, even when strokes overlap one another.

▷ FIGURE 8-2

Pencil, Smooth, Path Eraser, and Blob Brush tools.

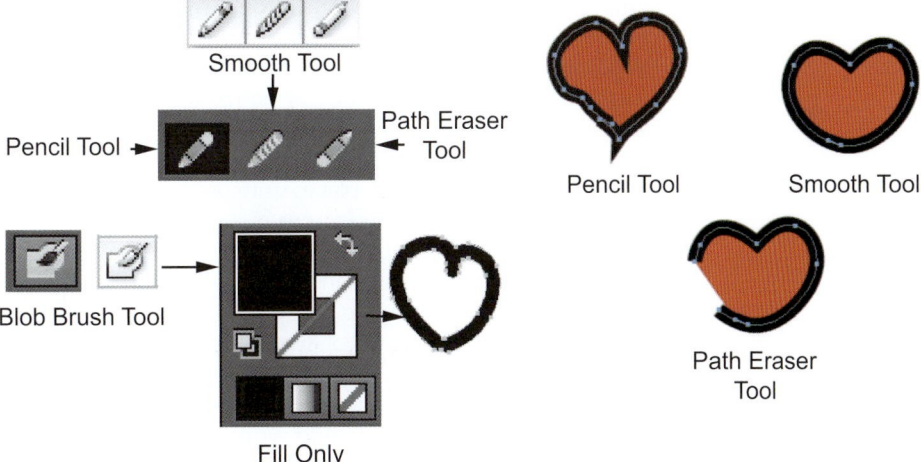

Smooth Tool

Pencil Tool →

Path Eraser Tool

Blob Brush Tool

Fill Only

Pencil Tool

Smooth Tool

Path Eraser Tool

These tools work in conjunction with the Direct Select, Path Eraser, and Smooth tools creating paths that can be merged as filled shapes of the same color. You can create variable widths to your stroke paths or use the default Uniform Profile for a consistent stroke.

THE DIRECT SELECTION TOOL

In addition to using the Selection Tool (V), which creates a bounding box around selected paths, there is also the Direct Selection Tool (A), which is used when you need to select specific segments, anchor points, or objects (Figure 8-3). You can then drag and reposition these selected paths and anchor points. In Illustrator CC, the Direct Selection Tool can also reshape corner points into curves using the **Live Corners** function. It is activated when the anchor point is selected.

▷ FIGURE 8-3

The Direct Selection Tool selects individual path segments and anchor points.

Direct Selection Tool

Live Corner

SYMBOLS, SYMBOLISM TOOLS, LIBRARIES, AND THE SYMBOLS PANEL

One of the nice features in Illustrator is the ability to create symbols, store them in the Symbols panel for later use, and modify them in your document with the various Symbolism tools in the Tools panel. **Symbols** are art objects that you can create from combinations of paths, text, images, or groups of objects, and you can save them for later use in the Symbols panel in your document. Symbols can also include brush strokes, special effects, blending of colors, and more. The **Symbols panel** is used to place, store, and create symbols. You can create repeating symbols or **symbol instances** of a particular symbol within a document. After a symbol is created, any instances on the artboard can be edited and changed if necessary. Using symbol instances in your artwork minimizes file size, because they are set up as links to the original symbol in the Symbol library. You can modify the size, color, and distribution of symbol instances using various **Symbolism tools** (Figure 8-4). Illustrator comes with a wide variety of preset symbols organized in collections called **symbol libraries**. When you open a symbol library or any library, it displays in a new panel. To add symbols, select from the symbol library and drag to the Symbols panel, or select Add to Symbols from the Library panel menu.

▷ FIGURE 8-4

Symbols, Panel Menu options, Symbol Library panels, and Symbol instances.

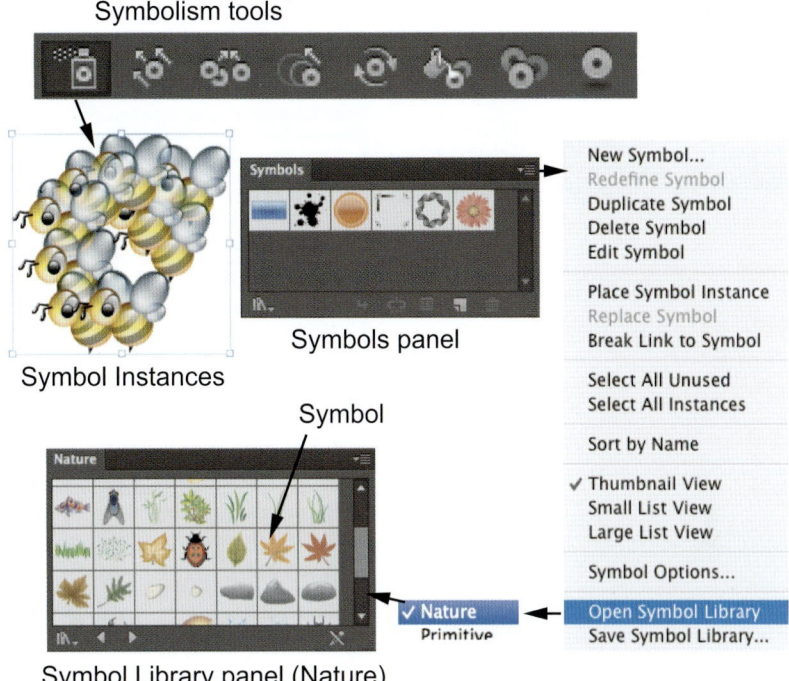

Symbolism tools

Symbol Instances

Symbols panel

Symbol

Symbol Library panel (Nature)

BRUSHES, BRUSH LIBRARIES, AND THE BRUSHES PANEL

Brushes allow you to apply freehand strokes of artwork in various ways to paths or objects. You can apply brushes to existing selected paths or use the Brush Tool (B) to create a path. Illustrator comes with a variety of preset brushes organized as **brush libraries**, which appear in a Brushes panel (Figure 8-5). You can create new brushes by selecting the object you have created in your document and dragging it to the Brushes panel. To apply a brush stroke with the Paintbrush Tool (B), select the tool first, along with fill and stroke settings, and then select a brush style from the Brushes panel. You can also select an existing path drawn by any tool, and then choose a brush style from the Brushes panel. You can create your own brush artwork and add it to the **Brushes panel** or use predefined brushes in five different categories: **Calligraphic Brushes, Scatter Brushes, Art Brushes, Bristle,** and **Pattern Brushes.** The **Bristle Brush** style allows you to create brush strokes with the appearance of a natural brush with bristles. In Illustrator CC, you can create brushes from bitmap images and photos. You can either select the Brushes panel from the Window menu (Window > Brushes) or from the Control panel when a brush stroke is selected. Double-clicking on any brush brings up the Art Brush Options dialog box for further adjustments.

DESIGN TIP

Libraries provide a vast selection of preset images a designer can use to create more complex images or to add to an existing image. Some of the libraries include symbols, brushes, swatches, and the new graphic styles used to apply special effects to selected objects.

Brush Control panel (path selected)

Calligraphic Brushes

Scatter Brushes

Art Brushes

Bristle Brushes

Pattern Brushes

New Brush...
Duplicate Brush
Delete Brush

Remove Brush Stroke

Select All Unused

✓ Show Calligraphic Brushes
✓ Show Scatter Brushes
✓ Show Art Brushes
✓ Show Bristle Brushes
✓ Show Pattern Brushes

✓ Thumbnail View
List View

Options of Selected Object...
Brush Options...

Open Brush Library
Save Brush Library...

Brush Libraries menu

New Brush

Delete Brush

WORKING WITH TYPE

The Type tools provide many functions in Illustrator (Figure 8-6). You can select the normal horizontal Type Tool (T), make selections from the Type menu, and then click anywhere to start typing normally. There are also Type tools that allow

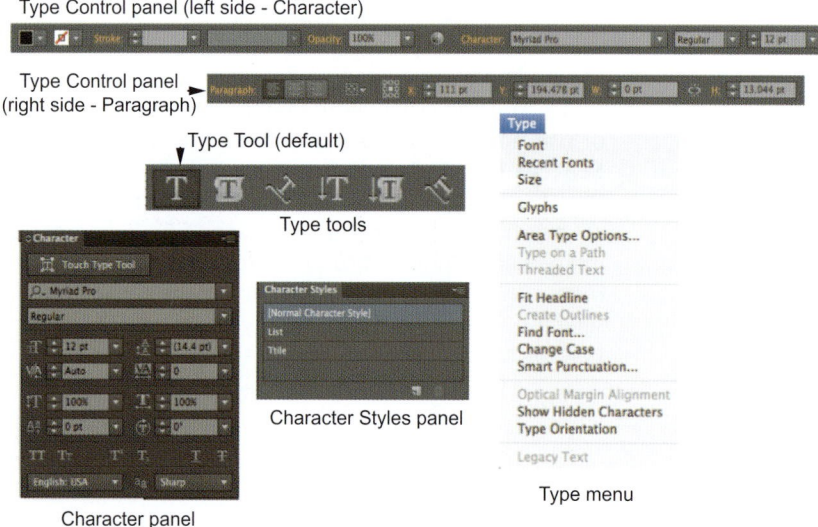

Type Control panel (left side - Character)

Type Control panel (right side - Paragraph)

Type Tool (default)

Type tools

Character Styles panel

Character panel

Type menu

you to type vertically, along a path, or within a shape. In Illustrator CC, there is a font search feature to look for fonts based upon a criteria you type in. You can instantly switch between type within a shape to point type, and you have the capability to manipulate type as individual objects. Type-related panels found under the Window menu (Window > Type) allow adjustments in character or paragraph formatting, tabbing, and creating and applying automatic formatting or styles to selected text. The Character panel and Character Styles panel apply formatting options to selected type. You can also apply formatting options to selected type by using the Control panel.

CLIENT ASSIGNMENT: Creating a Tourist Map

The owner of Magic Bus Tours, Mike Nelson, wants you to help him create a map of Cape Cod lighthouses in Massachusetts that he wants to print on parchment-type paper for his summer bus tours. He wants to use it as a visual reference for his clients, showing lighthouse locations with some cities and towns labeled. Symbols of lighthouses would be placed around the map and numbered so they could be identified in a list placed beneath the map for reference. The two main highways to the Cape, U.S. Highway Route 6 and State Highway Route 28, would be placed on the map for further reference. He gives you a sketch of Cape Cod with lighthouse locations marked with an "x" to scan into your computer and a document for the text information to include for each lighthouse. Knowing this would be best done in Illustrator, you tell Mike you will trace the map and create lighthouse and highway symbols, and then place the list of lighthouses beneath the map shape. You tell Mike it will be ready at the end of the week.

ACTION ITEMS OVERVIEW

To use a sketch, a designer must first scan the sketch into Photoshop and save it in Grayscale mode to be used as a template to trace. Color is not important here, because the template will be grayed out for tracing. This has already been done, and the template is in your *Chapter 8* folder. In Illustrator, the image needs to be traced with drawing tools, and symbols and brushes must be created and applied for the map elements (Figure 8-7). All chapter files for any tutorials are available at *www.CengageBrain.com*, if you haven't already downloaded them (Chapter 1).

Here is what you need to do:

- Place the scanned image in a new Illustrator print document using portrait orientation and the default CMYK color mode.
- Trace the document using the Pencil Tool (N) and adjust the paths with the Smooth, Eraser, and Selection tools.

Sketch of map
of Cape Cod, Massachusetts

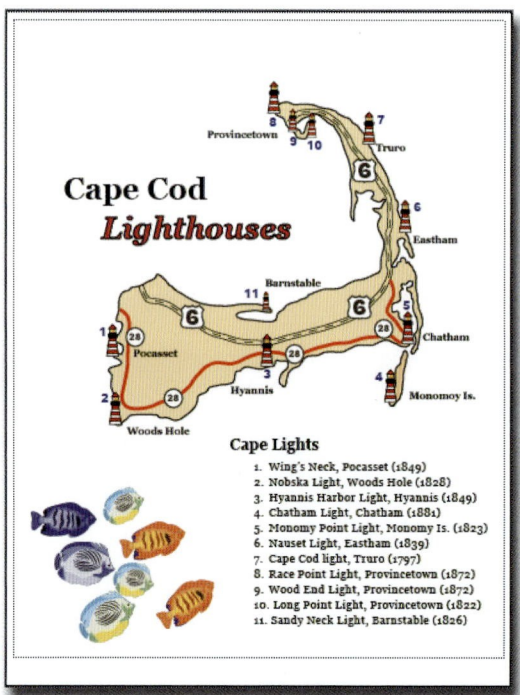

Completed map

▷ FIGURE 8-7

**Creating a tourist
map from a
drawing sketch.**

- Create the highway roads as brushes and apply them to the highway template outlines.
- Create the U.S. Highway symbol using the Image Trace command.
- Place lighthouse and highway symbols.
- Type in titles, numbers, and lighthouse descriptions on the map. Use formatting techniques and apply styles for consistency.
- Edit symbol instances with Symbolism tools.
- Save as EPS for service provider and backup AI formats.
- Package artwork, images, and fonts for service provider, and manage the artwork in Creative Cloud.
- ADVANCED USERS: Placing Logos Created by the Blob Brush onto Multiple Artboards.

PREPARING THE MAP IMAGE FOR TRACING

Before tracing and applying brushes and symbols to the map, it needs to be brought into Illustrator as a template to use as a guide for tracing. Since the template will be dimmed when placed in Illustrator, you can scan the image into Photoshop and save it in Grayscale mode to keep the file size down.

SCANNING LINE ART INTO PHOTOSHOP

Line art can be any drawing or sketch created by traditional drawing utensils, like pencil, pen, charcoal, and so on. To bring line art into the computer to use in Illustrator, it still needs to be scanned into an image-editing program like Photoshop. After any adjustments are made, the image can then be "placed" into a new document created in Illustrator. Using a scanner, always preview the scan first, drag a marquee around what you want to keep, then select to scan, which should import the new digital image into Photoshop. Most office printers have a scan feature where the document can be scanned directly into the computer, or onto a flash or portable hard drive, which can then be opened in Photoshop.

Optional Exercise: In this exercise in scanning line art, you can print the *Map* file from your *Chapter 8* folder, and then scan and adjust the image into Photoshop. If you do not have access to a scanner, you can proceed to the next exercise, "Clearing the Background…" and just use the same prescanned map.

DESIGN TIP

If you are scanning a pencil or charcoal sketch, use the Grayscale Mode option (Image > Mode > Grayscale) in Photoshop or on your scanner to capture the subtle shading of these types of drawings and to keep the file size down. With line art, you can scan at 300 dpi.

1. Open Photoshop and open the *Map* file in the *Chapter 8* folder within the *Illustrator* folder on your drive (Illustrator > Chapter 8 > Map).

2. Print the sketch using the default portrait orientation, which displays the document vertically (File > Print > Portrait Orientation). Your printer settings may be worded differently.

3. Place the printed document of the map on your scanner glass face down; using Photoshop, select File > Import > Images from Device… > then select your scanner, or office printer if connected by USB cable.

4. On the scanner, make sure you have Reflective, or Document, as the document setting—something indicating you are scanning a document for print, not transparency or film, because this indicates scanning slides or film negatives—and that you are scanning as 8-bit or 256 colors of gray (grayscale), and set the resolution of your scanner to 300 dpi (Figure 8-8). On an office printer, plug in your flash drive or device and select to scan.

5. On the scanner select Preview: when the image is displayed, drag the marquee around the map sketch area to delete as much white space as possible, and click Scan to bring the image into Photoshop. If you are using an office printer, wait until the scanning process has completed, plug in your device into your computer, then locate and open the file in Photoshop.

6. With a scanner, in most cases, you can close the scanner software and you will find the image in Photoshop. If your scanner software is different, save as a TIF file to your *Chapter 8* folder, and then launch Photoshop to open it. Leave the image open in Photoshop for the next exercise.

Scanner menu

EPSON Scan   Mode: Professional Mode

File

New...	⌘N
Open...	⌘O
Browse in Bridge...	⌥⌘O
Browse in Mini Bridge...	
Open as Smart Object...	
Open Recent	▶
Close	⌘W
Close All	⌥⌘W
Close and Go to Bridge...	⇧⌘W
Save	⌘S
Save As...	⇧⌘S
Check In...	
Save for Web...	⌥⇧⌘S
Revert	F12
Place...	
Import	▶
Export	▶
Automate	▶
Scripts	▶
File Info...	⌥⇧⌘I
Print...	⌘P
Print One Copy	⌥⌘P

Variable Data Sets...
Video Frames to Layers...
Images from Device...
Notes...

Photoshop menu

Drag Marquee around what you want to keep

▷   FIGURE 8-8

Scanning line art or sketches into Photoshop as 8-bit grayscale.

CLEARING THE BACKGROUND WITH THE MAGIC ERASER TOOL IN PHOTOSHOP

When scanning line art, most of the cleaning up of the paper background and spots should be done in Photoshop before placing the image in Illustrator. Using the **Magic Eraser Tool (E)** removes the unwanted background colors and spots to make the background transparent.

 TOOLKIT TIP Drawings or sketches that are scanned into Photoshop to be used in Illustrator are generally saved as TIF files, which are better for tracing, because they are the most accurate when recording detail.

Now you will use the Magic Eraser Tool (E) to clear out the background area.

1. If you completed the previous optional exercise, the scanned *Map* file should be open and displayed on the Photoshop desktop. If not, launch Photoshop and open the *Map* file in the *Chapter 8* folder within the *Illustrator* folder on your drive (Illustrator > Chapter 8 > *Map.tif*).

2. In Photoshop, select the Magic Eraser Tool (E) entering a Tolerance of 32 pixels; click all the white areas of the map to make them transparent or absent of color, so the background does not interfere with painting in colors later (Figure 8-9).

▷ FIGURE 8-9

Making the background transparent with the Magic Eraser Tool, and adjusting the brightness and contrast for clarity.

DESIGN TIP

Using the Magic Eraser Tool in Photoshop allows the designer to remove the white paper background, or any single colored background, so that when the line art is placed into Illustrator, it is "clear"; only the line art is displayed.

3. To darken the drawing lines, adjust the Brightness to minus 30 and the Contrast to 30 (Image > Adjustments > Brightness/Contrast). Click OK.

4. Check to make sure the mode is set to Grayscale (Image > Mode > Grayscale). Do not forget it is going to be a gray template anyway, so color does not matter. Use the Crop Tool (C), if needed, to crop the image down to just the map itself.

5. Save the file as *MapSCAN.tif* in your *Illustrator* folder (*Chapter 8*) with default settings. If you get a message that saving as a TIF with layers will increase file size, click OK.

6. Close the file, and then quit Photoshop. It is time to bring your map into Illustrator.

SETTING UP FOR CMYK COLOR IN ILLUSTRATOR

In Illustrator, color defaults to the CMYK mode, which is used mostly for illustrations going to press. RGB colors are the colors best used for electronic display and for limited printouts from an ink-jet printer. When there will be a large quantity printed, leaving the default CMYK mode intact allows the map to be printed fairly inexpensively by a local print shop.

You will now create a new document for print in portrait orientation with CMYK color mode.

1. Launch Illustrator and create a new document in CMYK Color, one (1) Artboard, Profile: Print, Units of Inches for measurement, set at Portrait Orientation, and Letter Size, with no Bleeds for this project (see Figure 8-10). Click on the Advanced arrow if all the display box is not displayed.

2. Name the file *MapPRINT*. Click OK.

3. Make sure Rulers are displayed (View > Rulers > Show Rulers), and leave this document open for the next exercise.

New document in CMYK color.

PLACING THE DRAWING AS A TEMPLATE LAYER

Before an image is traced, a template layer must be created, which dims the image. **Template layers** are nonprintable representations that allow you to trace a sketch or drawing. By using the **Place command**, any sketch or drawing can be made into a template for tracing manually by either the Pencil or Pen Tool (P). When the Place dialog box comes up, and the Template option is checked, the scanned image can be placed in a new document created in Illustrator and is automatically dimmed 50%. A drawing layer is automatically created on top of the template layer for tracing the drawing. You can lock and unlock the template layer or any other layer by clicking on the Lock Icon to the left of the active layer. Layers can be named and options set by double-clicking on a layer's name.

1. In Illustrator, make sure the Layers panel is displayed. If not, make sure it is checked in the Window menu (Window > Layers). Click on the Selection Tool (V) on the Tools panel.

2. With the *MapPRINT* file open, select File > Place and locate the *MapSCAN.tif* file created in the *Chapter 8* folder in the last exercise. Select the *MapSCAN .tif* file.

3. Make sure that the Template box is checked in the Place dialog box when the file is selected to create a template layer for tracing. Leave the Link box unchecked to embed the file (Figure 8-11).

▷ FIGURE 8-11

Placing the map sketch as a template.

Make sure Template is checked

4. Select Place in the dialog box. If a TIFF Import Options dialog box displays, choose to "Flatten Layers to a Single Image," and then select OK. The image will be centered in the new document and automatically dimmed, with a drawing layer named *Layer 1* added above the italicized *Template MapSCAN.tif* layer in the Layers panel. A template layer is identified by the square icons (multi-shapes in previous versions) in the far left column of the layer panel, and the type is italicized.

▷ FIGURE 8-12

Layer options, renaming layers, and moving and locking layers.

5. To move the map image, you will notice a lock on the *Template MapSCAN.tif* layer in the Layers panel; click on the lock to make the layer editable, and then select the *Template MapSCAN.tif* layer itself (Figure 8-12).

6. With the Selection Tool (V), select the map; use your mouse or the arrow keys to move it until the top is about 1½ inches from the top of the document. Remember, you can always drag a guide from the top ruler to ensure accuracy.

7. Click the lock icon again in the template layer to prevent accidently drawing on the template layer or moving the template image.

8. Double-click the icon next to the *Layer 1* text above the template layer to display the Layer Options dialog box.

9. Name the layer *Map Outline* (Figure 8-12). Leave the default settings as they are, and click OK. The working layer *Map Outline* is ready for tracing.

TOOLKIT TIP Any layer can be a template layer by double-clicking the layer thumbnail. When the Layer Options dialog box comes up, check the Template box and the image will gray out. You can also turn a selected layer into a Template layer using the Layers panel submenu. To create a working layer above the template layer for tracing, click the Create new layer icon at the panel bottom.

TOOLKIT TIP When placing files in a single-page document or small job that may be sent to a service provider for printing, leave the Link box unchecked. This way, the graphic will be embedded in the document, and you will not have to worry about remembering to supply the original as well. Linked files need to have the original template file along with the document, but this keeps the document size smaller. Make sure you have placed the template or object where you want it before accepting its position. You can unlock a template layer and move the scan around. Even if you link the scan, you can always delete the template layer when you are done with the image. When the placed object or template is accepted, it becomes a permanent part of the document, or it can be deleted if no longer required.

TRACING THE MAP OUTLINE USING DRAWING TOOLS

The Pencil Tool (N) allows the designer the freedom to draw complex outlines of images by creating paths. These paths can then be modified with any of Illustrator's tools and features that apply to paths. There is no worry about making an outline in one stroke when using the Pencil Tool (N). When you finish drawing a section and you are ready to continue, simply move the Pencil Tool (N) close to the still-selected path (the * below the Pencil Tool (N) cursor should disappear) and continue drawing to add to the path. The reconstructed Pencil Tool (N) in Illustrator CC provides more accuracy in creating paths and allows flexibility to create curves, straight lines, and use less anchor points. You can also use the Live Corners feature with the Direct Selection Tool (A) to edit the corners of shapes and paths.

TRACING WITH DRAWING TOOLS

When tracing an image, the Pencil Tool (N) allows you to create freehand paths. You can modify a path by drawing over the path with the Pencil Tool (N) again, which replaces the existing path with the newly drawn path. The Smooth Tool is used to edit or smooth out crooked path segments, while the Eraser Tool (Shift + E) will remove path segments. Use the scroll bars (or hold your spacebar) to move around your image and take your time tracing the outside of the map. If you mess up, use Edit > Undo Pencil to delete that portion of the path, redraw it, and then use the Smooth and Eraser tools to adjust and complete the basic outline, if needed. The default Uniform Profile is used for a consistent stroke path, whereas you can also create variable widths.

DESIGN TIP

When using the Smooth Tool, the amount of smoothing can be controlled more precisely when you zoom in on an image's path, creating more subtle results. When the image is zoomed out, the Smooth Tool deletes more points.

TOOLKIT TIP Be careful when using the Eraser Tool (Shift + E) because it might remove paths and anchor points that you need. Save the file frequently, and zoom in to at least 200% or closer in a given area to view the results.

In this exercise, you will trace the map image with the Pencil Tool (N).

1. Select the *Map Outline* layer on the Layers panel.

2. Zoom in to 400% or even closer for more detailed work.

3. Set your workspace settings from the default Essentials on the Application bar (or frame) to Painting (Window > Workspace > Painting) to bring up common panels for painting.

4. Select the Pencil Tool (N), with a Fill of None and a black Stroke of 2 pt. Use the default Uniform on the Control panel to keep a consistent brush stroke path. This will allow you to trace the template without a fill color, which could cover your template as you draw.

5. Start at the upper left and draw carefully, staying close to the template lines.

6. Continue tracing the outline of the map with the Pencil Tool (N). If you stop, you can resume where you left off by clicking on the last anchor point or watch the cursor change to a slanted line "/" under the tool before you start tracing again. Trace only the outline as a single shape; do not include the roads.

7. Continue as the same path by clicking on the ending anchor point of the selected path. That way you will be creating a series of connected paths (Figure 8-13). Keep saving the file and continue drawing until you reach the upper left side of the map with a long curve (Figure 8-14) which we'll create in the next exercise.

8. Use the Smooth Tool to go over crooked lines to help smooth them out; use the Path Eraser Tool to remove any clusters of anchor points that may be generated.

▷ FIGURE 8-13

The Pencil Tool creates open freehand paths. To continue with the path, start at the end anchor point and keep drawing.

▷ FIGURE 8-14

The Pencil Tool in Illustrator CC provides options for creating long curves.

CREATING LONG CURVES WITH THE PENCIL TOOL

Illustrator CC has rebuilt the Pencil Tool for accuracy in creating long curves and straight lines. When you double-click the Pencil Tool icon in the Tools panel, a dialog box displays with lots of options. One of these, Fidelity, allows you to adjust for close accuracy which is the default you have been using, and you can adjust to create a long path between anchor points in creating graceful curves. In the left side portion of the map there is an area that you would need the smooth tool to create a long curve in earlier versions. With this new version, you can adjust the Fidelity to Smooth and create a long curve in one stroke.

Here, you will change the Pencil Tool's Fidelity setting to Smooth and generate an easy curve to complete your map.

1. Double-click the Pencil Tool icon on the Tools panel to bring up the Pencil Tool Options display box. You will notice the Fidelity is defaulted to the left side for Accurate, which is what you have been using when tracing over your map.

2. Adjust the slider to the right side to Smooth and click OK (Figure 8-14).

3. From the point on the left side of the map click and drag from that anchor point to the right towards the peninsula and connect to the next anchor point, creating a long curve, although your movements with your mouse may not have been that accurate. It keeps the line nice and steady.

4. When the map path shape is ready to be connected, the cursor under your Pencil Tool will display a link icon to indicate it is ready to close the path.

5. Finish with the Pencil Tool and close the path. Don't forget the island on the right side of the map.

6. Double-click the Pencil Tool icon again in the Tools panel, change the Fidelity back to Accurate, and click OK.

FINE-TUNING WITH THE DIRECT SELECTION TOOL

The Direct Selection Tool (A) allows the designer to select single path segments or anchor points and move them around independently of the rest of the path. Dragging the **direction lines** extending from anchor points modifies a curve or path with precision. Use this tool to fine-tune and accurately match the template outline.

TOOLKIT TIP When using the Direct Selection Tool (A), always click outside the path first to deselect it, and then select the path segment or anchor point to work on.

▷ FIGURE 8-15

The Direct Selection Tool allows you to select individual anchor points, direction lines, or path segments to make adjustments, and use Live Corners to round points.

Here you will use the Direct Selection Tool (A) to make any final adjustments.

1. For fine-tuning, zoom in to 300% or better, select the Direct Selection Tool (A), and click away from the path. Then click on the portion of the path you want to edit to display the anchor points and direction lines from those points.

2. Drag anchor points and direction lines to make the path match the outline of the shape template. Direction lines help to steer a path segment's bending direction (Figure 8-15).

Dragging path segment inward

Adjusted path segment

Direction line

Anchor point

Path segment

Live Corner handle

3. In Illustrator CC, when zoomed in, if you click on an anchor point you may also find a blue circle indicating a Live Corner that allows you to round off a point or corner connection by dragging that associated path or anchor point. Feel free to use this feature as well.

4. Save the file in your *Chapter 8* folder on your drive in the native Illustrator .AI extension format.

WORKING WITH LAYERS AND SUBLAYERS

When you use drawing tools, every time you create a closed or open path, a "path" layer or sublayer is created under the initial layer in the Layers panel. You can select the circle to the right of the sublayer thumbnail to select that particular path to work on. A template layer is locked (which can be toggled on or off), and it displays a shapes icon instead of the eye icon in the Layers panel. To hide the template, click the square icon to toggle the template view off, and then click again to see it.

DESIGN TIP

If you are concerned whether all paths are connected to make one complete path, a good indicator is to check the subpaths layers. Click the triangle next to the layer to see sublayers. If your paths are all connected, you will see one path displayed, rather than multiple, disjointed sublayers.

TOOLKIT TIP To select large areas or combinations of paths, drag a diagonal box over the area with the Selection Tool (V), or use the Lasso Tool (Q) to draw a free-hand selection intersecting the paths to be highlighted. To join separate paths as one, draw a circle between open paths with the Lasso Tool (Q), and then select Object > Path > Join (or Average > Both).

Next, you will hide the Template layer to see your progress, and then observe how to select paths you created.

1. To see the progress of your outline by hiding the template display, click on the square icon, which reads as Toggle Visibility (Cmd-click to toggle view mode) on the *Template* layer.

2. Select the *Map Outline* layer and then select the triangle on the left side, where you may notice a series of path sublayers. If you connect the entire map outline correctly, it will display as one large closed path, with the island as an additional closed path (Figure 8-16).

▷   FIGURE 8-16

Displaying and hiding the template layer and selected paths.

Select circle on the right to display highlighted path

Click triangle to view a layer's sublayers

Displays sublayer

Icon hides or displays template

Locked Template Layer

Delete Selection
Create New Layer
Create New Sublayer

3. To highlight a path to display, select the circle to the right of the thumbnail. It displays a bounding box around the path on that sublayer.

4. To make your outline more accurate, select the various paths you want to work with and edit them with the Direct Selection, Smooth, and Pencil tools.

5. Save the file in your *Chapter 8* folder when you have completed the outline.

CREATING AND APPLYING BRUSHES

In the Brushes panel, you can create your own brushes or use predefined brushes in four different categories: Calligraphic, Scatter, Art, and Pattern. You can apply any brush stroke with the Paintbrush Tool (B) to create a path or apply brush strokes to existing selected paths by choosing a brush style from the Brushes panel. Any special stroke or combination of shapes and lines can be created and saved in the Brushes panel to be applied as a brush style. In Illustrator CC, you can also create brushes out of bitmap images or photos.

CREATING U.S. AND STATE HIGHWAY ART BRUSHES

One of the techniques a cartographer might use in Illustrator is to create various brushes of topographic mapping elements or symbols for roads, railroads, waterways, and boundaries, using a combination of various tools and shapes, and then saving them in the Brushes panel to use again. The Line Segment Tool (\) is used to create straight lines at any angle. The Stroke panel is used to change the properties of lines, including their weight and style, and comes with the option to create dashed lines. In Illustrator, you can create stroke paths with variable widths and precise arrowheads, and control the alignment of dashes, including around corners. The default stroke profile is the Uniform setting on both the Stroke and Control panels. A single line element can be copied by selecting the line with the Direct Selection Tool (A), and then dragging while holding the Option/ALT. Saving artwork as an Art brush stretches it evenly along a path.

TOOLKIT TIP In Illustrator CC, you can also use the Pencil Tool to create a straight line by pressing down the Option/ALT key while drawing. If you hold down the Shift key, you will create perfect straight lines with the Pencil Tool at 45 degree intervals.

Now you will create two different highway brushes and save each in the Brushes panel.

1. To create the U.S. Highway brush, zoom in to 200%. Make sure nothing is selected.

2. Set the Fill to None and the Stroke to black with a 1-pt Weight.

DESIGN TIP

If the panels temporarily seem to get in the way as you are drawing, press the Tab key to remove them, and then press again to toggle them back on to display.

DESIGN TIP

When first creating brush styles, it is a good idea to keep the initial stroke weight to a minimum; when you need to apply the brush, you can alter it at that time.

**Using the Line
Segment and the
Direct Selection
tools to create the
U.S. Highway brush.**

Line Segment Tool

Drawing tools

Line Segment Tool Options

Direct Selection
Tool

Creating U.S. Highway

Fill None

Black Stroke

3. Select the Line Segment Tool (\) and click once, away from the map image (Figure 8-17), to access the Line Segment Tool (\) options.

4. For the first line, enter 1 inch for the length and 180 for the angle; click OK.

5. To make two more copies underneath one another, use the Direct Selection Tool (A) to select the line; then, while holding down the Option/ALT key, select and drag twice to copy two more lines directly underneath the original.

6. Make the lines equal distances apart but close together. Use the arrow keys for positioning.

7. To create a dashed centerline, use the Direct Selection Tool (A) to select the middle line and set the Stroke to 1 pt with 10-pt gaps and 10-pt dashes with a Uniform Profile (Figure 8-18). If the dashed line options are not showing, select Show Options from the Stroke panel's submenu, or click the arrows at the top right to toggle through the layer views until they appear.

**Using the Stroke
panel to create a
dashed line for the
highway center.**

Click to display
panel options

Select
Middle Line

Result

8. To group all three lines together, Shift-select all three lines with the Direct Selection Tool (A), or drag through the lines with the Lasso Tool (Q).

9. Select Object > Group.

10. With all three lines selected, select the Brushes panel (Window > Brushes) and select the New Brush icon at the panel bottom or from the Brushes panel menu.

11. Select Art Brush in the dialog box and click OK.

12. When the Art Brush Options dialog box appears, name the brush *US Highway;* choose the right arrow in the Direction section, leaving all the other defaults as they are, and then click OK (Figure 8-19). The brush will display in the Brushes panel.

13. Delete the selected graphic on the artboard. It is now saved in the Brushes panel. Save the file.

▷ FIGURE 8-19

Creating highway brushes.

1. Select Artwork

2. Select new brush type, set options, and name the brush.

3. Brush is saved in the Brushes panel.

14. To create the state highway in red, set the Fill to None and the Stroke to red with a 2-pt width. Make sure the Dashed Line box is NOT checked in the Stroke panel.

15. Select the Line Segment Tool (\), click on the artboard to display the dialog box, and enter a 1-inch segment with 180-degree angle line.

16. With the new line selected, open the Brushes panel and select the New Brush icon at the panel bottom or from the panel's submenu. You can also simply drag the selected line into the Brushes panel.

17. Select Art Brush for the type and name the brush *State Highway.* Choose the right arrow in the Direction section, and then click OK.

18. Delete this line graphic on the artboard and save the file.

APPLYING BRUSHES

Creating paths with brush styles usually involves the Paintbrush, Pencil, or Pen tools. To apply brushes using the Paintbrush Tool (B), you choose a brush from the Brushes panel first and then draw the paths you need. You cannot use a brush style with the Pen Tool (P) or the Pencil Tool (N) until you draw a regular path first and then apply the brush style to it. You apply brushes to existing paths by selecting the path first; then choose a brush in the Brushes panel.

It is time to create a separate layer for the highways, and then paint the U.S. highway using the Paintbrush Tool (B) and the state highway using the Pencil Tool (N), so you can see how each works with brush styles (Figure 8-20).

1. To create a layer for the highways, make sure the *Map Outline* layer is highlighted, and select the Create New Layer icon at the bottom of the Layers panel. Make sure the Map template layer is turned on.

2. Double-click this layer and name it *Highways.*

DESIGN TIP

Before selecting drawing tools or brushes, set the stroke and fill colors first; then set the stroke weight in the Stroke panel or Options bar.

▷   FIGURE 8-20

Painting the highways with Paintbrush and Pencil tools.

3. Select the Paintbrush Tool (B), and then click on the new *US Highway* brush in the Brushes panel. Carefully trace over Route 6 on the template. To continue to add to the path, click on the end anchor point of the previous path. Once you have completed the path, choose Select > Deselect.

4. For the state highway, select a Fill of None and a black Stroke of 2 pt, and then select the Pencil Tool (N).

5. Trace over Route 28 on the template.

6. To apply the red *State Highway* brush, click on the *State Highway* brush in the Brushes panel to apply the red color brush. To remove a brush stroke, in the Brushes panel, choose Remove Brush Stroke from the panel menu, click the Remove Brush button at the bottom of the panel, or select Basic Brush from the Brushes panel or Control panel.

7. Toggle the square Toggles Visibility icon on the *Template* layer to see the results of the map. Use the Direct Selection Tool (A) to create the lines to accurately follow the template.

8. Save the file and then minimize the document window.

CREATING AND APPLYING CUSTOM SYMBOLS

In Illustrator, a designer has the ability to create symbols. Symbols can be any graphic that you create that can then be used as repeated symbol instances on your document. Symbols are not applied to paths and do not create paths like brushes; these repetitive symbols are placed onto a document with the Symbol Sprayer Tool (Shift + S). Symbol instances on the artboard can be edited and changed if necessary, using the various Symbolism tools. This allows you to create variations of the same basic symbol on your document. Symbols are saved for later use in the Symbols panel. You will be making lighthouse and highway symbols to be placed on the map.

USING THE IMAGE TRACE FUNCTION TO MAKE THE U.S. HIGHWAY SIGN

Symbols can also be created from scanned drawings or sketches or with Illustrator's tools. A sketch can be traced, scaled to size, and saved in the Symbols panel for future use. Illustrator has an **Image Trace** (Live Trace in earlier versions) function that interprets the contours and outlines of drawings and bitmap images, translating them into vector drawings. In the Control Panel, you can choose from various preset tracing options to trace a variety of images, including sketches, drawings, photos, and even templates. You also have the ability to set your own options for tracing. Image (Live) Trace is located in the Object menu. In order to trace any object, it has to be selected first. To create a simple trace without anchor points and paths outlined for future editing, select the Make command. To convert the tracing outline to a series of connected paths, you select the **Expand command**. You will be using more of this powerful new function in Chapter 10. Although the Image (Live) Trace function does a nice job in accurately reproducing a sketched outline, you can modify any path it generates with the Direct Selection Tool (A), if you choose the Expand command to create anchor points and path outlines.

Using the Image Trace function, you will trace a template file of a U.S. highway sign. Remember to make sure the object is selected before applying the Image (Live) Trace function.

1. To create the U.S. highway sign, open the *Sign* file in your *Chapter 8* folder. You can trace this even though it is set up as a template.

2. Select the Zoom Tool (Z) and zoom in 200% to 300%.

▷ FIGURE 8-21

In Illustrator, the Image Trace command allows you to trace over preset drawings, sketches, and bitmap images with accuracy.

3. To trace the *Template* layer in this document, in the Layers panel, click on the padlock to unlock the template layer, and make sure that layer is highlighted.

4. Select a Fill of White and a black Stroke weight of 2 pt; then with the Selection Tool (V), select the drawing, which will display a bounding box around it.

5. Select Object > Image Trace > Make to create a solid stroke closed path of the highway sign (Figure 8-21).

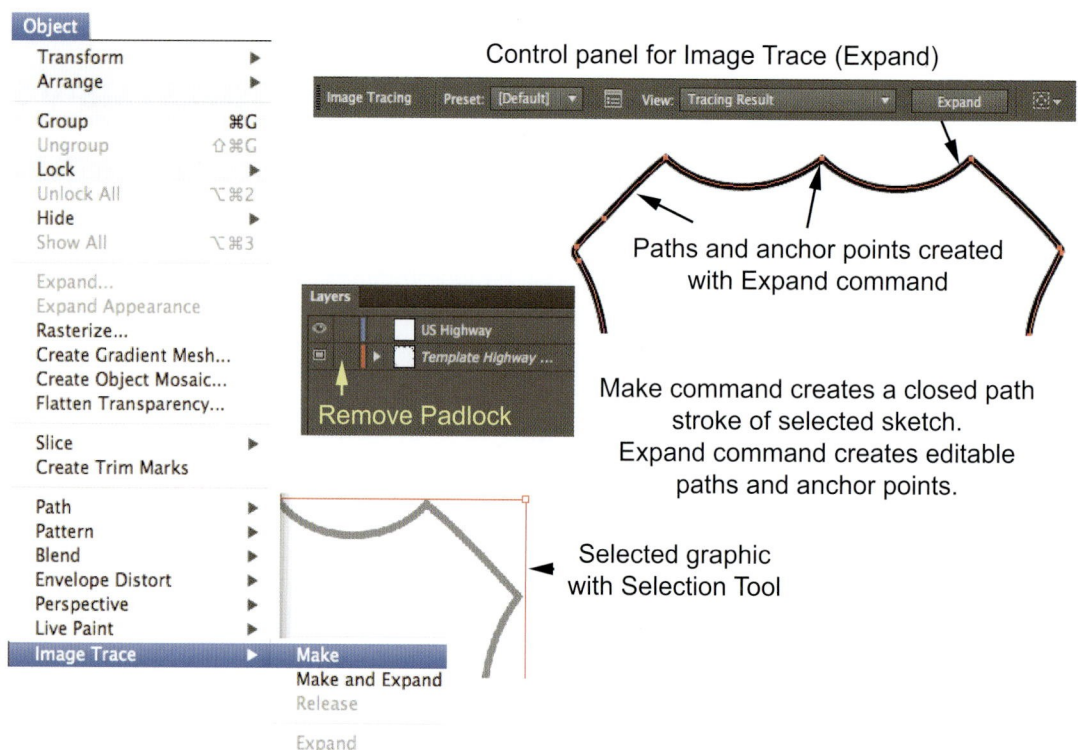

6. To convert any tracing to paths, select Expand from the Control panel, or use Object > Image Trace > Expand. You will notice a closed path line with anchor points ready to be edited or selected.

7. Optional: If you wish to modify the path outline, zoom in 200% to 300% and use the Direct Selection Tool to make your adjustments (see Toolkit Tip).

8. To make sure all the paths are connected, select Object > Group.

9. With the U.S. Highway sign selected, copy it (Edit > Copy).

10. Close the *Sign* file (File > Close). Do not save the file.

11. Maximize the *MapPRINT* window to display the map document again.

12. Paste the *US Highway* graphic outside the map outline (Edit > Paste). Leave it selected.

13. To scale down the selected graphic, select Object > Transform > Scale and enter a Uniform scale of 40%. Uncheck the Scale Strokes and Effects box to keep from scaling the stroke weight (Figure 8-22). Click OK.

14. Save the file as *Map PRINT.ai* again in your *Chapter 8* folder and leave it open for the next exercise in creating symbols.

▷ FIGURE 8-22

Use the Type Tool to type the route numbers in 36-pt Arial Black font.

Type Tool

DESIGN TIP

When creating headings or basic labels, it is good practice to use a universal sans-serif font, like Arial Black, that can easily be viewed.

TOOLKIT TIP Although it will not be necessary here, if you needed to modify the highway shape, you can select a path and then click and drag individual anchor points or click and adjust the shape of line segments using the Direct Selection Tool (A). You do this by clicking outside the path to deselect everything; then select the portion of the path to display anchor points and direction lines. Drag anchor points and direction lines to make adjustments. Feel free to experiment and then choose File > Revert to have Illustrator go back to the previous save.

TOOLKIT TIP When scaling an object to a smaller size, sometimes it is better to leave the Scale Strokes and Effects option unchecked to avoid creating hairlines that may not print well. When enlarging an object, place a check in the Scale Strokes and Effects for consistency and sharpness. Sometimes, however, the lines get so wide compared to the rest of the image that they obliterate it.

USING TYPE IN SYMBOLS

The Type tools contain many functions in Illustrator. You can select the default horizontal Type Tool (T), make selections from the Type menu, and then click anywhere to start typing normally. You can type inside an area and type vertically as well. Type can also be used in a graphic and made into a symbol. You can always view what the font looks like before you use it in your project, and in Illustrator CC, you can use the Font Search feature to find fonts and styles that match criteria you choose. We'll also turn on Scale Strokes and Effect to see the changes made.

Here you will add text to the U.S. Highway Route 6 sign and create the State Highway Route 28 sign as well.

1. To create the U.S. Highway Route 6 sign, select the outline of the highway sign with the Direct Selection Tool (A), and change the stroke weight in the Stroke panel to 4 pt. Select the Type Tool (T) from the Type menu or use the Control panel to find an Arial Black font with a size of 36 pt.

2. Click inside the U.S. Highway sign and type the number "6."

3. Use the Selection Tool (V) to select the text and center it with the arrow keys.

4. Press the Shift key and select both text and shape to display a bounding box around both.

5. Select Object > Group to combine both text and shape together as one.

6. To scale down the *US Highway* graphic further to be used as a symbol, select Object > Transform > Scale and scale the image to 40% Uniform. This time place a check in Scale Strokes & Effects. Click OK and then choose Select > Deselect. The graphic outlined stroke has been scaled down.

7. To make the State Highway Route 28 sign, choose a Fill of white or a light color, and a black Stroke of 2 pt, and then select the Ellipse Tool (L).

8. Click on the artboard to display the dialog box, and then enter a 1-inch by 1-inch circle.

9. Select the Type Tool (T) and use the Type menu to select Arial Black with a Size of 36 pt.

10. Click inside the circle and type "28" (Figure 8-22).

11. Repeat steps 3 through 5 to group the type and shape.

12. To scale down the *State Highway* graphic, make sure it is selected and use Object > Transform > Scale and scale down the image to 20% Uniform (not shown). Keep the Scale Strokes & Effects checked.

13. Save the file.

MAKING HIGHWAY SIGNS AND THE LIGHTHOUSE GRAPHIC SYMBOLS

A designer can create a graphic, copy it, and then paste it into another document. The selected graphic can then be saved as a symbol in the Symbols panel for later use. Any object can be made into a symbol, which can then appear as a graphic thumbnail in the Symbols panel (Figure 8-23). Once a symbol is created, it stays in the Symbols panel for use whenever it is needed in the document. You can create

New Symbol

Select Graphic

Choose as Graphic
and Symbol Name

Graphic placed as new symbol

New Map Symbols

▷ FIGURE 8-23

Symbols panel with new symbols created for the map.

DESIGN TIP

Storing graphics as symbols is a great way to create and reuse artwork for multiple projects without having to recreate the same artwork over again. Since they are stored as vector images, they can be resized to fit any dimensions needed.

multiple versions of the symbol, called *symbol instances*, by dragging it from the Symbols panel to the artboard. Once it is placed in your document, you can resize or edit it. Illustrator allows you to name your symbol and determine whether it will be used as a graphic or as part of a video or animated sequence.

Now that you have created the highway signs, you will turn them into symbols. You will then bring in the copy of the *Light* graphic of the lighthouse that you created in Chapter 7 (Digital Toolkit Extra), and paste it into the *MapPRINT* file to be used as a map symbol. If you missed that exercise, open the *Light2* graphic in the *Chapter 8* folder and use that instead.

1. Select the U.S. Highway Route 6 graphic with the Selection Tool (V).

2. Open the Symbols panel and select the New Symbol icon at the bottom of the panel. When the Symbol Options display opens, select the "Graphic" option under Type, and then name the symbol *Hwy 6* and click OK. You will notice a thumbnail representation of the U.S. Highway Route 6 symbol in the Symbols panel (Figure 8-23).

3. Repeat the process to make the State Highway Route 28 sign (name it *Hwy 28*); then deselect the Route sign and reset the Fill box to black on the Tools panel.

4. To make the *Light* graphic a symbol, open the *Light* file you created in last chapter's Digital Toolkit Extra in the *Chapter 7* folder. If it is not available, open the *Light2* graphic in the *Chapter 8* folder instead. You can also select File > Open Recent Files to locate the file.

5. Use the Selection Tool (V) to select the lighthouse.

6. Copy the graphic (Edit > Copy) and then close the *Light* file without saving it (File > Close).

7. Paste the selected lighthouse graphic outside the map outline in the *MapPRINT* file (Edit > Paste).

8. With the lighthouse graphic still selected, select the Symbols panel and click on the New Symbol icon at the bottom of the panel. Name the graphic *Lighthouse*.

9. You now have a lighthouse symbol and the two highway signs that will be used on the map later. Delete the lighthouse graphic and the highway signs from the artboard—they are now permanent symbols in this file.

10. Save the file *MapPRINT*.

PLACING THE HIGHWAY SYMBOLS

Before placing the symbols you created onto the map, it is a good idea to create another layer for just the symbols. Placing symbols is done by dragging the symbol onto the artboard or by using the Symbols panel Place Symbol Instance icon. The placed symbols, called *symbol instances,* can be resized using the bounding box or modified with the Symbolism tools. Although not needed here, you can also create sublayers for symbols in symbol editing mode.

 TOOLKIT TIP You can stack symbol instances by selecting the Place Symbol Instance icon at the bottom of the Symbols panel and then dragging each to its appropriate location with the Selection Tool (Figure 8-24).

▷ FIGURE 8-24

Dragging symbols from the Symbols panel and placing on the map image.

Place Symbol Instance

Create New Layer

In this exercise, you will create a layer for the symbols and place both highway symbols as instances on the map.

1. With the *MapPRINT* file open, select the *Highways* layer in the Layers panel; then click the Create New Layer icon at the bottom of the panel. Make sure the new layer is the topmost layer; if not, click and drag it to the top.

2. Rename the new highlighted layer *Symbols* (Figure 8-24).

3. Select the *State Highway Route 28* symbol from the Symbols panel and drag it into position on one of the places where *28* is written on the template (or use the Place Symbol Instance icon on the Symbols panel). This creates an instance of the symbol in your artwork. Drag additional instances of this symbol on the map as indicated in the template. You can also click on the symbol and copy it by holding down the Option/ALT key.

4. Repeat the same process for the *US Highway Route 6* symbol.

5. Delete any extra highway symbols outside the map area and save the file.

PLACING AND NUMBERING THE LIGHTHOUSE SYMBOLS

An instance of the lighthouse symbol needs to be dragged from the Symbols panel and placed on each *X* on the map. Consecutive numbers will be typed next to each lighthouse, starting from the top left side and positioned counterclockwise around the map outline until all the lighthouses are numbered. These numbers are important, because they refer to the numbered list that will be placed under the map for the viewer to follow.

For this exercise, you will create an instance of the lighthouse symbol, number it, and then place it by each *X* on the map.

1. Click and drag the lighthouse symbol onto the artboard or use the Place Symbol Instance icon on the Symbols panel.

2. Use the Option/ALT key to copy the selected graphic and drag the instance to the first *X* on the left side of the map near the Route 28 symbol.

3. Use the Option/ALT key to make copies; repeat the same process until lighthouse instances are placed on all eleven marks (Figure 8-25).

4. Select the Type Tool (T) (default setting) with a Fill of a deep blue color and a Stroke of None.

▷ FIGURE 8-25

Placing and numbering the lighthouse symbols along the map.

5. In the Type menu, select the Arial Black font at 14 pt.

6. Type the number "1" to the left of the first lighthouse; position it with the Selection Tool (V).

7. Select the number and use Option/ALT to copy it, moving the copy over to the second lighthouse position, as shown in Figure 8-25.

8. Select the Type Tool (T), highlight the number *1* and type "2."

9. Continue the same process, numbering all the lighthouse symbols consecutively (Figure 8-25).

10. To resize the lighthouse graphics as shown in Figure 8-25, select the graphic to be resized with the Selection Tool (V), which will place it inside the bounding box (View > Show Bounding Box), and press the Shift key while dragging inward or outward to resize it proportionately.

11. Save the file.

LABELING THE MAP

Using text in an image can provide contrast to the artwork as well as adding information about the image. Labeling the map defines the map as a reference tool. This map is going to be used by tourists with a focus on lighthouses, indicated by the map's title "Cape Cod Lighthouses." Because of Illustrator's capability to use stroke and fill colors for text as well as graphics, lettering can be enhanced to provide focus. Labeling some of the cities and towns on the map will help to give it perspective and distance. The list of lighthouses to be visited, already created in a word processing application, will be "placed" below the map image. You can then format the list for consistency using Illustrator's Character panel.

TYPING THE TITLE, TOWNS, AND CITIES

DESIGN TIP

Since the map image is made of lots of curved paths, using a serif font like Georgia for the title and labels complements the image.

The main title of the map will be placed diagonally within the empty area inside the cape "elbow," as shown in Figure 8-26. Since the emphasis is on the lighthouses, making the word *Lighthouses* red with a darker black stroke color italicized will help to bring focus to the purpose of the map. The towns, cities, and the lighthouse list will be labeled with the same Georgia font in Bold style for continuity. In Illustrator, a designer can get a quick visual of the font in the Character panel or using the Type > Font menu before selecting one to use in the document. In Illustrator CC you can also use the Font Search feature to locate specific fonts that match the criteria you type in. You can also sync fonts in Creative Cloud between computers, and you can find special fonts from Adobe's online Typekit library.

TOOLKIT TIP You can also use the Control panel to apply type formatting commands easily.

▷ FIGURE 8-26

Labeling title, headline, cities, and towns.

Next, you will create the main title, headline, and label the cities and towns.

1. To create a layer for text, select the *Map Outline* layer in the Layers panel and click the Create New Layer icon at the bottom of the panel.

2. Select the *Layer 5* text in the new layer and rename the layer *Text*.

3. Select the Type Tool (T), and use the Type menu to select Georgia Bold (or something similar) in a 36-pt size. You can also use the Control panel.

4. Click in the elbow area of the map and type *"Cape Cod"* and then press the Return/Enter key to make a new line.

5. Select the Type Tool (T), and choose the Georgia Bold Italic font with a red Fill and a black Stroke; type "Lighthouses," tabbing over to offset it (Figure 8-26). To provide some space between the characters, you can select the Character panel (Window > Type > Character) and put in a tracking of 75 for starters. Deselect the text. Tracking provides spacing between characters.

6. To label the towns, change to Georgia Bold with a size of 12 pt. Change the color to a stroke of None with a black fill.

7. Type counterclockwise around the map the towns: *Pocasset, Woods Hole, Hyannis, Monomoy Is., Chatham, Eastham, Truro, Provincetown,* and *Barnstable* without having the type overlap the lighthouses or route symbols. To stop typing one line to start the next, select another tool, such as the Selection Tool (V), and then select the Type Tool (T) again to start another type line. When clicking on the map with the Type Tool (T), be careful not to click too closely to any highways or paths or the text will align itself to the path.

8. To place the headline *Cape Lights* under the map for the lighthouse list, select the Type Tool (T) and type "Cape Lights" in 18-pt Georgia Bold using the Hyannis town label as a guide for position.

9. The *Template* layer is no longer needed, so drag it to the Trash icon at the bottom of the Layers panel.

10. Save the file. The map is labeled; now it is time to bring in the lighthouse list.

PLACING AND FORMATTING IMPORTED TYPE IN ILLUSTRATOR

Creating bulleted or numbered lists is difficult within Illustrator. To solve this problem, Illustrator allows you to import text from other documents created in Microsoft Word (**DOC**), as plain text files (**TXT**), or Rich Text Format files that maintain formatting commands (**RTF**). Using the **Place command** for text imports the copy into its own text block so it can easily be moved into position and edited. Illustrator has a Character panel and a Paragraph panel to format selected type. This is helpful when you need to format large amounts of text or specialized titles and headlines. In the Character panel, you can apply character formatting techniques to selected characters or lines of text, while in the Paragraph panel, you can apply paragraph formatting commands to selected paragraphs.

To finish the map, you will place the lighthouse list from a Word document into the *MapPRINT* file. You will then format the text using the Character panel.

1. Select File > Place, and locate the file *Lighthouses.doc* in your *Chapter 8* folder. Select the Place button on the display box and put in check marks on the Microsoft Word Options box as shown in Figure 8-27 and then select OK to place the document text into the *MapPRINT* document. If a dialog box displays regarding swatch conflict, choose Merge and click OK to accept.

▷ FIGURE 8-27

Using the Place command to import a text document into the Illustrator document.

2. Use the Selection Tool (V) to select the text block; use the middle resizing handles to shrink the box and crop out the blank space below the text if needed.

PROBLEM If the list is spread out horizontally, you will need to select the Type Tool (T), click before each number on the list, and press the Return/Enter key to create a numbered list. Continue until all 11 lighthouses are set up as a numbered list.

3. Move the text box to the right side under the *Cape Lights* heading.

4. Make sure the Character panel is displayed (Window > Type > Character).

5. With the type box still selected, to use the Font Search feature, type a "G" in the font box and you'll find all the fonts that start with that letter. Select Georgia, with the Font Style as Regular, Size 14 pt, Tracking at 25 to separate the letters a little, and Leading at 18 pt in the Character panel. Leave the other settings at their defaults, and deselect the type to see the formatted type lines (Figure 8-28).

6. Save the file. You now have an easy-to-read map.

▷ FIGURE 8-28

Using the Character panel to format selected type.

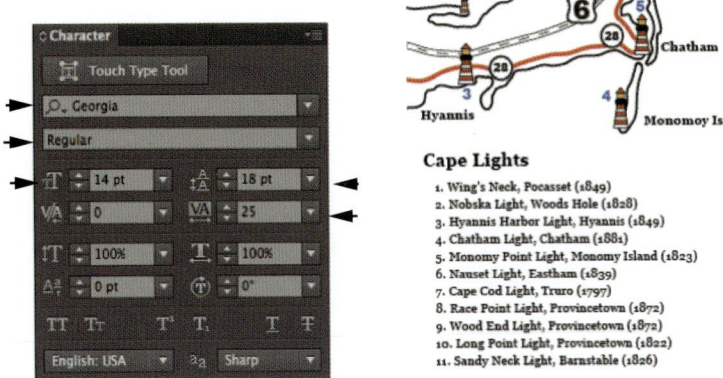

THE LEGACY TEXT COMMAND

Illustrator includes the Legacy Text command, which uses the Adobe text engine to provide the highest quality text output. If your intention is to edit or modify text elements from a document created in a previous version of Illustrator, the text needs to be updated for consistency. When you open an older file containing text, a dialog box usually displays, asking whether to update the legacy text (this will also occur when opening older files with type in Photoshop). When a previous version of text is updated, you may notice various changes in character position or words shifting. To avoid these changes, you can choose not to update the text if you do not plan to make any changes. This command is also located under the Type menu. As a general rule, it is better to update the type in your project when sending it for proofing or to a commercial printer. When in doubt, if the dialog box comes up, choose to update your text.

WORKING WITH TYPEKIT FONTS

As a Creative Cloud subscriber, you can sync special **Adobe Typekit fonts** to your desktop through the Creative Cloud desktop, using these chosen fonts in any application. In Illustrator's font menu in the Control panel, and from the Type menu, you can filter fonts and determine which fonts are from the Adobe Typekit library with a special green "T" icon. The Typekit website is at *www.typekit.com*. From the type menu, select Add fonts from Typekit to download your chosen fonts. This service may be an additional paid subscription.

USING SYMBOLISM TOOLS AND THE SYMBOL LIBRARY

You can select symbols from a variety of preset symbols organized in collections called *symbol libraries.* Illustrator has provided a vast selection to choose from. When you open a symbol library from the Symbols panel menu, it displays in a new panel. To add symbols to the Symbols panel from the library, just select it in the symbol library; it will automatically be placed in the Symbols panel. Placing symbols on the artwork creates symbol instances, which can be resized and modified using the various Symbolism tools. To make any changes to a symbol instance, it needs to be selected first. To adjust the size of a graphic, you can use the **Symbol Sizer Tool.** The **Symbol Spinner Tool** is used to vary the direction of the selected symbol instance. You can change the color of symbol instances with the **Symbol Stainer Tool** and apply other effects to symbol instances with the other Symbolism tools. You can experiment with the Color Guide panel to change color combinations on various selected symbols.

TOOLKIT TIP Always select the symbol instance before using any Symbolism Tool. Placing symbols individually allows the designer to modify each differently. Short clicks on the symbol instance work well with some of the Symbolism tools since they change the properties of symbol instances rapidly.

PROBLEM If the Symbolism tools are not working, make sure that the graphic is selected. After applying a Symbolism Tool on a selected symbol, choose the Selection Tool (V) again before choosing another Symbolism Tool or symbol instance.

Next, you will place and adjust a few fish symbol instances from the Nature Symbol library using some of the Symbolism tools. Feel free to practice this exercise in a new document before adding the graphics to the *MapPRINT* file.

1. From the Symbols panel, use the panel submenu to select Open Symbol Library > Nature (Figure 8-29).

2. Select the Fish 2 symbol, or any fish symbol, to place the symbol in the Symbols panel.

3. Drag the symbol to the left of the list of lighthouses. Repeat this until you have placed four fish on the artboard.

4. Select a fish with the Selection Tool (V), select a fill color, and then select the Symbol Stainer Tool to change its color. The color changes the whole fish. The Symbol Stainer Tool can be found in the Tools panel underneath the Symbol Sprayer Tool.

5. Select two fish and vary their size using the Symbol Sizer Tool. Hold the Option/ALT key to decrease the size.

Symbol Sprayer Symbol Scruncher Symbol Spinner Symbol Screener

Panel menu

Open Symbol Library
Save Symbol Library...

Symbol Shifter Symbol Sizer Symbol Stainer Symbol Styler

Nature Symbol Library panel

▷ FIGURE 8-29

Symbolism tools, and symbol libraries.

6. Select one or two fish and try the Symbol Spinner Tool to vary their direction.

7. Drag a couple of other fish symbols by the other fish; select and make adjustments with the Symbolism tools.

8. Experiment with other libraries and symbols, but be careful not to overdo, less is usually more. Feel free to experiment with the Color Guide panel to find other interesting color groups to change the fish symbols into.

9. Save the file *MapPRINT* again in the *Chapter 8* folder when you have finished playing with the Symbolism tools and libraries. You are now a cartographer! (Figure 8-30).

▷ FIGURE 8-30

Completed map.

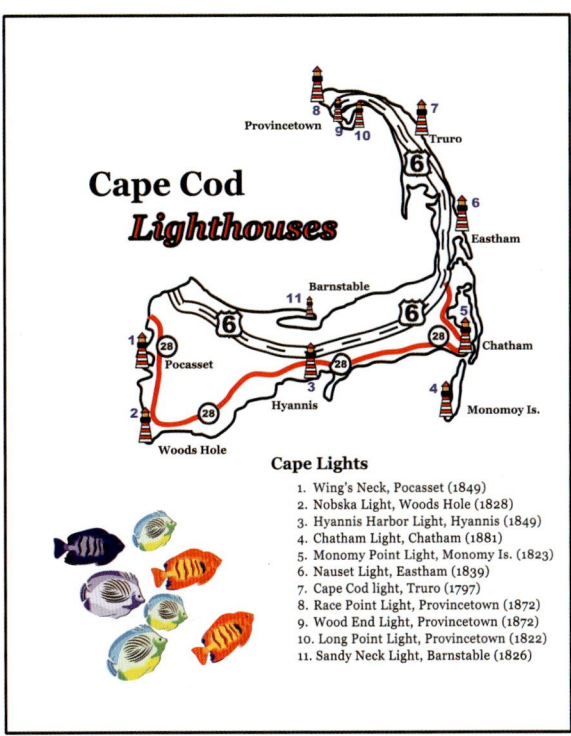

APPLY FILL COLOR IN MAP BY JOINING PATH END POINTS

Let's say you don't mind using more ink and want to fill in the land portion of the map of Cape Cod Lighthouses with a light sandy brown "beach" color. First you would need to check for path sublayers in your Map Outline layer and find any disconnected paths; then you can draw over the path with the Pencil Tool (N), which will sometimes recreate the path and connect the disjointed paths. Then smooth over the anchors points with the Smooth Tool. If this does not work, use the Object > Path menu to connect the end points of paths to make a large, closed path. To connect path end points and make a single smooth path, use the **Average command** (Object > Path > Average) in the Object menu. The **Join command** (Object > Path > Join) makes sure that end points that are apart are joined together as one. To select just the end points of the two paths to be joined together, draw a freehand selection around both end points with the Lasso Tool (Q). Once you have all paths joined, select with the Selection Tool (V) and find an appropriate color from groups of special swatch libraries supplied with Illustrator. Apply the fill color to fill in your complex shape.

TOOLKIT TIP The best way to connect points on a complex drawing in order to create a closed path is to go over the end points with the Pencil Tool (N) and then smooth over multiple anchor points in one area with the Smooth Tool. Using the Average and Join commands from the Object menu after drawing around end points with the Lasso Tool (Q), should only be done after the previous has already been tried.

Here you will go over the path segments and combine any suspected gaps between paths. You'll then select a color from the Beach swatch library to apply to your complex shape (Figure 8-31).

DESIGN TIP

It is a good habit to use the Average command first to align end points on top of one another, and then to use the Join command, if needed, to join them correctly as one anchor point. If you do not average the points first, Illustrator simply draws a straight line between the two selected end points.

1. First, turn off all layers except the *Map Outline* and *Template* layer in the Layers panel to see if there are multiple path sublayers. If the Cape Cod map and the island (Monomoy) are the only paths that display, both paths are closed and you can skip to step 6. If there are sublayers, click on the circle to the right of each sublayer, which will highlight as a larger blue square on the Layers panel, and display the highlighted path on your artwork. This way you can see where there is a disconnection between paths. Zoom in to 400% to 600% to look closely at the paths.

2. If you find a gap between the two paths, select the paths with the Direct Selection Tool (A). Try going over the path anchor points with the Pencil Tool (N) first to try to connect them and then use the Smooth Tool to smooth out the sharp corners or connections.

3. If they won't connect, select the Lasso Tool (Q) and draw a freehand circle around the open area between the two paths, including the end points, to make a selection.

4. Select Object > Path > Average. When the Average dialog box pops up, select Both to let the distance be averaged on both the horizontal and vertical axes.

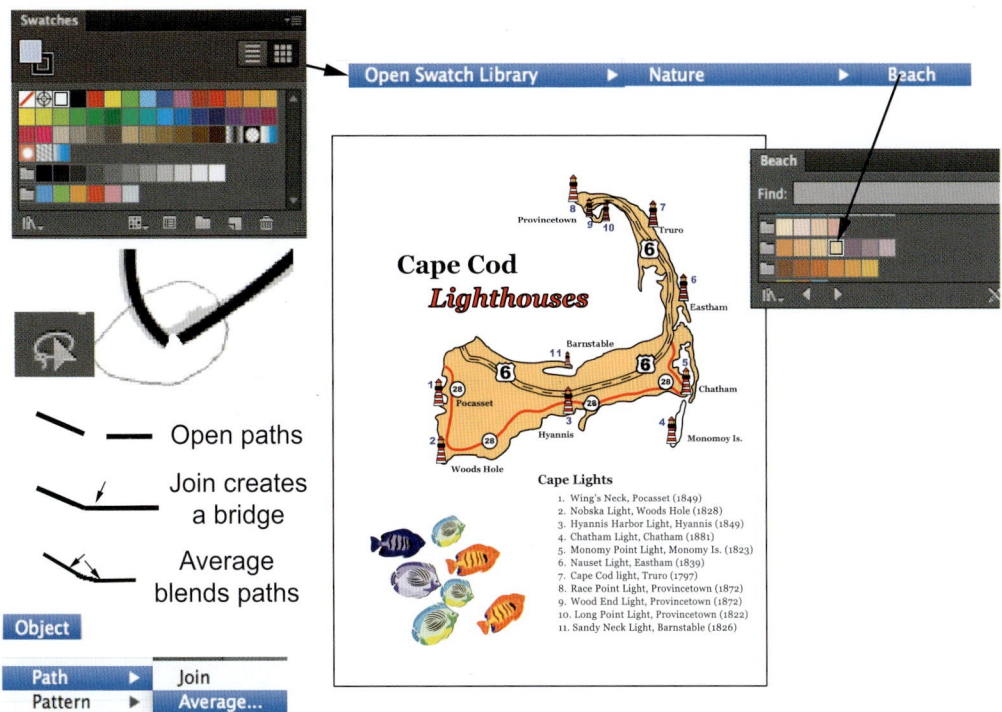

▷ FIGURE 8-31

Closing paths to apply a beach fill color in the map.

5. If you find two paths disconnected but overlapping, draw a circle between both selected path end points with the Lasso Tool (Q). Select Object > Path > Join to add a line segment to bridge the paths to make sure they are joined properly as one point. When the Join dialog box displays, choose Corner or Smooth, depending on the type of path you are connecting. Feel free to use the Control panel; it contains the same settings and is easier to access.

6. To see if you have a completely closed path after you have connected them all, select the entire map outline with the Selection Tool (V) and change the Fill to any color instead of None. If the color displays inside the outline you just created, congratulations! If not, check for open paths, and repeat the steps above.

Ⓧ **PROBLEM** When you are trying to join end points and an Error dialog box comes up when you apply either the Join or Average commands, just click OK. It means the end points are already connected; it could also mean more than two anchor points are selected.

7. With your path closed, it's time to select a special color from one of Illustrator's Swatch libraries. With the map outline selected with the Selection Tool (V), click the Fill color in the Tools panel, and, from the panel menu in the Swatches panel, select Open Swatch Library > Nature > Beach.

8. Select a swatch with the color values displayed as C=2, M=12, Y=49, K=0, or find a light brown sandy color as the Cape is famous for its beaches. You should find your map filled nicely if you were able to create a closed path. It may take a few tries, or redrawing the map to create the closed path.

9. When you are finished, turn off the template layer and turn on all the other layers to see your new map nicely filled with symbols, brushes, and text you created earlier.

10. Save the file in your *Chapter 8* folder.

SAVING YOUR ARTWORK IN EPS FORMAT

Saving Illustrator files in EPS format allows them to be viewed universally by many graphics applications (Figure 8-32). EPS files handle text and graphic elements very well and are used predominantly in the commercial press industry. You can also save individual artboards as separate EPS files. You can include options like embedding fonts and displaying thumbnail previews, although doing so will also increase file size. You can save EPS files using the current version or earlier versions. If you save to an earlier version, you may see various warnings and functions grayed out in the dialog box; this is because some of Illustrator current features may not have been available in a previous version.

DESIGN TIP

For files used in the printing industry, save files as EPS whenever graphic objects, illustrations, and text are used in the same graphic. You can edit an EPS file the same way you would an AI file. For photographic images only, saving files in TIF format is universally used.

▷   FIGURE 8-32

Saving the document in the universal EPS format with options.

TOOLKIT TIP   Before saving and sending your work to a service provider, always check first to see what version they are using. If they are using an earlier version than you are working with, save to their version, and in most cases, although you may receive a warning about saving backwards, there may not be an issue.

Here you will save the file in EPS format with default settings.

1. Choose File > Save As > and navigate to your *Chapter 8* folder.

2. Name the file *MapPRINT* and select Illustrator EPS for the format; then click the Save button.

3. When the EPS dialog box comes up, save to the version you are currently working in. If you save to an earlier version, you may see some warnings regarding possible editing or font issues. Do not worry about this for this assignment. With most all versions, select an 8-bit color TIF Preview to display a thumbnail preview of the document. Leave the rest at the default settings (Figure 8-32).

4. Select OK to save the file in the *Chapter 8* folder as *MapPRINT.eps.* You now have two files; a map ready for print (*MapPRINT.eps*) with the EPS extension and a backup in Illustrator's native .ai extension (*MapPRINT.ai*).

TOOLKIT TIP To create an interesting map without using much ink from a home printer, instead of filling in colors, you can print on parchment paper, which you can get at any stationery store. Parchment paper provides a "treasure map" background because the "white document" of your EPS file actually prints as if transparent.

PACKAGING AND SYNCING YOUR ARTWORK AND SETTINGS TO CREATIVE CLOUD

Illustrator Creative Cloud (CC) allows designers the ability to take their artwork and create a package-ready folder that includes their document, their linked images if applicable, any fonts used in the document, and a report of what components are in the folder for the service provider. If you subscribe to Adobe Creative Cloud (CC), on the Creative Cloud desktop on your computer you can select the link to Sync Files to Creative Cloud to place your artwork online, which can be shared between other professionals using the free Behance portfolio site, or you can access your work on another computer. You can also sync your Illustrator settings, brushes, symbols, and other elements between computers.

PACKAGING YOUR IMAGES, FILES, AND FONTS FOR COMMERCIAL PRESS

Illustrator Creative Cloud (CC) has a Package feature that allows designers to auto package their files, images, and fonts in one folder to send to a commercial printer. This comes in handy, especially with fonts to make sure the service provider can use those same fonts for your document by simply installing them on their computer. If your work is linked to original files, a copy of the original is packaged so you don't have to worry about locating your original files for the printer. It also generates a report for your service provider as well.

Here you will package your map as if ready to send to a commercial printer. This is always the last step, after you have checked spelling, alignment of images and text, etc.

▷ FIGURE 8-33

Using the Package feature in Illustrator CC to prepare your artwork, fonts, and images for your service provider.

1. Open your *MapPRINT.eps* file if it is not already displayed.

2. Select File > Package, and when the Package dialog box displays, choose Location: Desktop (or choose where you want the folder to be placed). Type in the Folder name: *Chap 8 Project-Map*, and leave all default boxes checked.

3. Select the Package button on the dialog box when you are ready. When a warning box appears regarding font usage and copyright, click OK (Figure 8-33).

4. The next dialog box will display indicating your Package was created successfully. To see your contents, select the Show Package button.

5. Your *Chap 8 Project-Map* folder will open up to display the contents. As there are no linked images since your images have been embedded in our map project, there is no folder for images. You'll find your *MapPRINT.eps* document. You'll also find a report, and a *Fonts* folder with all the fonts used for your map project (Figure 8-33).

6. Now you're ready to send everything packaged to your service provider, knowing you have everything for them in a digital "suitcase."

MANAGING YOUR ARTWORK IN CREATIVE CLOUD

Assuming that you have already installed Creative Cloud (Chapter 3 Advanced), as you did with Photoshop, you can submit and access your artwork from the Creative Cloud storage between computers. The service is provided for free for 30 days, and is free to all paid subscribers. The real purpose of using this is not so much for permanent storage, but for use as part of your intended workflow. You can upload additional images with thumbnails displayed, and download your image(s) from Creative Cloud.

In this optional exercise, you'll use Creative Cloud to submit your *MapPRINT.eps* file, and then access the file to download to your computer.

▷ FIGURE 8-34

Submitting and retrieving your map document.

1. On your computer, if it isn't already active, launch Creative Cloud as you would any other application from your Applications (Mac) or Programs (Windows) folder (in Windows 8 you can also type in "Creative Cloud" from the Start Screen).

2. With the Creative Cloud desktop active, click on the icon and select the Files tab to display the folder icon (Figure 8-34).

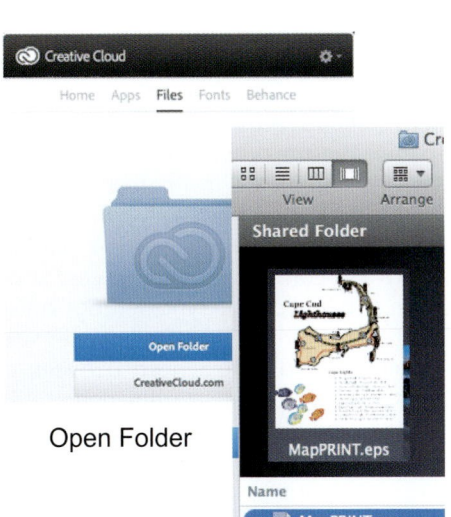

Open Folder

Drag file into folder,
file synced to Creative Cloud

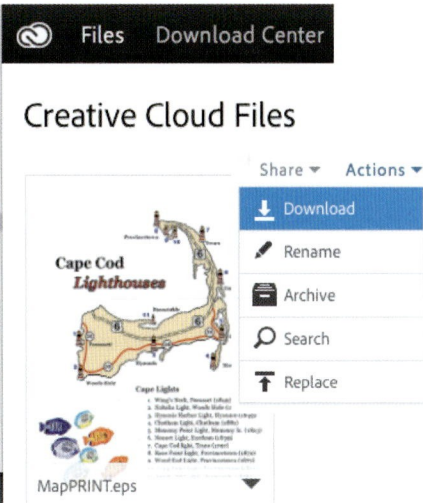

Access file in Creative Cloud

3. Click Open Folder and drag your *MapPrint.eps* image file you just created into the open folder, which may read Creative Cloud Files in the title bar.

4. To access your files on the Creative Cloud server, click on the *CreativeCloud .com* button.

5. From the Creative Cloud website, select the Files tab. Your image file should display as a thumbnail. Click on the thumbnail to expand the screen view.

6. In the Actions panel, with the image expanded, select Download and your expanded image will be downloaded onto your computer, even if Creative Cloud is not installed on that computer. As long as you have an Adobe ID you can access your image file on the Creative Cloud suite and download your image file to most any computer or device. Note: If you have Creative Cloud installed on multiple computers, you can access your image file, edit it, and then send it back up to the Creative Cloud, where it will replace the older version. That way your image version stays current.

7. To minimize back to thumbnail view, click on the Creative Cloud Files link above your expanded image.

8. You can also upload your image files from your computer to the Creative Cloud site. To upload files, with the image thumbnail(s) displayed, select Actions > Upload and load up another image file of your own or one of the images from the past exercises into the Cloud. You can also drag an image from the desktop into the Files tab window in Creative Cloud.

9. When you select the arrow under the image thumbnail, or in the Actions panel you'll find lots of other actions you can accomplish like sharing and syncing files, and syncing application settings in Creative Cloud.

10. Log out of the website when done.

SYNCING ILLUSTRATOR SETTINGS IN CREATIVE CLOUD

Now that you're finished creating brushes and symbols, and have worked with various tools and panels, you may want to use these items and settings on another computer. As was completed in Photoshop (Chapter 6 Advanced Users), Illustrator Creative Cloud lets you not only sync and share you artwork between computers to keep the most current version available, but also sync your Illustrator settings between computers. The process is basically the same for any application, you can either click the Sync Settings button at the bottom of your document, or select Sync Settings from Preferences where you can have choices as to what you would like to have synced between computers. When you select to Sync Settings, your settings are uploaded to the Creative Cloud online.

 PROBLEM When ready to sync your settings to the Creative Cloud, if you cannot find your Adobe ID displayed in the Illustrator (Mac) or Edit (Windows) menu, you'll need to sign out of Illustrator, and then sign back in again. Go to Help > Sign Out… to sign out. Choose Help > Sign-in… to sign in again. Quit Illustrator, and then launch Illustrator again. Sync Settings should then be enabled.

Optional Exercise: Let's sync the Illustrator settings from the *MapPRINT.eps* file you just created. If you have access to two computers, you'll sync settings from your current computer you created the map on so that you can use the same settings on another computer.

1. Select Illustrator (Mac) or Edit (Windows) and make sure your Adobe ID (email) is displayed. Note: If your Adobe ID doesn't display follow the directions in Problem section above.

2. At the bottom of your map document window you'll find a gear-like icon. When you click on the icon, your Adobe ID will display and a button named Sync Settings Now. Select Sync Settings Now to push your settings related to what you used in creating your document to Creative Cloud (Figure 8-35).

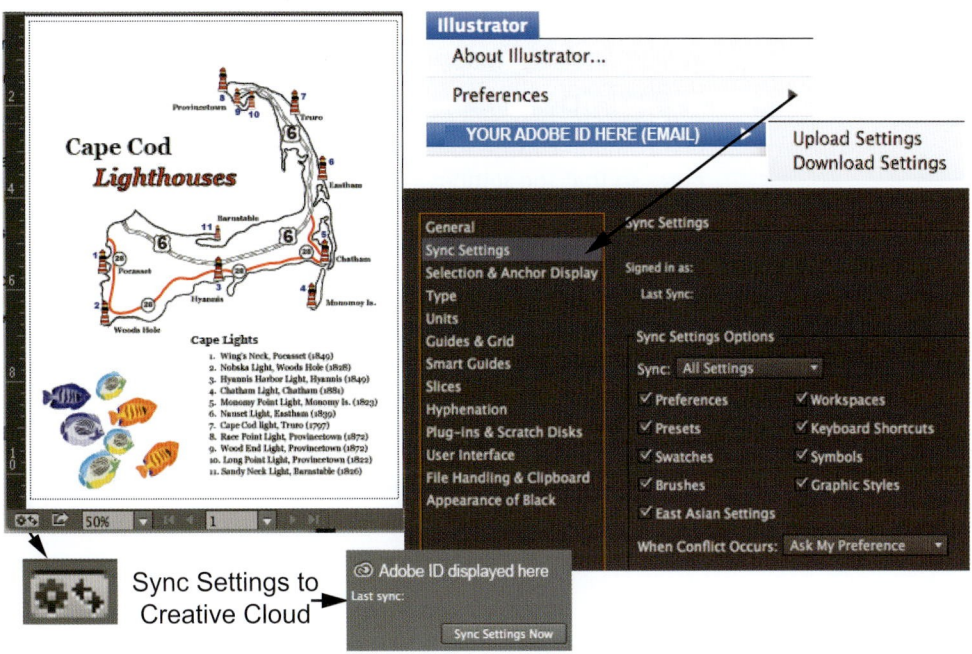

▷ FIGURE 8-35

Syncing Illustrator settings between computers.

3. Open your other computer (computer B), then launch Illustrator, making sure you are logged in with your Adobe ID again. After closing all documents, choose Download Settings (or Manage Sync settings) from Illustrator's Adobe ID link.

4. If a dialog box displays as Updated settings are ready, select Apply Now to bring the settings from the Creative Cloud onto your other computer. Your new settings, synced from Illustrator on your initial computer, will display on the second computer when you open a new document. If needed, restart Illustrator again to apply the settings.

TOOLKIT TIP For more control of what settings you would like to sync, if you choose Preferences > Sync Settings (Figure 8-35), you can choose options of what to sync instead of the default to sync everything possible. After closing any open documents or files in Illustrator, select Upload Settings (or Manage Sync Settings) in the Illustrator (Mac) or Edit (Windows) menu. It will automatically send all your settings to the Creative Cloud. Make selections, then select Upload (or Download if downloading from the Cloud server) to start the process. It will also display a log of what is being completed. Click OK when done.

EXPORT AND IMPORT SETTINGS IN A FOLDER

In Illustrator CC, You can export or import Illustrator settings like workspaces, profiles, color settings, and more by packaging your settings in a simple file that you can carry between computers. This is helpful to manually export settings from one computer to be imported into another copy of Illustrator on another computer so that the settings will match. Select a location where you would like the settings saved on the initial computer with Illustrator CC, say your desktop, and then export the settings available onto that computer (Edit > My Settings > Export Settings). A file will be created displaying the Illustrator version with the word "Settings" and the creation date in the file name that can now be shared. Once you have the packaged settings, you can copy, email, FTP, or use any portable device to bring the file to another computer. You can then use Illustrator CC on another computer to import settings from the package file (Edit > My Settings > Import Settings). A warning dialog box will appear indicating that Illustrator needs to be restarted after you choose the settings package file to import, just click OK and your settings will be applied.

ADVANCED USERS: Placing Logos Created by the Blob Brush onto Multiple Artboards

Suppose you have a client who is developing a successful kid's play center and wants a simple kid-like logo on various pieces of media for advertising and on letterhead. Illustrator has a couple of cool features that just invite you to play and increase your production workflow. The Multiple Artboards feature allows a designer to create up to 100 multiple artboards to show a potential client various sizes and types of media that the artwork created can be used for. Whereas the Brush, Pen, and Pencil tools create stroke paths and anchor points from the inside out, the Blob Brush Tool (Shift + B) creates paths of a Fill color with no stroke with paths and anchor points on the outside creating shapes from anything you draw.

USING MULTIPLE ARTBOARDS

Multiple artboards are useful for creating a variety of things such as multiple-page PDFs, printed pages with different sizes or different elements, independent elements for websites, etc. Designers can use and save multiple artboards within one document, or export each artboard to its own file. Double-clicking the Artboard Tool (Shift + O) opens the Artboard Options dialog box, as does clicking the Artboard Options button in the Control panel. You can adjust dimensions of a selected artboard using the Control panel or by using the Artboard Tool (Shift + O) (Figure 8-36). You can also have independent ruler guides set up for each artboard to help with your sizing.

Multiple artboards

Artboards with completed logo

▷ FIGURE 8-36

Using multiple artboards to place logo created by the Blob Brush Tool.

You can create multiple artboards for your document, but only one can be active at a time. Each artboard is numbered for easy reference. You can edit or delete an artboard at any time, and you can specify different artboards each time you print or export. You can specify custom names for your artboards using either the Control panel or new Artboards panel.

In the New Print Document dialog box, you can set the bleed of your artboards so if they are going to be sent to a commercial printer, the **bleed** can be used as a trimming guide to avoid problems. A slight shift in paper going through the press might cause a white line to appear on the color background print. A good default setting for documents is 0.125 or one-eighth inch bleed. With this project you really don't need to set a bleed, but it's good practice. The bleed shows as a red box outside the document area. Using the multiple artboards feature allows a designer to define uniform bleed for all artboards being created.

THE ARTBOARD TOOL

The **Artboard Tool** (Shift + O) controls how you move, resize, and edit artboards, with one artboard selected at a time. To set an artboard as the active artboard, click it. When you have multiple artboards defined, you can view them all by selecting the Artboard Tool. Double-clicking the Artboard Tool opens the Artboard Options dialog box, as does clicking the Artboard Options button in the Control panel.

To start your new document, you are going to create four artboards for a logo you will later create with the Blob Brush. The artboard sizes will be for a letterhead, CD front cover, business card, and direct mail piece. You will also have a 0.125-inch bleed around each artboard document as if the artboards were going to press. A bleed extends beyond the trim edge of a document to ensure good color coverage at the edges of printed material. This is especially useful when artwork contains solid color boxes or artwork itself extends to the edge of the document. It is a good habit to get used to, even though, as in this exercise, it may not be totally necessary.

▷ FIGURE 8-37

New document settings for four artboards with bleeds.

1. To create a new document, select File > New. Then, in the display, choose to create four artboards, which you'll adjust later (Figure 8-37). Use a bleed of 0.125 inches all around. Set up as a Portrait Orientation, and Units to Inches.

2. Name the document *Sun Logo* and click OK. Your four artboards will display as equal sizes.

Bleed marks in red

Create new Illustrator document with multiple artboards and bleed   Four artboards created

3. We want rulers and guides displayed. To have the artboard rulers display for each selected artboard, choose View > Rulers > Change to Global Rulers. Make sure Smart Guides is also checked in the View menu (View > Smart Guides). For additional help with resizing, make sure the Info panel is displayed (Window > Info).

4. Select the Artboard Tool (Shift + O) and click on the top left artboard designated as number 1 in the top left area. We'll use this as the main artboard on which to create the logo. Notice the ruler guides display for that artboard along the edge of the document. This will be the letterhead artboard at 8.5 x 11 inches so we won't make any adjustments here.

5. To create the CD cover dimensions, with the Artboard Tool selected, click on the number 2 artboard to the right and notice the ruler guides now display for this artboard. Drag for the CD cover using the ruler and smart guides, which will display as you drag so that you have a square measuring 4.75 by 4.75 inches. Notice the bleed follows along with the changes you make.

6. To create the direct mail piece, click on the number 3 artboard and drag to create a 4.25 Height x 5.5 Width dimension.

7. To create the business card, click on the number 4 artboard and create a 2.0 Height and 3.5 Width.

8. You can move artboards around, not only with the Selection Tool (V), but also with the Artboard Tool (Shift + O). Click on the direct mail piece and drag underneath the CD cover; then click on the business card and drag under the mail piece to maximize the work space (Figure 8-38).

9. As an additional note, you can also use the Artboard Tool (Shift + O) to click and drag on the gray canvas and automatically create an artboard. To remove an artboard, just click on the "X" in the upper right corner of the artboard.

10. Save the file as *Sun Logo.ai* in your *Chapter 8* folder. All the multiple artboards can be saved as one document.

▷ FIGURE 8-38

Using the Artboard Tool to select, edit, resize, and move artboards to suit various client needs.

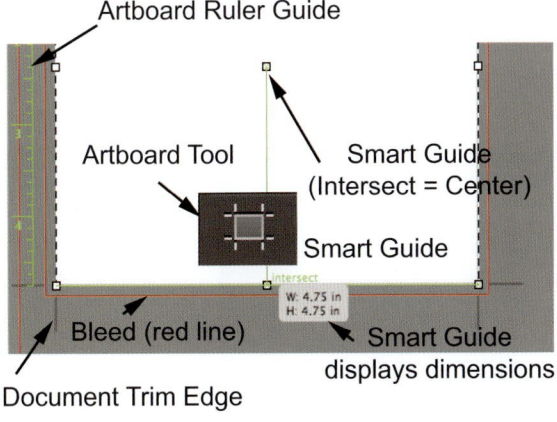

Artboard Ruler Guide

Artboard Tool

Smart Guide (Intersect = Center)

Smart Guide

Bleed (red line)

W: 4.75 in
H: 4.75 in

Smart Guide displays dimensions

Document Trim Edge

Resizing artboard

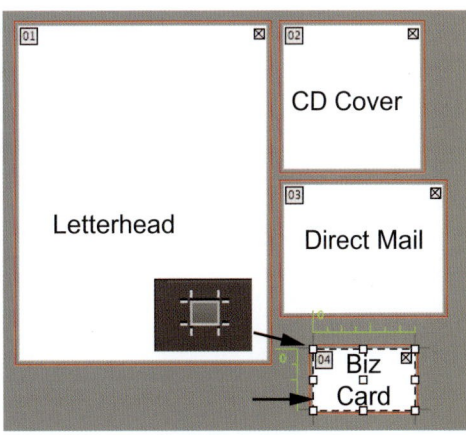

CD Cover

Letterhead

Direct Mail

Biz Card

Adjusted artboards

TOOLKIT TIP Pressing the Option/ALT key while creating or resizing an artboard will keep the center of the artboard fixed. Pressing the Option/ALT + Shift keys while creating or resizing an artboard will keep the width and height of the artboard in its original proportion (constrained scaling) while keeping the center of the artboard fixed.

NAMING THE ARTBOARDS AND USING THE ARTBOARDS PANEL

You can use the Artboard Tool (Shift + O) to name and orient your artboards using the Control panel. There is also an Artboards panel, which allows you to create new artboards, reorder artboards, rearrange artboards, and create duplicate artboards. This helps to keep track of your artboards and edit your work quicker.

Here you will use the Artboard Tool (Shift + O) to rename each artboard using the Control panel. You can then see the names displayed on the Artboards panel for quick reference to access your work.

1. With the *Sun Logo.ai* document open, show the Artboards panel by selecting Window > Artboards.

2. Select the Artboard Tool (Shift + O), and then select the letterhead artboard you created. It is labeled in the top left corner as the default *01 - Artboard 1*.

3. You will notice that the same name displays on the Control panel. Type in the box "Letterhead," then press the Return/Enter key. You can also adjust each artboard's orientation, which is not needed for this exercise. You will notice the name will automatically change in the Artboards panel from *01 - Artboard 1* to *Letterhead*. (You can also double-click the text in the Artboards panel as well.)

4. Repeat the same so that all four artboards are labeled correctly.

5. As you see in the Artboards panel, all four artboards are labeled. You can then select an artboard from the panel to highlight and edit. Check out the panel menu and see the options available in the panel (Figure 8-39).

6. Save the file when done.

▷ FIGURE 8-39

Using the Artboard Tool to name each artboard or create orientation. The Artboards panel provides options for your individual artboards.

Artboard Tool

Artboards panel

ILLUSTRATOR'S DRAWING MODES AND THE BLOB BRUSH TOOL

Illustrator's **Blob Brush Tool** (Shift + B) allows a designer to draw merged paths as fill shapes. Instead of a regular paintbrush stroke, you get a filled compound path. You can use the Blob Brush Tool (Shift + B) to paint filled shapes that you can intersect and merge with other shapes of the same color. The key here is same color shapes. The Blob Brush Tool (Shift + B) uses Fill colors with a Stroke of none. Different colors create different or independent shapes or object paths. The Blob Brush works alongside the Direct Selection, Smooth, and Path Eraser tools to smooth out or erase parts of the shape paths created by the Blob Brush. To see brush options, double-click on the Blob Brush Tool (Shift + B). Near the bottom of the Tools panel, you have Drawing mode options. You have been working in the default Normal Drawing mode all along. Using the Draw Behind mode, you can draw behind all artwork on a selected layer if no artwork is selected; otherwise if artwork is selected, the new object is drawn directly beneath the selected object. Draw Inside mode allows you to draw inside a selected object.

In this exercise you'll create a simple playful logo using the Blob Brush Tool, place a playful font underneath, and then copy, resize, and place your logo on all the artboard media you created.

1. Set your workspace settings from the default Essentials on the Application bar (or Application Frame) to Painting to bring up common panels for painting.

2. Double-click the Blob Brush Tool (Shift + B) to bring up the Options display. Make sure Keep Selected is checked so you can see the shapes you are creating. Leave all the rest of the settings as shown. The lower half of the display shows brush settings mainly with a graphics tablet. Select OK.

3. Select the first top artboard and zoom in at 100%.

4. Select an orange color stroke with a fill of None. Select the Blob Brush Tool (Shift + B) and paint a sun outline rising over the horizon as shown in Figure 8-40. Don't worry about the size of your logo since you'll resize it later. Notice that any shapes of the same color merge together as one shape, and those not touching any shape have their own individual shape.

▷ FIGURE 8-40

Using the Blob Brush Tool and drawing modes to create and place freestyle shapes.

5. To paint the yellow sun, deselect the orange outline you created, choose the Selection Tool (V), and click on the artboard area; then select the yellow stroke color.

6. Select the Blob Brush Tool (Shift + B) and paint inside the sun outline. Notice the new yellow color creates a whole new shape that does not blend with the orange color. Feel free to get more creative if you like.

7. If the yellow color overruns the orange, just select the yellow shape you created with the Selection Tool (V) and select Object > Arrange > Send to Back. Use the Path Eraser, Direct Selection, and Smooth tools to adjust as you like it.

8. To create a cloud behind the sun, using the Draw Behind mode, deselect the selected shapes by choosing the Selection Tool (V) and click on the artboard. Then select a light blue color, select the Draw Behind mode near the bottom of the Tools panel, and paint again with the Blob Brush. The cloud should appear behind the sun as shown in Figure 8-40. Use the bracket keys on your keyboard to adjust the size of the brush to fill in the color of the cloud. Before creating a different colored shape, remember to deselect the shape you just created. Select the default Normal Drawing mode when done.

9. Use the Direct Selection (with the arrow keys), Path Eraser, and Smooth tools to refine your creation to the way you like it for a simple logo. Go ahead and play!

10. Use the Type menu (Type > Font) to see what all fonts look like. Find a fun font for this logo. We chose a sans-serif font called Stencil.

11. Type "Rising Sun Play Center" underneath.

12. You can now select the whole logo with the Selection Tool (V) and choose Object > Group to put everything together.

13. Hold down the Option/ALT key and copy the logo to the other artboards, or with the selected, logo, choose Edit > Copy and then Edit > Paste. With the logo selected, hold down the Shift key and drag the corner to resize the logo proportionately to each media piece as shown in Figure 8-41. Feel free to put in appropriate text lines for each type of media on your own.

14. When finished, save your work as *Sun Logo.ai* again in the *Chapter 8* folder.

15. Feel free to create a symbol of the logo you created, as you learned in the previous map project, for future use.

▷ FIGURE 8-41

Simple logo created with Blob Brush Tool, copied, resized, and placed in artboards.

RISING SUN PLAY CENTER

Completed Logo

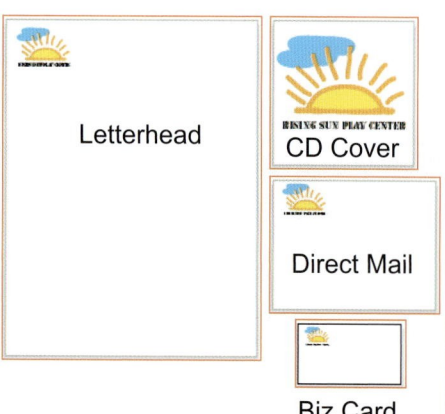

Letterhead

CD Cover

Direct Mail

Biz Card

TOOLKIT TIP Note: Options called Paste in Place and Paste on All Artboards paste the object at the same position as the copied objects referenced from the active artboard at the time of copying, which would not work for this exercise.

SAVING AND PRINTING MULTIPLE ARTBOARDS

When saving multiple artboards, you can save, as you have been doing, as one document, which will display as multiple pages in Bridge. There can be up to 100 artboards displayed. You can also export a range of different artboards or choose individual pages. Saving your work as a PDF file will display multiple artboards within the same document name.

When you create a document with multiple artboards, you can print the document in a variety of ways. You can ignore the artboards and print everything on one page, or you can print each artboard as an individual page. You can have artboards automatically rotated to print to a particular media size. There is also a feature called 9-pt referencing that allows you to set reference points for artboards to hinge a corner or center of an artboard while it is being changed. When you print artboards as individual pages, you can choose to print all artboards or a range of artboards. To print all artboards as separate pages, select File > Print > All. You can see all the pages listed in the preview area in the lower left corner of the Print dialog box. To print a subset of artboards as separate pages, select Range, and specify the artboards to print. To print the artwork on all the artboards together on a single page, select Ignore Artboards. If the artwork extends past the boundaries of the page, you can scale or tile it. You can also specify other print options, and then click Print.

Here you'll print all the completed artboards as separate pages for a potential client.

1. With the multiple artboards saved as *Sun Logo.ai,* select File > Print.

2. Select the General tab on the left side and then select the printer you are using.

3. Make sure All is selected under Copies and leave the rest as defaults for now (Figure 8-42). We'll cover more of these settings in depth in future chapters.

4. Select Print to print your copies as separate pages.

▷ FIGURE 8-42

Options for printing multiple artboards.

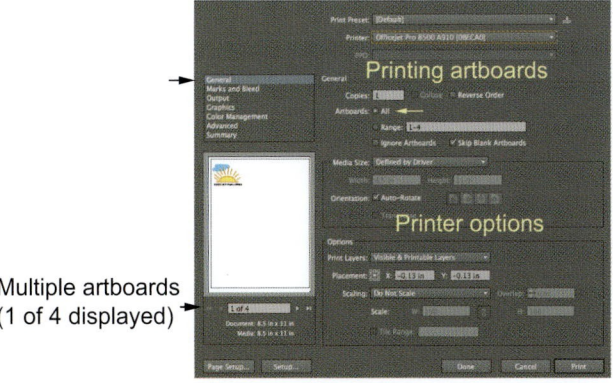

Multiple artboards
(1 of 4 displayed)

DIGITAL TOOLKIT EXTRA: Using 3D Effects and Mapping the Label

Here is a great function in Illustrator that you will really enjoy. You can create 3D effects from 2D artwork. You can also control the appearance of 3D objects by adjusting the lighting, shading, rotation, and other properties. To create these effects, use the Effects > 3D menu where you can **Extrude** a 2D object, like a circle, into a cylinder; **Rotate** a 3D object; and **Revolve** a 2D outline along an open or closed path around an axis to create a 3D object. In addition, you can map artwork onto each surface of a 3D object to design packaging and other 3D objects. **Mapping artwork** is done in the 3D Options dialog box to precisely match the artwork to the contours of the 3D surface. The **Appearance panel** is used to edit the appearance attributes of an object, group, or layer. Strokes, fills, and corresponding effects are stacked in order for future editing. The Appearance panel also displays properties of selected 3D objects. Any characteristics of an object, from its color to special effects, can be edited directly in the Appearance panel. Click on links, and display boxes from previous commands regarding fill, stroke, or effects are automatically opened up for editing without having to open up their corresponding panels. For this assignment, you will create a 3D wine (or juice) bottle, using the 3D Revolve function; then create the label, using symbol and brush library graphics; and map the label to the wine bottle surface (Figure 8-43). The Color Picker lets you select an object's fill or stroke by choosing from a color spectrum, defining colors numerically, or clicking a swatch.

▷   FIGURE 8-43

Creating the 3-D Revolve effect on the outline of the bottle.

CHOOSING COLOR IN THE COLOR PICKER AND OUTLINING THE BOTTLE

To prepare for creating any 3D effects, an outline needs to be created of half of the shape in order to create the 3D effect. Use the **Line Segment Tool (\)** while holding down the Shift key for straight lines and the Pencil, Pen, and Selection tools to create and adjust the curves. When this is completed, you will have an open path before applying the 3D effect.

TOOLKIT TIP When creating the path for a 3D effect, use a Stroke color with no fill for most work. If you revolve an open path that has a fill, the fill is revolved in addition to the stroke color and may produce unexpected results. The process of applying the effect may also slow down your system significantly.

Here you will trace a template already created of the wine bottle.

1. Launch Illustrator and Open the file *Wine* located in your *Chapter 8* folder. The image has already been scanned and a template created for tracing; if you want, feel free to draw your own, scan it, and place the scanned image into Illustrator.

2. Select View > Rulers > Show Rulers if the rulers are not displayed, and make sure Smart Guides is checked in the View menu. If they are displayed as points, select Illustrator > Preferences (Mac) or Edit > Preferences (Windows). Select Units, and in the General box, switch to inches for this exercise. You can also Option/Right-click in the ruler and select inches from the contextual menu.

3. Select the *Wine* layer in the Layers panel to use as the working layer, not the Template layer (Figure 8-44).

4. Zoom in 100% or closer and drag a vertical guideline from the left side ruler to the left side of the wine sketch to be used as the axis for the 3D revolve.

5. Double-click the Stroke box to display the Color Picker and select a deep purple, 1-pt Stroke with no Fill; there should be a red line through the Fill square. The Stroke becomes the fill when revolving a 3D object.

TOOLKIT TIP You can click on any color, or move up the color scale to choose a color, and it will display its six-digit identity number, although this number is used mostly for colors for the web on older computer monitors. Make sure the color will display for the intended output: if a yellow triangle displays, it may not print accurately; if a box displays, it may not display properly on the web. By selecting either warning icon, the display will select the next closest color.

6. Zoom in to 200%. Select the Line Segment Tool (\) and hold down the Shift key to create straight lines to trace over the bottle base, starting on the guideline. Release the Shift key first and then the mouse. Click on the end points as you continue to draw to keep the path a single element. Do not draw to the left side of the guideline (Figure 8-44).

▷ FIGURE 8-44

Creating the outline of the bottle with the Line and Pencil tools.

7. Select the Pencil Tool (N) to draw the curve. In Illustrator CC, double-click the Pencil Tool icon in the Tools panel and change the Fidelity setting to Smooth. Adjust with the Direct Selection Tool (A) using the arrow keys if needed. Use the Smooth Tool if needed to lengthen the direction lines and decrease the amount of anchor points.

8. Although you can use the Line Segment Tool (\) again, you can create straight lines with the new Pencil Tool (N) by holding down the Shift key to complete the bottle neck. Use the smart guides to find the anchor points and for aligning the bottom of the bottle with the top edge. This may take a few attempts to get it right.

9. When completed, zoom back out and Save the file as *Wine.ai* in Illustrator's native format in your *Chapter 8* folder, using the default settings for whichever version you are using.

APPLYING 3D EFFECTS

You can revolve an open or closed path around an axis up to 360 degrees for a closed, solid object or make it appear that a slice is removed by using less than 360 degrees. The 3D Revolve Options dialog box allows the designer to not only preview the effect but also control lighting, shading, and other properties. The process of having the computer figure out and apply a 3D effect to an outline is called *rendering*. Use the Appearance panel to open the 3D Revolve Options dialog box if you need to make any changes.

TOOLKIT TIP When you want to make any changes or delete the 3D object you created, select the 3D object and then double-click the effect in the Appearance panel. With the bottle still selected after applying the Revolve effect, you can experiment with applying different colors in the Stroke box.

It is show time! Next we see how this 3D effect can be used for your future projects.

▷ FIGURE 8-45

Creating the 3D Revolve effect on the outline of the bottle.

1. With the entire bottle path selected, select Object > Group; then choose Effect > 3D > Revolve to display the 3D Revolve Options dialog box.

2. Use the settings shown in Figure 8-45 to create your wine bottle or use the default settings. Make sure the "Turn cap on for solid appearance" button is selected to apply a solid effect to the wine bottle.

Provides more options for
lighting and shading effects

Appearance panel
with bottle not selected

Appearance panel
with effect applied

3. Select the More Options button to display light qualities and other properties you can apply. Click the Preview box to render the sketch and see what your bottle will look like. Click OK when you are ready to accept the graphic.

4. To experiment with lighting and position of the selected bottle, you can make adjustments while creating the effect, or click the 3D Revolve link in the Appearance panel to reopen the 3D Revolve Options pane. You can adjust the lines to change the shape of the bottle directly on the artboard. In our example, we created a small lip below the neck of the bottle. If you deselect the bottle, you'll find the Appearance panel will display Stroke and Fill links to change colors on the fly if you want. Any changes you make to the object on the artboard are recognized and re-rendered. Be patient while it is rendering each change.

5. Deselect the bottle when you have finished. Save the file.

CREATING THE WINE LABEL USING SYMBOL AND BRUSH LIBRARIES

Here you will use a special symbol and brush from their respective libraries to create the components of the wine label. The Transform command in the Object menu can be used to reflect and copy any object to create a symmetrical design. Symbol and brush libraries store graphics under specialized categories for future use. To apply a straight decorative Art brush from the brush library, you will need to create a straight path using the Line Tool, while holding the Shift key to make a straight line. Before mapping the label to the 3D bottle, it has to be made as a symbol.

Here is a little review of using some symbols and brushes by creating a simple wine label (or feel free to change the label for juice, cider, soda, etc.).

1. Create a new layer in the Layers panel for the wine label and name it *Label.*

2. Double-click the Fill box in the Tools panel, and select a very light cream color in the Color Picker display. Double-click the Stroke box; select a deep blue, and set the stroke to 2 pt in the Stroke panel as shown in Figure 8-46.

DESIGN TIP

Objects that are revolved around an axis for 360 degrees appear solid, and objects less than 360 degrees will appear sliced or cut into. In the 3D Options dialog box, select Revolve Cap On to make the object appear solid throughout; select Revolve Cap Off to make the object appear hollow.

▷ FIGURE 8-46

Creating the label background.

Create New Layer

Fill (#F9F9EF)

Stroke (#00033)

Label background

DESIGN TIP

For small text (less than 24 pt, depending on the font) avoid using any stroke colors, so the type does not appear blotchy and hard to read.

3. Select View > Rulers > Show Rulers if they are not displayed, and select the Rectangle Tool (M).

4. Click (don't drag) on the document above the wine bottle and enter a 2-inch Width by 1.5-inch Height, select OK, and zoom in to 200%.

5. Select the rectangle with the Selection Tool (V) to display a bounding box. Drag a vertical guideline to the center point of the rectangle (Figure 8-46).

6. Open the *Decor.ai* file in your *Chapter 8* folder, which contains the Arabesque 4 symbol; select and copy the symbol, and then paste it onto your wine document. You can also locate a different graphic if you want, or you can create your own in a separate file. Select the graphic you will use and then click the New Symbol icon in the Symbols panel to add the symbol to your Symbols panel.

7. Position the graphic along the top right edge of the rectangle; then hold down the Shift key and resize it from the right corner toward the middle of the label. Make sure the graphic does not touch the stroke borders.

8. To create the other side, choose Object > Transform > Reflect.

9. From the dialog box, select a 90 degree Vertical Axis rotation, and then click Copy, but *do not* click OK.

10. Drag the copy with the Selection Tool (V) and position it at the left side of the label.

11. To apply a decorative Art brush, select Open Brush Library from the Brushes panel menu and select Decorative; then select the Decorative Banners and Seals library.

12. Select the Banner 16 brush to place it automatically in the Brushes panel, or choose something similar in style.

13. To apply the brush, select the Paintbrush Tool (B). While holding the Shift key to make a straight line, draw across the label about two-thirds of the way up. You can also try to use the Line Segment Tool (\) and apply the brush style to it afterward.

14. Reposition the sizing handles to center the graphic as shown in Figure 8-47.

15. To enter the text, select the Type Tool (T) and click outside the label, not on the brush. Use the Character panel and choose a Century Old Style (Mac) or Century Schoolbook (Windows) font, or another serif font, in Italic style. Set the size to 18 pt, with a black Fill and no Stroke.

16. Type "Fine Wine," or create your own title, and use the Selection Tool (V) to drag the text on top of the Art brush graphic. Deselect the text.

17. Select the Type Tool (T), click on the artboard, and change the Fill color to deep red with no Stroke; set the Size to 14 pt with a Regular Style. Type "Cabernet Sauvignon" below the brush graphic, or create another title in the wine label and center it.

18. Select all the elements in the wine label with the Selection Tool (V) and choose Object > Group.

19. To make the label into a symbol, click the New Symbol icon in the Symbols panel and name the symbol as *Label*. Make sure, in the Symbol options, you set it as a graphic, not a movie clip.

**Creating the label
for the wine bottle.**

Banner 16 Decorative Brush

20. Delete the label if you want, or leave it next to the bottle for comparison or in case you want to modify it later.

21. Save the file. Your wine label is finished and ready to be placed on the bottle.

OPTIONAL: CREATING YOUR OWN DECORATION USING THE BRISTLE BRUSH

In Illustrator, there is a brush library called Bristle. Bristle brushes create brush strokes with the appearance of a natural brush with bristles, and you can also vary the width of a stroke or select from a preset group of variable width brushes. When working with brushes, keep the fill color to none and choose colors for Stroke only. In this exercise, try to create a decorative piece of artwork that can be used as a symbol, using the *Decor* artwork file as a guide for starters. You will use the Bristle brush library of brushes. To display options for making adjustments to your brushes, just double-click on the Definition box that shows your brush.

This exercise will show you how to select and use the Bristle brushes. We'll start off making a copy of the *Decor* file, which has an elegant series of lines.

1. In Illustrator, open the *Decor.ai* file, and then create an additional new print-able document with one artboard and leave the rest as default settings.

2. Resize both windows so they are next to one another. If you don't want to draw freehand, you can Place the *Decor* file as a template (File > Place > Template) and paint on top of it.

3. Select the Paintbrush Tool (B) and choose a Fill color of None and a Stroke color of dark blue, deep red, or golden.

4. To select from the Bristle Brush Library of brushes, make sure the Brushes panel is open (Window > Brushes), and from the panel menu, select Open Brush Library > Bristle Brush > Bristle Brush Library. You can also select Window > Brush Libraries > Bristle Brush > Bristle Brush Library.

5. With the selection of brushes, you can see there are quite a few different brush styles. Hover your cursor over each brush to display each one's name. Choose Cat's Tongue, Angle, or Dagger style brushes for starters, and you'll see the brush style displayed in the Control panel's Brush Definition box.

6. Double-click on the brush chosen in the Brushes panel to display the many brush options available for your selected bristle brush (Figure 8-48).

▷ FIGURE 8-48

You can select pre-set variable stroke widths, or create and save your own. Double-click the Bristle Brush Definition Box to display plenty of options.

Preset stroke widths

Bristle Brush
Options display
(partial)

7. To choose a variable stroke width, select the Width Profile 1 preset variable width (located directly under the Uniform width).

8. The rest is just playing. Try to duplicate the style of the *Decor* file; play with different brush styles. Don't forget to use the Eraser, Smooth, and Direct Selection tools to help you create the path shapes you are looking for. If you are happy with your new artwork, save as a new symbol, and drag onto your wine bottle project.

9. Save the file as *Decor2.ai* in your *Chapter 8* folder.

10. To save your brush with its settings, choose Save Brush Library from the Brushes panel menu, and place the new library file in the Bristle Brush Library so that it will appear in the Brush Libraries menu when you restart Illustrator.

MAPPING ARTWORK TO A 3D OBJECT

Mapping artwork involves wrapping the artwork around the projected surface of an object to match what it would look like on an actual 3D product. This process can be used when designers are showing products packaged in containers or applying labels to bottles and so on. In Illustrator, any artwork to be mapped onto a 3D surface has to be stored in the Symbols panel. You can apply any artwork that has been converted into a symbol around any surface of any 3D object.

The Map Art feature is located in the 3D Revolve Options dialog box and is easily accessed by double-clicking on the 3D Revolve effect in the Appearance panel. The Appearance panel allows editing directly from the panel itself. Click on links from previous commands regarding fill, stroke, or effects and the corresponding display windows are automatically opened up for editing without having to open up their corresponding panels. You can also adjust the opacity settings for each effect applied and have direct access to live effects to see results on the fly.

TOOLKIT TIP To edit 3D objects, the object must first be selected to display attributes and properties on the Appearance panel. Double-click on the 3D list item in the Appearance panel to make changes, like adding mapped artwork to the object, changing lighting, and adjusting object properties.

Now you will Map the label to the wine bottle.

1. Select the wine bottle with the Selection Tool (V).

2. In the Appearance panel, double-click the 3D Revolve link to open the 3D Revolve Options dialog box; drag it to the side so you can see the bottle.

3. Click the Map Art button. Do not worry if the color on the bottle disappears. Be patient, as it takes a while to render all the surfaces.

4. Click the Next Surface arrow to page through the surfaces. Select the Surface that displays as a light gray gridline on the right side, as shown in Figure 8-49, to display the front of the wine bottle.

5. Make sure the Preview box is checked to view the results and that the Shade Artwork box is checked to display the label correctly.

6. In the Map Art dialog box, select the new layer symbol from the Symbol dropdown menu and position the bounding box to align the label on the bottle; observe the preview to check the effect.

PROBLEM If it is taking very long to process, you may have saved the Label symbol as a movie clip instead of a graphic.

7. If you make a mistake, just select the Clear button on the display box and repeat steps 3 through 5 until you have it positioned the way you want it.

8. When you are satisfied, click OK to exit the Map Artwork window; then click OK again to return to your document and observe your work. Pretty cool, huh? Delete the Template layer when your work is finished.

9. Save the file in the native Illustrator AI format as *Wine.ai*

10. You are now designing in 3D!

PROBLEM If the text on your bottle appears faint or disappears, the Shade Artwork box in the Map Art dialog box was not checked to display the text correctly. Double-click the effect in the Appearance panel to fix it.

Make sure this is checked

Select the label symbol just created

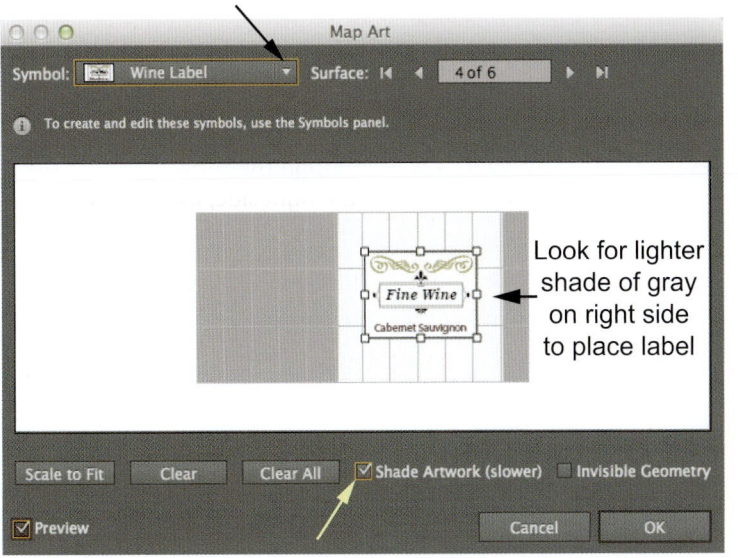

Look for lighter shade of gray on right side to place label

Shade Artwork needs to be checked to display all shading

Indicates area for mapping (red)

Label mapped

▷ FIGURE 8-49

Mapping the wine label to the 3-D bottle.

TOOLKIT TIP Try experimenting with different lighting settings to get the look you want. You can also apply 3D effects using the 3D library from the Graphics Style panel. 3D objects can be rotated using the Rotate command in the Effect menu (Effect > 3D > Rotate). The Graphic Styles panel has been greatly enhanced, so you can preview applied styles on the fly on a large thumbnail display to determine if an effect works for you. You can also save your 3D effect for future use in the Graphic Styles panel. Use the Help menu to find more ways to use 3D effects and lighting.

CHAPTER SUMMARY

In this chapter, you learned that you could trace any sketch or image brought into the computer by creating a nonprintable template layer that dims the image so you can trace the outline on a second layer. Creating various elements on separate layers isolates them, so they do not affect other layers unless you choose. Brushes allow the designer to apply strokes with predesigned brushes, brush libraries, or custom brushes that can be created and saved in the Brushes panel. Graphics can be made into symbols and added to the Symbols panel, or they can be selected from various preset symbol libraries. Symbols can be placed repeatedly on a document to create symbol instances, which can be modified with the Symbolism tools. Illustrator also allows the designer to create or place text from other documents into the artwork. Text can be edited by applying formatting commands. In the Advanced Users section, you explored the purposes of using multiple artboards, and created a logo using the Blob Brush Tool. For the Digital Toolkit Extra you created a tutorial to see how Illustrator gives the designer the ability to create 3D objects from 2D drawings and apply lighting and shading properties. Artwork can also be mapped to 3D surfaces for precise alignment for packaging and design applications. Do not forget to check out the *Extras & Goodies* folder on *www.CengageBrain.com* for more projects and ideas.

REVIEW QUESTIONS

1. Why would you use Grayscale mode when scanning line art?

2. Explain the EPS formats when saving Illustrator files.

3. Explain two ways templates can be created.

4. Explain uses of the Pencil, Smooth, Eraser, Selection, and Direct Selection tools.

5. Explain the differences between using symbols and brushes.

6. Describe styles, symbol instances, and libraries.

7. What is the purpose of the Appearance panel for 3D effects?

8. Explain mapping.

9. What is the difference between paths created by the Paintbrush or Pencil tools and those paths created by the Blob Brush Tool?

10. Explain the purpose of the Artboard Tool.

Sketch of map
of Cape Cod, Massachusetts

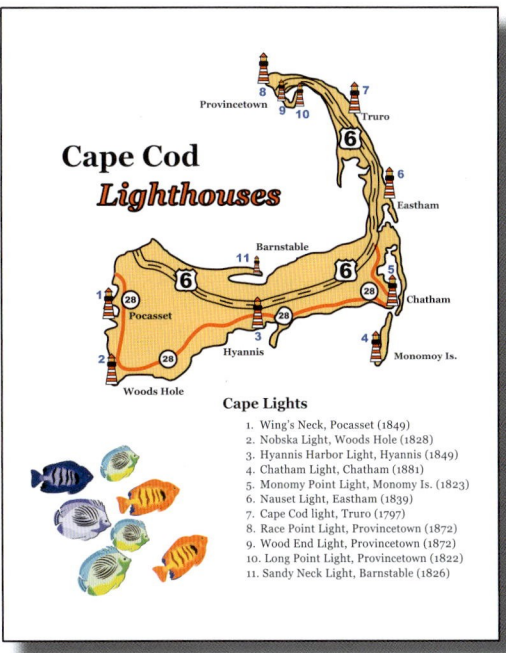

CHAPTER 8
Creating a scalable tourist map from a drawing sketch in Illustrator. Using symbols for visual enhancement.

CHAPTER 8 ADVANCED
Freestyle shapes with the Blob Brush. Placing logo on multiple artboards.

CHAPTER 8 EXTRA
3D bottle shape with label created and mapped onto bottle.

▷ FIGURE 8-50

CREATIVE CLOUD EDITION

CHAPTER

9

Precision with the Pen Tool

CHAPTER OBJECTIVES: To understand the use of the Pen Tool (P) as a precision instrument, and to see how it is used with other drawing tools, in this chapter you will:

▷ Create a custom tools panel for most frequently used tools for this project.

▷ Master the use of the Pen Tool (P) to create straight lines and Bézier curves.

▷ Combine paths created with the Pen Tool (P) and other drawing tools to create complex shapes.

▷ Connect separate paths using the Lasso Tool (Q), and then align and join end points with Average and Join commands.

▷ Label and arrange layers of complex shapes in creating final artwork.

▷ Create special shape combinations with the Pathfinder panel.

▷ Learn to create and adjust type on paths.

▷ Save files in Illustrator's native format as a backup and in EPS format for commercial printing.

▷ ADVANCED USERS: Create professional business cards.

▷ DIGITAL TOOLKIT EXTRA: Create a clock face using guides and gradients.

Although the Pencil Tool (N) is easier for drawing lines and editing freehand lines, the Pen Tool (P) is used for creating paths that demand precision. With the **Pen Tool (P)**, the designer can create perfectly straight lines between anchor points by clicking from one point to the next and can also create complex shapes from special Bézier curves of path segments. **Bézier curves** are created by setting anchor points with the Pen Tool (P) and dragging the mouse to define the shape of the curve. Special purpose Pen tools can be used to add and delete anchor points, to change smooth curves into sharp corners, or to change sharp corners into smooth curves.

PEN TOOL BASICS

The Pen Tool (P) allows the designer to work on images that require precision paths. It takes a little getting used to, but it becomes a very useful tool to the digital designer. The Pen tools are also used in Photoshop and other applications as well. Pen tools can be used in conjunction with other drawing tools to combine paths. Pen tools work well for tracing outlines of complex shapes and images and for creating complex lines from scratch. Pen tools have symbols under the pen cursor to provide feedback as to what function you are about to perform (Figure 9-1). For instance, a "*" ("x" in earlier versions) under the Pen Tool cursor indicates you are starting a new object, and a circle indicates a path will become closed. You will find many adjustments with anchor points and paths can be done using the Control panel with selected tools, and in Illustrator CC, there is a Path Segment Reshape feature when you use the Pen Tool and hold down the Option/ ALT key. This feature allows you to click and drag path segments to accurately adjust curves to match any template sketch. If you like, open the template file called *Pentools* in your *Chapter 9* folder inside your *Extras & Goodies* folder found online at *www.CengageBrain.com* and practice with this great tool.

▷ FIGURE 9-1

Pen tools with cursor feedback, Control panel options.

CREATING STRAIGHT LINES

When you click the first time with the Pen Tool (P), the first anchor point is created. When you click a second time, a caret—an upside down *V*—appears next to the Pen Tool (P) cursor, indicating that you can continue creating more anchor points. If you click the secondary point without dragging, a single straight line is created (Figure 9-2). When using any of the Pen tools, you must end the path before you can draw other lines that are not connected to the path. To end any path with the Pen Tool (P), select the Pen Tool (P) icon again or hit the Return/Enter key.

▷ FIGURE 9-2

The Pen Tool creates straight lines between anchor points when clicking from one point to another.

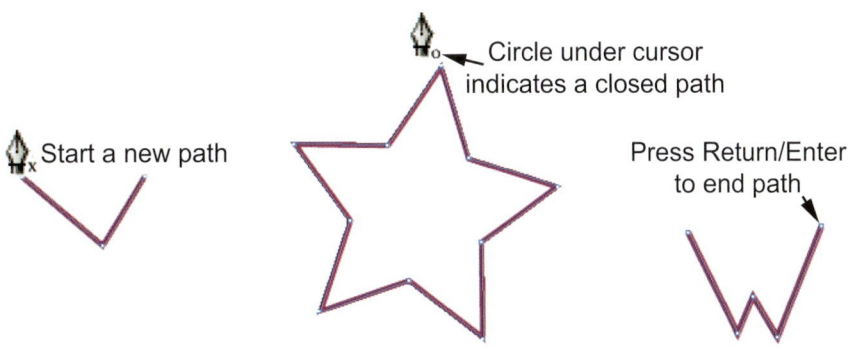

Circle under cursor indicates a closed path

Start a new path

Press Return/Enter to end path

DESIGN TIP

To create perfect horizontal or vertical straight-line segments or perfect straight lines at 45 and 90 degree angles, hold down the Shift key before clicking the next anchor point.

TOOLKIT TIP You can also end a path with Select > Deselect (Command/CTRL Y), or by selecting the Command/CTRL key and clicking away from the line you created. The Command/CTRL key toggles from the selected tool to the last-used selection tool. If you select Edit > Undo Pen or press the Delete key, it will remove the last selected path segment.

DRAWING BÉZIER CURVES

You can make Bézier curves by setting anchor points with the Pen Tool (P) and dragging the mouse to define the shape of the curve (Figure 9-3). Instead of drag- ging the Pen Tool (P) to draw the curve, as you would with the Pencil Tool (N), you drag it to set the starting point or anchor point and the direction of the curve. Path shapes are then created when the anchor point is dragged in a specific direc- tion, creating **direction lines**. Dragging two anchor points in the same direction creates an "S" curve, while dragging two anchor points in the opposite direction creates a "C" curve. The anchor points and direction lines do not print with the artwork. Holding down the Option/ALT key while dragging with the Pen Tool also generates the Path Segment Reshape cursor to reshape any selected paths. Use the Direct Selection Tool (A) to edit your paths for even more precision.

TOOLKIT TIP You can set Preferences of how anchor points and paths are dis- played in the Selection and Anchor Point Display option. When you select a point, Illustrator now selects the closest point.

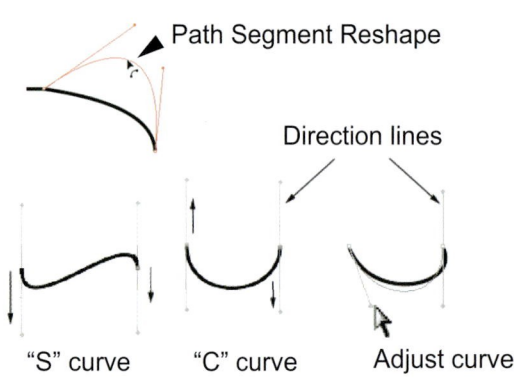

Path Segment Reshape

Direction lines

"S" curve   "C" curve   Adjust curve

MAKING CORNERS FROM CURVES

A smooth curve anchor point can be converted into a corner point and vice versa with the **Anchor Point Tool (Shift+C)**, originally named the Convert Anchor Point Tool. A corner point can be created from a smooth point by clicking again, not double-clicking, on the last anchor point drawn with the Pen Tool (P) as shown in Figure 9-4. You will notice the convert symbol under the Pen Tool cursor; it looks like an upside down V.

TOOLKIT TIP Holding down the Option/ALT key converts any Pen Tool (P) into an Anchor Point Tool (Shift+C).

▷ FIGURE 9-4

Curves can be made into corners and vice versa with the Anchor Point Tool, or by clicking a second time over the selected anchor point using the Pen Tool to display the convert symbol underneath.

DIRECT SELECTION AND LASSO TOOLS

The **Direct Selection Tool (A)** works in conjunction with the Pen Tool (P) to precisely adjust the shape of a path the Pen Tool (P) creates by adjusting its anchor points and direction lines, and in Illustrator CC, its path. There is a Path Segment Reshape function where you can use the Direct Selection Tool to drag and reshape the actual path itself. There is also the ability to take advantage of the Live Corners feature to change corner points into curves. The **Lasso Tool (Q)** is great for quickly making a freehand selection in a small area between end points of paths to be joined (Figure 9-5).

▷ FIGURE 9-5

The Direct Selection Tool adjusts the shape of a path, while the Lasso Tool selects path segments and anchor points.

PATH TYPE TOOLS

In Illustrator, there are two **Path Type tools** that allow the designer to place type on any path created. One allows the type to be placed horizontally along the path, and the other allows placement vertically (Figure 9-6). These tools provide plenty of flexibility to apply type along any path, shape, or object created.

TOOLKIT TIP To practice using the Pen Tool (P) before starting the project, open the *Pentools.ai* document in the *Chapter 9* folder. If an update legacy text dialog box displays, select Update and open the file.

▷ FIGURE 9-6

Horizontal and vertical path type tools.

CLIENT ASSIGNMENT: Creating a Logo

The manager of Captain Jack's Sailing, Richard Zeigler, needs a new, scalable logo created that can be used for various promotions and signage for his business. He is looking for a simple, playful logo for adults and kids to enjoy the adventure of sailing. He provides a simple sketch as a guide and indicates he would like a square logo, and a circular one for various types of media they would use. A slogan for the logo is chosen: Come Play! A playful wide font is chosen for the business name to match the curvature of the sailboat in the waves. After summarizing how the logo will look, an appointment is made for the final logo approval.

ACTION ITEMS OVERVIEW

The drawing has been scanned and a template created for recreating the image in Illustrator. The Pen Tool (P) will be used to create straight lines and smooth curves. Any closed paths are to be filled in with color, so any disjointed paths can be connected using the Lasso Tool (Q) and the Object menu. To accurately match the final curves to the sketch template, final adjustments are made with the Direct Selection Tool (A). If you haven't downloaded the files needed for this chapter, you can find them at *www.CengageBrain.com*.

Here is what needs to be done:

- Create a custom tools panel to provide quick access to the most frequently used tools for this project.

- Use the Pen Tool (P) and Smooth Tool to create smooth lines and curves and adjust them with the Direct Selection Tool (A).

- Join separate paths and end points of the outline using the Average and Join commands in the Object menu.

- Label and organize complex shapes using the Layers panel.

- Create the type along horizontal and circular paths to complete the logo.

- Save in EPS format to be used by various applications.

- ADVANCED USERS: Make the logo into a business card and use the Transform command to scale, copy, and position graphic elements accurately for a sheet of business cards.

CREATING COMPLEX ARTWORK FROM A TEMPLATE

▷ FIGURE 9-7

Creating sailboat logo from sketch to completion.

Vector images can be scaled to any size needed. Creating long, smooth lines with the Pencil Tool (N) is pretty difficult, whereas the Pen Tool (P) can do this with ease. To fill in shapes with color, the paths must be created as closed paths. Creating various layers from these paths provides the designer an opportunity to move layers around for each closed path to produce the desired effect in the artwork (Figure 9-7).

Original sketch placed in Illustrator

Completed Standard Logo

Modified Logo

PLACING THE SCANNED IMAGE AS A TEMPLATE

You will create a new document, and, to help as a review, you're going to take a sketch of a sailboat that has already been scanned and edited in Photoshop and use the Place command to create a template in Illustrator to create your artwork. The key again with the Place command is to make sure that you check the box next to the Template so the sketch will automatically have the template layer created (Figure 9-8).

▷ FIGURE 9-8

Setting up the document and placing the image as a template for tracing.

You will create a new document and then create a template of the sketch of a sailboat.

1. Launch Illustrator; make sure the Layers and Stroke panels, Rulers (View > Rulers > Show Rulers), and Smart Guides (View > Smart Guides) are displayed.

2. Select File > New to create a new document. You want a letter-size document, Units: Inches, Orientation: Portrait, Bleed: 0.0125 inch all around, in CMYK Color Mode. Name the file *Sailing* and click OK.

3. Select File > Place. Locate the *Sail.tif* file in your *Chapter 9* folder that is a thumbnail sketch of a sailboat in waves, and click on it. Make sure that you check Template in the Place dialog box so the image will be brought in as a dimmed template layer. Leave the Link box unchecked (Figure 9-8).

4. Select Place. When the TIFF Import Options dialog box displays, select to Flatten Layers to a Single Image. Although not necessary, it is the default. Click OK.

5. The image should come in with a template layer labeled as default *Template Sail.tif* and a layer above named *Layer 1*.

 PROBLEM If you forgot to check the Template box to create a template layer, you can also convert the new layer in your Layers panel to a template by selecting Template from the Layers panel menu, and then select New Layer to create the working layer above the template layer.

6. For our purposes, you don't need to unlock the template layer and move the image. The idea is to leave space for text, like for a flyer. If you need to position the template centered nearer to the bottom, click the lock by the *Template Sail.tif* template layer to move the template image into place using the Selection Tool (V) as shown in Figure 9-8. When in place, click the lock again to secure it.

7. Leave the default template name; double-click the *Layer 1* text layer above, and rename as *Boat*.

8. Save the file as *Sailing.ai* in your *Chapter 9* folder.

CREATING A CUSTOM TOOLS PANEL

With so many tools available in Illustrator it can be sometimes frustrating to locate specific tools that you may use quite frequently in a given project. Illustrator CC has solved this problem by allowing designers to create their own custom tools panel to increase their workflow. The project that you are creating in this chapter is a prime candidate for creating a custom tools panel, as you will be using a select group of tools, namely, the Pen tools, Selection tools, Type tools, and Lasso Tool. Once a custom tools panel is created, it can be closed and reopened to use on another document, regardless of which document is open, as well as docked and saved on a workspace. The panel becomes a free-floating panel you can put anywhere on your document.

▷ FIGURE 9-9

Creating a custom tool panel for tools that will be used in this project.

In this exercise, you will create your own custom tools panel for the sailboat project.

1. To create a custom tools panel for your sailboat project in this chapter, select Window > Tools > New Tools Panel (Figure 9-9).

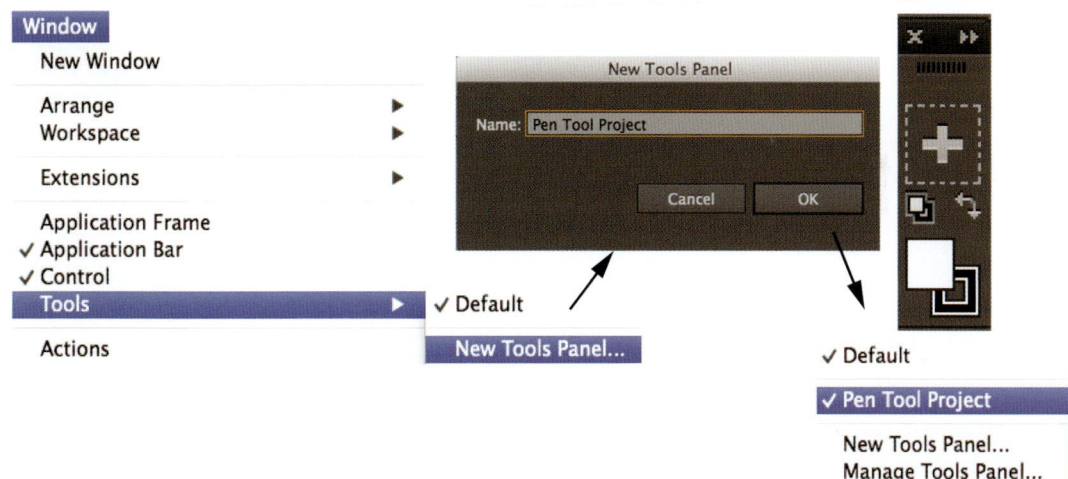

2. When the dialog box displays to name the panel, type "Pen Tool Project" and click OK. The tool panel displays as a free-floating vertical panel with a plus-sign icon to add tools. If you select Window > Tools, you'll find the custom panel listed (Figure 9-9).

3. To add tools into your custom tools panel, for starters, select the Selection Tool icon on the main Tools panel and drag to the plus (+) icon in your custom panel. When the cursor displays as also a "+" underneath, release the mouse to add the new tool. A copy of the Selection Tool icon will display on your new Pen Tool Project tools panel.

4. To add more tools, make sure the tool icon displays on the main panel, and drag under the previous tool in the Pen Tool Project tools panel. You will see a blue line displayed underneath when it's ready to accept another tool, much as if you were moving around layers in the Layers panel. Select the Direct Selection Tool and drag over to your custom panel (Figure 9-10).

Drag until blue line is displayed

Main Tools panel

Pen Tool Project tools panel completed

5. In your custom panel, click the double arrow pointing to the right at the top to display your Pen Tool Project tools panel as two columns of tools.

6. Let's add the rest of the tools needed for this project. Select the Lasso Tool and drag, then select each of the four types of Pen tools, and drag over. You'll need to select each Pen tool so that it displays in the main Tools panel, and drag each individually over to your new panel.

7. To finish up, select the Type Tool and drag over, and then the Type on Path Tool and drag over to your Pen Tool Project panel.

8. You're all set for your project with quick access to the tools you will need (Figure 9-10). You can choose to close your main Tools panel if you like.

TOOLKIT TIP To remove your custom Tools panel select Window > Tools > Manage Tools Panel and select the tools panel name and click the Delete Tools Panel trash can icon, then click OK. The tools panel will be removed.

CREATING STRAIGHT LINES USING THE PEN TOOL

Before tracing, make sure you are creating your drawing on the working layer above the italicized template layer. One of the first things to practice with using the Pen Tool (P) is to create straight lines for the boat mast and body. The mast will be created as an open path with a wide Stroke, and the body of the boat as a closed path, using straight lines. Using Smart Guides helps align points and paths for straight vertical and horizontal intersection. The trick here is *not* to click and drag, just click once to create an anchor point, and then continue to click to create straight lines. To close the path, the tool cursor needs to display an "o" over the initial anchor point, and then click.

In this exercise, you will first create the mast, and then a separate graphic sublayer to create the boat body, using straight lines with the Pen Tool (P).

1. Make sure the *Boat* layer is selected above the *Template Sail.tif* layer to use as the working layer where you will draw the lines.

2. To start creating an open path for the mast, select the Pen Tool (P), with a light brown 6-pt Stroke selected from the Swatches panel (C=25, M=40, Y=65, K=0), and a Fill of None.

3. Click just under the circle of the boat image, hold down the Shift key to keep the tool at a vertical position, or use the green Smart Guides for assistance, and then click at the point where the mast meets the boat deck to create a straight vertical line. (Note: You could also use the Line Segment Tool (\) and just make the Fill color light brown instead.)

4. Press Return/Enter to deselect.

 PROBLEM If you cannot draw with the Pen Tool (P), or a line displays across the cursor, you have the template layer highlighted as the active layer. Make sure the *Boat* layer is highlighted as the active layer in the Layers panel.

5. To place a circular shape on top of the mast, select the Ellipse Shape Tool (L), and switch the Fill color to the same light brown, and no Stroke. Hover your mouse and use the green Smart Guides to click on the center of the circle. When the dialog box displays, type in "0.2" inches for measurements, as shown in Figure 9-11. Use the Selection Tool (V) if needed to move the circle above the mast you just created.

6. Press Return/Enter to deselect.

7. To create the boat body, use a deep red Fill color from the Swatches panel (C=15, M=100, Y=90, K=10), with no Stroke (Figure 9-11).

8. Select the Pen Tool (P), click on the right side first, then hover your mouse downward, and click in the waves. Do not worry about exact placement as the bottom of the boat will be covered by the wave layers applied later.

9. Click as shown in Figure 9-11, and when the mouse hovers over the initial anchor point, displaying an "o" on the cursor, click to close the path. It should fill in with your red color. Click the Selection Tool (V) to deselect the boat.

Labeling paths

▷   FIGURE 9-11

Using the Pen Tool to create straight lines for the mast and boat body.

LABELING YOUR PATHS AND FINE-TUNING ANCHOR POINTS

To increase your workflow by saving time, it's a good habit to label your subpath layers located under your main layer. This helps you keep organized as you continue adding paths, or if you need to locate a particular sublayer path to edit. You can also use the Direct Selection Tool (A) for precise adjustments when moving selected anchor points by using the arrow keys on your keyboard.

1. Click the arrow next to the *Boat* layer on the Layers panel to display the three sublayer paths you have just created.

2. Double-click on the "<path>" text line in each of the three sublayers and name "Top," where you created the circle; "Mast," where you created the line to the boat; and the "Deck," where you created the boat body (Figure 9-11).

3. If needed, to straighten out your lines by adjusting your anchor points, use the Direct Selection Tool (A), click on the anchor point, and move using the arrow keys on your keyboard.

4. Save as *Sailing.ai* in your *Chapter 9* folder. We'll create the sails next.

BASIC BÉZIER "C" CURVES USING DIRECTION LINES AND PATH SEGMENT RESHAPE FUNCTION

Before tracing, make sure you are creating your drawing on the working layer above the italicized template layer. Long and short smooth curves called **Bézier curves** are best created with the Pen Tool (P). To make a path outline of the sails, start with the Pen Tool (P); click first, then drag the direction line created in the direction you plan to go. To create a "C" curve, you need to drag one direction line one way and the other line in the opposite direction. Using the direction lines and expanding them creates longer curves, and then you can adjust the direction of the curve by the direction of the line. You also have the option in Illustrator CC to use the Pen Tool while holding down the Option/ALT key or the Direct Selection Tool by itself to click and drag on the selected path segment you want to reshape. Making sharp corners can also be done with the Pen Tool if, after drawing a direction line, you click the last anchor point again; a convert anchor point symbol is displayed under the Pen Tool (P) cursor. You can also use the Anchor Point Tool, originally named the Convert Anchor Point Tool (Shift+C), to turn smooth lines into sharp corners and vice versa. The Pen Tool (P) may take some practice, so plan on making a few attempts to get it right.

TOOLKIT TIP If the path is way off, or you make a mistake, press the Delete/ Backspace key to remove the last path segment. Click on the end anchor point or end of the path with the Pen Tool (P) to start again. Also, a good habit when tracing over a template in creating paths is to create a 2-pt black Stroke with no Fill to create the path first, and then, to fill in with color, change the Stroke to None and apply the Fill color.

DESIGN TIP

Curves are adjusted by altering the angle of a direction line with the Direct Selection Tool (A), and changing the length of the direction line as well.

In this exercise, you will create and connect Bézier curves with the Pen Tool (P) to create the front sail and use the direction lines to control the length of the curve and its direction. You will create corner points as well.

1. Make sure the *Boat* layer is the active layer in the Layers panel and the *Template Sail.tif* layer is displayed to trace. Select the Pen Tool (P).

2. Set up a 2-pt Stroke and a Fill of None to create the path outline to follow.

3. With the Pen Tool (P), click the top portion of the front sail; then click the bottom of the sail and drag downward toward your left, following the contour of the curve by dragging the direction line quite a distance, as shown in Figure 9-12.

Ⓧ PROBLEM If you seem to be covering up the template with white or some other color when drawing with the Pen Tool (P), make sure the Fill box is NOT set to None.

4. Click the anchor point again to create a corner point. Notice the Pen Tool (P) cursor turns into a convert point icon underneath (looks like an inverted "v" or caret).

5. Click on the upward slope of the bottom of the sail and drag upward; then click on the rightmost anchor point at the bottom of the sail and drag downward. Again, drag the direction line to match the "C" curve of the template. Click the anchor point to make another corner point.

Click and drag

Close path

Adjust direction line downward

handle

Drag with Direct Selection Tool

Click and drag

Extend the direction line

Create corner points, click anchor point again

Use Direct Selection Tool to adjust path segment or direction lines

▷   FIGURE 9-12

▷   FIGURE 9-12

To create curves with the Pen Tool, click and drag the direction lines. Click the anchor point again to generate corner point. Adjust path segments or direction lines with the Direct Selection Tool.

6. To create a closed path of the sail, hover your mouse over the initial point you started up top, and when the cursor displays a "o" underneath, click to close the path and drag to the upper left to bend the curve to create a "C" curve to match the template drawing (Figure 9-12).

7. Press the Return/Enter key to end the path.

8. You will find that the curve is difficult to match the template for the right side of the sail. You will need to either use the Direct Selection Tool to adjust the path directly, or you can adjust by dragging the opposite direction line.

9. To make adjustments to match the curves of the template sail, select the Direct Selection Tool (A) and, as you hover your mouse over the path the Path Segment Reshape cursor displays. Click and drag on the path to adjust the curve. Alternate option: You can also create a curve by dragging the direction lines; click outside the image; then select the top anchor point or path segment to bring up the direction lines and anchor point to adjust. To make a longer curve, extend the bottom direction line outward, and turn the direction line to adjust the direction of the curve (Figure 9-12).

10. When you have matched the sail in the template, select the closed path with the Selection Tool (V); then change the Stroke to None and a turquoise tone of color (C=78, M=10, Y=45, K=0) from the Swatches panel, or something with a little blue-green in the color mix.

11. Save the file as *Sailing.ai* in your *Chapter 9* folder.

TOOLKIT TIP Try to adjust the curves by moving the anchor points or direction lines with the Direct Selection Tool (A) before attempting to adjust any path segment. Path segments can sometimes be difficult to adjust and can cause problems if adjusted too much. In Illustrator CC you now have the option to use the Direct Selection Tool to create smooth curves by dragging on the path segment. You can also do this using the Pen Tool on a selected path while holding down the Option/ALT key.

OPTIONAL: AVERAGING AND JOINING PATHS

If you are having trouble with closed paths, sometimes it may be that you have open end points. Use the Object > Path menu to connect end points of paths to make one closed path. To connect path end points and make a single smooth path, use the Average command (Object > Path > Average) in the Object menu. The Join command (Object > Path > Join) makes sure the end points from multiple open paths are joined together as one. To select just the end points of the two paths to be joined together, draw a freehand selection around both end points with the Lasso Tool (Q). Illustrator provides the option to join two or more open path segments using the Selection Tool (V) to select the open paths and clicking Object > Path > Join (Command/CTRL + J). Illustrator adds a line segment to bridge the paths to join.

TOOLKIT TIP A good rule of thumb is to use the Average function to connect end points, and use the Join function to connect separated path segments as a direct line segment, or for ones that are overlapping. Sometimes it's easier to use the Average command first to align end points on top of one another, and then use the Join command if needed, to join them correctly as one anchor point. If you want to create a straight line between two select end points, use the Join command first.

This is an optional exercise if you find you are having problems creating closed paths at any point in this chapter. Here you can use the Object > Path command to join end points so you can create closed paths to fill with color.

1. Zoom in to find where paths are not meeting; then select the Lasso Tool (Q) and draw a freehand circle around the open area between the two paths, including the end points, to make a selection (Figure 9-13).

2. Select Object > Path > Join to create a straight line between the end points if that's what you need. If a Join dialog box displays, select Corner or Smooth, depending on the type of path you are connecting. If you select Object > Path > Average, let the distance be averaged by selecting Both on the dialog box.

Selecting end points with the Lasso Tool. Averaging and joining end points using the Object menu.

Control panel for path and anchor point options

PROBLEM When you are trying to join end points and an Error dialog box comes up, just click OK. It may mean the end points are already connected somehow; it could also mean more than two anchor points are selected.

3. You can also use the Control panel for quicker access. Here you can convert anchor points to smooth, create corners, and join selected end points.

4. Use the Direct Selection Tool (A) for final adjustments and save the file when done.

USING ANCHOR POINTS TO CREATE CORNERS AND ADJUST CURVES

As done in the previous exercise with the sail, you can initially make long, smooth curves with the Pen Tool (P); then, after drawing a direction line, you click the last anchor point again to create a corner point. In Illustrator CC, you can also use the Path Segment Reshape function with the Pen Tool by holding down the Option/ALT key and dragging the selected segment. Sometimes you may need to add an anchor point to complete a special task in generating the correct shape. Use the Add Anchor Point Tool (+) to add anchor points. Remember, fewer anchor points are usually preferred. Anchor points can also be used in conjunction with the Direct Selection Tool (A) and the arrow keys on the keyboard to further adjust a tricky curve to accurately match the template drawing. When you have completed the sailboat, you'll lock the layers to prevent any inadvertent editing.

In this exercise, you will create and connect Bézier curves with the Pen Tool (P) to create the back sail. To generate a special curve, you will use the Add Anchor Point Tool (+) to add an additional anchor, which will be adjusted with the Direct Selection Tool (A) and the arrow keys on your keyboard.

1. Make sure the *Boat* layer is the active layer in the Layers panel and the *Template Sail.tif* layer is displayed to follow; then select the Pen Tool (P).

▷ FIGURE 9-14

Creating curves with the Pen Tool. Adding anchor point, and adjusting with the Direct Selection Tool and arrows on your keyboard.

2. Set up a 2-pt Stroke and a Fill of None to create the path outline to follow.

3. With the Pen Tool (P), click the top portion of the back sail; then click the bottom right point of the sail and drag downward toward your right, following the contour of the curve by dragging the direction line as shown in Figure 9-14.

Add Anchor Point Tool

Creating the back sail   Completed boat

4. Click the anchor point again to create a corner point. Notice the Pen Tool (P) cursor turns into a convert point icon underneath.

5. Click on the upward slope of the bottom of the sail and drag upward; then click on the leftmost anchor point at the bottom of the sail and drag downward to create a gentle "C" curve. Again, drag the direction line to match the curve of the template. Click the anchor point to make another corner point.

TOOLKIT TIP To change a smooth anchor point to a corner point with the Pen Tool (P), hold down the Option/ALT key and click the point. You will notice a convert anchor point symbol under the Pen Tool cursor. You can also use tools on the Control panel to adjust, add, or remove anchor points.

6. To create a closed path of the portion of the sail, hover your mouse over the initial point your started at, and when the cursor displays an "o" underneath, click to close the path and drag to the upper left to bend the curve to match the template drawing.

7. Press the Return/Enter key to end the path.

8. You will find that the curve is difficult to match the template for the left side of the sail. You will need to create an additional anchor point, and then adjust using the Direction Selection Tool (A) and the arrow keys. With the path closed, select the Add Anchor Point Tool (+) on the middle of the path on the sail outline as shown in Figure 9-14.

9. Select the Direct Selection Tool (A), and click outside the image; then click on the anchor point you just made. Use the arrow keys on your keyboard to adjust the anchor point to bring the curve inward to match the template drawing.

10. If the curved path segments still don't match the template, use the Path Segment Reshape function with the Direct Selection Tool. Click and drag the path segment to match the curve in the template.

11. When you have matched the sail in the template, select the closed path with the Selection Tool (V); then change the Stroke to None and a light yellow Fill color (C=3, M=0, Y=55, K=0) from the Swatches panel.

12. Select the sublayer for each sail, double-click the "<path>" text, and name each sail. Type "Front Sail" for the front and "Back Sail" for the back.

13. Your boat is done. Lock the *Boat* layer and sublayers to prevent any editing mistakes, and click the eye icon to hide the layer to create the waves in the next exercises.

14. Save the file as *Sailing.ai* in your *Chapter 9* folder.

COMBINING CORNERS AND CURVES

This set of exercises involves further using the Pen Tool (P) to create waves using Bézier curves. Be wary that if you create too many anchor points, your path will appear choppy or segmented. Remember, you are looking for gentle smooth lines with the Pen Tool (P). Here is where you can also use the Path Segment Reshape function by holding down the Option/ALT key with the Pen Tool, to adjust the curves of path segments. Again, to create corner anchor points, click on the anchor point a second time and you'll find the convert point icon on the Pen Tool (P) cursor, or you can also use the Anchor Point Tool (Shift+C) to turn smooth lines into sharp corners and vice versa. To create 90-degree angles for square corners, you can hold down the Shift key while clicking for anchor points, and use the Smart Guides to help as well. Using fewer anchor points is better in most circumstances. If there are too many anchor points, use the Delete Anchor Point Tool (-). Feel free to try the same functions on the Control panel for smoothing paths and converting paths to corners. Creating sublayer paths allows you to move your layers as needed for the desired effect, and turning off sublayers allows you to focus on your existing artwork.

In this exercise, you will use the Pen Tool (P) to create the waves in the drawing. Where these closed paths will be overlapping one another, it's easier to create the paths first with no fill, and then go back to fill in with color after the paths are created. You'll create simple corner points to create a closed path using the Pen Tool (P), using the Smart Guides to create 90-degree angles. You'll then fill the color in the closed path and adjust the path outline using the Direct Selection Tool (A).

1. In the Layers panel, click on the Create New Layer icon at the bottom of the panel, and label the new layer as *Waves*.

2. Make sure the *Waves* layer is placed above the *Boat* and *Template Sail.tif* layers to use as the working layer where you will draw the lines.

3. Click the eye icon by the *Boat* layer to hide the artwork to focus on the *Waves* layer, and make sure the template layer is displayed.

4. So that you can view the path outlines, set the Fill to None and the Stroke to 2 pt in black. The trick here again with the Pen Tool (P) is to click and drag for creating curves. If you click, and click again without dragging, you'll create a straight-line connection between the two points.

5. To create the first bottom wave, select the Pen Tool (P), and click once on the beginning of the line on the left side, as shown in Figure 9-15; then click once and drag on the bottom portion of the wave, following the slope as it matches the sketch line.

▷ FIGURE 9-15

Creating Bezier curves for the top portion of the wave.

6. At the top of the wave, click once and drag following the slope upward of the wave, again to match the curvature of the sketch. Continue until you reach the right edge of the line. With the path still selected from drawing with the Pen Tool, hold down the Option/ALT key and drag any selected path segments that need to be adjusted to match the template.

7. Click the anchor point with the Pen Tool again to stop the path and make a corner (Figure 9-15); you'll see the convert point icon displayed on the cursor.

8. With the right anchor point clicked twice to display a convert anchor point on your Pen Tool cursor, move your cursor down about an inch along the green line of the Smart Guides; then click once to create a right side corner point.

9. Continue to the left side, using the green Smart Guides to help, until it reads "intersect," matching with the right side point and the initial anchor point you started. Click once.

10. Move your cursor upward along the green Smart Guides, until when you hover over the initial anchor point, the cursor displays an "o" indicating this will be a closed path. Click on the initial anchor point (Figure 9-16).

11. Press the Return/Enter key to end the path.

12. To apply color, use the Selection Tool (V) to select the path, and change the Stroke color to None.

13. Double-click the Fill color to bring up the Color Picker. Type the number "C1D2EC" for the color number, or select a very light blue color. If the wave shape doesn't fill, repeat the previous steps to create a closed path.

Click once

Click once

Smart Guides (intersect)

Click once

Adjust anchor points, path segments, or direction lines with the Direct Selection Tool

▷ FIGURE 9-16

Create corner points with the Pen Tool. Fill in color in closed path. Adjust with the Direct Selection Tool.

DESIGN TIP

When applying same tones of color as in the exercises here in creating waves, having light to dark shapes or varying tones helps to give the artwork some dimension and depth.

14. To further adjust the curves if needed, use the Direct Selection Tool (A) to make adjustments.

15. Save the file in your *Chapter 9* folder.

REARRANGING PATH SUBLAYERS FOR DESIRED EFFECTS

Just as you have been able to label your layers to help in organization and move around layers for different effects, you can also perform the same operations with path sublayers in the Layers panel in Illustrator. One of the great aspects of this is that you can build various paths or shapes on top of one another, turn on and off layers to help with drawing and organizing, and rearrange your sublayers as needed for the desired paths to display fully, or partially, on your artwork. To help you see your work, you can again use a black Stroke with no fill, create your intended shape, and then fill in the color with no Stroke afterwards to see the completed path. To edit a sublayer to make it active, just select and you'll find a blue square on the right side to indicate it is active.

In this exercise, you will continue to create the waves using the Pen Tool (P) and label each closed path as needed, and then rearrange the path "shapes" to create the waves for the artwork. You will create the back most exposed wave, move the layer so it displays behind the front wave layer, and then create the middle wave, which you will also move in the Layers panel, to place it between the front and back waves.

1. Locate the path of the first wave you just created under the *Waves* layer by clicking the right side arrow. Double-click the "<path>" text line and rename as *Front*.

2. So that you can view the path outlines for the back wave you are going to create, set the Fill to None and the Stroke to 2 pt in black.

3. Select the Pen Tool (P), use the green Smart Guides to align with the previous shape, and as you did with the first front wave, from the left side, click and drag from the top of the wave, and then click and drag at the bottom of the slope, continuing to the right side. To reshape any selected path segments, hold down the Option/ALT key and drag.

▷ FIGURE 9-17

Labeling, creating, and repositioning layers.

4. On the right anchor point, click twice with the Pen Tool (P) to create a corner point and, following the green Smart Guides, move your cursor downward and click a little above the line you created in the first wave. This portion is going to be hidden behind the other waves so it is important to *not* have this bottom line display below the first wave line (Figure 9-17).

Label layer as *Front*

Back layer

Front layer

Move *Front* layer above *Back* layer

Back layer positioned behind *Front* layer

5. Complete the path as done previously, making sure when the cursor hovers over the initial anchor point you created, it displays an "o" to indicate a closed path. Click the initial anchor point.

6. Press the Return/Enter key to end the path.

7. To apply color again, change the Stroke to None, and double-click the Fill to display the Color Picker. Choose a medium blue color, or type in the digits "799FC5." You'll notice the fill color completely covers the front area.

8. In the Layers panel, open the new path sublayer you just created, double-click on the "<path>" text line, and rename as *Back*.

9. As you can see, the *Front* wave layer doesn't display because it is covered by the *Back* sublayer you just created. Move the *Front* layer above the *Back* layer in the Layers panel to display both (Figure 9-17).

10. Zoom in a little with the Zoom Tool (Z), and use the Direct Selection Tool (A) to make final adjustments to your *Back* wave by clicking outside the path first; then select the direction line or anchor point to adjust the curve's shape.

TOOLKIT TIP In many instances a designer would create the larger shapes first and place smaller ones on top. The procedure for this project is to show how you can move around layers to get the desired effect you are looking for. To make longer sloping curves using the Direct Selection Tool (A), click on the end of the direction line and expand it out or click on the selected path segment to generate the Path Segment Reshape function; then adjust to match the contour of the sketch. To display the direction lines, just click on the anchor point. You can also move the anchor point slightly by selecting it with the Direct Selection Tool (A) and then adjusting using the arrow keys on your keyboard. If you find the anchor points are difficult to place or move around exactly where you want them, turn off the Snap to Point function under the View menu.

11. To create the middle wave, click the eye icon of the *Back* wave on the Layers panel to hide it so you can observe what you are doing; then, using the Pen Tool (P), follow the same procedure as outlined in the previous steps, with a 2-pt Stroke and no Fill again.

12. When your closed path is completed, find a light blue color in between the two colors you have selected, or type in "A4B9E0" in the Fill Color Picker with no Stroke to fill in. Rename the new sublayer as *Middle*, click the eye icon of the *Back* sublayer to display it again, and then move the *Middle* sublayer in between the other two (Figure 9-18).

▷ FIGURE 9-18

Creating, coloring, and positioning the middle wave.

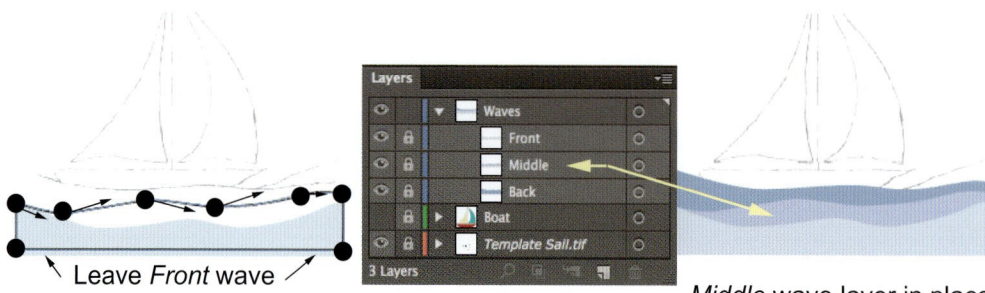

Leave *Front* wave layer bottom exposed

Middle wave layer in place

13. If you have additional path sublayers in the Layers panel, check to see if they are important by turning off these additional path sublayers and looking for any changes; if not, drag into the Trash icon.

14. There is also a portion of a wave in the far back. Repeat the same process and fill with the light blue color you used for the *Front* wave layer. Feel free to add additional waves to give you more practice with the Pen Tool (P). Remember to offset the colors with the additional waves to add dimension.

15. Once you have created the waves exactly as you would like, lock the *Waves* layer to keep all sublayers from moving or being edited, and then turn off the template layer. Turn on all layers to see your work.

16. Make any final adjustments with the Direct Selection Tool (A) if needed.

17. Save the file again as *Sailing.ai* in your *Chapter 9* folder.

MOVING AND ADJUSTING COMPLEX SHAPES

As what you have been working is a sketch template, with your sailboat and waves created as vector shapes, you can make further adjustments without need of the template. You can use the Object menu to group and ungroup selected shapes with the Direct Selection Tool (A) and then use the Selection Tool (V) or, for more precision, the arrow keys on your keyboard, to move your selected group of objects.

In this exercise, because the original sketch had the boat very much on the left side, you are going to move the boat itself a little further to the right, but still

DESIGN TIP

In most artwork or photography, designers and photographers use the rule of thirds concept where the artwork is divided visually horizontally and vertically into thirds, making the main subject(s) off centered, not completely centered. It provides a more pleasing experience for the viewer.

remaining off center, so it is still pleasing to the eye and looking like it is still going into the waves, and not going out of the picture. You will need to do this, as text will be added later, and the image will be cut as a circle. You will need to group together all related shapes that encompass the boat with the Direct Selection Tool (A), and use the arrow keys on your keyboard to move the boat over the waves.

▷ FIGURE 9-19

Selecting, grouping, and moving the boat graphic over the waves.

1. Make sure the *Waves* layer is locked in the Layers panel to prevent any problems in editing, and the *Boat* layer is unlocked, including all sublayers. The template layer should also be hidden.

2. With the Direct Selection Tool (A), or the Selection Tool (V), click and drag diagonally over ONLY the boat parts, not the waves, to highlight only the boat (Figure 9-19).

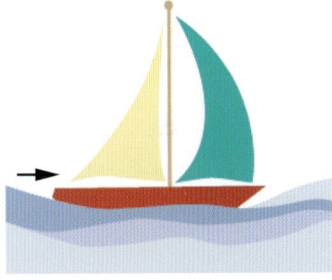

Original artwork   Select and group the boat   Move the boat slightly to the right

3. With the boat highlighted, select Object > Group to group all the boat-related shapes together.

4. Use the right arrow key on your keyboard and press about 15 times to move the boat over the locked waves. Although the change is slight, you will notice it is still slightly off center.

5. Because we want to keep the original *Saling.ai* file for backup, save this adjusted file as *Sailing Circle.ai* in your *Chapter 9* folder as we make changes in the next exercises.

CREATING TYPE ON PATHS

With Path Type tools in Illustrator, you can place type along any path or shape created by drawing tools. The Path Type tools let you click on a path and set the text to flow along the perimeter of the path. When type is placed on the path, the path itself loses its Stroke and Fill colors and is nonprinting. It simply becomes a guide for the type to follow. To reposition the beginning of the text, use the Direct Selection Tool (A) to drag the path type I-beam, which looks like a vertical line. Formatting type can be done either by using the Type menu, the Type Control panel, or by selecting the Character panel from the Window menu (Window > Type > Character).

DESIGN TIP

To create a playful look for the logo, choices for wide serif fonts can include bold and italic styles. On a Mac, look at these fonts: Gadget, Baskerville, Bookman Old Style, Goudy Heavyface, Minion Pro, and Minion Black. For Windows, try Goudy Stout or Minion Pro, also in bold style. These can be used as informal fonts.

TOOLKIT TIP The Arc Tool is another Illustrator tool that can be used for specific curved paths. Once the path is created with the Arc Tool, the Direct Selection Tool (A) can be used for selecting and editing the path by adjusting the direction lines. The Arc Tool can be found under the Line Segment Tool (\).

TOOLKIT TIP When making any adjustments to a path of selected type, select only the I-beam and drag carefully with either the Direct Selection Tool (A) or Selection Tool (V). You will know that you are clicking on the right place when a small *T* appears next to your cursor.

First you will create a new layer for text; then using the Type Tool (T), you will type the introduction line *Come Play!* Then you will type the Captain Jack's Sailing title using the Path Type Tool (T) along a circular path created by the Ellipse Tool (L).

1. In your *Sailing Circle.ai* file, select the *Waves* layer in the Layers panel, and click the Create New Layer icon at the bottom of the panel.

2. Rename the new layer *Text*. This will be your text layer to add and edit type.

3. Select the normal Type Tool (T) and then select a deep red Fill with a Stroke of None for the slogan line.

4. Select Bookman Old Style Bold Italic (Mac), shown in Figure 9-20, or choose a wide type font like Goudy Heavyface Italic, Minion Standard Black, or Goudy Stout Italic (Windows). Select a 24-pt size from the Type menu, Control panel, or the Character panel (Window > Type > Character). Remember the Character and Control panels contain most of the formatting commands you may need for your text.

▷ FIGURE 9-20

Using Type tools to create type on paths and to format selected type using the Character panel or Control panel.

Type on a Path Tool

Select I-beam with Direct Selection Tool, drag outside of circle

Company Title

5. Now you are going to create two separate lines of text that can be adjusted separately with the Selection Tool (V). First, click on the artboard and type "Come." Select the Type Tool (T) again, click on the artboard, and type "Play!" Position as shown in Figure 9-20 with the Selection Tool (V). Deselect the text.

6. To make the Captain Jack's Sailing name, select the Ellipse Tool (L). Make sure you choose a Fill of None and a Stroke of None, and then click once on the artboard to bring up the dialog box.

7. In the dialog box, enter a Width and Height of 6 inches (or 440 pt) for the circular path.

8. Position the circle, using the Selection Tool (V) and arrow keys, so that the boat graphic fits inside, as shown in Figure 9-20.

9. Select the Type on a Path Tool, and click on the left side of the circle. Try the same font you chose in the intro line, but if the characters are touching, try adjusting the tracking by 25 or 50 on the Character panel.

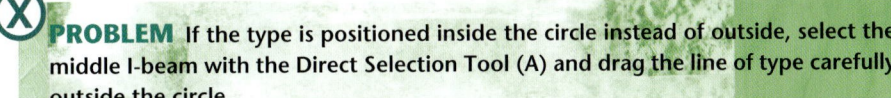

ⓧ PROBLEM If the type is positioned inside the circle instead of outside, select the middle I-beam with the Direct Selection Tool (A) and drag the line of type carefully outside the circle.

10. Using the Character panel, Type menu, or Control panel, set the point size to 36. You may need to adjust the tracking to a 25 or 50 setting to add space between characters, depending on the font you use. Select a deep blue fill from the Swatches panel (C=100, M=100, Y=25, K=25) and a Stroke color of None and type "Captain Jack's Sailing" along the path.

11. Zoom back out, and with the Direct Selection Tool, select the vertical I-beam that appears on the type path. Drag along the curve to balance the type line. This may take a few tries.

12. Save the file again as *Sailing Circle.ai* in the *Chapter 9* folder.

USING THE PATHFINDER PANEL TO CREATE A CIRCULAR LOGO

The Pathfinder panel allows the designer to combine, exclude, or crop various overlapping shapes to create another composite shape. It is a powerful tool for the designer who needs to create artwork other than a four-sided document. Here, you can use the Pathfinder panel to create a circular cutout of the artwork to balance out the circular type path.

In this exercise, you will create another circular selection, select the artwork, and crop into a circular logo.

1. With the type and graphic positioned as needed, make sure all layers are unlocked, including sublayers, and create another new layer above the Text layer and name it as *Circle*.

DESIGN TIP

Italicized type is primarily used for emphasis, and is best used in small amounts.

DESIGN TIP

When designing logos with type and graphics, having components near or overlapping each other helps to form a connection within the composition.

2. First, the front wave needs to be extended, as this will be a circular logo. With the Direct Selection Tool (A), click on the bottom corner anchor points of the front wave, and press the down arrow key 20 times to add more depth to the shape of the front wave.

3. Select the Ellipse Tool (L), and create a circle 7 inches in diameter, with a Stroke of 1-pt black to view your position and a Fill of None, and then click on the graphic.

▷ FIGURE 9-21

Using the Pathfinder panel to crop the logo into a circular piece of artwork.

4. Use the Selection Tool (V) or the arrow keys to carefully position the circle so that it is balanced as best as possible between the title and the bottom line of the first wave (Figure 9-21).

Extend the front wave graphic and create a 7-inch circle for cropping

Completed circular logo

5. Make sure the Pathfinder panel is displayed (Window > Pathfinder) and the cutting circle is still selected. Very carefully, with the Direct Selection Tool (A), drag over only the pieces of the boat graphic and all the waves. Hold the Shift key if needed to click on all graphic layers.

6. Select the Crop button on the Pathfinder panel to create a circular logo. If it doesn't work, make sure that the outside 7-inch diameter circle and the graphic elements are selected, and try again. It may take a few tries.

7. When you have the crop completed, change the stroke color to None, and save the file as, *Sailing Circle.ai* in your *Chapter 9* folder.

PROBLEM If the crop doesn't occur using Pathfinder, make sure you have created a separate layer as outlined in Step 1. Then select the circle that provides the cutout. With the Direct Selection Tool (A) carefully select all the graphics, and then select Crop in the Pathfinder panel.

SAVING IN EPS FORMAT

Saving an illustration in EPS format allows the designer to use the graphic universally in most graphic applications. This format works well with scalable vector graphics that are going to press, and along with other options, it can provide thumbnail previews and permanently embeds the fonts, so the viewer does not need the actual fonts. In Illustrator, a designer can save to a previous version, although some editing features may not be backwards compatible. Warnings will display if you save to an earlier version, especially when type is involved. For the purposes of this exercise, save to your current version of Illustrator.

 TOOLKIT TIP It is always a good habit, when space allows, to keep a backup copy of a file in its native format, such as Illustrator's .ai format, before saving in other formats.

To save the file in EPS format, here is all you have to do.

1. Select File > Save As > Illustrator EPS.

2. Save the file in your *Chapter 9* folder as *Sailing Circle.eps* in the version of Illustrator you are using.

3. Use the default options settings, as shown in Figure 9-22. Include thumbnails and document fonts to embed any information to a CMYK PostScript printer.

4. You should have three files created at the end of this project; *Sailing.ai* as the backup file with square logo, *Sailing Circle.ai* as the logo cut out as a circle, and *Sailing Circle.eps* for sending to a commercial printer.

5. Print the file with the default settings. You now have a logo for future use.

▷ FIGURE 9-22

EPS format options settings.

ADVANCED USERS: Creating Professional Business Cards Using Logo Just Created

Here is where you will put the logo to good use. As long as the completed drawing is saved in either Illustrator's default format (AI) or the universal Illustrator EPS format (EPS), it can be scaled to any size needed by the client. To create a logo for a business card, you only need to Place the image in your document, and then scale down the image using the Scale command in the Object menu (Object > Transform > Scale). Other sizes can be used for other promotional materials. When a graphic that contains text is scaled down considerably, as for a business card, text lines may need to be adjusted to help maintain emphasis on the graphic logo. To properly align these cards with text lines and the logo, drag horizontal and vertical guidelines from the rulers. Using guidelines promotes consistency in the layout of the design. Remember, they are nonprinting. Once you position the lines of type and the graphic, you can modify them to balance out the card. We will show you some variations of the same theme.

TOOLKIT TIP Besides using the Transform command to scale objects, you can also double-click the Scale Tool (S) in the Tools panel to bring up the same dialog box. The Scale Tool (S) scales from a center default reference point of the selected object. Option/ALT clicking with the Scale Tool (S) lets you position the reference point for scaling.

Here you will resize the logo, create layout guidelines for text placement, and create the initial business card.

1. Create a new CMYK color document 8.5 × 11 inches, no bleeds, portrait orientation, named *Sailing Cards.* Set the view to 100%.

2. Display the rulers for making guides (View > Rulers > Show Rulers).

3. Place the *Sailing Circle.ai* file into the new document (File > Place). Leave the Template and Linked boxed unchecked. If a Place PDF display box appears, select Art or Media, and then select OK. Note: If you were unable to create the circle logo, use the square *Sailing.ai* file instead.

4. With the graphic and text selected, choose Object > Transform > Scale.

5. Make sure the Scale Stroke and Effects option is checked to adjust line weights as the graphic is resized to maintain continuity throughout (Figure 9-23).

6. Enter 20% in the Uniform box to scale the graphic proportionately. Select OK and then deselect the graphic.

7. Select the "Come Play" type lines with the Type Tool (T), change the size to 6 pt, and move if needed. You don't need to change the title, but you will notice that selecting with the Type on a Path Tool you would have to select each individual letter to change.

8. To help with positioning the cards and the left margin for text, click inside the vertical ruler and drag vertical guides to the ¾-inch and 1-inch marks using the horizontal ruler to mark the positioning of the card edge and start of type lines.

▷ FIGURE 9-23

Scaling the logo to size.

9. To position cards and lines of text, zoom in to 200%, click in the horizontal ruler, and drag horizontal guides to quarter inch intervals at ½, ¾, 1, 1¼, 1½, 1¾, 2, 2¼, 2½, 2¾, and 3-inch vertical marks (Figure 9-24).

10. Lock the guides once you have them all laid out (View > Guides > Lock Guides).

▷ FIGURE 9-24

Using guides to align the logo, card, and text.

Click and drag from horizontal ruler along vertical ruler to create horizontal guidelines

TOOLKIT TIP To move guides or edit guides, use the Direct Selection Tool (A) and drag. Many business cards can be made a little smaller in height and width with dimensions of 2.25 inches by 3.25 inches. You can also create cards with these dimensions if you prefer.

11. Select the Rectangle Tool (M) with a Stroke of 1-pt black and a Fill of None. Click on the document to bring up the dialog box.

12. Enter 3.5 inches Width and 2.5 inches Height for a business card–size rectangle. Select OK.

13. Using the arrow keys or Selection Tool (V), carefully move the box into the upper left corner of the document, as shown in Figure 9-24.

14. Select the resized logo with the Selection Tool (V) and position it in the right corner of the box, with the top aligned near the 1½ inch guide.

15. To make the *Your Name* line, select the Type Tool (T) and choose a deep blue from the Swatches panel that matches the company title color, and 14-pt Arial Bold Italic font from the Character panel, the Type menu, or the Control panel.

16. Type your name on the top line.

17. For all other lines of text, use black 10-pt Arial Regular from the Character panel. Feel free to substitute your own information and make changes. After each line of text, click the Text Tool (T) in the Tools panel, and then start another line. This allows you to select each line separately in case you need to make changes later.

18. Fill in the remaining lines as shown and align them flush left at the 1-inch vertical guide.

19. To view your work without guides, select View > Guides > Hide Guides.

20. Now you have a business card. You can select individual text lines with the Selection Tool (V), or highlight them with the Type Tool (T), and type in new information. You can also move the type around, making adjustments to balance out the card.

21. Feel free to use the card you just created, or look at the other options shown in Figure 9-25. Create, combine ideas, or copy what you feel makes the best card design using the graphic logo, title, and intro lines. Feel free to reposition the graphic logo as well.

22. When you have completed the card you want to use, save your file before the next exercise, in which you will create a sheet of these cards.

DESIGN TIP

A person's name is the most important line on the business card; it should always stand out by either changing the size, style, and/ or color of the font. Some logos display the company name in large letters, while others are subtle—to make the viewer pay attention to the card, as has been done in this project. Another option would be to remove the business name above the graphic and place it underneath as shown in Figure 9-25.

▷ FIGURE 9-25

Other options to create business cards on the same principal logo design.

Option B: Remove title and place to the left side at top for balance

Option C: Remove title, open up full scale and create an 8-inch circle, for 48-pt text line for title underneath graphic

TOOLKIT TIP When changing logo graphics for specific or alternative media needs, making adjustments in placement of text and graphics can be a challenge. Figure 9-25 shows the other alternative business cards. To remove the title (Option B) that will be used as a larger type line on the card, you will need to select each letter in the title with the Direct Selection Tool (A) and delete. For the other card (Option C), you will need to reopen the original full-scale file, create an 8-inch circle, and use the Type on a Path Tool to create the title on the bottom. Use the Direction Selection Tool (A) to adjust the I-beam from the inside. This graphic may be the more challenging of the alternatives. In creating the business card sheet, I have chosen to use Option B.

TOOLKIT TIP Part of designing is coming up with possible alternatives, because creating a logo or other graphic image may not work appropriately with all types of media. In the case of the business card, the title above the graphic may not seem to balance with the rest of the card, or the font used may be too distracting. Creating alternatives in addition to what the client has asked for, as shown in Figure 9-25, gives them a chance to become more involved in the process. We are choosing to remove the title from the graphic and place it on the initial title line on the card. Feel free to modify your card now before creating a sheet of cards.

OPTIONAL: CREATING AN ACTION FOR MULTIPLE BUSINESS CARDS

As was done in the Chapter 6 Digital Toolkit Extra section, you can create actions of repetitive tasks. Here you will use the Transform command to take a business card you created and have the card copied to equidistant locations to generate eight business cards on a normal sheet ready for printing. By creating an action, you can perform the same complex task with any future business card with ease. After you complete an action, you can uncheck those parts of the actions that you don't want to include, and keep checked those actions to perform. You can also add action components for multitasking, and actions stay with the application so you can use them on future projects.

In this optional exercise, you will set up the action to perform the following exercise in creating eight business cards on a sheet.

1. Make sure your business card is placed on the sheet along the guidelines created, and then make sure the Actions panel is displayed (Window > Actions).

2. Select Create New Action at the bottom of the panel, and name the new Action *Business Cards*. Click Record (Figure 9-26). It will display on the Actions panel and a red record button, Begin Recording, will display showing actions are being recorded.

3. Follow the steps in the next exercise carefully. If you run into a problem, or whenever you want to stop recording, click on the Stop Playing/Recording square icon to the left of the recording button on the Actions panel.

Create New Action

Begin Recording

Play

THE TRANSFORM COMMAND

To make multiple copies of the business card to fit on a letter-sized page, use the **Transform command** in the Object menu to accurately position copies vertically and horizontally.

Now you will use the Transform command to copy and paste the card to make eight copies.

1. With the Selection Tool (V), select the rectangle that defines the size of the business card, and change the stroke to a dashed black Stroke by simply clicking the Dashed Line box in the Stroke panel. This will create a line that can be used for trimming purposes. To move all the elements in the business card, choose the Selection Tool (V) again, and drag diagonally over all the text and objects, including the now-invisible rectangle. Make sure the guides are still hidden, or locked.

2. Group them together (Object > Group). Make sure the card stays selected.

3. Select Object > Transform > Move to get the dialog box. Since the height of the card is 2.5 inches, the card will be copied vertically downward 2.5 inches.

4. Since you are going to copy downward vertically, type "2.5 inches" in the Vertical field of the dialog box. Keep the other settings as shown in Figure 9-27. Click inside Distance and both of the other settings will automatically appear.

5. Click Copy (NOT OK) to place a copy below the original. A duplicate will be made.

6. While the new card is still selected, choose Object > Transform > Transform Again.

7. If you have set up to create this process as an action you can see the action components being created in the Actions panel.

8. To copy the fourth card, select Object > Transform > Transform Again with the same settings once more to make four cards on the left side.

9. To make four cards on the right, choose Select > All to select all four cards on the left side.

▷ FIGURE 9-27

Use the Transform command to copy the card vertically and horizontally.

Vertical Copy Transform Settings

Horizontal Copy Transform Settings

10. Select Object > Transform > Move to open the dialog box. Since the width of the cards is 3.5 inches, the cards will be copied to the right across 3.5 inches. Enter 3.5 inches in the Horizontal dialog box, and 0 inches in the Vertical dialog box, and hit the Tab key for the rest to appear.

▷ FIGURE 9-28

Completed business card and sheet of cards.

11. Click Copy (NOT OK) to duplicate the cards to the right.

12. You now have eight aligned business cards (Figure 9-28).

First business card design created   Chosen design for final printing

13. Optional Action: If you had chosen to create an action of this procedure, click on the square icon reading Stop Playing/Recording to stop recording and complete the action.

14. Select the Name line with the Selection or Direct Selection Tool (A), and then select the Type Tool (T) to highlight and type in any new information. That's it!

15. Save the file in the Illustrator EPS format as *Sailing Cards.eps* using the default settings and the version of Illustrator you will be using most often. Leave it open for the next exercise.

16. Optional Action: If you had created the action for creating multiple business cards on a sheet, first set up margin guides on a new document as in this tutorial, and copy/paste one of your business cards along the guides. To play the action, highlight the card with the Selection Tool (V), click on the Business Cards action on the Actions panel, and select the Play button. Your action should copy the cards duplicating the exercise you just created beforehand (Figure 9-29). If it worked, congratulations! Save the file as *Action Cards.eps* in your *Chapter 9* folder.

▷ FIGURE 9-29

Action completed to create multiple business cards on a sheet.

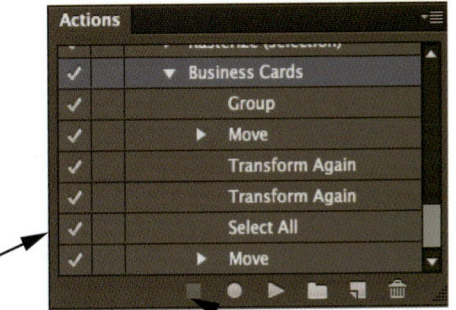

Leave each action checked to perform action component

Stop Playing/Recording

SEPARATIONS PREVIEW PANEL

You can preview CMYK color separations and overprinting using the new Separations Preview panel. Previewing separations on your monitor lets you preview spot color objects in your document, and check for rich blacks or process black (K) ink mixed with color inks for increased opacity and richer color. The panel also checks for overprinting when the color CMYK plates are laid on top of one another to observe blending and transparency effects for the particular output device. To observe the sailboat business cards you just created, select the Separations Preview panel (Window > Separations Preview) and then select the Overprint Preview icon to observe CMYK plate effects. The CMYK plates display as separate layers on the panel. To hide a separation ink on screen, click the eye icon to the left of the separation name, and then click again to view the separation. To view all process plates at once, click the CMYK icon. To return to normal view, deselect Overprint Preview. Previewing separations on your monitor can help you detect problems without the

DESIGN TIP

Any files that are to be used for commercial printing must be saved as either EPS, PDF, or TIF files and must be set up in CMYK color mode. There are functions in the Print dialog box that can be set for commercial printing as well.

expense of printing separations; it does not let you preview trapping, emulsion options, printer's marks, and halftone screens and resolution. Previewing CMYK inks to be visible or hidden on screen in the Separations Preview panel does not affect the actual separations process—it only affects how they appear on your screen during the preview. This will be covered more in depth in the Unit 3 Review.

CREATING A PROOF SHEET FOR PRESS

In Illustrator, there is a very detailed print dialog box, specifically designed to generate any information a service provider in a commercial press environment might need. Since a sheet of business cards has been created, the next step for a designer would be to generate a proof for client approval, which can also be used as a guide for the service provider (Figure 9-28). This proof sheet will be larger than the document to show the necessary printer's marks including:

- The position of the **registration marks**, which will allow for precise placement of individual color plates.

- **Trim marks** to show where the document will be trimmed.

- **Color bars** to show the accuracy of colors to be used.

- Other page information to help with the printing process.

- **Bleeds**, which extend solid color boxes of graphics beyond the trim edge of a document to avoid any paper color lines (not needed for this project).

Here you will create a basic proof sheet with printer's marks included in the document.

1. Place an 11 × 17 inch sheet of paper in your printer; you will need the larger size to display the printer's marks.

2. With the *Sailing Cards.eps* file open, select File > Print to display the Print dialog box.

3. Select the Marks and Bleed option; then select the Page Setup button. If you get a warning about using the Adobe Print dialog box, click continue.

4. Set the Paper Size to tabloid (11 × 17 inches). Select the color printer you want to print to. Click OK to close the Page Setup window.

5. Click on the Printer's Marks box to select all the basic information for the proof sheet. Leave the other settings at their defaults (Figure 9-30).

6. Select Print to print the proof sheet. That's all there is to it!

▷ FIGURE 9-30

Creating a proof sheet to include printer's marks.

DIGITAL TOOLKIT EXTRA: Creating a Clock Face

▷ FIGURE 9-31

Creating a scalable
clock face using
guides, drawing
tools, and the
Gradient Tool
and Gradient
panel.

Here is a simple method of using guidelines and shape tools to create the numbers on a scalable clock face (Figure 9-31). The hands are created using the Pen and Ellipse tools. The **Pathfinder panel** will be used to create custom shapes. You will also learn to work with gradients, which transition one color to another—a necessary ingredient in any digital designer's toolkit.

▷ FIGURE 9-31

Creating a scalable clock face using guides, drawing tools, and the Gradient Tool and Gradient panel.

CREATING THE CLOCK HANDS WITH PEN AND ELLIPSE TOOLS

The hands of the clock are made by making straight lines for the minute hand and by combining straight lines and Bézier curves with the Pen Tool (P) for the hour hand. The circular point that connects the two hands together is made with the Ellipse Tool (L).

Here is how to create the hands using the Pen and Ellipse tools.

1. First you will create a working layer for drawing above the template layer. In Illustrator, open the file *Hands Template.tif* in your *Chapter 9* folder for the dimmed template of the clock hands that you will trace with the drawing tools. In the Layers panel, create a duplicate layer, which will be used to draw on. Select the original Hands template layer and select Template from the panel menu to create a template layer that can be locked in place. Select the new layer above and name it *Hands*. Now you are ready to draw.

2. Select the Ellipse Tool (L) and click on the document to enter a 0.6-inch Width and Height with a black Stroke and Fill.

3. Place the selected circle on the minute hand and Option/ALT copy the second circle onto the hour hand.

4. For the minute hand, click straight lines with the Pen Tool (P), and then select and group the paths with the circle (Object > Group).

5. For the hour hand, follow the guides in Figure 9-32 to create the straight lines and Bézier curves.

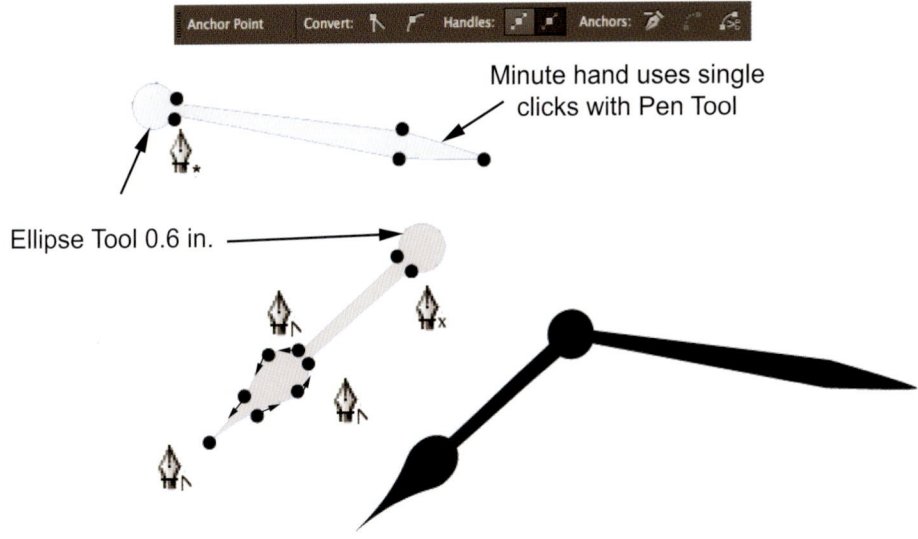

Minute hand uses single clicks with Pen Tool

Ellipse Tool 0.6 in.

6. Adjust the curves with the Direct Selection and Smooth tools to make them symmetrical.

7. Using the Selection Tool (V) and arrow keys, move both hands so the ellipses are overlapping, and then group them together (Object > Group).

8. Save the file as *Hands.eps* in the *Chapter 9* folder, using the default settings.

9. Minimize the document window, leaving the file ready for the next exercise.

SPACING FOR NUMERALS: USING GUIDELINES AND THE POLYGON TOOL

To create the clock face and set up accurate placement of the clock numerals, you need to use guides. Guides help to place objects in a document with precision. They can be locked, shown, or hidden from view to help you with your document layout. Guides can also be created using shapes to position text or graphic elements and then removed after everything is set. You can create a shape with any number of equidistant sides outlining a particular radius with the **Polygon Tool**.

In this exercise, you will place guidelines to position and type the numerals and add the hands.

1. With the *Hands* file minimized and out of the way, create a new CMYK color document, letter Size with Portrait Orientation, and Units in Inches. Name the file *Clock*.

2. Make sure rulers are displayed; if not, select View > Rulers > Show Rulers.

3. Select the Polygon Tool (located with other shape tools) and set a black, 1-pt Stroke with no Fill.

4. Click once on the artboard and enter 12 Sides and a 2.5-inch Radius in the dialog box. This will be the outer shape.

5. With the Selection Tool (V), select the shape to show the bounding box and center the shape inside the document.

6. Drag a vertical guide and a horizontal guide through the center points on each side of the bounding box to mark the center of the shape, as shown in Figure 9-33 (step 1).

▷ FIGURE 9-33

Aligning shapes and guidelines for placing numerals.

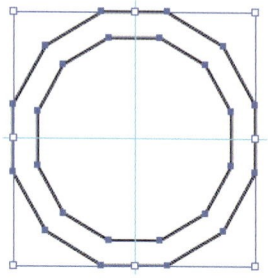

1. Create the two 12-sided shapes with the Polygon Tool

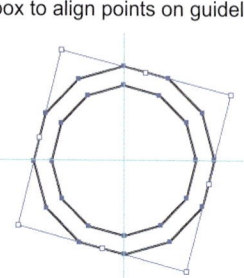

2. Select and rotate bounding box to align points on guidelines

3. Drag guidelines along inner points for placement of numerals

DESIGN TIP

Using the vertical and horizontal guides, the arrow keys on the keyboard, and various shapes as guides such as the Polygon Tool provides the designer the ability to position any element within the artwork with true precision. A keystroke option to turn the polygons into guides here is Command/CTRL 5.

7. To make the inner shape, select the Polygon Tool again, and use a black, 1-pt Stroke with a Fill of None. Enter 12 Sides and a 2-inch Radius this time.

8. Select the new polygon and center it using the guides, as shown in the first drawing of Figure 9-33.

9. Hold down the Shift key and select both shapes with the Selection Tool.

10. Group the polygons together (Object > Group).

11. Use the Selection Tool (V) and move the cursor to just outside one of the corners of the bounding box to display a bent arrow; then click and drag to rotate it until the points of the shape rest on the guidelines, as shown in the second drawing of Figure 9-33.

12. Ungroup the two polygon shapes (Object > Ungroup) and deselect them.

13. For placing the numbers, drag horizontal and vertical guidelines along each point in the inner shape, as shown in the third drawing of Figure 9-33.

TOOLKIT TIP Here is an advanced way to use shapes as guides. Designers can create guides from shapes and lines, not just from the rulers. Another way to create guides for the numbers would be to draw a vertical line, and then use the Rotate Tool to make a copy, rotated to 30 degrees; use Command/CTRL D (redo) a few times to create six lines like spokes (you could use the Align panel to center them to each other if necessary). Select them all and press Command/CTRL 5 to turn them into guides.

14. Create a new layer in the Layers panel and name it *Numbers*. This way, you can adjust the numbers later without affecting any other layers. Lock the bottom layer with the polygons and guides so as not to accidently alter or draw on it.

15. Select the Type Tool (T) and choose 36-pt Arial Black, or some other font, and align it centered. You can use the Paragraphs panel or the Control panel to set the paragraph alignment.

16. On the top guide, where the number 12 should go, type "3" instead, and position the middle of the number accurately on the guidelines, using the Direct Selection Tool (V) and arrow keys. This number works great for the initial setup.

17. Option/ALT copy the number 3 and place copies all around the clock accurately. Use Smart Guides if needed. See Figure 9-34.

18. When all the 3s are positioned, select the Type Tool (T) and type in the proper numbers all around. Select the numbers 10, 11, and 12; reposition them slightly, as shown in Figure 9-34.

▷ FIGURE 9-34

Placing numbers and hands to complete the clock face.

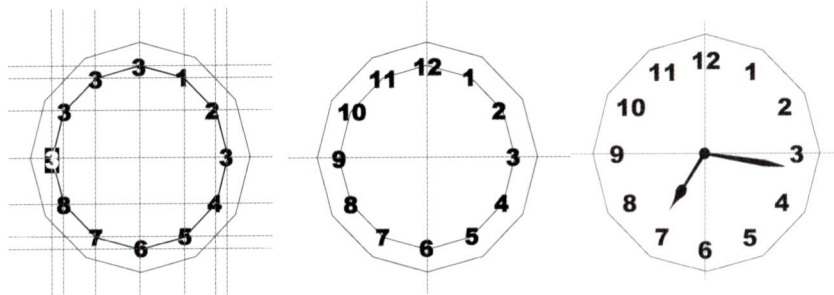

COMPLETING THE CLOCK FACE

To complete the clock face, we will reopen the minimized window of the clock hands created earlier. The hands will be copied and pasted into the clock face document, and then resized proportionately to fit the clock (hold the Shift key while dragging one of the corner resizing handles inward to resize proportionately). Use guides to position the hands exactly as desired.

To complete the clock face, you will position the hands.

1. To set up guides for placing the hands, drag a vertical and horizontal guide from the rulers, intersecting the center of the clock again.

2. Open the *Hands* file by selecting it at the bottom of the Window menu; select and copy (Edit > Copy) the hands, and then close the *Hands* file.

3. Paste (Edit > Paste) the hands artwork onto the *Clock* document.

4. To resize the hands to fit inside the clock face, use the Selection Tool (V) and hold down the Shift key. Click near a corner-resizing handle, and drag inward.

5. Use the Selection Tool (V) and arrow keys to move the hands into position.

6. Unlock the original layer and delete both polygon radius shapes; you will not need them anymore.

DESIGN TIP

Whenever a designer needs to resize a graphic from its original size in perfect proportion, hold down the Shift key while clicking and dragging the graphic.

7. Select all the numbers and clock hands and group them so any editing can be done to all the numbers at once (Object > Group). Deselect everything.

8. Save the file as *Clock.eps* in your *Chapter 9* folder.

CUSTOM SHAPES USING THE PATHFINDER PANEL

The Pathfinder panel allows the designer to combine various shapes by adding, subtracting, excluding, or intersecting overlapping shapes to create a composite shape. Once the shape is created, it can be filled with gradients or solid colors.

Now that you have created the clock face, let us create the outer clock body using the Pathfinder panel.

1. Make sure you can access the Layers, Swatches, Color, and Pathfinder panels.

2. With the *Clock* file open, create a new layer in the Layers panel called *Outershape*.

3. Select the Ellipse Tool (L), set with a 1-pt black Stroke and a Fill of None. Click on the artboard and enter a 6-inch circle for the outer dimension.

4. Use the Selection Tool (V) to select the center point of the circle (not the bounding box) and position so that it is centered where the guides meet. The cursor will display as an arrowhead.

⊗ PROBLEM If the clock face is covered, the Fill is not set to None.

5. Select the Ellipse Tool (L) again, with a black Stroke of 1 pt and a white Fill to view what happens next.

6. Click on the artboard and enter a 5-inch circle. Position it so that it is centered inside the larger circle. If you Option/ALT click in the center, the circle will be automatically centered.

7. Use the Selection Tool (V) to select both circles while holding down the Shift key.

8. Open the Pathfinder panel and, with both circles selected, select the Exclude Overlapping Shape Areas option (first row, fourth icon from the left) to remove the inner clock face area (Figure 9-35).

9. Choose View > Guides > Clear Guides to remove the guides. If the guides do not clear, unlock the layer and then clear the guides.

▷ FIGURE 9-35

Using the Pathfinder panel to create the outer portion of the clock.

Selecting "Exclude"

USING THE GRADIENT PANEL AND TOOL

Gradients provide one of the more artistic tools in a designer's digital toolkit. A **gradient** is a transition or blend of one color into another. There are two types of gradients: *linear* and *radial.* **Linear gradients** are applied in a straight line at a given angle, while **radial gradients** spread out from an inner position to the outer edges of an object. Gradients can be created using the Gradient Tool (G) and then selecting a linear or radial gradient type from the Gradient panel. The **Gradient panel** is the control center for creating the gradients. Gradients can be faded into transparency. Colors can be selected from the Swatches or Color panels and dragged into the gradient bar to create color gradient sliders, which can be adjusted to blend in special colors. You can choose from a few preselected gradients in the Swatches panel and modify them. You can even select a gradient color mode to work in from the Tools panel.

TOOLKIT TIP You can create gradients at any angle, depending on the direction in which you drag with the Gradient Tool (G).

Adding gradients will provide a sense of depth to the clock.

1. To make sure the Gradient panel is displayed, select Window > Gradient, double-click on the Gradient Tool (G) in the Tools panel, or click the gradient box under the Color Picker in the Tools panel. To display all the gradient options, click on the double arrows at the top left of the tab.

2. Make sure the Color and Swatches panels are also open, and then select a deep blue color from the Color panel using the color spectrum bar at the bottom.

3. To add the blue color to the gradient bar, click and drag the blue color from the Fill box of the Tools panel to the right side of the gradient bar on the Gradient panel (you will notice a small square or plus sign displays); then release the mouse. It will appear as a new color gradient slider next to a black gradient slider. The Fill box in the Tools panel will display the new gradient (Figure 9-36).

▷ FIGURE 9-36

Adding color and dimension to the clock with gradient colors from the Gradient panel, and using the Gradient Tool.

White and blue gradient sliders with Linear gradient

Gradient Tool

White, yellow, and black gradient sliders with Radial gradient

4. Select the Linear Gradient type in the Gradient panel.

5. Click and drag the black color gradient slider down and off the bar of the Gradient panel. This will create a linear gradient with white on the left side and blue on the right. If there is a black gradient slider in addition to the white and blue sliders, drag it downward to remove it.

6. To apply the gradient, select the circles, and click on the gradient in the Gradient panel. This will create a light highlight on the left side of the clock, fading to the blue on the right. You can adjust the direction of the gradient by selecting the circles, selecting the Gradient Tool (G), and dragging across a new direction to apply the new gradient. Deselect the object when you have finished with the gradient. You will also find an adjustment bar across the shape with the same color sliders, which you can adjust to taste.

7. For the inner clock face area, select the Ellipse Tool (L) and create a 5-inch circle, 1-pt black Stroke with a Fill of None, and drag it on top of the other 5-inch circle. Use the arrow keys to position it precisely.

8. Drag the *Outershape* layer below the *Numbers* layer to position it behind the numbers (you can rearrange individual objects using Object > Arrange).

9. Select the black swatch from the Swatches panel and drag it to the right side of the gradient bar. The left side should have a white color slider. If no colors display, select the Default CMYK library from the Colors panel submenu.

10. Select a yellow color from the Swatches panel, and it drag onto the right side of the gradient bar next to the black slider color to give a slight shadow.

▷ FIGURE 9-37

Creating gradients that can be saved in the Swatches panel. Dragging color from the Swatches panel to create color stops for gradients.

11. Select Radial gradient for the gradient Type, and click on the center of the clock to make a central radius (Figure 9-37).

12. Use the Selection Tool (V) to drag a diagonal across the whole clock face to select it, and then choose Object > Group to group all elements together.

13. Save the completed file as *Clock2.eps*.

14. This can serve as a template for any clock face with different fonts, outer shapes, and colors. Experiment with different gradient settings and combining different shapes with the Pathfinder panel. Have fun!

Drag to add color
gradient slider

Gradient Color
Mode   Swatch Libraries menu

▲Show Swatch
Kinds menu

Color gradient
sliders

Double-click on gradient slider
to choose colors from display

SAVING AND OPENING TEMPLATES

Illustrator has the ability to save documents as templates and to open these templates to use as new documents (File > Save As Template). This function lets you develop documents with common settings and design elements, which can include symbols, imported artwork, brushes, libraries, and document window settings, without having to start from scratch each time. Illustrator templates are saved with an Adobe Illustrator Template **AIT extension.** To create a new document using a template, use the New from Template command (File > New from Template). Illustrator creates a new document with the template settings, while leaving the original template file in its original location. Illustrator includes many preset templates in a variety of layouts and formats that a designer can select from in the Templates folder.

To save a template copy of the clock face, here is all you have to do (Figure 9-38).

Save as Template in *Chapter 9* folder

Save as Template in Illustrator's *Templates* folder with preset templates.

▷ FIGURE 9-38

Saving the clock as a template.

1. Make sure all panels, the document window, and the desired artboard size are set up for the workspace you want to save as a template.

2. Select File > Save As Template to save the file as *Clock Template.ait* in your *Chapter 9* folder. The template is now saved and can be used as a guide for future documents.

3. Feel free to look at the variety of preset templates by selecting File > New from Template and locate the *Templates* folder (Adobe > Illustrator > Cool Extras > en_US (your own country and language) > Templates). These templates can be opened and edited to suit a designer's needs.

CHAPTER SUMMARY

Some of the most important universal tools a designer can learn to master are the Pen tools. By using the Pen Tool in combination with other drawing tools, any curve or line can be changed into a path or group of paths to create complex shapes. The Direct Selection Tool (A) plays an important role in shaping paths created with the Pen tools by adjusting path segments, anchor points, and direction lines. Illustrator documents, when saved in the universal EPS format, can be used in most graphic applications and can provide previews. Type tools can place text along any given path or shape. Guides are nonprinting and provide consistency and accuracy in the layout of any image. The Gradient Tool (G) and Gradient panel are used to create a transition or blend of colors within a shape. Documents can be saved as templates to be used for future artwork. Do not forget to check out the *Extras & Goodies* folder on *www.CenageBrain.com* for more projects and ideas.

REVIEW QUESTIONS

1. Explain when to use the Pen Tool (P) and when to use the Pencil Tool (N).
2. Explain the purpose of the Average and Join commands in the Object menu.
3. What is the difference between using the Direct Selection Tool (A) and the Lasso Tool (Q)?
4. Describe the "feedback" for the four cursors displayed by the Pen Tool (P).
5. Explain how to adjust the position of type placed on a given path.
6. What is the purpose of saving Illustrator documents as EPS files?
7. Explain the use of the Transparency, Transform, and Pathfinder panels.
8. Explain how to create gradients using the Gradient Tool (G) and the Gradient panel.

Original sketch

Completed standard logo

Modified logo

CHAPTER 9
Logo created from sketch using the
Pen Tool and type paths in Illustrator.

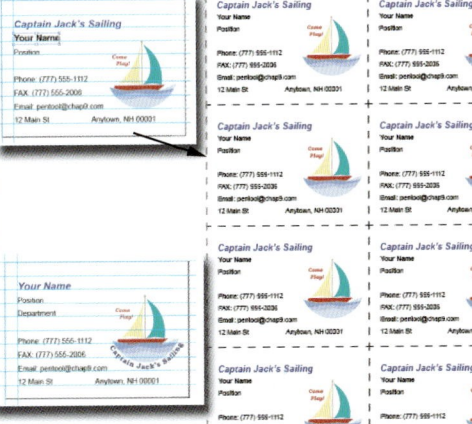

CHAPTER 9 ADVANCED
Creating business cards with graphic
logo and type; with alternative options.
Using the Transform command to create
aligned sheet of business cards.

Chosen design for final printing

CHAPTER 9 EXTRA
Clock face created in Illustrator
using guidelines, and the Gradient
Tool and Gradient panel.

▷ FIGURE 9-39

Integrating Photoshop and Illustrator Files for Web Use

CHAPTER OBJECTIVES: To understand how to integrate Photoshop and Illustrator files and to learn what their possibilities and limitations are, in this chapter you will:

▷ Understand the difference between linking and embedding images.

▷ Work with gradients within both applications.

▷ Place, paste, and export graphic images that have varying opacity and transparency.

▷ Set and optimize composite images for use on the web.

▷ Save in various graphic file formats for specific purposes.

▷ Create Smart Objects for nondestructive editing.

▷ ADVANCED USERS: Save files in PDF and EPS formats.

▷ DIGITAL TOOLKIT EXTRA: Use Image Trace and Live Paint to convert bitmap images into scalable vector artwork.

Integrating Illustrator and Photoshop gives a designer the flexibility to combine bitmap artwork and line art into composite images for a variety of effects. Bringing Photoshop's images into Illustrator allows the designer or photographer to trace and create compound paths and apply stroke and fill effects that transform these images into scalable line art. The designer can also bring Illustrator's vector-based line art into Photoshop to apply a variety of special Layer Style effects. In this chapter, you will set up composite web headers using both applications and become familiar with the more common uses and considerations of each. This chapter is a review of some of the techniques and functions in each application as well.

COMBINING ILLUSTRATOR AND PHOTOSHOP GRAPHICS

Before combining graphics from these applications, it is important to decide what factors will affect the final product. The designer needs to know what media the final design will be used for. The image's final size (dimension), resolution, and color depth should be determined ahead of time, as this may affect the size of the file. Back-up copies should always be made. The graphic format or extension in which the file is saved determines the file size, how it can be used, what components can be edited, and how it will record details for use in various media. Careful planning creates a much easier work flow along the way.

TOOLKIT TIP When designing web pages, there are differences between creating web headers, banners, and logos. **Logos** are the graphic that is used to identify a company or website. **Web banners** are usually considered in the development of marketing advertisements that may display vertically or horizontally on a web page, or may be used for strictly informative uses. **Leaderboards** are a popular type of banner advertisement usually placed between headers and the page content, originally used in sports pages as a sign board. **Web headers** today are the images that are usually placed on top of the website, displayed horizontally, and include a logo and tagline among other elements. The color of the website header is also used to set up the look and feel of the website. Although the terms for banners and headers are used interchangeably, we will refer to your projects as headers in this chapter.

VECTOR IMAGES VERSUS BITMAP IMAGES

Illustrator creates vector graphics that contain sharp, crisp lines that define shapes or objects. A designer can create artwork that uses a limited number of colors in Illustrator, so the file size remains small. Illustrator is used for illustrations, logos, and type that can be scaled to any size based on mathematical calculations. In general, use Illustrator if you need to create scalable graphics or when working with type or outlines that need clean, crisp lines. Photoshop creates pixel-based bitmap images and have a high color bit depth (millions of colors) to display subtle gradations of color. This typically generates larger file sizes. These images, usually photographs or paintings, are called **continuous-tone images**. They should not be enlarged without adding pixels between existing pixels through a process called *interpolation.* With interpolation, the images start to deteriorate in quality and may appear jagged. Use Photoshop for images that require a large color depth, such as photographs, and for editing pixels and creating special effects, such as drop shadows, beveling, and embossing (Figure 10-1).

▷ FIGURE 10-1

Vector images are scalable to any size for illustrative work, whereas bitmap images are nonscalable and cannot be enlarged but are better for continuous-tone images, like photos.

Vector image enlarged 300% of original size

Converted bitmap image enlarged to 250% of original size

SETTING UP FILES FOR THE WEB

When creating files to be used for the web, the measurement settings should be in pixels, the color mode in RGB color, and the orientation is usually landscape mode. Using a measurement of pixels instead of inches makes it easier to lay out graphics for web documents. This can be set ahead of time in the Preferences area (Illustrator/Photoshop > Preferences for Mac; for Windows, use Edit > Preferences). Determining the size of the web page itself will also help to create the final composite graphics, such as the web banner. Computer screen resolutions in measurements of 800 × 600, 1024 × 768, and 1600 × 1200 px (the first number represents width) are the most standard settings. Screen displays have changed with the introduction of wide screen displays. Screen resolution still always displays at 72 px per inch, so if you increase your screen resolution, you will notice the icons and images

DESIGN TIP

Although scrolling vertically is acceptable, a user should not have to scroll horizontally through a well-designed web page.

all get smaller. The more pixels being displayed, the smaller images become to fit 72 ppi. Web pages can be created to grow and shrink to a user's screen size by setting the tables (created with a web page application like Dreamweaver) within the page to shrink and expand based on percentages, depending on the monitor screen being used, in your web application software. Graphics that extend across the screen horizontally will need some marginal blank space on both sides, usually about 5% of the screen size, so as not to cut off the graphic. The table below displays the maximum width allowed for horizontal graphics for various computer screen resolutions.

COMPUTER RESOLUTION	MAXIMUM HORIZONTAL WIDTH
800 x 600 pixels	760 pixels
1024 x 768 pixels	980 pixels
1600 x 1200 pixels	1520 pixels

▷ FIGURE 10-2

Selecting Web Safe RGB (Illustrator) or Web Color Sliders (Photoshop) in the Color panel menu ensures web-safe colors. If a cube displays indicating color is not web safe, simply click it to find the nearest web color.

WEB COLORS

Files to be used on the web are usually set up in landscape orientation and in RGB color to display accurate colors on the web. Although not as necessary today with monitors capable of displaying millions of colors, web-safe colors are sometimes used in HTML CSS as a hexadecimal notation for consistency of colors between all monitors, or for a specified color. To make sure all colors are web safe if necessary, set the initial document to RGB color mode; then in the Color panel menu, select Web Color Slider in Photoshop or Web Safe RGB in Illustrator (Figure 10-2).

Selecting Web Safe Colors (Illustrator)

Cube indicates incorrect color display for the web

Click on the cube to find the nearest color

Selecting Web Safe colors (Photoshop)

Cube in Photoshop shows incorrect web color display

Nearest color found

SAVING GRAPHIC FILE FORMATS

Using Illustrator and Photoshop files saved in their native formats (AI and PSD, respectively) allows them to work nicely together and maintains layers for further editing, but native file formats may not be able to be imported or placed in other applications. Still it is a good habit to save a file in its native format as a backup and for future editing when necessary. Saving Illustrator files in universal formats (SVG, EPS, and PDF) and Photoshop files (EPS, TIF, JPG, GIF, PNG, and PDF) gives these files more flexibility when used with other graphics programs. Although they have larger file sizes, EPS and TIF files work best for desktop publishing, while JPG, GIF, and PNG files are used on the web. For artwork with limited flat colors (no continuous tones or gradients) that may be used for the web or in animation programs, save as either a GIF or SVG file. PDF files are used for electronic communication nowadays between designers and service providers; low-resolution PDFs are sent electronically for review with low-res graphics, and then can be set up for high-resolution printing.

The table below gives an overview of the most common file formats.

FORMAT	ADVANTAGES	CONSIDERATIONS
JPG	Compressed format used in photo images or images that need detail in shading and tones. Universal format read by all graphic applications and browsers. Used for web and proof printing (before going to press).	Data is thrown out each time the image is saved and may gradually deteriorate the quality. Flattens layers in files. Does not support background transparencies. Not recommended for use when documents will be printed commercially.
PNG	PNG files can include detailed transparencies in files without losing detail. Used in photo images.	Cannot be read by older browsers. Larger size files images record detail most accurately. Compressed for the web.
GIF	Used for logos, illustrations, and animation. Compress without losing data. Records with transparency settings. Read by most graphic applications.	GIF files have only 256 colors. Not suitable for continuous-tone images or gradients.
SVG	Used in vector-based graphics for the web and animation. Files can be enlarged on screen without sacrificing sharpness. Embeds fonts for the web. Cannot be read or created in Photoshop.	Limited color depth. Files are not compressed and can be edited in Illustrator.
PDF	Embeds fonts and graphics for electronic distribution and the web. Can be read by most graphic applications or read with the free Adobe Reader. Can sometimes be edited in Illustrator. Compresses files without losing detail. Used for both electronic communication and high-resolution printing.	Adding embedding and preview characteristics may increase file size. Cannot be edited except through application Adobe Acrobat, only viewed by other applications (except Illustrator, where it can still be edited).

continues

continued

FORMAT	ADVANTAGES	CONSIDERATIONS
TIF	Most accurate record of detail in continuous-tone images. Nonscalable. Used primarily for print output.	Largest file size. Not used for the web.
EPS	Can be imported by most graphic applications and still edited in Illustrator. Vector graphics can be still be scalable. Preferred method when combining graphics and fonts. Used extensively for print output.	Large file size. Does not handle transparency in files created in older versions of Illustrator or Photoshop. Not used for the web.

CLIENT ASSIGNMENT: Creating Web Banners

The marketing manager of E-Music Corporation, Christine Santelli, comes to you to design a couple of web headers to choose from to promote their classic rock radio station. After listening to her describe the station and creating a number of sketches and roughs, two possibilities are decided upon. You summarize the conversation to confirm her needs. Both headers will have a black to deep blue gradient background. The first web header, initially created in Illustrator, will have the characters of the station title, with a rock image inside each character. The same header will have a glowing image of a guitar snapshot photo, supplied by Christine, enhanced in Photoshop, placed in the banner and rotated. "Classic Rock!" and "All the Time!" will be typed in two lines along a slanted path to match the angle of the guitar neck. The second web header, created initially in Photoshop, will have the station title and the intro line "We're Talking . . ." added to the graphic using a chiseled layer style effect created in Photoshop. A guitar photo, traced in Illustrator and filled with a black, red, and yellow color gradient with the slogan "Classic Rock" typed inside the guitar, will be brought into Photoshop and a drop shadow effect added. Christine cannot wait to see the banners and leaves very excited (Figure 10-3).

ACTION ITEMS OVERVIEW

- Create a gradient black-to-blue color background for each web header.
- For the first header, create a rock image in Illustrator in the shape of the letters of the station title by creating a clipping mask of the type and the rock photo.
- Create a glow effect on the guitar photo in Photoshop, and save in PNG format so that transparency and effects are retained in Illustrator.

Header 1: Integrating Photoshop images and effects with Illustrator

Header 2: Integrating Illustrator graphics into Photoshop

▷ FIGURE 10-3

Completed web headers.

- Place the image into Illustrator, and then rotate it inside the header for an angled effect.
- Create a path with the Pen Tool (P) along the guitar neck; type the lines "Classic Rock!" and "All the Time!"; reposition them to complement the guitar.
- Save as *Header1* in Illustrator's native format, and then optimize the file for the web.
- For the second header, use the Layer Style effects in Photoshop to create chiseled type of the station title and the intro line for the guitar illustration.
- Use the Pen Tool (P) in Illustrator and trace a closed path for the guitar, filling it with a black, red, and yellow gradient.
- Type the slogan "Classic Rock!" with a yellow fill and black outline, and then warp it inside the guitar graphic to match the guitar shape.
- Export the new guitar image into Photoshop.
- Save in Photoshop's native format; then optimize the second header for the web.
- ADVANCED USERS: Save graphics in EPS and PDF formats for later use.

INTEGRATING PHOTOSHOP IMAGES WITH ILLUSTRATOR

Web headers are the titles across the top of web pages that identify the page and the site; they are also sometimes referred to as banners, although banners are used mainly these days for advertising or marketing purposes. Headers are the eye-catchers that make someone decide whether it is interesting enough to explore the page or site or go to another site. Photographic images or paintings brought into Illustrator are brought in as bitmap images. Before bringing an image from Photoshop into Illustrator, adjust the size and the resolution in Photoshop's Image > Image Size menu. You can then create a template in Illustrator to use as a guide for tracing images and placing type. You will be creating scalable compound paths with Illustrator's drawing tools.

SETTING PREFERENCES AND CUSTOM SIZE IN ILLUSTRATOR

Illustrator takes the guesswork out of what you will need for universal settings for various media. A designer can select preset document profiles for print, web screen (full size), mobile devices like tablets and smart phones, video and film, as well as basic RGB and CMYK profile settings; and you can also create your own custom size profile, which we will do here for your web header. Setting up your document for RGB color and measuring in pixels helps to ensure the accuracy of your electronic artwork.

TOOLKIT TIP If you were to design for an entire web page, you would choose a preset document profile of 1024 × 768 px or 1280 x 800 px for example to accommodate many computer screens. This size header can be integrated into any web page adjusting to the web page size, providing the web designer adjusts to percentages within tables being created for the web page. To measure dimensions for the web, use pixels. Graphics that extend across the screen horizontally will need some blank space on both sides so as not to cut off the graphic; allow about 5% of the screen size. Screen displays are constantly changing with the introduction of wide screen displays and mobile devices.

Here is what you need to do to set up a new document in Illustrator for the web header:

1. Launch Illustrator and select the Illustrator menu in Mac OS X or the Edit menu in Windows.

2. Select Preferences > Units; change the General measurement to Pixels, because we are creating for the web (Figure 10-4). Click OK.

3. Select File > New to bring up the New Document dialog box, or if the Welcome screen displays, select Create New > Web Document.

4. Select Profile: Web, and type in a custom size of 980 px Width by 90 px Height (Figure 10-4). This provides some margins when placed in the client's web page. This will accommodate older and newer computers that will display a web page size of 1024 x 768 px.

5. Select Pixels as the Units from the drop-down menu.

6. Select RGB Color, and then select the Landscape orientation icon. Do not select Align New Objects to Pixel Grid for this assignment.

7. Name the file *Header1*, and then select OK.

8. To make sure the rulers are displayed, choose View > Rulers > Show Rulers. You should also make sure Smart Guides (View > Smart Guides) and Snap to Grid (View > Snap to Grid) are checked to help with quick alignment.

9. Zoom to about 200%, click on the vertical ruler, and drag a vertical guide to about the 36-pt mark for aligning text later.

10. Open the Color panel; then select Web Safe RGB from the panel submenu.

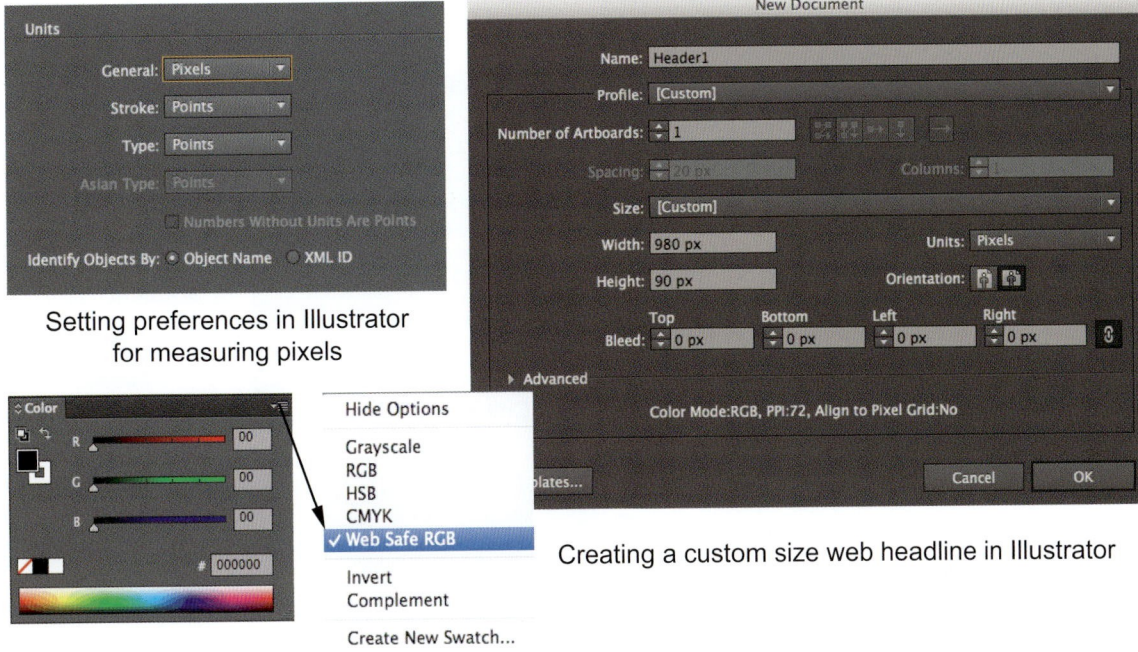

Setting preferences in Illustrator
for measuring pixels

Creating a custom size web headline in Illustrator

▷ FIGURE 10-4

Setting up the file for use on the web with a customized header setting in the New Document dialog box.

TOOLKIT TIP The Align to Pixel Grid feature in Illustrator only works with web-based objects that have straight vertical of horizontal path segments that can be aligned, as was used in the Checkerboard assignment in Chapter 7. You cannot pixel-align objects that contain special effects like drop shadows, or text objects, because such objects do not have real paths, as will be created for this assignment. If an object with the Align to Pixel Grid option is selected, and the pixel-aligned object is moved or transformed using the Transform panel, the object is then realigned to pixel grid according to its new coordinates.

CREATING A GRADIENT WEB BACKGROUND IN ILLUSTRATOR

Gradients provide variety in color shapes and backgrounds. The Gradient panel is the control center for creating gradients. You can select colors from the Swatches or Color panels and drag them to the gradient bar to create color Gradient Sliders that can be adjusted to determine how colors are blended. You can even select a gradient color mode to work in on the Tools panel. In Gradient color mode, you can double-click on any color slider to display the Color panel; select another color, and that color will replace the previous color slider (see Figure 10-5). But first you need to create a shape the size of the header to place the color in.

Web Safe colors

Rectangle

Width: 980 px

Height: 90 px

Cancel   OK

Color Gradient Sliders

Gradient

Gradient
Tool

Web Header
Gradient

▷ FIGURE 10-5

**Creating a gradient
for the Web header
background in
Illustrator.**

DESIGN TIP

If you are using the
standard RGB color
mode, rather than
Web-Safe RGB, in
the Color panel, and
a cube displays, it is
a warning that the
chosen color may
not display accu-
rately on the web.
Click on the cube
to automatically
find the nearest
replacement color.
Selecting Web-Safe
RGB from the Color
panel eliminates this
problem.

Here you will create the web header's background using gradients and the Gradient Tool (G).

1. In Illustrator, select Gradient from the Window menu (Window > Gradient) to display the Gradient panel. Click on the right side of the color bar to display gradient sliders (a white slider displays on the left, and a black slider displays on the right) where you will place a new color (Figure 10-5). Click on the right side (black) gradient slider.

2. Select the Gradient color mode at the bottom of the Tools panel, if it isn't already selected, under the Fill and Stroke color boxes.

3. Double-click the Fill color in the Tools panel to display the Color Picker.

4. Select a deep blue color on the color bar (try entering #0000FF) and then click OK. The right color slider on the Gradient panel will now become the deep blue color. If not, just drag the new blue color displayed in the Fill color box in your Tools panel to the color stop at the right in the Gradient panel.

5. On the Gradient panel, click on the left side (white) gradient slider; then select the black swatch from either the Color or Swatches panel to change the left side gradient slider to black. You can also drag a black swatch to the left side instead. Drag any other color sliders displayed downward to remove them from the gradient bar. You will find a gradient from black to blue displayed in the fill box.

6. On the Gradient panel, adjust the middle, diamond-shaped position slider (on top of the bar) about two thirds over toward the blue slider for the desired effect. Select Linear Gradient as the type. Notice the gradient color also displays on the Tools panel fill box (Figure 10-5).

7. To apply the gradient, select the Rectangle Tool (M), and click on the artboard to display the dialog box.

8. Enter the same size as the header, 980 px Width and 90 px Height; click OK to display the gradient rectangle, and position it over the blank header with the Selection Tool (V), or use the arrow keys on your keyboard if necessary. You may notice that the blue gradient color shown in the figure in your text may look quite different than what is shown on the screen, because this book was printed using CMYK color, while your screen is displaying RGB.

9. If the rectangle does not display the new gradient, select the Gradient Tool (G) and drag from left to right on the rectangle shape.

 TOOLKIT TIP Solid colors can be selected in the Color panel or from the Color Picker and simply dragged onto the Gradient panel to become color sliders.

LINKING FILES OR EMBEDDING FILES

Files from Photoshop can be opened, copied, pasted, or placed in an Illustrator document. Photoshop images placed in Illustrator can be either **linked** or **embedded**. The main benefit of linking a Photoshop file before placing it into Illustrator is that when you update the image in Photoshop, any changes made are automatically updated in the linked file in the Illustrator document. This also keeps the file size small. The only drawback is that if you move the location of the linked file, the link will be broken, and changes cannot be updated easily, unless you place the image again. Also, if you are sending the file to another person, both the Photoshop and Illustrator files must be included. **Embedded files** are added permanently, which will increase the file size, and any changes made to the image in one document will not be updated in the other (Figure 10-6). The advantage of embedding is that there is no need to worry about dealing with linked files in different locations.

▷ FIGURE 10-6

Embedded documents paste graphics, and changes can only be made on the document itself while linked documents update one another when changes are made.

Embedded Documents

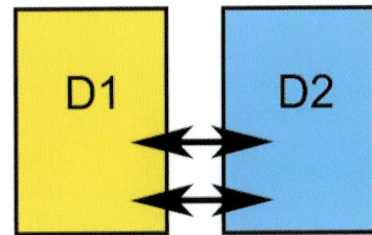

Linked Documents

PLACING PHOTOSHOP IMAGES INTO ILLUSTRATOR

To bring Photoshop files into an Illustrator document, the Place command may be the preferred method (File > Place). When an image is placed, it can be rotated and resized before pressing the Return/Enter key. You can do this with a pasted image as well; pasted images are automatically linked. Browse to find the Photoshop file, and check the Link check box in the Place dialog box to link the placed file for future editing. Uncheck the Link check box to embed the image into the Illustrator document (Figure 10-7). You can also copy illustrator artwork into a Photoshop document as a "Smart Object" (and vice versa) that can be edited as a linked object. This will be covered in depth later.

TOOLKIT TIP If you are working in a smaller document size, crop the images to the smaller size before placing them into the header document. Do not place images larger than the header or banner size; you may have problems with excess space beyond the document size if its used in a regular web page. The Rock image was first cropped to the size of the web header in Photoshop beforehand to avoid problems.

▷   FIGURE 10-7

Placing an image as embedded (link unchecked).

DESIGN TIP

For images to be used on the web, set the resolution of the image width to 72 dpi (or ppi) as the standard resolution, and display the image at 100% in Photoshop when making any changes. **Browsers** display web images full size. While you can alter the image size in a web file, it is best practice to create the image in the exact size needed.

In this exercise, you will place a Photoshop image into the Illustrator document and type the header title over the image with the Type Tool (T) before clipping the image.

1. With Illustrator open, select File > Place and locate the *Rock.jpg* image inside the *Chapter 10* folder.

2. In the dialog box, make sure the Link and Template boxes are *unchecked* (Figure 10-7), so the image will be embedded and can be transported without needing the original image. The file size is small enough that embedding will not affect download time. Click Place.

TOOLKIT TIP If an error comes up about an Embedded Profile Mismatch, select the Use Embedded Profile option and Illustrator will closely match the colors in the file. It will have no effect on your screen. When saving an image, check the ICC Profile—if it displays—in a Save dialog box. An **ICC profile** describes a file's colors so that Illustrator can interpret the profile and keep the colors consistent throughout.

3. Select the image with the Selection Tool (V) and move it to the left side alongside the edge of the gradient shape as shown in Figure 10-8. Deselect the image.

▷ FIGURE 10-8

Type positioned over the image.

4. Select the Type Tool (T) and click on the image, and choose a wide, rigid font, such as Arial Black, from the Type menu; if you want to try another wide, rigid font instead, try Franklin Gothic Heavy or ITC Eras Bold.

5. Use a black Fill and a Stroke of None.

DESIGN TIP

One of the concerns a designer needs to keep in mind is the download time of images. Keeping file sizes to a minimum is one of the best ways to achieve this.

6. Select a Size of 48 pt for the title text.

7. Starting on the left guide you created, type in capital letters, "ROCK 99.2"; press the Return/Enter key to start a new line (Figure 10-8).

8. Select a Size of 24 pt and type "WABW" or any four capital letters starting with a "W." Why not use your own initials?

9. Select the text lines with the Selection Tool (V) and position as shown in Figure 10-8.

10. If needed, select the rock image and reposition it so that it is behind the text.

MAKING TEXT IMAGES: CREATING A CLIPPING MASK IN ILLUSTRATOR

▷ FIGURE 10-9

Creating a clipping mask to make text images.

In Illustrator any shape, type, or closed path placed on top of a graphic can become a window to the image underneath. To do this, you create a **clipping mask** of the selected images (Figure 10-9). Clipping masks can be created from any closed path shape. They can also be created from text typed into the document, so the image fills the shape of the letters.

Next you will create a clipping mask by using the type to create a window through which you will see the rock image.

1. Select the text lines with the Selection Tool (V), and then Shift-click to select the rock image underneath and *not* the blue gradient box.

2. Select Object > Clipping Mask > Make to combine the two into a text image.

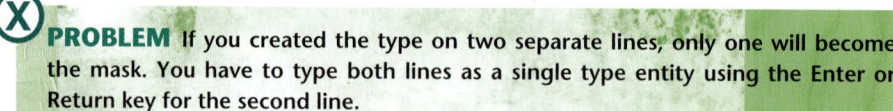

PROBLEM If you created the type on two separate lines, only one will become the mask. You have to type both lines as a single type entity using the Enter or Return key for the second line.

3. Position the new type image, if needed, with the Selection Tool (V); then deselect by clicking outside the image. Remove the guides by selecting View > Guides > Clear Guides.

4. Save the text image as *Header1.ai* in Illustrator's native format in your *Chapter 10* folder. Leave the file open, and leave Illustrator open.

USING THE TOUCH TYPE TOOL TO SELECT TEXT CHARACTERS AS OBJECTS

Illustrator CC has a Touch Type Tool (Shift+T) in the Tools panel (Type Tool section) that enables you to work with letters or characters as individual objects. You can now select a character or letter, a single word, or a series of words; change the font; and then scale, rotate, and move your selection using the familiar bounding box–like interface. Above the selected letter object a white circle displays. As you hover your mouse over, the cursor displays a bent arrow so you can rotate your object. This tool not only works with a mouse or stylus, but also is compatible with multi-touch devices, or computers with touch screen capability.

As this is a "rock" station you're going to slightly rotate some of the text characters in the station headline to make the station headline a little more informal.

1. Select the Touch Type Tool (Shift+T) in the Type Tool section of your Tools panel.

2. Select the letter "R" in ROCK and hover your mouse over the top until you can see a circle icon and your cursor turns into a bent arrow. Slightly rotate as shown in Figure 10-10.

3. Select and rotate the "K" towards the station number. If you want to rotate any of the other letters, do so only slightly as you have a limited space with the image clipped underneath. Be careful not to clip the "2" in the station number.

4. For the station initials, as you would with any object, to constrain proportions, hold down the Shift key and drag from the corner of the object selected by the Touch Type Tool. Here we enlarged the letter initials (Figure 10-10). It's that easy!

5. Save the file in your *Chapter 10* folder and leave open.

▷ FIGURE 10-10

The Touch Type Tool in Illustrator CC allows you to select individual characters and adjust as objects.

▷ FIGURE 10-11

Copy and paste the selected guitar into a new document the same size as the selection.

PASTING AN IMAGE COMPONENT TO A SELECTED SIZE IN PHOTOSHOP

For images that only need to be duplicated or copied into another document, or when only a portion of an image needs to be copied, the Paste command works well. When an image is pasted into a new document in Photoshop, it is on its own separate layer and can be edited independent of the background. In Photoshop, when an image is selected with the Rectangular Marquee Tool (M) and copied, a new document can be set to the same size as the copied selection, and the selected image can be pasted into this new document. When a selected graphic is copied, it is stored in a temporary place in the computer's memory called the computer's clipboard, mentioned in earlier chapters. It remains there while the computer is on until something new is copied to replaced it. You can then paste the selection into various documents.

In Photoshop, you will select a guitar from a photo with the Rectangular Marquee Tool (M) and copy it, then paste it into a new document the same size as the selection (Figure 10-11).

Selection on its own same size document

1. Launch Photoshop and open the *Guitars.jpg* file in your *Chapter 10* folder.

2. Draw a diagonal marquee selection around the blue guitar with the Rectangular Marquee Tool (M).

3. Select Edit > Copy to copy the one guitar, and then close the *Guitars.jpg* file.

4. To paste the guitar into a new document the same size as the selection, select File > New, name the file *Guitar,* and select OK to the Preset > Clipboard settings that match the size of the selection (Figure 10-11).

5. Select Edit > Paste to paste the guitar into the new document.

6. Save the file as *Guitar* in Photoshop's native PSD format (Save As > Photoshop) in your *Chapter 10* folder, which will keep the two layers in this file intact.

TOOLKIT TIP If you receive a dialog box warning about maximizing compatibility, leave the Maximize Compatibility unchecked, then select OK. Usually, if file size is an issue, or if you are opening your files only in Photoshop, unchecking or turning off Maximize Compatibility reduces the file sizes significantly. Leaving it checked saves a composite (flattened) image along with the layers of your document. If you edit or save an image using an earlier version of Photoshop, unsupported features are discarded.

APPLYING EFFECTS AND TRANSPARENCY IN PHOTOSHOP

Designers need to make sure that backgrounds of objects intended as transparent maintain their transparency when brought into web pages. The background needs to be removed to make it transparent in Photoshop before it is placed in a document. Layer Style effects can then be applied to the Photoshop image before placing into Illustrator. If, when using the Magic Eraser and Eraser tools (E) to remove the background, part of the image to keep is removed, you can select the History Brush in Photoshop to paint back areas to their previous state.

In this exercise, you will make the background transparent and apply an Outer Glow Layer Style around the guitar image.

DESIGN TIP

Saving graphic elements that contain transparency and gradient settings as PNG files preserves these effects. If the guitar graphic was saved as a JPEG, the background would be automatically converted to white.

1. In Photoshop, you will notice that the *Guitar* file you just created has two layers; one contains the guitar and the white *Background* layer. Drag the *Background* layer into the Trash icon in the Layers panel; it is not needed.

2. Use the Quick Selection Tool (W) at 10 px, and create a selection that stays outside the guitar image, but outlines it accurately. This is a typical snapshot image a client on a limited budget may provide you.

3. With the background selected, press the Delete key, to create a transparent background.

4. If any part of the background is still displayed, use the Magic Eraser Tool (E) with a tolerance of either 5 or 10 px, and click on the background area. If you notice part of the guitar is missing, select the History Brush with a few pixels and paint back what was removed.

5. To soften the edges, use the Refine Edge command (Select > Refine Edge) and select about 5 px Smooth effect.

6. Zoom back out to observe the effect you are going to apply on the guitar. Deselect the selection.

7. To make a red glow around the guitar, click the Layer Style ("fx") icon at the bottom of the Layers panel, and select the *Outer Glow* layer style.

8. When the Layer Style display box opens, click the Color Box next to the Gradient bar to display the Color Picker. Select an orange red color, making sure no cube appears to warn of web-color issues; if it does, click on the cube to display the nearest color match. Enter the settings shown in Figure 10-12 to create an outer red glow effect (Spread 30%, Size 20 px). This gradient fades from the red color to transparency.

▷ FIGURE 10-12

Applying layer style effects to create an outer glow effect.

9. Before you click OK, check the Drop Shadow box in the Styles display to add a little depth to the guitar. Click OK. If there are any white areas after the glow effect has been applied, zoom in to around 300% and use the Eraser Tool (E) with a small brush to drag over and remove any stray background areas around the guitar.

10. Leave it open for the next Photoshop exercise. Optional: If you want to have further editing of effects later on, you can save the file as *GuitarGLO.psd*, Photoshop's default format (Save As > Photoshop), and then close the file.

SAVING IN PNG FORMAT IN PHOTOSHOP

The **PNG format** supports varying levels of transparency and also preserves gradients. It is effective at compressing continuous-tone images without losing detail, called **lossless compression**, but it may create a larger file size than

JPEG compressed images. JPEG uses a **lossy compression**, where details are thrown out every time the image is edited and saved. The disadvantage of PNG formats is that they cannot be read by older browsers, which may be a consideration when you are advertising to a particular market. Saving the file in PNG format saves the image as a Copy and leaves the original where you saved it originally; the PNG can be saved to a different location. Later, you will use the Save for Web command to observe different settings for various graphic extensions, including PNG.

The guitar image contains a transparent background and various levels of opacity in the guitar glow effect. You will save the image in PNG format to preserve these effects (Figure 10-13).

▷ FIGURE 10-13

Saving a document of varying opacity and effects with the PNG extension.

DESIGN TIP

If a designer uses a lot of images on a web page, checking the Interlaced box causes the images to display in successive detail, as if coming into focus as they download. This helps to keep the viewer's interest without having to wait for the entire image to download. Because an entire header usually displays quickly, however, the choice here would be to select None when the PNG Options box comes up.

1. In Photoshop, use Save As (File > Save As) to save the file as *GuitarGLO.png* in your *Chapter 10* folder; then click Save in the dialog box. This will keep the background transparent and the Layer Style settings accurate.

2. When the PNG Options dialog box comes up, leave the default of None for Interlacing options, because this will be part of the web header and should display at once. Leave the default option of compression to Smallest, to decrease the file size a little without losing any important details, especially where this graphic wlll be scaled down and used in a small area. Click OK.

3. It will automatically be saved as a copy of the original *Guitar.psd* file in the *Chapter 10* folder.

TOOLKIT TIP Files saved with a GIF extension are also used for transparent backgrounds, and have a smaller file size. However, they have a limited color depth of only 256 colors, which usually will not display gradients, and Layer Style effects with smooth transitions between colors.

PLACING LINKED PHOTOSHOP IMAGES INTO ILLUSTRATOR

Placing layered Photoshop images into Illustrator re-creates those layers in the Illustrator document, leaving them intact for making further changes. When these images are ready for the web, all the layers will need to be combined as one, or flattened, to keep the file size small. Linking images makes the file size even smaller, especially with rasterized or bitmap images like the guitar; so linking helps speed up the download time, as long as the linked image is stored in the same place on the host server for the website as the original image. In Illustrator, you can double-click on the selected graphic to display **Isolation mode** in the Layers panel, where surrounding graphics are faded out. Isolation mode allows you to edit a symbol or graphic. On the Control panel, you will find the selected graphic as linked, options for editing, and you can isolate it as well. You can also create smart object links, which we'll cover later.

TOOLKIT TIP If changes need to be made to the placed file that is linked, you can select the Photoshop image in the Illustrator document and select Edit > Edit Original. This will launch Photoshop. You can then make the changes and save the file in Photoshop. The new changes will appear in the linked Photoshop image in Illustrator. You can also use the Link panel to do this.

Now that you have created the guitar in Photoshop, it is time to put the image into the Illustrator web header.

1. Open the Illustrator window with the *Header1.ai* document and zoom to 100% and select File > Place.

2. Locate and select the *GuitarGLO.png* file you just created; leave the Link option checked to provide a link in case you need to make changes to the guitar image later; click Place. Click the thumbnail on the right side of the web header, to display the large image inside a bounding box.

3. *Do not* press the Return/Enter key; use the Object > Transform menu to scale down 30%, or use the Selection Tool (V) while holding down the Shift key, and drag inward so the graphic is minimized.

4. Rotate the selected guitar –80 degrees (Object > Transform > Rotate > –80 degrees > OK) and position as shown in Figure 10-14.

5. Drag the guitar up to the header's right side with the Selection Tool (V) or use the arrow keys. Resize it to fit inside the banner by holding the Shift key down and dragging inward on one of the bounding-box handles to constrain proportions.

6. Optional: With the graphic selected, double-click to display it in isolation mode in the Layers panel. Notice the surrounding graphics are faded out. You won't be editing here, so double-click on the banner to return to normal mode, or select the Exit Isolation Mode option in the Layers panel menu.

7. Save the file as *Header1.ai* in Illustrator's native format in the *Chapter 10* folder. Deselect.

Placing the guitar image linked, scaling the image, and rotating 80 degrees.

TEXT PATHS IN ILLUSTRATOR

Illustrator's variety of drawing tools provides the means to create a path to place type on. The Pen Tool (P) not only creates precise curves; it also creates straight lines between two points (two clicks).

Next you will create an angular path for the slogan type to follow.

1. In Illustrator, create a new layer in the Layers panel for the text and name it *Type*. Zoom in close at 200% and select the Pen Tool (P) with a Stroke and Fill of None. Click a long straight path between two points along the outside of the guitar to match the same angle as the guitar neck. If you run into problems with aligning the path, select the path with the Direct Selection Tool (A) and use your eyes to adjust, or use the Transform command (Object > Transform > Rotate) to rotate by 1 degree (or minus one degree) increments.

2. With the Selection Tool (V) select the path only and position it to the left of the guitar. Then select the path and hold down the Shift key to enlarge the bounding box proportionally to make a diagonal longer path line across the banner from top to bottom; longer than necessary is okay.

3. Select the Type on a Path Tool, click on the bottom of the path you created with the bottom diagonal line of the type tool cursor aligned with the path you just created, and then select a red Fill and a Stroke of None. Pick the same font you chose for the *ROCK 99.2* title; we used Arial Black.

4. Change the Size to 24 pt from the Type menu or Control panel.

5. Type "Classic Rock!" (or your favorite type of music) along the path. If, after you type not all the type displays, and you see a plus icon at the end of the path, the path is too short and you will need to lengthen it.

6. You can also use the Direct Selection Tool (A) to reposition the text by dragging the middle I-beam, which looks like a vertical line on the path. If the text is upside down, drag the I-beam to the other side of the baseline to flip it. Save the file.

7. To make a copy of the angled line, make sure the path line is selected, and hold the Option/ALT key, dragging downward.

8. Select the Type on a Path Tool again and change the words to "All the Time!"

9. Use the Selection Tool (V) to provide some spacing between the two type paths for the slogan. Position the paths and guitar as shown in Figure 10-15.

10. After the guitar and text are all positioned accurately, with the Selection Tool, drag diagonally to select all the objects in the header and group (Object > Group). The header is ready to be saved as one unit.

▷ FIGURE 10-15

Placing type on a path so that it aligns with the guitar neck.

Use vertical I-beam to position type on path

Type on a Path Tool

USING THE SAVE FOR WEB COMMAND IN ILLUSTRATOR

Illustrator and Photoshop both provide a Save for Web command to optimize a flattened copy of the file with the fastest download time while maintaining image quality for web display. Using this feature allows the designer to preview the results of different settings at one time to determine image quality before they are applied. Layers are flattened on the saved copy to keep the file size small. The original layered image is not affected.

Here you will save the file in PNG format to maintain the transparency settings in the guitar glow effect. PNG format provides the best accuracy for images of varying opacity or transparency.

1. In Illustrator with *Header1.ai* still displayed, save in Illustrator's native AI format first as a backup; then select File > Save for Web.

2. Select the 2-Up tab on the dialog box to compare quality with two different settings for the header image.

3. Zoom in to 200%; then use the Hand Tool (H) to drag one of the images to display the guitar, as shown in Figure 10-16.

4. Select each image, and then try different settings using the options at the right. Observe what happens to the image, especially in the glow around the guitar. Click the Preview button to see how it would actually display as if on the web.

DESIGN TIP

All bitmap images need to be set at 72 dpi (ppi) resolution for web use. When optimizing a web header, one of the things a designer needs to keep in mind is that using a bitmap image within the graphic can increase the size of the file, because it generally uses more colors, as opposed to using all vector graphics.

▷ FIGURE 10-16

Optimizing the banner by saving it as a PNG file to preserve transparencies.

5. Select PNG-24 to save the image and preserve all opacities, gradients, and transparencies. The quality is what is needed here, but you can try PNG-8 also (notice a difference in file sizes). You can look at GIF, but you may notice the glow around the guitar may be too choppy looking. The JPEG has a white background, because it cannot record transparent backgrounds.

6. Zoom to 100% to see the actual size; this is what the your monitor will see. Make sure the PNG preview is selected, and then click Save.

7. Save the file name as *Header1.png;* choose Images Only for the format, and if PNG Options displays, leave it set at None; this will tell the browser to display the header all at once. This is a copy, saved for use on the web (the guitar graphic is also embedded in the header) in your *Chapter 10* folder, while the original is still open in Illustrator.

8. Save the original image in your *Chapter 10* folder as *Header1.ai.* Using the AI extension will preserve all the layers intact for editing, and the file can be used as a back-up copy. You now know how to place images with effects from Photoshop into Illustrator.

TOOLKIT TIP Illustrator's **Raster effects** are effects that generate pixels on bit-map mages, rather than vector images. Raster effects include all of the effects in the bottom section of the Effect menu, and the Drop Shadow, Inner Glow, Outer Glow, and Feather commands in the Effect > Stylize submenu. The **Resolution Independent Effects (RIE)** capability in Illustrator makes it possible to make changes with these effects resulting in very little, if any, change in the appearance of the effect. This will only work with embedded files, not linked graphics as was done in this project. For example, this might have been helpful if the client wanted to change the size of the header, in which case you would have had to embed the guitar graphic instead of linking it. For this project, the linked guitar graphic can also be adjusted and edited in Photoshop, with the new linked graphic displayed in the header.

INTEGRATING ILLUSTRATOR IMAGES INTO PHOTOSHOP

Any Illustrator graphic placed in Photoshop will become rasterized and cannot be enlarged after that point without losing quality. Because Illustrator uses paths to outline objects, and sharp lines are needed for type, a designer must create this art in Illustrator first, and then export that graphic as a PSD file to keep the layers and effects intact. For this second web header, you will create the gradient background and header in Photoshop. You will then export a composite guitar graphic with outlined type created in Illustrator to be added to the Photoshop web header. Special layer style graphics will be used in Photoshop to enhance the illustration.

SETTING PREFERENCES FOR PIXELS IN PHOTOSHOP

You will need to set the Photoshop header to the same size it was in Illustrator. Since you will be creating the same size banner in Photoshop, you will need to enter the settings using the Custom preset. Photoshop provides a wide selection of preset sizes, not only for web pages and print but also for film, video, and for mobile electronic devices.

TOOLKIT TIP In the Advanced section, you will notice settings at various Pixel Aspect Ratios, depending on the media format. For our purposes, we will stay with Square Pixels format.

First you will set the preferences and set a custom web header size in Photoshop.

1. Launch Photoshop, and then select the Photoshop Apple menu in Mac OS X or the Edit menu in Windows.

2. Select Preferences > Units & Rulers. Change the Rulers measurement to pixels, and then click OK to return.

3. Select File > New; choose a preset size of Custom, and enter 980 Width by 90 Height in pixels to accommodate for universal 1024 x 768 screen size. Click on the Advanced section; in the Pixel Aspect Ratios area, select Square Pixels format for our purposes here.

4. Select a Screen Resolution of 72 px, RGB Color Mode, and white for background contents in the dialog box (Figure 10-17). Name the file *Header2* and click OK.

5. Make sure View > Rulers is checked in the Menu to display the ruler.

6. When the document displays, zoom to 200%.

Photoshop preferences for pixels

Custom web header size

▷   FIGURE 10-17

Setting preferences and web header size in Photoshop.

CREATING THE WEB HEADER USING GRADIENTS IN PHOTOSHOP

Gradients in Photoshop use a transition from foreground to background colors. To apply gradients in Photoshop, select colors and apply them with the **Gradient Tool** (G). The colors have to be selected in the foreground and background color boxes before using the Gradient Tool (G). When the Gradient Color bar is clicked in the Tool Options bar, the **Gradient Editor** dialog box displays to select various preset gradient combinations, which can also be customized. You can adjust, add, and remove **Color Stops** in the Gradient Editor to create custom gradient combinations. **Opacity Stops** vary the amount of color applied.

In this exercise, you will create the gradient background for the header by selecting the foreground and background colors for the gradient, using the Gradient Editor to set up the type of gradient, and then applying the gradient using the Gradient Tool (G).

1. Make sure the Color panel is set to Web Color Sliders. Click the Foreground color box on the Tools panel to display the Color Picker, and select a black foreground color (#000000) first.

2. Click on the bent arrow on the Tools panel to display the background color box in front or press the X key to switch to the Background color, and click to select a dark blue background color from the Color Picker (try #0000FF, which was used in Illustrator). Do not forget: the bright RGB color blue on your screen will display differently than the blue you see in CMYK mode in this textbook.

3. If the cube displays, click it to find the closest web color, or check the Only Web Colors box in the Color Picker. Press the X key to bring the black Foreground color in front of the blue Background color. Do not worry if a triangle displays; that is for printing.

▷ FIGURE 10-18

Selecting a fore-ground to back-ground gradient from the Gradient Editor, then apply-ing the gradient with the Gradient Tool.

4. Select the Gradient Tool (G) to display the Gradient toolbar in the Tool Options bar. If the Paint Bucket Tool (G) is displayed in the Tools panel instead, hold down the mouse on the Paint Bucket icon to access the Gradient Tool (G).

5. Select Linear Gradient with the Blend Mode set to Normal in the Tool Options bar.

6. Click the Gradient Color bar in the Tool Options bar to open the Gradient Editor, and select the Foreground to Background Preset box (first box, top left). Click OK (Figure 10-18).

7. With the colors displayed in the Tools panel, click and drag the gradient across the header from left to right to display the gradient. Hold down the Shift key to ensure you are dragging the gradient horizontally.

8. You can click the Gradient Color bar in the Tool Options bar to adjust the color stops in the Gradient Editor the way you want, and then use the Gradient Tool (G) to drag the new gradient.

9. Zoom in to 200% and drag a vertical guide to the 35-px mark as a guide for setting the radio station title in the next exercise.

10. Save the file as *Header2.psd*, Photoshop's native format (Save As > Photoshop), in your *Chapter 10* folder for editing; if you get a Maximize Compatibility warning, click OK for now. We will adjust the file size for Web use later.

CREATING TYPE EFFECTS IN PHOTOSHOP

A large variety of special effects can be created using Photoshop's Layer Style effects in the Layers panel, including effects on type as well as images brought into Photoshop. These effects can also be applied to type and objects from Illustrator.

For this exercise in Photoshop, you will create a chiseled effect on type to identify the rock station and the intro line to the guitar illustration, which will be brought in later.

1. In Photoshop, with *Header2.psd* open, select the Type Tool (T) and set the font to 48-pt Arial Black in black with a Strong Anti-alias; you can also try fonts like Eras Bold ITC or Franklin Gothic. Make sure the paragraph alignment is set to align left.

2. Click on the 35-px guide and type "Rock 99.2." With the cursor still blinking after typing the "2," change the size to 24 pt; press the Return/Enter key to start a new line, and type "WABW," or choose your own call letters beginning with *W*. The type will appear very dark but will change when you add the effect.

3. Make sure the text layer on the Layers panel is highlighted, and use the Move Tool (V) to position the text as shown in Figure 10-19.

4. Select the Add a layer style icon at the bottom of the Layers panel, and then select Bevel & Emboss from the drop-down list to bring up its dialog box.

5. Select an Inner Bevel Style with a Chisel Hard Technique and a Gloss Contour of Cone (second square) to give a chiseled effect to the type (Figure 10-19). Set the Depth to 100%, and the Size to 5 px. Feel free to experiment. Click on the Drop Shadow box to add dimension to the type, then click OK.

6. To create an intro to the upcoming graphic, select the Move Tool (V); then select the Type Tool (T) again to create another type line. Use the same type font, but change the size to 30 pt; if the text layer is still selected, choosing a different point size will change the existing text.

7. Click near the 400 px mark and type "We're" for the first line; press the Return/ Enter key for the next line, press the space bar to align under the letter "e", and type "Talking…."

8. Highlight the two lines of type, and create the same layer effects used in steps 4 and 5 to create the same chiseled effect for consistency. You can also select the effects you just created using the Layers panel; hold down the Option/ALT key, and drag the effects in the *Rock 99.2* layer to the new type layer.

▷ FIGURE 10-19

Creating special layer style effects on type.

9. Remove the left vertical guide (View > Clear Guides) and save the file in your *Chapter 10* folder, again as *Header2.psd*.

10. Minimize the *Header2* document window.

CREATING THE GUITAR GRAPHIC IN ILLUSTRATOR

Illustrator creates paths for complex shapes using a variety of drawing tools. The Pen Tool (P) is the most effective tool for drawing smooth lines and curves. Here is a little review for using the Pen Tool. In Illustrator, you will use the Place command to import the guitar image created earlier in Photoshop and then trace the guitar to create a graphic of the guitar. Gradients will be applied, and text created along a path will be placed inside the guitar; the new graphic will then be brought into Photoshop.

TOOLKIT TIP If you are working in Illustrator, and you are using the Place command to import a Photoshop (PSD) or layered image, a Photoshop Import Options dialog box will open up, allowing you to choose to flatten all layers or convert layers to objects to edit in Illustrator. Illustrator will also allow Photoshop images with Layer Comps to be imported.

TOOLKIT TIP Remember, to edit paths in Illustrator, click on the circle to the right of the layer or sublayer to select that path to edit.

It is time to use the *GuitarGLO.png* image you created earlier in Photoshop to use as a template in Illustrator. You will use the Place command to set the guitar image as a template to trace with the Pen Tool (P) in Illustrator.

▷ FIGURE 10-20

Setting up the document to place the guitar image as a template.

1. Launch Illustrator; create a new web document, RGB Color, 800 x 600-px landscape orientation. Name this document *Guitar2*; it will be used to place the *GuitarGLO.png* template image in the next exercise. Click OK.

2. In Illustrator, with the *Guitar2* document open, locate and Place (File > Place) the *GuitarGLO.png* file from your *Chapter 10* folder as a template (check the Template box and uncheck the Link box). This will create a dimmed template layer with a working layer above it (Figure 10-20).

Illustrator New Document size for *Guitar2* document

3. Click the lock next to the template layer on the Layers panel to unlock it. Select the template guitar graphic and, while holding the Shift key, use the Selection Tool (V) to select a corner and drag inward until it fits in the document you just created.

TOOLKIT TIP When placing images as templates, it is a good idea to use flattened files. If you are using Illustrator, and the Photoshop Import Options dialog box displays, select the option Flatten Photoshop Layers To A Single Image before placing the file in Illustrator.

4. In Illustrator, double-click on *Layer 1* in the Layers panel and rename it *Outline*. Deselect the guitar.

5. With the new *Outline* layer highlighted, select the Pen Tool with a 4-pt blue Stroke and a Fill of None.

6. Place anchor points along the guitar's outline to create a closed path. Use the dots on the image in Figure 10-21 as a guide.

▷ FIGURE 10-21

Tracing an outline of the guitar image using the Pen, Direct Selection, and Smooth tools.

Guitar image traced by the Pen Tool

7. Edit with the Direct Selection and Smooth tools to get a good outline. Zoom in close for editing details. Use the Path Segment Reshape function by dragging the selected paths with the Direct Selection Tool (A) to match template curves.

8. To join end points, use the Direct Select Lasso Tool (Q) to select the end points.

9. Using the Object menu, select the Path command to Average, and then Join any end points (Object > Path > Average > Join). There is a cool shortcut for this—Command Option Shift J—that does both in one step.

10. When you have created a closed path for the guitar, select it with the Selection Tool (V). It is time to apply the gradient effect.

APPLYING GRADIENTS IN ILLUSTRATOR

In Illustrator, the Gradient panel is the control center for creating custom gradients. Select colors from the Color or Swatches panels, and drag these colors to the gradient color bar to create gradient color sliders. These sliders can be moved around to vary the amount of colors for different effects. In Illustrator, you can have gradients that can be adjusted to fade to transparent, apply special gradients in real time, and move them around. You select the object, then the Gradient Tool (G), and click. A gradient bar displays to edit the gradient effect by dragging and rotating the gradient bar around the selected object. The new gradient can be saved in the Swatches panel. You can also make edits from the Appearance panel.

With the guitar graphic selected as a closed path, you will apply a gradient color inside the graphic.

1. In Illustrator, open the Gradient panel; then select the Gradient Color Mode in the Tools panel.

2. Select a red Foreground color from the Swatches or Color panel, and drag it to the middle of the gradient bar on the Gradient panel (Figure 10-22).

3. Select a yellow Foreground color and drag it from the Swatches panel to the right side of the gradient bar on the Gradient panel (Figure 10-22).

DESIGN TIP

Applying a stroke outline on type can work nicely as long as the type is over 18 pt in size; it must provide enough width for both fill and stroke elements.

▷ FIGURE 10-22

Applying gradients for the guitar illustration.

Gradient Sliders

Gradient Color Mode

In Illustrator, gradients can be adjusted live. Select the guitar, then the Gradient Tool, and click. A bar displays to edit your gradient by dragging and rotating the gradient bar.

Gradient bar

4. Drag a black swatch onto the gradient slider to the left, and drag any other color sliders downward to remove them.

5. Select the Gradient Tool (G) and drag across the guitar from bottom to top.

6. Adjust the gradient sliders for desired effect on the guitar outline (Figure 10-22). You can edit the gradient by rotating or dragging the gradient bar, and by adjusting the gradient sliders. Select the guitar, then the Gradient Tool (G), and click.

7. Drag the Template layer onto the Trash icon in the Layers panel to delete it from this file.

8. Save the file as *Guitar2.ai* in the *Chapter 10* folder. You can also save it as a symbol for future use in the Symbols panel.

APPLYING GRADIENTS TO STROKES

You can apply gradients not only to the Fill color in shapes, but also to Stroke color as well. You can choose to apply gradients within a stroke, alongside a stroke, and across a stroke. The Gradient on Stroke feature also allows you to choose the style of gradient (Figure 10-23).

▷ FIGURE 10-23

Applying gradients to strokes.

In this optional exercise, you are going to increase the Stroke color size and apply gradient colors to outline the stroke of the guitar.

1. Select the *Guitar2* graphic with the Selection Tool (V), and change the size of the Stroke to 6 pt.

2. Select the Stroke color in the Tools panel, and select the Gradient mode.

3. To get started, click on the down arrow, select the Summer gradient as a starting point, and select Linear type.

4. Click and drag colors to create depth in the guitar outline, as was done in the Fill color.

5. Observe how the outline looks and adjust to taste.

6. Save the file again as *Guitar.ai* in your *Chapter 10* folder.

WARPING TYPE IN ILLUSTRATOR

Although type can also be warped in Photoshop, in this case using a light-colored type with a black-stroke outline in Illustrator helps to make it stand out within the guitar's gradient color. With Illustrator's stroke colors, type can be easily outlined in any color and weight. To warp type in Illustrator, you can use either the Effect menu (Effect > Warp), or use the Object > Envelope Distort > Make with Warp command. To make the identity of the radio station stand out, the words *Classic Rock!* will be typed inside the guitar and warped using the Flag effect to match the guitar shape.

▷ FIGURE 10-24

Warping type to match the inside of the guitar shape.

Now you will create two lines of text inside the guitar, and then warp them to match the guitar's shape (Figure 10-24).

1. In Illustrator, select the *Guitar2* image with the Selection Tool (V).

2. Rotate the selected guitar minus 90 degrees to make it horizontal (Object > Transform > Rotate > Angle –90 degrees). Resize if necessary.

3. Select the Create New Layer icon on the Layers panel, and rename the new layer Type to use it as a text layer.

4. Select the Type Tool (T), click the artboard, and then set the type to 36-pt Arial Black with a Fill color of yellow and a 2-pt black Stroke using the Type menu and the Color panel.

5. Type the word "Classic," and then select the type line with the Selection Tool (V) and position it within the guitar body.

6. Select Effect > Warp > Flag. Drag the Horizontal Bend arrow to the left until it matches the curve at the top of the guitar. Check the Preview box to see what is happening while you make the adjustments. Click OK; then deselect the text.

7. Select the Type Tool (T) to make a separate second line and click just below the guitar.

8. Select a 48-pt Arial Black with a Fill color of yellow and a 1-pt black Stroke outline from the Type menu.

9. Type "Rock!" or another type of music you listen to; select the type and position it within the guitar, toward the bottom, with the Selection Tool (V).

10. Select Effect > Warp > Flag. Position the Horizontal Bend to the right so that it matches the bottom curve of the guitar. Keep the Preview box checked. Click OK when you are satisfied.

11. Use the Selection Tool (V) and hold down the Shift key to select the guitar and the text.

12. Use the Object menu to Uniform scale the guitar and text to 40% (Object > Transform > Scale > 40%). It is a good idea to scale it before it is brought into Photoshop.

13. Save the file again as *Guitar2.ai* in Illustrator's native format. This will be the back-up copy as you prepare to bring the artwork into Photoshop in the next exercise.

EXPORTING ILLUSTRATOR ARTWORK TO BE OPENED IN PHOTOSHOP

Not only can you open layered Photoshop files in Illustrator, you can also save layered Illustrator files and open them in Photoshop. If a designer wants to work with an Illustrator file in Photoshop, it can be exported in Photoshop's PSD bitmap format. Here are some considerations when exporting files from Illustrator into Photoshop.

- Exporting Illustrator files in the Photoshop format saves most Illustrator layers so they can be edited; it maintains background transparency and gradients so long as the Write Layers option is selected in the Photoshop Options dialog box when you export. With Illustrator, you can export multiple artboards as well.

- You can open the new exported file, edit layers, copy, and paste it into the artwork.

- Resize and rotate the image as needed *before* exporting it into Photoshop, which converts images into unscalable bitmap images.

- Exporting the guitar graphic or any artwork with layers allows the graphic and text to be edited for special effects using Photoshop's Layer Style effects.

 TOOLKIT TIP To keep the Illustrator type layer editable in Photoshop, it must be on the topmost layer by itself and not on a layer containing other artwork. Area type, type on paths, or multicolored type in Illustrator can then be exported to Photoshop to be edited.

Here you will export the resized and rotated guitar image with separate text layers created in Illustrator into Photoshop for special effects.

1. In Illustrator, make sure the original guitar image is saved as *Guitar2.ai* in your *Chapter 10* folder in case it needs to be resized or edited later.

2. To export the *Guitar2.ai* file to Photoshop, select File > Export > Photoshop PSD > and save it in your *Chapter 10* folder. Name the file *Guitar2PSD.psd* and click the Export button.

3. When the Photoshop Export Options dialog box comes up, choose RGB Color Model, set the Resolution to Screen 72 ppi, select Anti-aliasing: Type Optimized (Hinted), to maintain consistency in the type and gradients, and check Write Layers to include all layers (Figure 10-25).

▷ FIGURE 10-25

Exporting Illustrator files into Photoshop to include layers, text, and color information.

4. Select OK and the PSD version will be placed in your *Chapter 10* folder, while the original *Guitar2.ai* will remain open.

5. Save and close the *Guitar2.ai* image. You are ready to open the new file in Photoshop.

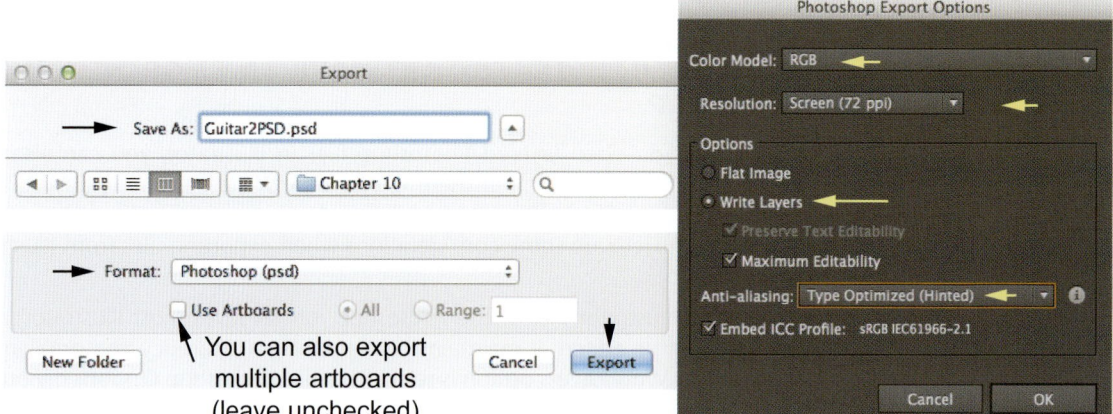

OPENING ILLUSTRATOR ARTWORK IN PHOTOSHOP VERSUS PLACING ARTWORK AS SMART OBJECTS

You have created a guitar graphic with layers and type in Illustrator. You exported the file as a Photoshop PSD file including all layers. Now it is time to bring the guitar artwork into the Photoshop header you created earlier. You can either Open the artwork or Place it into the Photoshop document. Here are some considerations to help you decide whether you want to open or place artwork created in Illustrator into Photoshop:

• When you use the Open command in Photoshop to open an exported PSD file, Photoshop rasterizes the vector objects created in Illustrator and keeps the background transparent although the image cannot be upsampled.

• When using the Open command in Photoshop, the illustration must be resized *before* bringing it into Photoshop to avoid having to enlarge it as a converted bitmap, creating pixeling issues. The key issue with this technique is to make sure the artwork has been resized beforehand and will not be needed for making changes later. The problem arises if the artwork needs to be resized to a larger size, the pixels have already been thrown out to create the reduced size, and therefore interpolation occurs creating a pixelated object.

- When using the Open command in Photoshop, most of the layers made in Illustrator are editable in Photoshop. Once you make changes to any layers in Photoshop, you can use the Copy Merge command in the Edit menu to paste a flattened copy of those edited layers as a new layer in the Photoshop image without affecting the original exported PSD file.

- Placing embedded files in Photoshop (File > Place Embedded) automatically flattens all layers into one with the background transparent, preventing any future editing other than applying effects around the image like drop shadows. However, it does allow you to resize the surrounding bounding box before pressing the Return/Enter key.

- Placing artwork as embedded Smart Objects creates a high-resolution copy of the original, so that when changes are made they are applied as high resolution and the quality remains intact.

- Placing artwork as a linked Smart Object allows you to make changes in the original Illustrator artwork, and the change is also applied to the linked copy, making your artwork and its associated documents versatile for making changes on the fly.

OPTIONAL EXERCISE: OPENING AND PASTING ILLUSTRATOR ARTWORK IN PHOTOSHOP

Using the Open command to bring in Illustrator artwork into Photoshop, the artwork is rasterized and cannot be enlarged any more than the size created before opening it. This technique works best for permanent situations where the work is at its final stages without any need for adjustments in the future. If the artwork needs to be upsampled afterwards, the result is usually a rather blurry or pixelated image, as the pixel data has already been removed before opening into Photoshop.

Since the image has already been scaled to the correct size, you will use File > Open to open the *Guitar2PSD.psd*, create a drop shadow effect in the outline layer, and then copy and paste it into the web header; or you can also just drag the guitar image onto the header. You'll also see what happens when you resize the image larger.

1. In Photoshop, open the *Header2.psd* image.

2. In Photoshop, open the exported *Guitar2PSD.psd* file that is in your *Chapter 10* folder. If the Photoshop Import Options dialog box displays, select Convert Layers to Objects and click OK to keep layers. You will notice the background remains transparent, and all graphics are intact, as well as the Illustrator layers.

3. Highlight the *Outline* layer in the Layers panel, and then click and hold the Add a Layer Style icon at the bottom of the Layers panel.

4. To give the guitar image a little depth, add a Drop Shadow effect with a Size and Distance of about 5 px. Click OK.

5. Select the entire image (Ctrl A, or choose Select > Select All).

DESIGN TIP

Always save the Illustrator file in its native AI format, or use the universal formats EPS or PDF before having the image exported to Photoshop, and you will always have a back-up copy for editing the artwork. Once the image is rasterized in Photoshop, it cannot be enlarged or have pixels added, otherwise the quality may deteriorate.

6. Use the Copy Merge command to copy a flattened version of the image (Edit > Copy Merged). This does not affect the actual layers in the document.

7. Click on the right side of the web header, and then paste it (Ctrl V or Edit > Paste). This will create a new layer. Name the layer as *Guitar*. The image should appear nice and sharp at the size you want, and artwork components have been flattened.

8. To resize the guitar to larger size, select Edit > Free Transform. Hold down the Shift key and drag the bounding box to make the image larger than the header. Press the Return/Enter key to apply the new size and you'll find the image looks blurry or pixelated. Carefully resize the guitar back to its original size, again using the Shift key and dragging inward to keep proportions constrained.

9. Use the arrow keys to position the guitar using Figure 10-26 as a guide. As you can see this method works more for permanent design solutions.

▷ FIGURE 10-26
Completed web header in Photoshop using Open and Paste.

CREATING SMART OBJECTS FROM ILLUSTRATOR INTO PHOTOSHOP

Smart Objects in Photoshop are layers that contain image data from raster or vector images, such as Photoshop or Illustrator files. These allow a designer to make changes while preserving an image's source data with all its original characteristics, enabling you to perform nondestructive editing to the layer. In Photoshop CC, you can select Place Embedded or Place Linked in the Fie menu, to create linked or embedded Smart Objects. The commands to choose to convert layer objects to Smart Objects, convert embedded objects to linked objects, and embed linked objects are also found under the Layer menu. Here are some characteristics of Smart Objects.

- Smart Objects allow a designer to scale, rotate, and warp Illustrator vector images without fear of pixeling or degrading the artwork.
- Illustrator images placed or pasted into Photoshop as Smart Objects remain live and scalable, allowing future edits made in Illustrator to automatically update in the Photoshop document.
- You can place a variety of EPS and PDF formats into a single layer or paste Illustrator's native format onto a single layer.
- You cannot alter pixel data such as painting, dodging, burning, or cloning, unless the Smart Object is converted into a regular layer, which will rasterize the artwork.
- Smart Objects are like Illustrator symbols: editing one linked copy will update all other linked copies automatically.
- Smart Objects can be created in Photoshop in different ways.

  A. Converting existing selected layers from embedded to linked Smart Objects and vice versa.

  B. Placing files inside an existing smart object.

  C. Duplicating Smart Objects to generate multiple versions.

  D. Dragging and dropping PDF and Illustrator artwork into a Photoshop document.

  E. Copying existing Illustrator artwork and paste it into Photoshop as a Smart Object.

  F. Using the Place Embedded or Place Linked commands, or Open as Smart Object in the File menu.

PLACING ILLUSTRATOR ARTWORK IN PHOTOSHOP AS EMBEDDED SMART OBJECTS

One of the main benefits of using Place Embedded is it creates a Smart Object of the image or a high-resolution copy of the original, so that when changes are made they are applied as high resolution and the quality remains intact. An example of this is if you decide to shrink an object that has been pasted, then saved as in the previous exercise, if you need to resize to back to its original size it is all pixelated because all of the pixels were discarded when the image was resized down. A placed embedded file with the same situation could be resized to the original larger object because a copy of the original was saved as a Smart Object. You can create embedded Smart Objects using either the Open as Smart Object or Place Embedded commands in the File menu, pasting data from Illustrator, or converting one or more Photoshop layers into Smart Objects.

Here you will place your guitar graphic as embedded, and slightly resize to stretch the graphic a little to accommodate the web header space, noticing the change is still sharp. You'll use the same *Header2.psd* image

1. In Photoshop, open the *Header2.psd* image. If you had performed the previous optional exercise in opening and pasting the guitar graphic, click the eye icon in the Layers panel to turn off the layer.

2. Select File > Place Embedded and locate the *Guitar2PSD.psd* file you created in your *Chapter 10* folder.

▷ FIGURE 10-27

Placed embedded graphic, when adjusted, still maintains sharpness.

3. A bounding box will display around the guitar graphic (if you enlarge it, the graphic will remain sharp). With the guitar graphic still selected at its normal size, select the middle resizing handle of the bounding box by the right side of the guitar neck and stretch a little to fill in some of the empty space in the header as shown in Figure 10-27.

4. Press Return/Enter to accept the change. The guitar image is still sharp. If you need to resize again, you can always select Edit > Transform. With the guitar graphic embedded in the document, the original does not change when you stretched the graphic in the web header.

5. To give the guitar image a little depth, add a Drop Shadow effect with a Size and Distance of 5 px.

6. Name the new layer as *GuitarEmbed*. Use the arrow keys to position the guitar using Figure 10-27 as a guide.

7. Click the eye icons of both "guitars" to turn on and off the effects to see which works best for you. We chose the slightly stretched guitar graphic that was embedded. Select the *We're Talking…* type layer and adjust to balance the composition.

8. Save the file as *Header2.psd* in your *Chapter 10* folder.

PLACING ILLUSTRATOR ARTWORK IN PHOTOSHOP AS LINKED SMART OBJECTS

In Photoshop CC, you can create linked Smart Objects whose contents are referenced from external image files. The contents of a linked Smart Object are updated when its source image file changes. With linked Smart Objects, you can use a shared source file across multiple Photoshop documents. Linked Smart Objects are particularly useful for teams or in cases where artwork might be reused across designs. Linked Smart Objects will have a link icon within the layer panel's Smart Object icon. You create linked Smart Objects by choosing File > Place Linked in the File menu, locating the file, and selecting Place. If your external or original file source has been changed, and if the linked document has been closed and is opened, the link in the Layers panel will display a yellow warning icon indicating the link to the document needs to be updated to match the original file change.

You simply update the document in the Layer menu (Layer > Smart Objects > Update Modified Content). You can also convert layers to Smart Objects from the Layer menu or the Layers panel menu, or right-click on the layer.

TOOLKIT TIP For changes made in Illustrator to display in an embedded Photoshop Smart Object layer, you need to first select the Smart Object layer to be edited in Photoshop, and then choose Edit Contents from the Layer menu (Layer > Smart Objects > Edit Contents). You can then make additional changes in Illustrator and save them. When the changes are saved, the image will be updated in the Photoshop document.

This exercise involves placing smart objects as linked for future editing on the fly. You will use the Place Linked command to locate the *Guitar2.ai* file you created, and place the artwork into Photoshop as a Smart Object, then create a drop shadow effect. You will then make changes to the graphic in Illustrator and save the Smart Object file to observe the linked change to the Photoshop document.

1. In Photoshop, make sure the *Header2.psd* file is open, make a duplicate copy of the *Header2* image (Image > Duplicate), and move the layer(s) with the guitar graphic into the trash.

2. Select File > Place Linked, then locate the *Guitar2.ai* file in your *Chapter 10* folder.

3. When the Open As Smart Object dialog box opens, leave at defaults and click OK. You will notice a new layer is created labeled as *Guitar2* with a bounding box around it (Figure 10-28). Do not press the Return/Enter key yet.

4. With the graphic still selected, if needed, hold the Shift key and drag one of the corner handles inward to make the graphic small enough to fit inside the banner. Use the arrow keys to position it. Press the Return/Enter key once the guitar is scaled and positioned accurately. You'll notice a link icon displays on the Smart Object icon in the Layers panel.

▷ FIGURE 10-28

To create a linked smart object layer, select File > Place Linked into Photoshop.

5. To add a drop shadow layer style effect, keep the Vector Smart Object layer selected; click the Add a layer style icon on the Layers panel, select Drop Shadow, and choose a Size and Distance of about 5 px.

6. To observe the effect of using Smart Objects by editing the graphic, highlight the Vector Smart Object layer and choose Layer > Smart Objects > Edit Contents (or double-click the Smart Object thumbnail in the Layers panel). A dialog box opens reminding you to save your changes, notifying you that the changes will be reflected upon returning to the smart object (Figure 10-29). Click OK.

▷ FIGURE 10-29

To edit a Smart Object layer, choose Edit Contents; make changes in Illustrator, save the new graphic, and observe the linked change in Photoshop.

Make changes in Illustrator

Linked change displays in Photoshop

TOOLKIT TIP Because you have created a Smart Object graphic in Illustrator that is linked to the Smart Object layer in the Photoshop document, both files must be kept in the same folder—in this case, *Chapter 10*—for existing and future edits, or you may not see any changes. Always keep files in the same location for links to work correctly.

7. The smart object is now linked back to Illustrator, opening up the program if it is closed to display the guitar graphic for editing.

8. Use Illustrator's Type on a Path Tool (T) to select the word "Classic"; change the word to "Metal" or another word. Adjust the type size to as needed; then use the Direct Selection Tool (A) and the arrow keys to move the type line into place. Feel free to make any additional changes to experiment with this feature.

9. Select the graphic, and save as *Guitar2.ai* in your *Chapter 10* folder.

10. With the new linked Smart Object document saved, switch back to the Photoshop banner image; you will notice that the linked smart object now appears with the changes you made in Illustrator. Both files have to be in the same location folder (*Chapter 10*) to work.

11. Save the new, adjusted duplicate Photoshop *Header2.psd copy* file with the different name in the guitar as *Header2B.psd* in your *Chapter 10* folder. Feel free to select Edit >Free Transform, to adjust the length of the guitar graphic to fill in some space, if you'd like. Close this file and leave the original *Header2* file open.

TOOLKIT TIP In Photoshop, to adjust the length of the guitar neck, select Edit > Free Transform to drag the middle resizing handle on the side of the bounding box around the guitar. Press the Return/Enter key to apply the change. When you check the guitar graphic in Illustrator, the change from Photoshop is not made because the linked Smart Object is only in Photoshop from Illustrator, not vice versa. If, however, you adjusted the guitar neck in Illustrator, the change would automatically appear in the Photoshop document. The link is in one direction.

ILLUSTRATOR'S GRAPHIC STYLES PANEL

Designers can use the Graphic Styles panel (Window > Graphic Styles) to create, name, and apply effects to graphic objects or text in conjunction with the Appearance panel. You can create the effect in the Appearance panel and drag the thumbnail, say the guitar gradient, as a new Graphic Style in the Graphic Style panel. You can also choose effects for objects and text from graphic style libraries, which are collections of preset graphic styles. When you open a graphic style library, it appears in a new panel, much like the Swatches panel. You select the object, graphic, or text before applying the style and then select the style to apply. Try creating a copy of the guitar graphic; then choose the Image Effects library and start applying various styles for fun. Select the type line and try different effects using the Type Effects library.

USING THE SAVE FOR WEB COMMAND IN PHOTOSHOP

The process for saving in Photoshop is about the same as in Illustrator, using the Save for Web command in the File menu. In Photoshop, the choices are .GIF, .PNG or .JPG. Any one of these formats will automatically flatten the *Header2.psd* file and save it as a copy of the original file, leaving the original file with its layers still open and intact. Since there are no transparencies used in this header, the JPEG option is the best choice for maintaining the quality and keeping the file size minimal. JPEG images are compressed, but cannot handle transparencies. You might also notice that since no continuous-tone images (photographs) were used, *Header2* has a smaller file size than *Header1*.

TOOLKIT TIP If an image like the guitar graphic, which has a curved outer edge, is saved as a JPEG file, the background would become white instead of transparent. This is why it is important to understand how to save a graphic for its intended purpose. GIF and PNG files allow transparent backgrounds, but JPEG images do not.

Next you will look at the different format options for optimizing the header, and then save it as a JPEG.

1. In Photoshop, with *Header2.psd* open, select the File > Save for Web command, choosing the 4-Up tab. If the header is not fully shown, select the original tab, and then select the 4-Up tab.

2. Select the gray box under each image one at a time, and change the settings to PNG-24, JPEG High, and GIF to observe the differences in the quality of the image, the file sizes, and download times compared to the original image.

▷ FIGURE 10-30

Optimizing the *Header2* image, observing different formats for quality and file size, and selecting the JPEG option.

3. Select the gray box with the JPEG High option; it has the fastest download time and will display all graphics accurately inside the banner. Each of these formats will flatten the header image.

4. Save the file as *Header2JPG.jpg* in your *Chapter 10* folder. The original *Header2* file remains intact with all its layers (Figure 10-30).

5. Compare the file sizes of the *Header1* and *Header2* images. You will see that when the file contains a bitmap, the file size increases. Compare the various files.

FILES AND FORMATS CREATED

In your *Chapter 10* folder on your drive, you will find the following files with extensions capitalized if you completed all the exercises. This list also includes those files downloaded and used in this tutorial, *Rock.jpg* and *Guitars.jpg*, that were found online at *www.CengageBrain.com*:

- *Rock.JPG* (text low-res online file)
- *Guitars.JPG* (text low-res online file)
- *Guitar.PSD* (pasting selected guitar photo in its own document, Photoshop backup)
- *Header1.PNG* (creating "glow" layer style settings in Photoshop with transparency)
- *Header1.AI* (created in Illustrator for back-up file with layers)
- *Header1.PNG* (final Illustrator web *Header1* file with "guitar glow" photo image with transparency)
- *Header2.PSD* (file created in Photoshop with layers for backup and where you created a pasted layer using the Open command, and an embedded Smart Object layer using the Paste Embedded command to choose from)
- *Guitar2.AI* (created illustration in Illustrator from photo and applied gradients)
- *Guitar2PSD.PSD* (exported from Illustrator into Photoshop with layers to be placed in *Header2* with Illustrator effects)
- *Header2JPG.JPG* (final web *Header2* flattened image in Photoshop containing all illustrative artwork)
- With the "Creating Smart Objects" exercises, you will have an additional file, *Header2B.PSD,* which you created to show how you can edit and have the change linked as a Smart Object from Illustrator to Photoshop.

The files you have been creating for these exercises have various purposes. Now you can compare various files and also see how you would organize them to set up a productive workflow. In the world of graphics, you will be creating and working with many types of files. You can also use Bridge or use the each application's Mini Bridge function to quickly observe info about each file and get a visual thumbnail representation of each.

PACKAGING AND CONVERTING TO CSS FOR WEB USE

Illustrator's Package command (File > Package) allows you to package not only image files and artwork that can be used by service providers of the printing industry, but also files for web use. Packaging provides an opportunity for designers as part of a team to transfer all related files between worksites by creating a simple folder "suitcase" to place all contents in. In Illustrator CC, you can also package linked Smart Objects.

Another feature in Illustrator CC is the ability to generate CSS HTML code that can easily be copied and then pasted into any web page document. It will even create the necessary code that also includes gradients created.

Just to show the power of these two features, you'll package the *Header1.ai* file that contains the linked placed guitar image from Photoshop, then you'll open the flattened *Header1.png* file and generate the required CSS HTML code as if ready to insert into a web page.

<table>
<tr><td>

▷ FIGURE 10-31

In Illustrator CC, you can package your web contents, and export artwork to CSS HTML format for web pages.

</td><td>

1. In Illustrator, open the *Header1.ai* file you created in your *Chapter 10* folder.

2. Select File > Package and in the dialog box, choose the location as your *Chapter 10* folder, name the Folder name as *Header1_Folder*, and keep all options checked. Click Package.

3. When the font warning dialog box opens, click OK, and then select Show Package in the next dialog box to view your content (Figure 10-31). You'll notice you have your report, images, fonts, and a Links folder that contains a copy of the original *GuiterGLO.png* you created.

4. Your artwork and associated files are ready to be transported if needed.

</td></tr>
</table>

Packaging the Header1 Web Header Contents

Exporting *Header1.png* file as CSS HTML Code

5. To create CSS HTML code to place in a web page with any web page creation program like Adobe Dreamweaver, using Illustrator, open the *Header1.png* file you created in Illustrator as a flattened file.

6. To save the file for CSS format, select File > Export and select Format: CSS. Save As the default *Header1.css* in your *Chapter 10* folder. Click Export.

7. When the Export Options dialog box displays, choose CSS Units as Pixels, check all boxes in Object Appearance and Options (options prepares for certain browsers). Click OK.

8. You'll find the file *Header1.css* in *Chapter 10* folder. At this point you would use Dreamweaver or your web creation software to open the document, then you can copy and paste the code (there's a lot of it) where you want it to display on a particular web page, saving time in writing complicated CSS code.

ADVANCED USERS: Understanding PDF and EPS Files

Two universal graphic formats, PDF and EPS, can be read by most other graphic applications, which comes in handy if someone does not have the same application in which the original document was created. Documents saved as either EPS files or PDF files have very much the same characteristics; it is up to the designer to decide what media they will be used for. In general, EPS files are used in the commercial printing process and for vector graphics that use text and images. PDF files are most useful in sharing documents over the web, through email, on CDs, and where minimal file size is needed. It should also be noted that with improved technology these days, many commercial printers can accept documents created from the original applications like Adobe products. PDF files are also used as proofs for commercial printers to check document layouts, fonts, and graphics, and these can also be used in the actual printing. This text was communicated between myself and the production team electronically from low-res PDF documents and then was printed from high-resolution PDF files.

SAVING PORTABLE DOCUMENT FORMAT (PDF) FILES

If you want to save your files for distribution via email, on CDs, on the web, or for electronic documents, Portable Document Format (PDF) files can be saved and read by most applications. If an application cannot read them directly, PDF files can be read on any computer using Adobe's free Adobe Reader program, which you installed as part of Chapter 1 of this text. Anyone can download it from Adobe's website (*http://www.adobe.com*) and install it easily. In Illustrator, the PDF Options dialog box provides many options for specifying compression, Marks and Bleeds for commercial printers, security, file summary, and advanced settings for color management. You will find the same display in the general section for both Illustrator and Photoshop with universal options in each (Figure 10-32). We will concentrate on the General functions. Here are some great features regarding all PDF files:

- When saving a PDF file, all fonts can be automatically embedded so that the viewer can read the document clearly without having the actual fonts installed on their computer.

- PDF files retain any transparency information in the file.

- To display web options, choose Optimize for Fast Web View (or Screen Optimize in earlier versions) from the Adobe PDF Options dialog box.

- When you check the Preserve Illustrator Editing Capabilities box in the Adobe PDF Options dialog box, the file can still be opened and edited as an Illustrator file.

- A Photoshop PDF file can be brought into Illustrator with type made into outlined paths if the Use Outlines for Text box is checked.

- Many commercial printers also prefer to receive files in PDF format from their clients as guides, proofs, and for the printing process itself.

- You can save to earlier versions of Adobe Reader with a description of considerations. The drawback of this option is that there are no editing capabilities in older versions.

- PDF files use lossless compression; no data is thrown out.

TOOLKIT TIP If you are not sure that the intended viewer has the most current version of Adobe Reader to view your PDF document, you can save your PDF document to an earlier version of Adobe Reader.

Illustrator's editable layers

Photoshop's editable layers

▷ FIGURE 10-32

Creating PDF files in Illustrator or Photoshop. Using options to allow future editing.

Let us bring in the headers you created and save them as PDF files to compare. As long as you select the option to Preserve Editing Capabilities, you can make adjustments to various layers later.

1. Launch Illustrator and locate the *Header1.ai* file in your *Chapter 10* folder and Save As > Adobe PDF (pdf). Select the General settings.

2. In the Adobe PDF Preset field, select the smallest file size; notice you can set for high-resolution and press-quality documents here. Make sure Preserve Illustrator Editing Capabilities, Embed Page Thumbnails for previews, and Optimize for Fast Web View boxes are all checked (Figure 10-32). The setting will add "modified" to the Preset, since you have changed some of the defaults.

3. Name and Save the file as *Header1PDF.pdf* in your *Chapter 10* folder.

4. Notice that all layers are editable, and vector type and gradients are still scalable. The guitar image is still a bitmap that can be scaled smaller but not enlarged.

5. Launch Photoshop and open the *Header2.psd* created earlier; choose Save As > Photoshop PDF, making sure that Save: Layers, and Color: Embed Color Profile are both checked. Click Save, and another dialog box will pop up with the settings shown in Figure 10-32; these options are identical in Photoshop and Illustrator.

6. Name the file *Header2PDF.pdf.* Notice the individual layers and sublayers are still separated, except for the guitar layer, which has been combined.

TOOLKIT TIP Photoshop also provides a Scripts function (File > Scripts) to send Layer Comps to clients, team members, or your boss. Layer Comps can be sent as specific files, electronic PDF files, or as exported layers to multiple files. This comes in pretty handy for those who need to document the progress of their project. It is also a time-saver when creating graphics for animation and rollover buttons for the web. Illustrator provides the option to save a document in the smallest file size as a compact PDF. When saving to PDF in the Save Adobe PDF dialog box, select the Smallest File Size option from Adobe PDF Preset. Make sure that you deselect the Preserve Illustrator Editing Capabilities check box to avoid saving the Illustrator resources along with the document.

ENCAPSULATED POSTSCRIPT (EPS) FILES

Encapsulated PostScript (EPS) files create file sizes that are too large for web use. EPS files are useful for documents that will be used in the commercial printing industry, when the image involves a combination of type and graphics. Here are some features of EPS files.

- EPS files can be imported into and read by most graphic programs. Documents saved as EPS files from other illustration programs can be edited in Illustrator and then saved as an Illustrator document.

- In Photoshop, files saved in EPS format are saved as copies to a designated location, while the original file remains open.

- The EPS file format is a good choice if you want to import graphics into a page layout program, word processing program, or other drawing programs when you are not sure what application the intended receiver is using.

- EPS files do not use compression; they produce large file sizes with precise accuracy, which is why they are used in printing but not for web design.

- EPS files are well suited when you need to combine bitmap and vector graphics. Photoshop, however, rasterizes its EPS files into nonscalable bitmapped graphics that cannot be enlarged but still maintain image quality.

INTEGRATING PHOTOSHOP AND ILLUSTRATOR PDF FILES

Documents saved as either EPS files or PDF files have very much the same characteristics. The designer needs to know what media the document will be used for. There is more flexibility bringing Photoshop PDF or EPS files into Illustrator than Illustrator files into Photoshop, especially with type. Here is a quick breakdown of what happens when you integrate PDF or EPS files in either Photoshop or Illustrator.

- Although Illustrator will flatten the Photoshop layers from either a PDF or EPS document, type is treated as individual outlined paths, which can be edited with the Direct Selection Tool (A).

- Illustrator PDF and EPS files can be brought into Photoshop, but they are rasterized and flattened into a one-layer bitmap image with a transparent background: Layer Style effects can only be applied to the whole image.

Here you will see that there is more flexibility integrating Photoshop PDF files into Illustrator than there is integrating Illustrator PDF files into Photoshop.

▷ FIGURE 10-33

Photoshop PDF (and EPS) files can have type converted to outlined graphics in Illustrator.

1. In Illustrator, open the *Header2PDF.pdf* file created in Photoshop. You will notice when you open it in Illustrator and click on one of the circles to the right of a sublayer, the type is outlined as a graphic and can be selected with the Direct Selection Tool (A) to be edited (Figure 10-33). The graphics are combined as a single image.

2. In Photoshop, open the *Header1PDF.pdf* file created in Illustrator. The file will be rasterized onto one layer. Any effects will be applied to that layer.

3. Try saving the *Guitar* and *Guitar2* graphics in PDF and EPS formats, and observe what happens when you open them in Illustrator and Photoshop.

4. As you can see, more flexibility is provided when working with PDF and EPS files in Illustrator if any rescaling or editing is needed, especially with type, while PDF and EPS files in Photoshop are useful for optimal detail in a certain preset size.

5. Go ahead; play around and see what you can and cannot do. Do not forget to take a look at the file sizes of the PDFs you just created, and compare them to the file sizes of the originals.

DIGITAL TOOLKIT EXTRA: Converting Bitmap Images to Vector Artwork Using Image Trace and Live Paint

In Illustrator there is a function that allows the designer to trace various types of bitmap images called Image Trace. It automatically follows the contours and outlines of drawings and various shades of bitmap images to create vector drawings consisting of many closed paths. The Live Paint Bucket Tool (K) creates Live Paint groups of closed paths for adding fill colors. The hours of work required to generate a complex set of paths can now be done quickly live. Creating vector illustrations from bitmap images enables them to be scaled to any size.

TOOLKIT TIP Image Trace and Live Paint are very powerful functions in Illustrator, and can be quite complex in their operations. For an introduction about these functions or as a review, go into Illustrator Help, search either Live Paint or Image Trace, and click on the links; or go to the Adobe website and view live video tutorials if you have a high-speed Internet connection.

IMAGE TRACING DIFFERENT BITMAP IMAGES

Image Trace, in Illustrator, automatically follows the contours and outlines of drawings and various shades of bitmap images to create vector drawings consisting of many closed paths. The more detailed the selection, the more complex the paths, depending on the tracing options you choose. Choosing certain tracing options can also create special effects. To trace any object, it must be selected first. To trace the image using the default tracing options, click the Image Trace button in the Control panel, or choose Object > Image Trace > Make. To set tracing options before you trace the image, select presets from the Tracing Options dialog box, which provides a variety options for different types of images, sketches, drawings, and photographs. You can also set up your own custom tracing parameters. To convert the tracing outline to a series of connected paths, select the **Expand** command (Object > Image Trace > Expand). There is also an option to complete both Make and Expand at the same time in the Object menu, and in the Control panel there is an Image Trace panel for precise adjustments.

TOOLKIT TIP If you know in advance that you plan to use the Live Paint Bucket Tool (K) to add color to fills and strokes, you can select the Live Paint button in the Control panel after selecting the tracing option.

TOOLKIT TIP Instead of using the Open command to open TIF and JPG files in Illustrator, you can create a new Illustrator document and use the Place command instead; then save the document as an Illustrator file.

Here you will trace a scanned-in painting as one type of bitmap image that can be used for Image Trace. You then will select the Expand command to create connected paths. In order to trace any object it has to be selected first.

1. Launch Illustrator and open the *Sailboat.jpg* file in your *Chapter 10* folder. This is a scanned file of a kitted cloth that, once traced, will allow you to change various colors to show different versions of the image as an illustration.

2. Select the image with the Selection Tool (V).

3. Set the color boxes in the Tools panel to the default black Stroke with a white Fill for neutral starting colors.

4. In the Control panel, select the down arrow next to the Image Trace button to display the Image Trace options (Live Trace in earlier versions).

TOOLKIT TIP You can also select a tracing option on bitmap images to create certain effects. Try bringing in a photograph and selecting Detailed Illustration or the Hand Sketch option to observe the changes.

▷ FIGURE 10-34

Using Image Trace in Illustrator to create vector illustrations from bitmap images.

5. Select the Low Fidelity Photo option to capture details in the shading. You will notice that the colors will appear to be painted in; however, the masts holding the sails need to be filled in more (Figure 10-34).

Original Image (scanned fabric)

Click Expand to create paths

Image Trace panel

6. In the Control panel, you can select the Image Trace button, which opens the Image Trace panel (or use Window > Image Trace), and make any fine tune adjustments, or leave at the default displayed. In earlier versions use the Control panel to change the Min Area of pixels from the preset of 10 px to 30 or more pixels for a better tracing. It will now display as a Custom Preset setting.

7. Select the Expand button to create the paths.

8. Leave this file open for the next exercise.

TOOLKIT TIP The more complex the tracing option, the longer it will take to convert to paths. The Photo High Quality option will take quite a long time to convert an image due to the complexity of reading shades and tones. Avoid using this unless you have plenty of time to wait for it to render.

LIVE PAINTING FACES AND EDGES

Live Paint detects and corrects gaps to create closed paths for fills and strokes for painting. It treats all paths as if they were on the same canvas without any layering. By creating a **Live Paint group,** all paths are fully editable, and fills can be adjusted as individual paths are adjusted. If you remove a path or adjust it with the Direct Selection Tool (A), the color simply fills in wherever changes were made. Live Paint groups can be painted along edges, like strokes, where the portion of the path intersects with other paths or inside faces, which would be the filled areas for color. You can select colors from the Color panel or various swatch libraries to get the tones of color you are looking for. In Illustrator, the **Live Paint Bucket Tool (K)** is used to create Live Paint Groups and to fill in the faces or color the edges. **Faces** are the inside areas, and **edges** are the stroke or outlined areas of the path. To paint faces and edges with the Live Paint Bucket Tool (K), you need to create a Live Paint Group first. Use the Paint Bucket cursor to paint in the faces. To paint the edges with stroke colors, hold down the Shift key to change the Live Paint Bucket to a Brush. You will find a vast selection of **Swatch libraries** for specific color combinations. Any colors you select are placed in the main Swatches panel for future use. These can be found by clicking on the Swatch panel submenu and selecting Open Swatch library. The **Live Paint Selection Tool** (Shift+L) lets you select and then delete faces and edges of a Live Paint group. When paths are deleted with the Live Paint Selection Tool (Shift+L) the color of the surrounding paths fills in the deleted path.

TOOLKIT TIP Once a Live Paint Group is created, you cannot delete a component path of a closed path very easily. Make path deletions and adjustments before creating the group to paint. You can use the Live Paint Selection Tool (Shift+L) to help select and delete faces and edges of a Live paint Group. Before applying any colors with the Live Paint Bucket Tool (K), always select the fill or stroke colors first, and then select the tool.

In this exercise, you will use the Live Paint Bucket Tool (K) to fill in edges and faces with color. Then you will use the Live Paint Selection Tool (Shift+L) to remove paths to fill in adjacent colors.

1. In Illustrator, open or maximize the window of the traced and expanded *Sailboat.jpg* image, and zoom in at 150% to 200% to observe the many paths created.

2. Make sure the image is selected with the Selection Tool (V) to select all paths.

3. Select the Live Paint Bucket Tool (K), located in the area of the Shape Builder Tool (Shift+M), and click on the brown sail to make the entire image part of the Live Paint group. (If a dialog box displays that you will not be able to edit the paths after a Live Paint group is applied, select OK). As you move the cursor over the image, you will find various closed paths highlighted in red. The brown sail will be filled in white.

4. In the Swatches panel menu, choose to Open Swatch Library and select the System swatch that matches the type of computer you are using, Macintosh or Windows, or choose another swatch library.

5. Select a light blue color to change the color of the sky. Select the Live Paint Bucket Tool (K) and click on the faces of the sky Live Paint group to apply the lighter blue tone.

6. Zoom in to 200% and click any dark remnants inside the red Live Paint group with the Live Paint Selection Tool (Shift+L); it will look like a dotted patch. Press the Delete key to remove it and keep the overall sky light blue. You also notice that both Fill and Stroke have defaulted to None.

7. Continue changing the face colors on the sails, if you like, for a lighter toned image (Figure 10-35). You now have another version of this graphic. Be careful not to change the colors of the edges unless that is what you are planning to do. Use the Lasso Tool (Q) to Average paths together in the Object menu (Object > Path > Average > Both) to paint smaller areas, and use the Live Paint Selection Tool (Shift+L) to remove fills and edges. Have fun and experiment!

8. Save the final sailboat image in your *Chapter 10* folder.

▷ FIGURE 10-35

Using the various Live Paint techniques to make a lighter-toned image.

Live Paint Bucket Tool
Click sail to make Live Paint Group

Sail is filled with color, and as mouse is dragged over, paint groups are highlighted in red

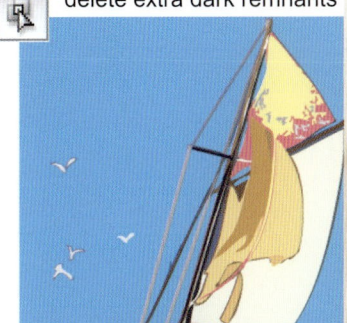

Live Paint Selection Tool to delete extra dark remnants

Image being painted with lighter toned colors

Live Paint Bucket   (K)

Live Paint Selection Tool   (Shift+L)

TRACING AND PAINTING COMPLEX DRAWINGS AND PHOTOS

▷ FIGURE 10-36

Tracing a photo with Image Trace for effects and applying paint groups.

Here is where the creative fun comes in. You can use Image Trace and Live Paint to save you hours of tracing scanned images using the Pen or Pencil tools. You can also trace a photograph to use as a starting point for artwork or to create special effects. You can take a complex scanned drawing and use Image Trace to set up the initial paths. Keep in mind that before creating Live Paint Groups or applying colors with the Live Paint Bucket Tool (K), the image first needs to be selected and traced with one of Image Trace's options to create the paths.

For more practice, you will open the Maine lighthouse photo and trace and color it using Live Paint groups and adding color as you see fit (Figure 10-36).

Original Photo

Sketched Art Trace
(only a few colors)

Simple Colors

Low Fidelity Photo Trace
(more paths, paint more color details)

TOOLKIT TIP If you want to paint the stroke edges, hold down the Shift key. As you move the cursor over the edges, it will turn from a paint bucket to a brush. Click on the edge to apply the stroke. If the brush displays an *X* in the cursor, you are over a face area and cannot apply the color.

1. In Illustrator, open the *Maine Lighthouse.jpg* photo image in your *Chapter 10* folder.

2. Select the image with the Selection Tool (V).

3. Using the Control panel, choose to Image Trace as 3 Colors or Sketched Art to see the special effects you can create. This is sometimes helpful if a client wants to create a simple logo out of a photograph.

4. Select the Live Paint Bucket Tool (K) to create the Live Paint groups and have some fun.

5. For the grand finale, with the same original image, *Maine Lighthouse* from your *Chapter 10* folder, select the image with the Selection Tool (V) and select the Image Trace button on the Control panel; select Low Fidelity Photo; and then click Expand to create the paths. You will notice the image has been traced quite nicely with good contrast in color.

6. Select the Live Paint Bucket Tool (K) and click on the image to generate lots of paint groups. You can almost look at this as creating your own digital multi-color oil painting.

7. Go ahead and get creative adding color to the paths. Experiment with different fills. Do not forget: if you want to paint the edges, hold down the Shift key. As you move the cursor over the edges, the cursor will turn from a paint bucket to a brush; just click on the edge to apply the stroke. If the brush displays an *X* in the cursor, you are over a face area and cannot apply the color.

8. Save both images in your *Chapter 10* folder, as *Lighthouse3CLR.ai* and *LighthouseMultiCLR.ai* to see your work. Go ahead and open the guitar photo you used for the web header and see what effects you can create. If you have a complex illustration, bring that it in to play with. Enjoy!

 TOOLKIT TIP Be very careful that you don't choose to Expand a photograph as high fidelity unless you have lots of time to wait for the process depending on your computer's system and memory, and the image size. Simplicity in using less color for less complicated paths is at times better with this powerful function.

CHAPTER SUMMARY

In this chapter, you were introduced to various methods of saving and importing graphic files and images between Illustrator and Photoshop. Here is a brief list to summarize what was covered; use this as a guide for projects you may do in the future.

- Always try to save Illustrator and Photoshop files in their native formats for a backup.
- Embed images when you do not want to worry about locating the original image. Understand that you may have a larger file size as a result, especially with bitmap or raster images.
- Use linking if you can keep the Illustrator file in the same place as the linked graphic, which will minimize the file size.
- Use the Place command when bringing Photoshop images into Illustrator, making sure you have created the final size in Photoshop first.
- Smart Objects allow you to make changes while preserving an image's source data with its original characteristics, enabling you to perform non-destructive editing to the layer.
- Embedded Smart Objects can be adjusted in the document and leave a copy of the original size document for future editing without throwing out pixels and data info. Linked Smart Objects allow you to make changes in the original artwork that automatically makes the change in the linked document.
- To open Photoshop artwork with layers into Illustrator, choose to convert to objects.
- Graphics saved as PNG files preserve transparency settings, whereas images saved as JPEGs do not; however, JPEG files are smaller in size.
- Export Illustrator files into Photoshop as PSD files to maintain the most layers and keep the background transparent.
- Photoshop will always rasterize images from Illustrator, so export at a larger size that can be reduced if necessary.
- Illustrator EPS and PDF files can be edited in Illustrator and saved in Illustrator's native format, whereas Photoshop EPS and PDF files are flattened.
- You can create text outlines in Illustrator as individual closed paths; Photoshop PDF and EPS files can have type converted to outlined graphics in Illustrator.

REVIEW QUESTIONS

1. As a designer, you want to maintain a transparent background in your image. What file formats would you choose in Illustrator to keep this effect? What format would you save in if you needed to bring an Illustrator file into Photoshop?

2. What command in Illustrator allows the background transparency of a bitmap image to be transferred from Photoshop to Illustrator?

3. Explain the difference between bitmap and vector images.

4. Explain the difference between placing and pasting a document within either application.

5. Describe the difference between linking and embedding an image and when one would be more appropriate over the other.

6. Explain when to use EPS and PDF files for each application.

Integrating Photoshop Images and Effects with Illustrator

Integrating Illustrator Graphics and Effects into Photoshop

CHAPTER 10
Web headers created by integrating
elements between Photoshop and Illustrator.

CHAPTER 10 ADVANCED
Understanding PDF and EPS files.

CHAPTER 10 EXTRA
Using Image Trace and Live Paint in Illustrator
to generate editable paths from various types of images, and apply color.

▷ FIGURE 10-37

Digital Illustration: Adobe Illustrator CC

CREATIV
CLOUD
EDITION

Most drawings created in Illustrator are combinations of various paths. Here you will learn the importance of layering paths to create compound shapes, how to use layers to isolate graphic components, build your skills using the Pen and Pencil tools, and use the Object menu for various edits. You will be creating an illustration from a sketch, building layered paths, and making type paths on a dark mug as part of a promotion. In this case, you will be creating a multicolor logo.

CLIENT ASSIGNMENT: Making a Promotional Mug Logo

Louise Ambler is the owner of Stage Fright Café, a local coffee shop where local musicians come and play on the weekends to entertain the crowds. She wants to promote the café and its local entertainment by creating promotional coffee mugs to be used at the café and for sale and marketing purposes. She brings you a very rough sketch of an acoustic guitar. She discusses with you how she wants the mug to be a royal blue color with the café name in yellow or yellow gold lettering in a circular path with the guitar in the center of the name. The guitar will be a gradient blend of yellow and orange with red and black details. You meet again with Louise to discuss how she will be given a proof of the logo inside a royal blue square that represents the mug color, and how you will also provide a 3D rendition of what the logo may look like when applied to the mug surface. You also discuss how you can show her what the logo may look like on other promotional pieces like a CD cover, business card, and direct mail piece. She leaves, excited to see the final results ready for press by the end of the week (Figure UR3-1).

▷ FIGURE UR3-1

Starting from a sketch, create a multi-shape guitar graphic, and then create a 3D mug to map the logo on.

ACTION ITEMS OVERVIEW

After tracing the sketch using Illustrator's drawing tools, primarily the Pen Tool (P), you will need to create a series of shapes to create the guitar graphic. You will then create the business name, Stage Fright Café, on circular paths separate from the guitar graphic. Once you save the graphic as a symbol, you will create a 3D view of the mug with the logo in it. Here is a breakdown of what needs to be done:

- Clean up the scanned sketch in Photoshop using the Magic Eraser Tool (E) and adjusting the brightness and contrast in the Image menu.

- Place the sketch as a template in Illustrator, and create working layers for different portions of the image.

- Use the Pen Tool (P) and the other drawing tools to create layered paths and various strokes and fill combinations for the logo.

- Add the Stage Fright Café name in capital letters using the Path Type Tool within circle paths, and adjust the position of the text with the Direct Selection Tool (A).

- Create the symbol of the logo for future use.

- Scale the logo to fit the mug and also create a symbol of the logo.

- Create a 3D mug illustration, and map the logo to the mug's surface.

- Apply the finished logo in multiple artboards format to include a CD cover, business card, and direct mail piece.

TRACING THE BASIC SKETCH LOGO

If an image is to be traced in Illustrator, there usually needs to be some preliminary work in Photoshop. If a sketch or drawing is on tracing or lightweight paper, the scan can create a very "dirty" background. Before scanning an image that is on tracing paper, use a copy machine to copy the traced image onto regular white paper to get rid of much of the background interference. When the image is scanned into Photoshop, adjust it by selecting Image > Adjustments > Brightness/Contrast, or Auto Contrast, or try Levels adjustments (Image > Adjustments > Levels) to further remove the background shadows. Use the Magic Eraser and Background Eraser tools to remove the background from the image, so only the actual drawing is left to be placed into Illustrator for tracing. This will prep the image to be placed in Illustrator for using drawing tools to create the basic acoustic guitar logo.

TOOLKIT TIP Because the image was scanned in Grayscale mode, you have access to the same adjustments as you would with a color scan. If it was scanned as black and white, you would find little or no adjustments could be made.

Next, you will take an image that was drawn on tracing paper, copied, scanned, and prepped in Photoshop to be placed in Illustrator for tracing.

1. Launch Photoshop and open the file *Acoustic.tif* in your *Unit 3 Review* folder. If you need the file, you can download it at *www.CengageBrain.com*.

2. Select Image > Auto Contrast to darken the lightly scanned-in lines. You can also try the Brightness/Contrast option in the Adjustments menu.

3. Zoom in to 200% and use the Magic Eraser Tool (E) to remove any excess spots so that the image can be traced in Illustrator. Clear out any white areas so that only the lines will show. Be careful not to delete the lines themselves.

▷ FIGURE UR3-2

Prepping the scanned, sketched image first using Photoshop's tools for cleaning up the image before bringing it into Illustrator for use as a template.

4. In Photoshop, select Image > Adjustments > Levels and increase the midtone slider in the Levels dialog box to the right. This will darken the lines significantly, and you can see if there are any dust spots to clean up, too. To remove dirty edges, use the Crop Tool (C) and select only the guitar area; crop out any extra space outside the guitar (Figure UR3-2).

5. Save the file in your *Unit 3 Review* folder and minimize the window. Do not be concerned with the roughness of the lines; this is a sketch we will bring into Illustrator as a template to create the required paths.

6. Launch Illustrator and create a new Print document. Select CMYK color, portrait orientation, letter size, 4 artboards with a 0.125 (1/8) inch bleed, and inches as the Units measurement. Name the document *CafeMug*. Click OK. When the four artboards display, choose the number 1 artboard to create the logo.

7. In Illustrator, use File > Place to first select the *Acoustic.tif* image you just fixed in the new document, to be placed into first artboard. Make sure the Link box is unchecked and the Template box is checked to create an embedded template layer and a working layer, *Layer1*, above it (Figure UR3-3). If a TIFF Import Options dialog box displays to convert or flatten layers, choose the default Flatten Layers to a Single Image. After you click OK, check your Layers panel to ensure that you have two layers.

8. If the Guitar is placed in the center of the 4 artboards, unlock the template layer in the Layers panel, and using the Selection Tool (V), select the guitar template image and drag into the first artboard. Zoom in to 100%.

9. Save the file as *CafeMug.ai* using the default options in your *Unit 3 Review* folder.

▷ FIGURE UR3-3

In Illustrator, placing the guitar image as a template.

CREATING THE GUITAR FACE USING THE PEN TOOL AND BÉZIER CURVES

Yep . . . it's baaack! That's right: the best tool for most of this job is the Pen Tool. Use this tool for smooth connecting lines and placing paths on top of one another, and you will realize just how great this tool really is. It is important to create closed paths when you want them to have a fill color. For making nonconnecting lines, like the turn screws or keys on the neck of the guitar, the Pencil Tool (N) may come in handy, or you can still use the Pen Tool. There are different approaches to building these shapes, you can create sublayers or simply move shapes from the work area with the Selection Tool (V). You can also experiment by using the Draw Behind drawing mode to bring selected path lines behind one another. The Draw Behind mode allows you to draw behind all artwork on a selected layer if no artwork is selected. If the artwork is selected, the new object is drawn directly beneath the selected object.

TOOLKIT TIP If you want to know which path you are selecting, check the Layers panel; you will notice a colored square will display next to the selected path sublayer.

TOOLKIT TIP Feel free to create a custom tools panel (Window > Tools > New Tools Panel) adding the various Pen and Selection tools, Scissors Tool, Pencil Tool, Ellipse Tool, and Type on a Path Tool for this tutorial. To assist with adding shapes you can create a series of sublayer paths, so you can draw one shape on top of another by selecting Create New Sublayer in the Layers panel.

First you will create the guitar shape, making sure that it is a closed path.

1. Rename *Layer1* above the template layer *Guitar Shape*.

2. Zoom in to about 200% and start using the Pen Tool (P) with a 1-pt black Stroke and a Fill of None to be able to see the paths you create. Create your Bézier curves carefully (refer to Chapter 9).

3. Create an outer outline (Figure UR3-4) by clicking and dragging with the Pen Tool. Use the Backspace key, or Command/CTRL Z to go back a step, and make sure the Pen Tool cursor has an *X* showing to continue the path. To make corner points, use the Pen Tool with the convert cursor or the Anchor Point Tool (Shift+C). When you approach the bottom neck of the guitar, just click to make straight lines. The last point will indicate an *O* on the Pen Tool cursor to indicate that you are about to close the path.

Use the Pen Tool to create accurate curves that meet the shape of the guitar

To create another shape below the guitar front, move the front face to provide work area, create a new sublayer or select Draw Behind and use the Pen Tool for precision

Draw Behind

▷ FIGURE UR3-4

Creating overlapping closed paths using the Pen and Selection tools and arrow keys.

4. To check to see if you made a closed shape, select a Fill color to see if it stays inside the path. If so, select None again to remove it for now. Save when you have made an accurate path.

5. Use the Direct Selection Tool (A) to adjust path components by clicking outside the path; then select anchor points and direction lines to adjust them or select highlighted path segments and adjust curves using the Path Segment Reshape function.

6. If needed, zoom in to 300% and select open end points with the Lasso Tool (Q), and then use Object > Path > Average > Both to join them into one path.

7. Check again to make sure the path is closed by selecting a fill color. Change the Fill back to None once this step is complete.

8. To create the side of the guitar, select Create New Sublayer in the Layers panel to start another sublayer path to add paths on top of one another, and use the Selection Tool (V) to move the guitar front off to the side. You can choose, instead, to select Draw Behind mode from the bottom of the Tools panel to try to draw behind the guitar face. Use the Pen tools to create a closed path of the guitar side. Try not to use too many anchor points, and keep saving the file periodically.

9. When you have checked to make sure you have a closed path for the side of the guitar, if the Draw Behind option worked it should locate directly behind the guitar face, otherwise use the Selection Tool to move back the guitar front over the side path you just created. Keep a black Stroke and Fill of None at this point to show your paths.

10. Do *not* group the two paths; keep them separate. Save the file in Illustrator's native AI format.

CREATING PRECISE OVERLAPPING PATHS FOR THE GUITAR FACE AND SIDE

Next, you will place part of one path on top of another. The key to good artwork is to do this without changing the width of the original stroke. This takes some adjusting with the Direct Selection, Selection, and Smooth tools to complement the paths created by the Pen Tool. The key when making overlapping paths is to zoom in close and adjust them so that the overlapping paths appear as one (Figure UR3-5).

▷ FIGURE UR3-5

Using the Direct Selection Tool and arrow keys to adjust the direction lines and anchor points for precise placement of overlapping paths.

Testing closed path with fill color, check overlapping path

Overlapping Path

Next, you will create overlapping paths so they appear as one.

1. Use the Selection Tool (V) to make sure the guitar face and side are in place, matching the template. Save frequently.

2. With the guitar face selected using the Direct Selection Tool (A), refine paths by adjusting the direction lines, and move anchor points so the paths start to line up where they meet at the side. If you are comfortable using the Draw Behind mode mentioned earlier, you may not have to make many adjustments.

3. Use the Direct Selection Tool (A) to select the side piece, and make adjustments as needed to create one path where they overlap.

4. Use the arrow keys to move anchor points into place. Save frequently.

5. Continue to check for closed paths by applying a fill color. Change Fill back to None, and leave the Stroke as black to outline the paths.

6. Select View > Outline to see if the overlapping paths are close to looking like a single path. You can then select View > Preview to go back to the original state.

7. If you want, select the guitar side with the Selection Tool (V) and then select Object > Arrange > Send to Back to place it underneath the guitar face (see Adjusting the Arrangement of Layers), if again, you were unable to use the Draw Behind function.

8. Feel free to group the two paths together for coloring later. You can always add fill by selecting each piece with the Direct Selection Tool (A), even if they are grouped.

9. Save, save, save!

TOOLKIT TIP In Illustrator CC, you can hold down the Option/ALT key while using the Pen Tool on selected path segments and adjust curves for accuracy.

ADJUSTING THE ARRANGEMENT OF LAYERS

You can use the Object menu to rearrange objects in any order. With Illustrator, objects are placed on top of one another to create a composite illustration. The Arrange function (Object > Arrange) provides the option to rearrange the stacking order of objects. If you select Send to Front or Send to Back, the object is brought either directly in front of all the other objects or directly behind all the other objects. If you choose Send Backward or Send Forward, you are sending the objects backward or forward one sublayer at a time. You can also send an object to a different highlighted layer by selecting the Send to Current Layer option.

TOOLKIT TIP You can also use the Layers panel to select objects on sublayers and drag them to another position. You can always create separate layers as well for easier navigation between objects.

CREATING THE GUITAR NECK WITH STRAIGHT AND BÉZIER PATHS

To create the guitar neck, you will use the Pen Tool (P) to click for straight lines, click and drag to create Bézier curves, and use the Anchor Point Tool (Shift+C) (or hold down the Option/ALT key with Pen Tool) to create corners. It may take a few tries, but mastering this technique will be a huge asset in your digital arsenal.

Now you will create the neck face of the guitar using the Pen Tool.

1. Use the Selection Tool (V) to Shift-select or drag diagonally across both guitar shapes you created, and move them downward so you can work on the guitar neck. If you had previously tried the Draw Behind mode, click on the Normal Draw (default) mode on the left side in the Tools panel.

2. In the Layers panel, add another layer above the *Guitar Shape* Layer and call it *Neck*.

3. Zoom in to 300% and start at the upper back end of the neck, placing anchor points until you reach the other side of the upper neck area (Figure UR3-6). Save the file.

▷ FIGURE UR3-6

Creating the face of the guitar neck using the Pen Tool to create straight lines, Bézier curves, and using the Anchor Point Tool for corners.

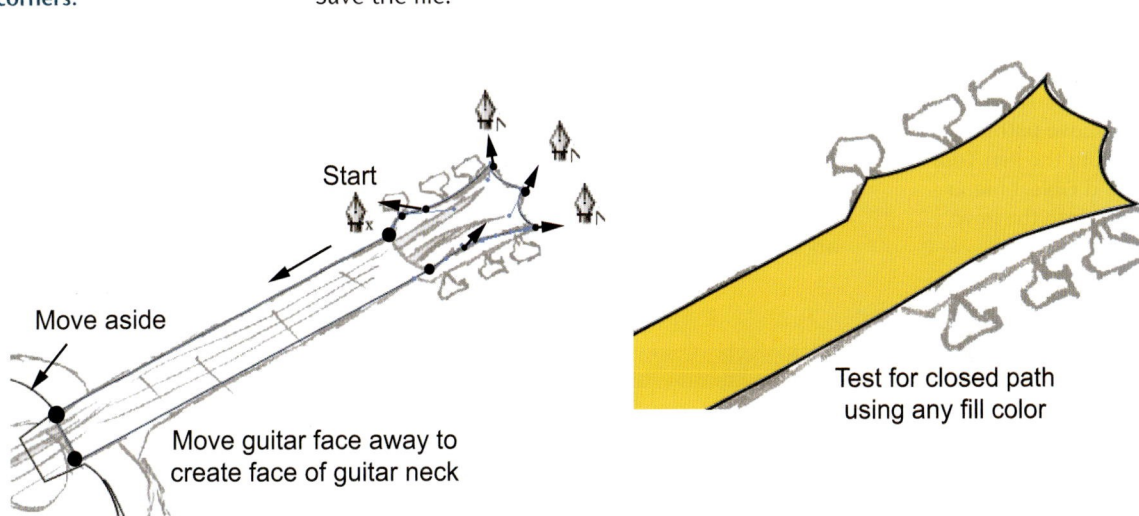

4. In Illustrator CC, with the lines still selected, hold down the Option/ALT key with the Pen Tool to convert to the Path Segment Reshape function to adjust the curves in the path segments.

5. You can also use the Direct Selection Tool (A) to adjust path segments and components by deselecting the path; then select anchor points to adjust their position and direction lines or select path segment and drag to create curves.

6. Zoom back in to 300% and select any unjoined end points with the Lasso Tool (Q); use Object > Path > Average > Both to overlap the selected points.

7. Check to make sure you have a closed path by selecting a Fill color. When the path is closed, change the back Fill to None.

8. Keep saving your work frequently.

USING THE SCISSORS TOOL TO REMOVE SELECTED PATHS

Here is another fun challenge. In this exercise, we want to create another shape the same as the head piece at the top of the neck of the guitar, called the *headstock*, and then close it and put it on top of the neck to apply a different color. You are going to copy the complex guitar neck you just created and use the Scissors Tool (C) to delete the portion of the path you do not need. You will use the Pen Tool (P) to close the path for the head to create another closed path and apply a different Fill color. The Control panel has a Cut path at selected anchor points function, too.

First, you will use the Option/ALT key to copy the selected guitar neck object you just created; then use the Scissors Tool (C) or the Control panel to cut the paths to isolate the complex head path. You will then use the Pen Tool (P) and Object menu to close the path.

1. Select the neck face you just created with the Selection Tool (V); then hold down the Option/ALT key and drag a copy to the side. Save your file.

2. Select the original neck face to see its anchor points.

▷ FIGURE UR3-7

Copying a complex object, using the Scissors Tool to remove paths, then using the Pen Tool and Object menu to close the new path shapes.

3. Use the Scissors Tool (C) located behind the Eraser Tool (Shift+E), and click the straight path of the neck as shown in Figure UR3-7 under the tuning keys. When you split the path in the middle of a segment, the two new end points appear on top of the other, and one end point is selected.

4. Do the same on the other side; or you can use the Direct Selection Tool (A) to select the anchor point where you want to split the path, and then click the Cut path at selected anchor points button in the Control panel. When you split the path at an anchor point, a new anchor point appears on top of the original anchor point, and one anchor point is selected.

5. Select the unwanted portions of the neck and use the Delete key to remove them. You now need to close the path, so you can apply a different fill color.

6. Use the Direct Selection Tool (A) to select the path, and then zoom in to 600%. Use the Pen Tool (P) to click on the back end of the path; it should have a slash icon indicating you are about to start drawing from that anchor point, and drag across the bottom edge to create a curve that matches the template. This may take a few attempts. Hit the Return/Enter key or select another tool to end the path segment.

7. If you did not close the path, select the two end points with the Lasso Tool (Q), and then select Object > Path > Average > Both to overlap end points.

8. Check to make sure you have a closed path by selecting a Fill color. When the path is closed, change the Fill back to None.

9. Drag the guitar neck you copied earlier back into position over the template, and use Object > Arrange > Send to Back to ensure it is behind your new head. Save your file.

CREATING THE UNDERSIDE OF THE GUITAR NECK

Here is where you may find you need to improvise a little. Sometimes clients cannot think in three dimensions when creating sketches, as is the case of this guitar. You still need to create an underside to the neck face so that it balances with the side of the guitar front. You will then need to overlap both neck paths or shapes. Again, the key here is trying to make the stroke weight as consistent as possible when paths overlap. Remember: the template is just a guide for the drawing.

 TOOLKIT TIP If you are nervous about moving the artwork to create the underside of the guitar, another option for those who want a little challenge would be to just create the second shape to overlap the neck, and then use the Pathfinder panel to divide it into the two pieces as you did in the Digital Toolkit Extra exercise in Chapter 9, to make the clock. If you do this, you can skip steps 1 through 3 below.

It is time to create the underside of the guitar neck using the Pen Tool (P) and the Direct Selection Tool (A) to overlap the paths accurately, as you have already done with the guitar face and side.

1. Using the Selection Tool (V), move the neck face you just created aside to create the underside closed path, or, select the Draw Behind mode in the bottom Tools panel.

2. Start underneath at the head end with the Pen Tool (P) and a 1-pt black Stroke and a Fill of None; start heading down the neck, placing anchor points a little beyond the line in the sketch to improvise an edge shape, and then work your way back up, as shown in Figure UR3-8.

3. Create a Bézier curve to match the curve on the guitar head, and then click to close the path.

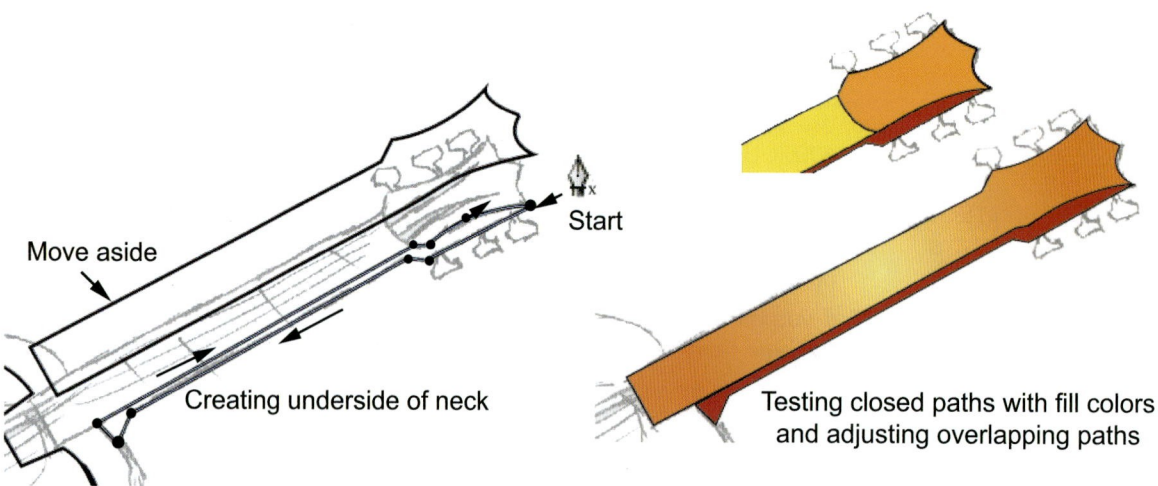

Move aside

Start

Creating underside of neck

Testing closed paths with fill colors
and adjusting overlapping paths

▷ FIGURE UR3-8

**Creating the under-
side of the neck
using the Pen Tool,
with a little impro-
vising. Making
overlapping
paths and adjust-
ments and testing
closed paths.**

4. Use the Direct Selection Tool (A) to adjust the paths by deselecting the path, and then select the anchor points and direction lines to refine the path. Use your arrow keys as well.

5. If needed, zoom in to 300% and select open end points with the Lasso Tool (Q); then select Object > Path > Average > Both.

6. Check to make sure the path is closed by selecting a Fill color. When the path is closed, change the Fill back to None.

7. Use the Selection Tool (V) to move the guitar neck back next to the neck side you just created. Keep saving frequently.

8. With the neck selected with the Direct Selection Tool (A), refine the paths by adjusting the direction lines and anchor points, so the paths start to line up alongside the side piece.

9. Use the Direct Selection Tool (A) to select the underside piece, and make adjustments as needed to create one path line where they overlap.

10. Use the arrow keys to move anchor points into place. Save frequently.

11. Check the closed paths by applying fill colors to see if any areas are "leaking" through.

12. When you are finished, change the fill back to None and leave the stroke black so you can see the paths. Select View > Outline to see if the overlapping paths are close to looking like a single path. Select View >Preview to toggle back to the original.

13. Group the two paths together for coloring later. If needed, select the neck underside with the Selection Tool (V), and then select Object > Arrange > Send to Back to place it underneath the neck face.

14. Keep on saving!

CREATING TUNING KEYS WITH THE PEN OR PENCIL TOOLS AND THE TRANSFORM COMMAND

In this exercise, you can choose to use the Pen and Pencil tools to create the tuning keys. You will use the Selection Tool (V) to select and move the keys into position under the neck; use the Option/ALT key to copy the keys to make them consistent. The Transform menu can be used to reverse the object to use it on the other side of the neck.

Now you will create the tuning keys using either the Pen or Pencil Tool (N), Option/ALT copy for consistency, and then use the Transform menu to flip the keys for the other side of the neck. You will only need to make one tuning key. You will use this tuning key to create the rest. Don't worry about matching the template sketch since it's just a guide, and accuracy is more important.

1. You may not need to move aside the neck, but feel free if it is easier. Zoom in to about 600% and either using the Pen or Pencil Tool (N), with a black, 1-pt Stroke, and a Fill of None, create the middle key of the guitar. Because this is a very small detail, you can be forgiving as to how the key looks.

2. Use the Direct Selection Tool (A) to adjust anchor points and direction lines. Use the arrow keys as well.

3. If needed, zoom in to 300% and select any open end points with the Lasso Tool (Q); then select Object > Path > Average > Both.

4. Check to make sure the path is closed by selecting a Fill color. When the path is closed, change the Fill back to None, and keep the Stroke black.

▷ FIGURE UR3-9

Creating a tuning key and copying it for consistency.

5. Using the Selection Tool (V), select the closed path of the tuning key, and hold down the Option/ALT key to drag copies to each side, as shown in Figure UR3-9. Create an additional copy to be reflected for the other side.

Copy for other side

Use Pen or Pencil Tool

Option/Alt copy the selected object

Check with Fill color

Zoom at 600%

6. To reflect the key for the other side, select Object > Transform > Rotate > 180 degrees to flip the object, as shown in Figure UR3-10.

7. Position the reflected key; then use the Selection Tool (V) and the Option/ALT key to make the two additional copies.

8. Use the Selection Tool (V) to move the keys into place. To place the keys behind the stroke of the guitar neck, select Object > Arrange > Send to Back. Zoom back in to 100% to check your work. There is no need to match the template sketch of the keys underneath. Keep saving frequently.

▷ FIGURE UR3-10

Using the Object menu to rotate the tuning key, copy, and position as shown.

FINSHING DETAILS WITH THE ELLIPSE, PEN, AND PENCIL TOOLS

The hard parts are done, so now it is time to use the Pen, Pencil, and Ellipse tools to provide the finishing details. First you will create the guitar sound hole with the Ellipse Tool (L) and then the bridge that holds the strings with the Pen or Pencil Tool, and the strings themselves using the Pen Tool.

1. Using the Selection Tool (V), move the guitar face and side together over the guitar neck you just created, matching the template for position; then select Object > Arrange > Bring to Front, so these objects are on top of the guitar neck.

2. Use the Direct Selection Tool (A) to adjust any paths as needed. Add fill colors to check for accuracy, and then select a Fill of None when done.

3. With a Fill of None you can see the template below. Select the Pen or Pencil Tool (the Pen Tool (P) may work best), and with a 1-pt black Stroke and a Fill of None, outline the bridge. If you use the Pen Tool, create a straight line across the top; then use the Anchor Point Tool (Shift+C) at the corner to create the curved bottom portion. Or, with the Pen Tool (P) selected, hold down the Option/ALT key. Use the Direct Selection Tool (A) to adjust the curves. Test with a Fill color to make sure the path is closed (Figure UR3-11).

4. To create the sound hole, select the Ellipse Tool (L) and click on the hole area. When the dialog box comes up, create a 0.75-inch circle, and move it below the neck as shown.

5. Select both the sound hole and the bridge, and select Object Arrange > Bring to Front to make sure they are on top of the guitar surface.

6. Add a light Fill color to the neck, so you can see how the strings will look, and use the Pen Tool (P) with a black, 2-pt Stroke and no Fill. Click from the bridge to the upper neck as shown in Figure UR3-11, and then press the Return key to end the path, so you can create the next string. Create only three strings, and keep them spaced equally. Remember: this will be used in a much smaller version on a mug, so you do not want many lines. If this were going to be for a poster, then you would create all six strings.

7. Open the Layers panel, and drag the Template layer to the Trash to remove the template. Save the file.

Pen Tool to
create bridge

Ellipse Tool for
the sound hole

Pen Tool
for strings

APPLYING COLOR AND GRADIENTS WITH THE SWATCHES PANEL

You can use the Swatches panel and select from the existing colors, or use the Swatches panel submenu to open up other swatch color libraries, and choose to add the swatches to the main Swatches panel. For instance, choose Open Swatch Library > Nature > Beach; you will find various matching color groups. Command/ CTRL click to select the individual swatches you want to add, and select Add To Swatches from the library's submenu, or drag one or more swatches from the library panel to the Swatches panel. You can also automatically add all the colors from selected artwork to the Swatches panel to create your own customized color group by selecting the default Include Swatches for Tints.

Now it is time to play with color. Since the background will be a deep blue, we want to use lighter colors for balance and contrast. For the neck and keys, a yellow or yellow gold may work fine. Use an orange color for the head. Select a deep red for the side of the neck, the bridge, and the side of the guitar. Use a radial gradient of yellow and deep orange for the guitar face. The sound hole will match the blue of the mug itself (Figure UR3-12).

▷ FIGURE UR3-12

**Applying fill colors
and gradients for
the final guitar
illustration.**

Beach Swatch Library

Gradient Panel

Libraries
Menu

Select Gradient
Mode

Completed
Illustration

Radial
Gradient Bar

TOOLKIT TIP Selecting stroke and fill colors for closed paths can be done with the Direct Selection Tool (A). If you grouped objects together and used the Selection Tool (V) to apply color, the color would be applied to all objects instead of to individual objects. If you do not know where the color you have selected is located on the Swatches panel, just select it and the swatch will be highlighted for you.

1. With all objects in position, it is time to fill in color. We will keep the 1-pt black stroke for all the objects. You can use the Swatches panel submenu to select Open Swatch Library and choose from various options for colors. Use your own combinations of colors if you like, but keep them light and balanced against the blue color of the mug. To add swatches from any open swatch library to the Swatches panel, just drag them from the library to the Swatches panel.

2. Use the Direct Selection Tool (A) to select and apply a yellow Fill color to the keys and neck face (try C5, M0, Y90, or K0).

3. Select the headstock with the Direct Selection Tool (A), and apply an orange fill (try C0, M50, Y100, or K0).

4. Select the side of the neck, the bridge, and the side of the guitar face and apply a reddish color (try C15, M100, Y90, or K10), or try a deep orange tone instead.

TOOLKIT TIP In Illustrator, you can have gradients adjusted to fade to transparent, apply special gradients in real time, and move them around. You select the object, then the Gradient Tool (G), and click. A gradient bar displays to edit the linear or radial gradient effect by dragging and rotating the gradient bar around the selected object. The results are viewed live. The new gradient can be saved in the Swatches panel. You can also make edits from the Appearance panel.

5. To create the radial gradient for the guitar face, use the Gradient panel first (Window > Gradient), and select the colors you want from the Swatches panel; stick with those you have already used for consistency. Drag one to each side of the Gradient panel to create gradient sliders. Select Radial for Type, and adjust the upper gradient slider to preview what it will look like. You can edit the gradient by rotating or dragging the gradient bar, and by adjusting the gradient sliders. To display the bar, select the guitar, then the Gradient Tool (G), and click.

6. Select the guitar face with the Direct Selection Tool (A), and click the Gradient Mode button or the Fill color picker to apply the gradient.

7. For the sound hole, select the circle you created and apply a royal blue color Fill that will be the same used for the mug (try C100, M100, Y25, or K25). If the hole is above the strings you created, select Object > Arrange > Send Backward; this will send it back one sublayer at a time. Keep doing this until it is under the strings but not under the guitar face.

8. After you have chosen and applied all your colors, you can save them as a group (Figure UR3-13). Just select the entire guitar graphic with the Selection Tool (V), and click the New Color Group icon at the bottom of the Swatches panel.

▷ FIGURE UR3-13

Creating a new color group from the selected guitar graphic.

New Color Group

New color group from selected guitar artwork

9. Name the color group *Guitar Colors*, select Create from: Select Artwork, leave the default Include Swatches for Tints selected, then click OK, and you will find your color group in the Swatches panel. Save the file.

TOOLKIT TIP To group all your objects together as one guitar graphic, use Select > All, then Object > Group. You would have created a vector graphic that can be scaled to any size. However, remember that grouping objects from several layers combines them all onto one layer, so saving your file first before grouping keeps the layers separate to provide further opportunity for editing.

TOOLKIT TIP Not sure what colors to use together? Select the colors using the Color panel, or open swatch libraries to display various color groups that work nicely together. You can also play with the Color Guide panel (refer to Chapter 7).

SCALING THE LOGO AND SAVING IT AS A SYMBOL

Now that you have spent some time creating you artwork, you can save it as a symbol to reuse whenever the need arises. Saving artwork as symbols allows you to create your own library of reusable, scalable artwork (Figure UR3-14).

Here is where you can save all your hard work as a symbol for future projects.

1. To make the graphic a little smaller, use the Selection Tool (V) to select all objects, and then use Object > Transform > Scale > 90%.

2. Select the guitar graphic; then click the New Symbol icon at the bottom of the Symbols panel.

3. Name the symbol *Guitar*, select Graphic, and click OK.

4. You will find a thumbnail of the guitar symbol in the Symbols panel.

TOOLKIT TIP After this project, try dragging the Guitar symbol out and play with the new Graphic Styles panel to observe preset effects applied that could be used as variations of the logo graphic you just created. You can also create your own effect and save it for future projects. You can also specify 9-slice scaling in Illustrator so that the symbols scale appropriately when used for specialized media like video.

▷ FIGURE UR3-14

Creating a reusable symbol from the guitar illustration.

New Symbol

DESIGN TIP

When placing type against a dark background, it is good idea to use a bold font.

DESIGN TIP

Sometimes varying the layout will create a different graphic feel appropriate for another market. Here, we are going for a more contemporary-alternative acoustic environment, but another idea may be to use a yellow circle with the type inside for a more country look. Go ahead, experiment and create a few variations.

CREATING THE TITLE ON CIRCULAR PATHS

With the guitar graphic complete, you will add the Stage Fright Café name on two separate circular paths to complete the logo. You will use a yellow color or another light color you may have used on the guitar for consistency, and place the text around a 6-inch diameter circle.

First we will create an 8-inch by 8-inch blue background, twice the mug size, to preview the type and logo to see how they will look on the mug. Then, we will put the Stage Fright Café name on a circular path.

1. In the Layers panel, add a new layer and call it *Type*. Move the *Type* layer under the *Guitar Shape* and *Neck* layers to make sure it will appear under the guitar illustration.

2. Select the Rectangle Tool (M) and create an 8-inch square in the same blue that will be used for the mug (we used C100, M100, Y25, and K25).

3. With the Selection Tool (V), select and drag the guitar illustration you created over the background. It should display on top. If it does not, use the Object > Arrange > Bring to Front option.

4. Select the Ellipse Tool (L), click on the artboard, and create a 6-inch circle and a 2-pt yellow or other light color Stroke with no Fill to use temporarily as the type path; it will disappear once you start typing. Use the Selection Tool (V) to move the circle into position as shown in Figure UR3-15.

5. Select the (Horizontal) Type on a Path Tool using 48-pt Copperplate Gothic Bold or another bold font in order for it to stand out against a dark background, and type "STAGE FRIGHT." Drag the vertical I-beam with the Direct Selection Tool (A) to center the type.

6. To make the other part of the title "Café" line, you need to create a new 6 × 6 inch circular path with the Ellipse Tool (L) using same settings. Position it as shown in Figure UR3-15.

Drag I-Beam

Drag I-Beam

▷ FIGURE UR3-15

Create a background, place the graphic, and create a type path for the title.

7. Select the (Horizontal) Type on a Path Tool using the same 48-pt Copperplate Gothic Bold Type, or whichever font you chose for the Stage Fright title. Type "CAFÉ"; use the Direct Selection Tool (A) to center the I-beam at the bottom of the circle. Drag the I-beam toward the inside of the circle to make sure the type is right side up.

8. To increase separation between characters, you can adjust the Tracking, which is located on the right side of the Character panel. Select the type with the Type on a Path Tool, and use 25 as a starting point in the Tracking settings on the Character panel (Figure UR3-15).

9. Make adjustments using the Selection Tool (V) to position the type and graphics. Feel free to save and experiment. As you can see, "Café" has been moved up closer to the neck of the guitar for a more pleasing effect.

10. Select all the objects, including the background (Select > All or Command/ CTRL A), and choose Object > Group to combine all objects together.

11. Use the File menu to Save As, and name this Illustrator backup version *CafeMug.ai*.

12. Now to scale the graphic to fit the mug, Select Object > Transform > Scale > 40%. Make sure the Scale Strokes and Effects option is checked for consistency. Click OK.

13. Open the Symbols panel, and then Option/ALT copy the graphic with text and background grouped together into the Symbols panel. Name the new symbol *Guitar Mug*. This prepares the graphic to be mapped to the 3D mug that you are about to create and will be used for the other three artboards.

CREATING A 3D MUG ILLUSTRATION TO MAP THE LOGO

One of the best features in Illustrator is the ability to create 3D objects and map 2D objects to 3D surfaces (see Chapter 8, Digital Toolkit Extra). Since the logo has been completed, you can show your client what it would look like on a mug. This feature will be a great asset for those who venture into the field of package design. Before placing the graphic onto a 3D object, it has to be made into a symbol.

TOOLKIT TIP When using the 3D Revolve effect, draw half of the intended object. In this case, the width of the mug is 3 inches, so you would draw horizontal lines at 1.5 inches before applying the effect. The height is the axis that the effect will use to revolve around and should be drawn at full length. You can adjust the size of the 3D effect using the Selection Tool (V) and the bounding box's resizing handles. To remove guides, hold down the CTRL key on your Mac and click, or right-click on the guide in Windows. Select Undo Ruler Guides or Hide Guides to temporarily hide the guides.

Now that the logo is created, it is time to see how it will look on a 3D mug surface.

1. Make sure the *CafeMug.ai* file is open and the logo selected with the Selection Tool (V); then move the logo so that there will be enough space to create the mug full size at about 5 inches tall.

2. Leave the logo on the artboard as a guide. The colors used in the logo should display in the Swatches panel, and the graphic itself is safely stored in the Symbols panel if you delete it by mistake.

3. Select View > Rulers > Show Rulers and drag two vertical guides, one to the 4-inch mark and another at 2.5 inches to set up the lines for the mug. Then drag two horizontal guides, placing them 4 inches apart.

4. To create the blue mug, make sure Fill is set to None; then select the blue that you used for the sound hole in the guitar from the Swatches panel for the Stroke color. Use a 4-pt Stroke weight. You can also reverse this and have a Fill color blue with a stroke of None. Either way will work.

5. Select the Line Tool (\); then while holding the Shift key down, draw a vertical, 4-inch line along the vertical guideline at the 4-inch mark. Then draw two horizontal lines at either end to the 2.5-inch guideline; hold the Shift key to ensure the lines are straight (see Figure UR3-16).

TOOLKIT TIP You can also try using the Pen Tool (P) instead, while holding down the Shift key, for straight lines; adjust with the Direct Selection Tool (A). This will eliminate the need to join end points.

> ▷ FIGURE UR3-16
>
> **Create a 3D mug of royal blue color by applying 3D effect using the 3D Revolve function.**

6. Use the Lasso Tool (Q) to select the corners; then select Object > Path > Join > Corner to make sure the corners are connected. Make sure the path is still selected.

7. Select Effect > 3D > Revolve to display the 3D Revolve Options dialog box. Select the Turn cap off for hollow appearance icon to make the mug appear hollow inside, and leave all other settings at their defaults.

8. Click OK to apply the effect.

 TOOLKIT TIP Before selecting OK to apply the 3D effect, you will notice that a warning may appear stating that spot colors will be converted to process colors. This will have no effect on the outcome of this project; the 3D effect is only used to give the client an idea of what the final product will look like.

Ⓧ **PROBLEM** If the mug cylinder displays as broken shapes, the paths are not connected. If it is taking considerable time to apply the effect, make sure the Fill and Stroke boxes do not both have color: one has to not be displaying any color. If you find this, cancel the operation, adjust, and apply again. The revolve process may actually be faster with the Fill color applied and a Stroke of None.

MAPPING THE LOGO TO THE MUG SHAPE

Once artwork is converted to a symbol in the Symbols panel, it can be mapped around any 3D object you create. The Appearance panel is used to display a hierarchy of fills, strokes, graphic styles, and applied effects. To edit 3D objects, the object must be selected so its attributes and properties are displayed in the Appearance panel. You can then double-click on the 3D item in the Appearance panel to make changes to the object, including mapping artwork, lighting, and object properties. The key to having the mapping operation work is to make sure the artwork to be mapped is saved as a symbol first.

Now you will map the logo to the mug surface.

1. To apply or map the logo to the mug surface, double-click the 3D Revolve item in the Appearance panel (Window > Appearance) to display the 3D Revolve Options dialog box again. Drag the window to the right side so you can view the mapping effect.

2. Click the Map Art button. Do not worry if the color on the mug shape disappears.

3. Use the arrows to find the surface that matches Figure UR3-17; it will display as a light gray gridline on the right side. The number of surfaces may differ than shown on Figure UR3-17.

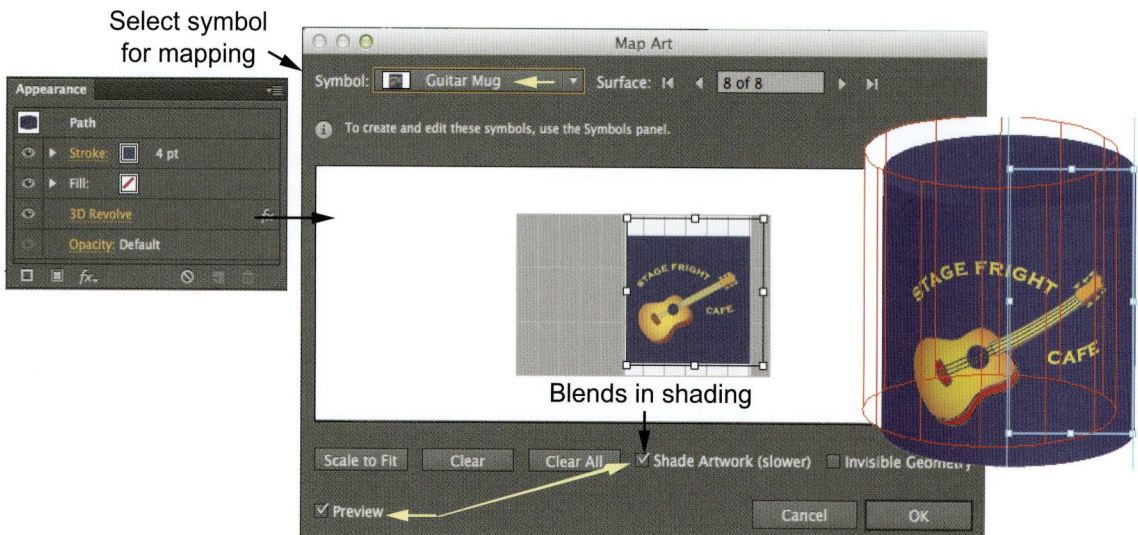

Select symbol for mapping

Blends in shading

▷   FIGURE UR3-17

Mapping the guitar label onto a 3D representation of the mug.

4. Make sure the Preview and the Shade Artwork boxes are checked to display the text correctly, along with the lighting properties.

5. In the Map Art dialog box, select the new symbol you created from the Symbols drop-down menu, and position the bounding box to align the logo while observing the preview to check the effect. Do not worry about the guides created by the Ellipse Tool (L) for your type; they will not display on the mug.

6. If you make a mistake, select the Clear button on the dialog box, and repeat the previous steps until you position it the way you want it. Select OK when you are satisfied.

 PROBLEM If the logo in your mug appears faint, the Shade Artwork box in the Map Art dialog box was not checked to display the text correctly.

7. Select OK, then OK again when you are done; observe your work. Pretty cool, huh?

8. To add a handle for your mug shape, select the New Art Has Basic Appearance icon in the Appearance panel to turn off the 3D effects and start a new art shape (Figure UR3-18). It toggles on and off.

▷ FIGURE UR3-18

Use the Appearance panel to reset for new artwork to add the handle to the mug for the final 3D effect.

9. Make sure the mug is not selected, and use a Fill color of None and a 25-pt blue Stroke. Create a path for the handle using one of the drawing tools and the Smooth Tool.

10. Use the Direct Selection Tool (A) for any path and anchor point adjustments that need to be made. When you have finished, select the mug and the handle, and group everything together (Object > Group).

11. Double-click 3D Revolve (Fx) again in the Appearance panel, and play with different views and lighting styles by selecting More Options in the 3D Revolve Options dialog box.

12. Save the file in your *Unit 3 Review* folder. Time for coffee!

EDITING THE LOGO ARTWORK WITH MULTIPLE ARTBOARDS

The Multiple Artboards feature allows a designer to create up to 100 multiple artboards to show a potential client various sizes and types of media that the artwork created can be used for. One of the nice benefits to this new feature is it allows a designer to make variations of the artwork to show to a client with ease, and they can be rotated, edited, and printed individually for a potential client. They are also useful for creating a variety of things such as multiple page PDFs, printed pages with different sizes or different elements, etc. Designers can use and save multiple artboards within one document, or export each artboard to its own file. Double-clicking the Artboard Tool (Shift+O) opens the Artboard Options dialog box, and allows you to move, resize, and edit artboards, with one artboard selected at a time. You can adjust dimensions of a selected artboard by using the Artboard Tool (Shift+O), or the Control panel. You can also have independent ruler guides set up for each artboard to help with your sizing. Each artboard is numbered for easy reference; each can also be given a custom name. The Artboards panel helps you to keep track of multiple artboards, reorder and rearrange artboards, create new artboards, and duplicate artboards. You can paste objects at a particular location on the artboard and paste artwork on all artboards at the same location using the new Paste in Place and Paste on All Artboards options. Multiple artboards can be saved as individual artboards with an Illustrator extension, available in the Illustrator Options dialog box. You will resize the three remaining artboards for a CD front cover, business card, and direct mail piece (Figure UR3-19). With the graphic already saved as a symbol, you can copy it over and resize or edit as needed.

▷ FIGURE UR3-19

Displaying edited versions of artwork logo on multiple artboards resized with the Artboard Tool for specific uses.

CD Cover

Direct Mail

Business Card

3D Mug and 2D logo

1. Before you resize the remaining three artboards, make sure rulers and guides are displayed. Make sure Smart Guides is also checked in the View menu (View > Smart Guides).

2. To create the CD cover dimensions, with the Artboard Tool (Shift+O) selected, click on the number 2 artboard to the right and notice the ruler guides now display for this artboard. Drag for the CD cover using the ruler and smart guides, which will display as you drag so that you have a square measuring 4.75 by 4.75 inches. Notice the bleed follows along with the changes you make.

3. To create the direct mail piece, click on the number 3 artboard and drag to create a 4.25 Height x 5.5 Width dimension.

4. To create the business card, click on the number 4 artboard and create a 2.0 Height and 3.5 Width.

5. You can move artboards around, *not* with the Selection Tool, but with the Artboard Tool (Shift+O). Click on the direct mail piece and drag underneath the CD cover, and then click on the business card and drag under the mail piece to maximize the work space.

6. To make the CD cover, select the flat graphic with the Selection Tool (V), not the final mug graphic, if you still have it displayed and Option/ALT copy it to the CD cover piece. Hold down the Shift key to adjust proportionately to adjust slightly larger than the bleed area.

7. Symbols can be edited by breaking the linked graphic components. To create the direct mail piece, open the Symbols panel (Window > Symbols) and drag out the Guitar Mug symbol from the Symbols panel onto the direct mail artboard or near to it.

8. Here you are going to remove the blue background from the symbol by selecting the entire graphic with the Selection Tool (V); then CTRL + click (Mac) or right-click (PC), and select Break Link to Symbol to create individual components of the artwork (Figure UR3-20).

▷ FIGURE UR3-20

Using multiple artboards to create variations of artwork for a potential client.

Original Artwork　Break Link to Symbol

Direct Mail Piece

9. Click outside the artwork to deselect, and then use the Direct Selection Tool (A) to select the blue background and drag away from the graphic.

10. To change the yellow text color to match the blue background, select the Type on Path Tool and highlight the Stage Fright title.

11. Select the Eyedropper Tool (I) and click on the blue background to change the color of the type. Choose the Selection Tool (V) and click outside the graphic to deselect and make sure the type is the deep blue color.

12. Repeat the same process with the Café type line using the Type on Path Tool and the Eyedropper Tool (Figure UR3-20).

13. Select the new artwork with the Selection Tool (V) and choose Object > Group. Drag into Direct mail piece, and then resize holding down the Shift key and dragging inward. Adjust for space in the top left corner.

14. You may find you may need to readjust the type to bring it closer to the guitar. Click on the type path with the Direct Selection Tool (A), making sure the path vertical I-beams display and not the direction lines. Adjust using the arrow keys on your keyboard.

15. To create a new symbol with the new changes, drag the graphic into the Symbols panel and name it Café Logo as another variation of the original graphic.

16. For the business card, resize the graphic and Option/ALT copy it to drag it into the artboard. Feel free to experiment with the type. You may want to resize the type only to make it 10-pt size as shown. You can always remove the circular type paths and type in the title as horizontal text; your call. You can use the Artboard Tool (Shift+O) to draw additional artboards to show other variations of the same logo. You can now go in and label each artboard to keep track of each one, and then use the Artboards panel to click each artboard and play. Go ahead and experiment!

17. Save the file when you are satisfied with your efforts.

THE SEPARATIONS PREVIEW PANEL

In Illustrator, you can preview CMYK color separations and overprinting using the new Separations Preview panel. Previewing separations on your monitor lets you preview spot color objects in your document, and check for rich blacks or process black (K) ink mixed with color inks for increased opacity and richer color. The panel also checks for overprinting when the color CMYK plates are laid on top of one another to observe blending and transparency effects for the particular output device. In this exercise you should only find CMYK ink plates.

To preview your artwork in CMYK in the Separations Preview panel:

1. Select the Separations Preview panel (Window > Separations Preview) and then select the Overprint Preview icon to observe CMYK plate effects. The CMYK plates display as separate layers on the panel (Figure UR3-21).

2. To hide the separation ink on screen, click the eye icon to the left of the separation name, and then click again to view the separation. You can see what the artwork looks like at various stages of laying out CMYK plates, or without a particular color.

3. To view all process plates at once, click the CMYK icon.

4. To return to normal view, deselect Overprint Preview.

5. Save the entire file with multiple artboards as CafeLogo.eps, selecting the version of Illustrator you are currently using. This would be the file format you would use to give the file to a commercial printer, although many commercial printers are accepting native Adobe formats as technology improves.

▷ FIGURE UR3-21

Completed graphic ready with multiple artboards for printing as a soft proof to show the client.

SAVING AND PRINTING MULTIPLE ARTBOARDS

When saving multiple artboards you can save, as you have been doing, as one document or as multiple individual documents, which will display as multiple pages in Bridge. You can also export a range of different artboards, or choose individual pages. Saving your work as PDF file will display multiple artboards within the same document name, or you can set to save as individual artboards.

When you create a document with multiple artboards, you can print the document in a variety of ways. You can ignore the artboards and print everything on one page, or you can print each artboard as an individual page. When you print artboards as individual pages, you can choose to print all artboards, or a range of artboards. To print all artboards as separate pages, select File > Print > All. You can see all the pages listed in the preview area in the lower left corner of the Print dialog box. To print a subset of artboards as separate pages, select Range, and specify the artboards to print. To print the artwork on all the artboards together on a single page, select Ignore Artboards. If the artwork extends past the boundaries of the page, you can scale or tile it. You can also specify other print options, and then click Print.

Here you'll print all the completed artboards as separate pages for the client.

1. With the multiple artboards saved as *CafeLogo.eps* in Illustrator's current format, select File > Print.

2. Select the General tab on the left side, and then select the printer you are using.

3. Make sure All is selected under Copies and leave the rest as defaults for now (Figure UR3-21).

4. Print the file using default printer's marks, as if you were going to show it to a potential client as a soft proof (File > Print > Marks and Bleed); then check All Printer's Marks (Figure UR3-21). We'll cover more of these settings in depth in later chapters.

5. Select Print to print your copies as separate pages.

6. To print as additional PDFs, select File > Print; in the General tab, choose Adobe PDF as the Printer, print All copies to print all pages, and leave all other settings as default.

7. Feel free to use the Illustrator Package utility (File > Package) to package your images, fonts, and generate a report as if sending it to a service provider.

UNIT 3 REVIEW
Create guitar graphic from sketch.
Set up logo for mug.
Create 3D version of promotional mug
with shading and lighting applied.
Edit artwork on multiple artboards for
various uses.

▷ FIGURE UR3-22

InDesign Fundamentals

CHAPTER OBJECTIVES: To understand the importance of InDesign's function as a desktop publishing program, in this chapter you will:

▷ Learn procedures to set up preferences for special settings with InDesign documents before bringing in graphic and text objects.

▷ Lay out guidelines for accurate placement of text and graphics.

▷ Place graphics and format type characters and frames using the Control panel and InDesign menus.

▷ Format spacing within a text frame and align vertically using the Text Frame Options dialog box.

▷ Apply color to selected type and stroke of frames.

▷ Save as the original document and as a template for future editing.

▷ Generate QR code for promotional purposes.

▷ ADVANCED USERS: Preflight, package, and print the final document for press. Sync InDesign files and job folder, and settings between computers.

▷ DIGITAL TOOLKIT EXTRA: Create a desktop photo calendar using tables.

InDesign is a high-end desktop publishing program used in today's print industry. Desktop publishing programs allow designers to bring in text and graphic objects or elements from other applications and assemble and lay out these items accurately inside boxes called **frames** in an organized manner. InDesign is used to create and prepare documents, brochures, and books for commercial printing. This chapter will focus on the basics of InDesign, techniques to create documents for press, and the importance of layout using text and graphics.

THE INDESIGN ENVIRONMENT

InDesign is Adobe's premiere desktop publishing program used in the printing industry (Figure 11-1). Documents saved for printing using InDesign documents have an **INDD extension** to identify them. Here are some key components that make up the InDesign workspace environment.

- The Menu bar provides commands to create and edit your documents. In the Menu bar, the Type and Object menus allow the designer to make modifications to text and graphic items and adjust the formatting of paragraphs, characters, and other elements within the page itself.

- InDesign's Layout, View, and Window menus allow you to create and navigate between various layout spaces, display different document views and guides, and access panels and special windows.

- The Tools panel contains the tools you need to create and lay out your document. As you select a particular tool, its options are displayed in the Control Panel above the Tools panel.

- InDesign panels provide commands and functions to help you modify your projects. As with all Adobe products, panels can be docked and minimized to conserve workspace and expanded when needed by clicking on the panel icon.

- The Application bar provides a tabbed interface for displaying multiple images, and a Workspaces menu (Essentials default) for retrieving essential information like basic tutorials, and for choosing specific media workspace settings.

- In the document window, you can view the **Pasteboard,** which is a space to store graphics and text outside the document page area; you can change the viewing size, measure with rulers, and navigate between pages.

▷ FIGURE 11-1

InDesign CC workspace.

TOOLKIT TIP Windows can read InDesign documents created on a Mac, and Macs can read InDesign documents created in Windows. Due to differences in fonts, it is wise to stay with the same operating system in which you create your document to avoid any problems later. For outputting to a commercial press, create your work on the Mac if possible for consistency; most commercial presses use Macs.

DESKTOP PUBLISHING VERSUS WORD PROCESSING

There is a difference between a **desktop publishing program** and a **word processing program**. To create documents of formatted text for reports, short articles, or single-page brochures with fixed inserted graphics that will be distributed in a very small volume (with the exception of electronic distribution over the Internet), a word processing program works best; but they are usually not suitable for printing on a commercial press, where high-volume printed material is needed for distribution for home or office use. Desktop publishing involves placing items from a more diverse group of source applications into boxes for text and images called *frames*. These **frames** serve as "containers" that can be easily resized, repositioned, reshaped, combined, and in the case of text, linked into other frames on other pages. When you look at a newsletter, articles may be continued to other pages to lead the reader on to other articles. Creating documents for mass production, advertisements, books, and other multipage documents is best done using a desktop publishing program. It becomes a place to lay out and reposition items and edit and format contents in a more controlled workspace ready for publishing.

TOOLKIT TIP When creating documents with lots of text, it is easier to use your word processor and then import the text into your InDesign document. Although you can type in InDesign, it may display slower and works best with single paragraphs.

MEASURING IN INCHES AND POINTS

Desktop publishing and word processing programs use points as a default measurement for sizing type fonts and spacing between characters and lines of type. Although many designers lay out text and graphic items using fractions and inches as standards of measurement, sometimes, on a commercial press, the preferred units of measurement are picas and points. Font sizes and spacing are measured in points; because 72 pt is the equivalent of one inch, and 36 pt equals one-half inch, you can see why using points is a more precise method of measuring for the smaller measurements. This will be covered more in detail in the following chapter.

THE INDESIGN CREATIVE CLOUD (CC) TOOLS PANEL

Look at the Tools panel: you should be familiar with some of these tools since some are the same as those used previously in Photoshop and Illustrator. Tools with a small black triangle display other tools when held down with the mouse (Figure 11-2).

▷ FIGURE 11-2

InDesign CC Tools panel.

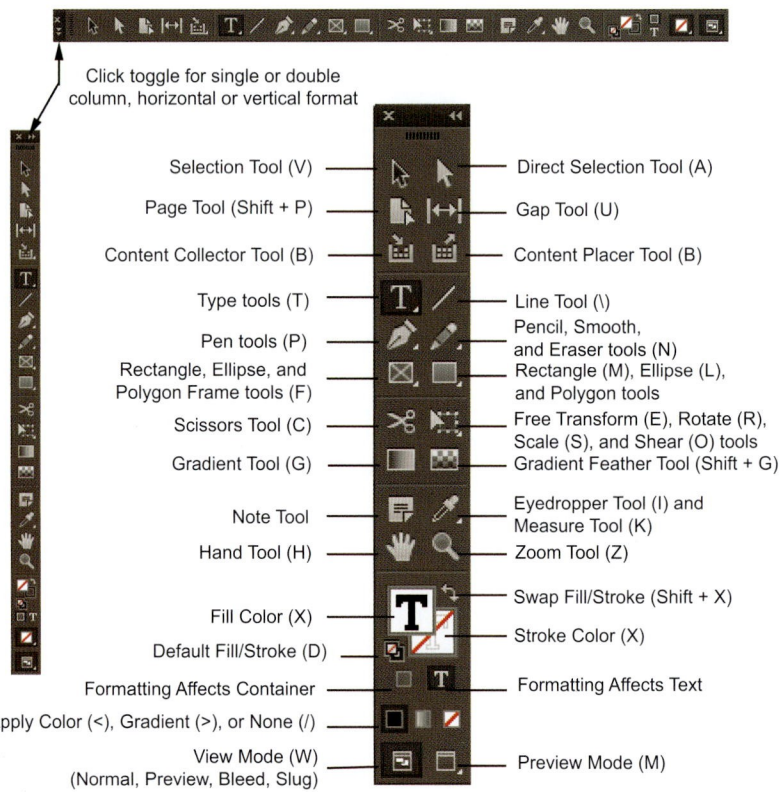

Click toggle for single or double column, horizontal or vertical format

Selection Tool (V) ——— Direct Selection Tool (A)

Page Tool (Shift + P) ——— Gap Tool (U)

Content Collector Tool (B) ——— Content Placer Tool (B)

Type tools (T) ——— Line Tool (\)

Pen tools (P) ——— Pencil, Smooth, and Eraser tools (N)

Rectangle, Ellipse, and Polygon Frame tools (F) ——— Rectangle (M), Ellipse (L), and Polygon tools

Scissors Tool (C) ——— Free Transform (E), Rotate (R), Scale (S), and Shear (O) tools

Gradient Tool (G) ——— Gradient Feather Tool (Shift + G)

Note Tool ——— Eyedropper Tool (I) and Measure Tool (K)

Hand Tool (H) ——— Zoom Tool (Z)

Fill Color (X) ——— Swap Fill/Stroke (Shift + X)

——— Stroke Color (X)

Default Fill/Stroke (D) ———

Formatting Affects Container ——— Formatting Affects Text

Apply Color (<), Gradient (>), or None (/) ———

View Mode (W) (Normal, Preview, Bleed, Slug) ——— Preview Mode (M)

The InDesign Tools panel includes a variety of handy tools.

- The **Selection Tool (V)** allows you to select entire objects, and the **Direct Selection Tool (A)** is used when selecting points on a path or contents within a frame. You can use these tools when you want to resize, move, or select the item.
- The **Page Tool (Shift+P)** allows you to resize pages within a document.
- The **Gap Tool (U)** provides a quick way to adjust the size of the gap between multiple items, or align several items at once.
- The **Content Collector Tool (B)** and **Content Placer Tool (B)** allow you to grab multiple pieces of content and place them to another area of the same document or onto other documents with ease.
- **Pen Tools (P)** create complex paths that require precision, and the **Pencil Tool (N)** provides free-form paths.
- The **Scissors Tool (C), Erase Tool,** and **Smooth Tool** are used for editing paths.
- The **Scale Tool (S), Free Transform Tool (E),** and **Rotate Tool (R)** all change the size of an object or its point of origin, and the **Shear Tool (O)** changes an object's perspective.
- The **Type tools (T)** create various shaped text boxes and type on selected paths.
- The **Rectangle Frame (F), Ellipse Frame**, and **Polygon Frame tools** create frames as containers to insert text and graphics. The **Line**, **Rectangle**, **Ellipse**, and **Polygon tools** are used to draw basic shapes.
- The **Eyedropper Tool (I)** samples color, and the **Gradient Tool (G)** and **Gradient Feather Tool (Shift+G)** blend one color into another.
- The **Measure Tool (K)** measures the distance between points along a path.
- The **Zoom Tool (Z)** magnifies the document view, and the **Hand Tool** is used to move the page document.
- The **Note Tool** allows designers to leave messages to themselves and to one another when working on a team project to help with workflow.

CREATING FRAMES

With InDesign, as with any desktop publishing program, the designer creates a text box, picture box, or path before placing text or images in the document. InDesign uses frames as the containers for type and graphics (Figure 11-3). Some considerations when working with frames follow.

- You can select the Type Tool (T) and diagonally drag a frame to start typing inside.
- Text and graphics can be put in either container, frame or shape. The Frame tools display a nonprinting X inside the shape. In the graphics industry, a box with an X has traditionally been used to show the location of an image or graphic.
- The empty frames created by the Rectangle, Ellipse, and Polygon Shape tools are generally used for text inserts, although with InDesign, both containers can be used for type or graphics.
- Understanding where to place type (empty container) and graphics (container with an X) can help with your workflow by communicating specific elements to team members.

▷ FIGURE 11-3

Creating various frames that can be used for type and graphics.

With InDesign, both types of frames can be used for either type or graphics. Many traditional designers use the Rectangle Frame tools (with x) for graphics only.

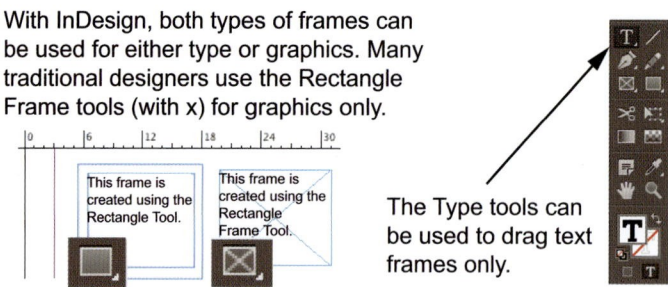

The Type tools can be used to drag text frames only.

DISPLAYING PANELS AND THE WINDOW MENU

For the convenience of providing additional space on your desktop, InDesign displays its panels as tabs, which you can click to expand or make active from the side as needed, then click again to contract when you are done, as has been done with the rest of the Creative Suite of applications. Sometimes when you click on a panel, it will be grouped with others for convenience. You can select a panel by its title bar or tab and pull it onto your document workspace. This process is called *undocking,* and the panel becomes free-floating. When you have finished using the free-floating panel, drag it back to the edge of the screen to *dock* it, or click on the X button to close it (Figure 11-4). When you see two small arrows, as in the Pages panel, you can click the arrows to expand or contract the panel.

▷ FIGURE 11-4

Displaying and minimizing (docking) panels and using the Window menu.

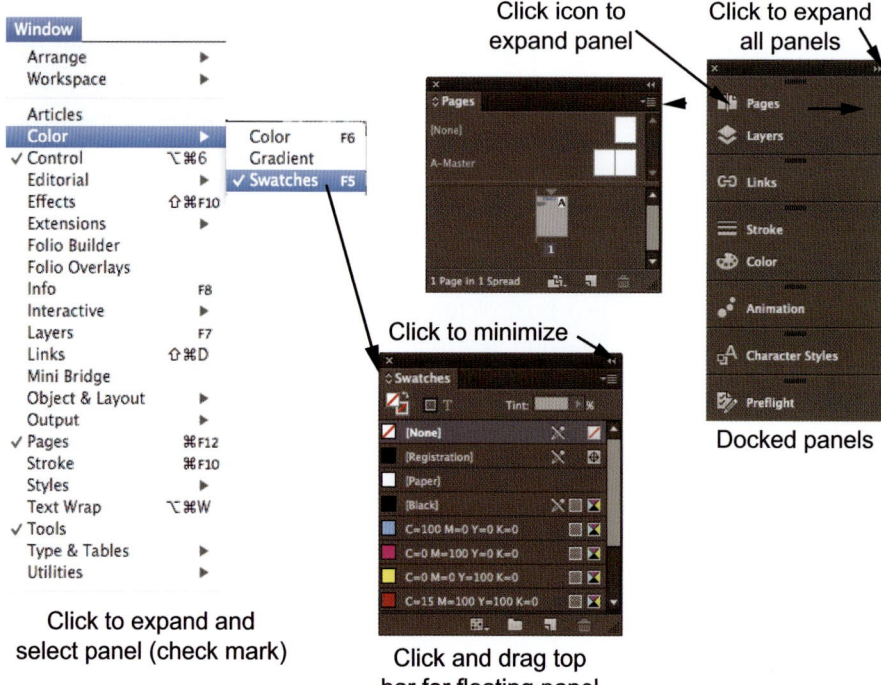

The Window menu also provides toggled check marks to expand or contract panels to the side of the desktop screen. Panels that are displayed or are expanded show a check mark to indicate they are active. In InDesign, the Window menu allows you to save a specified workspace, choose preset buttons for web pages, printed documents, or for creating interactive PDFs, and to display and hide documents. As mentioned with other Adobe products, InDesign has an Application bar that provides a tabbed interface for displaying multiple images, and a Workspace menu (Essentials default) for choosing preset work space settings, or you can select panels and save your own customized workspace. Function keys, which are usually the F function keys, can be used to display or hide the panels as well. For instance, the F5 key toggles to display or hide the Swatches panel.

THE CONTROL PANEL AND PAGES PANEL

The two panels you will use most often are the *Control panel* and the *Pages panel* (Figure 11-5). The **Control panel** is context sensitive, and it displays the most frequently used commands for a selected item or tool. With the selected frame box containing type, select the Type Tool (T) and highlight the type to be edited, and you will find frequent commands to format selected type. Click on the Rectangle Tool (M) and drag a diagonal box on the document, and you will find coordinates and formatting commands displayed. Functions that are displayed in the Control panel will vary, depending on the selected object or tool.

▷ FIGURE 11-5

InDesign Control panel and Pages panel.

The **Pages panel** provides information about pages and allows you to control the layout of pages, spreads, and master pages. When you set up a document and the Facing Pages option is *not* checked, the Pages panel displays pages as individual pages and you can view thumbnail representations of your work on each page. When the Facing Pages option *is* checked when creating a new document, the pages are put together as left and right pages and is called a *spread.* The Facing Pages option is useful in projects such as books, in which you are creating spreads; otherwise, leave this option unchecked when you create a new document.

Master pages contain items that repeat from page to page, such as headers, footers, page numbers, and graphic elements. Master page elements appear in the same location on every page, creating layout consistency from page to page. For instance, the layout in this text has master pages set up for the table of contents, chapter introduction page, chapter body, glossary pages, and so forth. You will use the Pages panel more in the following chapter.

TYPOGRAPHY BASICS

When an intended reader receives an advertisement, magazine, or coupon, it only takes a split second for that person to decide to read it or put it in the trash. Choosing the right typeface to enhance the graphic elements can help with the success of that document. The terms *typeface* and *font* are used interchangeably; however, the term **type family** refers to a collection of all the related typefaces, such as Arial, Arial Black, and Arial Narrow. Type should create an appealing path that leads the reader in; it should also play a supporting role for graphic elements, and it helps determine the personality of a document.

What follows is a brief review of typography terms we discussed back in Chapter 2 (see also Figure 11-6).

▷ FIGURE 11-6

Typography basics and terminology.

- A *family* is a group of fonts that share a basic character construction, like the Arial family, which comprises Arial Black, Arial Narrow, and Arial Alternative. This collection of characters is like having your family of uncles, aunts, cousins, and grandparents over for the holidays.

- A *font* or *typeface* is an individual member of a type family, such as Arial Black or Arial Narrow, both members of the Arial type family.

- Type falls into two main categories: *serif* and *sans serif.* Serif type displays foot-like extensions at the top and bottom, like Times Roman or Minion; sans serif has no extensions, like Arial or Helvetica. Sans serif works nicely as a starting point for headlines and subheadlines, whereas serif type is easier to read in the body of a document.

- A font *size* is the measurement of type in points instead of inches (1 pt = $\frac{1}{72}$ inch). When you open an InDesign document, the default size is usually 12 pt.

- InDesign does not allow you to create "fake" typefaces by clicking a bold or italic style button. When you specify a bold or italic typestyle, you are using an actual bold or italic font, not a stylized imitation.

- *Tracking* adjusts the spacing between characters and words. Adjusting the tracking of words too tightly in a paragraph can make it difficult to read, whereas adjusting too loosely can create "rivers" of white spacing in a paragraph. Justified alignment of type can also be the culprit, creating rivers of white.

- *Kerning* is a technique used for pairs of characters in titles or headlines that may need to be brought closer together for a more consistent look.

- *Leading* refers to the spacing between lines of text. Usually the default leading is 120% of the letter size for most documents. In long articles or newsletters, less space between lines of text tends to darken the document, whereas more space will lighten it up. The end result of what kind of message or mood you want to convey will determine how you will set up your text and what fonts you will need.

- The style or arrangement of setting type is called type *alignment.* Left aligned flushes type to the left and is easy to read; right aligned flushes type to the right side, as you might see in return addresses or columns of numbers to be added. Centered lines of type are used in some headlines or titles, and justified alignment places text equally on the left and right sides in a column.

TOOLKIT TIP To display text formatting controls in the Control panel, a text frame needs to be selected in the document.

WELCOME AND HELP SCREENS

Like the Help menu described in Illustrator and Photoshop, choosing Help in InDesign opens the Adobe Help and Support Center to search for tutorials, resources, and additional expert information and resources online, including documentation and community support from peers (Figure 11-7). There are also links to watch video how-to clips. You can select Help > InDesign Help and access various ways to get help, including an index, a search field, and various tutorial and web links. When you launch InDesign, you'll find a "What's New" welcoming dialog box of current features.

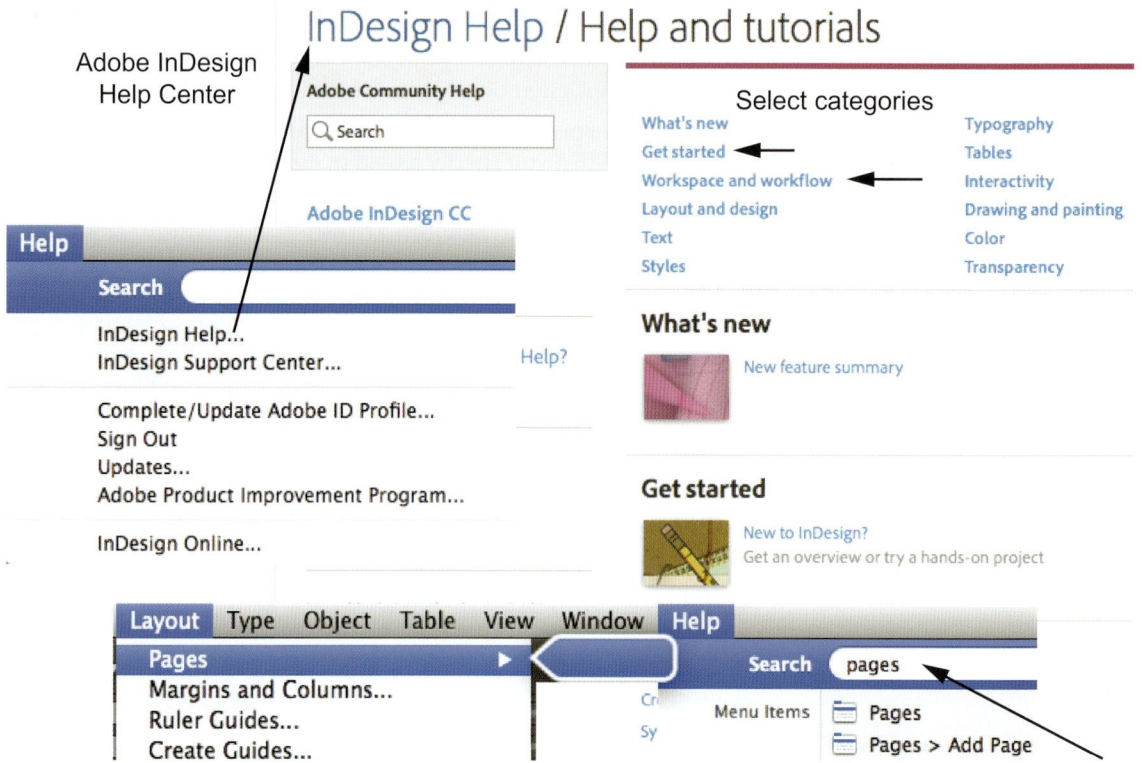

Let us view a tutorial in using the Adobe Help Center for a quick review:

1. Launch InDesign, and select Help > InDesign Help. When the Adobe Help website opens with a list of links, select the *Get Started link,* and then observe some beginner video tutorials to get a sense of the power of this application.

2. When completed, select the back arrow on your browser to return to the Adobe Help Center.

3. From the list of categories select *Workspace and workflow > Workspace basics* and look at the first two links to get a feel for the InDesign desktop. Close the website when done and select the Help menu in InDesign.

4. In the Search box, type "pages" to bring up related help to this topic. Get comfortable with this powerful feature, and feel free to browse around.

CLIENT ASSIGNMENT: Creating a Coupon Advertisement

Maria Dilorne wants to create a direct mail coupon for her pizzeria business. She contacts you and discusses the basic layout; it consists of an image of a pizza loaded with toppings surrounded by cheese and vegetables, the restaurant name, some text with the phone number underneath, and four coupons to entice customers to come visit the restaurant. The coupon will be included inside a direct mail envelope, which includes coupons from other businesses in the community. It will be mass mailed to the surrounding area, so Maria will not need to have the customer address on the back side. She also mentions that she would like a template made so that all she has to do is change the specials on the coupon and keep the original layout. You tell her you will have the ad completed by the end of the week for her to look over (Figure 11-8).

▷ FIGURE 11-8

Completed coupon advertisement.

DESIGN TIP

When creating coupons or any advertisement for a client, it is important to understand the target market to make sure the ad reaches the intended audience for maximum success. How the ad will be distributed and the volume that will be generated also needs to be considered.

ACTIONS ITEMS OVERVIEW

- You will need to create a custom-size coupon measuring in inches.
- You will place and accurately position a graphic for the advertisement.
- Coupons will be created using dashed outlines from the Stroke panel for cutting edges.
- You will enter text and format using the Control panel's character formatting function.
- The text will need to be centered and justified using the Text Frame Options function.
- For displaying the "cents" as smaller type in the pricing, you will create superscripts for emphasis.
- You will learn to add and apply new swatches using Pantone Process colors.
- A graphic will be placed behind the entire coupon to become the new background and add a sense of warmth and a QR code will be created for advertising.
- A template will be created for future editing and an IDML and PDF version for those who may not have the current InDesign installed.

SETTING UP THE COUPON ADVERTISEMENT

After discussion with the client and designing thumbnails and roughs, a designer should have a pretty good idea of what the final project will look like in the overall layout of the piece. Before laying out text and graphic items, preferences need to be set, and the final size and margins need to be set up. Note: If you haven't downloaded the files for this chapter yet, they are located at the publisher's website at *www.CengageBrain.com*.

CREATING AND ORGANIZING FOLDERS FOR OUTPUT

When you are going to be sending your materials to a commercial printer or web designer, you need to keep all documents, images, and fonts required in folders to be included with your InDesign document. This is crucial: without these elements, images may not print at full resolution and fonts may be substituted. It is also just as important to keep these folders with your InDesign document on your hard drive or on the same portable media, like a flash drive or final CD. All changes or saves to files will be made in these folders. Consider this as packing a suitcase to make sure you have everything you need for where you are going. Later on, you will be introduced to InDesign's Package utility for packaging document files.

TOOLKIT TIP InDesign has a series of utilities for checking links and spelling and for packaging images, text, documents, and fonts; these are covered in the Advanced Users section of this chapter, but it is still a good habit to make sure you are organized before you start your project.

Here you will create a folder to place your document and other folders in one area.

1. On your drive, locate the *Chapter 11* folder in your *Toolkit > InDesign* folder.

2. Create a new folder called *Coupon* (File > New Folder) that will become your main folder for your InDesign coupon project.

3. Create the folders *Images*, *Fonts*, and *Text* inside the *Coupon* folder. Now you have all the "suitcases" that you will need for your trip to the press.

4. Here is a look at your directory structure: *Toolkit > InDesign > Chapter 11 > Coupon > Images/Fonts/Text* (Figure 11-9). The InDesign coupon document project will also be saved inside the *Coupon* folder.

5. Drag the Pizza and Parchment image files that are inside the *Chapter 11* folder to the desktop, and then drag them to the new *Images* folder you just created inside the *Coupon* folder. Now you are organized.

▷ FIGURE 11-9

Creating images, fonts, and text folders inside the main *Coupon* folder for press.

PREFERENCE SETTINGS

Setting preferences provides a convenient way to adjust settings and parameters in your work environment to work on your document productively. There are two types of preferences: **application-level preferences** affect work on all documents, and **document-level preferences** affect only the active document. When you change preferences with InDesign launched but no document open, you are changing the application preferences. When you change preferences with a document open, those changes apply only to that document. Preferences in InDesign should always be set up first before creating a new document. In Mac OS X, the InDesign Application menu is where you would set Preferences; in Windows, Preferences are set in the Edit menu. The settings in Preferences will still remain, even when you turn off the computer, until you go in to change them again. In InDesign CC, you can sync your settings between computers which we'll complete later.

Here you will set up the measurements preferences in your coupon ad (Figure 11-10).

1. In Mac OS X, select InDesign > Preferences > Units & Increments; in Windows, use Edit > Preferences > Units and Increments.

2. Change the Ruler Units for Horizontal and Vertical document measurements to Inches.

3. Leave all other defaults as shown. Select OK.

▷ FIGURE 11-10

Setting InDesign document preferences for Ruler Units to display in inches.

THE FILE MENU

The **File menu** is where you save, print, place text and graphics, and export to special files; it is also where you determine what kind of file you are going to create, such as documents, books, or libraries, which are used to store graphics. When you create a new document, you need to input information to describe the page layout. You will notice in the New Document window, choices display for margin and column sizes, gutter width, the layout name, and the document orientation, either portrait or landscape (Figure 11-11). There is also a convenient link icon that allows you to type one dimension for margins, for instance, and it will change all the other margins to the same measurement.

▷ FIGURE 11-11

InDesign new document settings for coupon ad.

TOOLKIT TIP To set all margins at the same measurement, type in the measurement you want in the first box, and then click on the link; the same dimensions will appear on the rest of the boxes. Margins and guidelines do not print out on your final document.

Next, you will set up margins and parameters for the Coupon assignment.

1. Select File > New > Document to open the New Document display box.

2. Select Landscape Orientation (right-side icon).

3. Type in an 8-inch Width and a 3.5-inch Height (see Figure 11-11).

4. To set the Margin guides as 0.25 inches all around, type in 0.25 in the first box, and click the link icon to make the margins all around 0.25 inches.

5. Uncheck the Facing Pages option and uncheck the Primary (or Master) Text Frame, because we are not creating a bound book or a magazine with long text articles. Keep all other default settings.

6. Click OK.

TOOLKIT TIP The Facing Pages option sets up the document for printing books with left and right sides. The Primary Textbox Frame option creates a page-size text box that includes the entire page for multiple-page newsletters with long, continuous articles.

SAVING INDESIGN DOCUMENTS

There are many choices for how you can save your InDesign document besides the traditional Save and Save As commands. InDesign saves its documents within the File menu with an **INDD extension.** When you save the InDesign document, all nonprinting guides and margins are saved as well. A designer can also use the **Save a Copy** command, which creates a duplicate of the document under a different name, leaving the original document still active. An **InDesign template** can also be saved (Save As > InDesign CC template) to use for future editing of a document without having to start all over from scratch. It saves the templates with an **INDT extension**. A template can contain settings, text, and graphics that you preset as a starting point for other documents. The **Revert** command will allow you to go back to the last time you saved your document to get you out of a possible jam. Feel free to use these features as you work on your assignment. If you need to save to the earlier version of InDesign CS6, CS5, or CS4, as long as the version is updated, you can export InDesign documents to the InDesign Markup Language as **IDML** extension. This format replaces the earlier version CS3 and CS4 formats called InDesign Interchange (**INX**). This IDML format allows you to open your current document in InDesign CS4 for direct editing.

Now you will save the new document in your *InDesign > Coupon* folder.

1. Select File > Save As and locate the *Chapter 11* folder inside the *InDesign* folder you created on your hard drive. Then save the document with the name *Coupon Ad* inside the *Coupon* folder; you can click on the right-side arrow by the Save As bar to expand the display box and locate the folder (Figure 11-12).

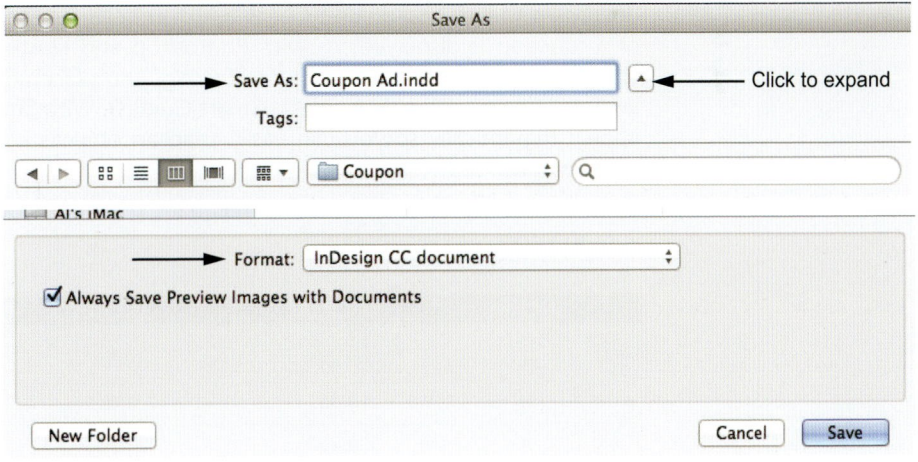

▷ FIGURE 11-12

Save as *Coupon Ad* in *Coupon* folder.

2. Select the InDesign document (not the template) and select Save using the Mac. It will automatically add the InDesign INDD extension to identify it as an InDesign document. For Windows users, Save As > InDesign CC Document.

TOOLKIT TIP With InDesign, saving a document also updates the metadata, or file information, that is part of the InDesign document. This metadata includes a thumbnail preview, fonts used in the document, color swatches, and all metadata in the File Info dialog box, all of which enable efficient searching. For example, you might want to search for all documents that use a particular color. You can view this metadata in Adobe Bridge and in the Advanced panel of the File Info dialog box.

USING GUIDES AND THE VIEW MENU

Guides are used to accurately lay out various text and picture items. **Margin guides** use purple lines as a default for measurements set up in creating the initial document. In the View Menu, it is good practice to show the top and left-side rulers for precise measurement by selecting View > Show Rulers if they are not displayed. This allows you to drag layout guides for placing text and picture boxes. **Layout guides** are usually green in color and are guidelines dragged out from the top and left-side rulers. The cursor will display a double arrow to indicate a selected guideline. To move or remove a layout guide, click it with either the Selection Tool (V) or Direct Selection Tool (A); when you observe a change in the cursor (double arrow with Selection Tool (V), arrow point with Direction Selection Tool (A)), drag back into the ruler or select View > Hide Guides to hide all guides (Command/CTRL R). Guides are nonprintable and can be set up in the View menu along with displaying rulers. You can also use the Control panel for exact placement by typing the location in the selected guide X- or Y-coordinate field (Figure 11-13). The View Menu provides all the various ways of displaying your document, rulers, and guides. Check marks indicate whether a command is active or a function is displayed. As with Photoshop and Illustrator, InDesign also has Smart Guides for precise alignment, resizing, and placement of multiple graphics and text (View > Grids & Guides > Smart Guides). With Smart Guides coordinates appear dynamically so you can easily snap an object's edge to other objects in your layout.

To help with converting inches to decimals, see the following table to help jog your memory.

INCHES	DECIMAL	INCHES	DECIMAL
1	1.00	½	0.50
⅞	0.857	⅜	0.375
¾	0.750	¼	0.250
⅝	0.625	⅛	0.125
		¹⁄₁₆	0.0625

▷ FIGURE 11-13

Creating guides for placement of text and graphics.

TOOLKIT TIP For the most accurate placement of guides, use the Control panel by dragging out the guide and typing in the exact measurement in the X and Y coordinates. It provides you the flexibility of moving guides quickly to experiment with your layout.

Here you will create guides to align picture and text frames for the coupon ad.

1. To make sure the rulers are displayed, you should see left and topside rulers outside your document. If not, select View > Show Rulers; it will toggle to display the rulers.

2. To make sure that frame containers you drag to create easily snap to the guides, select View > Grids & Guides > Snap to Guides to make sure a check mark displays; if not, click it. To use Smart Guides, select View > Grids & Guides > Smart Guides.

3. To create the coupons to be cut out, drag vertical guides at the 3.5 (3½) inch and 5.625 (5⅝) inch marks to separate the two coupons. As you drag, the coordinates display by your cursor. You can also use the Control panel and type in the horizontal coordinates as X coordinates for exact measurement (Figure 11-13).

4. To split the amount of coupons offered to four, drag a horizontal guide to the 1.75 (1¾) inch mark. You can also use the Control panel and type in the vertical coordinate as a Y coordinate for exact measurement.

5. Save the file. You are now ready to insert graphics and text.

CREATING GRAPHIC AND BOX FRAMES

When inserting graphics, typing in text, or importing text documents, you can create a frame box or container to put the contents in (Figure 11-14). With InDesign, designers may use the various shape or frame tools to place type or graphics or they may select the Type Tool (T) and drag a rectangular box to place type only. It is generally accepted practice in the industry that if you have created a blank box where you intend to insert type, a box with an *X* in it created by one of the frame tools will usually be used for placing graphic elements. Graphics and type can also be placed without any container in InDesign. Clicking the mouse will drop the text or image on the document, with or without a box. This feature is one of the greatest efficiency features in InDesign—creating frames as you place. You can then make adjustments to the box and format the text or adjust the coordinates, stroke weight, and format a selected frame using the Control panel.

▷ FIGURE 11-14

Setting up text and graphic boxes. Creating dashed lines for coupons.

Ⓧ **PROBLEM** If an *X* does not appear and you have used the Frame Tool, select **View > Extras > Show/Hide Frame edges.**

You will create frames to put text and graphics in for the coupon ad.

1. To create the frame for the graphic, select the Rectangle Frame Tool (F) with a Stroke and Fill of None, and drag from the top-left inside margin to the 3.5-inch ruler guide, and then downward to the 1.75-inch guide. It should feel like it's "snapping" in place. You will notice the box will have an *X* inside.

2. Select the Type Tool (T) and drag a text box under the graphic frame from the left margin to the 3.5-inch guide for the restaurant information along the bottom margin guide. You'll notice a blinking cursor displays in the left corner to start typing. You can select this transparent box with the Selection Tool (V) later. Note: The Rectangle Tool (M) can also be used instead; you just create the frame, select the box, and then click inside the box with the Type Tool (T).

3. Use the Rectangle Tool (M) to create the four coupon boxes. Drag carefully to create the four boxes that will be used for the coupons on the right side. An arrow displays under the cursor when you start on a guide corner edge. The Snap to Guides option you selected in the previous exercise will help to align the boxes with precision. Smart Guides will display coordinates and its smart dimensions features will display arrows and center lines when the boxes are aligned.

TOOLKIT TIP You may notice light green dimension-like arrows displaying alongside the boxes to help you with proper alignment. This is the Smart Dimensions feature. As you resize an object next to another object, Smart Dimensions creates a line segment with arrows at each end that lets you snap the object to the same width or height as the adjacent object.

4. To create the coupon boxes with a dashed stroke, make sure the Control panel is displayed (Window > Control), zoom in to 200%, and then select each of the four boxes with the Selection Tool (V), clicking inside each text box frame or on the margins while holding down the Shift key. A dot will display at the center of each selected frame. As in Illustrator, there is also a Stroke panel you can use instead of the Control panel.

5. Change the Stroke thickness or weight to 2 pt; change the line type to a Dashed (3 and 2). The 3 and 2 setting is a ratio between the dash line (3) and the black space between the dashes (2).

6. Although Snap to Grid should have all four boxes aligned, if not, use the Selection Tool (V) and arrow keys to overlap the boxes if needed so the dotted lines appear as one. Make sure your alignment is accurate then save the file.

TOOLKIT TIP In InDesign CC, a frame or box selected with the Selection Tool will display a yellow handle in the top right corner. When clicked you have the Live Corners feature to create curves from corners as was used previously in Illustrator and Photoshop.

DESIGN TIP

Dashes in a coupon ad are universally accepted as proposed cutting lines to take the coupon back to the vendor.

PLACING GRAPHICS IN AN INDESIGN DOCUMENT

You can create all kinds of picture-box shapes using these shape tools. As mentioned previously, an empty picture box should display an *X* inside the box after it is drawn for communicating that this will be used to insert graphics. Here are some other considerations when placing graphics files:

- Bring in or import images by selecting the Place command in the File menu. The Place command will provide the most accurate reproduction, although it can also copy and paste graphics or drag and drop from one document to another.

- The image that is Placed in the document will display as a low-resolution image. It is linked to the original, high-resolution image and may look pixeled on your computer screen. This makes it easier to move the image around in the document for placement on your monitor. (If you want to see a high-resolution version of the image, go to View > Display Performance > High Quality Display.)

- When the document is given the command to Print, InDesign replaces the linked, low-resolution image with the original, high-resolution image, located in the folder from whence you retrieved the file when you used the Place command.

- When a graphic is placed in a document, a thumbnail representation is displayed in the Links panel and a link reference icon is displayed on the image. You can use the Links panel to identify, select, monitor, and update files that are linked to external files. Each object in the Links panel is represented with a thumbnail that provides more detailed information when clicked such as scale, rotation, and resolution, among other attributes. Click on the text or graphic link and find more info about that file.

- If an image covers the area up to the edges of a document, a designer may create a bleed that overflows the image outside the document's trim area to avoid a white line from trimming due to the shift of the paper sheets as they were transferred on the press.

- InDesign offers support for Illustrator's multiple artboards. You can place any selected artboard from Illustrator in its native format into your InDesign document.

- InDesign also provides an Edit With command (Edit > Edit With >) that allows a designer to choose the application to edit a placed item instead of relying on the operating system to default to a particular application.

- InDesign uses the Links panel for keeping track of graphics, with their related info, that are used in a given InDesign document by providing direct links to those objects for easy access, and to be able to relink missing objects.

DESIGN TIP

When importing images into a frame, the frame is only a "window" display. If the image is larger than the frame, then only the exposed portion of the image will display in the frame. If you cannot afford to crop portions of the image, resize your image in Photoshop to the picture box size before you bring it into InDesign.

TOOLKIT TIP When placing graphic images, InDesign will display on the computer as low resolution for easier maneuvering of the image in the document. If a designer needs to see what the final design will look like when printed, InDesign provides commands in the View menu to see various resolutions, such as Display Performance (High Quality Display). If you move the image from the location where you had originally used the Place command in the document, InDesign will be unable to locate the high-resolution image, because you have broken the link between the low-resolution copy and the high-resolution original image, and it will display a dialog box asking for the whereabouts of that image. Whenever you are changing the location of the image, you need to Place the same image again into the document for InDesign to locate that high-resolution image when it is ready to print.

REPOSITIONING SELECTED LARGER GRAPHICS

With InDesign, graphic frames that contain content now display a transparent "doughnut" shape called a **Content Indicator** when you use the Selection Tool to select and reposition a graphic. This feature is effective when you have a larger graphic behind a frame window and need to view the entire image dimensions for repositioning. When you hover your mouse over the doughnut in the center of the image, the cursor turns into the familiar hand icon for moving around. You can use it to reposition content within its frame by simply clicking and dragging on the doughnut to move the graphic where you want it within the frame. When you let go, your content is repositioned. This feature replaces the Position Tool in earlier versions, which worked by the same principle. Clicking on the Content Indicator will select the content, but also keep the Selection Tool (V) active. This allows the designer to see the complete dimension of an image with a bounding box and to place the image within the frame with precision. A bounding box appears to show outer dimensions of the graphic (Figure 11-15).

Image placed within graphic frame window. The *Pizza* file is shown in the Links panel.

Adjusting the image area with the Content Indicator and Selection Tool

▷ FIGURE 11-15

Placing and positioning the graphic displays graphic thumbnails and related info in the Links panel.

Let us insert the pizza graphic. You will use Figure 11-15 as a guide to move the image around using the Selection Tool.

1. With the Selection Tool (V), select the rectangle frame box with the *X* to place the graphic.

2. Select File > Place and locate the *Pizza.tif* file in your *Chapter 11* (*Coupon*) *Images* folder, where you are keeping your images for the printer. Click Open.

3. You will notice that the larger image is placed under the frame window as shown in Figure 11-15.

4. You will also notice the Pizza image has a link icon on the ad and it is displayed as a layer in the Links panel (Window > Links). You can use this panel to monitor and update files linked to your document.

5. Select the graphic using the Selection Tool (V).

6. To see the full image to move around, when you hover your mouse over the center the cursor turns into a hand. Click and drag on the center position Content Indicator (doughnut). You will see the area outside the graphic appear as a bounding box, but it can still act as guide to make an accurate placement of the image.

7. When you let go and select the image again, you will see a bounding box that surrounds the entire image area inside and out to get an idea of its size.

TOOLKIT TIP The Links panel is used to identify, select, monitor, and update files that are linked to external files. All files placed in a document are listed in the Links panel and they display as thumbnails for quick reference. The Links panel also provides more detailed information when clicked such as scale, rotation, and resolution, among other attributes. You can also click on the page number displayed to go directly to that file. Links can be files, text, graphics, or hyperlinks from local disks or from those managed on a server.

TOOLKIT TIP InDesign also allows the designer to import many graphic file formats. TIF image formats are used extensively with photographs, and EPS formats work best using illustrations or when combining type, illustrations, and photographs. Many commercial printers now accept native format files from Adobe applications. A placed PDF page displays at the best resolution possible for the given scale and screen resolution and is also acceptable to use in an InDesign document and for a service provider.

PLACEMENT AND FORMATTING OF TYPE

The Type commands on the Control panel have character formatting in the A button from a selected graphic, and paragraph formatting commands, like alignment of blocks of type within text boxes, use the paragraph symbol button, which looks like a backwards *P*. The Type menu allows the designer to observe what the actual font looks like in a font sample display, instead of trial and error in choosing. The type frame must be selected and the copy highlighted before editing. InDesign CC's Font Search feature quickly filters your choices as you start to type a font's name or style. You can also have instant font preview with your selected text for a quick visual of selected fonts as you scroll.

DESIGN TIP

The most important pieces of information that must appear in the ad are the company name, phone number, address, web address, email, or other type of contact information, with the coupon displaying the sale amount for this type of ad. To emphasize the importance of these elements, increasing the type size and using color can go a long way toward grabbing the reader's attention.

TOOLKIT TIP When creating a document for commercial press, a good designer needs to use fonts that have the style in their name, like Minion Pro Bold. Artificially applying a style such as bold by clicking the letter *B* may not duplicate exactly at the press, causing spacing problems. If an italicized font style is desired, look for font names with the word "italic" or "oblique" in them. Try to keep various font use to a minimum in any given project. Keep in mind—less is more!

Next, you will place all the text information first; then we will format it.

1. Use the Selection Tool (V) to activate the type frame under the graphic; then select the Type Tool (T) and click inside the box. The Control panel (or Character panel as another option) will automatically select the character formatting button A. Choose the Align center button (Figure 11-16).

2. Select a 24-pt Minion Pro (or similar font) with a Bold and Italic Style and a black Fill. Type in "Mamma Di's Pizzeria." You'll notice as you type the name of the font the Font Search feature filters the font choices.

▷ FIGURE 11-16

Entering type using the Type Tool. Character formatting using the Control panel.

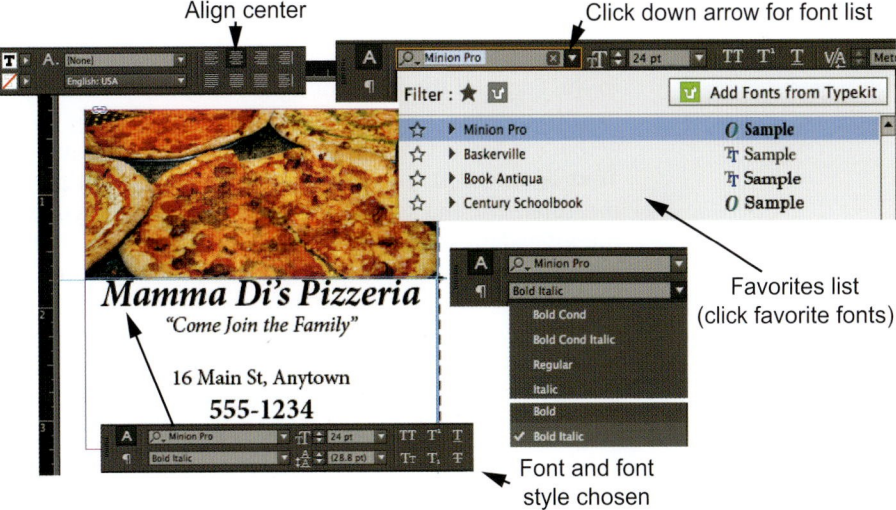

Align center

Click down arrow for font list

Favorites list (click favorite fonts)

Font and font style chosen

3. Press Return/Enter for the next line.

4. For the slogan, select a 14-pt Minion Pro font (or your own choice), Italic style (no Bold), and type with quotes "Come Join the Family." Press Return/Enter twice to skip a line; a better method of adding space between paragraphs will be introduced later.

5. For the address, use the same size font, in Regular style, and type "18 Main St., Anytown" or put in your own info. Press Return/Enter.

6. For the phone line, increase the font size to 18-pt Minion Pro with a Bold Style and type "555-1234." If you observe a "red cross" being displayed or the line just disappears, it indicates the type is too big for the space. Decrease the font size until you can see your phone text line.

7. Deselect the text, and then save the file in your *Chapter 11 > Coupon* folder. You will further format the color and placement of the type in relation to the graphic later.

DESIGN TIP

When working with italics, especially in traditional methods of design, they should only be used for emphasis. It's a good habit to keep a "less is more" attitude when applying this style.

LOCATING, PREVIEWING, AND GENERATING FAVORITE FONTS IN ILLUSTRATOR CC

InDesign CC has some special features for locating, previewing, and saving fonts or typefaces. Highlight the title line in your Coupon Ad document, then click the down arrow inside the font search box within the Control panel and use the arrow keys on your keyboard (don't click) to scroll down to see what other fonts look like using InDesign's Instant Font Preview feature. The highlighted title will display each font as you scroll down. If you find font typefaces you like, maybe Baskerville, Century Schoolbook, or Book Antiqua, when you click on these fonts, they will display to the top of your font list as a favorites list for quick access (Figure 11-16). This also works if you use the Character panel instead of the Control panel. You will also notice, as a paid subscriber, you have access to Adobe Typekit fonts (for a trial period, then as an additional subscription) that you can easily select and sync to your computer for quick access (typekit.com).

WORKING WITH TYPE WITHIN A FRAME

As a general rule, a designer would not want to have type placed directly next to the edges of the frame or against a graphic object. In this case, some space is needed between the pizza graphic and type for the title and where type is placed within the dashed frame of the coupons. In the Object menu, you can choose the **Text Frame Options command.** In this dialog box, you can specify an "inset" measurement that keeps copy away from the edge of the frame. After you specify the inset dimension, a guide will be visible inside the frame when it is selected with the Selection or Direct Selection Tool. In the Vertical Justification > Align area of the Text Frame Options dialog box, you can align the copy to the top, bottom, or the center of the frame. You can also justify the copy, which spreads the lines of type from the top frame edge or inset to the bottom frame edge or inset. You can also use this function on non-rectangular frames like rounded corners.

DESIGN TIP

When type is placed in a text frame, it defaults to the top portion of the frame and is against the frame outline. Especially when frame outlines or stroke weights are used and colored, type should not be set against the frame line. Always provide space for easy readability and a professional look. For headlines or for centering within a type box, select Vertical Justification > Align > Center to make the type centered within the frame.

> **TOOLKIT TIP** You can also use the key combo Command/CTRL B to access the Text Frame Options dialog box or Control click for Mac (right-click for PC) to display the context menu to choose Text Frame options.

Here you will use the Text Frame Options command to vertically center the type in the Restaurant information and to create spacing between type and the dashed outline within the coupons.

1. Using the Type Tool (T), select the type lines you created earlier under the pizza graphic.

2. Choose Object > Text Frame Options (or Command/CTRL + B) and select the General tab.

3. In the Vertical Justification area, select Align as Center, Columns as Fixed Number, to preserve the adjusted columns, and make sure the Preview button is checked. This will center the type within the type box (Figure 11-17). Click OK.

▷ FIGURE 11-17

Using the Text Frame Options box to control vertical center alignment and spacing between type and the frame.

Vertical center alignment
for restaurant info

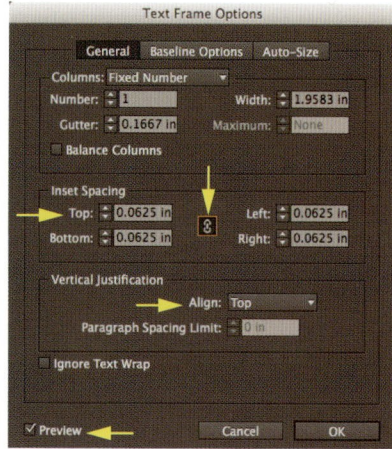

Text spacing for inside
coupon frame boxes

4. Choosing Minion Pro Regular 12-pt font, or a font that matches the restaurant info, type in the lines of text to indicate the specials inside the coupons as shown in Figure 11-18. Do not use decimal points for displaying cents in the dollar amounts. We will format them and the type in the next exercise.

▷ FIGURE 11-18

Placing type in the coupon boxes, ready for formatting.

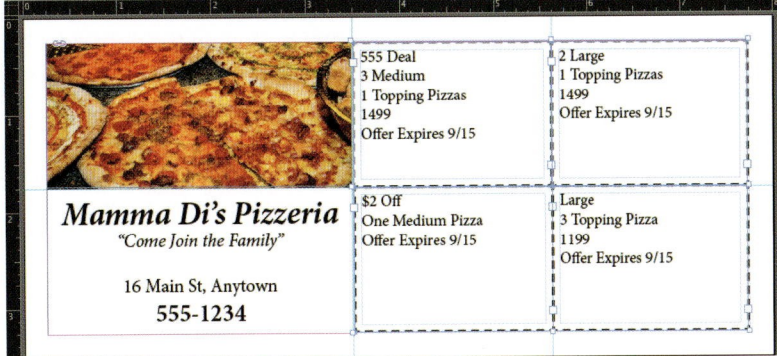

5. Deselect the text, then use the Selection Tool (V) and while holding down the Shift key, select all four coupon boxes.

6. To create breathing space between the type to be entered and the dashed line, choose the Text Frame Options dialog box again and enter in the Inset Spacing area "0.0625," the equivalent of $\frac{1}{16}$th of an inch, on all sides as shown in Figure 11-17. You can click on the center link icon to get this measurement. Click OK.

7. Note: To see a small thumbnail representation of your coupon document at this point, open the Pages panel (Window > Pages). We'll cover this more in depth in the next chapter in creating a newsletter.

Ⓧ **PROBLEM** If you find that the dashed lines are not overlapped as one, select inside the box with the Selection Tool (V), and then uncheck Fixed Width in the Text Frame Options dialog box to make your adjustments.

FORMATTING TYPE AND VERTICAL ALIGNMENT

DESIGN TIP

It is good practice to create text margins within a frame before typing text, both for easier readability and to give the designer an idea of the allotment of space when using a particular font.

To make the specials stand out, you can select a different font, change the font size, or select color, all of which you will do in the next exercise. This exercise will help you review how to use the Control panel to format and center align selected type using Character formatting, and use Text Frame Options to center the copy vertically inside the frame. For the coupons in this exercise we are going to use Bookman Old Style Bold font for easier reading, with Italic style added for pricing lines to make them stand out. To adjust the vertical spacing of the lines of type inside each coupon evenly from top to bottom, select Vertical Justification > Align >Justify in the Text Frame Options dialog box.

TOOLKIT TIP Fonts to try for the headings and prices may also include Cooper Black, Minion Standard with Black Style, or Copperplate Gothic Bold. A font with a Black style fills in the font to make it wider.

Next, you will format the type inside the coupons to make the specials display for easy reading.

1. First, to center align the type, select the Type Tool (T), highlight all the lines of type *except* "Offer Expires 9/15," which we will keep as left aligned; click the Character Formatting Controls (A) button on the Control panel.

2. Select the Align center button on the right side of the Control panel and perform the same operation for each coupon.

3. Use the Type Tool (T) to change all type lines *except* the expiration line and price lines to the Bookman Old Style Bold font, or stay with the same font you used under the pizza image changing to Bold style to make the coupons stand out. You may notice the chosen font appears at the top of the "Favorites" font list for quick access.

4. Change the type size in all coupons to 14 pt, with the exception of the expiration lines.

5. Change the price in each coupon, including the $2 Off line, to a 24-pt size, with a Bold Italic style. Make sure the style term is named with the font you are using because this is the most important attention getter. Change the line "555 Deal" to your selected font at 18-pt size in the Bold Italic style.

6. Select the *Offer Expires 9/15* line in each coupon, and change the size to 8 pt. This will stay left aligned for attention.

PROBLEM If you can't click in front of the type line, then you may have a frame on top of another frame. Use the Selection Tool (V) to select and then delete the extra box so you can access the type lines.

7. To position the expiration lines near the bottom left of each coupon, click in front of each *Offer Expires 9/15* line, except in the first frame, and press Return/Enter once to separate it. If the line disappears, you have put too much space and the line is outside the box.

8. To make sure the *Offer Expires 9/15* line is consistent along the bottom of each coupon, and to provide consistency in display of various lines of type in each coupon, you will use the Justify Alignment command in the Text Frame Options dialog box.

9. Highlight all lines in the first coupon and select Object > Text Frame Options to bring up the dialog box. Select Vertical Justification > Align > Justify. It should space all lines evenly along a vertical axis (Figure 11-19). Click OK.

10. Repeat the same procedure with the other three coupons. The expiration line should be consistent along the bottom of each coupon.

11. In some coupons, there is a significant gap between the expiration line and the offer. You may also notice that the top lines may also seem too close to the cutting edges or dashed lines. To adjust, select only the top line of each,

except the "555 Deal," with the Type Tool (T), and then select Object > Text Frame Options. Make sure alignment is still "Justified," and the Inset Spacing link is "broken" by clicking on it; then click on the Top inset up arrow a couple of times without losing the expiration lines. Click OK. Use Figure 11-19 as a guide.

▷ FIGURE 11-19

Formatting the type in each coupon, and justifying vertical alignment.

Using Justify for position of expiration line

Adjusting spacing for first line from top

APPLYING SUPERSCRIPTS

All type sits on an invisible line called a **baseline**. As you look at this line of type, you are reading along the baseline that the type sits on. A designer can use certain formatting techniques, like superscript and subscript, to shrink to a percentage of the font or to change how the font is positioned in alignment with the top of the font or on the baseline. To create the cents portion of the price, select the T1 (Superscript) button where the "1" is showing above the "T" on the Control panel. It will display the cents portion so that it aligns with the top portion of the font. A **superscript** is a percentage of the original font size and will display aligned with the top of the font. **Subscripts** are also percentages of a font that are displayed on or below the baseline of the font.

Here you will apply a superscript to shrink the cents portion of the prices to display aligned with the top portion of the font (Figure 11-20).

1. Highlight only the cents portion of each price with the Type Tool (T) and select the "Superscript" option to shrink the cents to align with the top of the font.

2. That is all there is to it. Save the file.

DESIGN TIP

In most cases the expiration date in any coupon should also include the year. For our purposes here, we removed the year in the coupon so as not to date the publishing of this book.

▷ FIGURE 11-20

Applying the super-
scripts option to for-
mat the cents in
each price.

Superscript ↓

↑ Subscript

TOOLKIT TIP When you have more text copy than the frame is able to contain, a red plus sign may appear in the lower right corner of the frame, indicating that the text is overset. You can make the overset text fit by increasing the size of the frame or decreasing the size of the text. You can also use Command/CTRL Z or the Edit menu to undo the action that caused the overset text to begin with.

CHOOSING AND APPLYING COLOR FROM SWATCH LIBRARIES

To apply color to type that is generally set without a stroke, select the Type Fill color box in the Tools panel, choose a color from the Swatches panel, or double-click the Type Fill color box in the Tools panel to bring up the Color Picker, where you can choose a particular color. You can select from a random color or use the Swatches panel to select from one of the color libraries. When sending a document to press, all colors need to be **CMYK process colors.** The swatch libraries contain libraries or process colors specific to print media like Pantone and also for RGB colors used for web media. Spot Colors used in print media are premixed, much as you would get at the paint store, and they use a numbering system to identify each specific color. You can then choose a color and save it in the Swatches panel for future use for that document; however, it does not perma-nently remain in the Swatches panel for all documents.

TOOLKIT TIP You can select from a range of color libraries that are used for com-mercial press or for the web. Some of these may include the Pantone Process Color System, Focoltone color system, the Trumatch color swatch system, and libraries created especially for web use. Before using swatches from a color matching system, consult with your prepress service providers to determine which ones they support. A word of caution: professional designers need to be careful choosing colors for commercial print using their monitors, although the technology in modern flat panel monitors using calibration devices is widely acceptable. A designer can use an actual print swatch book to be used in conjunction with the digital swatch libraries to be extremely accurate. For our purposes in these exercises, we will use digital colors.

For the colors for type and dashes in the coupon ad, you will select from the Pantone-coated library colors. Some of the naming of Pantone colors will be slightly different between the current version and earlier versions; both options are provided.

1. Choose New Color Swatch in the Swatches (Window > Color > Swatches) panel menu (click the lines in the upper right corner to open the panel menu).

2. Make sure the Color Type is Process Color in the display; from the Color Mode list, choose Pantone + CMYK Coated, as the library in which to choose colors.

3. For a deep red color, select Pantone P 60-8 C (or in earlier versions try DS 61 1 C) as shown in Figure 11-21. You can also type "60-8 C" in the Pantone dialog box. This will be used for the restaurant title, phone number, and coupon prices.

Fill color only

Indicates a process color

4. Select the Add button, and the color you chose will automatically be added to the Swatches panel. Do *not* click OK or Done yet, so you can add another color. If you have, just repeat Steps 1 and 2 before going on to the next step.

5. For a deep green color, add Pantone P 138-14 C (or try 261 1 C in earlier versions) to the Swatches panel. This will be used for some of the type descriptions. Click Add.

6. With both colors selected, click OK (or Done) on the dialog box to indicate that you have finished your choices.

7. To use the colors, highlight the *Mamma Di's Pizzeria* title with the Type Tool (T), and select the red Pantone P 60-8 C (DS 61-1 C in earlier versions) in the Swatches panel. Make sure the type Fill color is displayed and the Stroke color is set to None in the Tools panel.

8. Repeat the same process with the phone number and prices in the coupons for consistency.

9. Highlight the line *555 Deal* and make it the green Pantone P 138-14 C (261-1 C in earlier versions). The rest of the colors can remain the default black.

10. If you want to change the color of the dashes in the coupon boxes, leave the Fill color to None and select the Stroke color on the Tools panel.

11. Use the Selection Tool (V) to select each coupon box.

12. Select the Pantone green color you added in the Swatches panel to apply it. The dashes will turn green; then click outside the coupon with the Selection Tool (V) to deselect the coupons.

13. Save the file.

ARRANGING PLACEMENT OF GRAPHICS

The Object menu in InDesign, as well as in all Adobe products, allows you to place multiple graphics in front of or behind one another, much like you would rearrange the stacking order of sheets of paper. The command Send to Back and Send to Front arranges the graphic to appear directly on top of or underneath all the other graphics. The Send Backward and Send Forward commands move the graphic behind or in front of one graphic at a time. The coupon you have created is on a white background at this point and would look more appealing with a warmer tone background. You can place an image to act as the background behind the type and pizza image or have the ad printed on special colored paper. Here you will use a graphic to place behind the other elements to act as the background. If you have the Links panel open, you will also notice that the Links panel displays both the Pizza and Parchment graphic objects as thumbnails for future editing or modifying if needed.

TOOLKIT TIP In InDesign, a bleed is usually added under Document Setup > More Options. Always add an eighth inch to each side that has a bleed.

In this exercise, to complete the ad and give it more color, you will place a scanned parchment color graphic to cover the entire document and send it behind the type and graphic objects to act as the background.

1. Select the Rectangle Frame Tool (F) and draw a diagonal box over the entire document so that it extends or "bleeds" beyond the edges of the document about an eighth of an inch (0.125). This will prevent white lines created from trimming or paper shifting on the press, which will be covered more in depth later.

2. Select File > Place and choose the *Parchment.tif* file located in your *Images* folder. Notice that the Links panel displays both the Pizza and Parchment graphic objects as thumbnails (Window > Links), and the link reference icons are shown on each image.

3. To move the graphic behind the other objects, use the Selection Tool (V) to make sure the graphic is selected, and then choose Object > Arrange > Send to Back. It will provide a warm tone background for those hot pizzas!

4. Look at the bottom of the window display of your ad you just created. If you see a green circle that reads "No errors" the automatic checker for graphics links assures you are ready to save and print a soft proof (Figure 11-22). If a red error dot displays, double-click, read the error, and fix as recommended. This will be covered more in depth in the Advanced section. Save the file when ready.

▷ FIGURE 11-22

Completed ad with parchment graphic placed behind all objects as the background.

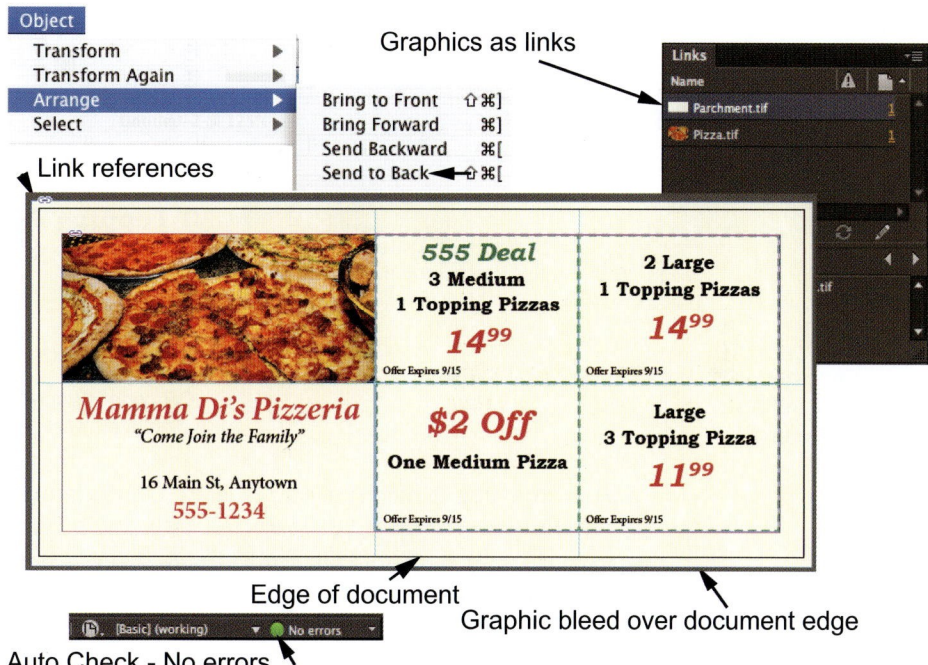

GENERATING QR CODES IN INDESIGN CC

QR codes are machine-readable printed representations of data for various industry uses, especially for advertising for many businesses. A consumer with a smartphone can install an app with a QR code scanner that can read and decode the URL information and redirect the phone's browser to a company website, where the company may have promotions. QR codes can also be created for business cards so the user can add the contact to their devices, or for email and text messaging.

You can now generate and edit high-quality independent QR code graphics from within InDesign CC. The generated QR code is a high-fidelity graphic object that behaves exactly like native vector art in InDesign. You can easily scale the object and fill it with colors. Once placed inside a document, the QR code is treated as a traditional EPS object, except that information regarding the code's contents appears upon hovering your mouse from your computer that originated it over the object, revealing the content details in the form of the embedded code. At any point, you can edit the QR code directly within InDesign.

As this business is providing promotional coupons, you are going to generate a QR code of a website address; scanning the code with a smartphone will take a customer to that website. This code will be placed on the right side of the coupon ad document, inside a frame for proper fit.

1. Select the Rectangle Frame Tool (F) with Fill and Stroke of None, and hold down the Shift key while dragging a square shape about 4 dashes in length on the bottom right side coupon. Make sure it does not overlap into the price. Keep it selected so the code will automatically be placed inside (Figure 11-23).

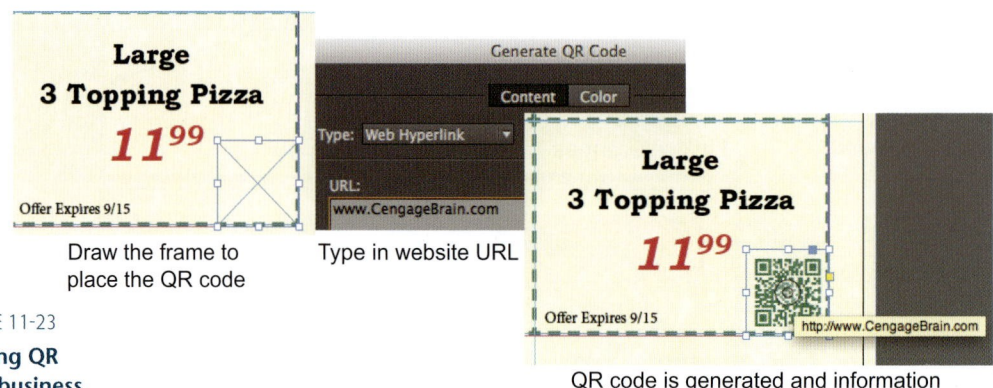

Draw the frame to place the QR code

Type in website URL

▷   FIGURE 11-23

Generating QR code for business promotion.

QR code is generated and information is displayed when mouse is hovered over

2. From the Object menu, select Generate QR Code to display the dialog box. Make sure the Content tab is selected and choose Type: Web Hyperlink.

3. Type in your favorite website URL, making sure you include the "www" if necessary. In our example we chose the publisher's website, *www.CengageBrain.com*. Don't press OK as we are going to add color to this code.

4. Select the Color tab, and choose the green Pantone P 138-14 C (or 261-1 C) color you created earlier from the Swatches panel. Click OK.

5. Instantly your code should be placed in the selected frame on your coupon. Hover your mouse over the center to display the Content Indicator, and the website address you chose should also display. This is helpful if, as a business, you wanted to send promotions online; it gives the user your website address and optionally plenty of other information that could be added. As a print it can be scanned on a smartphone with the code reader app for the user. Note: If you notice in the Links panel that the QR code does not display, it is because it is embedded in the document without any link to an original file as the other two graphic images.

INDESIGN'S LAYERS PANEL

In InDesign, there is a Layers panel that behaves much the same way as the Layers panel in Illustrator. Each document layer now has a disclosure triangle that can be expanded to reveal the objects and their stacking order on that given layer. This allows you to click on a particular layer to display the objects or graphics created. Simply dragging the item name in the list and dropping it where you want it within the panel can change the stacking order of objects. You can even drag and drop items into and out of groups, buttons, and multi-state objects. The Layers panel also provides you the ability to now toggle the visibility of individual page items, as well as the ability to lock and unlock them, providing choice as to what components can be edited or not. This behavior matches Illustrator in that a locked item cannot be edited, or even selected, without first unlocking it.

To see the locking features of the Layers panel, you'll lock the graphic objects.

1. In InDesign, select the Layers panel (Window > Layers).

2. You can see on the Layers panel that *Layer 1* is displayed. Click on the left side arrow next to the *Layer 1* text to display sublayers of the individual graphics and text boxes under the initial layer.

3. Click to toggle a lock next to the three graphic sublayers, Pizza, QR code, and Parchment, as shown in Figure 11-24.

Graphic sublayers locked

▷ FIGURE 11-24

InDesign's Layers panel for locking text and graphic objects.

4. Try adjusting either graphic and you'll find you can't edit either graphic because it is locked. Leave these two graphics as locked as they will not need to be edited in future coupons.

5. Lock one of the text boxes, and then try to edit it. You should not be able to make any edits. You can see how useful this could be when you want to edit only some objects. We'll cover more on the Layers panel later.

6. To see the completed work without most guides, select View > Grids & Guides > Hide Guides (Figure 11-24). Remember, guides do not print.

7. Save the file when finished.

TOOLKIT TIP To view what the proof will display, select View > Screen Mode > Preview. To bring back the guides for editing, select View > Screen Mode > Normal, which is the default. To remove the non-printing guidelines, select View > Extras > Hide Frame Edges.

CREATING A TEMPLATE FILE IN INDESIGN

If you are working on a design that may need to be used or duplicated later, saving your document as a template allows you to bring up what you have created as a new starting point that you can edit later without starting from scratch (Figure 11-25). InDesign saves the template file with an INDT extension so that it can be opened as a regular InDesign file ready to edit later. A template file can contain settings, text,

▷ FIGURE 11-25

**Saving the document
as a template file.**

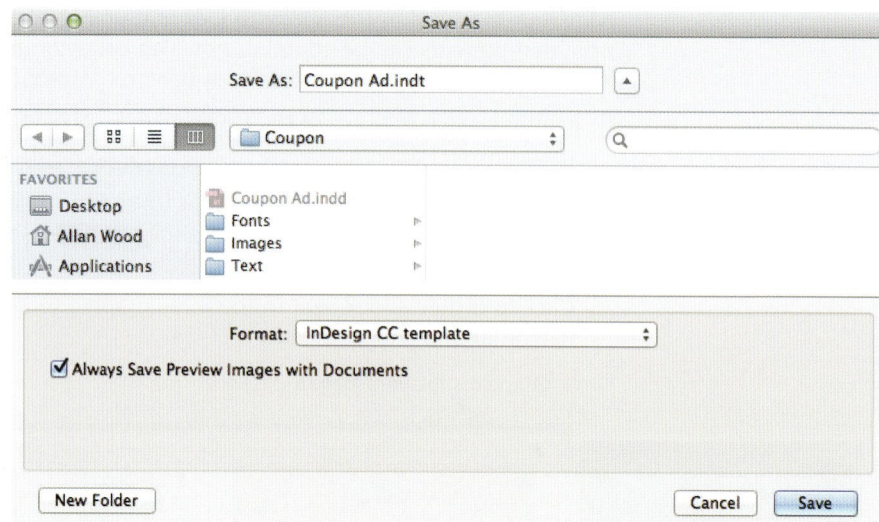

and graphics that you preset as a starting point for other documents. Normally, if you are providing your file to someone who has an earlier version of InDesign, they will not be able to read your document successfully. Always keep this in mind when transferring files. Find out your client's version.

Next, you will save the final document as a template for future editing.

1. With the document active, select File > Save As > InDesign CC template.

2. Save it in your *Coupon* folder in the *Chapter 11* folder.

You are all set at this time with the coupon ad. Time for a pizza break!

TOOLKIT TIP You have images in your *Images* folder; although text is not necessary here, any documents would go in the *Text* folder. To put your fonts you used in your *Fonts* folder you created, you would use the Font Book application (Mac users), select the font(s) used, and select File > Export Fonts to copy all used fonts into the folder. Windows users would locate the Appearance and Personalization link in the Control panel, then click on the Fonts link, then drag the selected font(s) into the *Fonts* folder. In the Advanced Users section you'll learn to package everything automatically using InDesign's Package utility.

TOOLKIT TIP InDesign has a feature that allows you to save the document so that a designer or service provider who has an earlier InDesign CS4 version can read and edit the document. This can be done by using the Export command in the File menu and exporting the InDesign CC, CS6, or CS5 document to InDesign Markup Language, which will convert it to an IDML extension. This is covered in the Advanced Users section.

ADVANCED USERS: Preflight, Packaging, and Preparing for Press. Syncing Job Folders and InDesign Settings.

Suppose you are planning to give this assignment, or any other for that matter, to a commercial press to have a volume amount of copies professionally printed. InDesign comes with a few handy utilities and features to help you check your work, package it for the printer, and create soft proofs for the printer or client to use and approve as needed. Here you will go through the process involved with the coupon advertisement you just created. Taking a little extra time for a proactive approach to make sure your work is ready goes a long way in this profession. You will also have few if any surprises and a more confident client in your work as a professional. With Illustrator Creative Cloud (CC), designers also have the opportunity to sync their job folders with their artwork, images, fonts, and text in their Creative Cloud account as paid subscribers. This provides another method of delivering work to a service provider, updating work to the latest version, and sharing work with colleagues or with other designers as part of a team between multiple computers. You can also sync settings between computers for consistency.

TOOLKIT TIP Always talk to your service provider or printer first before sending anything. They may have specific requirements and suggestions that could help your project go more smoothly. Requirements for publishing on a commercial press will be different from publishing for a website. For both media, all required electronic files should be placed inside one titled *Folder* to keep them organized for the service provider. These include the InDesign project documents with images, text, and fonts placed inside their own folders.

DESIGN TIP

Images saved with a .JPG extension for the sake of compression need to be converted to .TIF files, because compressed files can create problems at the press and cause delays.

PRINT PUBLISHING GUIDELINES

When sending a job to be printed on a commercial press, care needs to be taken to include a laser proof for accurate CMYK colors to show precise placement of all items, which should be larger than the trim size of the paper to show trim and registration marks. All electronic files need to be checked for up-to-date accuracy, and hard copy laser proofs should be provided with a job output report.

TOOLKIT TIP The actual page layout size should also be the trim size of the document.

As a general rule, when the job is ready to be handed over to the service provider for print publishing, it should contain the following components:

- Updated electronic files in organized folders.
- All items should be set in CMYK color mode for press inks. Native PSD and AI documents can also be used. Photographs, painted images, and detailed drawings can be saved as TIF images, while illustrations and images with text can be saved as EPS files. High-resolution PDF files are also acceptable and keep formatting consistent.

- The most up-to-date laser proof needs to be included, labeled with name and date to provide hard copy confirmation of how the final layout should appear. It should also include trim and registration marks for the printer to follow.

- If you have a color laser PostScript printer, you can print separate color proofs as a guide for creating the color plates for the printing press. InDesign allows you to create these proofs, but we will not create them for this exercise.

- Folder and files, the document, and a report file generated by InDesign's Package utility provide all the files, fonts, and basic job information needed including the print specifications.

 TOOLKIT TIP When sending projects to a commercial press, use fonts that have the style built into the name instead of selecting style buttons in your toolbar. This will ensure proper spacing of text in InDesign. When a bold or italic style is applied in InDesign, it is using the actual font. If the actual font is not available, the style will not be changed. For an italicized font, look for the word *Oblique* or *Italic* in the font name.

CHECKING FOR SPELLING

Although this assignment should not contain any spelling errors, it is always a good habit to walk through the process to understand the importance of spell checking. InDesign has a spelling checking feature in the Edit menu that not only allows you to check for spelling errors, but also to autocorrect and add special words in the dictionary (Figure 11-26). When you check for spelling and a questionable word comes up, InDesign provides options or other words to take its place, or you can type in the correct word.

▷ FIGURE 11-26

Using the Check Spelling utility.

Here you will misspell a word and use the spell check to correct it.

1. Launch InDesign and open the *Coupon Ad.indd* file you just created.
2. Add an extra *Z* in the word *pizza*.

3. Select Edit > Spelling > Check Spelling.

4. Choose the word *pizza* spelled correctly from the list of choices, and click on the Change button.

5. Select Done when you have finished and you are all set. You can see how this can be a great help when you are creating multipage documents or books with lots of text.

6. Save the file.

TOOLKIT TIP One of the biggest issues an amateur designer faces is forgetting to make sure that image and font files are stored in the same location as the document when taking the document to a client or printer. If you are transporting your document to another computer on a portable storage device, make sure you have the images also on that device and that the same fonts are on the other computer you have chosen. Use InDesign's Preflight and Package operations to gather all the elements needed for production.

DESIGN TIP

Do not use more than three different type families in a document. It is acceptable to use numerous font members from one type family in a single document, such as Myriad Light, Bold, Condensed, Italic, and so on. The spacing between characters and lines of text also determines how that type looks on your document. Usually the default leading is 120 % of the letter size for most documents.

CHECKING GRAPHIC LINKS USING THE LINKS PANEL

Before sending any file or completed document, always check to see if your links are up to date. One way is to use the Links panel. Here is where the Links panel we so quietly mentioned in the coupon assignment comes to our aid. By double-clicking the file you are checking on the **Links panel**, you will find plenty of information, including file size and color mode, all kinds of descriptive attributes, and the file's location, so you can make your edits accordingly (Figure 11-27). Each object in the Links panel is represented with a thumbnail that provides more detailed additional information when clicked such as scale, rotation, and resolution, among other attributes. You can use the Links panel to find, sort, and manage all of your placed objects. For instance, if you are sending everything to commercial press, then you would want all your graphic files in CMYK color. If you found one in RGB mode, you could simply open it in its application, such as Photoshop or Illustrator, and change the mode to CMYK. Using the Links panel, you can also select the Relink icon to find where you put the file that is linked in the document. The Go To Link icon shows you the actual graphic's location in your document. The Update Link icon lets you update the link location.

TOOLKIT TIP When you open a document and a warning dialog box comes up regarding the need to update or looking for links to graphics, select to automatically fix the links. If this does not work, you probably moved the file away from its original position and it is trying to find the links to the graphics and fonts it was using. Find where the graphics and text are located and relink to the document. You can also do this by selecting the items manually from the Links panel. If you need to edit the graphic, select Edit > Edit With > and choose the application you want to use for editing.

▷ FIGURE 11-27

**Using the Links panel
to check file link and
detailed information.**

FIGURE 11-27

Using the Links panel to check file link and detailed information.

Let us check the links from the coupon ad you just created.

1. Make sure the Links panel is displayed (Window > Links).

2. Double-click on the *Pizza* graphic link layer to see information about it. If there is a yellow sign next to either graphic, the link has been broken and needs to be updated.

3. If both are linked correctly, you will see no warning signs or dialog boxes. If not, use the Links panel to locate and update the file.

PREFLIGHT

Before you send any work to a client or the **service provider**, which can be your commercial printer, web developer, or other professional who will provide a service for setting up your document for whatever output media you intend to use, you need to go through a process called **preflight** to check for any errors. With InDesign, the default preflight settings are to "Enable Preflight for All Documents" and "Preflight Document," which are located at the bottom of the window display. While you were creating the coupon ad, InDesign was checking graphics and text from your work behind the scenes. InDesign also has a live Preflight panel to work along with the Links panel in identifying and correcting errors on the fly. With this new feature, a designer doesn't have to wait until the document is near completion before finding errors. There should be no problems displayed on the panel for your advertisement (Figure 11-27). The Preflight panel (Preflight utility in earlier versions) warns of problems, such as missing files, graphics, or fonts. This is especially helpful in working with long documents as you will be creating in the next chapter. You have just performed initial preflight operations in the previous assignments, so now you will check the document using the Preflight panel. You can always perform preflight during various stages of your project.

To check the coupon ad you just created, do the following:

1. Launch InDesign and open up your *Coupon Ad* document, not the template, you just created. If you are using earlier versions, you would choose File > Preflight.

2. Select the Preflight panel option at the bottom of the window display; you should not see any errors, as shown in Figure 11-28. If you have any errors, it may be having to locate the graphic link. Use the Links panel to help find the graphic. In earlier versions, choose the Summary panel in the Preflight dialog box (File > Preflight) as a guide; you can select various menus to check fonts, links, graphics, and other information. A yellow sign alert icon indicates problem areas.

3. Although you can use the Preflight panel menu to generate a PDF report to give to a client, you'll be creating an in-depth report using the Package utility in the last exercise, so leave this alone for now and make sure all links are correct.

▷ FIGURE 11-28

Live preflighting to check files, fonts, and images.

PREPARING THE PROJECT FOR PRINTING

With the project checked for spelling and appropriate fonts and images updated for accuracy and placement, it is time to get ready for press. Usually the commercial press you send your document and information to is called your *service provider* or *service bureau*.

THE POSTSCRIPT LANGUAGE

The commercial printing industry operates on a **page description language (PDL)**, created by your desktop publishing application and your computer, that defines precise position and composition of the images, text, and other elements in your document by mapping each pixel for the high-resolution output of your pages. The **PostScript language** is the most widely accepted and used PDL in the commercial printing industry. When you print your document to a disk file, a PostScript printer, or an output device, you are creating a PostScript language file that is processed by that device. PostScript functions as a computer programming language and a page description language (PDL). PostScript printers or image-setter devices also use a **raster image processor (RIP)** as an interpreter to convert the page information from the PostScript language into a bitmap image pattern for film or paper output.

TECHNICAL INFORMATION REGARDING POSTSCRIPT, TRUETYPE, AND OPENTYPE FONTS

Fonts fall into one of three types: *PostScript, TrueType,* and *OpenType*. OpenType is the standard most widely used in the commercial printing industry today. Most commercial printing service providers can handle fonts you supply or will find a suitable replacement. This is why it is important to include fonts as part of your packaging to the printer in case they need to install your fonts in their system. You can observe the type of font you are using when you look down the font list of any Adobe product. With technology in the printing industry today, you can usually use different types of fonts if needed. Always check with your service provider first.

PostScript fonts are bitmap-type fonts that contain two files: one for screen display and one for printer display. They are the most clear for printing and are preferred when sending to press. They also have set sizes, because they are bitmap files and cannot be resized without causing deterioration in quality. They were created initially by Adobe. Fonts that are PostScript are designated with a red *a*. PostScript fonts and files are divided into levels, with Level 1 being an older level. These levels help to specify compatibility with the interpreters in PostScript output devices. Level 2 will often improve the printing speed and output quality of graphics printed only on a PostScript Level 2 or greater output device. Level 3 provides the best speed and output quality, but requires a PostScript 3 device.

TrueType fonts, designated by an icon displaying two *Ts*, are scalable and were initially created by Microsoft. When you open a Microsoft Word document and can quickly select the font size without any deterioration, usually that is a TrueType font. Although they are extremely popular, they can cause production problems with older RIP processors by slowing down production time. Most newer systems handle TrueType fonts without any problem.

OpenType fonts are the newest members and are also scalable and may include a number of additional features, such as swashes and discretionary ligatures found in many foreign languages, that are not available in current PostScript and TrueType fonts. They are designated with the letter *O* italicized. Looking in your Fonts directory, you will usually find these fonts and their designated icons next to them to identify their type. OpenType fonts are cross platform, eliminating the font issues that occur when moving documents between Mac and Windows operating systems.

PREPARING GRAPHICS

Before any graphics are sent to press, they may be saved as either an EPS for vector artwork or images with text or as a TIF file for photographic images or paintings. They can also be saved in their native formats, or as high-quality PDF files. If an illustration is a composite of more than one graphic element, all the original files must be included in the delivery. Illustration and image files in TIF or EPS format are imported or placed so that the low-resolution preview appears on the page layout with a low-resolution link to the original high-resolution graphic. At print time, the low-resolution link locates the original high-resolution image and is immediately replaced to provide the high-resolution graphic data to the intended output. High-resolution PDF files are used quite often for both text and graphics.

- Save graphics in uncompressed formats; no JPEGs. Use PDF files for communication, or if the service provider requests final proofs.

- Convert RGB images to CMYK. Make a duplicate RGB file first, and then convert to CMYK to have two separate files.

- Do not change graphics file names unless you first relink them in InDesign.

PRINTING A FINAL PROOF

With the work completed, it is time to create a proof that can be used as a communication tool between you, your client, and the service provider you are working with. This exercise will provide insight about the printer settings or printer's marks for you to communicate the layout of the document, color accuracy, registration marks, and trim marks. The first thing is to make sure your "suitcase" of images is in the same place as your document and has not changed; otherwise, you will only be able to print the low-resolution copy, because the link to the original image has been broken. You will need to set up the *Coupon Ad* document to be printed as centered on legal-size paper in landscape orientation. This provides space for you or your client to write any information. **Printer's marks** include **registration marks**, which provide a place for pin registration of plates for the press (they look crosshairs in a rifle sight), and **color bars** to balance and check the color. **Crop marks** indicate where the cutting of the paper will be. If you are setting crop marks and want the artwork to contain a bleed or slug area, make sure that you extend the artwork past the crop marks to accommodate the bleed or slug. The **bleed area** is the part of text or objects that extends beyond the page boundaries after trimming, and the **slug area** is an area outside the page and bleed that contains printing instructions or job sign-off information. Also make sure that your media size is large enough to contain the page and any printer's marks, bleeds, or the slug area.

TOOLKIT TIP It is best to print to a sharp and clear color laser printer; for this exercise try to print from a color ink-jet printer if a color laser printer is unavailable. Print to a black-and-white laser printer if you need to look at layout only.

For this exercise you will need to make sure you have your images in your folder linked to the *Coupon Ad.indd* document. The same fonts you used to create your coupon ad should be on the computer you are going to print from or you may find either a dialog box to ask you for replacement fonts or it may substitute some evil font that will mess up your creation.

1. Since you have completed preflighting your document, your *Coupon Ad.indd* file is ready to print. Select to Print the file (File > Print) and select the General tab from the menu.

2. Select the printer you wish to use. Consult with your instructor to choose the printer.

3. To set up the positioning of the document in relation to the page, select the Setup tab, set the Paper Size to Letter, choose Landscape Orientation, and a Page Position of Centered, as shown in Figure 11-29. Leave all other default settings. You will see the coupon page icon displayed in the window.

▷ FIGURE 11-29

Creating a proof with printer's marks.

4. Finally, select the Marks and Bleed category, and then check All Printer's Marks to observe special printer's marks (Figure 11-29).

5. To print the document with printer's marks, select the Print button at the bottom of the display and check your work. You should have a nice proof ready for approval by your client or to hand off to your service provider.

TOOLKIT TIP This exercise regarding setting up printer's marks may be used for client approval. The service provider would never waste so much space on an actual print run; they would combine copies of the coupon to fit on whatever size sheet of paper they intend to print on to utilize as much print space as needed to run the job economically. This exercise is created to give you some exposure to the process.

PACKAGING YOUR DOCUMENT

One of the first good habits you made earlier in the chapter was to create folders to put your images, text, and fonts in for easy access and to maintain links to the document. If you are planning to transport all the information on a flash drive or other removable media, you will need to make sure you copy all the folders and files from your hard drive to the type of media you intend to take to the service provider. You can do this manually, or InDesign has a handy utility called **Package** that will do it for you. When you package a file, you create a folder that contains the InDesign document, any necessary fonts, linked graphics, text files, and a customized report. This report, which is saved as a text file, includes the information in the Printing Instructions dialog box from the Preflight dialog box; a list of all used fonts, links, and inks required to print the document; and print settings. You should get in the habit of using InDesign's Preflight and Package utilities for all your documents to be organized and checked for accuracy. Usually, when you send a client a Fonts folder they would have to install the fonts onto their system manually if they didn't have the same font or same version. When you choose to include the fonts used in a document or file when using the Package command, InDesign will now generate a folder named "Document Fonts." This way when you as the receiver, or your client, may need to open an INDD file, InDesign will automatically install these fonts for you. Document installed fonts, however, are not the same as fonts available from the standard operating system font locations. They get installed for only that document when it is opened, and are subsequently uninstalled when the document is closed. In Illustrator Creative Cloud (CC), you also have the option to Package a copy of your document as a PDF and IDML version for those who may not have the current InDesign CC.

TOOLKIT TIP When you are packaging a document, InDesign automatically performs an up-to-date preflight check, making it unnecessary to perform a separate preflight check as described earlier. If problem areas are detected, a dialog box appears. However, it still helps to understand the process here.

TOOLKIT TIP Once a job is packaged, it creates a final copy of the document inside the packaged folder. When users still have the original document open and make changes, they do not realize that those changes will not be reflected in the document included in the package. Unless they do a Save As and replace the document in the package, they will actually be sending the printer an older version. That is why packaging should always be the last step.

In this exercise you will go through the process of packaging your folders, files, and document into another folder within your *Chapter 11* folder, or you can try to use this utility to transport to a removable media such as a flash drive.

1. Select File > Package, and using the Summary panel in the dialog box as a guide, you can select various menus to check fonts, links, graphics, and other information. There should be no errors before packaging.

2. With everything checked out OK, select Package; when the Printing Instructions dialog box comes up, put in all relevant information including contact information that will become part of the report, as if you were sending this document as a job to the service provider. Select Continue.

Using the Packaging utility to place the job contents, files, images, and report in one folder.

3. When the Create Package Folder dialog box comes up, save the publication in your *Coupon* folder as *Coupon Job,* or save it with all your other files on your removable drive media. Keep the first three boxes checked (default) in the dialog box and in Illustrator CC, check the boxes to also create a PDF and IDML version in the folder as well (Figure 11-30), and then click on the Package button.

Select links for info and check for errors

Font Warning

4. When a Font Alert dialog box comes up reminding you of copyright issues, select OK for this exercise, unless your instructor advises against copying your fonts.

5. The Package utility will generate a folder that contains a copy of your document, related files or an *Instructions.txt* file, fonts in a Document Fonts folder, and images in a Links folder, ready for press. You will also see a job report to provide instructions to the printer. Close that file when done.

6. That is all there is to it.

TOOLKIT TIP InDesign can also convert the files, graphics, and document for web use and also allows you to send a client a PDF version of your document.

EXPORTING INDESIGN CC DOCUMENTS FOR EVERYONE ELSE

Some clients may not have InDesign CC installed on their computers. Another way you can show a client a potential layout or bring an electronic proof of your work to a service provider or commercial press is to have a PDF created of your project that can be burned on CD or sent by email to your client. Also, InDesign CC, users have a feature that can export their document for earlier version InDesign CS4 users to read as an **InDesign Markup Language (IDML)** document (File > Export > InDesign Markup (IDML)). With both of these avenues available, most anyone should be able to view your creations. You'll be shown how to create an IDML document very soon.

CREATING A PDF DOCUMENT FOR ALL TO READ

Since some of your clients may not have InDesign CC installed, it normally would mean they could not read the document. With InDesign, if a universal proof is needed that embeds all fonts and graphics to provide to a printer, a designer can use the Export command to create a PDF document. This can be read by the free Adobe Reader available on the Adobe site (Adobe Reader was installed on your computer in an exercise in Chapter 1 of this text) and other graphic applications as well. InDesign also allows you to select the quality of the PDF file you wish to create. Press Quality is always the best for distributing to a commercial press, but if you want to send a document through email for a preliminary proofing, you may want to choose Smallest File Size under the Adobe PDF Preset pulldown menu. You can quickly choose to select Adobe PDF (Print) for press, or Adobe PDF (Interactive) for electronic distribution.

 TOOLKIT TIP A PDF document cannot simply be opened in InDesign. It can only be placed in a document using the Place command.

Next, you will create a PDF file from the coupon ad you just made (Figure 11-31).

▷ FIGURE 11-31

Setting up to export an InDesign document as a press-quality PDF.

1. Open the coupon advertisement you just completed, and, with links checked and updated if needed, designate Press Quality by selecting File > Adobe PDF Presets > Press Quality.

2. Select Save for the PDF document to be saved and exported in your *Coupon* folder. You can also just select File > Export > Adobe PDF (Print).

3. When the Export Adobe PDF dialog box appears, select the Press Quality pre-set with a compatibility set for Adobe Acrobat 5 or 6 to cover most users since the coupon ad involved no specialized creations. Leave all other defaults.

4. To display all kinds of printer's marks for the press (which we will cover in more detail in the next chapter), select the Marks and Bleeds from the left side menu and select All Printer's Marks to display color calibration, trim marks, and registration marks on your document. Leave all other defaults.

5. Select Export to create the PDF version in your *Coupon* folder while the original InDesign file stays on the desktop.

6. You can double-click the new *Coupon Ad.pdf* file to open it in the free Adobe Reader or in the Adobe Acrobat application which comes with Creative Cloud, CS6, or any suite of applications, if it is installed on your computer; because Adobe Reader is the universal means to view any document, and the Reader is free, most computers have some version installed already.

7. You will notice the various printer's marks added to your document for the press to read for accuracy in color, registration of the plates, and trimming marks.

8. Print the PDF document and close it when you are done.

EXPORTING INDESIGN CC DOCUMENTS TO SAVE BACKWARDS

Normally, if you are providing your file to someone who has an earlier CS4 version of InDesign for further editing (unlike PDF files which are read only) in InDesign itself, they will not be able to read your document successfully. To open an InDesign CC, CS6, or CS5 document in InDesign CS4, you will need to do two things. First, in InDesign CC, CS6, or CS5, export the document to the InDesign Markup Language as **IDML** (File > Export). In Illustrator CC, you can also use File > Save As > InDesign CS4 or later (IDML). This format replaces the earlier version CS3 and CS4 formats called InDesign Interchange (**INX**). Second, the user can make sure that their computer running InDesign CS4 is updated with appropriate plug-ins so that it can be able to open the exported IDML file. To check, simply select Help > Updates to install any updates, or go to the Adobe website and choose Support > Updates, and then go to the InDesign Downloads page. Opening a document in a previous version of InDesign is also referred to as "saving down." It must also be noted that content using features that are specific to only the CC, CS6, or CS5 version may be modified or removed when you open the IDML document in InDesign CS4.

Next, you will save your Creative Cloud (CC) document so that it can be opened by those using InDesign CS6, CS5, or CS4.

1. Launch InDesign and open the InDesign document of the *Coupon Ad.indd* file you just created if you had previously closed it.

2. Select File > Save As. Then, from the File Type (Windows) or Format (Mac OS X) menu, select InDesign CS4 or later (IDML), or, if choosing File > Export, select InDesign Markup (IDML).

3. Select to save the file in the *Coupon* folder. Choose Save when done.

4. The document will have an IDML extension to indicate that it can be read in version CS6, CS5, or CS4. You can then open the *Coupon Ad.idml* file in InDesign CS6, CS5, or CS4, to convert it to an untitled InDesign document for viewing and editing in InDesign CS6, CS5, or CS4.

5. In your *Coupon* folder, you will find the *Coupon Ad* files with extensions INDD, INDT, IDML, and PDF. Note: If you have the most current version of InDesign CC, there is also the option when packaging files for a job, to create IDML and PDF versions of your current document.

SYNCING YOUR INDESIGN DOCUMENTS AND SETTINGS TO CREATIVE CLOUD

If you subscribe to Adobe Creative Cloud (CC) products, on the Creative Cloud desktop on your computer you can select Sync Files to Creative Cloud to place your artwork online, which can be shared between other professionals using the free Behance portfolio site, or you can access your work on another computer. You can also sync your InDesign settings such as workspaces, PDF Presets, and customized menus between computers.

MANAGING YOUR INDESIGN FOLDER OF ARTWORK, FONTS, AND IMAGES IN CREATIVE CLOUD

With Creative Cloud installed as a paid subscriber, you can submit and access your documents and artwork from the Creative Cloud storage between computers. The real purpose of using this is not so much for permanent storage, but for use as part of your intended workflow. You can upload additional images with thumbnails displayed, and download your image(s) from Creative Cloud. Where you have images that are linked to your *Coupon Ad.indd* file and others, you can submit the entire *Coupon* folder of InDesign documents, graphics, text, and fonts up to the Creative Cloud for access by a team of designers, client, or even service provider. This way everything is still in its digital suitcase for any future editing.

In this optional exercise, you'll use Creative Cloud to submit your *Coupon* folder, and then access the file to download to your computer.

1. On your computer, if it isn't already active, launch Creative Cloud as you would any other application from your Applications (Mac) or Programs (Windows) folder (in Windows 8 you can also type in "Creative Cloud" from the Start Screen).

2. With Creative Cloud desktop active, click on the icon and select the Files tab to display the folder icon (Figure 11-32).

3. Click Open Folder and drag your *Coupon* folder you just created into the open folder, which may read Creative Cloud Files in the title bar.

4. To access your files on the Creative Cloud server, click on the *CreativeCloud .com* button.

5. From the Creative Cloud website, select the Files tab. Your *Coupon* folder should display as a thumbnail. To open a folder or expand a file click anywhere on the thumbnail. Click on the thumbnail to open the *Coupon* folder to view your files and folders inside. You can continue to click on down arrows to display contents of folders, rename, move, archive, or send links to your files (Figure 11-32).

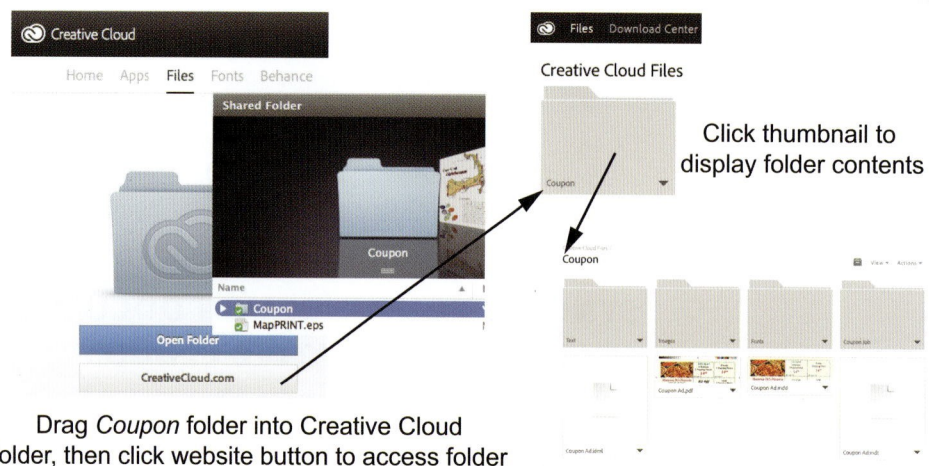

Click thumbnail to display folder contents

Drag *Coupon* folder into Creative Cloud
folder, then click website button to access folder

▷ FIGURE 11-32

Managing InDesign folder of artwork, fonts, and images between computers using Creative Cloud.

6. To minimize to the original thumbnails, click on the Creative Cloud Files link above your *Coupon* text.

7. In the Actions link, select Upload to upload additional InDesign artwork (or any Adobe files) from your computer.

8. To access your folder from another computer with Creative Cloud installed, in the Actions panel, with the folder or document selected, select Download and your expanded image will be downloaded onto your computer. You can edit the document and then send it back up to the Creative Cloud, where it will replace the older version. That way your image version stays current. You can also drag an image from the desktop into the Files tab window in Creative Cloud.

9. Log out of the website when done.

SYNCING INDESIGN SETTINGS BETWEEN COMPUTERS WITH CREATIVE CLOUD

InDesign has the Creative Cloud feature to not only sync and share your artwork between computers to keep the most current version available, but also the availability to sync your InDesign settings between computers. The process is basically the same for any application, you can either click the Sync Settings button at the bottom of your document (gear-like icon), or select Sync Settings from Preferences where you can have choices as to what you would like to have synced between computers.

ⓧ PROBLEM When ready to sync your settings to the Creative Cloud, if you cannot find your Adobe ID displayed in the InDesign (Mac) or Edit (Windows) menu, you'll need to sign out of InDesign, and then sign back in again. Go to Help > Sign Out... to sign out. Choose Help > Sign-in... to sign in again. Quit InDesign, and then launch InDesign again. Sync Settings should then be enabled.

When you select to Sync Settings, your settings are uploaded to the Creative Cloud online. With InDesign, you can sync settings from a previous version as well.

Optional Exercise: Let's sync the InDesign settings from the *Coupon Ad.indd* file you just created. If you have access to two computers, you'll sync settings from your current computer you created the coupon on so that you can use the same settings on another computer.

1. Select InDesign (Mac) or Edit (Windows) and make sure your Adobe ID (email) is displayed. Note: If your Adobe ID doesn't display follow directions in the Problem section above.

2. Choose Preferences > Sync Settings (Figure 11-33), where you can choose options of what to sync instead of the default to sync everything possible. Close your *Coupon Ad.indd* file and any other open documents or files in InDesign, then select the Upload Settings (or Manage Sync Settings) in the InDesign (Mac) or Edit (Windows) menu. It will automatically send all your settings to the Creative Cloud. Click OK when done.

▷ FIGURE 11-33

Syncing InDesign settings between computers with Creative Cloud.

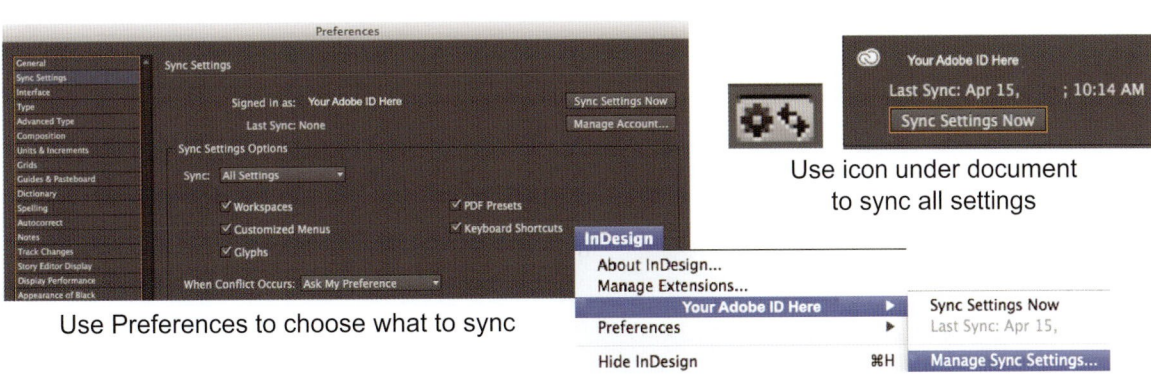

Use Preferences to choose what to sync

Use icon under document to sync all settings

Sync settings from Creative Cloud to other computer

3. Open your other computer (computer B), then launch InDesign, making sure you are logged in with your Adobe ID again. After closing all documents, choose Download Settings (or Manage Sync settings) from InDesign's Adobe ID link.

4. If a dialog box displays as Updated settings are ready, select Apply Now to bring the settings from the Creative Cloud onto your other computer. Your new settings synced from InDesign on your initial computer will display on the second computer when you open a new document. If needed, restart InDesign again to apply the settings.

TOOLKIT TIP If you want to automatically sync all settings between computers, at the bottom of your coupon document window you'll find a gear-like icon. When you click on the icon, your Adobe ID will display along with a button displayed as Sync Settings Now. Select Sync Settings Now to push your settings related to what you used in creating your document to Creative Cloud (Figure 11-33).

DIGITAL TOOLKIT EXTRA: Creating a Photo Calendar with Tables

This assignment will demonstrate how to create a calendar template that can be used on your desk with your favorite image while displaying the current month using a table. A **table** consists of rows and columns of cells. A **cell** is like a text frame in which you can add text, inline graphics, or other tables. Tables provide a powerful tool for proper alignment and distribution of evenly spaced columns and rows or containers containing text and graphics. When you create a table, it fills the width of the container text frame that you create. A table is inserted where you place the cursor insertion point. Tables can be created by using the Table menu to set up formatting and specifics. You can also create tables by using the Convert Text to Table command. In this extra assignment, you will create a calendar using both methods to see which you prefer (Figure 11-34). As always, with InDesign and most applications, there are many ways to create a project. Any selection of table cells or contents to be edited requires highlighting with the Type Tool (T).

▷ FIGURE 11-34

Completed calendar.

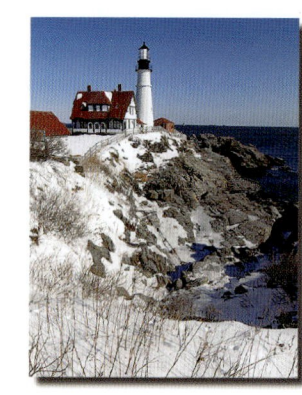

SETTING UP THE DOCUMENT

First, you will set up the document as two columns in landscape letter-half mode to create a desk calendar (Figure 11-35). The left column will be used to place the month, and the right column will be used for the table to place the days. You will create a large gutter width of one inch in between the columns to act as guide for the margins. A **gutter** is the space between two columns. Gutters are used with layout guides, folding guides, and sometimes to help with margin guides.

It is time to set up the new document parameters.

1. Create a folder inside your *Chapter 11* folder named *Calendar*. Move or copy the *Portland Light.tif* file that we'll use later into the folder. Launch InDesign, making sure the Units and Increments settings in preferences are set for Inches (InDesign > Preferences [Mac], or Edit > Preferences [Windows]).

▷ FIGURE 11-35

Document layout for desk calendar.

2. Select File > New > Document. When the display opens, make sure the Intent is set to Print, and the Facing Pages options and Primary Text Frame options are *not* checked, because we are not creating a book or newsletter.

3. Set up the document in letter half size in landscape orientation, as 2 columns, with half-inch margins all around; you can click on the Link icon to make all measurements the same.

4. Create a half-inch gutter and leave all other defaults. Select OK.

5. Save the file in InDesign's native INDD format as *Calendar* in your *Calendar* folder within your *Chapter 11* folder.

SETTING UP THE LAYOUT GUIDES

Here you will set up some layout guides as preliminary guides to split the gutter visually to match the half-inch margin guides, and then you will set up guides for placement of the month, days of the week, and start of the table for the days of the month (Figure 11-36).

Next, we will set up the guidelines to make things easier.

1. Make sure rulers are displayed (View > Show Rulers). Also make sure Smart Guides is checked (View > Guides and Grids > Smart Guides).

2. Drag a vertical guideline from the left side ruler guide to the 4.25-inch (4¼) mark to split the gutter visually.

3. For the month title, year, days of the week, and start of the table for the days of the month, drag horizontal guides or use the Control panel (Y coordinate for horizontal lines) for precision by entering at 1.25 (1¼), 1.5 (1½), 1.75 (1¾), and 2-inch marks.

▷ FIGURE 11-36

Layout guides for calendar.

4. You can resize your document window to display your document spread proportionately by selecting Fit Spread in Window in the View menu; then drag the bottom right corner of the window. Save the file.

FORMATTING AND COLORING TYPE

There are many different ways to enter type, whether in a table or in individual text frames. Sometimes having different text frames provides a little more flexibility when editing than having everything within a table. Here, you will put the title and year in their own text frame. Instead of creating a text frame with the Shape or Frame tools, you can also use the Type Tool (T) to create its own text frame.

 TOOLKIT TIP To create individual text frames for headings, select the Type Tool and create the text frame, type in the line, deselect by selecting the Selection Tool (V) or one of the tools on the Tools panel, and then select the Type Tool (T) and draw another text frame. This way they can be edited individually.

Here, you will create frames using the Type Tool (T) and type in the month and year, center it horizontally and vertically, and color the text.

1. Select the Type Tool (T) and drag a diagonal box in the right-side column between the half-inch margin up top and the 1.25-inch horizontal guide. This will be for the month title.

2. Using the Type Tool (T), make sure that you have a Stroke color of None and black Fill color in the Tools panel. You will select colors later.

3. Select from the Control panel a 36-pt Copperplate Gothic Bold font, and type "January." You will center this later.

4. To start another text box, click on the Selection Tool (V) to reset; then select the Type Tool (T) again and drag another text box, this time diagonally up from the 1.5-inch horizontal line up to the 1.25-inch line. You may notice InDesign's Smart Dimensions displaying as dimension arrows when the two type boxes align together.

5. Select from the Control panel 24-pt Copperplate Gothic Bold font (you may notice the font is already displayed up top as a favorite list for quick access), and type in the year 2016 (or whatever year you want to use).

6. Highlight the text in the title with the Type Tool (T) and select the Character Formatting Controls button on the Control panel as shown in Figure 11-37. Select the icon to Align center the text. Repeat with the year text.

▷ FIGURE 11-37

Formatting type lines and setting up color to add to the Swatches panel.

7. To vertically center the type line, highlight the title line, *January,* and select Object > Text Frame Options > Vertical Justification > Align Center, then click OK. Repeat with the year text. There are also vertical adjustment buttons on the Control panel for quick access instead.

8. To select color for your type, choose either a deep blue, green, or red by double-clicking on the Type Fill color and then selecting the color you want to use.

9. To add the color to the Swatches panel, select New Color Swatch from the Swatches panel menu and enter your color; we chose a deep red (CMYK) of C29, M100, Y100, and K40. Select Add to include the color in the swatch; then select Done to close the dialog box. You can also do this after you have set up the type in your type line.

10. Highlight the *January* text line, and tag the new color you chose in the Swatches panel (Figure 11-38). You can leave the year as black as shown, or choose another color.

▷ FIGURE 11-38

Creating the month title and year.

TOOLKIT TIP When you want to color the cell itself or the text in the cell, under the Fill and Stroke colors are two icons. One is for coloring the cell (square) and one is for coloring the text (T). You can switch back and forth to choose what you want to color.

TOOLKIT TIP Use the Type Tool (T) to select rows and columns to place text into. You can use the Selection Tool (V) to double-click inside a cell to bring up Type Tool options.

CREATING A TABLE

To place the weekdays and numbers in the month, you will create a table to distribute the information equally in the document. The easiest way to set up a text frame to place the table in is to use the Type Tool (T) again. You can then insert the table at the insertion point after creating the text frame. You will want to create the table on the right-side column of the document, because we will be putting an image on the left side later. To delete or move a table, use the Selection Tool (V).

This is one method for creating the table.

1. Using the Type Tool (T), draw a new text frame from the upper left corner on the right-side column from the horizontal guide at 1.75 (1¾), not 2-inch mark, and drag to the bottom right margin guide; make sure you drag to the bottom right margin guide and not just between the two horizontal guidelines. You will notice the blinking insertion point will display at the beginning of the text frame. Click on the Character formatting button to make it active; change the type size to 10 pt as a minimum size with the same Copperplate Gothic Bold font.

2. Choose Table > Insert Table.

3. You need to specify the numbers of rows and columns. Enter *7* body rows and *7* columns. Leave all other defaults and select OK (Figure 11-39). Although most months would fit in six rows including the days of the week titles, there are a few rare times when seven rows are needed (as in the year 2016).

> **TOOLKIT TIP** If you are creating tables of various row or column widths and heights, you can always create a table for each type and use the arrow keys to position accurately. If your table spans more than one column or frame, specify the number of header or footer rows in which you want the information to be repeated.

RESIZING ROWS AND COLUMNS

Before editing any cells within a table, the cells need to be highlighted. For most editing, you can highlight cells with the Type Tool (T) and use the Control panel or Table menu to make an exact measurement. For almost any modifications, you need to use the I-beam from the Type Tool (T). When you change the width of rows and columns, the external dimensions of the table change. To resize rows or columns proportionally, hold down Shift while dragging the selected row or column. To resize rows or columns without changing the table width, hold down the Shift key while dragging an inside row or column edge (not the table boundary). One row or column gets bigger as the other gets smaller. Holding down Shift while dragging the right table edge will resize all the columns proportionally; holding down Shift while dragging the bottom table edge will resize all rows proportionally. To drag all rows or columns, select the right table border or bottom table edge.

Here you will use the Shift key to resize the cells for the days of the week, and then drag the rows for the numbers to be distributed evenly to the bottom margin (Figure 11-40).

1. Select View > Grids & Guides and uncheck the Snap to Guides command here to freely drag the guidelines.

2. Make sure the Type Tool (T) is selected. Hold down the Shift key and click on the bottom horizontal line of the table you just drew when the cursor displays as a vertical double arrow, dragging the table straight downward very close to the bottom margin. If you drag to the margin, you may find one of the rows will disappear. We will adjust these in Step 4.

3. To create the cells for displaying the weekdays, hold down the Shift key again and click on the second horizontal line of the table; drag up to the 2-inch guideline mark. You may notice that the second row for the first week's

▷ FIGURE 11-40

**Creating and resizing
the table cells.**

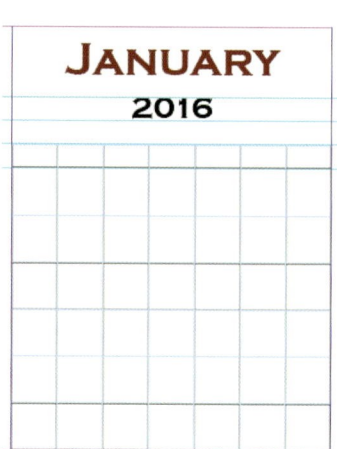

numerals is unequal to the rest. If the bottom row is moved away from the bottom margin, repeat Step 2.

4. To make all the cells that will display a number for the days of the week equal, highlight all the cells that will have the numbers with the Type Tool (table rows 2-7) and select Table > Distribute Rows Evenly. You are ready to enter the numbers.

 PROBLEM If all your rows are different sizes, you can click and drag each row upwards to its original state, and then Shift-drag all rows again or reinsert the table. Do not drag all the way to the bottom margin.

 TOOLKIT TIP To select cells in the columns and rows you want to resize, you can also specify Column Width and Row Height settings in the Table panel or choose Table > Cell Options > Rows and Columns; specify Row Height and Column Width options, and then click OK. To move or copy a table, select the entire table, place the insertion point in the table, and choose Table > Select > Table. Choose Edit > Cut or Copy, move the insertion point where you want the table to appear, and then choose Edit > Paste. In InDesign CC, designers have the option to "drag and drop" table columns and rows.

FORMATTING CONTENTS AND CELLS

To place the days of the week, you will highlight all the cells in the first row and set the type to Myriad Pro Bold font for easy readability. To go from one cell to another, it is best to use the Tab key once between each cell, or you can try and click in each cell with the mouse. You can then center align the type in each cell using either the Cell Options function in the Table menu, or simply highlight the type and cells you want to edit, and make the formatting changes using the Control panel (Figure 11-41).

▷ FIGURE 11-41

Using the Control panel to format cell contents.

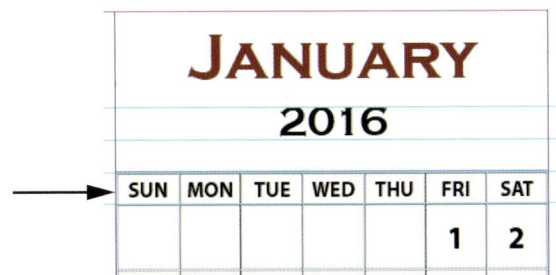

Next, you will use the Control panel to center-align the days of the week and the numbers in the calendar.

1. Select the Type Tool (T), highlight the cells for the days of the week, and choose a 12-pt Myriad Pro Bold font, or choose the same Copperplate Gothic Bold font, or some other fairly wide font. Highlight the cells for the numbers and change the size of your font to 18 pt.

2. Type in the three letters that signify the days of the week. Use the Tab key to move from one cell to the next. If you see only a red dot display in the cell, the type is too big for the cell. Reduce the size to 10 pt.

3. Find the month of January in the particular year you want to create this calendar and start typing the number "1" in its correct place as shown here for the year 2016. Use the Tab key to go to the next cell to type in the next number. Tabbing will also take you to the next row.

4. To center the days of the week and numbers within the cell, highlight the cells with the Type Tool (T), which will change the Control panel display options; select the Align Center and vertical Align Center buttons on the Control panel. You can also use the individual Character panels on the right side of the desktop for more formatting functions.

5. Save the file.

TOOLKIT TIP If you want the numbers to align right and at the top of each cell, highlight those cells with the Type Tool (T), and select the Align Right for paragraph and vertical Align Top buttons on the Control panel. There are vertical justification buttons on the Control panel you can also use. Using the Text Frame Options inside the Object menu, you can now choose to have InDesign automatically balance across columns in a multiple column frame by turning on the Balance Columns option to evenly distribute the text across a number of columns. InDesign CC provides designers the ability to drag and drop columns and rows into documents.

APPLYING FILLS AND TEXT COLOR USING CELL OPTIONS

DESIGN TIP

When coloring type in most cases, unless you are looking to outline a very light colored type, you would keep the stroke to None to maintain the exact shape of the font you are using.

The **Cell Options command** gives you the flexibility to format text; rows and columns; strokes and fills, including tints; and diagonal lines. Under the color boxes on the Tools panel are two formatting icons: one indicates a Formatting Effects Container, which could be the cell or a frame, and the other looks like a *T*, which indicates Formatting Effects Text. These can be used with selected cells to edit the cell itself or the type within the selected cell. When placing graphic images, InDesign will display on the computer as low resolution for easier maneuvering of the image in the document. If a designer needs to see what the final design will look like when printed, InDesign provides various commands in the View menu to see various resolutions, such as Display Performance (High Quality Display).

TOOLKIT TIP To adjust a cell's color fill, click the Container formatting icon in the bottom Tools panel (Figure 11-42). To adjust a text color, click on the Text Formatting icon. You can easily go back and forth between the two types of formatting by clicking these icons.

Here you will add a little more color to your work using the Cell Options command; then you will add the final image.

1. To add a fill for the days of the week, highlight the row SUN through SAT with the Type Tool (T). Select Table > Cell Options > Strokes and Fills.

2. Click on the Color button by the Cell Fill area, and select the deep red color you chose for the month of January as the Cell Fill; set up with 100% Tint and 1-pt black stroke weight for the outline of the cell (Figure 11-42). This will be used to fill color into the cells for the days of the week. Select OK. We will change the color of the type next.

▷ FIGURE 11-42

Formatting cells and contents using the Cell Options command.

Deep red color created previously and saved in Swatches panel

3. Highlight the days of the week cells again with the Type Tool (T), and select the *T* formatting icon (Formatting affects text) located underneath the Fill color box.

4. If you kept a very deep color, click on the Swatches panel and select the standard yellow color with a 30% tint, as displayed in Figure 11-43, or select the white or "Paper" color to make the days of the week stand out. Try other combinations of fills for a good balance of color. Click on the Selection Tool to deselect the text.

▷ FIGURE 11-43

Formatting type using Text formatting options on the Tools panel, and adjusting tint using the Swatches panel.

5. Be careful if you want to increase the stroke weight, because this will probably cause the bottom row of the table to disappear, and you will have to readjust the table.

6. If you want to change the color of the type in the days of the month, select the type, and then select the *T* formatting icon (Formatting affects text) located underneath the Fill color box. Then choose an appropriate color.

7. It is time to place the graphic for the month of January; you can also use your own graphic. To place a graphic on the left side to balance the calendar, draw a frame using the Rectangle Frame Tool (F) between the left side, top and bottom margin guides, and the 4-inch vertical guideline. It should display an *X* in the frame.

8. Select File > Place and place the *Portland Light.tif* file, from either your *Chapter 11* folder or the *Calendar* folder you created earlier into the selected frame; you can also use your own graphic image. Use the arrow keys or the center doughnut (Content Indicator) on the image with the Selection Tool (V) to move the image around if needed. If you do not want the white page background, try to copy and insert your own graphic as a background (there are plenty for free on the Internet) and send to the back (Object > Arrange > Send to Back).

9. Optional: To apply a drop shadow effect on the image, select it with the Selection Tool. Choose Effects > Drop Shadow from the Object menu. Leave the default drop shadow effect or go ahead and experiment to add dimension to the image.

10. When you are set, select View > Grids & Guides > Hide Guides to view your work without the layout guides you used earlier. To remove all frame edges not previously drawn with stroke weight, select View > Extras > Hide Frame Edges. To view how the calendar will look at high resolution for print, select View > Display Performance > High Quality Display.

11. Save the file as a regular InDesign document in your *Calendar* folder. It will have still have an INDD extension. Use the Links panel to check for links, and use the Preflight panel (near bottom of the window where there should be a green circle) to make sure there are no errors.

12. You can now create a monthly calendar template by choosing File > Save As > InDesign Template in your *Chapter 11* folder. It will have an INDT extension (Figure 11-44).

13. Save and Print the final file. Check with your instructor to choose whether to include crop marks and other printer's marks.

▷ FIGURE 11-44

Placing the graphic, removing frame and guidelines, and saving as a template for future documents.

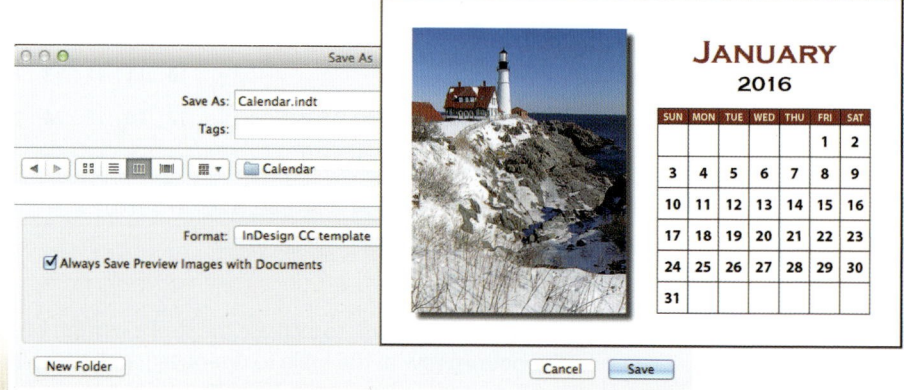

14. To create a package of all fonts and the lighthouse graphic to be copied into a folder, including other info mentioned in the Advanced section, select File > Package; then select Package. Put in any print instructions and select Continue. Name the new folder as *Calendar Job* and Save inside your *Calendar* folder. The graphic and fonts will be copied over for you. Nice and organized!

TOOLKIT TIP When ready to place a full-sized image into the frame window, unless you are fine with having a portion cropped, resize the image or graphic ahead of time in Photoshop before placing it in an InDesign document.

TOOLKIT TIP As a final note, in the next chapter you will be working with master pages. You can come back to the calendar document you just made and create the other 11 documents for each month from the master page; then simply place images or designs for each month and the appropriate numbering for each month. Use the Layers panel and save the layer you just created as January. You can then duplicate and create 11 more layers, labeling each for each month. Then just edit for each month.

CONVERTING TEXT TO A TABLE (OPTIONAL)

Another method to create a table is either by importing text from a spreadsheet or by entering data using the Tab key to generate columns and then using the Return/Enter key to generate rows.

1. Set up preferences and the document layout as you did before.

2. Start typing in the numbers of days of the week; hit the Tab key once after each word or number to create the columns, and then use the Return/Enter key to make a paragraph return to create the rows.

3. To create the table, select Table > Convert Text to Table. The cells of rows and columns will be created around your type.

4. Size the rows and apply formatting as described in the earlier exercises. Have fun.

TABLE AND CELL STYLES

A more advanced function allows you to create cell and table styles that serve as mini templates that contain all formatting, so you could create a cell style and then save that cell style to have the formatting copied to other cells. The same can be created using a table style, where you can also include cell styles within table styles. These styles are in their own Table Styles and Cell Styles panels, and you would use the panel menu to create new styles. Check in InDesign Help to view the tutorials for using these styles; we will look more at styles in the next chapter. You can also create inline notes in tables to other workers. You can store your notes linked to specific text in a table as well.

CHAPTER SUMMARY

You learned that in a desktop publishing program, you can create frames by using Shape tools or the Type Tool (V), or by clicking the mouse in the document for inserting text and graphics. You learned how to control the container contents using stroke and fill effects, and to use the Text Frame Options command and the Control panel to control formatting. In the advanced section, you were able to go through the process of preflight, packaging, and preparing a final proof of your document for either final client approval or for the service provider. You also generated a special promotional website QR code, and synced your coupon advertisement and InDesign settings using Creative Cloud. Do not forget to check out the *Extras & Goodies* folder on *www.CengageBrain.com* for more projects and ideas.

REVIEW QUESTIONS

1. Explain the differences between word processing and desktop publishing.
2. Explain the differences between margin guides and layout guides.
3. Explain at least three different extensions InDesign can create and what purposes they serve.
4. What is the purpose of the Links panel?
5. Explain briefly the process of the preflighting and the Package utility.
6. Describe the following printer mark terms: *bleed, slug, crop, color bars,* and *registration marks.*

CHAPTER 11
Creating a direct
mail coupon ad
using InDesign.

CHAPTER 11 ADVANCED
Preflighting, packaging, and preparing for press.
Syncing a job folder and InDesign settings in Creative Cloud.

CHAPTER 11 EXTRA
Creating a desktop
calendar using tables.

▷ FIGURE 11-45

Working with Multipage Documents

CHAPTER OBJECTIVES: To understand the importance of using InDesign to create effective multipage documents, in this chapter you will:

▷ Learn procedures to set up multipage InDesign documents for importing text and graphics.

▷ Set up a master page as a template for layout and design consistency.

▷ Navigate and edit the document using the Pages panel.

▷ Apply stroke and fill techniques for specific press-ready Pantone colors.

▷ Import text into multiple columns and multiple pages. Create jump lines into multiple pages.

▷ Create precise alignment columns using tabs.

▷ Apply special formatting techniques for headlines, body text, drop caps, rules, and pull quotes.

▷ ADVANCED USERS: Special editing techniques and designing alternative layouts.

▷ DIGITAL TOOLKIT EXTRA: Creating interactive PDF documents.

One of the main uses that a desktop publishing program like InDesign provides is the ability to create multiple documents like newsletters, books, and other printed media with consistency in layout. Text documents created in another application can be easily imported into the project without having to retype the content. In this chapter you will create a four-page newsletter to learn the process of importing text and graphics and providing consistency in layout and design. You will learn how to automate repetitive tasks to save time and increase your productivity by using master pages as document templates, importing text into multiple columns and multiple pages, and applying styles for consistency in formatting of text.

DESIGNING MULTIPAGE DOCUMENTS

Multipage documents include many types of documents, from booklets to newsletters. The key when working with multipage documents is consistency in layout, design, and character or paragraph formatting. The reader's eye can easily pick out a mistake or error if formatting is inconsistent. In creating newsletters or multipage documents, you may have various articles all vying for the reader's attention. Employing certain techniques discreetly helps to introduce or lead the reader to various articles within the multipage document, which heightens a reader's interest. Some of these techniques, such as filling a couple of text boxes with color, establishing visual hierarchy in headings, continuing an article to a later page to entice the reader to view other articles as they are turning to that page, and providing an index sheet all help to promote a positive reading experience. All pages created in InDesign can be accessed as thumbnail representations through Adobe Bridge or through the Mini Bridge application within InDesign.

NAMEPLATES AND CONTINUING BANNERS

Nameplates are the identifying sections located on the first or front page that usually consist of a company logo or identifiable graphic, the formatted title of the newsletter, and a color text box consisting of information such as the issue or volume number, edition description, and author or editor. Nameplates are also referred to as **mastheads**, although technically mastheads are found on the section of a newsletter that lists the name of the publisher and other pertinent data that may include staff names, contributors, subscription information, addresses, a logo, and so on. **Continuing banners** or **headers** are found in the top portion of the additional pages and have a continuing color scheme, text format for the title, and sometimes an identifiable company logo (Figure 12-1). The nameplate and continuing banners are used in each newsletter to identity them to the reader.

▷ FIGURE 12-1

Newsletter with nameplate and continuing banners.

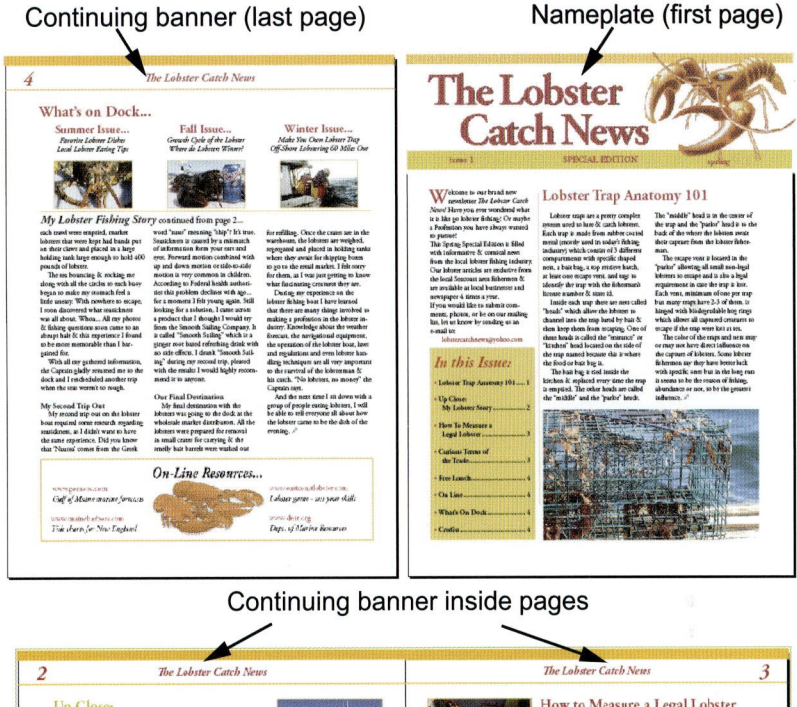

Continuing banner (last page)

Nameplate (first page)

Continuing banner inside pages

Newsletter text and photos courtesy of Shelly Britton.

TYPE DESIGN FOR MULTIPAGE DOCUMENTS

When you are creating a document for printed media that contains articles or lots of paragraphs, in many cases choose a serif typeface for text in the body of the document; it helps to lead the reader's eyes from one line to the next.

- The default size for body text is usually 10 pt, but it may be increased to 12 pt depending on your target audience and the type of information you are printing.

- Using serif and sans-serif headings and subheadings may depend on the body text being used. The purpose of a font or style—such as bold, which widens the letter shape—is to distinguish it from the body text, and also complement the body text. Increasing the size or using color will also promote visual distinction.

- In a document that is going to be used electronically, such as on the web, for the body of the text, choose a sans-serif option that is at least 2 to 4 pt larger than you would use in the printed text body so that the text displayed electronically will read easier.

- When working with sentences, do not double space between sentences.

TOOLKIT TIP Nowadays, whether to use serif or sans-serif text may also depend on what context it will be used in. For this book, as it is technology based, contains much terminology, and uses many exercises, sans-serif text is more appropriate for users or readers that may need to go over steps or terms repeatedly to help in understanding processes or techniques.

CONVERTING INCHES TO DECIMALS OR PICAS AND POINTS

Although most designers create and align items in their documents in inches or fractions of inches, the designer who works at or for a commercial printing establishment may use points and picas as the standard of measurement for more precision. One inch is the equivalent of 72 pt, whereas 12 pt equals one **pica**. Six picas equal an inch. Points are used universally for measuring font sizes and spacing between text characters and text lines. In the printing industry, when measuring with picas and points, the designation "3" *before* the "p" indicates 3 picas, whereas "9" *after* the letter "p" indicates 9 pt. The measurement "3p9" for instance, indicates 3 picas and 9 pt, or the equivalent to ⅝ of an inch.

Here is a table to get you comfortable with this conversion.

INCHES	DECIMAL	POINTS	PICAS
1	1.00	72	6p
⅞	0.875	63	5p3
¾	0.750	54	4p6
⅝	0.625	45	3p9
½	0.500	36	3p
⅜	0.375	27	2p3
¼	0.250	18	1p6
⅛	0.125	9	p9
1/16	0.0625	4.5	p4.5

MASTER PAGES AND THE PAGES PANEL

There are two main sections in the **Pages panel**. The top section, or global level, contains icons for using **master pages**, which are used as guides or document templates with the same parameters and formatting for selected documents. They affect changes globally in the document. In a book for example, a designer might want to create separate master pages for a table of contents, a chapter introduction page, body text, glossary, and index. You can apply master pages by simply dragging the master page icons onto the document page icons below those documents that you would like to contain that master page format, or you can use the Panel menu display as in all Adobe panels. Because they are set as formatting guides or document templates, master pages can be edited or built upon previous master pages after they have been applied to a document. The bottom portion of the Pages panel, or local level, contains the document icons that represent the actual document pages being created and allow you to edit individual documents. This also helps you navigate through multiple pages, and these can be set up as individual documents, as was done in the previous chapter, or as facing pages for multiple documents. Multiple pages butted next to one another or viewed together, such as the two pages visible in a book or magazine, are referred to as a **spread**. In a master page spread, there is a left-hand and right-hand facing page with the first page of a spread on the right side (Figure 12-2). At the local level, as you create frames of graphics and text on your pages, you will see thumbnail graphic representations with master page letters displayed on each individual page for quick reference. In previous versions, if a user has a number of designs with different page sizes, they would have to create separate documents. In InDesign, designers can use the Edit Pages function at the bottom of the Pages panel to define different page sizes for pages within a document. This works quite nicely for advertising campaigns where the user can create a number of different sized pieces (business cards, post cards, letterheads, envelopes, etc.), which would all share the same design elements and the designer could manage as one file.

▷ FIGURE 12-2

Pages panel contains master pages and documents individually and as spreads.

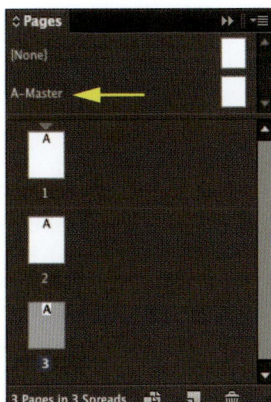

Individual documents
(no facing pages)

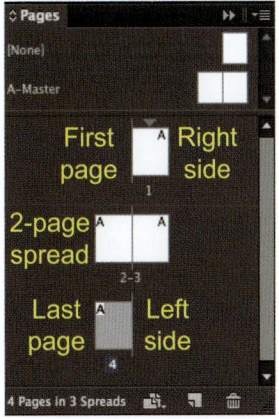

Facing pages spread
(one master page)

Multiple master pages
(A and B)

TOOLKIT TIP Take a piece of paper, fold it in half lengthwise, and open it as a four-page booklet. Number the pages front and back to give yourself a visual of the layout. In this example, the front cover would be page 1 (right side), the opened spread comprises pages 2 and 3, and the last page is the back cover (left side).

CMYK PROCESS AND SPOT COLORS

Every color in the InDesign Swatches panel is defined as either a process color or a spot color. Commercial printers use inks that are percentages of a subtractive process of the colors cyan, magenta, yellow, and black (CMYK). The color black (K) is added last as a fourth color for purity in shadows and improved contrast and tones. These four colors are used in four separate plates during the printing process, hence the term CMYK **process colors**. Use process colors when a job requires so many colors that using individual spot inks would be expensive or impractical. This is the universally accepted and default method when designing with color for print. A **spot color** is a special premixed ink that is used instead of, or in addition to, CMYK process inks, and it requires its own printing plate on a printing press. Use spot colors when few colors are specified and color accuracy is critical. The Coca-Cola Company, for instance, uses a special spot color when printing its special red color used in its logo. Spot colors are easily converted into process color equivalents and are printed as CMYK plate separations rather than on a single plate (Figure 12-3).

▷ FIGURE 12-3

CMYK process colors use percentages of cyan, magenta, yellow, and black inks with each color etched on its own plate for the press. Spot colors are premixed colors that use an additional plate during the printing process.

CMYK process colors

Spot color

TOOLKIT TIP Any RGB color graphic images that are to be printed on a press need to be converted to CMYK color mode before they are imported into the InDesign document. Before converting, create the CMYK as a separate file to retain the RGB color in the original file in case you may need to edit it in the future. If you must use a special spot color, like Coca-Cola would use a special spot color for the red in their cans, keep the number of spot colors you use to a minimum. Each spot color you create will generate an additional spot color printing plate for a printing press, which will increase your printing costs.

CLIENT ASSIGNMENT: Creating a Multipage Newsletter

Shelly Britton, a student editorial photographer at a local college, has been asked by the local newspaper to create a quarterly four-page newsletter insert that gives tourists to the area a glimpse into the life of lobstermen and fishermen. She has gone out on a few trips with a local lobsterman and has created the photographs and written a series of articles for this premier edition. Shelly has asked you to design the layout for her to give to the newspaper. You discuss that the layout will be set up in a three-column format with an index section, a story continuing on within the newsletter, line and fills applied to add color and dimension, and reference sections for special terms, websites, and upcoming issues. You lay out a rough idea of what the nameplate will look like to identify the newsletter and for future newsletters, which she approves. You tell Shelly you will have the layout completed by the end of the week for final approval (Figure 12-4).

ACTION ITEMS OVERVIEW

- Set Preferences to Pica measurement for more precision in your layout.
- Lay out the document with guides for text and graphics.
- Select specific four-color premixed Pantone colors to apply consistent color to text, continuing banners, and frames.
- Create a master page template that contains continuing banners with a continuing theme and automatic page numbering.
- Edit the front page document to include the nameplate to identify the newsletter.
- Place graphics into specific areas set by guides.
- Import text articles using the Place command into multiple columns and into multiple pages.
- Create jump lines to specify "Continued to" and "Continued from" between pages with the same article.
- Use the Tabs panel to align columns for index page and text frames.
- Create rules to separate articles and for use as pull quotes.
- ADVANCED USERS: Baseline alignment and automation with styles and object libraries. Using Liquid Layout to create alternative layouts for use on devices like iPads and iPhones.
- DIGITAL TOOLKIT EXTRA: Create an interactive PDF document.

LAYOUT USING FACING PAGES AND PICA MEASUREMENTS

To give you an idea of how to work with more precise measurements, you will need to set the preferences to picas for this assignment and then set up the document using facing pages. When you select the Facing Pages option in the

Newsletter text and photos courtesy of Shelly Britton.

▷ FIGURE 12-4

Completed newsletter.

File > Document Setup dialog box, document pages are arranged in spreads. Selecting the **Primary Text Frame option** in the New Document dialog box flows large articles over a series of pages. For this assignment we will not need to have that option checked. Every InDesign spread includes its own **pasteboard**, which is an area outside a page where you can store objects that are not yet positioned within the active page. Each spread's pasteboard provides space to accommodate objects that bleed, or extend past the edge of a page, when the bleed setting is created under the document set up.

TOOLKIT TIP Six picas are equal to an inch, and 12 pt equals 1 pica. When measuring with picas and points, the designation "4" in front of the letter "p" indicates 4 picas in measurement, whereas a "6" after the letter "p" indicates 6 pt. The measurement "4p6," for instance, indicates 4 picas and 6 pt, the equivalent of 0.75 (¾) of an inch (Figure 12-5).

▷ FIGURE 12-5

Conversion table for inches, decimals, points, and picas.

Conversion Table			
12 Points = 1 pica	Example: 3p4 = 3 picas 4 points		
Inches	Decimal	Points	Picas
1	1.00	72	6
7/8	.875	63	5p3
3/4	.750	54	4p6
5/8	.625	45	3p9
1/2	.500	36	3
3/8	.375	27	2p3
1/4	.250	18	1p6
1/8	.125	9	p9

DESIGN TIP

When working with spreads, the inside margins generally are smaller in width than the outside margins. Pica measurements work quite nicely when more precision is needed; this is the measurement that a designer might use when sending complex or multipage documents to press.

Next, you will set up the newsletter document. All files needed for this chapter can be downloaded at *www.CengageBrain.com* if you haven't already done so.

1. To make sure you are using picas to measure margins and gutters, go into InDesign Preferences (InDesign > Preferences > Units & Increments [Mac] or Edit > Preferences > Units & Increments [PC]) and change the Horizontal Ruler Units and the Vertical Ruler Units to Picas for more precision in this assignment. Click OK.

2. On your drive, locate your *Chapter 12* folder inside your *Toolkit > InDesign* folder.

3. Locate the *Newsletter* folder inside your *Chapter 12* folder. Inside the *Newsletter* folder, you will find the folders *Images* and *Text*. You will copy fonts later.

4. Here is a look at your directory structure:

   Toolkit > InDesign > Chapter 12 > Newsletter > Images/Text

   The InDesign document project you will be working on here will also be saved as *Lobster* inside the *Newsletter* folder.

5. Select File > New > Document and enter the following information: Pages = 4, Facing Pages On, Page Size is letter with portrait orientation and Intent of Print, Columns = 3, Gutter = 1p0 (1 pica), Margins = picas. First, click the link icon to break it so you can put in these individual amounts: Top = 4p6 (equal to 0.75 inches), Bottom = 4p6, and Inside = 3p0 (equal to 0.5 inches), and Outside = 4p6. Click the Bleed and Slug button and add a "0p9," or one-eighth inch, bleed along the outside edges. Click OK. Use Figure 12-6 as a reference.

▷ FIGURE 12-6

Organizing folders and setting up the document for the newsletter with Facing Pages option and pica measurement.

6. Save the file as *Lobster* inside your *Newsletter* folder. You can see the master page and document icons in the Pages panel.

7. At the bottom of the document window next to the green circle, click on the downward arrow and check that you have enabled Preflight options in the Preflight menu to have the document checked dynamically as you add text and graphics. Display the Preflight panel (Window > Output > Preflight).

SETTING UP THE MASTER PAGE TEMPLATE

Master pages allow the designer to set up guides, page numbers, color fills, and text formatting on a page that can be used as a formatting guide for documents and to build other master pages upon. Master pages provide one of the best ways to create consistency in layout when using multipage documents, and they save time in developing individual documents. In newsletters, the first page contains a nameplate to identify the set of documents. A continuing banner or header may be used in the following pages to continue with the theme of the newsletter. A continuing banner may contain the same colors or logo used, the newsletter title, and a formatted page number. By creating a master page, you can make changes to the template, such as creating the continuing banner for the following pages and removing it for the nameplate on the first page. You will first create the continuing banner master page template with components on the left side, and then duplicate the same components to the right side for accurate placement. When working with facing pages, each master page spread has a left- and right-hand page; elements such as page numbers that should appear on all pages should be placed on both the left and right master pages of a spread.

TOOLKIT TIP When you work with facing pages, you must make the same measurements and formatting to both the left and right side of the master page.

MEASURING LAYOUT GUIDES IN PICAS

Measuring layout guides in picas and points is much more accurate than using inches. You can also enter any decimal equivalent in the guide field. The smaller increments of the point measurement system are easier to visualize than inches as decimal equivalents. For instance, 24 pt is easier to visualize for most people than 0.3472 inches. To create a continuing banner in the master page document to apply the template to all documents, use layout guides to position the newsletter title, page numbers, rule, and top color bar for a consistent look (Figure 12-7).

TOOLKIT TIP The top left black edge of the document is usually displayed as the zero point on the ruler guides (default). To create a zero point, drag from the corner where the guides intersect to the black corner edge of the document. The red outline outside the document edge is the bleed area.

TOOLKIT TIP You can also change preferences in measurement to inches on the fly then back to points or picas by Control clicking (Mac) or right-clicking (Windows) on the rulers to toggle and select different units of measurement.

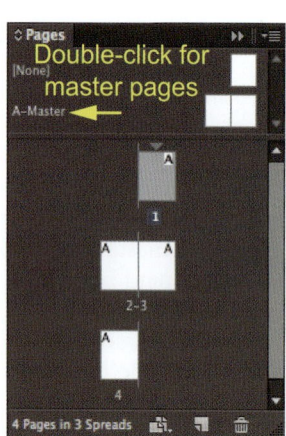

Drag from corner until zero point matches
document edges, drag from ruler guides downward

▷ FIGURE 12-7

Setting up horizontal guides for the master page continuing banner.

In this exercise, you will create the guides for the left and right side for the continuing banner on the master page.

1. Double-click the A-Master text on the global upper portion of the Pages panel. This will display both left and right master pages centered on your screen. If you select the icons, they will move to the selected side (Figure 12-7).

2. Zoom in to 100% or closer to see your work.

3. To start the edges of the document at zero, or to create a zero point, drag from the left corner where the ruler guides intersect until the edges of the document read as "0" on the vertical and horizontal ruler guides.

4. To set up guides for the continuing banner and the starting guide for the text frames, make sure Rulers display (if not, select View > Show Rulers), and Snap to Guides is checked (View > Grids & Guides > Snap to Guides); Smart Guides and Lock Column Guides should also be checked in there as well. Choose the Selection Tool; then, to make sure the guides span across both master page documents, hold down the Command (Mac)/CTRL (PC) key while dragging horizontal guides at pica measurements of 1p0, 3p0, 4p0, and 6p0 from the ruler guides into the master pages. As you drag, you will notice the coordinate will display above your cursor. As an alternative, you can also use the Y Location box (horizontal axis) on the Control panel to help with exact measurements. For easier accuracy, you can start to drag out each guide, and then type in the coordinates, pressing the Return/Enter key afterwards to put the guide in place.

5. With the document set at Facing pages, this will set up the continuing banner on all odd and even pages of your project.

DESIGN TIP

Some fonts to choose from are Garamond, Georgia, Times Roman, or Bookman Old Style. Whatever typeface you choose, be consistent with the text body and the overall look of the newsletter.

TOOLKIT TIP To move identical guides across two facing pages, using the Selection Tool, hold down the Command (Mac)/CTRL (PC) key and drag from the ruler guide. The guide line will span across both pages. To move guides to one page simply drag from the ruler guide using just the Selection Tool (V).

 TOOLKIT TIP To remove guides, select the guide with the Selection Tool (V) (a black square displays under the cursor) and press Delete. You can also drag them back into the ruler.

NEWSLETTER TITLE ON THE CONTINUING BANNER

The continuing banner continues the style, color, and theme of a multipage document throughout the pages. You can continue the formatted name of the newsletter and page numbers to help the reader identify what they are reading. The newsletter title can be formatted for consistency on all pages with the same look (Figure 12-8).

▷ FIGURE 12-8

Creating the continuing banner title.

Here you will type and position the newsletter title, *The Lobster Catch News,* on the master page continuing banners.

1. To create the newsletter title for the continuing banner, zoom in at 100% or more and select the Type Tool (T), dragging a text frame on the left side of the master page document between the 1p0 and 3p0 pica measurements and the document edges.

2. Select Adobe Garamond Pro Bold Italic font (Mac) or another serif font that specifies Bold and Italic in its name; select a size of 18 pt, and type "The Lobster Catch News."

3. Select the Character formatting icon on the Control panel and Align center the text line.

4. With the cursor still in the text frame, select Object > Text Frame Options and change the Vertical Justification Alignment to Bottom (Figure 12-8). Click OK. Now the text line should sit on the 3-pica guide.

5. Repeat the same process on the right-side master page, except drag the type frame box diagonally from the right side toward the left vertical line. The Smart Guides will display as arrows when you reach the left vertical line without overlapping onto the other text frame. To make sure you have just created this type line on Master Pages, click on the Pages panel and double-click on any thumbnail representation to see the type line on all four pages. Double-click the A-Master text in the Pages panel to display facing pages.

CREATING AN AUTO PAGE NUMBER MARKER

InDesign provides the designer with lots of options in the Type menu to insert special characters. You can add a **page number marker** to your pages to specify where a page number sits on a page and how it is formatted. Because a page number marker updates automatically, the page number it displays is always correct, even as you add, remove, or rearrange pages in the document. Page number markers can be formatted and styled as text. To create one, make sure you have the master page selected; then select the Type Tool and drag the text frame until it is large enough to hold the largest number and any additional text you would like to include. Use the Insert Special Character > Markers > Current Page Number commands in the Type menu to display the master page prefix *A*, in this case on both the left and right sides. When you click on a document, it will automatically indicate the sequential page number you have created.

TOOLKIT TIP If you want a page number to appear on all pages based on a master, double-click the master in the Pages panel as was done in this exercise. If you want the page number to appear on a specific page only, double-click the page in the Pages panel. If the automatic page number is on a master page, it displays the master page prefix, such as *A*. On a document page, the automatic page number displays the page number.

In this exercise, you will use the Insert Special Character command in the master pages to automatically format the page numbers (Figure 12-9).

1. To create the text frame for the page number, make sure the master page section is selected in the top portion of the Pages panel (A-Master). Select the Type Tool and drag from the document edge at the 4p0 guide up (not down) to the 1p0 guide over to the 6 pica horizontal ruler mark (6p0) on the top left side of the left side document; the gray measurement cursor box should read W: 6.0 and H: 3.0 (Figure 12-9).

Left side
(drag text box upwards)

Right side
(drag text box upwards)

▷ FIGURE 12-9

Using the Type > Insert Special Character menus for creating auto pages in master page documents.

2. To create an automatic page number, change the size of the font you used for the newsletter title (The Lobster Catch News) to 30 pt, and select Type > Insert Special Character > Markers > Current Page Number. An *A* will appear to show it is a master page number (A-Master displays in the Pages panel). If the text disappears and a red cross is displayed, the type is too big; decrease the size.

3. To center the Page number in the text frame, select Object > Text Frame Options and change the Vertical Justification Alignment to Center. Click OK. Select to Align Center to center the text horizontally by clicking the icon in Character formatting on the Control panel.

4. Repeat the same process on the right-side master page, but have the page number marker created on the right edge of the document. Draw the text frame box from the edge of the document up (not down) between the 4p0 and 1p0 pica guides to the horizontal ruler 96-pica mark. The gray measurement box guide should read W: 6.0 and H: 3.0.

5. To see the effect, double-click one of the documents in the lower document section of the Pages panel; you will notice the document number will display instead of the master page number, and the title line. Double-click the A-Master text, when you are done in the Pages panel, to continue working on the master page banner.

6. Save the file.

TOOLKIT TIP The Pages panel can display absolute numbering—labeling all pages with consecutive numbers, starting at the first page of the document—which is the default. It can also display section numbering to label pages by section, such as the preface, table of contents, text body, glossary, or index. Changing the numbering display affects how pages are indicated in the InDesign document and in the Pages panel and the page box you create. However, it does not change the appearance of page numbers on document pages. Click on the arrow above the document to see your numbering choices.

CREATING RULES AND COLOR BARS

Rules are lines that are used to help separate sections of articles in a pleasing way, and they can be created using the Line Tool (\) while holding down the Shift key. There are also paragraph rules that are used for pull quotes in long articles, which we will discuss later. Whenever working with graphics that involve a very wide stroke weight for color bars, you may find it easier to use one of the frame tools and create a graphic box to fill in the color. Color bars are technically not rules but may be used as a decorative touch. You can use the Control panel to set stroke and fill settings with a pop-up Swatches panel for quick access to color.

Here you will create a rule along the 4p0 layout guide to both edges of the document, and then use the Rectangle Frame Tool (F) to create a color bar at the top of the document (Figure 12-10).

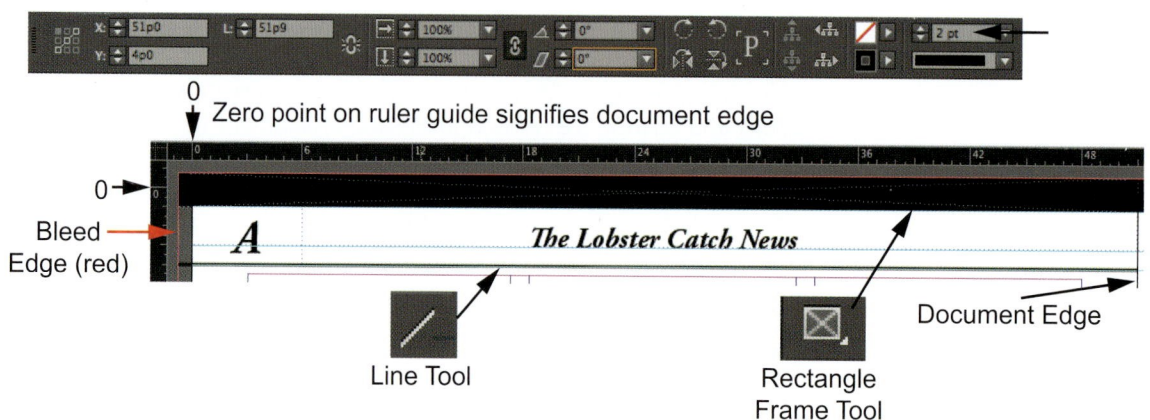

Zero point on ruler guide signifies document edge

Bleed Edge (red)

The Lobster Catch News

Line Tool

Rectangle Frame Tool

Document Edge

▷ FIGURE 12-10

Creating rules and color bars for a continuing banner.

1. Make sure you are still working with a master page document (double-click A-Master) and Snap to Guides is checked (View > Grids & Guides > Snap to Guides).

2. Select the Line Tool (\) in the Tools panel. Using the Control panel (or Stroke panel), choose a 2-pt stroke weight. Make sure the Stroke is set to the default color, usually black, and the Fill color is set to None. Leave the default color; you will change it later. Make sure the entire document displays.

DESIGN TIP

When sending a document with rules to the printer, avoid creating rules that are less than 1 pt, sometimes referred to as *hairlines*, as they can cause problems and may not print clearly.

3. Hold down the Shift key and drag carefully on the left-side master page document along the 4p0 layout guide to create a perfectly straight line from the left side red bleed edge of the document to the right edge, making sure you don't overlap to the other document. You will notice when you are at the edge of the document that an arrow will display under the cross cursor. The gray measurement cursor box will also display L: 51.9. Release the mouse first, and then release the Shift key.

4. Create another rule the same way on the right side. Do not drag across both documents or overlap the graphics; this will not allow you to edit the rule on one document without affecting the other document when working with spreads. Select the Selection Tool (V) and click on the outer pasteboard to deselect the Line Tool (\).

5. Optional: To delete the 4p0 guide, not the line, to see your work, move the Selection Tool (V) until it displays a black square underneath. Select the guideline and press the Delete key.

6. For the top color bar on the continuing banner, make sure the Fill color box is selected in front with the default black color and the Stroke color set to None.

7. Select the Rectangle Frame Tool (F) and drag up the left-side bleed edge of the master page document from the 1p0 horizontal guide along the top bleed guideline (0p9 or ⅛ inch). Drag to the right edge of the document. Do not worry about the color; you will add that later. The dimensions should read W: 51p9 and H: 1p9.

8. Carefully repeat the same process on the right-side document to stay consistent. Do not overlap onto the left side color bar.

9. Use the Selection Tool (V) if needed to select and adjust the resizing handles of the selected box to extend the color over to the bleed edge.

10. Save the document.

SETTING UP PANTONE PROCESS COLORS

Just as you would select colors at a paint store, InDesign provides an almost limitless assortment of colors from various color-swatch manufacturers in what are called **color libraries**. Most of the commercial print industry in the United States uses color swatches by Pantone. You can install additional color libraries and load swatches from them in InDesign (Figure 12-11). Pantone Colors are one of the worldwide standards for color reproduction, and Pantone color guides and chip books are printed on coated, uncoated, and matte paper stocks to ensure accurate visualization of the printed result and better on-press control. You can print a solid Pantone color in CMYK. In InDesign, the settings you have in other Adobe applications can all be synchronized with InDesign for consistent color management. Before applying colors, it is best to select colors and add them to the Swatches panel for future use on your document. You will also notice that the box icon displaying the four CMYK colors to the right of each color will display the process CMYK color percentages when the cursor hovers over it. Remember that pros in the field do not rely solely on the monitor to display the correct color; they also may use print color swatches to check for color accuracy. As was discussed in using Illustrator colors, designers can access the Adobe Kuler color libraries to explore, create, and share various color themes, from this online community. Themes can be easily downloaded and moved into your Swatches panel. You can also use the Control panel to set stroke and fill settings with a pop-up Swatches panel for quick access to color. As you add new colors to the Swatches panel, they are also added in the swatches pop-up menu in the Control panel. In InDesign CC and CS6, the Pantone color libraries have been updated with the new Pantone Plus series of colors.

▷ FIGURE 12-11

Selecting Pantone colors from the Color library to add to the Swatches panel.

TOOLKIT TIP When you are looking for Pantone color reference numbers, they are sequential in terms of the first digits and in color tone. For instance, if you are looking for the number 1235, you need to be within numbers that start with 12; look past the first three digits, and you will find number 126 followed by colors in four digits, up to 1235.

Here you will select Pantone+ Solid Coated, or in previous versions, Solid to Process Coated inks for the banner color bars, rules, and to fill text boxes (Pantone 1235 C, 1935 C, 612 C).

1. To add premade Pantone process colors, it is easiest to create a new color swatch from the Swatches panel menu.

2. To access the Swatches panel, choose Window > Color > Swatches or press the F5 key. Choose New Color Swatch in the Swatches panel menu.

3. When the New Color Swatch dialog box opens, from the Color Mode list, choose the library file *Pantone+ Solid Coated* in the current CC or CS6 version, or *Pantone Solid to Process* in previous versions.

4. Type in 1235, then click Add, NOT OK; then type in, 1935, click Add, and 612; click OK (or Done) after selecting all needed colors (Figure 12-11).

5. You will notice the new swatches you have selected will display on the Swatches panel to use for your newsletter.

6. Save the file in your *Newsletter* folder inside your *Chapter 12* folder.

TOOLKIT TIP In InDesign and other Adobe applications you can share most of the solid swatches you create in one Adobe application with any other Adobe application by saving a swatch library for exchange. The colors appear exactly the same across applications as long as your color settings are synchronized. In the Swatches panel, create the process and spot-color swatches you want to share, and remove any swatches you do not want to share. Select Save Swatches from the Swatches panel menu, name the swatches, and save in an easily accessible location. The Load Swatches command retrieves swatches used in other InDesign documents.

TOOLKIT TIP When you set up color management using Adobe Bridge or Mini Bridge within the application, color settings are automatically synchronized across applications. This synchronization ensures that colors look the same in all **Adobe Creative Suite** applications. If color settings are not synchronized, a warning message appears at the top of the Color Settings dialog box in every Creative Cloud application. To synchronize color settings through the suite of applications, click the Go to Bridge icon on the Control panel, or File > Browse in Bridge; then choose Edit > Suite Color Settings. Select a color setting from the list and click Apply.

APPLYING COLORS USING THE SWATCHES PANEL

The Swatches panel is the most productive way to apply accurate color. You only need to select the frame, text, or object to apply the color, or tag the color in the Swatches panel to apply it. When this is done within a master page, the color is universally applied with any formatting to all pages that are based on that master page. When applying color to fill a frame, use the Fill color in the Tools panel or in the Control panel with the selected graphic or text; when applying color to a rule, make sure the Stroke Color box is selected and that the fill color is set to None (Figure 12-12). The same Stroke and Fill operations are duplicated in the upper left corner of the Swatches panel. Using the Swatches panel to apply stroke and fill is usually faster than returning to the Tools panel. In Illustrator CC, you can create color groups of selected swatches for quick access. When you create a color group in the Swatches panel, the same color group is duplicated and displayed in the Fill and Stroke color buttons in the Control panel.

Swatches panel

Color   Rule   Text
bar

Text Fill button from
Control panel

▷   FIGURE 12-12

**Using Stroke and
Fill settings to
apply colors to the
continuing banner.**

Next, you will apply color to the continuing banner and text to complete the
master page.

1. With the Master Page A document active, select the top color bar on the left-
   side document with the Selection Tool (V). Check the Tools panel color boxes
   or boxes displayed on the Control panel, and make sure that the Stroke is set
   to None and the Fill color is in front.

2. Select the golden Pantone 1235 C (or Pantone 1235 PC labeled in earlier versions) color in the Swatches panel. The color bar will become that selected
   color without a stroke border.

3. Repeat the same process with the right-side color bar.

4. Apply Pantone 1235 C to the bottom rule at the 4p0 guide mark. Select the
   rule, and make sure the Fill color is set to None and the Stroke color is active
   in the Tools panel.

5. To apply the red Pantone 1935 C color to the text, highlight the Auto Page
   "A" on the left master page with the Type Tool (T). The type fill icon on the
   Tools panel should be on top, or active, and the stroke icon underneath
   should display a red diagonal line through the icon. Apply Pantone 1935 C to
   the auto page number on the right-hand master page, as well as The Lobster
   Catch News header on both pages. Feel free to try using the Control panel
   instead of the Tools panel.

6. Congratulations: you now have your master page set up. Feel free to double-
   click your page documents on the lower portion of the Pages panel; click the
   tab to display the panel to see the continuing banner applied with text formatted and the appropriate page numbers displayed.

7. To create a color group in the Swatches panel, highlight the three Pantone colors you just created, and select New Color Group at the bottom of the Swatches panel (Figure 12-13). When the dialog box displays, name the color group Newsletter and click OK. Your Pantone colors are now grouped together. They can be moved around the panel like layers if needed, and the operation is duplicated with the Stroke and Fill color buttons in the Control panel.

8. Save the file again as *Lobster.indd* in InDesign's INDD format.

> **ⓧ PROBLEM** If you cannot select the rule or have trouble applying the color, you may have created a fill color with the Line Tool (\\) instead of using a stroke color. Deselect the rule and redraw it again making sure Stroke is selected.

▷ FIGURE 12-13

Creating a color group of Pantone colors.

New color group

Color group displays on Swatches panel and on Control panel

> **ⓧ PROBLEM** If you notice, when you click on the page 1 or page 4 thumbnail, that the color bar or rule extends the length of an additional document, it is because the graphics are overlapping. Readjust in Master Pages view, and then recheck the pages.

EDITING THE MASTER PAGE ITEMS AND PLACING THE NAMEPLATE OR MASTHEAD

What happens if you want to only use a portion of the master page layout for the front page of the newsletter? In that case, you would need to remove the continuing banners and replace them with the newsletter nameplate. You can do this by a process called *overriding the master objects*. The **master page items** are the individual components you created that together make the continuing banner. If a master page contains most of the elements you want, but you need to customize the appearance of a page or a few pages, you can override master page objects on that page or those pages instead of removing the master. On the document level, master page items are displayed with a dotted guideline. To override a single master page item on the document level and not the master page itself, press Command Shift (Mac)/CTRL Shift (PC) as you click the master page item. Change or delete the object as desired.

The Place command in the File menu is best used to bring in graphics. You can carefully reposition a larger graphic within the frame window using the Selection Tool (V) and, as you hover your mouse over the image center, a non-printable guide that looks like a shaded doughnut graphic called the **Content Indicator** displays. When adjusting the graphic, use the Selection Tool (V) with the shaded doughnut shaped graphic in the center to view the graphic behind the frame window; then, when the graphic is in position, adjust the resizing handles to align with the edges of the graphic.

ABOUT THE FRONT PAGE

The first page of a newsletter is the initial eye-catcher that entices the reader to take a look at various articles. A newsletter has a nameplate that identifies the newsletter and what the reader may expect. It may also include relevant information like the author or editor, issue number, and additional information the reader might need. It usually contains a graphic or logo with a formatted title to make it stand out. The *nameplate,* sometimes called the *masthead,* identifies the newsletter and carries important information like the issue number and the formatted logo. Technically, the **masthead** is on one of the other pages that list the publisher, subscription rates, and so on. A small index box may be included to help the reader navigate through various articles. A **drop cap** is a larger letter that drops down to extend over more than one line of text to start off an article. This technique is used frequently in the front page's first article.

TOOLKIT TIP To override all master page items, target a spread and then choose Override All Master Page Items in the Pages panel menu. You can now select and modify any and all master page items as you wish. To remove a master from document pages, apply the None master from the masters section of the Pages panel. When you remove a master from a page, however, its layout no longer applies to the page. To delete a master from a document, drag a selected master page or spread icon to the Delete icon at the bottom of the Pages panel.

TOOLKIT TIP References to pages such as page 1, or document A-1, technically refer to the document as Master Page 1, based on Master Page A. Please keep this in mind when working on various pages.

To prepare for the nameplate, you will remove the continuing banner master page objects from the first page document. You will then import the *Nameplate.eps* file using the Place command, and then use the Content Indicator doughnut with the Selection Tool (V) to move it into place.

1. In the Pages panel, go to the Panel menu and select Override All Master Page Items. Then double-click on the A-1 page in the local formatting level on the bottom of the Pages panel, where the A designates the master page "A" applied (default) and the "1" indicates the first page in the document. This will open up the first page of the newsletter indicated by the page number 1 on the right side.

2. Zoom in about 150% and with the Selection Tool (V), press Command/CTRL + Shift as you select the rule, color bar, and text on the continuing banner master page objects. Also select the bottom of the "1" auto page number.

PROBLEM If you cannot select anything with the Selection Tool (V), go to the Panel menu in the Pages panel and select Override All Master Page Items for that document.

3. Press the Delete key to remove the objects. That's it! It only affects the first page you were working on.

4. Using the Selection Tool (V), drag a horizontal guide to the 15-pica mark.

5. Before placing the *Nameplate.eps* file on a spread, first select the Rectangle Frame Tool (F) and drag upwards from the 15-pica mark on the vertical ruler guide from the left bleed edge (not margin) over to the right bleed edge of the document up and over the document bleed edge.

6. Select File > Place and locate the *Nameplate.eps* file in the *Images* folder within your *Chapter 12* folder on your drive. Select Open to place the graphic in the document.

7. Use the Selection Tool (V) to move the graphic into place by clicking on the Content Indicator that looks like a central doughnut. You will notice the lobster antennae will stick out above the document; position so the bottom line of text displays with spacing and the color bars meet at the bleed edges (Figure 12-14).

8. If needed, with the Selection Tool (V), drag the top middle resizing handle above the document and adjust the graphic to fit in the window as shown in Figure 12-14. Do not worry about the margins; they will not print.

9. Align the top color bar to the bleed edge of the document. You will notice that the graphic may appear pixeled, because it is displaying as a low-resolution image for easier maneuvering. When it is ready to print, it will link to the high-resolution file for accurate sharp printing.

10. If adjustment is still needed, when the graphic is positioned, use the Selection Tool (V) and select the horizontal sizing handles to adjust the graphic frame to align with the bleed edges outside the document, eliminating the extra lobster antennae. Remember that whatever displays through the graphic "window"

DESIGN TIP

The title "The Lobster Catch News" contains red text overlaid on top of black text that is offset slightly to provide a slight shadow-like appearance for depth. This technique is used quite often for titles in magazines and newsletters

▷ FIGURE 12-14

**Removing master
page objects
to place the
nameplate graphic.**

Graphic displays as low resolution link to original graphic

will print. Whatever is outside the document edge and not in a bleed dimension will not print. You should have artwork sized beforehand to extend out to the specified bleed dimension. Deselect the graphic when you are done.

11. Save the file. You will notice the *Nameplate.eps* file and related info is also displayed in the Links panel (Window > Links).

(X) **PROBLEM** If the image only displays as a gray box, especially if you are using Windows, open the file in your Illustrator program and resave the image onto your drive (not CD) as an Illustrator EPS file as the original. Place the file again in your frame and the image should be displayed.

GUIDES, GRAPHIC FRAMES, AND PLACING GRAPHICS

If you have laid out your design in a rough draft for positioning of text and graphics, and you have received client approval, you will need to size your graphics to approximate the specifications you set up in your design. Before placing text, try to place your graphics to get a feel for the layout. Here the graphics have already been sized for the newsletter. Dragging layout guides helps in positioning of graphics. The Rectangle Frame Tool (F) sets up the window for the graphics to display, but the Place command is still the best way to import graphic images. You can use the Selection Tool (V) to further adjust the size of the graphic window to accommodate the text flowing around it later. You can reposition a larger graphic within the frame window using the Selection Tool (V) and the shaded "doughnut graphic."

PLACING GRAPHICS IN PAGES 1 AND 2

In page 1 you will place a graphic that continues across two columns. On the second page you are going to place a graphic that extends halfway over to the second column. This will be used to accent a very long article and to wrap text around the outside of the graphic. Using graphics that face in toward the document lead the reader into articles they may want to read. InDesign has a Layers panel that works much like the one in Illustrator. You can create individual layers of your document to match your pages and lock the graphics or text frames so they cannot be adjusted by mistake. You can also right-click on the layer item to select it on the document, which helps when you have lots of items on a page. Each layer here will represent one page. For that layer to be active and to observe its contents, you will need to select the page in the Pages panel first.

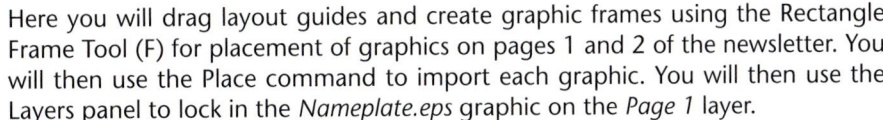

TOOLKIT TIP If precision is needed when dragging guides, hold down the Shift key and drag slowly to move the guide in 1-pt increments. You can also select the guide with the Selection Tool (V) and type the number you wish to move to the Y box of the Control panel. To remove these guides, click on them using the Selection Tool, and then press the Delete key.

Here you will drag layout guides and create graphic frames using the Rectangle Frame Tool (F) for placement of graphics on pages 1 and 2 of the newsletter. You will then use the Place command to import each graphic. You will then use the Layers panel to lock in the *Nameplate.eps* graphic on the *Page 1* layer.

1. For the front page, document A-1 (page 1), drag (or type 46p0 in the *Y*-axis box) a horizontal guide to the 46-pica mark. Using the Rectangle Frame Tool (F), drag a graphic frame—with a Fill of None and a 1-pt Stroke of Pantone 1235 C (or PC) from the Swatches panel—from the second column at the 46-pica mark to the bottom corner margin of the third column as shown in Figure 12-15. You can also use the Rectangle Tool (M), which has a 1-pt stroke as a default; then only the stroke color needs to be changed.

2. Select the frame and place the file *Trap.tif* in the frame (File > Place). Page 1 is now done. Open the Layers panel (Window > Layers) and rename the *Layer 1* layer (double-click *Layer 1* text) as *Page 1*. When you click on the downward arrow next to that layer you'll notice both graphics. Click to lock just the *Nameplate.eps* graphic; then create a new layer naming it *Page 2* for the next step.

Page 1   Page 2

Photos courtesy of Shelly Britton.

▷ FIGURE 12-15

Layout of guides, using Rectangle Frame tool for graphic frames, and placement of graphics for pages 1 and 2.

DESIGN TIP

The boat image with the front area (the bow) facing into the document helps to lead the reader's eye back to the document.

3. For the A-2 document (page 2), double-click the A-2 document icon in the Pages panel to bring up the second page. Zoom in at 100% or larger making sure page 1 is not displayed. Check to make sure *Page 2* in the Layers panel is highlighted.

4. Using the Selection Tool (V), drag horizontal guides to the 19-pica and 33-pica marks. Drag a vertical guideline to the 23-pica mark to place the graphic overlapping into the second column or type in 23p0 in the *X*-axis box on the Control panel.

5. Using the Rectangle Frame Tool (F), create a graphic frame in the third column with a Fill of None and a 1-pt Stroke of Pantone 1235 C between the 6-pica and 19-pica marks to the right margin guide.

6. Create a second frame in the first column with same color stroke from the 33-pica mark down to the bottom margin and over to the 23-pica mark halfway into the second column, as shown in Figure 12-15.

7. Select the frame you created in the top right with the Selection Tool (V) and place the *Boat.tif* file in the upper third column; then use the Selection Tool and center "doughnut" to position the larger graphic within the frame so that boat displays. Place the *Hauling.tif* file in the bottom left corner as shown (Figure 12-15). Page 2 is now all set. Use the Selection Tool (V) to delete the guidelines used for placing the graphics to avoid confusion.

TOOLKIT TIP Made a mistake with your guidelines or just want to remove them? The easiest way is to select guides with the Selection Tool (V) and when you observe a black square under the cursor, press Delete to remove the guide. Another method is to click on the guidelines with the Selection Tool and drag the guides back to the ruler area.

TOOLKIT TIP The Layers panel will show both images when you open the *Page 2* layer. If you want to access the layer corresponding to a particular page, select the page document using the Pages panel first. References to pages such as page 1, or document A-1, technically refer to the document as Master Page 1, based on Master Page A. Please keep this in mind when working on various pages.

PLACING GRAPHICS ON PAGE 3

On page 3, you will use graphics to accent two very short articles to also help to frame the text. You will also create a *Page 3* layer in the Layers panel.

Here you will drag layout guides and create graphic frames to place graphics on page 3 of the newsletter.

1. For the A-3 document (page 3), double-click the A-3 document icon in the Pages panel to bring up the third page. In the Layers panel, create two more empty layers and rename them as *Page 3* and *Page 4,* respectively, as you had done with the first two pages. Make sure *Page 3* layer is highlighted.

2. Drag (or type in the Control panel) in horizontal guides to the 18-, 21-, 30-, and 42-pica marks.

▷ FIGURE 12-16

Placement of graphic frames and importing graphics into page 3.

3. Create the following rectangle graphic frames with the Fill of None and a 1-pt Stroke color, Pantone 1235 C, from the Swatches panel. First, in the first column between the 6-pica and 18-pica marks; second, from the 30-pica and 42-pica marks across the first and second column; and last, in the third column, between the 21-pica and 42-pica marks (Figure 12-16).

Page 3

4. Select the upper left frame and place the *Tools.tif* file in the upper rectangle frame in the first column (Figure 12-16). Select and place the *Ondeck.tif* file in the frame that stretches across the first two columns. Select and place the *Mable.tif* file in the third column frame. Adjust the images using only the center doughnut of the Content Indicator and Selection Tool (V) as needed, and delete guidelines used for graphics.

5. Open the *Page 3* layer in the Layers panel to observe the graphics. Page 3 is all set.

PAGE 4: USING SMART GUIDES AND SMART SPACING WITH GRAPHICS

With Smart Guides turned on, you can not only have X and Y coordinates appear dynamically, but you can easily find the central points of multiple objects or shapes by aligning their center lines. To align items to match, Smart Spacing and Smart Dimensions (which are features turned on when you select Smart Guides) arrow indicators appear as you move your selection. Smart spacing evenly spaces multiple items by snapping objects into position. When the arrows display and center lines appear, you have perfect alignment with other objects. When you stop, the guides disappear, so your layout remains uncluttered. If you need to move your objects in relation to the others you want to match, Smart Dimensions will highlight when the dimensions match the others. With these new tools you get immediate feedback with precise positioning. You can also use align icons for selected tools in their tool's option bar.

For page 4, you'll have the opportunity to duplicate the same size frame for consistency in declaring what will be appearing in forthcoming issues. You'll then align the graphic using Smart Guides for precision. You will then lock the three images using the Layers panel to keep them from being moved in future editions. You will also place an illustrative graphic near the bottom of the page for balance of the text that will be imported to the middle of the document.

1. Make sure Smart Guides is checked on (View > Grids & Guides > Smart Guides). Double-click the A-4 document icon in the Pages panel to bring up the fourth page, making sure it is only displaying. Make sure the *Page 4* layer is highlighted in the Layers panel.

2. Drag or type in horizontal guides to the 13-, 19-, 21-, and 51-pica marks.

3. First, you are going to create three rectangle graphic frames of equal size in each of the three columns. In the first column, select the Rectangle Frame Tool (F) as before, but instead of dragging to create a frame, click on the document to bring up the Rectangle Frame dialog box (Figure 12-16).

4. Enter a Width of 10p2 (10 picas, 2 pt) and a Height of 6p (6 picas). Click OK. Create a 1-pt Stroke color of Pantone 1235 C and a Fill of None.

5. Position the graphic frame with the Selection Tool (V) so it is centered in the first column between the 6p and 16p6 marks on top and between the 13 and 19 horizontal pica guides you just made (Figure 12-17). With Smart Guides turned on, you will find a vertical center line display when the box is in between the guidelines.

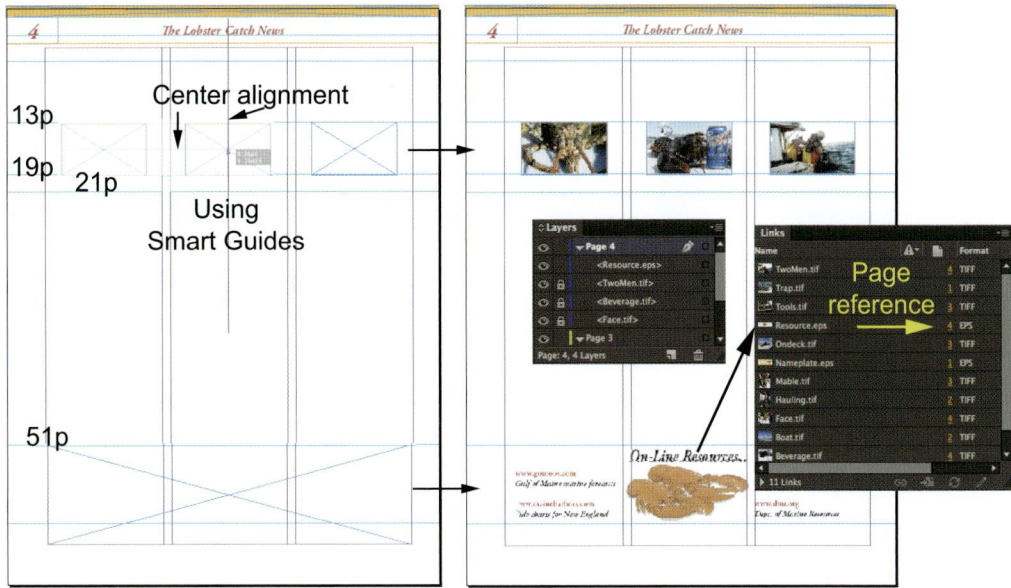

Photos courtesy of Shelly Britton.

Page 4

▷ FIGURE 12-17

Placement of graphic frames and importing graphics into page 4.

6. Use the Edit menu or Option/ALT to copy the graphic box size two more times so that each frame lines up within the same horizontal guidelines in the second and third columns. Using Smart Guides, when you drag the second box into position, you will find the green horizontal center line intersecting with a blue vertical center line, indicating you have perfect alignment (Figure 12-17).

7. When you select and move the third frame into position, not only will you see the horizontal center line displayed, but when the frame is equidistant from the other two objects, you'll find green arrows displayed (Smart Dimensions) under the other two frames for precise alignment.

8. Select and place the file *Face.tif* in the first column frame, the file *Beverage.tif* in the second column, and the file *TwoMen.tif* in the third column graphic frame. Adjust from the center Content Indicator with the Selection Tool (V) as needed.

9. For the *Resource.eps* graphic box, which contains an illustration and text, drag a rectangle graphic frame green across the three columns between the 51-pica horizontal guide and the bottom margin.

TOOLKIT TIP The Gap Tool (U) on the Tools panel provides a quick way to adjust the size of a gap or resize between multiple items that have commonly aligned edges all at once, while keeping the gaps between them fixed. Just hover your mouse over the gap area you want to adjust, and then click and drag to resize the items aligned to the gap. Also, when distributing multiple selected objects, and you want to resize the space between the selected items instead of resizing the actual items, use the Selection Tool to drag the bounding box resizing handle while holding down the space bar on your keyboard.

10. Place the *Resource.eps* graphic file in this graphic frame; adjust with the Selection Tool (V) to align the baseline of the email addresses on the 59-pica line; you can also click on the images to toggle between the Selection and Direct Selection tools to make adjustments. Change the Pantone 1235 C Stroke color to a 2-pt weight. Deselect the graphic and lock the three graphics aligned at the top in the *Page 4* layer of the Layers panel. Page 4 is all set for graphics.

11. If you look at the Links panel, you will notice all graphics are placed there for future reference, including the associated page numbers for updated linking, and editing of graphics if needed. The graphics on the Links panel are all set as thumbnails for quick reference. Click on the graphic for more related information, which will display in the Link Info panel underneath.

12. Save the file. Make sure you do not change where these graphics are kept, or you will break the link to the original files. What you will see on your document at this point are the low-resolution copies of the originals so they will look blotchy.

TOOLKIT TIP If a red circle with a question mark displays next to the file in the Links panel, it doesn't know where the file is. This usually occurs if the document has been moved without the original files. Click on the question mark, and locate the folder where the files are kept. If you have multiple missing files in the same folder, it will update all of those missing as well.

TOOLKIT TIP You will also notice that when you lock a graphic in the Layers panel, that it is outlined with a padlock icon on it on the document page. This way it can't be edited until you unlock it. To view one of the pages and toggle the locked graphics, you must select the page in the Pages panel first; then you can access the components of that layer. Using the Layers panel you can also right-click on the item and choose to select it, which comes in quite handy when you have lots of items in a page. Note: These images are medium resolution at 150 dpi for these exercises. When using actual images for a document that will go to press, maintain a high resolution of 300 dpi.

TOOLKIT TIP When placing graphics and text in InDesign, you can place PSD and PDF layered graphics in a document. You can selectively display and output layers and layer comps from Photoshop (PSD) and layers from PDF files, and you can modify layer visibility in placed graphics. Graphics appear in the Links panel after they have been imported. You can reuse InDesign layouts by creating and placing *snippets,* which are portions of a document, or by placing the entire InDesign document into another InDesign document. All the links remain intact, and InDesign lets you know if any changes are made.

INDESIGN'S EFFECTS

InDesign allows the designer to create Photoshop-like effects, such as drop shadows, bevels, and embossing. It also provides other great effects using InDesign's Effects panel. You can use the Effects panel (Window > Effects) to specify the opacity and blending mode of objects and groups, isolate blending to a particular group, knock out objects inside a group, or apply a transparency effect. These effects can also be accessed from most of the tools as part of the appropriate tool's menu bar or in the Control panel bar. If you want, try creating drop shadow effects on the three images you placed in page 4 to see if the effect may accent the final newsletter, or try applying this effect afterwards when all text is placed in the newsletter. InDesign provides corner effects on the fly if you want to create accented corner effects. To view these live, you will see a yellow square which, when you click on it, will display yellow diamond shapes on each corner. If you click and drag on a corner box, you can create a rounded radius effect on all corners. Hold down the Option/ALT key while clicking on the diamond to view other special effects. Although we will not be using this technique in the exercises, go ahead and unlock the graphics in the Layers panel and play if you want. With InDesign CC, there is improved accuracy in scaling effects proportionally.

TYPING AND IMPORTING TEXT

Text and graphic components need to complement one another. Text provides the description or identifies what the images are trying to convey to the reader. The images provide the visual representation of what the text message defines to the reader. In this section, you will not only type in text elements and apply basic formatting; you will learn to import text articles using the Place command to flow into multiple columns and into multiple pages. Although the Control panel handles many of the most widely used character and paragraph commands for text, the Type menu provides all the essential commands and features you will need, such as inserting special characters, displaying specific panels—like Tab, Character, and Paragraph formatting—including style panels for consistency in formatting. The Type menu provides a central location to apply any formatting needed to text. Sometimes when you place type into a frame container, there is no type that appears, only a red plus sign. This is called an **overset** symbol. It is a text "overflow" symbol indicating too much text is in the frame container.

TOOLKIT TIP All text for articles in this newsletter have been created in Microsoft Word's default text format. With InDesign CC and CS6, the most recently used fonts now appear at the top of your font list for quick access. If you have a pretty good idea of the kind of font you wish to create, you can open each document in Microsoft Word if it is available, highlight the text, and format to your chosen font and font size (try 10 or 11 pt size); then save the document before placing the text in your InDesign document. It is important when doing this that you are using the same operating system, and InDesign has the same font as your chosen Word font.

TYPING IN TEXT INFORMATION

As you were doing in the previous chapter, you can type in text and apply formatting when small amounts of type are called for in a given section; afterward, you will also see how easy it is to import text from a document created in another application. This will serve as a brief review of using the Character formatting buttons on the Control panel when the Type Tool (T) is used. To create a true ellipsis (which indicates "and so forth"), which are three evenly spaced dots, select the Option/ALT key and then press the semicolon key.

Because this is a quarterly newsletter, you will type in brief information in the upcoming quarters and format it using the Control panel.

DESIGN TIP

To help with work-flow, if you have the three type lines formatted in the first type box, you can copy those lines into the other two text boxes, and then simply type over the changes. The formatting will remain the same.

1. Notice the Pages panel displays thumbnail views of the placed graphics for a quick visual reference. Double-click on the A-4 document to bring up the fourth page in the document if it is not already open. Zoom in to around 150% and scroll to the top. Make sure the *Page 4* layer is highlighted in the Layers panel.

2. Using the Selection Tool (V), drag horizontal guides to the 8-pica and 12-pica marks.

3. To create the headline, use the Type Tool (T) to drag a text frame across the columns between the 6-pica and 8-pica marks; then type in "What's on Dock…" with the font you have chosen (we are using Adobe Garamond Pro) using the bold style. Use the Option/ALT key followed by a semicolon to enter a "true" ellipsis. Or, you may open the Glyphs panel and double-click; an ellipsis will appear at the insertion point of the text cursor.

4. Highlight the text with the Type Tool (T) and change the Fill color to Pantone 1935 C in the Swatches panel, and resize to 24 pt.

5. Select the Type Tool (T) and create three separate text frames above each photo between the 8-pica and 12-pica marks and the column margin edges. If you are having trouble drawing frames, make sure your text cursor displays a white arrow at the starting corner.

6. In the First column frame, type "Summer Issue…" making sure to create a "true ellipsis," as described above. Select the text with the Type Tool (T) and change the Fill color to Pantone 1935 C in the Swatches panel, and format type to 16-pt or 18-pt Bold style in the font you have chosen. We used the Adobe Garamond Pro font here.

7. Click at the end of the ellipse dots to display the blinking cursor. Press Return/Enter to create another line; change the size to 11-pt or 12-pt size, depending on the font you are using, with a black Fill and Italic style and type "Favorite Lobster Dishes"; press, Return/Enter, and then type "Local Lobster Eating Tips" on the next line.

8. To center the text in the frame, select all three lines of text and choose the Character Formatting icon on the Control panel. Select the Align Center button (Figure 12-18).

9. If the type disappears, or the red plus overset text sign appears, adjust the text size to display the new formatted text lines.

▷ FIGURE 12-18

Typing and formatting text components.

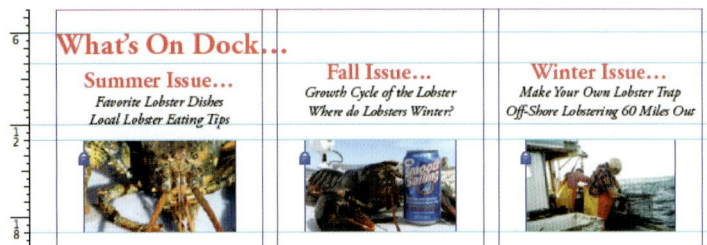

What's On Dock...

Summer Issue...
Favorite Lobster Dishes
Local Lobster Eating Tips

Fall Issue...
Growth Cycle of the Lobster
Where do Lobsters Winter?

Winter Issue...
Make Your Own Lobster Trap
Off-Shore Lobstering 60 Miles Out

Newsletter text and photos courtesy of Shelly Britton.

10. To place the lines of text along the bottom guideline of the text frame, with the text highlighted, select Object > Text Frame Options. Select the Vertical Justification of Align Bottom then click OK.

11. Repeat the same process with the Fall and Winter issues, as shown Figure 12-18.

12. Notice on the Layers panel (Page 4) the text also displays in addition to the image files. Save the file when done.

TOOLKIT TIP If the guides are making your work appear too cluttered, you can click on the line with the Selection Tool (V) and when it shows a black square under the cursor, drag it back to the ruler guide bar. You can also select View > Grids & Guides > Hide Guides.

IMPORTING TEXT INTO TEXT FRAMES

One of the great features of any desktop publishing program like InDesign is the ability to import text from other documents into individual text frames and to connect multiple text frames together, flowing text into multiple columns (Figure 12-19). When importing text, the Place command is again the most appropriate command to use. To use the Place command, you can use the key combination Command D/CTRL D or select File > Place. When placing text, a space needs to be created between the bottom of the text line within the text frame and sometimes above the top line, to allow for breathing space so that text does not sit on the edges of the text frame. In the Object > Text Frame Options command, you can adjust the inset spacing within each text frame. Creating an **inset** provides space for the text so that type is not placed next to a graphic frame or one that may have a stroke weight or is filled with color. Inset settings apply to all text in a text frame. The space between columns is called the **gutter**.

DESIGN TIP

When working with body text in various articles, use the same size and font throughout; remember that serif fonts work best. Keep the point size at a minimum of 10 pt or a maximum of 12 pt for easy reading, depending on the placement of the articles. Here we used an 11-pt Adobe Pro Garamond (serif) font for easier reading throughout.

TOOLKIT TIP Any frame can be converted to a text frame by clicking inside the frame with the Type Tool (T). When the Place dialog box opens, select Replace Selected Items to replace the contents in the text frame with the placed text. A good production habit is to deselect the previous frame before placing the next image or text file. Selecting Show Import Options controls how different versions of a text document are to be handled. Keep these options unchecked in these exercises.

▷ FIGURE 12-19

Importing text into selected frame, providing inset spacing at the bottom.

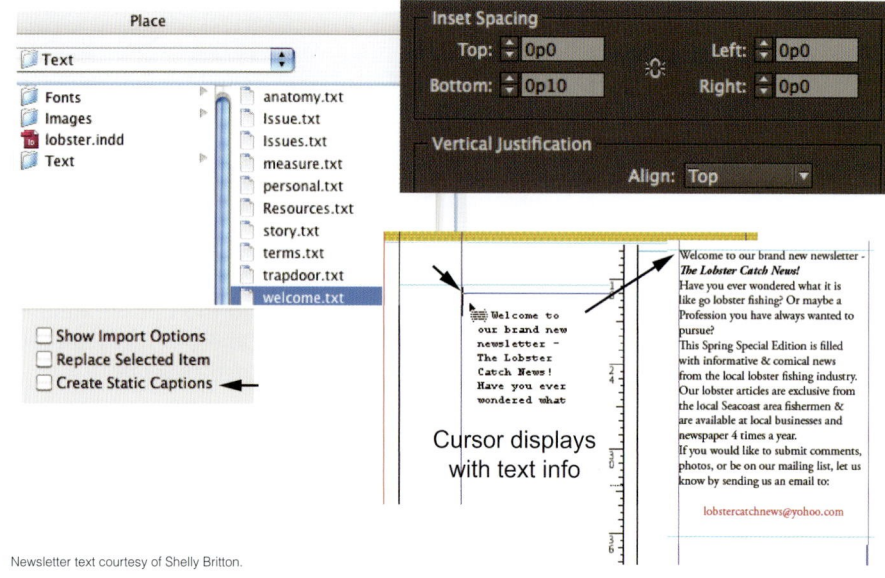

Newsletter text courtesy of Shelly Britton.

Here, you will import a small text file into a single text frame on the front cover.

1. Make sure the document A-1 (first page) is selected, not the top master page. Make sure *Page 1* in the Layers panel is selected.

2. Drag a horizontal guideline to the 17-pica and 38-pica marks.

3. Select the Type Tool (T) and drag diagonally to create a text frame—do not just click in the first column—from the vertical 17-pica mark about halfway down to the 38-pica mark between the left margin and first gutter.

4. Select File > Place or Command/CTRL D and locate the *Welcome.doc* text file in your *Text* folder. Leave Replace Selected Item, Create Static Captions, and Show Import Options Select unchecked here. Select Open to import the text.

5. The cursor may display a thumbnail view of the text first lines. Click in the top left corner of the text box and the text will flow into the column. If you see a red plus sign (overset symbol) at the bottom or end of the article, more text needs to be displayed. Choose the Selection Tool (V), select inside the frame, and drag the bottom resizing handle down to display all text.

6. Select all the text with the Type Tool (T) and change to the font you have chosen in its Regular style to an 11-pt size for easier reading. We have chosen Adobe Garamond Pro Regular to continue with this document. You may decide with your chosen font to use the standard 10 pt size.

7. Select the text with the Type Tool *The Lobster Catch News!* in the first sentence and change it to a Bold Italic style to identify the title of the newsletter.

8. Select the email address and change the color to the red Pantone 1935 C, and then Align center the email line using the Control panel. Click in front of the email line, and press the Return/Enter key to create a line space as shown in Figure 12-19.

DESIGN TIP

When inserting paragraphs of type, keep the same font and size consistent for easier readability between columns and multiple documents. A font size of 10 pt is a standard size used in most documents.

9. To create a space for the bottom of the text frame, with the text frame first selected using the Selection Tool (V), select Object > Text Frame Options and enter Inset Spacing Bottom of 10-pt (0p10) with Top, Left, and Right Insets set at 0. Use Vertical Justification to Align Top then click OK. Make sure the frame meets the guides you created, again, use the resizing handles with the Selection Tool (V) if necessary.

10. Save the file.

MANUALLY THREADING TEXT FRAMES

To import text into multiple columns manually, you do not need to create text frames. You can create a text frame before placing text, or you can manually flow text between columns and adjust the frame dimensions using the Selection Tool (V); the text flow will adjust automatically. The space between columns is called the **gutter**. The process of creating linked text frames is **threading text**. After threading has been completed, the frames are linked. You can flow text between linked columns in different pages and in adjacent multi-column text frames. When placing imported text into a text frame, a loaded text cursor displays—which will look like lines of type inside a dotted page outline—indicating that text is ready to be dropped into a frame. Click on the text frame to dump the text that needs to be displayed. If a red plus sign displays, this is called the **overset symbol**, which indicates that there is more text. Click in the next column to continue flowing the text, and adjust the frame using the Selection Tool (V) to cause the text flow to adjust automatically, giving you room to experiment with formatting and placing graphics; this perceptual technique may be used instead of creating inset spacing, although it may look inconsistent in the document.

Although headings are included in the original text document for identification, you can cut and paste them on a separate text frame that spans across the columns, connected to the text body frames. When using text, sometimes it makes better sense to create separate text frames for the headings of an article, especially if the heading is to expand across multiple columns. This allows you to format the headings or lines of type without adversely affecting the text body in the article.

TOOLKIT TIP References to pages, such as page 1, or document A-1, refer to the document as Master Page 1, based on Master Page A. Please keep this in mind when working on various pages.

In this exercise, you will manually import and place text files in multiple columns in page 1. You will place the headings into separate text frames for formatting later.

1. For a headline text box, with Document A-1 (page 1 based on Master Page A) displayed, select the Type Tool (T) and drag a box from the 17-pica mark in the second column over to the right-side margin (third column) and down to the 20-pica mark. Your gray box coordinate will display as H: 3p0. Zoom in close if needed.

2. Use the Type Tool (T) to create another frame only in the center second column extending from the 20-pica mark to the 45-pica mark above the *Trap.tif* graphic. You may need to select the text box with the Selection Tool (V) and move the resizing handles to make sure it starts at the 20 pica mark inside the column.

3. In this second frame, select the Place command and click the *Anatomy.doc* file from your *Text* folder in the top left corner of the box.

4. Observe the overset text symbol at the bottom of the text column which appears as a red plus sign; in the next step, you will now flow the copy into the next text frame. Note: If the text flows to the bottom of the column, use the Selection Tool (V) and drag the bottom resizing handle in the box upwards to align at the 45-pica mark. The red overset symbol should display.

5. Using the Type Tool (T), drag another text frame in the third column, again from the 20-pica mark to the 45-pica mark as done in the second column. With the Selection Tool (V), click on the overset symbol in the text frame in the middle column. This process creates a *loaded text cursor.*

6. Click the loaded cursor on the upper left corner of the third column at the 20-pica mark, below the text box for the headline (don't click inside the headline text box), which may display a link icon; click and flow the remaining text into that column. Don't worry if the text is not all displayed with your chosen font; you will remove the title to make room in the next exercise. Click the Selection Tool (V) to reset.

TOOLKIT TIP Note: In most cases, InDesign will automatically create a text frame that fits between the column guides flowing into the next column in most instances as well. It's still a good habit to draw out your text frames ahead of time for practice.

DESIGN TIP

In most cases, in traditional design, you will want to have a space between the paragraphs or type lines, and the graphic nearby.

7. Select the Type Tool (T) and highlight the "Lobster Trap Anatomy 101" headline; then cut (Edit > Cut) the headline out of the first column. Then click and Paste the heading into the headline text box you created above, in the second column; you will format it later. Click inside the top second column underneath and delete the line space until the paragraph rests at the top of the text body frame (Figure 12-20).

8. Select all the text (Command/CTRL + A) and format to the same font you chose in the "Welcome" column. In our example we are using an 11-pt size Adobe Garamond Pro font throughout. Choose a point size of 10, 11, or 12 that fills both text columns depending on the font, and keep the same size throughout. Don't forget the headline as well.

9. With each text frame selected, select Object > Text Frame Options and enter Inset Bottom settings of 10 pt (0p10) with top, left, and right insets set at 0 and a Vertical Justification of Align Top. This provides space between graphic and text.

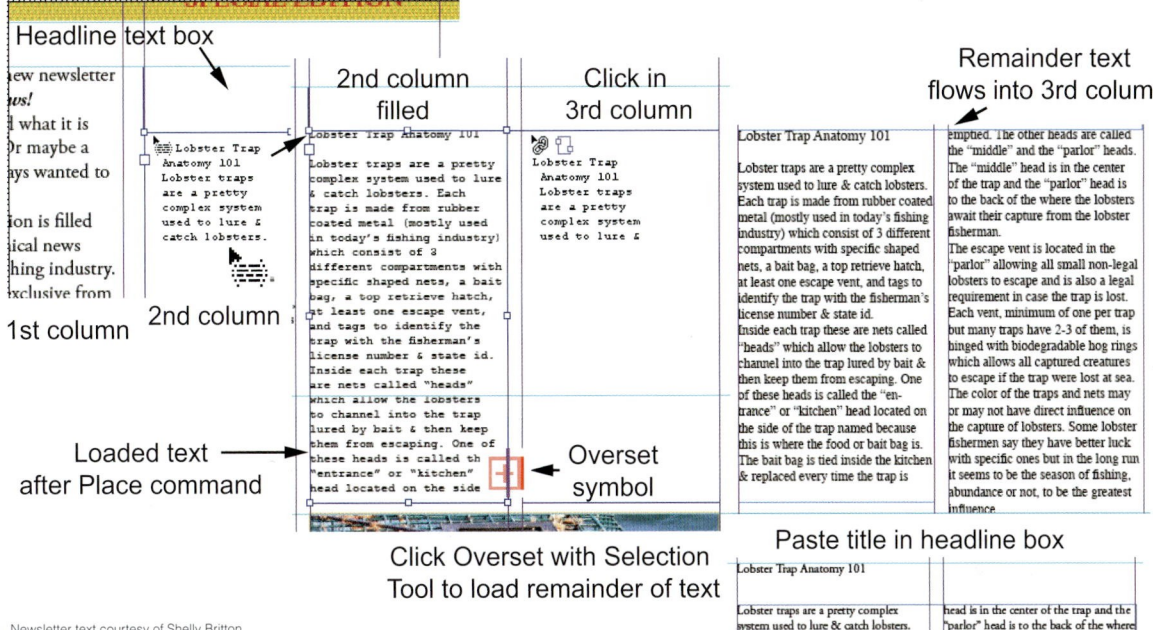

Headline text box

1st column

2nd column

Loaded text after Place command

2nd column filled

Click in 3rd column

Overset symbol

Remainder text flows into 3rd column

Click Overset with Selection Tool to load remainder of text

Paste title in headline box

Newsletter text courtesy of Shelly Britton.

 ▷ FIGURE 12-20

Threading text manually across multiple columns.

10. Using the Selection Tool (V), adjust the text in the columns until they appear balanced, or have one line more on the left side. Use the frame resizing handles to shorten or lengthen the depth of the text frames to balance out the columns (Figure 12-20). You can also select the resizing handle of the trap graphic below and include a little more of the image if too much negative space displays. Check the Layers panel and you can see that the individual text frames are displayed. Leave as is.

11. Save the file.

TOOLKIT TIP If the text cursor still displays text, and you know you have added all the text lines, click on the Selection Tool (V) on the Tools panel to reset the cursor. Did you inadvertently put text frames on the wrong layer in the Layers panel? Just like in Photoshop or Illustrator, you can rearrange the stacking order or simply move sublayers from one layer (or page in this instance) to another. You can also drag sublayer items into and out of groups, buttons, and multi-state objects. Be aware to get in the habit to select the document in the Pages panel first.

UNTHREAD TEXT FRAMES

If you make a mistake threading text frames, you can unthread the frame to start again. When you unthread a text frame, you break the connection between the frame and all subsequent frames in the thread. Any text that previously appeared in the frames becomes overset text with all subsequent frames left empty; no text is deleted. To unthread a frame using the Selection Tool (V), double-click on the out-port arrow at the bottom of the text frame that indicates a thread to another frame, or click the in-port arrow on the top left of the second or additional frame. You can also position the loaded text icon over the previous or next text frame to display the unthread icon, which looks like a broken link; then click in the frame.

FLOWING SHORT ARTICLES ACROSS COLUMNS USING THE RECTANGLE FRAME TOOL

Text can be placed in text frames or frames created by the Rectangle Frame Tool (F). When placing text documents in the corner of the frame as was done in the previous exercise, the text will generally flow to the bottom of the column as the default. When text is placed in the middle of either the text frame, or the rectangle frame, not in the upper corner, the text will stay within the frame created. The remainder text can be flowed to other framed columns when the red overset symbol is clicked on by the Selection Tool (V) to load the cursor with the rest of the text. Traditionally the Rectangle Frame Tool (F) is used to help designers place graphics as you have done in the previous exercises. This tool is also helpful as a text box "container" to place text in. On the third page, you will repeat the process you used for the first page except you will create text box frames using the Rectangle Frame Tool (F). Make sure that the text is balanced across columns and that there is sufficient space between the images and the text. You can also view the text threads between columns by selecting Show Text Threads in the View menu. This display is non-printable.

Now you will manually import and place text files to thread between multiple columns in document A-3 (page 3), and then place the headings into separate text frames for formatting later.

1. For document A-3, double-click the document A-3 on the local section of the Pages panel to bring up the third page of the document. You will notice a "3" will appear in place of the automatic page number created from the master page. Make sure Page 3 is highlighted in the Layers panel.

2. Drag horizontal guidelines at the 6- (if it isn't already there), 9-, 19-, and 22-pica marks for the headlines and the articles.

3. Use the Type Tool (T) to create a frame that stretches across the second and third columns between the 6-pica and 9-pica horizontal guides. Type in the headline, "How to Measure a Legal Lobster."

4. For the body text, select the Rectangle Frame Tool (F) and start by drawing a frame between the 9-pica and 18-pica guides in the second column; then create another frame in the third column. Use the Selection Tool (V) if needed to drag sizing handles.

5. With the Selection Tool (V) click the first text box frame, then select the Place command and locate the *Measure.doc* text file. Select Open.

6. Click in the middle of the frame you created in the second column under the headline text frame around the 9-pica mark. The text will flow into that column (Figure 12-21). Note: In the event the text flows beyond the frame use the Selection Tool and drag the excess upwards using the resizing handle to align with the bottom guide you created.

7. With both of the text frames selected, select Object > Text Frame Options and enter Inset Bottom settings of 10 pt (0p10) with top, left, and right insets set at 0 and a Vertical Justification of Align Top. Click OK.

▷ FIGURE 12-21

Manually importing and threading text into multiple text frames.

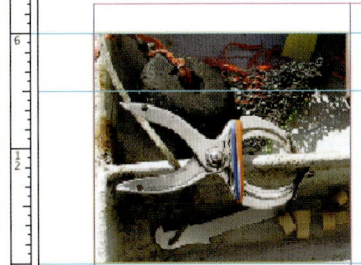

Place loaded cursor in middle of text frame

How to Measure a Legal Lobster

Every lobster taken from the trap has specific size requirements in order to be saved for market.
Each lobster is measured with a tool called the "e zwinkler" and must be at least 3 inches in size but not larger than 5 inches. For a correct measurement, the "e zwinkler" tool is placed

on the topside of the lobster with one end placed at the eye socket and the other end at the end of the shell or at the base of the tail.
Once a reading is determined, the lobster is either returned to the sea or secured for storage in the holding tank.

Article threaded

Every lobster taken from the trap has specific size requirements in order to be saved for market.
Each lobster is measured with a tool called the "e zwinkler" and must be at least 3 inches in size but not larger than 5 inches. For a correct measurement, the "e zwinkler" tool is placed on the

topside of the lobster with one end placed at the eye socket and the other end at the end of the shell or at the base of the tail.
Once a reading is determined, the lobster is either returned to the sea or secured for storage in the holding tank.

Newsletter text and photos courtesy of Shelly Britton.

Text shown threaded

8. Select the second column text frame with the Selection Tool (V). Click the red overset plus symbol; then click the loaded text cursor (displays a link icon with text) in the middle of the frame the third column, creating a thread over the third column. If it doesn't flow, drag another frame again in the third box, and place the text in the column.

9. Change the font and font size to match the rest of the document, and adjust the resizing handles to even out both columns of text if possible.

10. To see the threaded text display, select View > Extras > Show Text Threads. With the Selection Tool (V), select both frames. You will see the connection made showing the threads between the two columns of text.

▷ FIGURE 12-22

Threading text for the Trap Door article.

11. For the next article, "Trap Door," create the headline text frame using the Rectangle Frame Tool (F) first across the first and second columns from the 19-pica and 22-pica guides (Figure 12-22).

Closing the Trap Door

Free Lunch!
Not all lobsters are lucky enough to have a free lunch but "Mable" and many of her friends have had the pleasure. Lucky for "Mable", she is carrying thousands of eggs and was returned to sea as

a breeding stock lobster. All female lobsters with eggs that are removed from a lobster trap, must be "V-notched" by all fishermen, which designates them as breeding stock.

Newsletter text and photos courtesy of Shelly Britton.

12. Using the Rectangle Frame Tool (F), drag the text frame for the body text between the 22-pica and 30-pica marks in the first column.

13. Locate and Place the *Trap door.doc* text file starting at the 22-pica mark in the middle of the frame under the headline text frame and in the first column to the 30-pica mark, click on the overset symbol with the Selection Tool (v); then click inside the middle of the frame second column to fill in the remainder of the text. Format the text lines and title line to your chosen document format and type size.

14. For inset spacing, select Object > Text Frame Options and enter Inset Bottom settings of 10 pt (0p10) with top, left, and right insets set at 0 and a Vertical Justification of Align: Top.

15. This time cut and paste the headline "Closing the Trap Door" above the body text. Even out the lines of text by adjusting with the Selection Tool (V) until they are both even, as shown in Figure 12-22. As you can see you can also cut and paste parts of text lines into selected frames.

16. Save the file.

TOOLKIT TIP With the headline included in the article, another method would be to use the Enter key to push the copy from one frame or column to the next. This function can also be found under Type > Insert Break Character or by holding the Control key (Mac) or right-click (Windows) to access the Context menu.

FLOWING TEXT INTO MULTIPLE PAGES

There are various methods that can be used to flow text into multiple documents. You can use the Manual method shown previously, in which text is added one frame at a time, but you will need to reload the Selection cursor each time. The manual loaded text cursor looks like a page with lines. There is also the Autoflow method for large articles, which adds pages automatically and frames into multiple documents until all the text is flowed into your project; this is done by holding down the Shift key and clicking into the area of the document to start. The semi-autoflow method, which you will perform in the next exercise, provides control and allows you to place the text in adjacent or nonadjacent columns (Figure 12-23). What is nice about this technique is that the cursor is automatically loaded each time a frame is covered with text, until all text is flowed into the project. The loaded text cursor here looks like a sideways "S" curve half solid and half dotted. With the Selection Tool (V) still active, hold down the Option/ALT key to set up for semi-autoflow.

Here you will place a large article to semi-autoflow between document A-2 and document A-4.

1. Double-click on document A-2 (page 2) of the newsletter on the Pages panel; then click once on the *Page 2* layer on the Layers panel.

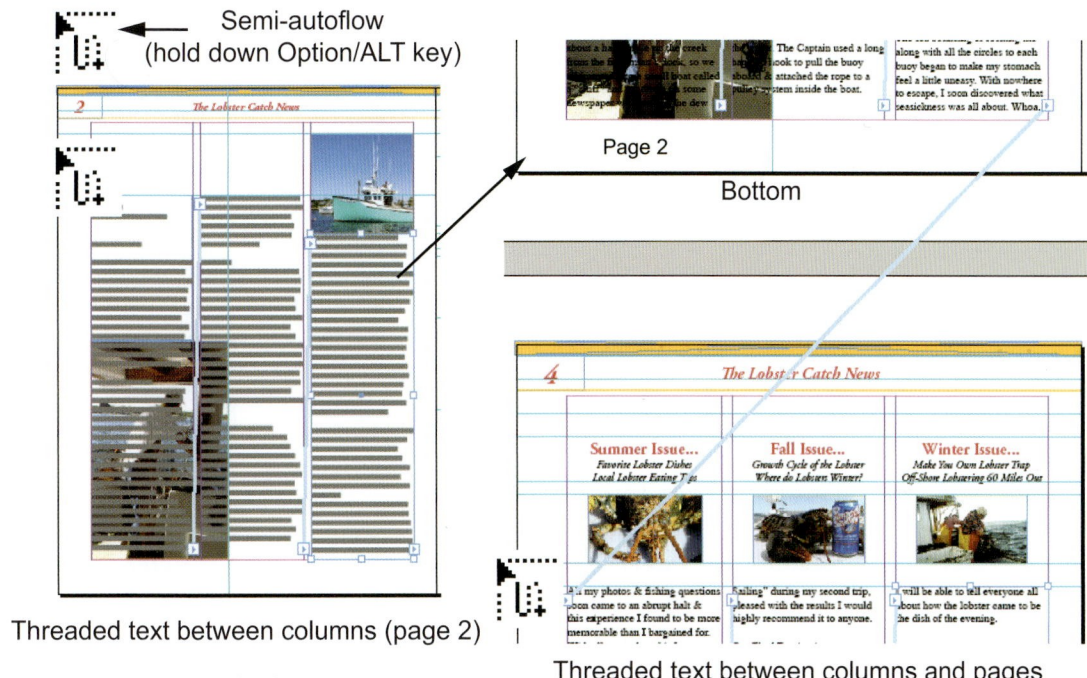

Semi-autoflow
(hold down Option/ALT key)

Page 2

Bottom

Threaded text between columns (page 2)

Newsletter text and photos courtesy of Shelly Britton.

Threaded text between columns and pages

▷ FIGURE 12-23

Using the semi-autoflow method to flow text between columns and pages.

2. Drag a horizontal guide to the 14-pica mark; then, using the Type Tool (T), drag a text frame in the first column from the 14-pica mark to the top edge of the graphic underneath.

3. Choosing the Selection Tool (V), choose File > Place and locate the *Story.doc* file in the *Text* folder. Select Open to bring in the file.

4. With the Selection Tool (V) still active, hold down the Option/ALT key to see the loaded text cursor show the sideways, half-solid, half-dotted "S" to indicate it is in semi-autoflow mode.

5. Click in the middle of the text frame in the first column of document A-2 under the 14-pica guideline.

6. Hold down the Option/ALT key, click the loaded text cursor into the upper left corner of the second column at the 14-pica guideline, and then do the same in the third under the boat graphic. If the loaded text cursor does not display, click the overset icon in the first column with the Selection Tool (V), and hold down the Option/ALT key again. Do not worry if the text flows over the graphic; you will fix that soon (Figure 12-23).

7. Select the A-4 document (page 4) of the newsletter by double-clicking on A-4 document in the Pages panel or by scrolling to the A-4 document. Click on the *Page 4* layer in the Layers panel.

8. The cursor should still display as loaded. Hold down the Option/ALT key; then click the loaded text cursor into the upper left corners of the first, second, and third columns under the graphic frame at the 21-pica mark. If the semi-autoflow does not show, click the frame with the Selection Tool (V), then the overset icon back in page 2 to load the cursor again (Figure 12-23).

9. The text is now threaded across multiple pages. If you have trouble with semi-autoflow, you can always employ the manual method you used earlier. Use the Selection Tool (V) to resize frames if needed. Notice with the "show text frames" option you set earlier you can select text frames to get a good visual of the flow you just created. These lines will never print but act as guides.

10. Double-click the A-2 document in the Pages panel, and click Page 2 in the Layers panel. For the "My Story" headline, select the Type Tool (T) and drag a text frame across the first and second columns between the 6-pica and 14-pica marks. Click the Selection Tool (V) to highlight the frame and using the Control panel, create a 1-pt stroke with a fill of None.

11. Using the Type Tool (T) select the text "Up Close: My Lobster Fishing Story by Shelly Britton" out of the first column; then from the Edit menu select Cut (Command/CTRL +X) then Paste (Command/CTRL + V) the heading into the text frame above the body text; you will format it later. Remove the blank spaces so the first line "My Story begins..." starts on the 14-pica guideline as the rest of the text.

12. To format the text with the rest of your newsletter, highlight all the text (click inside the story text frame and press Command + A for Mac, or CTRL + A for Windows; it will highlight text frames flowing between both documents) and change the font (Adobe Pro Garamond for this example) and font size (11 pt) to match the rest of the document body text. Use the Selection Tool (V) to resize text frames as needed around the graphics. We'll take care of the "lob-sterman" graphic that is halfway into the second column of Page 2 next.

13. Save the file.

TOOLKIT TIP After clicking on the overset symbol with the Selection Tool (V), you can also hold down the Shift key to thread text automatically over columns and create new pages. A threaded set of frames is called a **story**. Designers have the ability to set text frames to automatically expand or contract using the Auto Size feature, based on specific criteria set in the Text Frame Options panel. For instance, by setting Auto Size to Height Only, the expansion only builds downward leaving the top height remaining in its original set position. There is also a Cross-references feature in the Type menu to help simplify production as content can be dynamically updated as it is changed or moved within a document.

FOOTNOTES AND CITING

With InDesign CC, designers can create footnotes (Type > Insert Footnote) that can become part of a text wrap feature around graphic objects, either as in internal text wrap, which will surround the selected object, or as an external text wrap around a non-anchored or floating object (Type > Document > Footnote Options).

For a more visual impact, designers can also create footnotes in non-rectangular frames. When creating footnotes to cite source material, always use sources that are validated and cannot be edited by just anyone. For instance, Wikipedia is not an accepted source for citing, especially for academic and professional documentation as it can be edited by any user without validation.

TEXT WRAP AROUND GRAPHICS

When importing graphics into a document, a designer needs to decide how to place text to support the graphic or object. He or she may need to apply a certain amount of space between the graphic object and the text or overlap the two. You learned to create an inset space for text within a text frame; there is another method, called **text wrap,** in which a space is created between the graphic and the text that surrounds it or overlaps the two frames or objects. To wrap text around graphics, InDesign has a Text Wrap panel in the Window menu that you can select to wrap text around the outside of a graphic using its shape or bounding box as guides, place it within transparent areas, or overlay the graphic itself (Figure 12-24). Here you will use the bounding-box method. Because the text frames have overlapped the graphics when performing a semi-autoflow, you can use the Selection Tool (V) and drag the text frame to the edge of the graphic to expose it.

▷ FIGURE 12-24

Setting text wrap options to allow space between graphics and text.

Photos courtesy of Shelly Britton.

TOOLKIT TIP For graphics inserted within columns, the columns themselves may provide enough spacing so that it is not necessary to insert a left or right offset. Because the columns are set at a 1-pica width, it makes sense to have the graphic edges facing the text frames at a 1-pica width for consistency.

In this exercise, using the bounding-box method on the selected graphic, you will provide a 1-pica space along some edges in documents A-2 and A-4.

1. Double-click on the A-2 document in the Pages panel and select *Page 2* in the Layers panel.

DESIGN TIP

Spacing of at least a pica between paragraphs and graphics provides breathing room for each to compliment one another.

2. Select the bottom of the text frame created in the first column and drag up to expose the bottom left graphic, *Hauling.tif,* which is a picture of a lobsterman. The text will flow into the other columns.

3. Choose Window > Text Wrap to display the Text Wrap panel; select the photo.

4. To wrap text to the rectangle formed by the graphic's height and width, choose the Wrap around bounding box icon.

5. Make sure the link icon is broken so you can specify individual settings. Set the Top Offset and Right Offset spacing to 1 pica (1p0). You will notice the text will space away from the graphic (Figure 12-24).

6. Select the lobster boat image in document A-2 (Page 2) and enter a Bottom Offset of 1 pica, or 1p0.

7. In document A-4 (page 4), and *Page 4* of the Layers panel, drag up the text boxes to expose the *Resource.eps* graphic.

8. Create a 1-pica Top Offset space between it and the remaining text. Adjust the graphic or spacing if needed to accommodate the text font you have chosen. You may have to decrease the offset space here instead.

9. Feel free to apply text wrap to any other graphic if needed, depending on the font choice. To remove the thread display, select View > Extras > Hide Text Threads.

10. Save the file.

TOOLKIT TIP You may find you may need to use the Selection Tool (V) and Content Indicator "doughnut" displayed in the center of the image to move the graphic to the left side to accommodate the text line in the second column. Do not use the resizing handles or this may distort the graphic.

Take a look in your Layers panel to view text and image frames. You can lock these to prevent further editing, you can edit each sublayer frame, and you can right-click on a sublayer to select a particular frame for editing. Much of the formatting in the next set of exercises will occur in those text frames already set up in the Layers panel and will display showing the changes made. You can see the many options you have using the Layers panel.

AUTOMATING AND APPLYING SPECIAL FORMATTING TECHNIQUES

Desktop publishing programs like InDesign have many special formatting techniques that allow the designer to automate repetitive tasks, so that when changes are made, the position or the formatting adjusts to the change. There are also special techniques that can be used to format text, break up articles, and insert special characters to grab the viewer's attention, including the ability to precisely align columns of information with the use of tabbing. Here you will use a sample of some of these powerful features.

ADDING JUMP LINES

Because the story on page 2 continues on to page 4 of the newsletter, you can let readers know where to locate the rest of the article. To do this you create a **jump line** that says "Continued on page 4." Use a jump-line page number to automatically update the number of the page containing a story's next or previously threaded text frame when you move or reflow the story's text frames. The jump line always needs to be in a separate text frame that is touching the linked frame it refers to. That way, the jump-line page number remains in position even if the story's text reflows. The page number automatically updates to reflect the current location of the next or previous frame of the story (Figure 12-25).

▷ FIGURE 12-25

Inserting automatic jump lines for continuing article to other pages.

Jump lines

Bottom of page 2   Top of page 4

Newsletter text and photos courtesy of Shelly Britton.

 TOOLKIT TIP The text frame containing the jump line must touch the frame-linked text for the automatic page number to work properly. For books and many page documents, if you insert an Auto Page Number character in the Find/Change dialog box, jump-line page numbers can also be found and changed.

Next, you will create a jump line to and from the designated pages in the newsletter article you just threaded.

1. Double-click the A-2 document (page 2) in the Pages panel. Zoom in to 200% and navigate to the bottom right third column.

2. Select the Type Tool (T) and drag a text frame with a Stroke of None and a Fill color of black *under* the bottom margin in the third column where you want the jump line to appear (Figure 12-25).

3. With the Selection Tool (V), position the new text frame about halfway into the document margin so that it touches or overlaps the text frame containing the story in the third column.

4. To add an automatic jump-line page number, select the Type Tool (T) and click an insertion point in the new text frame.

5. Select Object > Text Frame Options and set Vertical Justification of Align: Bottom to set the jump line at the bottom of the frame. Click OK.

6. Type "Continued on page " and make sure to leave a space after the last word; then choose Type > Insert Special Character > Markers > Next Page Number. This inserts the number of the page containing the story's next frame; in this case, page 4 (Figure 12-25).

PROBLEM If your jump line does not read "Continued on page 4," and may still read page "2" or another number, try overlapping the frame box. If not, do not use the autoflow method and click in each column's offset symbol instead to manually flow the text.

7. Select the jump line text with the Type Tool (T); then on the Control panel, select Align right formatting to place the text on the right edge of the text frame (Figure 12-25).

8. Change the font to the body text font you are using and include an Italic style while increasing the font size to 14 pt to make it noticeable to the reader. If the jump text line disappears, increase the size of the text frame with the Selection Tool (V).

9. To create an automatic page number to display as "continued from" on page 4, double-click the A-4 document from the Pages panel to display page 4. Make sure the *Page 4* layer is selected in the Layers panel.

10. Select the Type Tool (T) and drag a text frame with a Stroke of None and a Fill color of black from the left margin between the 19-pica and 21-pica marks across *both* columns to the right side of the second column.

11. With the Selection Tool (V), position the new text frame so that it touches or overlaps the text frame containing the story.

12. To add an automatic jump-line page number, select the Type Tool (T) again and click an insertion point in the new text frame above the first column.

13. Type "My Lobster Fishing Story continued from page "; make sure to leave a space after the last word. Then choose Type > Insert Special Character > Markers > Previous Page Number. This inserts the number of the page containing the story's previous frame, which is in page 2.

14. Select Align left, if needed, on the Control panel to place the text on the left side of the text box.

15. The page number 2 automatically displays to reflect the current location of the previous frame of the story.

16. Select the jump line and change to the font you are using for the body of your document. Change the "My Lobster Fishing Story" phrase to 18-pt Bold Italic, while keeping the "continued from page 2" line as an italic style 14-pt size.

17. To have the type sit on the bottom of the text frame, select Object > Text Frame Options > Vertical Justification > Align Bottom. Make sure Ignore Text Wrap is checked and then click OK.

18. To create some spacing between the "continued from" jump line and the body text, you can choose to create a guide line at the 22-pica mark, use the Selection Tool (V) resizing handles and drag the text frames in the three columns to the 22-pica mark, or you can create a Top Inset space of 1 pica in each of the three text frame columns in page 4. You'll notice the text will easily reflow as you make adjustments.

19. Save the file.

TOOLKIT TIP To prevent the story from being moved without its jump line, Shift-select the frames with the Selection Tool (V); then choose Object > Group.

CREATING DROP CAPS

Drop caps are used to lead the viewer into an introductory article or into an article that may span multiple pages or columns. You can add drop caps to one or more paragraphs at a time. The drop cap's baseline sits one or more lines below the baseline of the first line of a paragraph. Drop caps should be used sparingly and not in every article or paragraph in a document to maintain a more professional look. To create a drop cap, you simply highlight the character or characters to edit in the paragraph where you want the drop cap to appear. In the Paragraph panel or Control panel, type a number for Drop Cap Number of Lines to indicate the number of lines you want the drop cap to occupy. In the next field to the right, select the number of characters to be dropped.

DESIGN TIP

As a quick reference, any text formatting that involves individual characters, type lines or titling, use Character formatting. Formatting that involves individual paragraphs, or sometimes paragraph components, like drop caps, use Paragraph formatting on the Control panel.

TOOLKIT TIP You may have to remove the line space between the email address line at the bottom and the "email to:" line, so it is directly underneath to accommodate the change. As a designer you may need to reconfigure and rearrange text and graphics components to achieve the overall best layout for the project.

Here you will create a single character drop cap for the initial "Welcome" article on the front page.

1. Select document A-1 (page 1) in the Pages panel to make it active. Zoom in to the first article on the top left side. Select *Page 1* in the Layers panel.

2. Select the Type Tool (T), highlight the first letter "W," and then select the Paragraph Formatting button on the Control panel.

3. Enter the number "2" in the Drop Cap Number of Lines box; then click on the Character Formatting Controls button on the Control panel, and select a Bold style for the font to make the character stand out (Figure 12-26).

Paragraph formatting for a two-line drop cap

Swatches pop-up menu
(Control panel)

Applying Bold style

Completed drop cap

Adjusted line

Newsletter text courtesy of Shelly Britton.

▷ FIGURE 12-26

Creating a two-line drop cap to introduce the newsletter.

4. With the letter still highlighted, select the Pantone 1935 C color from the Newsletter color group you created on the pop-up Swatches panel on the Control panel, or use the Swatches panel. Remove the word "brand" from the first sentence so that the newsletter title "The Lobster Catch News!" will stand out as its own line (as a designer, you may have to ask permission to do this from the author in some cases).

5. If the email address disappears and a red plus sign displays indicating too much text and space in the text frame, you will need to adjust the spacing to bring it visibly back. Save the file.

USING RULES FOR ARTICLE SEPARATION

Rules are thin lines, usually 1 pt or slightly wider in weight, that can be used to provide a separation between specific articles. To create rules, the Line Tool (\) works nicely. To create perfectly straight lines vertically, horizontally, and at 45-degree angles, hold the Shift key while you drag with your mouse.

 TOOLKIT TIP To see colored rules instead of the guidelines they are drawn over, select **View > Grids & Guides > Hide Guides** to observe your work. Toggle to **Show Guides** when you are ready to continue.

You will create a vertical rule to separate articles on page 1; then you will create a horizontal rule to separate the continued article onto page 4.

1. Double-click on the A-1 document on the Pages panel if needed.

2. Zoom in 100% and drag a vertical guide using the Selection Tool (V) to be placed in the middle of the gutter that separates the first and second columns to around the 17p4 mark for starters, or type it into the X-coordinate field in the Control panel. With Smart Guides you will see the arrow indicators split to two arrows to display the center of the gutter space.

▷ FIGURE 12-27

Applying vertical and horizontal rules to separate articles.

3. Select the Line Tool (\) and hold down the Shift key to create a straight vertical line from roughly the 17-pica mark to the 58-pica mark. Release the mouse first before the Shift key. You have now separated the "Welcome" article (Figure 12-27).

Vertical rule applied between articles

Horizontal rule applied to separate issues and continued story

Newsletter text and photos courtesy of Shelly Britton.

DESIGN TIP

Use pull quotes sparingly within a multipage document. Too many can become a distraction to the reader. Usually you will find only one pull quote used in a long article.

4. With the rule still selected or active, apply a Pantone 1235 P Stroke color from the pop-up Swatches panel (Fill color None) and a 1-pt weight in the Control panel.

5. To create a rule to isolate the continuing article on page 4 from the Coming Issues section above, double-click document A-4 in the Pages panel or scroll to display Page 4.

6. With the Selection Tool (V) drag a horizontal guide at the 19p6 mark or type in the Y coordinate in the Control panel.

7. Using the Line Tool (\) while pressing the Shift key down, drag a horizontal line across the three columns along the guide. Release the mouse first before the Shift key.

8. With the rule still selected or active, apply a Pantone 1235 C Stroke color from the pop-up Swatches panel (Fill color None) and a 1-pt weight in the Control panel.

9. Save the file.

CREATING PARAGRAPH RULES AS PULL QUOTES

DESIGN TIP

When creating pull quotes from paragraph rules, provide enough space to avoid text line bleeds. The text inside should also be larger than the body text and is usually italicized to grab the reader's attention.

The width of a paragraph rule is determined by the width of the column. Rules are used in the creation of pull quotes. **Pull quotes** are used in long articles to "pull" a line or comment out of an article that helps to identify that article to the reader. Pull quotes are inserted in between two paragraphs with enough offset spacing to make them stand out. The **Paragraph panel** provides most of the formatting essentials to type lines, including paragraph rules you will need, and it is selected in the Type menu (Type > Paragraph), or in the Window menu (Window > Type & Tables > Paragraph). The Control paragraph panel also contains these features. You can use the Control paragraph panel or Paragraph panel to control the amount of space between paragraphs. If a paragraph begins at the top of a column or frame, InDesign does not insert extra space before the paragraph. In such a case, you can increase the leading of the first line of the paragraph or increase the top inset of the text frame in InDesign by adjusting the appropriate values using the Space Before and Space After options in the Paragraph panel or the Control panel.

To create a pull quote from the multipage "My Lobster Fishing Story" to identify the article, here is what you need to do.

1. Double-click on page 2 in the Pages panel and zoom back out to 100%. Make sure the Paragraph panel is displayed (Type > Paragraph).

2. In the third column, there is a subheadline that reads "Bringing In the Lobsters." Using the Type Tool (T), select the last line of text that includes the words "inside the boat." In the Paragraph panel (Figure 12-28) or the Control panel, select the Space After function to enter 2p0 to increase the leading. Click at the end of the "boat" sentence of the last line and then press the Return/Enter key to create a line space. Then, using the Type Tool (T), type in the line *with* quotes "It's not easy to be steady on a lobster boat."

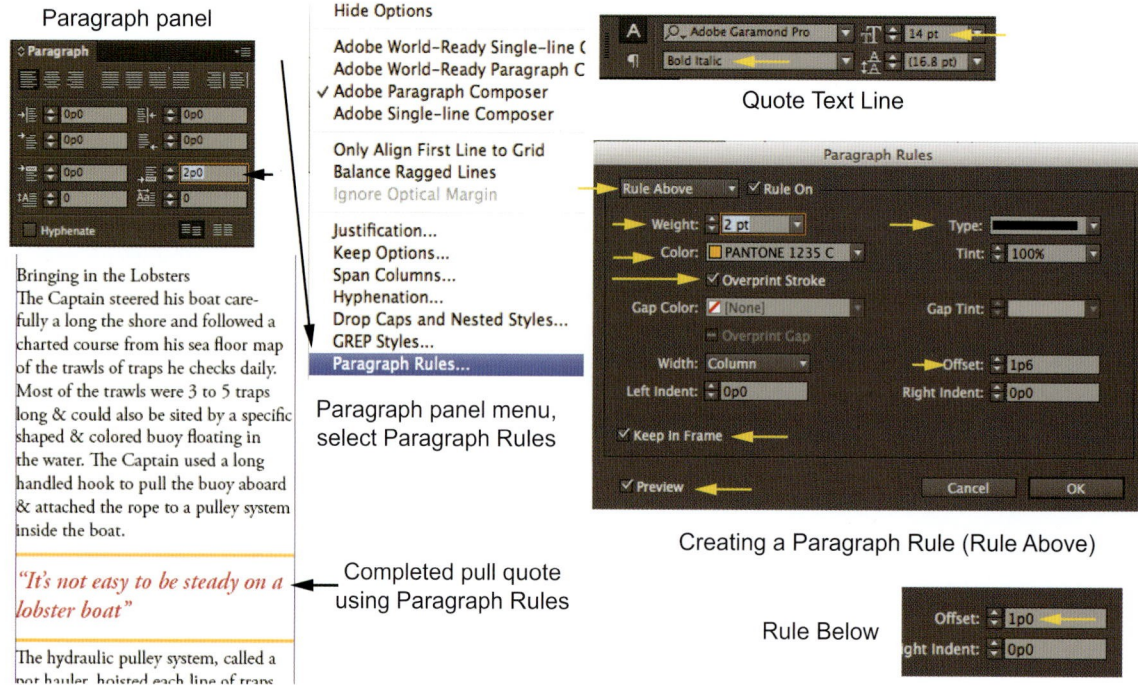

Newsletter text courtesy of Shelly Britton.

▷ FIGURE 12-28

Creating pull quotes using Paragraph Rules.

3. Change the Space After to 1p0 in the Paragraph panel, hold the Shift key, and press the Return/Enter key to create a line space below the line.

4. Highlight the text line in quotes, select the Character Formatting Controls (A) in the Control panel, and change the font to Adobe Garamond Pro Bold Italic or a similar style to match the font you are using, and then increase the font size to 14 pt with the Fill color of Pantone 1935 C from the Newsletter group in your Swatches panel to apply the lobster color theme.

5. To create the rule above the text line, choose Paragraph Rules in the Paragraph panel menu or Control menu on the far right of the Control panel. At the top of the Paragraph Rule dialog box, select Rule Above and then select Rule On. Type in an Offset of 1p6.

6. For Weight, choose 2 pt; then select the Pantone 1235 C color in the Newsletter color group in the Swatches panel for Color.

7. Select Preview to see what the rule will look like. Select Overprint Stroke to make sure that the stroke does not knock out underlying inks on a printing press, and check Keep in Frame, to avoid overlapping. Select OK to accept the rule (Figure 12-28).

8. For the bottom rule, choose the Paragraph Rules in the Paragraph panel menu again, select Rule Below, and then select Rule On. Repeat the same procedure, but type in an Offset of 1p0. Click OK.

9. Save the file.

 PROBLEM If the display box is grayed out, make sure the Rule On box is checked.

 TOOLKIT TIP You have the ability, when in a multi-column text frame, to use the Span Column feature in deciding whether a paragraph should span all columns or a maximum number of columns using either the Paragraph panel menu (Figure 12-28) or using the Paragraph formatting function in the Control panel and clicking on that right side panel menu to observe your options. This feature also helps in balancing text between frames.

USING TABS TO CREATE THE INDEX BOX

The index box lets the reader know what articles are in the newsletter and where they are located. The page numbers are aligned properly using tabs. **Tabs** are important for creating accurate columns of data. Here are some considerations when working with tabs:

- When you are planning to tab data, do the typing first, making sure you press the Tab key once between columns of data. It may not look correct, but that will be adjusted afterwards when you set what are called *tab stops.*

- In the Tabs panel you will notice various methods of setting tabs using the tab arrows to align flush left, right, centered, or on special characters, such as decimal points, or the "=" sign of an equation.

- For multiple lines of tabbing, and to help keep the data focused, you can create leading characters, such as periods, in the Leader box that lead the viewer to the tabbed information, like you would see leading up to page numbers in a table of contents. To create indents without any lead characters, make sure the Leader field is blank.

- The Tabs panel also contains a Magnet icon to align the tab ruler with the selected text. This provides a visual for the designer to properly align the tabbing arrows with precision. The Tabs panel is displayed using the Type menu (Type > Tabs).

- It is a good habit to only tab once between columns of information that need to be tabbed.

- You can observe if you have tabbed correctly by showing **hidden characters**. These are nonprinting characters that display spaces, tabs, ends of paragraphs, index markers, and ends of stories. These special characters are visible only in a document window on the screen and can be toggled on or off in the Type menu.

- When setting tabs, an inset space can be used to provide space for the text so that type is not placed next to a graphic frame that may have a stroke weight color or be filled with color. Inset settings apply to all text in a text frame.

DESIGN TIP

Adding dot-leader fills to tabbed copy assists readers in tracking across columns of type.

TOOLKIT TIP If you do not get the Tab locations correct the first time, you can select the Tab Stop icon in the ruler and drag to the location you desire, or select the icon and type the location in the X-value box. To remove a tab, click on the tab and drag it up and out. To change alignment you can Option/ALT click on tab stops.

Here you will set up the Index box with appropriate tabbing to align articles corresponding to the pages they start on using the Tabs panel in the Type menu. You will also format the text frame.

1. Display the front page document by clicking on the A-1 document in the Pages panel and zoom in to around 125%. Select *Page 1* in the Layers panel.

2. Choose Type > Show Hidden Characters to display nonprintable hidden characters; they can also be toggled off by selecting Type > Hide Hidden Characters. Tabs will display as double arrows, paragraphs will display as a backwards *P*, and so on.

3. Select the Rectangular Frame Tool (F) and drag from the 37-pica mark to the bottom margin. Select a Stroke of None and a Fill of Pantone 612 C selected from the Swatches panel or pop-up Swatches panel in the Control panel. Adjust the Tint in the Swatches panel to 75%.

4. Select the Type Tool (T) and click in the top corner of the frame.

5. Select Object > Text Frame Options and click the link icon to make all settings the same link; enter an inset setting of 6 pt (0p6) for all edges. Under Vertical Justification, select Align Center, then click OK (Figure 12-29).

6. Use the Place command to locate the *Index.doc* file in your *Text* folder. Select Open to insert the text, and click in the rectangle frame you just created. The text has already been tabbed once in each category for the page numbers, although you may need to make further adjustments. You can also type and tab the list on your own instead to get a feel for the layout.

▷　FIGURE 12-29

Setting tabs for alignment of page numbers and second line indents.

Left　Right

Center　Special

Left Justified Tab (1p0)
Second line indent

Right Justified Tab (12p0)
Align for page numbers

Position tabs panel above
text frame and click magnet

Newsletter text courtesy of Shelly Britton.

7. Format the text to the font you are using in body of the document with a Bold style, choosing the same size you are using for the document (we use 11-pt Adobe Garamond Pro), and then highlight all lines of text except the first line, "In This Issue."

8. To open the Tabs panel, select Type > Tabs and you will see the Tabs panel above the selected type.

9. On the right side of the Tabs panel, click the Magnet icon (labeled as Position Panel above Text Frame) to align the tab ruler with the selected text (Figure 12-29). If the magnet is grayed out, it is already aligned. The magnet does not work when the view is magnified if the frame edges extend beyond the viewable area.

10. To make the tabbed page numbers right aligned, click on the Right-Justified Tab icon.

11. Click inside the blank gray box *above* the ruler number 12 to display the right justified arrow and to set the distance for the page numbers as shown in Figure 12-29. Make sure you select inside the blank gray box. You can then move the right align tab stop arrow to place it accurately, or you can type in a 12p0 coordinate in the X-coordinate box; then press Return/Enter.

12. The tabs leading to the page numbers will be created with dotted lines called **dot leaders**. To create a dot leader to the pages numbers, type a period and a space in the Leader field and press Enter or Return. Make sure all page numbers are aligned accurately.

DESIGN TIP

Dot leaders are frequently used for quick reference to page numbers and other info when indexing, providing definitions, etc. They help the viewer to focus attention by leading their eye to the intended information.

13. To create a second line indent, click in front of the word you want to use to start the second line (click in front of the M in "My Lobster Story") and press Return/Enter (Figure 12-30). In the Tabs panel select the Left justified tab arrow; then type 1p0 in the X-coordinate box, remove the dot in the Leader box, and press Return/Enter. Make sure you use the Left justified tab or it will not work.

Newsletter text and photos courtesy of Shelly Britton.

▷ FIGURE 12-30

Creating the second line indent at 1 pica.

14. Click in front of the second line and press the Tab key once to tab over 1 pica. The second line should align under the second character of the first line. Repeat this same procedure with the other two lines as shown in Figure 12-29.

15. If a line space is not already displayed between the text lines, click after each page with the cursor and press the Return/Enter key to make space between the lines or article names as shown in Figure 12-29.

16. Select the headline "In This Issue" and change the type to a 24-pt Bold Italic style font with a Pantone color of 1935 C at 100% tint.

17. To make bullets for emphasis, click in front of the first line of type, and select Type > Insert Special Character > Symbols > Bullet Character (or press Option + 8 on the Mac). Press the space bar once after the bullet to create a space between it and the first word. To make the bullets stand out, highlight each and select the Pantone 1935 color (Figure 12-29).

18. To hide the hidden character display to view your work, select Type > Hide Hidden Characters. Toggle to display when finished.

19. Save the file.

TOOLKIT TIP If you need regular circle bullets or universal special characters such as copyright symbols, trademark symbols, and so on, you can find these in the Type menu (Type > Insert Special Character > Symbol). Another option is the Glyphs panel. A **glyph** is a specific form of a character. For example, in certain fonts the capital letter A is available in several forms, such as swash and small cap. You can use the Glyphs panel to locate any glyph in a font. Choose Type > Glyphs or Window> Type and Tables > Glyphs. You can also use the Glyphs panel to view and insert OpenType attributes such as ornaments, swashes, fractions, and ligatures.

DESIGN TIP

Creating color bullets to match the title color helps to provide consistency within the index box.

SETTING TABS FOR TERMS AND DEFINITIONS

This is basically the same process as creating the index, except this time you are aligning to two columns; the term on the left and its definition on the right use leading dotted lines again. When placing text across multiple columns in a page, or to ignore wrapping around a graphic, you can place a check mark in the **Ignore Text Wrap** box in the Text Frame Options display box. This will ensure the text will flow across columns in the length or width determined by the text frame drawn. You will also see how to remove the leader characters between lines for tabbing multiline definitions. You will also adjust the background fill color in the Swatches panel to a 30% tint to lighten up the background.

DESIGN TIP

Setting fill characters, like the period, creates a dotted line that leads the eye to the page number or definition as examples in the newsletter. They can also be used for menu items, for instance. This technique provides easier reading, especially when listing many items.

TOOLKIT TIP This exercise poses another solution to a problem. If, as in the case here, you want to use a dot leaders to align the term with the definition, the Tabs panel will also do this if you have more than one line for a definition, making the layout look sloppy with too many tabbed periods. To be able to have a tab align in the second definition line without the dot leaders you created for the initial line, you need to insert an Indent to Here nonprinting character using the Type Tool (T); click the insertion point where you would like to indent (choose Type > Insert Special Character > Other > Indent to Here), and the text line will be properly aligned under where you placed the Indent to Here insertion point. The Indent to Here, also called a *hanging indent,* should be used to indent the second line of the definitions.

In this exercise, you will create a light-toned background, place the lobster terms, and align the columns using the Tabs panel. Then you will apply formatting.

1. Double-click page 3 in the Pages panel, select *Page 3* in the Layers panel, and then drag horizontal guides to the 43-pica and 46-pica marks for two text frames for the headline and terms with definitions.

2. If hidden characters are not displayed, choose Type > Show Hidden Characters if you want to check your work.

3. Select the Rectangular Frame Tool (F) and drag from the 43-pica guide across the three columns and to the right side and bottom margins; depending on the placement of your lobster graphic, allow about 1 pica of space. Fill the frame with a Stroke of None and a Fill of Pantone 612 C selected from the Swatches panel.

4. Using the Swatches panel to change the Fill color to a 30% tint, select the arrow next to the Tint box and drag the slider to 30% as shown in Figure 12-31.

▷ FIGURE 12-31

Settings for placing terms and definitions across columns.

Swatches panel

5. Select the Type Tool (T) and drag a text frame across the three columns between the 43-pica and 46-pica marks for the headline.

6. Select Object > Text Frame Options, click to break the link icon, and enter Left Inset and Top Inset settings of 6 pt (0p6) with the rest at 0 pt. Set a Vertical Justification of Align Top. To make sure the text runs across the columns, click in a check mark in the Ignore Text Wrap box. Select OK.

7. With the Type Tool (T), drag a second text frame from the 46-pica mark to the margins across the three columns for placement of the terms and definitions. Use the Selection Tool (V) if needed to adjust resizing handles so both boxes touch.

8. Select Object > Text Frame Options, click the link icon to make all settings the same, and enter inset settings for a space of 6 pt (0p6) all around, with a Vertical Justification of Align Center. To make sure the text runs across the columns, click to put a check mark in the Ignore Text Wrap box. Select OK.

Ⓧ **PROBLEM** After you Place the text in the box, if it appears empty with only the overset icon (red cross) displayed, go back to step 8 and make sure you have the Ignore Text Wrap box checked.

9. Select the Type Tool (T) and choose File > Place to open the file *Terms.doc*. Click in the lower text frame to display the contents.

10. Highlight the headline "Curious Terms of the Lobster Trade" and select Edit > Cut; click inside the headline text frame you created, and select Edit > Paste to place the headline in its own frame; to create a true ellipsis, select the three periods; then hold down Option/ALT and press the semicolon key.

11. Click inside the second text frame below the headline, and delete the top space to bring the text lines near the top of the frame; then delete the extra line space between each line of text to display all terms within the text box.

12. Highlight the text terms and definitions and select Type > Tabs for the Tabs panel to display above the selected type. Click the Magnet icon to align the ruler with the selected text.

13. To apply tabs, click on the Left justified tab stop and click in the blank gray box above the ruler number 10, or type 10p0 in the X-coordinate box to set the distance for the definitions, or drag over to the 10-pica mark the stop created earlier. Press Return/Enter. Understand that this example is one of the few times a left tab stop is used with a leader.

14. To create a dot leader to the definitions, type a period and a space in the Leader field and press Enter or Return. Remove the dash after each term; then click in front of the definition and press tab. The definitions should align to the 10 pica (10p0) mark you just created with dots leading to each definition. Use Figure 12-32 as a starting guide.

15. Change the font size to 14 pt to stand out. If the text box is empty, you can either adjust the text frame height to include all the text, or change the size to 12 pt, depending on the font you chose.

16. To create an indented second line without lead dots, click in front of the first word "A" across from the Skiff term; then choose Type > Insert Special Character > Other > Indent to Here to align the words "lobster boat" underneath (Figure 12-32).

▷ FIGURE 12-32

Tab settings for terms and definitions and applying formatting.

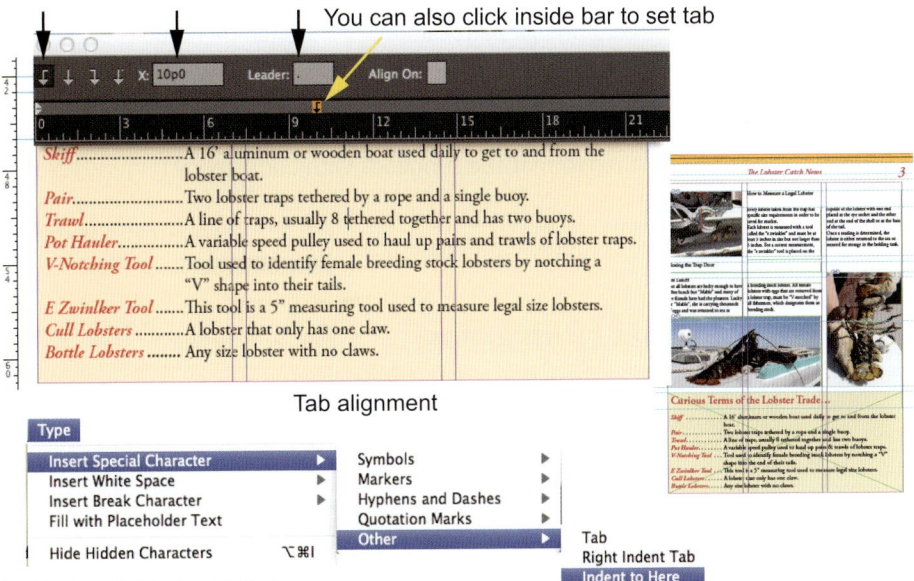

Newsletter text and photos courtesy of Shelly Britton.

DESIGN TIP

Using special techniques for headlines, like increasing font size, applying a style, and adding a universal color that is utilized in the theme of the newsletter, helps to grab the reader's attention. Make sure you are using a consistent font throughout the project. Leave subheads left aligned to stand out over indented paragraphs.

17. Repeat the same for the "V-notching tool" term.

18. To format the headline, highlight the "Curious Terms of the Lobster Trade" headline, and change the font to a Bold style, increasing the size to 24 pt with a Pantone color of 1935 C at 100% tint.

19. To format the terms with the same red, select each term and change the font style to Bold Italic; then choose Pantone 1935 C to make the terms stand out with the lobster color theme, as shown in Figure 12-32.

20. To remove the hidden characters, select Type > Hide Hidden Characters. Save the file.

FINAL FORMATTING AND LAYOUT ADJUSTMENTS

It is time to format headlines that stand out to grab the reader's attention by increasing the size, adding a style, such as Bold, and adding color. **Subheads** or subheadlines are used to break components of a large article into smaller parts to keep the viewer focused. In the Advanced section, you will learn about setting up paragraph and character styles to apply the same formatting easily to any characters or paragraphs in the document. You will also create a drop cap to start off the feature article. As a design feature, you can also end each article with a symbol or character to let the reader know they have finished the article. This works nicely when there are many articles to read. Selecting a symbol in the Wingdings font is a starting point. Paragraphs should also be indented for easier reading. This can be done using the First Line Indent field in the Paragraph formatting controls. When finishing final formatting techniques, you may need to readjust text frames and graphics to provide consistent spacing and accommodate all text. Selecting text frames and making adjustments in the Text Frame Options box can help, along with using the Selection Tool (V) and to adjust graphics. Be careful not to leave widows or orphans when splitting paragraphs between columns or pages. A **widow** is a single or partial line of a paragraph that falls at the bottom of a column or page. An **orphan** is one line of a paragraph that falls at the top of a column in a page, although it should be noted that these two terms are constantly defined interchangeably. Adjust frames or use the Control panel to make sure widows or orphans do not occur in the final document.

First, you will apply the same formatting to the headlines in the newsletter, and then format the subheads with consistency (Figure 12-33).

▷ FIGURE 12-33

Applying formatting for headlines and subheadings. Reflowing text to remove widows.

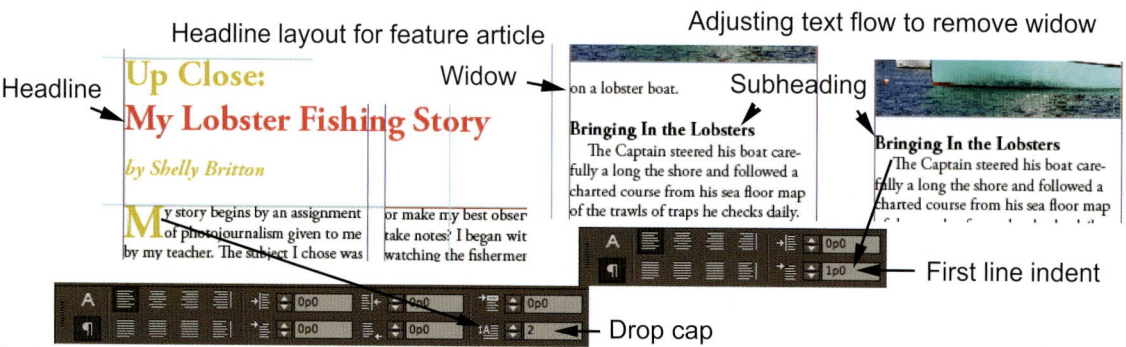

Newsletter text courtesy of Shelly Britton.

1. Display page 1, select the Type Tool (T) and highlight the "Lobster Trap Anatomy 101" headline. Choose a Stroke color of None and a Fill color of Pantone 1935 C in the Newsletter color group in the Swatches panel.

2. Select the Character Formatting icon in the Control panel, and select the font you have been using for your newsletter in a Bold style; increase the size to around 24 pt, depending on the font. If the text disappears, or if the overset icon appears, the text size is too big in the frame; decrease the font size.

3. To align the text to the top of the frame, if it is not top aligned already, select Object > Text Frame Options > Vertical Justification > Align Top.

4. Repeat the same process for the lines on page 2, "My Lobster Fishing Story," and page 3, "How to Measure a Legal Lobster," and "Closing the Trap Door."

5. On page 2, select the headline "Up Close:" and increase the point size to 24 or 28; use the Pantone 612 C color to indicate it as the feature article.

6. For the author line "by Shelly Britton," create a line space if needed, and increase the size to 14 pt in the font you are using with a Bold Italic style with a Pantone color of 612 C to make it stand out.

7. In the story below, create a two-line drop cap using the Paragraph Formatting button in the Control panel of the first letter "M" to start the story. Use a Bold style with a Pantone color of 612 C.

8. To create the subheadings in page 2 and page 4, highlight the following subheading lines and add a Bold style to make them stand out: *Sunrise on the Dock*, *Out to Sea*, *Bringing In the Lobsters*, *My Second Trip Out*, and *Our Final Destination*. If you increase the subhead size to 12 pt, you may need to decrease the leading space between the subhead and the first line for consistency.

9. On page 2 of the "My Lobster Fishing Story" article, you may notice a single line with "lobster boat" in the third column under the boat picture. This is a widow that needs to be adjusted. Drag a horizontal guideline to the 13p6 mark, and adjust the first and second column text frames up to reflow the text. If this still does not work, adjust the headline frame and decrease the text line "Up Close:" to reflow the text. This may take a few adjustments to flow the text so that the "Bringing In the Lobsters" subhead appears below the lobster boat graphic (Figure 12-33).

10. On page 4, you may notice the overset symbol displayed in the third column, indicating more text to be displayed; select each text frame and drag up to the 50-pica mark above the Resources graphic. Choose Object > Text Frame Options. Place a check in Ignore Text Wrap and change the Vertical Justification to Align Bottom.

11. To indent the paragraphs (except those with a drop cap), using the Type Tool (T), click in front of the line to indent, select the Paragraph Formatting button in the Control panel, and type in a 1p0 setting in the First Line Left Indent box (Figure 12-33). Press the Return/Enter key. Repeat for all paragraphs (you will learn to create a paragraph style for convenience in the Advanced Users section).

12. Optional: Feel free to type a subtle symbol, like an anchor or something, to go with the theme at the end of each article to signify the ending. The F key on the keyboard created an anchor using the Wingdings font.

13. To view your work without guidelines, you can click on the Preview icon on the bottom right of the Tools panel; pressing *W* will hide your guides and gray out the pasteboard, or you can select View > Grids & Guides > Hide Guides. Also select View > Hide Frame Edges to remove nonprinting frame guides. This also allows you to check to see if there are any stray frame stroke weights that were colored instead of set as transparent.

14. Make final adjustments for consistency of spacing and layout between text frames and graphics, and you are all set. Feel free to check your sublayers in the Layers panel; right-click to select text frames. Use the Links panel to make sure all you graphics are still correctly linked.

15. Save the file as an InDesign Document (INDD) and as an InDesign Template (INDT) to use as a guide for future documents.

TOOLKIT TIP You can choose Edit > Spelling > Dynamic Spelling to check for misspellings on the fly. There is a new all language user dictionary (Edit > Spelling > Dictionary) feature that allows you to add a custom word or name to a user dictionary and all languages will treat the term as correctly spelled. Use the Links and Preflight panel features to check for graphic and text links and related info. You can also apply special page transitions using the Page Transitions panel for special presentation effects that you can then output to PDF pages (Window > Interactive > Page Transitions). The Package command will create a folder and copy all documents and graphics files, and the document copy with a report for the service provider.

16. To prepare for the printer, as described in the previous chapter, Edit > Spelling > Check Spelling to make sure spelling is correct, although there will be lots of terms and words you will simply choose to skip or ignore. Select the Preflight menu panel at the bottom of the document window to check to make sure graphics are still linked, correct fonts are displayed, and images are set to CMYK colors for press.

17. Choose File > Print and use all the printer's marks to create proofs of the four pages. This is the soft proof you would look at and have your client check for any problems before setting up to package all files and documents.

18. After checking for any problems, you can package for press; select File > Package and create a folder within the *Newsletter* folder or on portable media to transport the image and text files, and name the new folder *Chapter 12 Newsletter*. With InDesign CC, you can also choose to package your newsletter in INDL format for those with earlier versions of InDesign, and in high-quality PDF format for all to read with Adobe Reader.

19. You can create a final additional PDF soft proof for press: choose File > Export > keep most defaults with Press quality, and place the PDF in the *Newsletter* folder. To create special transitional effects for your pages, try playing with the Page Transition panel (Window > Interactive > Page Transitions). Then create another PDF as the smallest file size for electronic presentation.

20. Congratulations! You have just completed a complicated and universally accepted project with many of InDesign's special features and with terminology that is used in the desktop publishing industry (Figure 12-34). If you would like to continue to the Advanced Users section, leave the document open for the next exercise.

▷ FIGURE 12-34
Completed newsletter with formatting.

Page 1

Page 4

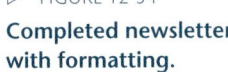
Page panel with
facing pages layout

Pages 2 and 3

Completed newsletter with formatting

Newsletter text and photos courtesy of Shelly Britton.

ADVANCED USERS: Special Editing Techniques and Designing Alternative Layouts

Some of the features in InDesign involve the flexibility to create alternate layout designs to meet not only print and electronic media, but also devices such as tablets and smartphones. With new linking features, artwork can be easily updated when the particular graphic or text in a document has had changes made to it within its original application. When working with multicolumn and multipage documents, a professional look can be acquired when the text lines align evenly across the columns in each document. This can be done by displaying baseline grids to align adjacent text frames. When multiple tasks or procedures are needed, InDesign provides various ways to save these repetitive tasks to apply in one step as opposed to recreating them through a multitude of steps. A designer can use character styles and paragraph styles to handle repetitive formatting and create object libraries to hold graphic and text objects for future use.

ADVANCED EDITING TECHNIQUES AND WORKFLOW IMPROVEMENTS

UPDATING GRAPHIC CONTENT WITH THE LINKS PANEL

With InDesign, the Links panel keeps track of all your images, text, and edits that you create in another program. When you make changes in the application, the graphic or text is created, and the Links panel will display an update warning, which allows you to double-click to update to the current edited version.

To show you the power of this new feature, you'll update the date of the *Nameplate.eps* file.

1. First, you'll change the date of the Newsletter nameplate in Illustrator. Launch Illustrator and open the *Nameplate.eps* in your *Chapter 12 > Newsletter > Images* folder.

2. Select the "Spring 2016" type line, and use the Type Tool (T) to change the season and the year from the current to "Fall 2016" for instance, or a future date. If you have trouble selecting the text, you may need to select the lobster graphic and move it first, as it may be overlapping a little.

3. Save the file in its original EPS format (*Nameplate.eps*) in the same folder, so the link is not broken to the Links panel.

4. In InDesign, make sure your newsletter you just created, *Lobster.indd,* is open displaying the first page, and have the Links panel displayed to show all the links created (Figure 12-35).

5. You should notice next to the *Nameplate.eps* link, a yellow triangle with an exclamation point displayed indicating as you hover your mouse over, "Modified. Double-click to update."

6. Double-click on the triangle as indicated, and you'll see the date change to the date you saved in the new edited *Nameplate.eps* (Figure 12-35).

▷ FIGURE 12-35

Editing and saving a linked graphic in its original application, then updating to the new version using the Links panel.

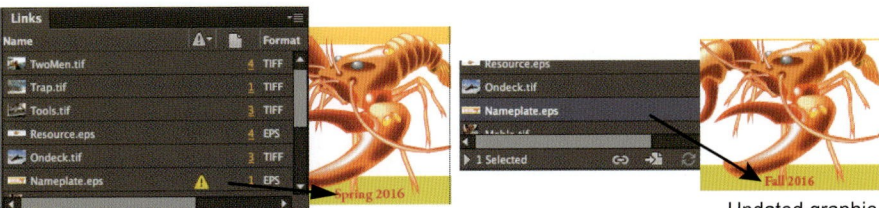

Double-click to update

Updated graphic

7. To have consistency in your newsletter, change the "What's on Dock…" progression of the titles on page 4, from *Summer*, then *Fall*, and then *Winter*, to *Winter*, then *Spring*, and then *Summer*.

8. Save the newsletter as *Lobster2.indd* with the new edited date.

TEXT ALIGNMENT USING BASELINE GRIDS

To help with final alignment of text lines in adjacent columns, you can select to display **baseline grids**, which align the baseline of the text from a starting point across the document for the designer to view how text aligns crosswise along columns to ensure a consistent look (Figure 12-36). Using a baseline grid ensures consistency in the location of text elements on a page. This is useful if you want the baselines of text in multiple columns or adjacent text frames to align. In the Paragraph panel or Control panel, click Align to Baseline Grid. You can view baseline grids by selecting View > Grids & Guides > Show Baseline Grid. To make incremental adjustments for consistency across columns, select the Text Frame Options display. Using the Text Frame Options display, you can experiment and enter values for your baseline grid in points to match text size and leading on selected paragraphs. With pull quotes, the Only Align First Line to Grid option is used from the Paragraph menu or Control panel menu. To ensure that the leading of your text does not change, set the baseline grid leading to the same leading value as your text.

▷ FIGURE 12-36

Adjusting to baseline grids to flow text lines evenly across columns.

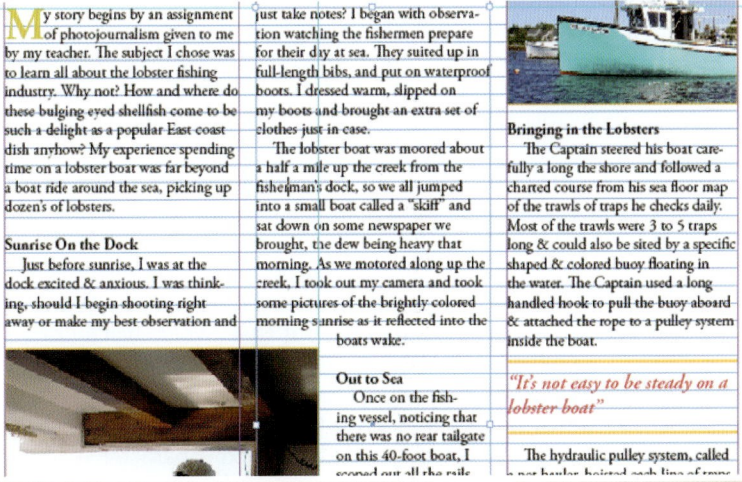

Newsletter text and photos courtesy of Shelly Britton.

You can view baseline grids and adjust the text frames for consistency in lines of text across columns in the document. Your baseline grid should begin with the same increment as the leading value.

1. To display nonprinting baseline grids, select View > Grids & Guides > Show Baseline Grid. Zoom into the document to 100% and observe whether the text line flows across fairly evenly.

2. Select text frames and make adjustments in the Text Frame Options display box using the General tab for the purposes of this exercise. If you want to venture into the Baseline Options tab to make adjustments, save the file first at this point and play; then choose File > Revert if you have experimented too far to return to the previous Save.

3. If you increased the subhead size to 12 pt, you may need to decrease the leading between the subhead and the first line for consistency. Your baseline grid should begin with the same increment as the leading value.

4. For the pull quotes, use the Type Tool (T) to highlight the second text line of the pull quote you created and the first line of the next paragraph that talks about the hydraulic pulley system; then choose Only Align First Line to Grid from the Paragraph menu or Control panel menu.

5. For paragraphs, select the paragraphs you want to align; then, in the Control panel menu or paragraph menu, you can click the Align to Baseline Grid icon to check for accuracy.

6. Try to use methods to have text align as evenly as possible across all columns; this can be a little time consuming to be precise, but the overall look will be very appealing to the reader and to your client.

7. Toggle to hide the baseline grids when you are finished.

FORMATTING USING CHARACTER AND PARAGRAPH STYLES

As you learned with other Adobe applications, to make workflow more productive, you can create character and paragraph styles for consistency in formatting. A **character style** is a collection of formatting attributes that can be applied to text that already has a paragraph style assigned. A **paragraph style** includes both character and paragraph formatting attributes, and can be applied to a selected paragraph or range of paragraphs. A paragraph style can be used for headlines as well. When you change the formatting of a style, all text to which the style has been applied will be updated with the new format. Paragraph styles can also include rules, tabs, spacing, and many other attributes. By default, each new document contains a basic Paragraph or Character default style that is applied to text you type. You can edit this style, but you cannot rename or delete it. After you create a custom paragraph or character style, you simply highlight the text, select the style you want, and the style is automatically applied. You can then add additional formatting to your style, which will automatically be updated in all text to which the style has been applied. You can base a style on an existing style to save time and for consistency. You can find the Styles panels in the Type menu and the Window menu (Window > Type and Tables), or you can use the F11 key for Paragraph styles and Shift + F11 for Character styles.

CHARACTER STYLES FROM FORMATTED TEXT

A designer can create a specialized format for a text line or characters by highlighting the formatted text and creating a paragraph or character style from it to apply to future documents. A new style is created by choosing New Character Style from the Paragraph or Character Styles panel menu. Character styles work within Paragraph styles to format selected copy or individual characters.

In this exercise, you will highlight the formatting you already created for headlines, subheads, drop caps, and terms to create individual character styles for future editing (Figure 12-37).

▷ FIGURE 12-37

Creating a character style from highlighted headline text. Completed character styles are displayed in the Character Styles panel.

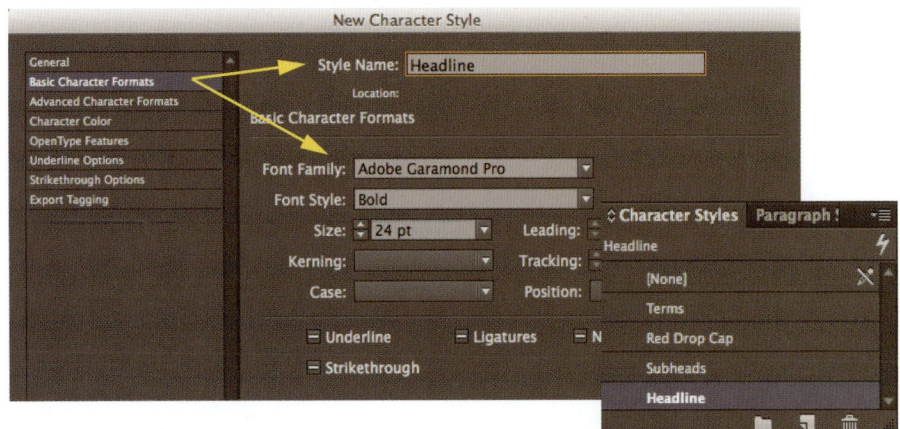

Character Styles created

1. Open the *Lobster.indd* document you created earlier in this chapter, then make sure the front page (page 1) is displayed, and highlight the *Lobster Trap Anatomy 101* headline.

2. To display the Character Styles panel, select Type > Character Styles, or Window > Styles > Character Styles.

3. From the Character Styles panel, click the panel menu, and select New Character Style. Another method is to hold the Option/ALT key and click the new style button in the lower right corner. This automatically opens the dialog box.

4. In the Basic Character Formats tab, you will notice that all the attributes of the highlighted headline are already displayed (the color of the formatted style is in the Character Color tab). Name the Style Name *Headline* and then select OK. The new style will display in the Character Styles panel.

5. Repeat the same procedure above for character styles for subheads, (red) drop caps, and the terms labeling each. If some of the information is missing in the Basic Character Formats tab, type it in and select OK when done.

6. Feel free to create additional character styles that you think might be a nice addition to your arsenal of formatted styles. Experiment!

7. To apply any style, just highlight the text you want to format and click on the style in the Character Styles panel to apply the formatting. That's it!

8. Save when done.

CREATING PARAGRAPH STYLES

Tired of indenting all the paragraphs in the newsletter project? Creating a paragraph style allows you to tag each paragraph to automatically apply the formatting. Applying a paragraph style will not remove any existing character formatting or character style applied to part of a paragraph, although you can remove existing formatting after you have applied the style. You have the option to apply the same style as the copy from which it is being created. A plus sign appears next to the current paragraph style in the Paragraph Style panel if the selected text uses a character or paragraph style and also uses additional formatting that is not part of the applied style. This additional formatting is called an **override**. Paragraph styles can also include formatted tabs, rules, and many other attributes.

▷ FIGURE 12-38

Creating a paragraph style for Garamond body text with a left indent.

Here you will create the body text style of the font you have chosen with an indented first line based on the default style that you will apply to headings in the newsletter (Figure 12-38).

1. Double-click on Page 1 in the Pages panel.

2. To display the Paragraph Styles panel, select Type > Paragraph Styles, press F11 or Command F11 (Mac) on your keyboard, or press the tab if it displays on the right side of your desktop.

3. To base a new paragraph style on the formatting of existing text, highlight the first few lines of the sample paragraph with an indented first line in the body text that contains the font and font size you plan to use. We used 11-pt Adobe Garamond Pro for our example.

4. Choose New Paragraph Style from the Paragraph Styles panel menu, and select the Basic Character Formats tab. For the Style Name, type "Garamond Body Text," or whatever font you have chosen to use, for your new style. Make sure the font information is displayed or type it in. In the general tab, choose Based On [No Paragraph Style]. When you base styles on another style, any changes to the style it is based on will affect the paragraph style. Leave the display open.

5. Select the Indents and Spacing tab (Figure 12-38); make sure the First Line Indent is set for 1p0 spacing. Name the style *Indent*, leave all other default settings, and select OK. Your paragraph style will display in the Paragraph Styles panel (Figure 12-38).

6. You can also create another paragraph style with another serif font to see what the newsletter will look like with that font.

7. To apply the style, you do not need to highlight the entire paragraph; just place the insertion point in the text line and click on the new *Indent* style on the Paragraph Styles panel.

8. Try to see if you can create a style based on one of the tabs you created earlier.

9. Save the file when done.

TABLE AND CELL STYLES

InDesign allows a designer to create cell and table styles that contain all formatting, so you can create a cell style and save it to have the formatting copied to other cells. The same can be created using a table style, where you can also include cell styles within table styles. These styles are in their own new Table Styles and Cell Styles panels, where you would use the Panel menu to create new styles. Check in InDesign > Help to view the tutorials in using these styles.

QUICK APPLY

You can use Quick Apply to locate a style quickly by typing part of its name. You can also use Quick Apply to find and apply menu commands and most other commands that use keyboard shortcuts. You will find the quick apply icon, a little lightning bolt on the Control panel right side, and the style panels to search for and apply formatting.

Here is a quick summary of how to use it.

1. Create a new document and use the Rectangle Frame Tool (F) to make a frame.

2. With the Selection Tool (V), select the text or frame to which you want to apply the style or menu command.

3. Choose Edit > Quick Apply or press Command Return (Mac) or CTRL Enter (Windows).

4. Start typing the name of the item you want to apply. The name you type does not need to be an exact match. Try typing "color" and you will find a bunch of choices.

5. Select the Tools > Apply Color option and the frame will be colored with the colors you have on your Color Picker on the Tools panel.

6. Go ahead and play. Close without saving.

OBJECT STYLES

Just as you use paragraph and character styles to quickly format text, you can use **object styles** to quickly format graphics and frames. Object styles include settings for stroke, color, transparency, drop shadows, paragraph styles, text wrap, and more; you can also assign different transparency effects for the object, fill, stroke, and text. You control which settings the style affects by including or excluding a category of settings in the definition. You can find the object style panel in the Window menu (Window > Object Styles). When creating styles, you can base one object style on another. When you change the base style, any shared attributes that appear in the "parent" style change in the "child" style as well. With any style, you select the object or item first, locate the style you want to apply, and select the style in the panel. Go ahead check out InDesign > Help to learn how to use this.

CREATING OBJECT LIBRARIES

Object libraries help you organize the graphics, text, and pages you use most often. You can also add ruler guides, grids, drawn shapes, and grouped images to a library. You can create as many libraries as you need: for example, you can create different object libraries for varied projects or clients. If an object library includes text files, make sure that the file's fonts are available and active on all systems that will access the library. When you add a page element, such as a graphic, to an object library, InDesign preserves all attributes that were imported or applied. For example, if you add a graphic from an InDesign document to a library, the library copy will duplicate the original, including the original's link information, so that you can update the graphic when the file on disk changes. If you delete the object from the InDesign document, the object's thumbnail will still appear in the Library panel, and all of the link information will remain intact. If you move or delete the original object, a missing link icon will appear next to the object's name in the Links panel the next time you place it in your document from the Library panel. When adding an item to an object library, InDesign saves all page, text, and image attributes automatically. Elements grouped in an InDesign document when dragged to the Library panel stay grouped when dragged out of the Library panel. Object libraries have an **INDL extension**. InDesign also provides support for 3D Photoshop artwork.

Next, you will create object libraries of some newsletter objects and the front page of the newsletter for future use (Figure 12-39).

1. With the *Newsletter.indd* document open, in the Layers panel for Page 1, make sure all graphics are unlocked (click the lock icon to unlock) so everything can be brought into the Library. Select File > New > Library and leave the default Library name, saving the file in the *Newsletter* folder. The Library panel will display.

2. To save the entire front page document as a guide for future issues, drag across the entire document with the Selection Tool (V). Drag the combined selection into the Library panel or select Add Items on Page 1 from the Library panel menu.

3. To rename the library object, double-click on the *Untitled* label in the object thumbnail to bring up the display box, and rename it *Front Page.* You can also put in a description as shown in Figure 12-39. Select Object Type as Page; then select OK.

4. To add individual components, make sure the *Nameplate.eps* layer is unlocked (click the lock icon to unlock) in the Layers panel. and then select the

Renaming object

Library objects

Panel menu display

Newsletter text and photos courtesy of Shelly Britton.

▷ FIGURE 12-39

Creating an Object library for frequently used objects and a front page for future use.

Nameplate.eps graphic in the front page. It will contain the name of the file *Nameplate.eps* in the thumbnail, which can also be edited. Select Place Item(s) from the Library panel menu of choices if guides and grids are still displayed. You could also select Add Item or Add Items on Page in the Library Panel menu display. Any graphic images or creations need to be unlocked in the Layers panel before bringing into the Library panel.

5. Go ahead and create separate objects for the *Resource.eps* graphic, any images you want to use for later, the "Index" text box, and the "Curious Terms" text box, so you will not have to tab over again. This is one cool feature!

6. To add any of these objects, including the entire front page, to a document, create the document and simply drag the object from the Object Library panel into the document window. The object is copied into the document (the same way symbols are used in Illustrator). Go ahead and give it a try.

7. To open the Object Library in the future, select File > Open and locate the name of the Library file (INDL). It will then display the Library panel again with object thumbnails.

8. If you have not already done so, to prepare the updated document for press as described in *Chapter 11;* select Edit > Spelling > Check Spelling to make sure spelling is correct, although there will be lots of terms and words you will simply choose to skip or ignore.

9. Use the Preflight panel menu at the bottom of the document window to check to make sure graphics are still linked, correct fonts are displayed, and images are set to CMYK colors for press. Check the Links panel as well.

10. Choose File > Print and use all printer's marks to create proofs of the four pages you could show to a client for final approval.

11. To package for press, select File > Package and create a folder inside the *Newsletter* folder, or save it on a portable medium to transport the files and name the new folder *Chapter 12 Newsletter*. Remember, whenever changes are made, always use the Package command to package the document as the last step before bringing it to your service provider.

12. To create a PDF soft proof for press, choose File > Export > and keep most defaults with Press quality; place the PDF in the *Newsletter* folder.

13. You now have a newsletter project with plenty of styles, libraries, and features for future issues without having to start over in layout or formatting from scratch.

CREATING ALTERNATE LAYOUTS WITH SAME CONTENT DESIGN

The projects you have been creating are based on a fixed design size. However, in today's industry, in what was predominantly a print publishing market, designers must also move into the realm of having their work configured to meet e-publishing demands, and for various electronic devices such as tablets and smartphones, in addition to meeting the demands of changes in sizes in the print market. InDesign has developed some new features to allow you to adjust your designs to meet the demands of using various hard copy content and screen sizes, without having to redesign your content from scratch. This new concept of design is known as fluid design or **liquid design**, in which the artwork is adjusted on the fly to meet the needs of the intended market. One thing to remember is to first choose the main output or target device with its corresponding dimensions and orientation as you normally would, and then base your design for that original output so that your layout, images, and formatting have been already established. Adobe incorporates rich text formatting to maintain consistency in text flow and quality as you adapt your layout to a particular screen size.

TOOLKIT TIP In the Links panel, if a red circle with a question mark displays next to the file, it doesn't know where the file is. This usually occurs if the document has been moved without the original files. Click on the question mark, and locate the folder where the files are kept. If you have multiple missing files in the same folder, it will update all of those missing as well. If a yellow triangle displays, it is an indication to update a file to its current version.

USING LIQUID LAYOUT WITH THE PAGE TOOL

A nice feature with InDesign is the use of Liquid Layout as one of the answers to the many changes in a particular layout in attempting to adapt your layout for different sizes that can be used for print, electronic, or interactive media. One of the benefits is that you can design a layout with the freedom of making changes, like scaling down or up your content layout without affecting the quality of workmanship, except for enlarging bitmap images. In most cases, where a designer may be targeting more than one device, the designer would select the page of content and add one of the optional Liquid Layout behaviors, like the ability for the entire page to scale, so the page can easily be dragged to be resized. Adjusting the size is best accomplished in coordination with using the Page Tool.

The Page Tool (Shift + P) can be used to resize selected document pages from any reference point to a specific size. It can be used to create special inserts for print, and adjust selected pages to various orientations. You can take these adjustments further with Liquid Layout and adjust to suit your needs. Here's a quick example of using this feature.

To give some exposure in using this feature, in this exercise, you will make a copy of your *Lobster.indd* newsletter, and set it up using Liquid Layout to be able to scale the newsletter down to about half size.

1. Open your *Lobster.indd* 4-page newsletter you created in Chapter 12 and save it as a copy (File > Save a Copy) in your *Chapter 12* folder as *Lobster3.indd*. This way you are not affecting the original newsletter for our purposes here in case you make any mistakes.

2. Check the Links panel to make sure the copy also contains all the links. If not (red circle with question appears next to file), click the *Nameplate.eps* graphic from page 1 to find where the image is and update all the rest of the links in the Links panel.

3. Zoom out to view the entire page 1 of the newsletter, and then using the Page Tool (Shift + P), click once on Page 1 to select all of Page 1. In the Control panel, select Liquid Page Rule: Scale, and check Objects Move with Page (Figure 12-40). This will have the entire page adjust to scale.

▷ FIGURE 12-40

Using the Page Tool to resize the page in coordination with scaling in Liquid Layout mode.

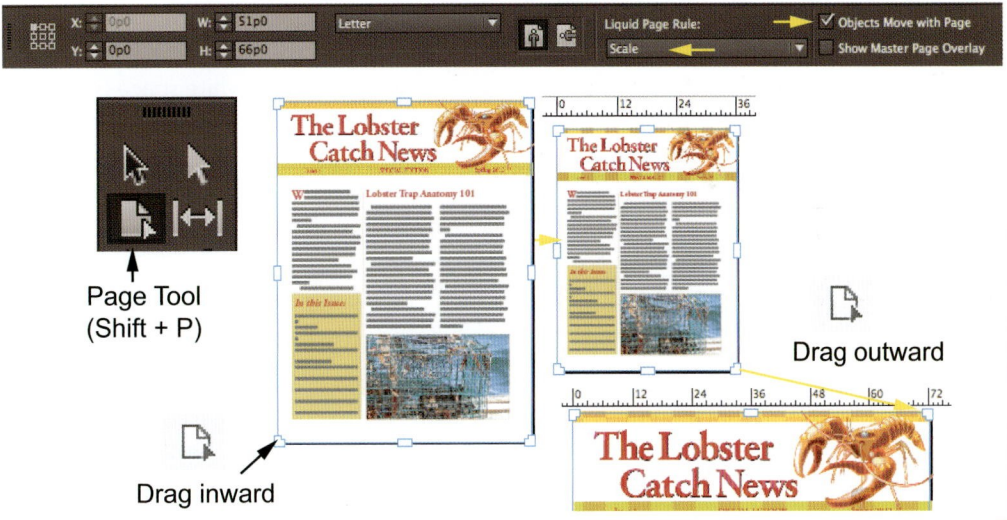

Page Tool (Shift + P)

Drag outward

Drag inward

Newsletter text and photos courtesy of Shelly Britton.

4. If you simply drag a corner with your mouse or pen, the page will stretch or expand to give you a quick preview, and then return back to its original position. To make actual adjustments to scale proportionately, hold down the Shift key *with* the Option/ALT key and drag a corner with the Page Tool (Shift + P).

5. Drag inward until the top aligns with the 36-pica size, and you'll find the text and graphics will be resized proportionately. Release the mouse first. The text should still be sharp.

6. Feel free to print just the page 1 to see the change in size and quality, which should not change.

7. You can also expand this same page to 72 picas by dragging the corner. Print to view the graphics. You may find the bitmap image of the trap may be lightly pixilated. This is important to be careful when expanding a document. As in Photoshop, create for your largest size first and then scale down when needed. Go ahead and play.

8. Don't save and undo (CTRL + Z) until you come back to the original page size (51 picas width, 66 picas height). Leave the *Lobster3.indd* file open for the next exercise.

Although liquid layout is actually more complicated as you can adjust individual components, it is beyond the scope of this book. However, here is a brief summary of some of the settings. Feel free to play and test out these features.

- Different types of selected objects and how they behave are called policies. For instance, in using the Scale policy in the previous exercise, you can scale selected items proportionately.

- Re-Center policy allows white space to be evenly distributed as you drag, although the selected content remains centered.

- Guide based policy allows you to place guides as behaviors where additional space is injected only on those page items or objects it touches. This works great with adjusting text to reflow while a neighboring images remains in the same position.

- Object based policy will create either a spring icon to allow flexibility of an object side or lock, which will keep the side at the original fixed dimension. This combination determines how much white space is equally distributed by clicking on the icons as a toggle, and how much of the object is adjusted from its original size.

- Be wary that using Liquid Layout to its full potential requires creating policies or rules (behaviors) as described that dictate how page elements move and change as different page sizes and dimensions affect them. This can also be time-consuming and the results will usually still need manual tweaking.

New Digital Publishing Document Layout

In addition to having the traditional settings for Print and Web dimensions, InDesign has a new document Intent or type called Digital Publishing that provides various screen sizes for devices like iPads, Kindles, and Androids to name a few. You can set up your designs for these devices and create custom sizes as new tablets and devices enter the market. Measurements represent physical sizes in inches with decimal points as opposed to pixel dimensions.

USING THE CONTENT COLLECTOR AND CONTENT PLACER TOOLS

The Content Collector and Content Placer tools are also convenient in InDesign. When you select the Content Collector Tool (B), a pop-up "conveyer" appears at the bottom of the screen; it allows you to grab multiple pieces of text and graphic content from any document and store it temporarily while the documents are still open, and then repurpose these objects within the same or separate created documents using the Content Placer Tool (B). Dragging the content out of the conveyer while choosing to keep or remove objects from the conveyer is a convenient way to replicate pieces of copy and graphics across multiple layouts and documents. You can use this feature with individual pieces, or with grouped pieces already put together in your document. This grouped set of objects is called a **set**, which InDesign remembers how you put them together to maintain the same layout. The time saver for this is that you can have a complicated formatted text frame created and reused over again in another document. As the properties of each frame or group of frames remain intact, you can readjust your design, like adjusting the reflow of text between frames with ease with the Selection Tool (V). To make proportionate adjustments of graphics to fit in an adjusted frame, there is also a Fitting command in the Object menu.

In this exercise, you will create a new Digital Publishing document for an iPad, use the Content Collector Tool (B) to grab some components from the open newsletter, *Lobsterr3.indd*, and use the Content Placer Tool (B) to place those elements into the new document.

1. Keep the *Lobster3.indd* newsletter open, from which you are going to collect items.

2. To create a new document to put the items to be selected from *Lobster3.indd* into, select File > New > Document, and select Intent: Digital Publishing. Choose Page Size: iPad with a landscape orientation. Leave all the other settings at their defaults. Click OK.

3. To grab items click to display the *Lobster3.indd* document with all four pages. Zoom in to about 75%.

4. Select the Content Collector Tool (B) on the Tools panel and you'll find a gray content conveyor at the bottom of the screen (Figure 12-41). If not, select View > Extras > Show Conveyor.

▷ FIGURE 12-41

Using the Content Collector Tool to select graphics and text to be placed on a new iPad document.

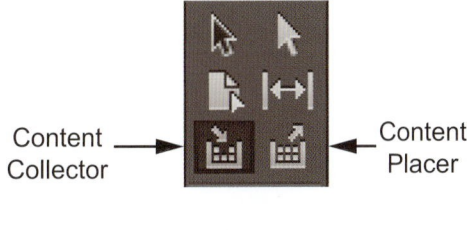

Content Collector ——→ ←—— Content Placer

Content Conveyor

Photos courtesy of Shelly Britton.

5. As you hover your mouse over boxes of content in the newsletter, you'll find them highlighted with a blue outline. Click to select the *Nameplate.eps* graphic from the top of page 1, and it will be displayed as thumbnail on the content conveyor.

6. On page 1, click and drag only the "Lobster Trap Anatomy 101" headline and text, not the lobster trap graphic. You'll find it is placed in the conveyor as a group item. You can also select headline and body text individually as well.

7. On page 2, select the image of the man hauling the trap on his boat, or select one of the other images that can be used in a vertical format.

8. On page 3, click and drag over the headline "Curious Terms of the Lobster Trade…" and terms in the colored box, which will also be deposited as a group. Imagine having to redo this tabbed formatting for another document. This is why this new feature is a great time saver.

▷   FIGURE 12-42

Placing content in to a new document with the Content Placer Tool. Adjusting frames with the Selection Tool.

9. Select as a group with the Content Collector Tool (B), the headline "How to Measure a Legal Lobster" along with the image and text with it as one group.

10. With the conveyor still displayed, select the new iPad document you just set up. Now you will place the content into the new document.

11. Select the Content Placer Tool (B), and click once on the first *Nameplate.eps* graphic and place it on the top portion of the new iPad document (Figure 12-42).

Click set number to display individual elements

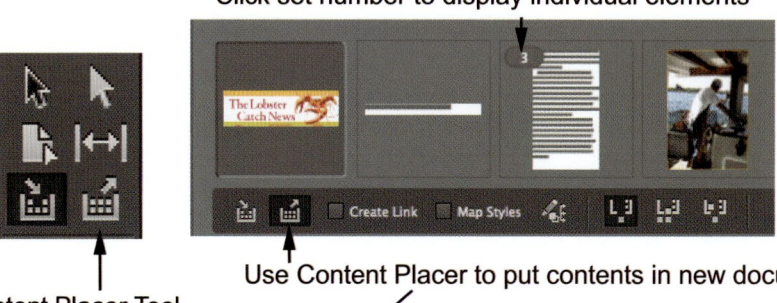

Content Placer Tool

Use Content Placer to put contents in new document

Object > Fitting to scale proportionately

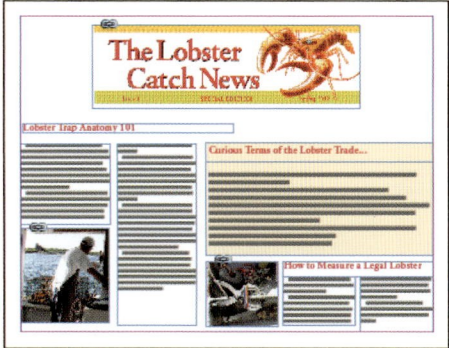

Use Selection Tool to adjust and resize content

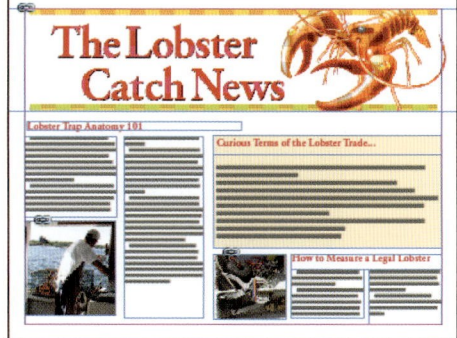

Photos courtesy of Shelly Britton.

12. Continue to use the Content Placer Tool (B) and put the items from the conveyor onto the iPad document. If you have a set or group of items, there will be a number above the thumbnail, which you can click to display all those items individually. If you have selected unwanted overlapping frames, you may want to adjust the frames and try again with the Content Collector Tool (B). Using these new tools takes a little practice.

13. Now, because all the formatting properties are still intact, you can use the Selection Tool (V) and resize and readjust the placement of your text and graphic frames to the desired design you'd like without having to worry about recreating the content all over again. Use Figure 12-42 as a guide or create your own layout.

14. Optional: If you feel the *Nameplate.eps* graphic is too small for the document, and want to extend it to both sides of the document proportionately, drag the guidelines to the margins or edge of the document and select Object > Fitting > Fill Frame Proportionately, and then adjust the graphic placement with the Selection Tool (V). You can always undo if this does not work for your design intent.

15. Save the document as *iPad.indd* in your *Chapter 12* folder.

TOOLKIT TIP Designers have the ability to set text frames to automatically expand or contract using the new Auto Size feature, based on specific criteria set in the Text Frame Options panel. These text enhancement technologies allow you to set text frames to expand, contract, or as the copy is adjusted. For instance, by setting Auto Size to Height Only, the expansion only builds downward leaving the top height remaining in its original set position. This can come in quite handy with changes in text content or when different text styles are applied in a given layout.

CREATING ALTERNATE LAYOUTS

Designers have the option to create multiple versions of the same document to include alternate layouts to fit various type of media, including iPads and other tablet devices. This feature takes a range of existing pages with content and automatically creates linked copies of the content on a set of new pages within the same document. To use this feature, you need to apply a liquid layout policy or behavior beforehand, if you plan or designing or more than one device. The layout will then create a new set of master pages and will link content with the original design you just created so that if you need to make changes, the content can be updated in all layouts within your design. Although this helps with your workflow, you may still need to go in and make manual adjustments.

TOOLKIT TIP To invoke the Alternate Layout feature, you have a few options: (a) choosing Layout > Create Alternate Layout..., (b) in the Pages Panel, CTRL/Right + Click on the inverted triangle that represents the Section marker, or (c) in the Pages Panel fly out menu, select Create Alternate Layout. Content will be automatically linked, so that when the original "source" page item is updated, all linked instances will inherit the change once the link is updated. You also preview various layouts beforehand using the Page Tool's Control panel to get an idea of placement, or make a quick conversion using the exiting dimensions.

In this exercise, we'll convert the iPad document size to an Android size by setting it up in liquid layout behavior to scale, and then using the Alternate Layout feature.

▷ FIGURE 12-43

To create an alternate layout of a design for multiple devices, set up the original as Liquid Layout, and then select to create an alternate layout within the same document.

1. With the *iPad.indd* document open, select the Page Tool (Shift + P), and in the Control Panel, select Liquid Layout of Scale for behavior or policy, and check Objects Move with Page.

2. You'll notice the iPad button on the Control panel. To see a quick preview with the same orientation for an iPhone, select the iPhone button and watch everything scale downward proportionately. This provides a nice preview.

3. Click the iPad button to bring back to its original document. Now you will create an alternate layout for the iPhone within the same document.

4. With the Page Tool (Shift + P) selecting the document, select Layout > Create Alternate Layout, and choose the settings for an iPhone using Figure 12-43 as a guide, and keep everything checked as shown. You'll also leave the iPhone in Landscape format just as you did with the iPad.

Preview new dimensions as Liquid Layout

Page Tool

Set up document as Liquid Layout first

Original iPad layout

Create Alternate Layout

Name: iPhone H
From Source Pages: iPad H
Page Size: iPhone
Width: 480 px   Orientation:
Height: 320 px

Options
Liquid Page Rule: Preserve Existing
✓ Link Stories
✓ Copy Text Styles to New Style Group
✓ Smart Text Reflow

Cancel   OK

Master Page (B) created
from iPhone alternate layout

Alternate layout created
in same document

iPhone
(converted as alternate layout)

5. You'll find the iPhone alternate layout as an additional page, and as an additional Master Page in the Pages panel. The alternate layout from iPad to iPhone is in the same document, scaling the same design, and all links are set up in the Links panel so that if there are any changes made to the original document, you can update them for the iPhone.

6. Save the document again in your *Chapter 12* folder. Click the Selection Tool (V) when completed to reset.

7. You can create additional alternate layouts based upon the original iPad layout and design. If you change the orientation from landscape to portrait, the alternate layout can be created, but you will need to use the Selection Tool (V) to resize and readjust the frames as needed; however, it creates a very nice starting point instead of having to redo the design all over again as was done before in previous versions.

8. Go ahead and play as a designer and make changes to your new layouts. Take advantage of this very powerful feature.

TOOLKIT TIP In the existing Text Frame Options dialog, there is a new option under Column: Resizing. This new option is "Flexible Width." The value here sets the maximum column width size to be reached before InDesign will automatically add a new column for you if the frame gets wider, or reduce the number of columns, as it gets narrower. This behavior is carried over into HTML, such that when there is more room for the column of text, more columns will be automatically added.

DIGITAL TOOLKIT EXTRA: Create Interactive PDF Documents

InDesign has the capability of creating interactive PDF documents that you can use to locate other documents, hyperlink to websites, and play movies and sounds. This is a valuable feature when you want to send a potential client available information, resources, movies, or sound clips in a universal PDF format. Here you will also learn to use the Buttons and Forms panel to create interactive buttons. As was discussed in previous exercises in creating documents with images and text, all components, including the InDesign document, should be in the same folder to keep everything together and linked as needed. In this section, you will create a map of directions that involves some review and some new techniques, an interactive PDF registration form, and finally a special interactive form that employs special button actions and rollover states (Figure 12-44). For images in this project, you can use the kayak image you completed in Chapter 5 and the Map illustration you created in Chapter 8.

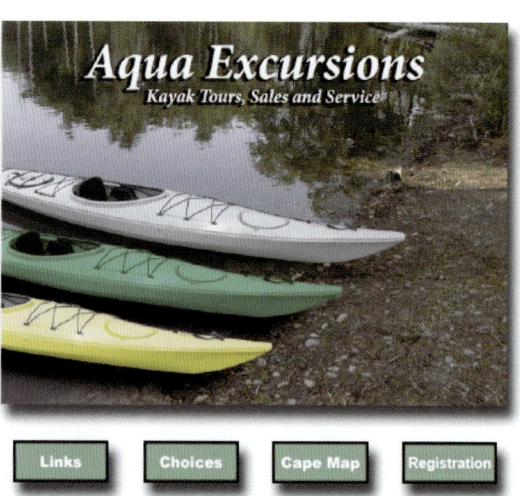

▷ FIGURE 12-44

Completed interactive PDF document.

CREATING THE CAPE MAP DOCUMENT

Before you create your interactive PDF, one of the documents you will need to create is a document that shows directions for a lighthouse tour. You can use the map you created in Chapter 8, removing all the text lines but the title, or use the map in the *Chapter 12 Extra* folder. This will help as review in placing graphics, and formatting text, and frames.

Here you will create a simple document that provides directions with a graphic for a reference.

1. Change InDesign preferences to inches. Create a new document with the Intent for Print at Letter - Half, and portrait orientation, with 0.5 (half) inch margins all the way around. Leave the rest at their defaults as shown in Figure 12-45 and click OK.

▷ FIGURE 12-45

Placing the map in a document, creating arrow line and slogan.

2. Select File > Place, and locate the *Map.pdf* document in your *Chapter 12 Extra* folder; then click Open. If you prefer, you can open the map illustration you created in Chapter 8, remove the fish symbols and text lines except the title, and save it as a PDF in the *Chapter 12 Extra* folder to be placed in the document.

3. With the cursor loaded, click in the top left margin to display the map and resize to fit within the margins.

4. Select the Type Tool (T), and create a text box underneath alongside the bottom of the image frame, typing in the line "Come join in the fun!" Use red or another color to help make it stand out (Figure 12-45). Choose your own font (we chose Minion Pro Bold). Deselect the text box.

5. To create an arrow to the site near Hyannis, select the Line Tool (\), with a 2-pt black Stroke; then select from the Stroke panel, the End of the line as a curved arrow. Drag towards Hyannis.

6. Create a Rectangular Frame box, then color with a 2-pt black Stroke and a yellow Fill with a 60% Tint from the Swatches panel. Use the Type Tool (T) and type the first line "Come Tour with Us" and second line "From Hyannis Harbor." Then use the Text Frame Options of Align: Center from the Object menu, and center both lines across the frame box using the Control panel.

7. Using the Rectangle Tool (M), create another large rectangle frame box between the margins, with a 2-pt black Stroke, and blue Fill with 20% Tint (Figure 12-46).

8. Select the Type Tool (T) and click inside the box; then select to place (File > Place) the contents of the document *Directions.doc* in the *Chapter 12 Extra* folder in the blue box you created.

▷ FIGURE 12-46

Completing the Cape Map with formatting frames and placing text.

9. Use the feature to insert bullets in front of each line using Type > Bulleted and Numbered Lists > Apply Bullets.

10. You should create a space from the text lines and the frame box, so select Object > Text Frame Options, then select a Top inset of 0.125 inches, and then select an inset of 0.0625 inches on the other three sides Click OK.

11. Format as needed and save the file as *Cape Map.indd* in the *Chapter 12 Extra* folder. The Cape Map document is done.

TOOLKIT TIP There are a variety of different ways to add bullets in InDesign. There is an Apply Bullets command (Type > Bullets and Numbering > Apply Bullets) that allows you to add and remove indented bullets quickly. In all versions you can also have special bullets or numbered lists created using the Bullet Character command (Type > Insert Special Character > Symbols > Bullet Character). You cannot use the Type Tool (T) to select any bullets or numbers in a list. Instead, edit their formatting and indent spacing using the Bullets And Numbering dialog box or the Paragraph panel. A quick way to create a bulleted or numbered list is to type the list, select it, and then click the Bulleted List or Numbered List button located in the Control panel. These buttons let you turn the list on or off and switch between bullets and numbers. You can also make bullets and numbering part of a paragraph style and construct lists by assigning styles to paragraphs.

CREATING AN INTERACTIVE PDF FORM

Another very helpful feature in InDesign is the ability to create an interactive PDF form that can be submitted to a designated email address. Once created, clients or vendors can put in their information inside text fields that you designate using the Buttons and Forms panel. The Buttons and Forms panel menu also includes sample buttons you can use, some with actions already built in so you don't have to create them from scratch.

SETTING UP THE REGISTRATION FORM

Creating the registration form involves placing graphics for visual effect and creating text fields and information for your user. Text fields need to be set up where a user can input information as needed to complete the form.

You will create the registration form by placing graphics, creating colored framed text boxes that will be used for input, and typing in text information. This will also help to serve as a bit of a review of some techniques covered previously.

▷ FIGURE 12-47

Setting up the registration form before making it interactive.

1. Create a new document with the Intent for Print at Letter - Half, and landscape orientation, with 0.5 (half) inch margins all the way around. Leave the rest at their defaults as shown in Figure 12-47 and click OK. This will provide use for all versions of InDesign.

2. Place (File > Place) the *Sandy Background.jpg* from the *Chapter 12 > Chapter 12 Extra* folder in the upper left corner of the document to create a neutral warm background.

3. Click outside the document with the Selection Tool (V) to reset, and then place (File > Place) the *Kayaker.jpg* from the same folder along the bottom right margin lines of your document.

4. Select the Type Tool (T) and drag a text box across the top area of the document to place the title and headline. Type "Aqua Excursions" in the first line at 36 pt, and then type "Registration Form" as a second line at 24 pt and center both lines. If the offset symbol appears, simply extend the text frame with the Selection Tool (V). Use Minion Pro Bold font for both, or use your own choices of a wide serif font. Use the Selection Tool (V) and Smart Guides to find the center at 4.5 inches. Color the font if you want or leave it at the default black. We chose a deep blue for the Registration Form line of text only (C=100, M=90, Y=10, K=0).

5. Using the Type Tool (T), drag under the headlines and across the document, and type three lines of text at 14 pt. First type "Register with us to receive information on special kayaking tours and events." Type for the second line "We will also email you discounts and coupons on equipment in our store." The third line should read "Any information provided stays with us and is never shared with any third parties." See Figure 12-47.

6. To create bullets in front of each line, click in front of each line and select Type > Bulleted and Numbered Lists > Apply Bullets. Adjust the text frame so that each line with bullets is only on one line, and then center the frame box in the document.

7. To create the text fields to put the information in, using the Type Tool (T), drag a text frame box with no Stroke or Fill about one-half inch height and 1-inch wide on the left side aligning with the top of the kayaker image. Use the Option/ALT key and the Smart Guides to duplicate and space evenly four additional boxes.

8. Type in the first box "Name"; second box, "Address"; third box, "City or Town"; fourth box, "State and Zip"; and last box, "Email" as shown in Figure 12-46. Use the Align Center in the Text Frame Options box (Object > Text Frame Options > Align: Center) to center the vertical height of each.

9. To create the form fields to enter data, using the Rectangle Tool (M), drag a box with 2-pt black Stroke and either white or a light color Fill (choose your own color), about 2½ inches wide by one-half (0.5) inches in height, aligning with the first Name box. As was done previously, duplicate the boxes and now you have your fields ready. Use the Type Tool (T) afterwards to click in each text box to indicate they will be text fields. Use the Control panel if any adjustments need to be made.

10. Save the file as *PDF Form.indd* in your *Chapter 12 > Chapter 12 Extra* folder.

CREATING INTERACTIVE TEXT FIELDS USING THE BUTTONS AND FORMS PANEL

In order for you to enter information electronically, you need to have the text field created using the Buttons and Forms panel. How you make it interactive is also determined by the event you choose. There are also PDF options available to set up security for input of information and sharing. For this exercise it would be that when you tap your mouse in the box, you can type in information.

1. Select the Buttons and Forms panel (Window > Interactive > Buttons and Forms).

2. On your document, using the Selection Tool (V), select the empty box you created next to the Name field.

3. Select Type: Text Field and Event: On Release or Tap. Make sure in the Name box on the Buttons and Forms panel you type in "Name" to identify it as which text field it is.

4. On your document, select the empty box you created next to the Address field.

5. In the Buttons and Forms panel, select Type: Text Field and Event: On Release or Tap. Identify your text field by typing in "Address" next to Name (Figure 12-48).

6. Repeat the same process with the City, State and Zip, and Email boxes.

7. The completed boxes will also display an icon indicating they are created as input text fields.

▷ FIGURE 12-48

Creating the text fields to input information electronically.

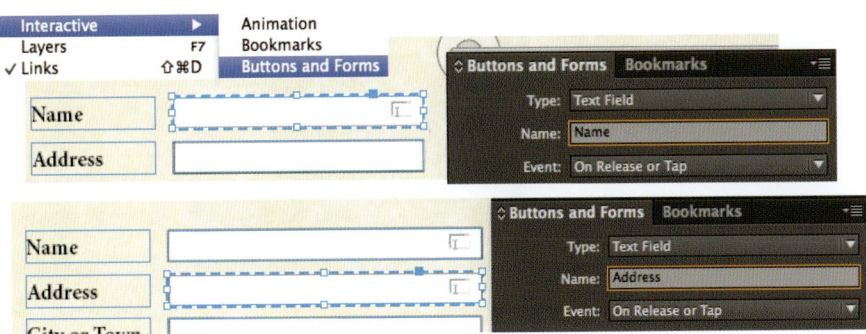

CREATING AN INTERACTIVE SUBMIT BUTTON

The Buttons and Forms panel has a panel menu that allows you to select premade interactive buttons and icons to use in your design. As was done in creating the text fields for your form, you can determine what happens as an Event when you choose to "Click "on the button by setting what is called an action. In this case you will create an action that will allow you to put in your email address using the "mailto:" command for a web browser to identify, to send the completed form to your designated email address.

1. From the Buttons and Forms panel menu, select Sample Buttons And Forms. Choose a rounded rectangle deep red button (we chose number 126) and drag it to the bottom center of the document, just below the margin line.

2. Select the Type Tool (T), with a 12-pt yellow Arial Black font to make it stand out, and type "Submit."

3. Center the text horizontally in the button shape using the Control panel and the Align: Center command in the Text Frame Options menu (Object > Text Frame Options > Align: Center).

4. Using the Selection Tool (V), select the button and you'll notice it displays options in the Buttons and Forms panel. Change the Name by typing in "Submit," and select the Event: On Click.

5. To add the Action to set up the email, click on the "+" symbol next to Actions, and then select Go to URL. Type "mailto:" to identify that it is email URL, and type in your own email address (mailto:name@email.com).

6. Uncheck the eye icon next to Rollover in the Appearance section, leaving just the Normal setting to keep the button the same (Figure 12-49). We'll create rollovers in the next section. Make sure your email address is still in the Normal appearance state.

Remove eye icon

▷ FIGURE 12-49

Creating a special Submit button to send form to a designated email address.

7. Your submit button is now ready.

8. Save the file as *PDF Form.indd* in your *Chapter 12 Extra* folder to serve as the original backup before you convert the form to PDF in the next exercise.

EXPORTING THE DOCUMENT AS AN INTERACTIVE PDF FORM

Here's where you will test your form. To set the document as an interactive PDF, you use the Export command to Adobe PDF (Interactive) to create an accurate PDF. Once the file is saved as an interactive PDF, you can open it in Adobe Reader, fill out the text fields, and then click the Submit button in any version to send the form to your designated email address.

1. With the form created, select File > Export > Adobe PDF (Interactive). Save as *PDF FORM.pdf* in capital letters in your *Chapter 12 Extra* folder (Figure 12-50). Select Save.

2. When the Export to Interactive PDF dialog box opens, make sure Forms and Media: Include All is checked, and do not check Open in Full Screen Mode (Figure 12-50). Leave the rest at their defaults and click OK.

▷ FIGURE 12-50

Exporting the registration form as an interactive PDF.

3. The form should automatically open in Adobe Reader, or you can simply launch Adobe Reader and open the file. You can input the text info to test it, and with all versions you can click on the submit button to send the form to your designated email address.

4. If the address doesn't work when submitting, check in the Buttons and Forms panel to make sure the mailto: and your address is typed correctly.

5. You are now ready to create a more complicated form using the Buttons and Forms panel.

CREATING A SPECIALIZED INTERACTIVE PDF DOCUMENT

In this section you will create a special interactive PDF document that provides specific buttons to access a website, a word document, the map document, and the registration form document you previously created. You will create buttons from scratch and use the Buttons and Forms panel to create specific events and behaviors when the mouse hovers over the button, and when the button is clicked.

Here you will create an interactive PDF document with buttons. You will set up the document with the *Kayak Ad* file you worked on in Chapter 5 without the sale text items, and then lay out guides for the buttons (Figure 12-51).

▷ FIGURE 12-51

Completed specialized buttons in interactive PDF document.

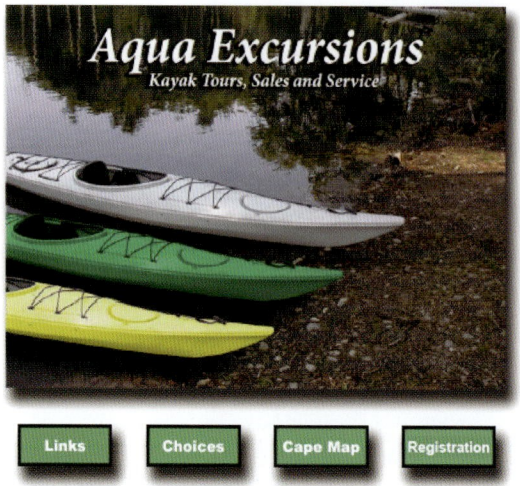

1. Change the workspace setting on your Application bar from Essentials to Interactivity to set up the appropriate panels. Set Preferences to Inches, and create a new letter size print document in landscape orientation with one column; set default margins at a half inch all around. Leave Facing Pages and Primary Text Frame unchecked, because this will be a single document. Select OK. Make sure Smart Guides is selected.

2. Name the file *PDF Ad.indd* and place it in the folder *Chapter 12 Extra* in the *Chapter 12* folder. Make sure at the bottom of the document window next to the green circle that you have enabled Preflight options to have the document checked dynamically as you add text and graphics.

3. Drag Horizontal guidelines at the 5.5-, 6-, and 6.5-inch marks. Drag vertical guidelines at the 2-inch and 9-inch marks to center the image and at 2.25-, 3.5-, 4-, 5.25-, 5.75-, 7-, 7.5-, and 8.75-inch marks to place the buttons.

4. Using the Rectangle Frame Tool (F), drag a rectangular frame in between the 2-inch and 9-inch guides to the 5.5-inch horizontal guide to place the image.

5. Optional: You can choose to launch Photoshop and open the *KayakAd* image you worked on in Chapter 5, creating a duplicate copy and removing the sale text lines, leaving the title and subtitle to identify the ad. Choose File > Place to place the image in the rectangular frame centered horizontally. If you want, you can select the title lines and italicize them as show in Figure 12-52.

6. The adjusted *Kayak Ad* file is located in the *Chapter 12 Extra* folder within the *Chapter 12* folder if you do not wish to perform step 5. Choose File > Place to place the image in the rectangular frame centered horizontally inside the frame (Figure 12-52).

7. Save the file.

Layout guides for image and buttons. Placing an image centered in the document.

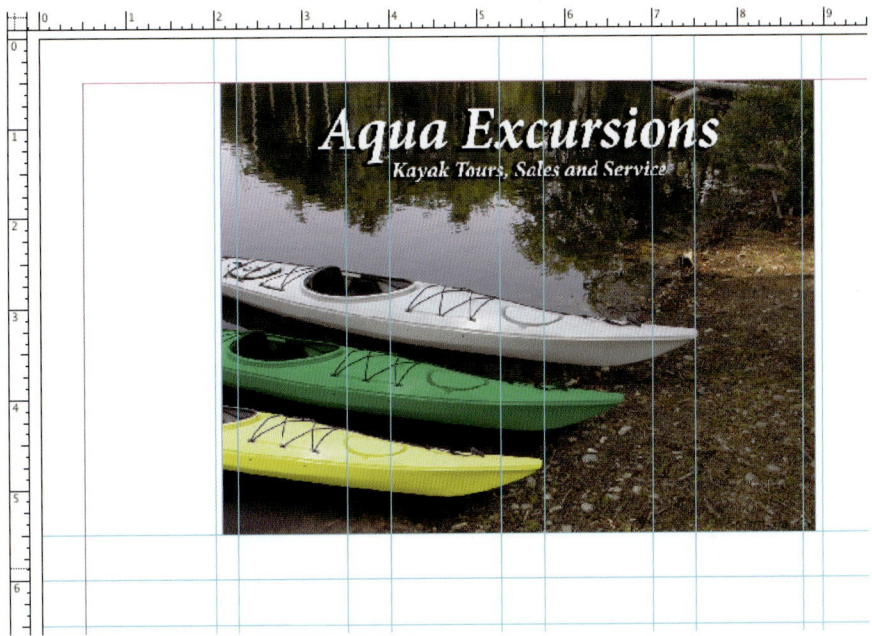

CREATING INTERACTIVE BUTTONS

The **Buttons and Forms panel** (Window > Interactive > Buttons and Forms) allows you to create interactive buttons for your document, and special forms. After creating a button, you make it interactive by selecting various **Appearances** or **States** to see what chosen Events need to occur with the mouse when it is either over the graphic (Rollover), away from the graphic (Normal), or clicking the graphic (Click). **Rollovers** are a change state that occurs when your mouse hovers over the button or graphic (Figure 12-53). You can change how text displays and other states when the mouse is over, clicking the button, and so on. Although the button icons display when creating these graphics, they are only guides and will not appear. There are a couple of ways to create buttons; creating your own shapes or by using the panel menu's Sample Buttons panel, which includes a number of pre-created buttons that you drag into your document, access these through the Buttons and Forms panel menu. To put in text headings, you need to create a text frame, type in the button name, then use the Character Formatting icon on the Control panel and the Text Frame Options command in the Object menu to center the text.

When creating your own interactive shape buttons, you will sample the green kayak color with the Eyedropper Tool (I), and then create rollover states that change the color of text for each button (Figure 12-53).

1. With the *PDF Ad* document open, select the Rectangle Tool (M) and drag between the 6-inch and 6.5-inch horizontal guides in between the 2.25-inch and 3.5-inch vertical guides.

Eyedropper Tool

▷ FIGURE 12-53

Creating rollover states for interactive buttons when the mouse is over the button graphic.

2. Select the Stroke color box on the Tools panel; then using the Stroke panel apply a black, 3-pt stroke; click to put the Fill color in front in the Tools panel.

3. Select the Eyedropper Tool (I) and sample the green kayak color to fill in the button.

4. Option/ALT copy the graphic to position the other three buttons equidistant from one another using the Smart Guides, Smart Spacing, and Smart Dimension features.

5. Select Window > Interactive > Buttons and Forms to bring up the Buttons and Forms panel.

6. Select the first graphic button with the Selection Tool (V), and click in the frame with the Type Tool (T). Using Arial Bold as the font, or another wide sans-serif font, type "Links" in a 14-pt size, choosing a white or light color to stand out over the green button color.

7. Center the text by choosing Center Align in the Character Formatting icon on the Control panel; then center vertically using the Text Frame Option command from the Object menu.

8. With the Links button selected, in the Buttons and Forms panel, select Type: Button, which will display the light text in the Appearance "Normal" state, as shown in Figure 12-53. If it does not, click outside the button with the Selection Tool (V), and then click the button again to bring up the Buttons and Forms panel. Name the button *Links* and make sure the Event is set at On Release or Tap.

9. In the Buttons and Forms panel menu, select the Rollover state for Appearance and select On Roll Over as the Event in the Buttons and Forms panel. With that Appearance highlighted, select the *Links* text line on the button and change the color to yellow or choose your own color as the Rollover state. Select the button with the Selection Tool (V); then select the two states in the Buttons and Forms panel to see how the button text changes.

10. Change the second Button name to *Choices*, third Button to *Cape Map*, and fourth Button to *Registration* (Figure 12-53). Repeat the same process in steps 6 through 9 with the other three buttons, creating rollover states. We'll create Actions (Behaviors) for each button in the next exercise.

11. Save the file.

SETTING BUTTON ACTIONS

Actions in InDesign identify what a button will do when it is selected with the mouse (open a document, locate a URL, play a movie, etc.). After creating a button, it makes good sense to determine the behavior of the button using the Actions display in the Buttons panel. This is what makes the document interactive. When you are locating documents or files that are *not* saved as PDFs, you will need to make sure you select Enable: All Documents to make all documents eligible for inclusion in the document when you locate these files. Files that are saved as PDFs will appear as Bookmarks as part of multiple PDF documents. InDesign allows you to Export multiple documents as PDFs, creating a Bookmark for each page.

Now you will link to a website, locate a document and the map illustration, and set up to play a sound file.

1. For the first button, you will link to a website for kayak resources. Select the *Links* button graphic with the Selection Tool (V), and then choose On Click, in the Event drop down list. Select the Click layer, and make sure the text of the selected Links panel is the same color as when it is a Rollover state; in our case we chose yellow. The Click state is set. In the Name box, type in the name "Links" if it is not already indicated in the Appearance box on the Buttons panel.

2. To set the action when the Links button is clicked, click on the "plus sign" in the Actions display on the Actions tab to locate the file. In the Actions drop-down list, select Go To URL and type in a local sporting site you may be familiar with or Google "kayak resources" to find a website you can use (make sure you type in "http://" before the address in the URL text box). You've created an action to locate the website upon clicking on the Links button (Figure 12-54).

3. To create the action that locates the File *Choosing.doc*, which contains information in choosing a kayak, when the button Choices is clicked, repeat the same process again from step 2, selecting the Choices button graphic to bring up the Buttons and Forms panel. In the Name box, change the name to *Choices* if it is not already indicated.

Links Button settings   Choices Button settings

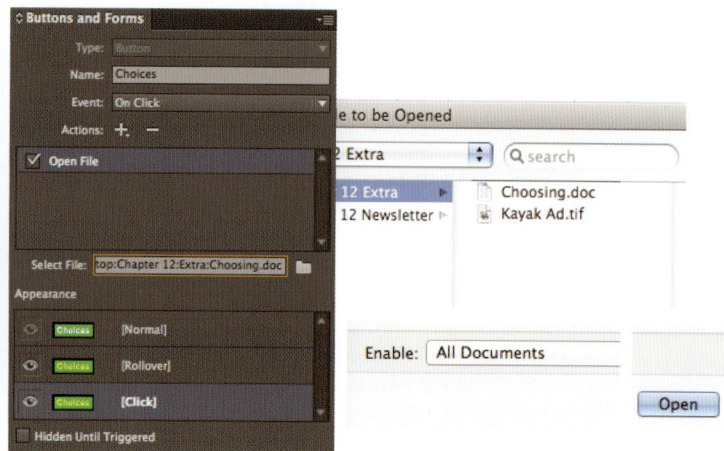

▷ FIGURE 12-54

Creating an action for Links and Choices buttons to locate URL and a document when clicked.

4. In the Actions drop-down list, select Open File; then click the folder in the Select File box to locate the *Choosing.doc* file in your *Chapter 12 Extra* folder. Select Enable: All Documents, to make all documents eligible, and then select Open to set up the link (Figure 12-54).

5. In the Control panel, when most any drawing or selection tool is active you can add special effects like drop shadows to your selected buttons (see Figure 12-55).

Cape Map Button settings   Registration Button settings

Special effects and functions

▷ FIGURE 12-55

Creating actions for the Cape Map and Registration buttons.

TOOLKIT TIP To deactivate actions (or behaviors), make sure the check box is deselected next to the action. You can change the order by dragging and dropping actions just as is done with layers.

6. Click on the graphic button Cape Map. Select the Buttons and Forms panel.

7. Locate the *Cape Map.indd* document you just created in the *Chapter 12 Extra* folder, and follow the same procedures as done with the Choosing button to add the action of locating the file when clicked to the button. Select Enable: All Documents to make all documents eligible (Figure 12-55). In the Name display on the Buttons and Forms panel, change the name to Cape Map if it is not already indicated.

8. For the fourth Registration button, you will need to select to open the file as done previously and locate the *PDF FORM.pdf* file in the *Chapter 12 Extra* folder. Make sure you have selected Enable: All Documents to make all documents eligible (Figure 12-55).

9. Save the file; it is time to check your efforts.

EXPORTING THE DOCUMENT AS AN INTERACTIVE PDF

Now that the buttons have been created with rollover states and events are set up, it is time to use the Export command to set the document to be created as an interactive PDF. It is important again to make sure all files are located in the same place as the document at this point. In order to play a sound file or a movie file, you must make sure when exporting the document that the Buttons and Media: Include All is checked, which you can save as a distinct Interactive PDF. With older versions when you export, make sure the Interactive Elements options is checked. For compatibility specify the appropriate PDF version and then click the Export command in the File menu. Then all you have to do is open the document using the free Adobe Reader that you can download off the Adobe website, click on the buttons, and step into the future of electronic documents!

 TOOLKIT TIP To play movies and sound clips, the computer in use must have QuickTime 6 or later installed. Use the Help menu and feel free to try creating a movie button from a movie file.

It is time to export your document to create an interactive PDF.

1. With the buttons created, select File > Export, Adobe PDF (Interactive). Save As *PDF Ad* in your *Chapter 12 Extra* folder with Format set as Adobe PDF Interactive format. Select Save.

2. When the Export to Interactive PDF dialog box opens, make sure you check Forms and Media: Include All, and do not check Open in Full Screen Mode. Click OK. For earlier versions, when the Export Adobe PDF dialog box displays, select Smallest File Size for the Adobe PDF Preset, as if the document would be sent over email or the Internet with Compatibility of Acrobat 6.0.

3. In the Include section, click check marks next to Hyperlinks, Bookmarks, and Interactive Elements. Click Export.

4. To check your work, launch Adobe Reader, and click on the buttons. You will notice that as you move the mouse over the button, the text will rollover to the new color you selected in the Buttons panel earlier. One word of caution: Open the Registration: *PDF FORM.pdf* last, because it is a PDF and replaces the interactive document you have just opened.

5. Have fun and try to create or change links for the buttons. All you have to do is make the changes and save the document to replace the existing PDF.

TOOLKIT TIP InDesign CC provides the ability to create intuitive hyperlinks, by simply right-clicking the selected text line to find commands to create and test hyperlinks. Desingers can manage hyperlinks and edit their names using the improved Hyperlink panel (**Window > Interactive > Hyperlinks**). Automatic styling features helps to easily spot hyperlinks within a given layout. InDesign CC also provides improved EPUB activity with special pop up footnote creations in electronic documents with a single tap.

INDESIGN'S GAP TOOL

The Gap Tool (U) provides a quick way to adjust the size of a gap or resize between multiple items that have commonly aligned edges all at once, while keeping the gaps between them fixed. The Gap Tool (U) ignores Master Page items and locked items so you can work freely to adjust multiple items around your white space area, instead of having to individually select page items and resize them. You use the Gap Tool (U) by hovering your mouse over the gap area you want to adjust, and then clicking and dragging to resize the items aligned to the gap. The gap is highlighted with transparent gray shading.

Although it is not necessary for this project, to give you an idea of the power of this tool, try to adjust the gap between the buttons and the image. You can use the Gap Tool (U) to drag between the action buttons you just created and the image dimensions to a set amount. You can also click between the buttons to resize between each button universally. Feel free to use the same *PDF Ad.indd* file you just created, go ahead and play with this tool, close when finished, and *do not save* the file unless you save as a different name. Create a series of aligned squares and try this tool. Have fun!

CHAPTER SUMMARY

You have just completed the most intensive chapter in the book. Not only did you work with creating master pages, layout graphics, and text components, along with formatting automated features like jump lines and automatic page numbering, but you also worked in the pica and points measurement format as opposed to the inches measurement you are probably more accustomed to. You learned an abundance of terminology used extensively in the desktop publishing and printing industries, you created rules and pull quotes, tabbed precisely for alignment of data and definitions, and threaded text between multiple columns and multiple pages. In the Advanced Users section, you learned to align text lines to a baseline grid for consistency across columns, automated formatting tasks using character and paragraph styles, and created object libraries for graphics, text, and the front page of the newsletter to be used in future documents. You also created alternate layouts and used the techniques of Liquid Layout to understand the use of fluid design technology with today's electronic publishing market.

REVIEW QUESTIONS

1. Explain the difference between spot and process colors.

2. What is the purpose of creating master pages?

3. Explain three uses of the Pages panel.

4. Explain the process of semi-autoflow of text into multiple text frames.

5. What is the overset symbol used for?

6. What is the difference between a widow and an orphan in desktop publishing?

7. What are jump lines?

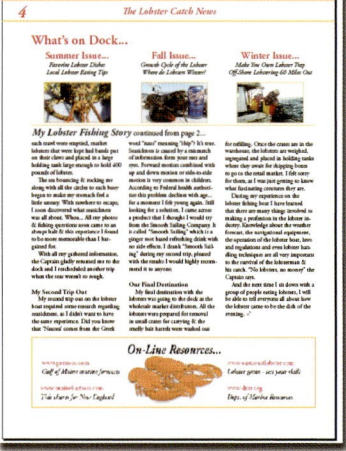

Newsletter text and photos courtesy of Shelly Britton.

▷ FIGURE 12-56

Baseline Alignment

Styles

Object libraries

Master Page (B) created
from iPhone alternate layout

Original iPad layout

iPhone
(converted as alternate layout)

CHAPTER 12 ADVANCED
Special editing techniques
and designing alternate layouts.

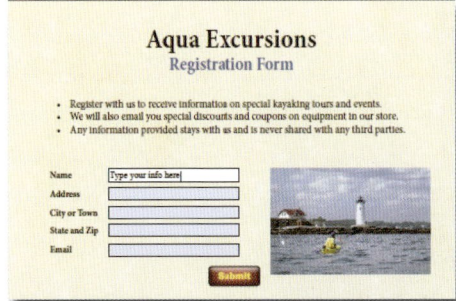

CHAPTER 12 EXTRA
Creating interactive PDF
documents using InDesign.

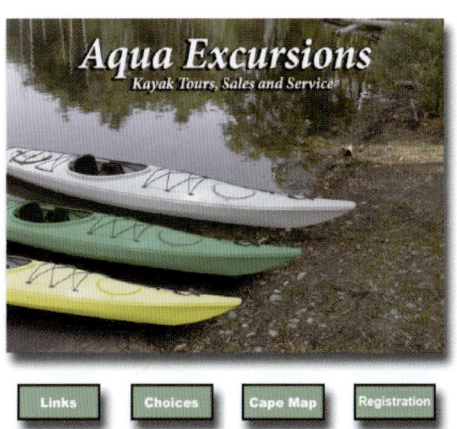

Newsletter text and photos courtesy of Shelly Britton.

▷ FIGURE 12-57

4

Digital Publishing: InDesign CC

One of the more popular assignments you will receive as a designer is creating brochures for clients. Here you will see how to set up and position guides, images, and text for a three-way folding brochure, or tri-fold. You will also use the map you completed in Illustrator in Chapter 8 and the images of the kayaks you completed in Photoshop in Chapter 5 to understand how using all the applications you have been working with interrelates in the creation and placement of imagery and text for specific purposes.

CLIENT ASSIGNMENT: Creating a Tri-fold Brochure

Alyce Powell, for whom you have previously created a direct mail ad piece for her business, Aqua Excursions, wants to create a tri-fold brochure to promote the business's kayak tours and kayak sales and service. She discusses using the brochure for display at various retail stores, restaurant establishments, and other places that promote local tourism. In discussing the layout of the brochure, she mentions that she wants the sections divided into the front section for the basic business information, the back section to display the directions and special tours, and the other sections to provide a business summary, information on various tours, special events, FAQs, and pricing for rentals. The brochure will contain various images for different types of kayak enthusiasts and will be printed commercially on glossy coated paper using four-color CMYK processing. Two fonts will be used, Myriad Pro Bold for the headlines and subheadlines, and Adobe Garamond Pro Regular for the body text. After getting her approval on a final rough you created, Alyce looks forward to the finished proof (Figure UR4-1).

Tour FAQs

How early do I need to get there?
You should arrive twenty minutes prior to your departure time so as not to delay the group.

Can we use our own equipment in any tour?
We are fully insured and we do offer a $10 discount if you have your own kayak and equipment.

What should paddlers bring?
Non alcoholic beverage or water, sun screen, shorts, extra T-shirt, shoes or sandals that will get wet, light rain gear, hat and some snacks.

How do I reserve my tour?
A 50% deposit is required to hold reservations and we do accept Visa/MasterCard. We have a 24-hour cancellation policy but reserve the right to cancel a reserved trip due to circumstances beyond our control like poor weather. Any cancellations will be cheerfully refunded.

Purchasing Your Boat

The process of selecting a canoe or kayak can be an overwhelming experience. Purchasing a boat involves a progressive process. For many consumers, their first boat is chosen as a result of the condition of each individual's developing interests and skills as a paddler. Begin looking for a boat by honestly determining:

- Why do you want to paddle?
- When do you want to paddle?
- Where do you want to paddle?

Here at **Aqua Excursions**, we'll help you to decide which boat is right for you and we provide workshops for you to not only learn the essentials of kayaking, but to try out different boats to find one that fits your needs and style. We provide service and repair to our boats. We carry wet suits, paddles, dry bags, regulation PFDs and camping gear. For kayaks we carry Necky, Perception, Ocean Kayak, and Wilderness Systems.

Special Tours

We offer informative, casual guided tours available upon request. We can customize a tour to fit your needs and experience. Call for scheduling.

Corporate Team Building Adventures
Get out of the office and see the other side of your staff as they enjoy special private guided tours. Call for scheduling.

Annual Cape Lighthouse Bus Tour
Join us in our three-day and two night's tour to visit all the coastal beacons on Cape Cod in Massachusetts during the month of August. You'll take lots of pictures and meet great friends.

Cape Cod Lighthouses

Provincetown, Truro, Eastham, Barnstable, Pocasset, Chatham, Hyannis, Monomoy Is., Woods Hole

Aqua Excursions Directions
From Route 95 take Route 1 from the Portsmouth rotary. Take a left on Ocean Road. Follow until you come to the harbor.

123 Ocean Road • Portsmouth NH 03801
508.555.1234
aquaexcursions.com

Aqua Excursions
Kayak Tours, Sales, and Service

123 Ocean Road • Portsmouth NH 03801 • 603-555-1234

A tour package for every taste...

Welcome to Aqua Excursions

We would like to welcome you to the exciting sport of kayaking. Our guides will instruct you in the basics of the sport and provide you with 2-4 hours of special adventures along the bay, along the ocean shoreline, and even in a quiet pond for those who just want to relax. The beautiful New England ecosystem in both a lake and ocean coastal environment provides a unique setting to explore this area rich in its natural beauty and maritime history up close with kayaks and canoes. We are fully insured to provide you with a safe and rewarding experience while enjoying this exciting sport.

Lessons
We also provide workshops to help you learn to enjoy the kayak and canoeing experience. Our specialists provide basic and advanced workshops for lake and ocean kayaking to help you feel comfortable and safe on the water. All lessons include kayak and equipment or feel free to bring your own.

Rentals
Take a daily or weekly rental to your favorite spot along the coastal shoreline or on your favorite lake. Includes kayak, paddle, personal floatation device, and delivery/pick up.

1/2 day (4 hours) (9am-1pm or 1pm-5pm) = $25.
Full day (8 hours) (9am-5pm) = $45.

Guided Wildlife Tours
These tours provide a relaxing view of natural wildlife and helps kayakers learn the basics of kayaking. Most tours can be taken with people who are considered beginners. Each trip includes boat and equipment.

The Wentworth Special
This tour is great for families. You'll be taken through Newcastle harbor outside of Portsmouth through quiet tidal waters while being introduced to the basics of sea kayaking.

Inland River (Salmon Falls)
This trip takes you up through the historical shipping lanes of the Piscataqua River to Dover, NH. The narrow river passage lets paddlers experience wild life up close as they head to the mills built in the 1800s.

Willand Pond Fishing Tour
This trip is for the beginner or the person who just wants to have a relaxing ride or fish along the pond with lots of wildlife. Canoes are also welcome on this excursion.

Ocean Adventure Tours
These tours are for intermediate paddlers who are at least 16 years of age and can paddle for 6 or more miles. Enjoy the beauty of coastal ocean kayaking and the smell of the sweet salty air. Each trip includes boat and equipment.

Lighthouse Tour
Enjoy coastal paddling along the Newcastle Island shoreline and experience the unique view of Portsmouth Harbor Lighthouse as sailboat and fishing boats go by. Depending on the conditions during low tide we may be able to paddle to nearby Whaleback Light and Jerry's Light station and have a picnic.

Sunset Tour
This tour allow you to watch the beauty of the sun setting along the coastal shoreline as you kayak through the quiet waters of inner Newcastle harbor area, just outside of Portsmouth. This trip gives you a wonderful experience to get you familiar with sea kayaking. You may even be able to enjoy outdoor theater arts at Prescott Park as you pass by.

▷ FIGURE UR4-1

Created tri-fold brochure.

ACTION ITEMS OVERVIEW

Here is a breakdown of what needs to be done to complete the tri-fold brochure.

- Create a folding dummy to show the layout and placement of graphics and text.

- For the master page, create a green color bar for the top and a gold color bar for the bottom for framing using Pantone color selections to add in the Swatches panel.

- Import graphics onto both pages and adjust them according to guides. (You can also use two images from previous projects you created in earlier chapters or use alternative images in the review folder.)

- Import and format text and create character and paragraph styles to apply formatting easily for a more productive workflow.

- Save the file as an InDesign document and as a template for future use and prepare the document for press.

SETTING UP THE BROCHURE PROJECT

After discussion with the client and designing thumbnails and roughs, a designer should have a pretty good idea of what the final project will look like in the overall layout of the piece. Before laying out text and graphic items, preferences need to be set, and the final size and margins need to be set up.

CREATING AND ORGANIZING FOLDERS FOR PRESS

When you send your materials to a commercial printer or web designer, you need to keep all documents, images, and fonts in folders to be included with your InDesign document in one main folder. Any font you use in a document should also be copied into a *Fonts* folder along with text and image folders. This is crucial, otherwise images may not print at full resolution or fonts may be substituted. It is also just as important to keep these folders with your InDesign document on your hard drive or on the same portable medium, like a flash drive or CD. All changes or saves to files will be made in these folders. InDesign provides preflight operations and the Package utility to take care of this for you.

Here you will locate the *Unit 4 Review* folder to place your document with the *Images* and *Text* folders in one area.

1. On your drive, locate your *Unit 4 Review* folder inside your *Toolkit > InDesign* folder. This folder already contains the *Images* and *Text* folders with content for the brochure assignment.

2. Here is a look at your directory structure:

   Toolkit > Unit 4 Review > Images/Text. The InDesign brochure project will also be saved inside the *Unit 4 Review* folder. Now you have all your "suitcases" that you will need to transport your work to the service provider.

CREATING A FOLDING DUMMY

To serve as a helpful guide for placement of items, a folding guide, or **folding dummy**, is made to provide a visual reference. This is where you would sketch in headlines and graphic elements, along with the type of fold you will use. This also helps to explain the layout to a client. The brochure that you are creating is based on what is called a *tri-fold design*. A **tri-fold** is simply a document divided into three sections folded toward the center, like a book. The individual sections of the document that are folded are called the **panels**. When designers create a folding document, they need to take into consideration the placement of items and text for easy reading and to keep the attention of the reader. The blank space between the columns is called the *gutter width.* For the brochure project, it also serves as the folding area. As shown in Figure UR4-2, you will notice that in the outside document, the front title piece is located on the far right panel, and the back piece is located in the center column.

▷ FIGURE UR4-2

Creating a folding dummy to observe layout, folds, and placement of graphics and text headlines.

DESIGN TIP

When designing
folded brochures,
placement of the
business name and
information is cre-
ated on the far right
panel of the first
page document.
The center panel
on page 1 describes
factual or special
information, hours
of operation, direc-
tions, or a business
summary or state-
ment. The far left
panel is folded to the
inside and is used to
promote specialty
items or events. The
three panels on page
2 describe the busi-
ness, what is being
offered, and what
the reader will find.

Here is how to make a folding dummy as a guide.

1. Place two pieces of 14 x 8.5 inch paper (legal size) and position length-wise (landscape).

2. Divide evenly and fold the left and right pieces into the center.

3. Sketch the headings as shown in Figure UR4-2 on both pages. Here is your guide.

INCH PREFERENCES AND NEW DOCUMENT SETTINGS

Setting preferences provides a convenient way to adjust settings and parameters in your work environment to work on your document productively. Because there is not much call for precise measurement here, we will use inches as the preferred measurement. If you would like to use picas, feel free to make the conversions. Preferences can be changed anytime while working on the document. Units of measure can be changed on the fly by holding down the Option/ALT key and clicking on the rulers. In Mac OS X, the InDesign Application menu is where you would set Preferences; in Windows, Preferences are set in the Edit menu. For the brochure project document settings, you will be creating two, nonfacing pages in landscape orientation with three columns. The two pages will constitute the inside portion of the brochure and the outside portion, and the pages will be set in legal size, 8.5 x 14 inch paper, to provide room for the graphics and text content to make the brochure stand out (Figure UR4-3).

▷ FIGURE UR4-3

**New document
settings for tri-
fold brochure.**

Here you will set up the measurements preferences to inches for your brochure.

1. Launch InDesign. In Mac OS X, select InDesign > Preferences > Units & Increments, and in Windows use Edit > Preferences > Units & Increments.

2. Change the Ruler Units for Horizontal and Vertical document measurements to Inches.

3. Leave all other defaults as shown. Select OK. Change the workspace to Essentials to bring up the panels that will be mostly used for this project.

4. Select File > New > Document to open the New Document display box.

5. Select Intent of Print. Select Page Size: Legal with Landscape Orientation (right side icon). The size will display as 14 x 8.5 inch paper. Enter one page for now.

6. To set the Margin Guides as 0.375 (⅜) inches all around, type in 0.375 in the first box, and click the link icon. Enter "3" for the number of columns.

7. Set the Gutter width at 0.75 inches. Uncheck the Facing Pages option and uncheck the Primary (Master) Text Frame, because we are not creating a bound book or magazine with long text articles. Maintain a 0.125-inch Bleed on all sides of the document.

8. Click on OK. Make sure Smart Guides is checked. At the bottom of the window of your document, choose to have Preflight Document checked from the Preflight menu. Display the Preflight panel (Window > Output > Preflight).

9. Save the document in your *Unit 4 Review* folder as *Brochure.indd*.

CREATING COLOR BARS FOR THE TOP AND BOTTOM

Color bars help frame a document with a particular color theme, like we did in the newsletter project last chapter. To match the outdoor theme, you will create a green color bar across the top margin and a gold color bar across the bottom margin. This green color theme will also be used for text headings and subheadings, with the gold for an initial drop cap. Because these will be considered graphics, you will use the Rectangle Frame Tool (F) and select the colors from the Pantone Swatch library. You will create the color bars in the master page section to be used for the second page as well. As you add new colors to the Swatches panel, they are also added in the swatches pop-up menu in the Control panel for quick access. Note: Pantone color libraries have been updated with the new Pantone Plus series of colors since InDesign CC. Choices for this and earlier versions are provided.

Now you will create the top and bottom color bars for the master page template. You will need to select the appropriate colors from the Swatch panel library first.

1. With the A-Master displayed (double-click A-Master in the Pages panel to activate the Master Page template) to create the color bars on a master template, select the Swatches panel (Window > Color > Swatches). Choose New Color Swatch in the Swatches panel menu.

2. In the display make sure the Color Type is Process, and then from the Color Mode list, choose Pantone + CMYK Coated, for InDesign CC and CS6, and Pantone Process coated for earlier versions as the library from which to choose.

DESIGN TIP

When setting gutter width, usually look at doubling the margin width as a starting point to accommodate folding, in this case 0.375 (⅜) inches doubled makes 0.75 (¾) inches.

▷ FIGURE UR4-4

Selecting Pantone color bars and headings.

3. For a green color select Pantone P 146-6 C for InDesign CC or CS6 version, (Pantone DS 284-2 C for previous versions), as shown in Figure UR4-4. Select the Add button and the color you choose will automatically be added to the Swatches panel.

4. For a gold color, add Pantone P 7-16 C for InDesign CC and CS6 (or DS 6-2 C for previous versions), to the Swatches panel. With both colors added, click on the Done button in the dialog box to indicate you have finished your choices.

5. To create a color group of your new colors, highlight both Pantone colors, then click the New Color Group icon on the Swatches panel. Rename the group as *Brochure*.

6. Select the rectangle Frame Tool (F) and drag across the top of the document from the margin to extend the frame to the bleed dimension an eighth inch away from the document's left, right, and top edges. Drag downward to the 0.375-inch margin line.

7. Choose the green Pantone P 146-6 C for CC and CS6 (or Pantone 284-2 C for previous versions) as the Fill color with a Stroke of None.

8. Select the Rectangle Frame Tool (F) and drag from the bottom margin to bleed out beyond the document edge. Choose Pantone P 7-16 C (or DS 6-2 C) as the Fill color from the Swatches panel with a Stroke of None.

9. Select the Layers panel, and rename the *Layer 1* default layer to *Page 1* to keep track of graphics and text frames. Save the file.

ADDING A PAGE TO YOUR DOCUMENT

You can add another page to your document by selecting the A-Master page and dragging it to the document level underneath page 1. Or click the Create New Page icon in the lower right corner of the Pages panel.

1. In the Pages panel, to add another page based on the A-master, select the A-Master in the upper panel and drag below the page 1, and release the mouse (Figure UR4-5). Page 2 will appear with an "A" at the top of the page, indicating that this new page is formatted with the A-Master. With the Pages panel selecting page 2, create a new layer in the Layers panel and name it *Page 2*.

▷ FIGURE UR4-5

Creating a new page based on the master page by clicking and dragging under the first document.

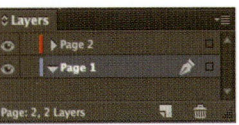

Create new page ▲

2. Click page 1 in the Layers panel to continue with the next exercises.

SETTING LAYOUT GUIDES AND ADJUSTING THE ZERO POINT

Designers use guides consistently to lay out various text and picture items with precision. Margin guides use purple lines as a default and are what you created previously in the initial set up. Layout guides are green in color and are guidelines dragged out from the top and left side rulers. To start your document with the margin edges set at a **zero point** for easier measuring, you can drag from the upper left-hand corner where the rulers intersect, and then release the mouse where the margins themselves intersect (Figure UR4-6). You can also use the zero point to set the measurements from where the margins intersect.

▷ FIGURE UR4-6

Setting zero point guides to measure from the margins instead of the edge of the document.

Zero point guide-
start at document edges

Drag for corner to
intersecting margins

Here you will set up the zero-point guides inside the margins as a point of reference for measurement and create guides to align picture and text boxes for the front and back of the first page.

1. Double-click document A-1 (page 1) in the Pages panel. Select Page 1 in the Layers panel.

2. To make sure the rulers are displayed, you should see left and topside rulers outside your document. If you do not, select View > Show Rulers; it will toggle to display the rulers.

3. To make sure that boxes easily snap to the guides, select View > Grids & Guides > Snap to Guides to make sure a check mark displays; if one does not, click it.

4. To create the zero point, click the box in the upper left corner where the two rulers intersect (dotted lines crossed) and drag to the intersection of the two margin guides. The zero point will remain in that position for document A-2 (page 2).

5. For guides to place upper and lower color bars, and for placement of the images on the first page for the front and back of the brochure, drag horizontal guides to place the logo image, select document A-1 in the Pages panel, click on the top ruler bar, and drag the horizontal guideline down to the 3.25, 3.75, 4.125, and 6-inch marks, or type in the Y coordinates for precision.

6. Draw one vertical guide in the center of the gutter between the first and second columns for a vertical rule later, or type "4.3" in the X-coordinate box.

7. Draw a second vertical line in the center of the gutter between the second and third columns to use as a guide for bleeding the images. Type "8.95" in the X-coordinate box. Both vertical guides serve as folding marks.

8. Save the file.

DESIGNING THE FRONT, BACK, AND SPECIAL PANELS (PAGE 1)

Use the paper folding guide you created earlier as a guide. The outside document, which is set up as Page 1 or document A-1 in InDesign, includes the brochure front, back, and specialty information panels. In designing this document, keep in mind that the "front page" panel of this tri-fold will be on the right side, and the "back" will be in the center of this tri-fold. The front panel identifies what the document is about; it is the attention-getter that sparks the reader's curiosity to continue reading the rest of the information. In a tri-fold, the back panel located in the center provides information that summarizes or complements the front page, and the specialty page located on the left side may include specialty information to entice the reader to look inside for what the brochure is about. You can also use the image of the kayaks completed in Photoshop (Chapter 5), and the map illustration you completed in Illustrator (Chapter 8) to see how these applications interrelate with one another for their intended purpose.

TOOLKIT TIP InDesign allows you to place layered graphics and edit them using the Links panel. With the application open, say Photoshop with the kayaks, you can make edits such as changing colors, and the changes are also made to the linked graphic in InDesign through the Links panel.

CREATING THE FRONT PANEL

The front panel will contain two images that contrast the type of kayaking offered with the Aqua Excursion logo on the top image. The images will be placed so they overlap into the gutter and bleed off the edge of the document. Here you can use the image of the kayaks you completed in Chapter 5, removing the sale lines, or a similar image from the *Images* folder within the *Unit 4 Review* folder if you prefer. If you are going to use the image of the kayaks, you will need to decrease the size using Photoshop to fit in the window, as a designer would have to do. You will also create a separating color bar between the two images that will display the address and phone number of the business in white text. When adding text in the color bar, you can insert a circle bullet as a special character between the address and phone (Figure UR4-7).

TOOLKIT TIP The images being used are low resolution for educational purposes here and may not appear clear when printed. They will, however, provide a guide as to what to expect in a layout. Normally, when sending images to the press, use a resolution of 300 dpi. Resize images ahead of time before placing them in the graphic frame window.

▷ FIGURE UR4-7

Completed front panel.

Right side front panel

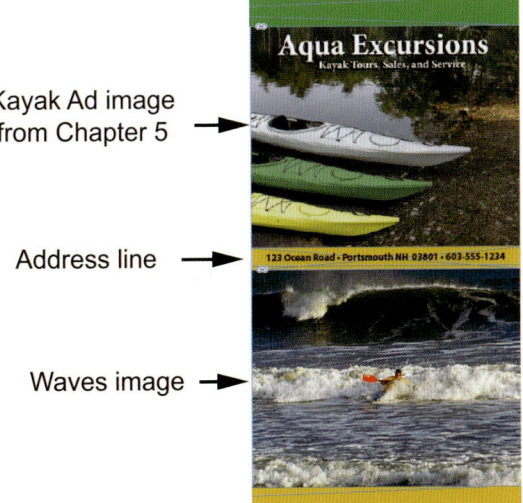

Kayak Ad image from Chapter 5 →

Address line →

Waves image →

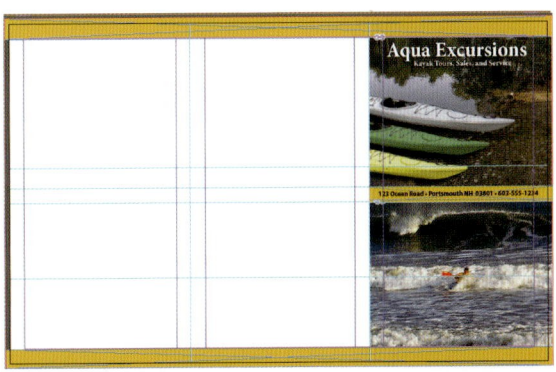

123 Ocean Road • Portsmouth NH 03801 • 603-555-1234

Bullets inserted as spacers between address lines

DESIGN TIP

Usually in most
cases of traditional
tri-fold brochure
design, the front
page is located on
the rightmost side of
the document.

DESIGN TIP

When centering text
lines on documents
with bleed edges,
adjust the inset
spacing usually with
the bleed dimen-
sions within the
frame to compen-
sate for the final
trim to ensure the
finished document
displays the text as
centered accurately.

TOOLKIT TIP If you would like to use the *KayakAD* image you created in Photoshop in Chapter 5, open the image in Photoshop, duplicate the image to make a copy,
remove the sale lines, choose whether to italicize the title lines or leave in their original regular version, resize the image to roughly 5 inches (width), and save the image
in the *Unit 4 Review/Images* folders where your document is. It is also a good habit
to flatten the completed file beforehand, although InDesign will allow layered files.

Next, you will create graphic frames and place the graphics in the front panel.
Then you will create the color bar to put in the business info.

1. Document A-1 (Page 1) should still be selected, but if it is not, display the
   Pages panel and double-click Document A-1, and then scroll to the right side
   of the page to create the front panel. Make sure you have Page 1 selected in
   the Layers panel as well.

2. Using the Rectangle Frame Tool (F), drag three graphic frames with a Stroke and
   Fill color of None: one from the gutter center vertical guide to the red bleed edge
   of the document to the 3.75 guide (providing you still have your zero point set
   on the margins and not at the edge of the document), a second between the
   3.75 and 4.125 guides for the color bar, and a third between the 4.125 guide
   and the bottom margin. Elements that bleed should be extended to the 0.125
   bleed guide outside the document's trim edges.

3. Select the top frame with the Selection Tool (V) and choose File > Place to
   locate the *Kayaks.tif* file in the *Images* folder inside the *Unit 4 Review* folder. The
   image has been resized to about 5.5 inches wide by 4 inches. Try using your
   own kayak image completed from Chapter 5 instead, removing the sale lines
   from the ad, and resizing it to fit in the window, extending the outer edge of
   the image to the bleed guide.

4. Use the Direction Selection Tool (V) to adjust the image so that the title is centered between the column margins.

5. Select the bottom frame and Place the file *Waves.tif* in the frame, adjusting as
   shown in Figure UR4-7.

6. Select the middle frame and fill with the gold color Pantone P 7-16 C (or
   Pantone DS 6-2 C) from the Brochure color group you created.

7. Using the Type Tool (T), drag a text frame inside the bar, choose a 12-pt
   Myriad Pro Bold or similar Bold style font, and type with a black Fill and no
   Stroke, "123 Ocean Road"; Leave a space after "Road" as shown (you can use
   your own address instead).

8. To place a bullet between address lines, select Type > Insert Special Character >
   Symbols > Bullet Character, and a bullet will be placed.

9. After another space, type "Portsmouth NH 03801"; leave a space after the zip,
   and insert another bullet and another space, and then type "603-555-1234";
   center the text horizontally.

10. Because the type line extends to include the 0.125 inch bleed edge, you will need to adjust the right inset spacing to compensate for the bleed so the trimmed brochure will have the text line as properly centered. Select Object > Text Frame Options > Align: Center, to center the type line vertically, then type in 0.125 in the Inset Spacing Right box. Click OK.

11. Your front panel is all set. Save the file.

CREATING THE BACK PANEL

The back panel describes the business, sometimes offers directions or relevant information, and usually provides a special promotion to attract the reader's attention. Here on the back panel, you can use the *Map* image you created in Chapter 8 in Illustrator to promote its annual lighthouse tour. You will also import a text frame into the panel using the Place command. If you are using the map illustration from Chapter 8, you will need to resize it, and save it in an EPS format, or use the alternative image in the *Unit 4 Review* folder.

TOOLKIT TIP When you are unsure of what kind of word processor your client is using, save the text documents as plain documents using either a TXT or RTF extension, which can be opened universally by any word processing application on any computer system (although most people are using Microsoft Word).

TOOLKIT TIP To use the Map image you completed in Illustrator (Chapter 8), resize the image to about 3.5 inches wide. For better accuracy, scale the image at 60% (Object > Transform > Scale), and make sure the Scale Strokes and Effects box is checked. You should also readjust the text to read at 8 pt, and select a few smaller lighthouse symbols to resize. Save it as an EPS file if you are going to use this image for placement into the InDesign document, or you can leave it in its native AI extension. Commercial printers usually accept native files.

DESIGN TIP

The back panel of a traditional tri-fold brochure describes the business, sometimes offers directions or relevant information, and usually provides a special promotion to attract the reader's attention.

DESIGN TIP

Always make the phone number and email address stand out a little by increasing their size or adjusting their color: these are important pieces of information for any business.

First you will place the map graphic, and then place two text documents for the back panel, leaving a top and bottom inset space of 0.125 inches. You will then format the headings. Click OK if a font warning appears when you place the text files (Figure UR4-8).

1. Using the Rectangle Frame Tool (F), drag a graphic frame between the 3.25-inch and the 6-inch horizontal guides and the column margins in the center column; an alternative method would be to click and drag a frame that extends to the guides before placing the image.

2. Select File > Place and import either the map illustration you created in Chapter 8 without bottom text lines and symbols (see previous Toolkit Tip), or the alternative *Map.eps* file in the *Unit 4 Review > Images* folder. For this example we used the Chapter 8 completed map file with filled beach color background here.

▷ FIGURE UR4-8

Completing the back panel using the map illustration and formatting text.

Rear panel   Front panel

3. Use the Selection Tool (V) to center the map in the frame and make slight adjustments to the graphic frame if needed.

4. To import text above the graphic, drag a text frame between the zero and 3.25 guidelines within the column margins with the Type Tool (T) and select File > Place. Locate the *Special.doc* file in the *Text* folder within the *Unit 4 Review* folder and import the text into the frame.

5. Select Object >Text Frame Options and set the Bottom and Top inset spacing to 0.125 (⅛) inches with the right and left at 0. Set the Vertical Justification to Top and select OK.

6. To create a vertical rule between the Special Tours panel and the Tour FAQs panel you will create next, select the Line Tool (\) with a Pantone P 146-6 C (or DS 284-2 C) green color Stroke of 2 pt. Using the Shift key, drag along the vertical guide in the center of the gutter at the 4.3 inch mark from the upper green color until it touches the gold color bar.

7. Drag a text frame using the Type Tool (T) from the 6-inch horizontal guide to the bottom margin.

8. Select File > Place, locate the *Directions.doc* file in the *Text* folder, and import it into the frame. Repeat the inset spacing settings in step 5 for consistency. If you get the overset symbol don't worry; we'll format the text next.

9. Format the text for both frames to 11-pt Adobe Garamond Pro Regular or choose alternative fonts, like Times New Roman or Georgia. Keep the same font throughout for body text.

10. To format the heading *Special Tours*, select the line of text with the Type Tool (T); change the font to 20- or 24-pt Myriad Pro Bold, or try Charcoal, Arial Rounded MT Bold, or Minion Pro Bold as alternatives, with the green Pantone P 146-6 C (or DS 284-2 C) color as the Fill color with a Stroke of None.

11. To format the subheadings (*Annual Cape...*, *Corporate Team...*, and *Directions*), highlight each subheading with the Type Tool (T) and change the size to 14-pt with the same font, style, and Pantone 146-6 C color you used in the "Special Tours" heading. Select and format the phone number as well with the same green color to make it stand out.

12. Horizontally center the address above the phone number, and apply 12-pt Myriad Pro Bold with black color.

13. Select Type > Insert Special Character > Symbols > Bullet Character to insert a bullet between the spacing from the street address and town.

14. Horizontally center the website address and apply an 11-pt Italic style with the same font. Adjust the frames if needed; then drag off some of the guides with the Selection Tool (V). Save the file when done.

TOOLKIT TIP Designers who need to create many thousands of copies that are to be folded mechanically will need to calculate paper thickness for exact placement of the fold on the vertical rule. For our purposes here, it is just used to separate two sections as a design piece that may be folded by hand or in a smaller quantity.

GENERATING QR CODE

As was completed in Chapter 11, for marketing purposes many businesses insert a QR code to bring potential customers to their websites where they find various coupons and deals. A consumer with a smartphone can install an app with a QR code scanner that can read and decode the URL information and redirect the phone's browser to a company website.

You are going to generate a QR code of a website address that can be used if a consumer scans it with his/her smartphone to go to the website address. This code will be placed on the bottom left side of the back panel, inside a frame for proper fit.

1. Select the Rectangle Frame Tool (F) with Fill and Stroke of None, and click (don't drag) on the bottom left of the back panel. In the Rectangle Frame Tool display, type in 0.5 inches for both Width and Height and click OK. Keep the frame selected and position with the arrow keys to the bottom left corner without overlapping the vertical rule or gold color bar. Make sure the frame is selected so the code will automatically be placed inside (Figure UR4-9).

2. From the Object menu, select Generate QR Code to display the dialog box. Make sure the Content tab is selected and choose Type: Web Hyperlink.

3. Type in your favorite website URL, making sure you include the "www" if necessary. Don't press OK as we are going to add color to this code.

DESIGN TIP

Many designers prefer to place QR codes in the back of a brochure document panel so as not to detract from the front panel. Here the QR code is placed on an empty space on the bottom back panel for quick access.

▷ FIGURE UR4-9

Creating a QR code to the client website.

DESIGN TIP

The left side panel of the outside page of a traditional tri-fold brochure, known at times as the special info panel, is used to help answer questions, and as its name implies, provides most relevant information to encourage a viewer to want to look at the rest of the brochure.

DESIGN TIP

Remember: the more you have set up the text info ahead of time, the less time you need for adjustments when placing text in the InDesign document.

4. Select the Color tab, and choose the green Pantone P 146-6 C (or DS 284-2 C) color you created earlier from the Swatches panel. Click OK.

5. Your generated QR code should be placed in the selected frame. Hover your mouse over the center to display the Content Indicator, and the website address you chose should also display. This is helpful if, as a business, you wanted to send promotions online, the user has the website address and plenty of other information that could be added.

CREATING THE SPECIAL INFO PANEL

This panel is important in that it is the inner folder panel that the reader will observe on the right side when opening up the brochure. This panel is located on the left side of the document page. This is a good place to have special information that may answer some potential questions that a reader might have and encourage them to read further. This panel also serves as a point of reference for acquiring needed information. In this brochure it provides answers to most frequently asked questions, or what is known as an *FAQ sheet*. It also provides information about choosing a boat, and it informs the reader what supplies the store carries. This is also known as a *soft sell panel*, because it is presented as a resource for the customer and does not attempt to jump out and convince the reader to buy merchandise (Figure UR4-10).

Here you will import the FAQ panel and perform a little tabbing and formatting.

1. Using the Type Tool (T), drag a text frame inside the entire first panel column.

2. Select File > Place and locate the *FAQs.doc* document importing it into the panel. If a font warning appears, click OK.

3. Use the same body text font and size as used in the back panel. In our example we used 11-pt Adobe Garamond Pro.

4. Format the headlines "Tour FAQs" and "Purchasing Your Boat" lines using the same font and formatting as you used for the "Special Tours" headline for consistency.

5. Under the "Tour FAQs" headline, highlight each question and apply an italic style using the same font you chose to make the questions stand out.

6. To create a special character bullet for the why, when, and where questions about paddling, under the "Purchasing Your Boat" headline, click before the first word, "Why," and then select Type > Insert Special Character > Symbols > Bullet Character. Don't put in space as you will create tabs next. Repeat for the other two lines.

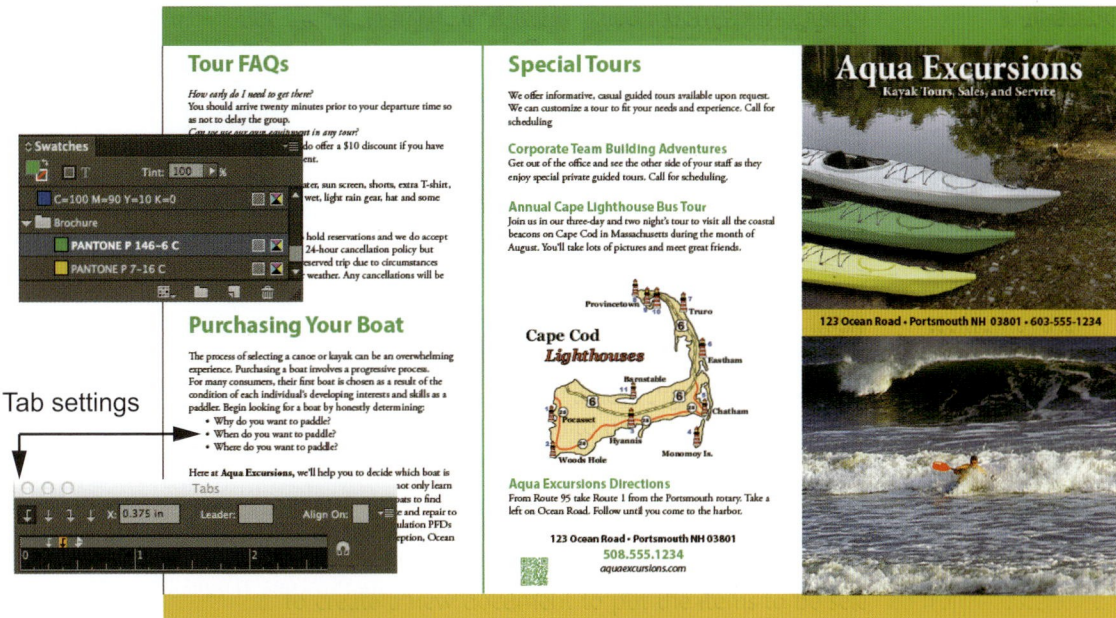

Special info panel   Back panel   Front panel

▷ FIGURE UR4-10

Completed page 1 InDesign document with front, back, and special information panels.

DESIGN TIP

Never use the space bar on your keyboard for spacing bullets on printed pieces for commercial use. Use tabs or insert special spacing characters from the Type menu for proper accuracy.

7. To create a tab for the bullet and a tab for the starting word, select the three lines; then select Type > Tabs to bring up the Tabs panel. Click on the Left Align arrow first, and set the type in the gray box above the rulers using a 0.25-inch tab that you type in the X-coordinate box. Click after the 0.25 and press Return/Enter after entering the amount.

8. Click on the 0.375 measurement on the gray box above the ruler display, or type it in again in the X-coordinate box. Make sure the Leader box contains no periods or characters.

9. For each line, click in front of the bullet and tab for the first measurement, and then click in front of the "W" and tab for the second measurement. Note: You can also create a left indent under the first line to achieve this.

10. In the paragraph underneath, apply a Bold style to the business name, Aqua Excursions.

11. Select the text frame, then select Object > Text Frame Options and set the Bottom and Top inset spacing to 0.125 (⅛) inches with the right and left at 0. Set the Vertical Justification to Top and select OK.

12. Adjust and edit any frames and text lines as needed to make everything fit within the panel. Save the file when completed. You now have page 1 completed.

CREATING CHARACTER AND PARAGRAPH STYLES

Here is where you have the opportunity to create styles from what you have made in the first page to apply in the next page to increase your production flow. You can apply character styles to selected lines of text or individual characters, while creating a paragraph style that may include character styles if desired; this allows you to tag each paragraph to automatically apply the formatting. You can also create a style based on the tabs you set in the last exercise. Remember, character styles are subordinate styles used within paragraph styles. The easiest way to set formatting is to simply highlight what is already formatted and name it as a style. To apply any style, just highlight the text you want to format and click on the style in the or Paragraph Style panel to apply the formatting. That's it!

In this exercise, you will highlight the formatting you already created for headlines, subheads, italicized questions, and bold style for the business name to create individual character styles for future editing. You will then create a paragraph style for tabs and for the body text.

1. Highlight the "Special Tours" headline.

2. To display the Character Styles panel, select Type > Character Styles.

3. From the Character Styles panel, open the panel menu, select New Character Style, or click the New Character Style icon in the lower right side of the panel.

4. In the Basic Character Formats tab, you will notice that all the attributes of the highlighted headline are already displayed, and the color of the formatted style is in the Character Color tab. Name the style *Headline*, and then exit out of the Character Styles panel.

5. Highlight the "Corporate Team Building" subheadline and repeat the same procedure above for character styles, naming it *Subhead.* Create a character style for the list of questions naming it *Questions,* and then create a character style highlighting the bold style applied to the bolded Aqua Excursions business name near the bottom of the FAQs panel, naming it *Business.* You are all set to apply these styles, or any additional styles you may wish to create and try out, to any selected text lines or characters. Highlight the copy first, and then apply the style you want.

6. To display the Paragraph Styles panel, select Type > Paragraph Styles.

7. To create a new paragraph style on the formatting of existing text, highlight the first few lines of any sample paragraph in the body text that contains the font and size you plan to use (Figure UR4-11).

8. Choose New Paragraph Style from the Paragraph Styles panel menu or click the New Paragraph Style icon in the lower right corner of the panel. Select the

▷ FIGURE UR4-11

Completed character styles and paragraph styles to use in the brochure.

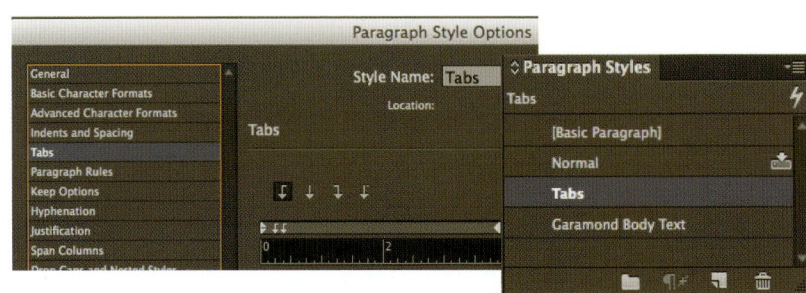

Basic Character Formats tab; then for the Style Name, type "Garamond Body Text," or whatever font you have chosen to use, for your new style. Make sure the font information is displayed or type it in. In the General tab, choose Based On: No Paragraph Style. Then select OK. Your paragraph style will display in the Paragraph Styles panel.

9. Optional: If you wish to use indents, in the Indents and Spacing tab, make sure the First Line Indent is set for 0.25-inch spacing. Leave all other default settings and select OK.

10. To create a paragraph style based on the tabs you created for the bulleted questions, highlight the three questions you created tabs for under the "Purchasing Your Boat" headline. Choose New Paragraph Style from the Paragraph Styles panel menu, select the Tabs section, and then for the Style Name, type "Tabs." Select OK to place the style in your Paragraph Style panel. (Note: This is an exercise to get you comfortable playing with styles. If you wanted to keep the tabbed section as part of the main paragraph style, you could also have highlighted more of the copy before making the style.)

11. Save the file. Your styles are ready to be applied in the next document page.

DESIGNING THE INSIDE PAGE FOR INTRODUCTION AND TOUR INFO

DESIGN TIP

The inside area of a tri-fold brochure gives the reader additional information as to what the business is all about.

Turning to the inside page document A-2 (page 2) is like opening a book to start reading the chapters. The reader wants to know what the brochure is about and what benefits he or she might find, so the content here is designed to encourage the reader to check out the business. The first panel on the left side is the introduction or welcome page that identifies the business with specific pertinent information. The following panels describe services and products being offered. In designing this inside portion, you will place the graphics and then import the text. Using the character and paragraph styles you created in the last exercise, you can apply simple formatting to text lines and paragraphs to provide consistency throughout the brochure.

PLACING THE GRAPHIC IMAGES

DESIGN TIP

Placing the graphics so they face into the document helps to focus the viewer's attention on the content at hand. Notice how the touring kayakers image will face the first "Welcome" introduction panel (Figure UR4-12).

Placing graphic images first helps to set up the text content that describes what the graphics are about. Again, both text and graphics need to complement one another. Using a touch of yellow color for the yellow kayak in the introduction panel is a great attention getter. Red is also used sparingly but grabs the viewer's attention. The bottom image spans across two columns, because the information is similar in both columns. It promotes a sense of continuity for the information being presented. You will note that one of these images are low resolution for our purposes here; for a job going to the press, you would need images at 300 dpi resolution, but these images will provide what you need for graphic layout and placement. A vertical rule will also be created to separate the introduction section and the section promoting the various tours.

Now you will drag guidelines and place the graphics for the inside of this page.

▷ FIGURE UR4-12

Placement of graphics in Page 2 (inside panels).

DESIGN TIP

The introduction or welcome panel on the left side panel identifies and summarizes the business.

1. Go to document A-2 (page 2) in the Pages panel, and double-click to make the second page active. Select *Page 2* in the Layers panel.

2. Make sure the zero point is dragged to start where the upper left margins intersect; then drag vertical guides to the 4.3-inch and 8.95-inch marks to mark center lines for the gutters.

3. For guidelines for placement of the graphics, drag horizontal guides to the 0.25, 1.875, and 5.5-inch marks.

4. In the left panel (introduction panel) using the Rectangle Frame Tool (F), drag between the column guides and the 0.25-inch and 1.875-inch guides. Use a 1-pt Stroke of Pantone P 7-16 C inside the Brochure color group you created in the Swatches panel, and a Fill of None.

5. Select File > Place and import the *Light.tif* file into the frame. Use the Direct Selection Tool (A) to adjust the size and position of the image so that the lighthouse and the kayaker fit in the frame window (Figure UR4-13).

▷ FIGURE UR4-13

Completed introduction panel with applied formatting.

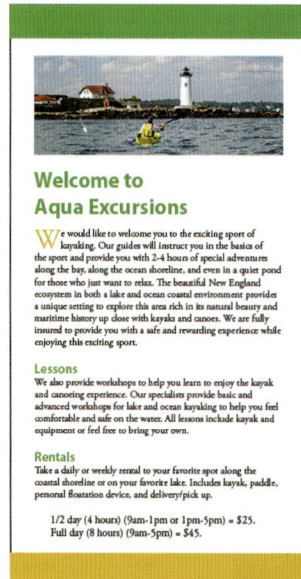

Welcome to Aqua Excursions

We would like to welcome you to the exciting sport of kayaking. Our guides will instruct you in the basics of the sport and provide you with 2-4 hours of special adventure along the bay, along the ocean shoreline, and even in a quiet pond for those who just want to relax. The beautiful New England ecosystem in both a lake and ocean coastal environment provides a unique setting to explore this area rich in its natural beauty and maritime history up close with kayaks and canoes. We are fully insured to provide you with a safe and rewarding experience while enjoying this exciting sport.

Lessons
We also provide workshops to help you learn to enjoy the kayak and canoeing experience. Our specialists provide basic and advanced workshops for lake and ocean kayaking to help you feel comfortable and safe on the water. All lessons include kayak and equipment or feel free to bring your own.

Rentals
Take a daily or weekly rental to your favorite spot along the coastal shoreline or on your favorite lake. Includes kayak, paddle, personal floatation device, and delivery/pick up.

1/2 day (4 hours) (9am-1pm or 1pm-5pm) = $25.
Full day (8 hours) (9am-5pm) = $45.

6. To place an image across two columns, drag a graphic frame using the Rectangle Frame Tool (F) between the second and third columns and between the 5.5-inch horizontal guide and the bottom margin. Use a 1-pt Stroke of gold color Pantone P 7-16 C in your Swatches panel and Fill of None.

7. Select File > Place and locate the *Touring.tif* image. Import the image into the frame and adjust to display the two kayakers.

8. To create a vertical rule to separate between what will be the Welcome panel and the Tour Package panels, select the Line Tool (\) with Pantone P 146-6 C (or DS 284-2 C) green color and Stroke of 2 pt. Using the Shift key, drag along the vertical guide in the center of the gutter at the 4.3-inch mark from the upper color bar until it touches the gold color bar. Release the mouse first, then select the Selection Tool to reset.

9. Save the file.

COMPLETING THE WELCOME PANEL

The introduction or welcome panel identifies and summarizes the business, and in this case, it supplies brief information regarding offering lessons and rentals. With the graphics in place, it is time to bring in the text. You can also apply formatting using the character and paragraph styles you created earlier, once the text is set up. You will apply styles to the subheads and pricing and create an initial drop cap (Figure UR4-13).

TOOLKIT TIP When designing brochures, be careful not to give too much information: the purpose is for the customer or client to contact the business. Be also wary of providing too many prices, especially if they are prone to frequent or seasonal changes.

You will place text and format character and paragraph styles, and you will create an initial drop cap.

1. With document A-2 or page 2 active, scroll to the left panel as displayed. This will be the welcome or introduction panel.

2. With the zero point at the intersection of the two upper margins, drag horizontal guidelines to the 2-inch and 2.75-inch margins to create a separate text frame for the main headline.

3. Using the Type Tool (T), drag a text frame between the column guides and the 2-inch and 2.75-inch guides.

4. Type in "Welcome to"; then press the Return/Enter key to create another line, and type "Aqua Excursions."

5. To apply the character style *Headline,* select Type > Character Styles to display the Character Styles panel. Highlight the two lines, and click on the *Headline* style. The color and formatting will be applied.

6. Select Object > Text Frame Options and make sure Vertical Justification is set to Align Top with no inset spacing needed. Click OK.

7. For the body text, drag a text frame with the Rectangle Frame Tool (F) from the 2.75-guide to the bottom margin. Select the Type Tool (T) and click in the frame.

8. Select File > Place and locate the *Welcome.doc* file.

9. Select Object > Text Frame Options and make sure Vertical Justification is set to Align Top with Top and Bottom Inset Spacing at 0.125 inches. Right and left need no inset spacing. Click OK.

10. Highlight the text and apply the body style text of the font you are using in the Paragraph Styles panel. Adjust (drag resizing handle downward) until the overset symbol is gone. We used Adobe Garamond Pro in an 11-pt size.

11. To create an initial drop cap, set your cursor in the first line of the paragraph, and specify a drop cap using the Paragraph Formatting button in the Control panel; create a two-line drop cap with a Bold style and the gold Pantone P 7-16 C (or DS 6-2 C) color.

12. Highlight the subheads "Lessons" and "Rentals," and apply the *Subhead* character style.

13. Highlight the two rental pricing lines near the bottom, and select the *Tabs* Paragraph style. Click in the front of both lines, and press the tab key once to indent each line according to the style. Increase the size of each line to 12 pt to make them stand out slightly.

14. Make any adjustments as needed, and save the file. The welcome panel is complete.

COMPLETING THE TOUR PACKAGES PANELS

The two inner panels are used to encourage the reader to check out special services and products, so they may call to get more information. Here is where you let the reader see what the business is mostly about. With the graphic displayed across the last two columns, you can create a major headline that also carries across both columns to tie the services in (Figure UR4-14).

Here you will create a headline across columns, and then import and format the text.

1. For the main headline, drag a horizontal guideline to the 0.75-inch mark with the zero point marked at the intersecting margins.

2. Using the Type Tool (T), drag a text frame from the 0.25-inch guide used for the image under the green color bar margin to the 0.75-inch mark across the second and third columns.

3. Type "A tour package for every taste…," (to create a true ellipse, which are three evenly spaced dots, select the Option/ALT key and then press the semicolon key); then apply Headline formatting with the Character Style panel (Type > Character Styles) as a starting point. Increase the size of the font to 30 pt and use a Bold Italic style font with a black color.

4. Select Object > Text Frame Options, and make sure Vertical Justification is set to Align Top with no inset spacing needed.

DESIGN TIP

The two other inner panels of a tri-fold brochure, located in the center and on the right side, are used to encourage the reader to check out special services and products, so they may call to get more information.

▷ FIGURE UR4-14

Completed tour services panels.

A tour package for every taste...

Guided Wildlife Tours

These tours provide a relaxing view of natural wildlife and helps kayakers learn the basics of kayaking. Most tours can be taken with people who are considered beginners. Each trip includes boat and equipment.

The Wentworth Special
This tour is great for families. You'll be taken through Newcastle harbor outside of Portsmouth through quiet tidal waters while being introduced to the basics of sea kayaking.

Inland River (Salmon Falls)
This tour takes you up through the historical shipping lanes of the Piscataqua River to Dover, NH. The narrow river passage lets paddlers experience wild life up close as they head to the mills built in the 1800's.

Willand Pond Fishing Tour
This trip is for the beginner or the person who just wants to have a relaxing ride or fish along the pond with lots of wildlife. Canoes are also welcome on this excursion.

Ocean Adventure Tours

These tours are for intermediate paddlers who are at least 16 years of age and can paddle for 6 or more miles. Enjoy the beauty of coastal ocean kayaking and the smell of the sweet salty air. Each trip includes boat and equipment.

Lighthouse Tour
Enjoy coastal paddling along the Newcastle Island shoreline and experience the unique view of Portsmouth Harbor Lighthouse as sailboat and fishing boats go by. Depending on the conditions during low tide we may be able to paddle to nearby Whaleback Light and Jerry's Light station and have a picnic.

Sunset Tour
This tour allows you to watch the beauty of the sun setting along the coastal shoreline as you kayak through the quiet waters of inner Newcastle harbor area, just outside of Portsmouth. This trip gives you a wonderful experience to get you familiar with sea kayaking. You may even be able to enjoy outdoor theater arts at Prescott Park as you pass by.

5. For the text about wildlife tours, drag a text frame using the rectangle frame tool from the 0.75-inch mark to the bottom of the margin in the second column.

6. Select the Type Tool (T) and click in the frame; then select File > Place and locate the *Wildlife.doc* file. Apply the body text formatting style in the Paragraph Styles panel.

7. Repeat the same process as in step 5 in the third column, and locate the *Ocean.doc* file to place.

8. For the "Guided Wildlife" and "Ocean" headlines, apply the *Headline* style; use the Space After command in the Command menu panel, if needed, to provide spacing after each line. Press Enter after each line.

9. Apply the *Subhead* style to all the tour titles.

10. Select Object > Text Frame Options, and make sure Vertical Justification is set to Align Top with top inset spacing of 0.25 of an inch (or 0.125 if needed)

11. Adjust the graphic frame of the kayakers to avoid too much empty white space.

12. To view your work free of guides and frames, select View > Grids & Guides > Hide Guides, and select View > Hide Frame Edges.

13. Look in your Layers panel, and see when you lock some of the frames or graphics that they cannot be edited until you unlock them. You can also right-click on the sublayers of your text frames or graphics to quickly select them.

14. Check your links in the Links panel to make sure your graphics show current locations. You can also click on the link graphic, and then select the Edit original button at the bottom of the Links panel to open the graphic in the default image editing program you have on your computer. Go ahead and play.

15. Save the file as a document and additionally as a template for future use in your *Unit 4 Review* folder (Figure UR4-15).

Page 1 (front, back, and "special" panels)   Bleed   Page 2 (inside panels)

▷ FIGURE UR4-15

Completed brochure pages for tri-fold format.

 TOOLKIT TIP If a body copy style is selected in the character mode of the Control panel when copy is placed, that copy will be assigned a character style, and the paragraph style will not override it unless the user does it manually. It is important that the word "None" is in the Character Style field of the Control panel when placing text.

 TOOLKIT TIP If you would prefer not to have a white background, try using the *Parchment* image file you used in the coupon ad in Chapter 11, and send the file behind the graphics and the text. Feel free to experiment.

READY FOR PRESS

In the final exercise here, you will again prepare the documents for press. Take note that the images used in this exercise are low resolution (75 to 100 dpi) for our educational purposes here; you would need 300 dpi for use on a commercial press. When getting ready for press, always check for spelling errors; then perform Preflight, print soft proofs for visual reference, and then Package all files. Your final proof will then be exactly what needs to be sent to the printer.

1. Save the file as an InDesign Document (INDD) and as an InDesign Template (INDT) to use as a guide for future documents.

2. To prepare your material for the printer as described in Chapter 11, select Edit > Spelling > Check Spelling to make sure spelling is correct.

3. Use the Links panel and the Preflight panel to check to make sure graphics are still linked, correct fonts are displayed, and images are set to CMYK colors for press.

4. Choose File > Print and use all printer's marks, creating proofs of the two pages.

5. To package for press, select File > Package and create a folder within the *Unit 4 Review* folder, or click "New Folder" and let InDesign create a separate folder located in a portable place that you specify to transport the files; name the new folder *InDesign Review*. In InDesign CC, check also to package as PDF and to INDL format for those who may have earlier versions of InDesign.

6. To create an additional PDF final soft proof for press, choose File > Export and keep most defaults with Press quality; place the PDF in your *InDesign Review* folder.

7. Congratulations, you have created a tri-fold brochure. Time to get outdoors!

Tour FAQs

How early do I need to get there?
You should arrive twenty minutes prior to your departure time so as not to delay the group.

Can we use our own equipment in any tour?
We are fully insured and we do offer a $10 discount if you have your own kayak and equipment.

What should paddlers bring?
Non alcoholic beverage or water, sun screen, shorts, extra T-shirt, shoes or sandals that will get wet, light rain gear, hat and some snacks.

How do I reserve my tour?
A 50% deposit is required to hold reservations and we do accept Visa/MasterCard. We have a 24-hour cancellation policy but reserve the right to cancel a reserved trip due to circumstances beyond our control like poor weather. Any cancellations will be cheerfully refunded.

Purchasing Your Boat

The process of selecting a canoe or kayak can be an overwhelming experience. Purchasing a boat involves a progressive process. For many consumers, their first boat is chosen as a result of the condition of each individual's developing interests and skills as a paddler. Begin looking for a boat by honestly determining:

- Why do you want to paddle?
- When do you want to paddle?
- Where do you want to paddle?

Here at **Aqua Excursions**, we'll help you to decide which boat is right for you and we provide workshops for you to not only learn the essentials of kayaking, but to try out different boats to find one that fits your needs and style. We provide service and repair to our boats. We carry wet suits, paddles, dry bags, regulation PFDs and camping gear. For kayaks we carry Necky, Perception, Ocean Kayak, and Wilderness Systems.

Special Tours

We offer informative, casual guided tours available upon request. We can customize a tour to fit your needs and experience. Call for scheduling

Corporate Team Building Adventures
Get out of the office and see the other side of your staff as they enjoy special private guided tours. Call for scheduling.

Annual Cape Lighthouse Bus Tour
Join us in our three-day and two night's tour to visit all the coastal beacons on Cape Cod in Massachusetts during the month of August. You'll take lots of pictures and meet great friends.

Cape Cod **Lighthouses**

Aqua Excursions Directions
From Route 95 take Route 1 from the Portsmouth rotary. Take a left on Ocean Road. Follow until you come to the harbor.

123 Ocean Road • Portsmouth NH 03801
508.555.1234
aquaexcursions.com

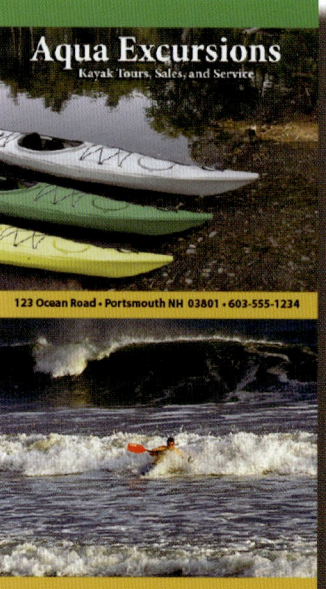

Aqua Excursions
Kayak Tours, Sales, and Service

123 Ocean Road • Portsmouth NH 03801 • 603-555-1234

Welcome to
Aqua Excursions

We would like to welcome you to the exciting sport of kayaking. Our guides will instruct you in the basics of the sport and provide you with 2-4 hours of special adventures along the bay, along the ocean shoreline, and even in a quiet pond for those who just want to relax. The beautiful New England ecosystem in both a lake and ocean coastal environment provides a unique setting to explore this area rich in its natural beauty and maritime history up close with kayaks and canoes. We are fully insured to provide you with a safe and rewarding experience while enjoying this exciting sport.

Lessons
We also provide workshops to help you learn to enjoy the kayak and canoeing experience. Our specialists provide basic and advanced workshops for lake and ocean kayaking to help you feel comfortable and safe on the water. All lessons include kayak and equipment or feel free to bring your own.

Rentals
Take a daily or weekly rental to your favorite spot along the coastal shoreline or on your favorite lake. Includes kayak, paddle, personal floatation device, and delivery/pick up.

1/2 day (4 hours) (9am-1pm or 1pm-5pm) = $25.
Full day (8 hours) (9am-5pm) = $45.

A tour package for every taste...

Guided Wildlife Tours

These tours provide a relaxing view of natural wildlife and helps kayakers learn the basics of kayaking. Most tours can be taken with people who are considered beginners. Each trip includes boat and equipment.

The Wentworth Special
This tour is great for families. You'll be taken through Newcastle harbor outside of Portsmouth through quiet tidal waters while being introduced to the basics of sea kayaking.

Inland River (Salmon Falls)
This trip takes you up through the historical shipping lanes of the Piscataqua River to Dover, NH. The narrow river passage lets paddlers experience wild life up close as they head to the mills built in the 1800's.

Willand Pond Fishing Tour
This trip is for the beginner or the person who just wants to have a relaxing ride or fish along the pond with lots of wildlife. Canoes are also welcome on this excursion.

Ocean Adventure Tours

These tours are for intermediate paddlers who are at least 16 years of age and can paddle for 6 or more miles. Enjoy the beauty of coastal ocean kayaking and the smell of the sweet salty air. Each trip includes boat and equipment.

Lighthouse Tour
Enjoy coastal paddling along the Newcastle Island shoreline and experience the unique view of Portsmouth Harbor Lighthouse as sailboat and fishing boats go by. Depending on the conditions during low tide we may be able to paddle to nearby Whaleback Light and Jerry's Light station and have a picnic.

Sunset Tour
This tour allows you to watch the beauty of the sun setting along the coastal shoreline as you kayak through the quiet waters of inner Newcastle harbor area, just outside of Portsmouth. This trip gives you a wonderful experience to get you familiar with sea kayaking. You may even be able to enjoy outdoor theater arts at Prescott Park as you pass by.

UNIT REVIEW IV
Creating a tri-fold brochure in InDesign.

Completed Projects and Tutorials

CHAPTER 1: WELCOME TO THE LAND OF OS

▷ FIGURE A-1

Macintosh OS X Mavericks desktop

Windows 7 desktop

CHAPTER 1
File management projects, and desktop fun using Macintosh OS X (top)
and Windows 7 (bottom) operating systems.

▷ FIGURE A-2

Windows 8 Start Screen

Windows 8 Desktop Screen

CHAPTER 1
File management projects and desktop fun with the Windows 8 operating system using the Start Screen and Desktop Screen.

CHAPTER 1 ADVANCED
Applications included in Mac OS X and Windows 7 used in creating electronic slide shows.

▷ FIGURE A-3

Photos App on the Start Screen displays images from Pictures Library   Slide Show

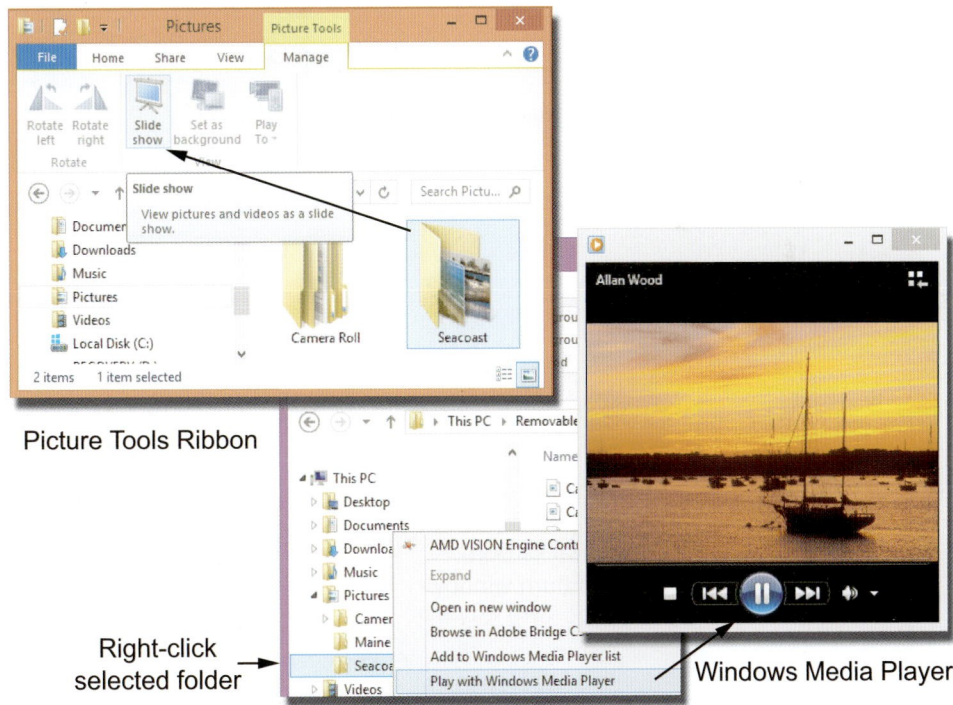

Picture Tools Ribbon

Right-click
selected folder

Windows Media Player

CHAPTER 1: ADVANCED
Applications in Windows 8 used in creating slide shows.

▷   FIGURE A-4

Select tracks, import to Library, then create Playlist. You can then drag the selected songs to your playlist.

Chapter 1: EXTRA
Creating music playlists in libraries to burn music CDs using iTunes (top) and Windows Media Player (bottom).

▷ FIGURE A-5

CHAPTER 2: DESIGNING FOR THE CLIENT

CHAPTER 2 ADVANCED: Identify design elements and principles in various ads.
CHAPTER 2 EXTRA: Internet resources.

▷ FIGURE A-6

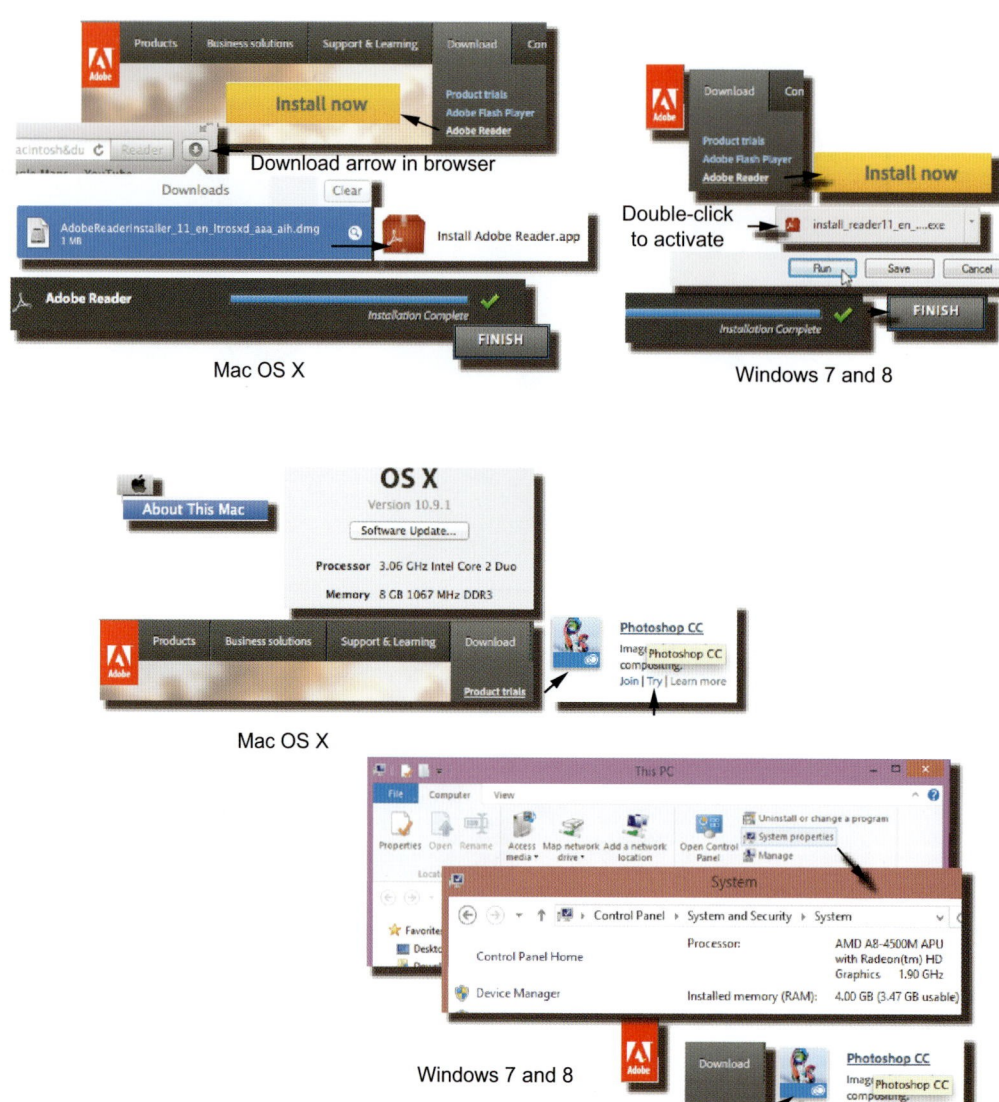

Download arrow in browser

Mac OS X

Double-click to activate

Windows 7 and 8

Mac OS X

Windows 7 and 8

UNIT 1 REVIEW
Downloading and installing Adobe Reader for both Max OS X and Windows.
Checking Mac OS X and Windows system information, and downloading Photoshop trial version of software.

▷ FIGURE A-7

CHAPTER 3: ADJUSTING IMAGES IN PHOTOSHOP

Originals

Adjusting
contrast, shadows,
and highlights

Converting colors for accurate
B&W tones

CHAPTER 3
Corrected images using special commands
in Photoshop's Image menu.

Adjusting color balance

CHAPTER 3 ADVANCED
Using histograms, levels, and curves adjustments in Photoshop to adjust
shadows, midtones, and highlights for quality images. Using Crop tools to adjust images.

▷ FIGURE A-8

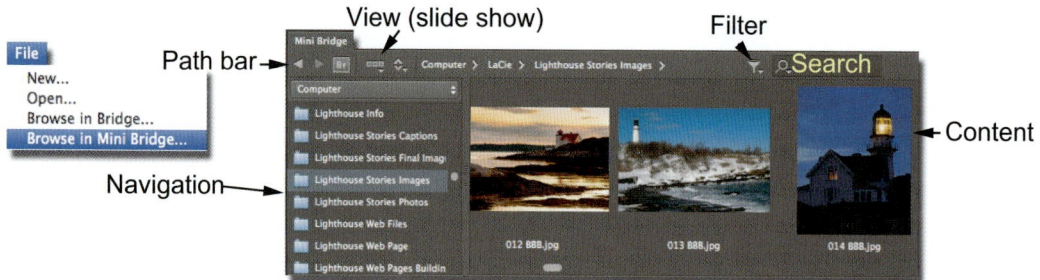

Adobe Bridge interface

Mini Bridge

CHAPTER 3 EXTRA

Using Creative Cloud to submit and access image files. Adobe Bridge and Mini Bridge, which is inside each Adobe application like Photoshop, allows you to import, retrieve, display, manage, and edit files.

▷ FIGURE A-9

CHAPTER 4: WORKING WITH SELECTIONS AND CHANNELS

Original image,
then selected image

Completed recolored image

CHAPTER 4
Using selection tools and techniques to change
a sports car's color while maintaining tonality.

CHAPTER 4 ADVANCED
Adding and subtracting selections
with precision using Quick Mask function,
Brush and Pencil tools.

Toggle Quick Mask
and Standard modes

Pencil Tool

Brush Tool

Quick Mask

CHAPTER 4 ADVANCED
Combining images for dramatic effects, selecting by Color Range,
then using the Paste Into command.

▷ FIGURE A-10

Original image

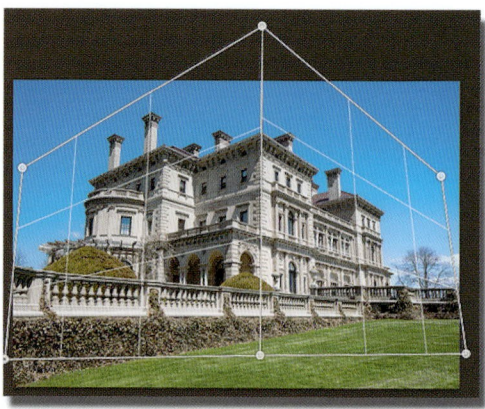

Align grids along corner axis

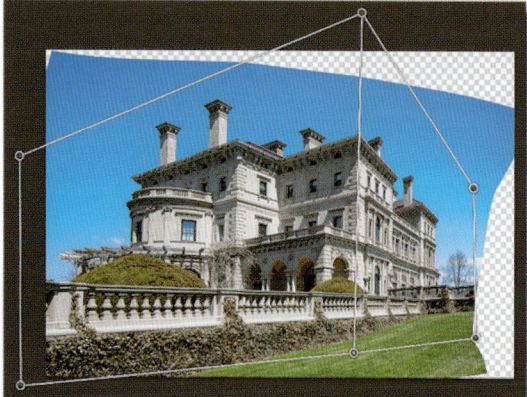

Warping to adjust perspective and vantage point

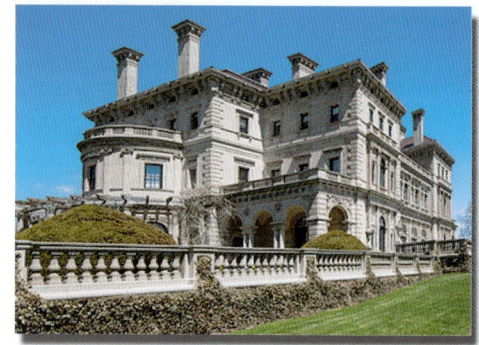

With Perspective Warp applied

CHAPTER 4 ADVANCED
Using the Perspective Warp function to adjust
three-dimensional perspective and vantage points.

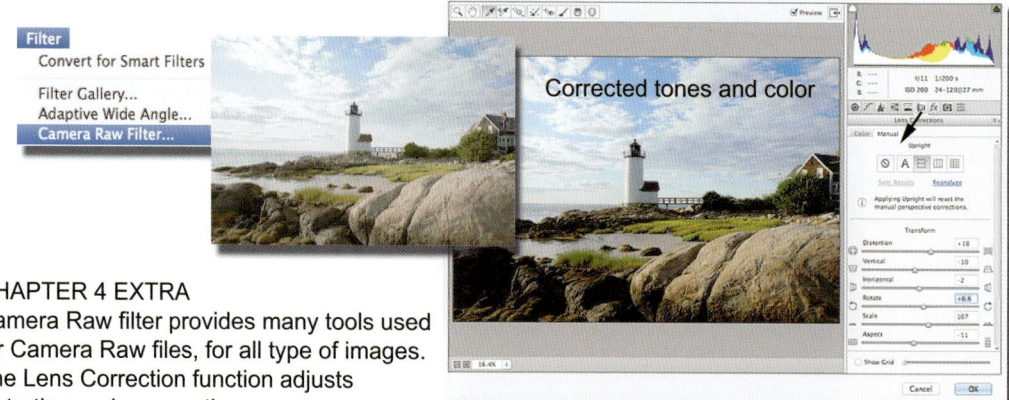

CHAPTER 4 EXTRA
Camera Raw filter provides many tools used
for Camera Raw files, for all type of images.
The Lens Correction function adjusts
distortion and perspective.

▷ FIGURE A-11

Original Camera Raw image

Basic and Tone Curve adjustments

Graduated Filter adjustments

CHAPTER 4 EXTRA
Taking a flat Camera Raw file from a digital camera and making precise adjustments using the Camera Raw functions and tools in Photoshop. The new digital darkroom.

Final adjusted Camera Raw image

▷ FIGURE A-12

CHAPTER 5: USING LAYERS

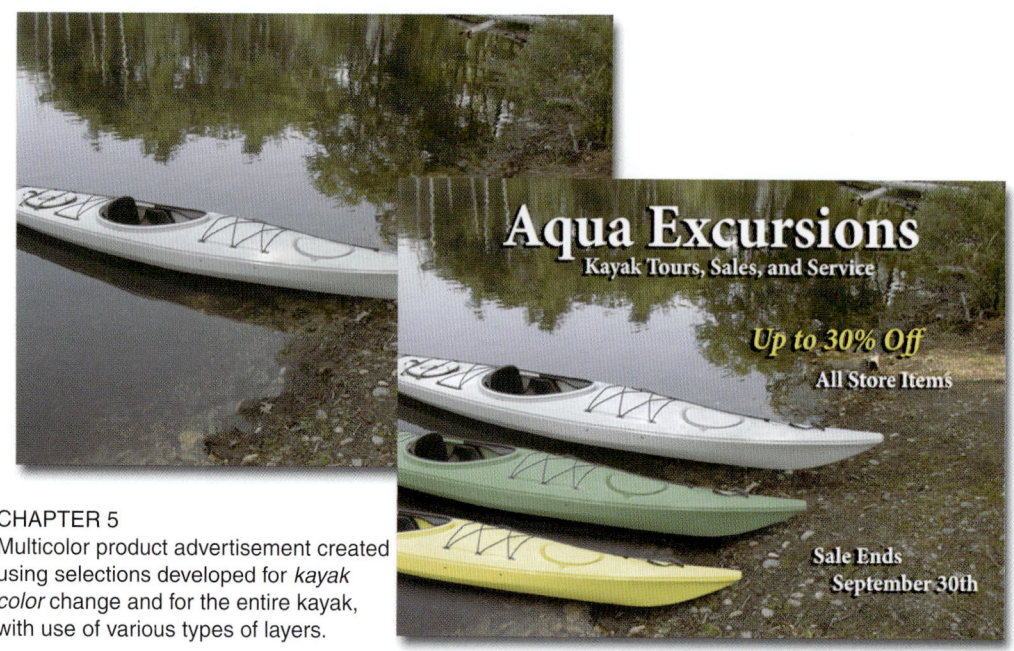

CHAPTER 5
Multicolor product advertisement created using selections developed for *kayak color* change and for the entire kayak, with use of various types of layers.

CHAPTER 5 ADVANCED
Using adjustment layers and layer masks to create special compositions. Creating a figure illustration using custom shapes.

▷ FIGURE A-13

CHAPTER 5 EXTRA

Using the Content-Aware Fill and Spot Healing Brush to remove unwanted distractions in an image (bridge).

Using Content-Aware Scale to resize important image elements with accuracy (lighthouse and red ship).

Using Content-Aware Move to reposition subject (birds).

Using the Eyedropper and Color Replacement tools to replace color in products and as corrective technique (back packs and stained lighthouse below).

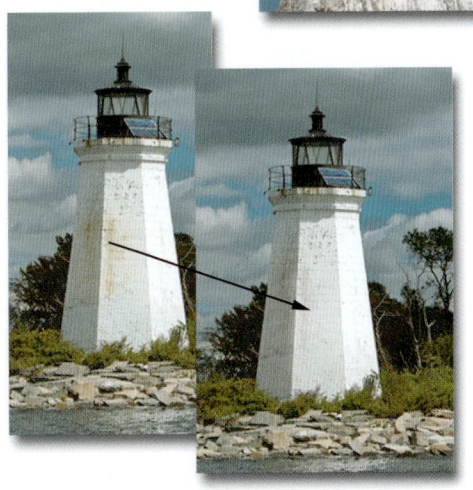

▷ FIGURE A-14

CHAPTER 6: RESTORING AND COLORING A BLACK AND WHITE PHOTOGRAPH

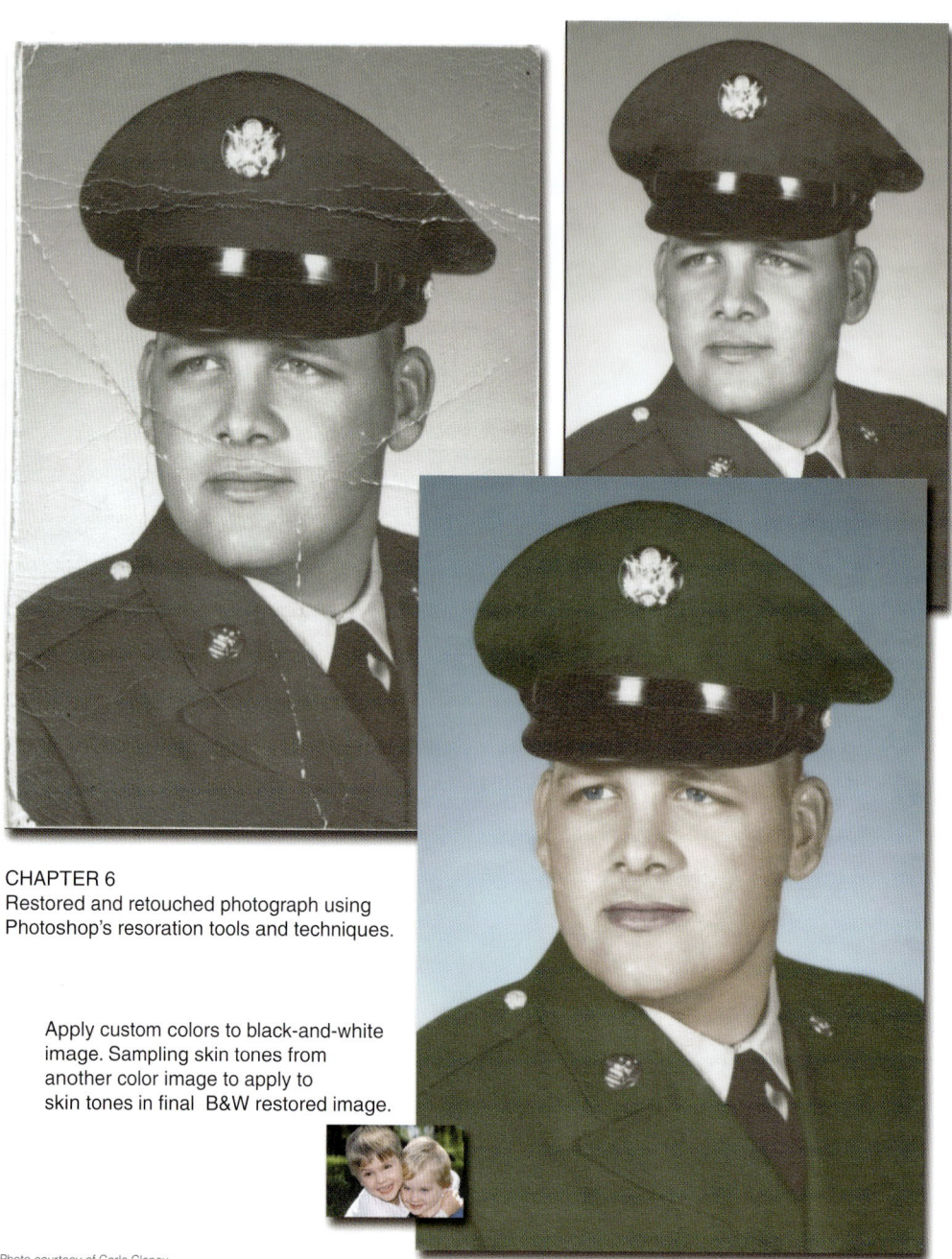

CHAPTER 6
Restored and retouched photograph using
Photoshop's resoration tools and techniques.

Apply custom colors to black-and-white
image. Sampling skin tones from
another color image to apply to
skin tones in final B&W restored image.

Photo courtesy of Carla Clancy.

▷ FIGURE A-15

Original Color Cast Image   Corrected Image

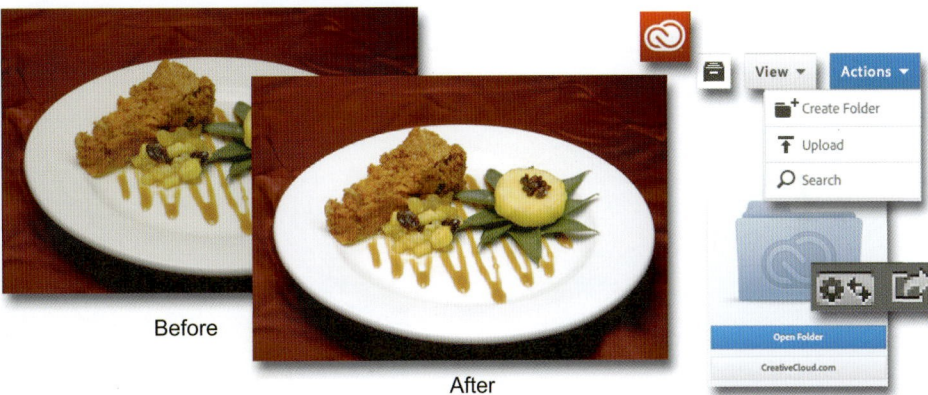

Before

After

Creative Cloud Settings

CHAPTER 6 ADVANCED

Neutralizing shadows and highlights to correct color cast images.
Using Creative Cloud to sync application settings and images between computers.

Play

Original Image   Action Applied

CHAPTER 6 EXTRA

Creating an action to place adjustment
layers on images for color and tone effects.
Batch processing action on multiple files.
Creating and working with 3D objects.

▷ FIGURE A-16

UNIT REVIEW 2: DIGITAL IMAGE EDITING: ADOBE PHOTOSHOP CC

Front Cover

Back Cover

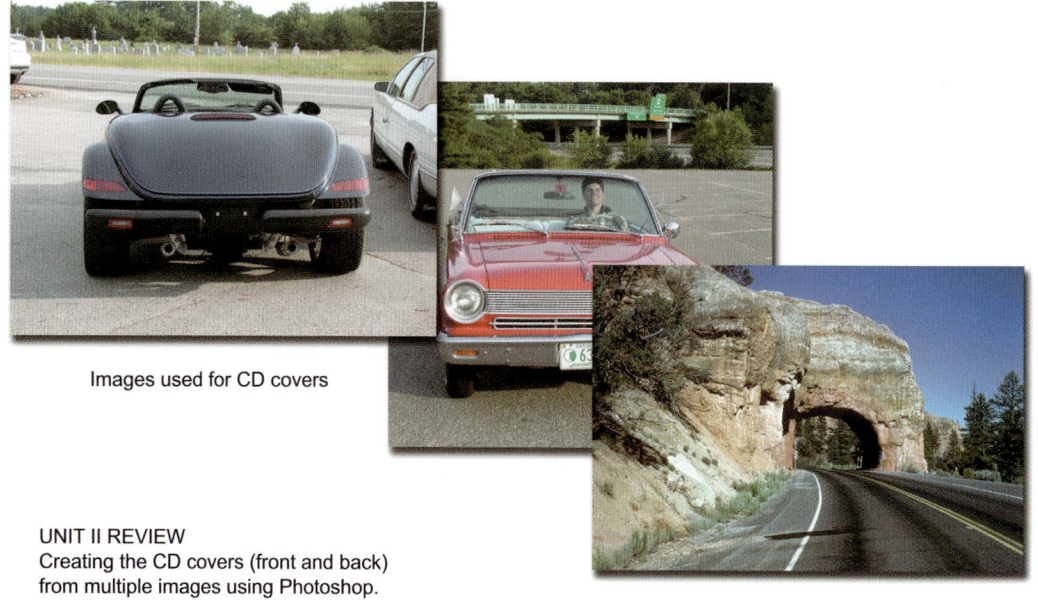

Images used for CD covers

UNIT II REVIEW
Creating the CD covers (front and back)
from multiple images using Photoshop.

▷ FIGURE A-17

CHAPTER 7: CREATING SHAPES WITH ILLUSTRATOR

CHAPTER 7
Electronic checkerboard created in Illustrator using shapes.

CHAPTER 7 ADVANCED
Building a lighthouse by creating and combining custom shapes. Creating a complex figure illustration to showcase Illustrator's Live Corners feature.

Selecting the shape with the Direct Selection Tool displays corner widgets — Round Corner — Inverted Round Corner — Chamfer Corner

Figure 7-XX
Double-clicking corner widgets with the Direct Selection Tool allows designers to create three types of Live Corners.

CHAPTER 7 EXTRA
Creating playing cards using custom shapes, Shape Builder Tool, and Object menu.

▷ FIGURE A-18

CHAPTER 8: WORKING WITH BRUSHES, SYMBOLS, AND LAYERS

Sketch of map
of Cape Cod, Massachusetts

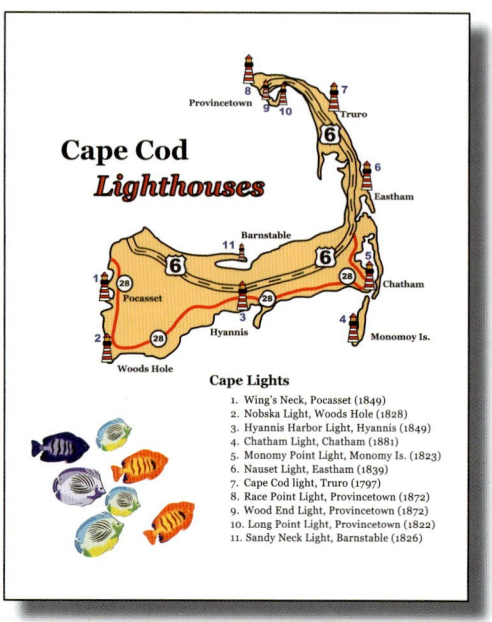

CHAPTER 8
Creating a scalable tourist map from a drawing sketch in Illustrator. Using symbols for visual enhancement.

CHAPTER 8 ADVANCED
Freestyle shapes with the Blob Brush. Placing logo on multiple artboards.

CHAPTER 8 EXTRA
3D bottle shape with label created and mapped onto bottle.

CHAPTER 9: PRECISION WITH THE PEN TOOL

▷ FIGURE A-20

Original sketch

Completed standard logo

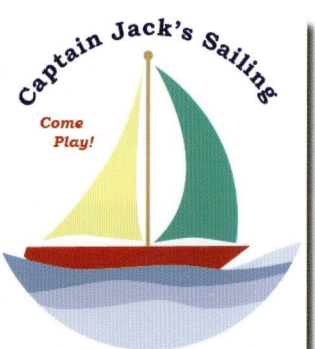

Modified logo

CHAPTER 9
Logo created from sketch using the
Pen Tool and type paths in Illustrator.

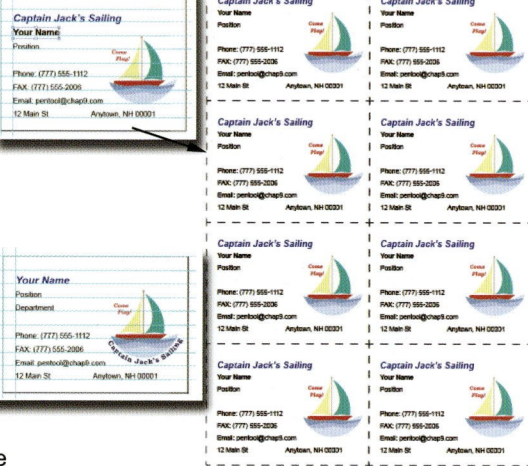

CHAPTER 9 ADVANCED
Creating business cards with graphic
logo and type; with alternative options.
Using the Transform command to create
aligned sheet of business cards.

Chosen design for final printing

CHAPTER 9 EXTRA
Clock face created in Illustrator
using guidelines, and the Gradient
Tool and Gradient panel.

CHAPTER 10: INTEGRATING PHOTOSHOP AND ILLUSTRATOR FILES FOR WEB USE

Integrating Photoshop Images and Effects with Illustrator

Integrating Illustrator Graphics and Effects into Photoshop

CHAPTER 10
Web headers created by integrating
elements between Photoshop and Illustrator.

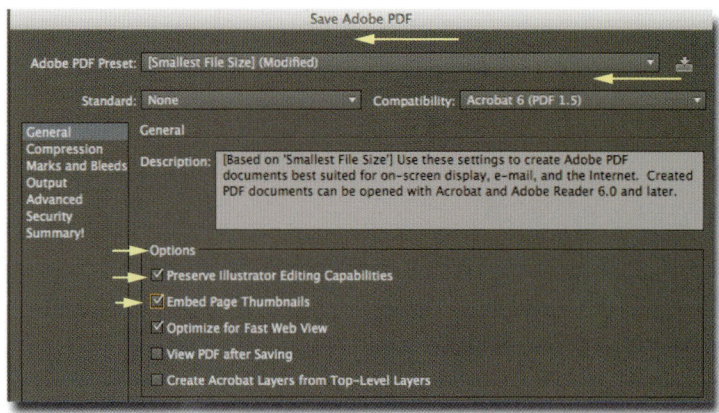

CHAPTER 10 ADVANCED
Understanding PDF and EPS files.

CHAPTER 10 EXTRA
Using Image Trace and Live Paint in Illustrator
to generate editable paths from various types of images, and apply color.

▷ FIGURE A-21

UNIT REVIEW 3: DIGITAL ILLUSTRATION: ADOBE ILLUSTRATOR CC

▷ FIGURE A-22

UNIT 3 REVIEW
Create guitar graphic from sketch.
Set up logo for mug.
Create 3D version of promotional mug
with shading and lighting applied.
Edit artowrk on multiple artboards for
various uses.

CHAPTER 11: INDESIGN FUNDAMENTALS

CHAPTER 11
Creating a direct
mail coupon ad
using InDesign.

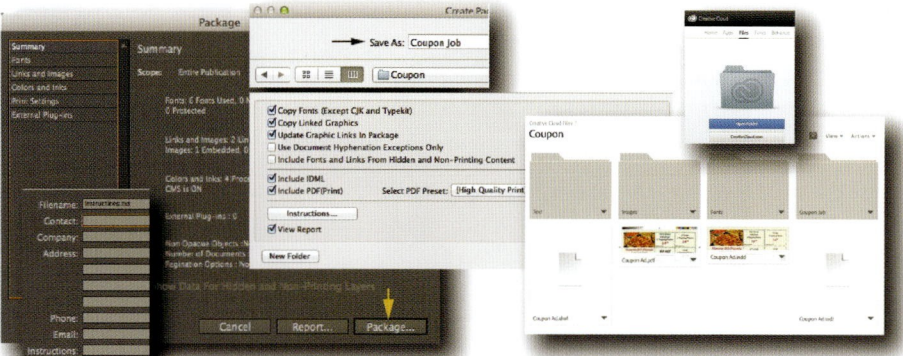

CHAPTER 11 ADVANCED
Preflighting, Packaging, and preparing for press.
Syncing a job folder and InDesign settings in Creative Cloud.

CHAPTER 11 EXTRA
Creating a desktop
calendar using tables.

▷ FIGURE A-23

CHAPTER 12: WORKING WITH MULTIPAGE DOCUMENTS

▷ FIGURE A-24

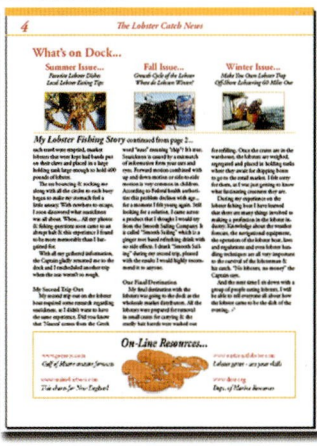

CHAPTER 12
Creating a 4-page Newsletter Spread using InDesign.

Newsletter text and photos courtesy of Shelly Britton.

My story begins by an assignment of photojournalism given to me by my teacher. The subject I chose was to learn all about the lobster fishing industry. Why not? How and where do these bulging-eyed shellfish come to be such a delight as a popular East coast dish anyhow? My experience spending time on a lobster boat was far a boat ride around the sea, pi dozen's of lobsters.

Sunrise On the Dock

Just before sunrise, I was a dock excited & anxious. I wa ing, should I begin shooting away or make my best observ

just take notes? I began with observation watching the fishermen prepare for their day at sea. They suited up in full-length bibs, and put on waterproof boots. I dressed warm, slipped on my boots and brought an extra set of clothes just in case.

Bringing in the Lobsters

Baseline Alignment

New Paragraph Style

Style Name: Garamond Body Text

- General
- Basic Character Formats
- Advanced Character Formats
- Indents and Spacing
- Tabs
- Paragraph Rules
- Keep Options
- Hyphenation
- Justification
- Span Columns
- Drop Caps and Nested Styles
- GREP Style
- Bullets and Numbering
- Character Color
- OpenType Features
- Underline Options
- Strikethrough Options

Location:

Basic Character Formats

Font Family: Adobe Garamond Pro
Font Style: Regular
Size: 11 pt   Leading: (13.2 pt)
Kerning: Metrics   Tracking: 0
Case: Normal   Position:

☐ Underline   ☑ Ligatures
☐ Strikethrough

Styles

Library

Beverage.tif   Front Page   Index

Nameplate...   Resource.eps   Resources

6 of 6 shown

Object libraries

Pages

[None]

A–Master

iPad H   iPhone_H

A   B

1   1

**Master Page (B) created
from iPhone alternate layout**

Original iPad layout

**iPhone
(converted as alternate layout)**

CHAPTER 12 ADVANCED
Special editing techniques
and designing alternate layouts.

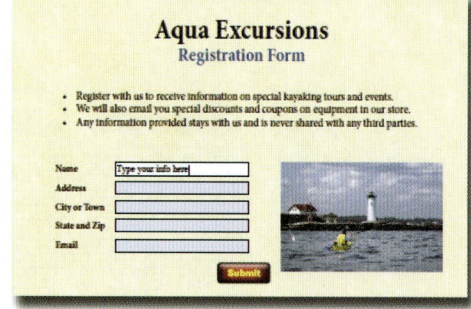

CHAPTER 12 EXTRA
Creating interactive PDF
documents using InDesign.

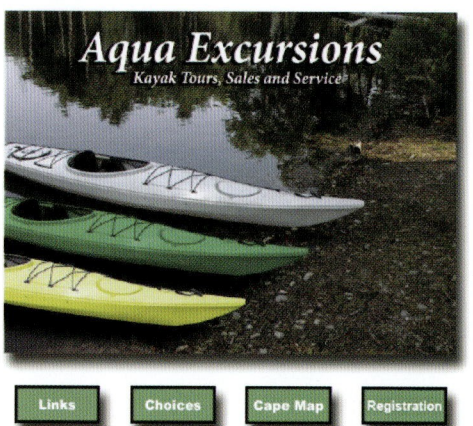

UNIT REVIEW 4: DIGITAL PUBLISHING: INDESIGN CC

UNIT REVIEW IV
Creating a tri-fold brochure in InDesign.

▷ FIGURE A-26

Glossary

A

3D application within Photoshop provides designers the opportunity to create complex 3D objects for both print and web media.

3D Axis Movement widget allows the object to be moved along the X-axis (width), Y-axis (height), and Z-axis (depth), and provides icons to rotate and scale objects along these axes.

3D Material Eyedropper Tool is used to sample 3D textures and shading.

3D objects are usually converted from 2D text, preset shapes, a selection on an image, or a layer mask.

3D panel in Photoshop controls layer selections of camera view, the lighting, the 3D workspace environment and current scene, and each surface or face of your object.

Absolute numbering involves labeling all pages with consecutive numbers, starting with the first page of the document.

Actions in Photoshop and Illustrator are little scripts or mini programs you can create for applying special effects, minimize repetitive tasks, and other creative methods of enhancing your workflow.

Actions in InDesign (referred to as behaviors in earlier versions) are interactive macros or mini programs that identify what the button will do when it is selected with the mouse (open a document, locate a URL, play a movie, play sound, etc.).

Adjustment layers within an image allow a designer to create a series of layered effects over the original image that are non-destructable, so that the pixels in the original image are not manipulated. Each adjustment layer is on its own individual layer, and can easily be edited.

Adjustments command in the Photoshop Image menu allows you the flexibility to select quite a variety of color adjustments for an image.

Adobe Bridge is the hub for retrieving and editing files and their information to help with file management and automation between files and those applications within the Adobe Creative Suite.

Adobe Creative Suite consists of Adobe products for all media (Photoshop, Illustrator, InDesign, Dreamweaver, Acrobat, with other special applications) and all work together in working with various types of files.

Adobe Help Center displays tasks, index help, and bookmarks of previously visited help areas. Topics can be searched by using keywords, an alphabetized index, or by selecting underlined text links. The Adobe Help Center also lets you seek help with other Adobe applications in a web-like format, and provides additional links to resources and expert product support.

Adobe Typekit fonts are a special library of fonts paid Creative Cloud subscribers may access for use with any of Abobe applications.

Aerial perspective is used to add drama to an image by using visual perspective from higher angles than a viewer's normal eye level.

.AI extension is Illustrator's native format extension.

Airdrop in Mac OS X allows a designer to share files over WiFi in any office or home network.

.ait (Adobe Illustrator Template) **extension** is the extension used for Illustrator templates.

Alias is a link or shortcut for Macintosh computers to drives, most frequently used applications, files, and folders that you can create on your desktop.

Align panel in Illustrator is used to align multiple selected items along a horizontal or vertical axis and along their centers. The Align panel can also be used to evenly space the distance between multiple objects.

All My Files in Mac OS X displays files in specific categories from music, to images, to spreadsheets.

Alpha channels in Photoshop are channels used to save and store selections of an image area permanently so they can be used and edited in the future.

Anchor links are links within a web page.

Anchor points are nonprinting marks that define where line segments begin and end on paths or objects.

Anti-alias keeps square pixel edges from looking jagged by softening the transition between colors.

Appearance panel in Illustrator is used to edit and display properties of selected 3D objects.

Apple menu in Macintosh OS X allows you to find information about your Mac system and files, which includes a listing of the most recently opened applications and files.

Application menu in Mac OS X contains commands for information about the application, changing settings, preferences, and quitting the application.

Application-level preferences affect work on all documents.

Applications are software programs for a particular use, such as Photoshop is an application used for digital image editing.

Applications command in the Macintosh Go menu displays all programs in the Applications folder.

Apps is an abbreviated term for applications.

Art Brushes in Illustrator stretch evenly along a path and are used for various types of art strokes, like the charcoal brush.

Artboard in an Illustrator document is the area inside the document where a designer creates and modifies illustrations.

Artboard Tool (Shift + O) in Illustrator controls how you move, resize, and edit artboards, with one artboard selected at a time.

Artboards panel in Illustrator allows the designer to create new artboards, reorder artboards, rearrange artboards, and create duplicate artboards.

Artwork is a term for an illustration or illustrations created in Illustrator using shapes, tools, paths, and panels.

ASCII type is an American type standard; it is not formatted and can be read universally by any application or computer.

Auto Color command in Photoshop looks for color casts in an image and adjusts any imbalanced colors for correct color.

Auto Contrast command in Photoshop works well with images that need lightening and darkening of highlights and shadows.

Auto Levels command in Photoshop adjusts the tonal balance of colors by rearranging an image's tones slightly to show detail in highlights and shadows.

Average command in the Illustrator Object menu connects path end points that need to be drawn in to make one smooth, flowing path.

B

Background layer is the initial layer of a Photoshop image that contains the original image. The Background remains locked at the bottom of the Layers panel until you double-click the "Background" text and rename it. It then behaves as a normal layer and can be moved around between other layers.

Baseline in typography is an invisible line that the type sits on.

Baseline grids align the baseline of the text from a starting point across the document for the designer to view how text aligns crosswise along columns for a consistent look.

Batch processing is a process where, after you have created an action, you can create a "factory" or assembly line where you take many images from one folder, apply the action, and place the "processed" images in another folder.

Bevel and Inflate widget creates surface adjustments that bevel and inflate on a 3D object.

Bézier curves are created by setting anchor points with the Pen Tool and dragging the mouse to define the shape of the curve.

Bi-fold is simply a document folded once, usually with the fold on the left side, like a booklet. This is used for mailers, brochures, menus, and other informational material.

Bitmap or **raster images** are photographs, paintings, or complex designs that use millions of colors to record subtle gradations of tone in the image and are nonscalable.

Bleeds extend solid color boxes of graphics beyond the trim edge of a document to ensure good color coverage at the edges of printed material so no white lines are generated from the graphic edge.

Blending modes in Photoshop allow the designer to determine how pixels in one layer blend with the underlying pixels in the image. Different blending modes produce different results between layers and allow a designer to create a variety of special effects.

Blob Brush Tool in Illustrator is used to paint filled shapes that you can intersect and merge with other shapes of the same color.

Blur Tool is used to smooth out pixels or imperfections of an image.

Bounding box in Illustrator is made when selecting objects to move or resize. It has resizing handles in its corners and can be used to reshape, copy, or rotate an object.

Brightness/Contrast command in Photoshop is used to remap highlight and shadow areas to maintain detail throughout the tonal range of an image.

Bristle Brush in Illustrator allows a designer to create brush strokes with the appearance of a natural brush with bristles.

Brush libraries contain a variety of organized preset brushes, which appear in a new panel and are added by selecting the brush and dragging it to the Brushes panel.

Brush tools are used for painting on an image.

Brushes in Illustrator allow you to apply various freehand strokes of artwork in various ways to existing paths or objects. Brushes can be applied to existing selected paths or used to create a path.

Brushes panel allows you to create your own brush artwork or to use predefined brushes in four different categories: Calligraphic, Scatter, Art, and Pattern.

Burn is a term meaning to write documents, images, video, and music onto recordable CDs using a CD recorder drive.

C

Cage is an outline that surrounds a 3D object when clicking once on any surface of that object.

Calligraphic Brushes give the appearance of hand-drawn strokes with an angled pen tip.

Camera Raw Files contain unprocessed picture data from a digital camera's image sensor. It lets photographers interpret the image data rather than letting the camera make the adjustments and conversions.

Camera Raw Filter in Photoshop allows you to use most of the Camera Raw tools and settings with not only Camera Raw files, but also files saved as JPGs, TIFFs, and PSDs.

Camera View widget is used in 3D space in conjunction with Photoshop's Move Tool, a grid is displayed as a reference plane that you can click and drag around to adjust how you want the 3D objects to be viewed.

Cell options command in InDesign is used to format text; rows and columns; strokes and fills, including tints and diagonal lines.

Cells are the individual "boxes" inside a table.

Channels in Photoshop are saved with the document and can be reopened and edited at any time. Channels store an image's color mode information in separate color channels, like RGB would store red, green, and blue channels.

Channels panel is used to store selections permanently and color mode information in separate channels in Photoshop.

Character styles panel in Illustrator and InDesign contains many formatting commands for setting text options and is used for applying character formatting techniques to selected characters or lines of text.

Charms bar in Windows 8 provides quick access to special related applications, tools, and features.

Clipboard is a temporary place in memory to store text and graphics that have been cut or copied before pasting them into another document or another location.

Clipping mask in Illustrator allows any shape, type, or path placed on top of a graphic to cut out that image below in the shape of the path above it, much like a cookie cutter.

Clone Stamp Tool in Photoshop allows you to sample a group of pixels from a source area and transfer or clone those pixels to a target area. Hold down the Option/Alt key and click a clean area to sample from.

Cloud-based services let designers build and publish websites, mobile apps, iPad publications, and content for any medium or device.

CMYK mode reflects the computer's secondary colors, which are cyan, magenta, and yellow, with "K" standing for the black used to increase contrast. Mix red and blue and you get magenta, for instance.

CMYK process colors comprise cyan, magenta, yellow, and black (CMYK). These four colors are used in four separate plates during the printing process.

Color Balance command in Photoshop allows you to replace colors opposite the color cast in your image using sliders for shadows, midtones, and highlight tones accurately, especially cyan and magenta color casts.

Color bars on a proof sheet show accuracy of colors to be used.

Color Guide panel in Illustrator provides quick access to color groups and to colors that complement one another, so designers can experiment with colors in their artwork, and then create custom groupings of colors.

Color libraries in InDesign are an assortment of colors from various color swatch manufacturers like Pantone.

Color modes in the Illustrator Toolbox below the Fill and Stroke boxes determine how color is applied to either the fill or stroke of an object or path. They are the Color (default), Gradient, and None (red line) modes.

Color panel allows the designer to select or sample any colors to use as either background or foreground colors in Photoshop or as stroke and fill colors in Illustrator.

Color Picker is displayed when the color boxes, background, and foreground in Photoshop or the Stroke and Fill boxes (located beneath the tool buttons) in Illustrator and InDesign are double-clicked. The Color Picker lets you select an object's color by choosing from a color spectrum, defining colors numerically, or clicking a swatch.

Color Range command in Photoshop is used for selecting same areas of color and color tones.

Color Replacement Tool in Photoshop replaces the color of a selected area with whatever the foreground color is.

Color Sampler Tool used to sample any color in an image and provide color information.

Color stops in Photoshop's Gradient Editor are used to adjust, add, and remove gradient combinations of colors.

Color tools in Photoshop, like the Eyedropper and Color Sampler tools, are used to sample any color on any image to make a new foreground color by default and provide color information.

Complementary colors are opposite colors on the color wheel.

Composite proofs (using the same page description language) allow the designer to create a single sheet that is an exact replica of the intended output.

Comps show exactly what the final design will look like when printed.

Constrain Proportions in Photoshop allows you to increase or reduce the image size proportionately to avoid distortion.

Content Aware Fill in Photoshop has the ability to remove an image element and replace it with details that blend in closely to match the lighting, tone, and noise of the surrounding area.

Content-Aware Move Tool (J) allows a designer to reposition a particular subject and have the background blend in with the change.

Content-Aware Scale function in Photoshop allows you to resize an image without changing the important elements like people, buildings, animals, etc., by affecting pixels in areas that aren't visually important.

Content Collector and **Content Placer tools** in InDesign allow you to grab multiple pieces of content and place them to another area of the same document or onto other documents with ease.

Content Indicator in InDesign displays a transparent "doughnut" shape to adjust graphic frames that contain content larger than the frame window. It is used with the Selection Tool to select and reposition a graphic.

Continuing banners are found in the top portion of the additional pages within a newsletter and have a continuing color scheme, text format for the title, and sometimes an identifiable company logo.

Continuous-tone images are usually photographs or paintings that have a high color bit depth (millions of colors), which display subtle gradations of shades of color, and generate large file sizes.

Control panel in Illustrator provides options and information based on selected artwork, including information regarding object dimensions and location, fill and stroke colors, opacity, and selecting the Bridge application.

Control Panel in Windows allows you to make modifications within your computer, like adding hardware, adding and removing programs, updating applications, and modifying system functions and monitor display.

Convert Anchor Point Tool is used to convert a smooth curve anchor point to a corner point and vice versa.

Creative Cloud (CC) is Adobe's current version of its suite of applications. It provides designers the ability to submit and manage files remotely from most any device.

Crop marks indicate where the cutting of the paper will be when sending a document to press.

Crop Tool allows you to draw rectangular selections inside the image area and crop the area outside the selection to trim the image.

Cross-platform files and applications can be read by different operating systems, like Vista and Mac OS X.

Curves adjustment allows the designer or photographer more precision in adjusting for toning in highlights, midtones, and shadow details using a system of plotting points in those areas that need adjustments.

Custom Shape Tool (U) in Photoshop provides a premade set of custom shapes in its custom display panel.

D

Dashboard is a feature of Mac OS X that contains small programs called **widgets** that have a wide variety of uses for everyday tasks such as checking stock prices, finding local or global weather information; some widgets are linked with larger applications, etc.

Decorative type is used sometimes in headlines to create a specific meaning.

Desktop is the screen displayed on your computer monitor. It displays your drives, and most frequently used applications, files, and folders.

Desktop publishing programs allow designers to bring in text and graphic items or elements from other applications and assemble and lay out these items accurately inside text and picture boxes in an organized manner.

Desktop Screen in Windows 8 provides all the functions as the earlier Windows 7 desktop without the Start menu button.

Device Central enables Photoshop users to preview how Photoshop files will look on a variety of mobile devices.

Devices charm in Windows 8 shows any hardware devices or peripherals that are connected to your computer, such as printers, monitors, or digital cameras.

Dialog box window appears and provides more commands or functions when you select a command or function.

Digital imaging involves scanning or importing images into the computer, which converts them into digital images.

Direct Select Lasso Tool in Illustrator is great for quickly making a freehand selection in a small area between end points of paths to be joined.

Direct Selection Tool allows you to select and move individual anchor points or path segments. It works in conjunction with the Pen Tool to adjust with precision the shape of a path the Pen Tool creates by adjusting its anchor points and direction lines.

Direction lines are nonprinting lines that extend from anchor points that can be dragged to modify a curve or any path with precision. Dragging two anchor points in the same direction creates an "S" curve while dragging two anchor points in the opposite direction creates a "C" curve. Anchor points and direction lines do not print with the artwork.

Directory structure is an organized method used to save files within folders, like having file cabinets with drawers to organize them.

Dithering is a process in which colors are substituted to simulate the missing color in the web panel, which can sometimes result in a spotty looking appearance.

DOC is the extension used to identify Microsoft Word documents.

Dock is used to display active applications, files, and folders on the Mac OS X operating system.

Document-level preferences in InDesign affect only the active document.

Dot Leaders in desktop publishing create a series of dotted periods or dots that lead the reader to info like page numbers.

Downloading files involves sending the files from the web host server to your hard drive for possible editing.

dpi (dots per inch) refers to measuring an image's resolution for print purposes.

Draw Behind mode in Illustrator allows you to draw behind all artwork on a selected layer if no artwork is selected. If an artwork is selected, the new object is drawn directly beneath the selected object.

Draw Inside mode in Illustrator allows you to draw inside the selected object. The Draw Inside mode eliminates the need for multiple steps to perform tasks such as drawing and altering stacking order or drawing, selecting, and creating a clipping mask.

Draw Normal mode is the default drawing mode in Illustrator.

Drawing Modes in Illustrator, located near the bottom of the tools panel, provide options to draw inside and behind artwork, eliminating multiple tasks.

Drop cap is a larger letter or group of letters that extend over lines of text to start off an article.

Duplicate command in Photoshop creates an exact image copy.

Dust & Scratches filter in the Photoshop Filter menu can help to smooth out and blend in pixels and remove small dust spots.

E

Edges referred in Illustrator's Live Paint command are the stroke or outlined areas of the path.

Edit menu allows you to work with text and graphics, including selecting all components in a document. It allows you to undo actions; copy, cut, and paste items; and see what is on the Clipboard.

Editing and retouching tools in Photoshop help to improve or enhance an image. They are the Color Replacement Tool, Healing and Path Brush tools, Eraser, Gradient, Paint Bucket, Blur, Smudge, Sharpen, Burn, Dodge, Sponge, Clone and Pattern Stamp tools.

Electronic media proof is used for website designers or multimedia designers. It shows indications for pixel dimensions, software used, resolution requirements, text and image locations, and information needed for publishing for the web, along with any special requirements.

Ellipse Frame tool in InDesign creates frames as containers to insert text and graphics.

Ellipses Tool (which means "and so on") are three evenly spaced dots, created by selecting the Option/ALT key followed by a semicolon.

Embedded files are added permanently to a file, which increases the file size, and any changes made to the image in one document will not be updated in any other documents.

Emphasis provides direction to various elements in a given design, promoting the concept that some things are more important than others.

Encapsulated PostScript (EPS) extensions are used in page layout programs for press. EPS files work quite nicely with text and graphic elements and are used predominantly in the commercial press industry, especially when vector graphics are needed to maintain sharpness and clarity.

Eraser Tool in Illustrator removes anchor points and path segments. In Photoshop it removes the background color.

Expand command in Illustrator Auto Trace function is used to convert the tracing outline to a series of connected paths.

Exposé is another mini application on the Mac in versions earlier than Lion that helps you move or copy items between different windows in an application and from one application to another; it is used quite frequently in combination with the Spaces.

Extract command in Photoshop works with very minute details searching for edge pixels, like a person's hair against the background. The Extract command provides a nice transition when placing various images together by removing distracting backgrounds.

Extrude command in Illustrator is used to take a 2D object like a circle and convert it into a 3D object like a cylinder.

Extrusion depth allows designers to control the "thickness" of text or a 3D object using the Properties panel.

Eye icon displayed on the Photoshop Layers panel indicates that the layer is visible. You can hide or show a layer by clicking the eye icon.

Eyedropper Tool is used to sample and place a color in the Color Picker. It can sample color from a current image or another image. From the sample you can read the color mode information in the Color panel if you need to record it.

F

Faces in Illustrator's Live Paint are the inside areas of a closed path or shape.

Fade command, in Photoshop's Edit menu, is used to adjust the amount of effect being applied.

File Explorer, in Windows 8, previously named Windows Explorer in earlier versions, is the central place where you can access any content on your computer to make changed and adjustments, retrieve information, or make deletions.

File menu allows you to create new folders, search for and get info about folders and files, duplicate items, and create links or shortcuts to files and folders.

Fill is the inside color of an object in Illustrator.

Fill box in Illustrator is used to fill color inside an object.

Filter Gallery in Photoshop's Filter menu allows the designer to preview and apply various specialized filter effects on an image.

Finder menu lets you organize how icons are displayed, much like a librarian organizes books. It can create, manage, and locate files and folders and navigate around the computer.

Flattening the image involves merging all the layers in a document into a single layer.

Focal point determines a component's size, shape, color, texture, or position in the layout as the most important feature.

Folding dummy is made to provide a visual reference for a brochure and is where you would sketch in headlines and graphic elements along with the type of fold you will use.

Font is the immediate family of characters with the same shape construction and style, such as Arial or Times New Roman.

Font size is measurement of type in points instead of inches.

Font style is applying a change to a character, such as bold, underline, or italics.

Formal balance places elements with equal distribution to convey trustworthiness and integrity, a technique financial institutions or insurance companies might use.

Frames in InDesign are boxes or containers that allow designers to bring in text and graphic objects or elements from other applications and assemble and lay out these items accurately in an organized manner.

Framing techniques are employed in which another subject surrounds the main subject for emphasis. Using tree branches in the foreground, for instance, provides emphasis to a distant subject.

Free Transform Tool changes the size of an object or its point of origin.

FTP (File Transfer Protocol) is the process of uploading your files to a web host server.

FXG extension format in Illustrator is useful when the need involves preserving maximum appearance and availability for accurate editing, and for animation purposes using Flash Catalyst.

G

Gadgets are mini programs in Windows that offer information at a glance and provide easy access to frequently used tools.

Gap Tool in InDesign provides a quick way to adjust and resize the gap between multiple selected items that commonly align edges.

Gaussian Blur filter is used to soften a matte surface or a portrait image.

GIF extension files do not use more than 256 colors and artwork can contain no applied gradients, but it allows transparency within the artwork and creates a small file size compared to a JPEG format.

Glyph is a specific form of a character. For example, in certain fonts the capital letter A is available in several forms, such as swash and small cap.

Go menu in Mac OS X lets you view your favorite places and folders and connect to a server to share information with other computers. You can jump to any location on your computer, the Internet, or on your network.

Gradient is a transition or blend of one color into another.

Gradient Editor in Photoshop displays to select various preset gradient combinations, which can also be customized and applied by the user.

Gradient Feather Tool blends one color into another.

Gradient panel in Illustrator is the control center for creating gradients. You can select colors from the Swatches or Color panels and drag these into the gradient bar to create color.

Gradient Sliders can be adjusted to blend in special colors. You can even select a gradient color mode to work in on the Toolbox.

Gradient Tool applies selected gradient colors in a linear or radial direction.

Graphic style libraries are collections of present graphic styles.

Graphic Styles panel (Window > Graphic Styles) is used to create, name, and apply effects to graphic objects or text in conjunction with the Appearance panel.

Grids comprise a network of intersecting horizontal and vertical lines that allow the designer to unify a series of designs to relate to one another. They provide a consistent framework for placing type and graphics.

Group Selection Tool in Illustrator selects paths in a group.

Guidelines are nonprinting lines used as a guide for laying out individual images or groups of images for composites.

Gutter is the space between two columns. Gutters are used with layout guides, folding guides, and sometimes to help with margin guides.

Gutter width is the blank space between the columns of text in a document.

H

Hand Tool in Photoshop is like moving a document with your own hands and is great for quick positioning.

Harmony (sometimes referred to as unity) establishes continuity with a variety of elements and promotes consistency within the piece to evoke a particular emotion from the viewer.

Headers are found in the top portion of the additional pages and have a continuing color scheme, text format for the title, and sometimes an identifiable company logo.

Healing Brush Tool works the same way as the Clone Stamp Tool by selecting a reference area while holding down the Option/Alt key; it then works like the Patch Tool and analyzes the texture, lighting, and color and blends that into the defective area.

Help and Support in Windows Vista in the Start menu is where you will also find all kinds of tutorials, troubleshooting, and maintenance information to help keep your computer performing optimally and to customize your settings; a box area also allows you to search for information.

Hidden characters are nonprinting characters that display spaces, tabs, ends of paragraphs, index markers, and ends of stories.

Histogram in Photoshop is a graph that shows the highlight, shadow, and middle tone properties of an image in the Levels dialog box. By adjusting the histogram you can control the amount of detail in the highlights and shadows by redistributing pixels to generate the full range of tones.

Histogram panel in Photoshop displays the before (gray) and after (black) histograms to show the changes made in an image.

History Brush Tool in Photoshop is used to paint back to a previous state in the History panel by erasing pixels back to a previous state.

History panel in Photoshop records previous actions in what are called states, so you can go backwards in a series of steps as if going through multiple undo commands. You can click on a previous state or drag the most recent states into the Trash.

Hue is the name of the color (red, green, blue, etc.).

Hue/Saturation command lets you adjust the hue, saturation, and lightness of an image or selected areas of an image. The Hue slider is used to select new colors, and the Saturation and Lightness sliders adjust color purity and intensity.

I

ICC profile is a color identity profile that defines colors and embeds the color information with the file.

iCloud allows you to sync your documents, music, and imagery with your multiple devices.

Icons are small picture representations of drives and most frequently used applications, files, and folders.

Ignore Text Wrap box in the Text Frame Options display box in InDesign ensures the text will flow across columns in the length or width determined by the text frame drawn.

Image menu in Photoshop contains commands for all kinds of image enhancements and modifications.

Image Size command within the Photoshop Image menu provides changing "Pixel Dimensions" for electronic media or "Document Size" for print output.

Image Trace in Illustrator is a complex tracing function that follows the contours and outlines of drawings and bitmap images to create vector drawings. You can set a variety of parameters for various types of images, sketches, and drawings to trace.

Import involves transporting text, artwork, or images into a document.

INDD extension identifies an InDesign native document.

InDesign Interchange (INX) allows you to save the document so that a designer or service provider who has the earlier InDesign version of CS3 or earlier can read the document. Using the Export command initiates this.

InDesign Markup Language (IDML) is InDesign's file extension in CS6 and CS5 for saving documents that need to be read by users who have the earlier CS4 version of InDesign.

InDesign template can be saved to use for future editing of a document without having to start all over from scratch. It saves the templates with an INDT extension.

INDL extension identifies an InDesign object library.

INDT extension identifies an InDesign template document.

Informal balance uses elements that counterbalance one another to create a harmonious composition. This type of balance gives the appearance of being casual, energetic, modern, and trendy.

Inset setting in InDesign provides space for the text so that type is not placed too close to a graphic frame that may have a stroke weight or be filled with color. Inset settings apply to all text in a text frame.

Instance in Photoshop 3D creates a clone of an existing object. This way when you make a change to the original (parent) object, the change will be applied to all instances of that object.

Intelligent Upsampling is a feature in Photoshop CC that allows interpolation of images to produce large resolution prints.

Interpolation adds pixels in between the actual pixels and deteriorates the image sharpness and quality. Scanning an image larger than its optical resolution causes interpolation.

Isolation mode in the Layers panel in Illustrator allows a designer to edit a symbol or graphic while graying out the surrounding area to focus on the graphic.

J

Job package needed by the service provider or printer contains all the necessary elements for outputting and verifying information about the project.

Join command in Illustrator makes sure that end points are joined together as one path.

JPEG format files generate smaller compressed files and are used primarily for the web or when smaller file sizes are needed. They are a universal format and can be read by most any graphic application.

Jump line is a line that indicates an article continues to or continues from another page.

Jump list in Windows 7 allows you to navigate around recent files, images, or tasks.

Justified alignment places text equally on left and right sides in a column.

K

Kerning is a technique used for pairs of characters in titles or headlines that may need to be brought closer together for a more consistent look.

Kuler panel allows a designer to explore online and download various color group themes that can be saved in the Swatches panel.

L

Landscape orientation displays a document in a horizontal format, where the width is greater than the height.

Lasso tools work well with selections that are needed as either freeform or complex selections.

Launchpad is on the left side of the Dock If you are using Mac OS X Lion version or later will also display applications when you click on it.

Layer Comps panel in Photoshop allows the designer to capture various stages or states of development of a document by recording layers with existing settings for visibility or opacity of layers and their effects on the previous layers, their position in the document, and various blending options.

Layer group is a number of layers grouped into one folder for ease of use.

Layer mask provide a window for various (adjustment) layer effects as they trickle down through the layers giving total control to the user.

Layer menu is used to display, modify, edit, copy, group, or delete layers and includes other various commands and options for layers and layer effects.

Layer Style effects allow you to create shadows, embossing and bevels, overlays, glow, and stroke effects on selected portions of an image and on text.

Layers in Photoshop are like stacks of transparent sheets with parts of an image laid one on top of another. Layers are used to modify selected portions of an image and to combine different images or selected areas together. Special effects can also be added to each layer.

Layers panel is used to display, modify, edit, copy, group or delete layers; includes various other commands and options for layers and layer effects. The Layers panel allows you to view thumbnails of the parts of the image displayed in each layer and to move layers for specific effects.

Layout guides are sometimes green in color and are guidelines dragged out from the top and left side rulers. They are used for exact placement of specified text and graphics boxes.

Leaderboards are a popular type of banner advertisement usually placed between headers and the page content, originally used in sports pages as a sign board.

Leading refers to the spacing between lines of text.

Leading lines is a design technique used to create the effect of depth perception.

Levels command in the Photoshop Image menu provides more subtlety and precision to images by making adjustments to display details in the highlights and shadows of an image.

Libraries in Illustrator provide a vast selection of preset images a designer can base complex images on or add to an existing image. Some libraries contain symbols, brushes, swatches, and the new graphic style libraries used to apply special effects to selected objects.

Libraries in Windows 7 and 8 can be used to gather content for special folders from various locations to be placed in certain categories of files.

Lighting Direction widget is where you can position the direction of your lighting by dragging the small ball in front in front of or around 3D objects.

Line art can be any drawing or sketch created by traditional drawing utensils, like pencil, pen, charcoal, and so on.

Line Segment Tool (\) in Illustrator is used to create straight lines at any angle.

Line Tool can be used to create perfect straight lines when used in combination with the Shift key.

Linear gradients are applied in a straight line at a given angle.

Linear perspective is where a horizon line is placed to approximate the eye level of the artist. Invisible lines or edges from within the image disappear into what are called **vanishing points** that lead the eye into the image.

Lines can be straight, angular, or curved as different line types drawn in horizontal, vertical, or diagonal directions. A line's visual quality determines how a line is drawn, whether thick or thin, broken or smooth.

Linked files will automatically update when the original file is edited. This keeps the file size small.

Links panel in InDesign provides information including file size, color mode, and whether the document is linked correctly to files and graphics, so you can update links if needed.

Liquid design, sometimes referred to as fluid design, in Indesign is a new technology in which the artwork is adjusted on the fly to meet the needs of the intended market.

Live Color in Illustrator is used by designers to find colors that complement one another or to experiment with colors in their artwork and then create custom groupings of colors.

Live Corners feature in InDesign allows a designer to apply different corner effects or corner radii on the fly.

Live tiles in Windows 8 display information on the Start Screen without clicking on the application tile, like the Weather tile or the News tile.

Live Paint in Illustrator detects and corrects gaps to create closed paths for fills and strokes for painting. It treats all paths as being on the same canvas without any layering.

Live Paint Bucket Tool in Illustrator is used to create Live Paint Groups and to fill in the faces or color the edges.

Live Paint group in Illustrator makes closed paths fully editable where filled-in colors can be adjusted as individual paths are adjusted.

Live Paint Selection Tool in Illustrator lets you select and then delete faces and edges of a Live Paint group. When paths are deleted with the Live Paint Selection Tool, the color of the surrounding paths fills in the deleted path.

Live Trace (Image Trace in new version) in Illustrator is a complex tracing function that follows the contours and outlines of drawings and bitmap images to create vector drawings. You can set a variety of parameters for various types of images, sketches, and drawings to trace.

Log In is used to set up your personal settings on the computer.

Logos are the graphic that is used to identify a company or web site.

Lossless compression is the process of compressing continuous-tone images without losing any detail, though this may create a larger file size.

Lossy compression images are compressed, usually in JPEG format, where details are thrown out every time the image is edited and saved. The file size is smaller than with lossless compression.

Luminosity is the quality of lighting and contrast in an image. Any adjustment doesn't affect color information.

M

Mac Help Center in Mac OS X provides answers to questions, instructions on how to perform various functions by clicking underlined links, and a list of topics to look for information.

Macintosh OS X is the most recent operating system used on Macintosh computers.

Magic Eraser Tool in Photoshop erases a single color background on the image to make it transparent.

Magic Wand panel in Illustrator is used to select the amount of similar colors based on a tolerance setting.

Magic Wand Tool selects parts of an image based on similar tints or shadings of colors. This tool is used for areas with difficult outlines or soft edges that cannot be traced with the lasso tools.

Make command in Illustrator provides a solid a quick trace of your image without displaying anchor points and paths for editing.

Mapping artwork in Illustrator is done in the 3D Options dialog box to precisely match the artwork to the 3D surface. It involves wrapping the artwork around an object's projected surface to match what it would look like on the actual product.

Margin guides use purple lines as a default and are created in the initial setup. They are used to create outer margins and for spacing between text and graphic boxes for folding and alignment.

Marquee tools in Photoshop select rectangular boxes, elliptical areas, and single pixel row or column selections.

Mask Edge command in the Masks panel in Photoshop is used to define the masks edges.

Masks in Photoshop are used to protect parts of an image from being changed the same way an auto body shop masks off parts of an auto not to be painted. Using a mask covers areas outside the selected area with a colored overlay. All exposed areas (unmasked or not red) display the image and are part of the selection made for making changes.

Masks panel in Photoshop CS5 and earlier versions, selects by color range or inverts a selection, and defines the selection edges using the Mask Edge function. It creates a layer mask that sits next to the thumbnail effect or image in the Layers panel.

Master page items in InDesign are the individual components you created that together make the continuing banner.

Master pages are document templates that a designer can modify to provide a consistency in placed items, page formats, formatting, and guidelines for multiple documents.

Master Text Frame option is used in creating booklets.

Mastheads are found on the section of a newsletter that lists the name of the publisher and other pertinent data, which may include staff names, contributors, subscription information, addresses, logo, etc.

Measure Tool measures the distance between points along a path.

Media Eject key is located on the upper right corner of the Macintosh keyboard and looks like an arrow with a line underneath. It is used to eject CDs.

Media Library in Windows stores selected audio tracks to be burned onto a recordable CD.

Median filter in Photoshop is used to get rid of dust and scratches or clean up solid color areas, like the blue sky in an image.

Menu bar contains commands from various menus that are specific to the desktop interface or for a particular application, like Photoshop.

Merge Visible command in Photoshop merges only those layers that display the eye icon.

Merging layers still maintains the image quality and allows you to group any combination of layers together.

Mesh, sometimes referred to as a wireframe or polygonal model, is the structural part of a 3D object or character before rendering is applied to create an accurate representation of the 3D object.

Mesh mode (default mode) in the Properties panel allows you to change the text even with 3D effects applied by selecting the Edit Source button.

Mini Bridge is an extension within an Adobe application, like Photoshop. It allows you to search for, sort, display thumbnails, batch process for multiple tasks, and also create slideshows from Mini Bridge's panel when you launch the application.

Mode Command in Photoshop's Image menu assigns different color modes and profiles for various output media.

Move Tool moves a selection onto another image or portion of the same image. It is used to drag selection areas within the image to create additional layers, or to drag selections created from other images onto the Layers panel of the image you are working on.

Multiple artboards in Illustrator are useful for creating a variety of things such as multiple page PDFs, printed pages with different sizes or different elements, independent elements for websites, etc.

N

Nameplates are the identifying section located on the first, or front, page that usually consists of a company logo or identifiable graphic, the formatted title of the newsletter, and a color text box containing information such as the issue or volume number, edition description, and author or editor.

Native file is a file created by an application that is saved with that application's exclusive extension to identify it.

Navigation in an image in Photoshop can be done with the Zoom Tool or Hand Tool.

Navigator panel in Photoshop helps the designer to see portions of an image.

Negative space, or space that is absent of visual elements, is a visual element that may promote luxury or elegance and sometimes a sense of mystery.

Nested styles in InDesign are multiple styles that can be applied to a line of text or paragraph with different styles of formatting, such as applying one character style to the beginning of a paragraph, then determining where that character style stops and where the next character style begins.

Note Tool allows designers to leave messages to themselves and to one another when working on a team project to help with workflow.

Notes and Annotation tools in Photoshop allow you to leave electronic or audio notes to yourself or other members of your team who are working on the same project.

O

Object libraries in InDesign help you organize the graphics, text, and pages you use most often. You can also add ruler guides, grids, drawn shapes, and grouped images to a library.

Object menu in Illustrator is used for editing, combining, and transforming objects to any specified option needed.

Object styles are used to quickly format graphics and frames. Object styles include settings for stroke, color, transparency, drop shadows, paragraph styles, text wrap, and more; you can also assign different transparency effects for the object, fill, stroke, and text.

Objects in Illustrator are vector images that have starting and ending points and determine the shape of an image. Objects can be closed, like circles, or open, like lines.

One-point perspective involves using converging lines to lead the eye to a subject or point along a horizontal line to provide depth in perspective within the image.

Opacity Stops in Photoshop's Gradient Editor vary the amount of blended colors.

OpenType fonts are designated with the letter O, are scalable, and may include swashes and discretionary ligatures found in many foreign languages that are not available in current PostScript and TrueType fonts. OpenType fonts are cross platform, eliminating the font issues that occur when moving documents between Mac and Windows operating systems.

Operating system, sometimes referred to as an "OS," makes sure hardware and software are working together nicely.

Optical resolution, which is set by the manufacturer, is what the scanner actually sees (i.e., 4000 dpi) or the original size of the image.

Orphan is one line of a paragraph that fall at the bottom of a column or page.

Outline view in Illustrator displays just the outlines of shapes for accurate placement.

Override is created as a plus sign (+) that appears next to the current paragraph style in the Paragraph Style panel if the selected text uses a character or paragraph style and also uses additional formatting that is not part of the applied style.

Overset symbol in InDesign indicates that there is more text that needs to be displayed. It displays as a red cross.

P

Package utility in InDesign creates a folder that contains the InDesign document, any necessary fonts, linked graphics, text files, and a customized report.

Page description language (PDL) used by the commercial printing industry is created by your desktop publishing application and your computer and defines precise position and composition of images, text, and other elements in documents by mapping each pixel for high-resolution output.

Page number marker in InDesign automatically adjusts page numbers as you move around documents. It specifies where a page number sits on a page and how it is formatted.

Pages panel in InDesign contains Master Page icons that affect changes globally in the document. The bottom portion or local level contains the document icons that represent the actual document pages being created and allows you to edit individual documents.

Paint Bucket Tool is used to fill an area with the foreground color for various background effects.

Painting and drawing tools in Photoshop allow you to apply brush or shape effects. They are the Shape, Brush, Pencil, History, and Art Brushes and the Pen, Path, and Direct Select tools.

Panel Menu button in Photoshop displays commands used for each particular panel.

Panels display many options, and help modify and control information about your project. Some panels or panels provide thumbnail representations of the project to help with your editing.

Paragraph panel in InDesign provides most of the formatting essentials to type lines, including paragraph rules.

Paragraph Styles panel (in Illustrator) **and panel** (in Photoshop) apply special paragraph formatting commands to selected paragraphs.

Paste Into command in Photoshop allows the designer to paste an image behind another image's selection "window."

Pasteboard is an area outside a page where you can store objects that are not yet positioned within the page.

Patch Tool in Photoshop samples patterns and textures of an image; it analyzes the texture and lighting and matches the source pixels to blend in with a destination area.

Path Segment Reshape function is used to create smooth selected path segment curves when used in conjunction with holding down the Option/Alt key with either the Pen Tool or Direct Selection Tool.

Path Selection Tool (A) can be used to select, move, and adjust selected vector shapes.

Path Type tools allow the designer to place type on any path created. One allows the type to be placed horizontally and the other vertically along the path.

Pathfinder panel in Illustrator allows the designer to combine various shapes by adding, subtracting, excluding, and intersecting overlapping shapes to create one composite shape.

Paths in Illustrator have starting and ending points and determine the shape of an image. Paths can be closed, like circles, or open, like lines.

Pattern Brushes in Illustrator paint in tiled sections along the middle, end, or corner of a path.

PCs are computers that use the Windows operating system.

Peek function, located as a small rectangle at the edge of the taskbar in Windows, gives you the opportunity to watch open windows instantly turn transparent to display only the Windows desktop.

Pen Tool (P) is where the designer can create perfect straight lines between anchor points by clicking from one point to the next and create complex shapes from special Bézier curves of path segments.

Pencil Tool in Illustrator allows the designer to draw freely or trace from a template any drawing or image. As a line is drawn, a path is automatically created with anchor points when the mouse is released.

Peripherals are outside hardware, like scanners, printers, digital cameras, and so forth that connect to your computer.

Perspective Warp in Photoshop allows designers to work in 3D space to adjust perspective and vantage, especially around architecture.

Photos app tile in Windows 8 allows users to play slide shows of selected images saved in the Pictures library.

Photoshop tools panel provides the tools to select, edit, manage, and manipulate image pixels and to draw or add type to images.

Pica is a measurement used by a printer where 12 points equals one pica. One inch is the equivalent of 72 points.

Pinning in Windows 7 allows you to pin your favorite programs or files to the taskbar.

Pixels are individual colored square dots and are the smallest picture elements on your computer screen.

Place command for text imports the copy into its own text block so it can easily be moved around into position and edited. When an image is placed, it can be rotated and resized before the Return/Enter key is pressed.

Place command in an Illustrator template allows any sketch or drawing to be made into a template, when the Template option is checked, so it can be traced manually by either the Pencil or Pen Tool.

Placing symbols is done by dragging the symbol onto the artboard or by using the Symbols panel option Place Symbol Instance. The placed symbols, called symbol instances, can be resized visually using the bounding box, or they can be modified with Symbolism tools.

PNG format supports varying levels of transparency and also preserves gradients. It is effective at compressing continuous-tone images without losing detail, called lossless compression, but it may create a larger file size than JPEG compressed images.

Point sample in Photoshop reads the average color vales of a pixel or pixel area.

Points are the measurement method for type and small graphics; one point is equal to 1/72 of an inch.

Polygon Frame tool in InDesign creates frames as containers to insert text and graphics.

Polygon Lasso Tool (L) creates straight edge selections between two points.

Polygon Tool in Illustrator allows the designer to create any number of equidistant sides to a shape outlining a particular radius.

Portable Document Format (PDF) is used for electronic publishing and can be read by Adobe Acrobat Reader or Adobe applications.

Portrait orientation is the vertical display of a document.

Positive space uses content to fill up space to identity or explain something in a particular page.

PostScript fonts are bitmap-type fonts that contain two files: one for screen display and one for printer display. They are the most clear for printing and are preferred when sending to press. They also have set sizes, because they are bitmap files and cannot be resized without causing deterioration in quality.

PostScript language is the most widely accepted and used PDL in the commercial printing industry. When you print your document to a disk file, a PostScript printer, or a PostScript output device, you are creating a PostScript language file that is processed by that device.

PPI (pixels per inch) refers to images measured at the screen resolution that you see on your computer monitor. All web pages are measured in pixels per inch, with 72 pixels per inch as the standard computer screen measurement.

Preflight utility in InDesign warns of problems, such as missing files, graphics, or fonts. It also provides helpful information about your document or book, such as the inks it uses, the first page a font appears on, and print settings.

Preview application in Mac OS X is used not only for slideshows, but you can also perform basic editing operations and you can view all kinds of documents, as well as images.

Preview view in Illustrator displays artwork with all colors, as it will look when printed.

Print proof is used to show indications for folding, cutting, bleeding, trapping, registration, or any special requirements.

Printer's marks are made on a proof sheet and include registration marks, trim marks, color bars, bleeds, and other color information a pressman might need.

Process colors use inks that are percentages of a subtractive process of the colors cyan, magenta, yellow, and black (CMYK). These four colors are used in four separate plates during the printing process.

Profiles determine what color will display most accurately based on which media the final image will be exported to.

Proof sheet shows the service provider how the final layout should look by providing color information, accurate layout of elements, and printer's marks.

Properties panel in Photoshop provides a one-stop place to change selection properties of layer masks and color toning properties of adjustment layers.

Prospective Crop Tool in Photoshop corrects issues regarding perspective in an image.

PSD extension is Photoshop's extension when saving an image. In the case of Photoshop, the extension would be as a native file. It can be read by other Adobe products or other Photoshop users and edited with ease without losing quality, but since it is generally not an extension that can be read by all graphic applications universally, some may not be able to read it.

Pull quotes are used in long articles to pull a line or comment out of the article that helps to identify that article to the reader.

Q

Quick Look function in Mac OS X looks like an eye icon to create quick slide shows. You can click on it to also observe a full screen preview of any selected image or document.

Quick Mask is used in creating complex selections by painting the mask to include and exclude areas within a selection. The red overlay mask acts much like taping those parts not to be painted in an auto body shop. Those areas not covered represent the selected areas to be edited.

Quick Selection Tool selects similar colors, tints, or shadings of colors and allows you to "paint" a selection of a predefined brush width you set in the Tool options bar, then looks for similar adjacent colors.

R

Radial balance arranges elements around a central point and is used to promote unity or separate-but-equal relationships. Teams of professionals may use these techniques.

Radial gradients spread out from an inner position to the outer edges of an object.

Raster effects in Illustrator are effects that generate pixels on bitmap images, rather than vector images. Raster effects include all of the effects in the bottom section of the Effect menu, and the Drop Shadow, Inner Glow, Outer Glow, and Feather commands in the Effect > Stylize submenu.

Raster image processor (RIP) is used by PostScript printers or image setter devices on a commercial press. It also acts as an interpreter to convert the page information from the PostScript language into a bitmap image pattern for film or paper output.

Raster images see *bitmap image*

Ray Tracing process will apply light to the 3D scene; the ray-tracer will render the materials, illumination, texture, and shadows, to create the final 3D object.

Rectangular Frame Tool in InDesign creates frames as containers to insert text and graphics into.

Recycle Bin stores and restores deleted files in Windows, much like the Macintosh Trash icon.

Refine Edge in Photoshop provides methods for handling the edges of selections. A designer can choose options, such as various masks, to view the effects or softening and sharpening selection edges.

Registration marks on a proof sheet allow for precise placement of individual color plates. They are used by the printer as guides for exact placement of plates so that colors are overlaid exactly on top of one another.

Removable media are flash drives, Zip disks, iPods, floppy disks, CDs, or portable external hard drives that can be transported to other computers.

Rendering is the process of having the computer figure out and apply a 3D surface effect to an outline.

Resample box increases or decreases its resolution either for print or for the web.

Resolution in an image determines the amount of detail in an image: the higher the resolution, the more detail in shading, highlights, and tonality; and the larger the file size.

Resolution Independent Effects (RIE) is the capability in Illustrator in the effect dialog box that makes it possible to make changes in the effect so that there is minimal or no change in the appearance of the effect. This will only work with embedded files, not linked graphics.

Revert command in InDesign allows the designer to go back to the last Save on the document to get out of trouble spots while working on a project.

Revolve command in Illustrator allows the designer to revolve an object around the axis of a 2D outline, along an open or closed path, to create a 3D object.

RGB mode colors are created by mixing the electronic primary colors red, green, and blue. Computers use an additive process to create color from the primary colors.

Rhythm is a visual pattern that creates a sense of movement between repeating elements. Variation in rhythm can be adjusted by changing the shape, size, color, spacing, and position of elements in a design.

Ribbon in Windows 8 groups similar functions, tools, and commands together and provides special tabs with more options or features on selected images, videos, music, and documents. For instance, select a photo, and you'll find a Picture Tools tab with lots of options in its ribbon you can select in regard to that selected image.

Ripping involves copying audio tracks from a music CD to convert audio music to a format that can be used on the computer.

Rollovers are a change state that occurs when your mouse hovers over a button or graphic.

Rotate Canvas command in the Photoshop Image menu allows the designer to flip or rotate a document 90 or 180 degrees.

Rotate Tool is used to change the size of an object, or rotate it from its point of origin.

Roughs are created as result of combining specific elements from each thumbnail, or they may be the result of one good thumbnail.

RTF or Rich Text Format files are universal text files with this extension that contain most formatting commands.

Rule of Thirds is a technique used by artists to visibly divide an image into thirds for placement of elements within the composition.

Rules are lines that are used to help separate sections of articles in a pleasing way.

S

Sans serif describes type characters without (*sans*) extensions or strokes at the top and bottom; these fonts are more legible for labeling illustrations, headlines, and titles.

Saturation describes the intensity of a color (bright red or dull red).

Save a Copy command creates a duplicate of the document under a different name, leaving the original document still active.

Save a Version command in InDesign is used to save different versions if you want to experiment while protecting the original document.

Save As command saves files with different extensions for various purposes, saves to different locations, and creates different file names of the same file.

Save as template option allows designers to save documents as templates in Illustrator for future projects.

Save command saves the file as the same name with the same extension and to the same location.

Save for Web and Devices command converts artwork for exclusive web or electronic use.

Scalable Vector Graphic (SVG) is a vector format that describes images as shapes, paths, text, and filter effects. The resulting files are compact and provide high-quality graphics that are used in the development of web pages.

Scale Styles box in Photoshop, if effects are applied, scales these effects proportionately without distortion when you are resizing.

Scale Tool changes the size of an object or its point of origin.

Scatter Brushes in Illustrator spread objects randomly over a path.

Scissors Tool in Illustrator is used to cut paths and shape lines.

Scratch area in an Illustrator document is the area outside the artboard area. This is a nonprinting area where you can store artwork components.

Script fonts are used in announcements or invitations and they have the appearance of being created with a pen or brush.

Scrubby Zoom feature in Photoshop allows you to zoom in and out of your image while holding down your mouse.

Search charm in Windows 8 lets you find applications, files, or settings on your computer.

Search Tools tab will open automatically when you enter something in the search bar opening the Ribbon for more advanced searches. This can be especially helpful when looking for recent searches, a specific file, file type, file by date, or even finding file sizes.

Secondary colors are orange, green, and violet, which can be further mixed for many color variations.

Section numbering involves labeling pages by section, such as the preface, table of contents, text body, glossary, or index.

Segments are curved or straight lines between various anchor points.

Select menu in Photoshop contains commands to edit selections on an image.

Selection mask in Photoshop displays areas that are exposed or selected (white) and areas that are hidden (not selected) are displayed in black.

Selection Tool in Illustrator creates a bounding box around selected paths.

Selection tools in Photoshop select and isolate image areas. They are the Marquee, Magic Wand, Lasso, and Crop tools.

Serif type characters have what look like extensions or strokes on the top and bottom and are used to convey a conservative look; serif fonts are easier to read with long articles or bodies of text.

Settings charm in Windows 8 lets you access general settings for your computer, as well as settings for the app you're currently viewing. This is where you want to correctly power down or shut off your computer without damaging data.

Service provider is an agency that will help set up and publish documents on a commercial press or as a web page document.

Set is part of a group of similar actions in InDesign, and a group of similar layers grouped together in Photoshop and Illustrator.

Shadow/Highlight command in Photoshop corrects overexposed or underexposed areas in photographic images.

Shake function in Windows works by clicking the window pane you want to focus on and give your mouse a shake. All other open windows will disappear except for your chosen window.

Shape Builder Tool in Illustrator allows a designer to create one complex shape out of a group of selected shapes.

Shape tools are paths created as vector shapes that can be resized without loosing any edge sharpness.

Shapes are usually considered to be closed forms or an outline of something. How a shape is drawn gives it a specific quality, like a curved shape or an angular shape.

Share charm in Windows 8 is a copy and paste feature that is designed to be as convenient as possible. It allows you to "copy" information (such as a photo or web address) and "paste" it into another app.

Shear Tool in InDesign changes an object's perspective.

Slug area in printing a proof for the service provider is an area outside the page and bleed that contains printer instructions or job sign-off information.

Smart Dimensions feature. As you resize an object next to another object, a line segment with arrows at each end lets you snap the object to the same width or height as the adjacent object.

Smart Guides are temporary snap to guides that appear when you create or manipulate objects or artboards. They help you align, edit, and transform objects or artboards relative to one another by snap-aligning and displaying X, Y location, and delta values.

Smart Objects in Photoshop allow a designer to scale, rotate, and warp Illustrator vector images within the layer without fear of pixeling or degrading the artwork. They allow the designer to make edits within Illustrator, which will be automatically updated in the Photoshop document.

Smart Sharpen filter in Photoshop provides additional sharpening controls over the Unsharp Mask filter. You can also control the amount of sharpening that occurs in shadow and highlight areas.

Smart Spacing in InDesign evenly spaces multiple items on your page by snapping objects into position working with Smart Dimensions and center line intersections.

Smooth Tool in Illustrator moves and deletes anchor points to help smooth out crooked freehand path segments.

Snap feature in Windows 7 allows you to resize open windows, simply by dragging them to the edges of your screen.

Snapshot is a saved state in the Photoshop History panel for later editing as long as the document remains open. It is removed when the file is closed.

Spaces used on a Mac allows you to organize your work in groups according to projects, applications used, or whatever by dragging the documents or images between windows.

Spatial recession is a technique in which varying the size of similar shape objects and blending tonal values to match the background gives the illusion of depth, as if objects were receding into the background.

Spot colors are special color libraries of premixed inks that will produce a certain color with one ink layer. Spot colors usually are designated by a title description and a number and are printed as a single ink plate rather than a combination of CMYK inks.

Spot Healing Brush Tool in Photoshop allows the user to simply click on smaller areas that need to be replaced without having to use the Option/Alt key to set the resampled area; it makes the change automatically.

Spreads are multiple documents viewed together, such as the two pages visible whenever you open a book or magazine.

Stacks in Mac OS X springs documents and folders from the Dock to display the contents when any folder placed on the Dock's right side.

Star Tool in Illustrator is used to created various pointed shapes.

Start charm in Windows 8 switches to the Start Screen. If you're already on the Start Screen, it will open the most recent app.

Start menu or icon is the control center for Windows 7. It can select from the most recently used applications, documents, stored images, and music and launch any programs on your computer, connect to the Internet, access email, use the Search command to locate files and folders, and look for help.

Start Screen in Windows 8 is where your applications are displayed as individual tiles, replacing the Start Menu button in Windows 7.

States are sequential recorded actions displayed in the Photoshop History panel, so you can go backwards in a series of steps, as if going through multiple undo commands.

States indicate in InDesign what changes if any occur with the mouse when it is either over the graphic, away from the graphic, or clicking the graphic. Up first, then Rollover, and then Down state.

States panel in InDesign is used to indicate how a button will react with the mouse (rollover, change type etc.).

Stop action involves the illusion of motion freezing something or awaiting use in a given time and space.

Story is a threaded set of text frames.

Stroke defines the outline or edge of an object.

Stroke box in Illustrator is used to fill the outline of an object.

Stroke panel in Illustrator determines the stroke thickness based on an entered value; it is also used to determine how stroke lines are joined, capped, or changed to dashed strokes.

Stroke weight determines the thickness measured in points of the outline or stroke of an object.

Styles apply automatic formatting commands to selected characters or paragraphs.

Subheads or subheadlines are used to break components of a large article into smaller parts to keep the viewer focused.

Subscripts are percentages of a font that are displayed on or below the baseline of the font.

Subtractive process comprises percentages of inks in the colors cyan, magenta, yellow, and black (CMYK) for commercial printers.

Superscript is a percentage of the original font size and will display aligned with the top of the font.

Swatch libraries in Illustrator are used for specific color combinations. You can select colors to be placed in the main Swatches panel for future use.

Swatches panel is a selection of predefined colors from which you can choose. Custom colors can also be created and saved in the Swatches panel.

SWF extension allows a document or graphic to be used as an animated web graphic to be read by computers that use Macromedia Flash.

Symbol instances in Illustrator are repeating symbol designs of a particular symbol within a document.

Symbol libraries in Illustrator are organized collections of preset symbols with a wide variety of symbols in each. When you open a symbol library or any library it displays in a new panel.

Symbol Sizer Tool in Illustrator is used to adjust the size of a graphic.

Symbol Spinner Tool in Illustrator is used to vary the direction of the selected symbol instance.

Symbol Stainer Tool in Illustrator changes the color of symbol instances.

Symbol type is a collection of related symbols used as bullets, map symbols, logos, and so forth.

Symbolism tools in Illustrator allow the designer to modify the size, color, and distribution of symbol instances.

Symbols are art objects that you can create from combinations of paths, text, images, or groups of objects and save for later use in the Symbols panel in your document. Symbols can also include brush strokes, special effects, blending of colors, and so forth.

Symbols panel in Illustrator is used to place, store, and create symbols.

Symmetrical balance places elements equally on both sides of the frame.

System Preferences program on the Mac within the Apple menu allows you to make modifications within your computer, like adding hardware, adding and removing programs, updating applications, and modifying system functions and monitor displays.

T

Table menu in InDesign creates specified tables. It creates a spreadsheetlike table that automatically divides into a specific number of rows and columns as entered.

Tabs in Mac OS X Mavericks and current versions allows user to locate files and folders in different locations and display as tabs in one window for quick access.

Tabs provide consistency in the alignment of numbers and text in columns. You can set tabs aligning flush left, right, or centered on special characters or by either decimal points or commas.

Tactile texture involves the actual feeling of a surface texture like a sculpture.

Tags in Mac OS X Mavericks and current versions can be used as a powerful way to organize files and folders by allowing users to search by color or custom keywords or phrases.

Taskbar in Windows is used to display minimized active files and applications, like the Dock on the Mac.

Template is a premade document or artwork that can be used as a starting point for other documents.

Template layer in Illustrator is a nonprinting, faded version of the original image that acts as a tracing guide for drawing tools. Illustrator also has customized template designs that can be edited to suit your needs.

Tertiary colors are created by mixing one primary color and one secondary color, like mixing blue and green to get blue green.

Text Frame Options command in InDesign allows the user to specify an "inset" measurement or spacing that keeps text copy away from the edge of the frame.

Text wrap is a process of creating space between the graphic and the text that surrounds it or to overlap two frames or objects.

Texture describes a surface quality, like rust, velvet, or sandpaper.

Threading text involves connecting text between selected frames in InDesign.

Threshold command in Photoshop works in conjunction with the Color Sampler Tool. You use the Threshold command to find the darkest blacks and whitest whites in an image.

Thumbnails are sketched variations of an idea. In software applications, they are small representations of documents, images, or image components in specific panel.

TIF format files can be edited repeatedly and still be as accurate as the original image. They can be edited in any graphic application without losing quality because they can be read by any graphic application. Graphic files saved with a TIF extension are preferred in the commercial printing industry. They also generate the largest file sizes.

Tile Control bar In Windows 8 displays on the bottom with options related to the app you are selecting when you right-click on any app tile.

Tiles are referred to for displayed applications on the Start Screen in Windows 8.

Title bar contains the file or function name and the icon boxes to close, minimize, maximize, and restore the window size.

Tolerance setting on the Tool Options bar for the Magic Wand Tool is important, because it determines the amount of similar colors selected; the lower the tolerance, the less similar colors are selected.

Tonal value involves the lightness and darkness of an image by varying its tone or value to the surrounding background.

Tones are low intensity versions of a color.

Tool Options bar in Photoshop displays options for each selected tool.

Toolbar displays special commands and functions from each application.

Tools panel in Illustrator contains all the tools to select, create, and manipulate objects.

Tracking adjusts the spacing between characters and words.

Traditional primary colors are red, yellow, and blue. These colors are the main colors that create all others, such as orange is created by combining red and yellow.

Transform command inside the Photoshop Edit menu and the Illustrator Object menu allows you to move, rotate, reflect, scale or shear an object to a specified size.

Transparency panel in Illustrator adjusts the opacity of a particular color.

Trash is a special function icon used for removing and restoring files and ejecting Zip disks and CDs. The Trash icon is located on the right side or bottom of the Dock on the Macintosh OS X computer. Within applications, it is used to remove unwanted images or layers and for burning data onto a CD.

Tri-fold is a document divided into three sections folded toward the center to open like a book.

Trim marks on a proof sheet show the edges of the document to be cut or trimmed.

TrueType fonts designated by an icon displaying two Ts are scalable and were initially created by Microsoft.

Two-point perspective involves a more natural approach, similar to how we view the world around us, at an angle with two edge points along the horizon line. In this view, vanishing points recede at either end of a horizontal line.

TXT is the extension for plain text files.

Type alignment is the style or arrangement of setting type.

Type family is a group of fonts that share a basic character construction, like the Arial family comprises Arial Black, Arial Narrow, Arial Alternative, and so on.

Type Tool in Photoshop creates its own text layer specifically for the text. Wherever you click, you can start to type on a path line.

Type tools bring text into your images with various type orientations and type masks.

Typeface or sometimes referred as a type family is a group of fonts that share a basic character construction, like the Arial family, which includes Arial Black, Arial Narrow, Arial Alternative, and so on.

Typography is the study and use of text styles in a document.

U

Unity is the organization of elements in a design so they appear to belong together. Unity establishes continuity with a variety of elements and promotes consistency.

Unsharp Mask filter is a filter that provides precision sharpening of an image or selected portions of an image.

URL is the address of a website or web page.

Use Global Light option in Photoshop, when checked, is used to cast all the shadows at the same angle so that all shadows in future layers will look like they have the same light source for visual accuracy.

V

Value is the shading, tonality, and tint of a color (light blue and dark blue). It determines depth and dimension of an element by its range of lightness or darkness.

Value contrast determines the relationship between different elements, producing both visual and emotional effects.

Vector images are illustrations, logos, drawings, or clip art that have a limited number of colors but can be enlarged to any size without affecting the quality of the original image.

Vibrance command in Photoshop controls the intensity of saturated colors. It adjusts the saturation so that clipping is minimized as colors approach full saturation.

View menu displays files and folders on various drives and disks. It lets you customize the toolbar and to change the way files look and are arranged on your system. Check marks and Hide displays indicate whether a command is active or if a function is displayed on the screen.

View tab on the Windows 8 ribbon, when using File Explorer, makes it easy to change the way files are displayed and sorted within a folder.

Visual texture is creating the illusion of texture using varying line qualities, patterns, or by adjusting the value and colors of an element.

W

Web banners are usually considered in the development of marketing advertisements that may display vertically or horizontally on a web page, or may be used for strictly informative uses.

Web headers today are the images that are usually placed on top of the website, displayed horizontally, and include a logo and tagline among other elements.

Welcome window provides links to tutorials, opens existing or starts new documents, and provides help.

White Balance tool, used in digital cameras, sets the color balance for various lighting conditions.

Widow is one line of a paragraph that fall at the top of a column in a page.

Window menu on the Macintosh desktop allows you to minimize any active window on the desktop into the Dock or maximize an active window to fill the screen.

Window Toolbar displays special commands and functions of each application. It provides Back and Forward buttons to navigate to previously opened windows.

Windows 7 is the most recent operating system for PC computers.

Windows 8 is Microsoft's current operating system that uses tiles to designate most common applications and live events. It has a Start Screen of tiles layered over its Desktop Screen.

Windows Media Player is an application in Windows that burns CDs from audio tracks, video files, and photos.

Word processing programs create documents of formatted text for reports, short articles, or single-page brochures with fixed inserted graphics. This is usually not suitable for printing on a commercial press, but it works well for home or office use.

Z

Zero point is used to set intersecting lines at "0" for easier measuring. You can drag from the upper left-hand corner where the rulers intersect, and then release the mouse where you want to start the measurement at zero.

Zipped files are files compressed together in one folder that becomes a file attachment for electronic distribution. Zipped files have a *.zip* extension.

Zoom Tool allows you to get in close and then zoom out to observe the whole image.

Index